Martine Schaer on Caribou Barbie (5.10a), Shelving Rock, Lake George. JIM LAWYER
© 2014 Patagonia, Inc.

Adirondack Rock
A Rock Climber's Guide
Second Edition, Volume 2

Jim Lawyer
Jeremy Haas

Adirondack Rock Volume 2
A Rock Climber's Guide
Second Edition

Published by: Adirondack Rock Press, LLC
2795 Henneberry Road, Pompey, NY 13138
www.adirondackrock.com

Copyright (c) 2014 by Jim Lawyer and Jeremy Haas
All rights reserved.
First edition published 2008
      Reprint, 2010
This edition published 2014

Printed in China
10 9 8 7 6 5 4 3 2 1

No part of this publication may be reproduced, stored in a retrieval system, or transmitted in any form or by any means—electronic, mechanical, audio recording, or otherwise—without the written permission of the publisher.

ISBN: 0-9814702-2-x
ISBN: 978-0-9814702-2-1

Written by Jim Lawyer and Jeremy Haas
Layout and design by Jim Lawyer and Jeremy Haas
Printed by Four Colour Print Group, Louisville, KY
Edited by Susan J. Cohan and Sara Catterall

Photographs by the authors unless noted otherwise.

Front cover: Art by Colin O'Connor.
Title page: *Hollow Stump*. Watercolor by Lucie Wellner.

Read This First

Rock climbing is an inherently dangerous activity regardless of your level of skill and experience. It requires that you constantly assess and manage risk. You alone are responsible for your safety.

This book is not an instruction manual for climbing. Information in this book has been collected from a variety of sources, and, despite efforts to verify it, the authors and publisher make no guarantees as to its accuracy or reliability. The routes in the Adirondacks change—vegetation reclaims critical protection placements, rockfall alters sections of routes, the freeze-thaw action in winter loosens rocks, and once-open rock slides grow in and become unclimbable. Fixed protection is unreliable—pitons loosen and pull out; bolts rust and weaken; and anchors become old, rotten, sunbaked, or are removed by other parties.

**THE AUTHORS AND PUBLISHER OF THIS GUIDEBOOK ASSUME
NO RESPONSIBILITY FOR YOUR ACTIONS AND SAFETY.**

If there is any doubt, if you are nervous and scared, then don't do it—seek instruction or hire one of the excellent local guides.

Emergency Information

Search and rescue is under the authority of the DEC forest rangers. In an emergency, call the DEC's 24-hour emergency dispatch center at:

518.891.0235

Make sure you have as much information as possible—name of the injured, time and location of the accident, nature of the accident, description of the injuries, who is present to assist, and what type of response to prepare for—high-angle rescue versus a litter carry.

Other important numbers include the following:

518.897.1300	Forest ranger headquarters
518.897.1200	DEC general information
518.897.2000	New York State Police in Ray Brook

You can call 911, but that requires extra rerouting of the information, and if you have a cell phone, depending on the receiving tower, you could be dialing 911 in Vermont.

Self-Rescue

Many of the remote cliffs in the park require that climbers be self-sufficient and get themselves out of tight situations. If you can safely evacuate the injured person to a vehicle, there are several hospitals in and around the park. Be warned that there are regions of the park where the nearest hospital is more than an hour from the trailhead. If you do self-rescue, be sure to let the DEC rangers know after the fact.

IN THE PARK
Here are the larger medical facilities in the park, each of which has a 24-hour emergency room:

Elizabethtown	Elizabethtown Community Hospital, 75 Park Street	518.873.6377
Lake Placid	Adirondack Medical Center, 29 Church Street	518.523.3311
Saranac Lake	Adirondack Medical Center, 2233 NY 86	518.891.4141
Star Lake	Clifton Fine Hospital, 1014 Oswegatchie Trail	315.848.3351
Ticonderoga	Moses-Ludington Hospital, 1019 Wicker Street	518.585.2831

OUTSIDE THE PARK
Just outside the park boundary are more options:

Glens Falls	Glens Falls Hospital, 100 Park Street	518.926.1000
Gloversville	Nathan Littauer Hospital, 99 East State Street	518.725.8621
Plattsburgh	Champlain Valley Physicians Hospital, 75 Beekman Street	518.561.2000
Potsdam	Canton–Potsdam Hospital, 50 Leroy Street	315.265.3300
Utica	St. Elizabeth Medical Center, 2209 Genesee Street	315.798.8100

MILEAGES BETWEEN GATEWAY CITIES AND DESTINATIONS IN THE PARK

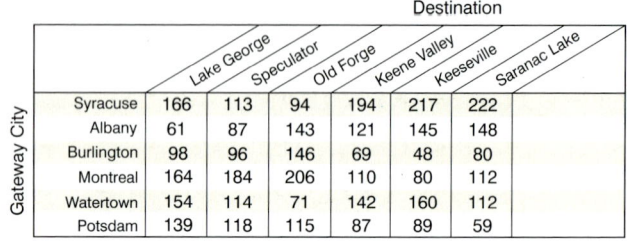

Gateway City \ Destination	Lake George	Speculator	Old Forge	Keene Valley	Keeseville	Saranac Lake
Syracuse	166	113	94	194	217	222
Albany	61	87	143	121	145	148
Burlington	98	96	146	69	48	80
Montreal	164	184	206	110	80	112
Watertown	154	114	71	142	160	112
Potsdam	139	118	115	87	89	59

A Grand Isle–Plattsburgh
B Charlotte–Essex

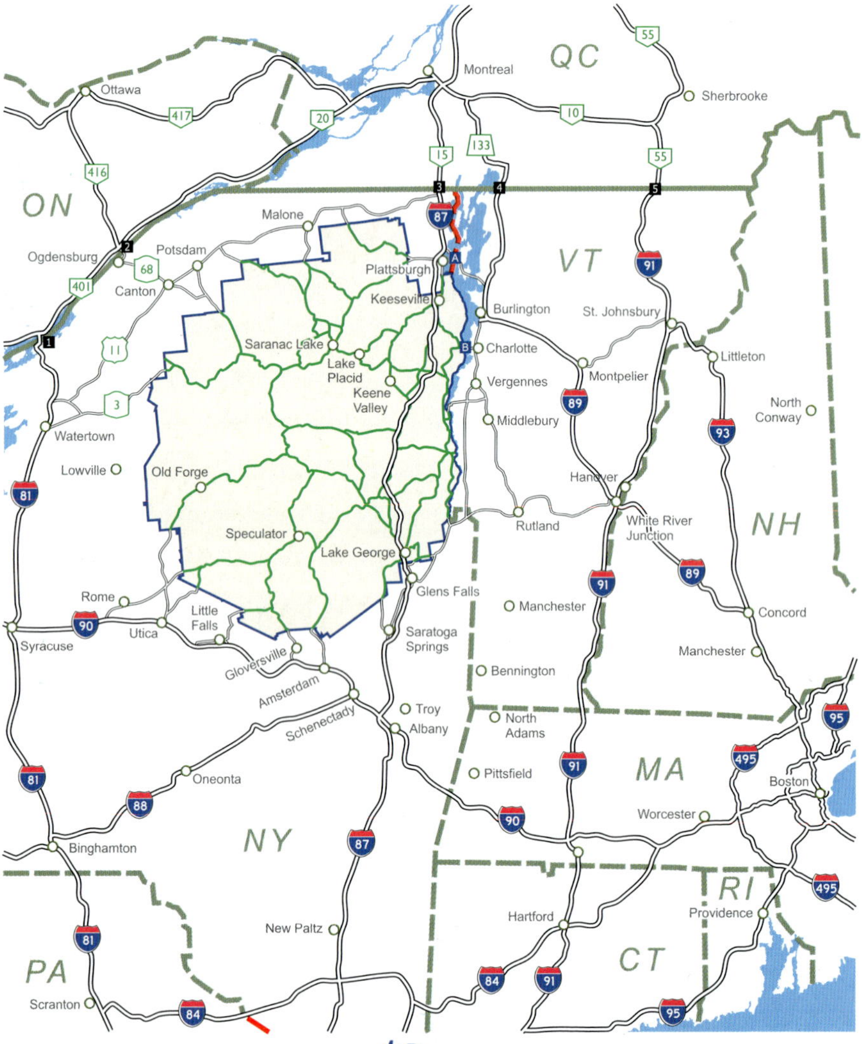

Border Crossings
1 *Thousand Island Bridge*
2 *Ogdensburg–Prescott Bridge*
3 *Lacolle / Champlain*
4 *Saint Armond / Highgate Springs*
5 *Stanstead / Derby Line*

#	Region	Page
1	Lake Champlain	vol. 1, 26
2	Chapel Pond Pass	vol. 1, 176
3	Keene	vol. 1, 318
4	Wilmington Notch	vol. 1, 382
5	High Peaks	vol. 1, 422
6	Lake George	34
7	Indian Lake	136
8	Southern Mountains	292
9	Old Forge	346
10	Cranberry Lake	384
11	Northern Mountains	402

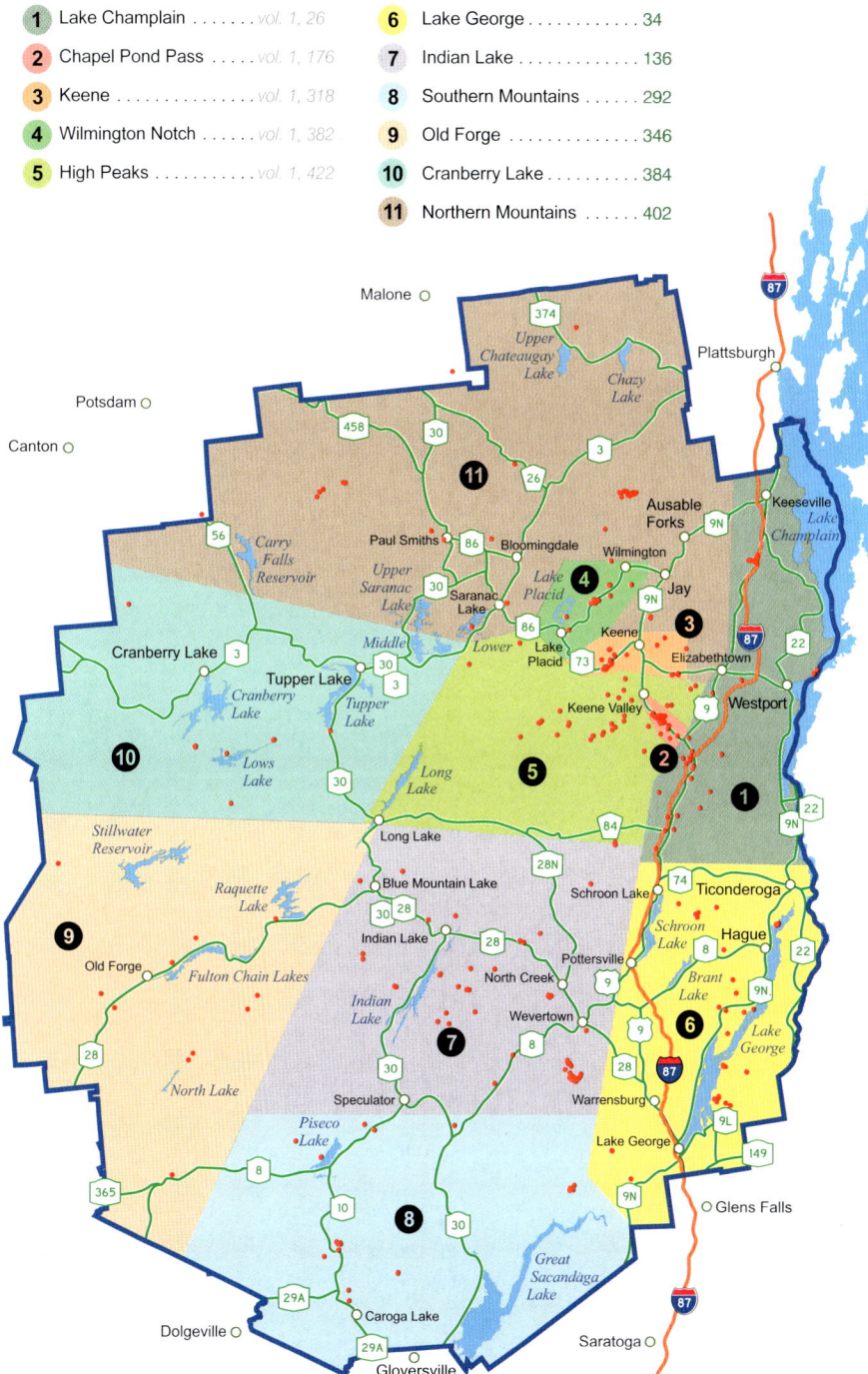

Contents

Read This First 3
Foreword 8
Introduction 11
The Area 12
Local Climbing Practices 17
Adirondack Geology 101: Rocks for Jocks 19
Using This Guidebook 21
Adirondack Climbing Chronology 28
Pushing the Grade 33

LAKE GEORGE 35
Shelving Rock 38
Ark Wall 60
Sleeping Beauty Mountain 64
Buck Mountain 67
    Upper Buck 67
    New Buck 69
    Eagle Cliff 72
Inman Pond Bluff 73
Pilot Knob Mountain 74
    Stewart's Ledge 74
    The Brain 78
Hudson River Crags 79
    Lower Cliffband 79
    Upper Cliffband 79
Potash Cliff 80
Rogers Rock 87
    Campground Wall 88
    Cove Wall 91
    Rogers Slide 92
Brown Mountain Cliff 102
Deer Leap 104
Wild Pines 106
Fly Brook Valley 107
    Wardsboro Cliff 108
    Catamount Main Face 109
Padanarum Cliff 109
Tongue Mountain Cliff 111
Barton High Cliff 117
Spectacle Ponds Cliff 121
Pharaoh Mountain 122
    Main Face 124
    Summit Cliffs *130*
    Upper Summit Cliff 131
    Lower Summit Cliff 131
Gull Pond Cliff 132
Devil's Washdish Cliff 134

INDIAN LAKE 137
Crane Mountain 140
    Crane West *144*
    Wayout Wall 144
    Beaverview Cliff 146
    Northern Knob 148
    Central Crane *148*
    Brown Slab 148
    Viewpoint Cliff 150

Tablerock Crag 152
Summit Cliffs *153*
Pondview Wall 153
Sweeper Wall 154
Firecamp Wall 156
True Summit 158
The Prows 159
Crane East *163*
Measles Group 164
    Above-the-Measles Wall 166
    Lower Measles Wall 168
    Upper Measles Wall 169
    Top-O-the-Measles Wall 170
    Below-the-Measles Wall 170
Belleview Area 171
    Belleview Slab 173
    Bellavista Slab 174
South Corner Cliffs 175
    Upper Walls 176
    Height of Land Wall 185
    Land of Overhangs 186
    TeePee Wall 188
    Long Play Wall 190
    Diagonal Ramp Wall 192
Pinnacle Overlook 193
Black Arches Wall 194
Slanting Cracks Wall 209
Waterfall Wall 211
East Nose 212
Caterpillar Cliff 213
Huckleberry Mountain 214
    North End 216
    Boneyard 216
    Corner Cliff 220
    Main Cliff 221
    White Slab 228
    No-Name Wall 228
    Last Wall 229
    Factory Slabs 229
Mill Mountain 229
Nameless Knob 229
Shanty Cliff 231
    Shanty Slab 240
Long Pond Cliff 240
Humphrey Mountain Cliff 247
Snowy Mountain 248
    Summit Cliff 250
    Lower Slabs 252
Baldface Mountain 253
    Summit Cliff 254
    Main Face 254
John Pond Cliffs 255
Kings Flow Cliff 255
Pine Peak Cliff 256
Chimney Mountain 257
    Chimney Summit 258
    Lookout Rock 259
    Caveman Wall 259
    True Summit Slabs 260
Puffer Mountain Cliff 261

Sugarloaf Mountain	263
Cedar River Crag	278
Ledge Mountain	278
Castle Rock	279
Tirrell Pond	280
McGinn Mountain	281
Starbuck Mountain	282
Black Mountain Cliff	285
Peaked Mountain	285
Gore Mountain	286
Dutton Mountain	290
Hayes Mountain	290

SOUTHERN MOUNTAINS 293
Pinnacle Mountain	295
Green Lake Cliff	301
Otter Lake Cliff	303
The Lost Crags	306
Lost T Cliff	306
The Annex	314
Lost Hunters Cliff	315
McMartin Cliff	319
Lost T2 Cliff	322
Good Luck Mountain	323
Good Luck Boulder	330
Summit Cliff	331
West Canada Cliff	331
The Black Wall	334
Panther Mountain	334
Echo Cliff	335
The Grotto	337
Summit Cliff	337
Fish Mountain Crag	337
Lake Pleasant Quarry	338
Toy Story Wall	339
Auger Falls	340
West Mountain	341
Gabe's Boulder	342
Rods & Guns Wall	342
Silver Bullet Band	345
Wave Wall	345
Whaling Wall	345

OLD FORGE 347
Ledge Mountain (Nobleboro)	349
Ice Cave Mountain	349
Fissure Face	351
Raven Wall	353
Middle Settlement Lake	353
Flatrock Mountain	355
Bald Mountain	356
Main Face	356
Summit Cliff	360
Moss Lake Slab	360
Mount Tom Cliff	362
Mitchell Ponds Mountain	362
Fox Mountain Crag	364
Eagle Falls	364

CRANBERRY LAKE 385
Lake Lila	387
Hitchins Pond Cliff	390
South Bay Roadcut	392
Grass Pond Mountain	392
Cat Mountain	396
West Cliff	397
Summit Cliff	398
Main Face	399
Twin Falls Cliff	399

NORTHERN MOUNTAINS 403
South Colton	406
Azure Mountain	408
Main Face	409
Planet Terror Face	414
Equinox Face	414
Santa Clara Tract	415
Deer Pass	417
Lost Key Crag	419
County Line Mountain	420
Jenkins Mountain	420
Charcoal Kiln Quarry	423
Blue Hill	424
Bluff Island	424
Baker Mountain	425
Inman Slabs	428
Deerfly Slab	429
Blackfly Slab	429
Panther Hill Cliff	430
Catamount Mountain	433
South Summit	434
Main Summit	435
Silver Lake	435
C Chimney Cliff	439
Never Never Land	445
Purple Rain Wall	446
Summit Cliff	447
Center of Progress Cliff	453
Tsunami Wall	461
Midway Cliff	464
Outback Slab	467
Wayback Cliff	469
Potter Mountain Cliff	470
The Burrow	484
Hydrogen Wall	485
Mud Pond Cliff	486
Silver Lake Mountain Summit Areas	490
Clements Pond Trail	490
The Towers of the Teeth	490
Fisherman's Wall	491
Titusville Mountain	492
Appendix A: Grade Conversion	494
Appendix B: Cliffs by Category	495
Appendix C: Private Land Crags	499
Appendix D: Advertiser Index	499
Appendix E: Local Resources	500

GRADED LIST OF CLIMBS 502
INDEX 522

Acknowledgements	544
About the Authors	544

Foreword

By Tad Welch

Fingertips and eyelids burn from shards of brittle lichen and topsoil spindrift settles into creases of exposed flesh. Warm evening light sends an exaggerated petroglyph shadow across unclimbed rock from the first climber up. The tug of war with a rope zig-zagged by stunted cedars and Chouinard ovals has been won.

A slithering descent leads to a cave behind a truck-sized block that has fallen away from the cliff's base. It's easy to imagine the past in a place like this, where nature is so overwhelmingly present. Adirondack miners drilled rock from similar ceilings, albeit in shafts hundreds of feet from sunlight where ore hauling mules lived their subterranean lives and went blind. When eyesight adjusts to the half-light, recesses are revealed, like the one that held an ancient clay pot of Mohawk origin.

The return to the forest brings more history. Broken barbed wire sprouts from either side of an aged beech tree scarred by black bear claws. Farther along, a bramble-choked skidder road and double-bladed axe head attest to multiple logging generations. At last, packs are tossed in the station wagon's backseat and blackflies climb aboard.

As this new edition of *Adirondack Rock* makes clear, it's not only days spent exploring, bushwhacking, and cragging that multiply as the years go by. New cliffs are "discovered" and exploratory routes are put up. Some are gems, while others (I must accept responsibility here) are less so. The current generation adds lines to familiar walls, ascents that were overlooked or unimagined by earlier pioneers. The amount of activity and quantity of data can begin to overwhelm. After all, this is a six million acre park, a playground the size of neighboring Vermont. It would take a stack of volumes the size of *A Climber's Guide to the Adirondacks*, which was first published in 1967 and barely the thickness of a Power Bar, simply to list directions to every cliff, never mind the route descriptions.

Obviously, a thorough accounting of what is needed to get us to and up a route is essential. We're fortunate that *Adirondack Rock* sets a high standard here with its accuracy and detail. Once you choose the cliff with a suitable approach, the ideal range of route grades, preferred height, the right number of starred routes, and amount of sun or shade desired, all of which are easily found in the guide, it will be surprising if you can't find your way up a chosen line - the reason being that either Jeremy or Jim has been there and very likely climbed the route. Now, think about it. Spread over millions of acres are 330 crags, the majority with little more than cairns or a faint footpath leading to them. All told, those cliffs host 3,100-plus routes and a total of more than 4,000 pitches. (That's over 65 miles of climbing, in case you're wondering.) The first edition of *Adirondack Rock* tallied 1,900 climbs. In the intervening six years many rock walls previously unknown to climbers have appeared and more than 1,200 new routes and variations have been added to the Park total. It's an incredible time commitment to compile such vast amounts of information and present it in written and illustrated form in two guide book editions in a way that comes as close as is humanly possible to meeting every user's needs. Knowing this can leave you wide-eyed at how Jim and Jeremy have also managed to author a combined 374 first ascents!

But a climbing region is more than the sum of its routes and grades, a fact that some guide books overlook. A sense of our shared history – who climbed what and when, and, by extension, upon whom to exact revenge for your latest epic - adds a rich dimension of meaning to our efforts. From in-depth historical overviews to brief essays penned by some of the key players over the decades to one-liners inserted into route descriptions, Jim and Jeremy have given us a valuable passage to our past. While always entertaining, this aspect of their work also offers a broader lens through which we are encouraged to see the uniqueness of the region where we climb. Whether it's a day on Silver Lake Mountain, Wallface, Crane, or any of literally dozens of similar places, the experience can't help but foster an awareness of the positive mix of the wild and human that is the essence of the Adirondacks. Of course there are other rock climbing areas that are equally or more wild. And you don't need to look far for destinations where the mark of humankind lies heavy on the land. But, there's an unquantifiable something that comes with a region like ours where the two merge in a relatively seamless and mutually beneficial way. Perhaps the something is the way that the past, present, and future don't exist separate from one another in the Adirondacks, as is too often the case in the rest of our lives.

When we summit the routes on Gothics Mountain or climb from Panther Gorge to Mt. Marcy's peak, we've journeyed hundreds of miles north and over 10,000 years back in time. The arctic ecosystem of the High Peaks, a fragile symbol of the alpine climbing realm, followed the glaciers' retreat and lives a tentative life in its 87 acres refuge on the tallest summits. Most Adirondack species will seek survival, if they can, by migrating to higher and cooler habitats in response to hotter temperatures. The mountain top flora has nowhere left to go. But a special opportunity comes with this knowledge. It's a new and broader perspective that encourages us to expand our energies beyond climbing's ethical controversies to issues of global significance. Like the climbing we do, it demands the best from us.

With the publication 48 years ago of the first climbers' guide, which listed a very modest 70-plus rock routes (fewer than exist on half of Poke-O's Main Face today!), Jim Goodwin wrote that, "...rock climbing has come of age in the Adirondacks." In the five subsequent decades each generation of climbers has been privileged to experience a new coming of age for Adirondack rock climbing with every advancement on Trudy Healy's foundational work. Following Healy was Tom Rosecrans' *Adirondack Rock and Ice Climbs*. It reflected the environmental ethic of the 1970s with its emphasis on clean climbing and stated hope that a guide book would prove "more helpful than destructive." Next was - and is – Don Mellor, who continues to author the area's ice climbing guide in addition to other Adirondack and rock climbing-related books. His writing captured the spirit of the climbers' world inside the Blue Line with three editions of *Climbing in the Adirondacks*. At its heart, Don's message is an eloquent reminder to embrace Adirondack climbing on its own terms, to relish the adventure and avoid taming the vertical landscape for the sake of convenience or personal ambition.

We're fortunate that the maturation of Adirondack rock climbing and that of its community has been nurtured, inspired, and shown the way forward without forgetting the past for nearly half a century by Trudy, Tom, Don, - and now Jeremy and Jim. Thanks to their cumulative efforts, we can head confidently away from civilization's insistent chatter and into the forest solitude to the places where past, present, and future come together to create the potential for the unforgettable. And depending on the weather, bugs, our abilities and sense of direction, we may succeed - or fail - in getting to the top. But, no matter what the outcome, we are ultimately the ones responsible for our safety and quality of experience. On a handful of days we'll climb as if gravity doesn't exist and wish for the moment to go on forever. It's then that we should give special thanks to the authors of *Adirondack Rock* and to their predecessors. Their generosity has given access to some of the best days of our lives.

Tad Welch.

Les Adirondacks

par Loïc Briand

Le parc des Adirondacks, familièrement appelé « les Adis » par de nombreux francophones qui le visitent chaque année – et « the Dacks », par les anglophones – est un harmonieux mélange de terres privées et publiques réparties sur plus de 24 000 km² (6 000 000 d'acres), soit la taille approximative de l'état du Vermont. Créé en 1892 dans le but de préserver les ressources forestières et les plans d'eau de la région, il est traversé dans son axe nord-sud par l'autoroute 87, le prolongement 15 Sud au Québec. Les forêts y sont riches et denses. La multitude de sommets de plus de 1 200 m (4 000 pi), de vallées et de falaises en font un endroit très prisé pour la pratique de la randonnée et de l'escalade.

La philosophie de développement du parc est exemplaire. Hormis quelques exceptions, les rares villages qu'il contient n'abritent à peu près aucune habitation de plus de trois étages. Les publicités envahissantes des grandes villes ou de leurs autoroutes connexes y sont absentes. On y trouve un peu partout, au détour d'un sentier, au confluent de deux ruisseaux, dans une clairière ou au pied d'une majestueuse paroi, « des petits miracles de silence, échappés du progrès[1] ». Il est crucial et impératif que tout visiteur qui s'y aventure respecte cette philosophie qui rend l'endroit tout à fait singulier.

Dès 1967, les grimpeurs ont la chance de pouvoir consulter un livre guide d'escalade décrivant le parc. En 1975, Tom Rosecrans publie Adirondack Rock and Ice climbs. Don Mellor, le doyen de la grimpe aux Adirondacks, produit la première édition de Climbing in the Adirondacks en 1983. Ce livre est revu et augmenté, puis réédité en 1986, en 1989, en 1994 et en 1995. Mellor décide ensuite de passer le flambeau à Jim Lawyer et à Jeremy Haas, en 2008, qui révolutionnent carrément le monde du livre-guide sur la côte Est, en publiant la première édition de Adirondack Rock, en un seul volume. Ce premier ouvrage, qui décrit l'ensemble du parc, est consacré uniquement à l'escalade de rocher et au bloc. Exhaustif, facile à consulter et très précis, il comporte les coordonnées GPS des

---

[1] La citation est tirée d'un article de Pierre Foglia (La Presse, septembre 2007)

parois, de nombreux détails historiques sur l'ouverture des voies et quelques récits des premiers ascensionnistes. Après une réimpression de l'ouvrage initial en 2010, ne reculant devant rien, forts de l'appui de nombreux collaborateurs motivés par l'incroyable travail de défrichage accompli, Jim et Jeremy poussent leur obsession jusqu'à de nouveaux sommets et décident en 2014 de scinder l'ouvrage en deux : le premier volume regroupe les régions de Keene, Chapel Pond, Wilmington, Lake Champlain et la région des High Peaks. Le second se penche sur les régions de Lake George, Indian Lake, Old Forge, Southern Mountains, Cranberry Lake, et les Northern Mountains. D'ailleurs, les auteurs ont accompli l'immense tâche de se rendre à la base de chacune des 3 100 voies réparties sur 330 sites et de les examiner toutes en détail. Il s'agit bien sûr d'un travail colossal ayant pris des années. De nombreuses photos aériennes et de multiples topos et croquis des parois rendent ces deux livres tout à fait remarquables. Si vous trouviez l'édition précédente déjà impressionnante, avec ses 672 pages, sachez que le nombre de parois développées et de voies ouvertes depuis lors a pratiquement doublé!

La proximité du parc avec la frontière canado-américaine en a fait un terrain de prédilection pour de nombreux Canadiens. Le développement de l'escalade aux Adirondacks a d'ailleurs largement été influencé par ces derniers au cours des décennies. De nombreux membres du club alpin du Canada, puis John Turner, Dick Wilmott, Claude Lavallée, Ben Poisson, Brian Rothery, Hugh Tanton, Dick Strachan, Rob Wood, Peter et George Bennett, Peter Baggaley, Peter Ferguson, François-Xavier Garneau, Bob Cartwright, Peter Gernassnig, Charles Pechousek, Pierre-Édouard Gagnon, Gelu Ionesco, Julien Déry, Louis-Philippe Ménard, Maxime Turgeon et Jean-Pierre Ouellet ont laissé leur empreinte sur la région en ouvrant de nombreux classiques.

La grimpe aux Adirondacks est surtout traditionnelle – c'est-à-dire protégeable avec des coinceurs – ou mixte. Ce n'est pas tout à fait le royaume de la moulinette, puisque la majorité des parois font plus d'une demi-corde. Pour bien apprécier les Adirondacks, il faut maîtriser l'art de poser tous les types de coinceurs. Cela dit, depuis la publication du dernier livre-guide de Don Mellor, les principaux ouvreurs ont équipé plus de voies que lors de tout autre époque. Les itinéraires sont à l'occasion très engagés, malgré tout, et nécessitent souvent un petit jeu de coinceurs. Une chose est certaine : bien que l'escalade sportive ou mixte soit en plein essor aux Adirondacks, il s'agit principalement d'un terrain de jeu d'aventure. De fait, en vertu des lois strictes de conservation du parc, il est interdit d'installer des protections fixes (plaquettes, scellements) dans la majorité des sites. Pour éviter toute interdiction de grimpe et par souci de préservation, veuillez respecter les règles concernant la modification permanente du milieu naturel. Le parc demeure un paradis des fissures classiques, parfois longues, sales, difficiles à protéger et soutenues. Les découvertes sont presque toujours au rendez-vous.

Les approches permettant d'accéder à plusieurs des parois décrites dans le guide sont parfois sauvages, impressionnantes, voire intimidantes. La pluie, les insectes et la recherche d'itinéraire sont régulièrement de la partie. Pour accéder aux parois de Wallface, l'une des plus hautes falaises des Adirondacks, avec ses quelques voies de plus de 250 mètres (800 pi), il faut marcher au moins 9 km par l'approche classique. Mieux vaut être bien préparé si on compte grimper l'une des nombreuses voies de la falaise et revenir à la voiture en une seule journée. Pour se rendre à Moss Cliff, il faut traverser un cours d'eau parfois glacial au printemps et à l'automne. Des voies sur les faces nord et sud de Gothics font près de 400 mètres (1 200 pi) de haut. Gravir de belles voies sur ces falaises rend l'aventure d'autant plus enrichissante.

Comme ailleurs, les voies les plus courtes et les plus faciles d'accès sont aussi les plus populaires. Il faut apprécier les approches plus longues ou complexes pour se rendre aux plus belles parois et éviter les foules. Les itinéraires les plus intéressants ne sont pas nécessairement les plus faciles à trouver; façonnez vos aptitudes à lire votre livre-guide et le rocher. Plusieurs cordées se sont fait surprendre par l'ampleur de l'épopée dans laquelle elles s'étaient lancées... et par leur manque de préparation.

Les auteurs ont produit deux ouvrages exceptionnels, à l'image des régions qu'ils décrivent. Vous avez l'embarras du choix, et il ne vous reste plus qu'à définir vos propres projets, vos propres rêves. Le plus formidable terrain de jeu du Nord-Est américain vous attend.

Loïc Briand.

Introduction

Splitter cracks, secluded crags, towering slabs and mazes of boulders— this is climbing in the Adirondack Mountains. The surrounding scenery of calm lakes, rocky stream beds and misty mornings carry you to the climbs, sometimes leading you across icy cold water to a high alpine face that sees only a handful of visitors each year. The variety, serenity, and solitude found here create a climbing experience that cannot be had anywhere else.

The year 1850 heralded the first technical climb on Adirondack rock—a bold solo on the remote Mt Colden. Much later, in 1916, John Case turned to the rope in order to safely seek out greater challenges, which marked the beginning of a steady increase in climbing activity. Presently there are more than 3,100 routes—1,240 new ones since the first edition—spread over 330 cliffs, 126 of which have multipitch routes, and 11 remote peaks with technical climbing.

Adirondack climbers are from all over—cosmopolitan cities, college towns, and neighboring Canada. This eclectic group's influence is felt at the crags with the array of cultures and climbing styles, yet the number of visitors remains low. The Beer Walls and Poke-O Moonshine are most popular, but at the peak of the season and even during a holiday weekend, the number of people at any one of these areas barely approaches 50. Perhaps the classic climb will have a queue of cordial and pleasant parties, but there are plenty more. This guidebook will direct you to them.

The Adirondack Park is a vast area, nearly 6 million acres, equivalent in size to Denali National Park in Alaska. Considering that half of the climbing destinations are located more than a half hour from the road, serenity reigns—the cliffs are as wild as the forests you pass through.

The Adirondack Park

The Adirondack Park was one of our nation's first protected areas (second to Yellowstone National Park). One of New York State's original missions in forming the park was to increase public landholdings until they comprised half of the total area. This goal, which promises more climbing opportunities, is getting closer with recent large land purchases. The blue line, as the park's boundary is called, surrounds public, private and municipal land—the towns located within have always been essential to the park's character. An early boom-and-bust period of logging and mining has now been replaced by tourism that consists of visitors who love the area's rich history and abundant outdoor activities. The small towns that have become popular vacation resorts struggle to provide year-round employment, living wages, and services for their residents, so by eating at the local restaurants, frequenting the gear shops, hiring one of the area's knowledgeable guides, or telling friends back home about your experience in the Adirondacks, you're doing your part to sustain this unique place.

Within the blue line, you find ski areas, colleges, factories, and busy towns. The park is unique in its capacity to encompass both the human and the natural and as metropolitan areas expand, the park's importance as a wilderness preserve becomes more apparent now than ever before. This is a place with remote expanses where you can hike for days without seeing another person.

This Guidebook

The number of cliffs and routes in the entire park far exceeds its climbers. Other than the popular spots in the park, the vast majority of cliffs have only a handful of visitors annually. If you want a wild experience, one that is far from the road and close to nature, you will have no difficulty finding such a cliff in this comprehensive book, and chances are you'll see little evidence that anyone else has ever visited.

Our primary goal is to get you to the base of a climb and give you the fine points of the ascent. You'll appreciate these details if you are a beginner climber or have chosen a route that is technically challenging. If you are a hardened adventurer, then our descriptions can be a springboard to your own explorations.

The climber's experience of the sport is captured by places visited, various partners, and challenges of particular routes, which add up to a rich backdrop of history. This guidebook continues the tradition established by previous guidebook authors by providing an extensive history inclusive of all routes—applauding and protecting the accomplishments of those who came before. With this clear documentation, you'll know where routes are located, their quality and grades, and who did the first ascents, allowing you to add new routes in a thoughtful and respectful manner.

This book shows the scope and potential of climbing areas in the park. There is a lot of undeveloped rock. By treading lightly on cliffs, it is possible to climb a route and leave little evidence of your passage. The Adirondack cliffs, like many natural resources, are finite and nonrenewable—they show scars much longer than a trampled forest, which can eventually regenerate. Many new crags discussed in this book are notable for their limited fixed protection and serve as a template, ideal, and guide for route development elsewhere in the park.

Undoubtedly there are undiscovered cliffs or ones that have been visited by climbers but whose history has been lost. We eagerly anticipate what the next generation of climbers will reveal.

The Area

Getting There

The Adirondack Park, roughly the size of Vermont, is hard to miss. It occupies nearly the entire upper portion of New York State. The primary points of entry are shown on the map (page 4) and accessed from the obvious interstate highways: the Northway (I-87), which runs north–south through the east side of the park; I-81, which runs north–south just west of the park; and the Thruway (I-90), which is to the south and runs east–west. Some popular tips and shortcuts are given here.

REFUEL OFTEN
There are few 24-hour gas stations, so plan accordingly.

NY 8 SHORTCUT
There are no fast east–west routes through the park: traveling from one side to the other can take 4 hr or more. (In other words, going through Old Forge is your last resort.) The exception is NY 8, the most convenient route for travelers coming from the west (e.g., Toronto, Buffalo, and Syracuse) aiming for the High Peaks and the southern areas. It is fast (shaving off an hour or more compared to going around the park through Albany), scenic, and has little traffic. There are few options for gas and groceries, though, so make sure you fill up first.

Take the Thruway (I-90) to Exit 33 in Verona, go northeast on NY 365, then northeast on NY 8 through Speculator and Wevertown. After Riparius, take US 9 north to Pottersville (24-hour gas), then get on the Northway (I-87).

DEALING WITH LAKE CHAMPLAIN
If you're coming from northern New Hampshire and Vermont, then all routes lead to Burlington. The Adirondacks beckon you from across the lake, but it takes more than an hour to get there. If you're going to Poke-O or Silver Lake, use the Grand Isle Ferry (www.ferries.com), as it is cheap, runs frequently, and avoids the hassles of south Burlington. Go north on I-89 to Burlington and continue north to Exit 17. Go east on US 2 to Grand Isle, then west on Ferry Road (VT 314) to the ferry dock. The ferry takes 12 min and runs every 15 min. Once you're in New York, follow NY 314 to the Northway (I-87) and go south. (This is Northway Exit 39 if you're reversing the route.)

If you're going to the Keene Valley area, head north on I-89 to Burlington, west on I-189 to its end, south on US 7 past Charlotte to Vergennes, south on VT 22A, then west on VT 17 to the Crown Point Bridge. Go north on NY 9N / NY 22 to Port Henry, west on Tarber Hill Road / Broad Street (CR 4), bear right onto Dugway Road (CR 4) to Moriah Center, northwest on Witherbee Road (CR 70) to Witherbee, then west on Tracy Road (CR 6) to the Northway and US 9 at Exit 30.

A popular alternative is to cross Lake Champlain on the Charlotte–Essex Ferry. In Charlotte, take Ferry Road (VT F5) west to the ferry dock. The ferry takes about 20 min and runs every 30 min; check the ferry schedule at www.ferries.com. Once you're in Essex, follow NY 22 to Wadhams, then take the Elizabethtown–Wadhams Road to US 9 in Elizabethtown.

COMING FROM CANADA
If you're coming from points along the northern shore of Lake Ontario, make your way to the Thousand Islands Bridge, then south on I-81 to Exit 48 in Watertown, east on NY 342, east on NY 3, east on NY 3A, then back on NY 3 to Cranberry Lake and Tupper Lake.

If you're coming from Ottawa, the best crossing is at the Ogdensburg–Prescott Bridge. Once you're across, take NY 68 to US 11 at Canton. Two options lead from here into the park: (a) south on NY 56, then east on NY 3 to Tupper Lake; or (b) east on US 11 to Potsdam, east on NY 11B, southeast on NY 458, south on NY 30 to Paul Smiths, then south on NY 86 to Saranac Lake and Lake Placid.

From Montreal, take AUT-15 south to the Lacolle–Champlain crossing. This is the largest border crossing and the delays can be considerable, with 20 min being typical. Early mornings are best, followed by late evenings. The alternatives (Rouses Point, Mooers) are less direct and usually not worth the extra time for the detour.

When to Come

Compared to the majority of the Northeast, the climate in the Adirondacks is wetter and colder than average—in fact, it's one of the coldest spots in the country. In the summer, the average daily temperatures are between 70°F and 80°F, with a range up to 25° (and as much as 30° in the High Peaks). Precipitation remains relatively constant throughout the summer at around 3"–4" per month. In general, it's wetter on the west side of the park than on the east side, and the High Peaks are colder and wetter than everywhere else.

The weather within the park can vary greatly, as conditions found online will illustrate. However, most of the current conditions that are reported at websites originate from stations located outside the park. Only a few locations, such as Old Forge and Saranac Lake, provide current conditions from within the park.

As early as April, although snow still blankets much of the region, climbing can begin at some south-facing cliffs. The Spider's Web always seems first on everyone's list, but there are plenty of other options—Hurricane,

Poke-O Slab, Potash Cliff, and Potter Mountain are great early season; see Appendix B, page 495, for more ideas). With no leaves on the trees, this is a good time to visit the harder-to-find cliffs, such as Lost Hunters, The Courthouse, or Pinnacle Mountain. Expect very wet approaches, and, for some cliffs, bring snowshoes. Optimal conditions continue until the middle of May, when the blackflies emerge.

The summer months range from perfect to hot and buggy. If it's hot, look for climbing up high (e.g., Wallface, Cascade Pass, Noonmark) or on north-facing cliffs (e.g., Avalanche Lake, Barkeater, Barton High Cliff, High Falls Crag, Cascade Cliff), or coordinate your climbing with the sun and chase the shade (Spider's Web and Upper Washbowl face toward the west; Poke-O Main Face and Chapel Pond Slab are oriented toward the east). South-facing slabs are best avoided on sunny days (e.g., Rogers Rock, Poke-O Slab). There's plenty of climbing near water (e.g., Bluff Island, Long Pond, Eagle Falls, Boquet River Crags, anything around Chapel Pond), providing ample opportunities to swim and enjoy the heat of the day (see Appendix B on page 495 for a complete list). Avoid bugs by sticking to the windy cliffs (e.g., Avalanche Pass, Poke-O Moonshine, Upper Washbowl, or Pitchoff Chimney Cliff) or those cliffs near BTI water treatment (anything near Chapel Pond). The insect population begins to decline in August.

The best months for climbing are September and October—the air is crisp and clear, all the cliffs are open, bugs are gone, snakes are hiding, summer vacationers have left, and daytime temperatures are perfect. Nights routinely dip below freezing. Even on cold days, the rock on the south-facing cliffs can be quite pleasant. As the season progresses toward winter, cliffs at lower elevations become better options (e.g., Potash Cliff, Stewart's Ledge, Shelving Rock, and Deadwater). The season continues into November with the occasional sunny day, but by Thanksgiving, it's time to break out the ice gear.

Rain and Rest Day Activities

If the rain is just starting, then the Spider's Web and King Wall stay dry longer than anywhere else. If it isn't absolutely pouring, you can go for a hike, perhaps investigating other cliffs. See Appendix B (page 495) for more ideas.

Summer recreational opportunities in the park are endless, and it seems only fitting to take advantage of what the region has to offer—mountains and lakes. You're really missing out if you haven't paddled down a remote winding bog or visited the alpine zones on the bare summits of the High Peaks.

For shopping, you can pass the time by visiting the shops in Keene Valley, Lake Placid, Lake George, and Old Forge. You can take the ferry to Burlington for shopping, restaurants, and a climbing gym.

The Keene Valley Library (518.576.4335, www.keenevalleylibrary.org) has a large collection of climbing-related materials contained in a special room in the basement, donated by John Case. It has computers, a copy machine, and free wireless high-speed Internet access. Check first, as its hours are unusual.

The Adirondack Museum at Blue Mountain Lake (518.352.7311, www.adkmuseum.org) is excellent, as is the Wild Center Natural History Museum (www.wildcenter.org, 518.359.7800) in Tupper Lake, and the Lake Placid Olympic Museum (www.whiteface.com, 518.302.5326). Historic forts are located at either end of Lake George: Fort Ticonderoga (www.fortticonderoga.org, 518.585.2821) and Fort William Henry (www.fwhmuseum.com, 518.668.5471). The Barton Garnet Mines in North River (www.garnetminetours.com, 518.251.2706) offer guided tours of this famous geologic site.

Layout of the Park

The Adirondack Park is unique in that it is a patchwork of private and public land. Out of approximately 5.8 million acres, roughly half the land is private. There is no climbing on private land unless you have the express permission of the landowner. Out of the remaining area, roughly 0.4 million acres are water (so no climbing there), and 2.5 million acres are public.

The public land is part of the New York State Forest Preserve, created in 1894 by a constitutional amendment, which requires that the lands be "forever kept as wild forest lands." There are several classifications of public land, broken down by the land's characteristics and ability to withstand use. The regulations are different for each classification. (The full set of regulations is contained in the Adirondack Park State Land Master Plan, on the Adirondack Park Agency website, www.apa.state.ny.us.) Even more confusing, each tract of land (wilderness, primitive, or otherwise) is managed according to a unit management plan (or UMP), and each one is different. (For example, climbing groups are limited in size and number of ropes in the Dix Wilderness Area but not in the High Peaks Wilderness Area.) The land classifications are as follows:

Wild Forest: Land that has a wild character but permits a higher degree of human use, such as biking, snowmobiles, and ATVs (although their use may be restricted by the UMP for the specific area).

Wilderness: Land where nature prevails and people are only visitors; land that has a primeval character, with the "imprint of man's work substantially unnoticed." Wilderness lands are the most regulated: no structures, no bikes, no motorized equipment, and tighter regulations on camping.

Primitive: Similar to wilderness but may have some inholdings (e.g., structures, roads, fire towers) or some other qualities that prevent it from meeting wilderness standards. Bikes are only allowed on existing roads and truck trails.

Intensive Use: Land where the state provides facilities for outdoor recreation, such as state campgrounds (e.g., Rogers Rock) and ski areas (e.g., Gore Mountain, Whiteface).

Where to Stay

There is a vast assortment of camping and lodging options that are simply beyond the scope of this book. Some general guidelines are offered here, with more specific options that are popular with climbers at the beginning of each chapter.

CAMPING

There is a basic set of rules for camping that apply to all forest preserve land. You can camp anywhere as long as it is 150' from a road, water, or a trail. Also, you can camp at any site designated with a yellow "Camp Here" disk. Fires are allowed using deadwood and downed wood, and you can bring pets as long they are under your control.

Groups up to 10 people can camp without a permit for up to three nights, beyond which a permit is required. Groups larger than 10 require a permit regardless of the length of stay. Camping is limited to two weeks at any location. Permits are obtained by calling the Forest Ranger Office in Ray Brook (518.897.1300) during business hours.

For disposal of human waste, the DEC encourages the use of the "leave no trace" principles (www.lnt.org)—e.g., 200' from a stream, buried 6"–8", toilet paper in the hole.

COMMANDO CAMPING

"Commando camping" is illegal camping, and every climber does it—sleeping at trailheads, pullouts, and other unsanctioned spots. The rangers know that climbers like to get an early start and probably won't bother you if you are discreetly sleeping a few hours *in your vehicle* before heading out at first light. Set up a tent, though, and you're asking for trouble. If you need to set up a tent or roll out a sleeping bag, then wander off 150' into the woods.

LODGING

A good resource for finding lodging is the Adirondack Regional Tourism Council (www.visitadirondacks.com). Its website has a search feature that allows you to narrow choices by a variety of criteria, including location and price.

The Adirondack Climbing Experience

Most of the cliffs in this guidebook have solid, climbable rock, but every cliff has its share of grunge—lichen; moss; pesky cedars; and grassy, dirt-filled cracks. The routes that see traffic stay cleaner, but even so, the Adirondacks have a way of reclaiming routes with alarming speed. Generally speaking, north- and west-facing cliffs are the dirtiest. For routes that aren't as well traveled, you should carry a wire brush to clean off the occasional key hold. For harder routes, you may want to inspect the line beforehand and do some cleaning. A nut tool for the leader is essential for excavating protection placements.

Approaches to cliffs in this guide can be a challenge, both from the perspective of navigation and from the sheer brutality of the bushwhack. For remote cliffs, a map and compass are essential and, for the gadget-minded, a GPS (or smartphone with GPS). Make sure you know how to use them. Unless you want scars, pants and a long-sleeved shirt should be considered for the more intense bushwhacks.

In the summer, there are the additional hazards of heat and insects. For the heat, check the aspect of the cliff so that you can avoid direct sun. For insects, a good repellent is essential; everyone has his or her own preference, but the ones with DEET tend to work longer. When the bugs are really bad, a long-sleeved shirt, pants, and thin socks work well. A head net is essential, especially for the belayer. The climate and terrain vary considerably in the park, as do the hatching schedules, so while climbers at Crane Mountain are hiding beneath head nets, those at the Spider's Web are climbing shirtless.

Black bears can be an issue when camping in the backcountry. Bear canisters are required for overnight camping in the High Peaks Wilderness Area. Outside that area, you'll still want to hang your food out of reach of bears. Poisonous snakes are a concern at some cliffs (see below), especially those around Lake George, and are noted in the cliff descriptions.

For remote climbs, hydration is very important, and you'll probably want more than you're willing to carry. Giardia bacteria have contaminated most of the water in the park, making it unsafe to drink without treatment. Backcountry climbers often carry a water filter or iodine tablets.

Poison ivy is a hazard at many lower-elevation cliffs, and it seems to be creeping in at the cliffs in the High Peaks as well. It's usually found in open, sunny areas near the base of cliffs and in the talus. Direct contact is required, but as little as a billionth of a gram of the oil is all that is needed to cause a rash, so know how to identify it and don't rub against it. The presence of poison ivy is noted in the cliff descriptions.

The Adirondack Rack: An "Adirondack rack" isn't all that unique, although, as with any other climbing areas, special gear is occasionally needed. For most climbing, a single set of cams up to 3.5", nuts, and microcams should suffice. For longer routes, double up on the cams. Specialized hardware includes larger cams (up to 6" for some of the off widths), slider nuts (especially at Rogers Rock), and RPs (especially at Poke-O).

Climbing and Endangered Species

PEREGRINE FALCONS

Peregrine sightings are one of the true pleasures of climbing in the Adirondacks. These majestic crow-sized falcons can be seen soaring around cliffs, diving at speeds up to 180 mph in pursuit of prey, transferring food midair, and performing aerial acrobatics during their courtship. They mate for life and often return to the same nesting site year after year, with a life span as long as 20 years. The peregrine population was all but wiped out due to exposure to DDT and other chemicals, and they were gone from the region by 1965.

Peregrine falcons returned to the Adirondacks as nesting birds in 1985, after an intensive, statewide restoration program. There are now over two dozen nesting pairs of peregrines present in the Adirondack region, which are closely monitored annually by the Department of Environmental Conservation (DEC) and by volunteer climbers and others. Rock climbers have been a great asset in this effort and have assisted the DEC with peregrine falcon protection and management for many years now by annually monitoring favored aeries (nesting sites) for occupancy; reporting new nest locations; advising on access points, climbing route designations, and cliff closures; and assisting with the occasional recovery of unhatched eggs or banding of young. Periodic cliff closures at some of the most popular climbing and nesting sites have been well respected and are essential to the successful nesting of the falcons. A single incidence of disturbance during the most sensitive period of incubation, or when a nestling is vulnerable to chilling, predation, or falling off the ledge before it can fly, can make all the difference between a successful and an unsuccessful nesting season.

In addition to heeding closure postings, the DEC asks that while climbers are climbing on open routes, they avoid disturbing peregrine falcons, not only for the sake of the peregrines but for climber safety as well. Peregrine falcons defend their nesting territories aggressively, vocalizing, circling overhead, and often diving at and even striking people (and predators) with their sharp talons. If you encounter such aggressive peregrine behavior, you should abandon your climb and report the incident to the DEC. The closures are generally posted on signs at trailheads, on approach paths used by climbers, and sometimes at the base of the cliffs, but consult the DEC website for more complete information. The closures sometimes apply to an entire cliff, or for larger cliffs like Poke-O, the signs may indicate a subsection of a cliff. All climbing activities are prohibited within the closed area. Access to the cliff or area immediately below for any purpose is prohibited when the area is closed, except for walking without loitering along the base to reach open areas or as otherwise specified by DEC.

The DEC makes every effort to ensure that the closures are focused on the cliff areas that affect peregrine activity and that cliffs are opened as soon as possible after the nesting season. Peregrine falcons are listed as an endangered species in New York State and are fully protected under state and federal laws. Climber assistance with this and other endangered species is vital for their continued recovery.

PETRA CLIFFS
Climbing Center & Mountaineering School
www.petracliffs.com
866-65-PETRA Burlington, Vermont
Indoor bouldering, top-roping & lead climbing
All ages & abilities; walk-ins welcome
Guided outdoor rock, ice & ski guiding;
avalanche education in VT, NY, NH and beyond

alpine
developmentkoncepts
www.alpinedevelopmentkoncepts.com
alpinedevelopmentkoncepts@gmail.com
518.524.3328
• Mountain Sports Education
• Guided Rock Climbing
• Rock Climbing Camps
• Alpine Ski Coaching
• Alpine Skiing Development Camps

ST. LAWRENCE UNIVERSITY
THIS IS YOUR CLASSROOM
St. Lawrence University Outdoor Program
Accredited courses
in outdoor leadership
and environmental
education
www.stlawu.edu/outdoor

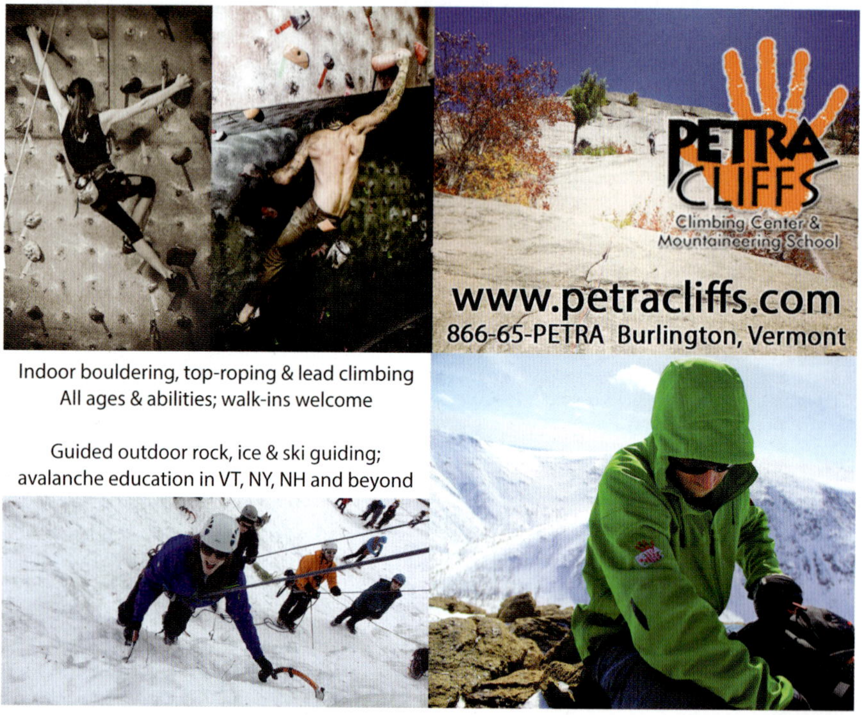

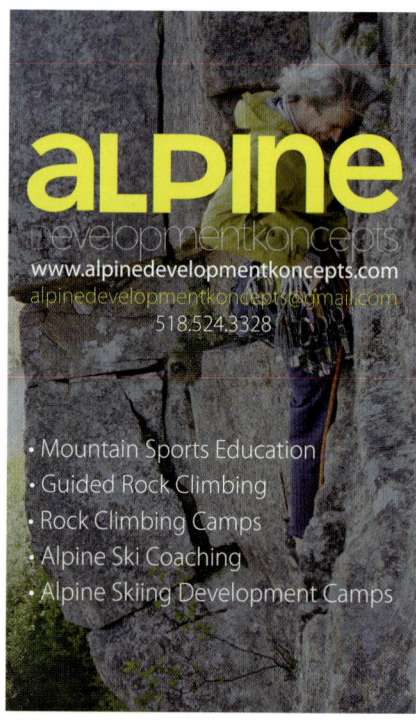

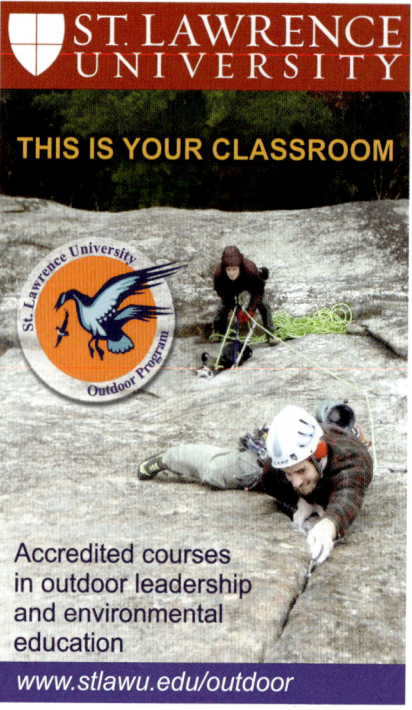

Local Climbing Practices
by Dominic Eisinger

The Adirondacks, like many other climbing areas of the world, have seen a variety of trends and styles with regard to the use of fixed protection and route preparation. A common philosophy of minimizing human impact in the Adirondack Park is shared by the Adirondack climbing community and will help ensure that we maintain our freedom, which is by its nature individualistic and free-spirited.

NEW ROUTES
If you are contemplating a new route and you can climb it from the ground up without placing fixed protection, fantastic! If the route requires a little cleaning, then so be it. If the route requires complete excavation, then keep a few things in mind. It's dirty for a reason, and it will grow back. Will it be a popular addition to the repertoire of climbs at that cliff? Will it be worth your trouble and the disruption caused by your cleaning?

The decision to place fixed protection requires further soul-searching. Fixed protection should only be placed if there *are no options* for natural protection, and for the benefit of the community as a whole. For this reason, toprope the route first and make every effort to make an informed decision. Have your friends climb it to double-check your decision. Research the history of the area: respect the style of new-route development that has occurred in that area and check with local climbers and the guidebook to make sure it has not already been climbed. Ask yourself a few questions: Is it a place others will climb, or is the route destined for obscurity? Is the route independent from its neighbors? Is the route good enough, and will it stay clean enough, to warrant the fixed protection? Can people of different body sizes reach the protection? Is it an untouched area with no signs of human influence, far from the road? How much of your motivation is driven by an ephemeral pleasure—altering the rock for your own self-interest on a marginal route that nobody will repeat? Maybe it's better left as a toprope first ascent.

ROUTE PREPARATION
Scrubbing lichen from holds, cleaning dirt from cracks for protection, breaking the occasional branch to squeeze by a tree, or removing a dangerous loose block are all accepted practices. Scrubbing an 8'-wide swath and cutting trees are not only illegal but aren't accepted by the climbing community. There's a fine line between what's necessary for climbing and what constitutes excessive behavior in the eyes of the management agencies, and we should always err on the side of minimal impact.

Keep in mind, plenty of adventure can be had by reclaiming existing high-quality routes from relentless Adirondack lichen. There is no shortage of routes that are presently too dirty to climb. The adventure of such rediscovery can fulfill an undeniable motivation for why we climb—total absorption in challenging one's ability, with mind and body coming together on a tremendous route.

FIXED ANCHORS
For existing routes, no additional protection or fixed anchors should be added without the consent of the first-ascent party. Fixed anchors have been installed by the climbing community where necessary for safety and preservation of fragile terrain and trees. When replacing or adding new anchor slings, black and gray webbing certainly blends into the background better than the bright colors of the rainbow. This is especially true at highly visible areas such as Avalanche Lake, where 100 hikers a day will see your webbing and complain.

HARDWARE
When new or replacement fixed protection is needed, use high-quality stainless-steel hardware manufactured specifically for climbing. Hardware should match the color of the rock.

Photo by Joel Dashnaw.

HERD PATHS
For popular cliffs, land managers often see "herd paths" as a good thing, as they confine impact to one place. To the extent possible, use existing herd paths and refrain from adding additional markings such as surveyor tape and reflector disks—these are litter and ruin the wilderness experience for others. If a new herd path is created, it is recommended that it be direct (easier to sight along), narrow (less invasive, better defined), and marked discreetly only with natural materials such as rock cairns.

Please respect and pay attention to preserving the special one-of-a-kind place that defines the Adirondack Park, a quality that makes climbing here so exceptional.

TIMBER RATTLESNAKES

Occasionally, another rare New York State species, the timber rattlesnake, might also be encountered while you're climbing in the Adirondacks, specifically in the Lake George or southern Lake Champlain region. The snake measures from 3' to 4.5' and has a broad triangular head. Two color phases are commonly found: a yellow phase, which has black or dark brown crossbands on a lighter background of yellow, and a black phase, which has dark crossbands on a dark background. The most distinctive feature is the rattle at the end of the tail, although the rattles regularly break off.

Climbers should be aware that they may encounter rattlesnakes, take appropriate safeguards to avoid them, and understand that they are fully protected as a New York State threatened species and should not be disturbed. Timber rattlesnakes are most active and likely to be encountered from mid-May until early October. The rocky talus slopes below the cliffs and open canopied basking spots above the cliffs (i.e., the areas that climbers pass through to approach a climb or descend from one) are the most problematic areas.

As a precaution, be aware of where you walk and where you set your pack down, especially around talus, bushes, and logs. Consider wearing pants and boots. If you walk at a normal pace, the snakes will generally move away, hide, or issue a warning with their rattles. Bites are rare and usually occur when a snake is cornered or surprised. Staying back 3' is usually enough to avoid a strike. In the event of a bite, immobilize the victim and transport him or her immediately to the nearest medical facility. Suction, incisions, alcohol, or drugs are no longer recommended treatments.

REPORTING

To report activity, or obtain further information on these or other New York State endangered and threatened species, visit the New York State Department of Environmental Conservation (DEC) website (www.dec.ny.gov) or call the Ray Brook Wildlife Office (518.891.1291) or the Endangered Species Unit (518.402.8863).

Opposite: Pen and Ink by Tad Welch.

Adirondack Geology 101: Rocks for Jocks

by Jason Brechko, with Dr. Don Minkel and Dr. Jim McLelland

This section illustrates how the geology of the Adirondacks has contributed to the variety of climbing that can be found in these mountains. It begins with an overview of the geologic history of the region, then follows up with a closer look at the rock that you pull on.

Don't you always wish you could go back, with all the knowledge that you have now? —Uncle Rico

Grenville Orogeny: 1.3–1.0 billion years ago: The Grenville Orogeny (*orogeny* means mountain-building event) was a series of tectonic plate collisions that happened along the east coast of ancient North America. Volcanic islands formed and crashed into the continent as the ocean floor subducted beneath it. Deeper in the earth, magma bubbled up, cooled before it reached the surface, and formed large masses of igneous anorthosite and various granites. Ultimately, on the surface, a mountain range formed that stretched from Newfoundland to Texas and was at least as magnificent as the Himalayas are today.

The colliding plates moved in from the southeast, compressed the rock (imagine the crumpling of a car in a head-on collision), and created fracture zones that run northeast to southwest, the same alignment of most of the major valleys and crags found in the park today.

These collisions distorted the rocks as they were buried up to 20 miles deep, heated to temperatures nearing 1000'C, and were put under extraordinary pressure. These extreme conditions recrystallized the igneous rocks into metamorphic rocks. Today over 99 percent of the rock in the park consists of this metamorphic rock that was formed during the Grenville Orogeny.

Erosion: 1000–560 million years ago: Mountain building stopped, and what followed was half a billion years of erosion. In that time, the 20 miles of rock that covered the metamorphic rock was washed into the ocean, and the Adirondack region rose from the released pressure, much like a spring-loaded dish tray at a buffet table, bringing the metamorphic rock to the surface. While it is staggering to think that the rock you climb on is a billion years old, it is mind-blowing to imagine 20 miles of rock being worn away. Erosion continued until most of the east coast of ancient North America was below sea level.

Deposition: 560–450 million years ago: The region was a seafloor that was getting buried by thousands of feet of sedimentary rocks. Nobody was climbing during this period because the region was underwater, the good rock was buried, and terrestrial life did not yet exist.

Faulting: 450–250 million years ago: A second series of continental collisions formed the neighboring Appalachians Ranges (the Taconic, Green, and White Mountains). In all likelihood, the Taconic Orogeny had the greatest impact on the Adirondacks by reactivating the ancient Grenville fracture zones and further weakening the rock.

When the continents pulled apart, long sections of rock in the southeastern and eastern Adirondacks sank along the fracture zones. Today, Lake George sits in one of these sunken (graben) blocks. The high (horst) blocks on either side of the lake form the cliffs of Rogers Rock and Pilot Knob.

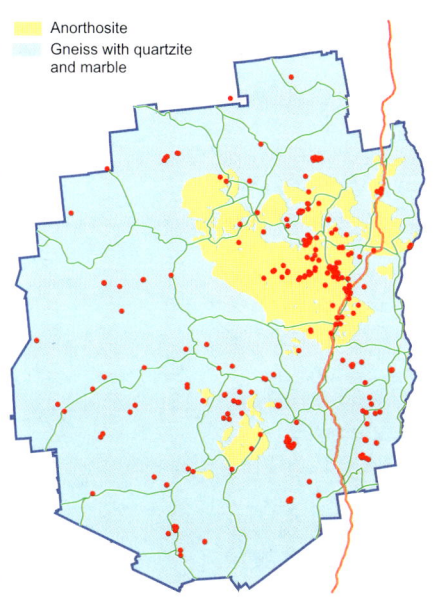

Uplift: 250–1 million years ago: While the Appalachians stood tall to the east, and the dinosaurs played their game, the Adirondack region was still buried by thousands of feet of sedimentary rock. The exact time of origin is still unclear, but sometime in the last 150 million years, the Adirondacks began to rise. The mechanism is also unclear, and some have suggested that a hot spot deep in the mantle, similar to Hawaii or Yellowstone, was rising beneath the Adirondacks.

Uplift resulted in steep slopes, the erosion of the sedimentary rock layer, and the unveiling of the billion-year-old metamorphic rocks. As the dome continued to rise, the metamorphic rocks were eroded along the fracture zones by water—not glaciers—to form the deep valleys found today.

Glaciation: 1 million years ago to the present day: The earth cooled and entered the Ice Age, during which at least four different continental ice sheets advanced over the Adirondacks. These 6000'-thick glaciers scraped away the soils, smoothed the slopes, and rounded the summits. Around 10,000 years ago, the glaciers melted and flooded the valleys. Evidence of these massive glaciers is everywhere: the thin soils and smooth rock slides on the mountains, and ancient lake sediments in the Lake Placid valley. Smaller valley glaciers both preceded and followed the continental glaciers. These glaciers followed the preexisting valleys and carved sharp features like the U-shaped valleys of Indian Pass, Chapel Pond Pass, and Cascade Pass, as well as the steep cirques of Gothics, Panther Gorge, and Whiteface Mountain.

Presently, permanent ice can be found in the rock crevices and talus caves of Ice Cave Mountain, Barton High Cliff, Grass Pond Mountain, and Indian Pass. The Adirondacks continue to rise, and mountain faces continue to slide.

Go find a cliff, identify the rock, and test if it's good for climbing

All of the rock climbing is on metamorphic rocks, with a single exception (discussed below). To the climber, most Adirondack rock is either meta-anorthosite or gneiss. Since geologists often refer to metamorphic rocks by their original igneous name, we, too, will call it anorthosite.

ANORTHOSITE: HIGH PEAKS AREA, SNOWY MOUNTAIN AREA

Formation: Magma solidified deep beneath the surface. Extreme pressure metamorphosed the resulting rock a billion years ago.

Characteristics: Green/gray in color when freshly exposed, darkens when exposed to air and biological activity. Composed largely of the mineral calcium feldspar and forms crystals a centimeter or larger in size. The crystals dissolve at different rates and create a very rough surface that is great for friction but bad for knuckles. Often it is these large crystals that enable a steep face to be climbed at a moderate grade.

Anorthosite is often called "moon rock," as it is nearly identical to the rock found in the light-colored regions of the moon. At times, anorthosite can be riddled with divots, grooves, and ridges. However, these textures can also be found in gneiss. The neat "moon rock" features that grace many of the cliffs are a result of different minerals in the rock dissolving at different rates, and this is not restricted to any particular rock type.

Anorthosite is a very massive rock, meaning it is devoid of cracks. This explains the scantily protected routes of the High Peaks and Snowy Mountain. This is in contrast to the fracture-zone cliffs of Chapel Pond Pass, where tectonic activity has produced an abundance of cracks in the anorthosite; the cracks, in turn, have produced the associated loose rock.

GNEISS: EVERYWHERE ELSE

Formation: Deep burial of rocks, during continental collisions, results in heat and pressure that causes metamorphism. Gneiss can form from sedimentary rocks (sandstone and limestone) or igneous rocks (charnokite and granite).

Characteristics: Smaller crystals make gneiss smoother in texture than anorthosite. The minerals in gneiss recrystallize into narrow bands that dissolve to form grooves and ridges, like the rails found at The Brain, in the Lake George region.

In the Lake George and Indian Lake regions, the gneiss alternates with layers of quartzite (ancient sandstone) or marble (ancient limestone). Since these rocks dissolve at different rates, a route that crosses these layers will likely span a long, horizontal roof.

IGNEOUS: DIKES AND SILLS

Formation: Liquid magma was thrust into the surrounding rock, where it solidified and formed vertical (dike) and horizontal (sill) intrusions. All these intrusions occurred after the Grenville Orogeny and were never metamorphosed.

Characteristics: The dark intrusions are typically basalt, and the white ones are largely composed of quartz. Intrusions usually fracture and dissolve more easily than the metamorphic rock through which they pass. As they erode, the intrusions create ledge systems capped by roofs (sills), and vertical chimneys (dikes). Poke-O Moonshine is littered with examples of both types of intrusions. The Trap Dike is another example of the rapid weathering of the weaker igneous intrusion.

BIBLIOGRAPHY

Isachsen, Y. W., E. Landing, J. M. Lauber, L. V. Rickard, and W. B. Rogers, eds. *Geology of New York State: A Simplified Account.* 2nd ed. New York State Geological Survey, New York State Museum, 2000.
    McLelland, James. "Rock of Ages." *Adirondack Life,* Jul–Aug 2001, pp. 64–69.
    Van Diver, Bradford B., PhD. *Roadside Geology of New York.* Mountain Press Publishing Company, 1997.
    Van Diver, Bradford B., PhD. *Rocks and Routes of the North Country.* W. F. Humphrey Press, 1976.

Using This Guidebook

The park has been divided into 11, and split into two volumes for convenience. The master map in the front of the book will orient you to the various regions and how they are split into the two volumes. Each region begins with information specific to that region, including a locator map, crag planning table, general driving directions, amenities, camping and lodging options, common trailheads, and access issues.

The fundamental organizational unit of the book is the cliff (a continuous face of open rock), and a region is simply a collection of cliffs within the same geographic area. Cliffs are sometimes organized into groups—for instance, when several cliffs are referred to by a single name or share a common approach or trailhead, such as the Beer Walls. To assist in locating routes along the base of a cliff, a cliff is often divided into named sections—for example, Poke-O is divided into 15 sections, including The Waterfall, Luther Wall, Nose Apron, and so forth.

Cliff Descriptions

Each cliff has a summary table that provides a quick overview of the cliff with the following information:

Location: Brief description of the cliff's location and from where it is approached.

Aspect: Direction in which the cliff faces.

Height: Height of the cliff in feet (not the length of the longest route).

Quality: 0 to 5 stars, with 5 stars being the best.

Approach: Length (in time) of the approach and difficulty.

Easy	A short approach, not strenuous, with simple navigation.
Moderate	Involves some bushwhacking, requires some compass work, and is moderately strenuous.
Difficult	Usually long, very strenuous, and can involve blind bushwhacking with complex orienteering.

Summary: A very brief description of the cliff.

Route Table: Distribution of free-climbing grades at a cliff, including the total number of routes at the cliff. Each grade has two bars: the red bar shows the total routes of that grade, and the gold bar shows how many of these are high quality (three stars or above). The total number of routes listed in this summary includes aid routes and uncompleted projects, so the numbers may not add up.

The summary table is followed by some or all of these entries:

Description: In-depth discussion of the cliff, what the rock is like, the type of climbing, and other notes.

History: Brief discussion of the history of climbing on that cliff.

Camping: Options for cliffs commonly visited as an overnight (such as Wallface) or ones with noteworthy camping nearby.

Directions: How to get to the cliff, including driving directions to the trailhead and a description of the hiking approach.

Driving directions are given from easy-to-find landmarks, like an exit on the Northway (I-87) or a prominent town or road intersection. At the point from which mile markers begin, the expression "(0.0 mile)" appears in the text. Subsequent mileages are provided in the text and increase from that starting location. Mileages are from our own car odometers, and since odometer readings can be affected by tire size and whatnot, you should expect some minor deviations.

Official designations are used for road names: "I" for an interstate, "US" for a U.S. route, "NY" for a New York State route, and "CR" for a county route. Some roads have names and route numbers, both of which are given. Some roads have multiple designations, such as when a road crosses into an adjacent county, and are often noted.

Hiking distances are often described in terms of time rather than mileage. This is obviously subjective, but it is difficult to quantify a bushwhack by mileage. The approach times assume a reasonably fit individual hiking at a moderate pace with no breaks. The directions "left" and "right" are provided with respect to the direction of travel. Times are given in hours (abbreviated "hr") and minutes (abbreviated "min"), as in "1 hr 20 min." Times are often accumulated from a starting point, marked by the expression "(0 hr 0 min)" in the text.

Descent Options: Lists the various walk-off or rappel descents for the cliff, when known. Some routes have their own descents, which are indicated in the route description.

Maps

Approach maps are provided for cliffs with involved or obscure approaches. These maps are usually oriented with true north at the top and are created to scale. Magnetic north is 14° west of true north. The maps in this book differ from USGS (United States Geological Survey) maps. First, the topographical lines are de-emphasized to allow you to focus on other landmarks while still getting a sense of the terrain. Second, the contours aren't labeled, but most maps use a contour interval of 6 m. Third, only features that are needed to get oriented and find the cliff are included, reducing the clutter found on the USGS maps.

> **Download Free Topos**
>
> If you're tempted to photocopy the topos, maps, and aerial photos—don't bother. You can download many of these in Adobe Acrobat PDF file format format from www.adirondackrock.com.
>
> Print them, fold them, shove them in your pocket, and take them up routes. There is no need to carry this heavy book up routes, tear pages out, or damage the spine of this book on a photocopier. Best of all, you can print them as large as you want.

A key to map symbols is provided on the inside back cover of the book.

Route Descriptions

The routes on a cliff are numbered and are always described from left to right, without exception. Admittedly, this is awkward for some cliffs, like those whose approach trail reaches the right end of the cliff. In these cases, you'll simply have to flip backward as you walk to the left. But at least you can open to any page and be sure of the orientation. The route numbers correspond to those used in the cliff photos and topos.

The typical entry for a route begins with a route heading with the route name, difficulty grade, protection rating, length, and quality. After the heading are entries for the start, each pitch (numbered P1, P2, and so on), gear list (if any), descent options, history, and first-ascent information. A difficulty rating, protection rating, and length are provided for each pitch. In some instances, this information wasn't available and is omitted. Toprope routes aren't described with the same level of detail and are shown in paragraph form, as are routes where information is scarce or where you can wander anywhere.

NCCS Grades

The National Climbing Classification System (NCCS), or commitment grade, indicates the time investment required for an average party to ascend the route. The scale goes from 1 to 7 and is always listed in roman numerals, I to VII.

The vast majority of the routes in the Adirondacks are grade I or II, which implies that they are less than five pitches in length and close to the road—not very committing. Many routes at Poke-O Moonshine, Moss Cliff, and Wallface are grade III—sustained and serious undertakings that can take the entire day to complete. Grade IV routes take a full day and are at least eight pitches in length with sustained and difficult climbing and may involve sections of aid climbing. There are several grade-IV routes, all on Wallface; these are the only routes in this guidebook shown with a commitment grade in the route heading.

There are no V, VI, or VII routes in the park.

Difficulty Ratings

The class system compares the technical difficulty of the hardest section of each climb. These grades assume dry conditions, clean rock, and favorable weather. At the least, the class system can offer a sense of difficulty relative to other sections for the climb. There are six classes: 1st class is hiking on and off trail; 2nd class is hiking on rough trails and low-angle slides; 3rd class is scrambling with exposure using holds, where a fall would be dangerous; 4th class is scrambling with exposure, where an unroped fall would be fatal; 5th class is technical free climbing using a rope for safety, further divided using the Yosemite Decimal System (discussed below); and 6th class is aid climbing, also further divided into an aid rating.

This book is concerned almost exclusively with 5th class climbing, although some noteworthy 4th class scrambles and 6th class aid routes are included.

Yosemite Decimal System (YDS): Routes and individual pitches are given difficulty ratings using the Yosemite Decimal System. The grades from 5.0 through 5.9 are further modified with a + or - for those pitches that are thought to be hard or easy for their grade. The grades 5.10 and above are subdivided with letter grades: a, b, c, and d (e.g., 5.11b).

The grade of a route is often that of the most difficult move on the most difficult pitch. For instance, P1 of Gamesmanship at Poke-O Moonshine has a short 5.8 crux move at the bottom, then decent rests for the remainder of the pitch, making the overall grade 5.8. As routes become harder, steeper, and more sustained, pump becomes an issue and is factored into the grade. For example, On The Loose at Spider's Web has no move harder than 5.9, but the sustained and pumpy nature of the climbing warrants a grade of 5.10a.

22

Older routes were not originally reported with letter grades; when no modern information is available for a route 5.10 or above, then the grade is shown without the letter subdivisions. Some routes were reported without pitch-by-pitch difficulty ratings, and in a few cases, we've simply omitted the pitch grades until this information becomes available.

Difficulty grades vary with the type of climbing. There is almost no correlation between a 5.10 crack climb and a 5.10 slab. Further, ratings are often relative to other routes on the cliff; for example, many believe Rogers Rock to have its own rating system.

Finally, ratings are highly subjective and provoke endless debate. The grades in this guide are often the result of our own personal experience and a consensus of other climbers. However, sometimes we have to rely on the raw data submitted by others with no verification. If the route feels too difficult and you cannot adequately protect it, then retreat and come back another day.

DON'T LET THE DIFFICULTY RATING LULL YOU INTO A FALSE SENSE OF SECURITY.

A grade-conversion chart, with international scales, is provided in Appendix A (page 494).

AID RATINGS

The rating of an aid pitch considers both the difficulty of making a protection placement and the fall potential if the placement were to fail. The grades in the park range from A0 to A4 and are further modified with a + or - for those pitches that are thought to be hard or easy for their grade. The sophistication of aid-climbing equipment increases as the grade increases. A climber can stand in slings on an A0 or A1 pitch but would need aiders, daisy chains, and hooks for A2 and harder. When a pitch has been climbed without using a hammer (i.e., no pitons, bashies, or rivets), then a C (for clean placement) is substituted for the A.

- A0 Pulling on a piece of protection, tension on rope, pendulums.
- A1 Aid on solid placements, including small wires and cams.
- A2 Awkward placements, or a few body-weight placements above solid placements.
- A3 Hooking, rivets, and thin pitons with a 30' fall potential.
- A4 Extreme aid, big fall potential, and the threat of hitting an obstacle.

PROTECTION RATINGS

Routes and individual pitches are given the now-standard protection ratings (G, PG, R, X). The ratings assume that you know how to place gear and have placed it correctly, that you have proper-sized gear at the right moment, and that you take advantage of the protection opportunities that are available. Protection ratings provide no information on how difficult or strenuous it may be to place protection, but rather the security offered by the placements.

- G   Good protection, closely spaced; small falls possible.
- PG Fair protection; moderate falls possible but not likely to result in serious injury.
- R   Poor protection with long falls possible; injury likely if you fall from the wrong place. Some well-protected routes have unfortunate ledge positions where even a short fall can be injurious; these get R ratings as well. An R rating can be due to a lack of gear or poor quality of the rock into which gear is placed.
- X   No protection; ground fall possible, with death likely if you fall from the wrong place.

Needless to say, you should be very solid at the grade before heading up an R- or X-rated route. Some excellent routes have no protection and are perhaps better recommended as a toprope.

A route's protection rating is that of the most difficult pitch. For R and X routes, we have attempted to determine the difficulty of the section of unprotected climbing, and, when known, the protection rating is further qualified. For example, the rating of **Space Walk** is "5.9 G (5.7 X)," which means that the most difficult climbing is 5.9 with good protection, but there's a serious fall potential in a 5.7 section. If the climb says, for example, "5.10b R," then you should assume the unprotected climbing is in a 5.10b section.

Protection ratings vary with the type of climbing. On a slab, falling on an R or X route may not be lethal but is certain to be an unpleasant, skin-abrading affair that should be avoided. On these types of routes, R and X are more an indication of how frequently you can place protection and the length of a potential fall rather than how messed up you'll be after the fall.

If you are unable to arrange adequate protection, then **DON'T ASSUME IT GETS BETTER** just because this guidebook doesn't give it an R or X rating. Every route is potentially an R or X route if, for example, you skip opportunities for protection, get off route, place your protection poorly, or fixed protection fails. Retreat and come back another day.

Protection ratings are often subject to other factors, like body height, having the right gear at the right time, and so forth. Critical placements, when known, are often noted in the route descriptions.

Quality Ratings

We have adopted a five-star system for rating routes and cliffs. The more stars, the better. A rough translation is as follows:

No stars: Not recommended. Either it's a nasty route, or we simply don't know and can't find anyone who's climbed it. Often a route is too dirty to climb and might otherwise be recommended if it were cleaned.

- ★ Worth doing if you're at the crag.
- ★★ Should do it if you're at the crag.
- ★★★ Good route for the cliff, worth traveling to the crag for this route.
- ★★★★ Excellent route, a classic.
- ★★★★★ Highly recommended, one of the best in the park.

The criteria for a "good" route are very subjective and make for great debate. Our criteria are based on consideration of the following: consensus from other climbers, quality of the movement, quality of the rock, position, exposure, views, history, comfortable belays, and general atmosphere at the cliff. An average route next to a beautiful swimming hole would get a couple of stars, whereas an average route at the end of a long bushwhack with no views would receive fewer stars.

Finding the Start of a Route

Route starts are described relative to easy-to-locate features along the base of a cliff. We avoid the syndrome in which every route is described relative to some other route; relative distances between routes are important and we've included those measurements, but rarely are those measurements the only way to locate a route. Major features include obvious corners, large boulders, low roofs, or anything that is permanent and readily recognized. We avoid using vegetation (e.g., the "double-trunked oak tree") as the only way to locate a route, since this tends to change over time.

Route locations often refer to the terrain along the base of the cliff. The term *lowest point on the cliff* refers to where the terrain is at its lowest point, and moving in either direction along the base involves going uphill. Another terrain term is the *cone-shaped dirt slope*, where the ground spills out from an abrupt, high indentation along the base of the cliff.

Left and Right

In route descriptions, the terms *left* and *right* are from a climber's perspective while facing the rock. In approach descriptions, however, *left* and *right* are from a hiker's perspective and are referenced from the direction of travel. When an approach meets the cliff, these terms switch from a hiker's perspective to that of the climber. If there is any ambiguity, the terms are further qualified by a compass direction or by some other means. The terms become especially confusing when a climber finishes a route, then turns around to descend a gully, facing downhill like a skier. At these times, *left* and *right* are further qualified with *(climber's)* or *(skier's)*, depending on whether you're facing the rock or facing downhill.

Other Climbing Terms

We use a collection of standard climbing terms to describe routes. Some of the important ones are listed here.

OVERHANGS

For overhangs, we've loosely adopted the terminology used by Dick Williams,[1] which takes the size of the feature into account:

overhang: A small overhang that protrudes 2' or less.
ceiling: A medium-sized overhang, roughly between 2' and 6'.
roof: A large overhang deeper than 6'.

CORNERS

There are many types of corners, and the terminology depends on the angle of the corner.
corner: The generic term *corner* refers to one whose angle is roughly 90°. A corner must face either left or right.
open book: A corner whose angle is obviously larger than 90°. An open book by itself faces out but can also be qualified as left- or right-facing.
V-corner: A corner whose angle is obviously less than 90°. A V-corner by itself faces out but can also be qualified as left- or right-facing.

---

[1] Dick Williams, *The Climber's Guide to the Shawangunks* (2004).

CRACKS
Cracks vary from very narrow seams to chimney.
crack: A generic crack that could be any size.
seam: A faint crack that may take small protection, but you can't get your fingers in.
tips crack: A crack into which only the tips of your fingers can be inserted.
fingercrack: A crack that accepts fingers.
handcrack: A crack that accepts a hand.
fistcrack: A crack that accepts a fist.
off-width crack: A crack larger than your fist but smaller than your body.
chimney: A crack into which you can squeeze some or all of your body.
stem-box: A very wide chimney that is bridged with your legs.

LEDGES AND EDGES
Ledges vary from tiny edges to larger spacious forested terraces.
edge: A small edge, part of the rock face, that you can grab or stand on. An edge by itself is horizontal but can also be qualified as left- or right-facing.
rail: A long edge that you can shuffle your hands along.
flake: Same as an edge, but it's detached from the main rock face (i.e., there is space separating it from the primary surface of the rock).
ledge: A larger horizontal on which you can shuffle or walk.
ramp: A ledge that rises left or right. As a ramp steepens, it eventually becomes a leaning corner.
terrace: A very large ledge. Sometimes you can unrope and walk around on a terrace.

POCKETS
Pockets can vary from smaller than a fingertip to room-sized voids.
divot: A shallow indentation.
pocket: Will accept a finger.
hueco: Will accept a hand.
pod: Will accept an arm or more.

Variations
Routes sometimes have alternate sections or pitches. A variation tag, such as "(V1)," appears within the route description at the exact point where the variation begins. Variations are described after the normal route and are identified with the same tag. The difficulty rating of a variation applies only to the climbing on that variation, not to the entire pitch as climbed with that variation.

Gear Suggestions
When known, some routes have gear suggestions—for example: To 3", 2 ea 0.5"–0.75". This means a standard rack that covers placements up to 3", with double cams in the range between 0.5" and 0.75". (The "ea" means "each.") You should always use your own judgment when selecting gear, but our recommendations can help you decide what to haul in to those remote cliffs. Some routes have brand-specific gear beta offered by the first ascent party, which we've preserved in some cases.

Pitches entirely protected by fixed gear are marked with a solid blue circle ● before the P1 or V1 entry. The Adirondacks has precious few sport routes, and those with a blue dot come close. Be warned that despite having entirely fixed protection, many Adirondack routes can have dangerous runouts. For example, **Bill Route** (5.6+) at Roger's Rock is entirely bolt-protected, but has 30' runouts. The Adirondacks has its own style of "sport" routes. Older routes were often climbed ground up, meaning that the leader climbed to the next stance before drilling, creating routes with substantial runouts. Also, fixed protection is used as a last resort, and only if no natural placements are possible. Hence, there are relatively few pure sport routes.

There are many routes that come oh-so-close to being a "sport" route, but have an optional or required trad placement. These pitches are marked with a hollow blue circle ◉ before the P1 or V1 entry, and the placements are mentioned in the gear list.

History and First Ascents
We believe that the history of a route adds an important perspective for those who follow. For this reason, each route has its own first-ascent information and occasionally a short history section. A historical summary for each cliff is also often provided. At a minimum, it adds an interesting human element to the route descriptions.

Route reporting is based on an honor system: if somebody says he or she did something, then, unless there's some obvious reason not to, we assume the claim is accurate. The first ascentionist names the route and provides the original description, difficulty rating, and other route details. (The difficulty rating may be adjusted by us or by community consensus.) Climbers are generally an agreeable lot, but even so, due to the lack of reporting, there are cases in which a route is known locally by one name but, upon further inquiry, it turns out that it was done years earlier and named something different. In these cases, the earlier name is used, and the more common local name is listed as an "aka" (also known as).

The first ascent (or "FA") of a route, when known, is provided at the end of each description. The date is given (as specific as is known) as well as the first-ascent party, listed in the order provided by the first-ascent party, which most often begins with the person who led the crux pitch. If the party shared equally in the climb, then we assume they've worked that out before submitting the route. A first free ascent (or "FFA") is listed when the first ascent is known to have been on aid. The term *as climbed by* (or "ACB") is used when the first-ascent party isn't sure if their ascent is the first, perhaps because they found some evidence of earlier passage (e.g., old pitons, slings on trees).

GPS Coordinates

This book contains GPS coordinates for every cliff and most parking areas. The coordinates are provided in UTM NAD-83 format. For example, the coordinate **619271,4917806** is UTM zone 18T (the entire park is in this zone), the x-axis (called "easting") 619271, and the y-axis (called "northing") 4917806. Coordinates are listed in the text next to the places to which they apply.

UTM coordinates are x,y values in a square grid of meters. They are easy to understand and use in equations; there's no degrees, minutes, seconds, or decimal values. The x and y values are in the same units (meters) in a square grid, not spherical polar coordinates. For example, **619272,4917806** is one meter to the right of **619271,4917806**.

With a handheld GPS system, these coordinates can be used to assist in blind bushwhacking to remote cliffs. GPS coordinates can often be used with a car navigation system to help reach trailheads. The directions provided in this book do not rely on these coordinates; they are presented only for those who prefer using these tools. Be aware that when you're bushwhacking in a thick forest canopy, a GPS will lose its signal, rendering it useless. Navigating with a GPS almost always requires a compass as a backup.

GPS coordinates can also be used as an adjunct to other tools. The following tricks are particularly useful for planning trips into the Adirondack backcountry.

USGS Maps (www.adirondackrock.com/map.htm): On the maps page, type in the UTM coordinate to see a USGS topographical map with the coordinate centered.

Google Maps (maps.google.com): Convert the coordinate to decimal latitude/longitude (e.g., 44.40372269709332, -73.50216000198026), then type the comma-separated pair into Google Maps to display a map centered on that coordinate. The same feature is available at Bing Maps (www.bing.com/maps). There are plenty of online tools that perform UTM coordinate conversion, including the Adirondack Rock web site (www.adirondackrock.com/map.htm).

KML file (/www.adirondackrock.com/cliffs.kml): The coordinates for all of the cliffs in this book are available in a KML file, a file used to display geographic data in earth browsers. Type the complete URL of the KML file into Google Maps to see a map of the entire Adirondack Park with markers for each cliff. This file can also be downloaded to your computer, then opened in Google Earth, allowing you to interactively browse the cliffs in the whole park.

SMARTPHONES

The popularity of smartphones with GPS has simplified backcountry navigation. Some popular apps are Topo Maps (by Philip Endicott, www.topomapsapp.com) and Gaia GPS (www.gaiagps.com). With these apps you can see your location on a USGS map, input GPS coordinates from this book, and navigate to them using the phone as a compass. Just like a normal GPS, though, watch the battery and your GPS signal in the forest canopy. Always carry a compass as a backup.

Cliff Photos and Topos

> Be sure to check out the free topos available on www.adirondackrock.com.

Line diagrams (or "topos") are included for many cliffs to assist in finding and following routes, and to help you better understand the detailed terrain, fixed gear, and the spatial relationships among routes. With few exceptions, these diagrams were created from aerial photos and are drawn to scale.

A photo can sometimes be an effective tool for orienting yourself to a cliff, so we've included many cliff photos overlaid with route lines. For cliffs with a large number of climbs, such as Poke-O, we've included both a cliff photo with a few route lines (enough to get oriented, but limited to avoid obscuring the cliff features in the photo) and an accompanying comprehensive topo that was drawn from the same photo.

A key to topo symbols is provided on the inside back cover of the book.

Conduct

We climbers tend to be responsible land users with a full appreciation for the environment in which we play. With our expanding numbers and the increased scrutiny of land managers, it is imperative that we continue to portray ourselves favorably to the outside world and minimize the petty squabbles that plague other climbing centers.

The Department of Environmental Conservation (DEC) somewhat controls our conduct with general rules that prohibit cutting of vegetation and defacement of rock. The DEC also limits group size and restricts camping. This section adds to the formal rules with the following suggested behaviors:

Safety: First and foremost, don't get hurt. Nothing inhibits climbing freedoms more than the public's perception of irresponsible land users who make poor decisions and endanger others. If you see your fellow climbers make errors that affect their safety or endanger others, then speak up respectfully and offer to help.

Minimize your impact: The impact of the climbing community is most noticeable at the base of cliffs, so make every attempt to tread lightly. Avoid "pack dumps" that force everyone else to tromp off trail around your stuff. Stay on the established herd paths. Rappel from existing fixed anchors to avoid damage to the fragile cliff-top environment.

The Leave No Trace Center for Outdoor Ethics (www.lnt.org) is a nonprofit organization committed to minimizing environmental impacts by recreationists. Their tenets and commonsense guidelines are: (a) plan ahead and prepare, (b) travel and camp on durable surfaces, (c) dispose of waste properly, (d) leave what you find, (e) minimize campfire impacts, (f) respect wildlife, and (g) be considerate of other visitors.

Litter: Pack out what you pack in, and pick up the careless litter of others. If you smoke, take your butts with you.

Noise: The cliff is a shared environment where people go to enjoy the wilderness, so keep your voice down and shouting to a minimum. If you choose to bring music to the cliff, keep it to yourself and use headphones. At the few crags with cell-phone reception, keep your calls short and quiet. Turn off your ringer.

Beta: Don't offer unsolicited climbing beta. For many people, part of the game is figuring out the moves for themselves. Don't assume that someone is going to welcome your telling him or her how to do a problem.

Red tagging: On newer cliffs sometimes you'll find climbs with a small red tag on the first piece of fixed gear. This marks a new route that is somebody's active project. Ask around and find out more before jumping on it.

Courtesy: Be respectful of the climbers around you. Don't step on their ropes or kick their gear. If you have a pet, keep it under control and prevent it from stepping on the ropes and gear of others. If your intended route is occupied, then make a polite inquiry. While you're waiting, climb something nearby until they're finished. This does, however, mean you've given up your spot—no reserving routes.

If people are waiting for the route that you occupy, be accommodating and get on with your climb.

Passing: For longer routes, let faster teams pass you. You won't feel pressured, and the party behind won't get antsy. If you're the faster party, be patient and polite, and pass at a point that doesn't endanger others.

Rappelling: If you're rappelling, clearly yell "ROPE!" listen for a response, then throw your rope. If others are below you, they have priority—make sure you have their attention and permission before you throw. Use established fixed anchors when available and deemed safe. Avoid rappelling directly from trees, as repeated use kills a tree, especially birches. Instead, use dark-colored webbing and rappel rings. There are many options for rappel rings, the best being the stainless-steel rings made for climbing, and the cheapest being links of 7000-lb chain.

Toproping: Topropers have the same right to climb a route as do leaders, but nobody has the right to monopolize a route. If you're camped out on a route, be willing to share or move your rope aside if somebody wants to lead it. Don't leave your ropes unattended to reserve a route.

Avoid toproping through existing rappel anchors, and never toprope through webbing. Create your own anchor following best practices for anchor building. At fixed anchors, attach your own quickdraws to the anchor. Not only does this put the wear on your gear, but it allows other parties to share the anchor.

At cliff tops, use extreme care not to dislodge loose rock. Always assume there are people below you.

Chalk and brushing: If you use chalk, try not to overdo it. If you add tick marks, be sure to clean them off afterward. Use a nylon brush to remove excess chalk. Nylon brushes don't polish the holds as much as metal brushes do.

Landowner permission: If you want to climb on a cliff on private land, then get the landowner's permission. In general, landowners in the Adirondacks are accommodating, but only if you ask first. Some approaches in this guidebook cross private land. If you encounter the landowner, don't run away. Be respectful, listen, and do what he or she says.

Emergencies: Offer to help in the event of an emergency.

Adirondack Climbing Chronology

1850: Robert Clarke and Alexander Ralph climbed the **Trap Dike** on Mt Colden in 1 hr 30 min from Avalanche Lake (vol. 1, 516).

1896: Newell Martin and Milford Hathaway climbed the **South Face** of Gothics, one of the earliest technical rock climbs in the United States, leaving an undershirt fastened high on the rock to mark their passage.

1916: John Case, born in 1892, vacationed around Keene Valley and roped up at Indian Head with his wife, introducing modern rock climbing to the Adirondacks. He was the former president of the American Alpine Club, and, although he used belay techniques, he felt that piton use was unsporting.

1920: Henry Ives Baldwin, Eastburn Smith, and George B. Happ ascended Wallface via a zigzag line surmised to be the **Case Route**, using a rope and belaying (vol. 1, 459).

1928: Jim Goodwin began technical climbing with John Case at Indian Head. Goodwin had many notable early ascents in the 1930s and wrote extensively about Adirondack climbing in the years to come (vol. 1, 506).

1933: Fritz Wiessner climbed **Empress** on Chapel Pond Slab. Wiessner climbed routes throughout the park through 1970, although many dates are unknown, and later helped Trudy Healy with the first guidebook.

1933: After many tries, John Case succeeded on a route up Wallface, a cliff Fritz Wiessner later described as unclimbable.

Sam Senior rappelling Roaring Brook Falls in the late 1940s. Photo by Stanley Smith.

1933: Three boys tried to make the "first ascent" of Wallface (ironically three days after Case's successful ascent) and precipitated a large-scale technical rescue (vol. 1, 457).

1941: Gerry Bloch made his first attempt on **Forty-niner** on Wallface, a route he took 49 years to complete.

1941: Edward C. Hudowalski summited Chimney Mountain, the first recorded technical climb outside of the High Peaks region.

1947: Jim Goodwin started a rock-climbing school for the Adirondack Mountain Club using Fritz Wiessner as an instructor.

1950: Dave Bernays and Stanley Smith climbed **Lost Arrow** (5.8, although aid was used) at the Lower Washbowl. Along with Donald LeBeau, these three local boys were the only game in town from 1948 to 1953 (vol. 1, 241).

Donald LeBeau and Sam Senior at Pitchoff Chimney Cliff, Sep 1950. Photo by Stanley Smith.

1958: The first 5.9 route in the park, **The Arch**, was climbed by Dick Wilmott and Brian Rothery on the Poke-O Slab.

1959: John Turner climbed **Bloody Mary** at Poke-O Moonshine, considered the most difficult and committing route for the next 10 years. Turner and the Montreal group dominated the Adirondack climbing scene from 1957 to 1960.

1965: The Penn State Outing Club began visiting, led by Craig Patterson, ascending routes in unlikely places, such as the West Face of Gothics, Wallface, and the Rainbow Slide. They stopped climbing here in 1966.

1967: The first guidebook appeared, Trudy Healy's *Climber's Guide to the Adirondacks*, published by the Adirondack Mountain Club, which documented about 73 rock climbs.

1967: The Adirondack Northway (I-87) opened, significantly improving access to the park for everyone, including weekend climbers.

1970: The Clarkson Outing Club began exploring Azure Mountain, the first technical climbing of consequence outside of the High Peaks.

1971: Dimitri Kolokotronis climbed **Little Finger** on Rogers Slide, the first significant technical climbing in the southern Adirondacks.

1972: Trudy Healy released the second edition of her guidebook, *A Climber's Guide to the Adirondacks*.

1972: Barbara McMartin published her first backcountry hiking guide, *Walks and Waterways*. Her guides (a series that now includes 11 books) opened up sections of the park to climbers as never before. She passed away in 2005.

1973: Tom Rosecrans climbed **TR** at the Spider's Web. Over time, Rosecrans participated in 116 new routes and continues to add routes today.

1974: Dave Cilley moved to Lake Placid and opened a branch of Eastern Mountain Sports, which became a climbing center. Cilley was responsible for bringing many outsiders into the area to climb, including Henry Barber, who, with Cilley, made significant ascents at the Spider's Web.

1974: Geoff Smith and the Ski to Die Club made their first first ascent at Poke-O, with the route **Opposition**, and dominated development at that cliff through 1980. Smith participated in 58 new routes spread out over the next 31 years (vol. 1, 79). He passed away in 2013, his last route being **Wedlock** at Notch Mountain.

1974: Ken Nichols climbed **Black Plague** on Wallface with Ed Webster. Over the years, Nichols participated in 127 new routes, most notably at the Upper Tiers of Poke-O Moonshine.

1975: The Mountaineer was built in Keene Valley and, over time, became a climbing center and place for new route reporting.

1976: Tom Rosecrans self-published *Adirondack Rock and Ice Climbs*, a pocket-sized affair documenting ice climbs and 110 rock routes (19 of which are on private land).

1976: The first 5.10 route in the park, **Fear of Gravity** at the Upper Tiers of Poke-O Moonshine, was climbed by Gary Allan, one of Geoff Smith's Ski to Die protégés.

1976: The first rappel-bolted route, **New Star** at the Poke-O Slab, was climbed by Geoff Smith and Dave Hough.

1976: Mark Meschinelli climbed **Southern Hospitality** at Poke-O Moonshine in the winter with Geoff Smith and became a Ski to Die member. Meschinelli was a strong influence at Poke-O for more than 30 years and participated in 62 new routes there. His photography increased awareness of climbing in the park.

Above: Mark Meschinelli on a winter ascent of **Pinhead**, *Poke-O Moonshine, in 1977. Photo by Dave Hough.*

Below: Dick Tucker. Photo by Jay Harrison.

1976: Bruce Bandorick published a hand-printed mini-guide to Bald Mountain. Despite having many routes in a section of the park otherwise devoid of climbing, it quickly fell into obscurity.

1977: Tad Welch climbed Toad's Traverse at Panther Hill, his first first ascent. Welch brought joy to groveling and was a driving force in backcountry exploration, participating in 160 new routes to date (pages 8 and 120). Over the next 36 years, he exhaustively explored remote corners of the park including Silver Lake, Sugarloaf, Cat Mountain, Chimney Mountain, Echo Cliff, Good Luck, Baldface, and Barton High Cliff.

1977: The first 5.11 pitches, both at Poke-O, were climbed: Firing Line by Jim Dunn, and Southern Hospitality by Geoff Smith and Gary Allan.

1977: Dick Tucker climbed his first first ascent, Black Dog Chimney at Blue Hill. Tucker, a north country local, was prolific in exploring moderate climbing on remote cliffs and participated in 100 new routes (with even more undocumented) over the next 23 years.

1978: Rock Morse and friends climbed the first routes at Sugarloaf, a predominately slab-climbing area. These routes were included in Mellor's 1983 guidebook, but were later removed due to access issues. The area became a clandestine climbing destination for the next 35 years.

1979: Don Mellor made his first first ascent, Mr. Spaceman at the UFO Wall. Mellor participated in 163 new routes through the years. His three guidebooks defined Adirondack climbing for the next 20 years.

Jim Cunningham at Mt Joe.
Photo Jim Cunningham Collection.

Don Mellor. Photo Mark Meschinelli.

1979: John Case donated his mountaineering collection to the Keene Valley Library.

1980: Labatt-Ami, the first route at the Beer Walls, was climbed by Bill Simes and Chuck Turner. This area was considered a major discovery and now boasts over 100 routes.

1981: Jim Cunningham climbed various ascents around the Lower Washbowl. Over the next seven years, he and the Red House Gang stacked up numerous new routes on a variety of cliffs in the Keene / Chapel Pond Pass region (vol. 1, 288).

1982: Patrick Purcell began climbing, with P1 of Elusive Dream at the King Wall. He uncovered routes on cliffs previously overlooked and, during his 16 years in the park, participated in 203 new routes, which stood as a record until recently (vol. 1, 292).

1983: Skyline Outfitters, Ma Schaefer's colorful store in Keene, closed its doors. It was the first store in the park to offer technical climbing gear.

1983: Don Mellor self-published his first guidebook, *Climbing in the Adirondacks,* with a hard blue plastic cover and insertable pages, documenting 250 rock climbs (17 of which are on private land).

1983: Tim Beaman climbed his first route in the park, The Fang at the Eighth Wall. Admired for his unassuming manner and crack-climbing skills, over an 18-year period, he quietly put up free routes (only 37 of which are known; the remainder even he can't recall) in the High Peaks region.

1986: Don Mellor wrote the second edition of his guidebook, this time published by the Adirondack Mountain Club.

1986: The Central New York Climbers (Jim Vermeulen, Eric Dahn, Bill Morris, and Stuart Williams) climbed three routes at Kings Flow and began a wave of cliff exploration in the Indian Lake area. (page 263).

1986: Tom DuBois climbed his first route in the Adirondacks, **Start Again** at Buck Mountain. Since then, this unassuming explorer has uncovered an enormous number of small crags throughout the park.

1987: Ed Palen came on the scene, climbing **Orchestra** at Poke-O with Patrick Purcell. Over the next 20 years, Palen emerged as the driving force behind backcountry rock climbing in the High Peaks, with 71 new routes.

1987: The park's first 5.12, **Bitter End**, was climbed by Ken Nichols at the Upper Tiers of Poke-O Moonshine.

1988: The park's first 5.13, **Salad Days** at Poke-O, was climbed by Dave Lanman, a Gunks local. This was 11 years after the first 5.13s in the country, **Phoenix** in California and **Phlogiston** in Wisconsin, and stood as the most difficult route in the park for 8 years, until Fred Abbuhl's **Elusive Trophy** at Lost Hunters Cliff in 1995. There are 21 routes of this difficulty in the park. (page 33)

1988: The most difficult multipitch route in the southern Adirondacks, **Stones of Shame Direct** at Pharaoh

Ed Palen. Photo by Tomás Donoso.

Mountain, was climbed by Felix Modugno and a New Paltz crew.

1991: Patrick Munn, another Ski to Die member and Smith protégé, got really good and completed his first of many long, hard free routes, **Calvary Hill** (5.12c) at Poke-O Moonshine. Over the next five years, Munn continued his streak of long, upper-end free routes at Poke-O. Over a 30-year period (beginning in 1975), he participated in 77 new routes.

1991: Don Mellor freed **Mental Blocks** at Wallface, a long-standing aid route, raising standards in the High Peaks backcountry to 5.12.

1991: Jay Harrison showed up at Crane Mountain and began his new routing spree. On this mountain alone he's participated in more than 250 new routes, variations, and soloes, and roughly 344 routes park wide, a record. And these are just the ones he's bothered to report.

1992: Fred Abbuhl visited Tongue Mountain and climbed seven excellent routes, but nobody noticed and the cliff fell into obscurity, only to be rediscovered later as one of the top crags in the Lake George region.

1993: Jeff Edwards and Don Mellor climbed the **Diagonal** on Wallface in 3 hr 14 min car-to-car, from the Adirondack Loj. Backcountry speed ascents have yet to catch on.

1993: **Meat Hooks** (5.13a/b) was climbed by Mike Emilianoff at the New New, the second route of this grade in the park. Around this period, more than 70 routes were climbed on this cluster of private-land cliffs.

*Jay Harrison on **Long Play** on the first ascent, Crane Mountain. Photo by Mike Prince.*

Craig Volkommer at Pinnacle Mountain.

1995: Dave Aldous climbed **Zippity Doo-Dah**, one of the first routes at the Campground Wall. Aldous participated in 35 new routes around the Lake George region. Together with Tom Rosecrans and Gary Dietrich, he demonstrated that Lake George has more to offer than Rogers Slide.

1995: Don Mellor wrote the third edition of his guidebook, published by the Adirondack Mountain Club, with 861 routes and variations.

1995: The first all-gear 5.13 route **Primal Scream** was climbed at Mosher by Frank Minunni. This cliff is on private land, but it still counts!

1996: Dave Aldous led the long-standing project **Zabba** (5.13a) after three weeks of effort. His ascent went unreported and many have subsequently claimed the free ascent.

Dennis Luther on **Macho**, *Poke-O Moonshine.*

1998: **Summer Solstice**, once *the* long route to do, fell into the talus at Poke-O Moonshine, the second major cliff-altering catastrophe in recent memory (the first was **T.V. Dinner** at Avalanche Lake).

1999: Hurricane Floyd cleaned off the upper slabs of Mt Colden and made room for **California Flake**, a 900' rock climb, demonstrating once again how climbs come and go in the park.

2002: Karl Swisher climbed **House of Cards** at Good Luck Mountain, which, at 5.13a, is the most difficult all-gear line on public land in the park (page 328).

2006: Pete Kamitses climbed **Illuminescence** (5.13d) at Moss Cliff, advancing the difficulty standards once again.

2007: Will Mayo climbed **Catatonic** (5.11d) at the remote Cat Mountain, the most difficult route in the Cranberry Lake region.

2007: Craig Vollkommer climbed **Old School**, the first route at Shelving Rock on the east shore of Lake George. Now with more than 70 routes, this is a major climbing destination.

2007: Arietta Climbing, a group led by Bill Griffith and Gary Thomann, resurrected Shanty Cliff from obscurity. With the intention of making the Southern Adirondacks into a major destination, they've discovered numerous crags including Lost T, McMartin, The Annex, Lost T2, and Pinnacle Mountain (page 308).

2007: Local climber and prolific route developer Dennis Luther died in a rappelling accident while preparing a new route at Poke-O. He pioneered more than 30 routes over the 23 years he was climbing in the Adirondacks, including routes at the Creature Wall, Poke-O Moonshine, Lower Washbowl, Wallface, Pharaoh, Moss Cliff, Deadwater, Hurricane Cliff, and Peregrine Pillar. His last route, **Under the Influence**, was completed two years later.

Bill Griffith. Photo by Ilkka Kaartinen.

2008: The first edition of *Adirondack Rock* was published, by Jim Lawyer and Jeremy Haas. This included 1,938 routes and variations on more than 240 cliffs, or 1,077 new routes.

2009: Matt McCormick climbed Wheelin' N' Dealin' (5.13c) at the Spider's Web, at the time the most difficult all-gear route in the park.

2009: Silver Lake opened to the public, adding a huge amount of available rock to climb. There are now more than 150 routes here.

2010: The second printing of *Adirondack Rock* was released, which included corrections.

2011: Pete Kamitses once again extended the difficulty standards, climbing Oppositional Defiance Disorder at Silver Lake, the first all-gear 5.14a route in the eastern U.S. There are only two other routes of that grade in the park, Ill Fire and The Highline, both by Kamitses at Moss Cliff (page 464).

2011: Michael Farnsworth climbed Four Ounces to Freedom (5.12d), presently the most difficult route at Crane Mountain.

2011: Rock climbing Pioneer Jim Goodwin passed away at age 101. He added routes all over the High Peaks beginning in 1928, including routes on Porter, Gothics, Pitchoff, and Rooster Comb (vol. 1, 506).

2012: Local climbing legend and larger-than-life personality Joe Szot passed away climbing in the Gunks. As a prolific ice climber, his bunkhouse known as The Bivy was central to the Adirondack climbing community.

2012: The route count (including variations) at Crane Mountain exceeded 200, making this a major climbing destination on par with Chapel Pond Pass and Poke-O Moonshine.

2012: Potash Mountain opened to the public. Although first visited in 1990, it remained off the public radar until 2012 due to access issues. It is now quite popular with almost 20 high-quality routes from 5.8 to 5.13a.

2014: Sugarloaf near Indian Lake was acquired by the state, adding a high-quality multi-pitch slab climbing destination near Indian Lake.

Pushing the Grade

The top grades were slow to be established in the Adirondacks. The first 5.13 (Salad Days) was 11 years after this grade was established in the U.S., and the first 5.14 (Ill Fire) was 22 years after the grade was established (La Rage de Vivre in Buoux, France). Here's the history of those pushing the top grade in the Adirondacks.

1988: Dave Lanman
Salad Days (.13a, sport), Poke-O Moonshine

1993: Mike Emilianoff
Meat Hooks (.13a/b, sport), New New

1995: Frank Minunni
Primal Scream (.13a, trad), Mosher

1995: Fred Abbuhl
Elusive Trophy (.13a, mixed), Lost Hunters

1996: Dave Aldous
Zabba (.13a, mixed), Spider's Web

2002: Karl Swisher
House of Cards (.13a, trad), Good Luck

2006: Pete Kamitses
Fire in the Sky (.13c, mixed), Moss Cliff

2006: Pete Kamitses
Illuminescence (.13d, mixed), Moss Cliff

2006: Mark Polinski
Mark's Blue Ribbon (5.13a, sport), Beer Walls

2008: Pete Kamitses
Ill Fire (.14a, mixed), Moss Cliff

2009: Matt McCormick
Wheelin' N' Dealin' (.13c, trad), Spider's Web

2010: Nathaniel Popik
Zabba Direct (.13b, trad), Spider's Web

2011: Pete Kamitses
Oppositional Defiance Disorder (.14a, trad), Tsunami Slab

2012: Michael Farnsworth
Sasquatch Hunting (.13a, sport), Potash

2012: Pete Kamitses
The Highline (.13d/.14a, mixed), Moss Cliff

2012: Pete Kamitses
The Sword of Deception (.13, mixed), Mud Pond

2012: Matt McCormick
The Great Escape (.13a, mixed), Alcatraz

2013: David Buzzelli
Mushu (.13d, sport), Little Johnson

2013: David Buzzelli
Dope-a-mean (.13a, mixed), Gull Pond

2013: David Buzzelli
Leap of Faith (.13b, sport), Makomis Mountain

2013: Peter Kamitses
Moonshine and Chronic (.13+, mixed), Mud Pond

Peter Kamitses. Photo courtesy of Peter Kamitses.

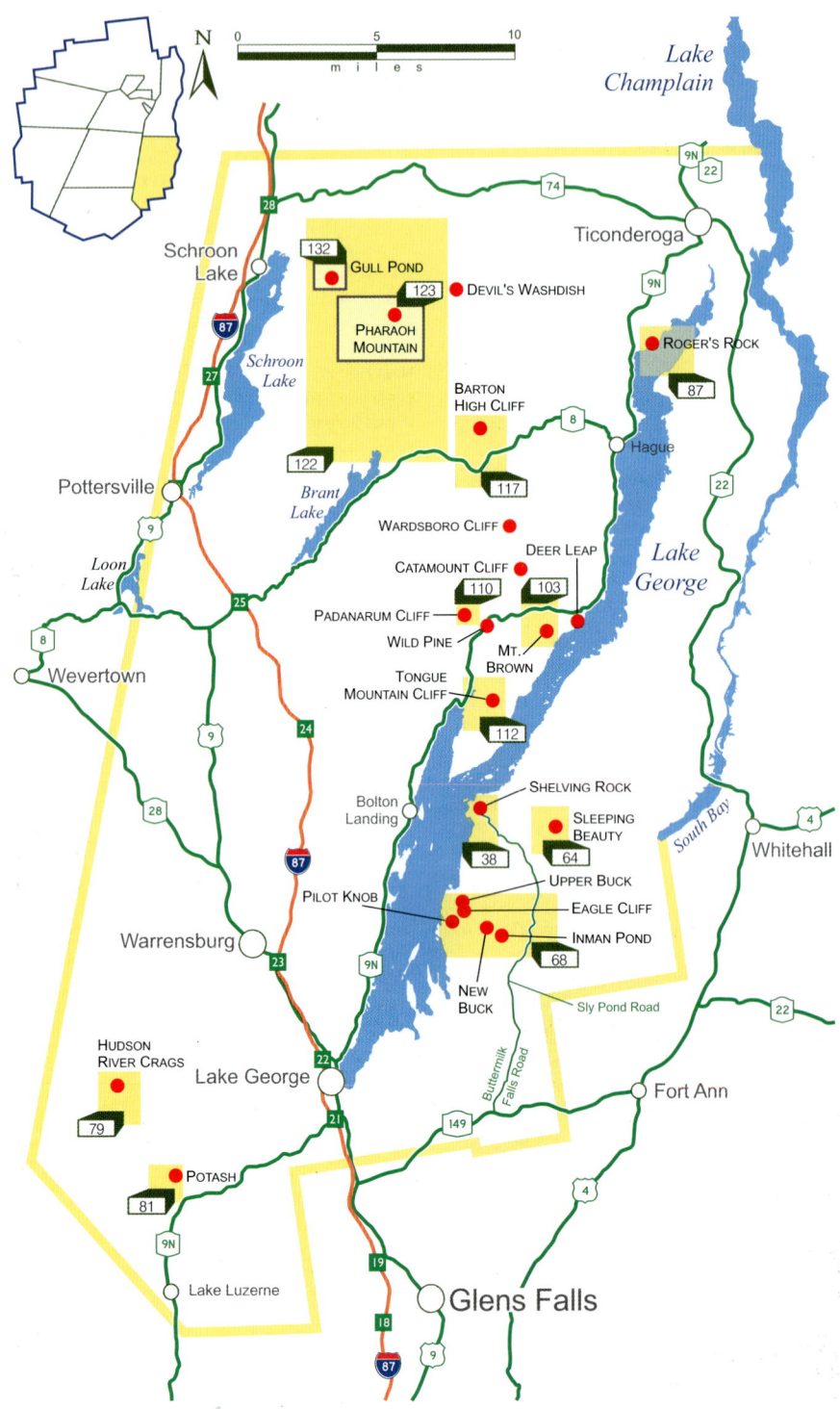

Lake George

The shoreline of Lake George, the archetype of Adirondack lakes, is flanked by mountains and cliffs. Thomas Jefferson described it as "the most beautiful water [he] ever saw."[1] Positioned between Lake Champlain and the Hudson River, the 32-mile-long Lake George has figured prominently in battles of the French and Indian War and the American Revolution. Historic forts sit at either end of the lake, and sunken warships can be glimpsed through its clear waters. For centuries, Lake George has been *the* summer destination in the Adirondacks, and it was only a matter of time before visiting climbers took notice.

The region is bordered by the lower Hudson River to the west and the park boundary / Vermont border to the east, and includes three lakes—Lake George, Schroon Lake, and Brant Lake. The hillsides along Lake George are particularly rugged and, together with the neighboring Pharaoh Lakes Wilderness, house a lot of rock.

The cliffs in this section are described from south to north along the Northway (I-87), beginning at the southern boundary of the park, near Exit 20. This exit accesses the east shore crags—Pilot Knob (Stewart's Ledge, The Brain), Buck Mountain (Upper Buck, New Buck), and the cliffs along Shelving Rock Road (Sleeping Beauty, Shelving Rock, and the Ark Wall). These crags offer mostly single-pitch climbing with a mixture of sport and traditional lines and are scattered in an area with many hiking trails and camping options.

To the north, Exit 21 provides access to Lake George Village (to the east) and Lake Luzerne (to the southwest) and the excellent single-pitch steep climbing mecca at Potash Cliff.

Farther north, Exit 24 accesses the west shore crags—the excellent ridgeline crag of Tongue Mountain Cliff, with some of the best rock in the park; the cliffs around Rogers Rock Campground, with multipitch slabs, steep faces, and cracks, in an idyllic lakefront setting; and Wild Pines, a quality road-side cliff.

Exit 25 accesses the trailheads for Pharaoh Mountain and Barton High Cliff. Although both are large, somewhat scruffy, and buried deep in the woods, they do offer excellent multipitch adventure climbing.

Exit 28, the northernmost exit in the region, accesses the sunny Gull Pond Cliff. This exit is also used by those coming from the north to access the north end of Lake George and Rogers Rock.

SEASON

The Lake George region has one of the longest climbing seasons in the park. In the early spring and late fall, this region is generally warmer than the rest of the park due to its low elevation and the moderating effect of Lake George. It's also located in a rain shadow, making it one of the drier places to visit. However, with warmth come pesky bugs. Ideal weather conditions are irrelevant when the bugs prevent you from even belaying, let alone climbing. Lakeside cliffs such as Roger's Slide, Stewart's Ledge, and Shelving Rock are breezy and have fewer bugs.

ACCESS

Annual closures for peregrine falcon nesting may affect Pharaoh Mountain, Barton High Cliff, Sleeping Beauty, the Campground Wall at Rogers Rock, the Main Face at Shelving Rock, and Potash Cliff. Shelving Rock Road is often closed during mud season (Apr–May), which affects access to Sleeping Beauty, Shelving Rock, and the Ark Wall.

DIRECTIONS   (MAPS PAGES 4 AND 34)

All of the cliffs are readily accessed from the Northway, via Exits 20–28. If you're coming from western New York, the quickest access is via the NY 8 shortcut (page 12). From northern Vermont, take the Crown Point Bridge (page 12), then south on NY 22N / NY 9N. (The ferry to Ticonderoga is slow and not recommended for crossing Lake Champlain.) From southern Vermont, follow US 4 to Whitehall, where the road splits to go toward either end of the lake.

WHERE TO STAY

Primitive car-camping sites can be found along the access roads to Hudson River Crags (River Road) and Shelving Rock (Shelving Rock Road). Most of the trailheads are on state land and are pleasant enough that setting up a camp, back in the woods, is an option.

Excellent backcountry camping is found in the Pharaoh Lakes Wilderness.

Campgrounds: No shortage of state campgrounds here, but even so, it can be busy during peak season, so call ahead for availability. Try Eagle Point, north of Exit 26 (518.494.2220); Hearthstone Point, near Exit 22 (518.668.5193); Lake George Battleground, in Lake George (518.668.3348); Luzerne, near Exit 21 (518.696.2031); Paradox Lake, near Exit 28 (518.532.7451); and Putnam Pond, near Exit 28 (518.585.7280). Rogers Rock, near Exit 25 (518.585.6746), is a huge campground and day-use area.

There are many options for other lodging (more than any other region), including cottages, motels, hotels, and luxury resorts. The Lake George Chamber of Commerce is a good place to start (www.lakegeorgechamber.com).

---

1 Sarah N. Randolph, *The Domestic Life of Thomas Jefferson* (1871), p. 201.

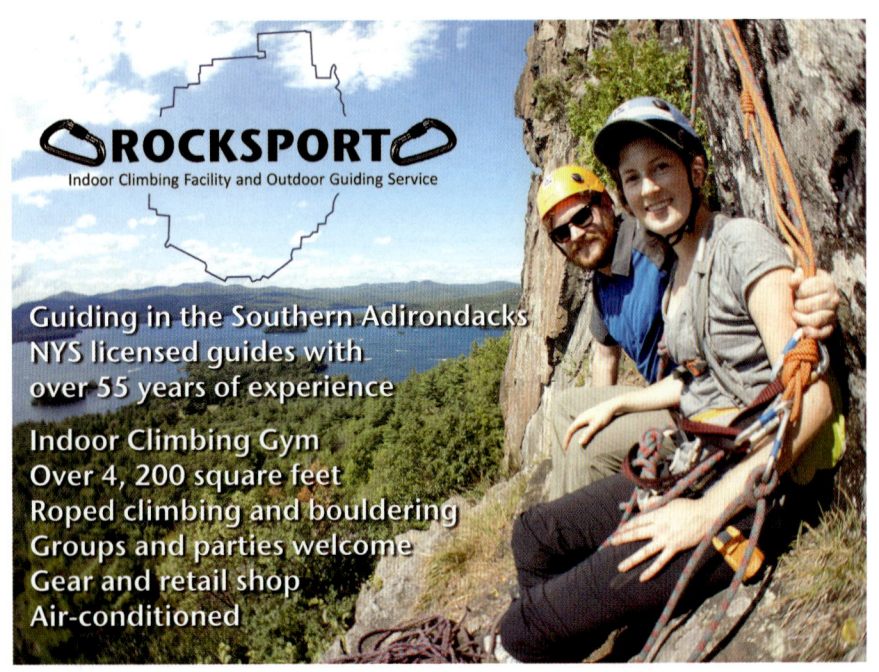

Lake George

ROCKSPORT
Indoor Climbing Facility and Outdoor Guiding Service

Guiding in the Southern Adirondacks
NYS licensed guides with over 55 years of experience

Indoor Climbing Gym
Over 4,200 square feet
Roped climbing and bouldering
Groups and parties welcome
Gear and retail shop
Air-conditioned

ROCKSPORTNY.COM   518-793-4626

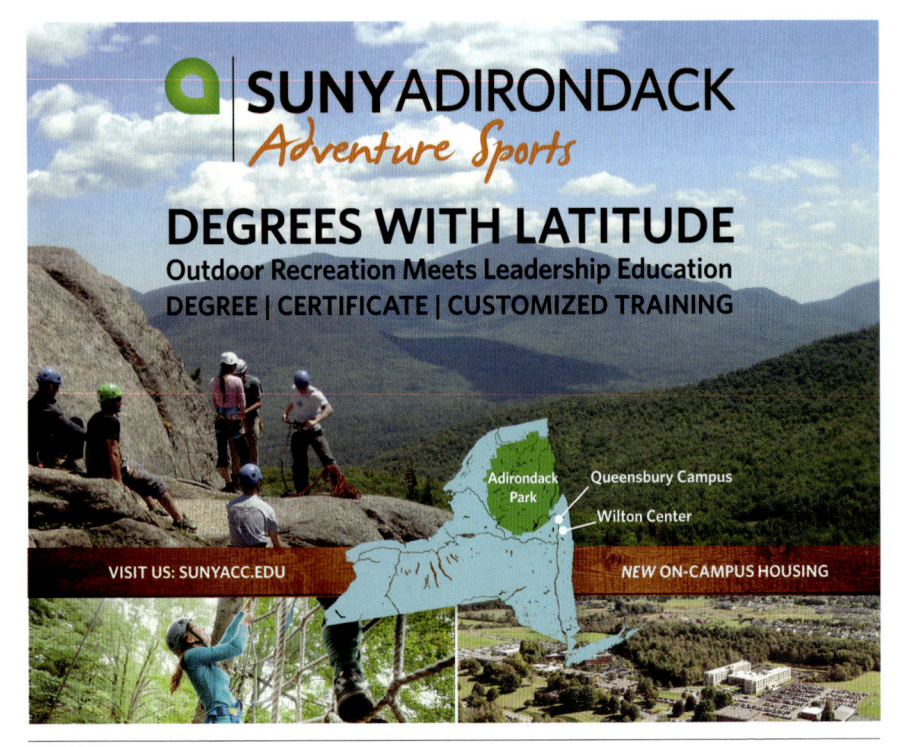

SUNY ADIRONDACK
Adventure Sports

DEGREES WITH LATITUDE
Outdoor Recreation Meets Leadership Education
DEGREE | CERTIFICATE | CUSTOMIZED TRAINING

Adirondack Park
Queensbury Campus
Wilton Center

VISIT US: SUNYACC.EDU   *NEW* ON-CAMPUS HOUSING

Lake George

PG	CLIFF	QUALITY	ASPECT	APPROACH		GRADES	#
38	Shelving Rock	★★★★	SW	4–20 min	easy	.6 .7 .8 .9 .10 .11 .12 .13	72
60	Ark Wall	★★★★	W	16 min	moderate	.6 .7 .8 .9 .10 .11 .12 .13	18
64	Sleeping Beauty Mountain	★★★	W	20 min	easy	.6 .7 .8 .9 .10 .11 .12 .13	19
67	Buck Mountain Upper Buck		W	30 min	easy	.6 .7 .8 .9 .10 .11 .12 .13	5
69	Buck Mountain New Buck	★★	W	40 min	moderate	.6 .7 .8 .9 .10 .11 .12 .13	28
72	Buck Mountain Eagle Cliff	★	W	50 min	difficult	.6 .7 .8 .9 .10 .11 .12 .13	8
73	Inman Pond Bluff		SE & S	35 min	easy	.6 .7 .8 .9 .10 .11 .12 .13	4
74	Pilot Knob Mountain Stewart's Ledge	★★	W	10 min	easy	.6 .7 .8 .9 .10 .11 .12 .13	21
78	Pilot Knob Mountain The Brain	★	W	40 min	moderate	.6 .7 .8 .9 .10 .11 .12 .13	6
79	Hudson River Crags	★	NW	5 min	easy	.6 .7 .8 .9 .10 .11 .12 .13	8
80	Potash Cliff	★★★★	SW	22 min	moderate	.6 .7 .8 .9 .10 .11 .12 .13	18
88	Rogers Rock Campground Wall	★★	SE	10 min	easy	.6 .7 .8 .9 .10 .11 .12 .13	16
91	Rogers Rock Cove Wall		SW	10 min	easy	.6 .7 .8 .9 .10 .11 .12 .13	2
92	Rogers Rock Rogers Slide	★★★★★	S	20 min	easy boat required	.6 .7 .8 .9 .10 .11 .12 .13	24
102	Brown Mountain Cliff	★	S	1 hr	difficult	.6 .7 .8 .9 .10 .11 .12 .13	4
104	Deer Leap		S	1 hr 20 min	moderate	.6 .7 .8 .9 .10 .11 .12 .13	1
106	Wild Pines	★	NW	5 min	easy	.6 .7 .8 .9 .10 .11 .12 .13	3
108	Fly Brook Valley Wardsboro Cliff		SE	45 min	difficult	.6 .7 .8 .9 .10 .11 .12 .13	4
109	Padanarum Cliff		S	20 min	moderate	.6 .7 .8 .9 .10 .11 .12 .13	5
111	Tongue Mountain Cliff	★★★	W	1 hr	moderate	.6 .7 .8 .9 .10 .11 .12 .13	27
117	Barton High Cliff	★★	NW	1 hr 15 min	moderate	.6 .7 .8 .9 .10 .11 .12 .13	13
121	Spectacle Ponds Cliff		W	33 min	moderate	.6 .7 .8 .9 .10 .11 .12 .13	2
122	Pharaoh Mountain Main Face	★★	SW	1 hr 35 min	difficult	.6 .7 .8 .9 .10 .11 .12 .13	16
130	Pharaoh Mountain Summit Cliffs	★	SW	1 hr 35 min	moderate	.6 .7 .8 .9 .10 .11 .12 .13	8
132	Gull Pond Cliff	★	W	20 min	easy	.6 .7 .8 .9 .10 .11 .12 .13	13

AMENITIES

There is no shortage of amenities, as there are many towns, most of which are easily accessed from the Northway. Glens Falls, located just south of the park (Exits 18–19), is a small city and has everything you could want, including a climbing gym (see Appendix E, page 500). Just inside the park and on the south end of Lake George is Lake George Village, a summerlong carnival of shopping, beachgoers, theme parks, and festivals. The other towns along the lake are also filled with summer tourists but have limited amenities during the off season (Columbus Day to Memorial Day). At the north end of Lake George, and just north of Rogers Rock, is Ticonderoga, a good-sized town with many options for groceries and gas. Pottersville, located at Exit 26, has 24-hour gas.

DIVERSIONS

There are lots of rest-day options in this region. Aside from the water recreation on Lake George, there is dam-released whitewater boating on the Sacandaga River near Lake Luzerne. Excellent hiking and trail running can be found in the trail systems around Shelving Rock and Tongue Mountain.

SHELVING ROCK

Location	North of NY 149 on the east shore of Lake George, accessed from Northway Exit 20
Aspect	Southwest
Height	200'
Quality	★★★★
Approach	4–20 min, easy
Summary	A wide range of difficulty and quality, with the greatest concentration of quality routes in the 5.10 range. Best for face climbing on incut edges. Dries quickly after the rain.

5	6	11	10	28	7	5	72
-5.6	5.7	5.8	5.9	5.10	5.11	5.12	5.13+	total

This long cliff rises above the eastern shore of Lake George and has mostly single-pitch routes. There are several multi-pitch routes, but few of them top out. Most of the routes are "modern trad", meaning fixed protection and gear; don't expect many clip ups. The rock is similar to that of nearby Sleeping Beauty and Ark Wall—featured, with incut edges and tiered overhangs, and not as sheer or low-angled as many Adirondack cliffs. Like many of the Lake George cliffs, Shelving Rock and its neighbors have one of the longest climbing seasons in the park. And you can't beat the location—full sun in the afternoon with outstanding views of Lake George.

Be aware that this cliff has a lot of choss. The routes documented here (mostly) stick to the better sections of rock, but even so the rock is brittle and breaks where you don't expect; treat it with caution, like desert sandstone. The routes are mostly well-protected, but sometimes bolts are placed off to the side in better rock, so carry some 2'-long runners to minimize rope drag.

Large talus fields and fresh rock debris litter the base of this cliff so watch your footing (and the poison ivy) as you approach your climbs. As with any recently developed cliffs, helmets are recommended for both the leader and belayer. Test your holds before weighting them and place protection often.

Thanks to a cell tower at the Sagamore Resort across the lake, the cliff and parking area have good cell reception.

Six different sections of the cliff have been developed. From left to right, they are the Carhartt Wall, Main

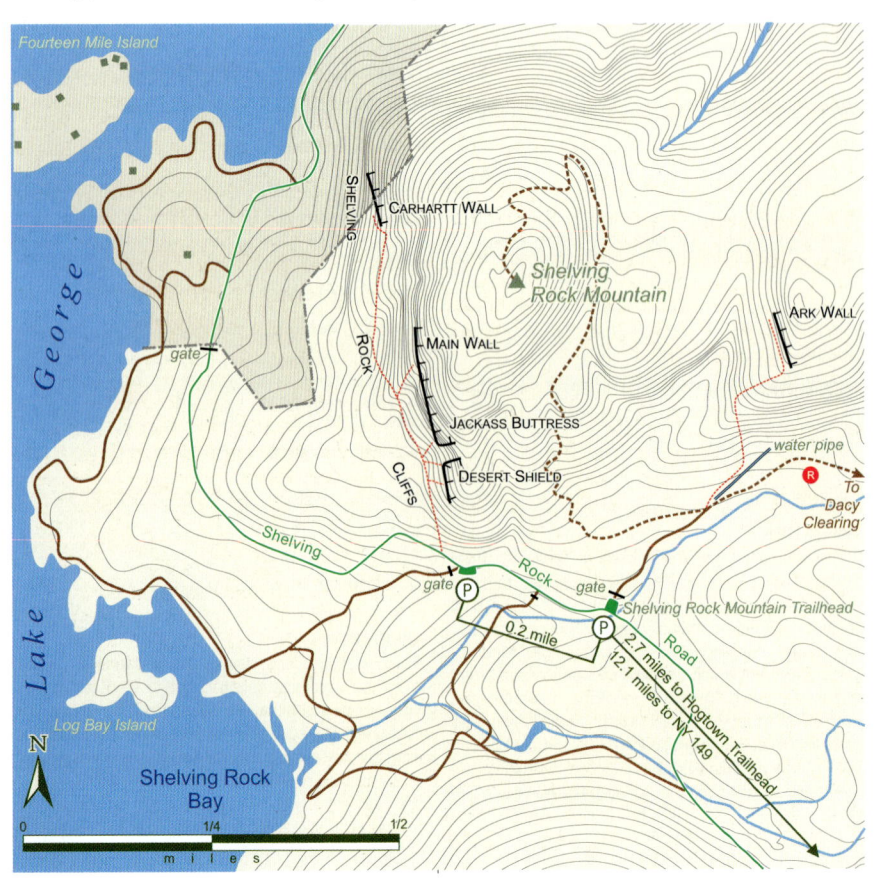

Lake George

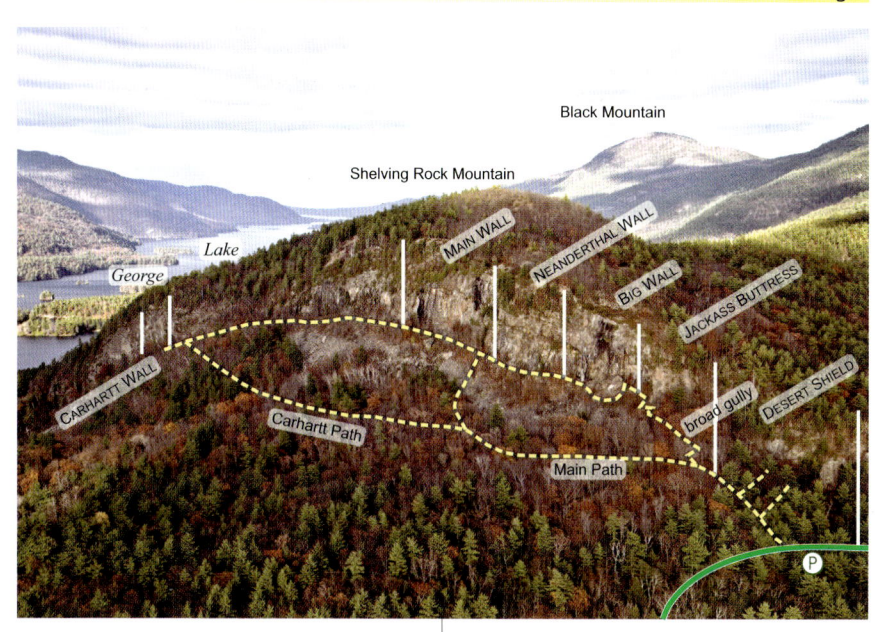

Labels on photo: Black Mountain, Shelving Rock Mountain, Lake George, MAIN WALL, NEANDERTHAL WALL, BIG WALL, JACKASS BUTTRESS, CARHARTT WALL, Carhartt Path, broad gully, DESERT SHIELD, Main Path, P

Face, Neanderthal Cave, Big Wall, Jackass Buttress and Desert Shield.

GEAR
Bring a standard trad rack with an emphasis on small cams and wires.

CAMPING
Sleeping Beauty and Shelving Rock are on a dead-end dirt road with excellent opportunities for car camping. Designated sites are posted on a map at a kiosk that is found at the Hogtown Trailhead, where the dirt road begins its steep descent from the large parking area on the right. There's also a good bivy spot at the base of the Main Wall' (no water).

DIRECTIONS   (MAP PAGE 38)
From the Hogtown Trailhead (page 64) continue on Shelving Rock Road. At 2.7 miles go past a bridge and the Shelving Rock trailhead on the right. At 2.9 miles, park at a parking area on the left; this is parking for a carriage road that leads to the shore, a large lot delineated with boulders 0612838,4823456, and signposted "Parking Area 4." Beyond the parking area, the road continues past several more parking areas before ending at private property (gated), 3.7 miles from the Hogtown Trailhead.

The last 4 miles of the road is a steep dirt road that is subject to closure during mud season (April–May) and can be impassable in midwinter after heavy snow.

From the parking area, continue down the road for 30', and look for a herd path on the opposite side of the road from the parking area. Follow the herd path north, contour uphill, and stay below the talus fields and cliff bands to the right. Specific spur trails are described in the approaches to the different cliff sections.

HISTORY
The cliff is situated above the former Knapp estate. In 1904, George Knapp, co-founder of Union Carbide Corporation, acquired 3500 acres of property, including Shelving Rock and about 6 miles of Lake George shoreline. New York State acquired most of this in 1941. The existing network of carriage roads were converted to a trail system that affords excellent hiking.

Early climbing history here is unknown. In the early 1980s Tom Rosecrans drove on the lake ice in search of ice and stopped to investigate the ice near Snake Charmer. He fled with a distinctly unfavorable opinion of the chossy rock. No doubt other climbers visited, only to be turned away by the lack of continuous crack systems or variable rock quality.

This all changed in 2007 with the arrival of Craig Vollkommer, a contractor from Glens Falls who developed routes at nearby Sleeping Beauty. Old School, a non-descript corner at the Jackass Buttress, was Vollkommer's first route here in 2007. Vollkommer was the right man at the right time—he had the patience, skills, and vision for dealing with the steep, chossy, unprotectable rock. In January 2008 Vollkommer returned with Jessica Donovan and established the first route on the Main Face, Monty Python. Many classic routes were climbed that year by Vollkommer, now joined by Warrensburg painting contractor Ian Measeck, most notably Rusty Lumberjack, Claim Jumper, Gong Show, Hackett Corner, Infinity and Beyond, and Wake and Bake. The cliff became a great year-round project area for Vollkommer and Measeck, who could be found hanging from ropes throughout the year. In fact, many of these early routes were first climbed in the middle of winter, which highlights how temperate the conditions can be at this cliff. In the fall of 2008,

39

Lake George

Vollkommer and Measeck invited a dozen climbers to visit, which opened a lot of eyes to the future of Lake George rock climbing.

With renewed enthusiasm (and 30 more years of new routing experience), Tom Rosecrans returned, finishing out the year with such pioneering ascents as **Cold Bare Report** at Jackass Buttress and **Obama Mama** at Desert Shield. Rosecrans, owner of the local climbing gym Rocksport, was on a quest to develop moderate routes for guiding, and his routes are generally well-protected in the easier grades for the area. In 2009, focus turned to a low section of cliff, the Neanderthal Cave, which started with Vollkommer and Measeck's contributions (**Protruding Forehead** and **Knuckle-Dragger**). Ultimately, it was Rosecrans's **Devo** that showcased what this section is best known for: good intermediate routes and a great place to start the day. Cliff-wide explorations continued, and 2009 ended with Kirby Girard's ascent of **Carhartt Confidential** at the more isolated Carhartt Wall.

Justin Barrett, an employee at Rocksport, raised the bar the next season with a slew of hard routes. These include **Vagtastic Voyage**, **Pinching One Off**, and **Infinity Crack**, all long routes on the tallest, steepest sections of cliff—Carhartt Wall, Big Wall, and Main Wall. Vollkommer and Rosecrans added some of the best 5.10 test pieces at these cliffs including **Die by the Drop**, **Johnny Tsunami**, **Three Degrees of Separation**, and **Cenotaph**.

Hard climbing at Shelving Rock peaked in 2011 at the Carhartt Wall when Vollkommer sent his long-standing project, **The Cosmic Ripple**, and visiting climber Michael Farnsworth freed Measeck's fine line, **The Fancy Cat**. Open projects remain today, many of them in the 5.13 range.

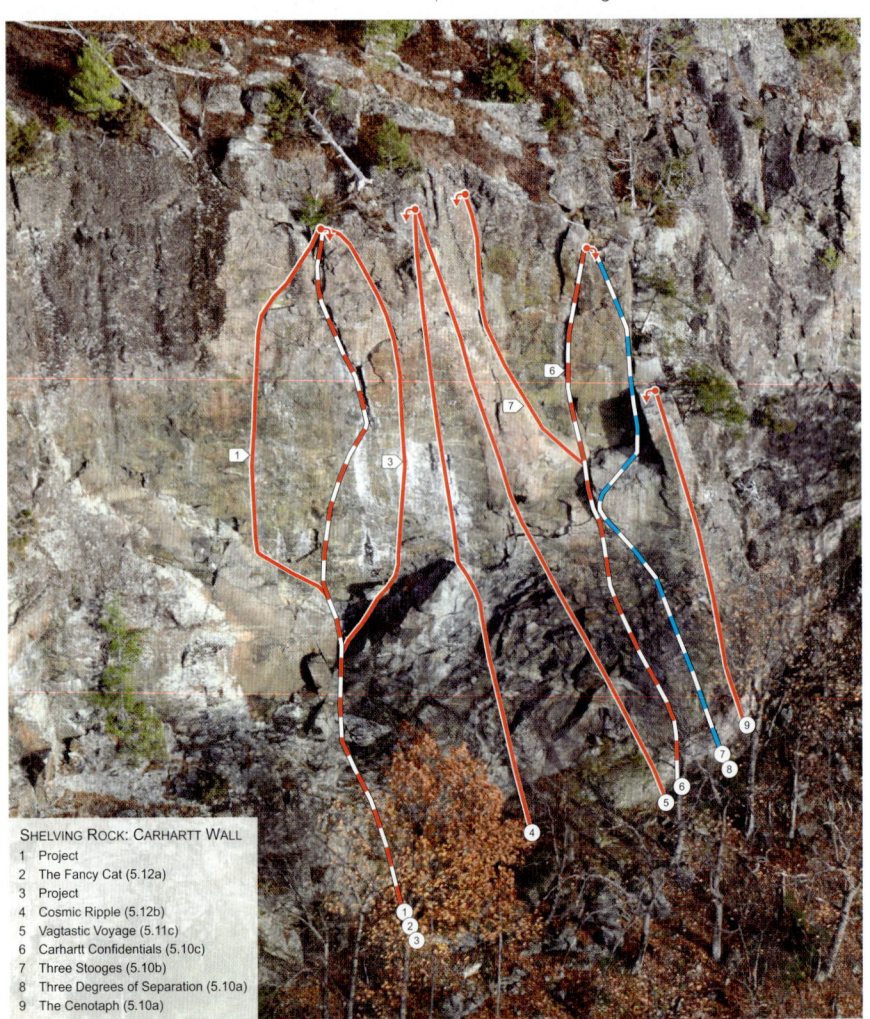

SHELVING ROCK: CARHARTT WALL
1. Project
2. The Fancy Cat (5.12a)
3. Project
4. Cosmic Ripple (5.12b)
5. Vagtastic Voyage (5.11c)
6. Carhartt Confidentials (5.10c)
7. Three Stooges (5.10b)
8. Three Degrees of Separation (5.10a)
9. The Cenotaph (5.10a)

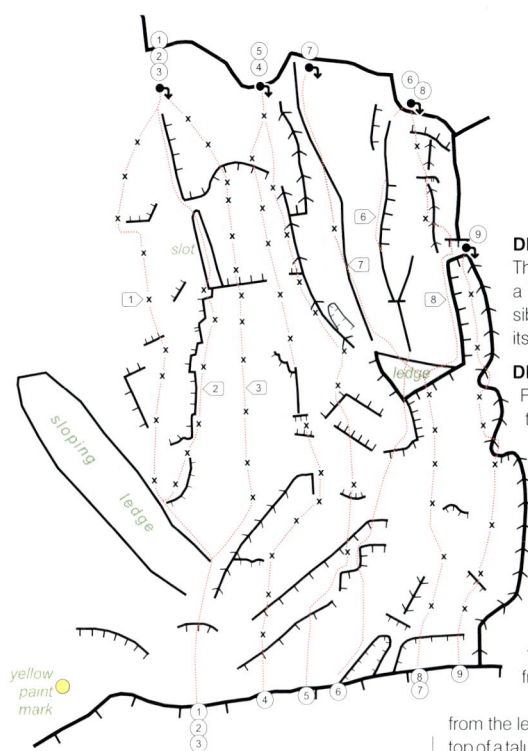

Lake George

SHELVING ROCK: CARHARTT WALL

1 Project
2 The Fancy Cat (5.12a)
3 Project
4 Cosmic Ripple (5.12b)
5 Vagtastic Voyage (5.11c)
6 Carhartt Confidentials (5.10c)
7 Three Stooges (5.10b)
8 Three Degrees of Separation (5.10a)
9 The Cenotaph (5.10a)

DESCENT OPTIONS

This is a tall wall that is best descended with a 70m rope. A rappel with a 60m rope is possible from **Three Stooges**, and the routes to its right.

DIRECTIONS (MAP PAGE 38)

Follow the path toward the Main Face. Continue past the turnoff for the Main Face 0612735,4823881 and stay below the talus until you reach a crest, then descend gently downhill for 400'. Next, ascend steeply for 150' to a long, semi-level bench (there is a campfire ring and view here 0612692,4824130). Walk along the bench to its far end, then go uphill across a short talus field to the base of the cliff. Walk left along the base of the cliff for 100' to reach the Carhartt Wall at its right end. Hiking time from the main path is 10 min.

Alternatively, follow the base of the cliff from the left end of the Main Wall. Hike for 5 min to the top of a talus field, then continue for another 100' to reach the Carhartt Wall at its right end 0612675,4824280.

1 Project

This closed project begins at the left end of the tree-covered ledge where 3rd class steps go up and left to a more exposed ledge. Scramble 3rd class ledges up and right to an open book that is right of the long, sloping, tan-colored slab, and left of the low, black arête. Go up the open book, then left above the sloping slab to a stance beneath a right-facing, left-leaning corner that begins 8' above the ledge. Work up the sheer face, stay right of the corner, go over a small overlap and then left past orange rock to the left end of a bulging wall. Climb around the left side of the bulge, and move rightward to a fixed anchor 5' below the top of the cliff. 110'.

2 The Fancy Cat 5.12a G 110' ★★★★★

Start: Go to the left end of the tree-covered ledge where 3rd class steps go up and left to a more exposed ledge. Scramble 3rd class ledges up and right to an open book, then left along the top of the slab to the base of a right-leaning, right-facing corner capped by a small overhang.

P1 5.12a G: Go up the corner, then move right to the base of the long, gently-overhanging, shallow, right-facing, right-leaning, blocky corner. Sustained climbing up the corner ends in a slot-crack system; follow this to a fixed anchor shared with **Project**. 110'
Gear: Standard rack to 2".
FFA Oct 18, 2011, Michael Farnsworth

Carhartt Wall

The leftmost section of the Shelving Rock cliff system is very wide and impressive, but most of it is on private property, thereby restricting climbing to a 50'-wide section on its far right end known as the Carhartt Wall. There are signs for private land on trees below the cliff, with occasional yellow DEC paint marks; there's also a 3'-tall yellow stripe on the cliff to the left of the routes marking the start of the private land.

The left side of the Carhartt Wall has a 100'-tall sheer face above a tan-colored slab. Most of this section is spectacular face climbing—the "Spider's Web of face climbing," as some have called it. A distinctive feature on this section is the shallow, blocky, right-facing corner of **The Fancy Cat**. To the right of the sheer wall (and just left of center on the wall) are two stacked arêtes—a lower, black arête that leans to the right, above which is a left-leaning arête (the route **Vagtastic Voyage**) that extends to the top of the cliff. The large right-facing, left-leaning corner to the right of the upper arête is the route **The Three Stooges** that begins at a sloping ledge halfway up the cliff's right side. **Carhartt Confidential** ascends the most prominent crack on the wall and begins from this ledge. The bottom of the cliff has a right-rising band of dike rock above a narrow ledge with several trees. All of the routes begin on this ledge and cross the dike rock.

41

Lake George

*Tom Rosecrans near the top of **Three Degrees of Separation** (5.10b) on the first ascent. Photo by Joel Dashnaw.*

3 Project
This open project starts as for **The Fancy Cat** and goes right and up a right-rising ramp, then up the overhanging face to the right of a low black streak. It continues through an overlap and up an orange face to a fixed anchor at the top.

4 Cosmic Ripple 5.12b G 110' ★★★
Start: Toward the left end of the tree-covered ledge, beneath the low, black arête and several, short right-rising ledges in dike rock.
● **P1 5.12b G:** Work up the ledges and a smooth wall to a long, right-rising ledge. Continue above the ledge on gray rock, and go around the left side of the black arête to its top. Pull onto the overhanging, sheer face and go past a small overhang to a stance below a discontinuous crack. Up the crack to a stance below a bulging wall. Work up the wall, stay right of a long overhang, and follow a right-rising seam in orange rock to a ledge where it joins **Vagtastic Voyage**. Climb a headwall and an arête on the right to a fixed anchor. 110'
Gear: 1 ea 0.75" cam.
FA Nov 13, 2011, Craig Vollkommer

5 Vagtastic Voyage 5.11c G 110' ★★★★
Start: In the middle of the tree-covered ledge, 10' left of a detached, hourglass-shaped pillar, below a right-rising ramp–ledge that begins 10' up.
● **P1 5.11c G:** Climb dike rock to the ramp–ledge which is followed right to short, left-facing corners with ledges. Up the corners and ledges to an overlap. Go past the overlap and up to a large, triangular ceiling. Work out the left side of the ceiling then move back right across a sheer face (crux) to a long, left-rising arête. Climb the arête past a large horn, then trend up the left side of the arête on a steepening face to a ledge below a headwall where it joins **Cosmic Ripple**. Climb the headwall (not easy) and an arête on the right to a fixed anchor. 110'
Gear: To 0.5".
FA May 5, 2010, Justin Barrett, Tom Rosecrans

6 Carhartt Confidentials
5.10c G (5.7 R) 110' ★★★
The original route on the wall. The name comes from the padding that was put in the sharp crack to protect the rope during its first ascent. The runout start can be avoided by climbing **Three Degrees of Separation** or **Vagtastic Voyage** to the sloping ledge.
Start: At the right side of the tree-covered ledge, next to a detached, hourglass-shaped pillar.
P1 5.10c G (5.7R): Climb the pillar, then up left-facing corners with ledges (small gear) to steep orange rock (5.7 R) and a left-facing corner. Go up the corner to a broad, sloping ledge beneath a prominent vertical crack that goes to the top of the cliff. The crack widens from finger to fist-sized, bends to the right and becomes a left-facing corner. Finish at a fixed anchor shared with **Three Degrees of Separation**. 110'
Gear: Standard rack, 2 ea of 3.5"
FA Nov 1, 2009, Kirby Girard

7 Three Stooges 5.10b G 110' ★★★
Start: Same as **Three Degrees of Separation**.
P1 5.10b G: Follow **Three Degrees of Separation** to the sloping ledge. Step left and go up a deep, right-facing, left-leaning corner. Move right (crux) at a vertical crack, then back left into a higher, right-facing corner that is climbed to the top of the cliff and a fixed anchor. 110'
FA Jul, 2010, Craig Vollkommer, Diane Dumouchel

*Opposite: Kirby Girard on the first ascent of **Carhartt Confidentials** (5.10c). Photo by Joel Dashnaw.*

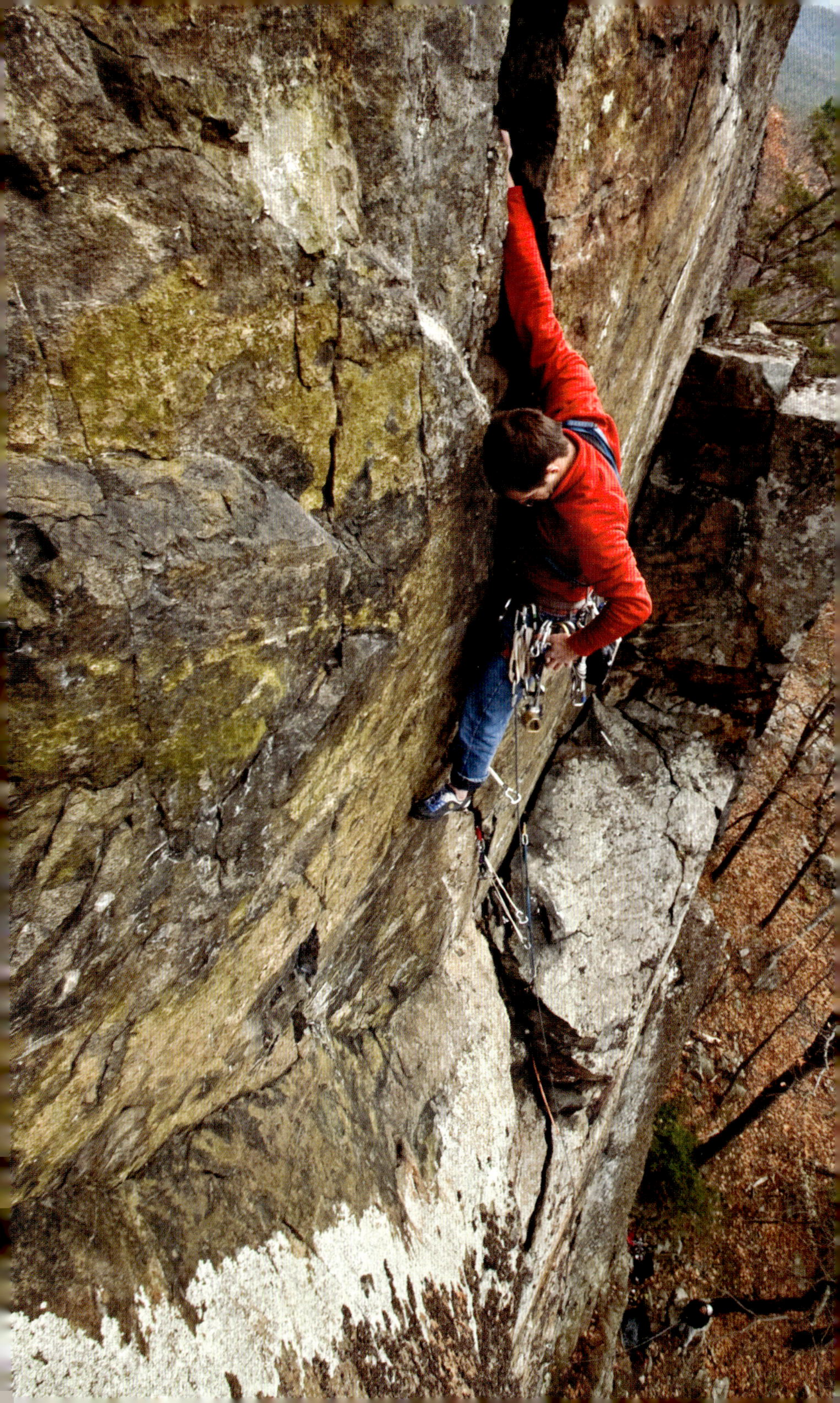

Lake George

8 Three Degrees of Separation
5.10a G 110' ★★★★

A tremendous pitch that ascends striking features on the right side of the wall. Exposed, sustained, with varied cruxes.

Start: At the right end of the tree-covered ledge, on a narrow ledge below blocky dike rock.

● **P1 5.10a G:** Climb steepening rock on generous holds, initially trending to the right then back left to the left end of a sloping ledge. Reach right to top out on the sloping ledge and then tackle a steep fingercrack in a left-facing corner. Exit the corner at an exposed stance on the right margin on the wall. Move up a step to the base of a high arête and start up its right side, then work left (exposed) to a small stance below the top. Finish at the fixed anchor shared with **Carhartt Confidentials**. 110'

Gear: Cams to 2"

FA Nov 17, 2009, Tom Rosecrans, Justin Barrett

9 The Cenotaph 5.10a G 75' ★★★★

Ascends the stepped arête, and tombstone-shaped pillar, on the right end of the wall.

Start: At the right end of the wall, at a level clearing along the cliff base.

● **P1 5.10a G:** Boulder up to the right end of a low ledge (start of **Three Degrees of Separation**), then move up and right across a sheer face to a stance on the arête. Step left and go up to a higher stance on the arête. Climb the tombstone-shaped pillar: use the arête, or zig-zag left then right, pull onto easier rock, and climb to a fixed anchor that is well below the top of the cliff. 75'

FA Nov, 2010, Tom Rosecrans, John Weston

Main Wall

This section of cliff is over 200' wide and rises above the highest stretch of talus field. The Main Wall was the first section to be developed, has seen the most climber traffic, and contains some of the best rock. The left end is at a height of land and has a very large, bottomless, right-facing dihedral 70' up, below which is a giant hanging cedar tree (climbed by **Lunar Manscaping**). Most of the routes are approximately 100' long and a few have second pitches that climb to the top of the cliff.

DIRECTIONS (MAP PAGE 38)

From the trailhead, follow the main path and, at 2 min, pass beneath a small talus field. Continue uphill to within 100' of the cliff 0612786,4823713. There is a spur path on the right that goes to the Desert Shield area, and 70' further, there is another spur path on the right that goes up a forested slope to the Jackass Buttress. Continue on the main path along a level bench and beneath a larger talus field below the highest section of the cliff (the Big Wall). Avoid the temptation to go up too early. Walk past several refrigerator-sized boulders, to a fork 0612735,4823881. Left goes to the Carhartt Wall; you go slightly right to a higher bench. From the higher bench, enter the talus field, cut directly uphill, and reach the cliff at the right end of the Main Wall 0612781,4823979, about 15 min from the trailhead.

SHELVING ROCK: MAIN WALL

Lake George

10 Protractor 5.8 PG 80' ★

Angular climbing with Gunks-style roofs and exposure. The final traverse, although easy, has sparse protection.
Start: 100' left of the start of Snake Charmer, and a bottomless right-facing dihedral 70' up, beneath a large open-book capped by a roof 20' up.
P1 5.8 PG: Climb the easy open-book to the roof, then traverse right along a roof crack. Follow the crack that becomes vertical to a higher roof. Traverse left along a wide crack (easy) to an exposed stance beneath a right-facing flake. Go up the flake (strenuous) to a ledge. Traverse right to fixed anchor. 80'
Gear: Standard rack plus an optional 5" cam.
FA Jun 16, 2009, Justin Barrett, Jeremy Haas, Tom Rosecrans

11 Lunar Manscape 5.8+ PG 85' ★

Climbs the deep, overhanging right-facing corner that is midway up the cliff.
Start: The left side of a 20'-tall blocky buttress, past the large clearing at the cliff base, beneath a big cedar bush 20' up.
P1 5.8+ PG: Make a bouldery move, then climb up easy rock to the top of the buttress. Step on the cedar bush to get onto a grey face, and climb it to a stance at a 1" horizontal crack. Protect in the crack, work up and left past a 2" left-leaning crack, to the base of the right-facing corner. Stem the steep corner to a fixed anchor on the right wall. 85'
Gear: Standard rack
FA Aug 22, 2013, Tom Rosecrans, Heather Neddo, Brie Livingston, Robert Livingston

12 Snake Charmer 5.9 G 95' ★★★

Start: Just right of the bottomless right-facing dihedral 70' up, at a blocky, right-facing, left-leaning corner.
P1 5.9 G: Up the blocky corner to a vertical, right-facing corner at its top. Climb the corner, with a crack that narrows from hand to finger size at an overhang. Pass the overhang (crux) and follow the fingercrack to a ledge. Above the ledge is an open book. Go up the open book, then step right to a fixed anchor. 95'
Gear: Standard rack; bring long slings.
FA May, 2008, Craig Vollkommer, Rick Hackett

13 Charming Hackett 5.10c TR 95' ★★

Uses the Snake Charmer anchor. Starts at the base of the Snake Charmer corner and climbs the face to its right.
FA (TR) Sep 2, 2013, Tom Rosecrans

SHELVING ROCK: MAIN WALL

11 Lunar Manscape (5.8+)
12 Snake Charmer (5.9)
14 Hackett Corner (5.10a)
15 Thunder Down Under (5.10c)
16 Grin and Bear It (5.8+)
17 The Price is Right (5.11a)
18 The Gong Show (5.9-)
19 Doodle Bug (5.9-)
20 Rock Lobster (5.9+)
21 Footloose (5.10d)
22 Dirty Dancing (5.10d)
23 Just Take It (5.11d)
24 Rusty Lumberjack (5.11b)
25 Claim Jumper (5.11b)
26 Project X (5.12a)
27 Infinity and Beyond (5.10b)
28 Infinity Crack (5.12a)
29 Monty Python (5.10b)
30 Knights That Say Neigh (5.11b)
31 Holy Grail (5.10c)
32 Project
33 Shake and Bake (5.8-)
34 Stake and Cake (5.10a)
35 Wake and Bake (5.10a)
36 Line of Fire (5.10c)
37 Princess Bride (5.5)

Lake George

*Climber on **Snake Charmer** (5.9). Photo by David Crothers.*

14 Hackett Corner 5.10a G 100' ★★★★
Steep, featured rock. Often wet.
Start: Same as **Snake Charmer**.
P1 5.10a G: Go halfway up the blocky right-facing corner, then up a shallow, right-facing corner in black rock (15' right of the **Snake Charmer** corner) to a right-facing slot. Up the slot, then work up and right, staying right of a pointed prow, to a right-facing corner. Follow the corner to a lone birch tree and a fixed anchor. 100'
Gear: To 2". A 2" cam protects the moves up to the shallow right-facing corner.
FA Sep, 2008, Craig Vollkommer, Ian Measeck

15 Thunder Down Under 5.10c G (5.7 R) 100' ★★
Although the initial corner has superb climbing that is independent of the neighboring routes, the upper half of the route is squeezed in. A top rope directional bolt is located between the fixed anchors of **Hackett Corner** and **Grin and Bear It**.
Start: Same as **Grin and Bear It**.
P1 5.10c G (5.7 R): Scramble up blocks to a shallow, right-facing, right-leaning corner that is 10' right of the **Hackett Corner**. Up the corner in fantastic black rock (small wires) to a ledge shared with **Grin and Bear It**. Move up and left (5.7 R) of an arête with a ceiling. Go over the ceiling and climb easier rock (5.7 R) up and right to the fixed anchor of **Grin and Bear It**. 100'
Gear: Small wires, gear to 0.5".
FA Jun 8, 2010, Justin Barrett, Tom Rosecrans, Adam Ostrander

16 Grin and Bear It 5.8+ G 100' ★★
Start: 10' right of the left-rising, blocky, right-facing corner of **Snake Charmer**, below a left-facing flake 20' up.
P1 5.8+ G: Scramble up blocks to the flake, then power to its top on good holds. Move right into shallow corners, then back left to a ledge below a deep right-facing corner (0.5" cam in corner). Move up and left off the ledge to a slab with a thin crack that is climbed to an overlap. Work past the overlap (crux, small wires and cams) and into an open book. Move up and right to a fixed anchor on a large cedar tree. 100'
FA May, 2008, Craig Vollkommer, Ian Measeck

17 The Price is Right 5.11a G 100' ★★★
Start: Same as **Gong Show**.
● **P1 5.11a G:** Start up **Gong Show** then go straight up a black slab to the right end of a long overhang. Pull the overhang and climb over a short overhang to a long slab with an arête at its top. Climb the slab and arête, then traverse right to the fixed anchor of **Gong Show**. 100'
FA Jul 18, 2009, Frank Minunni, Theresa Connolly, Richard Felch

18 The Gong Show 5.9- G 100' ★★★★
A short crux with lots of moderate climbing above makes this route a popular warm up.
Start: 25' right of the left-rising blocky corner of **Snake Charmer**, below the left end of a long ceiling 20' up.
● **P1 5.9- G:** Scramble up blocky terrain to the ceiling. Break through the ceiling on its left side at a jug (crux), then right onto the face above the ceiling. Go straight up to a left-facing corner formed by a huge "gong" flake. At the top of the flake, move up and left across a beautiful, clean face to a fixed anchor. 100'
Gear: 1 ea 2–3" cam.
FA May, 2008, Craig Vollkommer, Ian Measeck

Lake George

19 Doodle Bug 5.9- PG 100' ★★

Sustained and varied climbing. Not as innocent as the name suggests. Often wet.

Start: 45' downhill and right of the left-rising blocky corner of **Snake Charmer**, at a short left-leaning crack that begins at head height with a right-facing corner to its right.

P1 5.9- PG: Up the crack (or corner) to a ledge with loose blocks. Step onto a steepening face with dark rock, and trend leftwards to a ledge. Reach into a high crack and follow it to a slab. Go up the slab to a right-leaning seam beneath an overhanging wall (small gear). Move up and right to a fixed anchor at the top of an orange streak. 100'

FA May, 2008, Craig Vollkommer, Ian Measeck

20 Rock Lobster 5.9+ G 100' ★★★

Start: At a right-facing corner, with stacked but secure blocks, 10' right of **Doodle Bug**.

● **P1 5.9+ G:** Up the corner, then work up and right to a broken, open book with a steep wall above it. Pull over the steep wall (crux) and go up to a right-rising arête. Either climb past the arête directly or pass it on the left (easier), to a slab below a prominent arête with an overlap in its left side. Go around the right side of the arête, then up it to an exposed move to the left at its top. Climb easy, but unprotected rock to the fixed anchor shared with **Doodle Bug**. 100'

FA Jun 8, 2010, Tom Rosecrans, Justin Barrett, Adam Ostrander

21 Footloose 5.10d PG (5.4 R) 180' ★★★

P1 has good stances from which to place overhead protection, and makes for a good warm up. P2 is long, involved, and has a desperate (but well protected) crux.

Start: 60' uphill and left of the lowest point of the cliff and 20' right of the **Doodle Bug** corner, at a right-leaning hand- and off-width crack.

P1 5.10a G: Up the crack to a ledge beneath tiered overhangs. Mantle onto a small ledge, then pull an overhang to a slab. Go over another overhang and traverse a slab to the right. Step up into a right-facing corner and follow a slab up and right to a fixed anchor. 90'

P2 5.10d (5.4 R): Continue up the slab and right-facing corner. Make a long reach to the right, and pull onto another slab and right-facing corner. When the slab ends, climb up through rotten rock (5.4 R) to a bottomless, right-facing corner. Climb the left wall of the corner (watch for rope drag) to an exposed stance beneath a right-rising fin. Layback the fin (crux) and pull onto a ledge beneath a deep V-slot. Stem the slot and exit left onto blocky terrain. Belay at a tree with a fixed anchor. 90'

Gear: Standard rack with many long slings.

Descent: Rappel 90' down the slot (on P2) to the fixed anchor at the top of **Just Take It**, then another rappel to the ground.

FA (P1) Sep, 2008, Craig Vollkommer, Ian Measeck
FA (P2) May, 2009, Craig Vollkommer, Ian Measeck

Craig Vollkommer on Gong Show (5.9-).
Photo by Diane Dumouchel.

22 Dirty Dancing 5.10d R 90' ★

Start: 15' left of **Just Take It** at an overhanging wall with right-leaning seams.

P1 5.10d R: Up the steep rock to a small ledge beneath a 4'-wide ceiling. Pass the ceiling on its left end, and move up a broad, square slab. Go up a steep orange wall (left of a ledge) to a short ceiling (crux). Pass the ceiling, and continue straight up a steep slab to the fixed anchor of **Footloose**. 90'

FA Aug 3, 2009, Justin Barrett, Tom Rosecrans

23 Just Take It 5.11d G 100' ★★★★

Takes the steepest line up the brilliant center section of the Main Face.

Start: 20' uphill and left of **Rusty Lumberjack** below a left-facing, light-colored flake.

● **P1 5.11d G:** Up the flake (2" cam), right through a bulge to a right-facing, right-leaning corner. Make a big reach up, and then work left to easier rock. Climb straight up to a ceiling, and make a bouldery move (crux) onto a ledge with a fixed anchor. 100'

Gear: 1 ea 2" cam.

FA Aug, 2008, Ian Measeck, Craig Vollkommer

24 Rusty Lumberjack 5.11b PG 100' ★★★★

Start: At a refrigerator-sized boulder at the lowest point of the cliff.

P1 5.11b PG: Up a sandy, flaky face, then up a right-facing open book to a ceiling. Break left, then up a right-leaning dihedral with a crack. At its top, go up an orange face to an overlap, then right to a fixed anchor shared with **Claim Jumper**. 100'

Gear: To 1.5".

FA Feb, 2008, Ian Measeck, Craig Vollkommer

Lake George

25 Claim Jumper 5.11b G 100' ★★★★

Start: 10' right of Rusty Lumberjack below a low ceiling with a shattered left-facing corner above it.
P1 5.11b G: Up the corner to a stance on the right, then muscle through an orange ceiling to an overhang. Through the overhang (crux), then make big moves to big holds on a clean orange face. Break right, then straight up a crack to a fixed anchor shared with Rusty Lumberjack. 100'
Gear: To 1.5".
FA Feb, 2008, Craig Vollkommer, Ian Measeck

26 Project X 5.12a G 100' ★★★

Start: 20' right of Rusty Lumberjack at a chest-high ceiling with a broken slab above it.
P1 5.12a G: Up the slab to the right end of a ceiling, then power through the ceiling on crimpy holds (1st crux) to a stance. Over a second ceiling, up an orange face, then follow a right-leaning crack to a fixed anchor. 100'
Gear: To 1.5".
FA Aug, 2008, Craig Vollkommer, Ian Measeck

27 Infinity and Beyond 5.10b PG 180' ★★★★

Although the first pitch has a reachy crux, two of the first ascentionists were less than 5'7".
Start: Below the left side of a large, detached flake, below a prominent right-leaning crack that defines the left side of a clean shield of white rock. This is where the terrain begins to slope steeply downward to the left.
P1 5.10b PG: Climb the left side of the detached flake then move left to the bottom of the crack. Follow the crack to an overhang that is passed on the right. Step back into the crack and go up through featured rock until it is possible to reach left to a left-leaning rail. Traverse left along the rail (wingspan dependent) and mantel onto a sloping stance below a vertical crack. Go up the crack to the fixed anchor shared with Project X. 90'
P2 5.10b G: Continue up the crack that leans to the right (crux). Move up and left across easier, but rotten, rock to overhangs below the final headwall. Pass the first overhang to its left, then weave right around the next. Make an exposed step to the right into a right-facing corner that is climbed to a fixed anchor at the top. 90'
Descent: Rappel the route.
FA (P1) Nov, 2008, Craig Vollkommer, Ian Measeck, Mira Schwartz
FA (P2) Nov, 2008, Ian Measeck, Craig Vollkommer, Mira Schwartz

28 Infinity Crack 5.12a G (5.8 R) 100' ★★★★

Start: Same as Infinity and Beyond.
P1 5.12a G (5.8 R): Climb the left side of the flake to its top, then step onto the cliff where the crack bulges. Follow the crack as it tappers to a seam. Make powerful underclings with poor feet (crux) along the crack. At its top (join Knights That Say Neigh), traverse right 10'

Amelia Whalen on Claim Jumper (5.11b). Photo by Craig Vollkommer.

until it is possible to break a ceiling, and move onto the face above. Follow a horizontal crack to the left, then go up a vertical crack to fixed anchors on a ledge. 100'
Gear: To 2".
FA Jul 1, 2010, Justin Barrett, Aaron Newell

29 Monty Python 5.10b PG 180' ★★★

Start: At the high point of the terrain, 10' right of a large, detached, blocky flake, and 25' left of the large left-facing corner of Shake and Bake.
P1 5.10a G: Up a gray face, then trend left to a right-leaning, left-facing ramp. Up the ramp to a left-facing flake. Follow the flake to its top, then angle right across the wall following a crack to a ledge beneath a headwall. Up the headwall to a left-facing corner, and climb it to a fixed anchor. 100'
P2 5.10b PG: Traverse 25' left on the ledge to the fixed anchor of Knights That Say Neigh. Go up and left to a small ledge, then up a clean corner with small crack. Work up the crack a few feet, then step left around an arête and continue up face to a fixed anchor. 80'
Descent: Rappel to Knights That Say Neigh anchor, then another rappel to the ground.
FA (P1) Jan, 2008, Craig Vollkommer, Jessica Donovan
FA (P2) Nov, 2008, Craig Vollkommer, Ian Measeck

Opposite: Craig Vollkommer on Kinghts That Say Neigh (5.11b). Photo by Tomás Donoso.

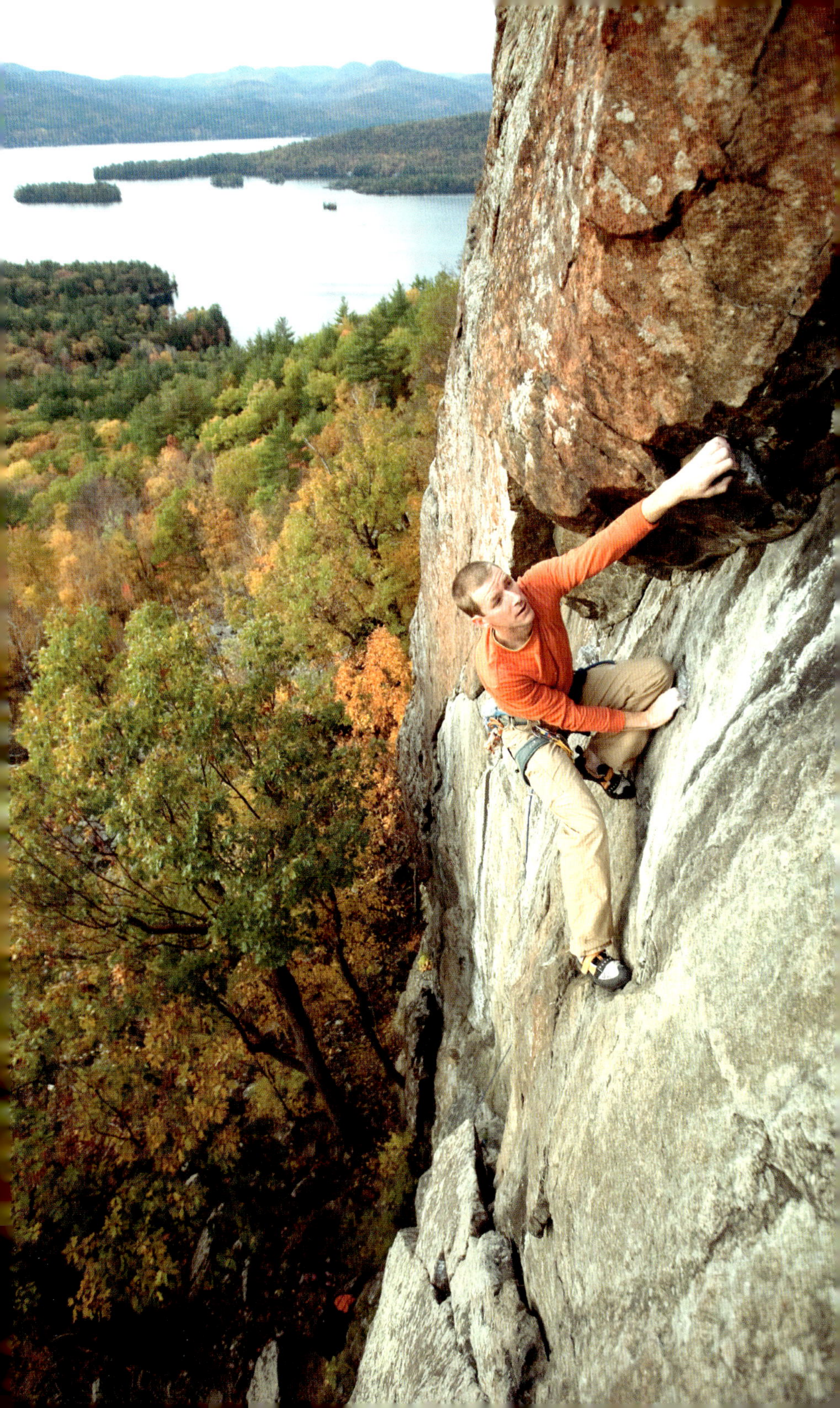

Lake George

30 Knights That Say Neigh
5.11b PG (5.8R) 90' ★★★
Start: Same as **Monty Python**.
P1 5.11b PG (5.8 R): Begin **Monty Python**: go up a gray face, trend left to a right-leaning, left-facing ramp. Climb a thin crack in a sheer face that is left of the right-rising slab of **Monty Python**. When the crack ends at a left-rising overhang, go over it and into the prominent right-rising ceiling that cuts across the cliff. Traverse right for 10' until it is possible to break the ceiling, and move onto the face above. Follow a horizontal crack to the left, then go up a vertical crack to fixed anchors on a ledge. 90'
FA Jun, 2009, Craig Vollkommer, Ian Measeck

31 Holy Grail 5.10c PG 100' ★
Start: On a table-sized boulder at the height of land, midway between a large, detached flake on the left, and a large, left-facing corner on the right.
P1 5.10c PG: Climb up to a ceiling that has a short, 5"-wide, parallel-sided slot. Go up the slot and climb a short open book to a vertical face. Work up the face past a vertical crack to a ledge, then join **Monty Python** up the headwall to a left-facing corner that is climbed to a fixed anchor. 100'
FA Jul, 2010, Ian Measeck, Craig Vollkommer

32 Project
This open project begins at the fixed anchors at the top of P1 of **Monty Python**. A line extends above the anchor and begins with a ledge, then follows right-facing flakes and overhangs.

33 Shake and Bake 5.8- G 80' ★
Often wet, but a convenient way to the top of the buttress.
Start: At the height of land, in a large, left-facing corner on the left side of a clean buttress.
P1 5.8- G: Up the corner to a fixed anchor at the top of the buttress. 80'
FA Apr, 2008, Craig Vollkommer, Ian Measeck

34 Stake and Cake 5.10a PG 170' ★★★
Start: Just right of the left-facing corner of **Shake and Bake**, below the prow of a clean buttress.
P1 5.10a PG: (V1) Up an open book in the prow of the buttress (5" cam on the left), then up the prow to another open book that is climbed to a fixed anchor at the top of the buttress. 80'
P2 + 5.9 PG: Go up a short corner to a ledge, and traverse to its right end. Move right over an overhang to the base of a right-leaning, right-facing corner. The corner defines the right end of the tall, black wall with tiered overhangs. Follow the corner until it is possible to break out left and climb to a fixed anchor. 90'
V1 5.8 PG: Climb the blocks to the right of the open book, then up a thin crack in face left of **Wake and Bake** to its end. Traverse left and join the arête above the crux.

Amelia Whalen on Monty Python (5.10b). Photo by Tomás Donoso.

Gear: To 1" plus 1 ea 5" cam.
FA (P1) Apr, 2008, Craig Vollkommer, Ian Measeck
FA (P2) Jun, 2009, Craig Vollkommer, Diane Durnouchel
FA (V1) May 1, 2011, Michael Gray, Kevin Heckeler

35 Wake and Bake 5.10a G 170' ★★★★
Climbs the clean face right of the prow of **Stake and Cake**.
Start: At the base of a right-facing corner, which is the next corner to the right of the large **Shake and Bake** corner.
● **P1 5.10a G:** Up easy rock to an overlap. Move right, then climb the center of the face until it is possible to make a move left (crux) to a rail, and then back right to the top of the buttress. Scramble to the fixed anchor shared with the neighboring routes. 80'
P2 5.10a G: Go up a short corner to a ledge and traverse to its right end (same as **Stake and Cake** P2). Start up a black-streaked wall with tiered overhangs, then up to a right-rising overhang that is above light-colored rock. Move over the overhang, then work left to a fixed anchor (shared with **Stake and Cake**). 90'
Gear: To 1".
FA (P1) Apr, 2008, Craig Vollkommer, Ian Measeck
FA (P2) Jun, 2009, Craig Vollkommer, Ian Measeck

Lake George

*Dillon Kovacs on **Wake and Bake** (5.10a).
Photo by Alex Wakeman.*

36 Line of Fire 5.10c G 90' ★★★
An alternate finish to **Wake and Bake**. The best of the upper pitches on the black wall.
Start: At the top of P1 of **Wake and Bake**.
P1 5.10c G: Climb a broken, right-facing corner to a stance at its top next to a cedar shrub. Pull onto a vertical face with superb water-worn crimps and knobs. Go up the face (crux) to an overhang and pass this on the right. Work back left, escape onto easier terrain, and follow it up and right to a shared fixed anchor. 90'
FA Jul, 2010, Craig Vollkommer

37 Princess Bride 5.5 G 90'
Start: Right of **Wake and Bake** in a broken corner.
P1 5.5 G: Climb stacked corners to face climbing past semi-dead pine, then step left onto rock steps that are climbed to a fixed anchor. 90'
Gear: To 3".
FA Aug 12, 2010, Tom Rosecrans, Sue Beadle

38 Kid Rock 5.9 TR 90'
Using the **Princess Bride*** anchor, climb the face between **Princess Bride** and **Wake and Bake**. Good climbing, but contrived.
FA (TR) Aug 12, 2010, Tom Rosecrans

Neanderthal Cave

This section of rock is 100' right of where the main herd path reaches the Main Wall.

DIRECTIONS (MAP PAGE 38)
From the right end of the Main Wall, go slightly downhill to a small talus clearing beneath a right-facing wall. The start of **Ghost Boner** is at this clearing. Downhill and right, the path levels out beneath the steep slab with several routes, including **Devo**. Immediately right of the slab is an overhanging, right-facing wall (climbed by **Protruding Forehead**) and the Neanderthal Cave.

39 Ghost Boner 5.10b G 70' ★★
Start: Above the talus at a vertical crack next to a tree.
P1 5.10b G: Climb up to a low roof and go left onto a slab. Move up and left (crux) to a crack in a slab. Follow the crack to its end then traverse right to a fixed anchor. 70'
Gear: to 2".
FA Sep 9, 2010, Justin Barrett, Craig Vollkommer

40 Left Out 5.8 G 70' ★
Start: Beneath a tall, right-facing wall.
P1 5.8 G: Go up the flake, step right onto slab, then back left to slanting corner. Up corner to near its top, then (V1) fun moves lead left to a fixed anchor. 70'
V1 Left In 5.7 G: Continue up right to the fixed anchor of **Breaking Bad**.
Gear: To 3".
FA Jun, 2012, Tom Rosecrans, Aaron Lizor

41 Breaking Bad 5.8+ G 70' ★★★
A popular route with good climbing. The bolts are somewhat widely spaced in the crux dihedral.
Start: At a low bulge next to a large oak.
● **P1 5.8+ G:** Climb a left-rising crack through the low bulge. Step into the slanting dihedral and climb it to its top. Climb easier rock to a fixed anchor beneath an overhang. 70'
FA Jun, 2012, Tom Rosecrans, Aaron Lizor, Heather Neddo, Lauren Richards

42 Dweezil 5.7+ G 65' ★
An awkward start with a high first bolt.
Start: Immediately right of a low, blocky corner.
● **P1 5.7+ G:** Up a shallow right-facing corner (better holds to the right) to an easy overlap beneath a slab. Go up and right across the slab, then reach left across a steep wall with jugs. Work over the wall to a ledge with a fixed anchor. 65'
Gear: Optional 1.5' cam
FA Aug 30, 2010, Clint McCarthy, Tom Rosecrans

43 Sub-Dude 5.7 G 75' ★★
Start: Where the path levels out, in the center of the steep slab.
● **P1 5.7 G:** Up steep slab to an overlap, which is climbed on the left to a good crack. Up the crack in a slab to a steep, right-rising ramp, which is followed to a fixed anchor. 75'
FA Aug 17, 2010, Tom Rosecrans, Brie Rosecrans, Robert Livingston

Lake George

SHELVING ROCK:
NEANDERTHAL WALL

44 Devo 5.8 G 95' ★★★
Start: Where the path levels out, beneath a right-facing overlap 15' up.
● **P1 5.8 G:** Climb face through two overlaps, then over a short, steep wall. Go right, cross *Diva*, and work up steep rock to a stance beneath a left-facing corner. Climb up a thin slab to a fixed anchor. 95'
FA Nov 5, 2009, Tom Rosecrans, Justin Barrett

45 Diva 5.10a G 95' ★★
Good climbing, especially up high, but beware of the rope-drag!
Start: At the low point of the cliff base, next to an overhanging arête.
● **P1 5.10a G:** Go over two bulges to a stem-box beneath a cedar. Go left and then over a steep wall (crux). Cross *Devo*, go left, and work up a blocky wall with good holds (harder for short climbers) to a fixed anchor. 95'
Gear: Slings and long quickdraws.
FA Jul, 2012, Tom Rosecrans, Aaron Lizor, Rhea Johnson

52

Lake George

Shelving Rock: Neanderthal Wall

- 39 Ghost Boner (5.10b)
- 40 Left Out (5.8)
- 41 Breaking Bad (5.8+)
- 42 Dweezil (5.7+)
- 43 Sub-Dude (5.7)
- 44 Devo (5.8)
- 45 Diva (5.10a)
- 46 Protruding Forehead (5.10d)
- 47 Project
- 48 Knuckle-Dragger (5.9)
- 49 Cro-Magnon (5.9+)
- 50 Homo (5.7)
- 51 Yabba Dabba Do (5.9)

46 Protruding Forehead 5.10d G 60' ★★★

Start: Midway along the overhanging wall and beneath an orange-striped flake with horn 15' up.

P1 5.10d G: Up the flake to the horn to gain a right-rising crack. Follow the crack to the right, through an A-frame overhang 25' up. Continue along the crack then work up the sheer face to a ledge. Step right to an overhanging left-facing corner that is climbed to a fixed anchor. 60'

Gear: To 1.5".

FA Apr, 2009, Ian Measeck, Craig Vollkommer

47 Project

This closed project begins left of **Knuckle-Dragger** and goes up a steep slab to a right-facing corner. Above the corner it climbs through a ceiling, then an overhang, to a fixed anchor.

48 Knuckle-Dragger 5.9 G 80' ★★

Start: At blocks that lead up to a sloping dirt ledge.

P1 5.9 G: Scramble up to a thin, vertical crack and climb it to the right end of a long, right-facing overhang. Go around the right end of the overhang and up to a stance beneath a long, right-facing corner capped by a ceiling. Climb flakes, and move around the right end of the ceiling (crux). Step left across a slab to regain the corner that is followed to its top and a fixed anchor on the right. 80'

FA Apr, 2009, Craig Vollkommer, Justin Barrett

49 Cro-Magnon 5.9+ PG 80' ★

Start: Same as **Homo**.

P1 5.9+ PG: Follow ledges to a slab beneath a right-facing corner. Move left to a thin vertical crack on the right side on a blunt arête. Up a thin crack (crux) that is followed by a shallow, right-facing corner and the fixed anchor shared with **Knuckle-Dragger**. 80'

FA Apr, 2009, Craig Vollkommer, Justin Barrett

50 Homo 5.7 PG 50'

Start: Scramble up blocks to a sloping dirt ledge next to a large flake.

P1 5.8 G: Follow ledges to a slab beneath a right-facing corner that is climbed to a fixed anchor. 50'

FA Apr, 2009, Craig Vollkommer, Justin Barrett

51 Yabba Dabba Do 5.9 G 80' ★

Start: 10' right of **Homo**.

P1 5.9 G: Go up and right to a sheer wall (bolt) that is climbed to a ledge below an overhang with a right-rising crack above it. Follow the crack to a slab and up to the base of a buttress. Work up the buttress to a fixed anchor at its top. 80'

FA Jul, 2010, Craig Vollkommer, Diane Dumouchel

Opposite: Ian Measeck on the first ascent of
Protruding Forehead *(5.10d). Photo by Diane Dumouchel.*

Lake George

SHELVING ROCK: BIG WALL

Big Wall

Located 200' right of the Neanderthal Cave and 200' left of the Jackass Buttress at the tallest section of cliff, this sheer wall has overhangs and ceilings that stretch across the middle of many of the routes. The cliff base is totally open with no trees, and has tons of debris with room-sized boulders. The open base provides the best views of the lake, but makes for a hot place to climb during the second half of the day. The rock here is blocky and difficult to read and requires a good deal of searching to find the best holds. Several of the cruxes involve powerful underclings.

DIRECTIONS (MAP PAGE 38)

The easiest approach is from the left end of the Jackass Buttress. From the trailhead follow the main path and, at 2 min, pass beneath a small talus field. Continue uphill to within 100' of the cliff 0612786,4823713. There is a spur path on the right that goes to the Desert Shield area and, 70' further, turn right on a spur path and go up a forested slope to the Jackass Buttress 0612820,4823788 at 8 min. Go uphill and left along the base of the cliff (near the start of **Gyroscopic Tendencies**), then drop down below three room-sized boulders and traverse to a small talus field below the left end of the Big Wall near the start of **Pinching One Off**. To reach **Die by the Drop** and **Johnny Tsunami**, scramble right over the middle and rightmost boulders.

54

Lake George

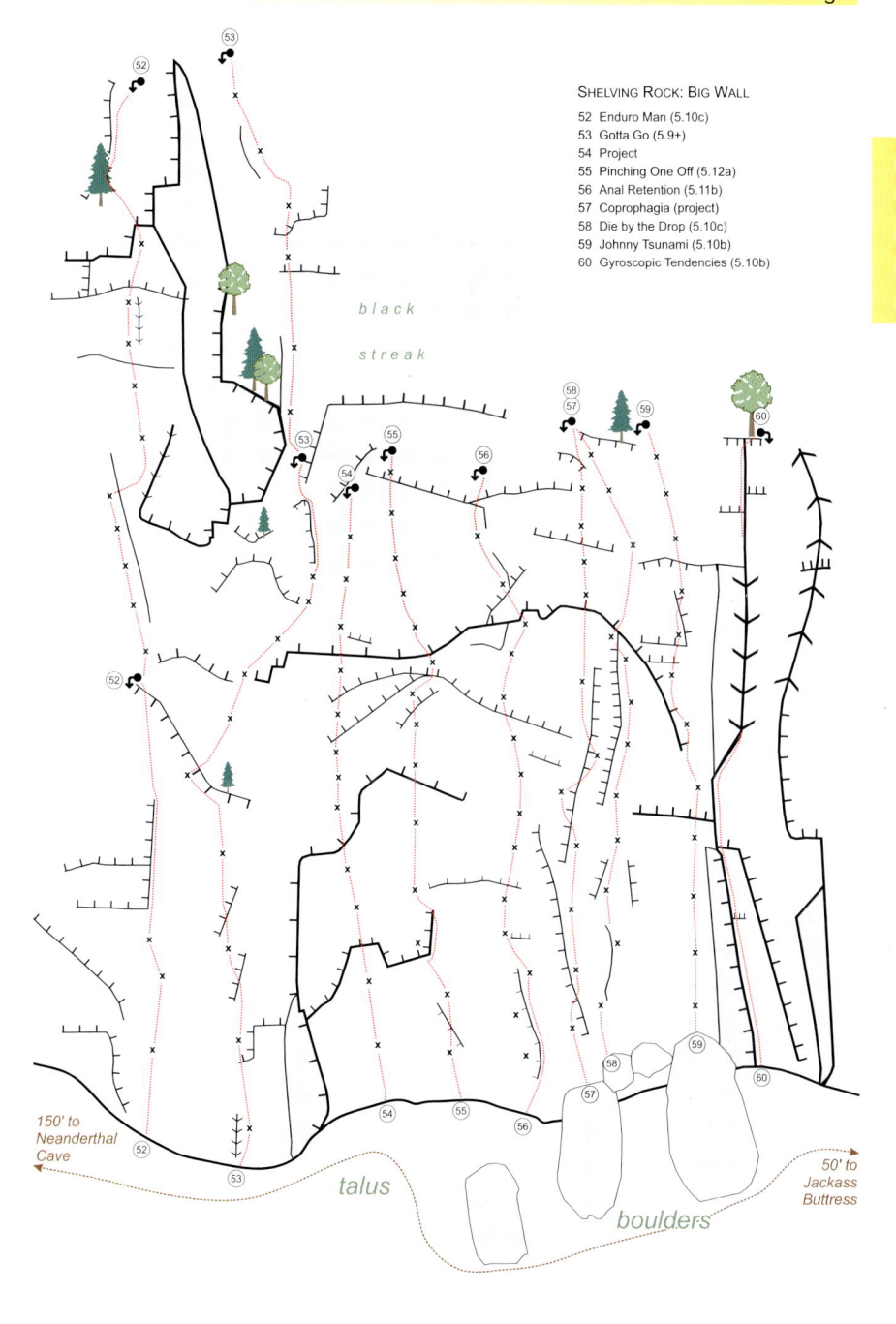

SHELVING ROCK: BIG WALL

52 Enduro Man (5.10c)
53 Gotta Go (5.9+)
54 Project
55 Pinching One Off (5.12a)
56 Anal Retention (5.11b)
57 Coprophagia (project)
58 Die by the Drop (5.10c)
59 Johnny Tsunami (5.10b)
60 Gyroscopic Tendencies (5.10b)

black streak

talus

boulders

150' to Neanderthal Cave

50' to Jackass Buttress

Lake George

52 Enduro Man 5.10c G 160' ★★★
Start: Lowest point of the wall, right of a blocky, overhanging, left-facing corner.
- **P1 5.10c G:** Climb a white calcite strip on overhanging rock to a small ledge 15' up. Move up and left across steepening rock to a right-facing, overhanging corner. Go up the corner, then pull over a bulge onto lower angled rock, and climb to a fixed anchor below a bulging wall. 60'
- **P2 5.10c G:** Go over the bulging wall and follow a left-rising seam, staying left of a large prow with a left-facing corner on its left side. Climb the corner then straight up a face, past a horizontal crack to a stance below a ceiling high on the cliff. Pull the ceiling on its left side, step into a left-facing corner, and follow it to a fixed anchor on the right. 100'

Gear: To 1.5".
FA Aug 6, 2010, Craig Vollkommer

53 Gotta Go 5.9+ G 195' ★★
One of the more exposed and adventuresome routes on the Big Wall. First route on the Big Wall.
Start: At a 6'-tall open book in a bulging buttress with a widening black streak on its right side.
- **P1 5.9+ G:** Climb the open book and go up a slab to a broken, overhanging wall that faces right and leads to a ledge. Move up and right to a long ceiling (climbed via a small crimp) that leads to rails. Follow the rails to an overhang on the right. Climb the overhang on its right side, then up easier rock to a right-facing corner with a fixed anchor at its top. 95'
- **P2 5.9+ G:** Traverse left across a grey slab to a deep, right-facing corner, and follow it to a face below a tiered ceiling. Climb the face, then go over a ceiling and follow a right-rising seam until it is possible to move up and right to a fixed anchor at the very top of the cliff. 100'

Gear: To 1.5".
FA Oct, 2009, Craig Vollkommer

54 Project
This open project begins at the top of the talus field and goes up a steep slab, and past a small overlap. It continues through tiered right-arching overhangs, and finishes across a black slab to a fixed anchor.

55 Pinching One Off 5.12a G 90' ★★★
Some say that underclinging the first ceiling is the crux, while others do battle at the second.
Start: At the top of the talus field, 20' right of a wet spot at the base of the cliff and 20' left of a boulder cave, at a left-rising rail 8' up.
- **P1 5.12a G:** Follow the rail to an overlap, then up steep, blocky rock to a ceiling. Make a powerful undercling move to clear the ceiling and continue up to a long right-rising ceiling in the center of the wall. Trend up and right, staying right of the bolts (spooky clips), until it is possible to step left over the ceiling and onto a black, low-angled face. Climb water-worn rock to a fixed anchor. 90'

FA Jun 17, 2010, Justin Barrett, Craig Vollkommer

56 Anal Retention 5.11b G 90' ★★★
Start: Left of the boulder cave, beneath a discontinuous, right-facing corner 8' up.
- **P1 5.11b G:** Up the corner for 25' to a short overhang then move left to easier climbing that is ends at tiered overhangs. Strenuous undercling moves and sloping footholds gain positive flakes on a sheer gray wall. Make a long reach left to a blocky roof, then work right to a broken, right-rising ceiling. Over the ceiling on its right end, then step left onto a slab and follow a left-facing corner to an easy ceiling with a fixed anchor above it. 90'

FA Jul, 2010, Craig Vollkommer

57 Coprophagia Project
This open project begins as for **Die by the Drop**, goes up an open book, then steps right and works up to the left side of an overhanging nose (crux). Lower-angled rock leads to a long overhang which is climbed to the right and finishes at the fixed anchor of **Die by the Drop**.

58 Die by the Drop 5.10c G 90' ★★★★
Start: On top of the middle boulder at a couple of chest-sized boulders, beneath a right-facing flake.
- **P1 5.10c G:** Climb the flake to shallow opposing corners. Exit the corners (crux) to the left to a stance beneath a prow. Move right beneath the prow into a right-facing, blocky corner. Go up the sustained corner to a left-rising overhang. Step right over the overhang to a ledge beneath an off-vertical face. Make a bouldery move up the face and then climb easily up and left to a fixed anchor left of a cedar tree. 90'

FA Jul, 2010, Craig Vollkommer

59 Johnny Tsunami 5.10b G 90' ★★★★
A great introduction to the Big Wall. This route features a gymnastic roof move (hang ten!), an exposed crux high above the ground, and a devious face climb to the anchor.
Start: On top of the rightmost boulder, 4' left of a deep, right-facing corner.
- **P1 5.10b G:** Up a blocky, vertical wall to the center of a ceiling with an overhanging wall beneath its right side. Go up the wall, then reach right to a jug at the lip and pull onto a slab in a deep, left-facing corner. Follow the corner to tiered ceilings with jugs. At the lip of the ceiling, make a hard move into a left-facing corner, and climb it to a ledge with a bulging black wall above it. Work up and left across the wall to a fixed anchor right of a cedar tree. 90'

FA Jul, 2010, Craig Vollkommer

60 Gyroscopic Tendencies 5.10b G 100' ★
Start: Right of the rightmost boulder, where the herd path first reaches the wall, beneath a clean right-facing corner that goes through two overhangs.
P1 5.10b G: Go up the corner and past the overhangs (crux), and continue up into a deep v-slot corner. Follow a widening crack, past an overhang on the left, to a ledge with a fixed anchor. 100'

FA Sep 11, 2010, Craig Vollkommer, Diane Dumouchel, Ian Measeck

Lake George

Jackass Buttress

This buttress forms the left (north) wall of a broad gully that separates the cliffband into two sections. The base of the buttress extends uphill to the left (towards **The O'Barrett Factor**), where it merges with the tallest section of the cliff, and uphill to the right (towards **Winds of Change**) where it diminishes in height at the top of the gully.

DIRECTIONS (MAP PAGE 38)

From the trailhead, follow the main path. At 2 min, pass beneath a small talus field. Continue uphill to within 100' of the cliff **0612786,4823713**. There is a spur path on the right that goes to the Desert Shield area and, 70' further, turn right on a spur path and go up a forested slope to the Jackass Buttress **0612820,4823788** at 8 min near **The Cold Bare Rapport**.

61 Old School 5.8 G 60' ★★

Vollkommer's first route at Shelving Rock.
Start: At the top of the hill, at a slab that is below a left-facing corner.
P1 5.8 G: Follow the corner to a tree with a fixed anchor. 60'
FA Nov, 2007, Craig Vollkommer, Jessica Donovan

62 The O'Barrett Factor 5.10a PG 100' ★★

Start: At the left side of the buttress, uphill and 40' left of where the approach trail reaches the cliff base, at a large cedar stump.
P1 5.10a PG: Climb an easy flake and go left to a short slab that is beneath a 1' x 1' overhang. Above the overhang is a tall, clean orange face; climb the left side of the face to a tree with a fixed anchor. 100'
FA Nov 12, 2008, Justin Barrett, Tom Rosecrans

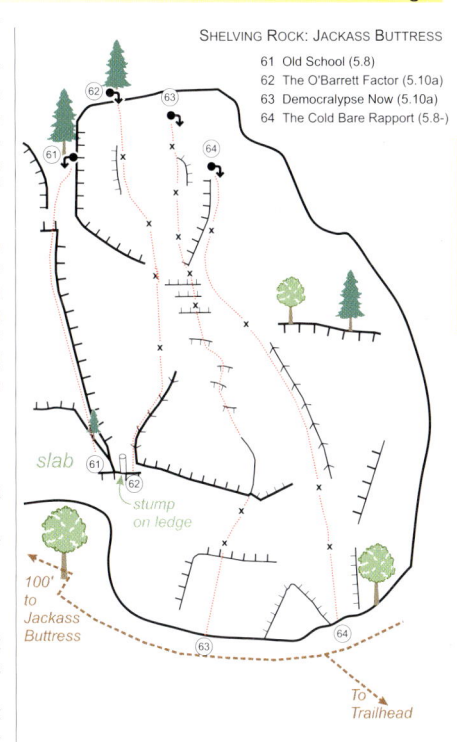

SHELVING ROCK: JACKASS BUTTRESS
61 Old School (5.8)
62 The O'Barrett Factor (5.10a)
63 Democralypse Now (5.10a)
64 The Cold Bare Rapport (5.8-)

Martine Schaer on **Caribou Barbie** (5.10a).

Lake George

63 Democralypse Now 5.10a G 100' ★★
Still some loose stuff to be cleaned.
Start: 15' left of where the spur path reaches the cliff at a chest-high, right-facing overhang beneath a 15'-tall slab.
P1 5.10a G: Climb the slab to a ceiling that becomes a right-facing corner. Move right over a bulge and into the right-facing corner. Exit left onto a slab and climb up to a steep wall with tiered overhangs. Work over the overhangs, then step left around a large right-facing corner to a tall, clean orange face. Climb the right side of the face to a fixed anchor. 100'
Gear: To 1".
FA Nov 8, 2008, Tom Rosecrans, Justin Barrett

64 The Cold Bare Rapport 5.8- G 90' ★★
Start: Between two, 8'-tall blocky pillars beneath a triangle-shaped face with a horn on top, where the spur path meets the cliff.
● **P1 5.8- G:** Climb the triangle-shaped face, and step left onto a slab that is crossed to its left side. Step left over the right end of tiered overhangs, move toward a right-facing corner, and climb up and right across a slab to a fixed anchor. 90'
Gear: 1 ea 0.5" cam.
FA Nov 8, 2008, Tom Rosecrans, John Weston

65 Indecision '08 5.7 TR 75'
Begin on the right side of the buttress, facing the gully, at a left-rising crack just left of **Winds of Change**. Climb the crack to the fixed anchor shared with **Winds of Change**.
FA (TR) Nov 3, 2008, Tom Rosecrans

66 Winds of Change 5.8+ G 75' ★★
Start: From where the approach trail reaches the base of the cliff, walk 30' right, then 30' up the gully along a steep herd path. Begin at three, 5'-tall, right-facing right-leaning corners below a jutting, diamond-shaped block.

P1 5.8+ G: Step up to the block and go over it to a featured face. Climb past a right-rising crack and a bulge to a left-rising crack that is followed to a ledge. Go up and right to a fixed anchor on top of the buttress. 75'
Gear: To 1".
FA Nov 11, 2008, Robert Livingston, Tom Rosecrans

Desert Shield Area

This section of cliff is very close to the parking area and has one spur path that goes to **Shelving Rock Earth Penetrator** and a second that goes to **Obama Mama**. **Shelving Rock Earth Penetrator** ascends a low-angled buttress 100' from the main path. Uphill and left are two steep walls separated by a low-angled corner with **Wolfshack Corner**. 200' to the right of **Shelving Rock Earth Penetrator** is a steep slab with three routes, including **Obama Mama**.

The routes **Shelving Rock Earth Penetrator**, **WMD**, and **Shock and Awe** are very easy and used by local guides. Long slings are recommended to reduce rope drag. There are several low anchors set on this wall for the convenience of toproping. The fixed anchors described here are at the top of the cliff and not visible from the ground.

DIRECTIONS (MAP PAGE 38)
From the trailhead follow the main path and, at 2 min, pass beneath a small talus field. Continue uphill to within 100' of the cliff 0612786,4823713. Locate a spur trail on the right, and follow this up to the Desert Shield Area near the base of **Shelving Rock Earth Penetrator**.

67 Rumney but Crumbly 5.9 G 60'
Steep and juggy.
Start: 120' left of where the spur path meets the cliff, beneath an overhanging 40' wall, at a notched ledge at head height.
● **P1 5.9 G:** Above the ledge, zig-zag up big holds to a bulge, then work around the left side and climb up to a tree with a fixed anchor. 60'
FA 2010, Justin Barrett, Adam Ostrander

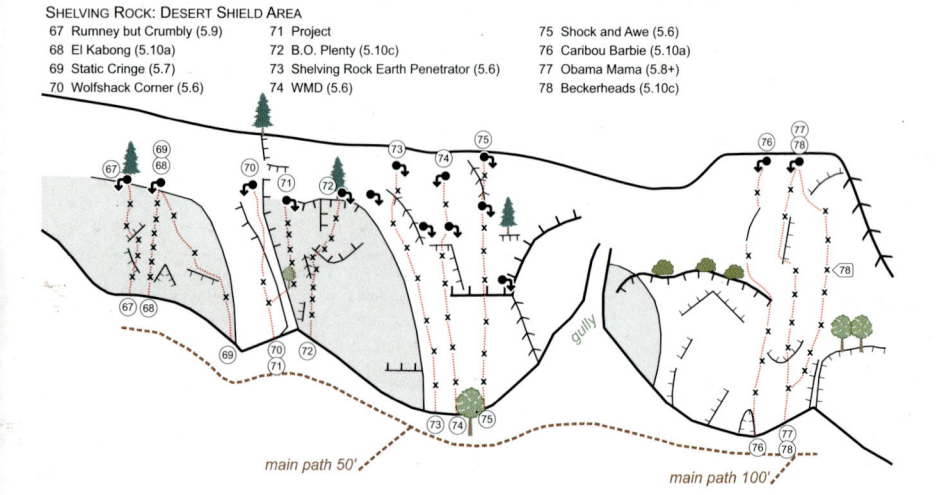

SHELVING ROCK: DESERT SHIELD AREA
67 Rumney but Crumbly (5.9)
68 El Kabong (5.10a)
69 Static Cringe (5.7)
70 Wolfshack Corner (5.6)
71 Project
72 B.O. Plenty (5.10c)
73 Shelving Rock Earth Penetrator (5.6)
74 WMD (5.6)
75 Shock and Awe (5.6)
76 Caribou Barbie (5.10a)
77 Obama Mama (5.8+)
78 Beckerheads (5.10c)

Lake George

68 El Kabong 5.10a PG 60' ★★
Start: Same as Rumney but Crumbly.
● **P1 5.10a PG:** Surf up right across a steep wall to a small ledge. Go up an overhanging face and around the right side of a bulge. Climb lower-angled rock to a fixed anchor at the top of the wall. 60'
History: Named for the block that came off on Van Evera's head on an early toprope lap.
FA 2011, Tom Rosecrans, Royce Van Evera

69 Static Cringe 5.7 PG 60'
Start: 100' from where the spur path meets the cliff, beneath a stepped arête to the left of Wolfshack Corner.
P1 5.7 PG: Work up a left-rising crack and wander up and left across a knobby face to the fixed anchor of El Kabong. 60'
FA Apr, 2011, Tom Rosecrans, Clint McCarthy

70 Wolfshack Corner 5.6 G 50'
Start: At a large left-facing corner 80' uphill and left of where the spur path reaches the cliff. The left wall is a slab, and the right is overhanging.
P1 5.5 G: Up slab for 20' then go into the corner. Up the corner past an overhang, then up the wall on the right and into a shallow right-facing corner of the overhanging wall. Follow the corner to a fixed anchor. 50'
Gear: To 2".
FA Apr, 2011, Tom Rosecrans, Clint McCarthy

71 Project
This closed project climbs Wolfshack Corner to a tree, then up right-facing flakes and blunt arête. Continue up blocky rock to a sloping ledge beneath an overhang, then pull the overhang. Fixed anchor.

72 B.O. Plenty 5.10c G 60' ★
Start: Immediately right of the start of Wolfshack Corner beneath a rust-colored wall.
● **P1 5.10c G:** Go up the steep wall to a right-facing flake. Climb the flake, and then work left to an overhanging arête. Climb the arête, move right, and climb a slab to an overhang. Pull the overhang and scramble to a belay at a tree. 60'
FA 2010, Justin Barrett, Adam Ostrander

73 Shelving Rock Earth Penetrator 5.6 G 70' ★
Start: Immediately left of a large oak tree.
● **P1 5.6 G:** Go past a low ledge to a shallow left-facing corner and pass an overlap to its right. Follow the corner as it deepens and becomes the left side of an arête. Step right onto the top of the arête, which has a fixed anchor. 70'
FA Oct, 2010, Tom Rosecrans, Clint McCarthy

74 WMD 5.6 G 80' ★★
Start: Immediately behind a large oak tree.
● **P1 5.6 G:** Go up a low-angled rib, past ledges to a good stance below a steep wall with an intermediate anchor. Go up the wall and onto lower-angled rock to a fixed anchor at the top of the cliff. 80'
FA Oct, 2010, Tom Rosecrans, Clint McCarthy

75 Shock and Awe 5.6 G 70' ★
Start: Same as WMD.
● **P1 5.6 G:** Work up and right on stepped rock to a ceiling (fixed anchor) that is passed on the left. Move back right and go up a steep wall to a ledge. Climb past a second intermediate anchor to a high arête and a fixed anchor at the top of the cliff. 70'
FA Nov, 2010, Tom Rosecrans, Clint McCarthy

76 Caribou Barbie 5.10a G 90' ★★★
Sustained with a steep start and a difficult-to-clip first bolt.
Start: Beneath a chocolate-colored streak that begins 8' up and a short, shattered pillar on the left.
P1 5.10a G: A committing start to a jug and a high first bolt, then easier climbing to a ledge beneath a short buttress. Go up the right side of the buttress (very close to Obama Mama) to another ledge. Climb a gray slab that is left of a long black streak, then move left to gain a right-rising, thin crack. Follow the crack to its end, and make a tough high step (crux) onto a bulging wall near the top. Fixed anchor. 90'
Gear: To 1".
FA Oct, 2008, Tom Rosecrans, Justin Barrett

77 Obama Mama 5.8+ G 90' ★★★
Watch the clip on the second bolt; after that, the route is 5.6.
Start: A few feet left of a vegetated chimney crack.
● **P1 5.8+ G:** Up steep juggy rock, moving left over a bulge to a thin face, then up a shallow left-facing corner to a fixed anchor. 90'
FA Oct, 2008, Tom Rosecrans, Brie Rosecrans, Robert Livingston

78 Beckerheads 5.10c G 90' ★★
Start: Same as Obama Mama.
● **P1 5.10c G:** up blocky rock to a hueco that is below and right of a smooth bulge. Move over the bulge (crux) and onto a slab where the climbing eases for 30' to an overlap with more blocky rock. Above the blocky rock is a sheer face. Make a high step onto the sheer face, then go left to a diagonal crack, and follow it to Obama Mama's last bolt and fixed anchor. 90'
Gear: 1 ea 1" cam.
FA May 21, 2010, Justin Barrett, Tom Rosecrans

79 Prima Facie 5.7+ G 75' ★★
This section of cliff, closest to the parking area, defines the extreme right end of the climbable rock. The name means "at first sight", as it was the first line in this section of cliff.
Start: 100' right of Obama Mama and 90' left of the extreme right side of the cliff at a short, waist-high ledge beneath a short overhang 15' up.
P1 5.7+ G: Work over the overhang, then go up a face past some huecos and pockets into a shallow, left-facing corner. Up the corner and face above to a fixed anchor. 75'
Gear: 2–3" cams
FA Jul, 2008, Randy Hibshman, Craig Vollkommer

Lake George

ARK WALL

Location	North of NY 149 on the east shore of Lake George, accessed from Northway Exit 20
Aspect	West
Height	70'
Quality	★★★★
Approach	16 min, moderate
Summary	Face climbing on a complex cliff with big roofs and steep buttresses; scenic with many good, easy routes.

	1	4	4	1	8			18
	-5.6	5.7	5.8	5.9	5.10	5.11	5.12	5.13+	total

Much like the other cliffs in the neighborhood—Shelving Rock and Sleeping Beauty Mountain—the Ark Wall has very good face climbing on steep rock with incut holds. The rock quality is uniformly better than Shelving Rock, and the routes have been cleaned well. That said, these routes are still fresh, so wear a helmet and watch for falling rock. There are views of Lake George from the top of the routes and the setting is more peaceful than nearby Shelving Rock (no noisy boat traffic). The cliff is 400' wide and has a relatively comfortable base with some open talus. The largest clearing is midway along the cliff where large talus blocks sit beneath impressive roofs.

There are three distinct sections. The left end of the cliff has steep arêtes capped by ceilings; the routes **Two Camels**, **One Hump** and **Two Pots to Piss In** weave through these ceilings. The middle section has a beautiful, High-Exposure-like buttress with a sharp arête (the route **Noah's Ark**) and a gently overhanging, sheer wall on its right side (the routes **Oracle** and **Two Evil Deeds**). Just right of this buttress is a wall capped by an enormous, wide roof. The right end of the Ark Wall has low-angled, stepped rock, with many well-protected, moderate routes.

DIRECTIONS (MAP PAGE 38)

Follow the directions for Sleeping Beauty Mountain to the Hogtown Trailhead (page 64, 0.0 miles). Continue on Shelving Rock Road. At 2.4 miles (and just past a bridge) is the Shelving Rock Mountain trailhead on the right 0613251,4823588. There is a large DEC sign marking this parking area. (If you continue past this trailhead approximately 0.5 mile, you will reach the large parking area on the left for the main Shelving Rock crags.)

From the parking area (0 hr 0 min), walk past the trail register and orange gate, then follow a jeep road to a T-junction with a trail marked with red discs (3 min) 0613434,4823632. (Left goes to Shelving Rock Mountain, and right goes to Dacy Clearing.) Go straight across the red-blazed trail and follow a lightly-worn herd path northeast. Stay left of a low ridge and follow an old, small-diameter water pipe. At 7 min, turn away from the pipe and follow cairns north up a ridge; after a few minutes the ridge merges with a steep hillside. At the top of the hillside 0613463,4823887 (0 hr 12 min), turn right (east) and ascend moderately past short rock ledges. At 16 min, reach a short talus field and the right end of the cliff 0613558,4824018.

Walk left along the base of the cliff; the rightmost route, **Tourista**, is 100' left from where the approach trail meets the cliff.

*Craig Vollkommer on **Messiah** (5.10c). Photo by Alex Wakeman.*

60

Lake George

ARK WALL

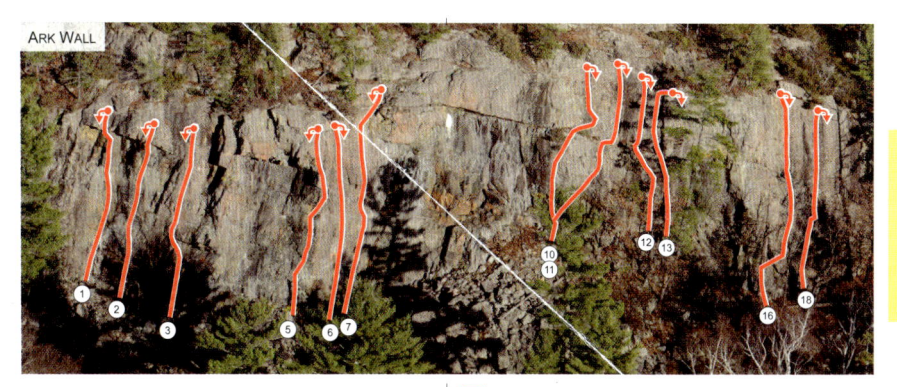

DESCENT OPTIONS
All routes have fixed anchors. It is possible to walk around either end of the cliff.

HISTORY
Craig Vollkommer and Ian Measeck first saw the Ark Wall and its impressive roofs while ice climbing at Shelving Rock in 2009. Vollkommer and Diane Dumouchel bushwhacked to the cliff in the fall of that year. A year later Vollkommer and Measeck established **Two Camels, One Hump**, and **Two Pots to Piss In**. Robert Livingston and Tom Rosecrans happened upon the cliff in the winter of 2011 during a day of skiing. They found Vollkommer's routes at the left end and Rosecrans began developing the right end the following summer.

1 Two Camels, One Hump 5.10a G 50' ★★★
Makes a good warm-up for the other 5.10 routes at the cliff, as the start is easy and the hardest moves are near the top.
Start: At the base of a right-rising ramp in a huge, right-facing corner with an orange-colored right wall.
P1 5.10b G: Go up the ramp that steepens into a vertical corner. Stem the corner for 20', then work out left to an overhanging arête. Follow the arête to a roof, then move left and pull through a notch to the top. Fixed anchor. 50'
Gear: Cams to 2.5".
FA Aug 14, 2010, Craig Vollkommer, Ian Measeck

2 Two Pots to Piss In 5.10b G 50' ★★★
Steep, thrilling, and safe.
Start: At a rock pedestal below an inverted staircase with a thin crack that begins 10' up.
P1 5.10b G: Make a strenuous, well-protected move up to the thin crack and pull onto a slab. Follow the crack, then traverse left to the base of an overhanging wall with black streaks. Work up and right toward an overhanging arête and make big moves to a ledge. Go up to the base of a ceiling and reach a long way (poor feet) to clear it at a short, right-facing corner. Fixed anchor. 50'
Gear: To 1".
FA Aug 14, 2010, Craig Vollkommer, Ian Measeck

3 Messiah 5.10c G 50' ★★★
Sustained vertical face climbing once you get past the low roof.
Start: Beneath a 5' roof 15' up. There is an offwidth in a left-facing corner above the roof.
P1 5.10c G: Go up easy rock (optional small cam) to a body-sized pillar on the left. Climb the pillar and make a hard step right to clear the roof. Work up a steepening face to a sheer wall with an arête on its left side. Use the arête to make a long reach across the face. Pull onto easier rock and a fixed anchor. 50'
Gear: Optional small cam.
FA Jun 1, 2013, Craig Vollkommer, Jeremy Haas

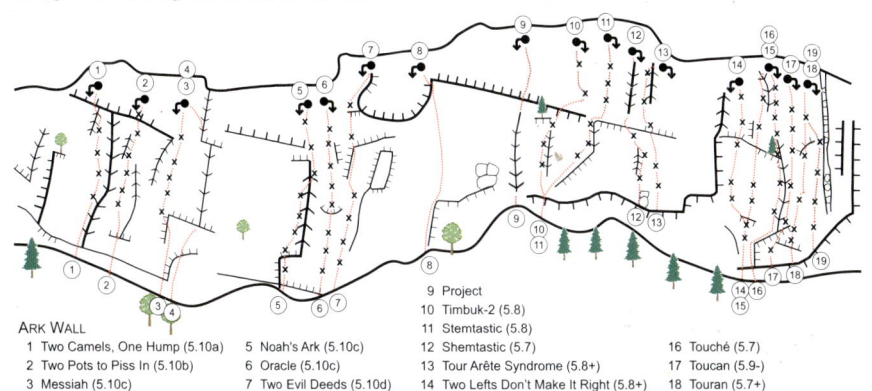

ARK WALL
1 Two Camels, One Hump (5.10a)
2 Two Pots to Piss In (5.10b)
3 Messiah (5.10c)
4 Gopher Wood (5.10a)
5 Noah's Ark (5.10c)
6 Oracle (5.10c)
7 Two Evil Deeds (5.10d)
8 Lost Ark (5.10a)
9 Project
10 Timbuk-2 (5.8)
11 Stemtastic (5.8)
12 Shemtastic (5.7)
13 Tour Arête Syndrome (5.8+)
14 Two Lefts Don't Make It Right (5.8+)
15 Tougastan (5.7)
16 Touché (5.7)
17 Toucan (5.9-)
18 Touran (5.7+)
19 Tourista (5.5+)

Lake George

4 Gopher Wood
5.10a PG 50' ★★
Start: Same as Messiah.
P1 5.10a PG: Scramble up to a low roof and climb a vertical fracture through its left side. Work up to the base of an offwidth crack in a left-facing corner and climb it to the top. Traverse left to the fixed anchor of Messiah. 50'
Gear: To 4".
FA Jul 28, 2013, Craig Vollkommer, John Whalen

5 Noah's Ark
5.10c G 70' ★★★
Start: Below the left side of a 50'-tall overhanging arête at an inverted staircase in a short, right-facing corner.
● **P1 5.10c G:** Make bouldery moves up the right-facing corner, then climb right across easier rock toward the arête. Follow the left-side of the arête past a smooth face, then straight up the arête to a stance with an overhang to its left. Pass the overhang on the right, work up and left to a stance below a headwall. Sidepull up and right, then make a long reach to the top. Fixed anchor. 70'
FA 2012, Craig Vollkommer

6 Oracle 5.10c G 70' ★★★
A bit looser than Two Evil Deeds with a low, powerful, deadpoint crux.
Start: Down and left of the high roof is a bush-filled, open book on the right side of the gently-overhanging face. Start beneath a right-rising rail in the center of this face.
● **P1 5.10c G:** Go up and left to a small ledge at 20'. Continue up and left to a bulge with pinches and underclings. Make a big reach over the bulge (crux) and work up past a quartz dike to a shallow, right-facing corner. Climb the corner on clean rock to easier terrain and a fixed anchor below a cedar tree. 70'
FA Sep 29, 2012, Craig Vollkommer

7 Two Evil Deeds 5.10d G 70' ★★★★
Stellar, pumpy climbing up the center of the sheer overhanging face; reminiscent of Doublissima in the Gunks.
Start: Just left of and below a bush-filled open book on the right side of the overhanging face and left of the enormous, wide roof that dominates the center of the cliff.
● **P1 5.10d G:** Boulder up to a jug-ledge next to the lowest bush. Work up the face to the left of the open book to a quartz band 35' up. Reach out left to a rail and traverse left to a fingercrack. Follow the crack into a right-facing corner and exit left (crux) onto a face. Up this to an easy crack and a fixed anchor. 70'
Gear: 1 ea Camalots #.5, #.75, #1.
FA Sep 22, 2012, Craig Vollkommer

8 Lost Ark 5.10a PG 70' ★
Climbs out the left side of the biggest roof.
Start: Beneath blocky orange rock.
P1 5.10a PG: Work left across the orange rock and go up a short, open book. Climb to the base of a deep right-facing corner and follow it to its top beneath the left side of the huge roof. Reach for a horizontal crack and traverse left to escape from beneath the roof. Climb easy rock to a fixed anchor. 70'
Gear: To 3".
FA Jul 28, 2013, Craig Vollkommer, John Whalen

9 Project
This closed project begins at a vertical crack in black rock and goes over the right end of the biggest roof.

Craig Vollkommer on Two Evil Deeds (5.10d). Photo by Alex Wakeman.

10 Timbuk-2 5.8 PG 60' ★

A zig-zag route with decent climbing that is separated by a bushy ledge.
Start: On the dirt-covered ledge above the cliff base, at the highpoint of the terrain.
● **P1 5.8 PG:** Scramble up to a TV-sized block right of a bulging arête. Stand on the boulder and reach up to a high ledge. Pull onto the arête and climb past a left-rising ramp to a steep, orange face below another arête. Step left and follow a crack to a high fixed anchor. 60'
FA Apr, 2013, Tom Rosecrans, Mikayla Tougas

11 Stemtastic 5.8 G 50' ★★

A tough clip at the second bolt.
Start: At a right-rising ramp, on a dirt-covered ledge that is above the cliff base. This ledge starts 15' right of the open talus area and is the highpoint of the cliff base.
● **P1 5.8 G:** Go up the ramp to a short, overhanging corner. Pull over and go up an easy open book to a tree ledge. Work up and left to a clean, black face, then up this to a fixed anchor. 50'
FA Jun, 2012, Tom Rosecrans, Clint McCarthy

12 Shemtastic 5.7 G 40'

The recommended finish (5.8+) is the steep arête of **Tour Arête Syndrome**.
Start: On a broad dirt-covered ledge uphill and right of the start of **Stemtastic**.
P1 5.7 G: Scramble up to a TV-sized block right of a bulging arête. Stand on the boulder and reach up to a high ledge. Pull onto the arête and climb to a left-rising ramp. Step left and follow a crack to a fixed anchor. 40'
Gear: To 2".
FA Jul, 2012, Tom Rosecrans, Aaron Lizor

13 Tour Arête Syndrome 5.8+ G 40' ★

The arête is short but has some good moves.
Start: 5' right of **Shemtastic**.
● **P1 5.8+ G:** Move up the face and slab to a left-rising ramp with a 15'-tall arête above it. Climb the face on the left side of the arête (ledge fall potential), make some tenuous moves to the top of the cliff, and reach right to a fixed anchor. 40'
FA Jul, 2012, Tom Rosecrans, Aaron Lizor

14 Two Lefts Don't Make It Right 5.8+ G 60' ★★

A devious start and an exposed crux at the top.
Start: At blocky rock below an eroded hand-size slot 8' up where the terrain begins to go uphill to the left.
● **P1 5.8+ G:** Up past the slot, then make an awkward reach up and left to get around the right end of a long fractured wall 25' up. Work up and right to a wall with a horizontal crack. Pull over the crack and go up to a stance beneath an overhanging headwall. Reach for right-facing, sidepull flakes and move up and left to a fixed anchor. 60'
FA Aug, 2012, Aaron Lizor, Tom Rosecrans

15 Tougastan 5.7 PG 60'

Start: Same as **Two Lefts Don't Make It Right**.
● **P1 5.7 PG:** Go up blocky rock (stay right of a hand-size slot) to a sloping stance 20' up. Climb straight up to a larger ledge with a small cedar tree (optional 3" cam eases the runout). Move up and right of a short arête and (nearly) join **Touché** for the last section to a fixed anchor (shared with **Touché**). 60'
FA Apr, 2013, Tom Rosecrans, Mikayla Tougas

16 Touché 5.7 PG 60' ★★★

Well-protected cruxes with widely-spaced protection.
Start: Same as **Two Lefts Don't Make It Right**.
● **P1 5.7 PG:** Go up rock steps, at the left end of a smooth bulge, to a shallow open book. Follow the open book up and left past a small cedar tree, then go up steepening rock to a headwall bulge. Reach over the bulge and climb to a fixed anchor. 60'
FA Jun, 2012, Clint McCarthy, Tom Rosecrans

17 Toucan 5.9- G 60' ★★

Start: On the right side of a low bulge, at a slab with left-rising ripples.
● **P1 5.9- G:** Climb the slab to the top of the bulge, then up an easy right-rising ramp and ledges to the right side of a sheer wall halfway up the cliff. Crimp up the wall to a jug, make a hard mantle onto the jug, then climb easily to a fixed anchor. 60'
FA Jun, 2012, Tom Rosecrans, Clint McCarthy

18 Touran 5.7+ PG 60' ★★

There are many variations including a 5.10a toprope start that goes straight up to the exit crack.
Start: At a clean, table-sized ledge below a left-rising overlap.
● **P1 5.7+ PG:** Up to the overlap, then reach right (crux) to a handcrack-slot. Climb onto a bulge and then up easy ledges to a slab below an arching overlap. Over the arch, then up low-angled rock to a fixed anchor. 60'
FA Jun, 2012, Tom Rosecrans, Clint McCarthy

19 Tourista 5.5+ G 60' ★★

Good rock quality, sometimes wet.
Start: At the bottom of a right-rising ramp that begins in the ground, 20' left of a short, chockstone-filled chimney.
● **P1 5.5+ G:** Step onto a ledge, then up and left to a higher ledge. Go up easy rock to the base of a prominent black streak on a vertical wall. Work left across the wall to join **Touran** above the arching overlap: up low-angled rock to a fixed anchor. 60'
FA Aug, 2012, Tom Rosecrans, Aaron Lizor

Lake George

SLEEPING BEAUTY MOUNTAIN

Location	North of NY 149 on the east shore of Lake George, accessed from Northway Exit 20
Aspect	West
Height	120'
Quality	★★★
Approach	20 min, easy
Summary	A tiered summit cliff near a popular hiking trail with many climbs on the lowest cliffband.

2	3	4	3	5	2	19
-5.6	5.7	5.8	5.9	5.10	5.11	5.12	5.13+	total

Sleeping Beauty Mountain is a popular day hike from the secluded trailhead known as Dacy Clearing. Below the summit ledges are several cliffbands; the lowest one contains more than a dozen routes. The summit hiking trail passes close to the lower cliffband and provides easy access to this impressive crag. The sunny aspect and views toward Lake George make this a pleasant place to climb.

ACCESS
The dirt road that goes to Dacy Clearing from the Hogtown Trailhead will often close in early spring due to muddy road conditions[2]. When the road is closed, park at the Hogtown Trailhead and walk—the hiking time to Dacy Clearing is approximately 30 min with little change in elevation.

Peregrine falcons nest on the cliffs (near **Sizzle Me**) and cause early season closures. Watch for poison ivy in the talus beneath the Gnar Wall and April Wall. Finally, Sleeping Beauty has a small population of rattlesnakes.

HISTORY
The first reports of climbing at Sleeping Beauty came from Steve Adler and Tom Dubois in 1990. The following decade saw the development of many routes by Steve Adler, Michael Christon, Tom Dubois, Russ Boudreau, and Bill Pierce. The specific location of a few of these routes is uncertain, but they are most likely near the April Wall. The cliff fell into obscurity until spring 2007, when Craig Vollkommer and Jessica Donovan began development at the left end. Recently, new route explorations have focused on the Gnar Wall and the Summit Cliffs.

DIRECTIONS   (MAP PAGE 64)
From NY 149, turn north onto Buttermilk Falls / Shelving Rock Road and drive 9.7 miles (partially paved, closed during mud season) to the parking area on the right known as the Hogtown Trailhead. At the far end of the parking area is a high-clearance 2WD road. Follow it for 1.5 miles to Dacy Clearing, a seasonal trailhead 616652,4822835. Hike the trail marked with yellow discs for 200' to a trail register. 300' further, where the yellow-disc trail veers left, leave the trail on the right near a campfire ring and cross a brook. Hike east uphill through open woods. Stay left of a short, wet cliffband, ascend a steep slope, and reach a hiking trail marked with blue discs at 12 min. Turn right and follow the trail along a level bench heading south beneath the cliffbands which are visible high above and left of the trail.

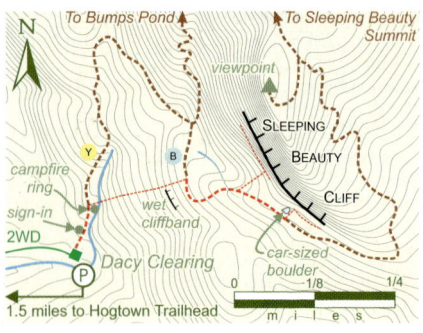

For the Tang and Circus Walls: At 15 min, the hiking trail crosses a small creek and turns right (south), uphill and parallel to the cliffband. Go left onto a herd path 617114,4822942 and follow this east past a small talus field to reach the center of the cliff near **Pine Nuts**, distinguished by a horizontal roof 20' up 617235,4822956.

For the Gnar and April Walls: Continue along the gradually-ascending hiking trail, parallel to the cliffs, for an additional 2 min or 1000'. The trail levels off near a car-sized boulder 100' off the trail and towards the cliff. Leave the hiking trail 0617220,4822894 and walk around the right side of the boulder. Continue another 150' to reach the cliff at **Thorn Forest** 0617270,4822921.

DESCENT OPTIONS
Most routes have fixed anchors.

SLEEPING BEAUTY: TANG WALL

1 Tang Corner (5.8)
2 Flight of the Falcon (5.9)
3 Frick (5.8)
4 Frack (5.8)
5 Good and Plenty (5.11c)
6 Fat Crack (5.7)
7 Sundowner (5.7+)
8 Not Long For This World (5.8)
9 Sizzle Me (5.6)

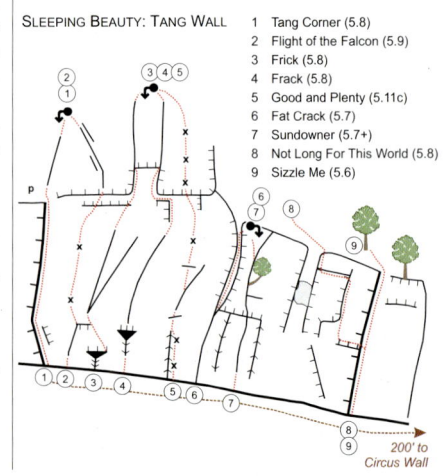

200' to Circus Wall

[2] Trail conditions are posted on the DEC web site at www.dec.ny.gov. Search for "sleeping beauty trail conditions".

Lake George

SLEEPING BEAUTY: CIRCUS WALL
10 Bouncy Bounce (5.10c)
11 Project
12 Crack 'n Corner (5.9)
13 High Wire (5.9+)
14 Hoops and Yo Yo (5.10a)
15 War of the Worlds (5.10a)
16 Pine Nuts (5.11a)
17 Falling Kaiser Zone (5.10d)

Tang Wall

From the end of the approach trail, hike 300' left along a ledge system beneath the cliff and past the Circus Wall. Landmarks for the Tang Wall are a tall, deep, right-facing corner at the left end (**Tang Corner**) and a long ceiling 60' up.

1 Tang Corner 5.8 G 80' ★★

Start: At a flared chimney-slot beneath a deep, right-facing corner at the left end of the wall.
P1 5.8 G: Go up the slot to a handcrack in the corner. Follow the handcrack to the left end of the ceiling, then move left onto a ledge. Make a hard move off the ledge to gain a vertical crack, then follow it to a fixed anchor. 80'
FA May, 2007, Craig Vollkommer, Jessica Donovan

2 Flight of the Falcon 5.9 G 80' ★★★

Start: Same as **Tang Corner**.
P1 5.9 G: Up a broken wide crack right of the flared chimney-slot to a stance on a pedestal. Up a smooth black face to the ceiling. Break through the ceiling at splintered cracks and follow them up and left to the fixed anchor of **Tang Corner**. 80'
FA Jun 10, 2007, Craig Vollkommer, Jessica Donovan

3 Frick 5.8 G 90' ★★★

Start: At a small open book beneath a ceiling 10' up and 20' right of **Tang Corner**.
P1 5.8 G: Up the open book, then right around the ceiling and up broken rock to a smooth black face. Follow the leftmost of two vertical cracks to the left side of a square notch in the ceiling 60' up. Through the left side of the notch and up a crack to a fixed anchor. 90'
FA Jun, 2007, Craig Vollkommer, Jessica Donovan

4 Frack 5.8 G 90' ★★

Start: Same as **Frick**.
P1 5.8 G: Up and right to a small open book beneath a ceiling 15' up. Over the ceiling to a zigzag crack in a smooth black face. Up the crack to the ceiling at 60'. Traverse left to the square notch and climb its right side. Follow a vertical crack above the right side of the notch to the fixed anchor shared with **Frick**. 90'
FA May 28, 2007, Craig Vollkommer, Jessica Donovan

5 Good and Plenty 5.11c G 90' ★★★

Start: 40' right of **Tang Corner**, at a gray arête.
P1 5.11c G: Up the arête to a smooth black face. Face-climb near the right margin of the black face to the ceiling 60' up. Pull the ceiling and onto the sustained headwall, then go left to the fixed anchor of **Frick** and **Frack**. 90'
FA Jun, 2007, Craig Vollkommer, Jessica Donovan

6 Fat Crack 5.7 G 50' ★

Start: 45' right of **Tang Corner** at a vertical handcrack.
P1 5.7 G: Up the handcrack, which becomes a flared off width and ends at a fixed anchor. 50'
FA Jun 10, 2007, Craig Vollkommer, Jessica Donovan

7 Sundowner 5.7+ G 50' ★★

Start: 50' right of **Tang Corner** at a flat block on the ground, beneath a fingercrack that begins 10' up.
P1 5.7+ G: Up to the crack, then climb it to a stance on an arête. Continue up the crack past a birch, then up and left to the fixed anchor shared with **Fat Crack**. 50'
FA Apr, 2007, Craig Vollkommer, Jessica Donovan

Pen and ink by Tad Welch.

Lake George

8 Not Long For This World 5.8 G 50'
The entire section of cliff is poorly attached to the rest of the mountain, hence the name.
Start: Same as Sizzle Me.
P1 5.8 G: Up the corner, then hand traverse left along a handcrack beneath an overhang and onto the front of a buttress. Climb a handcrack past a loose block to the top of a short left-facing corner. Hand traverse left to a stance at a birch tree stump. Pull on vegetation to reach the tree belay of Sundowner. 50'
Gear: Doubles from 1-1/2" to 3"
FA Nov 19, 2009, Jay Harrison, Jamie McNeill

9 Sizzle Me 5.6 G 70'
Start: 80' right of Tang Corner, beneath a right-facing corner with orange rock on the left wall.
P1 5.6 G: Climb the corner past a loose block 30' up. Move left past a roof on the right to a ledge with birch trees. Go up to a cedar tree belay. 70'
FA 1992, Tom DuBois, Steve Adler

Circus Wall

From the end of the approach trail, hike 100' left along a ledge system beneath the cliff to the base of the Circus Wall, the tallest and steepest section. Two landmarks for locating routes on this wall are a narrow black streak on the left and a 25'-tall perched slab at the base of the wall on the right side.

10 Bouncy Bounce 5.10c G 90' ★★★
Start: 15' left of the black streak, at a right-facing hollow flake.
P1 5.10c G: Up the flake to a seam in a shallow right-facing corner. Follow the corner, then step right of the black streak to a larger right-facing corner. Up the corner, then left to a ceiling at 40'. Break the ceiling and climb the smooth overhanging face to the left end of tiered overhangs. Traverse right through the overhangs, then up a face to the fixed anchor. 90'
FA Sep, 2007, Craig Vollkommer, Jessica Donovan

11 Project
This open project climbs an enticing right-facing corner and tiered ceilings to the anchor of Bouncy Bounce; in the 5.12 range.

12 Crack 'n Corner (aka Romper Room) 5.9 PG 120' ★★★
Start: 30' right of the black streak, at the left side of a 25'-tall slab that rests against the cliff.
P1 5.9 PG: Up an unprotected face (5.7+) to a left-leaning ramp that becomes a right-facing corner beneath a prominent roof 50' up. Traverse left beneath the roof, then up to a spacious ledge with a fixed anchor. 70'
P2 5.6 G: (V1) Continue up the corner above the belay to the top. 50'
V1 5.9 G (5.7 R): Go right across the ledge, then up a face (5.7 R) to discontinuous cracks that lead to a fixed anchor.
FA 1992, Steve Adler, Tom DuBois
FA (V1) Jul, 2007, Craig Vollkommer, Jessica Donovan

Craig Vollkommer on Bouncy Bounce (5.10c). Photo by Jessica Donovan.

13 High Wire 5.9+ G 120' ★★★
Start: At the right side of the 25'-tall slab that rests against the cliff.
P1 5.9+ G: Go up right to a slab with twin vertical cracks. Follow the cracks, then move left into an open book beneath a ceiling at 60'. Pass the ceiling on the right and move up to tiered overhangs. Go up and left of the overhangs to a fixed anchor. 120'
Descent: A 70-m rope is required to lower off.
FA Sep, 2007, Craig Vollkommer, Jessica Donovan

14 Hoops and Yo Yo 5.10a G 120' ★★★
Start: Same as High Wire.
P1 5.9 G: Move right and go up a slab–face to an arête. Work left to a groove, and follow it to a ledge with a fixed anchor. 70'
P2 5.10a G: (V1) Go right to the bottom of a left-facing corner-overhang. Climb up the corner to a fixed anchor. 50'
V1 Side Show 5.9 PG ★★★: Climb left to the base of a right-rising crack. Follow the crack through the center of the face to the fixed anchor.
FA Sep 24, 2007, Craig Vollkommer, Jessica Donovan
FA (V1) Sep, 2007, Craig Vollkommer, Jessica Donovan

Lake George

15 War of the Worlds 5.10a G 170' ★★★

Start: 45' right of **High Wire**, beneath the tall face above the approach path.
P1 5.9 PG: Go up the face to a right-facing corner. Follow the right-arching corner to its end at a ledge. Traverse right across the ledge to a fixed anchor. 80'
P2 5.10a G: (V1) Follow a wide crack beneath a large, left-rising roof to its top. Move right and go up a right-leaning crack. Face climb past horizontal cracks to a fixed anchor. 90'
V1 Vendetta 5.10b G ★★★: Go straight up to the roof, pull through and face climb up to a shallow, left-facing corner. Work up the corner, then up a face to the fixed anchor.
Gear: To 4".
FA Oct 7, 2007, Craig Vollkommer, Jessica Donovan
FA (V1) Oct, 2007, Craig Vollkommer, Jessica Donovan
FFA (V1) Aug, 2008, Craig Vollkommer, Ian Measeck

16 Pine Nuts 5.11a R 80'

Start: Where the approach trail reaches the cliff, beneath a roof 20' up.
P1 5.11a R: Climb a shallow left-facing corner that leads toward the right end of the roof. Go over the roof and onto a ramp beneath a left-facing wall. Follow a discontinuous crack on the left-facing wall, then traverse right to the fixed anchor of **Falling Kaiser Zone**. 80'
History: Christon had been eyeing the line with the intention of adding fixed protection. In a moment of clarity, Bill Pierce led the route ground-up.
FA 1996, Bill Pierce, Michael Christon

17 Falling Kaiser Zone 5.10d G 60' ★★★

Start: 20' right of the roof that is above the approach trail, beneath a sheer wall that is between opposing corners 20' apart.
● **P1 5.10d G:** Up a featured, clean face with small corners to a bulge. Move left across the bulge to a ledge with a fixed anchor. 60'
FA 1996, Michael Christon

Gnar Wall

The left end of this wall is a low buttress with **Thorn Forest**, above where the herd path reaches the cliff. Uphill and right is a black arête with a steep orange wall to its right. Several top-rope ascents have occurred here, and lead routes are likely to be established soon.

18 Thorn Forest 5.10c PG 70' ★★★

Climbs a vertical fingercrack through a sheer wall 30' up.
Start: Where the herd path reaches the cliff, at a right-leaning seam above a low bulge.
P1 5.10c PG: Boulder up to the seam and make increasingly difficult moves up the seam to a sloping ledge. Hand traverse left, then stand up. Follow the fingercrack and pull up to a stance beneath an overhang. Make a long reach right to a tight handcrack. Climb the handcrack and work back left to a fixed anchor. 70'
Gear: To 2", small wires.
FA Mar 31, 2011, Craig Vollkommer

April Wall

From the base of **Thorn Forest** where the herd path reaches the cliff, go right 100' and above a talus field to a high point along the cliff base. The deep left-facing corner of **Sweaty April** is 200' further right.

19 Easier Than Expected 5.6 G 50'

Start: Above the high point of a talus field with two cleaved truck-sized blocks. Start to the right of an orange wall with a large detached flake.
P1 5.6 G: Up the continuous right-rising crack, for which the route is aptly named, to the top of the cliff. 50'
FA Apr, 1990, Tom DuBois, Steve Adler

20 Sweaty April 5.7 G 50'

Start: At the right end of the talus field are two large left-facing corners. Start beneath the left-hand and higher corner with an off-width crack in the right wall.
P1 5.7 G: Climb the off-width crack to the top of the cliff. 50'
FA Apr, 1990, Steve Adler, Tom DuBois

BUCK MOUNTAIN

Location	North of NY 149 on the east shore of Lake George, accessed from Northway Exit 20
Summary	An assortment of walls scattered on the southern slopes of Buck Mountain; Mostly bolt-protected routes on good-quality rock.

13	7		5	2	7	4	2	41
-5.6	5.7	5.8	5.9	5.10	5.11	5.12	5.13+	total

Buck Mountain, located on the east shore of Lake George, is a popular hike with excellent views toward Vermont, Lake George, and beyond to the High Peaks. Low on its southwest flanks are two crags, Upper Buck, accessed from the west via Pilot Knob Road, and New Buck, accessed from the east via Sly Pond Road. The two cliffs offer predominantly bolt-protected routes on good-quality, less than vertical rock.

Buck Mountain
UPPER BUCK

Aspect	West
Height	50'
Quality	
Approach	30 min, easy
Summary	A small cliff easily seen from a popular hiking trail.

	2			1	1			5
-5.6	5.7	5.8	5.9	5.10	5.11	5.12	5.13+	total

This small trailside cliff is halfway to the summit of Buck Mountain. It has a couple of hard face climbs, a moderate handcrack, and an aid route.

HISTORY
Tom Dubois reported climbing **Start Again** in 1986 with Steve Adler. Nearly a decade later, Dave Aldous

67

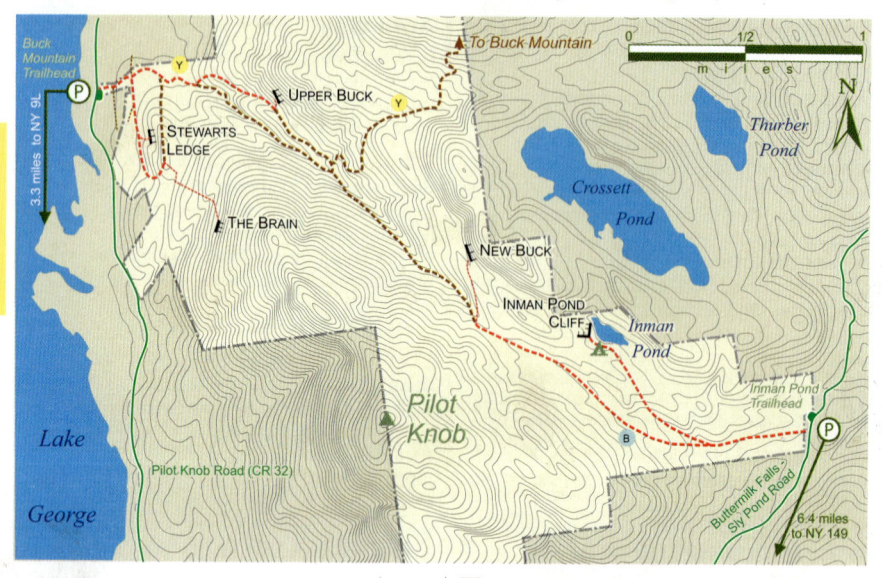

Lake George

equipped the two face climbs on the sheer face but never redpointed **Captain Crimper**.

DIRECTIONS (MAP PAGE 68)
Park at the Buck Mountain Trailhead, located on Pilot Knob Road, 3.3 miles north of its intersection with NY 9L. From the parking area, follow the hiking trail and take a left at the first signed junction. After crossing a creek, the trail switchbacks to the right at 20 min. Steady uphill hiking leads to the cliff, visible 100' left of the hiking trail, reached at 30 min 611894,4818140.

1 Fat Toad 5.7 G 35'
Start: On the left side of the cliff, at the top of the gully and under a large roof.
P1 5.7 G: Traverse right on a ledge. Round the corner on hand and foot rails to a vertical fist crack. Take this to the top where you may find a fat toad. 35'
FA Jun 16, 2009, Jason Brechko, Simon Cording

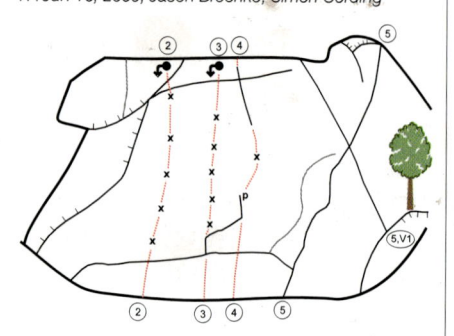

2 D Squared 5.10d G 50' ★
A hold broke near the bottom of the route, making the start a bit harder.
Start: 20' from the left end of the cliff, at a horizontal crack at chest height.
P1 5.10d G: Jump for the starting hold, or traverse in from left, then go up the face to a fixed anchor. 50'
FA Aug, 1995, Dave Aldous, David Hindson

3 Captain Crimper 5.12d TR 50' ★
In the center of the face is a zigzag crack above a horizontal crack at chest height. Go up the face, making long reaches between small edges, to a fixed anchor.
FA (TR) Sep, 1995, Dave Aldous

4 Mad Cow Disease A3 50' ★
Start: 35' from the left end of the cliff at a vertical seam.
P1 A3: Follow the thin seam up and right past fixed protection and bat-hook placements to a vertical seam that goes to the top. 50'
FA 2001, Christian Fracchia, Charlie Dickens

5 Start Again 5.7 G 50' ★★
Start: At the right end of the cliff below a right-leaning handcrack.
P1 5.7 G: (V1) Follow the handcrack, which widens to fists then off width near the top. 50'
V1 5.8 G: The fingercrack start to the right is a bit harder.
FA 1986, Tom Dubois

BUCK MOUNTAIN: UPPER BUCK
2 D Squared (5.10d)
3 Captain Crimper (5.12d)
4 Mad Cow Disease (A3)
5 Start Again (5.7)

Lake George

Buck Mountain
NEW BUCK

Aspect	West
Height	80'
Quality	★★
Approach	40 min, moderate
Summary	Steep slabs with clean bolt-protected face climbs that span a range of difficulties.

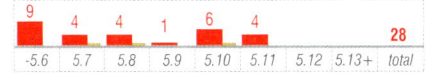

9	4	4	1	6	4		28
-5.6	5.7	5.8	5.9	5.10	5.11	5.12 5.13+	total

New Buck is a short cliffband situated on a forested bench above Lake George with a sunny aspect that affords a long climbing season. However, it does seep with moisture. This is a good introductory cliff with several easy cracks and moderate slab routes. With easy access around the right end and plentiful trees, this is a good cliff for building toprope anchors. For the more ambitious and capable, the harder routes are clean, varied, and well protected. Despite the amount of fixed protection, you should still carry a small rack. Interesting garnet crystals and solution pockets dot many of the routes at New Buck.

New Buck is described in two sections, New Buck Left and New Buck Right, which are separated by a 30'-wide wet depression of choss.

HISTORY
The cliff was visited by Dave and Lois Legg, who did some toproping in the early 1980s. It was rediscovered by Gary Dietrich, who named it the Solarium because of its sunny aspect. That name fell out of favor, and names like Back Buck were considered before the present name came into favor. The first route was **Pick Pocket**, which follows the garnet-filled pockets that are common to this cliff. Tom Rosecrans was a dominant developer here, adding routes for the duration of New Buck's existence as a climbing venue.

GEOLOGY
Common to New Buck are garnet lenses—pockets filled with red crystals. These lenses form deep underground when water trapped in the rock creates a space for uncrystallized garnet to move around and clump together during metamorphism. Garnet fractures easily, and the crystals eventually fall out of their pocket, leaving behind a perfect handhold like those found on the route **Pick Pocket**. Mining of this mineral continues today at the Barton Mines, near North River, which is one of the largest suppliers of abrasives for the sandpaper and sandblasting industry.

DIRECTIONS   (MAP PAGE 68)
You can access New Buck from the west via the Buck Mountain Trailhead (same parking as for Upper Buck) or make a shorter approach from the east via the Inman Pond Trailhead.

From the Inman Pond Trailhead: This trailhead is located on Buttermilk Falls–Sly Pond Road, 6.4 miles north of its intersection with NY 149. From the parking area, hike to the intersection with the Inman Pond Trail, reached at 5 min. Take a left and cross a creek, then follow blue markers to a beaver pond (25 min). Hike past the pond and over the height of land to a cairn on the right side of the trail that marks the start of the herd path (30 min). Leave the trail and go right (north) across a level bench to the right end of the cliff 613231,4817176, which is on the right and is reached at 40 min.

From the Buck Mountain Trailhead: The Buck Mountain Trailhead is located on Pilot Knob Road, 3.3 miles north of its intersection with NY 9L. From the parking area (0 min), hike to an unsigned trail junction, which is reached at 5 min. The left trail heads toward the summit of Buck Mountain and Upper Buck. Take the right-hand trail, which goes uphill, toward the Inman Pond–Inman Pond Trailhead, and at 45 min, reach the herd path, which is just before the height of land.

DESCENT OPTIONS
Many routes are equipped with fixed anchors; otherwise, walk off toward the right.

New Buck Left

6 Thin Soles 5.10b G 30' ★
The lone bolt to the left is used for a toprope directional and is not on this route.
Start: On top of high ground with a discontinuous crack 10' up.
● **P1 5.10b G:** Smear the shallow cracks until they disappear, then smear to the top of the cliff. 30'
FA 2002, Tom Rosecrans

7 Team Rocksport 5.5 G 30' ★
Team Rocksport is a junior competitive team that occasionally trains at this cliff.
Start: Below the leftmost of three full-length parallel cracks at the left end of the cliff.
P1 5.5 G: Up the left and middle cracks to the top. 30'
FA Jul, 2007, Team Rocksport

8 Coffee Break 5.1 G 30'
Start: Below the rightmost of three full-length parallel cracks at the left end of the cliff.
P1 5.1 G: Up the crack on the right past several ledges to the top. 30'

9 Pick Pocket 5.8+ PG 40' ★★★
Pick the right pocket and the crux won't be as hard.
Start: On the face left of a left-leaning ramp near the ground.
● **P1 5.8+ PG:** Up a run-out face to a stance, then up the pocketed upper face to a fixed anchor. 40'
FA 1998, Gary Dietrich

10 Pocket Pool 5.11b G 40' ★
A bit reachy since a hold broke off.
Start: At the base of a left-leaning ramp.
● **P1 5.11b G:** Make a long reach across the slab, then up a right-facing corner to a stance. Continue up a slab (crux) to a fixed anchor. 40'
FA 2000, Tom Rosecrans

Lake George

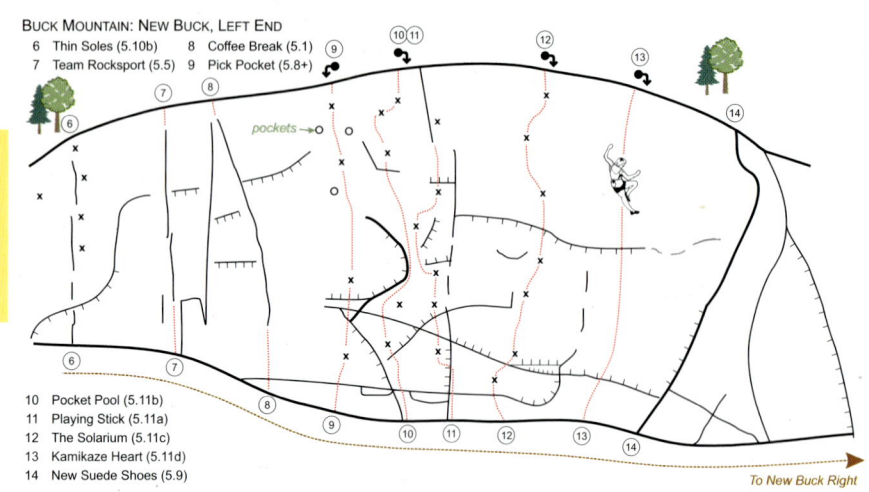

BUCK MOUNTAIN: NEW BUCK, LEFT END

6 Thin Soles (5.10b)
7 Team Rocksport (5.5)
8 Coffee Break (5.1)
9 Pick Pocket (5.8+)
10 Pocket Pool (5.11b)
11 Playing Stick (5.11a)
12 The Solarium (5.11c)
13 Kamikaze Heart (5.11d)
14 New Suede Shoes (5.9)

To New Buck Right

11 Playing Stick 5.11a G 40' ★★
Very close to the previous route. Often wet.
Start: At a right-facing corner to the right of the left-leaning ramp of **Pocket Pool**.
● **P1 5.11a G:** Up the short, steep corner, then move up and left to a stance beneath a vertical handcrack. Climb the strenuous crack to a fixed anchor shared with **Pocket Pool**. 40'
FA 2000, Tom Rosecrans

12 The Solarium 5.11c G 40'
Start: 20' left of the steep crack of **New Suede Shoes**, beneath a low bolt.
● **P1 5.11c G:** Up to a triangle flake, then follow crimps to the right and up a thin slab to finish. 40'
ACB 2005, Robert Livingston, Jon Strazza

13 Kamikaze Heart 5.11d TR 50'
Start on the steepest part of the face 10' left of the steep crack of **New Suede Shoes**. Climb shallow pockets and crimps (crux) to a handcrack finish. Often wet.
FA (TR) Sep, 2006, Robert Livingston

14 New Suede Shoes 5.9 G 60'
You'd appreciate some thicker skin as you jam this crack.
Start: At the overhanging finger- and handcrack that is left of the broken midsection of the cliff.
P1 5.9 G: Climb the widening crack past a jug and an easy exit left to the top. 60'
FA Sep, 2005, Jeremy Haas, Robert Livingston, Sid Perkins

New Buck Right

15 Wednesday Wisecrack 5.7 G 50' ★
Start: At a left-leaning crack that is right of the broken midsection of the cliff.
P1 5.7 G: Up the crack, then traverse right across the face to a left-facing flake. Continue up and left to a fixed anchor. 50'
FA Jul, 2007, Tom Rosecrans, Denny Davis

16 Tuesday Layback 5.7 G 50' ★★★
One of the best routes on the cliff.
Start: Below a ledge 7' up and 10' left of the **Autopilot** handcrack.
P1 5.7 G: Mantel the ledge, face-climb left past bolts, then layback a flake to a fixed anchor at the top. 50'
FA 1999, Gary Dietrich

17 Devil Wears Prana 5.10c PG 50' ★★★
Take care clipping the second bolt or you'll risk a ground fall.
Start: Same as **Tuesday Layback**.
P1 5.10c PG: Mantel the ledge and traverse right. Go up a thin face to a horizontal crack, make a long reach, then climb easier rock to a fixed anchor. 50'
FA 2004, Tom Rosecrans, Tom Lane, Justin Minder

18 Autopilot 5.6 G 50' ★
This route starts with a perfect handcrack.
Start: At the centermost crack on the cliff that is left of a sheer orange face.
P1 5.6 G: Up the crack to a fixed anchor. 50'
FA 1998, Tom Rosecrans

19 Low-Rise Thong 5.8 G 50' ★
Start: Below a vertical crack in a right-facing corner that begins 10' up.
P1 5.8 G: (V1) Gain a horizontal crack (easier from the right) and follow it left to the corner. Climb the sustained, but easier, crack to the top. 50'
V1 5.8+ G: Start beneath the right-facing corner and climb straight up. Somewhat dirty.
FA Jun, 2006, Robert Livingston

20 High-Rise Tightie Whities 5.10a G 50' ★★
Delicate climbing and a hidden solution pocket at the crux.
Start: 10' left of the vertical handcrack of **Train Wreck**, 70' from the right end of the cliff.
P1 5.10a G: Climb flakes up and left, then make a delicate step over a bulge at solution pockets to a fixed anchor. 50'
FA 1998, Tom Rosecrans, David Hindson

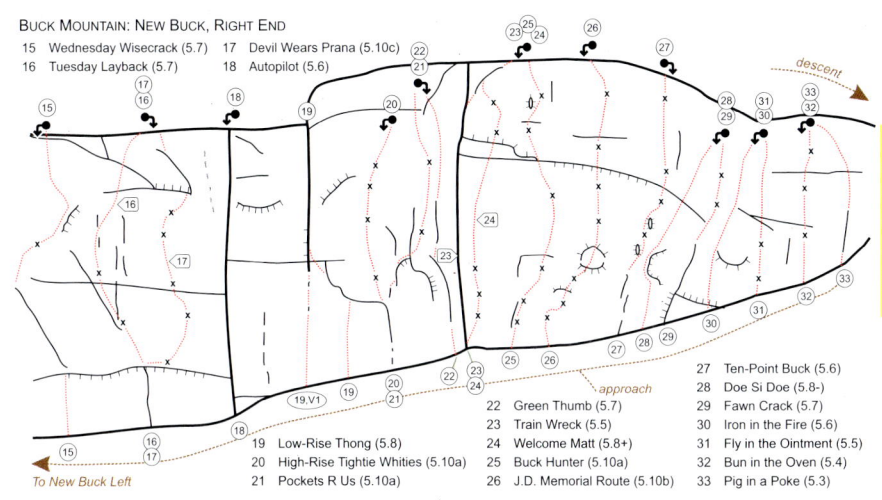

Lake George

BUCK MOUNTAIN: NEW BUCK, RIGHT END

15	Wednesday Wisecrack (5.7)	17	Devil Wears Prana (5.10c)
16	Tuesday Layback (5.7)	18	Autopilot (5.6)
19	Low-Rise Thong (5.8)		
20	High-Rise Tightie Whities (5.10a)		
21	Pockets R Us (5.10a)		
22	Green Thumb (5.7)		
23	Train Wreck (5.5)		
24	Welcome Matt (5.8+)		
25	Buck Hunter (5.10a)		
26	J.D. Memorial Route (5.10b)		
27	Ten-Point Buck (5.6)		
28	Doe Si Doe (5.8-)		
29	Fawn Crack (5.7)		
30	Iron in the Fire (5.6)		
31	Fly in the Ointment (5.5)		
32	Bun in the Oven (5.4)		
33	Pig in a Poke (5.3)		

21 Pockets R Us 5.10a PG 60' ★
Start: Same as **High-Rise Tightie Whities**.
P1 5.10a PG: Flakes lead up and right to a bulge with pockets. Over the bulge, then up a slab (stay left of the vertical crack of **Train Wreck**) to fixed anchors. 60'
FA 1998, Tom Rosecrans, David Hindson

22 Green Thumb 5.7 TR 50'
Climb the face, crack, and flake just left of **Train Wreck**, to the fixed anchor shared with **Train Wreck**.
FA (TR) Sep 10, 2010, Tom Rosecrans, Robert Livingston

23 Train Wreck 5.5 G 70' ★
Once the worse climb at New Buck, this has cleaned up nicely.
Start: Beneath a handcrack 60' from the right end of the cliff.
P1 5.5 G: Up the crack, over an overhang, then go right to fixed anchors. 70'
Gear: To 3".
FA Jul, 2007, Denny Davis

24 Welcome Matt 5.8+ G 80' ★★
Start: Same as **Train Wreck**.
P1 5.8+ G: Face-climb to the right of the crack, then run it out to the overhang. Break the overhang, then move left to the fixed anchor shared with **Train Wreck**. 80'
FA 2003, Tom Rosecrans, John Weston, Matt McGarvey

25 Buck Hunter 5.10a G 80' ★
Start: 50' from the right end of the cliff at a discontinuous crack that begins 10' up.
P1 5.10a G: Face-climb up to the crack, then up to an overhang. Break the overhang and go right to a crystal-filled pocket below a fixed anchor. 80'
FA 2000, Gary Dietrich

26 J.D. Memorial Route 5.10b G 80' ★★
Start: Below an overlap 15' up and 40' from the right end of the cliff.
● **P1 5.10b G:** Make hard moves past the overlap, then go to a shrub-filled hole. Follow easier rock to a fixed anchor. 80'
FA 2002, Tom Rosecrans

27 Ten-Point Buck 5.6 G 80' ★★
Secure climbing, sustained difficulties, and good protection make this the best route on the slab.
Start: At a discontinuous crack 20' from the right end of the cliff.
P1 5.6 G: Up the secure crack to a sustained thin face that ends at fixed anchors. 80'
FA 2000, Gary Dietrich

28 Doe Si Doe 5.8- TR 75'
Begin just left of **Fawn Crack**. Go up to a left-pointing flake, then up the **Fawn Crack** anchors.
FA (TR) Jul 2, 2010, Tom Rosecrans, Brie Rosecrans

29 Fawn Crack 5.7 G 80'
Start: Right end of the cliff at a right-leaning crack.
P1 5.7 G: Follow the crack through an overhang to easier rock and a fixed anchor. 80'
FA 2000, Gary Dietrich

30 Iron in the Fire 5.6 TR 70'
Begin just right of where an overhang meets the ground. Go up thin cracks, flakes, huecos, and around the left side of a depression. Go straight up to the anchors of **Fly in the Ointment**.
FA (TR) Jul 2, 2010, Tom Rosecrans, Brie Rosecrans

31 Fly in the Ointment 5.5 G 75'
Start: 20' right of the right-leaning crack of **Fawn Crack**, beneath a smooth slab.
P1 5.5 G: Climb straight up. Stay right of a depression and go past horizontals to a fixed anchor. 75'
Gear: To 1".
FA Jun 20, 2010, Tom Rosecrans, Lyle Farren, Ryan Konopinski

Lake George

32 Bun in the Oven 5.4 G 80' ★

The first ascentionists were expecting there first-born child.

Start: 30' right of **Fawn Crack,** at a short vertical crack.

P1 5.4 G: Climb the face right of the crack using huecos for protection. Move up to a horizontal, then up left to a fixed anchor. 80'

Gear: Small gear.

FA May 30, 2010, Tom Rosecrans, Tanya Mamedalin, Stuart Koonce

33 Pig in a Poke 5.3 G 55'

Start: Left of a gully beneath cracks that start 15' up.

P1 5.3 G: Follow intermittent cracks to the fixed anchor shared with **Pig in a Poke**. 55'

Gear: To 0.5".

FA Jun 20, 2010, Tom Rosecrans, Lyle Farren, Ryan Konopinski

Buck Mountain

EAGLE CLIFF

Height	65'
Aspect	West
Quality	★
Approach	50 min, difficult
Summary	Small cliff with short, single-pitch trad routes.

4	1	1	1		1		8
-5.6	5.7	5.8	5.9	5.10	5.11	5.12	5.13+	total

Beautifully situated on the ridge overlooking Lake George, Eagle Cliff is the tallest of the cliffbands that litter the steep slopes above Upper Buck. It is essentially one large dihedral, with the chimney of **Disappearing Act** in the middle facing the lake. The left side is sheer and split by a fingercrack (**Chingacrack**), and the right side has lower angled crack climbs.

DIRECTIONS

Once rough and nondescript, there is now a decent path to this cliff.

From Upper Buck (30 min), walk left (west) past the base of the cliff for 200' until it is possible to scramble to the top near a short gully. Go left (north) and switchback uphill a couple hundred yards and work left toward a blunt ridgeline. Continue uphill, going right (northeast) and pick up a faint trail (cairns) that arrives at the right side of the cliff 611872,4818419.

HISTORY

This crag has been "discovered" on three separate occasions with **Drama Queen** being reported three times! The earliest was Ryan Crochiere in 1997.

34 Annie's Crack 5.5 G 65'

Climbs a slab along the side of the sheer, left wall.

Start: 50' left of the chimney (**Disappearing Act**), at a short, left-facing corner.

P1 5.5 G: Go up the corner to a large ledge that is beneath two vertical handcracks. Go up the right handcrack, through a v-slot, past a blocky section, and finish to the right of a small tree. 65'

FA Jun 27, 2011, Michael Gray, Eric Sointio

35 Scorpion Bowl 5.9+ G 65' ★★★

Start: 40' left of the chimney (**Disappearing Act**).

P1 5.9+ G: Boulder up to a small ledge at 8'. Climb a right-rising ramp, move left past an arête, then join **Annie's Crack** at its blocky section. Finish to the right of a small tree. 65'

FA Jul 4, 2011, Michael Gray

36 Chingacrack 5.12a G 50' ★

The most obvious line on the cliff, a right-leaning fingercrack to the left of the chimney. The bottom 20' is very good, but some of the crux holds are crumbly and the jams are painful.

FA (TR) 1997, Ryan Crochiere

37 Disappearing Act 5.8 G 50' ★

Start: At the obvious chimney in the center of the cliff.

P1 5.8 G: Boulder past low chockstones (crux) to a ledge 15' up. Enter the chimney, pass behind a high chockstone, and climb to its top. 50'

FA Jul 15, 2011, Michael Gray, Valerie Bachinsky

38 Cross Dresser 5.7 G 60' ★★

A short, well-protected crux.

Start: 50' right of the chimney (**Disappearing Act**), at stacked blocks beneath a long ceiling near the ground.

P1 5.7 G: Go up the blocks, then up a short, left-leaning crack to a ledge on the left. Move to a higher ledge and traverse left to the left of three parallel cracks on the wall. Do the crux move to a horn and continue along the widening crack. Finish either left (above the chimney) or go right to a fixed anchor on a tree. 60'

FA Jul 11, 2011, Michael Gray

39 Devine 5.6 G 50' ★★

Start: Same as **Cross Dresser**.

P1 5.6 G: Climb up **Cross Dresser** to the center of the three parallel cracks on the wall. Go up the crack to its end then step right and climb to a fixed anchor shared with **Cross Dresser**. 50'

FA Jul 16, 2011, Kevin Heckeler, Valerie Bachinsky

40 Drag Queen 5.6 G 60' ★★

Start: Same as **Cross Dresser**.

P1 5.6 G: Climb up **Cross Dresser** to the right of the three parallel cracks on the wall. Go up the crack, past a flare, to a thin crack that goes up and right. Follow the thin crack up a steep wall and go to a fixed anchor shared with **Cross Dresser**. 60'

FA Jul 11, 2011, Todd Paris, Michael Gray

41 Drama Queen 5.5 G 60' ★★

Climbs the low-angled arête on the right end of the cliff

Start: 70' right of the chimney (**Disappearing Act**), at a mossy ledge beneath opposing corners.

P1 5.5 G: Stem up the opposing corners, then climb vertical fins to lower-angled rock, and follow it to the top. 60'

FA 1997, Ryan Crochiere, Peggy Drinkwater

INMAN POND BLUFF

Location	East shore of Lake George, accessed from Buttermilk Falls/Shelving Rock Road
Aspect	Southeast and south
Height	50'
Quality	
Approach	35 min, easy

2		1	1				4
-5.6	5.7	5.8	5.9	5.10	5.11	5.12	5.13+	total

Inman Pond Bluff has a handful of crack climbs beneath a pretty overlook popular with hikers. The rock is surprisingly clean and the existing routes are pretty good. At the left end is an impressive roof with a blocky slab to its right. Starting at the slab are several crack lines with the rightmost ones being near-vertical. The section of cliff facing the pond is broken by ledges and has no routes. The far right end has a vertical wall with crack climbs. A well-traveled herd path goes around the left end to the top.

DIRECTIONS (MAP PAGE 68)

Park at the Inman Pond Trailhead located on Buttermilk Falls-Sly Pond Road, 6.4 miles north of its intersection with NY 149. This is the same trailhead as for New Buck. From the parking area, hike to the intersection with the Inman Pond Trail, reached at 5 min. Go right and follow the trail to the south end of Inman Pond. Continue on the trail, heading north along its west shore, to its end at a camping site. Follow well-worn paths to the rock bluff 0614056,4816648 that is 80' from the north shore of the pond.

1 CLN 5.4 PG 50'
Named after Camp Little Notch, a neighboring girls camp.
Start: At a low overhang at the left end of the slab.
P1 5.4 PG: Go over the overhang and up a mossy right-facing corner to a vertical crack. 50'
FA 2009, Tom Rosecrans

2 SWAPS 5.6 PG 50'
Named after a girl scout keepsake.
Start: Center of the slab, at a low overhang.
P1 5.6 PG: Go over the overhang and climb a left-leaning crack through a bulge. 50'
FA 2009, Tom Rosecrans

3 Leader Line 5.8+ TR 30' ★
Start at the right end of the cliff at a short, sheer wall with a handcrack that begins at head height. There are two chest-sized boulders at the base. Go up the crack past a 6"-square slot to the top.
FA (TR) Jun 7, 2010, Michael Gray

4 Backer Line 5.9 TR 30' ★
Begin 10' right of Leader Line at a right-leaning finger-crack. Follow the crack that jogs left and joins parallel cracks.
FA (TR) Jun 7, 2010, Michael Gray

Craig Vollkommer on Crackatoa (5.9+). Photo by Jessica Donovan.

Lake George

PILOT KNOB MOUNTAIN

Location	North of NY 149 on the east shore of Lake George, accessed from Northway Exit 20
Summary	Two cliffs with mostly bolt-protected face climbing.

3	1	4	7	9	3		27
-5.6	5.7	5.8	5.9	5.10	5.11	5.12	5.13+	total

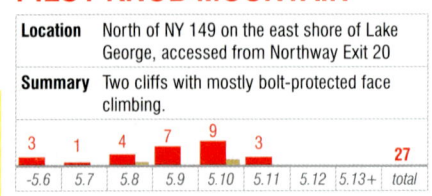

Located on the east shore of Lake George, the two small cliffs of Pilot Knob Mountain offer predominantly bolt-protected routes on less than vertical, high-quality rock with a sunny exposure. The approaches are relatively short (from 10 to 45 min).

HISTORY

Christian Fracchia and Al Hammel cleaned and to-proped the routes on the Lower Left Wall in 1989. Shortly afterward, they returned, with Ross Erskine and Craig Kennedy, and climbed the crack routes on the left side of the Main Face. The cliff went unnoticed until 1995, when Dave Aldous established the remaining routes with various partners. In 1996, Aldous caught a glimpse of the cliff that would become The Brain and added a collection of featured face climbs to the area. In the following decade, Stewart's Ledge, due to its easy approach, saw heavy use, while The Brain fell into obscurity.

DIRECTIONS (MAP PAGE 68)

The various cliffs on Pilot Knob are accessed from the Buck Mountain Trailhead, located on Pilot Knob Road (CR 32), 3.3 miles north of the intersection with NY 9L.

Pilot Knob Mountain

STEWART'S LEDGE

Aspect	West
Height	80'
Quality	★★
Approach	10 min, easy
Summary	Bolt-protected face climbing with easy to-prope access and lakeside views.

3	1	4	4	6	3		21
-5.6	5.7	5.8	5.9	5.10	5.11	5.12	5.13+	total

Stewart's Ledge is a short cliffband located a few minutes from the east shore of Lake George. Most of the routes ascend steep slabs, intricate corners and roofs, or shallow cracks. Despite the number of bolts, climbers are advised to carry a small rack. Access to the top is straightforward for toproping.

DIRECTIONS (MAP PAGE 68)

Follow the Buck Mountain Trail for 200 yards, take the second right (south), and follow an unmarked hiking trail. At 5 min, a fork is reached. Silly Slab is up from and left (northeast) of this intersection. To approach the main walls of Stewart's Ledge, go left at the fork and continue on the trail. The trail passes beneath a cliffband on the left. At 10 min, leave the trail and hike up and left, through some boulders, reaching the cliff in the vicinity of Dog Pounder 611043,4817931, at a bottomless corner above a low ceiling.

DESCENT OPTIONS

A 3rd-class descent is located between the Lower Left Wall and the Main Face (not the gully between the Main Face and the Right Buttress). The hiking trail continues rightward to the top of the cliff. Most routes are equipped with rappel anchors.

Silly Slab

A dirty slab 150' uphill from and left of the fork in the trail.

1 Slipshod 5.5 R 30'

Start: Left of a tree that is 8' up.
P1 5.5 R: Up the slab, past a left-rising crack, to the top. 30'
FA 1997, Ryan Crochiere, Jess Barr, Peggy Drinkwater

2 One Hold 5.7 X 40'

Start: At the low point of the slab at its right end.
P1 5.7 X: Up past right-rising seams (no protection) to the top. 40'
FA 1997, Ryan Crochiere, Jess Barr, Peggy Drinkwater

Lower Left Wall

The following routes are located close to the hiking trail where a short approach trail heads up to the center of this wall (near Dog Pounder).

3 The Curly Shuffle 5.10a G 40' ★

Despite a dirty start, this climb finishes with some aesthetic arête climbing.
Start: At a dirty crack and corner, 40' left and uphill of where the approach trail reaches the cliff.
● **P1 5.10a G:** Climb the crack (V1) then move left across a slab to the left side of the arête. Step up, then work right to pass tiered overhangs. Make a long reach back to the left side of the arête. Follow the arête to a fixed anchor. 40'
V1 5.7 G: Continue up the broken crack past several trees to the top.
Gear: 1 ea 1/5" cam.
FA May, 1997, Dave Aldous
FA (V1) 2007, Jason Brechko

4 Exit Cracks 5.11b PG 60'

The final cracks and seams were named after the final pitches of the Eiger's North Face.
Start: At the face left of a vertical slot that is immediately left of the approach trail.
P1 5.11b PG: Pull through an overhang and onto the face, then up past seams to a ledge. Climb thin cracks (crux) to a fixed anchor. 60'
Gear: Small wires.
FA Oct, 1996, Dave Aldous

5 Revolver 5.10b G 60' ★

The puzzling crux can be bypassed on the right.
Start: Beneath a vertical slot in a ceiling at head height, immediately left of the approach trail.

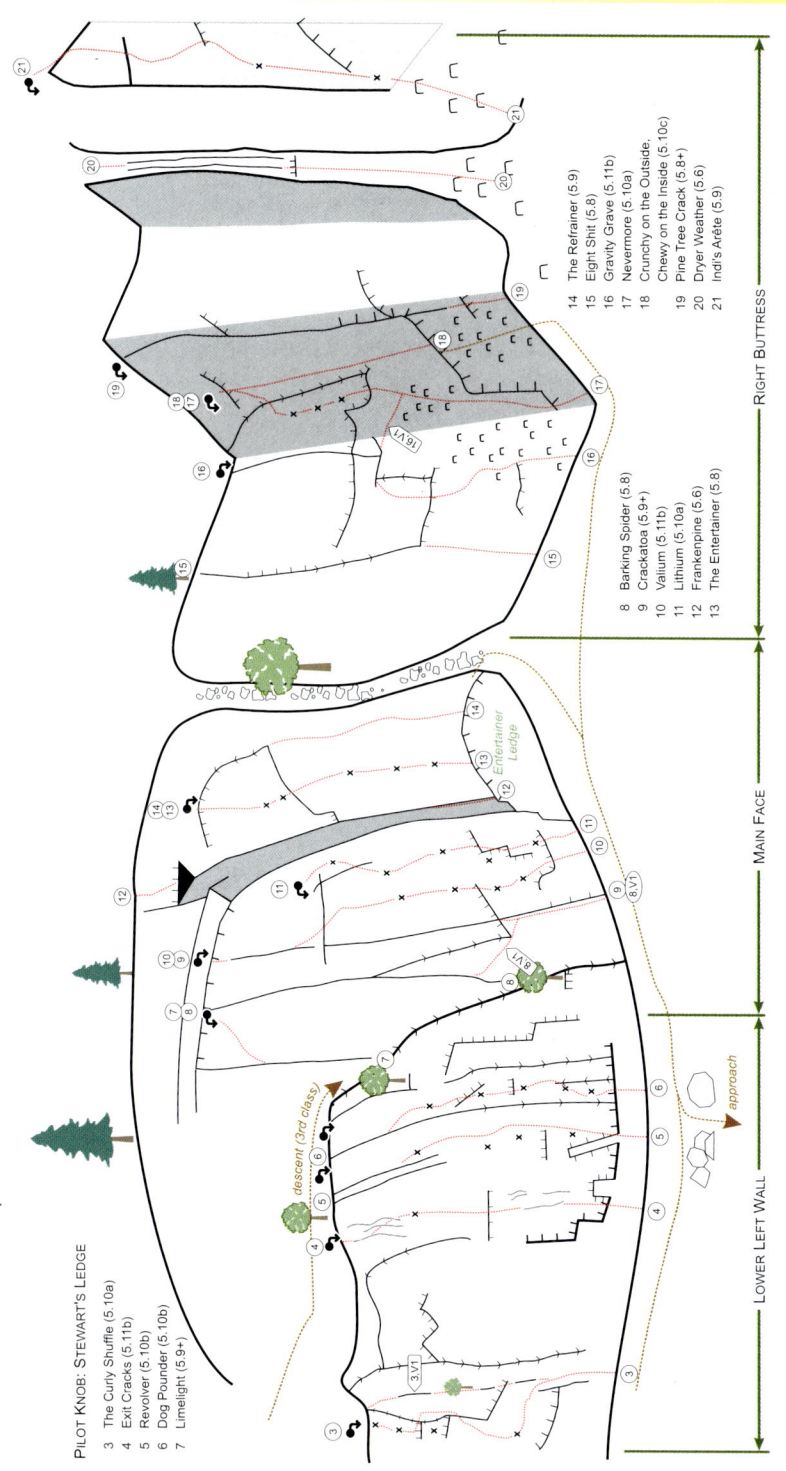

Lake George

PILOT KNOB: STEWART'S LEDGE

3 The Curly Shuffle (5.10a)
4 Exit Cracks (5.11b)
5 Revolver (5.10b)
6 Dog Pounder (5.10b)
7 Limelight (5.9+)
8 Barking Spider (5.8)
9 Crackatoa (5.9+)
10 Valium (5.11b)
11 Lithium (5.10a)
12 Frankenpine (5.6)
13 The Entertainer (5.8)
14 The Refrainer (5.9)
15 Eight Shit (5.8)
16 Gravity Grave (5.11b)
17 Nevermore (5.10a)
18 Crunchy on the Outside, Chewy on the Inside (5.10c)
19 Pine Tree Crack (5.8+)
20 Dryer Weather (5.6)
21 Indi's Arête (5.9)

LOWER LEFT WALL — MAIN FACE — RIGHT BUTTRESS

Lake George

P1 5.10b G: Pull up into the slot (V1) and work right to a bulge. Pull over the bulge (crux) to easy, blocky terrain. Scramble up and left to a handcrack in a steep wall. Climb the crack to a fixed anchor. 60'
V1 5.8 PG: Step left and follow an incipient crack over the bulge. Work back right to the handcrack in the steep wall.
Gear: To 2.5".
FA Oct, 1996, Dave Aldous
FA (V1) Apr, 2008, Jason Brechko, Simon Cording

6 Dog Pounder 5.10b G 60' ★★★
Steep climbing on high-quality rock. One of the better routes at Stewart's Ledge.
Start: Where the approach trail reaches the cliff, at a bottomless corner above a low ceiling.
● **P1 5.10b G:** Make a tricky press to get established in the corner. Stem the corner, then work right to a sloping ledge. Go up tiered overhangs and pull onto a slab. Climb easy rock to a fixed anchor. 60'
Gear: Optional small cam at the top.
FA 2000, Christian Fracchia

Main Face

The tallest section of the cliff has a 3rd-class scramble at its left end and a dirty gully at its right end. At the right end of the Main Face is a ledge 10' up known as Entertainer Ledge.

7 Limelight 5.9+ PG 30' ★
Start: Halfway up the 3rd-class descent at a shallow crack.
P1 5.9+ PG: Step right to gain the crack, then follow it to its end beneath a bulge. Make an unprotected traverse right to the fixed anchor of **Barking Spider**. 30'
Gear: To 2".
FA 1989, Christian Fracchia, Al Hammel, Ross Erskine, Craig Kennedy

8 Barking Spider 5.8 G 70' ★★
Start: At the left side of the Main Face, at the base of the 3rd-class descent.
P1 5.8 G: (V1) Scramble 10' up the descent ledges to reach the bottom of a vertical handcrack. Follow the crack to a fixed anchor at its top. 70'
V1 5.9 PG: Start up **Crackatoa** to the overhang. Traverse left past a left-rising crack to reach the handcrack.
Gear: To 3".
FA 1989, Christian Fracchia, Al Hammel, Ross Erskine, Craig Kennedy

9 Crackatoa 5.9+ PG 80' ★★
The prominent vertical crack on the Main Face.
Start: Beneath a left-facing corner, 10' right of the 3rd-class descent.
P1 5.9+ PG: Boulder up the unprotected corner to the base of the crack. Follow the crack through an overhang and past ledges. Work right to a thin vertical crack that disappears (crux) in a steep wall. Climb to a fixed anchor. 80'
FA Jun, 1995, Dave Aldous, Keith Chadwick

10 Valium 5.11b G (5.9+ PG) 80' ★★
This climb is a popular toprope after lowering off of **Lithium**. This route is 5.10b if you don't climb the slab directly.
Start: At the face 8' right of the **Crackatoa** crack.
P1 5.11b G (5.9+ PG): Climb steep rock to gain the crux slab. Up the steep slab, then past an overlap to easier climbing. Continue up and left to the finish of **Crackatoa**. 80'
Gear: To 1.5".
FA May, 1995, Dave Aldous

11 Lithium 5.10a G 65' ★★★
A popular route.
Start: Below the left end of Entertainer Ledge, the ledge 10' up at the right end of the Main Face.
● **P1 5.10a G:** Climb right-facing flakes (crux). Go up to a small ledge, then up a crack on the blunt arête to a fixed anchor. 65'
FA Apr, 1995, Dave Aldous, Gary Dietrich

12 Frankenpine 5.6 PG 60'
The Frankenpine is the neighboring cell-phone tower disguised as a pine tree, and the subject of some local controversy.
Start: Same as **Lithium**.
P1 5.6 PG: Scramble up to Entertainer Ledge. Clip the first bolt of **The Entertainer**, then step left into a right-facing corner and climb to its top. 60'
FA Jun, 1995, Dave Aldous, Keith Chadwick

13 The Entertainer 5.8 G 40' ★★★
A short but sustained route. Popular.
Start: Same as **Lithium**.
● **P1 5.8 G:** Scramble up to Entertainer Ledge. Climb the sustained face using edges and pockets to a fixed anchor. 40'
FA May, 1996, Dave Aldous, Scot Carpenter

14 The Refrainer 5.9 R 40'
Typically toproped off of the anchors of **The Entertainer**.
Start: At the right end of Entertainer Ledge.
P1 5.9 R: Climb the blunt arête to the anchors of **The Entertainer**. 40'
FA 2000, Christian Fracchia, Jason Brechko

Right Buttress

Right of the Main Face is a dirty gully; right of this is broken rock beneath a bulging buttress that has an overhanging wall on its right side.

15 Eight Shit 5.8 G 40'
Climbs past a ledge with a huge turkey vulture nest, which has been very active in recent years.
Start: Just right of the dirty gully.
P1 5.8 G: Scramble up to a ledge. Follow a crack, then move right to a giant flake. Climb the flake to the top. 40'
FA May 28, 2012, Lorenzo Sanguedolce, Michael Gray

Lake George

*Jeremy Haas on **Limelight** (5.9+). Photo by Andrew Linke.*

16 Gravity Grave 5.11b PG 70' ★
Good climbing on steep rock. Too bad it only has 25' of sustained climbing.
Start: On the left side of a broken buttress 25' right of the dirty gully.
P1 5.11b PG: (V1) Up and left on broken rock to a ledge below an overhanging face. Hand traverse right to gain the flaring hand- and finger-crack. Climb to a fixed anchor. 70'
V1 5.11b PG: Start on **Nevermore** and hand-traverse left to gain the crack.
FA Jul, 1996, Dave Aldous, Alex Astrom

17 Nevermore 5.10a G 70' ★★
A steep corner with an exciting exit.
Start: On the right side of a broken buttress 25' right of the dirty gully, below a dihedral that begins 30' up.
○ **P1 5.10a G:** Climb easily with poor protection to the base of the dihedral. Up the dihedral (crux) to a rightward hand traverse that leads to a fixed anchor. 70'
Gear: A couple cams to 1".
FA Aug, 1996, Dave Aldous, Gary Dietrich

18 Crunchy on the Outside, Chewy on the Inside 5.10c G 60'
Named after the loose rock encountered on the first ascent. (Bolts missing.)
Start: 50' right of the dirty gully, on a ledge beneath an overhanging wall.
P1 5.10c G: Steep face climbing ends at the **Nevermore** anchor. 60'
FA Jul, 1995, Dave Aldous

19 Pine Tree Crack 5.8+ PG 60' ★
Start: 50' right of the dirty gully, on a sloping ledge beneath a left-facing corner.
P1 5.8+ PG: Go up the corner to a steep handcrack. Climb the crack that tapers to a seam at a stance on a ledge. Pull over a steep wall to a fixed anchor. 60'
Gear: To 2.5".
FA Jun, 1995, Dave Aldous, Gary Dietrich

20 Dryer Weather 5.6 PG 40'
Start: At sloping ledges at the right end of the cliff beneath a steep gully.
P1 5.6 PG: Up easy terrain past an overhang to double cracks; climb these to the top. 40'
FA Apr, 2008, Jason Brechko, Simon Cording

21 Indi's Arête 5.9 PG 45' ★
This route has ledge fall potential.
Start: Same as **Dryer Weather**.
P1 5.9 PG: Go up and right on easy stepped terraces to a left-facing wall beneath a sharp overhanging arête. Climb the left-facing wall (dirty) to a broad, sloping ledge. Make a big reach to a sloping rail with a short left-facing corner above it. Work up to a good horizontal, then up the right side of the arête (small cams). Step left onto a slab and climb to a fixed anchor. 45'
Gear: To 1.5".
FA Apr 17, 2011, Jason Brechko, Simon Cording

Lake George

Pilot Knob Mountain
THE BRAIN

Aspect	West
Height	80'
Quality	★
Approach	40 min, moderate
Summary	A few low-angle face climbs on featured rock. Beautiful views of Lake George.

-5.6	5.7	5.8	5.9	5.10	5.11	5.12	5.13+	total
			3	3				6

The Brain is a steep slab that is hidden on a hillside with many broken ledges. The cliff gets its name from the convoluted features of the rock, such as ribs, huecos, and knobs. The small bluff in front of the cliff affords nice views out over the lake. Because of the bushwhack approach and nondescript location, The Brain sees far fewer climbers than Stewart's Ledge.

DIRECTIONS (MAP PAGE 68)
Follow the Buck Mountain Trail for 200 yards, take the second right (south), and follow a yellow-blazed hiking trail. Go left at a fork and continue on the trail past the base of Stewart's Ledge (10 min) until the switchback (left) leads to the top of Stewart's Ledge. At the top of the switchback near a chest-sized boulder, hike downhill on a bearing of 120° to a depression. Cross the depression and hike gently uphill on a broad ridge, following a line of small boulders to the left end of a rocky hillside (20 min). Turn right and hike a level bench along the base of the hillside to its right (south) end. Turn left and hike on a bearing of 120° up the steep and rocky slope to its top at a wooded knoll. Cross over the knoll and the small drainage area behind it. On the other side of the drainage area, turn right on a bearing of 180° and head uphill over small cliffbands, to reach The Brain on its left end (40 min) 611500,4817409.

DESCENT OPTIONS
Most routes have fixed anchors, or walk around either end of the cliff.

22 National Federation of the Blind
5.9 G 30' ★

On the approach, Aldous found a cane with a federation logo stuck in a snowbank.
Start: 30' from the left end of the cliff, at a short left-facing corner.
P1 5.9 G: Over a bulge to a horizontal crack, then past another bulge to a fixed anchor. 30'
FA Apr, 1996, Dave Aldous

23 Where's My Cane? 5.10b PG 80' ★
Start: 50' from the left end of the cliff at rock ribs and horizontal cracks at head height.
● **P1 5.10b PG:** Follow the left-arching crack, then wander up and right to a small ledge and a final slab that leads to the cliff top. 80'
FA Apr, 1996, Dave Aldous

24 This is Spinal Tap 5.10b G 80' ★★
Start: Between **Where's my Cane?** and **Corpus Callosum**.
P1 5.10b G: Start up a right-rising crack, then up a left-rising, intermittent crack (crux) to low-angled rock. Go straight up to a fixed anchor. 80'
Gear: 1 ea 2" cam; small gear.
FA Apr 25, 2010, Tom Rosecrans, John Weston

25 Corpus Callosum 5.10b G 80' ★★
The best climb on the crag splits The Brain in half.
Start: Beneath the highest part of the cliff, at a vegetated head-high shelf with a horizontal crack 3' above it.
● **P1 5.10b G:** After a hard friction move, the climb becomes steeper and more featured. Continue past a horizontal crack to a fixed anchor. 80'
FA Apr, 1996, Dave Aldous

26 Medulla Oblongata 5.9 G 60' ★
Start: Near the left end of a ledge in the center of the cliff and 20' up.
P1 5.9 G: Up a thin crack to a horizontal break beneath the bulging wall, then left to a discontinuous crack. Follow the crack to the top. 60'
FA May, 1996, Dave Aldous

27 Splitting Headache 5.9+ G 60' ★
The most prominent crack on the cliff had a mysterious piton.
Start: Same as **Medulla Oblongata**.
P1 5.9+ G: Climb clean low-angle rock to a 4" horizontal crack beneath the bulging wall, then face-climb up to the vertical crack. Exit right to a fixed anchor. 60'
ACB May, 1996, Dave Aldous, Keith Chadwick

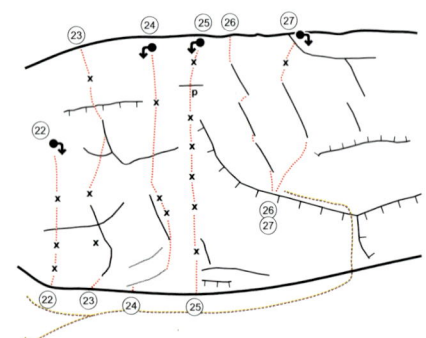

▲ To Stewarts Ledge (25 min)

PILOT KNOB: THE BRAIN
22 National Federation of the Blind (5.9)   25 Corpus Callosum (5.10b)
23 Where's My Cane? (5.10b)   26 Medulla Oblongata (5.9)
24 This is Spinal Tap (5.10b)   27 Splitting Headache (5.9+)

Lake George

HUDSON RIVER CRAGS

Location	North of NY 9N near Lake Luzerne, accessed from Northway Exit 21
Aspect	Northwest
Height	40'
Quality	★
Approach	5 min, easy
Summary	A few short climbs in a popular recreation area along the Hudson River. Easy access if the road is passable.

2	1	1	4		8
-5.6	5.7	5.8	5.9	5.10 5.11 5.12 5.13+	total

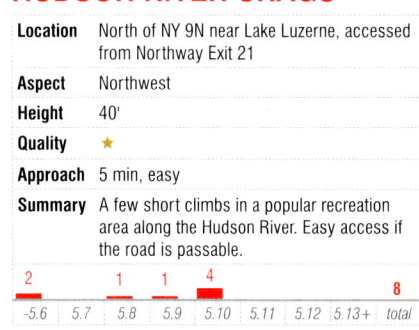

The Hudson River Recreation Area is a popular destination for car camping, swimming, flat-water paddling, mountain biking, and the Bear Slides—a short hike to a smooth-bottomed brook. The approach to the cliffs is very short, but the trailhead is reached via an improved dirt road that may not be maintained in its entirety. The routes are short, vertical, and ascend parallel-sided cracks. Conifer trees provide shade but prevent the cliffs from drying out quickly.

HISTORY

Jim Gilman and Carl Harrison discovered Hudson River Crags while camping in this popular recreation area. Not thinking too highly of its quality or potential, they made sporadic returns to clean and climb their routes. Paying a visit on his birthday, Jeremy Haas climbed a few of the obvious lines, including the off-width testpiece **Birthday Spanking**.

DIRECTIONS (MAP PAGE 79)

From Northway (I-87) Exit 21 (0.0), drive south on NY 9N to the intersection with Mill Street in Lake Luzerne next to the school, at 10.0 miles. Turn right and follow Mill Street to its intersection with Wall Street at 10.1 miles. Turn right and follow Wall Street / River Road along the Hudson River past a parking area on the right (16.9 miles) and a circular turnaround (18.8 miles) before reaching a parking area next to the river on the left at 19.3 miles 591043,4808394. The last 3.0 miles are dirt road and may not be passable until April. The herd path is across the road (southeast) from the parking area.

Hudson River Crags

LOWER CLIFFBAND

DIRECTIONS (MAP PAGE 79)

Follow the herd path uphill for 300' to a short, broken cliffband 591166,4808357.

1 Carl's New Baby 5.10b G 35' ★

Start: On the tallest section of the cliffband, beneath a right-rising overhang 10' up.
● **P1 5.10b G:** Climb up to the overhang from the left, then move left (crux) to a ledge. Up past a horizontal crack to a fixed anchor on top. 35'
FA Jun, 2005, Jim Gilman, Carl Harrison

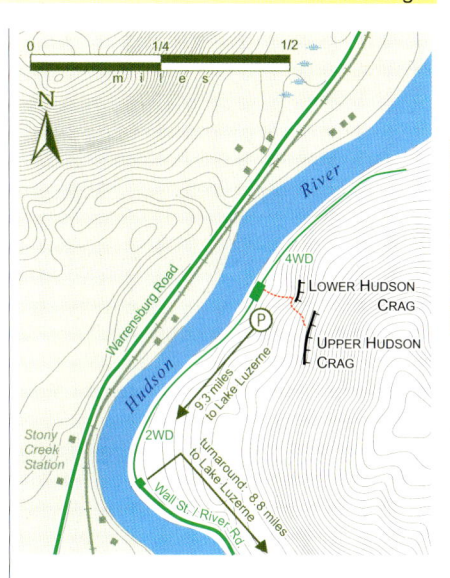

Hudson River Crags

UPPER CLIFFBAND

DIRECTIONS (MAP PAGE 79)

From the lower cliffband, hike right, then up for another 300' to a second cliffband with no climbing. Hike right, then up through a gully to reach the upper cliffband 100' farther 591217,4808296.

2 Asher Crack 5.6+ G 40' ★

Start: At the left end of the cliffband, at a vertical handcrack that begins at an overhang at waist height.
P1 5.6+ G: Up the crack, which narrows to hand size. Fixed anchor. 40'
FA Jun, 2005, Jim Gilman, Carl Harrison

3 Summer Party 5.9 G 40' ★

Start: At the left end of the cliffband, 5' right of a vertical handcrack (**Asher Crack**), at a vertical fingercrack with a ledge at chest height.
P1 5.9 G: Climb the crack, which widens to finger size at fixed protection 15' up (crux). Continue in the widening crack past a ledge to the fixed anchor shared with **Asher Crack**. Sustained crack climbing. The crack to the right is part of the route. 40'
FA Jun, 2005, Jim Gilman, Carl Harrison

4 Rosemary's Baby 5.10b TR 40' ★

Where the herd path comes up the gully and reaches the base of the cliffband is a blunt arête. Climb a disappearing fingercrack with a hand-sized pod 20' up, then face-climb left to a hollow flake and top out at a horizontal overlap.
FA (TR) Jul, 2007, Jim Gilman, Carl Harrison

5 Birthday Spanking 5.10d G 50' ★★

Start: In the middle of the cliffband, behind a freestanding tower.
P1 5.10d G: Up the clean, deep off width that widens from 5" to 12". 50'

Lake George

6 Dreams of the Desert 5.8 G 30' ★
Start: At the right side of the tower, on a face with vertical seams and a horn at waist height.
5.8 G: A tricky nut placement protects the move up to a horizontal crack. Using the small tree to the right is cheating. Creative rope work is necessary for the descent. 30'
FA Aug 16, 2007, Jeremy Haas, Stuart Linke

7 Back to School 5.10c G 30' ★
Start: At the left end of a sheer wall that is at the right end of the cliffband, beneath a fingercrack 8' up.
P1 5.10c G: Reach the widening fingercrack from the left and climb to a belay at the low tree. 30'

8 It's a Boy 5.4 PG 80' ★
Start: At the right end of the crag, beneath a deep chimney.
P1 5.4 PG: Up the widening squeeze chimney, past a thin horizontal crack, then step left onto ledges and follow them to the top. 80'
FA Aug 16, 2007, Jeremy Haas, Stuart Linke

POTASH CLIFF

Location	Near Lake Luzerne, 8 miles from Northway Exit 21
Aspect	Southwest
Height	95'
Quality	★★★★
Approach	22 min, moderate
Summary	A small crag with many face climbs on compact rock, and tricky footwork.

-5.6	5.7	5.8	5.9	5.10	5.11	5.12	5.13+	total
		3	2	4	6	2	1	18

Potash Mountain is a small, rugged peak with a cliff band along its base. The rock routes are tightly clustered on the tallest and steepest section of this cliff band. Above the tallest cliff band are numerous smaller bands linked by a mountaineering route that finishes on the summit ledges.

Potash Cliff is a great cragging destination because of its compact size, abundant fixed anchors, and clean, steep routes. Although it's small, it packs a punch, with thought provoking, exposed, and featured routes that take full advantage of the many roofs, dihedrals and arêtes. There are a few notable cracks—**Eat Dessert First**, **Double Diamond**, and **Fear of a Flat Planet**—but the majority of the routes are face climbs on compact rock with positive handholds and tricky footwork; **El Regalo**, **Endless Journey**, and **Iron Cross** are examples.

Potash is climbable for most of the year due to its sunny exposure, summer tree cover, and steep, dry walls. Quick access from the Northway makes it a convenient after-work crag, or an easy stop on the way through the Lake George region.

Although it is on public land, access concerns have created a unique situation for climbers: the state land is completely surrounded by private land, and there is no public right-of-way on record anywhere. Thankfully, there is a private nature preserve that allows climbers to access the cliff. Prinpaw Preserve (www.prinpaw.com) encompasses 300 acres of the northern side of Potash Mountain. Prinpaw hosts private retreats, maintains a network of trails, and preserves the natural beauty of the mountain.

The generosity of the Prinpaw owner can not be overstated. She wants climbers to enjoy the mountain, and we are indebted to her openness to let us pass through. All efforts need to be made to be good stewards to the mountain, respect the privacy of the neighbors, and preserve access to Potash for future generations of climbers. In short, the parking and approach directions must be followed exactly by all climbers visiting Potash Cliff.

DIRECTIONS (MAP PAGE 81)
From Northway (I-87) Exit 21 (0.0 mile), go south towards Lake Luzerne on NY 9N for 7.0 miles to the hamlet of Fourth Lake. Turn right (north) onto Potash Road which is opposite the entrance to the Fourth Lake DEC Campground and next to Harris Grocery. At 8.4 miles there is a dirt driveway on the right (east) that goes past an orange gate to the parking area. The entrance to the driveway is 200' before a bridge and immediately before a "Narrow Bridge" sign. (Note, this bridge has been "out" since Hurricane Irene; as of 2014, it's not possible to drive to the parking from Old Stage Road.) Follow the driveway for 200' (past a neighboring brown house with threatening dogs) to a parking area in front of a green garage. There is a designated parking area on the right for six cars. Do not drive or park past the green garage 0594217,4803547. There is a register at the trailhead which you need to sign.

The approach trail begins to the right of the garage door (0 hr 0 min). Follow the trail as it climbs at a moderate grade and curves toward the right (southwest). At 3 min reach the base of a steep hill where the climber trail intersects with an ATV trail. Turn left and go steeply up the ATV trail for 100' then turn right and continue up the climber trail. Go over two rocky sections to where the trail levels at the crest of the hill (7 min). Descend at an easy grade and reach the power line at 10 min. Diagonal across the power line and head downhill past pole #72 to two boulders. Go between the two boulders and continue on the trail as it contours to the state land boundary (yellow-blazed trees) at 13 min. Follow the trail and state land boundary, and drop below a broad open talus field on the left. From here, continue level and across a wooded talus field staying well below cliffbands uphill and to the left. Bear left away from the state land boundary and continue to contour through talus to reach the left end of the cliff at 22 min. Continue for 150' to the first route, **Eat Dessert First**, a right-rising finger- and hand-crack on a steep, 30'-tall wall 594825,4803138.

ACCESS
The local snowmobile club has the right-of-way from December to April for the uphill (east) shoulder of Potash Road and the driveway that goes to the parking

Lake George

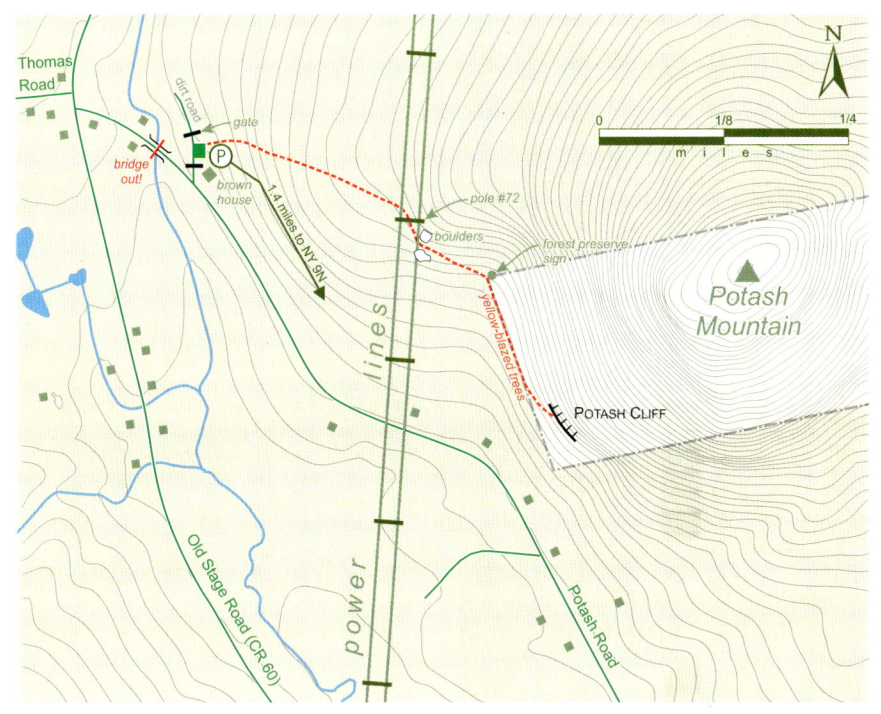

area. During the snowmobile season, climbers must park on the shoulder of Potash Road opposite the entrance to the driveway (the west side). Be prepared to dig out a parking space because the shoulder is narrow.

The approach to Potash Cliff crosses private property. Specifically, the parking area, the trail to the power line, the power line, and the short section of trail between the power line and state land boundary. The landowner generously allows climbers to access the state land by way of this trail. Avoid loitering at the parking area and along the trail to state land. Under no circumstances are climbers permitted to park beneath the power line and hike directly to the trail or cliff! Access and guidelines may change at any time. Be aware of all notices, postings or signs. All entry to the property is done at your own risk.

Peregrine falcons regularly nest at the far right end of the cliff between March and July. Currently there are no climbing restrictions and the birds continue to nest successfully. It is imperative that you do not walk past **Black Dog** (the last route on the main face of the cliff) during these months or whenever the birds are present. The climbs are out of sight from the nest, so climbers and peregrines have been able to share the cliff for many breeding seasons.

HISTORY

Tom Rosecrans, Doug Hamblett and Joel Clugstone did the earliest known climbing in the late 70's. Rosecrans recalls starting up a route on the main face but a lack of cracks, and an unfriendly exchange with a now deceased landowner discouraged him from coming back. In the early 1990's, Dick Tucker and Jim Bender made one visit to Potash. Much like the previous climbers, they were disappointed by the lack of cracks, but managed to climb the obvious plum, **Eat Dessert First**, at 5.8 A1. In the spring of 2003 Jeremy Haas made his first visit to the cliff when a friend suggested that he check out the "rugged little peak" outside of Lake Luzerne. He rapped a wide, open book in the center cliff, which would become the first in his collection of routes on this face: **El Regalo**. Haas developed most of the routes during the following three seasons with the last two routes being added in 2008-2009 by Jonathan Nickel and Bill Pierson. **Sasquatch Hunting** (5.13a), despite numerous attempts by notable climbers, was finally climbed in October 2011 by Michael Farnsworth.

1 Eat Dessert First 5.10d G 30' ★★

Short and desperate, this route is located where the approach trail first reaches the cliff. Tape your hands!
Start: At the left end of the cliff at a left-rising, moss-covered ramp, with a right-facing flake/handcrack that begins at its right end.
P1 5.10d G: Go up the flake and follow the crack as it narrows to finger-size and diagonals right. Go past a pod (crux) and continue up the fingercrack to a ledge with a fixed anchor. 30'
Gear: To 2".
FA (5.8 A1) 1990, Dick Tucker, Jim Bender
FFA 2003, Jeremy Haas

Lake George

2 Anopheles 5.8 G 80' ★★★

The route name is the scientific name for the mosquito.
Start: 50' right of **Eat Dessert First** beneath a left-rising dike–ledge that begins 10' up.
● **P1 5.8 G:** Scramble up a slab to a short, open book beneath the dike. Cross the dike, and go up a steep wall with a left-facing flake. Climb the flake and continue up low-angled rock to a second, left-rising dike. Go past the dike (crux) to the base of an enormous arrowhead block. Move around the left side of the block, and up a steep corner to a stance with a fixed anchor. 80'
FA 2003, Jeremy Haas

3 Pulled Tooth 5.8+ G 40' ★★

Start: 20' right of **Anopheles** at a ledge 7' up, and beneath an open book.
● **P1 5.8+ G:** Reach up to the ledge, then move left onto a blocky buttress and up to a left-rising, eroded dike. Make a big reach out right and above the dike to a horn (the tooth) and pull onto a right-facing arête. Climb the arête to a ledge with a fixed anchor. 40'
FA 2003, Jeremy Haas

4 Sunset Crack Project

Begin on a ledge above the fixed anchor of **Anopheles**. Go up a sheer orange face then move right to a left-arching, fingertip crack. Follow the crack to a severely overhanging wall that is climbed to the top. In the 5.12 range.

*Jim Bender on the first ascent (5.8 A1) of **Eat Dessert First** (5.10d), with Seth Haskins belaying. Photo by Dick Tucker.*

POTASH CLIFF
2 Anopheles (5.8)
5 La Frontera (5.11c)
7 Cara Bonita (5.11b)
11 Double Diamond (5.10d)
15 Fear of a Flat Planet (5.11c)
16 Iron Cross (5.11c)

Lake George

5 La Frontera 5.11c G 95' ★★★★
Ascends the tallest prow on the cliff which has a left-rising roof halfway up. Spanish for "the boundary".
Start: At a left-rising slab below a ceiling that formed from an eroded dike.
P1 5.11c G: Go up the slab and reach above the ceiling. The gymnastic crux goes past geometric corners and a jutting flake to a hand jam in a v-slot. Climb to a left-rising ledge and up a vertical fingercrack in a left-facing corner. Follow the crack past the right end right of the roof (technical crux) to a rest beneath a right-facing open book. Work up the exposed open book, mantle onto a ledge, and climb easily to a fixed anchor at the top of the prow. 95'
Gear: To 2".
FA Jul 29, 2004, Jeremy Haas, Jim Lawyer

6 El Regalo 5.10c G 85' ★★★★★
Steep cedar-pulling, guano-covered ledges, and sporty distances between gear add to this fine route. **El Regalo** follows a vertical fracture in the wide open book on the left side of the cliff. Spanish for "the gift".
Start: From the center of the cliff, scramble up a left-rising slab-ledge to a belay stance next to a car-sized boulder that is 20' above the ground and 20' below a cedar tree that grows out of a vertical crack.
● **P1 5.10c G:** Step up onto the boulder, and make an awkward move up a short, right-leaning corner to a small cedar tree. Enjoyable climbing on incut holds ends at a stance below a steep, left-facing corner. Stem the corner and mantel a ledge covered in bird guano. Launch out left onto the overhanging face (crux), and work up to a vertical crack in a shallow left-facing corner. Climb the crack past a jutting block to an easy handcrack that ends at a fixed anchor. 85'
FA 2003, Jeremy Haas

7 Cara Bonita 5.11b PG 85' ★★★★
Although the crux involves a dyno off of a single finger, leading the steep crack is "thrilling". Easily toproped from the **El Regalo** fixed anchor after clipping the piton as a directional. Spanish for "pretty face".
Start: Same as **El Regalo**.
P1 5.11b PG: Step up onto the boulder, and start up the awkward right-leaning corner. Step left onto a ledge, and reach for small holds that lead to incut flakes and easy climbing. Pull onto a steep slab, diagonal up and left along a stepped seam, then make a big move (crux) to a sloping ledge that is beneath a right-rising fingercrack. Follow the overhanging crack (piton) to its end, and join El Regalo at its crux. Finish as for **El Regalo**: work up to a vertical crack in a shallow left-facing corner. Climb the crack past a jutting block to an easy handcrack that ends at a fixed anchor. 85'
Gear: To 1.5".
FA 2003, Jeremy Haas

8 Endless Journey 5.11a G 95' ★★★★★
Climbs the deep, left-facing corner that starts 50' up the center of the cliff. The perplexing crux is well-protected and the remainder of the route is exposed—and sustained—5.10.
Start: Same as **El Regalo**.

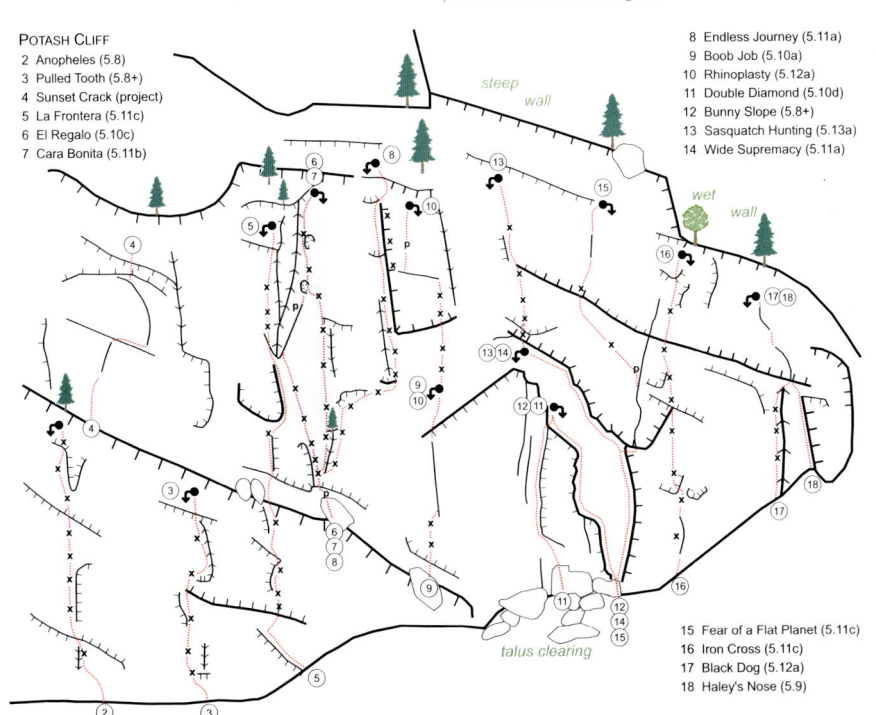

POTASH CLIFF
2 Anopheles (5.8)
3 Pulled Tooth (5.8+)
4 Sunset Crack (project)
5 La Frontera (5.11c)
6 El Regalo (5.10c)
7 Cara Bonita (5.11b)
8 Endless Journey (5.11a)
9 Boob Job (5.10a)
10 Rhinoplasty (5.12a)
11 Double Diamond (5.10d)
12 Bunny Slope (5.8+)
13 Sasquatch Hunting (5.13a)
14 Wide Supremacy (5.11a)
15 Fear of a Flat Planet (5.11c)
16 Iron Cross (5.11c)
17 Black Dog (5.12a)
18 Haley's Nose (5.9)

Lake George

Joel Dashnaw on Endless Journey (5.11a).

● **P1 5.11a G:** Follow **El Regalo** to the cedar tree: step up onto the boulder, and make an awkward move up a short, right-leaning corner to a small cedar tree. Go right around the cedar tree, and hand-traverse right across a sloping ledge to the base of a 10'-tall, overhanging arête. Move right beneath the arête, and reach above an overhang to a fingercrack on its right side. Make a strenuous pull to clear the overhang, then work up the right side of the arête to a stance. Step right to gain the base of a tall, deep, left-facing corner. Follow the corner past a left-facing flake on the left wall to an overhang. Climb the overhang, and continue up the corner to a ceiling near the top of the cliff. Escape out right and scramble around the ceiling to a fixed anchor. 95'
FA 2003, Jeremy Haas

9 Boob Job 5.10a G 45' ★

Like many alterations (a large flake was removed) this one is glaringly obvious. This route is used to access **Rhinoplasty**.
Start: From the center of the cliff base, scramble up a left-rising slab-ledge to a belay next to perched blocks that are beneath a vertical wall with a detached shield of rock.
P1 5.10a G: Grab the detached shield, and make a big move right to right-facing flakes in a shattered, right-facing corner. Go up the corner to a vertical crack. Work up and left along the crack, and finish on a right-rising ledge with a fixed anchor. 45'
Gear: To 1".
FA 2005, Jeremy Morgan, Jeremy Haas

10 Rhinoplasty 5.12a G 50' ★★★★

For safety reasons, this route got some plastic surgery above the ceiling. Clip the belay anchor as a first point of protection.

Start: At the fixed anchor atop P1 of **Boob Job**.
● **P1 5.12a G:** Follow a vertical seam up an overhanging wall (crux) to a stance below the right end of a long ceiling 60' up. Continue up the seam and over the ceiling to a horizontal fingercrack. Traverse left, along the crack, and mantel onto an exposed stance on an arête (the edge of the Endless Journey corner). Climb a slab up and right to a fixed anchor. 50'
Gear: To 1".
FA (TR) 2005, Jeremy Haas, Jeremy Morgan

11 Double Diamond 5.10d G 40' ★★★

Climbs the laser-cut, left-facing corner that begins 20' up. Stays dry in the rain.
Start: On talus blocks to the right of wet, moss-covered cracks.
P1 5.10d G: Go up a sloping ledge and reach left to a block above an overhang. Pull over the block and into a thin, vertical crack. Follow the crack into the left-facing corner where it narrows to tips. Stem the sheer corner and a vertical crack on the left wall, until the tips crack ends at a ledge with a fixed anchor. 40'
Gear: 1 ea to 2", doubles of 0.3".
FA 2003, Jeremy Haas

12 Bunny Slope 5.8+ G 40' ★★★

Climbs the right edge of an enormous, detached wall that sits beneath the most overhanging section of the cliff. Stays dry in the rain.
Start: 20' right of **Double Diamond** at chest-sized blocks that lean against the cliff.
P1 5.8+ G: (V1) Climb a thin vertical crack (0.2" cam, crux) to a sloping ledge. Hand traverse to the left, then follow a fingercrack past a jutting flake that is beneath a prominent horn. Reach for the horn and hand jam left along a crack to the fixed anchor shared with **Double Diamond**. 40'
V1 5.6 R: Start up a right-facing, friable flake that is 5' left of the start. Join the route at the sloping ledge.
Gear: Small cams to 3.5".
FA 2003, Jeremy Haas

13 Sasquatch Hunting 5.13a G 50' ★★★

Climbs the bulging prow at the top of the cliff. A hard, short, well-protected route with an exposed position.
Start: At the fixed anchor at the top of **Wide Supremacy**. Climb either **Bunny Slope** or **Boob Job** and continue up easy rock to a stance on top of the detached wall.
● **P1 5.13b G:** Step onto the main face, reach left into a handcrack, and follow it to an overhanging wall with stepped overhangs. Go past the overhangs and reach right to left-facing, vertical ribs (crux). Move right across a vertical face, then up easier rock to a fixed anchor. 50'
History: The route name comes from an encounter with a sasquatch hunter (seriously) when Mark Polinski and Ian Measeck were working the route in 2006.
FA (TR) Dec, 2006, Mark Polinski
FFA Oct 24, 2012, Michael Farnsworth

Opposite: Jeremy Haas on Cara Bonita (5.11b).
Photo by David Le Pagne.

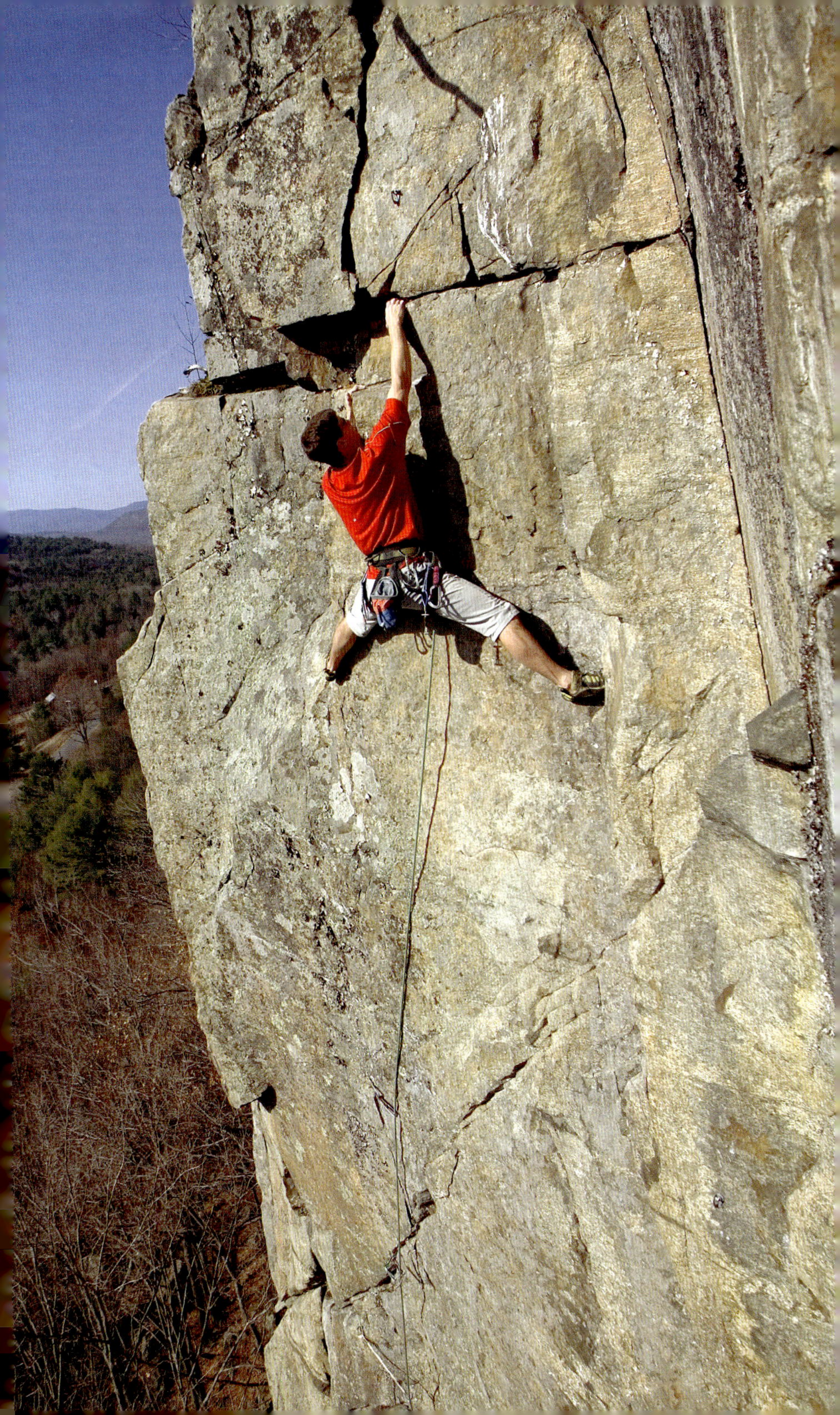

Lake George

14 Wide Supremacy 5.11a G 60' ★
Climbs the left-arching wide crack in the center of the cliff. Awaits a clean, no-falls lead.
Start: At a wide crack in a left-facing corner, just right of **Bunny Slope**.
P1 5.11a G: Follow the easy corner to the base of a roof, then go left, following a 6–10" crack that starts vertical and parallel-sided, then goes horizontal and funky (crux). Traverse left to a fixed anchor on top of the enormous detached wall. 60'
Gear: 1 ea to 8", doubles of 5" to 7".
FA (TR) Jul 29, 2004, Jeremy Haas, Jim Lawyer

15 Fear of a Flat Planet 5.11c G 85' ★★★★
Double ropes and long slings recommended. The crux roof is harder if you are short.
Start: Same as **Wide Supremacy**.
P1 5.11c G: Follow the easy corner to the base of a roof then move right to a fingercrack that goes through the roof. Go out the crack and past an arête to the lip of the roof. Pull over the roof (crux) and continue up the fingercrack splitting a sheer face. When the crack widens and eases (pin), traverse left across a face with left-facing flakes to a high, stepped ceiling. Pass the ceilings on the left (at a jutting block that faces left) and make strenuous moves until it is possible to step right onto a slab. Climb a vertical crack to a fixed anchor. 85'
Gear: To 3"; doubles to 1".
FA Jul 29, 2004, Jim Lawyer, Jeremy Haas

16 Iron Cross 5.11c G 70' ★★★★★
Brilliant face-climbing with a strenuous, low crux, and a balancy sequence beneath the open book.
Start: 15' right of the chest-sized blocks that lean against the cliff, where the base of the cliff begins to climb uphill, at a right-facing flake 4' up.
● **P1 5.11c G:** Go up the flakes, move left across an overhanging wall, and do an iron cross to reach a right-facing flake. Climb up sloping edges to a stance beneath a steep slab, in an overhanging, right-facing open book. Decipher some puzzling moves that go up and left across the open book to a right-rising flake in the right wall. Exit the open book at a ledge with a right-rising crack. Above the ledge, move up left-facing flakes to the right side of a long ceiling. Pull past the ceiling, then work up and left across a face to a ledge with a fixed anchor. 70'
FA 2003, Jeremy Haas, Jim Gilman

17 Black Dog 5.12a G 50' ★★★
A high stick-clip was employed during the first ascent. The initial moves out of the corner are reachy.
Start: At the right end, 30' uphill of the chest-sized blocks that lean against the cliff, at a left-facing corner beneath tiered ceilings.
P1 5.12a G: Start up the left-facing corner, reach out right to an arête and climb it (crux) to a sloping ledge. Continue up the left side of the arête and rock onto a higher sloping ledge. Step right beneath a ceiling to a vertical crack, which is climbed to a fixed anchor. 50'
Gear: To 3".
FA Mar, 2009, Jonathan Nickel, Bill Pierson

*Jeremy Haas on **Double Diamond** (5.10d). Photo Alex Wakeman.*

18 Haley's Nose 5.9 PG 50'
Start: 8' right of **Black Dog**, at opposing corners in a shallow chimney.
P1 5.9 PG: Work up the chimney to a ledge on the right. Step left to a vertical crack and join **Black Dog** to a fixed anchor. 50'
Gear: To 3".
FA 2008, Bill Pierson, Jonathan Nickel

19 Goes Both Ways 5.9 PG 80' ★
A popular winter route, that is worthwhile when the bottom is dry.
Start: 200' uphill and right of the chest-sized blocks that lean against the cliff, immediately right of a wet section of cliff, at a mossy right-facing corner with a ledge 10' up.
P1 5.9 PG: Scramble to the right to gain the ledge, then reach up and left into a vertical crack. Climb the crack and a short left-facing corner to its right (crux) to a wide ledge beneath a deep, left-facing corner 40' up. Follow a steep crack on the right wall of the corner, past a sloping ledge, to a ledge out right. Scramble to a fixed anchor that is 20' below the top. 80'
Gear: To 3".
FA Aug 18, 2007, Jeremy Haas, Stuart Linke

ROGERS ROCK

Location	Rogers Rock Campground on the West shore of Lake George, accessed from Northway Exits 24 and 28.
Summary	Several steep walls, and a boat-accessed multi-pitch slab.

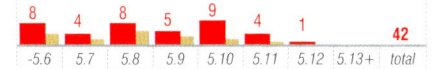

8	4	8	5	9	4	1	42
-5.6	5.7	5.8	5.9	5.10	5.11	5.12	5.13+	total

Rogers Rock rises above the western shore of Lake George, and, on its flanks, are several distinct cliffs. This picturesque setting and proximity to the water make for a truly unique climbing experience.

Just south of the mountain is Rogers Rock Campground, the largest state campground (and a nice one, too). The Campground Wall sits above the north end of the campground, with Cove Wall to its right. Rogers Rock is the hill above the campground, and the east side drops directly into the water and has two separate sections—the Jolly Roger Slab and Rogers Slide—both of which are approached by boat.

DIRECTIONS (MAP PAGE 87)

Access to the various cliffs at Rogers Rock is from the Rogers Rock Campground.

From the south: From Northway (I-87) Exit 24 (0.0 mile), go east on Bolton Landing–Riverbank Road to NY 9N (4.7 miles). Turn left (north) on NY 9N and continue past the town of Hague to the campground entrance on the right, reached at 25.4 miles.

From the north: From Northway Exit 28 (0.0 mile), go east on NY 74 to its intersection with NY 9N in Ticonderoga (17.2 miles). Turn right and go south on NY 9N to the campground entrance on the left, reached at 23.1 miles.

Pay the fee ($6.00 as of 2009, from early May through Columbus Day) at the entrance station, then go left and follow the road down to the large parking area for the boat launch. Park here and use the launch if you have a boat trailer; otherwise, continue past campsite #260 to a small parking area in a small cove used by scuba divers 622880,4850251. This parking area, which is used for the approach to all of the cliffs, shortens the paddle out to Rogers Slide and is suitable for launching a canoe.

CAMPING

Roger's Rock Campground is large with some very good sites, but like all campgrounds, there are some noisy, less-private sites too. Preferred sites include 4, 7, 8, 10, 11, 12, 13, 27, 29, 54, 55, 68, 74, 120, 125, 128, 145, 146, 153, 174, 175, 176, 205, 225, 234, 259, and 260.

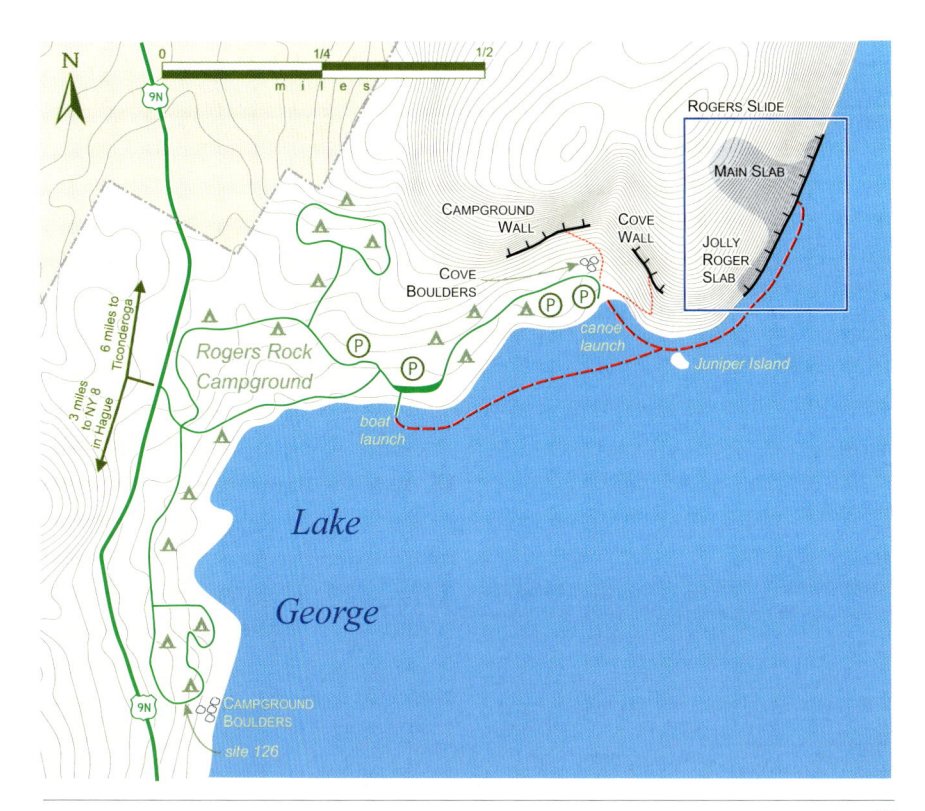

Lake George

Rogers Rock
CAMPGROUND WALL

Aspect	Southeast
Height	300'
Quality	★★
Approach	10 min, easy
Summary	Beautiful lakeside setting with a combination of steep and low-angle face climbing.

1	1	1	6	4	1	16
-5.6	5.7	5.8	5.9	5.10	5.11	5.12	5.13+	total

This cliff looms over the cove and parking area. It is tall with high, blocky roofs; prominent black streaks; and a deep right-leaning slash up the middle.

The cliff has several sections. At the left end, down in the trees, is the Psycho Slab, with a few low-angle face routes. Above this is a broad ledge accessed by a 3rd-class approach, above which is the Black Triangle Wall, which you can recognize by the black streaks and an A-shaped triangle at the base. Uphill from and right of the Psycho Slab is The Apron, another slab that leads to the steeper upper section of the cliff. The Psycho Slab and The Apron offer convenient single-pitch crag routes. Although many of these climbs are bolt-protected, most of them have a touch of adventure, whether it's overgrown cracks, questionable anchors, or stout climbing.

Despite being situated in a busy campground, the cliff is seldom visited and has a wild feel to it. Watch out for poison ivy on the approach.

HISTORY
The first reported route, **Pere-o-grins**, was climbed in 1991. In 1994, prior to the release of the third edition of *Climbing in the Adirondacks*,[3] Sean McFeely spent a few days solo aid climbing up the tallest section of the cliff, at a time when Dave Aldous and Tom Rosecrans had been working the same line (**Grace and Commitment**) as a free route. The cliff got busy in 1995 with Aldous, Rosecrans, and Gary Dietrich as the principal developers, who together established **Zippity Doo-Dah** and **Brothers in Arms**, two of the better routes on the cliff. Also during that year, R.L. Stolz climbed a two-pitch route (5.10) on the right side of the cliff. New routing at the cliff fell into dormancy after the 1997 ascent of **The Plunge**, and few climbers reported climbing at the cliff until the research for this book began in 2006.

ACCESS
This cliff is subject to seasonal closures due to peregrine falcon nesting.

DIRECTIONS (MAP PAGE 87)
From the parking area, walk into the woods that contain the Cove Boulders. Right of the largest boulder is a set of small boulders. Follow a line of cairns behind the small boulders to a herd path that goes uphill and right of the cliff. Traverse left to reach the base of the cliff near The Apron 622978,4850128. Alternatively, you can head up the talus field left of the cliff and traverse right to the Psycho Slab.

DESCENT OPTIONS
Except for the routes on the Psycho Slab, rappel all routes and expect to find some old anchors.

Psycho Slab
The following routes are located on a slab at the base of the cliff that is left of the tallest section and left of a steep, tree-filled gully that can be used as a descent. The routes end at a tree-covered ledge above the tree-filled gully.

1 Raging Queen 5.6 G (5.4 R) 70'
Appealing rock that leads to a dirty slab.
Start: 50' uphill from and left of the low point of the wall, below a pedestal 15' up.
● **P1 5.6 G (5.4 R):** A steep start leads to a dirty, unprotected slab. Belay just above on a tree-covered ledge. 70'
FA Jul, 1996, Tom Rosecrans, Brie Rosecrans, Erin Rosecrans

2 Psycho Slut 5.10b G 70'
A good cleaning would make this climb more enticing.
Start: Beneath a vertical wall left of the low point.
● **P1 5.10b G:** Deceptively difficult climbing leads to a dirty slab finish. 70'
FA Apr, 1995, Gary Dietrich, Dave Aldous

3 Pod Puller 5.11a G 70'
A harder start to the previous route.
Start: Beneath an overhanging face at the right side of the wall and left of the tree-filled gully.
● **P1 5.11a G:** Up the overhanging face to a dirty slab (joining **Psycho Slut**), then follow **Psycho Slut** to a tree-covered ledge. 70'
FA Apr, 1995, Dave Aldous, Gary Dietrich

Black Triangle Wall
You can access the following routes by ascending the tree-filled gully on the right side of the Psycho Slab. The section of the gully that is above the Psycho Slab is 3rd-class. The leftmost route begins at open ledges below a 50'-tall triangular buttress of black rock—Black Triangle Buttress. The open ledge has a fixed anchor on a tree for rappelling over the Psycho Slab.

4 Satisfaction Guaranteed 5.11b G 200' ★★★
Climbs the Black Triangle Buttress and the high, exposed roofs to the top of the cliff.
Start: Scramble up to a stance on the left side of the Black Triangle Buttress.
● **P1 5.11b G:** Stem the left-facing corner and layback to a stance below a headwall. Sidepull a rail and climb left of an overhang. A shallow slot leads to a narrow belay ledge with a fixed anchor. 70'
● **P2 5.10d G:** Step left and over a bulge. Thin face climbing up a rounded arête ends at a comfortable belay ledge. 70'

---
[3] Don Mellor, *Climbing in the Adirondacks* (Adirondack Mountain Club, 1995).

Lake George

ROGERS ROCK: CAMPGROUND WALL
1. Raging Queen (5.6)
2. Psycho Slut (5.10b)
3. Pod Puller (5.11a)
4. Satisfaction Guaranteed (5.11b)
5. Uncle Remus (5.12a)
6. Black Triangle Right (project)
7. Dangle 'n Whack Lad (5.6 A2)
8. Zippity Doo-Dah (5.10a)
9. Flake 'n Bake (5.11c)
10. Rangers' Run (5.7)
11. Black Watch (5.10a)
12. The Plunge (5.10d)
13. Pere-o-grins (5.9)
14. Brothers in Arms (5.10a)
15. Gu-man-chu (5.10d)
16. Grace and Commitment (5.8 A3)
17. Project

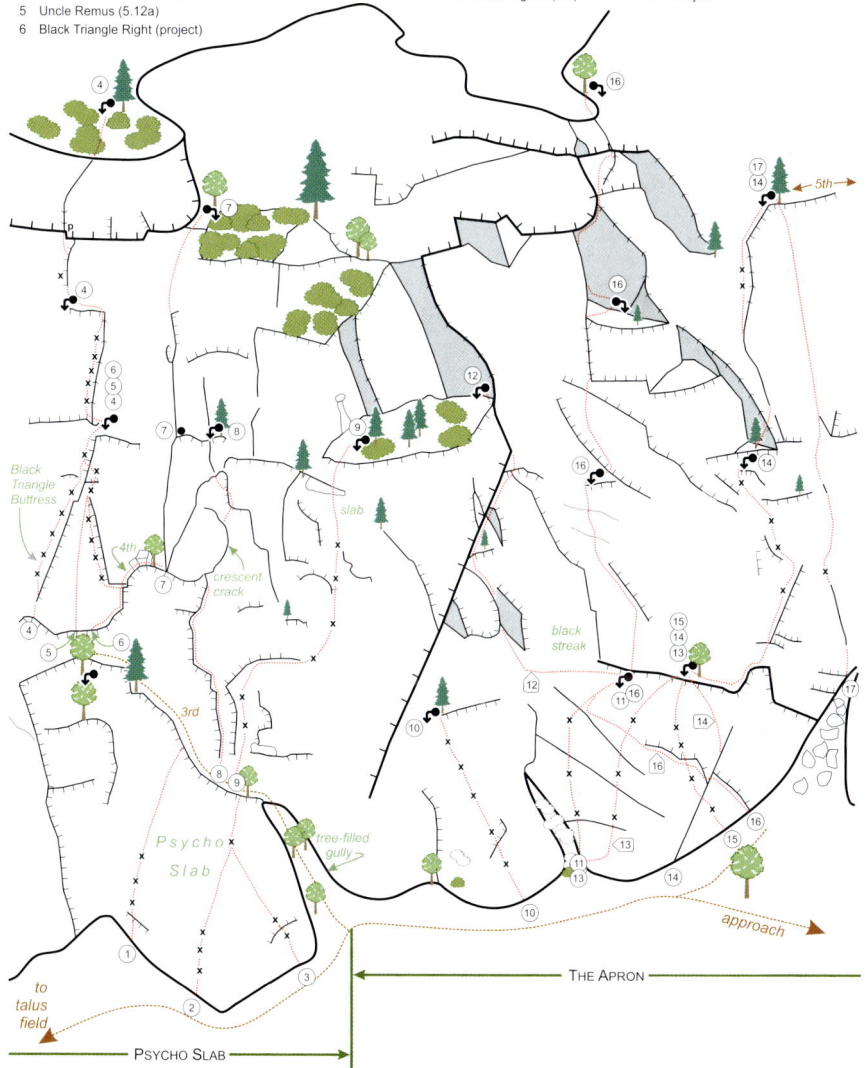

P3 5.9+ G: Up a vague right-facing corner to a stance beneath a slot that breaks the roof. Climb the slot through the roof (fixed protection) to the top of the cliff and a tree belay. Your satisfaction is guaranteed on this pitch. 60'
FA May, 1996, Dave Aldous

5 Uncle Remus 5.12a TR 70' ★
Up the center of the Black Triangle Buttress and finish on **Satisfaction Guaranteed**.
FA (TR) Oct, 1995, Dave Aldous, Alex Astrom

6 Black Triangle Right 5.11c G 70'
This open project awaits a lead.
Start: At the open ledges below the right side of the Black Triangle Buttress.
● **P1 5.11c G:** Up blocks and traverse vegetation left to the base of a right-facing corner. Stem the lower section until it is possible to traverse left onto the face. Climb up under the ceiling, step left, and finish on **Satisfaction Guaranteed**. 70'

Lake George

7 Dangle 'n Whack Lad 5.6 A2 150' ★

A continuous thin crack with great free-climbing potential.
Start: From the base of the Black Triangle Buttress, scramble up and right (4th-class) to a tree ledge.
P1 A2: Up a thin vertical crack behind a tree to a narrow ledge with a dead cedar tree. 50'
P2 5.6 A2: Continue up the vertical crack past a left-facing flake until it is possible to free-climb to a tree-covered ledge with a fixed anchor. 100'
FA Nov, 1995, Dave Aldous (solo)

8 Zippity Doo-Dah 5.10a G 90' ★★

On a cliff with few cracks, this one is obvious. This aesthetic crescent crack is visible above the tree-filled gully on the approach to the Black Triangle Wall. Sustained.
Start: At a right-facing, left-arching flake that is halfway along the tree-covered ledge and before the 3rd-class section that leads to the Black Triangle Wall.
P1 5.10a G: Ascend the first flake and hand-jam steeply over the next flake. A right-facing layback leads to a stance (exit left possible to the base of **Dangle 'n Whack Lad**) below the crescent crack. Jam the crescent, then layback and reach right to gain another crack. The exit crack (crux; small gear) ends at a belay on a narrow ledge with a cedar tree. 90'
FA Apr, 1995, Dave Aldous, Gary Dietrich, Tom Rosecrans

9 Flake 'n Bake 5.11c G 110' ★★

Double ropes are recommended.
Start: At a large tree halfway along the tree-covered ledge and directly above the Psycho Slab.
P1 5.11c G: Up a right-facing corner (crux; don't use the tree) to a right-arching overlap that becomes a crack. Move right from the crack to a bolt (long sling recommended), then up past thin flakes. Move right to a tree terrace in the middle of the cliff. 110'
FA Jul, 1996, Dave Aldous

The Apron

The Apron is a slab that sits below the tallest section of the cliff that is first encountered if you approach from the right. The lower section of the slab has several clean routes, a few of which have been extended up the steeper face above. The left margin of The Apron is defined by the tree-filled gully that leads to the Black Triangle Wall above the Psycho Slab.

10 Rangers' Run 5.7 G 75' ★★

Surrounded by vegetation, this route ascends a clean face past some interesting features.
Start: 50' right of the tree-filled gully and immediately left of a vegetated depression.
● **P1 5.7 G:** Up a 10'-tall blunt arête, then go right along the edge of the face. Traverse left onto a smooth face, then up to a tree with a fixed anchor. 75'
FA 1996, Tom Rosecrans, Gary Dietrich

11 Black Watch 5.10a PG 80'

Climbs the prominent black streak on the left side of The Apron. Harder than it looks.
Start: Immediately right of a vegetated depression at an often-wet black streak.
● **P1 5.10a PG:** Paddle up the slab to an easier (but run-out) finish. Belay at a fixed anchor on the right. 80'
FA 1996, Tom Rosecrans

12 The Plunge 5.10d G 75' ★

Starting near the tree-filled gully and partway up the cliff is a right-rising slash that splits the main face. This slash is a deep, overhanging right-leaning wall with a right-rising crack in the back. The first ascent was completed in winter and began at the vegetated depression at the left end of The Apron. The route described here avoids the vegetated depression by starting at the top of **Black Watch**. (You can also start on top of **Rangers' Run**, then traverse right to the flakes on P1.) Named after Chadwick's "Nestea plunge" lead fall.
Start: At the fixed anchor at the top of **Black Watch**.
P1 5.10d G: Traverse left over large flakes, then up a steep corner to a crack. Follow the crack into the large right-leaning overhanging corner, then up the strenuous crack past a higher A-shaped ceiling to a large grassy belay ledge with fixed anchors. 75'
FA Jan, 1997, Keith Chadwick, Dave Aldous
FFA May, 1997, Dave Aldous, Keith Chadwick

13 Pere-o-grins 5.9 PG 80' ★★

The most attractive pitch on the lower apron, **Pere-o-grins** avoids the bulging right side and climbs a direct line.
Start: Same as **Black Watch**.
● **P1 5.9 PG:** Up the slab, traverse right, then work past a couple of seams to a stance. Make a committing move (5.8), then climb a bulge (crux). Scramble to a tree with a fixed anchor. 80'
FA 1991, Tom Rosecrans, Ken Wright

14 Brothers in Arms 5.10a PG 220' ★★★

The sheer and tallest section of the cliff has defeated most free-climbing efforts. **Brothers in Arms** finds a surprisingly moderate way through the imposing verticality.
Start: At a right-rising crack right of the black streak of **Black Watch**.
P1 5.8+ G: Up the crack through the bulging right side of The Apron to easy slab climbing. Belay at the tree with a fixed anchor. 70'
P2 5.9+ G: Traverse right to the top of a pillar beneath a left-facing, right-leaning corner. Go up to the corner and follow it to a jug and a long reach. Excellent friction goes left, then straight up to a stance beneath a headwall. Make a strenuous move (either layback or mantel) to a ledge with a fixed anchor. 80'
P3 5.10a PG: Work right, then up a crack through a bulge (crux). Move up and right along a blunt arête to a tree with a fixed anchor. 70'
FA Oct, 1995, Dave Aldous, Tom Rosecrans, Gary Dietrich

15 Gu-man-chu 5.10d G 80' ★★

Climbs The Apron bulge directly, crossing the crack of **Brothers in Arms**.

Start: Below the right-rising crack of **Brothers in Arms** and 10' left of a left-facing corner (of **Grace and Commitment**).

● **P1 5.10d G:** Up past the right-rising crack (of **Brothers in Arms**). Layback a left-facing corner that is left of the bulge until it is possible to step right onto the crux slab. Smear up to a tree with a fixed anchor. 80'
FA Aug, 2006, Robert Livingston, Tom Rosecrans

16 Grace and Commitment 5.8 A3 320' ★

The roofs near the top of the cliff have excellent crack-climbing potential, but getting there involves hard aid climbing (such as this route) or rappelling in from the top.

Start: At the base of an arching left-facing corner that crosses the right-rising crack of **Brothers in Arms** 15' up.

P1 A2+: Up the left-facing corner, which becomes a discontinuous left-rising crack below an overlap. Cross **Pere-o-grins** and continue up and left across the slab to a vertical crack on the left side of The Apron. Join **Black Watch** here and go up and right to a fixed anchor. 100'

P2 A3: Over a bulge to a shallow left-facing, left-leaning corner. Follow the corner to its end, then up past several small left-rising slashes to a fixed anchor on a small ledge. (This pitch was freed on toprope at 5.12c.) 80'

P3 5.8 A1: Over a bulge (5.8 PG), then go left and up to a vertical groove (dirty) and follow the groove to a spacious ledge with a fixed anchor on the right. 60'

P4 A1: Up the large left-facing corner to a 2" crack that leads out the right side of the first roof. Step right and follow a 1" crack through a second roof to a tree belay with a fixed anchor. 80'

History: The first ascent was climbed ground-up and solo over three consecutive days. Dave Aldous, Tom Rosecrans, and Scot Carpenter had been free-climbing sections of the route prior to McFeely's ascent and were on the cliff during his ascent. McFeely left his pitons, hoping that attempts to free-climb the route would continue.

Gear: New-wave A3 rack, cams to 5", ball nuts, 0.5" tricam, and a cheater stick.
FA Oct, 1994, Sean McFeely
FFA (P2, toprope) 1996, Scot Carpenter

17 Project

Although the climbing is reported as excellent, hollow rock has halted efforts to establish this climb as a lead. Begin in a boulder-filled gully at the right end of The Apron. Go up to a left-leaning crack, past a bolt, to a ledge. The ledge is situated below an unprotected face, which is climbed to a tree with a fixed anchor at the top of **Brothers in Arms**. The tree can be accessed by 4th- and 5th-class climbing from the extreme right side of the cliff.

Rogers Rock
COVE WALL

Aspect	Southwest
Height	130'
Quality	
Approach	10 min, easy
Summary	Small, steep cliff with a couple routes.

This is the small, steep cliff that is visible above the parking area. It has a couple of impressive roofs and the beautiful right-facing dihedral of **White Lightning**.

DIRECTIONS   **(MAP PAGE 87)**
From the parking area, go northeast along the shore of the cove on a herd path. Scramble (3rd-class) over the right end of a cliffband, then go left and uphill over wooded ledges to a car-sized boulder. The cliff is 200' behind the boulder.

18 Up 5.10a PG 150'

Good looking features with a manky topout.

Start: The left side of the face is broken and ledgey. Right of this is a huge right-leaning open book, the left wall of which is interrupted by three large roofs. Begin just right of the broken rock at a black streak that leads to the first roof 30' up.

P1 5.9 G: Climb up to a right-rising horizontal, then up to the roof. Go around the roof on the right, then up the right-rising open book to the second roof. Leave the corner and traverse left following parallel cracks to a stance below a vertical crack. 80'

P2 5.10a PG: Up the vertical crack (crux) to a ceiling. Break the ceiling just right of a tree, then up a very dirty low-angle slab to trees. 70'
FA Jun, 1993, Jamie Brownell, R.L. Stolz

*Jamie Brownell on P1 of **Up** (5.10a) on the first ascent. Photo by R.L. Stolz*

Lake George

19 White Lightning 5.8 A1 120'

Start: In the center of the face and 15' left of a left-facing corner, beneath a wall with black streaks.
P1 5.8 R: Up ledges to a shallow right-facing corner (5.8 R), then follow the corner for 25' to a ledge with a small cedar tree. 40'
P2 A1: Above the tree, climb a deep right-facing dihedral to the top. 80'
FA (P1) 1979, Dave Szot, Joe Szot, Tom Rosecrans
FA (P2) 1979, Dave Szot

Rogers Rock
ROGERS SLIDE

Aspect	South
Height	650'
Quality	★★★★★
Approach	20 min, easy; boat required
Summary	A unique climbing experience combines an approach by boat with a clean slab that rises out of the water.

7	3	8	4	2		24
-5.6	5.7	5.8	5.9	5.10	5.11	5.12	5.13+	total

Unlike other slabs in the Adirondacks, this one requires a boat for the approach. The paddle provides a sense of commitment and solitude. Don't underestimate the challenge of paddling this lake on a windy day—although the distance is short, the sheer cliffs provide few landings and create dangerous waves. This is a beautiful place and truly is one of the most extraordinary climbing experiences to be had in the Adirondacks.

The rock quality is very good and quite clean. All of the routes have well-equipped anchors, and most of the protection bolts are modern. Numerous seams provide protection, albeit small and marginal.

Typical of most slab routes, the protection is sparse but adequate, and the protection grade is relative to the other routes here. A route that has four bolts in 170', with some supplemental gear placements, is considered PG. Similarly, the difficulty grade given to a slab route is relative to the other routes here; the psychological difficulty is often greater than the technical difficulty. With long, committing runouts, it's easy to go beyond your comfort.

Little Finger is the exception because it follows an obvious, continuous, and easy crack and is justifiably very popular. Be prepared to wait for this route or, better yet, plan on climbing one of the other excellent routes.

It is a misconception that this is a good cliff to visit on a hot summer day. Although the swimming is excellent, the risk of burning your feet on the hot rock (and losing control on lead) is very real. Be cautious when mooring your boat. When the wind picks up in the afternoon, you'll be comforted to know that it isn't getting banged up by the waves (at least one party sank their boat here).

Canoe and kayak rentals are available in Bolton Landing and just north of the entrance to the campground.

HISTORY
The first technical encounter with the slide was a hoax, which is now a Lake George legend. During the French and Indian War, U.S. major Robert Rogers was mounting a sneak attack on Fort Ticonderoga during the winter of 1758. His attack didn't go as planned, and he suffered heavy losses before retreating over the mountain known today as Rogers Rock. Caught at the top of

---

Rogers Rock

For me, Rogers Rock is a magical place, and late autumn, when the campground is closed, is my favorite time to visit. You put in at the cove where the walls soar above—the Campground Wall, capped by those eyebrow roofs; and the Cove Wall, with its alluring geometry and that leaning corner that looks just so good. Looking southeast, you see the prow of Anthony's Nose and can't help but wonder if there are any routes.

If it is your first time, you're probably headed around to the slabs that rise out of the water. The paddle can be class I or the crux of the day, depending on wind velocity and direction (always be the rear paddler). I remember being a lot less engaged on the first ascent of Slip Tease–Skid Row (back when it only had one bolt) than I was this last November when my canoe began taking on water.

I first learned of Rogers Rock in a woodcut that I saw in the library. The image offered few details, but the apparent size rivaled the best in the Adirondacks. A short time later, I learned of Jim [Demetri] Kolokotronis's routes there and decided to visit. I began with Little Finger and Two Bits—great experiences back then with EBs (and the requisite leather side panels), some corded hexes and stoppers, a few pins, and some faith in those little 0.25" bolts. With various partners, I returned again and again, filling in lines, climbing almost everywhere. Those were the days of bold routes—the runouts were just a reflection of the times. I do admit with some embarrassment that I put in the protection bolt on Slip Tease–Skid Row on rappel, guiltily, swearing Joel to secrecy. It was a big deal back then. I even tapped a #1 stopper in the little corner above the initial slab, but being gripped, made a bashie out of it thinking it would hold better.

There has been a fair bit of fixed protection added to existing routes in the past decade, and with the advantage of modern gear and rubber, the commitment just isn't what it used to be. There are some "new" routes here now (but how much is really new?) with adequate protection and solid anchors. Even though slab climbing is out of fashion—"Friends don't let friends climb slabs," I think the saying goes—I still enjoy it. I know the numbers aren't big and the climbing isn't cutting-edge, but the movement is elegant, the setting spectacular, and for me it is the quintessential Adirondack climbing experience.

- Tom Rosecrans

the slide, Rogers got clever, strapping his snowshoes on backward and walking away from the precipice to suggest that he had made the tumble down to the lakeshore. Hence the name Rogers Slide.

The next climber to visit Rogers Slide perpetrated no hoax. Demetri Kolokotronis hailed from the Gunks and was climbing 5.10 in 1973. He speculates that he first visited the slab while skiing on the lake and returned at a later date with Bob Perlee to climb the plumb line on the cliff, **Little Finger**. He reported the route in *Climbing* magazine,[4] describing a 1200' slab and extolling its merits. On later occasions, he added **Directissima** (known today as **Screaming Meaney**) and **Two Bits**, of which he thought **Directissima** was the best line on the slab. Kolokotronis once said, "I banish fear with two words: You lead."

When you look at the original black-and-white photos that Tom Rosecrans used in *Adirondack Rock and Ice Climbs*,[5] it is evident how much time he spent climbing on Rogers Slide. Black lines crisscross the photo like strands of spaghetti on a plate. There is even a girdle traverse halfway up the slab. Rosecrans climbed at the slab in pulses, beginning with the fieldwork for his guidebook, then again the midnineties when the Campground Wall was being developed, and recently with the development of the Jolly Roger Slab and resurrection of forgotten routes such as **Parallel Dreams**. Spanning three decades of slab climbing, Rosecrans has seen the changes at the slab firsthand. Prior to 2007, he had placed only one bolt on the entire slab.

GEOLOGY

Slickensides are thin layers of crystalline rock, smooth in one direction and coarse in another, that occur on fault lines where one block of rock moves past another. The orientation of the slickenside can indicate how the blocks shifted to reveal the cliff upon which you're climbing. Rogers Slide was formed in this fashion, and slickensides are evident on most of the routes.

DIRECTIONS   (MAP PAGE 87)

If you have a boat trailer, then use the boat launch that is next to the large parking area. Otherwise, continue past campsite #260 to a small parking area in a small cove used by scuba divers that is suitable for launching a canoe. Paddle north past Juniper Island and follow the sheer cliffs of the west shore. The Jolly Roger Slab is encountered before the Main Slab and plunges directly into the water. Farther north is a small wooded knoll at the left end of the Main Slab that is used for mooring boats. The climbs begin 100' right of the landing and are reached by a traverse (3rd-class in places) above the water.

Another option is the boat launch at the Ticonderoga Town Beach on the other side of the lake 625801,4851109. The beach is located on Black Mountain Point Road, and has an impressive view of the slab.

[4] "CAIRN," *Climbing*, no 11 (Jan–Feb 1972), p. 24.
[5] Thomas R. Rosecrans, *Adirondack Rock and Ice Climbs* (1976).

DESCENT OPTIONS

The Main Slab requires two 60-m ropes to rappel from fixed anchors. The Jolly Roger Slab requires a single 60-m rope for rappel. Hiking off or descending the vegetated ledges and gully along the sides is not recommended. With the exception of **The Matrix**, climbers who reach the very top of the Main Slab should be prepared to create their own rappel anchors.

There are two recommended rappel routes.

Rappel Option 1: From P3 of **Little Finger**, rappel 180' to the P1 anchors of **Still Bill** which are located on a spacious ledge to the right of the **Little Finger** crack. Next, rappel 100' straight down to the P1 anchors of **Bill Route**. Finally, rappel 170' to the base of the slab about 30' right of the start of **Little Finger**.

Rappel Option 2: Begin at the fixed anchor 30' right of the P3 anchors of **Little Finger**. Rappel 185' to the P1 anchors of **Prints of Darkness**. Next, rappel to the P1 anchors of **Pieces of Eight**. Finally, rappel 170' to the base of the slab about 60' right of the start of **Little Finger**. On the second rappel, it is possible to go to the base by diagonaling right for 200' (across **Roger That**) to the ledge near the start of **Slip Tease-Skid Row**.

Gear: Micronuts, slider nuts, and small cams are recommended. Extra slings are useful for managing rope drag. Consider bringing a couple of shock-absorbing quickdraws for marginal placements.

Jolly Roger Slab

This is the small, steep slab left of the Main Slab. It rises directly out of deep water and would be great for deepwater soloing if it were only steeper. Land your boat on the rock to the right of the slab; this requires calm water and a long bowline so that your canoe can be hauled out of the water and tied to the tree. Alternatively, the top of the slab can be accessed by traversing in from the left end of the Main Slab; two rappels are required to reach the tree at the start of **Walk the Plank**.

ROGERS SLIDE: JOLLY ROGER SLAB
1 Walk the Plank (5.10a)   3 Castaways (project)
2 Shiver Me Timbers (5.9) 4 Shipwrecked (5.10a)

Lake George

1 Walk the Plank
5.10a G 130' ★★★

Not too many pitches like this one in the Adirondacks! This route traverses across the bottom of the slab a few feet above the deep waters of Lake George.
Start: On the right side of the slab, scramble up a right-rising slope to a tree that is 10' above the water.
● **P1 5.10a G:** Go left past vertical cracks, then step down to a narrow, sloping ledge and follow it across the face to a small stance with a fixed anchor. 50'
● **P2 5.9 G:** Move up and right to the left end of an overlap, then up and left across a slab with thin cracks to a belay at a fixed anchor. 80'
Descent: Make a right-diagonaling rappel to the start of the route.
FA Aug 20, 2007, Robert Livingston, Tom Rosecrans, Brie Rosecrans

2 Shiver Me Timbers
5.9 PG 40' ★★

Start: On a vegetated ledge midway up the left side of the slab. This route can be reached only by rappel and is best approached by rappelling from the top of **Walk the Plank**.
P1 5.9 PG: Move right, then back left to gain a thin vertical crack. Climb the crack to a belay at the fixed anchors of **Walk the Plank**. 40'
FA Jul 13, 2007, Tom Rosecrans, Brie Rosecrans

3 Castaways Project
Climbs a thin vertical crack that begins midway along the traverse pitch of **Walk the Plank**.

4 Shipwrecked (aka Sweet Sunday)
5.10a PG (5.6 R) 100' ★

The first-ascent party didn't consider the consequences of leaving their boat tethered to the base of the slab. The boat was severely damaged by waves, and the climbers were in jeopardy of being shipwrecked.
Start: Same as **Walk the Plank**.
P1 5.10a PG (5.6 R): Up and left for 10' to a discontinuous, thin vertical crack, then climb the crack (crux) to a short right-facing corner. Go up the short corner, and the larger right-facing corner above (5.6 R), then up and left to a vertical crack with fixed protection. Up the crack, then go right to another vertical crack and follow it to a fixed anchor. 100'
FA 1981, Dave Szot, Joe Szot

*Robert Livingston on P1 of **Walk the Plank** (5.10a) on the first ascent. Photo by Brie Livingston.*

Main Slab

5 Le Petit Slab 5.6+ G 110' ★★

This pleasant pitch provides a convenient approach to **The Grand Game**.
Start: On a tree-covered ledge below a thin crack in a slab.
P1 5.6+ G: Up the crack to an easy corner, then left on flakes to a thin crack. Continue up to the tree at the base of **The Grand Game**. 110'
FA 2007, Tom Rosecrans

6 The Grand Game 5.6 PG 205' ★★★

This rope stretcher takes the first section with **Tone-Bone Tennys** and continues to the overlap.
Start: Same as **Tone-Bone Tennys**.
P1 5.6 PG: Up small left-facing features (small gear and bolts), then up cracks to the large overlap. 205'
FA Nov, 2007, Tom Rosecrans, Erin Rosecrans

7 Tone-Bone Tennys 5.7 R 500'

A historic route on the seldom-climbed left side of the Main Slab. The route crosses the left-rising tree-filled depression that bisects the left side of the Main Slab. Tony Goodwin went by the nickname "Tone Bone," hence the name.

Lake George

*Jim Gilman on **Little Finger** (5.5). © NYSDED, photo by Darren McGee.*

Start: 100' right of the landing is a low tree ledge below an overlap 25' up. Hike up and left in the vegetated corner, then left across a ledge for 50'. Three separate starts have been climbed. The easiest one, which is described here, begins at the highest point on the ledge.
P1 5.6 R: Up the water streak, aiming for a tan scar with a flake. 100'
P2 5.6 R: Traverse right to a cedar shrub in the left-rising tree-filled depression. 130'
P3 5.6 R: Straight up past several horizontals to a belay at a small ledge. 140'
P4 5.7 R: Continue straight up the steep wall (crux; poor protection) to the top. 130'
FA 1975, Tom Rosecrans, Tony Goodwin

8 Brinksmanship 5.5 R 270' ★★

Start: Between **The Grand Game** and **Crucible of War**.
P1 5.5 R: Up the slab following small left- and right-facing features to the white scar between **The Grand Game** and **Crucible of War**. Traverse right to the **Crucible or War** fixed anchor. 125'
P2 5.5 PG: Traverse back left to the white scar, then straight up to overhang. Traverse right to the fixed anchor of **Kings and Desperate Men**. 145'
FA Oct 8, 2008, Tom Rosecrans, Royce Van Evera

9 The Crucible of War 5.6+ PG 210' ★★★

Start: At a pine tree beneath small corners, 45' downhill and right of the highest point on the ledge.
● **P1 5.6+ PG:** Go up and right to a shallow right-facing corner that is climbed to a slab. Follow the slab to a ledge with a fixed anchor on the left. 140'
● **P2 5.5 PG:** Easier rock leads to a fixed anchor (shared with **Kings and Desperate Men**) under the right end of the big overlap. 70'
FA Nov, 2007, Tom Rosecrans, Robert Livingston

10 Kings and Desperate Men 5.8 PG 450' ★★

Start: At the lowest point of the ledge, 35' downhill and right of **The Crucible of War**.
● **P1 5.8 PG:** Up to a bolt 25' up. Go up some easier features, then friction straight up to a fixed anchor. 175'
● **P2 5.6 G:** Work up and left to a fixed anchor (shared with **The Crucible of War**) under the right end of the large overlap. 110'
● **P3 5.7 G:** Up over bulge at bolt, then straight left to a fixed anchor below a small overlap. 35'
● **P4 5.6 PG:** Continue left to a clean black streak (bolt), then up past a crack to a "bathtub" stance (gear). Continue up the cleanest rock in the black streak to a fixed anchor. 130'
FA Nov, 2007, Tom Rosecrans, Erin Rosecrans

Lake George

Lake George

ROGERS ROCK: ROGERS SLIDE

1. Walk the Plank (5.10a)
2. Shiver Me Timbers (5.9)
3. Shipwrecked (5.10a)
5. Le Petit Slab (5.6+)
6. The Grand Game (5.6)
8. Brinksmanship (5.5)
9. The Crucible of War (5.6+)
10. Kings and Desperate Men (5.8)
11. The Matrix (5.8-)
12. Screaming Meaney (5.8)
14. Parallel Dreams (5.8)
15. Little Finger (aka New Moon) (5.5)
17. Bill Route (5.6+)
18. Still Bill (5.8)
19. Two Bits (5.7)
20. Pieces of Eight (5.8-)
21. Prints of Darkness (5.9)
23. Slip Tease–Skid Row (5.9)
24. Last Hurrah (5.9+)

Lake George

11 The Matrix 5.8- PG 660' ★★★

This route crosses **Ziprod** (5.7) and **Noslom** (5.6), two forgotten, poorly protected, and seldom-climbed routes documented in Mellor's guidebooks.

Start: 100' right of the landing at a low tree ledge below an overlap 25' up. This is also 25' left of the **Little Finger** crack.

● **P1 5.8- PG:** Up to the leftmost of two vertical seams, then follow the seam to the overlap. Go over the overlap, then up and slightly left past shallow seams to a small ledge. Move up and left to a sustained slab and climb it (runout) to a fixed anchor, or climb the crack and left-facing corner to the right of the slab. 180'

● **P2 5.8- PG:** Stem above the belay (crux), then go right and avoid the left-facing corner on the left. Pull over a bulge and climb dimpled rock to a ledge with a fixed anchor. 170'

● **P3 5.6 PG:** Up the slab above the belay, then easier climbing up and right to a left-facing corner and a ledge with fixed anchors on the left. 160'

● **P4 5.7 G:** Move right past the left-facing corner, then up to an overhang with a left-facing corner above. Climb the corner to a tree ledge, then straight above the ledge to the exit overhang. Positive holds lead up and right to a fixed anchor. 150'

Descent: Rappel, angling right, to the fixed anchor at the top of **Screaming Meaney**. Three additional rappels end at the base of the Main Slab.

FA Apr 7, 2006, Jim Gilman, Carl Harrison

12 Screaming Meaney (aka Directissima) 5.8 PG (5.4 X) 515' ★★★★

An exceptional and classic route that represents the climbing on the slab better than **Little Finger**. Each pitch is increasingly more challenging, with P3 being both difficult and committing. Originally this route had only one bolt.

Start: Start as for **The Matrix**.

P1 5.7- G: Up the rightmost of two vertical seams to the right side of an overlap 25' up. Go over the overlap, then move left on ledges. Friction up to a fixed anchor below the left end of a long overlap. 170'

P2 5.7- G: Up to a fixed pin at the left end of the overlap, then work up and left to a seam and follow it to a stance. Move left to a crack and climb it to a spacious ledge with a fixed anchor on its right end. 160'

P3 5.8 PG (5.4 X): Traverse right for 40', then up to a small stance below an overlap. A short section of thin slab (crux) gains a ledge. Above the ledge (last protection), climb clean rock left of a water streak (5.4 X) to a ledge with a fixed anchor. 185'

Descent: Rappel the route.

History: Kolokotronis climbed this direct line to the top of the cliff, placed a single belay bolt at the end of P1, and considered this to be a better route than **Little Finger**. A few years later, Rosecrans et al., not knowing of the previous ascent, repeated P1 and continued up. Their P3, which traverses 40' to the right, was a new addition and is the standard line of ascent today. They did go to the top of the cliff but traversed right to the top of **Little Finger**. New to the sport, Meaney did not enjoy the ascent, and the route is named in recognition of her distaste.

FA (P1, P2) 1973, Demetri Kolokotronis
FA (P3) 1976, Tom Rosecrans, Joel Clugstone, Pat Meaney

13 Screaming Matrix (linkup) 5.7 G 660' ★★★★

This linkup combines the best pitches of **Screaming Meaney** with the easier pitches of **The Matrix** for a quality route that tops out.

P1 5.7- G: P1 of **Screaming Meaney**. 170'
P2 5.7- PG: P2 of **Screaming Meaney**; belay as for **The Matrix** at the left end of the ledge. 180'
P3 5.6 G: P3 of **The Matrix**. 160'
P4 5.7 G: P4 of **The Matrix**. 150'

14 Parallel Dreams 5.8 G (5.4 X) 500' ★★★

P1 is very close to **Screaming Meaney**, making it hard to decipher which bolts pertain to which route.

Start: 100' right of the landing at a narrow ledge above the lowest point on the slab. This is also 15' left of the **Little Finger** crack.

P1 5.7+ PG: Climb an unprotected slab, staying right of the overlap 25' up. Above the overlap, friction up and slightly left (hard moves) to a right-rising crack, then follow the crack (excellent climbing) to a fixed anchor. 180'

P2 5.7 PG: Up a right-rising seam above the anchor to a 4'-tall overlap. Make a long reach and a high step to clear the overlap. Go up and left to a right-rising crack in a right-facing corner. Follow the crack to its top, then step right and go up a black streak to a fixed anchor. 140'

P3 5.8 G (5.4 X): Up the increasingly steep slab with incipient cracks to a bulge. Over the bulge (crux), then up an unprotected slab to a short, vertical crack (last protection). Step left to the right end of a ledge (joining **Screaming Meaney** here) and up the unprotected, 100'-long clean streak (5.4 X) to a fixed anchor. 180'

Descent: Rappel the route.

History: Portions of this route had been lead on different occasions by Tom Rosecrans (P2) and R.L. Stolz (P3).

FA Jun 8, 2007, Tom Rosecrans, Brie Rosecrans

15 Little Finger (aka New Moon) 5.5 G 490' ★★★★★

A continuous crack line, **Little Finger** is out of character for a slab route in that it has good protection and positive holds; very popular. The **Direct Finish** variation is the single best pitch on Rogers Slide, as it has well-protected cruxes, exciting climbing, and fantastic position. The first-ascent party opted for a more challenging topout and climbed **Direct Finish**. The conventional finish—up the right-rising crack—was climbed on a subsequent visit.

Start: Unmistakable—at the base of the right-rising crack that bisects the slab and begins at the first black streak encountered along the base.

P1 5.4 G: Up the crack; after some initial challenges, the climbing eases. Belay at a small ledge with fixed protection. 180'

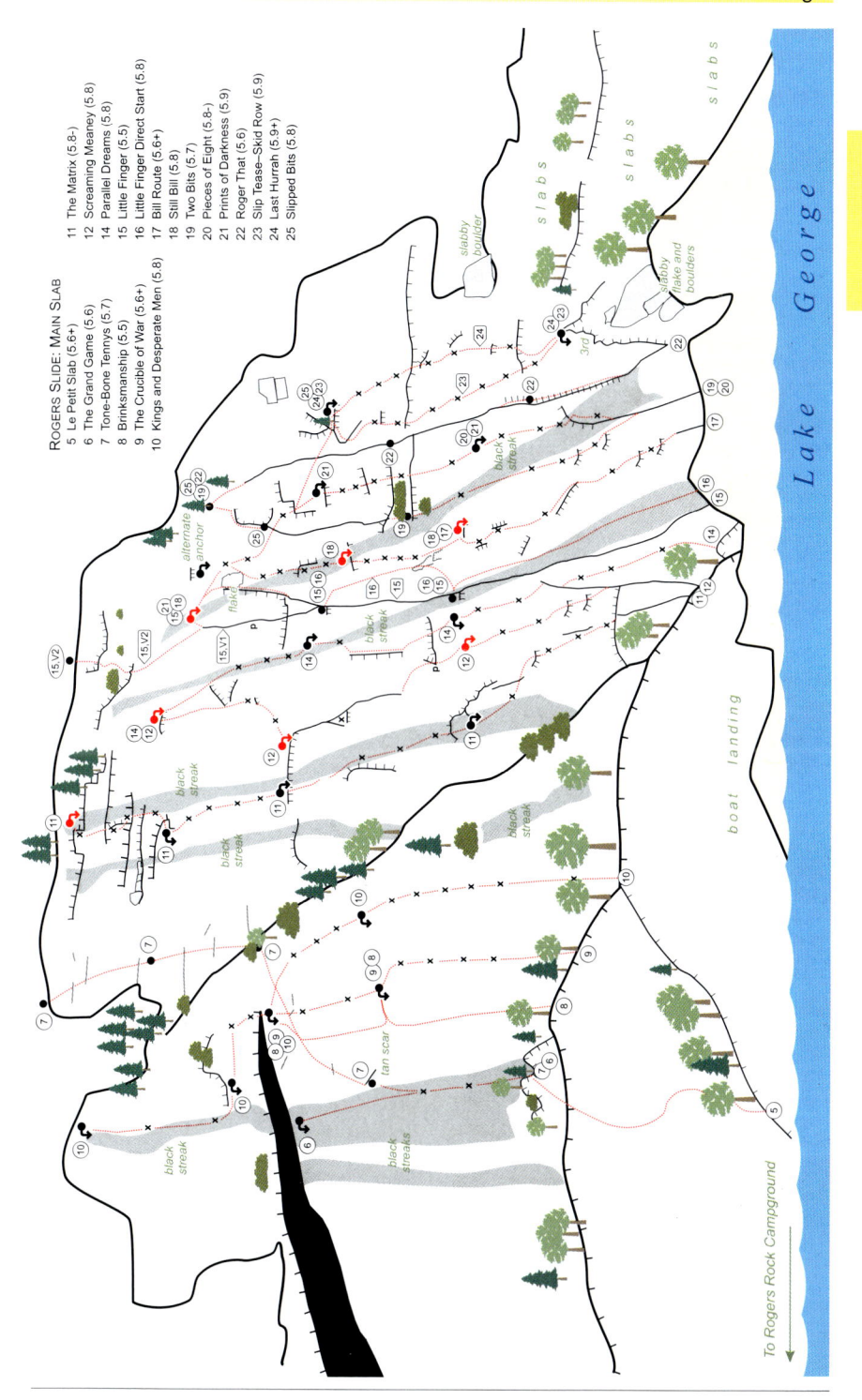

Lake George

Rogers Slide: Main Slab

5 Le Petit Slab (5.6+)
6 The Grand Game (5.6)
7 Tone-Bone Tennys (5.7)
8 Brinksmanship (5.5)
9 The Crucible of War (5.6+)
10 Kings and Desperate Men (5.8)
11 The Matrix (5.8-)
12 Screaming Meaney (5.8)
14 Parallel Dreams (5.8)
15 Little Finger (5.5)
16 Little Finger Direct Start (5.8)
17 Bill Route (5.6+)
18 Still Bill (5.8)
19 Two Bits (5.7)
20 Pieces of Eight (5.8-)
21 Prints of Darkness (5.9)
22 Roger That (5.6)
23 Slip Tease—Skid Row (5.9)
24 Last Hurrah (5.9+)
25 Slipped Bits (5.8)

Lake George

P2 5.5 G: Continue up the crack past a low challenging section to belay at a stance below a large overlap. 130'

P3 5.5 G: (V1) Up and right around the right end of the overlap (crux). Continue up the crack to its end and belay at a fixed anchor (V2). 180'

V1 Direct Finish 5.7+ G: Pull over the ceiling and into the vertical crack that is left of the **Little Finger** crack. Continue up the crack to its end, then move right and belay at the fixed anchor of **Little Finger**.

V2 Line of Fire 5.8- R: Move up to the right end of an overlap. Pass the overlap through a V-slot, step right, and then move up a steep face (crux) with a detached flake to the left and shrubs on both sides. Lower-angle rock leads to an overhanging headwall that is right of a left-facing corner. Belay at a tree at the top of the slab.

History: Although the new-route report was published in *Climbing* magazine,[6] the details of the first ascent were never recorded in previous Adirondack climbing guidebooks. Kolokotronis and Perlee reported climbing a 1200' slab (the top 600' being 3rd-class), in nine pitches, via a crack the size of a little finger. Above the main slab, Perlee fell, was injured, and Kolokotronis descended to their boat and went to the campground ranger for a rescue. At the end of the day, they were greeted by a new moon, hence the route name.
FA (P1, P2) Jul 17, 1971, Demetri Kolokotronis, Bob Perlee
FA (P3) Demetri Kolokotronis
FA (V1) Jul 17, 1971, Demetri Kolokotronis, Bob Perlee
FA (V2) Aug, 2006, Ken Nichols, Fausta Esguerra

16 Little Finger Direct Start 5.8 X 310'

Certainly the boldest line on the Main Slab. If you want to re-create the old-school experience of climbing a difficult, boltless slab route, then this one's for you.

Start: Same as **Little Finger**.

P1 5.7 X: Up the face immediately right of the **Little Finger** crack, following a black streak. Belay as for **Little Finger**. 180'

P2 5.8 X: Move right and climb up a detached pillar. Go up the unprotected slab, then join **Little Finger** at the end of P2. 130'
FA (P1) 1975, Tom Rosecrans, Joel Clugstone
FA (P2) 1993, Bill Dodd

17 Bill Route 5.6+ PG 170' ★★★

Start: 50' right of the **Little Finger** crack at a seam that leads to a mantel ledge.

● **P1 5.6+ PG:** Make a difficult move up to the ledge, then sustained climbing in between stances leads to a belay at a fixed anchor. 170'
FA 1980, John Bill, Herb George

18 Still Bill 5.8 PG 285' ★★★★

This is a continuation of **Bill Route**.
Start: The top of **Bill Route**.

● **P1 5.8 PG:** Climb straight up between a small, left-facing corner on the left, and a right-angling, right-facing corner on the right, ending at a spacious ledge with a fixed anchor. 100'

● **P2 5.7+ PG:** Up the right side of a right-leaning black streak to beautiful, gold face, climbing between **Little Finger** and **Two Bits**. This leads to the right side of the prominent flake, then straight up to the fixed anchor on **Little Finger**. 185'

Gear: Small gear (e.g., RPs).

History: Rosecrans avoided this part of the wall for 25 years, thinking it was too steep. It turned out to be easy, fun, and required no cleaning.
FA Sep 9, 2010, Tom Rosecrans, Justin Barrett

19 Two Bits 5.7 PG 400' ★★★

Recent inspection (and cleaning) has clarified the route-finding on P1, and restored the excellent crack climbing on P2.

Start: 75' right of the start of **Little Finger**, at a finger-crack in a black streak.

P1 5.7- PG: Up the fingercrack for 30', then step left and climb up flakes past two old (original) bolts. Go up to a stance next to a right-facing, orange flake, then work up and right to a discontinuous thin crack. Follow the crack into a prominent black streak, then climb easier rock past the right side of a sloping ledge with cedar trees. 200'

P2 5.7 G: Stem off of the trees to reach the bottom of a crack in a left-facing overlap (crux). Go up the widening crack to a good rest beneath a steep headwall. Continue up the steep crack to its end (possible belay), scramble to a tree belay on the right edge of the cliff. 200'

History: The name comes from the notion that the route had two bits of crack, one at the start and the second on the steep headwall. Oddly, P1 leaves the crack just above the ground and wanders way left. Before 200' ropes, the only suitable belay for P1 was a narrow ledge and left-facing flake that required some creative protection (Vise-Grips?). This historic route was often called **The Bolt Route** because it was unusual for slab routes to have mid-pitch bolts.
FA 1972, Demetri Kolokotronis, Bob Perlee

20 Pieces of Eight 5.8- G 170' ★★★

Start: Same as **Two Bits**.

P1 5.8- G: Up the fingercrack of **Two Bits**, which becomes a right-arching seam. At the end of the seam, step right across a sloping ledge to a bulge. Over the bulge (crux), avoid the loose flake on the left, and up an easy slab. Go up and right to a fixed anchor. 170'
FA May 22, 2007, Tom Rosecrans, Brie Rosecrans, Jon Melcher

21 Prints of Darkness 5.9 G (5.5 R) 285' ★★★★

This route is an extension of **Pieces of Eight**.
Start: At the P1 anchor of **Pieces of Eight**.

P1 5.9 G (5.5 R): Up and slightly right (no pro, 5.5) to a bulge with a black streak. Over the bulge to the overlap. Work up, then slightly left (crux), to easier climbing that ends at a nice ledge and fixed anchor. 100'

---

6 "CAIRN," *Climbing*, no 11 (Jan–Feb 1972), p. 24.

*Opposite: Climber on **Little Finger** (5.5).*

Lake George

101

Lake George

P2 5.8 G: Straight up to series of overlaps (small cams). Step left above a square block to a slab. Go left across the slab to the crack of **Two Bits**. Up a few feet, then left on a smile-shaped rounded ledge. Straight up pure friction to easier rock and the fixed anchor at the top of **Little Finger**. 185'
Gear: To 1".
FA Oct 10, 2008, Tom Rosecrans, Brie Rosecrans

22 Roger That 5.6 R 430'
More a landmark than a route, this corner system bisects the right side of the slab and is crossed during the rappel from **Little Finger**.
Start: 100' right of **Little Finger** is a gully. Start on the left side of the gully.
Route Description: Several pitches lead toward the steep wall, where the crack becomes dirty and wet. Join P2 of **Two Bits**: scramble to a tree belay on the right edge of the cliff.

23 Slip Tease–Skid Row 5.9 G 190' ★★★★
The first-ascent party placed only one bolt on rappel. Most mortals will appreciate the additions. Clean and sustained.
Start: 100' right of **Little Finger** is a gully with a narrow buttress to its right. From the top of the buttress, scramble (3rd-class) 20' to the start at a fixed anchor.
● **P1 5.9 G:** Increasingly difficult friction leads to a good ledge. Above the ledge is a more moderate slab. Climb it to a fixed anchor at the left end of a tree ledge. 190'
FA 1976, Tom Rosecrans, Joel Clugstone

24 Last Hurrah 5.9+ PG 190' ★★★
Similar to **Slip Tease–Skid Row**, but it wanders a bit and has some longer runouts.
Start: Same as **Slip Tease–Skid Row**.
● **P1 5.9+ PG:** Go right and climb over a couple of overlaps, then run it out to the right end of the tree ledge and belay at the fixed anchor shared with **Slip Tease–Skid Row**. 190'
FA Nov, 1994, Dave Aldous, Tom Rosecrans

25 Slipped Bits 5.8 PG 160' ★
An older route that follows similar terrain as P2 of **Prints of Darkness**.
Start: At the P1 belay ledge at the top of **Slip Tease–Skid Row**.
P1 5.8 PG: From the left end of the ledge, move up and left to the vertical crack climbed by **Roger That**. Cross the crack and work up and left to tiered overlaps and join **Prints of Darkness**: step left above a square block to a slab. Go left across the slab to the crack of **Two Bits** and follow it to its end. 100'
P2 5.3 PG: Finish as for **Two Bits**: scramble to a tree belay on the right edge of the cliff. 60'
FA Sep 19, 1994, R.L. Stolz, Roman Kostrubiak, Ed Peithman

BROWN MOUNTAIN CLIFF

Location	In the Tongue Mountain Range on the west side of Lake George, accessed from NY 9N
Aspect	South
Height	200'
Quality	★
Approach	1 hr, difficult
Summary	A long cliff in a high and wild location with only a few routes and potential for many more.

-5.6	5.7	5.8	5.9	5.10	5.11	5.12	5.13+	total
			2					4

DESCRIPTION
At the northern end of the Tongue Mountain Range below the summit of Brown Mountain is a 1/4-mile long cliffband facing Lake George. The rock is compact and sheer, with smooth faces and steep corners. This cliff has only recently been visited by climbers and, as a result, there are only a handful of routes—all single pitch with fixed anchors—and several projects.

Woodland Corner is a prominent right-facing corner located in the middle of the cliff, on the right side of a prominent buttress. **Karate Crack** is an off-width crack several hundred feet uphill and left. 300' right of **Woodland Corner** (and past an area of rockfall below orange right-facing corners) is a 25' scramble (3rd class) up to the left end of the tree-covered Patio Ledge. High above the left end of Patio Ledge are a pair of roofs with a blocky chimney system to the right. **Ramps of Deception** starts on the Patio Ledge.

There is a high probability of rattlesnakes at this cliff, especially in the talus field, between May and September.

DIRECTIONS (MAP PAGE 103)
From Northway (I-87) Exit 24, drive 4.7 miles east on the Bolton Landing–Riverbank Road to its end, where it makes a T with NY 9N. Turn left onto NY 9N and drive north 9.4 miles to the parking area for the Tongue Mountain/Deer Leap Trailhead 0617322,4835285.

From the trailhead (0 min) follow the trail marked with blue discs to Dear Leap Junction at 15 min. (The left-hand, yellow-disc trail goes to the top of Deer Leap.) Turn right and go uphill on the trail for 200' to a point where the trail swings to the right (west) along the crest of the ridge. Leave the trail 0617148,4834675 and head southwest (on a bearing of 220°) toward the lake side of the ridge. Stay on 220° and make a slightly descending traverse across easy slopes to a talus field (30 min). Go south downhill and around the talus field to a level bench beneath broken cliffbands uphill to the right. Continue south and, at 45 min 0617013,4833920, turn west and go uphill toward a small talusfield beneath the right end of the cliff. Ascend the talus and reach the cliff at 1 hr 0616770,4834019. The rightmost

Lake George

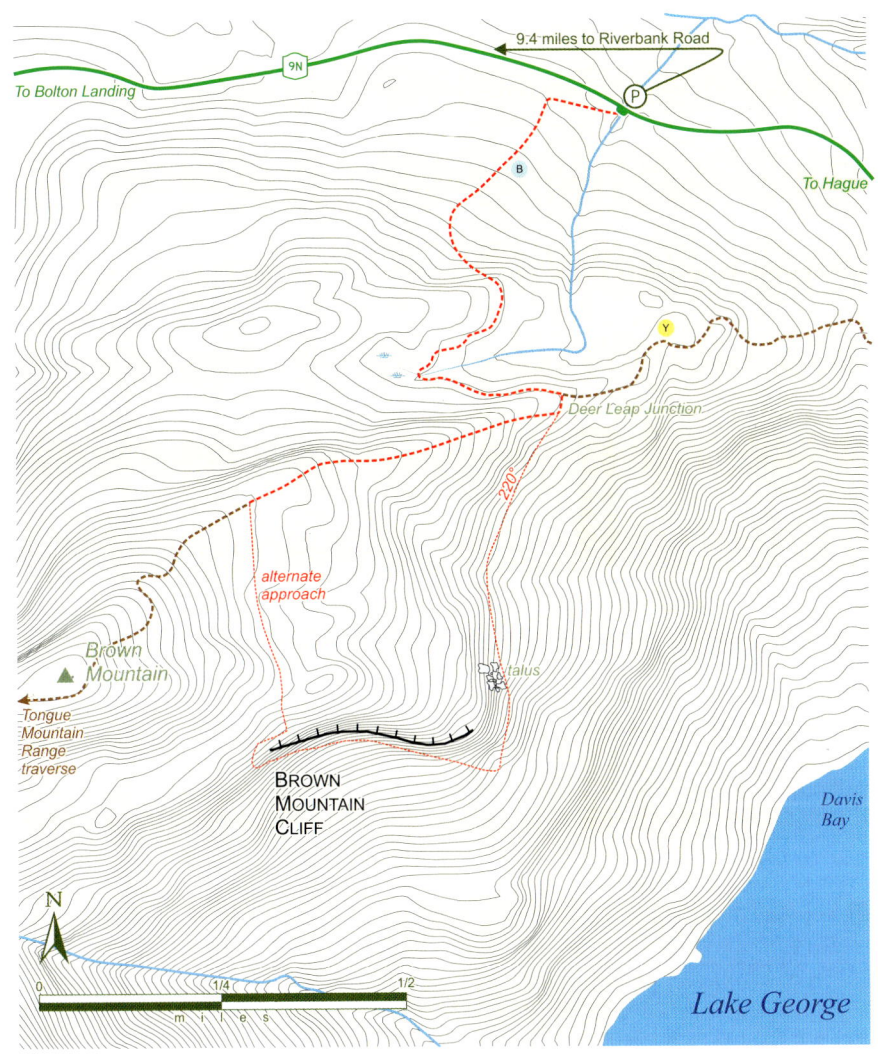

routes are 200' left on Patio Ledge; to reach them, walk left below broken cliffs for 150' to a scree field, then go up the scree and a 3rd-class step beneath black rock with wedged blocks.

An alternate approach to the left end of the cliff is possible. From the Dear Leap Junction at 15 min, continue west on the blue-disc trail to waypoint 0616475,4834482 (30 min). Leave the trail and go due south, downhill over easy terrain to the top of the cliff near Woodland Corner 0616575,4833980 (45 min). Turn right (west) and walk around the west end of the cliff to the base.

DESCENT OPTIONS
All routes are equipped with fixed anchors.

HISTORY
Scott Meyer scouted the cliff in September of 2012 and returned two weeks later with Craig Vollkommer who did the first route, Darklord, ground up.

1 Positive Progression 5.9 C1 90' ★★
Start: The left end of the cliff has a 60'-tall right-facing corner in black rock. Immediately to the right is a sloping tree-covered ledge 40' up. Begin at the right end of this, behind an oak tree.
P1 5.9 C1 G: Up a vertical fingercrack and into a left-facing corner where the crack widens to fist-size. The corner switches to right-facing (6" cam), then pinches down to a flared crack with intermittent protection. Follow the crack to a fixed anchor on a white pine. 90'
Gear: To 6".
FA Apr, 2013, Scott Meyer

Lake George

2 Karate Crack 5.10b G 95' ★★★★
Start: Beneath a right-facing wall with a vertical 5" crack 40' up that narrows and then leans right. To the right is a broad black slab.
P1 5.10b G: Go up the corner to a ledge 35' up. Follow a right-rising crack around an arête, and then hand traverse the crack right (crux) to the base of a vertical offwidth. Up this to a small ledge, then continue up the crack as it narrows and leans right. Reach out left to a vertical crack, leave the main crack, and then work back right across a face to a fixed anchor. 95'
Gear: Doubles to 5"
FA Oct 13, 2013, Craig Vollkommer

3 Woodland Corner Project
Closed project. This is a striking, full-height, right-facing corner on the right side of a buttress. The right-facing wall has orange rock and the main wall is black. There is a refrigerator-sized block at the bottom of the corner. Climb easy rock to the base of the corner. Follow a crack that forks and runs parallel up the orange wall to a stance beneath the steepest part of the corner. Above the steep section, the corner eases and leans to the left. There is a fixed anchor on a White Pine tree 120' up.

4 Darklord 5.10a G 95' ★★★
Continuously difficult crack climbing and the first reported route at the cliff.
Start: 50' right of Woodland Corner at opposing corners above blocky rock.
P1 5.10a G: Work up to a left-facing corner–flake and climb a wide crack into a slot. Follow a steep handcrack in the left-facing corner past an overhang. Continue up the crack on a slabby face, then leave the crack and climb left to a fixed anchor. 95'
Gear: To 4"
FA Oct, 2012, Craig Vollkommer, Scott Meyer

5 Ramps of Deception 5.10 C1 90' ★★
Start: At a left-rising ramp at the left end of the Patio Ledge, 100' right of twin roofs.
P1 5.10 C1 G: Go up the ramp then up to a higher ramp at the base of a sheer wall. Work over the wall to a small ledge with a 8'-tall vertical seam. Follow the seam to a right-facing alcove and right-facing flake. Move left from the alcove to a left-rising ramp. Climb above the ramp to a fixed anchor on a cedar tree. 90'
FA Oct, 2013, Craig Vollkommer

6 Project
Closed project. Start on the Patio Ledge and climb a finger- and handcrack in a left-facing corner past a dead tree.

7 Project
Closed project. Start 8' right of the previous project. Go up a vertical crack to a prominent horizontal crack. Traverse right along the crack and across black rock 2/3 of the way up the wall.

DEER LEAP

Location	East of NY 9N on the west shore of Lake George, accessed from Northway Exit 24
Aspect	South
Height	400'
Quality	
Approach	1 hr 20 min, moderate
Summary	A big chossy cliff that even John Turner couldn't resist.

This is a very large cliff that is not well suited for rock climbing. Its size and dramatic position above the most rugged stretch of Lake George has lured climbers to its base since the early 1960s. At 400' tall and 0.5 mile

Lake George

BROWN MOUNTAIN CLIFF
1 Positive Progression (5.9 C1)
2 Karate Crack (5.10b)
3 Woodland Corner (project)
4 Darklord (5.10a)
5 Ramps of Deception (5.10 C1)
6 Project
7 Project

long, this could be the largest choss pile in the Adirondacks. The right side of the cliff is overhanging and sheer, while the left side has a few left-facing corner systems that rise above broken ramps and ledges. If the lousy rock isn't a big enough deterrent, the abundance of rattlesnakes surely is.

HISTORY

John Turner climbed two routes on this cliff in the early 1960s with Craig Merrihue. Merrihue's parents had a "distinctly lavish cottage" farther up the lake from which Turner and Merrihue boated down to Deer Leap for two ascents—**Guermantes** (5.6) and **Méséglise** (5.6). These routes follow, in Turner's words, "the only two obvious lines on a not very impressive cliff." Tragically, Merrihue and his partner perished a couple of years later in a fall down Pinnacle Gully, Mount Washington, on Mar 14, 1965. Local climbers Tom Rosecrans and Ken Jackson made the only other reported ascent of Deer Leap in 1977. It is possible that **Mad Dogs and Englishmen** follows a route similar to either **Guermantes** or **Méséglise**. Rosecrans recalled scoping out the cliff during the winter when he drove his new car down the lake ice between Hague and Bolton Landing.

DIRECTIONS

From Northway (I-87) Exit 24, drive 5.0 miles east on the Bolton Landing–Riverbank Road to its end at NY 9N. Turn left onto NY 9N and drive north 9.3 miles to a parking area on the left that is across from the Deer Leap Trailhead. Hike the trail marked with yellow discs past an intersection (the intersecting trail goes south across the range) to its end (1.6 miles, 40 min) at a rocky shoulder with a view over the lake 618511,4834746. Bushwhack downhill and north (toward the road), then go right (east) and pass beneath small cliffbands until the lake is visible below and the profile of the cliff can be seen to the southeast. Cross a talus field and hike down along the base of the cliff, past the overhanging section with a black streak, to the lowest portion of the cliff near its left end, reached at 1 hr 20 min 618547,4834400.

1 Mad Dogs and Englishmen 5.7 PG 460'

The only redeeming qualities of this route are that it is long and has nice scenery.
Start: At the left end of the cliff, locate a deep open book that begins 50' above the top of a talus field that extends down to the lakeshore. Begin at the right side of the right wall of the open book.
P1 5.5 G: Up discontinuous cracks on the low-angle wall. Move left on broken rock toward the main wall. Belay beneath a tall right-facing corner that is right of the main wall. 120'
P2 5.5 G: Go up the corner and through a block-filled depression to a belay on a broad sloped terrace. 100'
P3 5.0 G: Scramble to the right end of the sloped terrace to a belay at conifer trees that are beneath stepped ledges on a fractured ridge that leads to the top. 100'
P4 5.7 PG: Climb stepped ledges up and right of the fractured ridge to a small left-facing corner with a vertical crack. Follow the corner to the top. 140'
History: Dismayed by the poor rock quality, nondescript features, and lack of protectable cracks, the first ascentionists settled for this route because the first 50' had the only attractive rock on the entire cliff.
FA 1977, Tom Rosecrans, Ken Jackson

Lake George

WILD PINES

Location	West side of Lake George, on NY 9N between Bolton Landing and Hague
Aspect	Northwest
Height	70'
Quality	★
Approach	5 min, easy
Summary	A small, easily-accessed cliff with mostly steep face climbs, and one exceptional crack, one of the best in the Lake George area.

	1	1	1		3
-5.6	5.7	5.8	5.9	5.10	5.11	5.12	5.13+	total

Wild Pines is a small cliff with only a few established routes, and several projects. The landmark feature is a 20'-deep corner with a right-rising fingercrack that begins 25' up (the route **Hysteria**). The left wall of the corner is sheer, overhanging, and has a massive roof at its left end; very impressive terrain. Left of the 20'-deep corner is a blocky steep wall that ends at a ledge beneath the roof (the route **Profusion**). Right of the 20'-deep corner is a blunt arête with the route **Thrill Ride**, and a sheer vertical wall split by a fingercrack (**Double Recracker**). Further right, the wall diminishes in height near a short corner with the route **Commotion**. Additionally, there is good bouldering in the talus blocks beneath the cliff.

The cliff is shaded most of the day due to the tall pine trees.

DIRECTIONS

From Northway (I-87) Exit 24, drive 4.7 miles east on the Bolton Landing–Riverbank Road to its end where it makes a T with NY 9N. Turn left onto NY 9N and drive north 6.5 miles to a small parking area on the left (north) side of the road, at a gap in a railing across from a roadcut 0613129,4834428. This is 2.9 miles south of the Tongue Mountain/Deer Leap Trailhead. There is room to park three cars.

The cliff is visible when traveling north on NY 9N, after crossing Northwest Bay Brook at a marsh and before the road goes uphill to the parking area.

Cross the road and walk uphill to the end of the roadcut. The herd path starts at a gap between the roadcut and a guardrail. Go up a steep vegetated slope and into an open conifer forest. Walk southeast for 500' over a low ridge and above a talus field to the left end of the cliff. Walk right across talus to reach the tallest section of the cliff near **Hysteria** 0613251,4834323.

DESCENT OPTIONS

Routes are equipped with fixed anchors.

HISTORY

Scott Meyer first visited the area in November of 2012 and did some bouldering. He returned with Craig Vollkommer in the summer of 2013.

1 Profusion 5.10c G 60' ★★

Start: 30' left and uphill of the start of **Hysteria**, at a car-sized block.
● **P1 5.10c G:** Clamber up the block to a stance beneath a vertical seam. Go up the seam, and work up and left on an overhanging face. Pull over an overlap, then step left to a steep face. Up the steep face and over a high overlap to a fixed anchor. 60'
FA Nov 17, 2013, Craig Vollkommer, Amelia Whalen

2 Untammed Stimulation Project

This closed project ascends the steep, left side of an overhanging arête. Start as for **Profusion**, then go right of the seam and work up wavy, overhanging rock (crux) to a ledge on the arête. Go up to a larger ledge on the arête, then continue up the left side of the arête to a ledge with a fixed anchor.

3 Wild Rumpus Project

A closed project. Begin at the low point of the cliff, 15' left of **Hysteria**. Scramble up and left to the right side of an 8'-tall square block. Climb to the top of the block and pull onto an overhanging, rippled wall. Make hard moves into a right-facing corner. Up the corner, then up a sheer face with a right-rising crack; follow the crack to the fixed anchor of **Untammed Stimulation**.

4 Hysteria 5.9+ G 70' ★★★

Start: Beneath a blocky wall with right-facing steps, down and right of the 20'-deep corner, the landmark feature of the cliff.
P1 5.9+ G: Go up the steps to a broad ledge, then scramble easy rock to the base of the corner. Climb a sustained fingercrack with good stems and fingerlocks beneath an impressive overhanging wall. Make a tough move at the top of the corner to a fixed anchor. 70'
FA May, 2013, Craig Vollkommer, Scott Meyer

5 Thrill Ride 5.11b G 70' ★★★

A closed project. Clean rock, big moves, and a high crux with two ways to the top.
Start: Same as **Hysteria**.
5.11b G: Work up and right past ledges to a stance on the left side of a blunt arête. Move left past two left-facing flakes, then work back right to a rest at a small ledge. Reach out right to the left end of tiered overhangs, then make a long reach to crimpy rails and finish at a fixed anchor. 70'

6 Double Recracker Project

A closed project. Begin 25' uphill and right of **Hysteria** at a slab below a crack that tapers to fingers. Follow this past an overlap with long reaches to twin cracks and a fixed anchor.

7 Commotion Project

A closed project. Start as for **Double Recracker**, then go up a low-angle, right-rising crack to a ledge with a tree. Climb the face left of a left-facing corner, then up the corner to a ledge with a fixed anchor.

Lake George

FLY BROOK VALLEY

Location	Between Brant Lake and Lake George, accessed from Northway Exit 24 and NY 9N
Summary	A collection of minimally-explored wilderness cliffs in a remote valley.

1	2	1			5
-5.6	5.7	5.8	5.9	5.10	5.11	5.12	5.13+	total

The Fly Brook Valley is a large hidden valley north of NY 9N and west of Lake George, in the same neighborhood as Tongue Mountain and Barton High Cliff. There are many cliffs in this valley, the vast majority of which are unexplored and undeveloped. Catamount Main Face and Wardsboro Cliff do have a small number of routes. The rock quality varies from bullet-hard to fractured and loose.

The area is heavily used by hunters during all hunting seasons. Despite this, the valley has a wild feel: the approach is long; there are thick fields of stinging nettles that guard the approach to Catamount Mountain and along the base of North Wardsboro Cliff; coyotes have been heard while climbing; and, while no snakes have been reported, there are known rattlesnake dens within a few miles of the cliffs.

HISTORY

Jason Brechko was first to explore these cliffs for climbing, which he discovered by studying topographical maps. He first visited Catamount Mountain, then later Wardsboro Cliff, which he saw from across the valley.

DIRECTIONS   (MAP PAGE 107)

From Northway (I-87) Exit 24, drive 5.0 miles east on the Bolton Landing–Riverbank Road to its end, where it makes a T with NY 9N. Turn left onto NY 9N and drive north 6.0 miles to Padanarum Road (0.0 miles). Turn left onto Padanarum Road, then right at 1.8 miles onto Wardsboro Road / Fly Brook Road. Park at a turnout on the right at 3.4 miles, just before the Wardsboro Cemetery and across from a red cabin 613100,4837732.

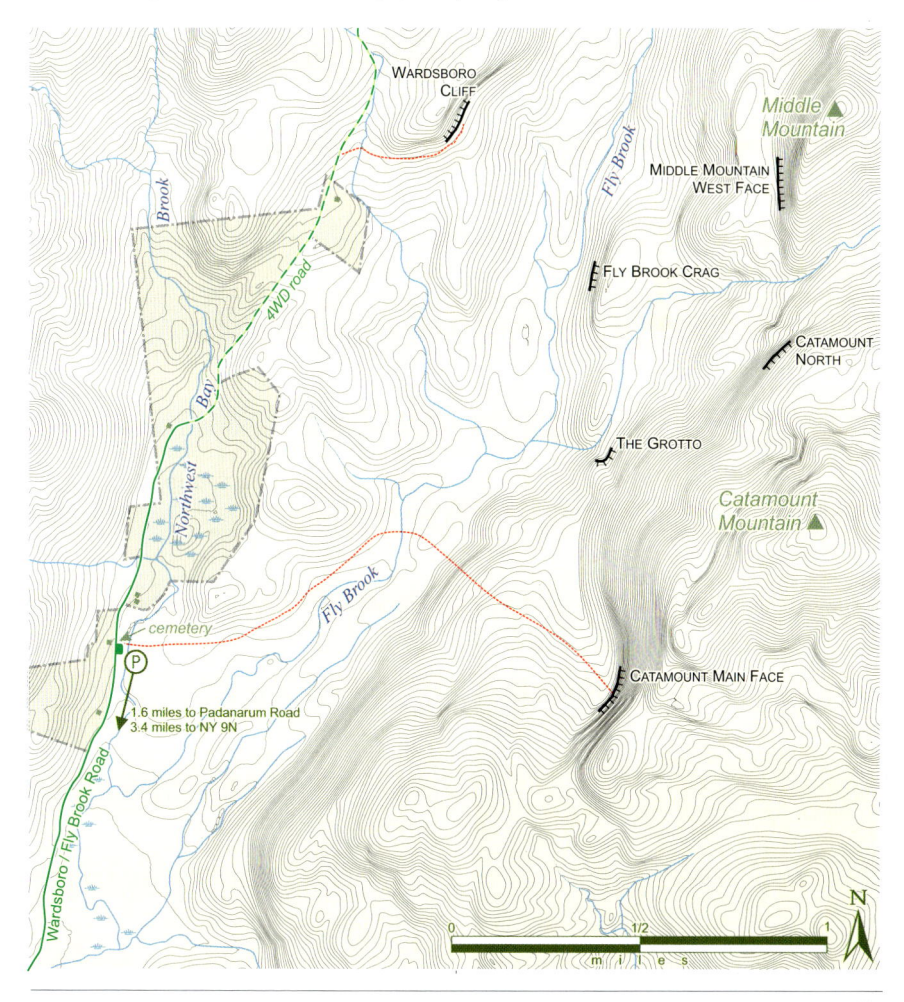

107

Lake George

Fly Brook Valley
WARDSBORO CLIFF

Aspect	Southeast
Height	150'
Quality	
Approach	45 min, difficult
Summary	Wild cliff with several crack routes and some new route potential.

	1	2	1					4
-5.6	5.7	5.8	5.9	5.10	5.11	5.12	5.13+	total

Wardsboro Cliff has seen the most attention in the Fly Brook Valley. The southeast-facing cliff is divided into two sections, the South Wall and the North Wall, separated by broad vegetated ledges. The top of the cliff is known as the Kenneth Palmer Lookout, identified by a memorial plaque bearing his name mounted on the side of a rock. The plaque is above the right end of South Wall, and on top of the route **Padanarum Crack**. From this lookout, you can see across the valley to the cliffs on Catamount Mountain.

DESCENT OPTIONS
Scramble down the vegetated ledges that separate the North and South Walls, or rappel with two ropes from large pine trees near the lookout.

DIRECTIONS   (MAP PAGE 107)
From the Fly Brook Valley parking, hike north along the road. At 0.6 mile there is a green house on the left, and the road becomes a 4WD track. At 1.3 miles there is a hunting cabin on the right. 90 yards beyond it is a cairn, and yellow blazes on trees marking a state land boundary. Continue on the track another 100 yards past the state boundary, then turn right on a bearing of 100°, following the contour of the terrain. Cross a drainage area and continue contouring to the cliff, the South Wall, which will be on your left 614588,4839983. It takes about 30 minutes to reach the cliff once you leave the 4WD track.

At the right end of South Wall is a cairn beneath a vegetated ledge system used to access Padanarum Crack. To reach the North Wall, make your way to the flat ground below the talus of the South Wall, then walk north until you can see the cliff on the left. The left end of the North Wall is identified by a large buttress with a huge roof 20' up, the location of **Bowling for Simon**.

WARDSBORO CLIFF
1 Padanarum Crack 5.9+
Kenneth Palmer Lookout

Photo by Jay Harrison.

Jason Brechko on the first ascent of **P8tience** *(5.8). Photo by Jay Harrison.*

1 **Padanarum Crack** 5.9+ G 120' ★★

Start: This route begins above the cliff base and at the right end of the South Wall. Scramble up right-rising, vegetated ledges for 100' to the base of a steep, 20'-tall dirty wall.
P1 5.9+ G: Up 10' to a small ramp. Work right on the ramp, then back left to ledges. Up the ledges, then step right to a protruding block. Face climb past two bolts (crux) to a right-facing corner. Climb a crack in the corner for 40' to where it forks (V1), then follow the wide left fork to a juggy, Gunks-like finish. 120'
V1 5.10 A0: Follow the direct fingercrack to the top.
FA Sep, 2007, Jason Brechko, Simon Cording
FA (V1) Sep, 2008, Jay Harrison, Jason Brechko

2 **Bowling for Simon** 5.7 PG 150'

Moderate climbing on loose rock.
Start: Near the left end of North Wall is a large buttress with a roof 20' up. Begin at a left-facing corner on the left side of the roof, behind a detached block.
P1 5.7 PG: Up the corner, then up the blocky face on the right to a large tree on a forested ledge. 150'
FA Sep, 2008, Jay Harrison

3 **P8tience** 5.8 G (5.2 R) 90' ★

Unique iron-rich rock with solution pockets.
Start: Near the center of North Wall is a large, orange, overhanging section of rock. At the right end of the overhanging section are two steep faces. Begin on the left of the two faces below a large figure-eight worn into the rock by natural weathering 25' up.
P1 5.8 G (5.2 R): Up the easy and fun face with the figure-eight to an overhang. Climb straight through the roof via a crack on the right edge of a large block, up 15' to a ledge, then head left over loose but easy terrain to a fixed anchor on an oak tree. 90'
FA Jul 10, 2007, Jason Brechko, Jay Harrison

4 Walking Fern Face 5.8 G 50' ★★

Good face climbing with several variations. Keep an eye out for the small fern with arrow-shaped leaves at 2/3 height (a walking fern), which is beautiful and rare.
Start: Right of **P8tience** is another steep face bordered on the right by a corner and roof system that arches over the face. Begin below the center of this face.
P1 5.8 G: Up the face using interesting solution pockets to an overhang, over this, then up the face to a fixed anchor. 50'
FA Jun, 2008, Jay Harrison, Jason Brechko

Fly Brook Valley
CATAMOUNT MAIN FACE

Aspect	Northwest
Height	70'
Quality	
Approach	1 hr 15 min, difficult
Summary	Remote cliff with a single exploratory route.

The only reported rock route is **Nettle Crack**, but there's a lot of potential here. Watch for poison ivy.

DIRECTIONS (MAP PAGE 107)
The approach is long and includes a sea of stinging nettles. From the parking, head east into the Fly Brook Valley, then northeast staying on the high ground above the brook. Eventually, cross the brook 614344,4838204, then head southeast and uphill to the cliff 615244,4837544 reached at 1 hr 15 min.

5 Nettle Crack 5.8 A0 70'
An incomplete route with no second pitch.
Start: At a right-facing corner, 50 yards up and left of the cliff's main left-facing corner and roof system.
P1 5.8 A0 G: Up the right-facing corner to a beautiful right-arching fingercrack hidden from below. 70'
FA 2007, Jason Brechko, Ryan Aleva

PADANARUM CLIFF

Location	Between Brant Lake and Lake George, accessed from Northway Exit 24 and NY 9N
Aspect	South
Height	50' - 150'
Quality	
Approach	20 min, moderate
Summary	Large cliff with some very steep rock and a moderate approach.

1		1	3				5
-5.6	5.7	5.8	5.9	5.10	5.11	5.12	5.13+	total

This large cliff is largely undeveloped and has good potential for more routes, although the rock is shattered and brittle. It's divided in three sections, the Left End, Center Section, and Right End. Additionally, there's a cliff above the Center Section called The Nightcap.

You can see the cliff from NY 9N, at a pullout 0.4 miles north of the intersection with Padanarum Road.

HISTORY
The cliff is close to the Old Bridge Boulder (aka Padanarum Boulder), and apparently had been ignored by boulderers. Tom DuBois was unaware of this boulder, and saw the cliff from NY 9N. Other climbers have explored the cliff, but DuBois was the first to report climbing in November, 2012.

DIRECTIONS (MAP PAGE 110)
From Northway (I-87) Exit 24 (0.0 mile), drive east on the Bolton Landing–Riverbank Road to its end at 4.7 miles, where it makes a T with NY 9N. Turn left onto NY 9N. At 10.4 miles, turn left onto an unmarked dirt road on the left: this is Padanarum Road (or Wardsboro Road depending on the map). There is a large gravel pullout on the left at this intersection. (This is 11.2 miles south of the intersection with NY 8 in Hague.) At 10.7 miles, cross the Northwest Bay Brook. At 11.2 miles, park on the left across from a yellow DEC state land sign on a tree 612550,4834793. If you miss it, 0.4 mile further is an intersection with the Wardsboro Road on the right.

From the parking area, walk west and cross the

*Tom Yandon on the first ascent of **Up Yanda** (5.8).*

109

Lake George

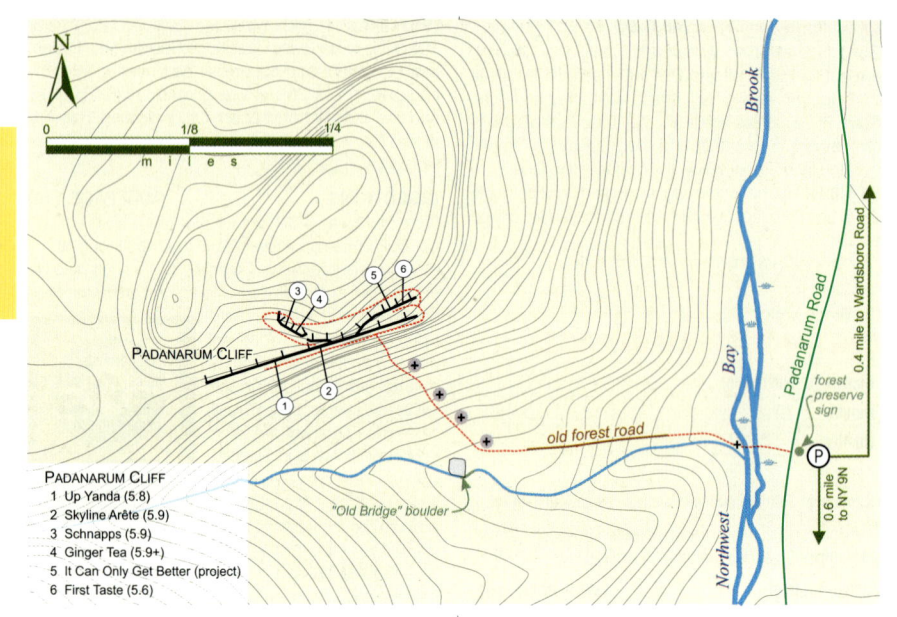

PADANARUM CLIFF
1. Up Yanda (5.8)
2. Skyline Arête (5.9)
3. Schnapps (5.9)
4. Ginger Tea (5.9+)
5. It Can Only Get Better (project)
6. First Taste (5.6)

braided river which runs parallel to the road (0 hr 0 min). In high water, the crossing may required wading. Once across, locate a seasonal rocky stream that enters from the west 612480,4834789. Follow this stream uphill, staying high on its right side; there's a good forest road that makes walking easy. The angle levels briefly at 7 min; from here, leave the valley, turn northwest, and follow cairns uphill to the cliff at the Right End, reached at 20 min 611920,4834944. It is easy to walk left along the base of the cliff.

Incidentally, the cliff is about 700' north and uphill from the Old Bridge Boulder 612092,4834772.

DESCENT OPTIONS

You can walk around either end of the cliff, but it is a long way. Alternatively, once you know where it is, there's a fixed anchor at the top of **Up Yanda** set up for a 100' rappel; rope up to reach this anchor, as it's very exposed.

Left End

The left end of the cliff is about 150' wide and 50' tall, and features mostly black rock. No routes here yet.

Center Section

The Center Section is about 500' wide and up to 150' tall. On its left end is a section of dramatic dihedrals and arêtes 611861,4834913. Right of this is a very steep orange and black-and-white-striped wave of rock 75' up, above which is a grass ledge (hidden from below). Right of the wave is a complex, vertical section with good potential for routes. The far right side of the Center Section is capped by a 20'-deep roof with a finger-crack 611970,4834915.

1 Up Yanda 5.8 G 100' ★★★

Excellent corner climbing. Named for a nearby farm on Lake George.

Start: 50' left of the very steep orange and black-and-white-striped wave of rock 75' up, and 4' right of a 10'-high chimney slot that begins 7' up, at a chest-high ledge. This is at the right end of a low, 50'-tall black-and-white striped wall with an open base.

P1 5.8 G: Go up and right on a staircase of ledges, then foot traverse right around an arête into a black V-groove. Stem up the groove to a ledge, then up to another ledge beneath a giant right-facing corner. Up the corner to a fixed anchor. 100'
FA Sep 4, 2013, Tom Yandon, Jim Lawyer

2 Skyline Arête 5.9 TR 90'

This route begins above the very steep orange and black-and-white-striped wave of rock at a hidden, difficult-to-access ledge. Walk to The Nightcap, then locate the double-trunked oak tree on the prominent prow. (This is a great place to be.) Lower in from the tree and climb the arête. This project was reported by Tom DuBois, and toproped and cleaned by Yandon and Lawyer; due to loose rock they decided to leave this as a toprope.
FA (TR) Sep 3, 2013, Tom Yandon, Jim Lawyer

The Nightcap

Above the Center Section is another small cliff about 100' back in the woods 611860,4834942. It's about 100' wide and 50' tall and has a 3'-deep roof in the center 20' up.

The easiest way to get here is to walk around the right end of the cliff, then back left. Go across the top of the upper tier of the Right End, then across the top of the Center Section. At the highest point along the top, you'll be standing on top of the Nightcap. Scramble down (skier's) right, then back (skier's) left to the base of this small wall.

There is a pleasant ledge above the Center Section here, and the rappel point for Skyline Arête.

3 Schnapps 5.9 TR 55'
Begin 22' uphill and left of the low point on the wall, at a short crack below the left end of the 3' roof. Go up the short crack, then up the left-facing corner, through a notch to an easy finish.
FA (TR) Aug 10, 2013, Tom DuBois

4 Ginger Tea 5.9+ TR 55'
Begin at the lowest point on the face at a rounded arête with a horizontal crack 8' up (this is 60' right of Schnapps). Climb the blunt arête past the horizontal to the right end of the roof. Break through at a V-notch to a sloping finish.
FA (TR) Aug 10, 2013, Tom DuBois

Right End

The Right End is about 200' wide, and has two tiers, separated by a grassy slope. The lower tier is 30'-50' tall and broken, with good rock only on its left end; the upper tier is 70' tall and features some black rock.

The reported routes are on the upper tier. Walk around the right end of the cliff, then back left on a grassy ledge. Look for is an 8'-tall, squat pedestal-shaped block resting on a slab, 75' left of the right end of the cliff; this is It Can Only Get Better.

5 It Can Only Get Better Project
An open project. Begin at the 8'-tall, squat, pedestal-shaped block resting against a slab. From the top of the block, go up to a left-facing flake, then left to a jug, then up to a crack that splits the black face. Go up the crack to where it disappears, then up to a ledge.

6 First Taste 5.6 PG (5.4 R) 70'
Start: Just left of a low, chossy roof below a short, dirty crack that begins 10' up, 60' right of It Can Only Get Better.

P1 5.6 PG (5.4 R): Scramble up easy rock for 10' to a grassy ledge. Go up the crack to where it fades, then up a blank section to a shallow left-facing open book where the crack continues. Up this to the top. 70'
FA Nov 4, 2012, Tom DuBois, Ellen DuBois

TONGUE MOUNTAIN CLIFF

Location	East of NY 9N on the west shore of Lake George, accessed from Northway Exit 24
Aspect	West
Height	140'
Quality	★★★
Approach	1 hr, moderate
Summary	One of the best crags in the Lake George region, offering high-quality single-pitch routes in an elevated, sunny, breezy setting with incredible views over Lake George.

4	4	6	8	3	2	27
-5.6	5.7	5.8	5.9	5.10	5.11	5.12	5.13+	total

Situated high above the waters of Lake George is one of the best cliffs in the Lake George region. The Tongue Mountain Cliff is blessed with a sunny exposure, a breezy position, and abundant crack climbs on excellent rock. Although the approach is neither short nor straightforward, the hike is a pleasant mix of easy trails and bushwhacking up an open hardwood forest. The Tongue Range is famous for its challenging trails with incredible views, and infamous because it houses the largest population of timber rattlesnakes in the Adirondacks. However, most snakes are sighted on the hiking trails, and the risk of encountering a den on the cliff is extremely low.

A forest fire swept across this hillside in 1950, and the evidence is still quite obvious. The trees across the top of the cliff are charred and weakened, but the destruction has resulted in great views over Northwest Bay and the mountains beyond.

TONGUE MOUNTAIN CLIFF
4   Sidewinder (5.8)
6   Tartar Control (5.10d)
10 Tongue-Lashing (5.11a)
14 Snake Charmer (5.8-)
21 Gridlock (5.9+)
25 Bear Claw (5.11a)

Lake George

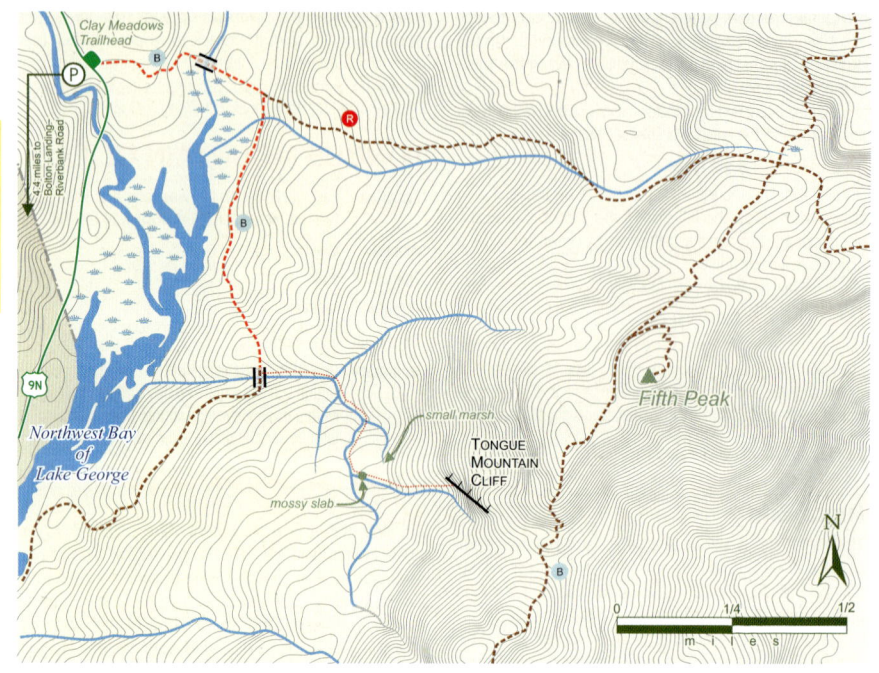

The cliff is situated on the southwest side of the ridge and is visible from the intersection of NY 9N and the Bolton Landing–Riverbank Road. Because the cliff base is sloped and forested, finding the start of a climb can be difficult. The distinctive features on the cliff are three left-facing walls that are over 100' tall and sheer: the Serpent Wall, the Project Wall, and the Lakeview Wall. These faces hold some sustained routes, both face and crack, moderate and severe.

The Serpent Wall, the leftmost wall, is encountered first on the approach. It has a full-length crack (**Sidewinder**) on its right edge. Downhill from and left of the Serpent Wall is a nondescript section of cliff with a single unmistakable feature—the splitter handcrack of **French Kiss**. To the right, the next left-facing wall is the Project Wall, followed by the Lakeview Wall. A 3rd-class chimney begins 100' right of the right edge of the Lakeview Wall and provides access to **Forked Tongue**, **Gridlock**, and the top of the cliff. Uphill from the access chimney, the cliff diminishes in height. A couple of routes are clustered at the right end of the cliff near a wall with diagonal-slashed cracks that is above a low ledge.

DIRECTIONS (MAP PAGE 112)

From Northway (I-87) Exit 24, drive 4.7 miles east on the Bolton Landing–Riverbank Road to its end, where it makes a T with NY 9N. Turn left onto NY 9N and drive north 4.4 miles to the Clay Meadow Trailhead on the right 612297,4831607.

From the trailhead (0 min), follow the trail marked with blue discs downhill, cross a large wooden bridge, then reach a trail junction. Go right and stay on the blue-disc trail, which heads toward Point of Tongue. The trail goes over a hill, then descends to a wooden bridge that crosses a creek, reached at 25 min 612859,4830593.

Leave the main trail and bushwhack upstream (left) in a moderately steep creekbed that levels out at the first stream junction. Take the right fork and follow the stream uphill to another level section and a second stream junction. Take the left (and larger) fork and follow it to a third junction 200' later. Take the right fork and follow it for 600' to a fourth stream junction. Take the left fork (130' SE), which has a 20-long mossy slab 50' above the junction. An orange blaze is located on the uphill (left) side of the creek. The creekbed climbs steeply; eventually the lower left end of the Tongue Mountain Cliff comes into view on the left above a talus slope. Hike to the right of the talus and then up to the cliff near **Sidewinder** (1 hr) 613580,4830078.

There are yellow and orange blazes along this approach. The newer orange blazes lead to the drainage area that contains the Tongue Mountain Cliff, whereas the yellow blazes ultimately continue to the ridge.

DESCENT OPTIONS

Fire damage has weakened many of the trees on top of the cliff. As a result, most of the routes have fixed anchors, and a single 60-m rope is necessary for descent. You can hike around either end of the cliff. The 3rd-class chimney behind the Lakeview Wall provides another option for descent.

HISTORY

Fred Abbuhl and Doug Douglas established many high-quality routes at the cliff in 1992. Although the routes were all recommended in Don Mellor's *Climbing*

Lake George

in the Adirondacks, the Tongue Mountain Cliff fell into obscurity. A lack of easy routes and a confusing approach may have deterred climbers. The cliff's potential, quality, and its beautiful setting were recognized by Jeremy Haas, who encouraged Lake George climbers to visit the cliff. A flurry of new routes was established, and several projects await completion.

1 French Kiss 5.9+ G 90' ★★★
Start: Near the left end of the cliff at an overhanging buttress capped by roofs below an open book with a splitter vertical crack in the left wall that begins 25' up.
P1 5.9+ G: Climb the open book to a ceiling, then up and left to an overhanging left-facing corner. Finish on a knob-covered bulge to a fixed anchor. 90'
Gear: 2 ea 1-2".
FA May 12, 2008, Jeremy Haas, Ben Uris

2 Bandaloop Dancers 5.9 TR 100' ★
Near the left end of the cliff is an overhanging buttress capped by roofs. Locate a horizontal crack that is below a right-rising ramp and some blocks that are perched on the ground to the right. Hand-traverse the horizontal crack left to a horn, then up the right-rising ramp. Follow the ramp, then move up to a left-facing corner and a sloping ledge. Go right past a wedged block to a stance. Move left, then step back right to a higher stance. Make an exposed traverse left, then up to the fixed anchors of **French Kiss**.
FA (TR) Nov, 2006, Jeremy Haas

Serpent Wall

The Serpent Wall is the leftmost of the three tall left-facing walls and is encountered first on the approach. It has a full-length crack (**Sidewinder**) on its right edge.

3 Anaconda 5.10d PG 100' ★★★★★
Committing, devious, and excellent; what a pitch!
Start: Same as **Sidewinder**.
P1 5.10d PG: Up the sheer face, then go left to a left-rising seam. Climb past a shallow horizontal to a large horizontal crack. Up and left to converging cracks, then climb them to a fixed anchor. 100'
Descent: Lower with a 60-m rope.
FA Nov, 2006, Robert Livingston
FFA Apr 7, 2008, Jim Lawyer, Emilie Drinkwater

4 Sidewinder 5.8 G 100' ★★
Sustained crack climbing after the crux ceiling near the beginning of the pitch. Extra runners are recommended for this sidewinder of a pitch.
Start: Centered on the Serpent Wall under a 15'-tall slab.
P1 5.8 G: Traverse right across the top of the slab, then up a right-rising crack-flake to a stance beneath a ceiling. Go left and over the ceiling to a vertical crack and climb it to a detached flake on the right edge of the wall. Up the flake to a second ceiling. Traverse left of the ceiling, then up converging cracks to the fixed anchor shared with **Anaconda**. 100'
Descent: Lower with a 60-m rope.
FA Apr 21, 2007, Tom Rosecrans, Robert Livingston

Project Wall

This is the middle of the three tall left-facing walls and has a tree-covered ledge halfway up that divides it into a lower and an upper wall. The upper wall has four routes that are best approached by climbing **Baywatch**.

5 Antivenom Project
Start beneath the centermost crack on the Project Wall that begins 30' up. Up a corner and through an overhang to a left-arching crack. Follow the crack to its end at a horizontal crack. Step right and climb a seam in the orange face to the tree ledge.

6 Tartar Control 5.10d PG 100' ★★
Start: At the right end of the Project Wall where the trail is pinched between the cliff and a car-sized block on the right, beneath a roof 8' up.
P1 5.10d PG: Up vertical cracks past either end of the roof. Move up and left across a face to an orange right-facing corner. Up the corner and over a ceiling to a handcrack, then climb the handcrack to a large ledge and a tree with a fixed anchor. 100'
FA 1992, Fred Abbuhl, Doug Douglas

7 Baywatch 5.7 G 70' ★
Provides easy access to the Project Wall Ledge.
Start: 10' right of **Tartar Control**, beneath a short offwidth crack that leads to a conifer on a sloping ledge.
P1 5.7 G: Up the offwidth, and across the sloping ledge to the bottom of a steep right-facing corner. Up the corner past two pesky trees to the right end of a large ledge. 70'
Gear: To 4".
FA Apr 15, 2008, Jamie McNeill, Jeremy Haas

8 Taste Buds 5.9 G 50' ★★★★
Start: On the vegetated ledge 80' up the Project Wall. Start 20' left of a horizontal slab at a vertical crack that comes out of the ground.
P1 5.9 G: Up the vertical crack to a horizontal crack with a converging crack on the right. Follow the right-hand crack (crux), then up to horizontal cracks (small gear). Fixed anchor on top. 50'
FA 1992, Fred Abbuhl, Doug Douglas

9 Rescue Breathing 5.10b G 80' ★★★★
Secure face climbing with a flared fingercrack finish.
Start: Same as **Tongue Lashing**.
P1 5.10b G: (V1) Move out of the pod at the bottom and into a left-rising crack with a dead tree. Go past the dead tree to a second pod. Hand traverse left along a horizontal to a piton, then face climb a vertical wall to a left-rising crack. Follow the crack to a horizontal dike and step left to a right-rising, flared fingercrack. Up the fingercrack, then traverse left to a fixed anchor shared with **Taste Buds**. 80'
V1 5.10d R: Start 15' to the left at a chest-sized block and beneath an A-framed overhang 10' up. A small cam on the left protects a hard move into the A-frame. Go over the A-frame to a horizontal crack and follow it to the piton on the right.
History: The first ascent climbed the difficult and poorly protected direct start. The recommended start and

113

Lake George

TONGUE MOUNTAIN CLIFF

1. French Kiss (5.9+)
2. Bandaloop Dancers (5.9)
3. Anaconda (5.10d)
4. Sidewinder (5.8)
5. Antivenom (project)
6. Tartar Control (5.10d)
7. Baywatch (5.7)
8. Taste Buds (5.9)
9. Rescue Breathing (5.10b)
10. Tongue-Lashing (5.11a)
11. Crotalusly Challenged (5.9)
12. Excalibur (5.8+)
13. Slip of the Tongue (5.12b)
14. Snake Charmer (5.8-)

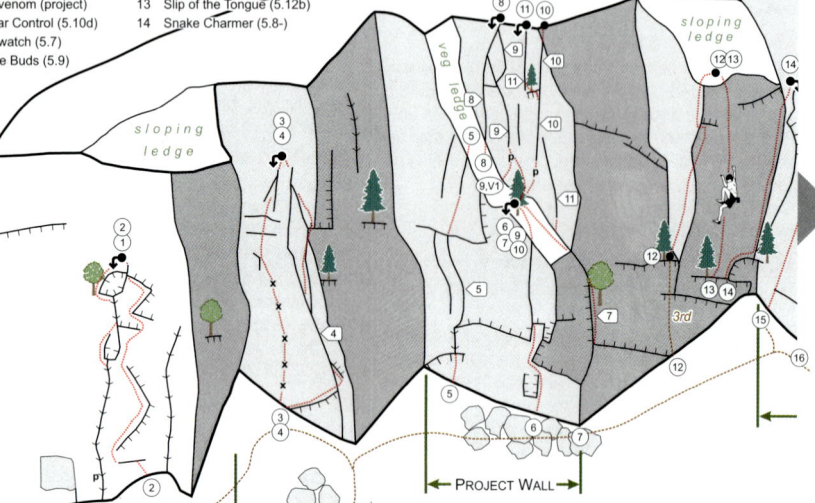

the piton were added two days later.
FA May 28, 2008, Jeremy Haas, Ben Uris, Tom Rosecrans
FA (V1) May 26, 2008, Jeremy Haas

10 Tongue-Lashing 5.11a PG 60' ★★
Start: On the vegetated ledge 80' up the Project Wall. Start 3' right of a horizontal slab at an 8'-long overhang 3' up.
P1 5.11a PG: An unprotected move off the ground gains a small vertical slot (gear placement). Move right across a face (crux) to fixed protection beneath an overhang. Follow a vertical crack through the overhang, then move left to a left-rising crack and climb it to the top. 60'
FA 1992, Fred Abbuhl, Doug Douglas

11 Crotalusly Challenged 5.9 G 90' ★★
Crotalus horridus is the species of timber rattlesnake.
Start: Right end of Project Wall Ledge, 10' right of the pine tree with a fixed anchor.
P1 5.9 G: Up a detached block–flake to a left-rising crack. Follow the crack to a ceiling (crux) that is above a raven's ledge. Continue up the crack to a small tree, then traverse left along a ledge to a vertical crack. Up the brilliant vertical crack to the top. 90'
FA Jun 14, 2008, Tom Rosecrans, Brie Rosecrans

End of Project Wall

12 Excalibur 5.8+ R 90' ★★
Although the arête is poorly protected, the crux is protectable.
Start: 40' left of the left end of the Lakeview Wall is an arête that begins 30' up. Scramble (3rd-class) up to the sloping ledge left of the arête and belay at a tree.
P1 5.8+ R: Up and right to the arête, then climb it (5.8 R) to a short left-facing corner. Climb the corner, then the ceiling above (crux). Step right to a fixed anchor. 90'
FA Mar 30, 2007, Mike O'Herron, Dan Skellie

13 Slip of the Tongue 5.12b TR 80' ★★
This toprope route begins 20' left of the left end of the Lakeview Wall. Scramble up to a tree-covered ledge at the left end of the Lakeview Wall and start at a flake that is beneath a sheer orange wall with a vertical seam. Up the seam to a small ledge. Face-climb (crux) to a left-rising rail, then past an overlap to a finish up and left at a belay with pitons.
FA (TR) 1992, Fred Abbuhl, Doug Douglas

14 Snake Charmer 5.8- G 80' ★★★★
Start: Scramble up to a tree-covered ledge at the left end of the Lakeview Wall and begin at a flake that is left of a large left-facing corner with a 6" crack.
P1 5.8- G: Climb the flake to the base of the corner. The wide crack quickly narrows to a sustained handcrack. Climb the handcrack to a stance in a large alcove. Continue up the steepening handcrack, past good holds, to an exposed flare, then climb the flare to a fixed anchor. 80'
FA Oct 25, 2006, Jeremy Haas, Robert Livingston, Joel Dashnaw

Lake George

#	Route	#	Route
15	Black Streak (5.10b)	22	Areticus Maximus (5.10a)
16	Tongue and Groove (5.10c)	23	Colossus of Tongue (5.10a)
17	Dark Venomous Dreams (5.8+)	24	Raindance Corner (5.7+)
18	Dark Venomous Reality (5.10b)	25	Bear Claw (5.11a)
19	Forked Tongue (5.7)	26	Foosa Territory (5.11a)
20	Snake Free (5.7+)	27	Kodiak (5.12b)
21	Gridlock (5.9+)	28	Teddy Ruxpin (5.9)

LAKEVIEW WALL

Lakeview Wall

This is the third and rightmost of the left-facing walls. To its left is a low tree-covered ledge and the start of **Snake Charmer**. Lakeview Wall has a high tier above a broad, sloping ledge. A 3rd-class chimney begins 100' right of the right edge of the wall and provides access to **Forked Tongue** and **Gridlock**.

15 Black Streak 5.10b TR 60' ★★
In the center of the Lakeview Wall is a black streak. Climb it to a fixed anchor.
FA (TR) 1992, Fred Abbuhl, Doug Douglas

16 Tongue and Groove 5.10c G 105' ★★★★
Start: At center of the Lakeview Wall, beneath a 5'-tall overhanging face with a horizontal crack above it.
P1 5.10c G: Up to the horizontal crack, then continue past shallow huecos to a left-rising crack. Follow the crack to a 6'-tall right-facing flare (3/8" cam crucial). Climb the flare, then up to a left-rising crack that leads toward **Black Streak**. Step right and reach over a bulge (crux), then move left and undercling a flake. Easy climbing up and right, past a ledge, gains a right-rising fingercrack. Follow the fingercrack to a fixed anchor. 105'
FA 1992, Fred Abbuhl, Doug Douglas

17 Dark Venomous Dreams 5.8+ PG 105' ★★★
Start: Near the right end of the Lakeview Wall, beneath a vertical crack that splits an overhang 10' up.
P1 5.8+ PG: Up the vertical crack and through the overhang. Move right, then up and left through chocolate-colored rock to a horizontal crack. Go right to a left-rising ledge with a tree and traverse it to the left. Move up and right to a vertical crack and climb it to an overlap. Undercling left (crux) and follow a vertical crack to a fixed anchor shared with **Tongue and Groove**. 105'
FA May, 2007, Tom Rosecrans, Robert Livingston

18 Dark Venomous Reality 5.10b G 100' ★★★
Climbs the right margin of the Lakeview Wall. Above the crux, don't pass up the gear opportunities if you want to keep the protection G.
Start: 15' right of **Dark Venomous Dreams** below a prominent roof 15' up.
P1 5.10b G: Up to the roof, then exit left to a crack. Climb the crack, then diagonal across a face and over an overlap (crux). Diagonal up and right, past discontinuous cracks to a stance below an overlap. Follow a bulging crack left of the overlap to a fixed anchor. 100'
Gear: To 1" with an emphasis on small cams and medium nuts.
FA Nov 9, 2009, Tom Rosecrans, Justin Barrett

19 Forked Tongue 5.7 G 50' ★★
Start: Above the Lakeview Wall is an upper tier that is approached via the 3rd-class chimney. Begin 20' uphill from and left of the exit from the chimney, where a dike shoots out of the ground toward the right.
P1 5.7 G: Climb the dike rock to a right-rising fingercrack, then follow the fingercrack to a ledge. Up a left-arching fingercrack to shallow vertical cracks. Climb the cracks (crux) through a steep wall, then step right to a fixed anchor. 50'
FA Oct 14, 2006, Jeremy Haas, Robert Livingston, Tom Rosecrans

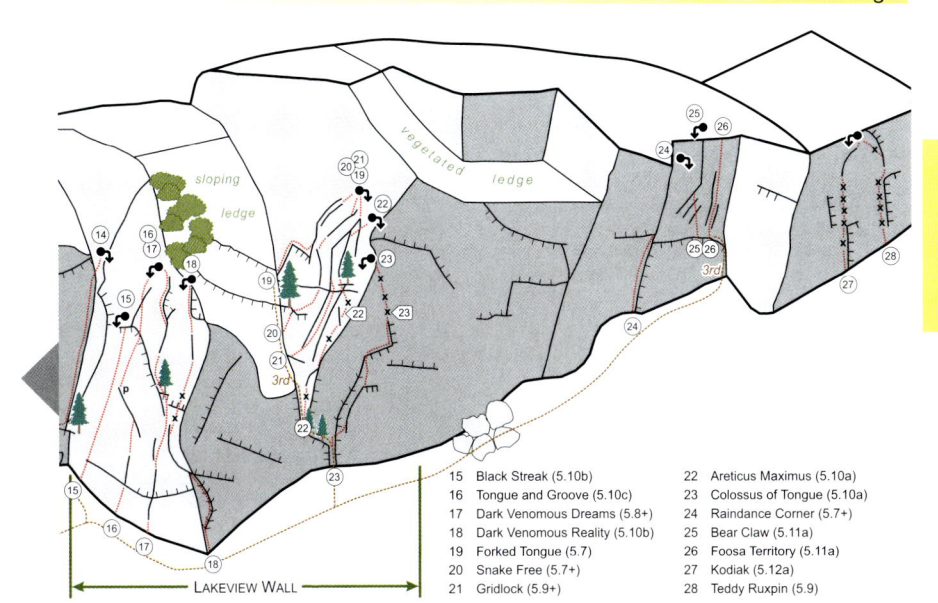

Lake George

20 Snake Free 5.7+ PG 60' ★★
This is the sister route to **Forked Tongue**, but a bit more feisty.
Start: Just left of the start of **Gridlock**, at a small tree above the access gully.
P1 5.7+ PG: Protect the bottom moves (crux) then move right along a ledge to a vertical crack. Follow the crack as it curves to the left, then work up and right across beautiful black rock to a short vertical crack in the headwall. Join **Gridlock**: scramble left up easy slabs to a fixed anchor shared with **Forked Tongue**. 60'
Gear: To 2".
FA Nov 9, 2009, Justin Barrett, Tom Rosecrans

21 Gridlock 5.9+ G 80' ★★★★
Start: Above the Lakeview Wall is an upper tier that is approached via the 3rd-class chimney. Start directly above the exit from the chimney, at a right-rising fingercrack that comes out of the ground.
P1 5.9+ G: Follow the fingercrack to a horizontal crack, then step left and climb a right-arching fingercrack (crux). (V1) Climb parallel right-rising cracks to the top, then step left to the fixed anchor of **Forked Tongue**. 80'
V1 5.9+ G: Make a long reach left to a jug, then climb a vertical crack to the top.
FA 1992, Fred Abbuhl, Doug Douglas

22 Areticus Maximus 5.10a G 90' ★★★
A low crux and a tricky topout. Dries quickly.
Start: At a ledge beneath the 3rd class chimney used to access the upper Lakeview Wall. The ledge begins 8' above the ground.
P1 5.10a G: Go up the chimney a few feet to a narrow ledge on the right. Start up a discontinuous crack that is left of a long arête. Make a crux move into the base of the crack where it is finger-sized. Go out right to the arête which can be climbed directly or on the steep face to the right. Make a long reach to the base of a right-facing flake that is on the left side of the arête. Climb the flake, then go back to the arête and climb it to a broken overhang. Traverse left and up to a ledge with a pine tree (the fixed anchor on the ledge is for **Colossus**). Work up and left to a crack that is left of a higher arête. Follow the crack past an awkward mantel to a fixed anchor at the top of the wall. 90'
Gear: To 1.5"
FA Jun, 2011, Tom Rosecrans, Robert Livingston, Jeremy Haas, Erika Schielke

23 Colossus of Tongue 5.10a G 80' ★★★
The opening dihedral is a prominent landmark. The alternate finish in the overhanging, left-facing ceiling is 5.10c.
Start: At the base of the approach to the 3rd class chimney used to access the upper Lakeview Wall.
P1 5.10a G: Scramble 8' onto a ledge at the base of a tall, deep, left-facing dihedral. Climb up a vertical fingercrack on the right wall of the dihedral to a sloping ledge. Step left into the dihedral and climb to a higher ledge, then traverse right to another left-facing corner. Start up the corner, and then exit out right onto a sheer face with a 3'-tall alcove beneath a ceiling. Pull over the ceiling on good holds, then run it out to a ledge beneath a wall with blocky rock. Move up and left to a horizontal dike. Follow the dike left (loose rock), reach up to a sloping ledge, and climb it to a fixed anchor on the right. 80'
History: The route was toproped and equipped by Justin Barrett.
FA Jun, 2011, Jeremy Haas, Erika Schielke, Tom Rosecrans, Robert Livingston

End of Lakeview Wall

24 Raindance Corner 5.7+ G 70' ★★★
Start: 250' right of the Lakeview Wall at a left-facing corner with orange rock on the left wall and a left-rising crack on the right wall.
P1 5.7+ G: Up the fingercrack in the corner to a ledge. Step right, then back left on flakes to reach the overhanging handcrack above the corner. The crack widens to 4" (crux) and ends at a fixed anchor. 70'
FA Sep 13, 2006, Jeremy Haas, Robert Livingston

25 Bear Claw 5.11a G 40' ★★★★
Start: 300' right of the Lakeview Wall is a low cliff beneath a ledge 30' up. Scramble around the right side of the low cliff. Begin beneath three right-rising parallel cracks.
P1 5.11a G: Climb the bulge (no protection) on the left to reach the right-rising cracks. Up the cracks to a jug, then reach left to the leftmost of the right-rising cracks. Follow the crack through a bulge (crux), then up the vertical fingercrack to a fixed anchor. 40'
FA May 7, 2007, Jeremy Haas, Joel Dashnaw
FFA May 9, 2007, Joel Dashnaw, Tom Rosecrans

26 Foosa Territory 5.11a TR 40' ★★
Start 10' right of **Bear Claw** and climb thin cracks to a horizontal crack below a thin face near the top.
FA (TR) May 2, 2007, Mike O'Herron

27 Kodiak 5.12a G 40' ★★★
Start: 75' right of **Bearclaw** and 110' left of the right end of the cliff, beneath an orange, left-facing corner.
● **P1 5.12a G:** Up the corner (harder for short climbers) to a rest on a sloping ledge. Above the ledge is a sheer, overhanging wall with several water-worn rails. The reach past the last rail to a horizontal crack is the crux (harder for tall climbers). Finish with a left-facing flake and a fixed anchor shared with **Teddy Ruxpin**. 40'
FA (TR) Aug, 2009, Jeremy Haas

28 Teddy Ruxpin 5.9 G 40' ★★★
Start: 100' left of the right end of the cliff, at a left-facing corner that starts 10' up.
● **P1 5.9 G:** Up easy rock to the corner, then up the corner to a ledge on the right. Go up a vertical crack, and step left to a fixed anchor shared with **Kodiak**. 40'
Gear: 1 ea 1"-2" cam.
FA Aug, 2009, Jeremy Haas, Rocco Mastrantoni

Lake George

BARTON HIGH CLIFF

Location	North of NY 8 accessed from Northway Exit 25 near Brant Lake
Aspect	Northwest
Height	280'
Quality	★★
Approach	1 hr 15 min, moderate
Summary	Predominantly multipitch, moderate routes on an expansive cliff in a wilderness setting.

1	3	3	3	3				13
-5.6	5.7	5.8	5.9	5.10	5.11	5.12	5.13+	total

The dark horse of Adirondack cliffs, Barton High Cliff is often mentioned, seldom seen, and more impressive than imagined. Invisible from roads or viewpoints, the cliff is guarded by an hour-long approach and a short climbing season. The off-trail hike, however, is quite pleasant—a beautiful brook draining from a large marsh teeming with wildlife. The cliff resides above a mountain pass and has an alpine aura, yet the elevation gain is modest. There is a lot of rock at Barton High Cliff, and plenty of promise for new routes, but the northern aspect ensures that the conditions will be cool and the lichen abundant. An open, sunny hillside sits opposite the cliff and affords great views of the routes. The left end has numerous low-angled dihedrals and buttresses. The landmark buttresses of **The Excellent Adventure** and **Final Frontier** are separated by a steep face with impressive roofs. The faces on the right end, including the Columbine Terrace Wall, are sheer with vertical cracks. **Final Frontier** and the left-end routes are cleaner than the rest.

HISTORY

Barton High Cliff is yet another discovery by Jim Vermeulen who visited the cliff and took a few photos, one of which inspired Tad Welch and friends to visit in 1989. With Chuck Yax, Welch climbed several of the less imposing lines near **Sunset Arête**. The central feature of the cliff—the buttress of **The Excellent Adventure**—was the obvious next target, climbed with Bill Widrig later that summer. The group continued exploring for a couple years until the work required to unearth the lines took its toll. Don Mellor made a brief visit here in 1994 climbing **Spit and Drivel**, but since then, no new routes have been reported.

DIRECTIONS (MAP PAGE 117)

From Northway (I-87) Exit 25 (0.0 mile), follow NY 8 east (past Palisade Road at 7.5 miles) to Spuytenduivel Brook at 9.8 miles. Park 200 yards past the brook by a wire guardrail on the north side of the road 610141,4844384.

Take the old jeep road that leaves the north side of NY 8 and follows the south side of Spuytenduivel Brook. After a few minutes, the trail crosses to the north bank. Follow it to a marsh. Cross back to the south bank and skirt the marsh and thickets by traversing on high ground to the north end, where a stream enters on the right (east) (50 min). Follow the north bank (left side) of the tributary as it climbs steadily. At 1 hr, the terrain levels. Locate a cairn that is 5' from the stream's north bank (left side). Head northeast (left) from the stream and hike up a small valley, staying on the open slopes on its left side (north). The first viewpoint (of the Columbine Terrace Wall) is from a moss-covered slab reached at 1 hr 10 min. The best view of the cliff is from a slab that is higher up on the hill, which you can reach by hiking up and left for a few minutes 612794,4845770. Approaches to climbs begin in the small valley beneath the talus field that stretches the length of the cliff.

Alternate Approach: A slightly faster approach, but with more complicated navigation. From Exit 25, follow NY 8 east for 11.3 miles to a large, paved parking area on the right. Walk to the east end of the parking area, then bushwhack north over chaotic terrain to reach a brook at 40 min. Continue north (downstream) to a minor brook, marked with a cairn on the right (east) bank,

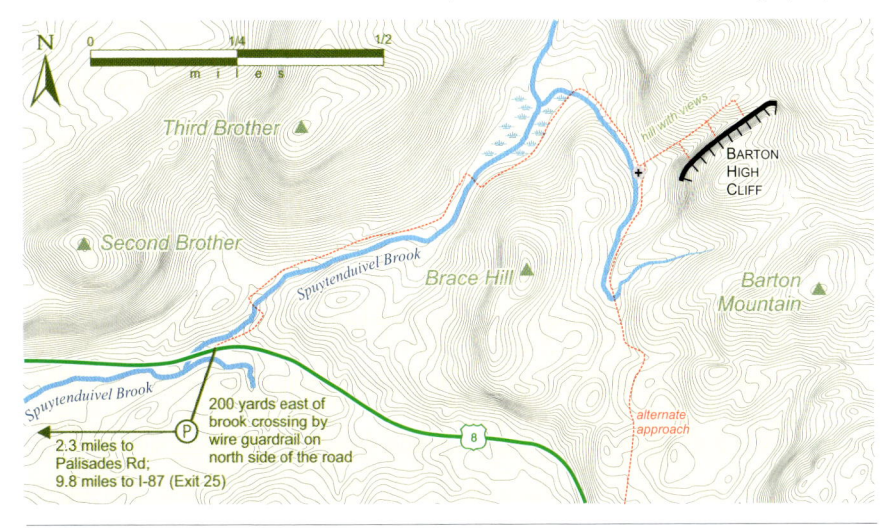

Lake George

BARTON HIGH CLIFF
3 Sunset Arête (5.7)
6 Reckless Endangerment (5.7)
7 The Excellent Adventure (5.9-)
9 Final Frontier (5.8+)

reached at 50 min. Go right (east) and follow a minor drainage area uphill to the cliff. Orange tape may be encountered along the brook.

DESCENT OPTIONS
Rappel with 2 ropes, as walking off isn't a good option. Although tree-covered ledges are abundant, don't expect to find established rappel anchors.

Sunset Arête Area

Sunset Arête, located at the far left end of the cliff, is an 80'-tall buttress that is low-angle on its left side and overhanging on the right. To approach, stay below the talus at the left end of the cliff, then hike up open talus.

1 Isosceles 5.8 G 50'
Start: 40' left of Sunset Arête at an 8'-tall left-facing corner with a white horn on top, above which is a smooth face with a long overhang at its top.
P1 5.8 G: Up the corner to the white horn. Above the horn, climb a vertical crack to the upper of two right-rising seams. Follow the seam up and right to its end at a tree belay on a ledge beneath an overhang. 50'
FA Sep, 1992, Tad Welch, Bill Widrig

2 Pythagoras 5.9- G 50'
Start: Same as **Isosceles**.
P1 5.9- G: Up the corner to the white horn. Above the horn, climb a vertical crack to the lower of two right-rising seams. Follow the seam up and right to its end at a tree belay on a ledge beneath an overhang. 50'
FA May, 1993, Tad Welch, Bill Widrig

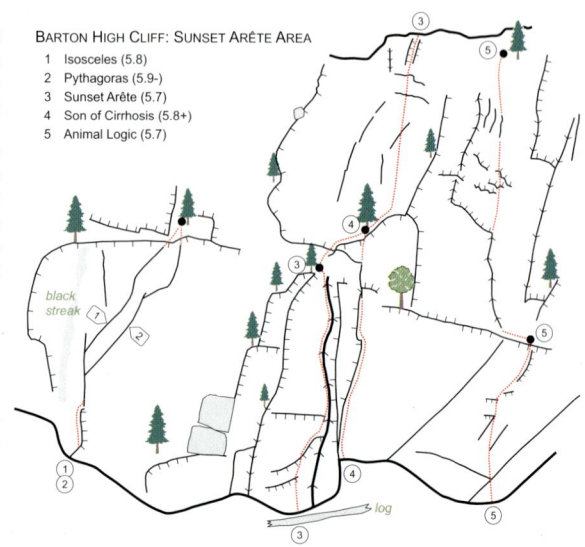

3 Sunset Arête 5.7 PG 150' ★
Start: On a dead tree left of the arête.
P1 5.7 PG: Climb the left side of the arête past a ledge, then up the arête. Belay on top of the buttress. 70'
P2 5.7 PG: Step right and climb the face between the large pine tree and the shrub-filled left-facing corner. Exit through the ceiling above, or left (easier). 80'
FA Apr 19, 1989, Tad Welch, Chuck Yax

4 Son of Cirrhosis 5.8+ G 60' ★
Start: Just right of **Sunset Arête** at a shallow right-facing corner that is immediately right of a large right-facing corner.
P1 5.8+ G: Up the clean, shallow corner, which widens beneath a ceiling 40' up. Pass the ceiling on the left and climb easily to a tree with a fixed anchor. 60'
FA Apr 19, 1989, Tad Welch, Chuck Yax

BARTON HIGH CLIFF: SUNSET ARÊTE AREA
1 Isosceles (5.8)
2 Pythagoras (5.9-)
3 Sunset Arête (5.7)
4 Son of Cirrhosis (5.8+)
5 Animal Logic (5.7)

Opposite: Bill Sacks on P2 of **Final Frontier** *(5.8+).*
photo Bill Sacks Collection.

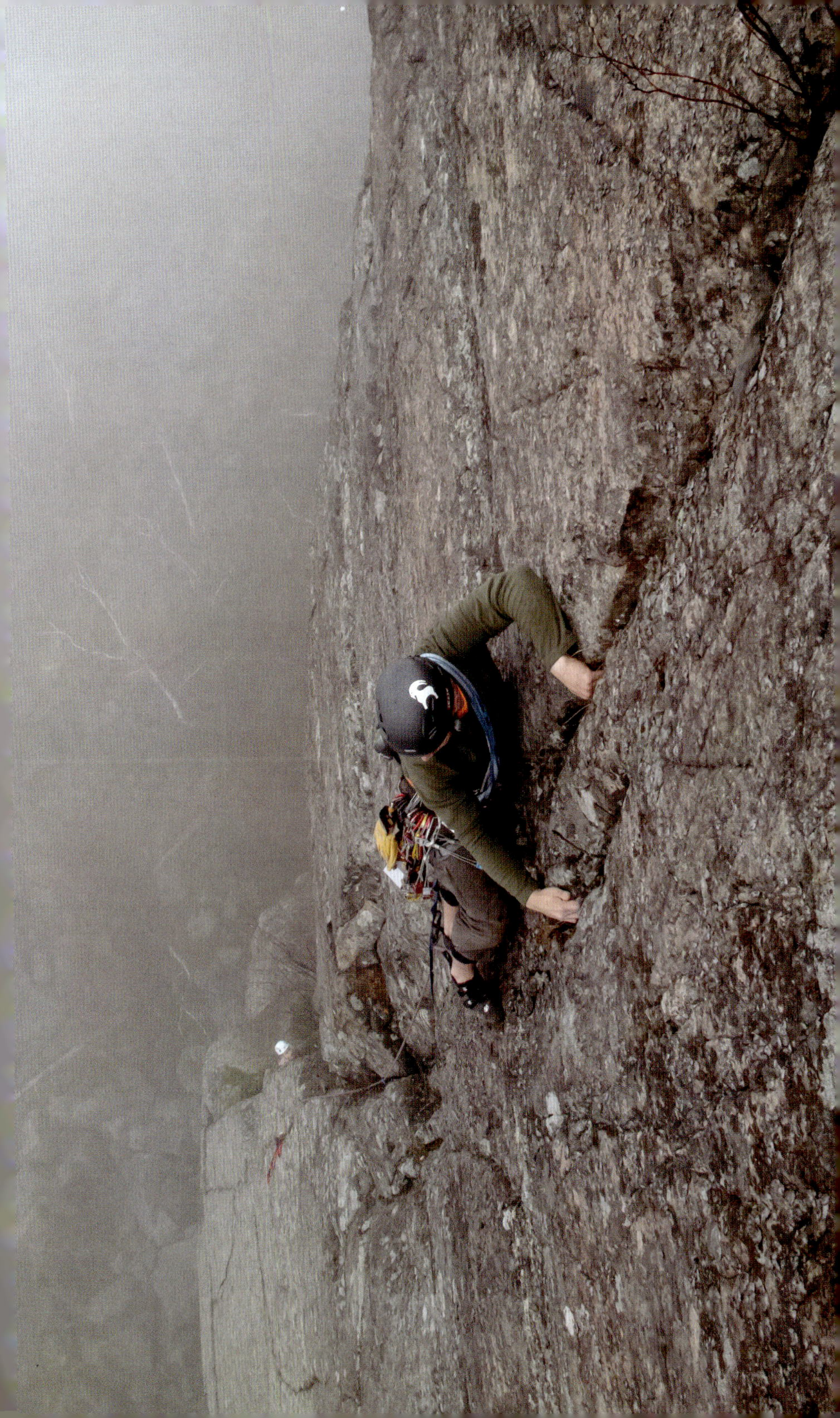

Lake George

The Nature of It

The moves off the ground were holdless, but a loop of cord dangled within reach. I pulled up on it. Then I fell, cratering into my parents' lawn—but not before the clothesline hanging from the birch tree hooked my lone front tooth and pulled it at a right angle to my jaw. It was a bloody introduction to climbing for a seven-year-old.

For me and a close group of friends, cliffs eventually replaced trees as objects of ascent, or nearly so—for there was never a lack of spruce or cedar sprouting from southern Adirondack jamcracks. As our interest in climbing on unknown crags increased, so did the amount of flora that we encountered. Manteling onto cushions of rock fern while black flies swam in our tear ducts became a part of new routing. We couldn't get enough of it. On most days, we returned to our packs at twilight, looking more like field hands than rock climbers. There were no bloody teeth to show for our efforts. Raw knuckles clotted brown with lichen were the tangible reminder of the day's work—that and our chalk bags of powdered twigs and fir needles.

Stillness blanketed the cliffs we explored: Echo, Good Luck, and others. Journal notes from a day at Barton mention hearing only the occasional raven and a pileated woodpecker from high on Final Frontier. At sundown, coyotes howled.

We were at our best in the all-encompassing wildness, and anything seemed possible. Sometimes the notion carried us to distant climbs on other continents. Yet even in those unlikely places, there were moments that evoked the crags we loved. Rope soloing (always a bad idea) a fissure at 18,000' near Mt Everest (an even worse idea) held memories of doing the same at Huckleberry Mountain. More often it was a piece of the foreign environment that spoke of the cliffs we knew best: a familiar wildflower beside the Strait of Magellan, the fragrance of balsam in a Himalayan gorge. These fragments of the Adirondacks made us treasure the fact that they exist in near-perfect entirety in one special place. We were always grateful to return home.

I am still a kid shinnying up a birch tree when I go climbing in the North Country. The impulse comes from a deeply rooted need to explore and embrace the natural world. And now I know never to let go.

- Tad Welch

5 Animal Logic 5.7 PG 160'
Start: 30' right of **Sunset Arête** at the left side of a low-angle wall that has diverging left- and right-rising cracks beneath rust-colored rock.
P1 5.7 PG: Up the low-angle face past small ledges to a right-rising seam that leads to a belay on a ledge beneath an overhang. 50'
P2 5.7 PG: Step left, then up a 30'-tall blocky arête to a face with several small overhangs. Climb the bulging wall above directly and finish more easily to the top of the cliff. 110'
FA Jun, 1989, Tad Welch, Chuck Yax

End of Sunset Arête Area

6 Reckless Endangerment 5.7 PG 80'
Start: Stay below the talus past **The Excellent Adventure** buttress and hike up moss-covered boulders to the base of the cliff. Locate an open book with a steep left wall containing right-leaning cracks. This wall is 40' left of a right-facing corner with a ceiling 15' up. Start beneath the leftmost of two cracks.
P1 5.7 PG: Climb a handcrack past a horizontal crack 15' up to an alcove where several cracks diverge. Climb the leftmost crack past a flared corner to its end at a grassy ledge halfway up the cliff. 80'
FA Apr 20, 1989, Tad Welch, Chuck Yax

7 The Excellent Adventure 5.9- G 200' ★★
This face offers a lot of climbing possibilities, with options of linking sections of different routes. Don't let the ugly complexion of P2 dissuade you; both the climbing and the position are first-rate. Shortened from **Bill and Tad's Excellent Adventure**, it is named after the 1989 popular comedic film *Bill and Ted's Excellent Adventure*.

Start: Across from the viewpoint slab is the razor-edged buttress of **The Excellent Adventure**. Walk down into the valley and up the steepest and tallest section of the talus field toward the right side of the buttress. Begin near the low end of the buttress at a right-leaning crack.
P1 5.9- G: Follow the right-leaning crack (steep and sustained) past a discontinuous section above the crux to a fixed belay at the right end of a long horizontal crack. 80'
P2 5.7 PG: Traverse left across the exposed face (very dirty) on a horizontal crack that extends to the prow of the buttress. Climb the edge of the prow (or easier farther left) to a belay beneath a corner on the prow. 80'
P3 5.7 PG: (V1) Step left and climb a shallow right-facing corner to the top. 40'
V1 5.7 PG: Climb right and up into a broken crack that exits the right side of the buttress.
FA Jun, 1989, Tad Welch, Bill Widrig, Chuck Yax
FA (V1) Aug 12, 1994, Don Mellor, Dave Furman

8 Spit and Drivel 5.10c PG 150' ★
Somewhat dirty and improbable looking.
Start: Same as **The Excellent Adventure**.
P1 5.10c PG: Follow the right-slanting crack for 30' to a clean, light-colored section of rock. Up the disappearing vertical crack, which is left of the leaning crack, then face-climb (crux) into another vertical crack and follow it to a belay at the traverse crack of **The Excellent Adventure**. 80'
P2 5.8 PG: Climb left along the traverse crack, then up a thin vertical crack that disappears before reaching the next horizontal break with a prominent vertical crack. Climb the crack and finish in a broken corner, right of the prow of the buttress. 70'
FA Aug 12, 1994, Don Mellor, Dave Furman

9 Final Frontier 5.8+ G 280' ★★★

Despite lackluster first and last pitches, the plumb-line fingercrack of P2 is outstanding.

Start: From the first moss-covered slabs that are encountered on the approach, the **Final Frontier** buttress comes into view. Walk up the talus to the cliff, aiming for the orange overhanging wall with right-slanting cracks. Begin in talus 100' up from and left of the base of the orange wall at a handcrack in a right-facing corner that is above a 4'-tall pedestal.

P1 5.6 PG: Up the right-facing corner to a 4th-class ramp, then follow it rightward to a belay ledge on the left side of the arête. 80'

P2 5.8+ G: Climb the arête (5.8), past a piton 20' up, to an overhang. Step right around the overhang, through a loose section, and up a vertical fingercrack. Sustained and exposed climbing with positive face holds leads to easier terrain. Head up and right to a belay ledge with an enormous tree stump. 120'

P3 5.5 PG: Step right and climb a short, steep face. Work up and left underneath ceilings to a stance on an arête, then up a loose tower of rock that is left of the arête to vegetation and a tree with a fixed anchor. 80'
FA Apr 24, 1990, Tad Welch, Bill Widrig

10 Ali-Kat 5.10b PG 130'

Presently very dirty.

Start: Directly across from the first moss-covered slabs you encounter on the approach is a steep wall. Locate a broken right-facing corner beneath a pine tree 40' above the ground. Begin left of the corner on a clean, knobby face.

P1 5.10b PG: Face climbing leads to an overgrown vertical crack. Follow the crack 10' left of the pine tree. The crux is level with the tree. 130'
FA May, 1993, Tad Welch, Bill Widrig

Columbine Terrace Wall

The first wall you see on the approach is a sheer, badge-shaped shield of rock broken by cracks. The wall is very distinctive, but the terrain at its base is nondescript. The climbs are accessed by a right-rising slope below the wall.

BARTON HIGH CLIFF: COLUMBINE TERRACE WALL
11 Columbine Crack (5.6)
12 Twinflower Traverse (5.9)
13 Bloodroot (5.10b)

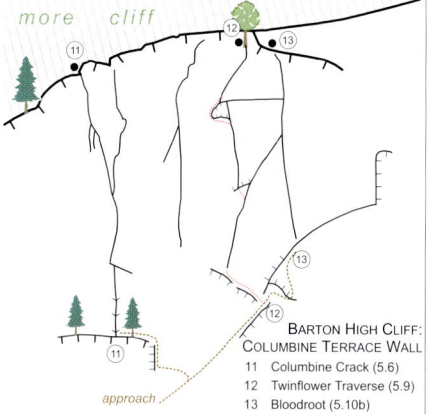

11 Columbine Crack 5.6 G 100'

Presently very dirty.

Start: Scramble up a right-rising slope, then step left to a right-facing corner (3rd-class) that accesses a hemlock-covered ledge 30' up. Begin beneath a V-slot.

P1 5.6 G: Up the V-slot, which becomes a vertical crack, past small birch trees, then head up and left to a clean handcrack. Follow the handcrack to the left end of a traverse ledge. 100'
FA May 19, 1991, Bill Widrig, Jamie Savage

12 Twinflower Traverse 5.9 G 120'

Presently very dirty.

Start: Scramble up a right-rising slope to its top at a broken left-facing wall. Belay next to ledges that head left across the face toward a vertical crack.

P1 5.9 G: Foot-traverse left to gain a vertical crack, then climb it to a horizontal break. Step left and climb another vertical crack to a left-facing flake. Undercling to the left and follow a right-slanting crack to the right end of the traverse ledge. 120'
FA Oct 1, 1991, Bill Widrig, Tad Welch

13 Bloodroot 5.10b TR 50'

Presently very dirty. Scramble up a right-rising slope to its top at a broken left-facing wall. Traverse right across the wall (3rd-class) to a forested slope beneath the upper right side of the cliff. Locate the vertical crack that is 30' left of a left-facing corner; climb this widening crack to the right end of the traverse ledge.
FA (TR) May 19, 1991, Bill Widrig, Jamie Savage

SPECTACLE PONDS CLIFF

Location	South of NY 8 accessed from Northway Exit 25 near Brant Lake
Aspect	West
Height	80' - 250'
Quality	
Approach	33 min, moderate
Summary	Broken, complex cliff with potential for adventure-style routes.

1		1					2
-5.6	5.7	5.8	5.9	5.10	5.11	5.12	5.13+	total

There is a large and complex array of rock on the hillside overlooking Spectacle Ponds, about 1000' wide. The general quality of the rock is good, with some unusual geology, but is broken up with no large continuous features. There is potential for more adventure-style routes.

HISTORY

The cliff was located by Tom DuBois in April, 2012 by studying satellite photos of the area. This cliff has some ice climbing—the central waterfall was climbed in winter 2012–13.

DIRECTIONS

From Northway (I-87) Exit 25, follow NY 8 east for 11.3 miles to a large, paved parking area on the right, the alternate approach to Barton High Cliff. At 11.6 miles, park on the left at a forest road; be careful not to block

Lake George

the forest road. Just past the road on the left is a hidden sign for Joseph Dixon Forest.

Walk back west about 150' along the south side of NY 8, and locate a blazed property line that runs south, perpendicular to the road, which serves as a guide for part of the approach 612691,4843214. Look over the embankment for rocks with yellow paint.

Walk down the steep bank to Swede Pond Brook (there are some nice dipping spots here, and further downstream). Cross the brook and follow the property boundary over the side of a small hill. At 10 min, reach a small brook (on the other side of the stream is the corner post for the property 612738,4842716). Stay left of the stream, go around the left side of a boggy meadow and pick up the stream on the other side. Follow the stream an additional 200' and locate several cairns. Follow a good cairn path on a bearing of 110° to the cliff.

The cliff is very broken up and obscured by foliage. The most obvious easy-to-find feature is a 25'-tall black wall with a seasonal waterfall (the winter route **Blue Spectacle**) and slide debris below, the bomb zone for falling ice and rock 613305,4842366. The routes are described relative to this waterfall.

DESCENT OPTIONS

It's a fairly long hike down from much of the cliff; rappel is the best option which, in some cases, requires two ropes.

1 Söt Torn 5.6 G 75'

Start: 75' left of the waterfall, on the right side of a 15'-wide buttress bordered on the left by a sharp-edged left-facing corner 12' up, and on the right by a right-facing corner 613315,4842398.

P1 5.6 G: Climb up and left a few steps, then go up the right side of the buttress past several small overhangs to the top of the buttress. There is a fixed anchor on a birch tree a few yards uphill. 75'
FA Oct 27, 2012, Tom DuBois, Ellen DuBois

2 Lakeview Arête 5.8- G 250' ★

Start: Walk right and uphill from the waterfall for 120' to a large right-facing corner with a square block at its base. Continue along the base of the cliff for 120' to a level section of terrain, and locate a blunt arête with several horizontals and wart-like knobs, and a 6'-wide ceiling on the left side 20' up 613326,4842295.

P1 5.8- G: Climb the arête past the right side of the roof (balancy crux), then up ledges to a wide open book corner left of large roofs. Up the open book to a spruce tree. 100'

P2 4th class: Step right from the tree and scramble up the blunt, loose arête to a small oak. 50'

P3 5.4 G: Step right from the oak and climb the corner and complex arête to the top. High on this pitch are good views of Lake George to climber's right. 100'

Descent: Walk 50' left to a fixed anchor on a large tree branch. 120' rappel over wooded ledges to a fine, flat mossy ledge. A fixed anchor on a tree at climber's right of this ledge provides a second 120' rappel down a brushy gully to the ground.
FA Aug 19, 2012, Tom DuBois, Ellen DuBois

PHARAOH MOUNTAIN

Location	North of NY 8 accessed from Northway Exit 25 near Brant Lake
Summary	Several small summit crags and a large, remote adventure cliff on Pharaoh Mountain.

1		3	2	8	8	1		24
-5.6	5.7	5.8	5.9	5.10	5.11	5.12	5.13+	total

The Pharaoh Lake Wilderness Area is a tract of land on the east side of the Northway (I-87), just east of Schroon Lake (Northway Exit 28) and north of Brant Lake. The area is littered with lakes (some having islands), ponds, hills, a mountain, and, of course, cliffs. Despite its accessible location and proximity to towns, Pharaoh remains one of the more remote and challenging climbing locales in the park. The approach is long (involving 4WD, hiking, and bushwhacking), the climbs are long, and the standards are difficult—mostly 5.10 and up.

The climbing at Pharaoh is either on the Summit Cliffs, two short single-pitch crags accessed from the west at the Crane Pond Trailhead, or on the Main

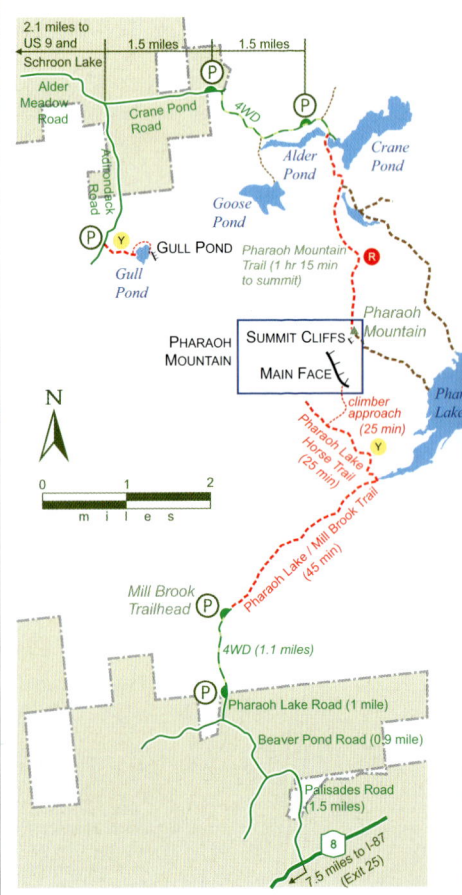

122

Lake George

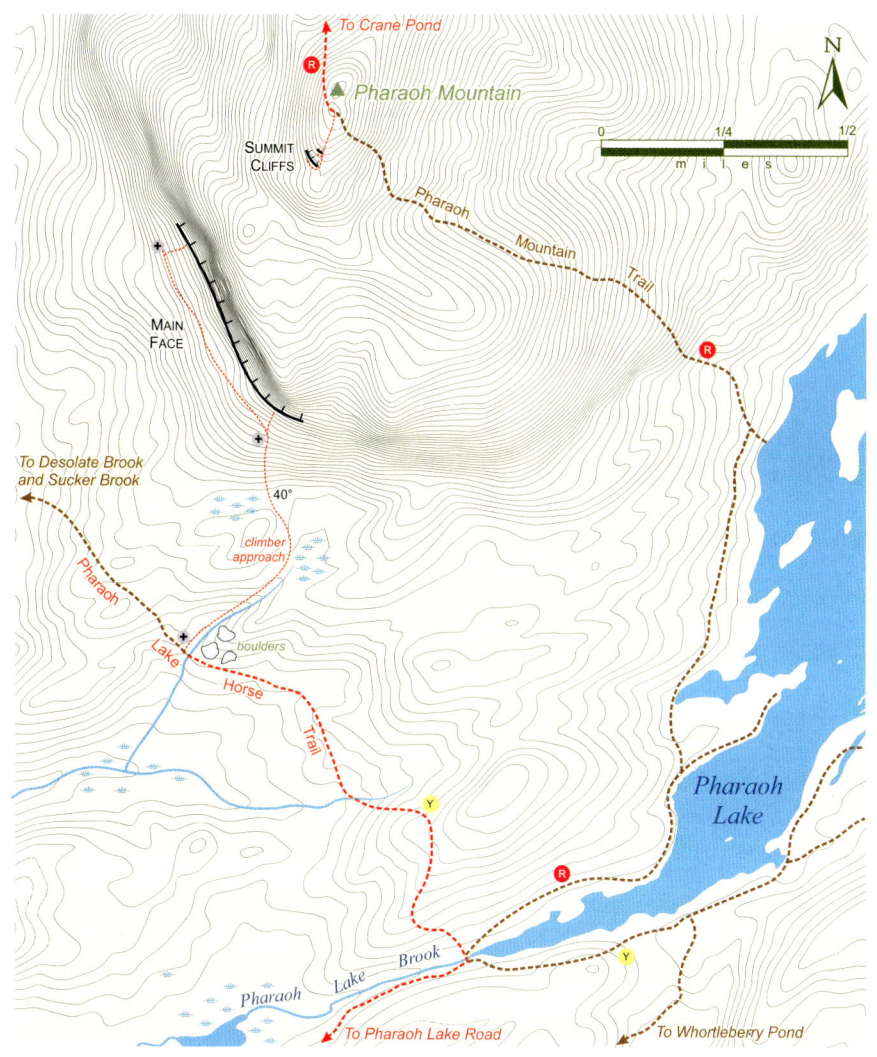

Face, a high, multipitch cliff accessed from the south off Pharaoh Lake Road. For a single day of climbing, it isn't advisable to attempt climbing at both cliffs, as navigation between the two cliffs is arduous. For multiday climbing, both cliffs can be accessed from the scenic Pharaoh Lake with excellent four-star camping and many lean-tos.

HISTORY

Pharaoh has seen development by three different groups of climbers. Patrick Purcell was the first to explore the cliffs here during his stint as a fire-tower ranger on the summit in 1983 (the fire tower was removed in the early 1990s). His climbs were mainly solo and restricted to the Summit Cliffs. He later returned in the 90s to add some routes on the Main Face, including the first routes at the South End of the cliff. The second group came to Pharaoh around 1987 from New Paltz, the main motivator being Felix Modugno, but also including Jim Damon, Bill Lutkus, Rich Romano, and Rich Gottlieb. Climbing at a high standard, they uncovered some severe lines, including the awesome **Stones of Shame**, which remains the longest and most difficult free climb in the southern Adirondacks. They eventually grew tired of the approach, thinking that they could climb at New River Gorge in the same amount of time it took to get to the base of Pharaoh. The third group arrived on the scene in 2000 and included Tom Yandon, Dennis Luther, and Tim Beaman. Camping for a week at a time, this group cleaned and explored many sections of the cliff. One of their most impressive achievements is undoubtedly **Flapjack**, a system of tiered roofs resembling a vertical stack of pancakes.

Lake George

BREAD LOAF AREA

STONES OF SHAME AMPHITHEATER

PHARAOH MOUNTAIN: MAIN FACE
3 Walk Like an Egyptian (5.10b)
5 Sphinx in the Face (5.12a)
6 Stones of Shame (5.11a)
9 Here Come the Pigs (5.11a)
10 Updraft (5.10a)
13 Trick or Treat (5.10)
15 Keep the Faith (5.10c)
16 Sands of Time (5.11d)

Pharaoh Mountain
MAIN FACE

Location	North of NY 8 accessed from Northway Exit 25 near Brant Lake
Aspect	Southwest
Height	400'
Quality	★★
Approach	1 hr 35 min, difficult
Summary	A large, remote cliff with many multipitch adventurous routes. Climbs have seen only a few ascents and can be dirty.

		2	7	6	1	16
-5.6	5.7	5.8	5.9	5.10	5.11	5.12	5.13+	total

The Main Face of Pharaoh is one of the largest cliffs in the southern Adirondacks. Located on the lower flanks of Pharaoh Mountain deep in the Pharaoh Lake Wilderness Area, this cliff typifies the Adirondack climbing experience: it is complex, somewhat dirty, very buggy (during bug season), difficult to reach, and has no easy routes.

The long routes here are major undertakings for a day trip, as you have to locate the cliff, locate the route, climb the route, descend the route, then reverse your way back out. The approach is especially involved, requiring a 4WD vehicle (to shave off a mile), a seldom-used horse trail, and blind bushwhacking. Many parties have opted to camp at Pharaoh Lake or bivy closer to the cliff where several good sites below the talus can be found with a fairly reliable water source.

The established routes follow the obvious lines, and there are wide expanses of unexplored rock between the routes (thus the potential for more routes). At the left end of the cliff is the Bread Loaf, a clean shield of rock shaped like a loaf of bread where the routes **Cleopatra**, **The Ten Plagues**, and **Walk Like an Egyptian** are located. Just right of this is the Sphinx Flake, a huge house-sized flake jutting into the skyline, below which are **The Mummy** and the awesome arête of **Sphinx in the Face**. Moving right, the next feature is an amphitheater with the square buttress of **Stones of Shame** that shares a start with the obvious inverted pancakes of **Flapjack**. Moving farther right, one encounters the next cluster of routes at the South End, including **Here Come the Pigs**, **Updraft**, and **Pharaoh's Phallus**. Right of this is a wet depression with a waterfall (of sorts) and the popular ice climb **Isis**. Walking right from here, you'll find a final cluster of shorter routes with, among others, **Halloween Cracks** and **Keep the Faith**; given some extra time, you can use these routes to round out the day before hiking out.

The cliff has no distinct top; rather, the cliff fades into steep, brushy terrain. Most routes end at fixed anchors or brushy ledges with trees from which you can rappel with double ropes. There is no toproping here.

Lake George

A final note about peregrine falcons, which are known to nest at the cliff: the state currently does not monitor the nesting sites here, so you're on your own regarding the birds. If you encounter peregrines (and they'll let you know by dive-bombing and screeching), then move to a different section of the cliff.

DIRECTIONS   (MAPS PAGES 122 AND 123)
There are several approaches for Pharaoh; the approach described here is not the shortest but is perhaps the easiest to follow.

The parking for Pharaoh is at the end of Pharaoh Lake Road. From the Northway (I-87) at Exit 25, drive east on NY 8, 7.5 miles to Palisades Road at the north end of Brant Lake. Turn left on Palisades Road and drive around the end of Brant Lake 1.5 miles to Beaver Pond Road. Turn right on Beaver Pond Road and drive 0.9 mile. Look for an unmarked dirt road on the right—Pharaoh Lake Road. Turn right onto Pharaoh Lake Road and drive 1 mile to a parking area 605518,4846053. Park here or, with a high-clearance 4WD vehicle, continue another very rugged 1.1 miles to the final parking area at the end of the road. (This last section is in wilderness land and may be closed by the DEC in the future.)

From the parking area, follow the Pharaoh Lake–Mill Creek Trail for 45 min to the bridge crossing the outlet of Pharaoh Lake. Immediately after the bridge, leave the hiking trail (which turns right) by continuing straight on the Pharaoh Lake Horse Trail (also known as the Sucker Brook–Desolation Brook Trail; the intersection isn't marked). Follow the horse trail for 30 min to a stream crossing with some very large boulders on the right 607472,4850885; several smaller streams are crossed, but this is the first stream that is substantial and has huge boulders on the right just beforehand. Cross the stream and turn right (cairn here), following the stream uphill for 10 min to a marsh. Staying left of the marsh, hike uphill on a bearing of 40°, past another marsh on the right, for 15 min to a cairn at the edge of the talus beneath the South End 607720,4851608.

From the cairn, the South End is a short bushwhack through the talus. If you aren't climbing at the South End, it's best to stay below the talus until you can see your route, then head up to the cliff. It takes about 15 min to hike to the Bread Loaf, on the far end of the cliff 607364,4852169.

Bread Loaf Area

The left end of the cliff is known as the Bread Loaf, since its upper wall is sheer and shaped as such.

1 Cleopatra 5.10b PG 150' ★★

Start: On a tree-covered ledge 100' up and 200' left of a gully at the left end of the talus field, beneath a bombay chimney on the right side of a perched flake.
P1 5.9 G: Up the chimney to a belay on the top of the flake (or skip this pitch by climbing its left side). 50'
P2 5.10b PG: Climb twin right-rising cracks until the right-hand crack jogs right into a right-facing corner.

125

Lake George

Face-climb up and left, over a bulge, to a thin crack. Climb the crack to broken rock and belay at the left end of the large ledge that splits the upper face. 100'
FA 1988, Felix Modugno, Rich Gottlieb

2 The Ten Plagues 5.11d PG 150' ★★★
You should have no trouble avoiding the 10 calamities on this good route (well, aside from the fourth one—getting attacked by flies).
Start: On a tree-covered ledge that is 100' above the cliff base and 100' left of a gully that is at the left end of the talus field. Start at an open book with a 10'-tall orange pillar to the right.
P1 5.11d PG: Climb a thin seam in the open book that arches to the right (crux). Belay at a small stance. 50'
P2 5.10a PG: Climb the right of two arching cracks that follow a right-facing overlap. Step left of the overlap to a shallow right-facing corner that is climbed past shrubs to a belay on the large ledge that splits the upper face. 100'
FA 1988, Felix Modugno, Rich Gottlieb

3 Walk Like an Egyptian 5.10b G 310' ★★
Start: On top of a small rock buttress at a left-leaning handcrack in an otherwise blank wall that is 20' left of a prominent right-facing corner and 100' left of **Sphinx in the Face**. The base of the route is best reached from the talus field on the right.
P1 5.10b G: Climb the handcrack to a chimney-sized V-slot capped by a square ceiling. Work up and left across a slab to belay at the base of a right-rising blocky overlap. 80'
P2 5.5 G: Angle up and right following the right-rising blocky overlap to its end, then up and left to a tree-covered ledge at the base of a sheer wall (the Bread Loaf). 80'
P3 4th class: Move the belay to the left end of the ledge below a chimney-pod in a right-facing corner. 30'
P4 5.10a G: Climb the chimney-pod to the ceiling at its top. Break through the ceiling via a crack, then follow the crack as it diagonals right across the face, past a vertical crack to a second vertical crack, which is followed to the top. 120'
FA Aug, 1987, Jeff Edwards, Patrick Purcell

4 The Mummy 5.11a G 210' ★★★
An excellent fingercrack. The first pitch has the only bolt ever placed by Modugno.
Start: Just right of the Bread Loaf is an enormous flake on the skyline—the Sphinx Flake—a house-sized wedge of rock that juts into the sky when seen from below. Below the flake is an arête that forms a large chimney on the right. Begin below the arête.
P1 5.9 PG: Climb the low-angle slab past a bolt and up to a ledge where the arête becomes steeper. 80'
P2 5.11a G: Climb down and left to a left-rising ramp, then up left to the base of a shallow right-facing corner. Climb up the corner, jog right around the overlap, and continue up the corner to reach a fingercrack that breaks the face on the right. Follow the fingercrack up to a belay on a sloping ledge. 80'
P3 5.7 G: Climb a left-rising ramp to a right-facing corner. Up the corner to a belay at a tree. 50'
FA 1987, Felix Modugno, Jim Damon

5 Sphinx in the Face 5.12a G 190' ★★★
This route climbs an amazing feature—a sharp arête that makes its way up to the Sphinx Flake.
Start: Same as **The Mummy**.
P1 5.9 PG: Same as **The Mummy**: Climb the low-angle slab past a bolt and up to a ledge where the arête becomes steeper. 80'
● **P2 5.12a G:** Continue straight up the arête following bolts to a final thin crack that leads to the top of the arête. Belay on a sloping ledge. 60'
P3 5.7 G: Same as **The Mummy**: Up a left-rising ramp to a right-facing corner. Up the corner to a tree. 50'
FA (V1) 1990, Jim Damon, Felix Modugno

*Jeremy Haas on P4 (5.10b) of **Stones of Shame** (5.11a).
Photo by Nick Wakeman.*

Stones of Shame Amphitheater

6 **Stones of Shame** 5.11a G 455' ★★★★

Stones of Shame and the Direct (described below) are the longest, hardest, most committing free routes in the southern Adirondacks. **Stones of Shame** has varied climbing on a steep wall with exposed positions in the tallest section of the Main Face. No fixed protection. The route is named for the boulders that blocked the Crane Mountain Road, put there by the state when designating the Pharaoh Lake Wilderness Area. In protest, locals moved the stones to the yard of a state official and posted a sign reading "Stones of Shame."

Start: Begin at the base of vegetated slabs, just left of a huge detached spire (the size of several tractor trailers).

P1 5.0 PG: Climb broken, vegetated slabs to a belay below a large open-book corner with white rock. 75'

P2 5.10c G: Climb the open-book corner, exiting up and left to a birch tree on a left-facing ramp. Sustained. 100'

P3 5.6 PG: Downclimb the left-facing ramp to a wide ledge. Move left 10' on the ledge and climb a left-rising, right-facing corner to a small ledge at its top. 60'

P4 5.10b G: Climb up and right into the large left-facing corner. Up the corner with small protection to the "guillotine" flake, underclinged left to a stance in the upper left-facing corner. A wild traverse to the right leads around the arête and onto the exposed face to a hanging belay at a thin crack in the middle of the face. 70'

P5 5.11a PG: Climb the steep, thin vertical crack for 10', then a desperate reach right gains another thin vertical crack. Up this crack (crux) to an overlap near the top of the arête, then swing right around the arête onto a right-rising zigzag crack. Up the zigzag crack via a series of mantel moves on sloped ledges. Make a long reach up and left to a horizontal crack on the headwall, then up a shallow open book to the tree-covered ledge at the top. 150'

Descent: Two 60-m ropes are required to rappel. The first rappel leads to a tree on the wide ledge of P3.

History: P2 and the upper buttress were originally climbed by the **Stones of Shame Direct** variation in 1988. It was thoroughly cleaned over a long weekend, excavated with garden tools. The route was then "rediscovered" by Tom Yandon and Bill Coryer in 1992 and thoroughly cleaned via a different line (i.e., the left-facing corner on the left side of the buttress), then climbed by Purcell and Mellor in 1994. The route described here (as **Stones of Shame**) is the Yandon-Coryer variation.
FA (P1, P2) 1988, Felix Modugno, Bill Lutkus, Paul Boissonneault
FA (P3, P4, P5) Aug 3, 1994, Patrick Purcell, Don Mellor

7 **Stones of Shame Direct**
5.11c PG 450' ★★★★

The original line on the buttress—direct and sustained, and although it probably hasn't seen a second ascent, the first ascentionist reported excellent climbing. The first ascent required two days of cleaning.

Start: Same as **Stones of Shame**.

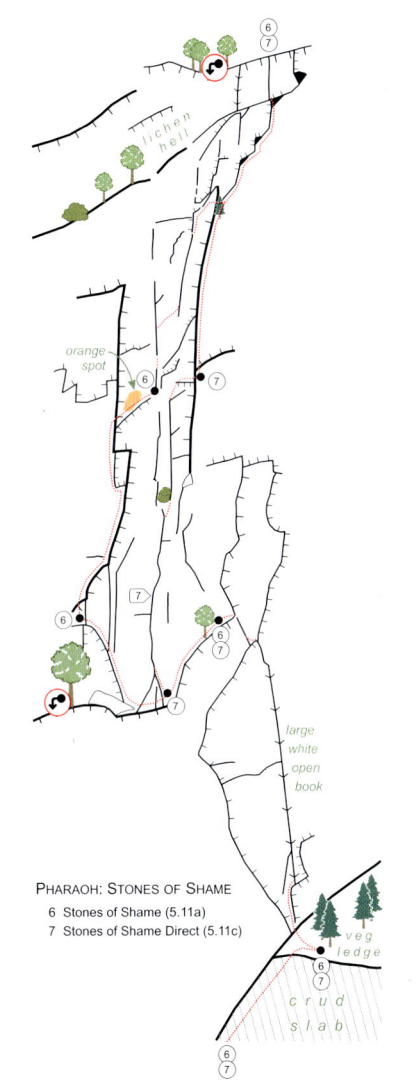

PHARAOH: STONES OF SHAME
6 Stones of Shame (5.11a)
7 Stones of Shame Direct (5.11c)

P1 5.0 PG: Same as **Stones of Shame**: Climb broken, vegetated slabs to a belay below a large open-book corner with white rock. 75'

P2 5.10c G: Same as **Stones of Shame**: Climb the open-book corner, exiting up and left to a birch tree on a left-facing ramp. Sustained. 100'

P3 5.6 PG: Reposition the belay—downclimb the left-facing ramp to a wide ledge and set up a belay below the cracks in the center of the buttress. 25'

P4 5.11c PG: From the ledge, climb the difficult thin crack to a beautiful handcrack that snakes up the buttress. At the top, undercling right to a belay at a stance at the base of a shallow right-facing corner. 100'

P5 5.11a PG: Up the right-facing corner to join **Stones of Shame** at the base of the right-rising zigzag crack.

Lake George

Up the zigzag crack via a series of mantel moves on sloped ledges. Make a long reach up and left to a horizontal crack on the headwall, then up a shallow open book to the tree-covered ledge at the top. 150'
Descent: Two 60-m ropes are required to rappel. The first rappel leads to a tree on the wide ledge of P3.
FA (V1) 1988, Felix Modugno, Bill Lutkus, Paul Boissonneault

8 Flapjack 5.10d PG 290' ★★★★★

An incredible feature of overlapping roofs that resemble a vertical stack of pancakes, or flapjacks. Climbing out the tiered roofs on P3 is like being in an airplane and having the floor drop out.
Start: Same as Stones of Shame.
P1 5.0 PG: Start as for Stones of Shame up the broken, vegetated slabs. Continue rightward to a decent ledge above spruce trees beneath a crack. 90'
P2 5.10a G: Climb a crack that heads directly for the "flapjacks," stopping at a nice ledge (with a fixed anchor) on the right just below the roof section of the flapjacks. 100'
P3 5.10d G: Follow the all-too-obvious crack through the flapjacks to a two-bolt anchor above. 100'
Gear: Standard rack plus 2 ea 2", 2 ea 3", 1 ea 4".
Descent: Two 60-m ropes are required to rappel.
FA 2000, Dennis Luther, Tom Yandon

Updraft Area

9 Here Come the Pigs 5.11a PG 240' ★★

Named for an experience of Yandon's in which he was harassed by pigs while camping at the base of the T-wall on an earlier climbing trip. P1 is quite good.
Start: Begin on the left side of a triangular face (which is defined on the right by a left-facing corner and on the left by a handcrack), 50' left of Updraft.
P1 5.10b G: Climb the handcrack on the left side of the triangular face up to a stem box with a roof at the top. Break the roof on the left and into a well-defined left-facing corner. Climb the corner past a bolt and through two smaller roofs to a two-bolt anchor. 100'
P2 5.11a PG: Traverse right (crux) to gain a right-rising ledge with the Updraft pine tree. Climb the pleasant face directly behind the pine via a thin crack to a tree ledge. Rappel from the Updraft anchor. 140'
FA (P1) Oct 12, 2000, Tom Yandon (roped solo)
FFA (P1) Oct 14, 2000, Tom Yandon, Will Mayo
FA (P2) 2001, Tim Beaman, Dave Boyden

10 Updraft 5.10a PG 230' ★★★

Named for the pattern of air movement that made cleaning the route a memorable experience. P2 is excellent and recommended.
Start: Find the clean left-leaning corner that defines P2, about 150' left of Pharaoh's Phallus, and begin below this corner at broken, unappealing rock.
P1 5.7 PG: Climb the broken, loose rock to a pine tree (V1). Continue up the right-rising ramp to a ledge at the base of the left-facing corner at a juniper bush. 140'
P2 5.10a G: Climb the left-leaning, left-facing corner to a two-bolt anchor under a juniper bush on the left face. 90'

Tom Yandon on P1 (5.10b) of Here Come the Pigs (5.11a) on the first ascent.

V1 5.10 PG: An alternative, more appealing start begins 15' right of the broken rock below an upside-down V-notch. Climb past the roof formed by the V-notch to a crack, then continue up to a second crack through an orange "spot." Tricky, unprotected moves left gain the juniper bush at the belay. 140'
Descent: Rappel to the pine tree, then to the ground.
Gear: Extra finger-sized gear.
FA 2000, Tom Yandon, Dennis Luther

11 Pharaoh's Phallus 5.9 R 250' ★★★

Start: About 100' down and left from the height of land, which is left of the Pharaoh waterfall (and ice climb), in a chimney area left of a left-facing corner. The distinguishing feature for the start of the climb is a phallus—a large protuberance projecting horizontally from the chimney 15' above the ground.
P1 5.9+ G: Follow a hand- and fistcrack that begins on the right-hand side of the phallus to a stem box below a roof. Instead of climbing the roof, step across to the right (fixed gear) and gain a crack that leads out of the chimney area to cracks in white rock on the face to the right, which are followed to a tree with an anchor. 130'
P2 5.9 R: Wander leftward behind large pines to a wide, rotten crack. Climb the crack (difficult to protect) to another pine tree, just left of a black roof. 120'
FA 2000, Tom Yandon, Dennis Luther

Opposite: Jeremy Haas on Keep the Faith (5.10c).

Lake George

Lake George

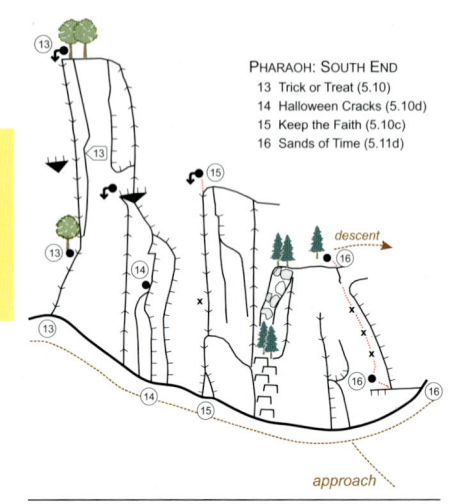

PHARAOH: SOUTH END
13 Trick or Treat (5.10)
14 Halloween Cracks (5.10d)
15 Keep the Faith (5.10c)
16 Sands of Time (5.11d)

descent

approach

South End

12 Tomb of the Falcon 5.9 PG 120'
An exploratory route, not recommended.
Start: A few feet left of **Trick or Treat** at the base of the left-rising ramp, just left of a deep left-leaning V-chimney.
P1 5.9 PG: Climb the left-rising arête to an alcove. Some detached rock. 60'
P2 5.9 PG: Continue up and left over fractured rock to the top of the left-rising arête past a juniper. Rappel from a juniper. 60'
FA Sep 7, 2000, Dennis Luther, Tom Yandon

13 Trick or Treat 5.10 G 120' ★★
Start: Locate the huge left-facing corner, 30' left and uphill from **Halloween Cracks**.
P1 5.8 G: Climb the corner to a birch tree below the overhanging crack on the right wall. 60'
P2 5.10 G: Climb the overhanging crack on the right wall to a ledge with several birches. 60'
FA Oct 31, 1992, Patrick Purcell, Ann Eastman

14 Halloween Cracks 5.10d G 50' ★
This route climbs cracks in pretty white rock to a fixed anchor. The route was extended (Tim Beaman, 2001) up the left-facing corner to the roof, then left around the arête up to a fixed anchor, but was never freed.
Start: 10' left of **Keep the Faith** at the base of several white-colored left-facing corners and flakes below a square-cut roof on the arête.
P1 5.10d G: Climb the cracks in the left-facing corners to a ledge with a nut anchor. 50'
FA Oct 31, 1992, Patrick Purcell, Ann Eastman

15 Keep the Faith 5.10c G 80' ★★★
A beautiful corner through red rock; well worth the effort.
Start: 50' left and uphill from the toe of the buttress below an orange open book.

P1 5.10c G: Climb up, making an awkward move to gain the base of the orange corner. Climb the corner, passing a bolt (crux) to the top of the corner at a two-bolt anchor. 80'
FA Sep 7, 2000, Tim Beaman, Tom Yandon, Dennis Luther

16 Sands of Time 5.11d G 80' ★
Short and stout. Success on this route depends on the slickness of the left-hand wall; bring a brush to touch up the foot placements.
Start: 40' right of the lowest point of the cliff below the left-facing, left-angling "hanging" corner (i.e., the corner doesn't reach the ground).
P1 5.9 G: Starting uphill from the crack, traverse left following an obvious horizontal crack to the base of the corner and a two-bolt anchor. Extremely short pitch but required to reduce rope drag in the upper corner. 20'
● **P2 5.11d G:** Climb the corner passing three bolts to a thin crack and ledge beyond. 60'
FA 2001, Tim Beaman, Tom Yandon

Pharaoh Mountain
SUMMIT CLIFFS

Location	East of Schroon Lake accessed from Northway Exit 28
Aspect	Southwest
Height	80'
Quality	★
Approach	1 hr 35 min, moderate
Summary	Two small crags near the summit of Pharaoh Mountain with mostly moderate cracks on clean rock.

	1		3		1		2		8
	-5.6	5.7	5.8	5.9	5.10	5.11	5.12	5.13+	total

The Summit Cliffs are located very near the summit of Pharaoh Mountain, elevation 2551'. The long approach, with an elevation gain of 1470', is rewarded by a pretty summit with good views. For the most part, the climbing is short, moderate, sunny, and on relatively clean rock; nearly all of the routes here are worth climbing. The cliffs are also manageable for toproping.

DIRECTIONS   (MAPS PAGES 122 AND 123)
The Summit Cliffs are approached from the summit of Pharaoh Mountain. There are several approaches, the shortest of which is from the Crane Pond Trailhead.

Crane Pond Trailhead: North of the village of Schroon Lake on US 9 (0.5 mile south of Northway [I-87] Exit 28), turn east onto Alder Meadow Road (0.0). Follow this road to an intersection with Crane Pond Road at 2.1 miles on the left. (Continuing straight, the road becomes Adirondack Road.) Go left onto Crane Pond Road and follow to a dirt pullout on the left at 3.6 miles. Park here or, with a high-clearance 4WD vehicle, continue to the trailhead at 5.1 miles. About 1 hr 15 min on the hiking trail takes you to the summit of Pharaoh Mountain.

Lake George

The summit area has several high points and a maze of small cliffs. To find the correct cliffs, first locate the highest point on the summit with the survey marker disk **607928,4852589**. Walk 50' southeast to the base of a small knob of rock. From here, walk on a bearing of 200° for 200' and drop down a small ledge. Another 200' on the same bearing leads to an erratic boulder that sits on top of the Upper Cliff. Drop downhill 50' to meet the right end of the cliff near the start of **Wilderness Work**.

To locate the Lower Cliff, continue another 200' on the same bearing, dropping down a gully, reaching the base of the cliff at its right end. Walk left along the base of the cliff for 100' to the rightmost route, **When Clouds Part 607910,4852425**.

Pharaoh Mountain ● Summit Cliffs
UPPER SUMMIT CLIFF

17 5756 in Service 5.8 TR 30' ★
At the left side of the cliff at a wet spot on the ground beneath a slightly overhanging wall is an open book with a vertical crack on the left side. Climb the crack to a horn 15' up, then out on the face to the right on featured steep face climbing.
FA (TR) Aug, 1983, Patrick Purcell

18 Wilderness Work 5.10d TR 30' ★
This route begins at the most obvious vertical crack just right of the arête that is in the center of the face. Climb the crack with a horn at head height to a small right-rising ledge 15' up. Move right to gain a crack in the middle of the face. At the top, step left to finish.
FA (TR) Aug, 1983, Patrick Purcell

Pharaoh Mountain ● Summit Cliffs
LOWER SUMMIT CLIFF

19 Shredded Wheat 5.11a R 80' ★
Start: Beneath a 20'-tall open book at the left end of the cliff. There is a horizontal dike leading right across the face.
P1 5.11a R: Hand-traverse right on the dike for 20' (first gear), up into a pod, then up to a higher horizontal. Mantel onto a sloping ledge, then work back left to a right-rising seam, which is followed to its end at a slab, which is climbed to the top. 80'
FA Aug, 1984, Patrick Purcell, Andy Zimmerman

20 Pharaoh Ocean Wall 5.7 A3 60'
Start: The left end of the cliff has a sheer wall broken by two horizontal dikes. This route begins at a 1' by 2' slab of rock on the ground beneath two rivets that lead to an incipient crack, 18' left of **Tuna Fish Crack**.
P1 5.7 A3: Climb the rivets to the incipient crack (fixed gear) to a mixed free and aid finish. 60'
FA Aug, 1984, Patrick Purcell (roped solo)

21 Tuna Fish Crack 5.11b G 65' ★★
A clean and continuous fingercrack.
Start: The left end of the cliff has a sheer wall broken by two horizontal dikes. This route begins at a vertical crack that starts 3' above the ground and 20' left of a chimney-recess at ground level.
P1 5.11b G: Climb the crack to the top. 65'
FA Aug, 1983, Patrick Purcell

22 Slippy Sliden' Away 5.8 G 65' ★
Start: At two parallel fingercracks about 1' apart in a left-facing corner, just left of the tiered ceilings on the right side of the cliff.
P1 5.8 G: Climb the parallel cracks past a ceiling at 20', then continue up the cracks to the top. 65'
FA Aug, 1984, Patrick Purcell, Andy Zimmerman

23 Pharaoh Winds 5.8 PG 65' ★
Start: At the right side of the cliff at a ledge at head height beneath tiered ceilings that begin 20' up.
P1 5.8 PG: Climb the face to the first ceiling, up through the ceiling into a left-facing corner to the second ceiling. Break through the ceiling to a handcrack finish. 65'
FA Jul, 1984, Patrick Purcell, Andy Zimmerman

24 When Clouds Part 5.6 G 65' ★
Start: 6' right of **Pharaoh Winds** at a vertical fingercrack that extends to the ground with a ledge at head height.
P1 5.6 G: Climb the vertical crack into a right-facing corner capped by a ceiling with a notch. Up through the notch into a right-facing corner, then up a prominent vertical fin that leads to the top. 65'
FA Aug, 1983, Patrick Purcell, Karen Bomba

Photo by Jay Harrison.

Lake George

GULL POND CLIFF

1 Big In Munchkin Land (5.7)
3 Crackerbox Palace (5.7+)
4 Up In Smoke (5.9)
6 Gull Pucky (5.10d)
9 Get Reborn (5.10a)
10 Toss Me My Nuts (5.11a)
11 Austin City Limits (5.12a)
12 Dope-a-Mean (5.13a)
13 Pull Up Your Pants (5.9)

GULL POND CLIFF

Location	East of Schroon Lake accessed from Northway Exit 28
Aspect	West
Height	100'
Quality	★
Approach	20 min, easy
Summary	Sunny cliff with near-vertical routes above a small pond.

1	2	1	3	3	1	1	1	13
-5.6	5.7	5.8	5.9	5.10	5.11	5.12	5.13+	total

Gull Pond is a high-quality location with great views of the High Peaks, abundant sunshine, and a short approach. It's also a popular camping and fishing destination. The routes are mostly single-pitch crack and corner climbs on good rock. Climber traffic is light on the handful of routes here, so expect some lichen. Left of the main cliff is a small outcrop—the Left End—with the route **Big in Munchkin Land**. The Main Cliff is 150' further. On its left side is a low wall with a ledge 20' up (the Terrace) and the starts of **Ugly as Sin**, **Crackerbox Palace**, **Up In Smoke**, and **Scales**. A deep open book with a ceiling 20' up is a landmark for locating the routes that start on the Terrace. In the center of the cliff are **Travisty** and **Dirty Little Corner**, which follow prominent corners to the highest section of the cliff. Right of **Get Reborn**, the obvious off-width crack, is a steep wall—the Toss Me My Nuts Wall—with some impressive climbing, and a short, clean fingercrack—**Pull Up Your Pants**.

HISTORY

Jay Harrison and Dick Tucker, the prolific developers at Crane and Huckleberry, were the first to report climbing here in 2001. A return visit with Jamie McNeill in 2007 encouraged Harrison to lead a few toprope routes and establish some harder projects.

DIRECTIONS   (MAPS PAGES 122 AND 132)

Gull Pond Cliff is accessed from the Gull Pond Trailhead. From Northway Exit 28, drive south on US 9. At 0.6 mile, turn left onto Alder Meadow Road. If you're coming from Schroon Lake (at the center of town near the school), drive north on US 9. At 1.8 miles, turn right onto Alder Meadow Road.

From US 9 (0.0 mile), head east on Alder Meadow Road. At 2.1 miles, the road forks; bear right onto Adirondack Road (aka East Shore Road). The trailhead is reached at 3.8 miles; there is a sign and a large parking lot on the left 603154,4854309.

Hike the trail marked with yellow discs for 10 min to Gull Pond, where the cliff is visible across the pond. Go back 200' on the trail and follow the yellow-disc trail towards beautiful campsites on the west shore. Continue clockwise (left) around the pond on a good herd path to the talus, then up to the base of the cliff, meeting it at the continuous off-width crack of **Get Reborn** 604048,4854082.

DESCENT OPTIONS

Rappel with a single 60-m rope. Fixed anchors can be found at the top of **Scales** and **Toss Me My Nuts**.

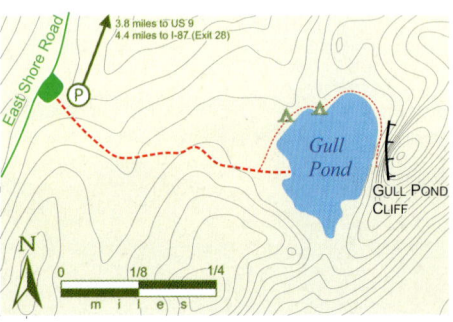

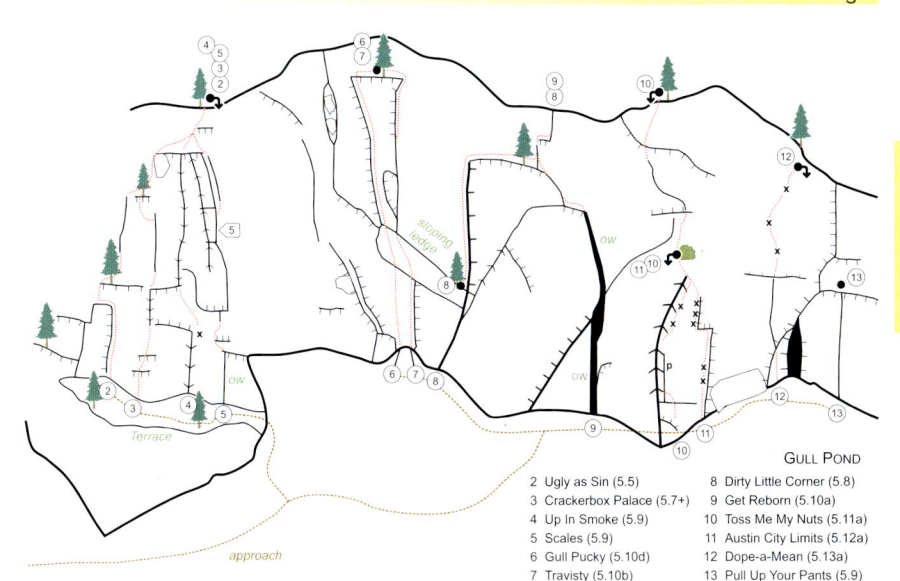

Lake George

2 Ugly as Sin (5.5)
3 Crackerbox Palace (5.7+)
4 Up In Smoke (5.9)
5 Scales (5.9)
6 Gull Pucky (5.10d)
7 Travisty (5.10b)
8 Dirty Little Corner (5.8)
9 Get Reborn (5.10a)
10 Toss Me My Nuts (5.11a)
11 Austin City Limits (5.12a)
12 Dope-a-Mean (5.13a)
13 Pull Up Your Pants (5.9)

Left End

This is the first cliff you come to as you walk clockwise around the pond. It is located very close to the water, just in the woods directly above the leftmost end of the talus, and about 150' left of the Terrace Wall.

1 Big In Munchkin Land 5.7 G 25' ★★

Start: In a right-facing large corner with a rectangular roof 20' up.
P1 5.7 G: Go straight up the corner system to the roof. (V1) Step right to a ledge in a smaller right-facing corner. Go up this, then step left to another ledge and fixed anchor on the face to the right. 25'
V1 5.11 TR: Break the roof on the right and continue straight up the major corner.
FA Jun 6, 2011, Will Roth, Monique Wicks

Terrace Wall

This is the wall that begins 25' up from a tree-covered terrace. Approach the base from the right.

2 Ugly as Sin 5.5 G 120'

Start: At the left end of the Terrace, 12' left of **Crackerbox Palace**, at a handcrack in a right-facing corner with a clump of birch trees.
P1 5.5 G: Climb the corner, then up and right past two large pine trees to a small pine tree with a fixed anchor. 120'
FA 2001, Jay Harrison

3 Crackerbox Palace 5.7+ PG 100' ★★

A sustained route with varied climbing.
Start: At the left end of the Terrace at an arête left of the large **Up In Smoke** corner.
P1 5.7+ PG: Up ledges on the arête and past the left end of the ceiling to the base of an open book. Up the open book to a ledge, then climb a thin vertical crack.

Move left to an arête and make a tricky move to a ledge with a large pine tree. Scramble up and right to a small pine tree with a fixed anchor. 100'
FA 2001, Jay Harrison, Travis King

4 Up In Smoke 5.9 G 60' ★★★

A well-protected corner with good jugs and wild stemming.
Start: At the large open book with a ceiling 20' up on the left.
P1 5.9 G: Go up a corner to a roof (crux). Wild stems lead past the roof on the right (bolt), then continue up the corner to a fixed anchor at the top. 60'
History: The FAers kept the bugs at bay by building a fire below the route such that the entire corner filled with smoke.
FA Jun 6, 2011, Will Roth, Kris O'Connor

5 Scales 5.9 G 90' ★★★

Diverse climbing and a fine line. **Scales** is the name of the resident milk snake that frequents this route.
Start: At the right end of the Terrace, at an off-width crack 10' right of **Up In Smoke**.
P1 5.9 G: Up the off-width crack to a stance beneath an overhang. Move left around the overhang (crux, small cams), then up to a ceiling with a crack on the right. Follow the crack onto a low-angle face with ledges. Climb twin cracks to the right of an arête and belay at a small pine tree with a fixed anchor. 90'
FA Sep 19, 2007, Jamie McNeill, Jay Harrison

Main Wall

6 Gull Pucky 5.10d TR 100'

Near the high point of the cliff base, climb the sheer wall left of **Travisty** to a sloping ledge. Finish in a long, clean right-facing corner with an orange wall on the right.
FA (TR) 2001, Travis King

Lake George

7 Travisty 5.10b TR 100' ★

Near the high point of the cliff base, climb a shallow left-facing corner to a sloping ledge. From the left end of the ledge, climb a vertical crack to a right-facing corner.
FA (TR) 2001, Jay Harrison, Travis King

8 Dirty Little Corner 5.8 G 80'

Start: 50' up the talus to the left from where the approach trail reaches the cliff at **Get Reborn**, 4th-class up sod and vegetation to a tree belay on a ledge beneath a deep left-facing corner.
P1 5.8 G: Up a steep, wide crack in the corner to a tree-covered ledge. Scramble up and right to a tree with a fixed anchor. 80'
FA Sep 17, 2007, Jamie McNeill, Jay Harrison, Ryan Clamp

9 Get Reborn 5.10a G 90' ★★

Start: Where the approach trail reaches the cliff at a 7" parallel-sided crack that begins 8' up.
P1 5.10a G: Protect in the 7" crack, move right along a flake, then move back left to join the wide crack at an alcove. Follow the left-hand crack out of the alcove. The crack narrows to fist-sized; at its top, step left onto low-angle rock and scramble up and right to a tree with a fixed anchor. 90'
FA Sep 19, 2007, Jamie McNeill, Jay Harrison

Toss Me My Nuts Wall

This is the remarkable, gently overhanging, tan wall 20' right of (and around the corner from) **Get Reborn**.

10 Toss Me My Nuts 5.11a PG 160' ★

Convoluted, as the climbing is on the left side of the arête, and the protection is inconveniently on the right side.
Start: Begin 12' right of the left side of the wall at a good handhold at head height.
P1 5.11a PG: Go up to a horizontal crack, traverse left to the arête, then up this to a good horizontal ledge. Mantel onto the ledge (crux), then continue up the arête to a slab. Angle right to a fixed anchor shared with **Austin City Limits**. 60'
P2 5.8- G: Go up and left to a wide crack in an overhang; up this, then up easier rock to the top. 100'
FA Jul 17, 2008, Jamie McNeill, Jay Harrison

11 Austin City Limits 5.12a G 55' ★★★

Formerly a toprope problem known as **Flaws of Physics**.
Start: 8' right of **Toss Me My Nuts**, at an overhanging, bottomless, left-facing corner and 3' left of a giant pointed flake.
○ **P1 5.12a G:** Make a hard boulder problem to gain the corner (V4, harder if you're tall), then up the corner system, around a small overhang, then up a shallow open book to where the angle eases.

Continue to a fixed anchor shared with **Toss Me My Nuts**. 55'
Gear: Small to medium cams, or medium nut.
FA May 10, 2011, Bill Pierson, Jonathan Nickel

12 Dope-a-Mean 5.13a G 60' ★★★★

Sustained. The crux is down low where the crack changes angle; pre-place gear in the crack here.
Start: At the right end of the large flake (the left end of which marks the start of **Austin City Limits**) and just left of a chimney at a black crack that rises above an alcove.
P1 5.13a G: Climb the severely overhanging crack (crux) to a wide 12"-deep overlap. Go up past the overhang to good holds, then up a face to a heartbreaker move rightward before the fixed anchor. 60'
History: Originally a Jonathan Nickel project named **Bakiri's Credo**. Finally redpointed by Buzzelli after 3 days of effort.
FA Sep 29, 2013, David Buzzelli

13 Pull Up Your Pants 5.9 G 25' ★★

Start: At the right end of the Toss Me My Nuts Wall is a short chimney. Begin 8' right of the chimney at a vertical fingercrack.
P1 5.9 G: Up the clean fingercrack to a tree-covered ledge. 25'
FA Jun 25, 2007, Jamie McNeill, Jay Harrison

DEVIL'S WASHDISH CLIFF

The Devil's Washdish Cliff is a remote cliff in the Pharaoh Lake Wilderness Area. The cliff is located above Devil's Washdish 611434,4853427, a small pond about 1.3 miles west of the south end of Putnam Pond, and is accessible only by bushwhacking. In the late 1970s, Steve Hayashi climbed two routes here, each two pitches and in the 5.4 range. He reported loose, dirty, but sound rock.

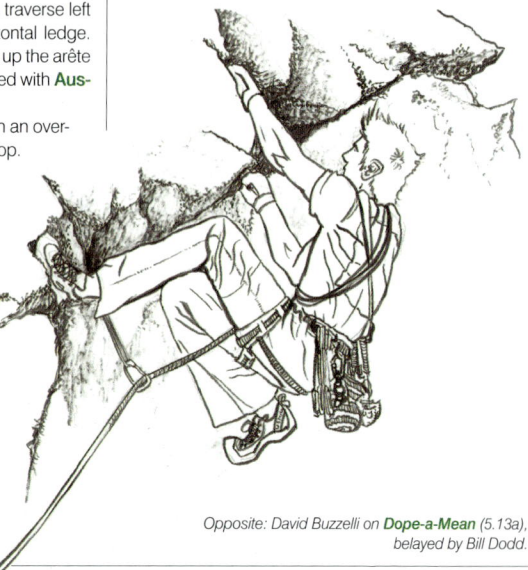

Pen and ink by Colin O'Connor.

Opposite: David Buzzelli on Dope-a-Mean (5.13a), belayed by Bill Dodd.

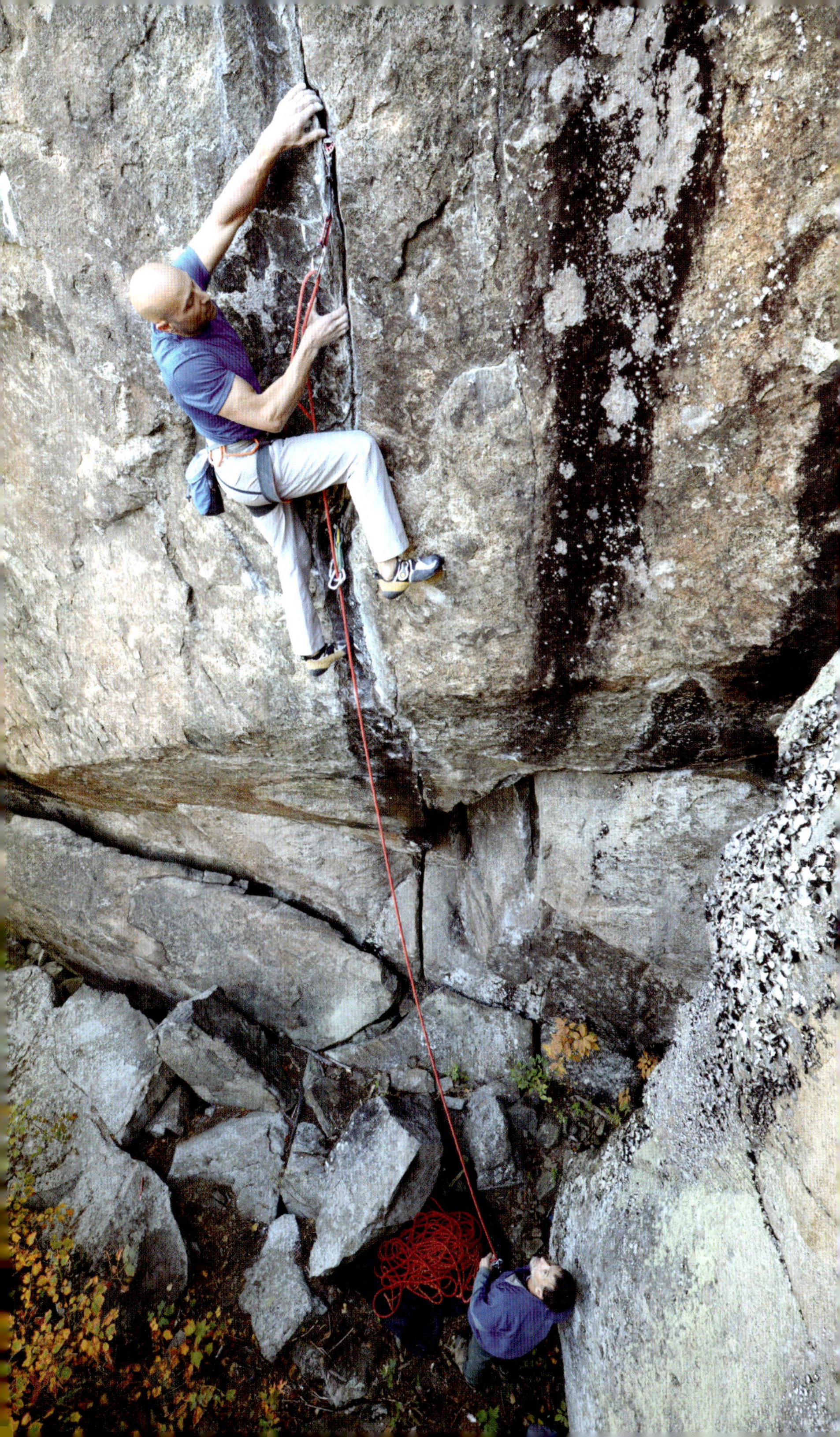

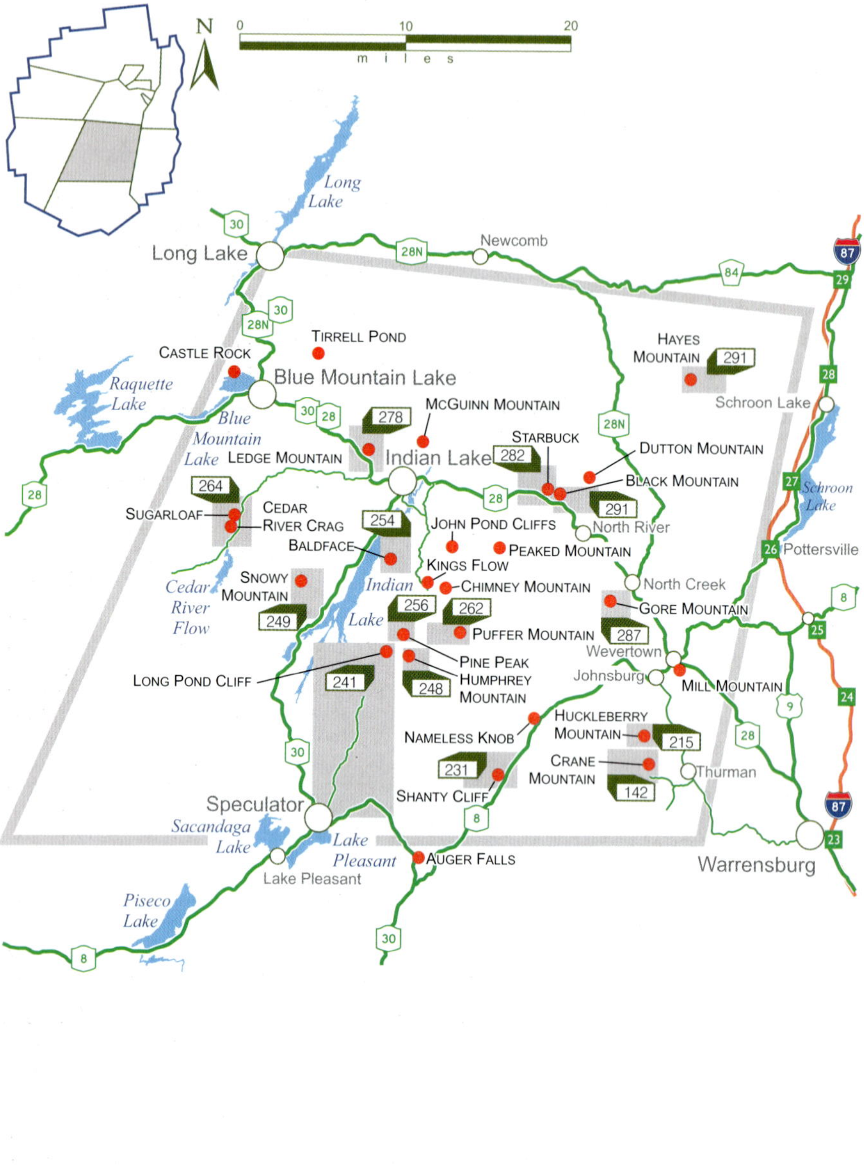

N
0
10
20
miles
Long Lake
Long Lake
Newcomb
Blue Mountain Lake
Raquette Lake
Blue Mountain Lake
Indian Lake
Tirrell Pond
Castle Rock
Hayes Mountain
291
Schroon Lake
278
McGuinn Mountain
Ledge Mountain
Starbuck
282
Dutton Mountain
Black Mountain
264
Sugarloaf
Cedar River Crag
254
Baldface
John Pond Cliffs
Peaked Mountain
291
North River
Schroon Lake
Pottersville
Kings Flow
Chimney Mountain
Snowy Mountain
249
Cedar River Flow
Indian Lake
256
262
Puffer Mountain
North Creek
Gore Mountain
287
Wevertown
Johnsburg
Mill Mountain
Long Pond Cliff
241
Pine Peak
248
Humphrey Mountain
Nameless Knob
Huckleberry Mountain
215
231
Shanty Cliff
Crane Mountain
142
Thurman
Speculator
Sacandaga Lake
Lake Pleasant
Lake Pleasant
Auger Falls
Warrensburg
Piseco Lake
30
28N
84
87
29
28
27
26
8
25
24
9
23

Indian Lake

Outside of the High Peaks, the Indian Lake region has the highest mountain (Snowy Mountain, 3899') and the highest towns (Speculator, 1739'; Indian Lake, 1706'). Located in the heart of the park, Indian Lake is sandwiched between the large wilderness areas of Siamese Ponds and West Canada Lake. The self-appointed "Moose Capital of New York," Indian Lake is as good a candidate as any for glimpsing this oversized ungulate. Much of this region lies within Hamilton County, which bears the distinction of having one of the lowest road densities east of the Mississippi River. Only a few places in Maine are more remote than the cliffs mentioned here.

With several exceptions, the cliffs here are raw and have difficult approaches. Although the history of climbing in this region is among the oldest in the park, many of the cliffs see limited activity. Climbers who like the road less traveled will be right at home in this region, and the descriptions that follow will help focus your next exploration.

North of the town of Indian Lake are several crags with completely different approaches and climbing experiences. The principle crag here is the impressive, multipitch, slab-climbing destination, Sugarloaf. This recently-opened gem has a short hiking approach, but does require a long drive on a seasonal dirt road. The other cliffs are obscure: the small and overshadowed Cedar River Crag; the difficult-to-locate Ledge Mountain with potential for many routes; the stunning but overgrown Tirrell Pond; and the bushwhack summit cliffs of McGinn Mountain.

The next grouping of cliffs is south of Indian Lake, on NY 30. Along the west shore of Indian Lake is the boat launch to Baldface Mountain, where a short hike ends at some good routes. Farther south is the popular trailhead for Snowy Mountain and the summit cliff, with its exposed position and excellent face climbs on the most featured rock in the park.

The Kings Flow area is an expansive wetland region, on the east side of Indian Lake. The overgrown multipitch routes of the Kings Flow Cliff are the only roadside climbs; everything else involves a moderate or difficult approach. Pine Peak is a small mountain with a chaotic (but clean) cliff that is reached by a level trail and a short bushwhack. Chimney Mountain is one of the few freestanding formations in the park and is easily reached by a good trail. Puffer Mountain Cliff wins the award for the most difficult approach in the park, and although there isn't much established climbing to write about, it has excellent potential and gets high praise from the few who have made this long march.

Entry to the Kings Flow area from the south end, near Speculator, follows a seasonal road to the trailhead for Long Pond Cliff and Humphrey Mountain. Long Pond is a popular day hike, and the cliff on the opposite shore has many routes—that is, once you get across the pond. Humphrey Mountain is seldom climbed (dirty) and has a tedious approach.

Shanty Cliff lies across the Sacandaga River from NY 8 and has an excellent concentration of single-pitch crack, slab, and steep face climbs. Farther north on NY 8 is the hamlet of Johnsburg and the road to Huckleberry Mountain and Crane Mountain. Huckleberry is an excellent cliff, but access is difficult and convoluted. Its neighbor, Crane Mountain, is where the action is. This complex area has a multitude of crags scattered across a broad area. Since the first edition, route development has exploded here, now with more than 200 routes from single-pitch clip-ups to multi-pitch slabs. The eastern side of Crane is especially popular and has a straight-forward approach.

A few small crags are located on the slopes of Gore Mountain Ski Area near the town of North Creek. Well north of town is the obscure and virtually unexplored Hayes Mountain. West of North Creek, on the pass toward Indian Lake, are a couple of obscure multipitch routes on Black Mountain. The recently developed Starbuck Mountain has an easy approach with some quality routes, a good first choice for those new to the region.

SEASON

All of the crags in this region have trailheads at high elevation. While the cooler temperatures are a blessing during the heat of summer, expect a shorter climbing season. The Crane Mountain Trailhead is above 2000' and is a great place to be in Aug but may not be accessible until the end of April due to lingering snow. Several seasonal roads exist in this region, including Cedar River Road and Elm Lake / East Road. This is snowmobile country, and snowshoes may be necessary to reach the higher elevations well into April.

DIRECTIONS (MAPS PAGES 4 AND 136)

The cliffs are clustered around Speculator and Johnsburg, accessed from the NY 8 shortcut (page 12), and around Indian Lake, accessed from NY 30 or NY 28. The cliffs around Johnsburg (Crane and Huckleberry) are the most accessible, being within 30 min from the interstate, whereas those around Speculator and Indian Lake are more difficult to reach.

WHERE TO STAY

Many primitive campsites can be accessed from trailheads and dirt roads in this region. NY 8, between Speculator and Bakers Mills, has excellent roadside bivy sites along the Sacandaga River. The trailhead

SWING IN BEFORE YOU CLIP IN
patagonia
MAMMUT
OR
OUTDOOR RESEARCH
Princeton Tec
Oboz
FOUNTAIN SQUARE OUTFITTERS
1 Ridge Street Downtown Glens Falls, NY (518) 932-8355
Facebook.com/FountainSquareOutfitters » @FSOutfitters

Indian Lake

PG	CLIFF	QUALITY	ASPECT	APPROACH		GRADES	#
144	Crane Mountain Wayout Wall	★	SW	1 hr 30 min	difficult	.6 .7 .8 .9 .10 .11 .12 .13	6
146	Crane Mountain Beaverview Cliff	★	S	1 hr	moderate	.6 .7 .8 .9 .10 .11 .12 .13	10
148	Crane Mountain Brown Slab	★	S	30 min	moderate	.6 .7 .8 .9 .10 .11 .12 .13	8
150	Crane Mountain Viewpoint Cliff	★	S	25 min	easy	.6 .7 .8 .9 .10 .11 .12 .13	10
154	Crane Mountain Sweeper Wall	★	SW	1 hr	difficult	.6 .7 .8 .9 .10 .11 .12 .13	8
156	Crane Mountain Firecamp Wall	★★	SW	1 hr 10 min	difficult	.6 .7 .8 .9 .10 .11 .12 .13	18
159	Crane Mountain The Prows	★★★	SW	1 hr 10 min	difficult	.6 .7 .8 .9 .10 .11 .12 .13	7
166	Crane Mountain Above-the-Measles Wall	★	S	20 min	easy	.6 .7 .8 .9 .10 .11 .12 .13	5
168	Crane Mountain Lower Measles Wall	★★	S	20 min	easy	.6 .7 .8 .9 .10 .11 .12 .13	10
169	Crane Mountain Upper Measles Wall	★★	S	20 min	easy	.6 .7 .8 .9 .10 .11 .12 .13	9
173	Crane Mountain Belleview Slab	★★	S	30 min	moderate	.6 .7 .8 .9 .10 .11 .12 .13	9
174	Crane Mountain Bellavista Slab	★	S	35 min	moderate	.6 .7 .8 .9 .10 .11 .12 .13	6
176	Crane Mountain Upper Walls	★★★★	SE	35 min	moderate	.6 .7 .8 .9 .10 .11 .12 .13	36
186	Crane Mountain Land of Overhangs	★★	SE	28 min	moderate	.6 .7 .8 .9 .10 .11 .12 .13	9
188	Crane Mountain TeePee Wall	★★★	SE	31 min	moderate	.6 .7 .8 .9 .10 .11 .12 .13	11
190	Crane Mountain Long Play Wall	★★★	SE	32 min	moderate	.6 .7 .8 .9 .10 .11 .12 .13	8
192	Crane Mountain Diagonal Ramp Wall	★★	SE	35 min	moderate	.6 .7 .8 .9 .10 .11 .12 .13	6
194	Crane Mountain Black Arches Wall	★★★★★	SE	35-40 min	moderate	.6 .7 .8 .9 .10 .11 .12 .13	36
209	Crane Mountain Slanting Cracks Wall	★★	SE	55 min	difficult	.6 .7 .8 .9 .10 .11 .12 .13	11
221	Huckleberry Mountain Main Cliff	★★★	SW	2 hr 30 min	difficult	.6 .7 .8 .9 .10 .11 .12 .13	27
231	Shanty Cliff	★★★★	SW	15 min	easy river crossing	.6 .7 .8 .9 .10 .11 .12 .13	45
248	Snowy Mountain Summit Cliff	★★★★★	SE	2 hr 30 min	difficult	.6 .7 .8 .9 .10 .11 .12 .13	6
258	Chimney Mountain Chimney Summit	★★	E & W	40 min	moderate	.6 .7 .8 .9 .10 .11 .12 .13	2
259	Chimney Mountain Caveman Wall	★★	W	35 min	moderate	.6 .7 .8 .9 .10 .11 .12 .13	2
260	Chimney Mountain True Summit Slabs	★★	S	45 min	moderate	.6 .7 .8 .9 .10 .11 .12 .13	3
263	Sugarloaf Mountain	★★★★	E & SE	10-30 min	easy	.6 .7 .8 .9 .10 .11 .12 .13	19
279	Castle Rock	★★	S	30 min	easy	.6 .7 .8 .9 .10 .11 .12 .13	3
282	Starbuck Mountain	★★	S	15 min	easy	.6 .7 .8 .9 .10 .11 .12 .13	13

Indian Lake

for McGinn Mountain Cliff is close to Indian Lake and has good designated tent sites located a short distance from the parking area. Crane Mountain Trailhead is secluded and adjacent to good bivy sites near the boulders.

Campgrounds: On NY 30 are the following state campgrounds: Moffitt Beach, in Speculator (518.548.7102); Lake Durant, near Blue Mountain Lake (518.352.7797); and Lewey Lake, near the south end of Indian Lake (518.648.5266).

AMENITIES

Speculator is the best option. Near the four-corners intersection in Speculator (www.adrkmts.com) are a general store, market, bank, and gas station. Supplies in Indian Lake (www.indian-lake.com) are somewhat limited by comparison. North Creek (www.goremtnregion.org) is another option to consider and boasts a good bakery on Main Street.

DIVERSIONS

The put-in for whitewater boating in the Hudson River Gorge is at the large parking area for the approach to McGinn Mountain Cliff (page 281). Gore Mountain Ski Area has a network of mountain bike trails (page 286). Some hikes to consider in the area include Crane Mountain, Peaked Mountain, and Tirrell Pond.

Jay Harrison, the "Mayor of Crane Mountain", follows P2 (5.7) of ***Polar Vortex*** *(5.8), East Nose, on the first ascent in 1997. Photo by Dick Tucker.*

CRANE MOUNTAIN

Location	South of Johnsburg, accessed from NY 8
Summary	Complex and extensive area with a few cliffs that see occasional traffic (Summit Cliffs and Slanting Cracks Wall) and some that have become extremely popular, the Southeast Corner Area.

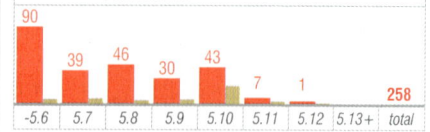

90	39	46	30	43	7	1	258
-5.6	5.7	5.8	5.9	5.10	5.11	5.12	5.13+	total

Crane Mountain, located near Johnsburg, has easy slabs, summit cragging, and many remote but good cliffs. A popular trailhead for day hiking, the Crane Mountain loop passes by a beaver pond, a natural bridge, an alpine lake, and an open summit. The cliffs are spread out over a vast mountainside, with some cliffs having only a few routes. Despite some long approaches, Crane has a little bit of something for everyone, potential for new routes, and excellent rock quality. Because of the southern exposure, the climbing season is long. However, biting insects and dense vegetation can make for a frustrating experience during the early summer months.

Much of the development at Crane has required cleaning, as the rock tends to be very dirty and vegetated. Despite the number of overgrown routes, crags such as Brown Slab, Summit Cliffs, and Slanting Cracks Wall are naturally clean. Other cliffs look as though they have never been climbed. Walk along the East Path and you'll begin to appreciate the thousands of man-hours spent preparing routes here.

Several cliffs have been omitted because information is insufficient or, in the case of the Putnam Farm Wall and Northernmost Wall, they are located on private property.

Cliffs are grouped into four areas: Crane West, approached by an old jeep road; Central Crane, approached from the summit hiking trail; Summit Cliffs, near the top of the mountain; and Crane East, approached by the East Path, a climber's trail. All approaches begin from the Crane Mountain parking area.

The older route descriptions in this section were adapted with his permission from Dick Tucker's meticulous notes[1]. Contributions were also made by Jay Harrison and his unpublished guide, "Cabin Country Rock."

HISTORY

Pre 1991: The early years: The early history of climbing at Crane Mountain is sketchy at best. Bob Gilmore, better known for his Gunks route **Junior** and his Whitehorse Ledge route **Sliding Board**, both in the early 1960s, was the first climber known to have explored the cliffs. He once co-owned the Putnam Farm, which is

---

[1] Richard E. Tucker, "Crane Mountain" (typescript, Adirondack Research Library, Niskayuna, N.Y., Jun 20, 1999).

near the Beaverview Wall, and would solo easy routes all over the mountain. If it was too hard or dangerous, he would downclimb or traverse off. Dave and Lois Legg explored a bit in the early 80s, toproping some lines on the Summit Cliffs. Around the same time, Bill Pierce climbed a "good route" at Tablerock Crag with an "undercling traverse near the top," thought to be near **Pine Tree Corner**.

1991–97: Exploration began in earnest in 1991 (coincidentally the same year Dick Tucker began his work at neighboring Huckleberry Mountain), when Jay Harrison read the descriptions from Barbara McMartin's *Discover the Southeastern Adirondacks*. **Chicken Flake**, his first new route at Crane Mountain, was climbed in 1991 during a weekend spent camping on the summit in lightning storms. Initial exploration centered on the Summit Cliffs, one of the more obvious attractions, but soon Harrison branched out all over the mountain. He was so impressed that in 1993 he relocated his family to Sky High Road, very near the trailhead, and Crane became his backyard. Within six years he visited (and climbed routes on) nearly every cliff. Dick Tucker was a frequent partner of Harrison during this period, and recalls that going someplace new was as much a part of the experience as the climbing. Out of the roughly sixty routes climbed during this period, more than half are no-star routes, and only five are destination-worthy; some were pretty bad, and both Tucker and Harrison agreed that even they wouldn't go back there. The better routes include **Thank You, Cindy** on the Firecamp Wall, **Cornerstone** on The Prows, and **Sun Dogs** on the Wayout Wall.

1998–2007: Crane climbed out: Harrison climbed by a strict set of rules—ground-up, trad, no previewing no fixed protection, and no prior cleaning. If there was no gear, Harrison would either solo it (which he did...a lot), or back off. Climbers elsewhere had been cleaning routes top-down for many years, but Harrison would have none of it. Crane was dirty and blank, and he was running out of projects that could be climbed in this fashion: Crane was climbed out. In the next decade, exploration slowed to a snail's pace—only 12 routes were put in during this period, roughly one per year, and all but one by Harrison, often solo. The third edition of *Climbing in the Adirondacks* was published in 1995 and, for the first time, included 26 climbs on Crane, but did little to increase its popularity. The place was simply too remote, too confusing, too dirty and too much work; in short, it was inconvenient. Harrison went in search of adventure elsewhere, adding routes at Hayes Mountain, Gull Pond, Gore Mountain, Huckleberry Mountain, Shanty Cliff, Wallface, and Fly Brook Valley.

2008 and onward: This all changed in 2008 when several things happened. First, *Adirondack Rock* was published, which provided better documentation for what was done up to that point, and how to find it. Second, Jamie McNeill came on the scene. McNeill brought a fresh perspective—the willingness to focus on a single area (in his words, "create a destination") and place fixed protection. McNeill's approach rubbed off on Harrison, and opened new opportunities in Harrison's own backyard. **Black Arch Arête** on the Black Arches Wall was a turning point—it was immaculately cleaned, employed some fixed protection, has a fixed anchor, and it's one of the best pitches in the Adirondack Park. The same techniques were employed with **Critical Crimps**, **Second Job**, and **Amphitheater Crack**; at first these routes went to the top, but convenience anchors were installed to make these more accessible.

Jamie McNeill.
Photo by Jay Harrison.

Finally, the East Path was constructed and cairned, and has since become a highway. While other cliffs on the mountain have idled, new route development on the east side of Crane Mountain has exploded, and accessibility from the East Path is a major reason. What was once an hour-plus, in-your-face bushwhack was reduced to a 30-minute, pleasant walk in the forest. In preparation for the Southern Adirondack Climbers Festival (which Harrison co-founded and hosted for many years), the trail was continuously rerouted until the approach time to the Black Arches Wall was reduced to 35 minutes. Since 2008, more than 180 new routes have been put in on this side of Crane, all along or above the East Path.

But even these factors cannot fully account for the frenzied pace of new route development at Crane. The climbing festival introduced new climbers to Crane, and beginning in 2009, the new routing party expanded to include Todd Paris, Kevin Heckeler, Valerie Bachinsky, Michael Gray, Mike Prince, Jason Brechko, and Ben Brooke. In 2010, Michael Farnsworth and Tom Lane joined the group. Farnsworth's contributions, while few in quantity, boosted the difficulty of routes at Crane, culminating in Crane's most difficult route, **Four Ounces to Freedom** (5.12d) at the Black Arches Wall. Farnsworth has moved away, but Tom Lane has had a more lasting presence. A retired police officer living near Northville, Lane has spare time, and with Harrison living right on the mountain, collaboration was inevitable. Together they have cleaned miles of crack, and acres of face, uncovering classic pitches such as **Oddy's Crack of Horror**, **Long Play**, **Broken Broom**, **Second Amendment**, and **Stand Your Ground**.

In September, 2012, Michael Gray published Storked Select Climbs at Crane Mountain, A Simple Guide—a fun, single-page, folded, mini-guide to selected climbs at Crane. It's jam-packed with hand-written descriptions and hand-illustrated maps and topos. All 37 routes described in this guide are on the east side of Crane, along the East Path.

Indian Lake

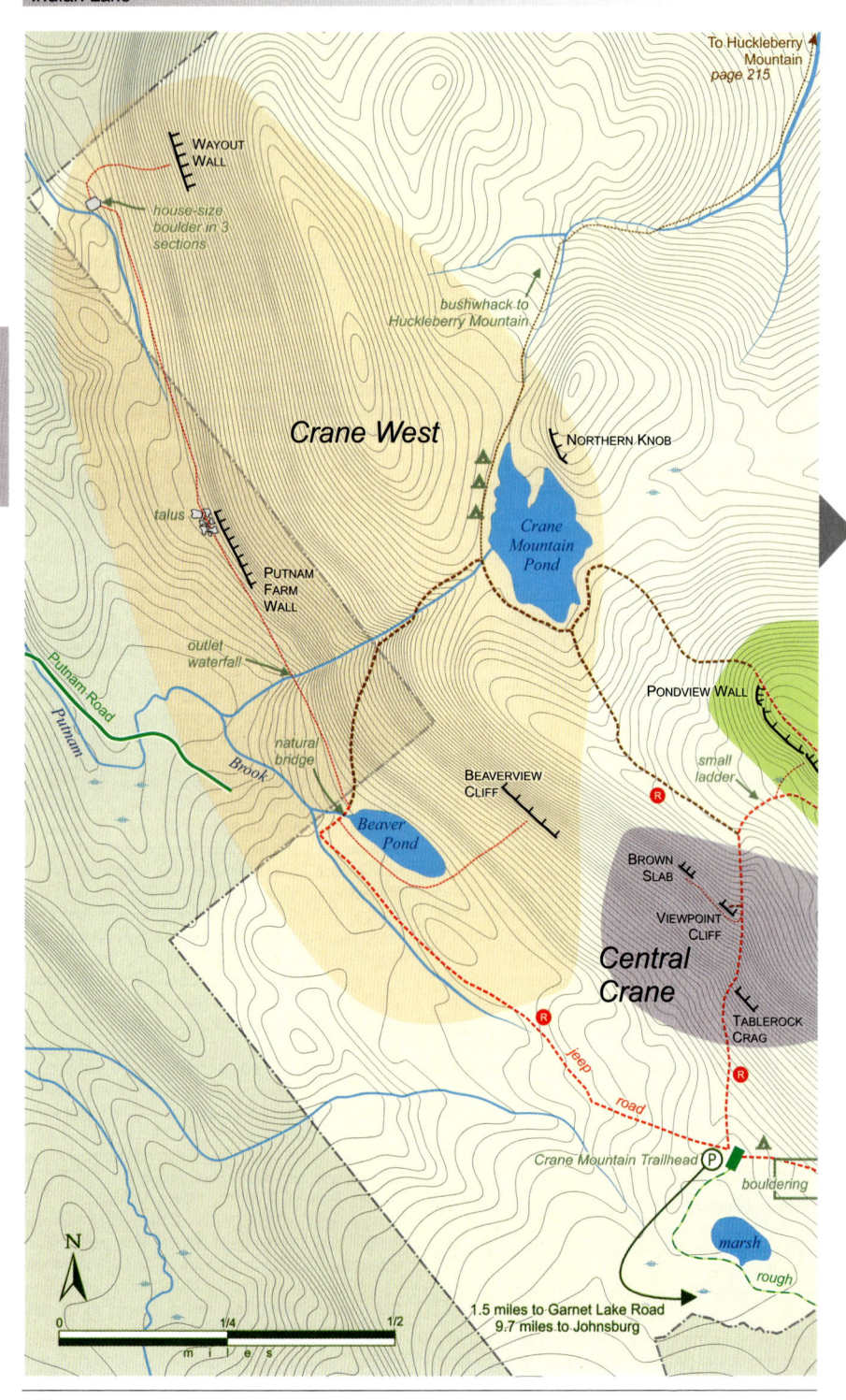

Indian Lake

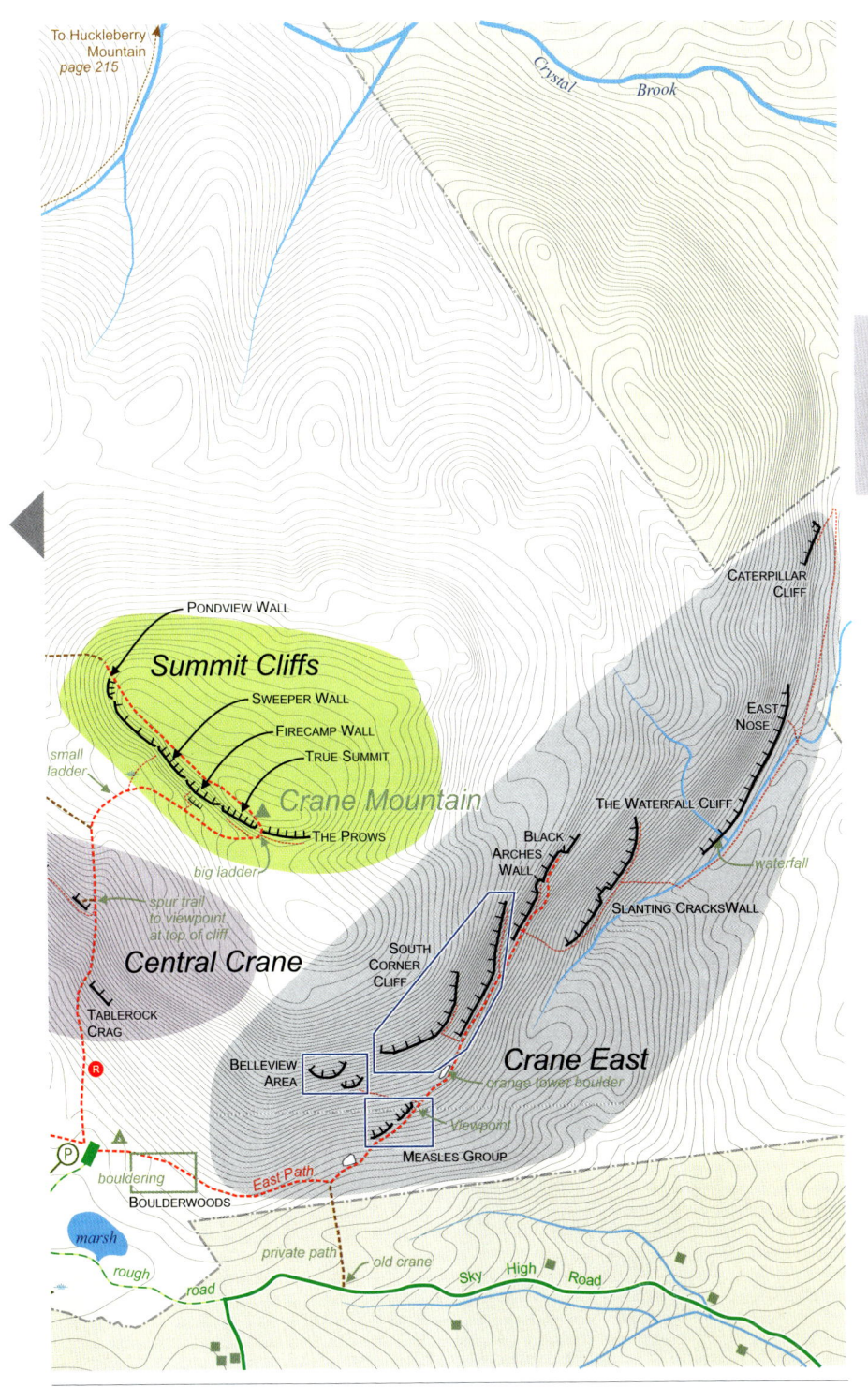

143

Indian Lake

DIRECTIONS (MAP PAGE 142)

Northway (I-87) Exits 23, 25, and 26 lead west toward Wevertown, located at the intersections of NY 28 and NY 8. From Wevertown (0.0 mile), go west on NY 8 to Johnsburg and the intersection with South Johnsburg Road at 1.7 miles. Turn left (south) onto South Johnsburg Road and drive to the intersection with Garnet Lake Road and a sign for Crane Mountain Trailhead at 8.6 miles. (Note: the sign for Crane Mountain Trailhead is stolen every few years.) Turn right (southwest) onto Garnet Lake Road and drive to the intersection with Sky High Road at 9.9 miles. (Note: this sign is also frequently stolen; replacements may read "Ski Hi," "Sky Hi," etc.) Turn right (west) onto Sky High Road, a steep dirt road, and drive to the end of the road and a large parking area at 11.4 miles, the Crane Mountain trailhead 583401,4821059. Late-season snow can make the last 0.2 mile impassable. This is the only public access for the south side of Crane Mountain.

CAMPING

There is a designated camping area near the trailhead. Follow the East Path (page 166) for 300'. The marked site is on the left. There are also some high-mountain camping sites at several points along the shore of Crane Mountain Pond.

Jay Harrison on the first ascent of Sun Dogs (5.9+). Photo by Dick Tucker.

Crane Mountain

CRANE WEST

Location	West side of Crane, accessed from the Crane Mountain Trailhead
Summary	The most remote and difficult-to-access side of Crane with tall, sparsely explored cliffs.

9	3	3	1				16
-5.6	5.7	5.8	5.9	5.10	5.11	5.12	5.13+	total

There's a lot of potential on the west side of Crane. The difficult approach and raw state of the routes keep people away, especially with the east side so tantalizingly close. So far, explorations have been limited to the Wayout Wall and Beaverview Wall. The Wayout Wall especially has many cracks ripe and ready for plucking (where "plucking" means exhaustive cleaning).

Crane Mountain • Crane West

WAYOUT WALL

Aspect	Southwest
Height	140'
Quality	★
Approach	1 hr 30 min, difficult
Summary	A steep, clean cliff with one very good 5.9 route as well as many unclimbed cracks and corners.

3	2	1					6
-5.6	5.7	5.8	5.9	5.10	5.11	5.12	5.13+	total

The Wayout Wall has one of the more strenuous approaches at Crane, but interesting in that it follows a unique brook past a natural bridge, and a slot canyon. There are only a few climbs here, most notably Sun Dogs, a beautiful system of geometric corners.
The wall has great potential for new routes.

DIRECTIONS (MAP PAGE 142)

From the trail register at the parking area (0 min), go left and take the trail marked with red discs that follows a jeep road to a junction (20 min) with a sign that points right for the pond and summit (the Crane Pond Outlet Trail). Go right and hike uphill for 300' to a natural bridge over the outlet stream from the beaver pond on the right. Cross the natural bridge, leave the trail, and hike left (northwest) along a level bench to a waterfall (25 min) on the right (east) that descends from Crane Mountain Pond. Cross the base of the waterfall and continue north on the level bench beneath a long cliffband (known as Putnam Farm Wall, on private land) on the right (east). The left end of Putnam Farm Wall is at a height of land with thickets and a talus field on the right (east). Pass over the height of land (40 min) and pick up a stream on the left (west) that drains to the north. Follow the stream past several house-sized boulders and a slot canyon to another talus field. At a house-sized boulder (1 hr 10 min) that is split into three sections, leave the stream and follow a tributary to the right (northwest) to a talus field. Cross the talus field to

Indian Lake

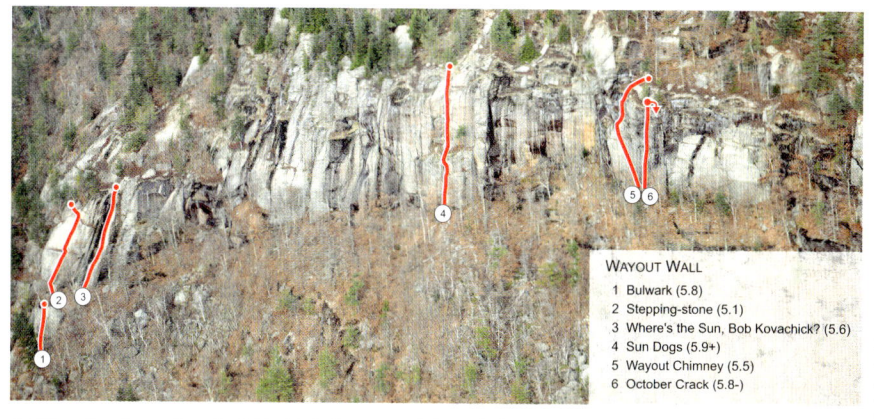

WAYOUT WALL
1 Bulwark (5.8)
2 Stepping-stone (5.1)
3 Where's the Sun, Bob Kovachick? (5.6)
4 Sun Dogs (5.9+)
5 Wayout Chimney (5.5)
6 October Crack (5.8-)

a cliffband, walk up along its right side to its top, and continue straight uphill to the Wayout Wall (1 hr 30 min) 582086,4823342.

1 Bulwark 5.8 G 25'

Start: At the left end of the cliff is a low-angle face with a short, steep cliffband at its base. Traverse down and left beneath the cliffband to a slab. Immediately downhill from the slab is a small cliff; approach by scrambling around its (skier's) left end. Begin below a left-facing corner in the center of the cliff.
P1 5.8 G: (V1) Up the clean corner to its top. 25'
V1 5.9 TR: Climb the left-hand corner.
Descent: Walk off to the right.
FA Aug 2, 1996, Jay Harrison, Dick Tucker

2 Stepping-stone 5.1 G 150'

Start: At the left end of the cliff is a low-angle face with a short, steep cliffband at its base. Traverse down and left beneath the cliffband to the base of a slab and begin at its left side.
P1 5.1 G: Up and left along a narrow, vegetated ledge, then up a vertical crack. Belay at a ledge on the left. 150'
Descent: Use the gully on the left.
FA Aug 2, 1996, Jay Harrison

3 Where's the Sun, Bob Kovachick? 5.6 R 130'

Start: 40' right of **Stepping Stone**, at a clean strip of slab bounded on each side by dark, dank stripes of moss.
P1 5.6 R: Go up near the left side of the clean slab (runout). At the end of the clean rock, step up and left through moss to belay at a tree. 130'
Descent: Two-rope rappel.
FA Oct 23, 2011, Garth Briscoe, Mike Prince

4 Sun Dogs 5.9+ G 150' ★★★

This route (and perhaps the unclimbed routes to either side) is the reason anyone would hike this far. Steep, geometric corners.
Start: Right of the low-angle face at the left side of the cliff are several right-facing corners beneath a tall, vertical wall. Begin at the leftmost of the right-facing corners that is 75' right of a ground-level slab, at a waist-high overhang and a triangular flake 15' up.
P1 5.9+ G: Up the right-facing corner to a stance beneath a ceiling in an orange-colored V-slot. Climb a crack out the left side of the ceiling to a tree belay on the vegetated ledge above. 80'
P2 5.8 G: Work up the rightmost of two parallel cracks to a left-facing corner, then follow it to an overhang. Belay at a tree 50' above the overhang. 70'
Descent: Rappel from trees using two ropes.
FA Jul 2, 1996, Jay Harrison, Rich Clifford, Dick Tucker

5 Wayout Chimney 5.5 G 95'

Start: At a chimney 200' right of **Sun Dogs**. This is 20' left of a 35'-tall, detached section of cliff with a cave behind it, and on its left side is a sweeping, right-rising edge.
P1 5.5 G: Chimney up to stacked blocks and climb easily up to the top of the chimney. Go up a wet slab to brushy slopes above. 95'
Descent: Walk up and right 40', then down to a pine tree in an alcove and rappel (same as **October Crack**).
FA Oct 11, 2011, Jay Harrison (solo)

6 October Crack 5.8- G 85'

If it wasn't for the stacked death-blocks at mid-height, this would be a decent route.
Start: Right of **Wayout Chimney**, at a fist–arm crack between **Wayout Chimney** and a detached 35'-tall mega-flake with a cave behind it and a sweeping, right-rising loft edge.
P1 5.8- G: Up the crack to a sloping stance below a block-filled alcove. Chimney up and climb left onto the outside corner to avoid blocks, then go up to another sloping ledge. Climb up to overhang and through it via a crack to a large, sloping ledge on the right, then step up and left onto the top. 85'
Descent: Rappel from pine tree.
FA Oct 11, 2011, Jay Harrison (roped solo)

145

Indian Lake

Crane Mountain • Crane West
BEAVERVIEW CLIFF

Aspect	South
Height	300'
Quality	★
Approach	1 hr, moderate
Summary	Multipitch moderate routes on a low-angle cliff.

6	3	1					10
-5.6	5.7	5.8	5.9	5.10	5.11	5.12	5.13+	total

Beaverview Cliff, easily seen from a beaver pond near the Crane Pond Outlet Trail, is a broad, tall, low-angle cliff capped by roofs.

DIRECTIONS (MAP PAGE 142)
From the trail register (0 min) at the parking lot, turn left and take the trail marked with red discs that follows a jeep road to a junction (20 min) with a sign that points right for the pond and summit (the Crane Pond Outlet Trail). Go right and follow the hiking trail uphill for 300' to a natural bridge over the outlet stream from the beaver pond on the right. Leave the trail before the bridge and hike around the beaver pond on its right (south) side, where the cliff is visible up and right. Continue to the far end of the beaver pond and follow the inlet stream for 200'. Follow cairns and a compass bearing of 60° directly uphill past a bench with boulders, a short cliff-band, and a final talus field with thickets beneath Dark Speed (1 hr) 582938,4821832.

DESCENT OPTIONS
Rappel with two ropes from trees left of the routes, hike down the right end of the cliff, or walk uphill to the hiking trail beneath the Summit Cliffs and go right.

1 Requiem Pro Patris 5.8- G 90' ★★
Start: About 250' left of the Dark Speed corner, on a small ledge above a 20'-high, very dirty slab, below a line of pockets along a left-rising seam. High above, a pine tree grows vertically from a 15' horizontal trunk.
P1 5.8- G: Climb face and pockets to a stance below a narrow face with several good, discontinuous vertical cracks. Climb this face via several cracks, passing left of the peculiar pine tree to a good ledge. 90'
Descent: Rappel from trees.
FA Oct 5, 2011, Jay Harrison (roped solo)

2 King and I 5.7 G (5.4 R) 140' ★★★
Start: 20' up from the low end of a slab, at a 15'-long crack that fades out 20' below a short, steep face. This is near the left edge of a lower-angled, 50'-wide, wetter section of slab, bracketed by large corners on either side. The ground to the right is covered with ferns. This is about 200' left of the Dark Speed corner.
P1 5.7 G (5.4 R): Go up the crack to its end, then climb a slab without protection up and right to the base of the headwall (V1). Climb the headwall stemming vertical cracks, then continue up along the edge of a corner using vertical cracks, past a short, low-angle, clean slab to an overhang. Pull directly through the overhang just left of an arête, up to a large, sloping ledge, then step left to belay at a large pine tree. 140'
Descent: Rappel into the fern glade to climber's right, then scramble down to the base.
V1 5.7 G: The runout slab near the bottom can be skipped by scrambling up the fern- and bramble-cov-

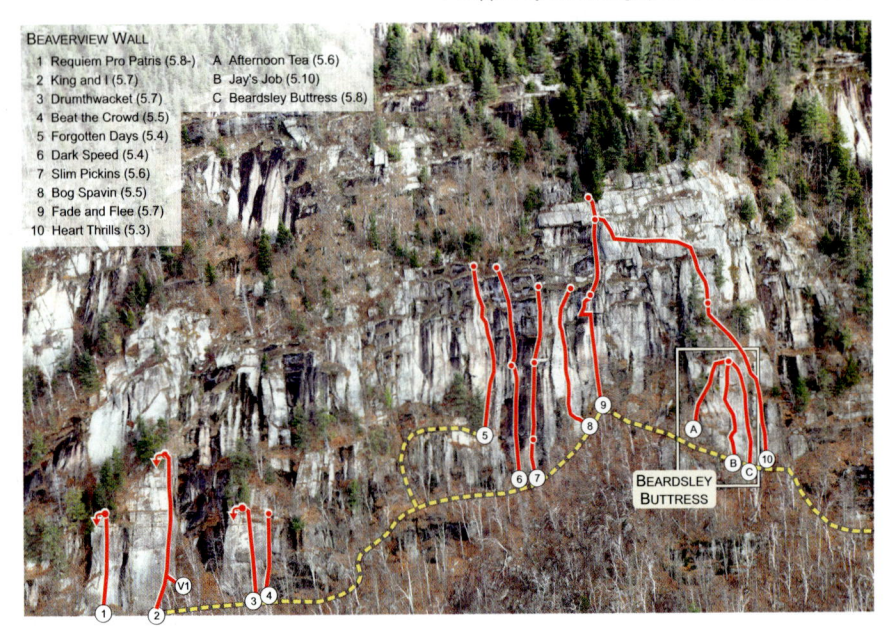

BEAVERVIEW WALL
1 Requiem Pro Patris (5.8-)   A Afternoon Tea (5.6)
2 King and I (5.7)   B Jay's Job (5.10)
3 Drumthwacket (5.7)   C Beardsley Buttress (5.8)
4 Beat the Crowd (5.5)
5 Forgotten Days (5.4)
6 Dark Speed (5.4)
7 Slim Pickins (5.6)
8 Bog Spavin (5.5)
9 Fade and Flee (5.7)
10 Heart Thrills (5.3)

BEARDSLEY BUTTRESS

Indian Lake

ered slope to a treed stance below a cave in the large inside corner. Move out left on good holds onto the main face, then follow the route as normal.
FA Nov 5, 2011, Jay Harrison, Travis King

3 Drumthwacket 5.7 PG 80' ★★
Start: 50' right of a fern patch below a slab bounded by corners facing each other, at a hand crack 10' left of a chimney.
P1 5.7 PG: Climb the crack to its end. Move up right for gear in another crack (possible to left as well), then up left to yet another vertical crack. Follow this up easier rock to a narrow ledge and walk 8' left to a pine tree. 80'
FA Nov 11, 2011, Tom Lane, Jay Harrison

4 Beat the Crowd 5.5 PG 80'
You won't have to stand in line for this one. If there were anti-stars, this would warrant a couple.
Start: At a chimney 60' right of the fern patch.
P1 5.5 PG: Climb a chimney past a large, dirty ledge, through an overhang, then up a brush-filled slope until level with pine trees to the left. 80'
FA Nov 11, 2011, Jay Harrison, Tom Lane

5 Forgotten Days 5.4 R 175'
Start: Locate Dark Speed. Scramble up the steep, tree-covered slope left of the 150'-high corner. Begin at a shallow right-facing, right-arching corner that is halfway between the start of Dark Speed and the highest vegetation on the upper slope.
P1 5.4 R: Up the corner, then face-climb up and left to a vertical crack (good gear). Step left and face-climb up, then right to another crack. Traverse left around an arête, then up moss-covered ledges to the top. 175'
FA Jun 9, 1999, Jay Harrison, Dick Tucker

6 Dark Speed 5.4 PG 235' ★★
Start: Locate an open grass-covered slope beneath a broad, tall, and clean slab 50' right of a 150'-high right-facing, right-arching corner. Begin in a smaller, shallow right-facing corner on the left side of the slab.
P1 5.4 G: Up the shallow right-facing corner to its end. 130'
P2 5.4 PG: Climb a slab to a zigzag handcrack. At its end, climb another slab and two overlaps to the top of the cliff. 105'
FA Oct 19, 1997, Dick Tucker, Jay Harrison

7 Slim Pickins 5.6 PG (5.4 X) 300' ★
Start: 10' right of the start to Dark Speed, beneath an overlap 40' up.
P1 5.6 PG: Up a left-rising seam to the overlap. 40'
P2 5.4 X: Face-climb past incipient seams and an overlap (protection) to a belay at a large pine tree. 170'
P3 5.6 G: Up to the left end of large roofs, then follow a large left-facing corner to the top. 90'
FA May 4, 2007, Jay Harrison

8 Bog Spavin 5.5 R 200'
Some good climbing, some bad, and some long runouts.
Start: 60' right of Slim Pickins, near the left side of the highest point of the terrain along the base of the main face, climb up a brushy ramp to a tree ledge with a large rectangular flake.
P1 5.5 R: Up cracks and flakes, then up a slab to connect with another series of cracks. Follow these to a bushy shelf under a huge roof. 200'
FA Oct, 2011, Tom Lane, Jay Harrison

9 Fade and Flee 5.7 R 300'
Start: Uphill from and right of the slab and right-facing corner of Dark Speed, on top of a 25'-tall buttress with a grassy stance and a table-sized flake on the right.

Tom Lane getting creative cleaning Drumthwacket (5.7). Photo by Jay Harrison.

P1 5.7 R: Climb a moss-covered depression into a V-slot that leads to a long overhang split by a vertical crack. Traverse around the left end of the overhang, up a corner, then back right (no protection) to a belay in the vertical crack. 150'
P2 5.7 PG: Work up and right beneath the lower of two roof systems at the right end of the cliff. Climb through the roof at the chimney-slot and belay at a small tree above. 100'
P3 5.3 PG: Step left of the vegetation and climb a slab to the top. 50'
FA Jul, 1995, Rick Villanueve, Jay Harrison

Beardsley Buttress

250' right of the slab of Dark Speed is a low-angle buttress with a left-facing corner on its left side. There are three toprope routes, each about 100' high, located on the center of the buttress: Afternoon Tea (5.6 TR; 95'; Oct 17, 1996; Dick Tucker) follows a zigzag crack, Jay's Job (5.10 TR; 95'; Oct 17, 1996; Jay Harrison, Dick Tucker, Rick Beardsley) climbs a flared fistcrack, and Beardsley Buttress (5.8 TR; 100'; Oct 17, 1996; Rick Beardsley) climbs incipient cracks of the right side. All the routes are dirty. The top of the wall can be accessed by climbing P1 of Heart Thrills or by scrambling up the left side (some 4th class).

End of Beardsley Buttress

10 Heart Thrills 5.3 PG 300'
Start: 50' right of Beardsley Buttress at a 20'-tall, low-angle left-facing corner.
P1 4th class: Climb the left-facing corner, then traverse left to the right-facing wall (formed by the right side of Beardsley Buttress) and climb the right-facing corner to the top of the buttress. 100'
P2 5.3 PG: Work up and left to an overhang; clear this (crux), then step left and follow a weakness in a headwall. Traverse left across the top of a chimney to the tree belay of Fade and Flee. 150'
P3 5.3 PG: Step left of the vegetation and climb a slab to the top. 50'
FA Jun, 1995, Jay Harrison

Crane Mountain • Crane West
NORTHERN KNOB

This is the southwest-facing cliff high on the hill north of Crane Mountain Pond, across from its outlet 583031,4822665. There's one reported route here, Garden Alone (5.3 PG; 50'; Aug 1996; Jay Harrison, solo), that climbs a left-facing corner high on the cliff.

Northern Knob.

Crane Mountain
CENTRAL CRANE

| Location | Mid-height on the mountain accessed from the summit hiking trail. |
| Summary | Mostly easier routes and topropes. |

14	1	5	1	1			22
-5.6	5.7	5.8	5.9	5.10	5.11	5.12	5.13+	total

The cliffs of Central Crane are positioned alongside and accessed from the summit hiking trail. So far this area has yielded easier routes and topropes. Good potential exists right of Tablerock Cliff, between it and the Upper Walls of the South Corner Cliff.

Crane Mountain • Central Crane
BROWN SLAB

Aspect	South
Height	250'
Quality	★
Approach	30 min, moderate
Summary	A clean, low-angle slab with several vertical cracks and seams.

8							8
-5.6	5.7	5.8	5.9	5.10	5.11	5.12	5.13+	total

The Brown Slab contains many vertical cracks and seams. Additional routes have been reported and were climbed solo or without protection. The routes described here are the better-protected ones. Expect to find grass-filled cracks and some mossy sections. The Brown Slab is divided into the Main Slab and the Father's Day Slab, which is below the left end of the Main Slab.

Some routes have been omitted because, as Jay Harrison notes, you can walk about the slab at will. These include Silly Willy (5.3 X; 170'; Sep 16, 1995; Dick Tucker), the third crack left of Silly; Sunday Stroll (5.4 X; 170'; Sep 16, 1995; Dick Tucker), the second crack left of Silly); and Fatal Ease (5.3 X; 200'; Sep 1995; Jay Harrison), between Badinage and Morning Stars.

DIRECTIONS (MAP PG 142)
From the parking area (0 min), follow the hiking trail uphill toward the summit, past a table-sized slab of rock in the trail at 15 min (the marker for Tablerock Crag) to an intersection with an arrow that points right (20 min). A short spur trail leads left (west) to the top of Viewpoint Cliff, where the Brown Slab is visible (northwest) from the left end of the viewpoint.

Indian Lake

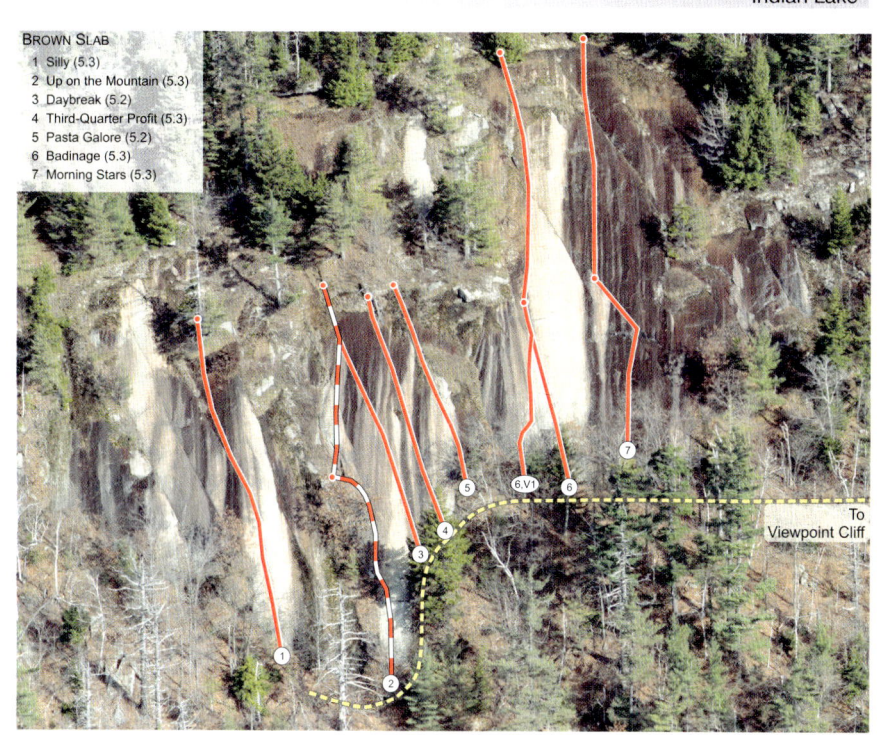

BROWN SLAB
1 Silly (5.3)
2 Up on the Mountain (5.3)
3 Daybreak (5.2)
4 Third-Quarter Profit (5.3)
5 Pasta Galore (5.2)
6 Badinage (5.3)
7 Morning Stars (5.3)

To Viewpoint Cliff

From this intersection, bushwhack west beneath Viewpoint Cliff at 25 min. Continue northwest over to the base of the Brown Slab, meeting it at its right end (30 min) **583299,4821713**.

DESCENT OPTIONS
Hike around either end of the slab.

Main Slab

Two vertical strips of vegetation divide the Main Slab into thirds, with **Silly** on the left slab; **Up on the Mountain**, **Daybreak**, **Third Quarter Profit**, and **Pasta Galore** on the middle slab; and **Badinage** and **Morning Star** on the right slab.

1 Silly 5.3 X 170'
Unprotected but easy climbing; starting left of the tree island is easier and offers some protection (5.2 R).
Start: At the left end of the Main Slab and right of a tree island 5' up.
P1 5.3 X: Up left-rising seams to an unprotected slab that leads to a tree belay at the top. 170'
FA Sep 16, 1995, Dick Tucker

2 Up on the Mountain 5.3 R (5.0 X) 250' ★★
Start: At the low point of the Main Slab between two vegetated ramps.
P1 5.3 R: Climb the dirty slab to an 8'-long overlap 20' up. Work up and left to gain a vertical seam, then climb it to a tree belay on the left. 120'

P2 5.0 X: An easy friction pitch heads up and right to the top of the slab. 130'
FA Jun, 1994, Jay Harrison

3 Daybreak 5.2 PG (5.0 X) 240'
Climbs the grass-filled crack in the slab between the two vegetated ramps.
Start: Between two vegetated ramps, 15' up from and right of the low point of the Main Slab, at a grass-filled vertical crack and right of an 8'-long overlap.
P1 5.2 PG: Follow the crack and belay at its top. 110'
P2 5.0 X: An easy friction pitch heads up and right to the top of the slab. 130'
FA Jun, 1994, Jay Harrison

4 Third-Quarter Profit 5.3 R 120'
Originally started from the lowest point of the Main Slab and climbed the initial section of **Daybreak**; the higher start described here makes more sense.
Start: Left of the rightmost of two vegetated ramps, at the highest point along the base of the slab.
P1 5.3 R: Up and left to a vertical crack. Follow the crack to its end and finish left of a fallen tree. 120'
FA Oct 1, 1995, Dick Tucker

5 Pasta Galore 5.2 G 100'
Start: At a vertical seam that is immediately left of the rightmost of two vegetated ramps, at the highest point along the base of the Main Slab.
P1 5.2 G: Follow the vertical seam to the top. 100'
FA Jun 15, 1997, Dick Tucker, Jay Harrison

Indian Lake

6 Badinage 5.3 R (5.0 X) 200'
Start: Right of the rightmost of two vegetated ramps at a vertical crack with an overlap to its left 15' up.
P1 5.3 R: Up the vertical crack, which becomes a right-facing corner, (V1) past the overlap, to a belay at the top of the crack. 100'
P2 5.0 X: Friction between two vertical flakes and up to the top. 100'
V1 Sword Breaker 5.2 PG: Undercling the overlap to the left, and layback the thin flake to its end. Traverse right to the vertical crack.
FA Sep 16, 1995, Dick Tucker

7 Morning Stars 5.3 PG (5.0 X) 200' ★★
Start: (V1) At the right end of the Main Slab, beneath a clean slab and a long overlap 50' up.
P1 5.3 PG: Unprotected climbing leads to the overlap split by a vertical crack. Climb the crack and belay at its top below a slab. 90'
P2 5.0 X: Climb to the top of the slab. 110'
V1 Golden Sheaves 5.2 X: An easier start begins 30' up and right and follows a seam to a long overlap.
FA Jun, 1994, Jay Harrison

Father's Day Slab

Located immediately below the left end of the Main Slab. To reach its base, scramble around the (skier's) left side of the slab. Two additional routes were climbed on the right side of the slab but are completely overgrown and unclimbable: **Dad's Day Off** (5.4 R; 110'; Jun 15, 1997; Jay Harrison, Dick Tucker), and **New Beginning** (5.2 PG; 90'; Jun 15, 1997; Dick Tucker, Jay Harrison).

8 Father's Day 5.4 G 110'
Start: Begin beneath a short right-facing corner near the low point.
P1 5.4 G: Climb up to the corner. Take the seam above, then step right and climb the slab past two hollow flakes to the top. 110'
FA Jun 15, 1997, Dick Tucker, Jay Harrison

Crane Mountain • Central Crane
VIEWPOINT CLIFF

Aspect	South
Height	130'
Quality	★
Approach	25 min, easy
Summary	Slab routes, some of which are topropes and all have poor protection.

3	1	4	1	1		10
-5.6	5.7	5.8	5.9	5.10	5.11	5.12	5.13+	total

You pass this 100' -wide cliff on the way to the Brown Slab. All routes begin on steep terrain, but finish on low-angle friction with sparse protection. All of the routes can be toproped.

HISTORY
This cliff was described in the first edition as a "minor cliff" with two routes mentioned, **Every Creature's Theme** and **Puzzle**, which Jay Harrison climbed early in Crane's history. He returned in 2008 to fill in the blanks.

DIRECTIONS (MAP PAGE 142)
You pass this cliff on the way to Brown Slab.
From the parking area (0 min), follow the hiking trail uphill toward the summit, past a table-sized slab of rock in the trail at 15 min (the marker for Tablerock Crag) to an intersection with an arrow that points right (20 min). A short spur trail leads left (west) to the top of Viewpoint Cliff. From this intersection, bushwhack west to the base of Viewpoint Cliff at 25 min 583358,4821628.
You arrive at the cliff at its right end. The easiest routes to identify are **Every Creature's Theme**, **Scenic Slip**, and **Puzzle**.

1 Every Creature's Theme
5.5 PG (5.2 R) 130' ★★
Start: At the far left side of the cliff below a left-facing corner that diminishes up higher to a rounded flap.
P1 5.5 PG (5.3 R): (V1, V2) Climb the corner to its end, then friction to the birch and spruce belay tree station on the far left edge of the Viewpoint Ledge. 130'
V1 5.7 TR: Friction up the slab left of the corner.
V2 5.4 G (5.3 R): Begin 8' right of the corner and climb a crack–corner on the right that joins the route 12' up.
FA Jun, 1993, Jay Harrison (solo)

2 Fifty-Foot Fright Fest 5.9+ TR 130'
Begin 5' right of the V2 variation of **Every Creature's Theme** (or 13' right of the start of **Every Creature's Theme**), at the lowest point of the slab. A bouldery lunge and mantle to small edges lead to tenuous friction climbing, staying 8' right of **Every Creature's Theme**. Belay as for **Every Creature's Theme**.
FA (TR) May, 2008, Jay Harrison

3 Slab Happy 5.8 TR 130' ★
The best exercise in pure friction at the cliff. Begin 8' right of the lowest point on the slab at a left-rising crack that fades 12' up. This is 20' right of **Every Creature's Theme**. Up the crack to its top, then up the right side of the blunt nose (crux) on continuously tricky friction for thirty feet to easier ground. Belay as for **Every Creature's Theme**.
FA (TR) May, 2008, Jay Harrison

4 The Good Book 5.8 TR 130'
Begin 4' right of the left-rising crack of **Slab Happy**, below a shallow, rounded open book. Climb up to and through the open book, then straight up the friction slab, meeting **Scenic Slip** just above the corner. Belay same as **Every Creature's Theme**.
FA (TR) May, 2008, Jay Harrison

5 Scenic Slip 5.7 PG 130' ★★
Start: 20' right of the left-rising crack of **Slab Happy** at a left-rising seam that becomes a sharply-defined, left-facing, left-slanting corner.
P1 5.7 PG: Climb the left-rising seam and left-facing corner to its top, then go straight up to Viewpoint

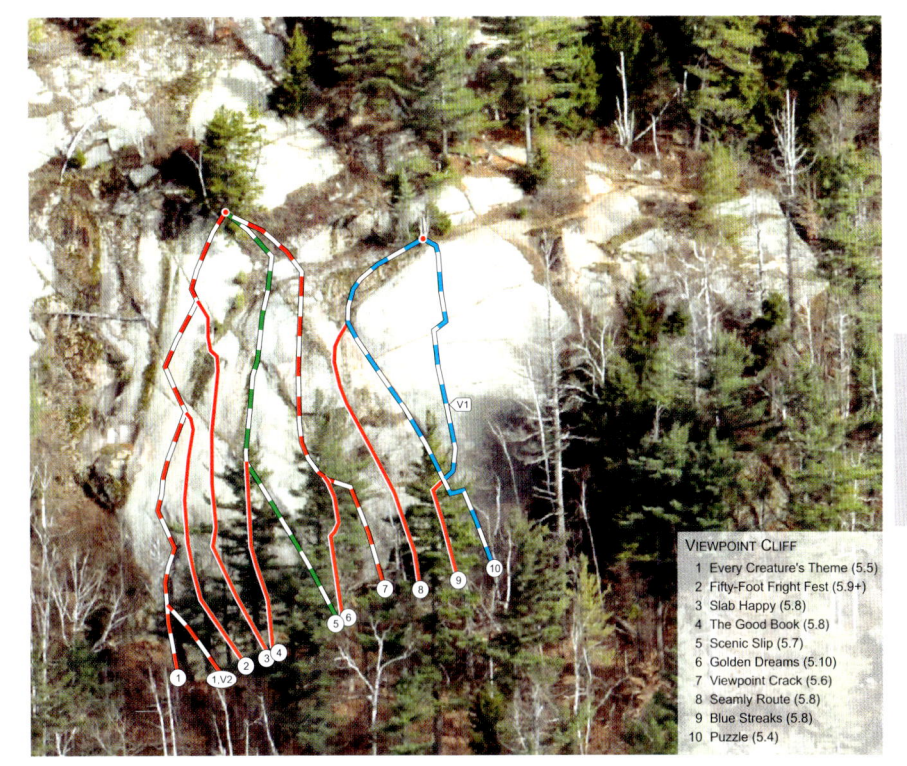

Indian Lake

VIEWPOINT CLIFF
1 Every Creature's Theme (5.5)
2 Fifty-Foot Fright Fest (5.9+)
3 Slab Happy (5.8)
4 The Good Book (5.8)
5 Scenic Slip (5.7)
6 Golden Dreams (5.10)
7 Viewpoint Crack (5.6)
8 Seamly Route (5.8)
9 Blue Streaks (5.8)
10 Puzzle (5.4)

Ledge. Belay as for Every Creature's Theme, or in the tree island on Viewpoint Ledge. 130'
FA May 28, 2008, Jay Harrison (solo)

6 Golden Dreams 5.10 TR 130'
Begin below the orange face 3' right of Scenic Slip at a double-edged flake. Up the flake onto the face. Work up the left edge of the orange rock, then move toward the center of the orange rock. Join Viewpoint Crack just before the overhang above the grass island.
FA (TR) May, 2008, Jay Harrison

7 Viewpoint Crack 5.6 PG 130' ★
Start: 13' right of Scenic Slip, at a left-leaning crack that begins at a small overhang 12' up.
P1 5.6 PG: Delicately gain the crack (crux) which is climbed to its top. Skirt the left edge of a grass island to the left edge of an overhang (Golden Dreams joins here). Break the overhang on the left side on knobs, then go straight up to Viewpoint Ledge. 130'
FA May 23, 2008, Jay Harrison (solo)

8 Seamly Route 5.8 R 110'
Start: At a pair of faint seams (one of which becomes a shallow crack above), 8' right of Viewpoint Crack and 5' left of Blue Streaks.
P1 5.8 R: Follow the seams up the steep wall past the brush island to where it becomes a crack. Continue up the crack through a small overhang in low-angled rock. 110'
FA Aug 20, 2008, Jay Harrison (solo)

9 Blue Streaks 5.8 R 125'
Start: 5' right of Viewpoint Crack and 7' left of Puzzle, below two blue–black water streaks under a flap.
P1 5.8 R: Initially tricky (and unprotected) moves lead to better holds, then to an undercling at the flap 18' up. Up over the flap to a narrow ledge, then straight up on a dirty, low-angle slab. 125'
FA Jul 7, 2008, Jay Harrison (solo)

10 Puzzle 5.4 G 120' ★★
The first route on the cliff and, with some cleaning, would be a worthwhile route.
Start: Near the right edge of the cliff (15' right of Blue Streaks) below the right of two parallel, left-slanting seams. The right seam reaches the ground and the left seam begins about 7' up.
P1 5.4 G: Climb the right seam until one can step left to use both seams. Go up to the right end of a small ledge and (V1) continue up and left in the crack. 120'
V1 5.4 X: Step right at the ledge and climb straight up the unprotected slab.
FA Jul 27, 1991, Jay Harrison (solo)

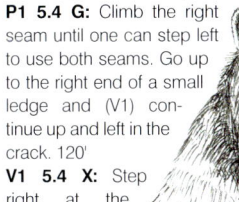

Pen and ink by Tad Welch.

Indian Lake

Crane Mountain • Central Crane
TABLEROCK CRAG

Aspect	South
Height	160'
Quality	
Approach	15 min, easy
Summary	An easily-approached cliff, with a couple of lower-quality, old routes.

```
  3       1                        4
 -5.6  5.7  5.8  5.9  5.10  5.11  5.12  5.13+  total
```

This minor cliff is directly on the summit hiking trail (this trail is also used to approach the Brown Slab and the Summit Cliffs). It is up from and right of a table-sized slab of rock in the trail. The cliff is reasonably tall but the routes aren't well protected and are of lower quality than those found elsewhere on the mountain, including those at the Viewpoint Cliff or the Summit Cliffs.

HISTORY
This cliff holds the some of the earliest climbing at Crane, namely Bill Pierce's lost route believed to be right of Pine Tree Corner.

DESCENT OPTIONS
Walk left to the hiking trail.

DIRECTIONS (MAP PAGE 142)
From the parking area (0 min), follow the hiking trail uphill toward the summit, to a table-sized slab of rock in the trail at 15 min. The cliff sits on the right side of the trail 583430,4821149.

1 Pinus Strobus 5.8 G 80'
The name is Latin for "eastern white pine". The start is unprotected 5.4.
Start: 25' left and up from Tablerock Corner (and the large, flat, table-like boulder that marks this route), below a low-angle 20'-tall slab leading to a ledge with trees on either end.
P1 5.8 G: Climb the unprotected slab to the ledge. Work up to an alcove formed by a left-facing corner and right-leaning crack. (This alcove is right of a large pine tree growing up against the wall.) Go up the alcove and overhang at its apex, then wrestle a sapling to gain the top. 80'
FA May 16, 2008, Jay Harrison (solo)

2 Feeble 5.3 G 80'
A line that heads towards, then avoids all challenge.
Start: At the table-sized rock.
P1 5.3 G: Head up and left from the table-sized rock toward a crack in the steep upper headwall. Escape to the right of the crack through an obvious, broken slot. 80'
FA Jun, 1993, Jay Harrison (solo)

3 Tablerock Corner 5.3 R 160'
Start: At the table-sized rock.
P1 5.3 R: Go up to a shallow left-facing corner and follow this to a ledge. Swing up and right to a large red pine tree, then (V1) continue up the funky (and often wet) open book. 160'
V1 5.6 R: The arête on the left provides a more exciting, unprotected finish.
FA Aug, 1993, Jay Harrison (solo)

4 Pine Tree Corner 5.3 G 60'
Start: Walk 120' right on a ledge just above the trail to a right-facing corner with a pine tree 30' up, just before a broken area.
P1 5.3 G: Climb the corner past the tree to the top. 60'
FA Aug, 1992, Jay Harrison (solo)

TABLEROCK CRAG
1 Pinus Strobus (5.8)
2 Feeble (5.3)
3 Tablerock Corner (5.3)
4 Pine Tree Corner (5.3)

Indian Lake

Crane Mountain
SUMMIT CLIFFS

Location	Below the summit ridge accessed from the summit hiking trail.
Summary	Steep hiking to scenic routes on broken cliffbands.

16	7	10	4	3		42
-5.6	5.7	5.8	5.9	5.10	5.11	5.12	5.13+	total

The summit of Crane Mountain is a long, open ridge with a discontinuous cliffband that rises above a level bench. Conveniently, the hiking trail traverses beneath the cliffband, breaks through it via a big ladder, and crosses the open ledges above the routes. Because of the exposure, the routes on the Summit Cliffs are naturally clean but contain sections of loose rock. In addition to the routes listed below, many toprope possibilities exist.

Since the first edition, more routes have been added and foggy memories refreshed. As a result, this section has been updated (in some cases routes have been moved), the various cliffs renamed, and directions simplified.

DIRECTIONS   (MAP PAGE 142)
From the parking area (0 min), head up the hiking trail, past the table-sized rock at 15 min (which marks the position of Tablerock Crag), past Viewpoint Cliff (on the left at 20 min), to a small ladder (four steps) beneath the level bench 583484,4821890 at 50 min. The small ladder is a landmark for the approach to the Sweeper Wall and the Firecamp Wall. The trail swings right (southeast) and breaks though the Summit Cliffs at a second 30'-tall ladder at 1 hr 583853,4821794. This "big ladder" is the landmark for approaching the True Summit Cliff and The Prows. You can approach Pondview Wall by continuing along the trail above the big ladder.

Crane Mountain • Summit Cliffs
PONDVIEW WALL

Aspect	West
Height	120'
Quality	
Approach	1 hr 30 min, difficult
Summary	Seldom-visited cliff facing Crane Mountain Pond; has a good steep clean wall on its left side.

1		1				3
-5.6	5.7	5.8	5.9	5.10	5.11	5.12	5.13+	total

Located at the left (northwest) end of the Summit Cliffs, Pondview Wall is steep, clean, and faces west toward Crane Mountain Pond.

DIRECTIONS   (MAP PAGE 142)
Above the big ladder (1 hr from the trailhead) the trail goes left (northwest) across the summit ridge at 1 hr 5 min. Before the trail descends steeply into the woods on the other side of the mountain, there is a spur trail on the left (south) that goes 50' to a viewpoint on top of Pondview Wall, reached at 1 hr 20 min. Continue downhill (west) on the hiking trail toward the pond for 50', turn left (south) and drop over two ledges, then turn left again (east) toward a left-facing wall. Follow the wall to a gully and cross this to the sheer left end of Pondview Wall 583478,4822125, reached at 1 hr 30 min.

PONDVIEW WALL
1 Pajama Sam (5.9)
2 Scruffy (5.2)
3 To Bee or Not to Bee (5.7 A0)

1 Pajama Sam 5.9 TR 60' ★
20' right of a short right-facing wall is a chest-sized block beneath a left-rising flake. Climb the flake to a vertical fistcrack that becomes a squeeze chimney.
FA (TR) Aug 30, 1997, Dick Tucker

2 Scruffy 5.2 G 60'
Start: In the center of the wall at wedged blocks between two opposing corners.
P1 5.2 G: Climb the blocks to a left-rising ramp, then follow it to the top of the cliff. 60'
FA Jun 18, 1996, Jay Harrison

3 To Bee or Not to Bee 5.7 A0 120' ★
Named in honor of some pesky bees.
Start: At the right end of the cliff at a small clearing beneath a sheer wall with a perched boulder 20' up.
P1 5.7 A0 G: Up discontinuous cracks to a belay on the ledge next to the boulder. 20'
P2 5.6 G: Move right and climb cracks and flakes on the face to the right of an arête. Climb to a ledge beneath an overhang and pass it on the left, then up to a stance beneath a steep wall. Go right along a rising ledge, then up vertical cracks to the top. 100'
FA Jun 29, 2003, Peter Bronski, Kelli Terry

153

Indian Lake

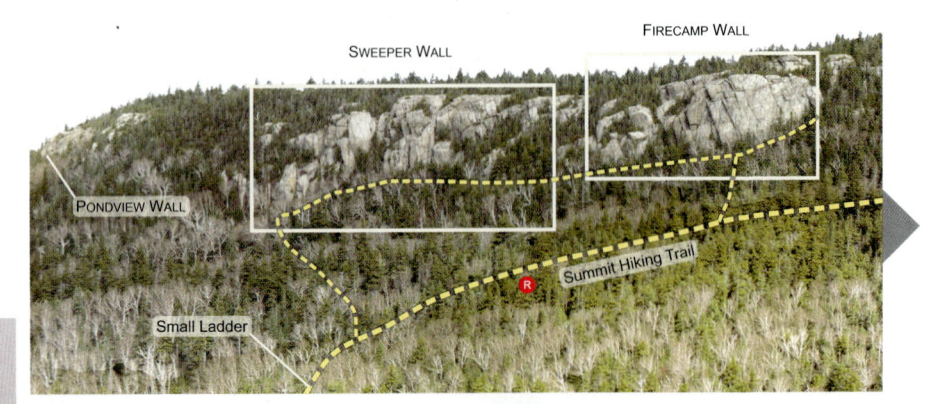

Crane Mountain • Summit Cliffs
SWEEPER WALL

Aspect	Southwest
Height	100'
Quality	★
Approach	1 hr, difficult
Summary	A wide, disjointed cliff with one really good route and excellent potential for more.

2	1	2	2	1		8
-5.6	5.7	5.8	5.9	5.10	5.11	5.12	5.13+	total

The Sweeper Wall[2] is the leftmost of the southwest-facing walls below the Summit Ridge Trail.

DIRECTIONS (MAP PAGE 142)
This wall comes into view just past the small ladder on the Summit Ridge Trail at 50 min. From the top of the small ladder, continue on the trail for 50' 0583246,4821735, then go left (north) into the woods and across a small marsh. Bushwhack steeply uphill, along the right side of an overgrown rockslide, to reach the left end of this low-angle, broken cliff, near an area of recent rockfall 0583789,4822194, reached 1 hr.

[2] In the first edition this was named the Dartmouth Wall.

DESCENT OPTIONS
Follow the Summit Ridge Trail to the (climber's) right (southeast) and down the big ladder.

4 Sweeper 5.5 G 90'
Start: At the extreme left end, in a slightly overgrown rockslide area, left of a sweeping left-facing corner, and below the right side of an overhang at head height.
P1 5.5 G: Climb through the right side of the overhang onto the face and up to a pair of left-arching cracks in orange rock. Up the cracks to their top, then scramble up easier rock to the top. 90'
FA May 29, 2008, Jay Harrison (roped solo)

5 Swept Away 5.8 G 90' ★
Start: 20' right of Sweeper, just left of a crack that sweeps up along the left side of a left-facing corner.
P1 5.8 G: Make a boulder move to gain a crack above blueberry bushes; follow this to its end. Step left around a bulge then up to a ledge. Continue up the crack in the corner to its top. 90'
FA May 29, 2008, Jay Harrison (roped solo)

6 Cripple Creek 5.8- G 110'
Start: Approximately 100' right of Swept Away. Walk right along the base of the cliff to a short, 12'-tall face split by a left-rising wide crack.

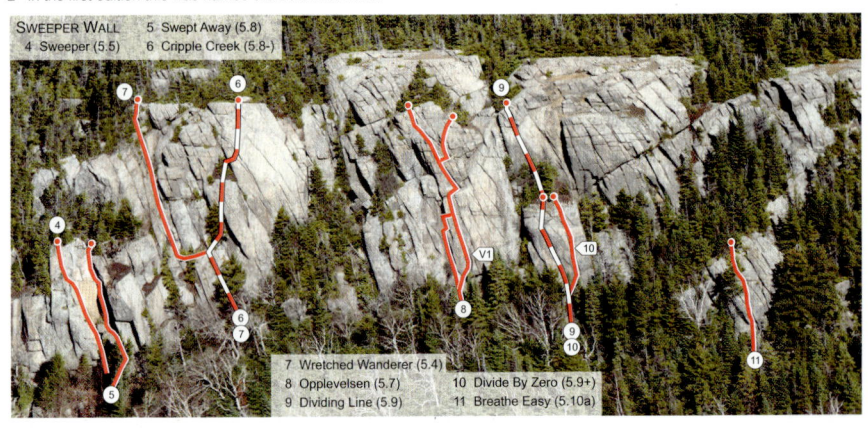

SWEEPER WALL
4 Sweeper (5.5)
5 Swept Away (5.8)
6 Cripple Creek (5.8-)
7 Wretched Wanderer (5.4)
8 Opplevelsen (5.7)
9 Dividing Line (5.9)
10 Divide By Zero (5.9+)
11 Breathe Easy (5.10a)

Indian Lake

True Summit Cliff   The Prows

Big Ladder

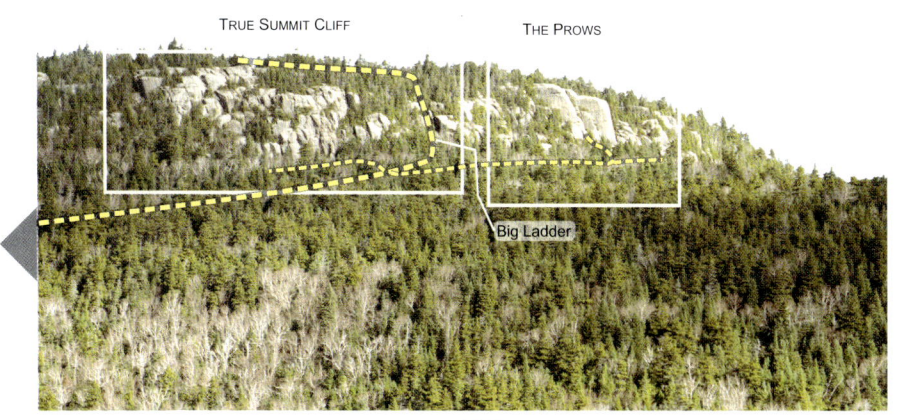

P1 5.8- G: Go up the crack to a dead spruce on a large ledge. Move right past a vegetated corner to a crack in a groove left of a large, brush-choked notch under an overhang. Go up this crack, under a bulging arête, and into a corner system. Continue up to a ledge, then make an airy traverse right onto a slab. Up this to the top. 110'
FA Apr 19, 2012, Jay Harrison

7 Wretched Wanderer 5.4 G 100'
Start: Same as Cripple Creek.
P1 5.4 G: Climb the crack to the ledge, then up a left-leaning, vegetated corner. Easier climbing leads to the top of the cliff. 100'
FA May, 1994, Jay Harrison

8 Opplevelsen 5.7 G 120' ★★
Currently dirty, but if cleaned, will be one of the better moderate routes on the Summit Cliffs.
Start: 50' left of Dividing Line at a cleared area with a large cairn, beneath a low-angled buttress with numerous cracks on its left side.
P1 5.7 G: (V1) Climb up the low-angled cracks left of a small, vegetated, left-facing corner. Scramble onto a boulder, step left around an arête and into a large, left-facing corner. Go up a wide crack in the corner to a stance with a horizontal crack leading out right. Take this onto the main face and follow vertical cracks to a sloping ledge. Go up a left-leaning, left-facing corner to an overhang. Traverse right to a wide crack and climb this to the top. 120'
V1 Opplevelsen Direct 5.8 G ★★★: Climb the vertical crack 10' right of the original start. Step left at its end to reach a crack breaking the overhang just right of the boulder. Climb the crack and join the original route: follow vertical cracks to a sloping ledge and go up a left-facing corner to an overhang. Pull through the final overhang and follow cracks to the top.
FA May 3, 2010, Jay Harrison (solo)
FA (V1) May 7, 2010, Jay Harrison, Bruce Monroe

9 Dividing Line 5.9 G 90' ★★
Start: 250' right of Sweeper, at a slab below a bulge 10' up. A striking handcrack cuts through the steep headwall above the bulge.
P1 5.9 G: Climb the short slab to a crack leading through a bulge, then up the handcrack in the steep headwall to a large sloping ledge. 50'
P2 5.2 G: Scramble up easy rock to the top. 40'
Descent: Rappel from trees, or descend a 5th class gully to the (climber's) right.
FA Jun 23, 2008, Jamie McNeill, Alysia Catalfamo, Jay Harrison

Jamie McNeill on the first ascent of Dividing Line (5.9). Photo by Jay Harrison.

155

Indian Lake

10 Divide By Zero 5.9+ TR 50' ★
Begin as for Dividing Line. Move up right to gain an offwidth crack. Up the offwidth to the rightmost crack that goes to the sloping ledge of Dividing Line.
FA (TR) Jun 23, 2008, Jay Harrison, Jamie McNeill

11 Breathe Easy 5.10a G 45' ★
Start: This route is easy to miss. From Dividing Line, walk right, cross a bush-filled gully, and traverse a steep, wooded slope beneath a short steep wall. Start beneath a crack in a left-facing, left-leaning corner 40' right of Dividing Line.
P1 5.10a G: Up the corner (crux) to its top, then traverse right 8' to a crack breaking an overhang. Over this to easier rock, to a belay in trees. 45'
History: Uphill and right of the P1 belay is a second pitch (Crusty; 5.6 PG; 35') up wide cracks. It's reportedly very dirty and not recommended.
FA May 7, 2010, Bruce Monroe, Jay Harrison

Crane Mountain • Summit Cliffs
FIRECAMP WALL

Aspect	Southwest
Height	120'
Quality	★★
Approach	1 hr 10 min, difficult
Summary	High-quality, moderate crack routes; the highest concentration of routes on the summit cliffs.

8	3	4	1	1		18
-5.6	5.7	5.8	5.9	5.10	5.11	5.12	5.13+	total

The Firecamp Wall[3] is visible while hiking between the small and big ladders, and is identified by a bulging face with vertical rock fins left of a large right-facing corner. It's named for the "firecamp", a sheltered campsite in a wooded pocket between the trail and the cliff face.

DIRECTIONS (MAP PAGE 142)
From the small ladder at 50 min, follow the trail for a few minutes past a few boulders on the left until you see a low cliffband 50' off the trail on the left 0583692,4821834. The deep corner of the Firecamp Wall (the route Free for All) is visible above the trail on the left. Leave the trail, hike around the left side of the low cliffband, and head directly uphill to reach the cliff at 1 hr 10 min. The landmark for the base of the wall is the Thank You, Cindy block—a 15'-tall block with a chimney on its left side that marks the start of Original Exploit 583707,4821861.

Alternatively, one can walk for 4 min from the right end of the Sweeper Wall (near Breathe Easy) to the left end of the Firecamp Wall (near Brighter Vision).

DESCENT OPTIONS
Rappel 80' from a tree with a fixed anchor located 25' right of the top of Carl's Climb. Alternatively, follow the Summit Ridge Trail to the right (southeast) and down the big ladder.

12 Brighter Visions 5.6 PG 60'
Start: Left of a forested dirt cone is a 30'-tall slab with a long, overhanging right-facing wall above it. Start at the longest, left-rising crack in the slab.
P1 5.6 PG: Up the left-leaning crack, which narrows to a seam beneath an overhang. Traverse right under the overhang, continue rightward past a notch, going under a bulge to a crack running up right of the bulge, and follow the crack to the top of the rock buttress. 60'
FA Sep, 1994, Jay Harrison, Gabe Linncourt

13 Darker Dreams 5.8 R (5.7 X) 65'
Harrison recollects this as "one of those things you're not quite certain you can get out of once you get in the middle of it."
Start: Below a left-rising seam 8' right of Brighter Visions
P1 5.8 R (5.7 X): Climb to the seam and up to the right edge of a large overhang. Climb directly through a notch to a ledge at the base of a steep wall with a left-rising crack that runs diagonal across the face. Up this crack a few feet, then reach right and step around onto the face of the arête. Climb this without protection to the top. 65'
FA Sep, 2008, Jay Harrison (solo)

14 Dartmouth Notch 5.8 PG 100'
You'll need a tetanus booster after climbing this one; not recommended.
Start: Immediately left of Gunga Din Chin at a cluttered gully leading to slabs and steeper rock.
P1 5.8 PG: Wallow through debris to a slab on the right side of the gully. Up this to a wide crack in a corner. Jam loose rocks through a steep bulge (crux) to a stance. Climb through the notch into a hellish tangle of small conifers, choss, and rusty wire onto a sloping dirty ramp between short walls, the right of which has "Dartmouth 1974" carved in it. Escape to the top. 100'
FA Apr 30, 2010, Jay Harrison, Bruce Monroe

15 Gunga Din Chin 5.10c TR 90' ★★
Begin 40' right of Brighter Visions below an overhanging arête with a V-notch 12' up. Climb the arête through the V-notch (5.8) and up using any of several cracks to a stance below the "chin." Up the buttress and out right onto the "chin" (crux), then up cracks and fins to the top.
FA (TR, upper section) Jul, 2008, Jamie McNeill, Jay Harrison
FA (TR, complete) Aug 21, 2008, Jay Harrison (toprope solo)

16 Paltry Show 5.2 G 150'
Start: Beneath a large, right-facing corner, down and right of an overhanging wall with vertical fins.
P1 5.2 G: (V1) Scramble up the bottom of the corner, then traverse left on a left-rising ramp beneath the overhanging wall. At the end of the ramp, step left across the top of the right-facing corner and continue leftward onto easier rock to the top. 150'
FA 1995, Jay Harrison

---
3 In the first edition this was named the Diagonal Wall.

Indian Lake

FIRECAMP WALL
12 Brighter Visions (5.6)
13 Darker Dreams (5.8)
14 Dartmouth Notch (5.8)
15 Gunga Din Chin (5.10c)
16 Paltry Show (5.2)
17 Mortal Strife (5.7 A1)
18 Free for All (5.6)
19 Knitel's Route (5.7)
20 Original Exploit (5.9)
21 Thank You, Cindy (5.7)
22 Amid the Flood (5.8-)
23 Carl's Climb (5.7)
24 Seam Ripper (5.8-)
25 Dairy Aire (5.5)
26 Cruise Crack (5.5)
27 Nervy (5.4)
28 Trouser Flute (5.5)
29 Exit Lite (5.5)

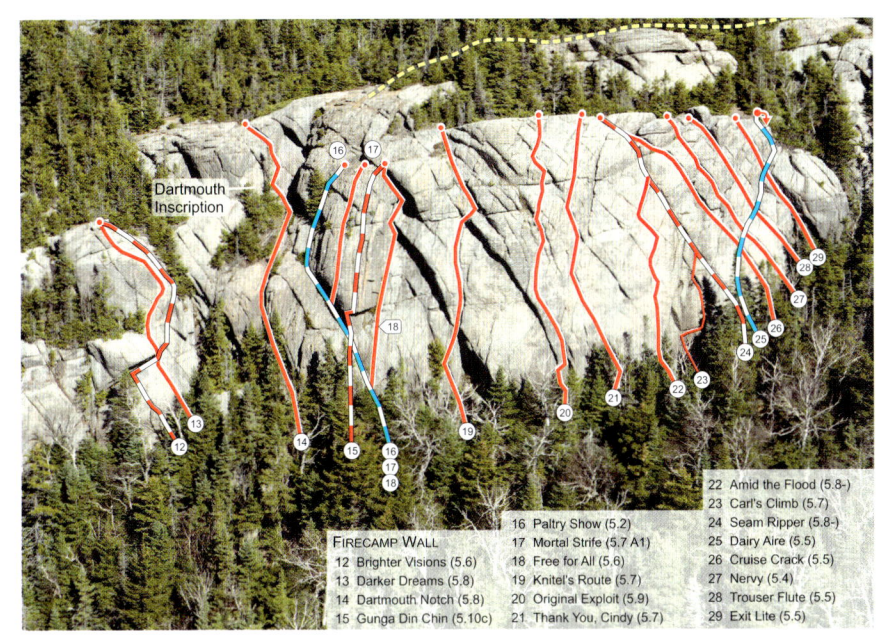

17 Mortal Strife 5.7 A1 170'
Start: Same as **Paltry Show**.
P1 5.7 A1 G: Halfway along the left-rising ramp of **Paltry Show** is a vertical crack. Climb the crack, with aid, to a low-angle finish. 170'
FA Jun, 1995, Jay Harrison, Gabe Linncourt

18 Free for All 5.6 G 150'
Start: Same as **Paltry Show**.
P1 5.6 G: Climb the large, right-facing corner to stepped ledges on the right wall. Go over the first step and continue up the corner. Escape to the left and climb to the top. 150'
FA 1997, Jay Harrison

19 Knitel's Route 5.7 G 100'
Start: Beneath an overhanging buttress with a low-angled corner–ramp to its left.
P1 5.7 G: Up the steepening corner. Move right into a corner with a wide crack, and follow this up along the right edge of the buttress to the top. 100'
History: Climbed by Neal Knitel thinking it was **Thank You, Cindy**.
FA 1996, Neal Knitel

20 Original Exploit 5.9 TR 90' ★★
Chimney up left side of the **Thank You, Cindy** block to a stance on top, then step left and climb a left-facing corner. Step right and climb the layback crack to the top.
FA (TR) 1993, Travis King, Jay Harrison

21 Thank You, Cindy 5.7 G 120' ★★★
Named in honor of Cindy, the belay slave on the route's first inspection.
Start: On the top, right side of the **Thank You, Cindy** block.

P1 5.7 G: Climb a left-facing corner past an overhang to a right-facing corner. Follow the corner, then climb a crack that goes left across a steep face and around a blunt arête to the top. 120'
FA Jun 15, 1991, Jay Harrison, Paul Medici

22 Amid the Flood 5.8- R 80'
A good line, but with ledge-fall potential.
Start: 6' left of **Carl's Climb** at a right-facing corner.
P1 5.8- R: Climb the corner 10' to a stance. Step up and left to a V-groove. Follow the groove its end, continue past several slanting cracks, and finish on the last moves of **Thank You, Cindy**. 80'
FA (TR) Sep, 1996, Jay Harrison, Carl Harrison
FA May 3, 2010, Jay Harrison (solo)

*Matt Wood follows **Thank You Cindy** (5.7). Photo by Jay Harrison.*

Indian Lake

23 Carl's Climb 5.7 PG 80' ★

Start: On a narrow grass ledge 25' up and right of the **Thank You, Cindy** block.
P1 5.7 PG: (V1) Climb a thin left-leaning crack, traverse right 4', and climb an overhang. Go up a crack through a notch and (V2) finish in a left-rising handcrack. 80'
V1 5.4 R: Used if the bottom seam is wet. Begin 4' right of the normal start (same as **Seam Ripper**) and climb up good holds for 8', then step left and join the original route beneath the overhang.
V2 Everywhere That Man Can Be 5.7 G: Continue straight to the top.
FA Sep, 1996, Jay Harrison, Carl Harrison
FA (V3) Sep 20, 1996, Jay Harrison, Carl Harrison

24 Seam Ripper 5.8- PG 70' ★★

Start: 4' right of **Carl's Climb** below a tight V-corner that ends 10' up.
P1 5.7 PG: Up the corner and onto the face above. Follow a left slanting crack to the top of **Thank You, Cindy**. 70'
FA Apr 20, 2010, Jay Harrison (roped solo)

25 Dairy Aire 5.5 PG 70' ★★

Start: 5' up and right of the tight V-notch of **Seam Ripper** where the face turns and begins slanting up a gully. A short crack is just out-of-reach up and left.
P1 5.5 PG: Up the orange face. Work back-and-forth across the wall (cross **Cruise Crack**), cross several left-rising cracks, to a short, steep headwall near the top. Make a tricky move right to gain wide cracks that go to an easy slab. Climb up and left to a fixed anchor. 70'
FA Apr 20, 2010, Jay Harrison (solo)

26 Cruise Crack 5.5 G 60' ★★★

Start: 15' uphill and right of **Seam Ripper**, at a clean, left-rising handcrack that begins just above the ground.
P1 5.5 G: Follow the crack to a large block. Above the block, continue up the crack as it widens through a steep corner, then easier climbing to the top. 60'
FA Apr 30, 2010, Bruce Monroe, Jay Harrison

27 Nervy 5.4 PG 55' ★

Start: 6' up and right from **Cruise Crack** at a small stance beneath a shallow crack.
P1 5.4 PG: Step up to reach the crack, then follow it over a large block at two-thirds height to the top. 55'
FA Apr 30, 2010, Bruce Monroe, Jay Harrison

28 Trouser Flute 5.5 G 40' ★

Start: At a crack behind a birch tree, 6' below a steep headwall and 6' above and right of **Nervy**.
P1 5.5 G: Follow the crack through a corner and up easier rock to the top. 40'
FA Apr 20, 2010, Jay Harrison (solo)

29 Exit Lite 5.5 G 30'

Start: At a wide crack in a left-facing, left-leaning corner.
P1 5.5 G: Climb through steep rock and follow the wide crack to the top. 30'
FA Apr 20, 2010, Jay Harrison (solo)

Crane Mountain • Summit Cliffs

TRUE SUMMIT

Aspect	Southwest
Height	120'
Quality	
Approach	1 hr 10 min, difficult
Summary	Disjointed cliff with exploratory routes directly below the actual Crane summit.

2	1	3					6
-5.6	5.7	5.8	5.9	5.10	5.11	5.12	5.13+	total

The True Summit[4] is the cliff below the actual summit of Crane Mountain. The cliff is divided into three sections depending on the approach.

Summit Face

DIRECTIONS **(MAP PAGE 142)**
From the big ladder, follow the trail to the summit, then scramble to the base of these routes at 1 hr 10 min. These are directly below the actual summit of Crane Mountain.

30 Little Buttress 5.8 G 20'

Hardly worth mentioning, except that it's fun.
Start: Scramble down, skiers right, to a ledge below a short steep prow 100' west of the summit marker. The left side of the prow is overhanging and featureless, and its right side is vertical and riddled with cracks.
P1 5.8 G: Up one of several crack lines on the prow. 20'
FA Aug 14, 2008, Jay Harrison (solo)

31 Gnarly 5.4 PG 60'

Start: 70' right of **Little Buttress**, at a ledge below a low-angle face with several open books. The route finishes 30' west of the summit marker.
P1 5.4 PG: Climb the open books, leftward at first, then back right to the top. 60'
FA 2008, Jay Harrison (solo)

Main Face

DIRECTIONS **(MAP PAGE 142)**
There is a level bench 100' below the big ladder and immediately above where the Summit Trail ascends past a short cliff. Turn left (west) and walk 100', through open spruce/fir woods to a view of the cliff. Go towards the cliff, easier on the right, and locate the hourglass constriction at the start of **Chicken Flake** and a deep chimney 30' to its left, 1 hr 10 min from the trailhead.

DESCENT OPTIONS
Follow the Summit Ridge Trail to the right (southeast) and down the big ladder.

32 Folly-Stricken 5.4 PG 130' ★

Start: 30' left of the start of **Chicken Flake**, at a deep chimney formed by a detached buttress.

---
4 In the first edition this was named Left of Ladder due to its rather vague position relative to the big ladder.

Indian Lake

TRUE SUMMIT CLIFF
30 Little Buttress (5.8)
31 Gnarly (5.4)
32 Folly-Stricken (5.4)
33 Pain and Pleasure (5.8)
34 Chicken Flake (5.7)

P1 5.4 PG: (V1) Up an offwidth and into the chimney. Climb the chimney to a small ledge, then traverse right beneath an overhanging buttress and above the car-sized block to a wide crack. 90'
P2 5.2 PG: Finish up and left. 40'
V1 5.4 PG: Start up the crack, then go left onto the face, and back right to enter the chimney.
FA Jul, 1995, Jay Harrison

33 Pain and Pleasure 5.8 G 100'
Start: Same as Folly-Stricken.
P1 5.8 G: Climb up and right into a squeeze chimney. Up the chimney as it narrows to offwidth to gain a series of ledges. Belay at the second major ledge. 60'
P2 4th class: Scramble right and up a gully, then through a thicket of tight trees to gain the summit trail. 40'
FA May 26, 2008, Jay Harrison (solo)

34 Chicken Flake 5.7 G 170' ★
Start: At an hourglass constriction formed by two opposing corners.
P1 5.7 G: Climb the detached flake to the hourglass constriction and up to the ledge above. Traverse left and up to the top of the cliff. 170'
FA Jun 15, 1991, Paul Medici, Jay Harrison

Ladder Area
Stay on the hiking trail to the big ladder at 1 hr.

35 Sweeping up to Glory 5.8 G 45'
Start: 8' right of the big ladder, just right of an arête.
P1 5.8 G: Stem up a short corner onto the face above. Up the left side of the face to an overhang, then move left around the corner, up a crack, then back right above the overhang to the prow, which is followed to the top. 45'

V1 5.7 G: Up the crack using the alcove just right of the big ladder.
FA Jul 12, 2008, Jay Harrison (solo)

Crane Mountain • Summit Cliffs

THE PROWS

Aspect	Southwest
Height	60'
Quality	★★★
Approach	1 hr 10 min, difficult
Summary	Most popular and cleanest cliff on the summit ridge with scenic, clean cracks and faces.

3	2	1	1			7
-5.6	5.7	5.8	5.9	5.10	5.11	5.12	5.13+	total

The Prows[5] are twin buttresses right of the big ladder—Rock of Ages Buttress on the left and Cornerstone Buttress on the right—and are the most popular of the summit cliffs. The routes are generally climbed by to-prope using a lower-in-climb-out approach.

DIRECTIONS (MAP PAGE 142)
There is a level bench 100' below the big ladder and immediately past where the Summit Trail ascends past a short cliff. (This is the same point on the trail where you leave to approach the True Summit Cliffs.) Turn right (east) and follow a herd path through open spuce/fir trees for 200'. Directly above the bench is a small cliffband with two short handcracks. Higher up are the two buttresses separated by the **Access Slot**—a steep

---
5 In the first edition this was named Right of Ladder due to its position relative to the big ladder, and the two buttresses were cleverly named Left Buttress and Right Buttress; too many lefts and rights.

Indian Lake

Jay Harrison belays John Juhl on Cornerstone (5.5). Photo by Autumn Harrison.

4th-class gully used to access the starts of several routes. Continue another 50', then head uphill to the two buttresses, 1 hr 10 min from the trailhead.

For toproping, continue 50' beyond the big ladder, then turn right into the woods and follow a well-worn herd path to the open ledges at the top of the buttresses.

DESCENT OPTIONS
Descend the gully (4th-class) or follow herd paths left (west) along the summit ridge to the big ladder.

Rock of Ages Buttress

The routes on this buttress begin in the gully that separates it from the Cornerstone Buttress. Head to the base of the Cornerstone Buttress, then walk up left along the base and into the gully.

36 Rock of Ages 5.7 PG 40' ★
Use caution, as the detached pillar will probably not hold gear or withstand an outward pull.
Start: Partway up the gully between the two buttresses.
P1 5.7 PG: (V1) Gain a crack on the right side of the Rock of Ages Buttress and face-climb to the top. 40'
V1 Rock of Aegis 5.9 TR: Traverse left and climb straight up the prow.
FA May 20, 2008, Jay Harrison (solo)
FA (V1) Aug 30, 1997, Dick Tucker

37 Stone Cross 5.8 PG 30'
Start: In the gully between the two buttresses, below a short corner and below the right end of a long horizontal crack. This is 15' right of Rock of Ages.
P1 5.8 PG: Gain the horizontal crack, then traverse left until under a short, small left-facing corner (8' right of the arête). Gain the corner and climb to a ledge, then follow a crack up and left to the top of the buttress. 30'
FA Aug 14, 2008, Jay Harrison (solo)

38 Foretaste 5.4 G 20'
Start: Near the top of the 4th-class descent gully at a vertical crack on Rock of Ages Buttress.
P1 5.4 G: Follow the crack to the top of the buttress. 20'
FA May, 1994, Jay Harrison

Cornerstone Buttress

The next buttress right of Rock of Ages Buttress.
There's another route right of Cornerstone which is now rendered unclimbable due to treefall: Dark Streets (5.3 G, 60'; Oct 1994; Jay Harrison).

39 Five Small Stones 5.5 PG 60'
Start: On a small prow sandwiched between Rock of Ages Buttress and Cornerstone Buttress (but closer to the Cornerstone prow), just up from Toiling Men.
P1 5.5 PG: Step onto the buttress, then go up and left on a slab to reach an arête. Up the arête using holds on both sides. Finish by scrambling up to the top of the gully, then doing a boulder move up a slanting crack. 60'
FA May 20, 2008, Jay Harrison (solo)

Indian Lake

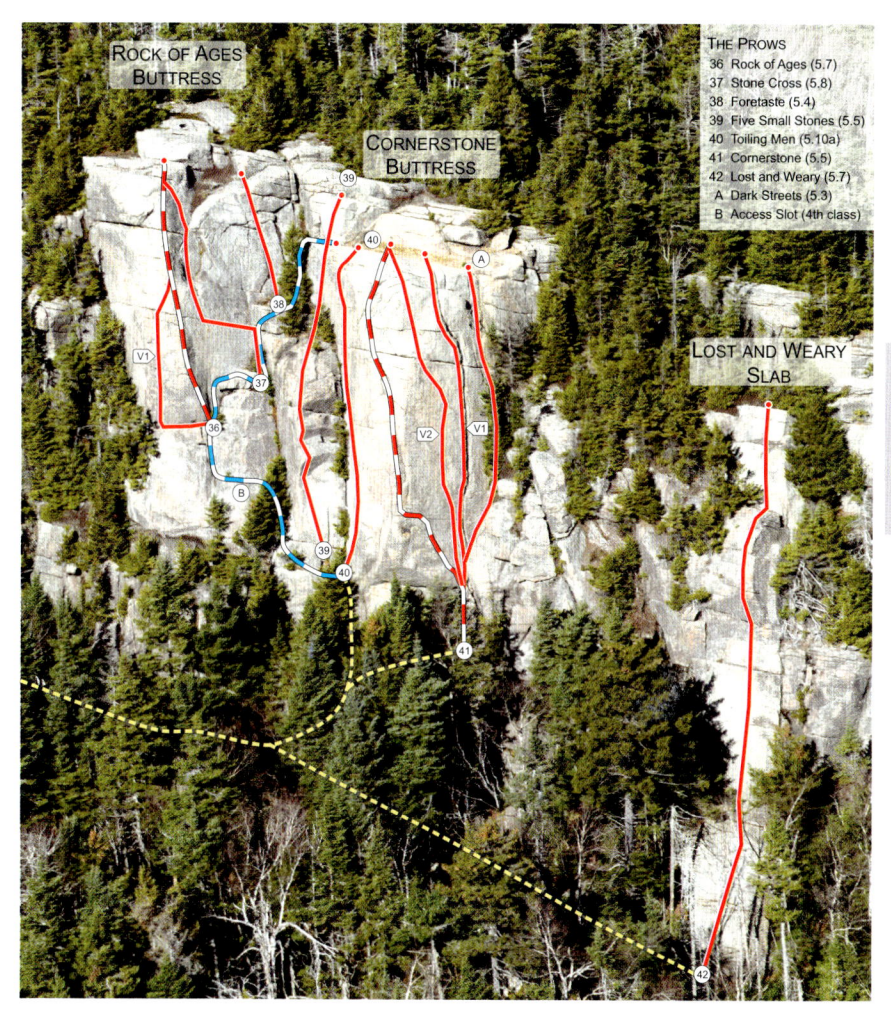

THE PROWS
36 Rock of Ages (5.7)
37 Stone Cross (5.8)
38 Foretaste (5.4)
39 Five Small Stones (5.5)
40 Toiling Men (5.10a)
41 Cornerstone (5.5)
42 Lost and Weary (5.7)
A Dark Streets (5.3)
B Access Slot (4th class)

40 Toiling Men 5.10a TR 60' ★★★

Climb the left-leaning crack on the left side of Cornerstone Buttress. Using the corner to the left is 5.8+.
FA (TR) Jun 8, 1996, Jay Harrison, Carl Harrison

41 Cornerstone 5.5 G 60' ★★★

Start: At a stance in front of a chockstone-filled chimney on the right side of Cornerstone Buttress.
P1 5.5 G: Climb the short chimney, (V1, V2) then traverse left to a vertical handcrack on the front of the buttress. Follow the handcrack to the top. 60'

V1 Lost in the Crowd 5.7 G: The first ascent of this variation was made by an unknown member of a 50-person church group. Above the chimney, follow the narrow, vertical handcrack on the right side of Cornerstone Buttress.

V2 Stoned in a Crowded Corner 5.10a TR ★★★: Climb the face between Lost in the Crowd and Cornerstone using small holds. Reportedly of a high quality with many delicate face moves.
FA Jul, 1995, Jay Harrison
FA (V2) Jul, 2008, Jamie McNeill, Jay Harrison

Lost and Weary Slab

The Lost and Weary Slab is 50' right of Cornerstone Buttress.

42 Lost and Weary 5.7 R 60'

Start: At the left end of the slab.
P1 5.7 R: Climb the left side of the slab (5.7 R), then up and right to the front of a buttress. Climb the buttress directly (crux) to its top. 60'
FA Nov, 1994, Jay Harrison

Mountainside Adventures

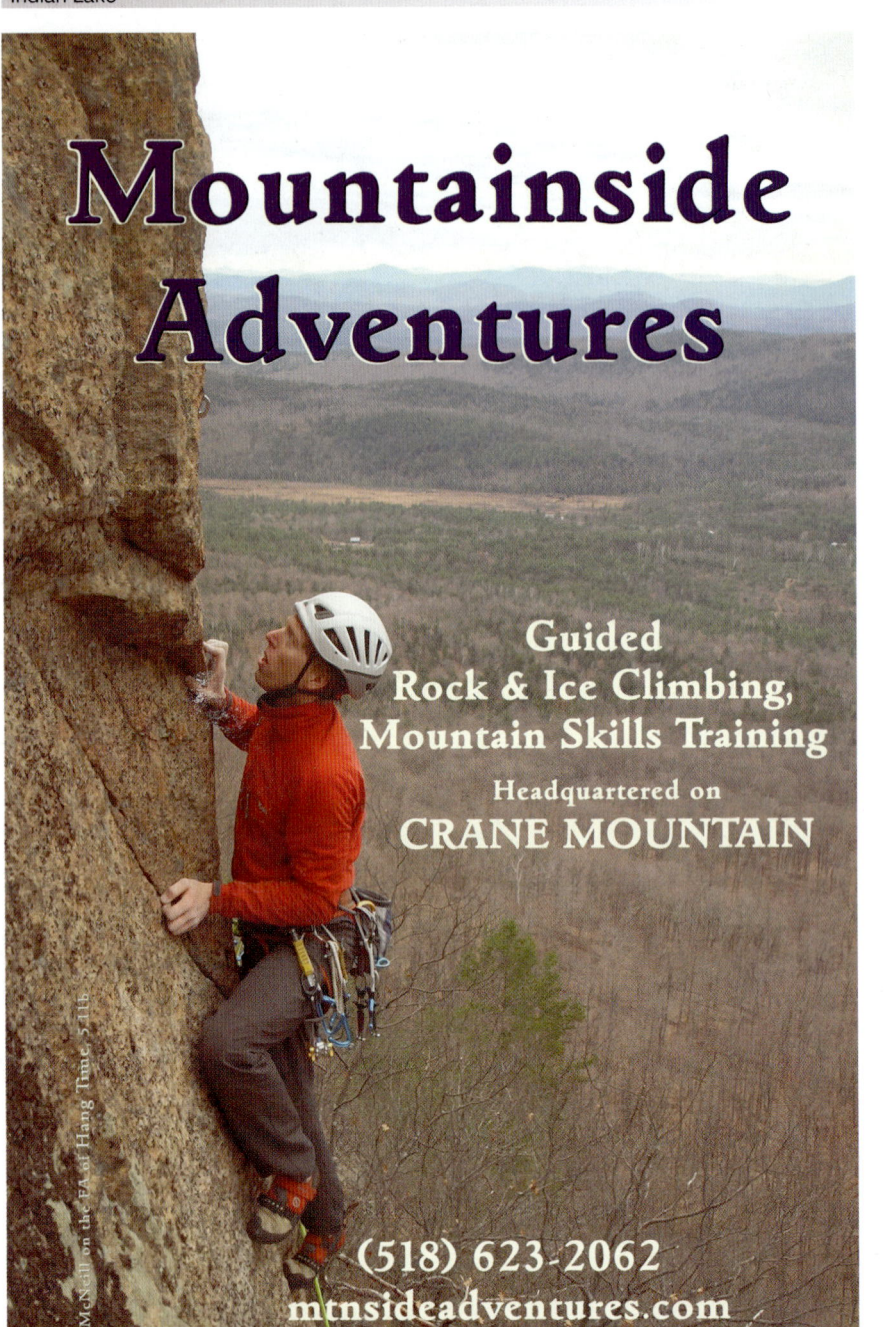

Guided
Rock & Ice Climbing,
Mountain Skills Training

Headquartered on
CRANE MOUNTAIN

(518) 623-2062
mtnsideadventures.com
jayclimbs@yahoo.com

Jamie McNeill on the FA of Hang Time, 5.11b

Indian Lake

Crane Mountain
CRANE EAST

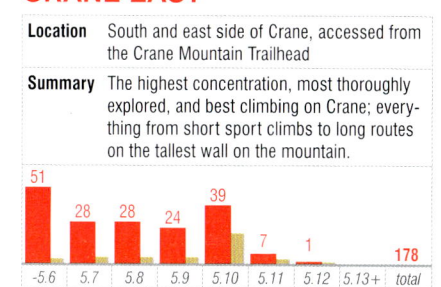

Location	South and east side of Crane, accessed from the Crane Mountain Trailhead
Summary	The highest concentration, most thoroughly explored, and best climbing on Crane; everything from short sport climbs to long routes on the tallest wall on the mountain.

-5.6	5.7	5.8	5.9	5.10	5.11	5.12	5.13+	total
51	28	28	24	39	7	1		178

These cliffs lie on the southeast slopes of Crane Mountain, and are visible from Johnsburg Road before you turn onto Garnet Lake Road, and from a vantage near the bottom of Sky High Road. Most of the cliffs are accessed from the East Path, the well-cairned climber's path that extends from the trailhead to the Black Arches Wall. These cliffs along the East Path are by far the most popular and accessible on Crane Mountain. There are some gems here that rank among the best in the park.

The first cliffs you encounter are the Measles Group, and just beyond is the turnoff to the Belleview Area. A short distance further is the Height-of-Land Wall and the turnoff to the Upper Walls. The Height-of-Land Wall morphs into the Land of Overhangs, then the Tee-Pee Wall, the Long Play Wall, and finally the Diagonal Ramp Wall. Right of this is the Black Arches Wall, and the end of the East Path.

Before the End of the East Path (just before the Black Arches Wall), you can drop down to a lower cliff-band and walk northeast to access the more remote

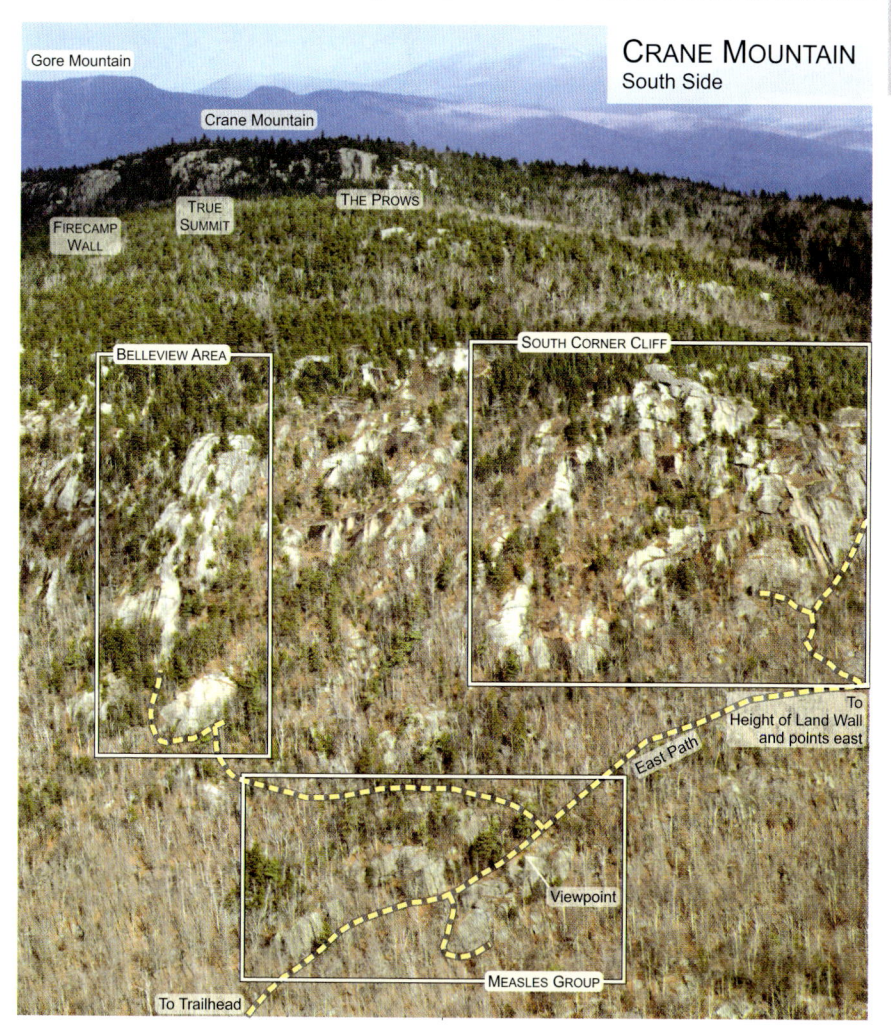

CRANE MOUNTAIN
South Side

163

Indian Lake

[Photo of Crane Mountain with labeled areas: Crane Mountain, The Prows, To Bellavista Area, To Trailhead, and numbered boxes 1–5]

Slanting Cracks Wall, Waterfall Wall, East Nose, and Caterpillar Cliff. These cliffs are more adventurous and raw than those along the East Path.

DIRECTIONS (MAPS PAGES 142 AND 166)

Locate the East Path—a herd path, not the summit hiking trail—that begins on the east side of the parking area and next to the wooden railing (0 hr 0 min). Follow the herd path past a designated camp site through Boulderwoods (a bouldering area) at 5 min. Follow cairns through a choke of boulders, crest a small hill, then descend to a level, fern-covered bench with logged clearings to the right. At 12 min reach an intersection: going right is a shortcut that goes through private land to Sky High Road. Go left (northeast) and follow the trail steeply uphill, past a very large boulder 584018,4821030, and arrive at the Measles Wall at 19 min 584103,4821102, the first cliffs along the East Path.

Crane Mountain ● Crane East

MEASLES GROUP

Location	Along the East Path on the south side of Crane Mountain.
Summary	Several small walls with unique pocketed rock and some sport climbs.

16	3	3	2	7	1		32
-5.6	5.7	5.8	5.9	5.10	5.11	5.12	5.13+	total

The Measles Group is a cluster of small cliffs situated along the East Path, and the first cliffs you encounter when approaching from the parking area. The Measles Wall is mentioned in the first edition of *Adirondack Rock* (and on the map on page 481), although no routes were included.

There are several reasons to climb here: the approach is easy (by Crane standards), the routes are easy to find, the cliff base is pleasant, top rope anchors are abundant, and the cliffs are sheltered and south

Indian Lake

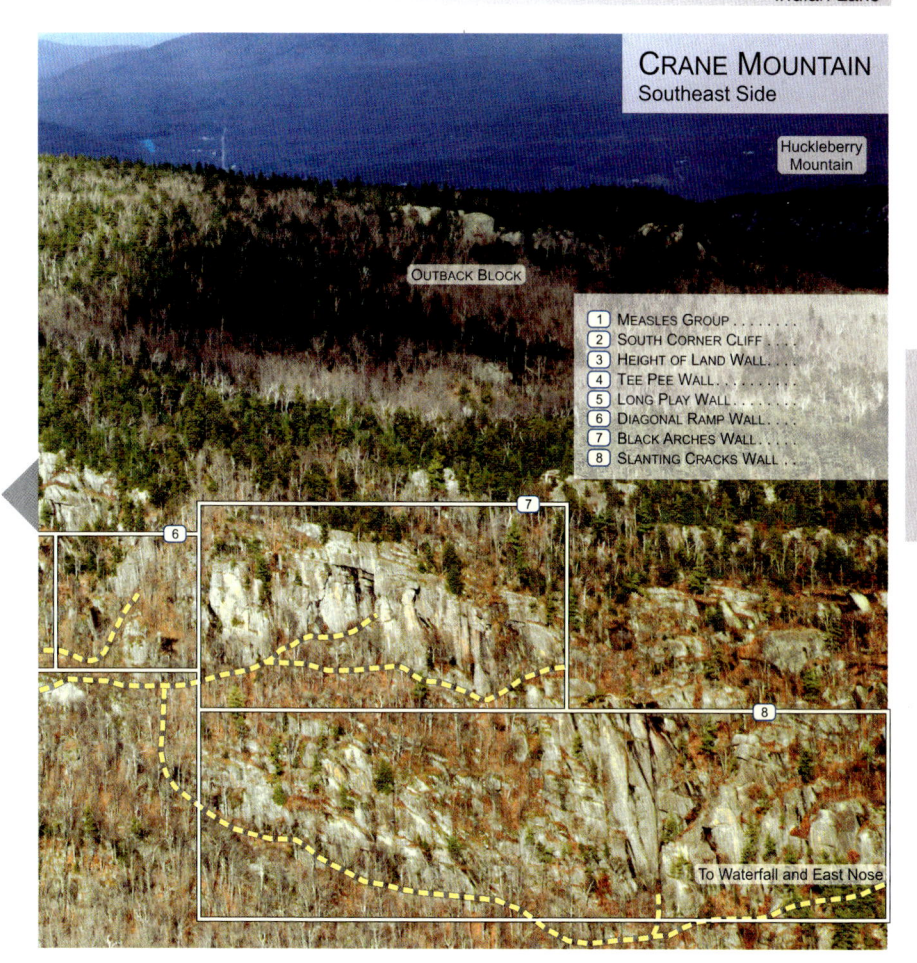

CRANE MOUNTAIN
Southeast Side

Huckleberry Mountain

OUTBACK BLOCK

1. MEASLES GROUP
2. SOUTH CORNER CLIFF
3. HEIGHT OF LAND WALL
4. TEE PEE WALL
5. LONG PLAY WALL
6. DIAGONAL RAMP WALL
7. BLACK ARCHES WALL
8. SLANTING CRACKS WALL

To Waterfall and East Nose

facing. The texture of the rock is unique: the rock feels grainy, like coarse sandstone, and the surface has weathered to form shallow pockets and divots, almost like a bad skin condition, or perhaps a bad case of the measles. Some of the walls are absolutely covered in divots, which makes for challenging route finding. If the angle were steeper, then many of these faces would be too difficult for most climbers.

The East Path goes along the base of the Lower Measles Wall and then the Upper Measles Wall. Situated above the left end of the Lower Measles Wall is the Above-the-Measles Wall. Top-O-the-Measles Wall is above the right end of the Upper Measles Wall. Below-the-Measles Wall is below the path, out of view, and accessed from the base of the Upper Measles Wall.

DIRECTIONS   (MAPS PAGES 142 AND 166)
From the parking area, follow a well-traveled path (not the summit hiking trail) which starts next to the wooden railing (0 hr 0 min). Hike past a designated campsite and through a choke of boulders to the four corners area of Boulderwoods (a bouldering area) at 5 min.

Pass through another choke of boulders, crest a small hill, then descend to a level, fern-covered bench with logged clearings to the right (south). At 12 min follow the path as it turns left (northeast) and goes steeply uphill. Hike uphill and diagonal to the right below several large boulders. At 19 min you'll reach a level section at the left end of the Measles Group, where you pass below the Lower and Upper Measles Walls; the path continues from there to the other cliffs accessed from the East Path.

DESCENT OPTIONS
There are a few fixed anchors on both the Upper and Lower Measles Walls. Otherwise these cliffs all have easy walk-offs.

HISTORY
Climbing occurred here prior to the first edition of Adirondack Rock—mostly solos and topropes by Jay Harrison—but it wasn't until the East Path was established that development began in earnest. Initially, Harrison considered these cliffs suitable for guiding and

Indian Lake

Crane East

BELLEVIEW AREA
1. O'Tom's Tick Twister (5.7+)
2. Chess Club Crack (5.4)
3. Discovered Check (5.8-)
4. Giucco Piano (5.8)
5. Belleview (5.9)
7. Lawyers, Guns, and Money (5.10c)
8. Belle Bottom Crack (5.6-)
9. Also Ran (5.7)
15. Bella Vista (5.7)

SOUTH CORNER CLIFFS
8. Blueberry Crumble (5.7-)
9. Madame Blueberry (5.6)
10. BLC (5.7)
11. Blueberry Tafone (5.6)
12. Second Amendment (5.10b)
14. Solar Grace (5.6+)
16. Never Alone (5.7)
19. Provando (5.7)
20. Riprovando (5.10b)
21. Fireworks (5.7)
24. Stand Your Ground (5.7-)
30. Animal Farm (5.10b)
34. Animal Charm (5.10c)
47. Stairway to Heaven (5.8)
52. Sauron's Bolt of Horror (5.10c)
55. A Peney for Your Freedom (5.8+)
59. Oddy's Crack of Horror (5.10b)
60. Yodellaybackloon (5.6-)

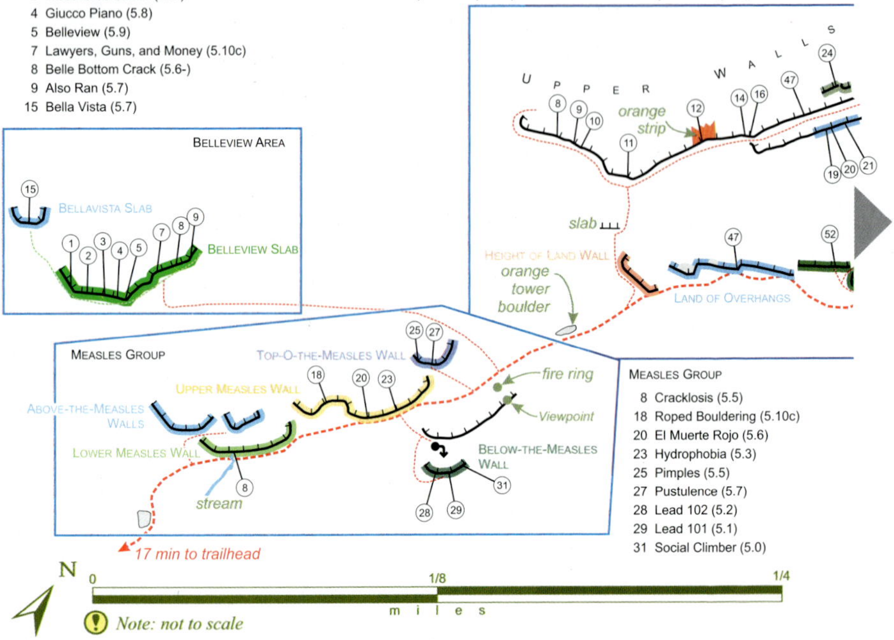

MEASLES GROUP
8. Cracklosis (5.5)
18. Roped Bouldering (5.10c)
20. El Muerte Rojo (5.6)
23. Hydrophobia (5.3)
25. Pimples (5.5)
27. Pustulence (5.7)
28. Lead 102 (5.2)
29. Lead 101 (5.1)
31. Social Climber (5.0)

Note: not to scale

ideal for setting top-ropes. But that changed with the route **I Am Lesion**, Harrison's nemesis that he tried repeatedly. Each time he would climb a little higher, then jump into a nearby beech tree when he got scared. On his last attempt, with the beech tree out of reach, he realized "this is stupid, nobody will ever want to do this." So he downclimbed, jumped into the tree for the last time, and rappel-bolted the route. This route was a transition where Harrison decided to create routes that others would want to repeat. This new way of thinking led to the post-2008 explosion of new routes at Crane.

CRANE MOUNTAIN: ABOVE-THE-MEASLES WALL
1. The Flu (5.5)
2. Trickagnosis (5.7)
3. Mixamotosis (5.9)
4. Resistant Strain (5.11a)
5. Jungle Rot (5.10c)

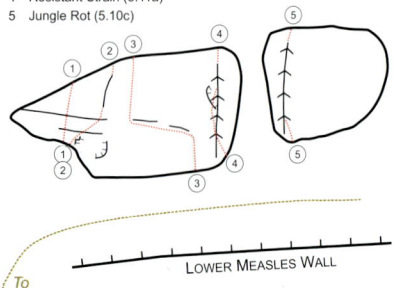

Crane Mountain • Crane East • Measles Group

ABOVE-THE-MEASLES WALL

Aspect	South
Height	55'
Quality	★
Approach	20 min, easy
Summary	A steep clean slab.

1	1		1	1	1		5
-5.6	5.7	5.8	5.9	5.10	5.11	5.12	5.13+	total

This steep, clean slab has the fewest pockmarks of the Measles Walls, making the routes here more typical of the region. Most of the routes are topropes on clean rock with no fixed anchors.

DIRECTIONS (MAPS PAGES 142 AND 166)
Follow the East Path to where it levels off at the mossy left end of the Lower Measles Wall—the first wall you come to on the East Path 584103,4821102. Go around the left end of this wall and up 80' along the path used

Indian Lake

SOUTH CORNER CLIFFS
63 Bodhi Tree (5.9)
64 Induhvidual (5.7)
66 Long Play (5.10a)
67 Moehammed, Larry, & Curly (5.9+)
68 Muckraker (5.9)
69 Kill It Before It Spreads (5.7+)
74 Leapin' Louie (5.10a)
75 Keystone (5.10a)

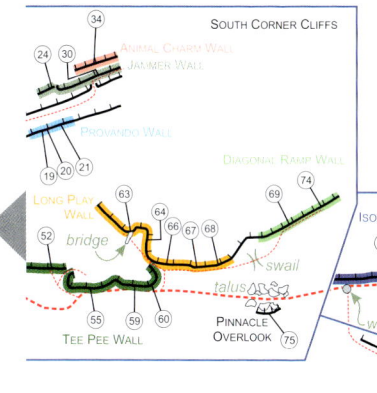

BLACK ARCHES WALL
79 Recuperation Boulevard (5.7)
87 Here I Go Again (5.6)
88 Amnesia Chasm (5.8)
89 Drive (5.9)
92 Amphitheater Crack (5.9)
96 Four Ounces to Freedom (5.12d)
97 Gun Show (5.10a)
98 Torcher (5.10b)
100 Hang Time (5.11b)
101 Black Arch Arête (5.10b)
102 Sleepy Hollow (5.8)
104 Parallel Passage (5.10a)
105 Plumb Line (5.11a)
107 Critical Crimps (5.10a)
108 Second Job (5.8)
110 Tilly's Trench (5.3)
112 Reducto Adductor (5.10c)

SLANTING CRACKS WALL
3 Straits of Fear (5.8-)
5 Fits and Arms (5.6)
6 Variety Crack (5.10a)
7 Slabmeister (5.11a)

To: The Waterfall Cliff, East Nose, Caterpillar Cliff

to access the top of this cliff; the Above-the-Measles Wall lies just above.

1 The Flu 5.5 PG 30'
Start: 15' right of the left end of the cliff, below a horizontal crack 5' up.
P1 5.5 PG: Up the rippled face past two horizontal cracks, then up the low-angle slab to the top. 30'
FA Oct, 2008, Jay Harrison (solo)

2 Trickagnosis 5.7 PG 40' ★
There are many variations including a 5.10a toproped start that goes straight up to the exit crack.
Start: Same as The Flu.
P1 5.7 PG: Go up a stepped, right-rising flake to a horizontal crack. Traverse right 15', then up a vertical crack to the top. 40'
FA Oct, 2008, Jay Harrison (solo)

3 Mixamotosis 5.9 X 55' ★★
A good toprope route.
Start: At a clean water streak and a 4'-tall bulge at the base of cliff.
P1 5.9 X: Make a boulder move off the ground, then friction up to a discontinuous, left-rising, horizontal crack. Follow the crack leftwards to a blunt arête, and climb this to the top. 55'
FA Oct, 2008, Jay Harrison (solo)

Todd Paris on the beautiful dimpled face of **H1N1** (5.8+). Photo by Jay Harrison.

Indian Lake

4 Resistant Strain 5.11a TR 55' ★★
Begin at the low-angled, blunt arête on the right side of the cliff. Go up the right side, then move to the lower-angled left side, and work up to a high bulge with a long left-facing flake. Make a crux move over the bulge, and climb easily to the top.
FA (TR) Oct, 2008, Jay Harrison

5 Jungle Rot 5.10c TR 40'
Begin 40' right of Resistant Strain on a separate cliff and below the right side of an arête. Climb flakes and knobs on a steep wall then finish on the arête.
FA (TR) Oct 27, 2008, Jamie McNeill, Jay Harrison

Crane Mountain • Crane East • Measles Group

LOWER MEASLES WALL

Aspect	South
Height	50'
Quality	★★
Approach	20 min, easy
Summary	Small slab with unique pocketed rock and some sport climbs.

4	1	5				10
-5.6	5.7	5.8	5.9	5.10	5.11	5.12	5.13+	total

This is a long, 50'-tall cliffband, the first cliff you reach on the East Path 584103,4821102. It is low and mossy at its left end. All of the routes begin on the path, which makes a nice open area to belay. At the low point on the cliff is a spring, near the start of Hypoxia; moving right the terrain rises gradually past a deep corner (Cracklosis) on the left side of the detached Cracklosis Block. The terrain on the right side of the cliff slopes steeply uphill below a steep, sheer slab uniformly covered in shallow pockets and dimples; several sustained routes ascend this face.

DESCENT OPTIONS
It is easy to walk off of either end of the cliff and there are many trees from which to anchor. There are fixed anchors on top of the right-hand routes.

6 Hypoxia 5.5 R 30'
On the most pocketed section of the cliff. Often moss-covered.
Start: Immediately right of the spring that flows from below the low point of the cliff.
P1 5.5 R: Up the face to an overlap. Move up and left over the overlap, then up to the top. 30'
FA 2005, Jay Harrison (solo)

7 Run for Rabies 5.6 R 35' ★
Start: 8' right of Hypoxia at a left-facing, left-leaning corner.
P1 5.6 R: Up the corner to a right-leaning crack. Step left and go over the crack, then climb to the top. 35'
FA 2005, Jay Harrison (solo)

8 Cracklosis 5.5 G 55' ★★
A good beginner lead. The variation makes for a good toprope introduction to pocketed face climbing.
Start: 25' right of Hypoxia at an offwidth crack in a left-facing corner, which is the left side of the Cracklosis Block.
P1 5.5 G: (V1) Up the corner to a ledge, then up a thin crack and slab to the top. 55'
V1 Scared for Life 5.8 X: Climb the face to the left of the corner and join Cracklosis at the ledge.
Gear: to 4"
FA 2005, Jay Harrison (solo)
FA (V1) 2005, Jay Harrison (solo)

9 Hamburger Face 5.10a TR 50'
Climbs the front of the Cracklosis Block. Go past a ledge at 7' then up a face to join Cracklosis at the top of the block.
FA (TR) 2005, Jason Brechko, Simon Cording

10 Measly Little Corner 5.3 G 45'
Start: The right side of the Cracklosis Block, at a wide crack in a right-facing corner.
P1 5.3 G: Up the corner to a ledge, then finish on Cracklosis: up a thin crack and slab to the top. 45'
FA 2005, Jay Harrison (solo)

11 Pox 5.10b G 35' ★★
As with the other routes on the face, the difficulties are sustained and insecure.
Start: At the left end of a ground-level overhang.
● **P1 5.10b G:** Go straight up the pocketed face to a fixed anchor. 35'
FA Dec 5, 2011, Jay Harrison

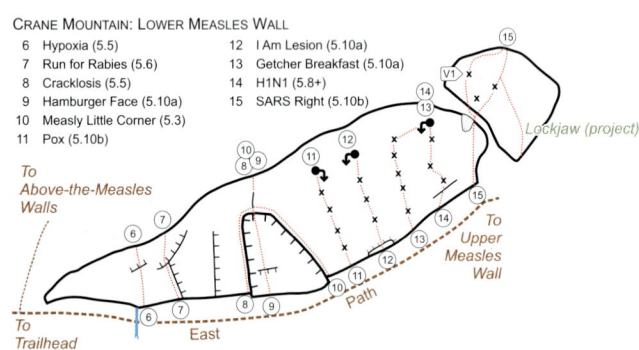

CRANE MOUNTAIN: LOWER MEASLES WALL

6 Hypoxia (5.5)
7 Run for Rabies (5.6)
8 Cracklosis (5.5)
9 Hamburger Face (5.10a)
10 Measly Little Corner (5.3)
11 Pox (5.10b)
12 I Am Lesion (5.10a)
13 Getcher Breakfast (5.10a)
14 H1N1 (5.8+)
15 SARS Right (5.10b)

12 I Am Lesion 5.10a G 35' ★★★
Start: At a 5'-long overhang at ground level, 10' uphill and right of Measly Little Corner.
● **P1 5.10a G:** Begin with tricky moves up shallow pockets and divots, then up the sustained face to the top. 35'
FA May 11, 2009, Jay Harrison, Todd Paris

Indian Lake

13 Getcher Breakfast 5.10a G 40' ★★★
A well-protected route with a secure start.
Start: Near a horizontal mineral band and a square-cut jug 6' up.
● **P1 5.10a G:** Go up the face, easy at first, then with more challenging route-finding in a sea of shallow divots. After the last bolt, traverse right to the anchors of **H1N1**. 40'
FA Jul 20, 2010, Neal Dunkley

14 H1N1 5.8+ G 30' ★★
Start: Below a right-leaning seam 7' up, where the path turns away from the cliff.
● **P1 5.8+ G:** Zigzag right to left on positive holds, then go straight up to a fixed anchor. 30'
FA Nov 18, 2009, Todd Paris, Jay Harrison

15 SARS Right 5.10b G 45' ★★
This route is effectively 15' of climbing, but it packs a punch. Take care clipping the crux bolt.
Start: 9' right or and above **H1N1** on a knobby face just left of a dirty, right-rising crevice.
● **P1 5.10b G:** Climb face up and right to a stance under a chest-high overhang right of a block lying on a slanting ledge. Use the block to clip a bolt, (V1) then step down, climb through the overhang right of the block. Follow right-rising seam to its end, make an intriguing move right to gain another seam, then move across right and head up to the top of the crag. 45'
● **V1 SARS Left 5.7+ G:** Consistent climbing, but avoids the best moves. From the block, pull the overhang, then move left up flakes, then step back right to ascend the slab to its top.
FA Nov 20, 2013, Tom Lane, Jay Harrison
FA (V1) Nov 20, 2013, Jay Harrison, Tom Lane

Crane Mountain ● Crane East ● Measles Group

UPPER MEASLES WALL

Aspect	South
Height	70'
Quality	★★
Approach	20 min, easy
Summary	Longest and tallest cliff in the Measles Group with unique pocketed rock.

5	1	1	1				9
-5.6	5.7	5.8	5.9	5.10	5.11	5.12	5.13+	total

This is the longest and tallest of the cliffs in the Measles Group. The left side has a wide roof 25' up (**Short Person's Disease**) above a broad ledge which continues across the cliff splitting it into a steep top section and a slabby, pocketed bottom section. The routes here are much like those on the right-hand side of the Lower Measles Wall—sustained for their grade, but more accessible due to positive holds, and a gentler angle.

DIRECTIONS (MAPS PAGES 142 AND 166)
Follow the East Path to the Lower Measles Wall—the first wall you come to on the East Path. From the right end of this wall, continue another 50' uphill along the path to this wall **584165,4821137**.

CRANE MOUNTAIN: UPPER MEASLES WALL
16 Little Fever (5.1)
17 Craterface (5.5)
18 Roped Bouldering (5.10c)
19 Short Person's Disease (5.8)
20 El Muerte Rojo (5.6)
21 Full Moon Fever (5.7)
22 Cat Scratch Fever (5.9)
23 Hydrophobia (5.3)
24 Chilblain (5.6)

DESCENT OPTIONS
It is easy to walk around either end of the cliff and there are many trees from which to build anchors. There are fixed anchors for the routes on the right end of the cliff.

16 Little Fever 5.1 G 35'
Start: 30' uphill of the East Path, below the left end of the long roof at a spruce tree.
P1 5.1 G: Follow a left-leaning crack 20' across an easy slab. Climb a broken, right-leaning crack to the top. 35'
FA Jun 7, 2011, Jay Harrison (solo)

17 Craterface 5.5 R 45'
Start: Same as Little Fever.
P1 5.4 R: Climb up through a rock notch below a spruce tree, then climb straight up the face above the spruce on excellent pockmarks. Cross a left-rising dirty crack and finish at the high point of the slab. 45'
FA Nov 9, 2011, Jay Harrison (solo)

18 Roped Bouldering 5.10c R 30'
With only four or five moves of climbing, this would be a bouldering problem if you had enough pads.
Start: Under the giant roof where an obvious crack splits its left side.
P1 5.10c R: Climb the thin overhung face to gain the roof crack. Make several moves to reach the end of the roof crack, then flip over the roof edge and climb the low-angle slab to trees above. 30'
FA (5.10c C2) Jul 14, 2012, Michael Gray, Peter Whitmore
FFA Nov, 2013, Kirby Girard

19 Short Person's Disease 5.8 G 50'
Start: 40' uphill of the East Path, below the right end of a long roof, at a huge, waist-high, horizontal flake.
P1 5.8 G: Crawl onto the flake and go right under the roof to a handcrack. Follow the crack around the right end of the roof, then step left and climb a slab to the top. 50'
FA Apr 17, 2011, Jay Harrison (roped solo)

Indian Lake

20 El Muerte Rojo 5.6 G 70' ★★

Start: On the East Path at a 3'-long overlap at ground level, next to a beech tree with a forked trunk.
P1 5.6 G: Climb to a series of vertical pockets 10' up. Follow the pockets to a 10'-long finger and handcrack. At the top of the crack, climb the face with shallow pockets (crux) up to a broad ledge. Step right to finish on **Full Moon Fever**: go up a short, left-facing corner to an overhang, and climb around its right end. Work up to a ledge, and then scramble to a large pine tree with a fixed anchor. 70'
FA Nov 13, 2009, Jay Harrison, Jonathan Losier

21 Full Moon Fever 5.7 G 70' ★★

Start: On the East Path, 6' right of **El Muerte Rojo** and 5' left of **Cat Scratch Fever**.
P1 5.7 G: Start up a sheer wall covered in shallow pockets. Zigzag left-to-right (V1), and gain a right-leaning handcrack. Follow the crack to a ledge. Go up a short, left-facing corner to an overhang, and climb around its right end. Work up to a ledge, and then scramble to a large pine tree with a fixed anchor shared with **El Muerte Rojo**. 70'
V1 5.8 R: Instead of going to the crack, move leftward (towards a bolt) toward **El Muerte Rojo** before reaching the ledge. From the ledge, go straight up to the left side of the overhang (no pro), then continue directly through it to the high point of the cliff.
FA Nov 8, 2009, Jay Harrison, Robin Harrison
FA (V1) Jun 18, 2010, Tom Lane, Maria Lane

22 Cat Scratch Fever 5.9 G 40' ★★

Start: On the East Path, 6' left of the right-leaning crack of **Hydrophobia** that begins 8' up.
● **P1 5.9 G:** Climb easy rock to a stance on a bulge. Move up, and slightly left, on shallow pockets. Diagonal up and right (V1) to a cruxy section below a broad ledge. Climb to the ledge and a spruce tree with a fixed anchor. 40'
V1 5.8 G: Go left to the handcrack of **Full Moon Fever**.
FA May 16, 2010, Jay Harrison
FA (V1) Mar 27, 2010, Jay Harrison, Dave Pomerantz, Todd Paris

23 Hydrophobia 5.3 G 40' ★★

Named for snowmelt in the upper crack during the first ascent.
Start: On the East Path, below a 20'-long, right-leaning crack that begins 8' up.
P1 5.3 G: Go up stepped ledges to the crack and climb to its end. Protect, and then traverse right to another handcrack, and follow this to an oak tree with a fixed anchor. 40'
FA Apr 3, 2010, Jay Harrison, Robin Harrison

24 Chilblain 5.6 R 30'

Start: Right of a last, left-facing corner. Very dirty.
P1 5.6 R: Climb dimpled rock without pro to the top, coming up 8' right of **Hydrophobia**. 30'
FA Nov 7, 2011, Jay Harrison (solo)

Crane Mountain ● Crane East ● Measles Group
TOP-O-THE-MEASLES WALL

Aspect	South
Height	60'
Quality	
Approach	20 min, easy
Summary	Tiny, dirty slab with some obscure routes.

1	1	1					3
-5.6	5.7	5.8	5.9	5.10	5.11	5.12	5.13+	total

This low, lichen-covered slab sits 50' uphill and right of the Upper Measles Wall.

DIRECTIONS (MAPS PAGES 142 AND 166)
Follow the East Path to the Upper Measles Wall. Continue uphill along the base of the cliff to near the viewpoint with a fire ring. Cut left uphill for 80' to the base of this wall 584171,4821146.

25 Pimples 5.5 R 45'
Currently dirty.
Start: 20' uphill and left of the low end of the slab.
P1 5.5 R: Climb an unprotected slab to a horizontal crack at 30'. Move up between two trees to the top. 45'
FA Apr 22, 2012, Jay Harrison

26 Halitosis 5.8 PG 60' ★
Start: Same as **Pustulence**.
● **P1 5.8 PG:** Go up a blunt arête using left-facing flake to a horizontal seam. Go straight up a slab with several difficult friction moves to the top. 60'
FA May 18, 2012, Mike Prince, Ben Brooke

27 Pustulence 5.7 R 60'
An exploratory climb that starts on **Halitosis** and finishes on **Pimples**.
Start: At the low point of the slab, below a left-facing flake.
P1 5.6 R: Go up a sloping, right-rising ramp to a horizontal seam. Follow the seam left for 15' and finish on **Pimples**. 60'
FA May 5, 2010, Jay Harrison (solo)

Crane Mountain ● Crane East ● Measles Group
BELOW-THE-MEASLES WALL

Aspect	South
Height	80'
Quality	★
Approach	20 min, easy
Summary	Long, low-angle slab with super easy routes.

5							5
-5.6	5.7	5.8	5.9	5.10	5.11	5.12	5.13+	total

Below-the-Measles Wall is positioned downhill of the Upper Measles Wall. It has a slabby bottom (with the routes **Lead 102** and **Lead 101**) and an overhanging top, above which is the viewpoint and fire ring that is along the East Path. The cliff base has been nicely terraced.

Indian Lake

DIRECTIONS (MAPS PAGES 142 AND 166)
Follow the East Path to the right end of the Upper Measles Wall near the start of **Hydrophobia**. Walk downhill on a spur path for 200' to the base of the slab 584193,4821114 on your left.

28 Lead 102 5.2 G 80' ★

Slightly wider spacing to the protection than its neighbor, and slightly more difficult climbing.
Start: 10' right of the left end of the slab, below a left-rising crack that begins 8' up.
● **P1 5.2 G:** Climb the face past a couple of cracks to a fixed anchor. 80'
FA Aug 19, 2012, Ryan Heffernan, Mike Prince

29 Lead 101 5.1 G 80' ★★

The easiest sport route in the Adirondacks. Bring a couple of cams if you really want to sew it up.
Start: Below a v-shaped flake 8' up, and a scoop 20' up.
● **P1 5.1 G:** Go over a low bulging wall, past two horizontal cracks, and join **Lead 102**. 80'
FA Aug 19, 2012, Mike Prince, Ryan Heffernan

30 Cooties 5.1 R 80'

An early exploratory climb, done before fixed protection was added to the cliff.
Start: At the lowest point on the slab, just left of center, and 6' left of **Social Climber**.
P1 5.0 R: Climb up and left to easier terrain and finish on **Lead 101**. 80'
FA Apr 11, 2010, Jay Harrison

31 Social Climber 5.0 G 50' ★

Start: 10' uphill and right of the low end of the slab, below a crack leading to a right-facing corner.
P1 5.0 G: Climb the corner to a ledge, then up and right to an oak tree belay. 50'
Descent: Walk climber's left along the ledge.
FA Oct 6, 2011, Jay Harrison, Robin Harrison

32 Social Pariah 5.3 R 50'

Start: On the face right of **Social Climber**.
P1 5.3 R: Go up the face past a left-rising wide crack, then past a series of discontinuous left-rising cracks to an oak tree belay. 50'
FA Aug 29, 2011, Jay Harrison (solo)

Crane Mountain ● Crane East
BELLEVIEW AREA

Location	South side of Crane Mountain accessed from a spur path from the East Path.
Summary	A tall, multi-pitch slab of moderate routes, and a steeper single-pitch cliff with routes in the 5.4–5.10 range.

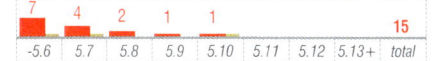

7	4	2	1	1		15
-5.6	5.7	5.8	5.9	5.10	5.11	5.12	5.13+	total

This area presently consists of two cliffs: a tall multi-pitch slab with moderate routes (Bellavista Slab); and a shorter, steeper, single-pitch cliff (Belleview Slab). Development has already started on cliffs left of Bellavista Slab.

DIRECTIONS (MAPS PAGES 142 AND 166)
Follow the East Path past the Lower and Upper Measles Walls to a viewpoint with a fire ring. Just past that, the trail turns sharply left. Immediately after this turn, turn left off the East Path and follow a smaller path uphill to a small slab above the Top-O-the-Measles Wall. Continue uphill and left, past the base of another slab, to arrive at the right end of the Belleview Slab near a left-facing corner with a crack (**Belle Bottom Crack**) 584045,4821212. The approach time is 5 minutes from the East Path.

HISTORY

At the time of the first edition, each of these two cliffs had a single route. On the Belleview Slab was **Belle Bottom Crack**, climbed solo by Jay Harrison in 1992, and on the Bella Vista Slab was **Belle Bottom Buttress** (now part of **Bella Vista**), climbed solo the next year. Since then, Harrison, often solo or with Tom Lane, resurrected these routes, and, after the lichen dust settled, added nearly 30 more pitches of climbing.

*Matt Wood on P2 of **Bella Vista** (5.7), the namesake route of the Bellevista Slab. Photo by Jay Harrison.*

Indian Lake

BELLEVIEW AREA
1. O'Tom's Tick Twister (5.7+)
2. Chess Club Crack (5.4)
3. Discovered Check (5.8-)
4. Giucco Piano (5.8)
5. Belleview (5.9)
6. Glee Club Crack (5.4)
7. Lawyers, Guns, and Money (5.10c)
8. Belle Bottom Crack (5.6-)
9. Also Ran (5.7)
10. Beautiful Dreamer (5.6)
11. Le Jour de Bon Heures (5.3)
12. Bon Chance (5.6)
13. Benediction (5.6)
14. Leftover (5.7)
15. Bella Vista (5.7)

BELLAVISTA SLAB

BELLEVIEW SLAB

To Viewpoint

Crane Mountain • Crane East • Belleview Area
BELLEVIEW SLAB

Aspect	South
Height	100'
Quality	★★
Approach	30 min, moderate
Summary	A tight concentration of moderate, low-angle crack and slab routes.

3	2	2	1	1		9
-5.6	5.7	5.8	5.9	5.10	5.11	5.12	5.13+	total

A good place for beginning intermediate climbers. The wall is quick to dry after wet conditions. Be aware that tentative leaders may want a stick clip.

1 O'Tom's Tick Twister 5.7+ PG 60' ★★
Start: Near the left end of the cliff at a 10'-high flake lying against the cliff that forms a right-facing arched opening.
P1 5.7+ PG: Up the flake, then up stepped rock. Go left and climb to the top of a flake, then go around the right side of the overhang and follow a crack up an easy slab to a white pine tree. 60'
Gear: #000 and #00 C3s were used for gear at a key placement just above the initial flake.
FA Jul 17, 2012, Tom Lane, Jay Harrison

2 Chess Club Crack 5.4 G 110'
Recommended if cleaned up.
Start: Same as O'Tom's Tick Twister.
P1 5.4 G: (V1) Up the flake, then traverse right on mossy slabs to a right-rising crack that goes up and right. Climb the crack to belay at an oak tree. 60'
P2 5.3 G: Continue up the widening crack, then move up to a right-rising crack and follow it to a large red pine tree at the top. 50'
V1 5.8 PG: Start 20' right at a smooth bulge below a 4'-tall right-facing corner 10' up. Pull over the bulge (crux), go up the corner, then straight up to the wide crack with a tree in it.
Gear: Large cams (#4 and #5 C4s) are required.
FA Dec 12, 2011, Jay Harrison

3 Discovered Check 5.8- G (5.4 R) 60' ★★
Start: 12' right of the starting flake of O'Tom's Tick Twister at a small crescent-shaped flake.
P1 5.8- G (5.4 R): Climb up to a short, left-facing corner (small cam), make a tricky move to get above it, then friction to an overhang. Climb over it and up a short right-facing corner. Step left and go up a line of knobs to the right of another overhang. Pull through a headwall, then up an unprotected slab to a white pine tree. 60'
FA Jul 17, 2012, Jay Harrison, Tom Lane

4 Giucco Piano 5.8 G (5.3 R) 60' ★
Start: At a clear swathe of slab between two mossy strips, 12' right of the starting flake of Discovered Check.

P1 5.8 G (5.3 R): Climb a clean slab to an overhang broken by a short vertical crack. Climb up via the crack to a stance below a steep slab. Up the slab (bolt) and through an overlap (bolt) to a ledge with an oak tree. 60'
FA Jul 17, 2012, Jay Harrison, Tom Lane

5 Belleview 5.9 G (5.2 R) 110' ★
A really hard couple of moves at the start, followed by much easier climbing.
Start: At the lowest point of the cliff base beneath a blunt arête.
● **P1 5.9 G (5.2 R):** (V1) Climb the blunt arête (crux) then work up an easy slab. Go up past a horizontal to a steeper slab, to another horizontal. Continue up the slab to a fixed anchor on a red pine tree. 110'
FA Jul 17, 2012, Tom Lane, Jay Harrison
V1 5.7 G: Begin 12' right of the low point at a 1'-long, left-rising foothold. Move up and left to reach the arête about 3' above the first bolt.
FA Jul 17, 2012, Jay Harrison

6 Glee Club Crack 5.4 G 100' ★★
Start: At a short vertical fistcrack leading to a ledge at head height.
P1 5.4 G: Up to the ledge, then make an awkward move onto a higher ledge on the left. Traverse left to a large, right-rising crack with pockets. Follow the crack past an oak tree, then face climb to the top. 100'
Gear: to 3.5"
FA Dec 12, 2011, Jay Harrison

Ben Cook just after the crux of **Lawyers, Guns, and Money** *(5.10c).*

Indian Lake

7 Lawyers, Guns, and Money
5.10c G (5.2 R) 100' ★★★

Has a perplexing slab move low, followed by sustained 5.9 face climbing for 30'. Quite nice. A good lead, or easily toproped after climbing **Belle Bottom Crack**.
Start: Same as **Glee Club Crack**.
● **P1 5.10c G:** Foot traverse up and right on a right-rising rail, up a slab to a bulge, then make a hard press-up over the bulge (crux). Move right, then straight up a sustained slab to where the angle eases. Run out easy slab to a large tree ledge. 100'
FA Jul 20, 2012, Jim Lawyer, Jay Harrison

8 Belle Bottom Crack 5.6- G (5.3 R) 90' ★★★

This route was mentioned in the first edition and has since been resurrected.
Start: At a left-facing corner with a hand crack, at the right end of the cliff.
P1 5.6- G: Climb up to crack–corner, and climb this to where the corner fades, and the crack veers sharply left. Climb the knobby face directly above the bend to an oak tree. 90'
FA Jul, 1992, Jay Harrison

9 Also Ran 5.7 G (5.3 X) 55'

Start: 20' right of **Belle Bottom Crack**, below a small, rounded, left-facing corner.
P1 5.7 G (5.3 X): Friction to gain the rounded corner, then move up to a horizontal crack. Work left and climb dirty knobs to a short, wide, right-rising crack (tricky #4 Camalot placement here). Continue up knobs on a slab to an oak tree. 55'
FA Sep 3, 2012, Jay Harrison, Tom Lane

Crane Mountain ● Crane East ● Belleview Area

BELLAVISTA SLAB

Aspect	South
Height	400'
Quality	★
Approach	35 min, moderate
Summary	A long, narrow, undulating slab positioned above and left of the Belleview Slab with long, moderate routes.

4	2					6
-5.6	5.7	5.8	5.9	5.10	5.11	5.12	5.13+	total

DIRECTIONS (MAPS PAGES 142 AND 166)
Climb something on the Belleview Slab then walk 150' (climber's) left. Alternatively, walk left along the base of the Belleview Slab and scramble up a steep gully to the base of the slab at its lowest point—the start of **Bella Vista** 584000,4821232. To reach the start of other routes, continue left and scramble up to an upper vegetated ledge 100' higher.

DESCENT OPTIONS
There's a line of fixed rappels on trees from the top of the cliff, possible with a single 60m rope.

10 Beautiful Dreamer 5.6 G (5.4 R) 480'

The lowest pitch is not memorable; the second has one decent move. The third is nice, and the final is the popular, shared final pitch of **Bella Vista**. A better linkup is **Bon Chance** to the oak tree under the headwall, then walk up and left 40' to the spruce tree belay below the last two pitches.
Start: 200' left of the start of **Bella Vista** and 40' left of (and below) the upper ledge of **Le Jeur de Bon Heurs**, at a 25'-tall, scruffy slab with a crack left of center.
P1 5.4 G: Climb slab, to crack, to top of slab. Move right to cracks that lead up a low-angle slab; follow these past several large loose blocks to a large pine tree (this tree is below and left of the oak tree rap anchor below the main headwall). 100'
P2 5.6 G (5.4 R): Move back left to a left-rising crack that leads to an oak tree growing from a break in the slab. Climb slab right of the oak tree and up trivial slab to a short flap. Step left and use a crack to mount this difficulty, then climb easy slab around several blocks to a tree belay below a steeper slab. 100'
P3 5.5 G (5.4 R): Climb crack and open book up and through a bulge, then continue up unprotected, easier slab to a spruce tree. 100'
P4 5.6 G (5.4 R): Go left around the spruce tree, continue up unprotected slab to a large flake lying on it, then finish same as **Bella Vista**: climb the crack in steep slab to its end, step left and go up seam and crack to below two small spruce trees, step right around these to the top. 180'
FA Aug 26, 2012, Jay Harrison, Robin Harrison

11 Le Jour de Bon Heures 5.3 G 460' ★★

Start: At the left side of the upper vegetated ledge, below a sharply-outlined, right-facing corner.
P1 5.3 G: Climb the corner to its end at the left end of a steep flap–overlap. Step up left and follow an incredible line of pockets and crack to an oak tree below and left of a headwall in the main slab. 100'
P2 5.3 G: Climb slab left of the headwall (stay left of a left-rising, left-facing corner) until you can climb up and right onto the main slab. Move up easily to a fixed anchor on a spruce tree. 80'
P3 5.3 G: Scramble up left of the spruce tree to a crack on the left edge of the slab. Climb this through a flap, then continue up easy slab to a clearing on the left. Step left into the clearing to belay. 120'
P4 5.2 G: Scramble up and left onto wide slab, then work upward along blocks, flakes, and cracks to the top. One can also scramble up a brushy ramp to the right of the slab, then work through a screen of spruce branches to reach the top. 160'
History: The name is a reference to Antoine Lavoisier, who described the chemistry research he did with his lab partner and wife as (translated) "the days of good hours."
FA Jun 25, 2012, Jay Harrison

Indian Lake

12 Bon Chance 5.6 G (5.4 R) 100' ★★
Start: There are three narrow bands of knobs leading down the slab right of **Le Jour de Bon Heures**. The first one is immediately right, the second about ten feet right, the third about 20' right. Begin at a large flake right of the third line of knobs.
P1 5.6 G (5.4 R): Climb up and left to the line of plates and knobs and follow them to an overlap. Climb through the overlap at a point where it is double-stepped. Go up and left to the oak tree belay at the headwall. 100'
FA Jul 5, 2012, Jay Harrison (roped solo)

13 Benediction 5.6 G (5.3 R) 450' ★★
Start: Near the right end of the upper ledge, below a left-facing open book that leads to the right end of the flap that crosses most of the slab above the ledge.
P1 5.6 G (5.3 R): Go up a crack that leads right into the open book, then go up this to the overlap. Work through this, then move up and right to belay at a low spruce below and right of the headwall. 110'
P2 5.5 G (5.3 R): Climb up either of two short cracks (left one is part of **Bella Vista**) to a ledge. Mantel up the short face left of a spruce tree to easier climbing to a fixed anchor on a spruce tree. 100'
P3 5.3 R: Go up narrow slab right of spruce tree to a ledge. Step left into a clearing in the woods and belay. 120'
P4 5.3 R: Continue up narrow slab on the right to its top. 120'
Descent: Either walk up and left to join the other routes, or scramble down and right into a steep gully that leads down to the base of the slab.
FA Jun 5, 2012, Jay Harrison

14 Leftover 5.7 R (5.6 X) 525'
Start: 15' left of **Bella Vista**, near the left edge of the low end of the slab. There are a few meager edges here that allow progress.
P1 5.7 R (5.4 X): Climb up a bulging start to easy, low-angled, dirty slab. Continue up to a pair of virtual seams (no gear) and go up, trending right, along the edge of the right-facing corner (cross **Bella Vista** where that route steps left onto the outside corner). Continue up to a flap below a mossy headwall, then traverse right to escape the slab. 125'
P2 5.6 R: Walk up and right to the base of a higher slab. Push through a small brush screen to a stance below a chimney formed by a large, left-facing flake 15' up. Climb up to and through the chimney to a stance on top of the flake. Traverse left 4' onto the slab and follow good knobs to a crack. Follow the crack to its end, then continue up a shallow open book past two horizontal shelves. Traverse left to a white pine for a belay. 200'
P3 5.6 X: Move back right onto the slab, and climb through a steep, unprotected section to easier ground. Continue up the slab to the top. (There are several brush screens and poorly-protected sections.) 200'
FA (P1) Aug 7, 2012, Jay Harrison (solo)
FA (P2, P3) Oct 8, 2013, Jay Harrison (solo)

15 Bella Vista 5.7 G 510' ★★★
The first two pitches are especially good; they can be combined with a 70m rope.
Start: At a hairline seam at the lowest point of the slab.
P1 5.4 PG: Go up and right on some fragile rock steps, then go up the slab, moving first up and right, then weaving upward along faint undulations and occasional hints of seam to a large, right-facing open book. Move left to a ledge with a gear anchor. 100'
P2 5.7 G: Move right to a crack through a bulge. Go up the crack to where it disappears, then make some pure friction moves (5.5) up a steep section (about 5' right of the open book of **Benediction**). Continue over an overlap, then up unprotected slab (cross to the left of **Benediction** here) to the left of two short cracks; up this to a small ledge on the right side of an orange headwall. Step left onto headwall, use another short vertical crack and some knobs to reach easy ground. Work up to a fixed anchor on a spruce tree. Two rappels with a 60m rope are possible from here. 130'
P2 5.3 R: Same as P3 of **Benediction**; 80'
P3 5.6 G: (The crack described here was originally **Belle Bottom Buttress**): Scramble up and left onto a wider, low-angle slab with a steeper section above. Climb up left of center to a vertical crack, make a tricky move to reach it, then climb the crack to its end. Continue up easy face, then go between two small spruce trees just before reaching the top. 200'
FA May 26, 2012, Jay Harrison
FA (P2) Jun 28, 2012, Tom Lane, Jay Harrison

Crane Mountain • Crane East

SOUTH CORNER CLIFFS

Location	South side of Crane Mountain accessed from the East Path.
Summary	Very developed collection of single-pitch crags along and above the East Path; some multi-pitch routes.

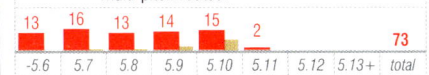

13	16	13	14	15	2		73
-5.6	5.7	5.8	5.9	5.10	5.11	5.12 5.13+	total

The South Corner Cliffs are a collection of tiered cliff-bands situated along (and high above) the East Path. Although its name suggests that it forms a corner, it does not; rather, these cliffs are situated on the broad southernmost shoulder of Crane Mountain. There are some very good single pitch routes (e.g., **Sauron's Bolt of Horror**, **Oddy's Crack of Horror**, **Long Play**), and multi-pitch moderates such as **Stairway to Heaven**. Six separate sections are described, four of which you walk past on the East Path: Height of Land Wall, Land of Overhangs, TeePee Wall, and Long Play Wall. The Diagonal Ramp Wall is an extension of the Long Play Wall accessed from a spur path. The final section—the Upper Walls—is positioned above these walls and consists of a series of slabs and cliffbands that extend hundreds of feet up the mountain.

Indian Lake

HISTORY

Jay Harrison and his family picked blueberries in this area in the 1990s, and Jay soloed a few routes in this area as well. He and Jamie McNeill made a roped exploration to the top of the Upper Walls in the fall of 2008. With the establishment of the East Path, development began at the easily accessed Land of Overhangs and TeePee Wall. Recent development has produced higher quality routes (e.g., **Long Play**) and those of greater difficulty (e.g., **Tighter Than Two**).

DIRECTIONS (MAPS PAGES 142 AND 166)

Follow the East Path past the Measles Group to a level section with a viewpoint and campfire ring on the right. Continue along the path, now going moderately uphill, to the Height of Land Wall **584312,4821350**, the leftmost of the South Corner Cliffs, 28 min from the trailhead.

Crane Mountain ● Crane East ● South Corner Cliffs

UPPER WALLS

Aspect	Southeast
Height	400'
Quality	★★★★
Approach	35 min, moderate
Summary	Some low-angled, multi-pitch exploration routes, and a collection of smaller, crag-like walls with a high concentration of routes.

9	10	5	7	5	36
-5.6	5.7	5.8	5.9	5.10	5.11	5.12	5.13+	total

This collection of lower-angled, short cliffbands and slabs is situated above the Height of Land Wall, Land of Overhangs, and TeePee Wall. Recent explorations have revealed some of the best single-pitch routes on Crane. Getting acquainted is another matter, as the cliff is complex with many treed ledges and vegetated gullies separating the open rock.

The left side has a long, tall, right-facing arch above a low slab—the route **McNeill–Harrison**. To its right is a short, steep slab with four blueberry-named routes. Further right is the tallest slab, which has the cleanest rock, and the excellent routes **Solar Grace** and **Second Amendment**. Right of **Second Amendment** are a number of sub-walls, each of which can be treated as a mini-crag of single-pitch routes. The Provando Wall and Jammer Wall are good destinations.

The upper pitches of **McNeill–Harrison** and **Lane–Harrison** have not been described. The first pitches of these routes have been described in order to point you in the right direction if you wish to continue upward.

DESCENT OPTIONS

Rappel anchors are found on trees at the top of **Madame Blueberry**, **Second Amendment**, **Provando** (P1 and P3), **Animal Charm**, and **Solar Grace**. You can also wander down 2nd class gullies with the occasional short rappel.

DIRECTIONS (MAPS PAGES 142 AND 166)

The Upper Walls are not visible from the East Path, and are best approached from the base of the Height of Land Wall. From the East Path, go left along the base of the Height of Land Wall to its left end, and locate the spur path. Hike steeply uphill and go right of a small slab to reach the base of the Upper Walls near the start of **Blueberry Tafone 584284,4821364**; this is 250' above the left end of the Height of Land Wall. The base of this route is a reference for locating the other routes in this section.

1 Mike's Mountaineering Route 5.8- PG 800'

An adventure link-up. Begin on the lowest cliff on the south side of Crane and climb **Lead 101**, then **Hydrophobia**, then **Halitosis**, then a small 20'-tall buttress known as **Garth's Solo Slab**, then walk up and right 300' to **Ben's Bump** (5.7+ PG, Ben Brooke, 2012)—the slab in the photo. Walk up left onto a long, low-angle slab and take it to its top. Move right and cross a steep gully to the base of **Sky High**, and finish on it.
FA Nov, 2012, Mike Prince, Jay Harrison, Darren Camp

2 Only the Lonely 5.7 R 450'

Soloed on Thanksgiving day to prepare for the overindulgence of the upcoming feast. Begin 50' right of **Ben's Bump**. The first pitch is runout, but can be skipped.
FA Nov 22, 2012, Jay Harrison (solo)

3 Sky High 5.2 G 30'

A short, quality finish to the other routes in this area.
P1 5.2 G: Climb the crack and flakes near the right end of the bushy ledge on the left side of the large buttress. 30'
FA Nov 22, 2012, Jay Harrison (solo)

4 McNeill–Harrison 5.9 G (5.7 R) 100'

Climbs over a long, right-arching, right-facing wall and continues up broken rock along the left side of the Upper Walls, to a poorly protected pitch (5.7 R) at the top. Only the first pitch is described; the overall length of the route is 540'.
Start: 200' uphill and left of **Blueberry Tafone**, at the bottom left end of a long, right-arching, right-facing wall that sits above a low-angled slab, at a right-leaning fingercrack on a vertical wall.
P1 5.9 G: Go up the fingercrack, then hand traverse left along a ledge to the top of an overhang. Go up a steep slab to the base of a low-angle, right-facing corner. Follow the corner to a horizontal crack (just before the corner becomes shrub-filled) and follow it left to a belay on a slab below the woods. 100'
FA Nov, 2008, Jamie McNeill, Jay Harrison

5 The Right Way 5.7 G 60' ★★

Start: At an 8'-high, scruffy, shallow chimney.
P1 5.7 G: Up the chimney to a horizontal. Move left along the horizontal, then up a vertical crack. Move left across a face to join the **McNeill–Harrison**. 60'
History: After climbing the runout, scruffy, and dangerous final pitch to their alpine route, McNeill pointed out this line to Harrison, surmising it would have been a better finish. He was right—this is the better finish to the **McNeill–Harrison**.
FA Nov 10, 2012, Jay Harrison, Tom Lane

Indian Lake

UPPER WALLS, LEFT SIDE
1 Mike's Mountaineering Route (5.8-)
2 Only the Lonely (5.7)
3 Sky High (5.2)
4 McNeill–Harrison (5.9)
5 The Right Way (5.7)
6 H2 Alpine (5.6)
7 Lane–Harrison (5.3)
8 Blueberry Crumble (5.7-)
9 Madame Blueberry (5.6)
10 BLC (5.7)
11 Blueberry Tafone (5.6)
12 Second Amendment (5.10b)
1 Ben's Bump
2 Eyebrow Overhang

6 H2 Alpine 5.6 R 400'

Start: 30' up the left edge of the Blueberry Ledge scramble, at a narrow rounded ledge leading 6' out onto the slab on the left. This is well below and right of the Eyebrow Overhang.

P1 5.3 R: Traverse to the end of the ledge and climb up scruffy slab, through a patch of hanging cherry shrubs and filth into steeply sloping woods. Scramble to rope's end below the foot of a long rib of low-angle rock. 200'

P2 5.6 G (5.2 R): Scramble up and right on scruff to the left edge of a band of trees, then move up and left to a chute right of a sharp-edged, blocky formation with a wide crack between it and the chute. Step left onto the block and make a rising leftward traverse to the block's edge, and follow it to a good ledge with a deep, horizontal crevice that is 3 1/2' tall. 80'

P3 5.6 R: Hop up onto the left edge of the slab above the crevice. Go up and reach a good edge to the right at a crack that points straight downward into the slab. At its end, climb easily to a lone, scraggly white pine at the base of a steep, smooth slab. Walk left to the edge, make dicey moves on friable holds through the slab to an overhang. Hand-traverse left to the edge of the overhang, then step back right and up more dicey slab to a block lying against the top slope. 120'

Descent: There are no trees close to the edge of the cliff; rappel via one of the spruces to the scruffy pine, rappel off that to the horizontal ledge. Rappel off a spruce on the right end of the ledge to the slope below. Scramble down and rappel to the Blueberry ledge, then either rappel to the base or scramble down the left-side chute.

FA May 27, 2013, Jay Harrison, Robin Harrison

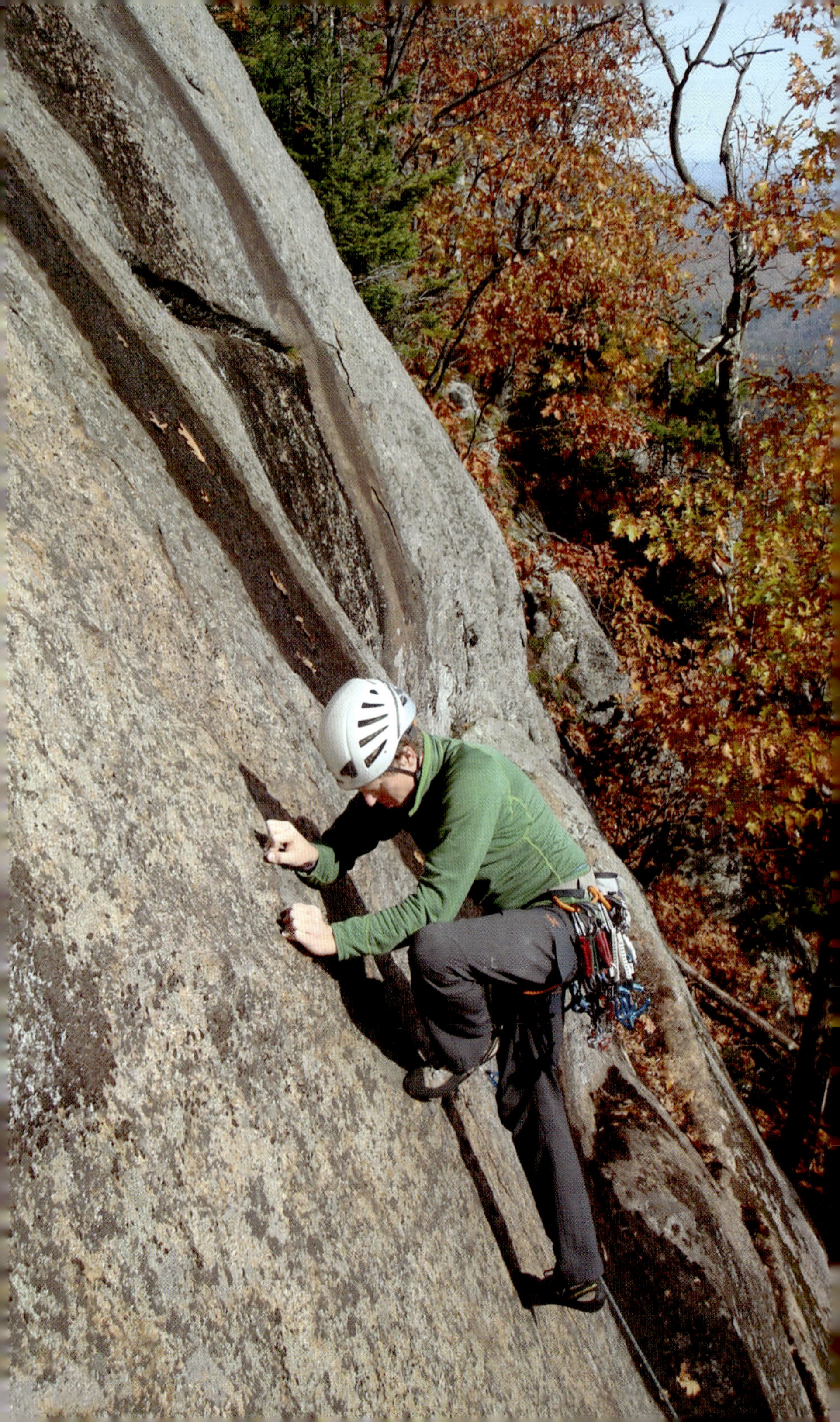

Indian Lake

7 Lane–Harrison 5.3 PG 190'
After the initial slab, this route avoids any hint of exposed rock. The full route is 450' long.
Start: At the belay ledge above **Blueberry Tafone**, below a short slab with a long, overhanging wall above it.
P1 5.3 PG: Go up a short steep slab to the overhanging wall, and go around its left end. Climb up a steep, brushy groove past a large spruce tree, over several short slabs, and move up and right of a large roof. Belay at a tree on the left end of a long ledge. 190'
FA Oct, 2010, Jay Harrison, Tom Lane

8 Blueberry Crumble 5.7- R 50' ★
Start: 100' uphill and left of **Blueberry Tafone**, below the center of a steep, 50'-tall slab, at a right-facing flake.
P1 5.7- R: Go up the flake to a stance, then make unprotected moves past right-facing flakes to a wide, left-leaning crack that is followed to a ledge with a fixed anchor on a tree. 50'
FA Nov 21, 2010, Jay Harrison, Todd Paris

9 Madame Blueberry 5.6 PG 50' ★
Start: 90' uphill and left of **Blueberry Tafone**, below a 50'-tall, steep slab at a right-leaning crack.
P1 5.6 PG: Go up the crack, then step left and follow a left-leaning, right-facing corner. (V1) Move right across a slab (crux) to a handcrack; go up this to a ledge with a fixed anchor on a tree (shared with **Blueberry Crumble**). 50'
V1 Blueberry Flapjacks 5.5 PG ★: Step left, go up a blunt arête, then finish at the ledge with a fixed anchor on a tree.
FA Nov 21, 2010, Todd Paris, Jay Harrison
FA (V1) Nov 21, 2010, Jay Harrison, Todd Paris

10 BLC 5.7 PG 70'
The name stands for Blueberry Ledge Chimney.
Start: 80' uphill and left of **Blueberry Tafone**, below a short chimney formed by a giant block perched on the slab.
P1 5.7 PG: Up the chimney (crux), then scramble up grassy ledges. Trend right and finish at a broad tree-covered ledge. 70'
FA Nov 15, 2010, Jay Harrison

11 Blueberry Tafone 5.6 PG 310' ★
This route trends up and left from the lowest point on the slab. A tafone is a pocket formed by the weathering of rock.
Start: At the low point of the Upper Walls, below a scruffy, diamond-shaped slab with a narrow, right-rising ledge that begins at the ground.
P1 5.6 PG: Follow the ledge for 20' to a left-leaning, zigzag crack. Go up the crack past a left-facing, left-leaning corner to a tall wall. Reach left and go over the wall to a hollow section of rock, then move up left along a horizontal rail to a pointed flake leading to a wide crack. Climb the crack to its end and finish at the broad tree-covered ledge. 140'

P2 5.5 R: Scramble right to the left edge of the **Second Amendment** slab, then make dirty, unprotected moves to reach sloping dirt. Claw up this to a large alcove, then clamber up left through a notch below an overhang and out onto the main face. Weave up the slab above, trending right to the top. 170'
FA (P1) Oct 31, 2010, Jay Harrison
FA (P2) 2012, Jay Harrison (solo)

12 Second Amendment 5.10b G (5.6 R) 200' ★★★★
When both variations are climbed, it eliminates both 5.10 moves and reduces the grade to 5.8+; known as **Bill of Rights**.
Start: 50' right of the start of **Blueberry Tafone**, and 20' right of a large, right-facing corner system, below a clean, dry streak of orange rock between two mossy wet stripes visible from the road.
P1 5.10b G (5.6 R): (V1) Climb up face to a shallow scoop. Continue up clean rock following knobs past two overlaps to a semi-hanging belay at a fixed anchor near a wide horizontal crack. 100'
P2 5.10b G (5.6 R): Climb up easy plates and knobs to an overhang, step right (V2) and climb through the overhang using a sloping, right-rising crack. Climb directly up a steep face, pull over onto an easy slab and scramble to a fixed tree anchor. 100'
V1 5.8+ G: Climb a right-rising crack, then traverse left to the scoop.
V2 5.8+ G: At the overhang, step left and climb straight up the left edge of a block–face, staying close to the left edge for gear.
Descent: Two rappels with a 60m rope.
FA Sep 20, 2012, Tom Lane, Jay Harrison
FA (V1, V2) Sep 23, 2012, Jay Harrison, Tom Lane

13 Tom's Daring-Do 5.9 R 25'
A stout and dangerous lead.
Start: From the top of **Second Amendment**, scramble left 60' to the right edge of a gigantic roof system.
P1 5.9 R: Follow a left-leaning crack out left above the overhang to the nose. Continue straight up a crack system (crux, unprotected) to the top. 25'
FA Nov 10, 2012, Tom Lane, Jay Harrison

14 Solar Grace 5.6+ R 90' ★★
Tricky gear placements in shallow, flared cracks.
Start: 50' right of the start of **Blueberry Tafone** at a moss-covered slab with a short, clean handcrack that starts 6' up.
P1 5.6+ R: Up the handcrack to a grass-covered ledge below a large, hollow flake. Follow a left-facing corner, then go back left across the top of the flake (5.6 R) to the base of a shallow, flared handcrack. Go up the crack past a horizontal on the left, then step left to the base of a pretty face covered with knobs. Go up the face, staying left of a short flared crack. Go past a horizontal and scramble to an oak tree with a fixed anchor. 90'
FA Nov 12, 2010, Jay Harrison, Tom Lane

Opposite: Jamie McNeill at the thin-slab crux of Second Amendment (5.10b). Photo by Jay Harrison.

Indian Lake

UPPER WALLS, RIGHT SIDE
2 Only the Lonely (5.7)
3 Sky High (5.2)
4 McNeill–Harrison (5.9)
5 The Right Way (5.7)
6 H2 Alpine (5.6)
7 Lane–Harrison (5.3)
8 Blueberry Crumble (5.7-)
9 Madame Blueberry (5.6)
10 BLC (5.7)
11 Blueberry Tafone (5.6)
12 Second Amendment (5.10b)
13 Tom's Daring-Do (5.9)
14 Solar Grace (5.6+)
15 Solo, Gracias (5.7)
16 Never Alone (5.7)
17 On the Fence (5.5)
18 Mad Cows (5.10b)
19 Provando (5.7)
20 Riprovando (5.10b)
21 Fireworks (5.7)
22 Robin's Rainy Day Route (5.0)

180

Indian Lake

23 Chokin' Chickens (5.8+)	34 Animal Charm (5.10c)
24 Stand Your Ground (5.7-)	35 Carnivore Crack (5.8)
25 Escalator to Heaven (5.1)	36 Ape X (5.9)
26 Reproof (5.9+)	40 Raindance Roof (5.8)
27 Firecracker (5.7)	42 Roofer Madness (5.10a)
28 Jammer (5.9-)	45 Spiral Staircase (5.5)
29 Blueberry Jam (5.9+)	46 Gray–Harrison (5.8)
30 Animal Farm (5.10b)	47 Stairway to Heaven (5.8)
31 Jug, Tug, and Jam (5.8-)	48 End of the Line (5.10a)
32 Little Jam (5.9-)	49 Crooks and Nannies (5.7+)
33 Blueberry Pie (5.8-)	50 Kissing Pigs (5.9-)
	52 Sauron's Bolt of Horror (5.10c)

1. HEIGHT OF LAND WALL
2. LAND OF OVERHANGS
3. PROVANDO WALL
4. JAMMER WALL
5. ANIMAL CHARM WALL
6. CHOKIN' CHICKENS WALL
7. MAD CROWS WALL
8. TEEPEE WALL

Indian Lake

15 Solo, Gracias 5.7 R 120'
Start: Same as **Solar Grace**.
P1 5.7 R: Climb up a mossy, right-facing corner, then burrow past spruce and oak shrubs. Commit to a dangerous face on the left (5.7 R), then move up and right to a crack. Follow the crack to a thin gong-flake. Up the flake and a crack to a ledge. Belay at an oak tree up and right. 120'
FA Jul 12, 2012, Jay Harrison (roped solo)

16 Never Alone 5.7 G 100' ★
Start: From **Solar Grace** go 40' up a dirt ramp to an oak tree next to a low overhang.
P1 5.7 G: Pull over the overhang and follow a left-rising crack to its end. Step up then follow a horizontal crack left 12' to a right-rising crack. Follow the right-rising crack to its end at a horizontal crack, step left to a vertical crack, and climb this to its end at another horizontal crack. Work up and left to a slab with knobs; climb then to an oak tree belay shared with **Solo, Gracias**. 100'
History: Never alone, and a good thing, too, as Harrison's rope rig jammed just shy of the top. He was forced to abandon it and finish the route unprotected.
FA Jul 13, 2012, Jay Harrison (roped solo)

17 On the Fence 5.5 G 95' ★★
Start: Same as **Never Alone**.
P1 5.5 G: Scramble a few feet up the right-rising ramp, then traverse left out a narrow ledge to another right-rising ramp. Follow right-rising ramp to a wide crack on the left wall. Up this to a horizontal crack, then traverse left to another vertical crack. Follow this as it swings right, then up to a ledge. 95'
FA Jul 14, 2012, Peter Whitmore, Jay Harrison

Mad Cows Wall

Another difficult-to-access wall on the South Corner Cliff. So far this cliff has one route.

DIRECTIONS (MAPS PAGES 142 AND 166)
Climb **Kissing Pigs** or **Sauron's Bolt of Horror** on the TeePee Wall, then walk 35' left. Alternatively, scramble up the chute leading to **Robin's Rainy Day Route** until you can walk climber's right along the base of the cliff.

18 Mad Cows 5.10b G 75'
Good face moves and a scary top out. Protection is available for the final moves, but strenuous to place.
Start: 35' left of the top of **Kissing Pigs** below a 6'-wide, down-facing crack. This is about 100' right of and below **Robin's Rainy Day Route**.
P1 5.10b PG: Reach up to the lower right edge of the eyebrow crack, then make a strenuous undercling traverse to its apex and climb through a flaring, shallow notch to a stance. Traverse left 6' on a rounded ledge, make a simple mantle up to another rounded ledge, step right and make a difficult mantle upward. Move left and up on good holds to a horizontal seam below a vertical line of small knobs. Follow these up and slightly right to a rounded, left-rising ledge. The short bulging wall above has enough holds (and one good horizontal pod for gear) to make the final moves safe. 75'
FA Oct 12, 2013, Tom Lane, Jay Harrison

Provando Wall

Several quality routes sit on this hidden wall above the Land of Overhangs with no easy approach.

DIRECTIONS (MAPS PAGES 142 AND 166)
There are three ways to reach the base of this wall: (a) from the P2 belay on **Stairway to Heaven**, walk right; (b) Follow the spur path to the Upper Walls near **Second Amendment**, then up and right to reach the narrow ledge at the top of the wall and rappel; (c) scramble up the slope right of the Land of Overhangs (not recommended). So far, most people rappel in.

19 Provando 5.7 G 160' ★★
Start: Below a vertical crack just right of a right-facing corner formed by stacked blocks. This is 50' right of the top of P2 of **Stairway to Heaven**, and 50' farther up the approach gully of **Robin's Rainy Day Route**.
P1 5.7 G: Climb the crack past a body-sized pod 20' up. Continue past steps on lower-angled rock to a tree belay on a broad ledge. 65'
P2 5.7 G: On the wall behind the tree belay, climb the right-leaning crack to the next tree ledge at the base of the Jammer Wall (on its left side). 30'
P3 5.6 G: (V1) On the left end of the wall (and right of the right-rising gully) is a right-leaning crack. Begin 6' right at a vertical crack that splits into 2 cracks at thigh-height, and rejoins into a single crack at head height. Follow the crack to a ledge 35' up. Step right and climb a vertical crack system to its end. Up face holds to a large tree ledge with a fixed tree anchor. 65'
V1 5.7 G: 8' right at a shallow vertical crack. Follow this to where it jogs left to a niche 7' up. Continue up a dual crack to join the normal route.
FA Nov 9, 2012, Jay Harrison

20 Riprovando 5.10b G (5.6 R) 80' ★★
Start: 6' right of **Provando**, 10' below the bottom of a left-rising mini-ramp.
P1 5.10b G (5.6 R): Use horizontal cracks to work up and right to a left-rising crack. Make a difficult move to get into it and follow it to a small stance. Move up and right on easier rock, then follow good knobs up a steepening wall. Make a difficult move, then follow a horizontal crack up and right to a tree belay on a broad ledge. 80'
FA Oct 13, 2012, Jay Harrison, Tom Lane

21 Fireworks 5.7 G 70' ★★
Start: 20' right of **Provando**, below an overhang with a short handcrack.
P1 5.7 G: Go up the handcrack then follow a right-rising ramp to an oak tree. Work up a slab, past a horizontal crack, then traverse right to a line of knobs. Follow the knobs, move right, climb an arête, and friction to a tree belay on a broad ledge. 70'
FA Jul 4, 2013, Jay Harrison, Tom Lane

Indian Lake

JAMMER WALL, ANIMAL CHARM WALL
19 Provando (5.7)
23 Chokin' Chickens (5.8+)
24 Stand Your Ground (5.7-)
25 Escalator to Heaven (5.1)
26 Reproof (5.9+)
27 Firecracker (5.7)
28 Jammer (5.9-)
29 Blueberry Jam (5.9+)
30 Animal Farm (5.10b)
31 Jug, Tug, and Jam (5.8-)
32 Little Jam (5.9-)
33 Blueberry Pie (5.8-)
34 Animal Charm (5.10c)
35 Carnivore Crack (5.8)
36 Ape X (5.9)
46 Gray-Harrison (5.8)
47 Stairway to Heaven (5.8)

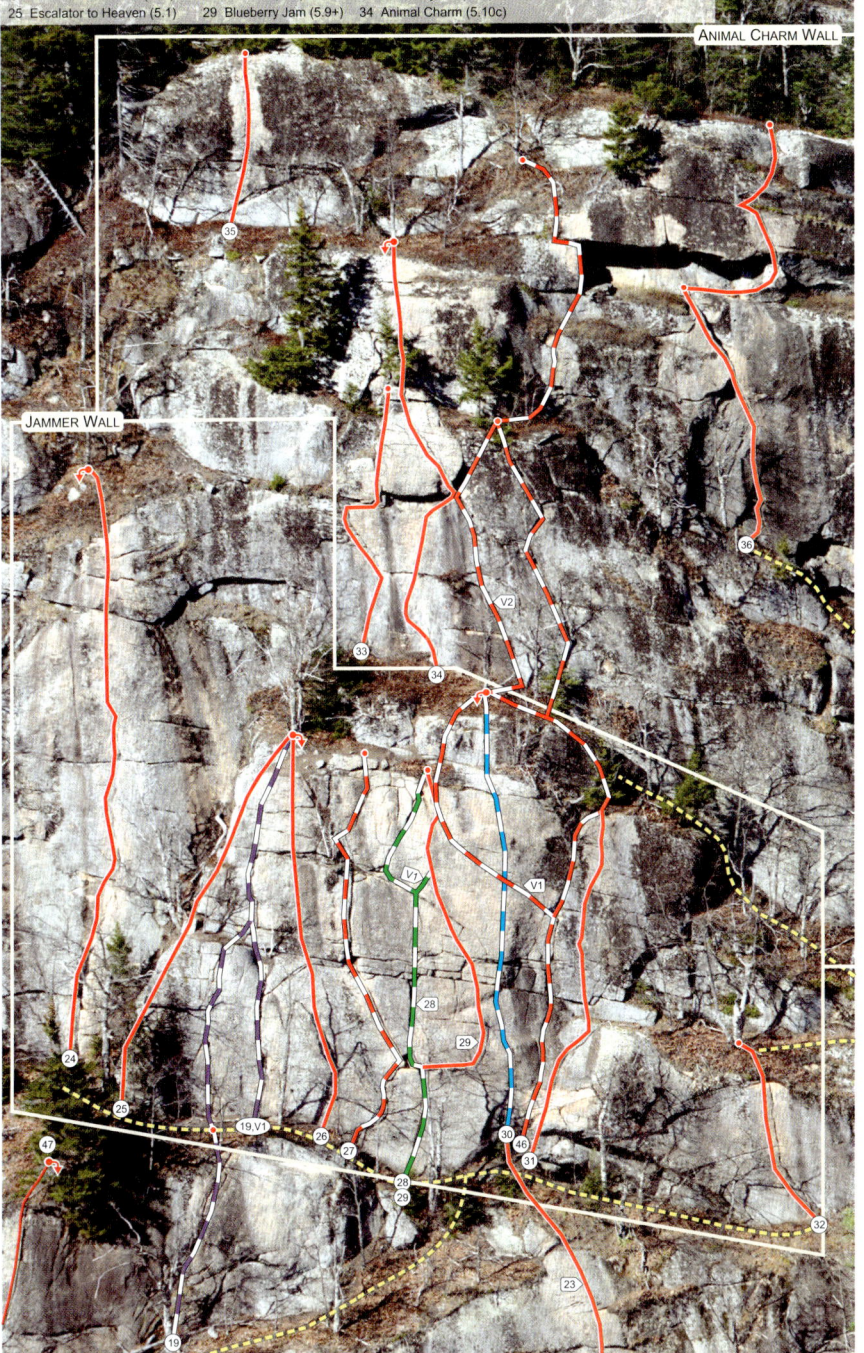

183

Indian Lake

22 Robin's Rainy Day Route **5.0 G 70'**
Much like the routes in the Upper Wall section, this one is in raw condition.
Start: Scramble up a wooded gully along the right end of the Land of Overhangs for 200' to a right-rising ramp that is above and right of the gully.
P1 5.0 G: Climb the rock ramp to a good ledge. 70'
FA Oct 30, 2010, Jay Harrison, Robin Harrison

Chokin' Chickens Wall

DIRECTIONS   (MAPS PAGES 142 AND 166)
You'll have to work to get here. There are a several ways to reach this wall: (a) Rappel from the base of Animal Farm; (b) Climb Kissing Pigs, then Mad Cows; (c) Move right from the oak tree part way up Fireworks; (d) Climb Robin's Rainy Day Route; and (e) Walk to the base of Bodhi Tree, then continue up and left on ledges.

23 Chokin' Chickens **5.8+ G 45'** ★ ★
Good knob climbing.
Start: 40' right of the left end of the ledge system, 6' right of an oak tree below a right-rising horizontal crack 7' up.
P1 5.8+ G: Reach up to the horizontal crack, rail right 5', then climb knobs up a face to another horizontal crack. Move left 4', then go up and left to the top. 45'
FA (P1) Sep 13, 2013, Tom Lane, Jay Harrison

Jammer Wall

This is the wall above the Provando Wall. Unlike many of the other sections of the Upper Walls, it's easy to walk here. Among the single-pitch routes on this wall is P3 of Provando (between Escalator to Heaven and Reproof).

DIRECTIONS   (MAPS PAGES 142 AND 166)
From Second Amendment, walk uphill and right to emerge onto an exposed ledge above the Provando Wall. Continue right and up a short scramble to an upper ledge at the base of this wall.

24 Stand Your Ground **5.7- G 105'** ★ ★ ★ ★
One of the best 5.7 routes at Crane.
Start: At the left end of the wall is a right-rising gully. Begin just left of the gully below a clean crack.
P1 5.7- G: Go up the clean crack system to its end. Continue up a face to easier ground. Scramble up the blueberry slope to a fixed anchor on an oak tree. 105'
Descent: Rappel with a 70m rope; with a 60m rope, rappel rightwards into the gully.
FA Jul 27, 2013, Tom Lane, Jay Harrison

25 Escalator to Heaven **5.1 PG 65'**
Start: At the left end of the wall below a right-rising gully.
P1 5.1 PG: Climb the outside corner of the ramp to a fixed anchor on a tree. 65'
FA Aug 25, 2013, Mike Prince (solo)

26 Reproof **5.9+ G 65'** ★ ★
Start: Right of the Provando P3 crack (and variation), at a point where the terrain steps down to the right, below a right-facing, left-leaning, rounded corner 10' up.
P1 5.9+ G: Step right onto the face, then move up into the corner (crux). Climb this until it begins to round off into a ledge, then move up the slab on the main face. Climb up to a black streak past several horizontal cracks to the top. 65'
FA Jul 24, 2013, Tom Lane, Jay Harrison

27 Firecracker **5.7 G 75'** ★ ★
Start: At the S-shaped crack.
P1 5.7 G: Climb the S-shaped crack to stance, then follow a left-rising vertical crack to a notch. Continue up the vertical crack to its end, then step right onto the face, and move up and left to a right-rising vertical crack leading to the ledge. 75'
FA Jul 19, 2013, Jay Harrison (solo)

28 Jammer **5.9- G 75'** ★ ★
Start: Just right of the approach path at vertical crack 10' right of Firecracker.
P1 5.9- G: Go up the vertical crack to its end. Step left onto a stance, then follow face holds right of a right-rising crack. Go up a vertical crack system to its end at a left-rising horizontal crack. (V1) Traverse left to a right-rising vertical crack and follow it to a large ledge. 75'
V1 5.9+ ★ ★ ★: Step up onto the sloping ledge of Blueberry Jam and follow that route to the top.
FA Aug 1, 2013, Jay Harrison (solo)
FA (V1) Oct, 2013, Jeremy Haas, Erika Schielke

29 Blueberry Jam **5.9+ G 80'** ★
This line links good crack systems that were curiously untouched by other routes.
Start: Same as Jammer.
P1 5.9+ G: Go up the vertical crack to its end, then traverse right along a horizontal crack 10' to a short, right-rising crack. Climb to its end, then move left and up to short vertical cracks. Follow these to a left-rising horizontal crack, and move slightly left and up onto a small sloping stance below a bolt. Climb past the bolt to a narrow horizontal crack, then step right to reach a left-rising vertical crack (this is the final crack of the Gray–Sointio variation of Gray–Harrison). Climb this to the ledge. 80'
FA Sep 17, 2013, Jay Harrison, Tom Lane

30 Animal Farm **5.10b G 75'** ★ ★
Start: At an overhanging notch just left of a head-high overhang and 15' right of the approach path. (This position is where P4 of Gray-Harrison begins.)
P1 5.10b G: Climb through a blocky notch, then step left and climb a thin crack to a sloped ledge. Go straight up an orange-tinted face past several horizontals (crux) to a ledge. Go up another 6'-tall wall to a ledge with a tree and fixed anchor. 75'
FA Aug 14, 2013, Tom Lane, Jay Harrison

Indian Lake

31 Jug, Tug, and Jam 5.8- PG 60'
Start: Just right of the overhanging notch of Animal Farm, on the left edge of a large, double overhang that begins at chest level.
P1 5.8- PG: Jug up and right through double overhang via a vertical crack. Walk up the slab above, following a right-rising seam to a ledge beneath a steep headwall. Climb the headwall using a network of vertical cracks linked by horizontal cracks, roughly parallel to (and 10' right of) Gray-Harrison. Make a tricky final move to reach a brushy ledge, then join Gray–Harrison for the final 15' to the top of the Jammer Wall. 60'
FA Oct 12, 2013, Jay Harrison, Tom Lane

32 Little Jam 5.9- G 25'
Short, but too good to pass up.
Start: Walk right on the ledge past a low overhang to a delicious left-leaning crack.
P1 5.9- G: Go up the vertical crack to a blueberry jungle ledge. 25'
History: The first ascent party had no rack, so they knotted slings and used small rocks (and a few slung bolt hangers) as gear.
FA Aug 2, 2013, Jay Harrison, Tom Lane

Animal Charm Wall

Access this wall by climbing any of the routes on the Jammer Wall.

33 Blueberry Pie 5.8- G 50'
Has some questionable blocks.
Start: At a 6'-tall left-facing corner left of a black streak.
P1 5.8- G: Climb up the corner to its top, and reach a crack at the point where it turns a corner. Move up left along the crack to a small overhang, then move right to another vertical crack that leads to a left-facing arête. Climb the face of the arête to a ledge just left of a spruce tree. 50'
FA Jul 27, 2013, Jay Harrison, Bruce Monroe

34 Animal Charm 5.10c G 80' ★★★
Start: On the right edge of a black streak below two horizontal cracks, the first is 12' up.
P1 5.10c G: Climb up good knobs to the first horizontal (#3 Camalot), then up past a bolt to a break beneath a roof. Traverse right under the roof 6' to a small right-facing corner left of a notch. (This notch is the Harrison–Haas variation to the Gray–Harrison.) Follow a left-rising crack that breaks the overhang (crux) to a ledge with a spruce tree. Go up a scooped slab to a horizontal crack (#2 and #1 Camalots); move past this (funky crux) to easier ground and a fixed anchor on a tree. 80'
FA Sep 13, 2013, Jay Harrison, Tom Lane

35 Carnivore Crack 5.8 G 35' ★
Recommended if you have a high tolerance for pain.
Start: Climb Animal Charm or Stand Your Ground and wander up to the base of this final buttress. Locate the sole vertical crack.
P1 5.8 G: Difficult moves gain the vertical crack, which is lined with some of the sharpest crystals in the Adirondacks. Wince and climb up to the top. 35'
FA Aug 7, 2013, Jay Harrison (solo)

36 Ape X 5.9 G 85' ★
The original intent was to climb the dramatic crack through the large roof directly above the P1 belay. Any takers?
Start: From the top of Little Jam, scramble up and right to a ledge below a steep wall with a large spruce tree growing in front of it. Walk up and left and go up a dirt ramp next to the cliff to a thin vertical crack with well-spaced finger-locks that goes up to the right end of an A-shaped overhang.
P1 5.9 G: Climb the vertical crack to the right side of the A-shaped overhang. Work up to the apex of the overhang and break through via a good handcrack. Follow the crack up and left to a large ledge. 45'
P2 40 5.5 G: Walk 15' right and climb the left side of a block to the lip of the overhang. Climb easily up a vertical handcrack to a horizontal crack, traverse right 8' to a thin right-leaning crack, and follow this to a notch in the upper slab. 40'
FA Oct 21, 2013, Jay Harrison, Tom Lane

Crane Mountain • Crane East • South Corner Cliffs

HEIGHT OF LAND WALL

Aspect	Southeast
Height	35'
Quality	
Approach	28 min, moderate
Summary	Very short wall right next to the trail, overshadowed by the better routes just a little further right; more of a landmark.

1	1	1					3
-5.6	5.7	5.8	5.9	5.10	5.11	5.12	5.13+	total

More of a landmark than a climbing destination, this cliff is 40' tall and 100' long. It has three routes toward its right end that are very close to the path and share a fixed anchor on a tree.

DIRECTIONS (MAPS PAGES 142 AND 166)
Follow the East Path past the Measles Group to a level section with a viewpoint and campfire ring on the right. Continue along the path, now going moderately uphill, to this wall 584312,4821350, situated very close to the path.

37 To Do 5.4 PG 35' ★
Start: 15' left of the arête that is near the path, at a left-rising ramp below a right-facing corner.
P1 5.4 PG: Climb the corner to an overhang, step right, then up the face to a tree with a fixed anchor. 35'
FA Apr 21, 2010, Jay Harrison (solo)

Indian Lake

38 Ta Da 5.8- R 35'
Start: At a left-rising flake at head height, immediately left of the start of Crane Fang.
P1 5.8- R: Go up the flake then up to a 4'-tall right-facing flake. Step left, then up the face to a tree with a fixed anchor. 35'
FA Nov 13, 2010, Jay Harrison, Robin Harrison, Tom Lane

39 Crane Fang 5.7+ R 35' ★
Start: 5' left of the arête that is near the path, at a 12'-tall fingercrack in a right-facing corner.
P1 5.8- R: Up the fingercrack to its end, then continue past a 4'-tall right-facing flake (the Crane fang) to easier rock and a tree with a fixed anchor. 35'
FA Aug 3, 2011, Michael Farnsworth, Connie Magee

Crane Mountain ● Crane East ● South Corner Cliffs

LAND OF OVERHANGS

Aspect	Southeast
Height	50'-500'
Quality	★★
Approach	28 min, moderate
Summary	Mostly single pitch routes, some of which break through impressive roofs; a couple of them have been extended way up the mountain.

1	1	4	2	1		9
-5.6	5.7	5.8	5.9	5.10	5.11	5.12	5.13+	total

Along the East Path, 100' past the Height of Land Wall, is the jutting buttress of Land of Overhangs. The left side of this buttress has a 15'-deep roof 20' up, and to its right is a huge, right-facing, block-filled corner where the buttress meets the main cliff (at the winter route Immigrant Song). The left end of the wall slopes steeply uphill and is the location of the zigzag line of Raindance Roof. Right of the buttress is a long roof 30' up with the routes Roofer Madness and Tight for Two. Further right is a clean narrow buttress with a squeeze chimney on its left side and the route Spiral Staircase. Beyond here the cliff diminishes in height and quality.

Unfortunately, some of the cracklines are natural drainage pathways and are growing back in.

DIRECTIONS (MAPS PAGES 142 AND 166)
From the Height of Land Wall, continue on the East Path. This is the next cliff on your left, very near the path, with many large overhangs 584321,4821366. The path is directly against the rock at the base of Stairway to Heaven.

40 Raindance Roof 5.8 PG 85' ★★
A zigzag route that follows the left edge of the cliff.
Start: Left end of a deep roof, at a fistcrack in a right-facing corner.
P1 5.8 PG: (V1, V2) Go up the fistcrack to the roof, and hand traverse left along a ledge. Move up left past another ledge then mantel (crux, tricky gear) onto a tree-covered ledge. Step left onto a steep face and climb enjoyable rock past an overlap to a tree with a fixed anchor. 85'
V1 Split Personality 5.8 PG: Start 10' left at a handcrack below a right-facing corner capped by a ceiling. Go right past the ceiling, then climb directly up the off-width crack to a sloping ledge.
V2 5.6 G: Begin 50' uphill and left, avoiding the bottom half of the route, and climb a right-leaning crack to the tree-covered ledge.
FA Sep 19, 2010, Michael Gray, Garth Briscoe
FA (V1) Nov 20, 2011, Tom Lane, Jay Harrison

41 Tom's Roof Project
This open project goes up a huecoed-face to an arête under the right side of the roof. Make a big reach to a horizontal crack that is above the roof, and follow it left to a discontinuous crack that goes to the top.

42 Roofer Madness 5.10a G (5.8 R) 80' ★★
A second pitch has been cleaned but not led.
Start: 20' right of the huge, block-filled, right-facing corner, below a left-facing, left-leaning corner.
P1 5.10a G (5.8 R): Go up the corner past two pitons to an overlap. Work around the left side of the overlap, then back right (5.8 R) and up a mossy slab to the base of the long roof. Go out a tapering fistcrack to the lip of the roof, pull over the roof, then step left to a left-leaning handcrack. Follow the handcrack to a spruce shrub and go around its right side to a belay at a birch tree. 80'
FA Nov 3, 2010, Michael Gray

43 Tighter than Two 5.11b G (5.4 R) 80' ★★
The roof crack appears to take a #2 Camalot, but it does not.
Start: Same as Roofer Madness.
P1 5.11b G: Traverse right along a foot ledge, then climb over a mossy bulge to a dirty slab (5.4 R). Up the slab to a stance below the right side of the long roof. Reach for a fingercrack that starts half way out the roof and climb to the lip. Pull the lip and follow a tapering fingercrack on a slab to a birch tree (same as Roofer Madness). 80'
FA Aug 3, 2011, Michael Farnsworth, Connie Magee

44 Misty Mountain Hop 5.8 G 50'
Start: 5' left of the start of Spiral Staircase at a left-facing flake near the ground.
P1 5.8 G: Reach and mantel (crux) onto a ledge 10' up. Go up a mossy face, past a horizontal crack, then past a ledge to another crack. Finish with a short slab that ends at a tree with a fixed anchor. 50'
FA Oct, 2010, Garth Briscoe, Ryan Heffernan

45 Spiral Staircase 5.5 G 50' ★
Start: On the East Path, at an offwidth crack in a short, left-facing corner.
P1 5.5 G: Follow the crack right past easy steps, then back left where it widens into a deep squeeze chimney. Climb this (crux) to a ledge and a tree with a fixed anchor (same as Misty Mountain Hop). 50'
FA Oct 4, 2010, Jay Harrison

46 Gray–Harrison 5.8 PG 535' ★

The lower pitches are uninspiring; the upper pitches have several interesting moves. Although the pitches are short and dirty, the climbing is sustained and the protection is adequate. This route was an eye-opener to the Upper Walls of the South Corner Cliff.

Start: Top of P1 of Stairway to Heaven.

P1 5.8 PG: Walk left to a large, dirty, right-facing corner. Climb a short way up this, move left around the corner to a small stance, then climb up a difficult crack to a ledge. Move left to a tree with a fixed anchor. 80'

P2 5.7 PG: Climb a dirty crack past a large, dead pine tree, then up a dirty face to a sloping ledge. Step up along a low-angle slab to a right-leaning, right-facing corner. Follow it to a short, steep headwall, then tunnel past dense trees to a steep wooded ledge. 75'

P3 2nd Class: Walk up and left to a right-rising, brushy ledge. Go right along this ledge, below P5 of Stairway to Heaven, to a low roof above the ledge. 175'

P4 5.7 G: Boulder up a broken, left-facing corner (which is left off the low roof) to a grassy ledge. Climb a steep crack that forks (V1). Follow the right crack past oak trees then scramble left to an oak tree with a forked trunk and a fixed anchor. 80'

P5 5.8- PG: (V2) Walk 10' right to a left-leaning crack and climb it for 30' to an overlap. Traverse right along the overlap to a vertical crack and follow it to a ledge and belay at a small birch tree. 65'

P6 5.8 G: Climb a steep fingercrack up a 12'-tall wall and make a tough move onto a grassy slab. Work up and right to a deep, right-facing corner capped by a roof. Climb up the wall on the left and make an exciting exit onto an easy slab. Tree belay at the top of the South Corner Cliffs. 60'

V1 Gray–Sointio 5.9 PG ★★: Stay left and follow a horizontal crack across a clean steep face then reach to a higher crack and follow it to its end. Reach into a shallow left-leaning crack and follow it (crux) to a vegetated ledge. Scramble up to the oak tree belay on the next ledge.

V2 Harrison–Haas 5.8 G (5.4 R): 5' left of the left-leaning crack is a long downward-pointing flake. Boulder up the left side of the flake, then move up and left to another long flake. Foot traverse left, then climb a face (5.4 R) to an overhanging, right-facing corner. Follow the corner and go over a steep wall (dirty) to the tree belay.

FA (5.8 A0) Oct 23, 2010, Michael Gray, Jay Harrison
FA (V1) May 22, 2011, Michael Gray, Eric Sointio
FA (V2) Aug 31, 2011, Jay Harrison, Jeremy Haas
FFA (P6) Aug 31, 2011, Jay Harrison, Jeremy Haas

47 Stairway to Heaven 5.8 G 245' ★★★

Clean, varied and enjoyable climbing for P1 and P2. From the top of P2, the best route to the top of the South Corner Cliffs is to walk right 50', climb anything on the Provando Wall, then continue as desired up the Jammer Wall.

Start: On the East Path, at the base of the clean, narrow buttress with a chimney on its left side and a birch tree 20' up.

P1 5.7 G: Go up to the first horizontal crack (unprotected, crux), then past a birch tree to the center of the narrow buttress. Go past horizontals to a belay on a ledge at an oak tree with a fixed anchor (same as Misty Mountain Hop). 50'

P2 5.7 G: Climb an S-shaped crack to a small oak tree. Move left to a ramp in an overhanging, right-facing corner. Follow the corner for 8' to a horizontal crack in the overhanging left wall of the corner. Work out left using the horizontal crack and a good sidepull to a small ledge. Climb a 5.4 slab to a belay on a tree-covered ledge. 60'

P3 3rd class: Scramble over a short wall above the ledge and walk for 60' up a steep wooded slope to the base of a short cliffband with a right-leaning crack. 70'

P4 5.8 G: Follow the crack, then make a long reach to a left-facing flake. Climb a short slab to a belay at a large oak tree on a long ledge. 30'

P5 5.7+ PG: Climb a right-leaning crack to its end, then step right to another crack and follow this to a belay at a spruce tree with a fixed anchor. 35'

FA (P1) Oct 3, 2010, Mike Prince, Garth Briscoe
FA (P2) Oct 8, 2010, Jay Harrison, Mike Prince
FA (P3) Oct 23, 2010, Jay Harrison, Michael Gray
FA (P4) Nov 12, 2010, Tom Lane, Jay Harrison
FA (P5) Nov 3, 2010, Tom Lane, Ryan Heffernan

48 End of the Line 5.10a G 40' ★★

Start: 20' left of Crooks and Nannies at a rock flake 6' up below a vertical line of knobs that fades halfway up the steep slab.

● **P1 5.10a G:** Climb up onto flake and step right and climb the vertical line of knobs to their top. Step up and left to a small, blocky open book and climb this to the top. Fixed anchor on a tree. 40'
FA Nov 20, 2013, Jay Harrison, Tom Lane

49 Crooks and Nannies 5.7+ G 30' ★

Start: Approach as for Robin's Rainy Day Route, but turn left before going up the steep gully, and locate a steep brown slab. Begin on the right edge of the slab at a vertical crack system.

P1 5.7+ G: Climb cracks to the notch at the top right edge of the cliff, or stay on the face left of the notch for a longer, more aesthetic finish. 30'
FA Oct 28, 2013, Jay Harrison (roped solo)

Pen and ink by Tad Welch.

Indian Lake

Crane Mountain • Crane East • South Corner Cliffs

TEEPEE WALL

Aspect	Southeast
Height	60'
Quality	★★★
Approach	31 min, moderate
Summary	Smallish wall with a couple of really good single-pitch routes; **Oddy's Crack of Horror** is especially noteworthy, and marks where the "good" trailside climbing really begins.

2	1	1	2	4	1		11
-5.6	5.7	5.8	5.9	5.10	5.11	5.12	5.13+	total

This wall is a long cliffband that starts above the right end of Land of the Overhangs. It has short, single pitch routes and nearly all of them start on the East Path. On the left side, the TeePee Wall reaches its highest point at **Sauron's Bolt of Horror**, a thin vertical crack on a cliffband 70' uphill from the East Path. Most of the climbing is concentrated near a bulging wall with the right-rising rail of **Half Man Half Wit**, adjacent to the trail. The right end, separated by a block-filled dirt ramp, has a tips crack on a steep slab—the route **Oddy's Crack of Horror**.

HISTORY
The name was originally TP Wall (the initials for Todd Paris), which later morphed into TeePee Wall.

DIRECTIONS   (MAPS PAGES 142 AND 166)
From the Height of Land Wall (the first wall of the South Corner Cliffs), continue on the East Path past Land of Overhangs to the next section of rock 584388,4821467. This is 3 min past the Height of Land Wall. The path is directly against the cliff at **A Peney for your Freedom**.

50 Kissing Pigs 5.9- G 65'
Interesting climbing with a couple scruffy ledges along the way.
Start: 60' left of **Sauron's Bolt of Horror** at a left-facing flake that is 3' left of a vertical handcrack and 7' left of a vertical seam in a steep wall. This is 40' right of a right-rising ramp.
P1 5.9- G: Climb the flake to its end, move left into the vertical crack. Follow it to a horizontal crack and traverse left 6' to a vertical seam which widens to a narrow, flared crack. Climb the crack to a large, thank-God shelf, move up a scruffy dirt slope past a large oak tree to a bulging overlap with a left-rising flake overhead. A hard pull gains a decent stance with a large, left-facing, left-rising flake to the right. Reach it and head up, once again scrounge through dirt, go past a spruce tree, and scramble up to safety. 65'
FA Oct 17, 2013, Tom Lane, Jay Harrison

51 Animal (linkup) 5.10c G 340' ★★★
This quality tour of the South Corner Cliff ascends all the "animal" routes, back-to-back, to the very top of the mountain. Sustained.
P1 5.9- G: Climb **Kissing Pigs** to the ledge. 65'
P2 5.10b G: Move 35' left on the ledge and climb **Mad Cows**. 75'
P3 5.8 G: Move the belay up and left and climb **Chokin' Chickens**, positioning you perfectly for the next pitch. Leave your approach shoes here at the top of this pitch, as you can rappel back to this point and walk off. 45'
P4 5.10b G: Climb **Animal Farm**. 75'
P5 5.10c G: Move the belay up to the top of the ledge and climb **Animal Charm**. 80'

52 Sauron's Bolt of Horror 5.10c G 60' ★★★
Follows a steep and continuous crack on a sheer face.
Start: 70' from the East Path, uphill and left of the start of **English Channel**. Approach from the left by following the base of the wall uphill to a 4'-wide grass ledge above a terraced belay stance.

*Michael Gray on the first ascent of **Sauron's Bolt of Horror** (5.10c). Photo by Jay Harrison.*

P1 5.10c G: Above the ledge is a vertical seam; follow this past the left end of an overlap to stepped ledges. Go up the ledges and continue up the seam as it widens and enters a left-facing corner on a bulging wall. Pull over the wall to a sloping stance in a right-facing corner. Up the corner and an overlap to a fixed anchor on a tree. 60'
FA Aug 27, 2011, Michael Gray, Tom Lane

53 English Channel 5.10a R 50'

Start: On the East Path, at the left end of the bulging wall, at a 1"-deep horizontal edge at waist height below a rock scar.
P1 5.10a R: Step up on the ledge, then up past a right-facing flake. Move left to a good horn (only pro in this section), work up and right to a short horizontal crack that turns vertical and becomes a fingercrack. Follow the fingercrack to a large ledge on the left. Step right onto a clean face with a right-facing flake, then go to a tree with a fixed anchor (shared with **A Peney for Your Freedom**). 50'
FA Jul 24, 2010, Michael Gray, Mike Prince

54 Rope Monster 5.11b TR 40' ★★

Climbs the face between **English Channel** and **A Peney for Your Freedom**. Go past a horizontal crack 20' up and up the steep slab above it.
FA (TR) Aug, 2010, Michael Farnsworth

55 A Peney for Your Freedom 5.8+ G 50' ★★

The short, steep crack above the ledge (5.10a) has been climbed on toprope.
Start: On the East Path at the most obvious feature on the cliff—the full-height C-shaped crack. This begins 20' left of a right-rising rail of **Half Man, Half Wit**.
P1 5.8+ G: Go through a flare to a jug below a thin crack (small cam). Follow the crack as it flares, bends to the right, and goes to a ledge. Follow the crack up and right in a right-leaning corner to a tree. Walk left to a larger tree with a fixed anchor. 50'
History: Named in memory of Jonathan K. Peney, who was killed in combat in Afghanistan.
FA Aug 24, 2010, Todd Paris, Tom Lane, Jay Harrison

56 Half Man, Half Wit 5.9 R 40'

Questionable rock and protection suggest that this is best climbed on toprope.
Start: On the East Path, at a right-rising rail below the bulging wall.
P1 5.9 R: Follow the rail around the bulging wall and work up parallel vertical seams to an overlap. Step left, and go back right to a belay at a tree. 40'
FA Oct 14, 2010, Tom Lane, Jay Harrison

57 Fool in the Forest 5.7+ G 35'

Start: On the East Path, 20' right of the right-rising rail of **Half Man, Half Wit**, at the leftmost of three left-leaning cracks.
P1 5.7+ G: Follow the crack past a chockstone in a slot to the right end of an overlap. Belay at a tree (same as **Half Man, Half Wit**). 35'
FA Jul 12, 2010, Jay Harrison

58 Woodland Idiot 5.6 PG 35'

Start: The rightmost of three left-rising vertical cracks before a gully that divides the TeePee Wall in half.
P1 5.6 PG: Climb crack to stance. Step left and climb through a blocky chimney to the top. 35'
FA Sep, 2011, Jay Harrison

59 Oddy's Crack of Horror 5.10b G 60' ★★★★

Good gear and stances from which to place it. Exceptional.
Start: On the East Path, at the right end of the cliff, at a sheer wall with a tips crack that begins 30' up.
P1 5.10b G: Climb up right-facing flakes to the right end of a horizontal crack. Work up and right past the crack to another horizontal crack. Continue up the tapering-to-tips fingercrack (crux) to a tree with a fixed anchor. 60'
FA Aug 26, 2010, Tom Lane, Jay Harrison

60 Yodellaybackloon 5.6- G 40' ★★

A meticulously-cleaned right-facing offwidth corner.
Start: 20' right of **Oddy's Crack of Horror** is a 30'-tall right-facing corner. Begin 30' right to access a ledge.
P1 5.6- G: Climb left to the base of the corner, then up the corner to its top. Place a 1" cam above for your second, then walk left to the fixed anchor on **Oddy's Crack of Horror**. 40'
Gear: A large cam (5") is nice for the top.
FA May 7, 2012, Valerie Bachinsky, Kevin Heckeler

Tom Lane on the first ascent of
Oddy's Crack of Horror (5.10b). Photo by Jay Harrison.

Indian Lake

Crane Mountain • Crane East • South Corner Cliffs
LONG PLAY WALL

Aspect	Southeast
Height	140'
Quality	★ ★ ★
Approach	32 min, moderate
Summary	High-quality face and crack routes with knobs and ribs; the face is split by left-rising horizontal cracks.

2		4	2		8
-5.6	5.7	5.8	5.9	5.10	5.11	5.12	5.13+	total

This tall, sheer wall is the rightmost of the South Corner Cliffs. The route **Long Play** ascends its greatest height. A vegetated gully on the left separates this cliff from the TeePee Wall, and the right end is separated from the Isobuttress by a tree-covered slope. As with many cliffs on Crane Mountain, there are knobs, flakes, and rib-like holds hidden beneath a thick carpet of lichen.

DESCENT OPTIONS

Rappel from a tree with a fixed anchor at the top of **Long Play**. One rappel can be made with a single 70m rope. Alternatively, make a long rightward rappel to an oak tree with a fixed anchor, then make a second rappel to the ground.

DIRECTIONS (MAPS PAGES 142 AND 166)

From the Height of Land Wall (the first wall of the South Corner Cliffs), continue on the East Path past Land of Overhangs to the Tee Pee Wall where the path is directly up against the cliff. Continue to its right end, then uphill to a fork in the trail in front of the route **Long Play** (a distinctive orange strip on a tall wall) 584390,4821516. This is 4 min from the Height of Land Wall.

From the fork, the East Path continues away from the cliff to cross open talus, at 34 min.

61 Paris–Harrison 5.7 PG 200'

Not technically on the Long Play Wall, but accessed from its left end. Much like the routes in the Upper Wall section, this one is in raw condition.

Start: Hike up the vegetated gully on the left end of the cliff. Go under a chest-sized block wedged between the cliff and a large boulder (start of **Bodhi Tree**), continue up and left to the base of a tall wall with a low ceiling on its left end.

P1 5.7 PG: Boulder up to a narrow vegetated ledge. Go left to the right edge of a low ceiling, and follow a bushy vertical crack to a broken ledge. Traverse left 60' to a large, right-facing corner. Up the corner to a moss-choked horizontal crack and follow it right (careful of rope drag), then up to a sloping vegetated ledge. Tree belay. 200'
FA Apr, 2010, Jay Harrison, Todd Paris

*Martin von Arx on the super textured upper face of **Long Play** (5.10a).*

Indian Lake

LONG PLAY AND TEE PEE WALLS

52 Sauron's Bolt of Horror (5.10c)	57 Fool in the Forest (5.7+)	62 Fifty Grades of Spray (5.10d)	67 Moehammed, Larry, & Curly (5.9+)
53 English Channel (5.10a)	58 Woodland Idiot (5.6)	63 Bodhi Tree (5.9)	68 Muckraker (5.9)
54 Rope Monster (5.11b)	59 Oddy's Crack of Horror (5.10b)	64 Induhvidual (5.7)	75 Keystone (5.10a)
55 A Peney for Your Freedom (5.8+)	60 Yodellaybackloon (5.6-)	65 Willie's Danish Prince (5.9+)	
56 Half Man, Half Wit (5.9)	61 Paris–Harrison (5.7)	66 Long Play (5.10a)	

62 Fifty Grades of Spray 5.10d G 130' ★★★

Challenging, well-protected crimping and slab climbing. Several gear placements require some creativity involving small TCUs and equalized small nuts.

Start: Same as Bodhi Tree.

P1 5.9 G: Climb P1 of Bodhi Tree to the fixed anchor. 50'

P2 5.10d G: Step left on the ledge and climb up to a horizontal seam 10' up (#000 C3, small nuts). Continue straight up the vertical wall on crimps to where the angle eases. Continue up a steepening slab to a horizontal break, then up more slab to an overlap (#0 C3, small nuts). Go over this, then angle up right to a fixed anchor on a tree (shared with Bodhi Tree). 80'

Gear: Camalots 1 ea #000, #0, #1, #0.75, and #0.5; small nuts.

FA Sep 9, 2012, Jim Lawyer, Jay Harrison

63 Bodhi Tree 5.9 G (5.5 R) 140' ★★★

Spectacular position and very good climbing. The low-angled finish is prone to seeping.

Start: 120' left and uphill from Willie's Danish Prince, go up a steep, vegetated gully to a casket-sized rock that bridges the gully. Begin on top of it, at a left-facing corner.

P1 5.9 G: Climb the widening finger crack in the corner (crux), it to its end at a broad sloping ledge with a fixed anchor. 50'

P2 5.8 G (5.5 R): Traverse right and beneath a bulging wall to an overhanging, left-arching crack. Climb the crack, which widens to 3", then go right and climb a plated face (5.5R). Work back left, past horizontal cracks, then up to a tree with a fixed anchor. 90'

Descent: A single rappel with a 70m rope, or make two rappels with a 60m rope.

FA Aug 25, 2012, Michael Gray, Keith Meister, Ben Brooke

64 Induhvidual 5.7 G (5.3 R) 50' ★

Start: 100' left and uphill from Willie's Danish Prince, go up a steep, vegetated gully to a narrow, treed ledge on the right. Follow this ledge rightwards under tiered roofs. Start to the right of the roofs and below a large right-facing corner.

P1 5.7 G (5.3 R): Climb a dirt cone to the base of a wide crack in the corner with a birch tree 7' up. Go up the wide crack (V1) 12' to a horizontal crack on the right wall. Follow this to an arête, and finish on an easy, unprotected slab that ends at a tree-covered ledge at the top of the wall. 50'

V1 Big Man's Bane 5.6 G: Continue up the crack, which widens to a squeeze chimney, to the top.

History: During the first ascent of the chimney finish, Lane refused to climb it, and opted to climb the outside edge.

FA Oct 13, 2010, Jay Harrison (roped solo)
FA (V1) Oct 14, 2010, Jay Harrison, Tom Lane

Indian Lake

65 Willie's Danish Prince 5.9+ PG 110' ★★★
It is, after all, his longest play.
Start: At a small, right-facing corner–flake, 20' left of where the trail reaches the cliff. This is 15' left of **Long Play**. There is a 7'-tall, loose rock pasted to the face just right of the corner-flake; don't touch it.
P1 5.9+ PG: Climb up onto the top of the flake, avoiding the loose rock. Climb up and step right on holds above the block. Make a tenuous move up, then right, then left, then up onto a ledge. Traverse right to a handcrack in a left-facing corner and follow it to a stance below an overhang, at a point where a vertical seam runs a few feet up the face above. Climb through the overhang here, step left, go up, then left, then up again to a good horizontal. Climb up and left on good holds, and easier-angled rock, to the ledge. 110'
FA Nov 3, 2011, Jay Harrison, Tom Lane

66 Long Play 5.10a G 115' ★★★★
Both a low and high crux. The middle section has more spaced protection, but with amazing, positive holds and clean rock.
Start: Where the East Path is closest to the cliff, below a steep, shallow, right-facing corner with a short fingercrack 7' up.
P1 5.10a G: Go up the corner, then make a tough reach to parallel cracks on the right (first crux). Follow the cracks to a broad ledge. Step right, go over a steep wall to a right-rising ramp (sling the flake on the left for only pro) and follow it past a horizontal crack. Go up and left past another horizontal to a long overlap. Above the overlap, work up a steepening wall past a horizontal crack, then crimp up a short face (second crux) to another horizontal crack. Work left past an overhang, and finish at a tree with a fixed anchor. 115'
Descent: A 70m rope is required to lower off.
Gear: Doubles to 2".
FA Jun 20, 2011, Jay Harrison, Tom Lane, Valerie Bachinsky, Mike Prince

67 Moehammed, Larry, & Curly 5.9+ R 180' ★★★
Varied climbing separated by ledges. P1 is a worthy objective by itself.
Start: 30' right of **Long Play**, below a vertical crack at head-height.
P1 5.8+ G: Make a hard move to gain the crack. Move up to an overhang and reach out left to a long, left-facing flake. Go up the flake and climb a short handcrack to sloping ledges at the base of a left-facing corner. Climb a fingertip flake (small gear) and make a long reach to a horizontal crack that turns vertical and goes over a bulge to a ledge (V1). Work up to an overhang with stacked flakes; pull over this, then go past a jutting block and scramble up to a fixed anchor. 110'
P2 5.9+ R: Scramble up the sloping ledge to a leftrising crack under a bulging face near the right end of a tapering overhang 12' up. Climb up and make unprotected, difficult moves up and right to a stance. Move up and left, following a series of intermittent cracks and sloping ledges, then up a shallow open book to a ledge. 70'

V1 Hail Mary 5.8- PG ★: Belay at the ledge below the overhang with stacked flakes. Go left along a ledge, then below an overhang, to a point where good holds are followed to a left-rising horizontal crack. Follow the crack, cross **Long Play** 15' below its headwall crux, and join **Induhvidual** at a blunt arête on the left end of the cliff. Finish on **Induhvidual**: climb an easy, unprotected slab that ends at a tree-covered ledge at the top of the wall.
History: Tom Lane, Worth Russell, and Doug Allcock climbed to the first ledge on Oct 19, 2010.
Descent: Rappel from fixed anchor at the top of P1. Fromm the top, rappel from a tree to the ledge, then rappel **Long Play** (70m rope).
FA Nov 29, 2010, Tom Lane, Valerie Bachinsky
FA (P2) 2011, Tom Lane
FA (V1) Oct 12, 2011, Jay Harrison, Bruce Monroe

68 Muckraker 5.9 PG 55' ★
Start: 40' right of **Moehammed, Larry, & Curly** at the leftmost of 3 vertical cracks that end at a right-leaning crack at head height.
P1 5.9 PG: Go up to a tenuous stance above the slanting crack and make a balancy reach to a good sidepull. Reach up to a right-rising crack (first pro), and climb this until you can make a move left to a right-facing corner. Up this to a ledge (V1). Advance over a triangular chockstone onto another good ledge. Go up the obvious crack to a sloping ledge finish. 55'
V1 5.10a TR: Climb the narrow seam-tips crack to its end. Bump to a good hold, then rejoin the normal route at the handcrack.
FA Apr 2, 2012, Jay Harrison, Tom Lane

Crane Mountain • Crane East • South Corner Cliffs

DIAGONAL RAMP WALL

Aspect	Southeast
Height	50'
Quality	★★
Approach	35 min, moderate
Summary	Short wall with some well-cleaned cracks.

	1	2	1	2			6
-5.6	5.7	5.8	5.9	5.10	5.11	5.12	5.13+	total

This short wall lies on the left side of a steep, wooded, right-rising ramp behind the Isobuttress. (This ramp is the start of the only nontechnical approach to Crane's summit from this part of the mountain.) The wall is 40' tall, and sports several good crack lines.

DIRECTIONS   (MAPS PAGES 142 AND 166)
Go to the route **Long Play**, which is 30' above the East Path. Walk right along the base of the wall. Shortly past **Muckraker**, drop into a small swale by a mossy wall (the winter route **DR Drip**), then reach the Diagonal Ramp—a steep, wooded slope rising behind the left side of the Isobuttress. The cliff begins a short way up the ramp, and runs along it to the top of the ramp 584409,4821594.

Indian Lake

69 Kill It Before It Spreads 5.7+ G 40' ★★
Start: On a dirt ledge at a vertical crack near the left end of the wall.
P1 5.7+ G: Climb the widening crack in a shallow right-facing corner to the top. 40'
Gear: To 4".
FA Aug 25, 2012, Valerie Bachinsky, Jay Harrison

70 Tun Tavern 5.8+ G 60' ★★
Start: Beneath the large, right-facing corner capped by a roof.
P1 5.8+ G: (V1) Go up a crack to the corner, (V2) break through the roof, then go straight to the top. 60'
V1 Fang Time 5.9+ G: Start 10' to the left at a short, vertical crack. Go up the crack then follow V2: a right-rising crack to the right-facing corner.
V2 5.7 G: Follow the corner for 20', then follow a right-rising crack. Move up and left behind a large flake, then right to finish at the fixed anchor of **Felonious Mopery**.
Gear: Standard rack plus doubles from #0.5 to #3 Camalot.
FA Jun 22, 2012, Tom Lane, Ben Brooke
FA (V1) Aug 22, 2012, Jamie McNeill, Ben Brooke
FA (V2) Jul 7, 2012, Ben Brooke, Mike Prince

71 Felonious Mopery 5.9- G 50' ★
Start: At a continuous vertical crack with a 6"-wide slot at chest height.
P1 5.9- G: Climb corner and cracks to overhang. Continue up a handcrack to a fixed anchor on a tree at the top of the cliff. 50'
FA Jun 14, 2012, Tom Lane, Jay Harrison

72 Norman's Crack of Joy 5.8 G 40' ★★
Start: At a pair of vertical cracks.
P1 5.8 G: Climb the cracks. There is a clean, but short, section of crack climbing before the top. Belay at a tree up and right. 40'
FA Jun 16, 2012, Kevin Heckeler, Jay Harrison

73 Kielbasy Posse 5.10a G 40' ★★★
Start: On the right side of an alcove between two opposing corners below a large chockstone.
P1 5.10a G: Bridge the gap of the alcove and climb up and over the chockstone. Follow a vertical crack to its top, then climb the excellent face (V1). Veer right to better holds, then up a final crack near the top. 40'
V1 5.10b G: Climb directly to the final crack.
FA Jun 16, 2012, Lukasz Czyz, Jay Harrison
FA (V1) Aug 22, 2012, Jamie McNeill

74 Leapin' Louie 5.10a R 35'
A one-move wonder that requires a #000 C3 to protect the initial crux moves. Named for the miniature poodle that fell 20' off a ledge during the first ascent.
Start: At a seam 6' right of the alcove of **Kielbasy Posse**.

P1 5.10a R: Climb the seam to a ledge, then up twin seams to a small open book. Go up the face left of the open book, then past cracks to the top. 35'
FA Jun 16, 2012, Jay Harrison, Lukasz Czyz

Crane Mountain • Crane East
PINNACLE OVERLOOK
This is a giant boulder-tower in the talus with a single route.

DIRECTIONS (MAPS PAGES 142 AND 166)
Follow the East Path past the Long Play Wall to a section of open talus, just before you reach the Isobuttress. Pinnacle Overlook is the large boulder on the right in the open talus 584395,4821539. Rappel to the base of the route from the fixed anchor on top of the boulder.

75 Keystone 5.10a PG 45'
The crux move is made with gear below your feet.
Start: Begin on the downhill side of the boulder, at a left-facing flake 10' right of the left edge of the boulder.
P1 5.10a PG: Climb the flake to a horizontal crack. Mantel this (crux), then step left to a gear placement under an overlap. Friction up past a bolt to the fixed anchor at the top of the boulder. 45'
FA Apr, 2012, Tom Lane, Ben Brooke, Jay Harrison

Tom Lane on the first ascent of Tun Tavern (5.8+), belayed by Ben Brooke. Photo by Jay Harrison.

Crane Mountain • Crane East

BLACK ARCHES WALL

Aspect	Southeast
Height	145'
Quality	★★★★★
Approach	35-40 min, moderate
Summary	Some of the most popular climbing at Crane—cracks and faces on delicious rock.

6	3	6	6	11	3	1		36
-5.6	5.7	5.8	5.9	5.10	5.11	5.12	5.13+	total

This steep, complex cliff is at the end of the East Path. A lot of work has gone into the terracing at the base, and several spur paths along ledges provide access to the different sections of the cliff. Those section are the Isobuttress, the Amphitheater, the Main Face, and the Right End Buttress.

*Jamie McNeill at the crux on P2 of **Carpenter & Das** (5.7). Photo by Jay Harrison.*

HISTORY

Typical of many of Jay Harrison's earlier explorations of Crane Mountain, **Tribulations** was done as a solo in 1993. While researching *Adirondack Rock* in 2006, there was no apparent path to the cliff and certainly no additional routes to document. The following year (and 15 years after **Tribulations**) Harrison and McNeill added the second route, **Eating Tripe and Lichen It**, one of the last new routes included in the first printing of *Adirondack Rock*. Since then 42 additional routes and variations have been climbed; Harrison was involved in all but 7 of them.

DIRECTIONS (MAPS PAGES 142 AND 166)

Follow the East Path past the Measles Walls and South Corner Cliffs. At the Long Play Wall (32 min), stay low (don't walk directly along the base of the wall) to a section of open talus with a view toward the Isobuttress, 34 min from the parking area. Continue on the East Path a short distance across wooded talus to reach the left end of the Isobuttress near the start of **Carpenter & Das** 584468,4821595, at 35 min.

DESCENT OPTIONS

There are several fixed anchors equipped for rappel with a 60m rope. The exception is **Black Arch Arête**, which requires a 70m rope. From the top of the cliff, go climbers right, and make short rappels down a tree-filled depression right of **Crossways**.

Isobuttress

The Isobuttress is the tallest and most distinct section of rock along the East Path. Short for "isolated buttress," the 35 min approach certainly adds to the isolation of climbing on Crane Mountain. It is bordered on the left by the Long Play Wall, and on the right by the Amphitheater. The base area is compact and comfortable, and the path conveniently diverges to the other sections of the Black Arches Wall, making the Isobuttress a good place to stage a day of climbing.

The Isobuttress has a couple of very good, two-pitch moderate routes and a few good single-pitch routes. Several of the routes are clean with excellent rock, and there's a good mix of climbing including pure friction, an exposed roof near the top, varied crack sizes, and face climbing on knobs and in-cut edges. At the base of the cliff is a 25'-tall, friction slab with a steep, cracked wall above it. Most of the first pitches end above the steep wall with the second pitches conveniently converging at a summit ledge. The upper pitches are lower angled, and make it easy to choose your own adventure and finish as you desire. The bottom left end, near **Carpenter & Das**, seeps during wet conditions, but the right end (near **E-Stim**) dries quickly.

HISTORY

Many of the routes were completed just in time for the 2nd annual Southern Adirondack Rock Festival which took place at Crane Mountain during the second weekend of September, 2009.

DESCENT OPTIONS

There is a fixed rappel anchor at the top of the cliff where **Carpenter & Das** and **E-Stim** finish. Make an 80' rappel to a fixed anchor on the spruce tree at the top of P1 of **Recuperation Boulevard**, then a second rappel (40') to the base. In addition, there are rappel anchors on top of **Adirondack Rehab** and P1 of **E-Stim**.

Indian Lake

DIRECTIONS (MAPS PAGES 142 AND 166)

After the Long Play Wall, continue on the East Path through some talus. This is the first cliff you come to, and the path is directly against the cliff **584468,4821595**, 3 min past the Long Play Wall.

76 Carpenter & Das 5.7+ G 150' ★★★

Memorable crack climbing on P2.

Start: Where the East Path reaches the base of the Isobuttress, at a 9'-tall steep wall left of a broad slab.

P1 5.7 G: Go left of the steep wall and up to a long, sloping ledge. Continue left to a prominent right-leaning crack and follow it for 5'. Step left and work up a vertical crack with a suitcase-handle flake to two right-arching cracks. Follow the cracks to a horizontal crack below a sloping ledge 60' up. Move up onto the ledge, then traverse to the left end of the ledge (a 3" cam is helpful to protect the second before the traverse). Belay at a horizontal crack with a vertical crack that rises above it. 70'

P2 5.7+ G: (V1) (V2) Use a 4'-tall flake to the right to gain a vertical crack which widens to hands. Follow the crack to a ledge on the left, then climb easy rock up a right-rising ramp. Go up a thin, vertical crack to a triangular roof (V3); pass this on the right via a right-facing corner with horizontal holds. Continue up the corner to a horizontal crack and follow this left to an arête. Up this easily to a tree-covered ledge with a rappel anchor below the ledge. 80'

V1 5.7 G: Step left and climb 8' up a manky open book. Hand-traverse right along a thin crack to the vertical crack above the belay.

V2 5.6 G: Move right and climb past the 4'-tall flake, then traverse back left to the vertical crack.

V3 5.5 G: Hand-traverse right under the triangular roof, then move back left to the horizontal crack.

History: Named in gratitude for Jay Harrison's physical therapist and surgeon. This was Harrison's first FA after shoulder surgery.

FA Jul 15, 2009, Jay Harrison, Todd Paris
FA (V1) Sep 18, 2010, Jay Harrison

77 Intensive Care 5.8 R (5.6 X) 120'

A direct route squeezed between **Carpenter & Das** and **Recuperation Boulevard**.

Start: At a tiny left-facing corner at head height, 4' right of a rock lying against the face (which marks the start of **Carpenter & Das**).

P1 5.8 R (5.6 X): Boulder up to the long, sloping ledge. Step right to the left end of a slab and friction (5.6 X) to the base of a steep wall. Go to a ledge, then up steep rock to the right end of the belay ledge on P1 of **Carpenter & Das**. Step right, go past an overhang, then up ledges to the right of the P1 anchor of **Recuperation Boulevard**. Go right and up clean rock to the right of a vegetated strip; continue up steepening rock right of the triangular roof on **Carpenter & Das**. Climb straight up (5.8 R) past a rappel station to the tree-covered ledge at the top. 120'

FA Jun 8, 2011, Jay Harrison (roped solo)

78 Outpatient 5.8+ PG 140'

The first pitch is a linkup of several routes and variations previously climbed.

Start: Same as **Intensive Care**.

P1 5.8+ PG: Make a bouldery move to a ledge. Walk right onto the slab of **Recuperation Boulevard**; use its second bolt for first pro. Follow **Recuperation Boulevard** through the niche to a horizontal crack running right; follow this crack rightwards to a left-facing corner (this is V2 of **Recuperation Boulevard**). Climb the corner to its top and traverse right to an oak tree on a ledge (the top of **Lane Change**). 60'

P2 5.8+ G: Climb the large right-facing corner and up the steep headwall. At the overhang, break right (very committing move). Either work back up left and traverse 30' to the anchors or walk up and right to the ledge at the top of **Post Op**. 80'

FA Apr 19, 2012, Jay Harrison, Ben Brooke

79 Recuperation Boulevard 5.7 G 125' ★★★

P1 is popular and is deceptively challenging. There are several toprope variations off of the P1 anchor. A lone bolt located left of P2 is not a part of any route (yet).

Start: Left end of the broad slab at a hollow flake at head height, where the path forks.

P1 5.7 G: (V1) Step up onto the flake and friction left along the left side of the slab. Go up a water-worn fracture to a steep wall. Step right and climb to a ledge under a ceiling. Move left to a left-facing corner; up this (V2) past a long overhang to a belay at a spruce tree with a fixed anchor. 50'

P2 5.5 PG: Go left and up to a vegetated ledge with a rectangular block. Step right and go up a vegetated strip to clean rock. Work up and right to a stance below a right-facing scoop. Go up the scoop past a left-facing flake to a horizontal crack. Step above the crack and up a clean face with good edges (5.5) to a sloping ledge. Continue to the spacious, treed ledge with a fixed anchor located directly below it. 75'

V1 5.10b G: Begin 10' left of the regular start and make a boulder move off a fingertip left-hand side-pull flake directly up to the first bolt and rejoin the normal route.

V2 5.8 PG: Traverse right to a left-facing corner, then up to good holds that are followed left to the spruce tree belay.

FA Sep 2, 2009, Jay Harrison, Todd Paris
FA (V1) Sep 25, 2011, Tom Lane, Michael Gray
FA (V2) May 2, 2011, Tom Lane, Jay Harrison

80 Adirondack Rehab 5.10a G (5.7 R) 80' ★★★

Start: 20' left of the right end of the Isobuttress, at the center of the slab under a long overhang 20' up.

P1 5.10a G (5.7 R): Friction up the slab (5.8+) to crumbly flakes under the overhang. Reach out past the overhang to an incut rail and pull up (crux) to a horizontal crack with a vertical, thin-hands crack above it. Follow the crack to a good stance below an arête with a steep wall to its left. Trend left across the wall (5.7 R) then up right to a fingercrack; go up this to a fixed anchor. 80'

FA Sep 19, 2009, Jamie McNeill, Jay Harrison

Indian Lake

BLACK ARCHES WALL: ISOBUTTRESS
76 Carpenter & Das (5.7+)
77 Intensive Care (5.8)
78 Outpatient (5.8+)
79 Recuperation Boulevard (5.7)
80 Adirondack Rehab (5.10a)
81 Scaredy Cat (5.11b)
82 Lane Change (5.9+)
83 E-Stim (5.6)
84 Post Op (5.9)
85 Full Recovery (5.6)

CRANE MOUNTAIN: BLACK ARCHES WALL: ISOBUTTRESS
76 Carpenter & Das (5.7+)
77 Intensive Care (5.8)
79 Recuperation Boulevard (5.7)
80 Adirondack Rehab (5.10a)
81 Scaredy Cat (5.11b)
82 Lane Change (5.9+)
83 E-Stim (5.6)
84 Post Op (5.9)

Indian Lake

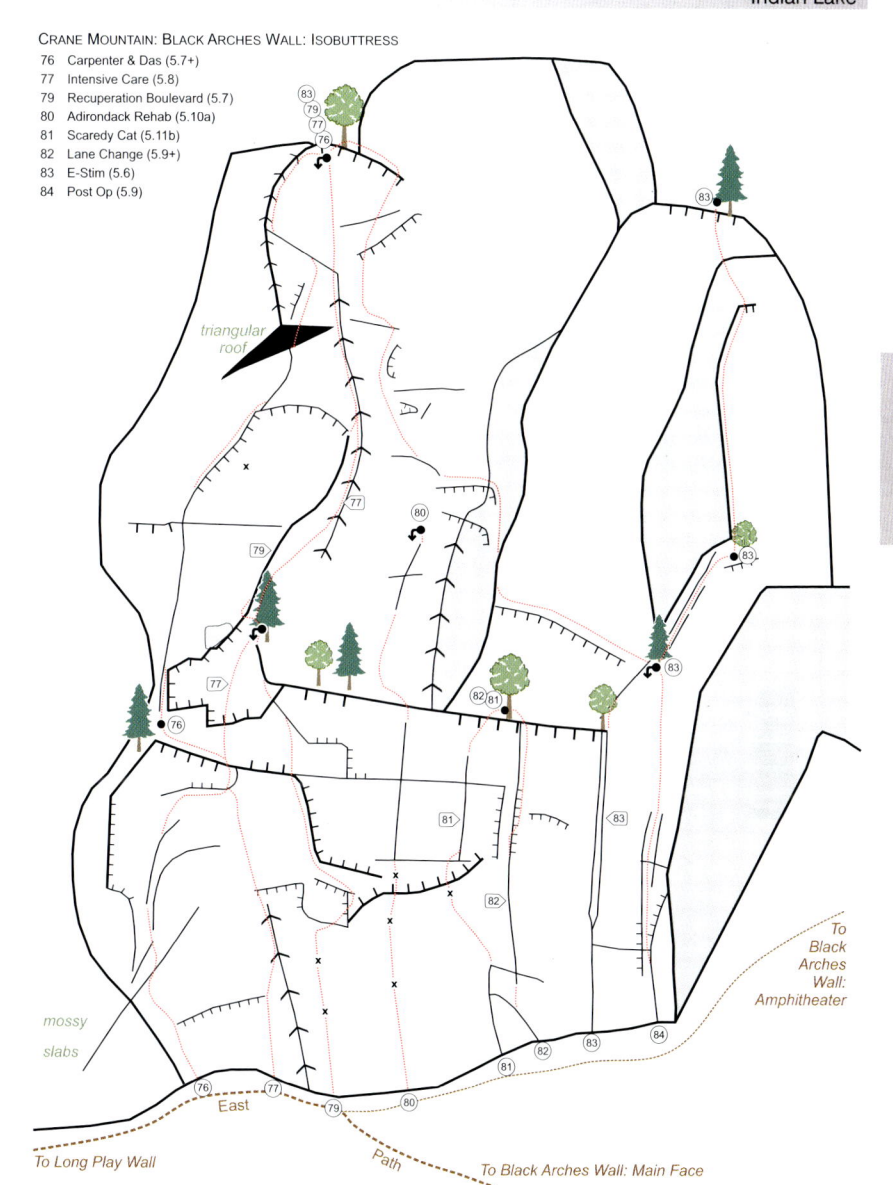

triangular roof

mossy slabs

East

To Long Play Wall

Path

To Black Arches Wall: Main Face

To Black Arches Wall: Amphitheater

81 Scaredy Cat 5.11b PG 45' ★★

Start: Below a flared handcrack and left-leaning crack that converge 8' up.
P1 5.11b G: Follow the cracks, then work left and up a slab to the right end of a long overhang. Pull over the overhang to a long horizontal crack (3" cam), then out right to a vertical seam. Reach to a higher horizontal crack and climb easier rock to a belay at an oak tree. 45'
FA Jul 28, 2011, Michael Farnsworth

82 Lane Change 5.9+ G 45' ★

A short crux on a short route. P2 is presently a closed project.
Start: Same as Scaredy Cat.
P1 5.9+ G: Up the left-leaning crack, then move right past a horizontal crack to a vertical fingercrack. Follow the fingercrack into opposing corners (crux) to a good ledge on the right. Belay at the oak tree on the left or join P1 of **E-Stim** to finish at a spruce tree with a fixed anchor. 45'
FA Jul 1, 2010, Tom Lane, Maria Lane

197

Indian Lake

AMPHITHEATER

ISOBUTTRESS

MAIN WALL

83 E-Stim 5.6 G 140' ★★★
Start: At a handcrack that becomes an offwidth 20' up, 10' left of the right end of the Isobuttress.
P1 5.6 G: Climb the widening crack on a steepening wall past good flakes and horns on the right to a small tree on a sloping ledge. Move left to a flared handcrack and follow it to a large spruce tree with a fixed anchor. 70'
P2 5.6 G: Traverse left on a ledge and go up to the base of a long, tall, right-facing corner. Follow the corner to the higher of two ledges that cut left across the steep wall. Hand traverse the ledge (5.6) to a stance on an arête and above the fixed anchor of **Adirondack Rehab**. Go up a pointed, right-facing flake to a right-facing scoop. Go up the scoop past a left-facing flake to a horizontal crack. Step left a couple of feet along the crack, then go directly up a clean face with good edges (5.5) to a sloping ledge. Continue to the spacious ledge with a fixed anchor located directly below its left end. 70'
Gear: Two 4" cams will adequately protect the offwidth on P1.
FA Sep 10, 2009, Todd Paris, Jay Harrison

84 Post Op 5.9 G 140' ★
Start: Right end of the Isobuttress, on the face just left of a right-facing corner that begins 7' up, 4' right of the **E-Stim**.
P1 5.7+ G: Make a boulder move to reach a horizontal and gain a handcrack. Up the handcrack to an easy slab. Go up the slab along the right edge of the cliff to

Indian Lake

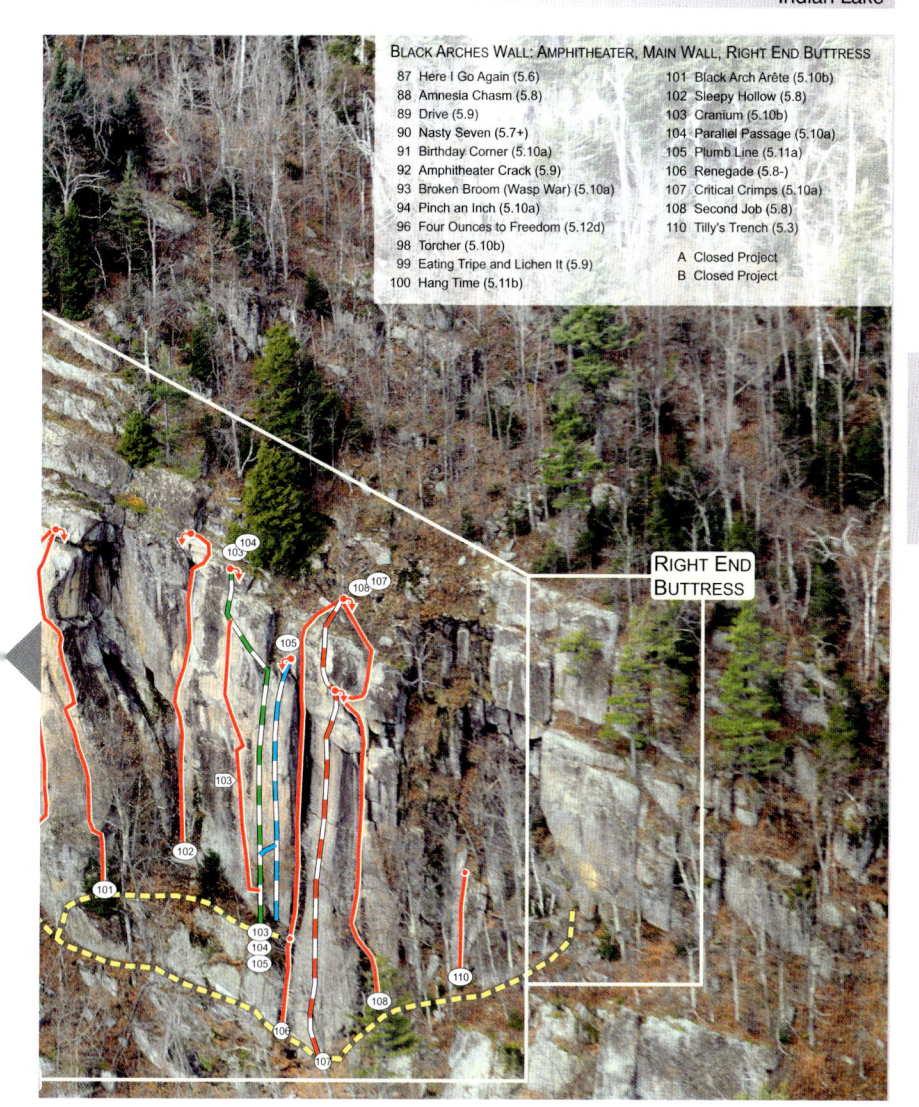

BLACK ARCHES WALL: AMPHITHEATER, MAIN WALL, RIGHT END BUTTRESS

- 87 Here I Go Again (5.6)
- 88 Amnesia Chasm (5.8)
- 89 Drive (5.9)
- 90 Nasty Seven (5.7+)
- 91 Birthday Corner (5.10a)
- 92 Amphitheater Crack (5.9)
- 93 Broken Broom (Wasp War) (5.10a)
- 94 Pinch an Inch (5.10a)
- 96 Four Ounces to Freedom (5.12d)
- 98 Torcher (5.10b)
- 99 Eating Tripe and Lichen It (5.9)
- 100 Hang Time (5.11b)
- 101 Black Arch Arête (5.10b)
- 102 Sleepy Hollow (5.8)
- 103 Cranium (5.10b)
- 104 Parallel Passage (5.10a)
- 105 Plumb Line (5.11a)
- 106 Renegade (5.8-)
- 107 Critical Crimps (5.10a)
- 108 Second Job (5.8)
- 110 Tilly's Trench (5.3)
- A Closed Project
- B Closed Project

RIGHT END BUTTRESS

the spruce tree at the top of P1 of **E-Stim**. Follow dual cracks to a belay at a tree on the right edge of the cliff and below a steep, right-facing corner. 90'
P2 5.9 G: Climb the corner to its top, step left onto a slab, and up past a large pine tree to the top. 50'
Descent: Go left for a short, easy pitch to get to the treed ledge with a fixed anchor directly below it.
FA Oct 3, 2010, Jay Harrison, Tom Lane

85 Full Recovery 5.6 G 165' ★★★

A girdle traverse that starts right of **Post Op** and finishes on **Carpenter & Das**. Starting on **E-Stim** is a popular option.
Start: Just right of **Post Op** at a blocky ramp.

P1 5.6 G: Go up ledges to the corner. Traverse left along a horizontal crack to a ledge near the top of the offwidth on **E-Stim**. Continue left across the ledge above the crux of **Lane Change**, then along the face under the 5.7 R section of **Adirondack Rehab**. Hand traverse a tree-covered ledge to the spruce tree at the top of P1 of **Recuperation Boulevard**. 75'
P2 5.6 G: Walk left along the belay ledge, then up and left onto a higher ledge. Continue left to the vertical handcrack on P2 of **Carpenter & Das**. Follow **Carpenter & Das** to the top using V3 to avoid the roof and keep the difficulty at 5.6. 90'
FA Sep 14, 2010, Jay Harrison, Robin Harrison

199

Indian Lake

Amphitheater

DIRECTIONS (MAPS PAGES 142 AND 166)
At the Isobuttress the East Path splits. Stay on the upper path which is against the base of the cliff. Contour rightwards to the Amphitheater 584499,4821635, about 1 min from the Isobuttress.

86 Project
This closed project is located at the left end of the Amphitheater Wall, at the high point of the cliff base, at parallel vertical finger cracks that go toward a blade of rock 50' up.

87 Here I Go Again 5.6 PG 70' ★
Start: 30' uphill and left from where the spur path reaches the Amphitheater Wall, 30' right of the left end of the Isobuttress, at an 8'-tall left-facing corner with a deep chimney to its right.
P1 5.6 PG: Go up the corner then step left and go up ledges, on an arête, to a pedestal that is separated from the main cliff by a wide crack. Tie off the pedestal, step across the crack and climb a steep face (crux) to a sloping, tree-covered ledge. 70'
FA Nov 8, 2009, Jay Harrison

88 Amnesia Chasm 5.8 G 75'
Named because, "it's forgettable, once the scars heal."
Start: At a chimney 40' right of the large, dank, broken corner formed by the Isobuttress and the Amphitheater face.
P1 5.8 G: Up the chimney and over a capstone boulder to a large, dirty ledge. Climb an arête on the right to a belay at a spruce tree on the left end of a ledge. 75'
Gear: Cams to 4".
FA Nov 17, 2009, Jay Harrison, Todd Paris

89 Drive 5.9 G 140' ★
The crux is getting off the ground, after which the climbing is interesting, varied, but easier. Still quite dirty.
Start: 30' left of **Amphitheater Crack**, on a ledge beneath a large right-facing corner. This is 5' left of an off-width crack, and 10' above the approach trail.
P1 5.9 G: Make a hard move up and around an arête to reach a good crack. Follow this to a large ledge that is above a deep chimney. 65'
P2 5.7+ G: Just left of an outside corner, climb face and intermittent vertical cracks left to a ledge with a spruce tree 20' to the left. Continue up a vertical crack to the top of the cliff. 75'
Descent: Walk up and (climber's) right to a spruce tree with a fixed anchor above the **Amphitheater Crack** fixed anchor. 2 rappels.
FA Jul 11, 2012, Jay Harrison, Tom Lane, Ben Brooke

90 Nasty Seven 5.7+ R 80'
Start: 15' left of **Amphitheater Crack**, at a slanting block lying in the spur path.
P1 5.7+ R: Go up a stepped left-rising ramp to an oak tree 20' up. Climb a thin crack in a right-rising ramp/left-facing corner. Climb crack and ramp to flakes and edges on a wet face 20' below a large roof. Climb right-rising tight seam with no pro to the right edge of the roof system (where **Birthday Corner** also meets this roof). Work around the corner, then traverse right to join **Amphitheater Crack** for the final moves to the anchors above **Broken Broom**. 80'
FA 2011, Jay Harrison (roped solo)

91 Birthday Corner 5.10a G 140' ★★
The start is often wet.
Start: 10' left of **Amphitheater Crack**, at stepped ledges below a right-facing corner 20' up.
P1 5.10a: Go up to the right-facing corner. Climb to top of corner and step right to a hold on the otherwise blank face, then work up and slightly left to a large roof and overhanging right-facing corner. Climb the corner to an overhang. Move left along the overhang and onto a high face. Belay at a large ledge. 75'
P2 5.7: Go up a bulging face to easier terrain and belay at an oak tree. 65'
Descent: Make two rappels with a single rope. Start at a spruce tree with a fixed anchor that is 20' right of the oak tree belay and rappel to the fixed anchors on top of **Amphitheater Crack**. Make a second rappel to the base of the cliff.
FA Sep 21, 2011, Jay Harrison, Tom Lane

*Jamie McNeill on **Amphitheater Crack** (5.9).*
Photo by Jay Harrison.

*Jay Harrison on **Broken Broom** (5.10a).*
Photo by Ben Brooke.

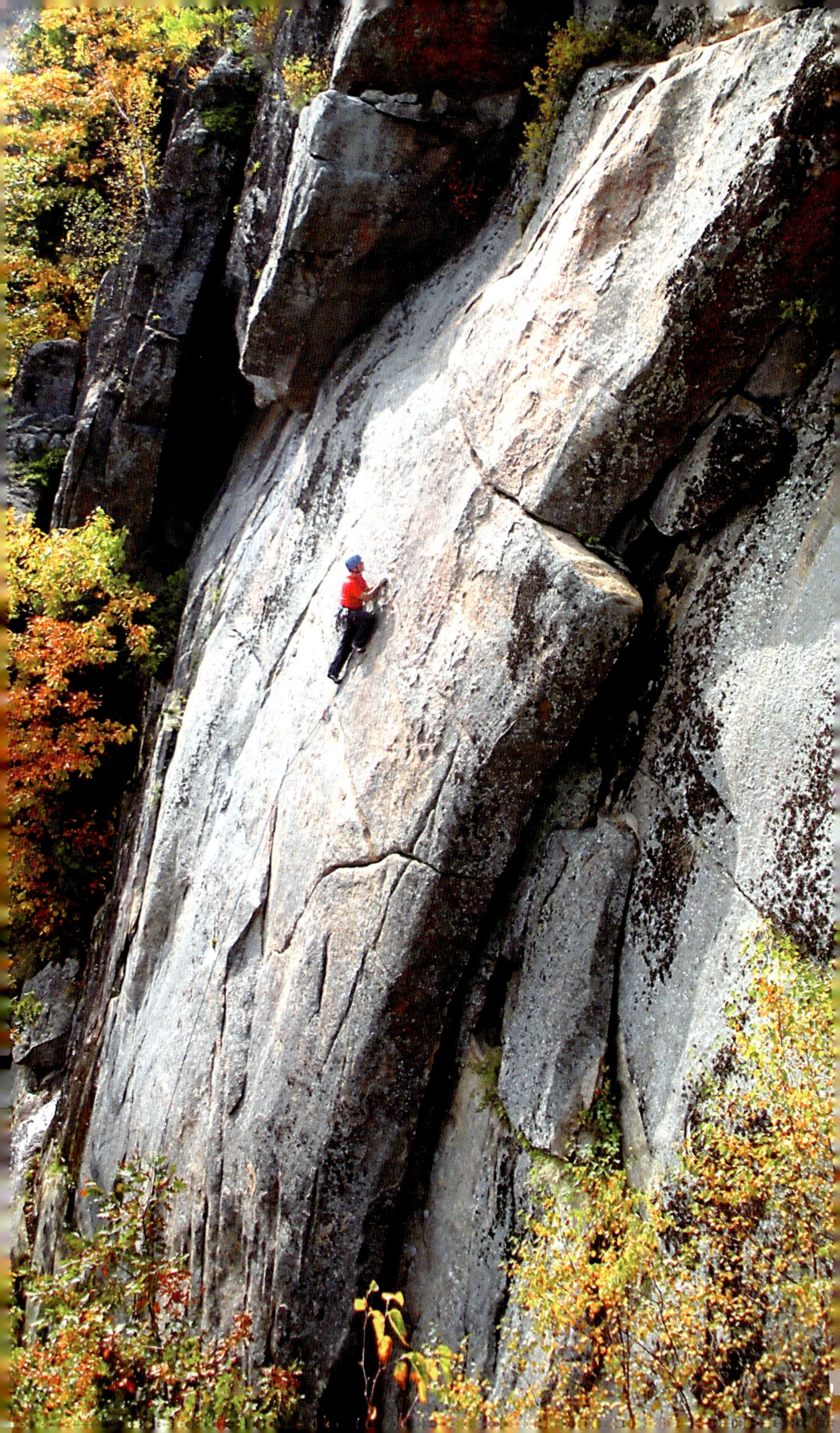

Indian Lake

92 Amphitheater Crack 5.9 G 70' ★★★★
Secure climbing with protection possible every inch of the way. Layback or jam? Hmmmm.
Start: 45' right of a block-filled chimney at the bottom of the leftmost, tall, right-facing wall, below a fingercrack that starts 10' up in a short right-facing corner.
P1 5.9 G: Go to the base of the crack and follow it as becomes a left-facing corner. Make a crux move into a scoop, then follow the crack as it angles right and narrows to fingertips. Go past a horizontal crack, move left onto a slab, go past another horizontal, then pick up another right-rising crack and climb this to a ledge with a fixed anchor. 70'
History: The first ascent continued to the top of the cliff by climbing the large right-facing corner–chimney to a large ledge, then up a slab and dirty crack to the top (5.6R).
FA Nov 14, 2010, Jamie McNeill, Bruce Monroe, Jay Harrison

93 Broken Broom (Wasp War) 5.10a G 75' ★★★★
Excellent crack down low, and well-protected face moves higher up.
Start: 15' right of **Amphitheater Crack** at a shallow, left-leaning, right-facing corner with a discontinuous fingercrack.
P1 5.10 G: Go up the fingercrack, then right on good knobs and plates to another left-leaning, right-facing corner. Go up the corner then work up to a left-rising ledge. Move left along the ledge, then face climb up to a horizontal crack. Continue up the face past a second horizontal crack to join **Amphitheater Crack** just before the ledge with a fixed anchor. 75'
FA Sep 21, 2011, Tom Lane, Jay Harrison

94 Pinch an Inch 5.10a R (5.6R) 70' ★★★
Start: 6' right of **Broken Broom** and 5' left of the large right-facing corner that defines the right edge of this wall at a shallow, left-leaning, right-facing with a discontinuous fingercrack. This is parallel to (and right of) **Broken Broom**.
P1 5.10a R: (V1, V2) Layback up the crack, then up onto a foot hold on the right (crux). Move back left onto another left-rising flake, then up slab to a right-rising crack. Follow a right-rising crack toward an arête on the right side of the wall. Go up a low-angled face with knobs (5.6 R) to a horizontal crack. Continue up the face and follow a right-facing scoop to a ledge with a fixed anchor shared with **Amphitheater Crack**. 70'
V1 Dexter's Dugout 5.8 PG: Begin 5' right and on a dirt ledge, below a fistcrack in a tall, right-facing corner. Go up the widening crack to a ledge with a perched block. Reach out left to a horizontal fingercrack and follow it to the arête.
V2 Impulse Drive 5.8- G: Begin 15' right at a 10'-tall right-facing corner. Go up the corner that becomes a left-rising ledge. Follow the ledge to the tall, right-facing corner, and climb a short, wide chimney to a prominent ledge on the arête.
Gear: To 3".
FA Jul 27, 2011, Jay Harrison, Michael Farnsworth, Tom Lane
FA (V1) Aug 23, 2011, Tom Lane, Jay Harrison
FA (V2) Aug 18, 2011, Jay Harrison, Tom Lane

95 Tribulations 5.5 PG 130'
Climbs a buttress that forms the right side of the Black Arch.
Start: Beneath a chimney on the right wall of the left-facing corner below the Black Arch.
P1 5.3 G: Up the chimney 15' to a stance inside it, then step out onto a brushy ledge (top of the Tripe Buttress). Climb the large, dirty corner to a ledge at the top of the buttress. 90'
P2 5.5 PG: Up and left to a ledge, then climb the face up and left to the trees. 40'
FA Sep 12, 1992, Jay Harrison

96 Four Ounces to Freedom 5.12d G 95' ★★★★
Start: Above the start of **Tribulations**, at a broad ledge below a sheer wall with an overhanging arête on its left edge.
● **P1 5.12d G:** Start up the wall (5.11a PG) and go to a 2' detached flake right of the arête. Follow the sharp, steep arête to its intersection with tiered roofs on the left. Move right and go up a sheer wall until the angle eases, and it is possible to move left to a right-facing corner. Follow the corner (5.10 PG) to a fixed anchor. 95'
Gear: 1 ea #2 Camalot.

Jay Harrison and Jamie McNeill (belaying) on **Gun Show** (5.10a). Photo by Alysia Catalfamo.

Indian Lake

History: After multiple periods of extended sickness, Farnsworth had a kidney transplant (donated from his mother) that allowed him to return to hard climbing. Four ounces is the average weight of a human kidney.
FA Oct 6, 2011, Michael Farnsworth, Connie Magee

97 Gun Show 5.10a G 95' ★★

A short, strenuous, excellent fingercrack, and the shortest route to the top of the cliff. This route stays sunny longer than the other routes on the wall.

Start: The right end of the Amphitheater at a left-facing, rectangular wall above a vegetated ledge.

P1 5.10a G: Climb the vertical crack past a pod (V1) to a ledge and exit right to a broad ledge with a fixed anchor. (You can walk off left from here.) 35'

P2 5.8 G: Step off a low block and reach left to a handcrack that begins 6' up a short buttress. Follow the crack, then climb easily to the top of the buttress and belay at trees. 60'

V1 Side Show 5.10b G ★★: Make a long reach right to a horizontal crack. Follow this across the top of the wall and finish on a blunt arête.
FA Jun 24, 2010, Jay Harrison, Matt Oakes
FA (V1) Jun 25, 2010, Jay Harrison, Jason Brechko

Main Face

The East Path leads to the base of the leftmost buttress of the Main Face with **Torcher**—an offwidth crack down low and a long ceiling/roof 70' up. (The route **Gun Show** is on the upper left side of buttress, but is accessed from the Amphitheater.)

Immediately right is the buttress of **Black Arches Arête**, and right of this is a tree-covered ledge—the Patio Ledge—that starts 20' up from the East Path and is accessed by a short, chockstone-filled chimney. **Black Arch Arête**, **Cranium**, **Parallel Passage** and **Plumb Line** begin from this ledge. Much smaller, but still striking in appearance is the buttress of **Plumb Line** that stands between the two tall, sheer, right-facing walls.

Below the access chimney to the Patio Ledge, the East Path drops steeply below and around a vegetated cliffband to the right side of the Main Face, and its lowest point. Here there is a broad slab with the route **Critical Crimps**. This is the tallest section with the longest routes, and has twin roofs near its top. Just below these roofs is a belay ledge know as Attic Ledge. Uphill and right of the slab are broken corners near the start of **Second Job** and **Crossway**. The cliff diminishes in height with a last buttress of rock—the Right End—and the short route **Suicidal Sydney**.

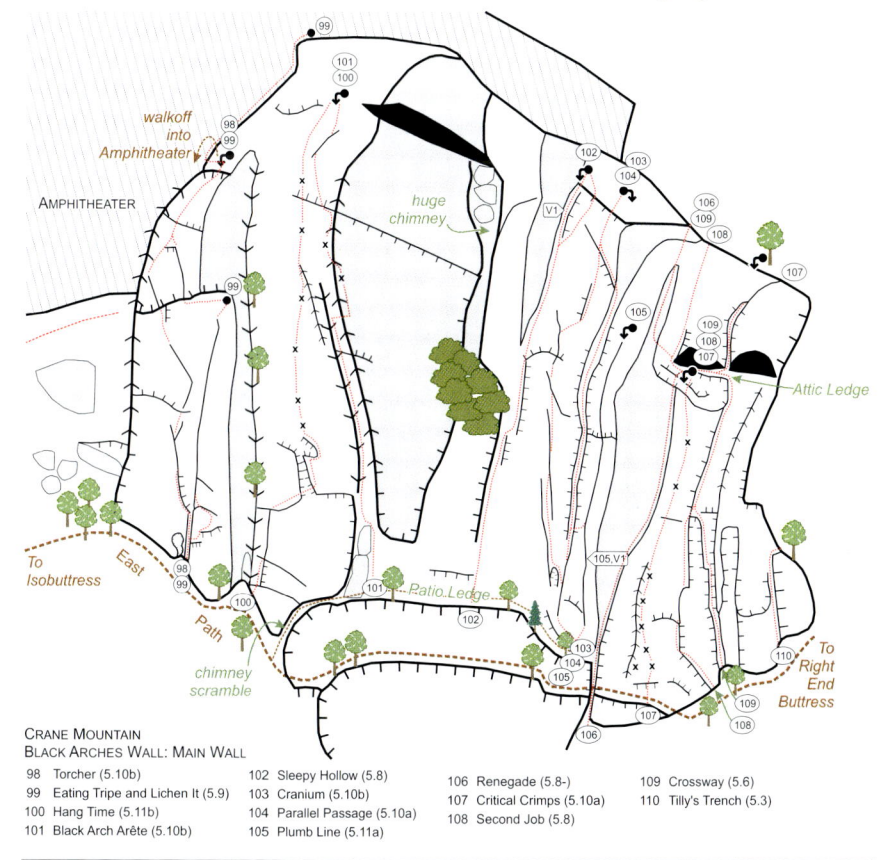

CRANE MOUNTAIN
BLACK ARCHES WALL: MAIN WALL

98 Torcher (5.10b)
99 Eating Tripe and Lichen It (5.9)
100 Hang Time (5.11b)
101 Black Arch Arête (5.10b)
102 Sleepy Hollow (5.8)
103 Cranium (5.10b)
104 Parallel Passage (5.10a)
105 Plumb Line (5.11a)
106 Renegade (5.8-)
107 Critical Crimps (5.10a)
108 Second Job (5.8)
109 Crossway (5.6)
110 Tilly's Trench (5.3)

Indian Lake

DESCENT OPTIONS
For routes that end at Attic Ledge, there is a fixed anchor here from which you can rappel with a 70m rope (or a 60m rope if you rappel diagonally to the right towards the start of **Second Job**).

DIRECTIONS (MAPS PAGES 142 AND 166)
At the base of the Isobuttress the East Path splits. The upper path stays against the base of the cliff and contours rightwards to the Amphitheater. Take the lower trail downhill to the reach the left end of the Main Face, 2 min from the Isobuttress, near the starts of **Torcher** and **Eating Tripe and Lichen It**.

Continue right to reach a 20'-tall, chockstone-filled chimney. Scramble up this to the Patio Ledge where the routes from **Black Arch Arête** to **Plumb Line** begin. To reach the remaining routes, follow an exposed ledge downhill to the lowest point on the face where **Critical Crimps** begins 584534,4821735, 4 min from the Isobuttress.

Jamie McNeill on the first ascent of **Plumb Line** *(5.11a). Photo by Jay Harrison.*

98 Torcher 5.10b G 105' ★★★★

Sustained and excellent; one of the better pure-trad routes at the Black Arches Wall. The move over the roof is wild, and getting established above is quite a puzzle.
Start: Same as **Eatin' Tripe & Lichen It**.
P1 5.10b G: Up the 8"-wide offwidth to a stepped overhang. You'll need a 5" cam to protect the start. Or, better yet, scramble easily up and right to protect in a horizontal crack, then step back left and climb the offwidth with protection from above. Go left along the overhang to a left-leaning fingercrack, then up this to a vertical seam. Climb the bulging seam (first crux) to a horizontal crack. Reach to a zigzag crack, and follow it rightward to its end. Traverse left 6' and climb up to the long ceiling at an A-frame with a fingercrack that shoots left from its lip. Make a strenuous move over the ceiling (second crux), then make a puzzling step up to a jug. Face climb straight up to a spacious ledge with a fixed anchor. 105'
Descent: Walk left across the ledge and scramble down a chimney to the base of the Amphitheater.
FA Jul 22, 2010, Jay Harrison, Jason Brechko

99 Eating Tripe and Lichen It 5.9 G 170' ★★

Start: 40' right of **Tribulations** is a large buttress; begin 10' right of this arête at a short mossy alcove leading to a 10'-high off-width crack.
P1 5.9 G: Up the mossy alcove, then move up and right 8' to a horizontal crack, and work back left to the top of the off-width crack where it narrows to fist size. Up the fist-sized crack to the right side of a ceiling; belay here. 60'
P2 5.8 G: Traverse left under the ceiling for 12' to a right-facing flake on the lip of the ceiling. Up the flake to its top, then up low-angle rock to a ledge. 40'
P3 5.5 PG: Walk left on the ledge and join the end of **Tribulations** to the top of that route, or climb P2 of **Gun Show**. 70'
FA Oct 25, 2007, Jamie McNeill, Jay Harrison

100 Hang Time 5.11b G 120' ★★★★

Consistently difficult face climbing with several good rests. The route almost touches **Black Arches Arête**, and can be toproped (with a 70m rope) from that anchor.
Start: 20' left of the Patio Ledge approach chimney, below a block-filled open book.
P1 5.11b G: Up the open book to a good horizontal on the right wall. Hand traverse right, then up to a fragile hourglass flake. Move up and right to a short right-facing corner, then straight up the orange face with plates and knobs. Move left to an overhang, then straight up a final bulge to a fixed anchor (shared with **Black Arches Arête**). 120'
Gear: Nuts and cams to 2"; doubles of #0.4 and #0.5.
FA Mar 24, 2012, Jamie McNeill, Tom Lane

Will Roth contemplates the crux moves on
Black Arch Arête *(5.10b). Photo by Jay Harrison.*

Indian Lake

101 Black Arch Arête 5.10b R 120' ★★★★★
Impeccable rock, equal parts of dihedral, arête, and face with a committing crux near the top; one of the best single pitch routes in the Adirondacks. The crimpy crux is scary with the risk of a big fall; a real mental testpiece.
Start: The left end of the Patio Ledge at the top of the chockstone-filled approach chimney, at a low roof with stacked blocks under it.
P1 5.10b R: Go up the blocks to the base of a 60' splitter handcrack in a clean dihedral. Climb this until the crack pinches down to finger-size. Reach out right to the sharp arête and pull around to a stance. Move up the right side of the arête past good stances, then directly up the arête to a horizontal crack under an overlap and bulging wall to the left. Step above the overlap and work up and left across the wall (crux) to a right-rising crack that is followed to a fixed anchor. 120'
Gear: 2 ea 1.5"–3.5".
Descent: Rappel 35m.
FA Oct 15, 2008, Jay Harrison, Jamie McNeill

102 Sleepy Hollow 5.8 G 100' ★★★
Many hidden holds, and tons of fun.
Start: 15' right and slightly uphill from **Black Arch Arête** at a right-facing corner with a crack system that widens to a chimney at 30'.
P1 5.8 G: Climb the corner and tight chimney to a ledge. Go up a handcrack in a left-facing corner. Work up to an overhang with a chimney on its left side. (V1) Undercling and move up and right to a jug. Climb though an overhanging face just right of the chimney on jugs to a fixed anchor. 100'
V1 5.9 G: Climb directly up the chimney to the anchors.
Gear: A full rack with doubles to 3". Wide gear is not necessary.
FA Aug 19, 2012, Ben Brooke, Gillian Herbert
FA (V1) Aug 20, 2012, Jay Harrison, Ben Brooke

103 Cranium 5.10b PG 95' ★★
Climbs the thin, left-leaning cracks on the overhanging face above the Patio Ledge. Small nuts protect the committing crux.
Start: The right end of the Patio Ledge, 60' right of the top of the chockstone-filled approach chimney, at an oak tree below the striking fingercrack of **Plumb Line**.
P1 5.10b PG: Start up a left-rising flake past a 2'-tall, detached flake below the slot of **Parallel Passage**. Work up a left-leaning crack-flake, then move right to a vertical crack. Go up the vertical crack and make a long reach to a horizontal crack that has a thin crack rising left from it. Follow the thin crack until it fades into a seam, and make another long reach (crux) to a crack in the overlap above. Pull the overlap, go leftward, step up and climb the right side of a small pillar, and finish on **Parallel Passage**: work up cracks and climb a steep face to fixed anchors. 95'
FA Aug 7, 2010, Jamie McNeill, Nathan Crain

104 Parallel Passage 5.10a G 100' ★★★★
Sustained difficulties with strenuous laybacks. Some parties traverse right after the initial difficulties and lower off of the **Plumb Line** anchor to avoid the serious rope-drag; despite this, the standard finish is recommended.
Start: Same as **Cranium** and **Plumb Line**, at the right end of the Patio Ledge.
P1 5.10a G: Go up to a 2'-tall flake that is below a slot with vertical walls. Follow the slot (crux) as it widens into a chimney and the angle eases. Follow a tight handcrack to a pointed overhang, then step out left and go up a left-rising ramp for 20'. Work up cracks and climb a steep face to fixed anchors shared with **Cranium**. 100'
Gear: To 3", doubles to 1.5".
FA Sep 10, 2009, Jay Harrison, Todd Paris

105 Plumb Line 5.11a G 80' ★★★★
A striking fingercrack on an overhanging buttress. When rappelling, take precautions to keep the rope out of the crack. In 2013, what was once a roof fell off, leaving a right-facing corner. Although the aesthetics of the line changed, the overall grade did not.
Start: Same as **Cranium** and **Parallel Passage**, at the right end of the Patio Ledge.
P1 5.11a G: (V1) Climb up **Parallel Passage** 12' to a stance on top of a 2'-tall flake. Traverse right on jugs to the fingercrack. Follow the crack to its end and make a few face moves to a horizontal crack under a small overhang and below a right facing corner. Pull into the corner, up this to its top, then follow a crack to a ledge with a fixed anchor. 80'
V1 Plumb Line Direct 5.11c G ★★★: Go directly up the tips cracks to join the normal route. Good protection can be obtained (micro cams and RPs).
Gear: To 3", doubles to 0.75".
FA Aug 3, 2009, Jamie McNeill, Alysia Catalfamo, Jay Harrison
FA (V1) Jul 3, 2010, Jamie McNeill

106 Renegade 5.8- PG 165'
This line is a challenging mixed route in winter. Cleaned up, it would be a decent rock route, but it is currently filthy.
Start: At the bottom of the wet gully left of the start of **Critical Crimps**.
P1 5.1 G: Climb up dirty corner system to Patio Ledge. 45'
P2 5.8- PG: Continue up corner system, through chimney, to the top of the cliff. 120'
FA Aug 24, 2012, Jay Harrison, Tom Lane

107 Critical Crimps 5.10a G 145' ★★★★
One of the first routes to tap the face-climbing potential on Crane Mountain.
Start: At the low point on the cliff, below a slab with a bulging wall that starts 12' up.
P1 5.10a G: (V1) Go up the slab and climb the right side of the bulging wall (1st crux), then move left and work up a blunt, low-angle arête. Begin up a steepening orange face, go past a thin horizontal crack, and decipher a crux sequence of crimps that ends at a wide horizontal crack under a ceiling. Haul out the ceiling and up a short, left-facing corner to a belay at a fixed anchor on Attic Ledge. 110'

*Opposite: Colin O'Connor on **Critical Crimps** (5.10a).*

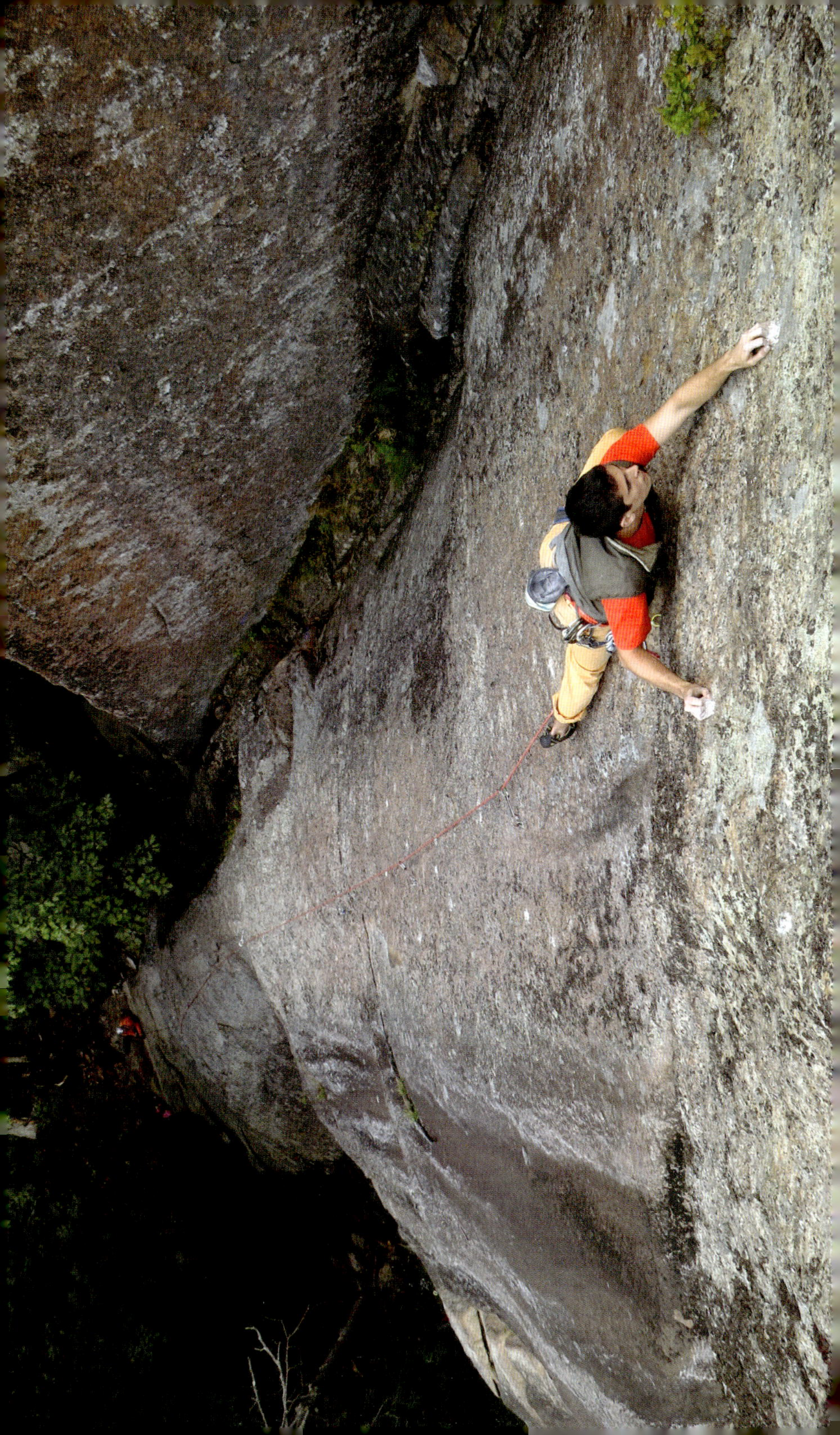

Indian Lake

P2 5.8 G: Step left and move around the left side of twin roofs to the top of the cliff. 35'
V1 Jay's Affliction 5.10a TR: follows a vertical dike on the left side of the slab then up the left side of the bulging wall to the blunt, low-angled arête.
Gear: Cams to 2"
History: Originally done as one pitch to the top.
FA Aug 27, 2009, Jamie McNeill, Jay Harrison

108 Second Job 5.8 G 145' ★★★

A low crux leads to an enjoyable handcrack. The top pitch is now largely ignored.
Start: 30' uphill and right of **Critical Crimps**, below a left-leaning ramp.
P1 5.8 G: Go up the ramp to the base of a left-facing corner. Work up the corner and around the right end of a ceiling (crux) to a stance below a right-rising handcrack. Follow the crack that turns vertical, and enters a deep, left-facing corner under twin roofs. Move up and left to Attic Ledge and belay from fixed anchors. 100'
P2 5.8 G: Traverse right to the offwidth crack that splits the twin roofs, and ascend the crack to the top of the cliff. 45'
V1 5.9+ TR: The flake to the right of the crux left-facing corner has been top roped.
FA Aug 27, 2009, Jamie McNeill, Jay Harrison, Todd Paris
FA (V1) Jun 8, 2010, Jay Harrison

109 Crossway 5.6 G 145' ★

Exciting traverse on P2. Can be used to access the fixed anchors on **Critical Crimps** and **Plumb Line**.
Start: Immediately uphill and right of **Second Job**, below opposing corners.
P1 5.6 G: Up the alcove, then follow steps up and left to join **Second Job** at the vertical handcrack that is followed to the fixed anchor on Attic Ledge. 110'
P2 5.6 G: From the left end of Attic Ledge, hand traverse left along a horizontal crack to a chimney (V1) that is followed up to the top. 35'
V1 5.6 G: Continue left, pass under a hollow (spooky) overhang, and go left to lower-angled rock. Belay at the fixed anchor on top of **Plumb Line**.
FA Aug 27, 2009, Jamie McNeill, Jay Harrison

110 Tilly's Trench 5.3 G 30'

Start: 20' right of **Crossway**, at a wide handcrack on the left side of a 30'-tall buttress.
P1 5.3 G: Climb the crack to the top of the buttress, and a belay at an oak tree. 30'
FA Aug 23, 2011, Tom Lane, Jay Harrison (both solo)

Right End Buttress

This buttress is 60' uphill and right of **Crossway**, and has a prominent left-facing wall with these routes. The buttress sits directly on top of the Slanting Cracks Wall.

111 Suicidal Sidney 5.9- G 30'

Start: 60' right and uphill of **Crossway**, at the top of a narrowing dirt slope, beneath a steep left-facing wall with an offwidth crack.
P1 5.9- G: Climb the offwidth crack to the top. 30'
FA Aug 30, 2011, Tom Lane, Jay Harrison

112 Reducto Adductor 5.10c G 40' ★★

Steep and sustained. Named for what it did to the leader on his first attempt. The successful assault had to wait for full healing.
Start: At a thin vertical crack 15' below and right of the offwidth crack of **Suicidal Sidney**.
P1 5.10c G: Climb the vertical crack, overhanging at first (crux) to a left-rising crack, then follow this (V1) to the top. 40'
V1 5.10c TR: After making the initial difficult moves up the left-slanting crack, climb directly up the face to the top.
FA Jul 11, 2012, Tom Lane, Jay Harrison

Martine Schaer on Second Job (5.8).

Crane Mountain • Crane East
SLANTING CRACKS WALL

Aspect	Southeast
Height	350'
Quality	★★
Approach	55 min, difficult
Summary	Tallest cliff on Crane with several very good cracks, and one excellent slab testpiece; excellent potential for new routes.

5	1	1		3	1		11
-5.6	5.7	5.8	5.9	5.10	5.11	5.12	5.13+	total

Several multipitch routes begin from a common start at the base of **Providence**, a towering left-facing corner. The left wall of the corner has the right-leaning crack (the wall's namesake crack) of **Straits of Fear**, which was once considered the best route at Crane Mountain (but is growing in from lack of use).

The left side of the cliff is known as the Underworld.

DIRECTIONS (MAPS PAGES 142 AND 166)
There is no established path yet. Begin near the left end of the Isobuttress, 100' before the start of **Recuperation Boulevard** at a wet section of the East Path 584447,4821576, about 35 min from the trailhead. 25' downhill of this wet section is a cairn. Go downhill (south) 200' to reach the (skier's) right end of a long cliff band. This is the far left end of the Slanting Cracks Wall known as the Underworld. Follow the base of this cliffband to the (climber's) right (east), which starts as a rocky creekbed. Go beneath an overhanging wall with a low cliffband below it. Continue past a broken section of cliff to reach the Slanting Cracks Wall near the base of **Providence**, 20 min from the East Path 584637,4821612, and 55 min from the trailhead.

Another option is to rappel from the right end of the Black Arches Wall; a 60m rope is required. Go to the Right End Buttress, which is on top of the Slanting Cracks Wall. Continue right 200' across the top of the wall to an oak tree with a fixed anchor. Rappel to the large sloped terrace (the top of P1 of **Providence**), then walk down and (climber's) left to the low point on the terrace. Make another rappel (the outside face, not down the **Providence** corner) to another ledge, the top of **Fits and Arms**. A final 100' rappel into the main corner lands you at the base of the cliff.

DESCENT OPTIONS
A rappel route has been established on the Slanting Cracks Wall, on the extreme right edge, using trees. The top anchor is 60' (climber's) right of the top of **Providence**. If you're using a single rope, rappel right to another large pine tree, then to the ground.

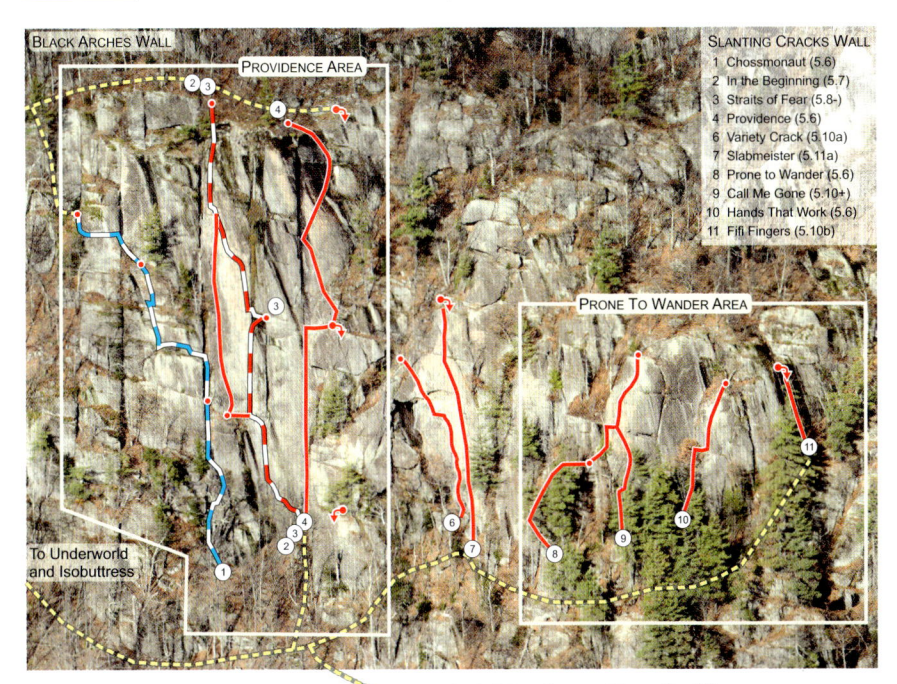

SLANTING CRACKS WALL
1. Chossmonaut (5.6)
2. In the Beginning (5.7)
3. Straits of Fear (5.8-)
4. Providence (5.6)
6. Variety Crack (5.10a)
7. Slabmeister (5.11a)
8. Prone to Wander (5.6)
9. Call Me Gone (5.10+)
10. Hands That Work (5.6)
11. Fifi Fingers (5.10b)

Indian Lake

Providence Area

1 Chossmonaut 5.6 R 270'
Contains a bit of everything that epitomizes Crane: clawing, scraping, scrubbing, and even some caving.
Start: 50' left of the large left-facing corner of **Providence**, at a large boulder pinned near the base of a wide chimney that forms a shallow cave.
P1 5.4 G: Climb up left of the boulder through a notch, then up right into a crevice. Squirm caving-style through a hole and up another tight section to open air 60' up. Belay at an oak tree in the chimney. 90'
P2 5.6 R: Continue up the gully for 30', then traverse left on a wide ledge for 20' onto the face. Go up a vertical row of knobs to another break, then up to a steeply sloping ledge with a large pine tree. 120'
P3 5.4 G: Move up and left to the highest point on the sloping ledge below a right-facing corner. Hand traverse left across a face to sloping ledge. 60'
Descent: Make a short rappel down to the woods, and walk up to the base of **Critical Crimps**.
FA Oct 28, 2013, Jay Harrison (solo)

2 In the Beginning 5.7 G 350'
Start: Same as **Straits of Fear**.
P1 5.6 G: Start as for **Straits of Fear** (up the flake and crack), then traverse left 20' across a narrow ledge and a slab to a tree belay beneath an overhang. 100'
P2 5.7 G: Climb the right side of the overhang into a right-facing corner and crack. Follow the widening crack, then left around an arête and up and right on flakes to an overhang beneath a birch tree. Belay at a stance above the overhang. 150'
P3 5.5 G: (V1) Follow the vertical crack to the top. 100'
V1 5.5 X: Step right and climb the knob-covered face, which becomes a slab.
FA Sep 19, 1993, Jay Harrison, Brian Westenberger

3 Straits of Fear 5.8- PG (5.4 R) 330' ★★★
Above the crux P1 is a rewarding pitch of secure face climbing on an exposed, knob-covered wall. A little overgrown now.
Start: 15' left of the **Providence** corner at a flake that leans left toward a vertical crack.
P1 5.8- PG: Up the flake and crack, then traverse left across a narrow ledge toward an orange flake. Climb the face right of the flake (crux) to a thin vertical crack through a bulge (loose rock). Continue in the crack (V1), up to a vertical fin (second crux), then to an awkward belay at a horizontal crack on a sloping ledge. 160'
P2 5.4 R: Step left past the vertical fin, climb the excellent knob-covered wall with discontinuous vertical cracks to an easy slab, and belay at the trees above. 170'
V1 5.8- PG: Traverse right 10' below the vertical fin to a right-facing corner, then follow it to the belay.
FA Sep 8, 1994, Jay Harrison, Brian Mosher

4 Providence 5.6 G 340' ★
Start: At the moss-covered base of a towering left-facing corner.
P1 5.6 G: Climb the sustained corner to its top. Belay at a spacious ledge. 180'
P2 5.6 G: Continue in the vertical crack, then climb up and right to a notch in an overhang. Through the notch to a left-slanting crack that leads to the woods. 160'
FA Sep 25, 1993, Jay Harrison, Brian Westenberger

5 Fits and Arms 5.6 G 65'
A hornets' nest kept the first ascentionists from completing the upper pitches.
Start: At the wide crack 10' right of the **Providence** corner.
P1 5.6 G: Climb the wide, flaring crack to a tree belay. 65'
FA Jul, 1995, Jay Harrison, Don Mellor, Ron Briggs

End of Providence Area

6 Variety Crack 5.10a G (5.5 R) 155' ★★★
Start: From the **Providence** corner, go downhill and around the base of the cliff to climber's right. Traverse right for 100' to tiered, left-facing, overhanging corners with a long slab to the right. Begin uphill at an 8'-tall, axe-shaped flake on the left-facing wall of the lowest corner.
P1 5.10a G (5.5 R): From the top of the flake, undercling left along a crack and into a tall, left-facing corner. Work up the corner, past a wide section (crux), to its end at 70'. Follow a thin horizontal crack left to its end, then move up to a stance that is below the left end of a long overhang. Move up to a short right-facing corner and climb a crack through the overhang. Follow a left-rising crack to a belay on a sloping ledge. 155'
Gear: Large trad rack with complete sets of C3s, C4s to #5, doubles of 1"-4" cams.
FA 2012, Jay Harrison, Tom Lane

7 Slabmeister 5.11a G (5.6X) 170' ★★★
Start: At stacked blocks at the base of a low-angled arête, 15' right and downhill of **Variety Crack**.
P1 5.11a G (5.6 X): Climb up blocks and slab to a stance below an overlap at a small right-facing corner. Climb through this and up a broad rib with knobs and discontinuous cracks. At 80' the angle steepens (crux). Climb to a good ledge, then over the right end of a long overhang. Go up an easy slab, then cross a dirty chute to a tree with a fixed anchor. (This is the same sloped terrace as P1 of **Providence**.) 170'
Descent: Either rappel with two ropes, or walk up and left to the Slanting Cracks Wall rappel.
FA Oct 18, 2012, Jay Harrison, Tom Lane

Prone to Wander Area

This cliffband is located several hundred feet to the right of the Providence Area. From the **Providence** corner, drop down and traverse right to the blunt, low-angled arête of **Prone to Wander**.

8 Prone to Wander 5.6 PG 140'
A right-rising traverse across a section of the cliffband.
Start: Above a narrow gully, directly above a wedged chockstone.

Indian Lake

P1 5.5 PG: Traverse left along a horizontal crack to an arête, then back right, following the arête to a ledge with a pine tree. Continue right, then downclimb 6' to a belay in an alcove. 70'
P2 5.6 PG: Go up and right toward the top of the cliff, then up the left side of a left-facing wall to an exposed perch. 70'
FA Apr, 1995, Jay Harrison, Gabe Linncourt

9 Call Me Gone 5.10+ TR 100'
Begin right of and around the buttress from **Prone to Wander** in the next large corner. Stem the corner and move left into a crack. Climb this to its top, then move right and climb a face to a horizontal crack-ledge (join **Prone to Wander** here). Finish up the face and fragile flakes to the top.
FA (TR) Oct 1, 1996, Jay Harrison

10 Hands That Work 5.6 PG 80'
Start: 200' right of the narrow gully of **Prone to Wander** at a large left-facing corner on the right end of a sheer wall with a right-arching crack.
P1 5.6 PG: Climb up the left-facing corner to a horizontal crack. Follow this rightward to a low-angled arête. Step right and climb to the top. 80'
FA Jun, 1995, Jay Harrison

11 Fifi Fingers 5.10b G 35' ★
Start: 150' right of the large left-facing corner of **Hands That Work** (and 350' right of the narrow gully of **Prone to Wander**) is a smooth brown slab 584695,4821777. Begin left of a left-rising ledge 6' up.
● **P1 5.10b G:** Delicate climbing follows a waterworn face to a fixed anchor. 35'
FA Jul, 1995, Mike Emelianoff

Crane Mountain ● Crane East
WATERFALL WALL

Aspect	Southeast
Height	290'
Quality	
Approach	1 hr 5 min, difficult
Summary	A couple long, discontinuous routes on textured, black rock under a seasonal waterfall, and some nearby short pitches.

3		1	1				5
-5.6	5.7	5.8	5.9	5.10	5.11	5.12	5.13+ total

Waterfall Wall is the most easily identified landmark on this side of the mountain—a seasonal waterfall that runs down a high-angle, black slab that keeps good sections of the routes naturally clean. As the rainy season tapers off, the waterfall dries up, revealing a textured face with good climbs.

Other topropes and soloes have been done here, including **Scout About** (5.3 X, 50'; Jul 1994; Jay Harrison) which ascends the scruffy leftmost slab.

DIRECTIONS (MAP PAGE 142)
From the Slanting Cracks Wall, walk east downhill to the stream that runs parallel to the wall. Follow the stream downhill 5 min to reach the base of a 100'-high waterfall that descends the clean, black slab on the left (north) and has a small pool at its base 0584818,4821738; about 10 min from the Prone to Wander Area.

DESCENT OPTIONS
Descent is easy and involves short rappels or easy downclimbs to the left of the waterfall.

1 Waterfall Left 5.6 PG 290' ★
Start: 20' left of the waterfall at a vertical seam.
P1 5.6 PG: (V1) Climb the seam. 90'
P2 5.4 PG: (V2) Ascend the vertical crack left of the

THE WATERFALL CLIFF
A Scout About (5.3)
1 Waterfall Left (5.6)
3 The Tempest (5.9)
4 Learning to Fly (5.5)
5 I'll Fly Away (5.10b)

Indian Lake

waterfall to its end. Continue on trivial but unprotected slab to the base of a steep face. 140'

P3 5.0 PG: Climb a vertical crack in the path of the waterfall. 60'

V1 5.7 R: Go straight up the slab left of the seam past a couple of pockets on the face, then move right to join the cracks near the top.

V2 5.7 R: Climb the slab to the right of the waterfall using a right-trending seam and knobs to reach a left-rising crack.
FA (P1) May, 1993, Jay Harrison
FA (P2, P3) Aug, 1994, Jay Harrison

2 Waterfall Center 5.6 X 90'

Clean but almost always wet.
Start: Directly above the pool.
P1 5.6 X: Climb the textured face with no gear to the top. 90'
FA Sep, 1996, Jay Harrison

3 The Tempest 5.9 R (5.5 X) 170'

Start: 20' right of the waterfall below a left-rising overlap.
P1 5.9 R: Climb the knob-covered slab to a left-leaning crack filled with vegetation. Work up the face left of the vegetated crack to a steep, vertical crack that splits the headwall. Belay from trees. 100'
P2 Footsteps of Fear 5.5 X: Traverse right to a 10'-high vertical black seam in a steep orange slab. Climb the seam and the sustained slab above to the top. 70'
FFA (P1) Sep 19, 1996, Carl Harrison, Jay Harrison
FA (P2) Jun, 1997, Jay Harrison

4 Learning to Fly 5.5 G 100'

This route is often climbed to set a toprope on I'll Fly Away.
Start: 150' right of the waterfall is a bulging wall with two chest-sized blocks on a ledge 4' up. Begin 30' uphill from and left of the blocks.
P1 5.5 G: Traverse right across the top of the bulge to a left-facing corner, then climb it to the top. 100'
FA Oct 1, 1996, Jay Harrison

5 I'll Fly Away 5.10b TR 40' ★★★

The face above the two chest-sized blocks is an excellent toprope. The anchor was a branch that nearly touched the cliff; it's gone now, so a gear anchor is required. The original ascent accessed the anchor by climbing Learning to Fly.
FA (TR) Oct 1, 1996, Jay Harrison, Carl Harrison

Pen and ink by Tad Welch.

Crane Mountain • Crane East

EAST NOSE

Aspect	Southeast
Height	250'
Quality	★
Approach	1 hr 20 min, difficult
Summary	A sprawling broken cliff with a tall, narrow, continuous section on the right side that has a few adventuresome, moderate crack routes.

	1	3					4
-5.6	5.7	5.8	5.9	5.10	5.11	5.12	5.13+	total

This cliff is located downstream from Waterfall Wall on an extension of the same cliffband. It's mostly a steep hillside dotted with small lumps of exposed rock, but there's an attractive tall, continuous section of open rock on the right side, perhaps the second tallest continuous open rock on Crane Mountain. Polar Vortex is a route of note, as P2 was once considered the best pitch on Crane (that was 16 years ago, so it may be overgrown now).

DIRECTIONS   (MAP PAGE 142)
Follow the outlet of the waterfall northeast. After 5 min, on the left, you will see Graphite Corner (5.9- TR; 80'; Aug 1, 1998; Dick Tucker, Jay Harrison), a large right-facing corner above a talus field that covers the streambed. Downstream (10 min from the waterfall), where the stream jogs right (southeast) away from the cliffs, head uphill to the left (northwest) for several minutes to the East Nose 585046,4822061, about 15 min from Waterfall Wall.

7 Vertical Ag & Tech 5.7 R 340'

P3 is reportedly quite good. You can approach it by hiking up right, then traversing left on a tree ledge.
Start: 150' from the jog in the stream are tiers of cliffs with woods in between. Begin at the right end of the low tier that has a right-facing flake.
P1 5.6 G: Up the left-rising crack to the right-facing flake. Unrope, and hike 100' through trees to the next tier. 150'
P2 5.4 G: Climb a right-facing corner formed by a large flake that leans against the cliff. Continue in a vertical crack to the top. 70'
P3 5.7 R: Step right, and climb a prominent right-facing corner. Exit the corner to the right on an unprotected slab. 120'
FA (P1, P2) Oct 18, 1997, Jay Harrison, Dick Tucker
FA (P3) Sep 6, 1997, Jay Harrison, Dick Tucker

8 Polar Vortex 5.8 PG 220' ★★

P2 was unearthed during a massive cleaning expedition. The first-ascent party considered the crack on P2 to be one of the best in the southern Adirondacks.
Start: 150' from the jog in the stream are tiers of cliffs with woods between (the start of Vertical Ag & Tech). Hike uphill and rightward past the low tiers of rock on the left. Beneath the upper and highest tier is a tree slope. Traverse the slope to the left 80' to its end. Begin at the left end of the tree slope, beneath a right-facing

Indian Lake

chimney, on a slab with a vertical crack that starts 5' up.

P1 5.8 PG: Climb the widening crack to its end then across a bulge to another vertical crack. At the end of the second crack, traverse left to a dirty corner and follow it to a tree belay beneath a ceiling. 130'

P2 5.7 G: Hand-traverse right above the ceiling to a vertical crack that jogs left. Follow the crack past a horizontal crevice to its end, then face-climb up and left to a knobby face finish. 90'
FA Oct 18, 1997, Dick Tucker, Jay Harrison

9 Weather Clown 5.8 G (5.6 X) 240' ★

Start: Approach as for Polar Vortex. Begin 20' left of the tree slope at a 15'-tall perched flake at the base of the face.

P1 5.8 G: Step left and climb a continuous right-facing corner through several overlaps until the crack splits. Climb the right-hand crack and belay on a ledge. 100'

P2 5.6 X: Above the belay is an overlap. Climb up and left 60' through the overlap to an unprotected slab and a 4"-wide crack (first pro). Follow the crack to its end, then up and right past a bulge to an easy finish. 140'
FA Sep 1, 1998, Jay Harrison, Dick Tucker

10 Upper Level Disturbance 5.8- PG 90' ★

Start: Same as Weather Clown.

P1 5.8- PG: From the tree behind the flake, step right and climb a small right-facing corner. At the top of the corner, step right and climb a thin vertical crack. Dodge the overlaps above by stepping right, then back left. Continue in the main crack system in the center of the wall and finish in the left-facing corner or the wide crack directly above. 90'
FA Aug 23, 1998, Jay Harrison, Dick Tucker

Crane Mountain • Crane East
CATERPILLAR CLIFF

Aspect	Southeast and northeast
Height	60'
Quality	
Approach	1 hr 35 min, difficult
Summary	A really-hard-to-get-to lump of rock with a single exploratory route and potential for more routes.

This northernmost public-land cliff at Crane has only recently been visited and needs further exploration. Great views from the top.

The cliff is comprised of two walls—a southeast-facing wall and a northeast-facing wall—that meet to form a large arête at the lowest point of the terrain. The northeast-facing wall severely overhangs.

DIRECTIONS   **(MAP PAGE 142)**

The approach is long. From East Nose, continue along the base of the mountain past the Northeast Cascade (winter climb), then drop down a bit to avoid some boulders. Walk parallel to the side of Crane, along the left edge of a marsh and below talus. At the far end of the talus, scramble up, then back left along the edge of

213

Indian Lake

the talus until you arrive at the low point on the cliff—the arête where the two walls meet 585164,4822494, about 15 min from the East Nose.

11 Caterpillar Chimney 5.5 G 60'

The approach and this route are exercises in self torment.

Start: Roughly in the center of the southeast-facing wall at a 16"-wide chimney that runs the full height of the cliff.

P1 5.5 G: Climb up the outside edge of the chimney. The crux is the move around an overhang formed by a block leaning across the chimney opening to a stance on the right. At its top, step right onto a block, then up a slab to the top. 60'

FA Oct 28, 2013, Jay Harrison (solo)

HUCKLEBERRY MOUNTAIN

Location	South of Johnsburg, accessed from NY 8
Summary	Many moderates mixed with a selection of quality 5.10s and 5.11s; many of the moderate routes are grown in.

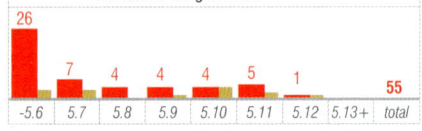

-5.6	5.7	5.8	5.9	5.10	5.11	5.12	5.13+	total
26	7	4	4	4	5	1		55

Huckleberry is a series of broken bands of cliffs on the south and west slopes of Huckleberry Mountain. It is a frustrating area with mystifying topography and very few clean features with which to identify routes. Many parties visit the cliff only to turn away unable to find any routes. Persistence pays off, as there are some high-quality routes here.

The approach to Huckleberry involves hiking over Crane Mountain to the Paint Mine Ruins Trail, a poorly marked, overgrown tote road in the valley high above Paintbed Brook between Crane Mountain and Huckleberry Mountain. Once on the trail, on the opposite side of the valley, you can glimpse the cliffs through the trees. It is possible to head up just about anywhere, but locating yourself at the cliff base would be difficult. First-time visitors are encouraged to follow the directions to the Main Cliff and begin explorations there, as this has the most distinguishable features on the cliff, such as the Great Dihedral and the Hard Guy Wall. Due to the difficulty in finding routes, the starts are especially descriptive in this section.

The leftmost section of rock is the North End, followed by the Boneyard to its right. These cliffs face west and are often very dirty and nondescript, but there are a few notable routes here, namely **Mr. Toad's Wild Ride**. Further right is the Corner Cliff, where the cliff line makes a bend to face southwest. Moving to the right, the next notable area is the Main Cliff, which begins with the Great Dihedral and extends southeast to the Hard Guy Wall; the Main Cliff holds the highest concentration of quality routes. High above the Main Cliff is the White Slab, a wide slab and perhaps the most intriguing feature when you view Huckleberry from a distance. As you move southeast from the Main Cliff, there are several smaller walls—No-Name; Last Wall; and, up by the ruins, the Factory Slabs. There are just a few climbs on these last walls, and nothing especially noteworthy.

A forest fire in 2003 affected areas of vegetation in the vicinity of the cliffs, most notably around the No-Name Wall and the Last Wall.

The route descriptions in this section were adapted from Dick Tucker's meticulous notes, with his permission.[6] Contributions were also made by Jay Harrison and his unpublished guide, "Cabin Country Rock."

HISTORY

The earliest reported climbing at Huckleberry was initiated by Dick Tucker, once again inspired by a photo in Barbara McMartin's 1986 guidebook and from a view of the White Slab from a rocky crag on Crane Mountain. Tucker recruited Hobey Walker, Jim Bender, and Jeremy Munson to make a reconnaissance in 1990 to find the White Slab and ended up thrashing around, finally climbing several routes on the Last Wall as a consolation prize. This initial visit sparked several years of rapid development, with Tucker being the main motivation behind the great majority of the routes. Another significant contributor was Walker, a local who had climbed in the Adirondacks since he was 12 years old. Walker was a design and production engineer for Summit Research (then later started Epic Software) in Schenectady and a talented climber. He returned with various partners, most notably Dave Furman; together they put in most of the difficult lines, including the beautiful **Insomnia** and the routes on the Hard Guy Wall. At around the same time, and by coincidence, Tad Welch visited the cliff and, with his cousin Bill Widrig, established several memorable lines. Eventually development ceased when Furman left for Colorado and Tucker developed elbow tendonitis from too much scrubbing, but it picked back up again in 1996 with the indefatigable Jay Harrison picking off more moderate lines, often with a still-recovering Tucker.

DIRECTIONS (MAPS PAGES 142 AND 215)

The traditional (and easy) approach from Hudson Street is closed to the public. Climbers now must approach from the Crane Mountain Trailhead, the only public approach to Huckleberry Mountain.

Park as for Crane Mountain (directions page 144). From the parking area (0 min), hike up the summit hiking trail (map page 142) to the intersection with the trail to Crane Mountain Pond (30 min). Turn left and follow the trail marked with red discs to the shore of the pond (45 min). Turn left and follow a hiking trail clockwise around the pond (map page 142). The trail crosses the pond's outlet and turns left 0582883,4822775; leave the trail and continue along the shore on a good herd path past several excellent campsites.

Bushwhack to the end of a long narrow bay at the northwest end of the pond to a moss-covered streambed (1 hr). Follow the streambed downhill and north

---

6   Richard E. Tucker, "Huckleberry Mountain" (typescript, Adirondack Research Library, Niskayuna, N.Y., Jul 18, 2002).

Indian Lake

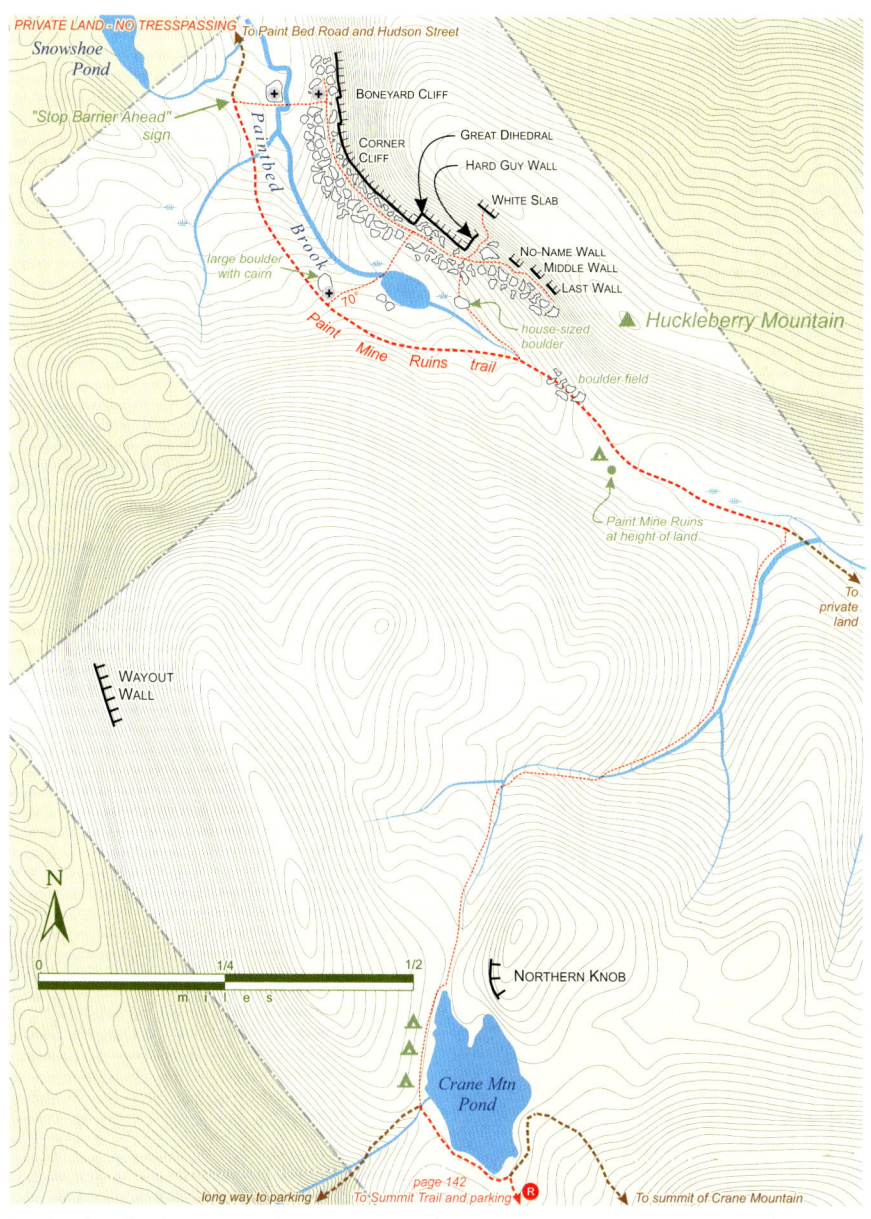

to a junction with a larger stream that enters from the left (1hr 20 min) 0583101,4823186. Continue east downstream past another stream junction that enters from the right (south) at which point the stream swings back toward the north. When the stream begins to level out and swings back to the east, leave the streambed and go north across level woods for 100 yards to a wide, double-track path, the Paint Mine Ruins Trail (2 hr) 0583666,4823748.

Turn left and hike the trail, which is unreliably marked, past a marsh on the right and over the height of land between Crane and Huckleberry Mountains. At 2 hr 15 min the trail passes through a boulderfield. Directions to the various cliffs are described relative to this boulderfield.

Indian Lake

Huckleberry Mountain
NORTH END

Aspect	West
Height	80'
Quality	
Approach	3 hr, difficult
Summary	Nondescript section of cliff with several exploratory routes.

3							3
-5.6	5.7	5.8	5.9	5.10	5.11	5.12	5.13+	total

The North End is the nondescript section of cliff farthest to the left (northwest). The three reported routes are exploratory in nature and are spread out over a wide expanse of choss broken by the occasional climbable bit. More exploration and development are possible.

DIRECTIONS   (MAP PAGE 215)
To approach, follow the approach to the Boneyard, then walk left. Eventually you'll come to a low, steep 40'- to 80'-high wall with steep buttresses and vertical cracks known as City of Cracks. There is some potential here for more difficult crack routes, but it is hardly the Mecca the name suggests. A cairn marks the base of this wall, and the first route is located at the right side of the wall 582552,4825069.

1 Little Jam 5.4 TR 20'
At the right end of the City of Cracks wall is a large block that forms a left-facing corner; the bottom of this block forms a low ceiling. Just right of this is a 20'-wide depression filled with bushes and trees. Just right of this depression is a smaller buttress of rock with a short, jagged crack on its left side, absolutely covered with large, leafy lichen. Climb the crack to a tree.
FA (TR) Oct 24, 1998, Dick Tucker

2 Indecisive 5.6 PG 40'
Start: 50' right of **Little Jam** is a steep slab with a "finger" that leans up against the face (a 5'-wide, 12'-high flake of rock that you can see behind). Begin at the left-facing corner formed by the left side of the "finger."
P1 5.6 PG: Climb up the left-facing corner onto the "finger." Traverse left on a vegetated ledge, then make a step left to gain a jagged crack. Up the crack as it bends left. Step back right and climb the vertical crack to the top. 40'
FA May 23, 1999, Jay Harrison, Dick Tucker

3 Trick or Treat 5.6+ G 70'
Start: 150' right of the "finger" that marks the start of **Indecisive** and 300' left of the 4'-wide straight-in chimney that shoots up the cliff is a cone-shaped slope that leads up to a very large right-facing chimney-corner capped by some blocks that form a roof. Begin at the top of this slope high in the right-facing chimney-corner.
P1 5.6+ G: On the right wall, climb dirty vertical cracks to a left-facing corner, then up to a ceiling with a jammed block. Traverse left under the ceiling to a right-facing block at the top of the chimney-corner. Over the blocks on their right side, then up to a pine tree at the top. 70'
FA Oct 31, 1998, Dick Tucker, Jay Harrison

Huckleberry Mountain
BONEYARD

Aspect	West
Height	200'
Quality	★
Approach	2 hr 45 min, difficult
Summary	Wide section of cliff with many once-cleaned multi-pitch moderate routes.

9	2	1					16
-5.6	5.7	5.8	5.9	5.10	5.11	5.12	5.13+	total

To the right (southeast), the next section of cliff with climbing is the Boneyard, so named for the pile of deer bones Dick Tucker found at the top of **Mr. Toad's Wild Ride** and for the porcupine bones found at the bottom.

300' to the right of **Trick or Treat** is an unusual 4'-wide straight-in chimney that shoots up the cliff, a useful locator. About 500' right of this is an intermittent waterfall that marks the beginning of the Boneyard. The waterfall spills down a black mossy streak at the left end of a steep wall cut by a 60'-wide ceiling 25' up.

DIRECTIONS   (MAP PAGE 215)
From the Main Cliff, walk left along the base of the cliff, past Corner Cliff, to reach the first landmark, **Broken Shovel Gully** (about 15 min).

A good landmark at the base of the cliff is Lunch Rock—a large, 4' by 8' flat-topped boulder slightly tilted away from the cliff with a large cairn 582567,4824694.

Dick Tucker, in action. Photo by Jay Harrison.

Indian Lake

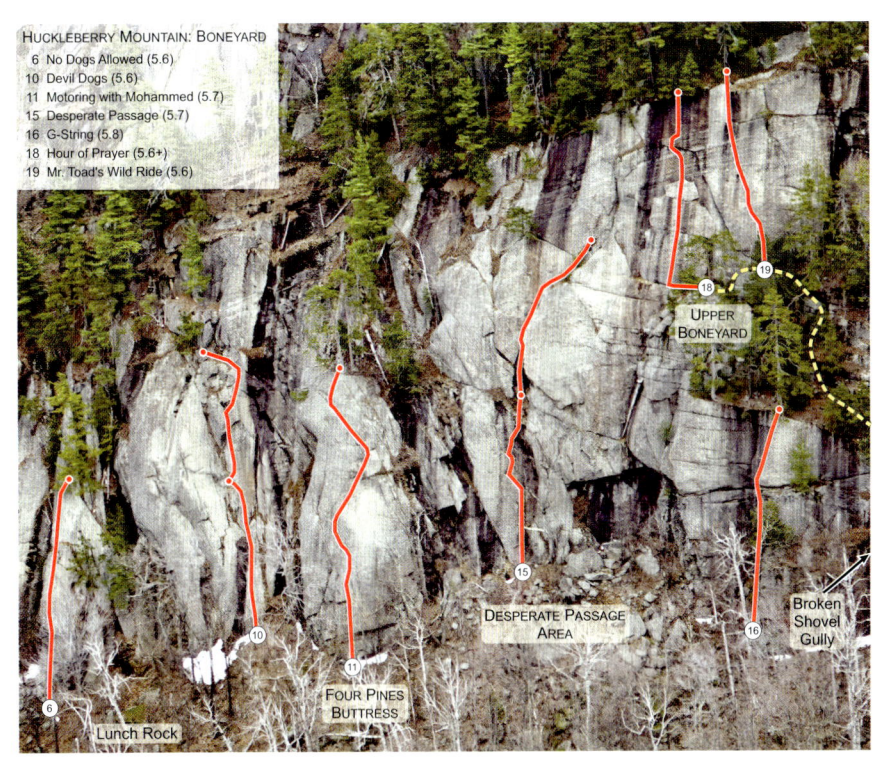

HUCKLEBERRY MOUNTAIN: BONEYARD
- 6 No Dogs Allowed (5.6)
- 10 Devil Dogs (5.6)
- 11 Motoring with Mohammed (5.7)
- 15 Desperate Passage (5.7)
- 16 G-String (5.8)
- 18 Hour of Prayer (5.6+)
- 19 Mr. Toad's Wild Ride (5.6)

This is used as a locator for routes such as **Le Petit Chien** and **Devil Dogs**. About 300' left of Lunch Rock is the intermittent waterfall. 60' right of Lunch Rock is a huge left-facing overhanging corner with some pine trees on top known as Four Pines Buttress (it used to be topped by four pine trees; at last count, three remain).

4 Lap Dog 5.3 G 100'
Start: 200' left of Lunch Rock and 100' right of the intermittent waterfall and at the high point of the terrain at the base of the cliff, at a narrow strip of clean low-angle slab with a black streak. This is just left of a 25'-high left-facing corner and 20' left of a huge orange left-facing corner that runs the height of the cliff (**Corner Scramble**).
P1 5.3 G: Climb the slab up to an hourglass flake. Step right and follow the black streak past two horizontals to a brushy ledge. A short, jagged crack leads to a tree ledge at the top. 100'
FA Jun 29, 1996, Tim Riley, Dick Tucker

5 Corner Scramble 3rd class 200'
20' right of **Lap Dog** is a large brush- and tree-filled left-facing corner that provides access to the top of the Boneyard. There is a nice flat rock covered with ferns at the base of the corner.

6 No Dogs Allowed 5.6 R (5.2 X) 190'
Start: At the left end of a slab and 10' right of a huge orange left-facing corner that runs the height of the cliff (**Corner Scramble**) below a short left-facing corner that leads to a ceiling 15' up.
P1 5.6 R: Up the corner to the ceiling, over this via a crack on its right side, and onto the slab above. Move left up the slab to a shallow left-facing corner, then up to a grassy ledge. Follow a dirty handcrack just right of the arête to its end, then traverse right via a fingercrack around a blunt arête to a huge pine (shared with **Le Petit Chien**). 110'
P2 5.2 X: Move left to the blunt arête and follow it with no protection to the top. 80'
FA Aug 10, 1997, Jay Harrison, Dick Tucker

7 Le Petit Chien 5.2 G 170'
Another "little" dog route.
Start: 20' left of Lunch Rock and 25' up from and right of **No Dogs Allowed** at a clean slab with a dirty vertical crack on the right side.
P1 5.2 G: Up the crack to a ledge, step right to a left-facing corner, and follow a wide crack up onto a slab. Friction up and right to a left-leaning brushy groove, follow it to a tree, then a little higher to a huge pine (shared with **No Dogs Allowed**). 90'
P2 5.2 G: Climb brown slab above the tree past a loose flake, then scramble up pine needles to the top. 80'
FA Aug 10, 1997, Dick Tucker, Jay Harrison

8 Lunch Rock Scramble 3rd class 200'
Above and right of Lunch Rock and 15' left of **Deviled Eggs** at a large tree is a left-leaning, low-angle left-fac-

Indian Lake

ing corner that leads to a huge chimney. This is **Lunch Rock Scramble**, which is used to access the top of the Boneyard.

9 Deviled Eggs 5.6 R 170'

Start: 15' left of **Devil Dogs** and 25' right of Lunch Rock, at a tree- and brush-filled left-leaning open book.
P1 5.5 G: Scramble up the open book past a couple of small trees. Above, the open book bends slightly left with a good crack. Climb this until the crack widens, then step right around the arête to a small ceiling. From the right end of the ceiling, follow cracks in the slab, staying right of the left-leaning arête, to a small stance at a tiny horizontal overlap. 100'
P2 5.6 R: Climb a crack to its end (last protection), then straight up the nose of the blunt arête to a pine behind a block (shared with **Devil Dogs**). 70'
FA Apr 25, 1999, Jay Harrison, Dick Tucker

10 Devil Dogs 5.6 G 160'

The first of the "dog" routes—i.e., routes named for Tucker's early adventure in which dogs accosted him on the approach, chasing him onto a large boulder. A well-thrown rock eventually encouraged them to find easier prey elsewhere. Lots of fixed gear on this one.
Start: 40' right of Lunch Rock, on a narrow, clean slab 20' left of Four Pines Buttress—a huge left-facing overhanging corner with some pine trees on top. The bolts on the P1 slab are another landmark.
P1 5.6 G: Climb up the initial slab past two bolts to a small sloped ledge. (V1) Continue up the slab left of a large left-facing corner to a bolt, then up and left to a grass-filled groove and belay at a small oak tree. 90'
P2 5.6 G: Move back right onto the slab and up to a small overlap (bolt). Climb up and left to a dirty chimney (bolt). Up the chimney, then angle up and left over vegetated rock to a pine behind a block (shared with **Deviled Eggs**). 70'
V1 5.6 G: Step right around the left-facing corner to a shallow left-facing corner, then follow it to its top. Angle up and left on a slab with cracks to join the normal route just above the chimney on P2.
FA Jun 13, 1993, Dick Tucker, Tim Riley
FA (V1) Jul, 2002, Travis King, Jay Harrison

Four Pines Buttress

About 60' right of Lunch Rock is a buttress with some pines trees on top. The left side of the buttress is defined by a huge left-facing overhanging corner. Unfortunately, the "four" pines seem to be dropping; at last count, there were three.

11 Motoring with Mohammed 5.7 G 140' ★★★

Once cleaned but now dirty, this zigzag line makes its way to the top of the Four Pines Buttress. The climb takes its name from a book written by Eric Hansen about his oddball adventures in Yemen.
Start: About 85' right of Lunch Rock (and 25' right of a huge left-facing overhanging corner that defines the left end of the Four Pines Buttress) are two left-leaning open books. Begin at the second (rightmost) open book, below the left end of a low, 20'-wide ceiling.
P1 5.7 G: Climb the open book to the triangular ceiling at the top. Break through the roof on its right side via a crack next to a tiny pine. Up the crack, then move up and left to gain two parallel cracks that diagonal up and right to the left end of a bushy ledge and a small ceiling. From there, step right, then up to another left-leaning crack; up this a short distance, then straight up to the top of the buttress. 140'
FA Sep 12, 1993, Dick Tucker, Tim Riley

12 Double Vision 5.6 G 125'

Presently very dirty and mossy.
Start: 40' uphill from and right of **Motoring with Mohammed**, at the left end of the Desperate Passage Area, at a large oak tree 6' left of a large block that leans up against the face (the top of this block forms a nice seating area).
P1 5.6 G: From the oak, climb up to a small ceiling broken by two cracks. Follow the left crack through the ceiling as it diagonals up and left to a bushy ledge (the same ledge as for **Motoring with Mohammed**). Climb straight up, then follow several left-leaning cracks to the top of the buttress. 125'
FA Aug 8, 1992, Dick Tucker, Tim Riley

13 Blueberry Scramble 4th class 200'

At the left end of the Desperate Passage Area and on the right side of the Four Pine Buttress is a bushy corner that provides access to the top of the buttress.

Desperate Passage Area

50' right of and uphill from **Motoring with Mohammed** is a level area beneath the left-facing blade of rock of P2 of **Desperate Passage**. There are several large partly buried boulders that provide level communal areas, and the terrain is relatively open. The right side of this section is defined by large left-facing, left-arching roofs with a black face below.

14 Bushwhacker 5.6 G 200'

Another long route that climbs to the top of the Boneyard.
Start: 30' left of **Desperate Passage** and 10' right of a block that forms a level seat, below a very shallow open book that leads to a thin seam and overlap 25' up.
P1 5.6 G: Climb the open book to the overlap. Step right and continue up the right-leaning crack to a blocky alcove beneath a ceiling with a slot in the center. Up the slot, then step right onto a narrow block, then right again onto the main face. Climb the face to a ledge, then step right to belay in a left-facing corner (just left of the P1 belay of **Desperate Passage**). 80'
P2 5.6 G: Climb the corner through a small overhang, then follow a left-slanting crack until you can traverse right 12' on sloping footholds to a short flake-pillar. Up this, then friction up the slab to a horizontal with a pine (this belay is off the pine on P3 of **Desperate Passage**). 80'
P3 5.3 G: Join **Desperate Passage** here: Up easier rock to two left-facing corners. Pick one and climb to the top. 40'
FA Jul 15, 2002, Jay Harrison, Kevin Bruce

Indian Lake

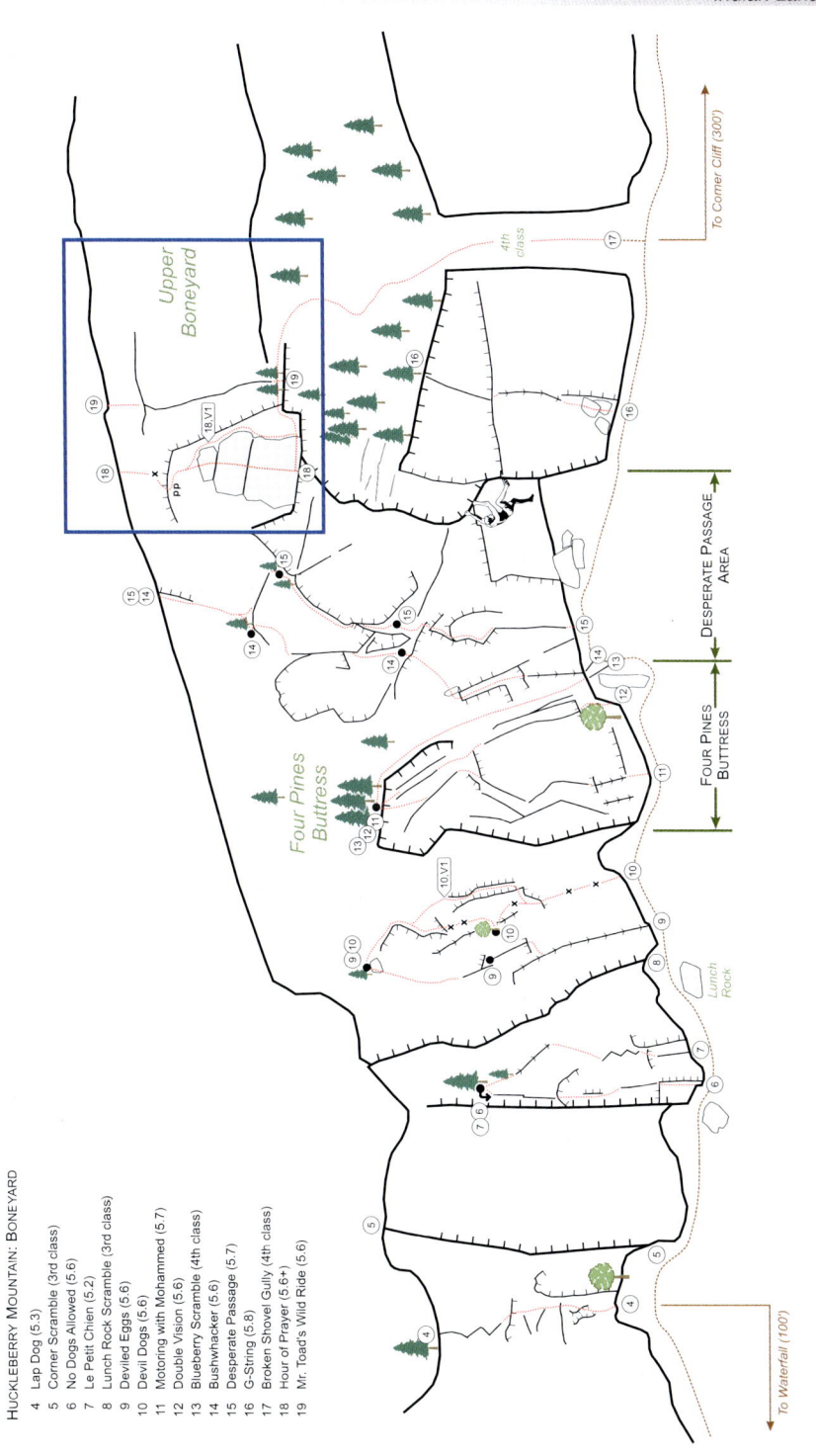

HUCKLEBERRY MOUNTAIN: BONEYARD

4   Lap Dog (5.3)
5   Corner Scramble (3rd class)
6   No Dogs Allowed (5.6)
7   Le Petit Chien (5.2)
8   Lunch Rock Scramble (3rd class)
9   Deviled Eggs (5.6)
10 Devil Dogs (5.6)
11 Motoring with Mohammed (5.7)
12 Double Vision (5.6)
13 Blueberry Scramble (4th class)
14 Bushwhacker (5.6)
15 Desperate Passage (5.7)
16 G-String (5.8)
17 Broken Shovel Gully (4th class)
18 Hour of Prayer (5.6+)
19 Mr. Toad's Wild Ride (5.6)

219

Indian Lake

15 Desperate Passage 5.7 G 230'
A longer route that climbs to the top of the Boneyard. Some grunge on P1 detracts from an otherwise pleasant route.
Start: Left of a large left-facing, left-arching corner and roof system is a chimney formed by a very distinctive, sharp-edged left-facing flake 120' up. Begin directly below this at an enormous tree on the left side of a large block.
P1 5.7 G: Climb a slab right of a bushy groove. Step left over the top of the groove and climb a right-facing flake—the "desperate passage" (crux)—to a right-rising ledge, then follow the ledge up and right to the base of the chimney and fixed anchor (one of the bolts is considered worthless). 90'
P2 5.7 G: Climb the chimney to its top, over a ceiling, and up to a ledge with a tree. 60'
P3 5.3 G: A handcrack leads out left to a pine, then easier rock to two left-facing corners. Pick one and climb to the top. 80'
FA Oct 9, 1993, Dick Tucker, Bob Hey

End of Desperate Passage Area

16 G-String 5.8 PG 100'
The route ends on ledges that are part of the Broken Shovel Gully approach to the Upper Boneyard.
Start: The right end of the Desperate Passage Area is defined by a large left-facing, left-arching corner and roof system, with a black face below. 30' right of this corner, but before the cliff turns mossy and lichen-covered, is a dirty open book with some blocks at the base that mark the start of this route.
P1 5.8 PG: Climb the open book, through the roof, then up the right-leaning flared off-width crack to a ledge with a tree. 100'
Descent: Rappel, or downclimb the gully to the right.
FA Nov 4, 1991, Jeremy Munson

17 Broken Shovel Gully 4th class 200'
This broad low-angle gully, right of G-String by 180', marks the end of the Boneyard. It is used to access the Upper Boneyard. At the base of the gully leaning up against a slab is a shovel, sans handle. The gully forms a natural drainage area from the slabs above and thus is often wet. Scramble up the first steep section, then trend left on ledges to the high ledge beneath Mr. Toad's Wild Ride.

Upper Boneyard
The next climbs begin on a ledge above the Four Pine Buttress and are guarded by a technical approach. The ledge can be accessed by traversing right from the end of P2 of Desperate Passage or, better yet, by scrambling up Broken Shovel Gully.
    Above the ledge is a left-facing corner that arches left into a ceiling. Below the ceiling and resting on the slab are three giant pancake flakes stacked one above the other 50' high.

18 Hour of Prayer 5.6+ PG 100' ★★
Start: In the center of the giant stacked pancake flakes that rest on the slab beneath the left-arching ceiling.
P1 5.6+ PG: (V1) Climb the crack-seam to the top of the flakes, then up the face to the arching ceiling (two pitons). Step left to mount the ceiling, move back right to a bolt, then friction up leftward following a shallow groove to finish. 100'
V1 Trav-Ass 5.6+ PG: Start at the right-facing corner formed by the right edge of the giant flakes, up the corner to its top, then step left to join the normal route.
History: On the first ascent, Harrison spent an hour above the lip of the arching ceiling rehearsing moves, up and down, repeatedly. After his "hour of prayer," he finally committed. The bolt and pitons were installed later by the first-ascent party.
FA Jul 11, 1996, Jay Harrison, Dick Tucker
FA (V1) Jul 10, 2002, Travis King, Jay Harrison

19 Mr. Toad's Wild Ride 5.6 G 110' ★★★★
Considered one of the best cracks at the Boneyard and on some of the cleanest rock. Tucker startled a crack-dwelling toad on the first ascent.
Start: At a crack 15' right of the left-facing corner that arches left into a ceiling, behind a clump of trees.
P1 5.6 G: Climb the left-leaning crack to its top at a horizontal, then up a pocketed face to the top. 110'
FA Oct 23, 1993, Dick Tucker, Karen Kuhn

Huckleberry Mountain
CORNER CLIFF

Aspect	Southwest
Height	100'
Quality	
Approach	2 hr 40 min, difficult
Summary	Very easy, exploratory routes where the cliff changes from west-facing to southwest facing.

3							3
-5.6	5.7	5.8	5.9	5.10	5.11	5.12	5.13+	total

About 300' uphill from and right of Broken Shovel Gully is a high point on the terrain below a slab known as Corner Cliff, named because this is the shoulder of the mountain where the cliff bends to become more south-facing. The terrain at the base is brushy and steep. The left side of the slab has a huge pine tree and a right-facing corner (there is a ceiling down low in this corner, then it leans left and has a ledge on top). There are roofs across the top of the slab. In addition to the routes described here, several toprope problems exist.

DIRECTIONS **(MAP PAGE 215)**
Corner Cliff is also located 300' left of the Great Dihedral Area.

Indian Lake

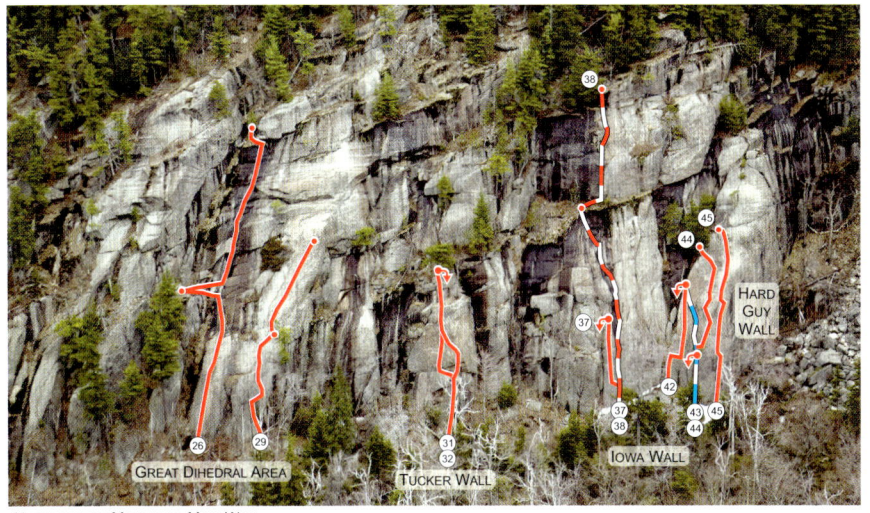

HUCKLEBERRY MOUNTAIN: MAIN WALL

26 Aunt Polly (5.6)
29 Jealous Dogs (5.7)
31 F.B.W. (5.10a)
32 Huckleberry Hound (5.10b)
37 I'd Rather Be in Iowa (5.7+)
38 Path to Iowa (5.8)
42 Geriatric Profanity Disorder (5.10a)
43 Darmok (5.7+)
44 Darmok Indirect (5.9-)
45 Insomnia (5.11a)

20 Sibiletto 5.3 G 135'
Start: At the base of the right-facing corner at the left side of the slab.
P1 5.3 G: Climb the right-facing corner to the ceiling, step right, then continue up the left-leaning corner to the bushes. Step left around the arête and up to a grassy ledge, continue up a crack in a smaller right-facing corner, then straight up through chocolate-colored rock and through two overhangs to a large tree ledge at the top. 135'
FA Sep 27, 1997, Dick Tucker, Jay Harrison

21 Malaise 5.2 G 100'
Start: 50' uphill from and right of Sibiletto, in the center of the slab, at a shallow depression that narrows to a single crack.
P1 5.2 G: Climb up the depression and the vertical crack to the right end of a ceiling. Break the ceiling on the right (under a horizontal pine tree) and continue up to the top. 100'
FA Sep 27, 1997, Dick Tucker, Jay Harrison

22 Falaise 5.2 G 100'
Start: 30' right of Malaise at a tiny left-facing corner with an alcove at the bottom.
P1 5.2 G: Climb the left-facing corner, then step left onto a slab to skip a jumble of rocks. Rejoin the corner and follow it up and left to a final block at the top. 100'
FA Sep 27, 1997, Dick Tucker, Jay Harrison

Huckleberry Mountain
MAIN CLIFF

Aspect	Southwest
Height	300'
Quality	★★★
Approach	2 hr 30 min, difficult
Summary	A mixture of single- and multi-pitch trad routes, and some sport routes on excellent rock.

6	5	2	4	5	1	27
-5.6	5.7	5.8	5.9	5.10	5.11	5.12	5.13+	total

The Main Cliff is the largest section of clean rock at Huckleberry and by far the most popular. The Main Cliff is defined by three large right-facing corners and walls. The leftmost of these is the Great Dihedral, a right-facing, right-leaning dihedral that extends up for 200'. Right of this is a right-facing corner whose left wall is the Teflon Wall. Farther right is the Hard Guy Wall, a steep, right-facing gently overhanging wall that marks the end of the Main Cliff.

DIRECTIONS (MAP PAGE 215)
After the boulderfield, the trail crosses a stream that flows to the west. Leave the trail and follow the stream as it goes downhill. At a house-sized boulder on the north side of the stream, leave the stream and go uphill through a talus field to the right end of the Main Cliff at the Hard Guy Wall, 2 hr 30 min from the parking area. (If you continue down the stream a few more minutes, you'll reach a marsh with excellent views of the Main Cliff.) Walk left along the base of the cliff to reach the Great Dihedral Area 582796,4824415.

Indian Lake

Great Dihedral Area

A central feature of the Main Cliff is a huge right-facing, right-slanting dihedral known as the Great Dihedral. The following routes are located near this feature.

23 Hat Rabbit 5.7 G 85' ★

Start: 4' left of the right-facing corner described in the start of **Weenie's Way**, at the base of the slab.
P1 5.7 G: Climb the slab and crack, staying parallel to the arête to the right, up to the trees. 85'
Gear: A #0 TCU and #1 slider are useful.
FA Oct 26, 1991, Dick Tucker, Jim Pittman

24 Mister Buzzárd 5.5 G 90'

In a memorable conversation overheard by Tucker at a store, a customer complained, "My name is Mr. Buzzárd, not Buzzard."
Start: In the right-facing corner described in the start of **Weenie's Way**.
P1 5.5 G: Climb the corner to its top, angling off right through the steep hay field. 90'
FA Jun 23, 1991, Dick Tucker, Bob Hey

25 Weenie's Way 5.5 PG 310'

Start: 50' left of the base of the Great Dihedral is a slab, the left side of which has a prominent sharp right-facing corner with a crack in it. Begin in cracks on the right side of the slab at its low point, right of the right-facing corner.
P1 5.5 G: Climb cracks up the edge of the slab, angling left to a left-facing corner. Up the corner to the top, then up grunge to trees. 120'
P2 5.2 PG: Step right and follow the edge of a slab to a short overhanging wall with an off-width crack. Step right and belay in a right-facing corner behind a pine. 90'
P3 5.5 PG: Climb the corner, then up nondescript slab to the trees at the top of the cliff. 100'
FA (P2, P3) Jun 23, 1991, Dick Tucker, Bob Hey
FA (P1) Nov 3, 1991, Dick Tucker, Hobey Walker

26 Aunt Polly 5.6 PG 275' ★★★

"Spare the rod and spile the child," as Aunt Polly said in Mark Twain's *Adventures of Tom Sawyer*. A good, moderate route on sound rock and relatively clean for this area.
Start: Begin at the base of a clean tan-colored slab, 20' left of the right-facing corner that defines the start of **Lucille**, and the first clean slab right of the Great Dihedral corner.
P1 5.6 PG: Climb the shallow crack in the slab (perhaps partially filled with grass) that leads to an unprotected slab section. Continue up chocolate-colored rock to a ledge; either belay in trees to the left or continue up to the overhang in black rock above. 130'
P2 5.5 G: Continue up to the overhang via a right-facing corner and through the roof at a notch with a good crack. Continue up the black slab to a tree in the Great Dihedral corner. 145'
FA Jun 8, 1991, Hobey Walker, Dick Tucker

27 Lucille 5.5 G 120'

The name Lucille adorned B. B. King's guitars throughout his career.
Start: At a face just right of a right-facing corner below a short, wide, shallow chimney capped by a ceiling.
P1 5.5 G: Climb up the face, then step left to the right-facing corner and up the chimney to the ceiling. Move through the ceiling on the left via a crack, then follow the crack up to a good horizontal. Continue up the face to a juniper island and step right to trees and a fixed anchor. 120'
FA Oct 20, 1991, Dick Tucker (roped solo)

28 Hammerdog 5.9 PG 260' ★★★

Start: At a slab with a vertical crack that leads to a horizontal crack (forming a cross), 10' left of the right-facing corner of **Jealous Dogs**.
P1 5.9 PG: Climb cracks in the slab to a horizontal, then up into a right-leaning crack and slab above to a ledge. 90'
P2 5.6 G: Continue up the obvious right-leaning handcrack (the leftmost of two parallel cracks) to an easy slab, over an overlap, then left to a tree ledge. 90'
P3 5.5 G: Climb the slab up and right to another overlap, over this, then up a slab to a thick flake-overlap that has two angular cutouts in the lip of the flake. Pass the flake-overlap via the left cutout and up to the tree ledge above. 80'
FA Jun 8, 1991, Hobey Walker, Dick Tucker

29 Jealous Dogs 5.7 G 150'

Jealous Dogs is named after a Pretenders song, in keeping with Tucker's "dog" theme. The initial chimney is easier and better than it looks, and the thin slanting crack on P2 is quite good. From the top, rappel, or climb easily up and left to join **Hammerdog** at the overlap on P2.
Start: At a tree-filled right-facing corner.
P1 5.6 G: Climb dirty cracks in the corner to its top, underclinging right into a chimney, then up a broken right-facing corner to a ledge. Move right to a tree belay. 80'
P2 5.7 G: Climb a slab and right-leaning fingercrack (the rightmost of two parallel cracks) to a lone pine. 70'
FA Oct 27, 1991, Tad Welch, Bill Widrig

Tucker Wall

Moving right from Jealous Dogs, you pass a section of scrubby cliff, which picks back up again at the distinctive buttress of **F.B.W.** and **Huckleberry Hound**. The wall is named for Dick Tucker, who was so influential to development here.

30 Bender's Chasm 5.8 G 100'

Uninspiring and not recommended. Used to access the top of **F.B.W.**
Start: At the base of a horrible-looking V-shaped chimney filled with giant boulders.
P1 5.8 G: Climb the V-chimney to its top. At this point, it is probably best to scramble rightward and rappel from the fixed anchor at the top of **F.B.W.** and **Huckleberry Hound**. 100'
FA Oct 27, 1991, Jim Bender, Jim Pittman

Indian Lake

HUCKLEBERRY MOUNTAIN: MAIN CLIFF

26 Aunt Polly (5.6)
27 Lucille (5.5)
28 Hammerdog (5.9)
29 Jealous Dogs (5.7)
30 Bender's Chasm (5.8)
31 F.B.W. (5.10a)
32 Huckleberry Hound (5.10b)
33 Teflon Wall (5.11b)
35 Dark of the Sun (5.7)
36 Escape from Iowa (5.12a)
37 I'd Rather Be in Iowa (5.7+)
38 Path to Iowa (5.8)
39 Potato-Chip Flake (5.11d)
40 Twenty-one (5.9)
41 Tallywhacker (5.4)
42 Geriatric Profanity Disorder (5.10a)
43 Darmok (5.7+)
44 Darmok Indirect (5.9-)
45 Insomnia (5.11a)
49 Horror Show (5.9+)

HARD GUY WALL
IOWA WALL
TUCKER WALL
GREAT DIHEDRAL AREA

Indian Lake

31 F.B.W. 5.10a G 90' ★★★
Climbs the left crack on the **Huckleberry Hound** headwall. Rumor is that the name stands for "flame-broiled Whopper," a Burger King specialty.
Start: Same as **Huckleberry Hound**.
P1 5.10a G: Climb a thin crack in a slab to a stance below a roof with a crack. Step left to the base of a fingercrack through orange rock, then follow the crack through the overhanging wall (crux) to the top. Scramble to a pine tree with a fixed anchor. 90'
FA Oct 27, 1991, Jim Bender, Jim Pittman

32 Huckleberry Hound 5.10b G 90' ★★★
One of the better cracks at Huckleberry. If the lower start is wet, it is possible to traverse left from the base of **Teflon Wall**.
Start: On a buttress between two boulder-filled chimneys, below a high roof with converging fingercracks.
P1 5.10b G: Climb a thin crack in a slab to a stance below a roof with a crack. Layback the fingercrack to gain the upper face, then traverse it left to a vertical handcrack finish. Scramble to a pine tree with a fixed anchor. 90'
FA Oct 30, 1993, Don Mellor, Dick Tucker

33 Teflon Wall 5.11b G 80' ★★
Climbs the center of the right-facing wall. The left side has been toproped (5.10d; Bill Pierce; Jul 25, 1993).
Start: Just right of **Huckleberry Hound** is a large right-facing corner in the Main Cliff. The back of this corner is a block-filled chimney, and the left wall of the corner is the Teflon Wall, which is split by several prominent horizontal cracks. Begin on a grassy ledge at the base of the wall.
P1 5.11b G: Climb up a dirty corner to gain the face and first horizontal. Sustained face climbing past several horizontals leads to the top of the buttress. Scramble to a pine tree with a fixed anchor (shared with **Huckleberry Hound** and **F.B.W.**). 80'
FA Nov 3, 1991, Hobey Walker

34 Last Dance 5.6 PG 215'
Start: Thirty-five feet right of **Teflon Wall**, at a section of dark, dirty rock with a good horizontal crack 4' up and a roof 50' up. Somewhat runout.
P1 5.6 PG: Climb up the middle of the dirty section following the left-rising flake through the steep section to a small ledge. Step right and, then follow an off width to a pointed boulder, then up to a ledge under the roof (2.5" cam helpful). Turn the roof at the handcrack in the center, then work up and right to a ledge. Go up a very clean black slab to a sloped vegetated terrace. 125'
P2 4th class: Walk left past a gully to a thin flake on a buttress of rock directly above **Teflon Wall**. 40'
P3 5.3 G: Up the flake, then zigzag up the obvious holds and cracks to the top. 50'
FA Oct 24, 1998, Jay Harrison, Dick Tucker

Iowa Wall

The right end of the Main Cliff, known as the Iowa Wall, extends from the small buttress with the "Iowa" climbs all the way to the Hard Guy Wall at its right end. This section of cliff holds the highest concentration of high-quality moderate climbs.

35 Dark of the Sun 5.7 G 150' ★★
Quite good, varied climbing on this one. Named for a 1991 Tom Petty song.
Start: At a tree that grows out of three stacked blocks at the base of a crack.
P1 5.7 G: Climb the crack past a pod (V1) to a birch tree ledge. 40'
P2 5.7 G: Continue up a right-facing corner to a ceiling; over this to a crack in black rock, then follow the crack to a tree with a fixed anchor. 110'
V1 5.10b G: At the pod, traverse right to a left-angling thin crack and follow it to the birch tree ledge. A bit overgrown.
FA Sep 28, 1991, Tad Welch (roped solo)
FA (V1) Oct 30, 1993, Bill Widrig, Ed Palen

36 Escape from Iowa 5.12a G 40' ★★★
Some unique and tricky moves on solid rock. Furman had just driven his van across the country from Yosemite with two people he'd never met because he couldn't afford gas. The trip turned into a nightmare, and Iowa became his euphemism for being stuck with these two across the middle third of the country, where everything was flat.
Start: At the base of the arête, 20' left of **I'd Rather Be in Iowa**.
● **P1 5.12a G:** Climb the arête to the tree ledge with a fixed anchor. 40'
FA Jul, 1994, Dave Furman

*Hobey Walker on the first ascent of **Teflon Wall** (5.11b). Photo by Dick Tucker.*

Indian Lake

37 I'd Rather Be in Iowa 5.7+ G 60' ★★★
A satisfying face climb.
Start: At a right-facing dirty corner with a wet spot.
● **P1 5.7+ G:** Climb the outside edge of the arête (which forms the right-facing corner) using rib holds to the first bolt. Move left onto the face and climb straight up to a fixed anchor. 60'
FA Jul, 1994, Dave Furman

38 Path to Iowa 5.8 PG (5.6 R) 230'
A good route that needs more cleaning.
Start: Same as **I'd Rather Be in Iowa**.
P1 5.8 PG: Climb the corner nearly to its end (you can bypass the grunge by moving right on the slab of **Potato-Chip Flake**). Move left onto a steep face, then up to a right-facing flake system and follow it up and left to a larger corner. At the top of this corner, step left onto the outside of the corner and climb easier rock to a tree ledge. 130'
P2 5.6 R: Climb the steep wall via a vertical handcrack, then step left and climb along a small right-facing flake. Step right and up to a horizontal crack, then up to the top. 100'
FA Jul 3, 1999, Jay Harrison, Dick Tucker

39 Potato-Chip Flake 5.11d G 60' ★★★
Climbs the incredibly delicate-looking flake pasted to the slab.
Start: 5' right of the right-facing corner of **I'd Rather Be in Iowa** on the face below the very obvious delicate right-facing flake.
P1 5.11d G: Difficult moves off the ground on small face holds gain the fragile flake. Follow the flake to its end, then up the face to a fixed anchor. 60'
FA Oct 16, 1993, Dave Furman

40 Twenty-one 5.9 G 50'
Furman had just turned 21, hence the name. This route is, in Furman's words, "schwag" and was used simply to get above **Potato-Chip Flake**.
Start: Same as **Tallywhacker**.
P1 5.9 G: Climb **Tallywhacker** until it is possible to climb up and left to a right-facing corner, up this, then move farther left to the fixed anchor at the top of **Potato-Chip Flake**. 50'
FA Oct 16, 1993, Dave Furman, Dick Tucker

41 Tallywhacker 5.4 G 240'
Provides access to the top of **Geriatric Profanity Disorder**, **Insomnia**, and the routes on the Hard Guy Wall, ending at the top anchor of **Horror Show**. The name is popular at rugger-bugger piss-ups. Slings have been found high above, so it is possible this route has a third pitch.
Start: At a left-facing corner formed by the left side of a pointed orange buttress (the buttress of **Geriatric Profanity Disorder**), on the left end of a terrace that drops dramatically on its right side.
P1 5.4 G: Scramble up the gully past a birch to a pine (the top of **Geriatric Profanity Disorder**), then step right and climb a short slab to a ledge. 140'

P2 5.3 G: (V1) Traverse 20' right, then climb up a slab (staying right of a pine tree) to a high tree ledge—the top of **Horror Show**. 100'
V1 Codswallop 5.6 G: Climb the fistcrack directly above the ledge and, at its end, continue up the left side of the slab to the high tree ledge—the top of **Horror Show**.
History: On the first ascent, Tucker and crew encountered some precariously stacked blocks at the top, which were decidedly unsafe. Since it was a remote, newly discovered area, they simply kicked them off without a second thought. To their horror, while rappelling to the base, they found Tad Welch standing there. Coincidentally, he was making his own explorations of the cliff and was equally surprised to find other climbers here.
FA Sep 28, 1991, Dick Tucker, Lois Legg, David Legg
FA (V1) Nov 2, 1991, Dick Tucker, Patty Li, Jim Bender

42 Geriatric Profanity Disorder (aka GPD) 5.10a G 80' ★★★
Beautiful face and thin-crack climbing up an unlikely face, and a local favorite. Named for one of the maladies listed in an infomercial (along with chronic nagging, indecisiveness, and darting eyes) shown on *The Simpsons*' episode "Bart's Inner Child."
Start: On the right side of the large boulder before the ground drops off to the right, below thin cracks.
P1 5.10a G: Climb the thin crack, hand traverse right, and make a blind reach into a widening crack. Climb the face via several cracks to meet the arête, then up the face to the top of the pointed buttress. There is a tree with a fixed anchor here. 80'
FA May 28, 1994, Dave Furman, Mike Dunkerly

43 Darmok 5.7+ G 100' ★★★
A nice initial handcrack with dirty climbing above. There is a fixed anchor after the good bits. The phrase "Darmok and Jalad at Tanagra," meaning to struggle together against a common enemy, is spoken by Dathon in an episode of *Star Trek: The Next Generation*.
P1 5.7+ G: Climb a clean handcrack to a tree 25' up with a fixed anchor. Above here, the climbing is very dirty: continue up the crack and through a wider section to the top of the buttress, where there is a tree with a fixed anchor (as for **GPD**). 100'
FA Oct 16, 1993, Dick Tucker, Dave Furman

44 Darmok Indirect 5.9- G 110' ★★
Start: Same as **Darmok**.
P1 5.9- G: Climb the initial handcrack of **Darmok** to the tree with the fixed anchor 25' up. Traverse right from the anchor following a crack across the face to meet a right-angling orange crack. Follow the crack up and right, then back left, then back right to where it fades into a dirty face. Good holds lead to a tree ledge with a fixed anchor. 110'
FA Oct 30, 1993, Don Mellor, Dick Tucker

225

Indian Lake

Hard Guy Wall

At the far right end of the Main Cliff, the cliff line turns into the mountain, forming the gently overhanging right-facing wall known as the Hard Guy Wall, named by Dick Tucker because he couldn't climb anything here. The real gem is **Barney Is the Antichrist**, but the other routes are also good.

45 Insomnia 5.11a G 140' ★★★★

A super route, one of the best at Huckleberry—long, varied, with several cruxes. Furman lost sleep trying to think of a good name for this route.
Start: Begin at the lowest point on the cliff left of the Hard Guy Wall below right-facing wafer flakes.
P1 5.11a G: Climb fragile right-facing flakes to an easy step right (bolt), then up cracks on the arête to their top and a second bolt. Climb thin face (crux) to gain a crack in orange rock. Climb the crack to the top, make a hard face move left, then up the lower-angle slab to a tree with a fixed anchor. From the top, rappel with one rope over the Hard Guy Wall. 140'
FA Oct 30, 1993, Dave Furman, Hobey Walker

46 Apollo Tucker 5.11a G 80' ★★

From the top of this route (and **Big Purple Rat**), it is possible to traverse right to link with the top of **Barney Is the Antichrist** for a longer pitch.
Start: At the left end of the Hard Guy Wall, near the low point of the buttress.
● **P1 5.11a G:** Climb a right-facing 10'-high corner, move left on good holds, then straight up on tiny edges (crux) to flakes. Angle up and right on the flakes to a short, 4'-high crack and on to a V-ledge, joining **Big Purple Rat** to the fixed anchor. 80'
FA Oct 16, 1993, Hobey Walker

47 Big Purple Rat 5.11a G 70' ★★

Another reference to Barney.
Start: 2' left of **Barney Is the Antichrist**.
● **P1 5.11a G:** Climb unstable flakes up the face, rail left, then up to a flake shaped like an eagle's head facing left. Climb up the eagle's-head flake to a V-ledge, then up the face to the top. 70'
FA Oct 15, 1993, Hobey Walker

48 Barney Is the Antichrist 5.10c G 80' ★★★★

Named after the annoying purple dinosaur of the popular children's show *Barney and Friends*. Superb, steep, and sustained climbing on great features and, in Walker's words, "some real moves."
Start: Begin at a flat boulder at an off-width pod beneath right-leaning cracks.
● **P1 5.10c G:** Step left to a fragile flake, then make a hard pull to gain a left-facing corner and an easy hand traverse right. The crux bulge ends at a jug and a hard layback move above. 80'
FA Jul 25, 1993, Hobey Walker

49 Horror Show 5.9+ G 130'

Never has a route name been more appropriate. Despite its appearance, however, you can face-climb around most of the off width.
Start: Uphill on the right side of the Hard Guy Wall is a wide right-leaning chimney that narrows to off width at its top. Begin at the base of this chimney next to two large trees and a large boulder.
P1 5.9+ G: Move left across the face and into the right-leaning chimney, then up a slab on the right edge of the chimney (RPs) until you're forced outside on the off width. Continue up the off width to its top and into a

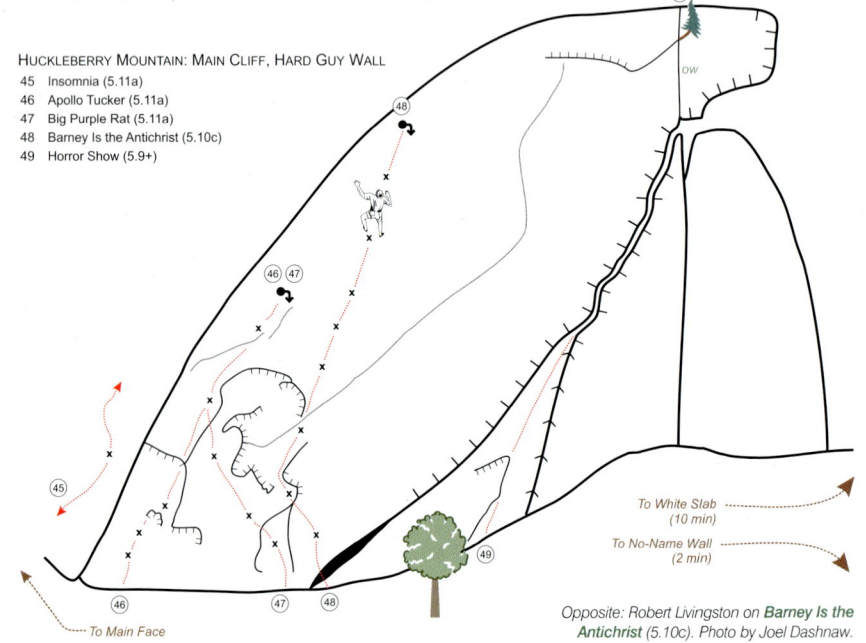

HUCKLEBERRY MOUNTAIN: MAIN CLIFF, HARD GUY WALL
45 Insomnia (5.11a)
46 Apollo Tucker (5.11a)
47 Big Purple Rat (5.11a)
48 Barney Is the Antichrist (5.10c)
49 Horror Show (5.9+)

Opposite: Robert Livingston on **Barney Is the Antichrist** (5.10c). Photo by Joel Dashnaw.

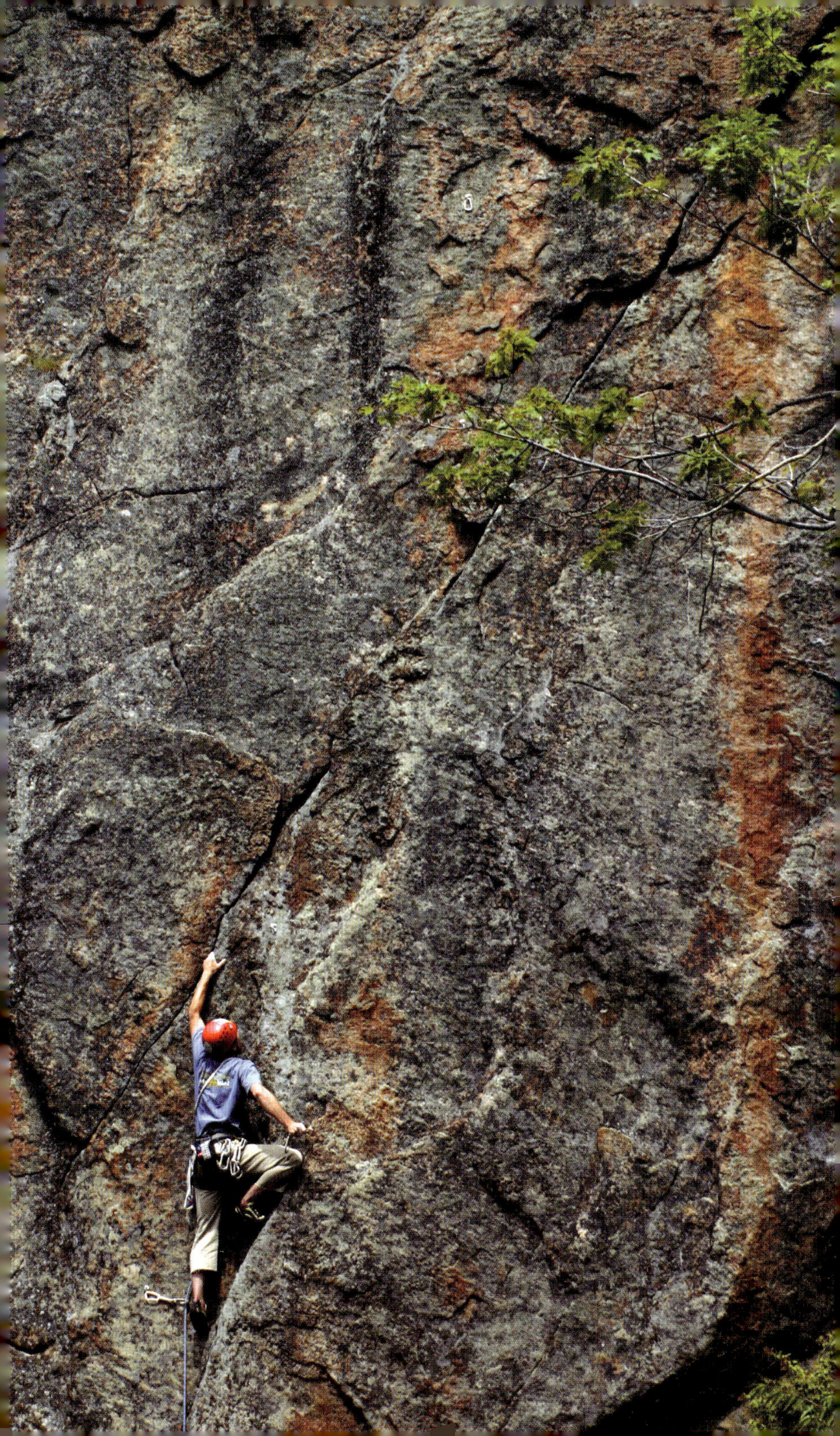

Indian Lake

right-facing corner. Up the corner to the roof, breaking through this via the off-width crack. Follow the crack past a horizontal with a small birch, then up to the top of the wall. Continue up and right on lower-angle rock to a tree ledge (the top of **Tallywhacker**). 130'
Gear: Up to 6".
FA Nov 3, 1991, Jim Bender, Patty Li

Hobey Walker on the first ascent of **Big Purple Rat** *(5.11a). Photo by Dick Tucker.*

Huckleberry Mountain
WHITE SLAB

Aspect	Southwest
Height	200'
Quality	★
Approach	2 hr 40 min, difficult
Summary	A long, white slab visible from a distance with single, high-quality slab route.

2						2
-5.6	5.7	5.8	5.9	5.10	5.11	5.12	5.13+	total

This is the slab that inspired the initial exploration of Huckleberry. It sits high above the Main Cliff.

DIRECTIONS (MAP PAGE 215)
Ascend the slope and gully right of the Hard Guy Wall. From the top of the gully, continue up and left to reach the base of the wide, clean slab with a prominent black streak.
    Another approach is to climb **Aunt Polly**, then bushwhack up and right through a steep band of trees to the base.

50 **Another Walk in the Sky** **5.1 X 100'**
Not recommended, but better than thrashing through the woods if you have to get to the top.
Start: Just right of a right-facing corner on the uphill left end of the slab.
P1 5.1 X: Friction up the cleanest line that you can find right of a corner to the top. 100'
FA Aug 4, 1996, Dick Tucker (solo)

51 **A Walk in the Sky** **5.1 X 200'** ★★★★
Named for a book by Nick Clinch that recounts the first ascent of Hidden Peak, the only American first ascent of an 8000-m peak. The climb is a mountaineering adventure in a unique position high on the ridge, providing a fun way to access the open ridge.
Start: At the black streak just left of center of the slab.
P1 5.1 X: Climb the slab following the black streak through a couple of bulging "waves" at the right end of a long overlap system, past a right-facing flake to low-angle terrain and on to the top. 200'
FA Oct 27, 1991, Tad Welch, Bill Widrig (both solo)

Huckleberry Mountain
NO-NAME WALL

Aspect	Southwest
Height	150'
Quality	
Approach	2 hr 40 min, difficult
Summary	An isolated blob of work with a single route.

DIRECTIONS (MAP PAGE 215)
On the right side of the Hard Guy Wall is a gully. Walk uphill and right from this gully; the first section of clean rock is No-Name Wall. The cliff is split horizontally by an overlap, and there is a prominent white streak on the right-hand side below this ceiling.

52 **Down in the Mall** **5.6 G 150'**
Not bad for its grade, albeit a bit scruffy. But, hey, even a second-rate route at Huckleberry beats shopping down in the mall. Named for a 1989 Warren Zevon song.
Start: On top of two blocks on the right side of the face, below a dirty crack.

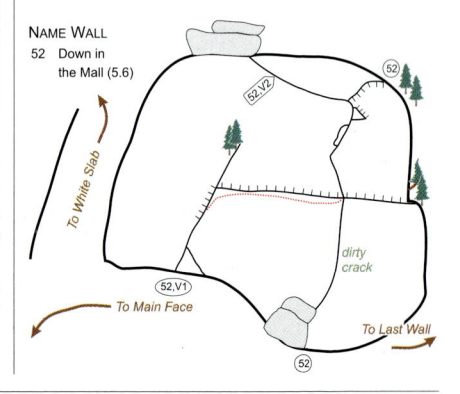

Indian Lake

P1 5.6 G: (V1) Climb the very dirty, weed-filled crack to the ceiling. Break through on the obvious handcrack up (V2) to some trees on the right-hand side of the face. 150'
V1 5.6 G: Starting on the left side of the face at a clean crack, climb the crack into the right-facing corner up to the ceiling, then traverse right to join the normal route.
V2 5.6 G: Head out left across the face and follow a crack to some stacked boulders at the top.
FA Oct 27, 1991, Bill Widrig, Tad Welch
FA (V1, V2) Oct 27, 1991, Bill Widrig, Tad Welch

Huckleberry Mountain
LAST WALL

Aspect	Southwest
Height	90'
Quality	
Approach	2 hr 42 min, difficult
Summary	Another tiny isolated wall with obscure routes.

2		1					3
-5.6	5.7	5.8	5.9	5.10	5.11	5.12	5.13+	total

From No-Name Wall, walk uphill and right about 100' to another dirty slab of rock, known as Middle Wall; there are no routes here. The bottom of Middle Wall is about even with the top of No-Name Wall. Another 100' to the right of Middle Wall is Last Wall, which has three routes. There has been some fire damage in this section of the mountain with a lot of down, charred timber and brush.

This was the first wall climbed at Huckleberry and a bit disappointing compared to the routes on the Main Cliff.

53 Demitasse 5.5 G 90'
Start: 15' right of a really dirty crack on the left side of the face below several solution pockets.
P1 5.5 G: Climb up the face past the solution pockets to a clean crack, then follow it to a horizontal. Traverse left, move up to a ledge with a small tree, then up an inverted V-notch to the top. 90'
FA Jun 16, 1990, Dick Tucker, Jeremy Munson

54 Barista 5.8 TR 90'
Perhaps the cleanest line on the face. Climb the face between the solution pockets (on the left) and a crack (on the right).
FA (TR) Jun 19, 1990, Hobey Walker

55 Opening Moves 5.6 G 90'
Noteworthy for being the first route at Huckleberry.
Start: At a crack on the right side of the wall.
P1 5.6 G: Climb the crack up to an 8"-deep overlap, then up to a corner, and angle right with increasingly dirty rock to a tree at the top. 90'
FA Jun 16, 1990, Hobey Walker, Jim Bender

HUCKLEBERRY MOUNTAIN: LAST WALL
53 Demitasse (5.5)
54 Barista (5.8)
55 Opening Moves (5.6)

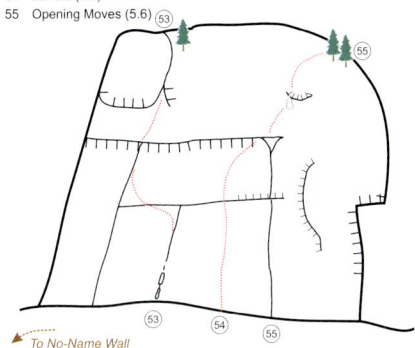

To No-Name Wall

Huckleberry Mountain
FACTORY SLABS

At the height of the pass on the Paint Mine Ruins Trail you'll see the ruins of an old paint mine. The red pigment in the soils, "Johnsburg Red," was once sought after for use on barns. Opposite the ruins is a slab known as the Southern Slab, 130' at its highest, with two toprope problems—**Johnsburg Red** (5.8 TR; May 10, 1992; Dick Tucker, Tim Riley), the crack above the roof on the left side of the slab, and **It's a Puzzle** (5.7 TR; May 10, 1992; Dick Tucker, Tim Riley), the offwidth crack on the right. Left of this (and out of sight from the ruins) is another slab with **Willy** (5.3; 60'; May 3, 1992, Dick Tucker) that climbs its right margin.

MILL MOUNTAIN

Wrapping around the south side of Mill Mountain 586168,4830608 are ledges and talus. There is a small, slabby cliff on the southwest side visible from South Johnsburg Road outside of Johnsburg (on NY 8). The cliffs aren't very inspiring, and the first ascentionist came away unimpressed, but only after climbing two routes: **Jay's Solo** (5.3; 100'; May 16, 1998; Jay Harrison) climbs the clean slab left of center, and, 50' left, **Mill Mountain Route** (5.3 G; 100'; May 16, 1998; Dick Tucker, Jay Harrison) climbs an attractive nose.

NAMELESS KNOB

Location	West of NY 8 south of Baker's Mills
Aspect	South
Height	60'
Quality	
Approach	20 min, easy
Summary	A collection of small walls with short routes.

1	1	4	1				7
-5.6	5.7	5.8	5.9	5.10	5.11	5.12	5.13+	total

Eleventh Mountain is a long ridge of summits that parallels the west side of NY 8 just south of Bakers Mills. Moving southwest, the ridge drops in several stages

229

Indian Lake

(eventually terminating in the East Branch of the Sacandaga River), forming several knobs and mini-summits. Nameless Knob is one of these, and is visible from a small pond on the west side of NY 8.

The area is a collection of minicliffs, some of which are fairly clean. There is potential for more short routes here.

DIRECTIONS

Park at the Kibby Pond Trailhead on NY 8 572418,4825513. From the north, this is on the left 10.8 miles south of the intersection with NY 28 in Wevertown (and 1.0 mile south of the Eleventh Mountain Trailhead). From the south this is on the right 12.6 miles north of the intersection of with NY 30. There is an even closer pullout on the east side of the road 0.1 mile north.

Across the road is a pond visible through a screening of trees. Walk north on NY 8 towards Wevertown to the end of the metal guard rail on the west side of the road, even with the north end of the pond 572533,4825753. Walk west (perpendicular to the road) across some blowdown north of the pond. Continue west up the hillside through open hardwoods with scattered boulders. Stay left of any exposed rock and boulders on the hillside to your right. At 20 min, reach the first cliff of any substance, the Lower Wall 572034,4825993, the right side of which is a left-rising rib. The cliffs are positioned just before the height of land.

HISTORY

The area was explored for ice climbing by Jay Harrison and Mike Prince in the winter of 2012. They returned in the spring to begin adding rock routes. The lower knobs and mini-summits between Eleventh Mountain and the river are nameless, hence the name of this cliff.

Tardis Wall

250' before the height of land where the terrain levels out is this 40'-tall rectangular cliff laced with cracks and seams and an attractive right-facing corner on its right side that breaks a wave of rock 12' up 571969,4826044.

1 Tardis Traveler 5.8 PG 35' ★

Start: In the center of a wall at a shallow, 12'-tall, right-facing corner.
P1 5.8 PG: Up the corner, then move up and left to a triangular depression. Follow a right-rising crack to its end, then up good holds to the top. 35'
FA Sep 2, 2012, Jay Harrison, Mike Prince

2 Dalek Connection 5.9 R 40'

Start: 6' right of Tardis Traveler at a larger right-facing corner, the right wall of which overhangs in a wave 12' up. **P1 5.9 R:** Go up the corner, then follow a right-leaning crack through the wave. Step left, then go up a left-rising crack to its top (where it meets Tardis Traveler). Good holds lead to the top. 40'
FA Sep 2, 2012, Jay Harrison

Upper Wall

This wall sits 130' above the top of the Tardis Wall. From the Tardis Wall, go 10' right of Dalek Connection and ascend a short 4th-class gully. Continue up the slope to a minicliff, around its right side, then back left to the base of this cliff at its lowest point.

From the low point, the terrain rises to the left along the base of a wide, short wall, and to the right is a steep slab.

3 Mountain Mist 5.3 G 90' ★

Start: At a left-rising groove 3' right of the low point of the wall. **P1 5.3 G:** Up the groove for 10' (just shy of a pine tree), then up and right to a thin crack in a flake on the blunt arête. Follow this to a ledge with a small birch. Continue up a corner to another ledge 50' up. Belay here, or continue for another 40' through a short headwall using a good vertical crack, then one more short headwall to reach the end of open rock. 90'
FA Mar 15, 2013, Jay Harrison, Mike Prince

4 Rain Delay 5.7 TR 35'

Begin 25' right of Mountain Mist and 8' right of a pine tree growing very close to the rock. Go up right-facing edges and flakes, then up the slab to the top.

Lower Wall

This is the lowest cliff on the hillside 572034,4825993. The right side of the cliff is defined by a left-rising rib (the route Instigator) and, 10' to the left, a crack on the face that parallels the rib (Troublemaker). The base of the cliff rises to the left to a jumble of smaller walls.

From the Tardis Wall, walk downhill to the right along the base of the rock to a prominent, 30'-tall, yellow, right-facing corner. Continue 150' uphill and right to reach the left end of this wall.

5 Crow's Nest 5.8 TR 55'

40' uphill and left of Troublemaker is a small blocky tower. Begin 20' left of this tower. Go up a short face to a ledge with a large evergreen tree. Fight past the tree to a dirty vertical crack, and climb it through an overhang to the top of the cliff. Could be nice if cleaned.

6 Troublemaker 5.8- G 60'

Start: 40' downhill and right of a small, blocky tower, at a wide, full-height, left-rising crack system parallel to the left-rising rib that defines the right end of the cliff.
P1 5.8- G: Climb crack to the top. 60'
FA Sep 2, 2012, Jay Harrison, Mike Prince

7 Instigator 5.8 PG 60' ★

Perhaps the best route at Nameless Knob.
Start: 5' right of Troublemaker and 4' left of a chimney, at a short, right-rising crack in clean rock. **P1 5.8 PG:** Go up the right-rising crack, then reach left to a small right-facing corner. Move up to a stance, then up to the rib, and follow this up and left to a narrow ledge below a small overhang. Move left 6' to a crack, and climb this to another ledge. Reach up to holds that lead to a thin vertical crack, and follow this to the top. 60'
FA Mar 7, 2012, Jay Harrison

Indian Lake

SHANTY CLIFF

Location	West of NY 8 south of Baker's Mills
Aspect	Southwest
Height	140'
Quality	★★★★
Approach	15 min, easy; river crossing
Summary	A small cliff in a pleasant setting with a selection of moderate routes on excellent rock.

17	8	6	4	4		45
-5.6	5.7	5.8	5.9	5.10	5.11	5.12	5.13+	total

Shanty Cliff lies on the southeast side of an unnamed peak (Peak 2048) south of Baker's Mills. In the middle of the summer, it's hard to see, but this cliff is actually the right side of an enormous eroded dike, one of the largest in the Adirondacks, that runs down nearly to the East Branch of the Sacandaga River. The setting at Shanty, while a bit thick with trees at the base, is quite pleasant. The top of the cliff has open ledges and slabs with pretty views down the river. About 100' in front of the cliff on its uphill end is an open area of slabs and ledges known as Lunch Rock, a great place to take the pack off and enjoy the view.

The cliff features excellent rock—relatively clean and solid with above-average friction properties—with slabs, cracks, roofs, and arêtes. Some of the routes feature incredible angular holds in the most unlikely and convenient places.

CAMPING

There are many excellent camping sites along the East Branch of the Sacandaga River; you just need to explore the many dirt-road offshoots of NY 8. An excellent alternative is the campsite on top of the cliff (on top of Blue Toes), with a fire ring, flat ledges, and excellent views, although you need to carry up water.

HISTORY

Shanty Cliff was discovered by Dave and Lois Legg, who brought it to the attention of Dick Tucker. Together, they made the first recorded visit in 1982, when they led one route and toproped several others. They weren't the first—during their visit, they encountered another party that had climbed on the cliff previous to that date. At any rate, the cliff was rediscovered in 1986 by Jim Vermeulen, who, with Stuart Williams, Eric Dahn, and Mike Cross, climbed many of the obvious lines over the next couple of years. Tucker reappeared several times (in 1990, then again in 1999 with Jay Harrison) and exhausted many more possibilities. Even so, there are still opportunities for new routes.

The summer of 2007 saw a flurry of activity by Arietta Climbing (page 308). The approach path was improved, and several new walls were developed, including the Shanty Slab and the Shanty Sports Arena.

Additionally, several top-quality routes were added in the vicinity of Gunky Route and Soweto. In all, eighteen routes were added.

DIRECTIONS (MAP PAGE 231)

Park on NY 8 at the trailhead for Cod Pond (and Cod Pond Flow, North Bend, and Baldwin Springs) 569056,4820031, 8.5 miles north of the intersection with NY 30. There are actually two trailheads for Cod Pond; this one is known as the Oregon Trail, and, from the south, it's the second one marked for Cod Pond and is located just before a small concrete bridge over Stewart Creek. From the north, the trailhead is 14.7 miles south of the intersection with NY 28 in Wevertown and 8.9 miles south of the post office in Baker's Mills.

The approach involves fording a river and some minimal bushwhacking. The worst part of the bushwhacking is near the river and the flat boggy sections on its far side; these directions minimize these difficulties by using a new approach path.

Walk north on NY 8 for 420' and turn left onto a dirt road just after the guardrail 569117,4820155. Follow the road for 100 yards to its end at a picnic/camping spot, then continue on a path to the river. Ford the river (calf-deep and slow-moving in the summer) and pick up the trail on the far side. Follow this trail for several minutes to a grassy meadow. 100' past the meadow, the trail forks; take the right fork and follow this uphill over a shoulder and into a broad gully—the base of the giant eroded dike. The trail ascends the gully on the left side to the base of Shanty Slab, then cuts across to the right side of the gully, where it continues uphill past a few short walls to the Shanty Sports Arena. The trail continues uphill, hugging the base of the right wall of the gully, to the main cliff 568574,4820719.

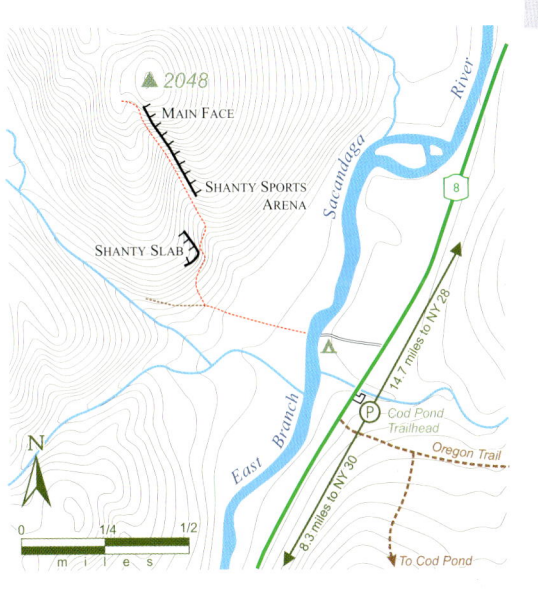

Indian Lake

Shanty Knob

Near the height of land on the opposite side of the dike from the Main Face is a delightful knob with two very short routes: **Thing 1** (5.6 G; 20'; Oct 10, 1994; Jim Vermeulen, Bill Morris), a right-rising crack, and **Thing 2** (5.5 G, 18'; Oct 10, 1994; Bill Morris, Jim Vermeulen), the right-hand crack.

Main Face

This is the largest section of rock situated high on the right side of the gully. It is located highest on the hillside, farthest from the parking area, and is divided into left and right sides by a deep chimney-gully with a giant chockstone at the top.

The main features include, at its upper end, a very long, low roof 6' up. Right of this is a cone-shaped dirt slope that leads to **Gullet**, an unpleasant chimney climb. In the center of the face is a large buttress-arête with a huge square roof 40' up; this is the location of **Soweto**. Just right of the buttress-arête is a large cone-shaped dirt slope that leads to the huge chimney with a giant chockstone at the top; several routes begin on the right side of this dirt slope, including **Little Gem Diner**. Downhill from and right of the buttress-arête is another set of roofs below which are two distinctive orange spots; **Gunky Route** and its neighbors climb through these roofs.

1 Sleepwalk 5.2 G 40' ★

Start: 15' left of where the low roof goes into the dirt below a straight-up fern-filled groove. There is a very large double-trunked birch tree at the base.
P1 5.2 G: Up the groove to near the top of the ferns, then traverse right following a crack to the center of the slab. Straight up to the lower of the two parallel left-leaning cracks in the headwall. Follow the lower crack up and left to the top. 40'
FA May 7, 1988, Jim Vermeulen

2 Bo Peep 5.4 G 90'

Start: At the left end of the low roof where it goes into the dirt, below two shallow cracks that begin 6' up.
P1 5.4 G: Climb the cracks onto the slab, then follow the upper of the two parallel left-leaning cracks in the headwall above. 90'
FA Jul 4, 1990, Dick Tucker (solo)

3 River View 5.7 TR 100'

Begin as for **Bo Peep** and climb straight up the headwall, crossing the two parallel left-leaning cracks.
FA (TR) Sep 19, 1982, Dick Tucker, Lois Legg

Shanty Cliff

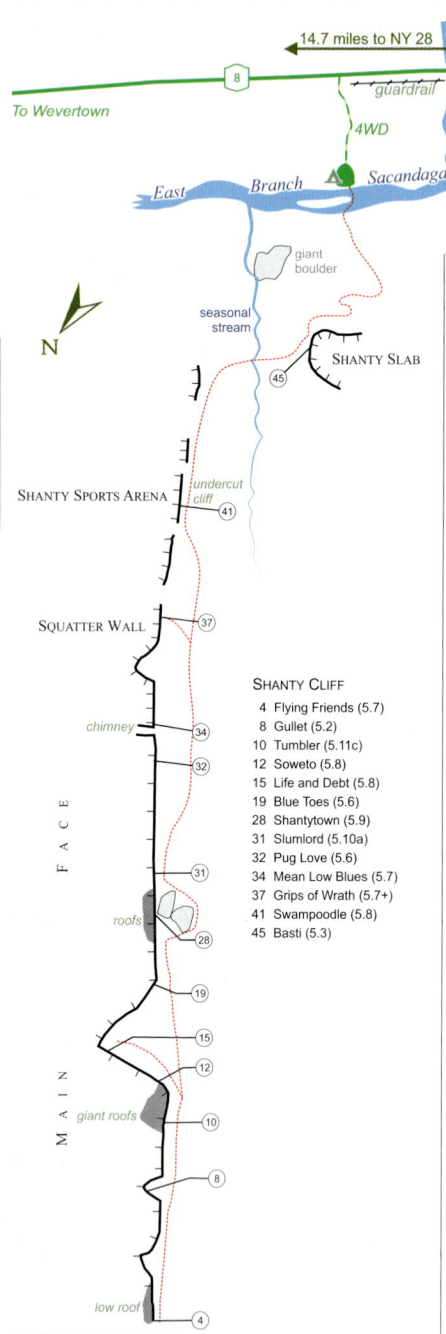

- 4 Flying Friends (5.7)
- 8 Gullet (5.2)
- 10 Tumbler (5.11c)
- 12 Soweto (5.8)
- 15 Life and Debt (5.8)
- 19 Blue Toes (5.6)
- 28 Shantytown (5.9)
- 31 Slumlord (5.10a)
- 32 Pug Love (5.6)
- 34 Mean Low Blues (5.7)
- 37 Grips of Wrath (5.7+)
- 41 Swampoodle (5.8)
- 45 Basti (5.3)

DESCENT OPTIONS

An easy descent involves walking left, then down a tree slope to the base of the cliff. Some of the newer routes have fixed anchors where you can lower back to the ground with a single rope.

Indian Lake

SHANTY CLIFF
1 Sleepwalk (5.2)
4 Flying Friends (5.7)
6 Circuitous Shit (5.4)
8 Gullet (5.2)
12 Soweto (5.8)
19 Blue Toes (5.6)
27 Gunky Route (5.8)
31 Slumlord (5.10a)
32 Pug Love (5.6)

4 Flying Friends 5.7 G 110' ★★★

Clean rock, a pumpy start, and a crux hand traverse make this one of the better routes here.

Start: 20' uphill from and left of Circuitous Shit, and 30' right of where the low roof goes into the dirt, below a good jamcrack that breaks the overhang.

P1 5.7 G: Climb up the crack to a slab, (V1) traverse left to a birch below a set of parallel left-rising cracks in the headwall above. Go to the upper crack, then follow a right-leaning crack to an arête. Hand-traverse right to a corner and follow it to the top. 110'

V1 Once a New 5.7 G: Continue straight up to horizontal crack in a steep face. Traverse left to a small mantel ledge, then finish up the arête of the normal route.

FA May 7, 1988, Stuart Williams, Eric Dahn, Jim Vermeulen
FA (V1) Aug 4, 1999, Jay Harrison, Dick Tucker

SHANTY CLIFF: MAIN FACE, LEFT SIDE
1 Sleepwalk (5.2)
2 Bo Peep (5.4)
3 River View (5.7)
4 Flying Friends (5.7)
5 Son of Circuitous Shit (5.6)
6 Circuitous Shit (5.4)
7 Cross-Eyed Orphan (5.3)
8 Gullet (5.2)
9 Wrong Side of the Tracks (5.9)
12 Soweto (5.8)

233

Indian Lake

5 Son of Circuitous Shit 5.6 G 110'

Start: 10' left of where the wide crack of **Circuitous Shit** breaks through the roof.
P1 5.6 G: Pull through the roof to a small face on the left with a crack. Follow the crack to a sloping ledge system with several trees. Step left and climb a chimney, exit right via a crack, and follow it to a left-leaning arête (the same arête as **Circuitous Shit**). Up the arête to the top. 110'
FA Aug 4, 1999, Jay Harrison, Dick Tucker

6 Circuitous Shit 5.4 G 140' ★

Start: 25' uphill from and left of the right end of the low roofs, at a wide crack that breaks through the low roof barrier.
P1 5.4 G: Climb the crack onto the slab. Traverse right 10' to a right-leaning crack and follow it to a left-leaning arête and slab that faces right. Up the arête to a vegetated ledge with a birch. At the top of the vegetation (and on the right-facing slab), climb an orange open book with a good crack to the top. 140'
FA May 7, 1988, Eric Dahn, Stuart Williams, Jim Vermeulen

7 Cross-Eyed Orphan 5.3 G 130' ★

Start: Halfway up the left side of the cone-shaped dirt slope that leads to **Gullet**, below some cracks in the arête.
P1 5.3 G: Up the cracks in the arête to a left-rising ramp. Follow this left to a slab (which is facing right, same as **Circuitous Shit**) and climb the slab via a crack to a small birch. Step left, up the face, then up the arête to the top. 130'
FA Aug 12, 1999, Dick Tucker, Jay Harrison

8 Gullet 5.2 G 110'

Start: Uphill from and left of the large roof on the **Soweto** arête, above the smaller of the two cone-shaped dirt slopes.
P1 5.2 G: Scamper up the chimney to some scary stacked blocks (V1, V2), then continue up the horribly vegetated chimney to the top. 110'
V1 Wanderer 5.4 PG: Walk up and left on the vegetated ledge to a groove. Climb the arête left of the groove to the top.
V2 Fizzle 5.2 G: Walk up and left on the vegetated ledge, past a groove to a shallow open book. Up the open book, then up and left, following cracks to the top.
History: Wanderer was the first nontoproped route at Shanty Cliff.
FA Jul 4, 1990, Dick Tucker
FA (V1) Sep 19, 1982, Dick Tucker, David Legg
FA (V2) Jul 4, 1990, Dick Tucker

Indian Lake

9 Wrong Side of the Tracks 5.9 G 120'
On the first ascent, Harrison dented his helmet when a 5-lb. hold pulled off and hit him in the head.
Start: On the right side of the cone-shaped dirty slope that leads to Gullet, at a right-facing corner capped by a 2' roof.
P1 5.9 G: Up the corner to the overhang, break it on the right, and continue up the right-facing corner to a face. Up the face, trending slightly left to a prominent overhanging block, then up to the top. 120'
FA (5.8 A1) Aug 12, 1999, Jay Harrison, Dick Tucker
FFA Sep 24, 2007, Jamie McNeill, Jay Harrison

10 Tumbler 5.11c G 50' ★★★
The name describes what you may turn into when you try to clip the last bolt.
Start: 10' up from and left of the toe of the arête beneath a bolt.
P1 5.11c G: Clip the first bolt and swing up onto the face. Climb the face (stoppers and small cams) to the large roof. Reach up for the thin crack under the roof, traverse left several feet to somewhat better holds, and pull yourself over the roof to a fixed anchor just above. 50'
FA 2007, Arietta Climbing

11 Get Over It 5.8+ PG 100'
Start: Find the arête with the huge roof 40' up. Begin left of the toe of the arête, 6' right of the huge right-facing corner, at a vertical crack.
P1 5.8+ PG: Up the crack to a horizontal, then move right 4' to incipient vertical cracks just left of the arête. Up the cracks (5.7) past a horizontal crack, then break right around the roof (same as Soweto V1) to a black open book. Step up and left into a vertical V-alcove and climb out its left side following a finger- and handcrack (crux) to easier ground to join Soweto to the top. 100'
History: The first half of this route was climbed in 2000 by Robert Livingston.
FA Sep 24, 2007, Jay Harrison, Jamie McNeill

12 Soweto 5.8 G 100' ★★★
Named for a shantytown in Johannesburg.
Start: Find the arête with the huge roof 40' up. Right of the arête is a large cone-shaped dirt slope with ferns and trees that leads to a large chimney with a huge chockstone at the top. Begin on the right side of the arête, 20' up from the toe, in the rightmost of two left-rising cracks.
P1 5.8 G: (V1) Climb the crack up and left to a black open book with a good crack. Follow the open book to the right end of the roof. Continue in the crack as it snakes up and right to a sloped shelf on the arête. Step left on a left-rising ramp to easier terrain and the top. 100'
V1 5.7 G: Start left of the toe of the arête beneath a right-facing corner that leads to the huge roof. Climb up to the roof, then right across the face (avoiding the raven's nest above) to the arête, joining the normal route.

History: The initial V1 corner was climbed by Williams in an attempt to aid the huge roof. That attempt was abandoned when the gear zippered.
FA 1989, Jim Lawyer, Stuart Williams, Eric Dahn

13 Rocinha 5.10c G 80' ★★★
A committing lead with good face climbing followed by the crux move at the top. Named for a slum in Rio de Janeiro.
Start: At the top of the cone-shaped tree slope where it becomes rocky. Belay from a tree.
P1 5.10c G: Scramble onto a ramp and the first bolt. Work up the face (5.9) past the right end of a sharp-edged overlap, work up and left to a right-facing flake, then up to a ledge. Over a bulge to another ledge, up a face to a right-rising horizontal, then to a left-rising horizontal. Follow a right-leaning fingercrack to a final crux move to reach a fixed anchor. 80'
FA Sep 22, 2007, Jonathan Nickel

14 Hard Times 5.11c G 80' ★★★
Nice face climbing with the crux near the top.
Start: Same as for Rocinha.
● **P1 5.11c G:** Climb Rocinha to the second bolt, then work right 6' to a hidden bolt. Straight up the face to a prominent horizontal, then up and right to a fixed anchor at the top. 80'
FA 2007, Arietta Climbing

15 Life and Debt 5.8 G 70' ★★
Start: 15' uphill from and right of Rocinha, below a giant chockstone in the chimney 40' up.
P1 5.8 G: Balance up the initial face past bolts to a right-leaning crack and follow it to the top. 70'
FA 2007, Arietta Climbing

16 Howdy Doody 5.2 G 80'
Start: On the right side, and 15' from the top, of the cone-shaped slope that leads to the large chimney with the huge chockstone at the top, at a left-leaning V-groove with stepped ledges at the bottom.
P1 5.2 G: Climb the V-groove, then up left on easy rock, nearly paralleling the ground until you're almost under the chockstone. Climb cracks up past a tiny birch, then up the slab, angling left between the cracks to the top. 80'
FA Jul 4, 1990, Dick Tucker

17 Little Gem Diner 5.6 G 110' ★★
Named for a well-known diner in the Syracuse area.
Start: About halfway up on the right side of the cone-shaped slope that leads to the large chimney with the huge chockstone at the top, at a left-leaning crack 2' right of the left-leaning V-groove of Howdy Doody.
P1 5.6 G: Climb the left-leaning crack (with a small right-facing arch at the top) to its top, then up and right to an overlap below a bulge broken by two cracks. Climb the left-hand crack, then up easier rock, angling left up the face to the top. 110'
FA Jun 14, 1987, Jim Vermeulen, Bill Morris

Opposite: Jamie McNeill on at the crux fingercrack of Rocinha (5.10c). Photo by Robin Harrison.

Indian Lake

18 Vernal Imperatives 5.6 G 100' ★
Start: 2' left of **Blue Toes** at a face with left-rising slash cracks.
P1 5.6 G: Climb the face to a bulge, angle left through the bulge, then continue up the face to the top. 100'
FA Oct 10, 1994, Jim Vermeulen, Bill Morris

19 Blue Toes 5.6 G 100'
So named because of the appendages numbed by an icy November ford of the Sacandaga.
Start: On the right side of the cone-shaped slope that leads to the chockstone-topped chimney, 8' downhill from and right of **Little Gem Diner**, below an A-shaped ceiling that leads to a fern-filled right-slanting crack.
P1 5.6 G: Climb up the A-shaped ceiling, then up the right-leaning fern-filled crack to its top. Step left to a tiny birch and climb a crack to the top of the face. Angle up and left on a slab to the top. 100'
History: Vermeulen was quite the explorer, and he thought Shanty Cliff was his discovery; he climbed this route the same day. Little did he know that Tucker had visited four years earlier.
FA Nov 9, 1986, Jim Vermeulen, Mike Cross

20 Bogus Dent 5.2 G 60' ★
Start: Downhill from and 25' right of **Blue Toes**, below a small left-rising arête that forms a left-leaning, right-facing corner filled with grass and ferns.
P1 5.2 G: Climb the left side of the corner to its top, paralleling the ground, then up a crack to the top of the small buttress. Step right and climb to the top of the pinnacle. 60'
FA Aug 18, 1999, Dick Tucker, Jay Harrison

21 Time Trials 5.7 G 60'
So named because the first ascentionists timed themselves with a stopwatch.
Start: 2' right of **Bogus Dent**, just right of the left-leaning, right-facing corner, below a left-leaning crack in brown rock.
P1 5.7 G: Climb the crack to the ceiling 15' up. Break this on the right via a sharp-edged off-width crack, then climb the crack to an A-shaped ceiling. Break through this at the apex and climb to the top of the pinnacle. 60'
FA Aug 18, 1999, Joel Bantle, Tim Bantle, Jeremy Cunningham, Joe Cunningham
FFA Sep 21, 2007, Jay Harrison (roped solo)

22 Shantyclear 5.5 G 70'
Start: At the bottom right side of the cone-shaped slope that leads to the chockstone-topped chimney is a right-rising ramp covered in trees used for descent (3rd-class). Begin at the base of the ramp.
P1 5.5 G: Climb broken rock up and right, paralleling the right-rising ramp, onto a slab, then follow the slab up and right to a wide crack in a left-facing corner. Up this crack, exiting left onto the slabs, which lead to the top. 70'
FA Aug 12, 1999, Jay Harrison, Dick Tucker

23 C & E 5.5 G 70'
Start: 50' uphill from and left of the orange spots beneath the large roofs, and 30' right of the right-rising 3rd-class ramp, at a grass- and fern-filled groove that leads to a ledge 12' up. There is a left-leaning off width above the ledge.
P1 5.5 G: Climb up the groove, traverse right on a small ledge, then up and right for 40' following a right-rising ledge. At its end, climb a left-facing corner, then continue traversing right to the base of a shallow chimney. Up the chimney to the top. 70'
FA Nov 9, 1986, Jim Vermeulen, Mike Cross

24 Soup Kitchen 5.10a G 40' ★
Start: 20' left of the serrated-topped boulder of **Gunky Route**, at a 4'-high right-facing corner on the left side of an overhanging wall.
● **P1 5.10a G:** Scramble up to a narrow ledge below the right end of a left-rising overlap. Over the overlap and bulging face above (crux, height-dependent) to a lower-angle face. Up easier rock to a fixed anchor (shared with **Breadline**). (You may need to move right on the top section to find gear.) 40'
FA 2007, Arietta Climbing

25 Breadline 5.11a G 40' ★★
Some people stick-clip the second bolt.
Start: 15' left of the serrated-topped boulder of **Gunky Route** and 5' right of **Soup Kitchen**, below an overhanging wall with a sloped shelf 10' up.
● **P1 5.11a G:** Up to the first bolt, then make a tricky move to stand on a sloping shelf (crux). Pull over a bulge on sloped horizontal holds, then up the easier face to a fixed anchor (shared with **Soup Kitchen**). 40'
FA 2007, Arietta Climbing

26 Skid Row 5.11a G 90' ★★★
Start: Left of **Gunky Route**, behind a large boulder below an orange slab with a bolt.
P1 5.11a G: Up slab (bolt), then move right across a left-facing corner (bolt) to a small slab below main roof. Move up to a jug (gear in left-slanting cracks above the lip), pull the overhang, then up moderate steep face (5.8) to a fixed anchor at the top of the cliff. 90'
Gear: To 2".
FA Jul 17, 2009, Jonathan Nickel, Randy Hibshman

27 Gunky Route 5.8 PG 100' ★★
This route sports Gunks-like holds.
Start: 80' right of the right-rising 3rd-class ramp is a section of low overhangs with two orange spots on the face below. There are two large boulders at the base, one with a serrated top.
P1 5.8 PG: Climb up the left-facing corner to a scary wedged block, up the overhanging arête on jugs, then hand-traverse right to the low-angle face to the right. Traverse right to a left-facing corner, up this to its top, then step right and climb up to an overhang with a protruding "snout." Over this, then up the easier face to the top. 100'
FA Aug 18, 1999, Jay Harrison, Dick Tucker

Indian Lake

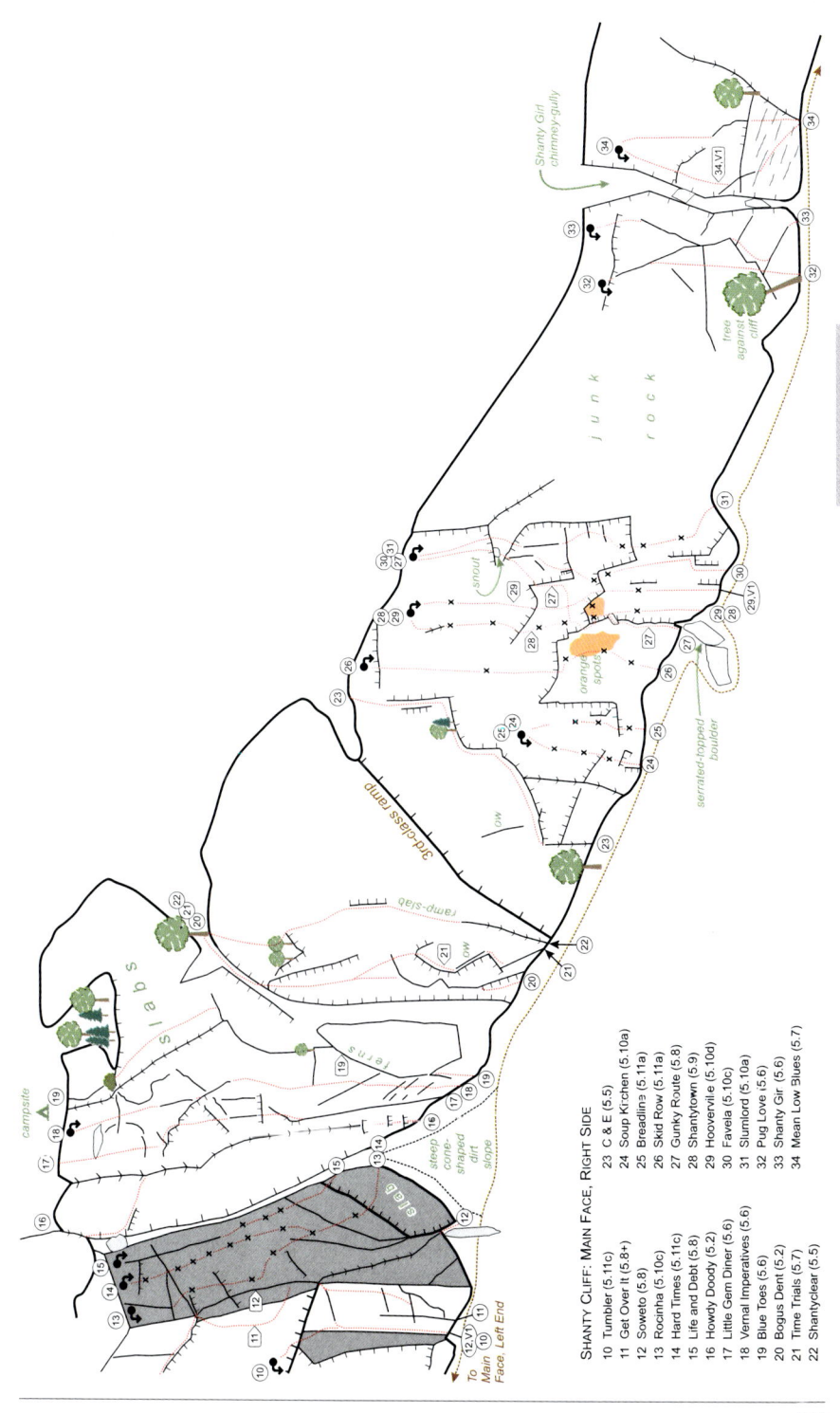

SHANTY CLIFF: MAIN FACE, RIGHT SIDE

10 Tumbler (5.11c)
11 Get Over It (5.8+)
12 Soweto (5.8)
13 Rocinha (5.10c)
14 Hard Times (5.11c)
15 Life and Debt (5.8)
16 Howdy Doody (5.2)
17 Little Gem Diner (5.6)
18 Vernal Imperatives (5.6)
19 Blue Toes (5.6)
20 Bogus Dent (5.2)
21 Time Trails (5.7)
22 Shantyclear (5.5)
23 C & E (5.5)
24 Soup Kitchen (5.10a)
25 Breadline (5.11a)
26 Skid Row (5.11a)
27 Gunky Route (5.8)
28 Shantytown (5.9)
29 Hooverville (5.10d)
30 Favela (5.10c)
31 Slumlord (5.10a)
32 Pug Love (5.6)
33 Shanty Girl (5.6)
34 Mean Low Blues (5.7)

Indian Lake

28 Shantytown 5.9 PG 100' ★★★★
Clean rock with a couple of pumpy, juggy sections through steep bulges.
Start: 4' right of the serrated-topped boulder that marks the start of **Gunky Route** below a slab with a bolt.
● **P1 5.9 PG:** Up the slab to the roof with white, scarred rock. On the left side of the roof, climb jugs on the overhanging arête (same as **Gunky Route**) to the slab above. (From here, **Gunky Route** heads right to the left-facing corner.) Straight up the slab to the left end of a second roof, then through this on jugs to another slab. Up the slab to a left-leaning open book. Climb the open book to its top (crux) and step right to a fixed anchor. 100'
FA 2007, Arietta Climbing

29 Hooverville 5.10d G 100' ★★★
The crux is a bit height-dependent. Named for a shantytown in Seattle.
Start: Same as **Shantytown**.
● **P1 5.10d G:** (V1) Climb up to the roof on **Shantytown**, then move right on tan rock under the roof to a corner, up to a jug (crux), then swing right around the corner onto the face. Continue up though the center of a second ceiling, then aim for the left side of a jutting fin of rock. Layback the fin to the fixed anchor (shared with **Shantytown**). 100'
V1 5.9+ G: Begin 5' right of **Shantytown** on top of a scrubby slab at a 3'-high left-facing open book. Climb up the face past a bolt to a thin crack that breaks the roof, just right of the large tan spot. Place gear and make a long reach to a jug at the top of the crack. Burly moves lead over the lip to join the normal route.
FA 2007, Arietta Climbing

30 Favela 5.10c G 100' ★★★
A short and strenuous crux on overhanging rock is followed by great face and crack climbing. The name is Portuguese for shantytown.
Start: 22' right of the serrated-topped boulder that marks the start of **Gunky Route**, below a wide left-facing open book that begins 20' up. The open book is capped by an overhanging wall with two bolts.
P1 5.10c G: Climb blocky rock to the base of the open book, then follow the open book to a good undercling crack at its top. Make a long reach straight up to a jug (crux), then another strenuous move left to good holds to gain a stance. Work up right to a ceiling and break through this at a right-facing edge. Follow the edge to a horizontal crack. Step up and right to a vertical crack that leads to a ledge, then join **Slumlord** up easier rock to a fixed anchor. 100'
FA Aug, 2007, Jonathan Nickel

31 Slumlord 5.10a PG 100' ★★★
Much easier than it looks, this route has a short crux on an unlikely overhanging wall.
Start: 40' right of the serrated-topped boulder that marks the start of **Gunky Route**, at the base of a slab that leads to an overhanging white-colored wall 20' up. This is 12' right of a shallow left-facing corner that leads to the overhanging white-colored wall.
● **P1 5.10a PG:** Mount the slab, step left, then up the slab (bolt) to the overhanging white wall. Up the overhanging wall (crux) on juggy sidepulls to a stance. Continue past two horizontal cracks, then step left to a vertical fingercrack and follow it to a ledge. Easier rock leads to a fixed anchor (shared with **Gunky Route**). 100'
FA Aug, 2007, Jonathan Nickel

32 Pug Love 5.6 G 30' ★★★
A good practice climb for new leaders.
Start: Below a bulge just right of an 8"-diameter tree that has grown up next to the rock, 12' left of the right-leaning **Shanty Girl** chimney-gully.
P1 5.6 G: Over the bulge, then straight up the face past many small cracks to a ledge with a fixed anchor. 30'
FA 2007, Arietta Climbing

33 Shanty Girl 5.6 G 40' ★★
Another good practice route for new leaders.
Start: 50' downhill from and right of **Slumlord** is a cleaned face with a right-leaning chimney-gully on its right side. Begin on the left side of the opening of the chimney-gully below a left-rising crack.
P1 5.6 G: Up the left-rising crack, then work back right to gain another left-rising crack. Up the crack to a ledge, then move up and right to a fixed anchor. 40'
FA 2007, Arietta Climbing

34 Mean Low Blues 5.7 R 50' ★★
Start: Downhill from and right of the **Shanty Girl** chimney-gully at the base of a right-rising groove with a birch tree 10' up.
P1 5.7 R: (V1) Climb up the groove for 5', then straight up to an overlap. Break the overlap on the right via a left-leaning crack, then straight up the face to a fixed anchor. 50'
V1 5.8 R: A good toprope after leading the normal route. Work up and left to a left-leaning crack, then follow the crack to the **Shanty Girl** chimney-gully. Stay just right of the arête and work up the face to the fixed anchor.
FA 2007, Arietta Climbing

35 Shaky Flake 5.7 G 50' ★★
Start: 36' right of right of **Mean Low Blues** and 5' left of two birch trees, below a right-rising ledge–ramp about 6' up.
P1 5.7 G: Move up to the ledge, then follow it up and right to where it becomes a right-leaning crack. Follow the crack to a blunt arête, the up this on jugs to a ledge (5.4, optional belay). Move up to a steep wall and climb an obvious, shallow, left-facing corner and flake to the top. 50'
FA Jul 17, 2011, Michael Gray, Valerie Bachinsky

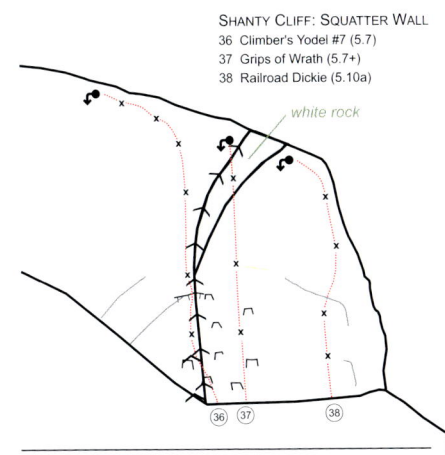

Indian Lake

SHANTY CLIFF: SQUATTER WALL
36 Climber's Yodel #7 (5.7)
37 Grips of Wrath (5.7+)
38 Railroad Dickie (5.10a)

Squatter Wall

This is the clean, shaded wall 150' uphill and left of the Shanty Sports Arena, and 100' downhill and right of **Mean Low Blues**. From the Shanty Sports Arena, follow the climber's path uphill for 150' until level with the base of the wall, then walk right 30'. There is a maple tree with 4 trunks centered on the wall, 1' back.

36 Climber's Yodel #7 5.7 G 60' ★★

Contrived, as the route gains length by traversing along the top of the cliff just below where you could otherwise walk. You finish 30' left of the start.
Start: On the left side of the open area, where the terrain goes steeply up left.
● **P1 5.7 G:** Go up a blunt arête on good, incut, blocky holds, staying 6' left of a black streak, then onto the face above. At the top, instead of standing up, traverse up and left for 20' staying just below the crest to a fixed anchor. 60'
FA 2011, Arietta Climbing

37 Grips of Wrath 5.7+ G 25' ★★★

Start: 4' left of the 4-trunked maple tree, on the left side of the black rock centered on the face, and 3' right of **Climber's Yodel #7**.
● **P1 5.7+ G:** Go straight up blocky incut rock into the black streak and up to a short overhanging face with white rock. Pull straight through on pumpy jugs to a hidden fixed anchor just above. 25'
FA 2011, Arietta Climbing

38 Railroad Dickie 5.10a G 25' ★

The second clip is difficult for short people.
Start: 4' right of the 4-trunked maple tree, and 8' left of the right side of the face, at an incut edge 6' up.
● **P1 5.10a G:** Climb straight up the face to a left-rising crack, then straight up to the top of the face. Instead of standing up, hand traverse left on hidden jugs for 10' to a fixed anchor. 25'
FA 2011, Arietta Climbing

Shanty Sports Arena

About 300' downhill from and right of the Main Face (and 250' right of **Mean Low Blues**) is the Shanty Sports Arena, a small, steep wall with several quality routes. It is the first wall with climbable rock on the right side of the gully as you approach from the road.

The face is about 40' high, overhangs at the bottom, and has a pleasant shaded open area at the base. On the left side is a small boulder pile, above which begins a left-rising roof that marks the start of **Swampoodle**. On the right side is a jammed block 15' up. The upper face is crisscrossed with cracks.

39 Shanty 101 5.8 G 35'

Start: 15' left of **Bidonville** at a slab with a high bolt, and directly below a pointed prow.
P1 5.8 G: Stick-clip the first bolt, then climb directly up a slab below the prow. Up over the pointed prow, then continue up the face to a fixed anchor. 35'
Gear: Above the prow, the route is 5.7 with trad protection.
FA May 25, 2008, Bill Griffith, Gary Thomann

40 Bidonville 5.7 G 35' ★

The name is the French word for shantytown.
Start: 5' left of the small block pile of **Swampoodle**, below the right end of a left-rising roof 10' up.
● **P1 5.7 G:** Reach up to a triangular jug on a wave of rock below the left-rising roof. Pull up to a stance and climb through the left-rising roof on good blocky holds. Continue straight up the wall past a left-rising crack to a fixed anchor. 35'
FA 2007, Arietta Climbing

41 Swampoodle 5.8 G 40' ★★

Named for a shantytown in Washington, DC.
Start: On top of a small block pile on the left end of the face.
● **P1 5.8 G:** Climb out right on overhanging rock and make a tricky reach to a jug (crux), then straight up the wall to a fixed anchor. 40'
FA 2007, Arietta Climbing

42 Corktown 5.9 G 40' ★★★

Named for a rough and tumble area of Ottawa that was dismantled in the 1950s.
Start: In the center of the face, 15' right of the small block pile of **Swampoodle** and 30' from the right end of

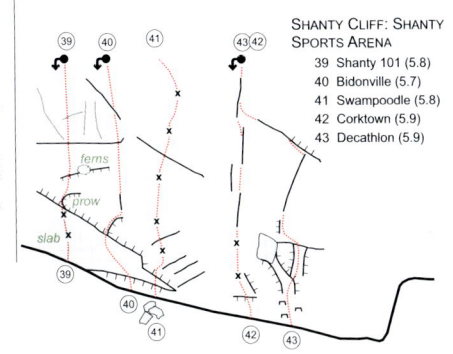

SHANTY CLIFF: SHANTY SPORTS ARENA
39 Shanty 101 (5.8)
40 Bidonville (5.7)
41 Swampoodle (5.8)
42 Corktown (5.9)
43 Decathlon (5.9)

Indian Lake

the cliff, at a narrow ledge 7' up that sits below a short, shallow left-leaning corner.

P1 5.9 G: Swing up onto the ledge (bolt), then up an overhanging wall on jugs to a stance. Continue straight up, following discontinuous cracks to a fixed anchor. 40'

FA 2007, Arietta Climbing

43 Decathlon 5.9 G 40' *

Start: At the right end of the cliff below a jammed block 15' up.

P1 5.9 G: Climb up blocky terrain, staying right of the jammed block, to a ledge. Step left and climb a right-leaning tips crack (crux) to a horizontal crack. Angle up and left to join the last 10' of **Corktown** to its fixed anchor. 40'

Gear: Double small TCUs up to 0.5".

FA Sep 5, 2007, Jim Lawyer

Shanty Cliff
SHANTY SLAB

Aspect	South
Height	120'
Quality	*
Approach	10 min, easy; river crossing
Summary	Low-angle slab with very easy friction routes.

2							2
-5.6	5.7	5.8	5.9	5.10	5.11	5.12	5.13+	total

This south-facing friction slab is the first rock encountered on the approach. It is situated on the left side of the gully near its mouth. Several routes can be climbed on this slab, all of which lead to one of two fixed anchors at the top.

44 Joe Hill 5.2 R 100' **

Named after a famous labor organizer and songwriter framed for a double murder during free speech struggles in Utah.

Start: Up from and left of the low point of the slab is a vegetated terrace with birch trees, about level with the vertical crack that begins 20' up **Basti**. Begin in the center of the terrace (15' left of its right end) below an overlap 12' up.

P1 5.2 R: Up scooped rock to the overlap, then wander up the slab to a fixed anchor. 100'

FA 2007, Arietta Climbing

45 Basti 5.3 G 120' **

The name is Indian for shantytown.

Start: At the lowest point on the slab below a vertical crack that begins 20' up.

P1 5.3 G: Friction up the slab to a vertical crack, then follow the crack to its top. Continue up to a bulge (gear), then up very textured rock, angling slightly leftward to a fixed anchor. 120'

Descent: A single-rope rappel returns to the base of **Joe Hill**.

FA 2002, Neal Knitel, Neal Lamphear

LONG POND CLIFF

Location	East side of Indian Lake, accessed from NY 30 in Speculator
Aspect	Southwest
Height	100'
Quality	**
Approach	2 hr, moderate; lake crossing
Summary	Crack climbs in an idyllic setting with excellent camping. Excellent rock, although very dirty.

6	4	2	1	2			15
-5.6	5.7	5.8	5.9	5.10	5.11	5.12	5.13+	total

Long Pond Cliff rises above the west shore of Long Pond, an isolated pond in a pristine setting. Access to the cliff is complex, involving a 2WD dirt road, a 1-hr hike, and a lake crossing, which takes a total of 2 hr or more. Although it's possible to climb here in a day, the beauty of the setting qualifies this cliff for an attractive multiday adventure.

When viewed from the pond, the cliff has three obvious features—the inverted L-shaped roof in the center and two cleaner-looking buttresses to the right. Most of the recorded climbing takes place on these three features. Unfortunately, the vegetation is thick near the cliff base, which obstructs the view and makes it difficult to find the starts of routes. The top of the cliff, on the other hand, is open, bare rock and offers views of Snowy Mountain to the west.

HISTORY

The first known climber to visit Long Pond was Bob Gwynn, who reportedly climbed nearly a dozen routes but has chosen not to report his work. The first recorded climbing was by Jim Vermeulen in 1988 on tips gleaned from Barbara McMartin's trail guides. As is typical with Vermeulen, the route, **Way of the Peckerheads**, is exploratory, adventurous, and nearly impossible to find. A year later, Dick Tucker added his grunge-fest route **Little Ado**.

In the mid-1990s, the main protagonist was Neal Knitel, who lived in nearby Speculator at the time, and various partners, including Kevin Crowl, Jonas Morelli, and Jared Thayer. Knitel, Crowl, and partners set up camp on the shores of the pond and exhausted many of the obvious lines, the most noteworthy being **Rodeo**, a route climbed on sight from the ground. More recently, Karl Swisher did some route preparation only to find that the lines had been climbed earlier.

DIRECTIONS (MAPS PAGES 241 AND 242)

There are several approaches to Long Pond.

From the south: Begin at the intersection of NY 8 and NY 30 in the center of the town of Speculator. Turn onto East Road (0.0, also signposted as Elm Lake Road) and head northeast. At the 1.4-mile mark, the pavement ends (no parking here); continue straight on the dirt road. The condition of the dirt road varies—a high-clearance vehicle may be required. At the 5.1-mile mark, there is a junction with a sign "Outhouse Cor-

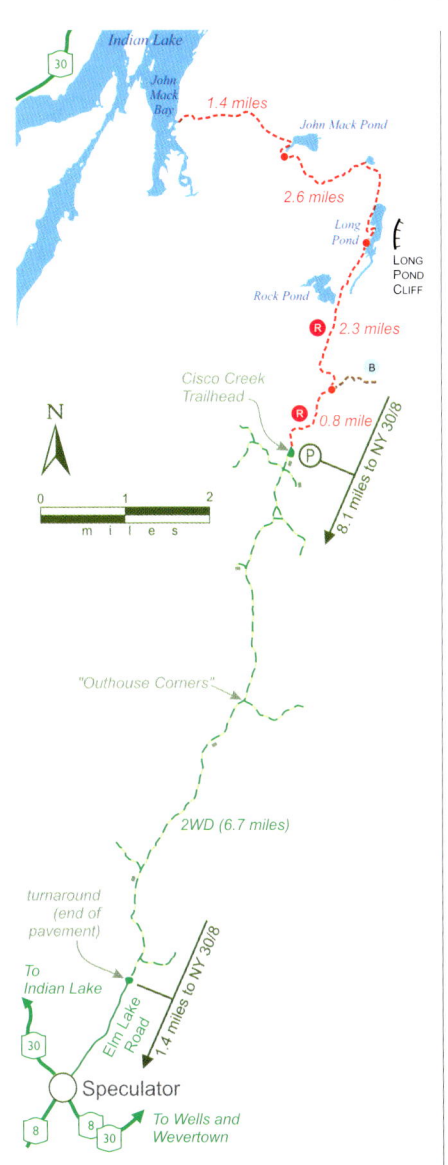

Indian Lake

Hike the shoreline of Long Pond roughly half the length of the lake to an excellent campsite with several rowboats 557311,4832143. The cliff is on the opposite side of the lake. There are several options for reaching the cliff: (a) swim across the lake (yes, climbers have done this), (b) use one of the leaky rowboats (duct tape helpful), or (c) hike around the north end of the pond, adding 45 min to the approach. (Hiking around the south end is boggy and not recommended.) Once you're across the lake, a short, 10-min bushwhack leads to the cliff; aim for the right end of the cliff, as the forest is more open 557667,4832162.

From the northwest: The second approach is from the northwest and begins by taking a boat across Indian Lake. The public boat launch is next to Lewey Lake Public Campsite on NY 30, 12.0 miles north of Speculator. Paddle across Indian Lake to John Mack Bay and pick up the John Mack Trail to John Mack Pond (1.4 miles). Just before the pond, there is a junction with the John Mack Pond / Long Pond Cross Trail. The currently marked trail is at times hard to follow (more of a bushwhack) and takes a route significantly different from that marked on the USGS map. Follow the trail another 2.2 miles to the north end of Long Pond. Another 0.4 mile takes you to the boat launch at the midpoint on Long Pond across from the cliff.

DESCENT OPTIONS

There is a two-bolt anchor at the top of **No Ifs, Ands, or Buts**; with a 60-m rope, you can reach the base. Walking along the top of the cliff is open and easy.

*Tom Cuminski on the second ascent of **Short-Term Memory** (5.6). Photo by Neal Knitel.*

ners"; continue straight. At the 7.9-mile mark, you come to a four-way intersection. For low-clearance vehicles, park here; otherwise, continue straight on an especially rough road an additional 0.2 mile (past a cabin on the right) to reach the DEC trailhead for Cisco Creek at the 8.1-mile mark 555758,4828147. The drive from Speculator takes about 25 min. (A permit is no longer required to reach the Cisco Creek Trailhead.)

From the parking area, hike north on the Cisco Creek Trail (red DEC markers). At 15 min, you reach an intersection; turn left onto the Rock Pond / Long Pond Trail, following red DEC markers. You'll reach Long Pond at 1 hr, hiking over mostly level terrain.

Indian Lake

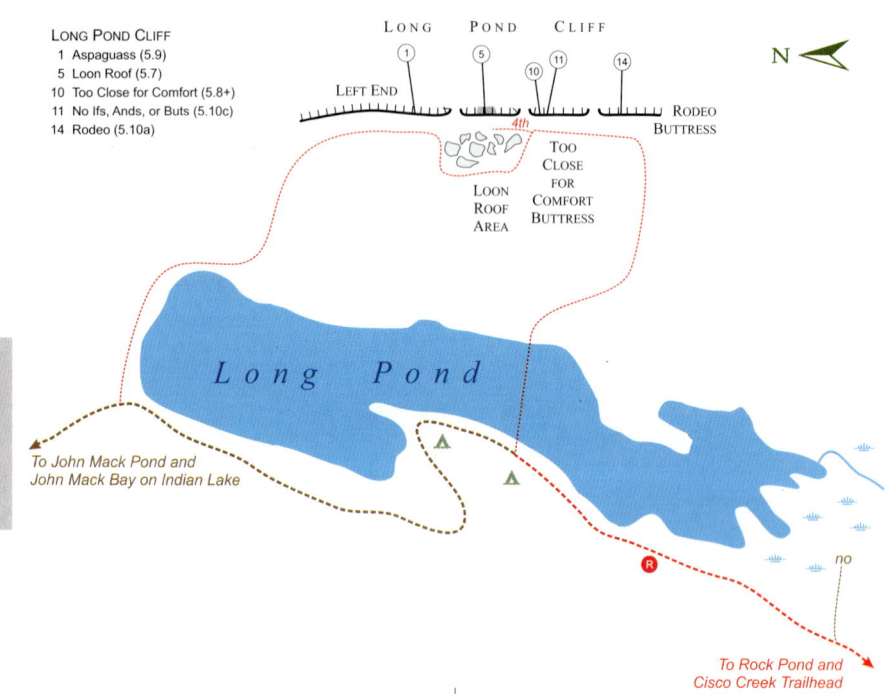

LONG POND CLIFF
1 Aspaguass (5.9)
5 Loon Roof (5.7)
10 Too Close for Comfort (5.8+)
11 No Ifs, Ands, or Buts (5.10c)
14 Rodeo (5.10a)

LONG POND CLIFF

LEFT END

TOO CLOSE FOR COMFORT BUTTRESS

LOON ROOF AREA

RODEO BUTTRESS

Long Pond

To John Mack Pond and John Mack Bay on Indian Lake

To Rock Pond and Cisco Creek Trailhead

Left End

1 Aspaguass 5.9 G 160'

Start: At the top of a vegetated ramp at the base of a large right-facing corner capped by a very large, square roof 30' up.
P1 5.7 G: Climb the crack in the corner to gain the block ledge below the roof. Out the roof on the right horizontal crack and into a right-facing corner above to an alcove with a pine. Continue up the overhanging wall (V1) above to a ledge with several small pines and a beautiful—but short—handcrack above. 120'
P2 5.9 G: Climb the handcrack, then straight up the face of the buttress to the top. 40'
V1 5.7 G: From the alcove, head left up the most apparent line to a ledge with a short right-facing corner at the back. Climb this corner (5.4), angling left up to the top.
FA May 25, 1997, Kevin Crowl, Jonas Morelli
FA (V1) May 27, 1997, Neal Knitel, Jared Thayer

2 Malcontent 5.6 G 150'

The name was influenced by a lack of communication between the leader and follower and rope drag caused by bad placements blamed on the belaying skills, causing both to be labeled malcontents.
Start: Left of a flake with a very small roof at the bottom, below a larger right-facing corner with a chimney 45' up.
P1 5.6 G: Climb up the ramp and pull the flake. Head left to the corner, up the corner, then up to a vegetated ledge. Continue up a dirty vertical crack. 150'
FA May 25, 1997, Neal Knitel, Jared Thayer

3 Leap of Flake 5.7 PG 120'

On the first ascent, a very large flake was pushed off the climb, hence the name.
Start: Below the orange arête about 25' left of **Pyromania**'s dirty gully-corner start.
P1 5.7 PG: Climb low-angle rock up to a vertical orange face, then up rightward to a ledge. From the right side of the ledge, go straight up slightly overhanging rock to gradually easier moves, finishing at a large pine at the top. 120'
FA Jun 29, 1996, Neal Knitel, Jared Thayer, Jane Pipkin

Loon Roof Area

The Loon Roof Area is accessed from the gully between it and the Too Close for Comfort Buttress. Bushwhack left and uphill along the base of the Too Close for Comfort Buttress to gain the slabs on left side of the gully. Make several 4th-class friction moves left across the slabs to gain the ledge at the base of the wall.

4 Pyromania 5.7 G 150'

Named for Knitel's mishap in which he ignited his fuel-soaked hands while camping across the pond.
Start: At the base of the huge corner below and left of the Loon Roof terrace.
P1 5.7 G: Climb the dirty corner to a ledge with a birch tree, then move out right to a left-facing corner. (This corner is left of the more prominent right-facing corner capped by a roof.) At the top of the corner, angle right to a ledge with a birch tree. 100'
P2 5.7 G: Up the crack in the right-facing groove. 50'
FA 1993, Neal Knitel, Neal Lamphear

Indian Lake

Long Pond: Left End
1. Aspaguass (5.9)
2. Malcontent (5.6)
3. Leap of Flake (5.7)
4. Pyromania (5.7)

5 Loon Roof 5.7 G 80'
Much less appealing, easier, and shorter than it looks.
Start: At the obvious right-facing corner below the roof.
P1 5.7 G: Climb the dirty corner to the roof, then left onto the face and up a crack to the top. 80'
FA Jul, 1995, Neal Knitel, Jonas Morelli

6 Short-Term Memory 5.6 G 60'
Start: At the base of the first crack right of the prominent **Loon Roof**. This crack angles left across the face.
P1 5.6 G: Climb the crack, which ends at the right end of **Loon Roof**, to the top. 60'
FA Jul, 1995, Neal Knitel, Jonas Morelli

7 Escape from Haiti 5.7 G 60' ★★★
This route has remarkably clean rock for the area.
Start: 20' right of the previous route, at the base of a fingercrack that starts 10' up, and just left of a giant flake that leans up against the cliff.
P1 5.7 G: Climb the slab to gain the parallel fingercracks, then climb them to the top. 60'
Gear: Standard rack to 2.5".
ACB May 8, 2006, Jim Lawyer, Chris Yenkey

8 Nut 'n Left 5.5 G 120'
Start: Just left of the tree-filled gully that separates the two buttresses. This is just below a large flake and at a point where you make a 4th-class move to reach the terrace below **Loon Roof**.
P1 5.5 G: Climb the slab using a left-leaning crack system to a stance. Straight up a crack, then right to another crack and up to the huge detached flake. Step right and follow a left-leaning ramp to a ledge with a lone pine. Rappel, or scramble to the top. 120'
FA Jul, 1995, Jonas Morelli, Jared Thayer

9 Little Ado 5.3 G 80'
Climbs the dirty gully between the Loon Roof Area and the Too Close for Comfort Buttress. According to the first-ascent party, it seemed "the worst possible route" and is probably most useful as a descent.
Start: At the highest point on the large, tree-covered talus slope between the two buttresses.
P1 5.3 G: Climb the chimney and rock rib left of the steep face on the right. There are three finishes: the chimney (5.0), the outside corner (5.6), and the handcrack on the left (5.8). 80'
FA Sep 16, 1989, Dick Tucker, Eric T. Laurin

Indian Lake

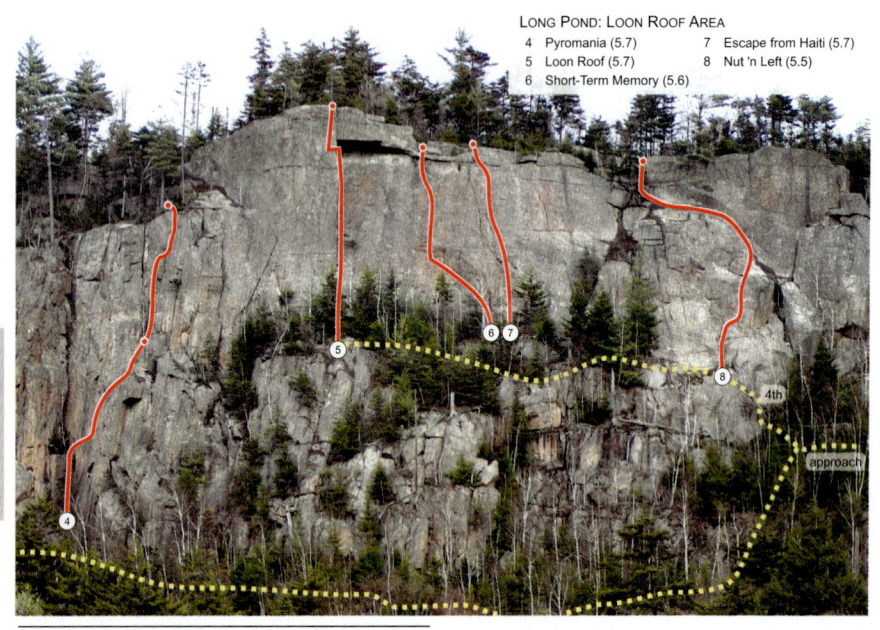

LONG POND: LOON ROOF AREA
4 Pyromania (5.7)
5 Loon Roof (5.7)
6 Short-Term Memory (5.6)
7 Escape from Haiti (5.7)
8 Nut 'n Left (5.5)

Too Close for Comfort Buttress

This buttress holds several quality routes. You can access the routes from a small tree ledge in the center of the buttress, which is reached by bushwhacking left and uphill along the base of the buttress until you're level with the ledge, then walking right and making a 3rd-class move to gain the ledge.

10 Too Close for Comfort 5.8+ G 110' ★★

Nice climbing, although a bit dirty. It is possible to climb the route as a single pitch.
Start: There are two right-facing corners (almost open books) that begin at the tree ledge. Start in the leftmost corner, from the left side of the tree ledge.
P1 5.6 G: Climb the corner to a ledge with a tree on the left. 50'
P2 5.8+ G: From the left end of the ledge, climb the fingercrack (V1) until it is possible to make a traverse left to a left-slanting fingercrack. Climb the fingercrack to the top. 60'
V1 5.9 G: Instead of traversing, continue straight up the finger- and handcrack to the top.
History: A piton of unknown origin was found below and to the right of the tree ledge.
FA 1993, Neal Knitel, Neal Lamphear
FA (V1) May 8, 2006, Chris Yenkey, Jim Lawyer

11 No Ifs, Ands, or Buts 5.10c G 100' ★★

Climbs the inverted V-slot in the center of the buttress. Can be climbed in a single pitch. The route was originally climbed at 5.8 A0. Seven years later, without knowledge of the first ascent, the route was recleaned and bolts were added to the crux section.
Start: There are two open books / grooves that begin at the tree ledge. This route starts in the groove in the center of the ledge.
P1 5.8 G: Climb the finger- and handcrack in the corner for 50'. Make a belay at a stance or move left to the comfortable tree ledge of the previous route. 50'
P2 5.10c G: Continue in the crack, then move slightly right and into the inverted V-slot, past two bolts. The slot narrows to hand size (crux); follow this to the top at a two-bolt anchor. 50'
Gear: Standard rack to 2.5".
FA May 26, 1997, Kevin Crowl, Neal Knitel
FFA 2004, Karl Swisher, Sid Perkins, Carlton Maricle

12 Yellow Paddles 5.8 G 40' ★★★

A clean, vertical handcrack with sharp jams. The route is named for the yellow plastic Fisher-Price children's paddle that was found beneath one of the rowboats on Long Pond. Unfortunately, there is no bottom pitch, so you must rappel in from the top or climb the first part of **Strike Zone**.
Start: At a ledge just left of the "Totem Pole" (the vertical wedge of orange, unstable blocks on the upper right side of the buttress). This ledge is at the same height as the base of the inverted V-slot of **No Ifs, Ands, or Buts**. Either rappel to the ledge or traverse in from the left from one of the other routes.
P1 5.8 G: Climb the handcrack to the top. 40'
FA 2004, Karl Swisher, Sid Perkins, Carlton Maricle

Indian Lake

Long Pond: Too Close for Comfort Buttress

10 Too Close for Comfort (5.8+)
11 No Ifs, Ands, or Buts (5.10c)
12 Yellow Paddles (5.8)
13 Strike Zone (5.6)

245

Indian Lake

LONG POND: RODEO BUTTRESS
14 Rodeo (5.10a)
15 Way of the Peckerheads (5.6)

13 Strike Zone 5.6 G 100'

The name was a reference to the loose rock on the route.
Start: On the left side of the tree ledge (as for **Too Close for Comfort** and **No Ifs Ands, or Buts**) at the base of a vertical fingercrack.
P1 5.6 G: Climb the fingercrack, past a huge detached block that rests on a sloped ledge. Continue up the crack system to the ledge. 70'
P2 5.6 G: Climb the fingercrack (V1) just right of **Yellow Paddles** to the top. 30'
V1 5.2 G: Step right to a chimney, ascend it to the top of the "Totem Pole," then scramble to the top.
FA Jul, 1995, Neal Knitel, Tom Cuminski

Rodeo Buttress

This is the cliff's prominent rightmost buttress, the right side of which is defined by a right-leaning orange crack. There is potential for several more crack lines on this buttress.

14 Rodeo 5.10a G 140' ★★★

A high-quality upper pitch. In 2004, Karl Swisher thoroughly scrubbed the route, which was thought to be unclimbed.
Start: Anywhere at the toe of the buttress.
P1 5.6 PG: Climb vegetated low-angle blocks and slabs to reach a flat, spacious ledge beneath the clean upper face of the buttress. It is also possible to reach this ledge by rappelling from a tree in the gully to the left. 60'
P2 5.10a G: Climb the right-facing, left-leaning flake above the ledge to its top. From here, a handcrack leads up and slightly right; when the crack fades, step left to a fingercrack and follow it to the top. 80'
Gear: Standard rack to 2.5".
FA May 24, 1997, Kevin Crowl, Neal Knitel

15 Way of the Peckerheads 5.6 G 190'

Named for the beer-drinking, gun-toting, bottle-breaking "peckerheads" who occupied one of the campsites during the first ascent. This was the first route climbed at the cliff and, like many exploratory routes, avoids many of the most dramatic features.

Jonas Morelli gearing up at Long Pond. Photo by Neal Knitel.

Start: At the top of the first rock band directly below the overhanging, right-leaning orange crack on the right side of the Rodeo Buttress.
P1 5.5 G: Climb the chimney to the birch tree, then past a wedged block until you're below the right-leaning orange crack. Step left and belay as for **Rodeo**. 90'
P2 5.6 G: Downclimb left from the ledge, then move up left to the top of the inverted V-slab. Climb the crack to the ledge (fixed rappel here). Step right and climb the crack to the top. 100'
FA Jul 9, 1988, Jim Vermeulen, Bill Morris

HUMPHREY MOUNTAIN CLIFF

Location	East side of Indian Lake, accessed from NY 30 in Speculator
Aspect	West
Height	200'
Quality	★
Approach	2 hr, difficult
Summary	Two routes on a broad cliff with a level approach on a seldom-used trail followed by a half-hour bushwhack. Located in a wild corner of the park that is popular with big-game hunters.

			1		1			2
-5.6	5.7	5.8	5.9	5.10	5.11	5.12	5.13+	total

Humphrey Mountain is a low peak surrounded by marshlands and is best known for a closed garnet mine that attracts hikers and prospectors. The cliff is visible from surrounding peaks but is hard to see during the approach from the Cisco Creek Trailhead outside of Speculator. Humphrey Mountain Cliff is a broad, broken band that has potential for multipitch crack climbs. The rock is good-quality but, in general, is somewhat dirty when compared to neighboring Pine Peak. The valley surrounding East Road and Cisco Creek Trailhead is popular with bear hunters and is also prime habitat for moose and deer. Several marshes are crossed on the approach, and the hiking trail, although well marked, is more of a bushwhack than a maintained footpath. Humphrey Mountain Cliff is fortified by stinging nettles, dense vegetation, and an army of biting insects, so plan your ambush carefully.

HISTORY

Karl Swisher spied the cliffs of Humphrey Mountain while climbing on the summit of Snowy Mountain. Swisher investigated Humphrey, visible east of the cliffs at Long Pond and apparently much larger, alone, then returned in October 2006 with Stan Czaplak and climbed **Dirty Boy**.

DIRECTIONS (MAP PAGE 248)

To reach the trailhead from the south, begin at the intersection of NY 8 and NY 30 in the center of the town of Speculator. Turn onto East Road (0.0, also signposted as Elm Lake Road) and head northeast. At 1.4 miles, the pavement ends (no parking here); continue straight on the dirt road. The condition of the dirt road varies—a

Indian Lake

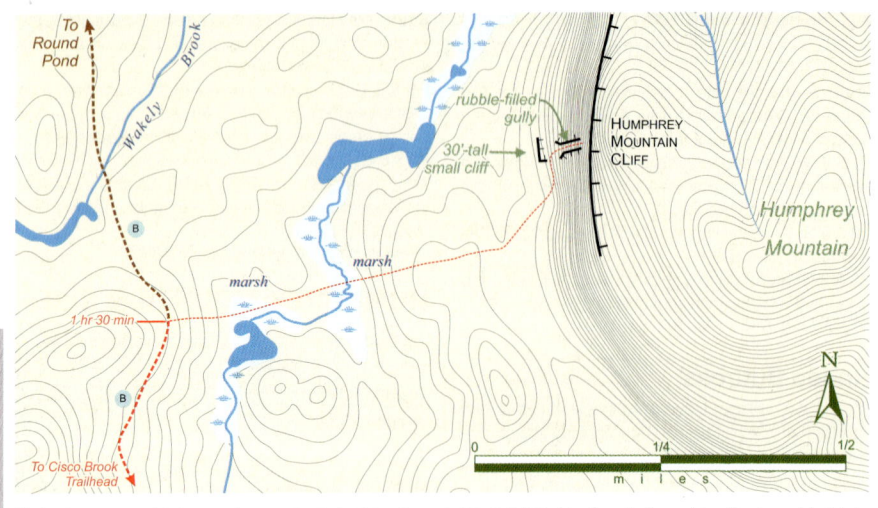

high-clearance vehicle may be required. At 5.1 miles, there is a junction with the sign "Outhouse Corners"; continue straight. At 7.9 miles, you come to a four-way intersection. If you have a low-clearance vehicle, park here; otherwise, continue straight on an especially rough road an additional 0.2 mile (past a cabin on the right) to reach the DEC trailhead for Cisco Creek at 8.1 miles 555758,4828147. The drive from Speculator takes about 25 min. (A permit is no longer required to reach the Cisco Creek Trailhead.)

From the parking area (0 hr 0 min), hike the red- and blue-marked trail to an intersection at 20 min where the red-marked trail goes left to Rock Pond and Long Pond. Go right and hike along the blue-marked trail to a large marsh, reached at 30 min. The blue-marked trail goes around the south end of the marsh to its east side; if conditions are dry, then cross to the east side of the marsh directly. Enter the woods on the east side of the marsh near a brook, reached at 40 min (last reliable water) and hike north along the blazed trail (overgrown, hard to follow).

At 1 hr 30 min, leave the trail and begin the bush-whack 558794,4831422 at a point where the trail is in open woods, near its highest point above the valley and before the trail descends and crosses Wakely Brook. Hike downhill to the east and reach a marsh at 1 hr 35 min. Cross the marsh and reenter the woods. A second, and smaller, marsh is crossed at 1 hr 45 min. At 2 hr, you reach boulders in open woods beneath the south end of the cliff 559821,4831771.

1 Dirty Boy 5.9+ G 180' ★★

Start: Hike north (left), through open woods with boulders, along a level bench well beneath the main cliff. Locate a 30'-tall cliff with a clean buttress that faces south. Go 200' uphill from and right of the small cliff to a rubble-filled gully. Follow the gully for 250' to open ledges beneath a wall with an orange rock scar 40' up. Begin below and right of the orange rock scar beneath a shallow slot.

P1 5.6 PG: Up the shallow slot with sloped holds to a stance that is right of the orange rock scar. Climb a steep wall with blocks and a vertical crack to low-angle terrain. Up sloping ledges past a final flared crack to a tree belay on the left. 80'

P2 5.9+ G: Move 10' right to a low-angle left-facing corner. Up the corner (5.8; small gear), which becomes steeper at its top. Follow a vertical finger- and hand-crack in a shallow left-facing corner, then move left across a sloping ledge to a flared crack. Up the flared crack on good holds to a belay at a large tree with a fixed anchor. 100'
FA Oct, 2006, Karl Swisher, Stan Czaplak

2 Nettle Highway 5.11a TR 90' ★★★

This route climbs the arête above the tree belay at the top of P1 of **Dirty Boy**, 10' left of P2 of **Dirty Boy** in a left-facing corner. Stem the corner to a ledge at head height, then up the arête on right-facing flakes. Step left, then up a dimple-covered face to a low-angle scoop. Follow the scoop to the tree with a fixed anchor. 90'
FA (TR) Aug, 2007, Karl Swisher, Jeremy Haas

SNOWY MOUNTAIN

Location	On the west side of Indian Lake, accessed from NY 30
Summary	A high-mountain face with sport climbs, and a beautiful lower slab.

1	3	1	1				7
-5.6	5.7	5.8	5.9	5.10	5.11	5.12	5.13+	total

Snowy Mountain, on the western side of Indian Lake, is the largest and best known of the southern Adirondack summits at 3899'. This popular peak lacks a bald summit but offers views from its reconditioned fire tower. Directly below the tower lies the Summit Cliff, clearly visible from Indian Lake and various points along NY 30 (when traveling north from Speculator). Below this are the Lower Slabs, a long open slab with a single slab route.

Indian Lake

Both cliffs are most easily accessed from the DEC hiking trail. This is a strenuous approach that gains 2106' in elevation.

CAMPING
The sites on Mason Lake are particularly convenient for those climbing at Snowy Mountain. These attractive sites are along Jessup River Road; from Speculator, drive 8.2 miles north (toward Indian Lake) on Route 30 to Jessup River Road. Turn left and drive 0.3 miles south. The lake is on your left.

*Emilie Drinkwater on **Redneck on a Rope** (5.10d).*

HISTORY
The first climbers to visit the face were Neal Knitel and Jonas Morelli, who attempted a route on the left side of the face in the mid-1990s. They never returned, as it was "too far and there was other stuff to do." In 2002, Karl Swisher and Sid Perkins began working on **Vertebrae**, and, coincidentally at the same time, Ed Palen and Bob Starinsky developed their routes on the left end. This must have been a productive summer, as Palen and Starinsky were also busy developing Deadwater. Swisher and Perkins returned the following year and climbed **Redneck on a Rope**.

249

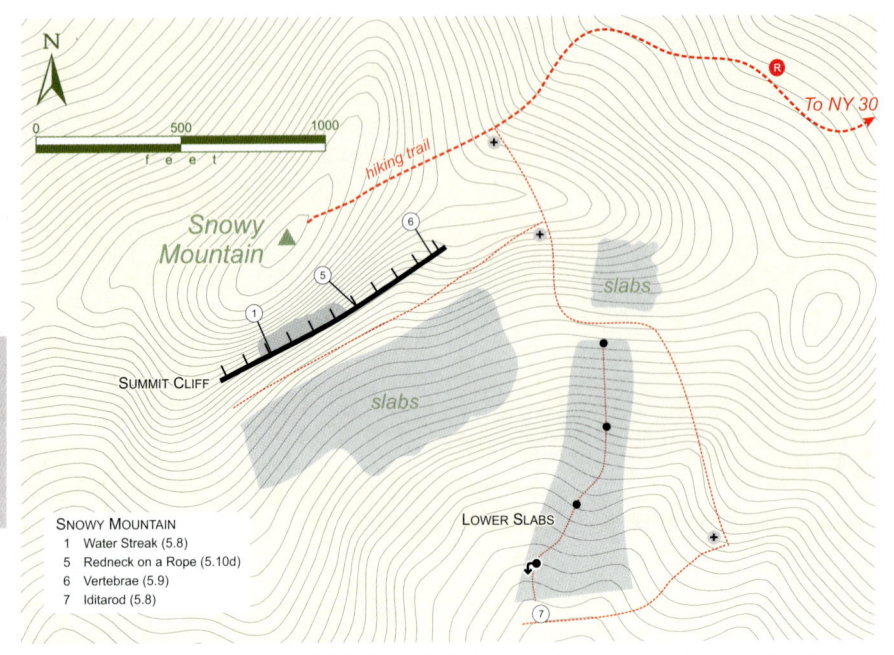

Indian Lake

SNOWY MOUNTAIN
1. Water Streak (5.8)
5. Redneck on a Rope (5.10d)
6. Vertebrae (5.9)
7. Iditarod (5.8)

DIRECTIONS (MAP PAGE 249)
Park on the east side of NY 30 553603,4838911, 7.0 miles south of Indian Lake (where NY 30 and NY 28 intersect) and 17.0 miles north of Speculator (where NY 8 and NY 30 intersect). The hiking trail (with red trail markers) begins across the road.

Snowy Mountain
SUMMIT CLIFF

Aspect	Southeast
Height	240'
Quality	★★★★★
Approach	2 hr 30 min, difficult
Summary	Bolt-protected face climbing on highly featured rock in a beautiful location with expansive views.

-5.6	5.7	5.8	5.9	5.10	5.11	5.12	5.13+	total
	1	2	1	1				6

This steep, off-vertical face sits directly below the summit and has some of the most featured rock found anywhere in the park—the "moonlike" rock, plates, huecos, and dike intrusions would seem more at home at Red River Gorge. Climbing aside, the idyllic location is perhaps this cliff's greatest asset.

All routes are well equipped; only 15 quickdraws and a 4" cam are needed.

DIRECTIONS (MAP PAGE 249)
Follow the red-marked hiking trail 3.9 miles toward the summit of Snowy Mountain. The last steep mile is well marked, heavily used, and eroded. Immediately after the trail reaches the ridge just before the summit, there is a small campsite on the left, and a small cairn 50' farther marks a blue-blazed trail on the left 549554,4838798. This poorly marked junction requires some searching, especially given the recent blowdown from Hurricane Irene. Follow the faint blue paint blazes downhill through open woods about 1 min to a large cairn on the right 549486,4838871. From this junction, the blue-blazed trail continues steeply downhill to the Lower Slabs.

Turn right (west) and contour slightly downhill to a steep grassy ledge that splits the lower slabs from the summit cliff. There is fixed protection (and often some fixed line) for leading across tricky sections to the base of the routes 549417,4838691.

DESCENT OPTIONS
Each route is equipped with a rappel anchor. Two ropes are required to rappel **Redneck on a Rope** and **Vertebrae**; otherwise, a single rope is sufficient.

1 Water Streak 5.8 G 45' ★★★
Start: Below a black water streak on the left end of the slab below the "eyebrow" roof 50' up. Often wet.
There is a dead-end route to the left that consists of two bolts (Neal Knitel, mid-1990s) and a piton (Karl Swisher, 2004).
● **P1 5.8 G:** Up the textured face to a fixed anchor. 45'
FA Sep, 2002, Ed Palen, Bob Starinsky

2 In the Buff 5.7 G 45' ★★★
Start: 5' right of **Waterstreak**.
● **P1 5.7 G:** Up the textured face to a fixed anchor. 45'
FA Sep, 2002, Bob Starinsky, Ed Palen

Indian Lake

Snowy Mountain

SNOWY MOUNTAIN
1 Water Streak (5.8)
2 In the Buff (5.7)
4 Buckwheat (5.9- A0)
5 Redneck on a Rope (5.10d)
6 Vertebrae (5.9)

Photo © Carl Heilman II.

3 Asteroid 5.8 G 45' ★★★

Start: Left of a black water streak, which is left of the obvious pillar that marks the start of **Redneck on a Rope**.

● **P1 5.8 G:** Up the textured face to a fixed anchor. 45'

FA Sep, 2002, Ed Palen, Bob Starinsky

4 Buckwheat 5.9- A0 120' ★★★★

A two-pitch adventure with a high-quality P2. To begin P2, you must aid through the "eyebrow" roof by pulling on bolts.

Start: Right of a black water streak, which is left of the obvious pillar that marks the start of **Redneck on a Rope**, below the right end of the "eyebrow" roof 50' up. Often wet.

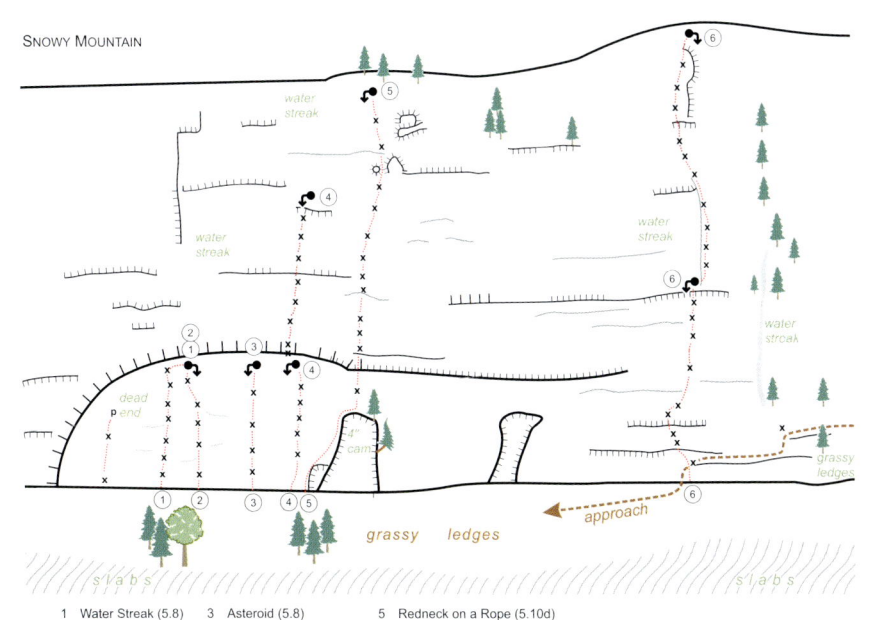

SNOWY MOUNTAIN

1 Water Streak (5.8)
2 In the Buff (5.7)
3 Asteroid (5.8)
4 Buckwheat (5.9- A0)
5 Redneck on a Rope (5.10d)
6 Vertebrae (5.9)

251

Indian Lake

Emilie Drinkwater on Vertebrae (5.9). Photo by Jesse Williams.

- **P1 5.7 G:** Up the textured face to a fixed anchor. 45'
- **P2 5.9- A0 G:** Pull past three bolts through the roof (A0), then up a vast garden of plates and knobs to a fixed anchor. 75'

FA Sep, 2002, Ed Palen, Bob Starinsky

5 Redneck on a Rope 5.10d G 190' ★★★★★

An amazing route in an amazing location, on a par with **Maestro** at Poke-O but longer, more scenic, and with more featured rock.
Start: At the base of an obvious pillar that leans up against the cliff and just right of the "eyebrow" roof 50' up.

- **P1 5.10d G:** Climb the pillar via the off width on the left side (5.8). From the top of the pillar, face-climb straight up a sea of crimps to a fixed anchor. 190'

Gear: A 4" cam protects the wide section to the top of the pillar.
Descent: Rappel with two ropes. Optionally, a single rope can be used to make a diagonal rappel to the first belay on **Buckwheat**.
History: The route was cleaned by Ed Palen, who never returned to complete the project.

FA May, 2003, Karl Swisher, Sid Perkins

6 Vertebrae 5.9 PG 240' ★★★★

This unique high-quality route climbs a backbone of rock littered with knobs, ribs, and undulations reminiscent of a spinal column in an alpine environment. From the top, you can continue to the fire tower or simply rappel the route. Often wet and reportedly growing increasingly mossy; if clean, it's definitely 5 stars.

Start: On the right side of the slab, above the second fixed rope on the approach, below an obvious line of bolts.

- **P1 5.9 PG:** Climb the face straight up to a small traverse left at a lip, then back right and straight up to a fixed anchor. 100'
- **P2 5.9 PG:** Mantel onto a ledge with soup-bowl dishes, then continue up a thin ribbon of plates and knobs on a steep wall to an overlap. Break the overlap, then up remarkable ribs past a second overlap to a flake finish. 140'

Descent: Two 60-m ropes are required to rappel this route.

FA 2002, Karl Swisher, Sid Perkins

Snowy Mountain
LOWER SLABS

Aspect	Southeast
Height	500'
Quality	★
Approach	3 hr, difficult
Summary	A long, open, clean slab with a single bolt-protected route.

The extensive south-facing slabs have a single long friction route.

DIRECTIONS   (MAP PAGE 249)

From the cairned junction, continue downhill on the poorly-marked blue-blazed trail for another 20 min to a second cairn, then turn right (west) and go a short distance to the base of the Lower Slabs.

Indian Lake

Jason Brechko on P1 of Iditarod (5.8). photo Jay Harrison

7 Iditarod 5.8 G (5.1 X) 500' ★

A long slab with a difficult P1 that can stand alone. A good outing would be to climb this route to its top, then walk over to the Summit Cliff to climb additional pitches.
Start: At the base of the lower slab on its left side 549748,4838554, below a line of bolts. Approach the slab from the blue-blazed herd path (see approach directions). P1 is wet early in the season.
● **P1 5.8 G:** Climb the slab to a fixed anchor. Rappel or continue to the top. 100'
● **P2–P3 5.1 X:** Angle rightward to anchors. 300'
● **P4 5.0 X:** Continue straight up to the trees that separate the two tiers of the slab. Break through the trees (about 20') and meet the blue-blazed trail. 100'
Gear: Many long runners.
FA 2004, Karl Swisher

BALDFACE MOUNTAIN

Location	East shore of Indian Lake, accessed from NY 30
Summary	Two cliffs rising above the scenic shoreline of Indian Lake that are broken and vegetated with a few quality lines.

1		1	1	2	1	6
-5.6	5.7	5.8	5.9	5.10	5.11	5.12	5.13+	total

Baldface Mountain faces the populated side of the lake with noticeable cliffs that look magnificent in the late afternoon light. Although you'll need a boat to access the trailhead on the eastern shore of Indian Lake, the extra effort is rewarded with a paradise of loose, vegetated, unexplored rock and some worthwhile lines.

The two cliffs on Baldface Mountain are split by the hiking trail. The larger Main Face is located south of the trail and higher up, just below the summit; Summit Cliff is to the north of the trail. The approach is easy, but getting oriented on the Main Face is challenging.

DIRECTIONS (MAP PAGE 254)
The trailhead to Baldface Mountain begins on the eastern shore of Indian Lake and is accessible by boat. Although an alternate land approach is described, it is only possible in low water (perhaps in the fall). The trailhead is marked with a large white circle painted on a rock in the back of a pinched-off bay known as Norman's Cove.

Approach by land: From where NY 28 and NY 30 intersect in Indian Lake (0.0 mile), drive south on NY 30. At 0.5 mile, turn left onto Big Brook Road; at 2.2 miles, turn right onto Jerry Savarie Road and follow it to its end at an old barn and parking turnaround (4.7 miles) 557582,4842930.

From the turnaround, walk past the barn through a gate to a three-way split. Take the middle fork, then make a left at the next fork, which leads to the shore. Follow the shoreline south for 30 min to Norman's Cove.

Approach by water: From where NY 28 and NY 30 intersect in Indian Lake (0.0 mile), drive south on NY 30. At 4.3 miles, turn left onto Lake Shore Drive (CR 9); Clark's Indian Lake Marina is on the left at 4.7 miles. There is a day-use fee for parking and putting in ($10.00 per canoe in 2007, open from May through October). Paddle across the lake (and slightly north) and enter the narrow neck of Norman's Cove, about 20 min.

If you are driving from the south, from where NY 30 and NY 8 intersect in Speculator, drive north on NY 30 for 18.3 miles to Lake Shore Drive. Turn right; Clark's Indian Lake Marina is about 0.3 mile on the right.

The lake, often calm in the morning, can become choppy and hazardous later in the day if the wind picks up.

HISTORY
The cliffs at Baldface Mountain were first explored by Tad Welch and Jim Lawyer in 1987. They cleaned and climbed a few routes at the Summit Cliff, then explored the disappointingly broken, overgrown, and nondescript Main Face, where they toproped a line. They deemed their experience too unremarkable to report any routes. Karl Swisher began exploring the Main Face in 2006 and uncovered some better lines by rappelling from the top, including the excellent **Keira's Thumbs**.

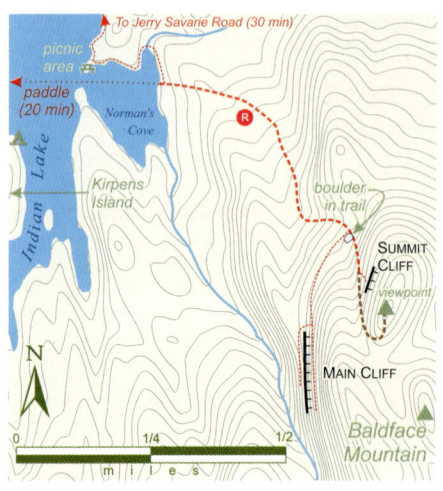

Indian Lake

2 A Tough Act to Follow 5.9+ G 80' ★★
Stemming, laybacking, jamming, and lunging, all in 40' of climbing. Could use a cleaning.
Start: 20' left of the blunt arête at the right end of the wall, at a right-facing, left-leaning corner that leads to a right-facing flake 20' up.
P1 5.9+ G: Climb up a crack just right of the corner to a ceiling at the bottom of the flake. Up the flake (4" cam) to a stance at its top. Make an unlikely lunge right 6' to a good rail, then up a fingercrack to a low-angle, lichen-covered right-facing corner. Up the corner, then traverse left 15' on a slab to a large tree. 80'
FA Nov 15, 1987, Jim Lawyer, Tad Welch

3 Caught in the Act 5.8 G 50' ★
Very dirty cracks; probably OK climbing if clean.
Start: 6' left of the blunt arête at the right end of the wall, below mossy parallel cracks, the leftmost of which begins 6' up.
P1 5.8 G: Up the double cracks, then ascend the slab to the trees. 50'
FA Nov 15, 1987, Tad Welch, Jim Lawyer

Baldface Mountain
MAIN FACE

Aspect	West
Height	140'
Quality	★
Approach	1 hr, easy
Summary	Large broken cliff with only a couple of routes, and great views; Keira's Thumb is especially good.

Down low, the Main Face is mostly a broken jumble of loose rock, gullies, and rock ribs, making it difficult to locate a route. The rock up higher improves in quality. The top of the cliff is appealing—sparsely forested with a soft bed of pine needles and views of Indian Lake and Snowy Mountain. Those familiar with the cliff will prefer to rappel into the routes from large trees conveniently perched at the edge, thereby avoiding the hassle of navigating the cliff base.

Once you are up on the cliff, the views and breeze add to a great outing.

DIRECTIONS (MAP PAGE 254)
Follow the red-marked trail to Baldface Mountain for 15 min to a large, 5'-high boulder in the trail. Leave the trail and contour right and slightly downhill for 5 min to reach the top of the cliff 558013,4840776.

DESCENT OPTIONS
Walk (climber's) left and descend forested ledges back to the base of the cliff.

Baldface Mountain
SUMMIT CLIFF

Aspect	West
Height	60'
Quality	★
Approach	1 hr, easy
Summary	A small cliff just off the trail with several quality lines, although they grow in fast. A Tough Act is especially good.

This face is below the summit of Baldface Mountain and has seen limited exploration. The documented routes are near the hiking trail, but the undeveloped cliff extends beyond this small face. The established, somewhat dirty routes follow difficult cracks.

DIRECTIONS (MAP PAGE 254)
Follow the red-marked trail to Baldface Mountain for 15 min to a large, 5'-high boulder in the trail (this is the marker for the turnoff to the Main Face). Continue up the trail 1 min to reach a small, overgrown cliffband visible through the trees on the left. Walk left through the trees under this lower cliffband, then cut right and up above it, until you reach a forested terrace 558187,4840980.

1 A Tough Act 5.11a G 60' ★★
A short, difficult crack route with excellent rock and protection.
Start: At two parallel cracks, 15' uphill from and left of A Tough Act to Follow and 10' right of a 12'-high leaning pillar.
P1 5.11a G: Up the left-hand crack, then make a big move to the right-hand crack (crux). Up this to a stance right of a small tree, then up easier rock to a large tree. 60'
FA Oct 11, 2013, Jim Lawyer, David Buzzelli

Indian Lake

4 **Justin Time** **5.10c TR 100'** ★★

Named for Swisher's son Justin. This route is located at the left end of the cliff, at the top of a gully capped by roofs. Scramble up the gully to its top; there is a comfortable position on its right side below a shallow left-facing open book. The left wall of the open book has white rock, and the right wall has a black streak. Climb up blocks to gain the left-facing open book, then climb it to a small ceiling. Step left, then up to a set of larger roofs in tan rock. Over this to a second downward-pointed roof; break this on the left into a short left-facing corner and climb it to a stance at its top. Continue up over another small ceiling to another stance, then step left into a left-leaning crack and follow it to the top.
FA (TR) 2007, Karl Swisher

5 **Colden's Corner** **5.6 G 140'**

This route, if you can find it, sports some nice sections intermixed with loose rock and grass. Named after Swisher's son Colden.
Start: 60' right of the Justin Time gully are three rock ribs, the center one being the best defined. Scramble up and right from these ribs for 40' to the high point of the terrain on top of a small, rocky perch. Above the perch is a large V-groove with a fin of rock 12' up.
P1 5.6 G: Climb up to the fin, then up an orange-colored crack in the right wall of the V-groove to a ledge with a large pine tree (optional belay). Angle up and right to a large right-facing corner. Climb broken rock on the left wall of the corner to its top, then move up into a low-angle right-facing corner and follow it to the trees. 140'
FA Sep 17, 2007, Karl Swisher, Jim Lawyer

6 **Keira's Thumbs** **5.10b G 170'** ★★★

Beautiful crack climbing on P1, followed by a spectacular airy roof on P2. Named after Swisher's daughter Keira.
Start: At the right end of the cliff (and 190' right of Colden's Corner), find a prominent orange-colored crack that snakes up the left side of a rock rib. Scramble up a gully below and left of the crack, then traverse right 15' to the base of an open book that leads to a ledge below the orange-colored crack. Belay at a tree at the base of the crack.
P1 5.10b G: Climb up the left-arching crack to where it becomes vertical, then straight up following a thin crack that widens to off fingers through a steep wall to the split boulder; over this to a ledge, then up a short lichen-covered wall to a wide, spacious ledge with two pine trees. 90'
P2 5.10a G: Traverse left 20', then up an open book to a small triangular ceiling (5.6 PG). Continue up to the large roof split by a crack. Through the roof via the crack and reachy jugs, then up easy rock to the top. 80'
Gear: To 2", including small nuts and TCUs.
FA Sep 3, 2007, Karl Swisher, Stan Czaplak

JOHN POND CLIFFS

John Pond is a largely unexplored series of east-facing cliffs located east of the village of Indian Lake. Most of the cliffs are between 40' and 100' and offer single-pitch slabs and large boulders (or fins) along the ridgeline. The rock is relatively clean and featured with small pockets and knobs, broken by a few cracks, and the setting is wild and scenic. The cliffs are reached from the John Pond Trailhead at the end of Starbuck Road 562738,4842357 by hiking to John Pond, then bushwhacking west, about 1 hr 30 min 563948,4841961.

The only known exploration here was by Daniel and Kate Mosny, who climbed Ahhh Autumn (5.5 PG; 40'; Sep 23, 2007), a prominent nose below the high point of the second ridge.

KINGS FLOW CLIFF

Location	East side of Indian Lake, accessed from NY 30
Aspect	West
Height	300'
Quality	
Approach	15 min, easy
Summary	Long cliffband with multipitch moderate routes that are close to the road. Very dirty.

2	2						4
-5.6	5.7	5.8	5.9	5.10	5.11	5.12	5.13+	total

An impressive-looking cliff that is visible when you're driving Big Brook Road, Kings Flow Cliff sports a handful of multipitch moderate routes that are very accessible. Unfortunately, the low-angle face and shady aspect are ideal for cliff grunge—this is a very dirty cliff, and the routes cannot be recommended in their current condition. The routes, however, follow notable features, such as the large corner of A Penguin's Progress and the chimney-flake of Wandering Window, and would be recommended if they were cleaned.

HISTORY

This cliff was explored by climbers from Syracuse, an informal group that called themselves the Central New York Climbers, which included, among others Jim Vermeulen, Eric Dahn, Bill Morris, and Stuart Williams. They investigated many southern cliffs (some others being Good Luck, Long Pond, Puffer, and Shanty Cliff), and their routes were always adventurous and exploratory in nature. This cliff typifies their climbs—dirty, wandering, and fun.

DIRECTIONS

From the center of Indian Lake (at the intersection of NY 28 and NY 30), drive south on NY 30 for 0.5 mile to Big Brook Road. Turn left (0.0). At 0.5 mile, you reach the Indian Lake DEC office. At 2.3 miles, you reach the intersection with Chamberlain Road (which comes in from NY 28). At 4.0 miles, you reach a Y-intersection with a "Chimney Mountain" sign; take the left fork. At 5.3 miles, you reach a confusing intersection with Moulton Road and Hutchins Road. Turn right, staying on Big

Indian Lake

Brook Road (although it isn't signposted) to a "Chimney Mountain—Private Property" sign at 7.1 miles; park before the sign 561461,4838477.

Cross the road and hike uphill (east) following the yellow-blazed state land boundary on the right (south). You'll reach the right end of the cliff within 10 min of the road 561597,4838628.

DESCENT OPTIONS

Two ropes are necessary for rappel. One option is to rappel from the top of the cliff to the tree belay at the top of P1 of **Lick 'Em & Stick 'Em**.

1 Bag It or Buy It 5.7 PG 280'

Start: Locate a continuous right-leaning dirty crack that separates the steep, dirty wall on the left from the clean slab on the right. Start beneath a left-facing corner 10' up and 30' right of the continuous crack.
P1 5.6 PG: Up the left-facing corner to a V-groove. Above the V-groove, go right and follow a right-arching crack to the belay. 140'
P2 5.7 PG: Friction past horizontal cracks, staying right of the left-facing overlaps, to a large overlap. Over the large overlap to a slab finish. 140'
FA 1987, Jim Vermeulen, Stuart Williams

2 A Penguin's Progress 5.6 PG 250'

Start: Below a large left-facing, left-leaning corner that is 150' above a tree-covered terrace.
P1 5.6 G: Above the terrace, climb a shallow left-facing corner to a shrub-covered ledge. Then up and left to a tree belay at the base of the large left-facing corner. 125'
P2 5.6 PG: Up the corner and through a notch at its top. Climb a right-facing flake to a belay on a ledge or continue up slabs to the top. 125'
FA Sep, 1986, Jim Vermeulen, Eric Dahn

3 Wandering Window 5.4 PG 250'

The Window is the chimney that is formed by an enormous mitten-shaped flake 100' above the start of the route. A less wandering P1 would climb the depression beneath opposing corners and belay at a lower ledge.
Start: 30' right of the tree-covered terrace of **A Penguin's Progress**, at a small, clean slab.
P1 5.4 PG: Across the slab and up stepped rock to a vegetated left-rising ramp. Up the ramp and shallow left-facing corner above to a ledge. Belay from a tree beneath the left side of a large flake. 100'
P2 5.4 PG: Climb through the window, then follow the vertical crack to the top of the cliff. 150'
FA May, 1986, Eric Dahn, Bill Morris

4 Lick 'Em & Stick 'Em 5.7 PG 250'

Start: 200' left of the state land boundary is a wide depression. Begin on the right side of the depression above a small slab.
P1 5.7 PG: Climb blocks to a squeeze chimney 25' up. Above the chimney, follow a long right-rising wide crack to a tree belay on a small ledge. 180'
P2 5.5 PG: Up the right-facing corner to the top. 70'
FA Sep, 1986, Jim Vermeulen, Stuart Williams, Eric Dahn

PINE PEAK CLIFF

Location	East side of Indian Lake, accessed from NY 30
Aspect	South to west
Height	200'
Quality	★
Approach	1 hr 45 min, difficult
Summary	A remote cliff with a flat approach and new route potential. **Pining for More** and **Hard Going** ascend clean corners with deep, wide cracks.

1		1		1			3
-5.6	5.7	5.8	5.9	5.10	5.11	5.12	5.13+	total

Pine Peak is a small, remote, rocky mountain surrounded by the marshes of Wakely Brook. The approach is level and involves minimal bushwhacking. New route potential is good, and the rock is fairly clean as a result of little seepage and a sunny aspect. However, the base of the cliff is broken, and getting to the good rock is somewhat punishing. The best views of the cliff are from the marsh below, where the west face is clearly visible. The overhanging orange wall near the top right end of the cliff is a key landmark. The large pine beneath the orange wall is the belay for the second pitches of **White Pine Fever** and **Pining for More**.

HISTORY

Karl Swisher investigated Pine Peak, having seen it from nearby Humphrey. He came in alone and cleaned **Hard Going**, then returned in 2007 with Jeremy Haas and climbed the three routes.

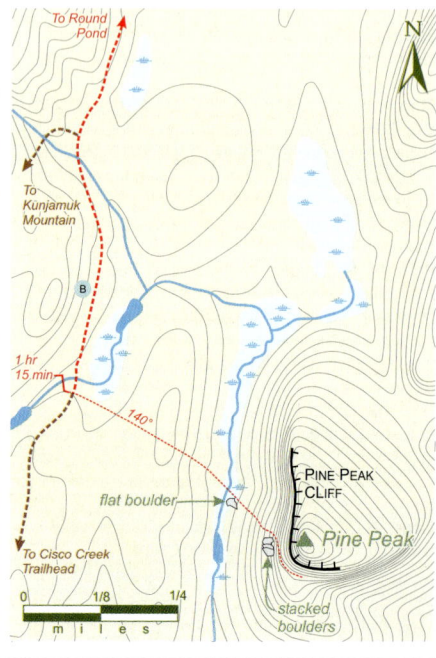

Indian Lake

DIRECTIONS   **(MAP PAGE 256)**

From the center of Indian Lake (at the intersection of NY 28 and NY 30), drive south on NY 30 for 0.5 mile to the Big Brook Road. Turn left (0.0). At 0.5 mile, you'll reach the Indian Lake DEC office. At 2.3 miles, you'll reach the intersection with Chamberlain Road (which comes in from NY 28). At 4.0 miles, you'll reach a Y-intersection that has a "Chimney Mountain" sign; take the left fork. At 5.3 miles, you'll reach a confusing intersection with Moulton Road and Hutchins Road. Turn right, staying on Big Brook Road (although it isn't signposted). At 6.3 miles, the road reaches an intersection on the right with a bridge over Big Brook. Cross the bridge and follow the high-clearance 2WD road. At a fork, go left and continue to the end of the maintained road at a parking area at 6.9 miles 560828,4838594.

From the parking area (0 hr 0 min), hike the blue-marked, unmaintained road past an intersection (go left), a cabin, then another intersection (go left, past the wilderness boundary) to Round Pond, reached at 30 min. At 1 hr 15 min, the trail crosses a small brook that flows east. Through the conifer forest, you can see the cliffs on the west face of Pine Peak across a marsh (to the east). Leave the trail and bushwhack southeast (140') to a marsh with a large, flat boulder, reached at 1 hr 35 min. Cross the marsh and enter the woods next to the flat boulder. Hike up and right to three stacked, room-sized boulders on a hill, above which is the cliff. At 1 hr 45 min, you'll reach the cliff at a large low-angle right-facing wall beneath the orange wall 150' up 559283,4833761.

1 White Pine Fever 5.5 G 200'

Start: 100' above the stacked boulders and right of the right-facing wall, directly beneath an arching roof 8' up.

P1 4th class: Up past the left end of the roof to the vegetated right-facing corner. Follow the corner to a belay at a large pine tree beneath the orange wall. 100'

P2 5.5 G: Up a left-rising crack beneath the orange wall to a right-facing corner with a short chimney above it. Climb the chimney and a left-facing wall with a broken crack to a tree belay. 100'

Descent: Traverse right across a tree-covered ledge for 50' to a tree with a fixed anchor at the top of Pining for More.

FA Jul 10, 2007, Karl Swisher, Jeremy Haas

2 Pining for More 5.10c G 170' ★★★

Start: Same as White Pine Fever.

P1 4th class: Same as White Pine Fever. 100'

P2 5.10c G: Up a right-rising handcrack past a small tree at 35' to a stance beneath a flared chimney in a roof. A boulder-problem crux (overhead protection with a large cam) gains the hanging chimney-slot; traverse 15' to the right to a chockstone. Exit the slot to the right and climb up to a tree with a fixed anchor. 70'

Gear: Up to 6", 2 ea 2"–3.5".
FA Jul 10, 2007, Jeremy Haas, Karl Swisher

3 Hard Going 5.8+ G 130' ★★★

Start: 300' right (south) of the stacked boulders, past a low-angle and broken section of cliff, is a wide depression clogged with downed trees. 200' up are two overhanging buttresses. Hard Going climbs the right-facing corner formed by the main wall and the buttress on the right. Follow the right-facing wall of the depression uphill for 150' to a belay beneath opposing corners and a chimney 50' up.

P1 5.8+ G: Up the opposing corners to the base the chimney. Climb the chimney and the crack above it, which narrows to 5" (crux), to low-angle rock at its top. Belay at a tree. 130'

Descent: Rappel from a pine tree that is 30' to the right of the belay. Make one rappel toward the right with a single 60-m rope.

Gear: Up to 6".
FA Jul 10, 2007, Karl Swisher, Jeremy Haas

CHIMNEY MOUNTAIN

Location	East side of Indian Lake, accessed from NY 30
Summary	A freestanding tower, some smaller walls, and a large south-facing slab.

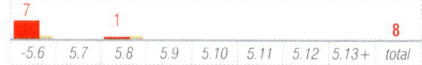

7		1					8
-5.6	5.7	5.8	5.9	5.10	5.11	5.12	5.13+	total

A small mountain (2700') with a high trailhead (1800'), Chimney Mountain is a popular hike in the Kings Flow area. Several spires and fins of metamorphosed sedimentary rocks dot Chimney Summit, with the largest formation being 100' (on its west side) and freestanding. Below this is a complex jumble of large blocks, cliffs, fissures, deep holes, and caves; the largest walls in this area are the west faces of Lookout Rock and Caveman Wall. East of Chimney Summit is the True Summit, a typical Adirondack summit of slabby open bedrock with good views.

More popular than rock climbing are the technical caving opportunities that this mountaintop also offers. On a busy weekend day, hoards of hikers wander through the complex landscape poking their heads into holes and exploring the fissures. Some have been known to explore the caves without proper equipment—lights, ropes, and so forth—necessitating numerous rescues, so be careful.

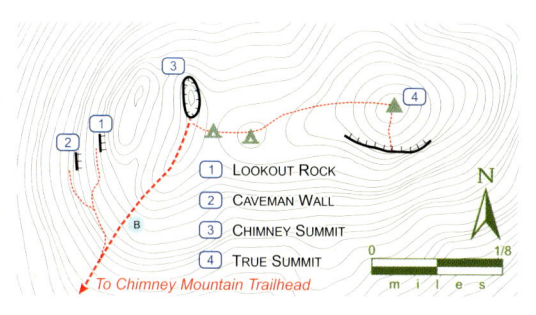

1. Lookout Rock
2. Caveman Wall
3. Chimney Summit
4. True Summit

Indian Lake

CHIMNEY MOUNTAIN
1. Southwest Ridge (5.6)
3. Overlap It Up (5.4)
4. Caveman Crack (5.8)
5. Caveman's Hairy Backside (5.4)

HISTORY
Because Chimney Mountain is small, inviting, and often visited by hikers, its first ascent may never be known. The first recorded ascent was by Edward C. Hudowalski, who tagged the summit in 1941.[7] Tempted by the challenging rock on the opposite side of the tower, members of Central New York Climbers made an ascent of the southeast ridge in 1980.

DIRECTIONS (MAP PAGE 257)
From the center of Indian Lake (at the intersection of NY 28 and NY 30), drive south on NY 30 for 0.5 mile to Big Brook Road. Turn left (0.0 mile). At 0.5 mile, reach the Indian Lake DEC office. At 2.3 miles, reach the intersection with Chamberlain Road (which comes in from NY 28). At 4.0 miles, reach a Y-intersection with a "Chimney Mountain" sign; take the left fork. At 5.3 miles, reach a confusing intersection with Moulton Road and Hutchins Road. Turn right, staying on Big Brook Road (although it isn't signposted) to the parking area at Chimney Mountain Wilderness Lodge 562031,4837511 at 7.9 miles.

The parking is on private land, and a $2 fee (as of 2013) goes in the drop box next to the DEC sign. The trailhead is 100 yards east beyond the parking lot. Follow the trail marked with blue discs towards the summit of Chimney Mountain, which takes about 40 minutes.

[7] Edward C. Hudowalski, "Chimney Mt.," *Cloudsplitter* 4, no. 7 (Oct 1941), pp. 2–3.

Chimney Mountain
CHIMNEY SUMMIT

Aspect	East and west
Height	120'
Quality	★★
Approach	40 min, moderate
Summary	Unique summit spire with unusual sandy rock.

2							2
-5.6	5.7	5.8	5.9	5.10	5.11	5.12	5.13+	total

This unusual spire-like summit is characterized by vertical and overhanging climbing on positive ledges. The easiest ascent of the main tower is 5.1 and climbs the shortest side, where the trail reaches the east face. The taller west face is best approached by descending a herd path counterclockwise around the tower. This side of the tower is much more impressive, as the rock is both taller and steeper.

DIRECTIONS (MAP PAGE 257)
Follow the blue-marked trail for 40 min to its end on the east side of the summit tower 563354,4838113. Herd paths lead around either side of the tower.

DESCENT OPTIONS
There is no fixed anchor on the top of the tower. Although downleading is an option, you can make a

Indian Lake

Eric Laurin on the main tower of Chimney Mountain after climbing the Standard Route (5.1) in 1977. This historic route was first climbed in 1941. Photo by Dick Tucker.

short rappel to the east by wrapping the rope around a block or horn.

1 Southwest Ridge 5.6 G 120' ★★
An engaging climb that ends at a small and exposed summit.
Start: 8' left of a deep chimney on the right side of the west face. A piton at 15' marks the beginning of the route.
P1 5.6 G: Up steep rock, then move right of the piton, and over a bulge. Go right and up (crux), then climb close to the ridge. Follow easier ledges left to the summit. 120'
FA 1980, Tad Welch, Eric Dahn, Chip Molton, Jim Vermeulen

2 Standard Route 5.1 G 40' ★
Hikers often climb this route and have epics trying to get back down.
Start: At a sandy spot beneath the south side of the tower.
P1 5.1 G: Up a flare and sloping ledges to the top. 40'
ACB 1941, Edward C. Hudowalski

Chimney Mountain
LOOKOUT ROCK

Aspect	West
Height	80'
Quality	
Approach	35 min, moderate
Summary	Severely overhanging wall in amongst a maze of fissures and boulders.

Far below the main cliff is a jumble of caves and fissures. There are two walls in this area roughly stacked on top of one another; this is the upper wall, is 100' wide, and the lower 40' overhangs with right-rising overlaps and cracks. There is a flat, sandy path running along its base. The top of this wall is a popular lookout. Good potential for more routes here.

DIRECTIONS   (MAP PAGE 257)
About 5 min before reaching the summit, the hiking trail steps over a right-rising 5'-tall rocky step. Just below this is a good herd path forking off left, the first such herd path you'll encounter, and by far the most well-worn and obvious. Take this left fork and contour the hillside. There are several forks in the path, you want to go uphill and stay on the well-worn path to reach the wall 2 min after leaving the main trail 563223,4838044.

3 Overlap It Up 5.4 PG 80' ★
Very nice top area with great views and easy set up of toprope anchors.
Start: At the left end of the wall (where it is merely vertical, not overhanging) below two 2' overlaps 10' up (the bottom overlap is formed by thin flakes), and 10' right of a tree clump growing against the rock.
P1 5.4 PG: Underclinging your way over the overlaps (gear) staying right of a small birch. Go up the relatively clean and easier, but sparsely protected slab to the blocky top. 80'
FA Sep 5, 2009, Daniel Mosny, Kate Mosny

Chimney Mountain
CAVEMAN WALL

Aspect	West
Height	40'
Quality	★★
Approach	35 min, moderate
Summary	Sheer orange face with a single crack and an amazing underclinging flake.

1	1						2
-5.6	5.7	5.8	5.9	5.10	5.11	5.12	5.13+	total

This brilliant orange and yellow wall cannot be missed. It's sheer, split in the middle by an amazing right-leaning handcrack. On its right side is another exceptional feature, an underclinging flake that runs the height of the cliff.

A toprope can be set with large gear (hexes) in a horizontal crack at the top.

Indian Lake

CHIMNEY MOUNTAIN: TRUE SUMMIT SLABS
6 Sunfall (5.6)
7 Ray's Ascent (5.5)
8 Bullhead (5.0)

DIRECTIONS (MAP PAGE 257)
Leave the hiking trail as for Lookout Rock. When the path forks, go downhill. The wall is positioned about 75 yards directly downhill and in front of Lookout Rock 563191,4838018, about 2 min from the hiking trail.

4 Caveman Crack 5.8 G 50' ★★★★
A striking right-leaning handcrack. What a feature!
Start: In the middle of the wall below the obvious right-leaning handcrack.
P1 5.8 G: Up the right-rising crack. After 30', the crack narrows to fingers through a bulge (crux). Continue up on small edges to the top. 50'
FA Oct 12, 2008, Daniel Mosny, Kate Mosny

5 Caveman's Hairy Backside 5.4 G 50'
Climbs the slab that forms the right side of the cliff. There's quite a bit of lichen (hence hairy backside) and some loose rock and flakes.
Start: 50' right of **Caveman Crack**, just around the corner from the giant flake that runs the full height of the cliff (with some unfortunate—but fading—graffiti) and 10' left of a small cave, below vertical parallel cracks.
P1 5.4 G: Climb up cracks to less steep climbing above, staying close to the corner to the left. Finish at a small birch on top. 50'
FA Aug 20, 2009, Daniel Mosny, Kate Mosny

Chimney Mountain
TRUE SUMMIT SLABS

Aspect	South
Height	300'
Quality	★★
Approach	45 min, moderate
Summary	Expansive summit slab that has seen little exploration; awful base area.

3							3
-5.6	5.7	5.8	5.9	5.10	5.11	5.12	5.13+	total

This slab is located east of Chimney Summit on the true summit of Chimney Mountain. The slab has good potential with the best rock yet found on Chimney Mountain—none of the characteristic sandy layers found on the other crags. The slab is quite large, open, and clean and you can scramble around the upper portions of it; the lower sections require a rope. Unlike the Chimney Summit and caving areas, you'll find few people on this summit, and nobody on the slabs below.

The base of the cliff is steep, complex, disorienting, and unpleasant. Since travel along the base is a challenge, a rappel approach is described, which deposits you within a few feet of the climbs. With use, perhaps the base will become better defined and easier.

DIRECTIONS (MAP PAGE 257)
Just before you reach the end of the hiking trail, you'll see a flat area down and to the right with a fire ring (there's good, legal camping here). Leave the main trail and follow a path to the campsite. On the far side of the campsite there three paths: take the leftmost path and follow it east to the true summit 563683,4838093, about 5 min from the hiking trail.

From the summit, the easiest approach to **Sunfall**

Indian Lake

PUFFER MOUNTAIN CLIFF
1 Cream Puffer (5.6)

is by rappel. Scramble down (south) and slightly right on the vegetated upper slab that grows increasingly steep as you descend. On the (skier's) left side of the cliff, locate a large pine tree 563688,4838027 with a 4'-wide horizontal crevice to its left; there are several large pines scattered around the cliff, this one is fairly high on the slab and is the only one with a horizontal crevice on its (skier's) left side. Crawl into the crevice and emerge out a rabbit hole onto a vegetated island below the pine tree. There is a fixed anchor on a pine tree on the lower end of this island. Rappel from here to the base of the slab; a 60m rope just makes it.

Since the routes are located on the (climber's) right end of the cliff, you can also walk down the steep terrain on that end.

6 Sunfall 5.6 G 170' ★★★

A nice climb, too bad the steep crack portion isn't longer. From the end of P1, a 3rd class scramble upwards with a 4th class move in the left-facing corner takes you to the top.
Start: Locate the large right-facing right-arching corner (of **Ray's Ascent**); scramble downhill to the base of this corner. 20' left of the corner, pull up onto a small ledge beneath a clean slab that scoops up into a steep wall where a right-rising crack T's into a long left-rising crack.
P1 5.6 G: Climb up the scooped slab, then follow the left-rising crack through the vertical wall to the slab above. Continue up this easier slab, moving towards the right to take advantage of cracks for gear, and over a couple of overlaps to belay just to the right of a pine tree in the middle of the slab. 170'
FA Sep 26, 2009, Daniel Mosny, Kate Mosny

7 Ray's Ascent 5.5 G 160'

A dramatic line that follows an impressive right-arching corner. Recommended if cleaner.
Start: From the rappel, walk left, scramble down a 10'-tall left-facing corner formed by a large boulder, then move 20' left to a 1'-deep corner that is 15' right of the major, overhanging, right-facing corner that arches up to a roof. This is 40' uphill and right of **Sunfall**.
P1 5.5 G: Straight up the small corner past two birch trees (V1) and up under the overhang. Traverse awkwardly right under the overhang, pass an offwidth crack that breaks the ceiling, and continue to a weakness in the wall directly below the rappel. Pull through the weakness to the rappel tree. 160'
V1 5.4 G: At the second birch, traverse right under an overlap with a good crack to its right side, then up to join the normal route.
FA Sep 19, 2009, Daniel Mosny, Kate Mosny

8 Bullhead 5.0 X 60'

Used to access the top, easier than scrambling around the right end of the slab.
Start: 50' right of the rappel.
P1 5.0 X: Climb straight up the slab to an easy exit. 60'
FA Sep 19, 2009, Daniel Mosny (solo)

PUFFER MOUNTAIN CLIFF

Location	East side of Indian Lake, accessed from NY 30
Aspect	South
Height	180'
Quality	★
Approach	3 hr 45 min, difficult
Summary	Medium-sized cliff with one route in a wicked remote, gorgeous setting.

Sections of the Siamese Ponds Wilderness Area are among the most remote places in the Adirondack Park; this is where you find (with some luck) Puffer Mountain Cliff. Although the approach to Puffer is not as rough and steep as the approaches to the High Peaks, the spartan trail network of the Kings Flow region discour-

Indian Lake

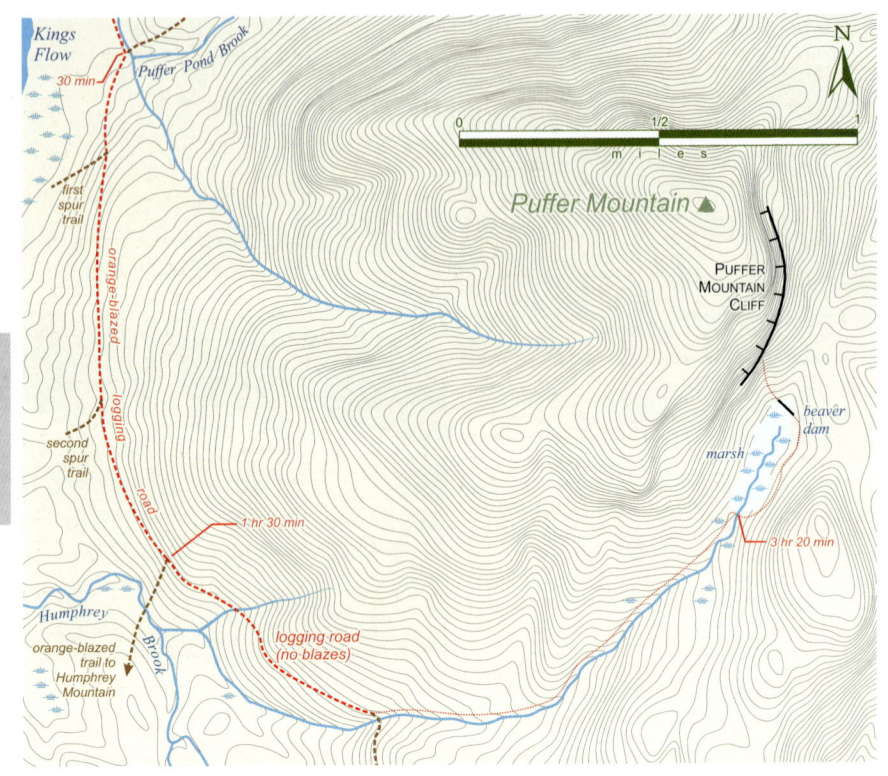

ages heavy wilderness use, and the solitude is very real. Moose sightings are common here, and the high-elevation marsh beneath the cliff lures both wilderness campers and wildlife. The cliff is both clean and undeveloped, with good potential for single-pitch crack climbs (right of **Cream Puffer**).

HISTORY

The route **Cream Puffer** is yet another exploration by Jim Vermeulen and cohorts, who got the idea from Barbara McMartin's *Discover the Adirondacks* book series. (See sidebar, page 263)

DIRECTIONS   **(MAP PAGE 262)**

From the center of Indian Lake (at the intersection of NY 28 and NY 30), drive south on NY 30 for 0.5 mile to Big Brook Road. Turn left (0.0). At 0.5 mile, you'll reach the Indian Lake DEC office. At 2.3 miles, you'll reach the intersection with Chamberlain Road (which comes in from NY 28). At 4.0 miles, you'll reach a Y-intersection that has a "Chimney Mountain" sign; take the left fork. At 5.3 miles, you'll reach a confusing intersection with Moulton Road and Hutchins Road. Turn right, staying on Big Brook Road (although it isn't signposted) to the parking area at Chimney Mountain Wilderness Lodge 562031,4837511 at 7.9 miles.

The parking is on private land, and a $2 fee (as of 2007) goes in the drop box next to the DEC sign.

A graded path begins at the flagpole next to the parking area and crosses a field before entering into the woods on the left side of the field. Hike south through the woods to the state land boundary. Continue south, across Puffer Pond Brook, to an intersection with the Puffer Pond Brook Trail (orange blazes), reached at 30 min. From the intersection, hike south along the orange-blazed logging road past two spur trails on the right (west). At 1 hr 30 min, you'll reach a third spur trail 562357,4833206, marked with orange paint, that goes sharply downhill to the right to the summit of Humphrey Mountain.

Leave the orange blazes and continue straight (south) on the logging road. There is considerable blowdown just prior to a large stream that flows over a smooth slab, reached at 1 hr 50 min 563169,4832623. Turn left (east), leaving the logging road, and follow the stream, staying on its north side. The stream climbs gradually but has dense vegetation. Choose the largest tributary—usually the one on the right—as the stream forks several times in this section. As the stream steepens and narrows, it swings toward the northeast and the forest becomes coniferous. You'll reach the south end of a large marsh at 3 hr 20 min 564724,4833445. The cliffs are visible up from and left of the height of land that is above the north end of the marsh. To reach the cliffs, hike right around the east side of the marsh to its north end and cross on a beaver dam, reached at 3 hr 30 min. Hike uphill (north) to the sheer left end of the cliff, reached at 3 hr 45 min 564767,4833982.

Indian Lake

Into the Heart of the Backwater

"Puffer Mountain Cliffs—Most difficult bushwhack, great views: The Puffer Mountain cliffs present the greatest challenge of any bushwhack in this guide. They should be attempted only by small groups with at least two guides who are familiar with the intricacies of bushwhacking." —Barbara McMartin and Bill Ingersoll, Discover the South Central Adirondacks

September 1988: It is late summer, and we don't want to yield to the conservative nature of autumn bushwhacking, so we veer off Kings Flow Trail and bushwhack along an indistinct branch of Humphrey Brook. Sweat breaks out, and the unmarked miles accumulate. In this place, upward momentum offers us more certainty than map and compass. Bill, Chip, and Mike are trusting me on this venture.

The unclimbed south-facing cliffs of Puffer Mountain are up there somewhere. As we thrash our way into terra incognita, I can feel the forest closing behind us, temporarily sealing off wives, children, and late mortgage payments. Puffer Pond Cliff is an obscure, remote place that, at this moment, no one cares a whit about except us.

Another mile of birch-beech-maple infighting and the sky opens to an unexpected high mountain meadow created by a double-tiered beaver pond. Above them angle the cliffs we had only imagined, a scraggly 200' swath of potential lines. But we're here, and the impending autumnal equinox dictates haste. Leaving some gear at our bivouac site, we push up to the cliff. Mike and Chip veer right, their afternoon destined to degenerate into exploratory scrambles that yield no roped climbing. Bill and I enjoy more luck, teasing an image of a route into reality as a gully scramble gives way to a left-facing crack and some delicate moves up a face to a small ledge. Years later, Bill remembers that lead "with someone below bitching about me sending down clumps of moss." I really don't recall bitching.

A second lead turns an overlap on its left and lands me in the summit scrub, where I bring Bill up. For a few moments, we enjoy those long, lonely views that McMartin earned by another route, then we cautiously rappel down into the gathering evening.

Camp accommodations that night consist of ground tarps, stars framed above the beaver ponds, and a lot of silly talk about the bear scat we've found nearby. With dawn and breakfast, no one professes much enthusiasm for more climbing, nor for a return bushwhack down Humphrey Brook. Chip suggests scrambling northeast beneath the cliffs until we can cross over and descend the back side of the mountain. The unknowns are quickly tallied. How brutal the scramble? Will we find Puffer Pond Trail easily? What if we somehow miss it?

We stuff our packs and begin walking toward the east. Hey, we'll figure it out. . . .

- Jim Vermeulen

1 Cream Puffer 5.6 G 180' ★★

The slab of **Cream Puffer** is beneath the highest buttress of rock, which is 800' right of where you reach the cliff at its left end.

Start: At a left-rising crack that begins 8' above the ground and is 20' left of stacked house-sized boulders.

P1 5.6 G: Up the left-rising crack to a right-rising crack, then follow it for 60' to a tree belay. 80'

P2 5.5 PG: Step left and climb a clean slab, then move left to a prominent right-facing corner. Follow the corner, past two steps, to the top of the cliff near a dead tree. 100'

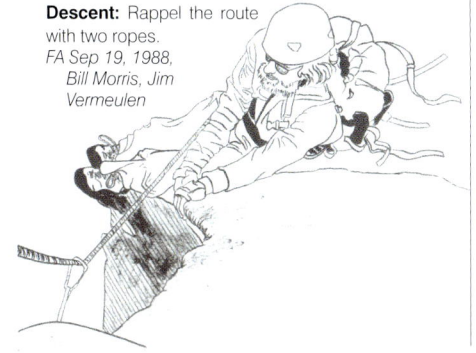

Descent: Rappel the route with two ropes.
FA Sep 19, 1988,
Bill Morris, Jim
Vermeulen

SUGARLOAF MOUNTAIN

Location	Off Cedar River Road, accessed from NY 28 / NY 30 west of Indian Lake
Aspect	East and southeast
Height	450'
Quality	★★★★
Approach	10-30 min, easy
Summary	Wide, tall cliff with many great, somewhat runout slab routes.

1	1	11	1	4			18
-5.6	5.7	5.8	5.9	5.10	5.11	5.12	5.13+	total

Sugarloaf is a major slab-climbing destination. It sits alone as an oddly-shaped hunched lump in the middle of a broad valley, the east side cleanly cleaved off, leaving a peppering of tree islands. The rock slabs upward, split horizontally by numerous overlaps and vertically by clean dimpled strips alternating with lichen- and moss-covered swaths.

The climbing is generally runout (especially on easy terrain) and links climbable features (e.g., clean slabs with holds, cracks, breaks in overlaps) with tree islands for belays. The trees often interrupt the aesthetic nature of the climbing, but they do provide shade and natural, mostly-solid anchors. Protection, when

Indian Lake

available, is often small, hence small nuts and micro cams are required. Be aware that some of the flakes and overlaps are expanding, and sometimes expand from the sun's heat. With some notable exceptions, the lower pitches, as they are down in the trees, are almost always dirty and unpleasant, but don't let that deter you from the excellent climbing above.

The terrain along the base of the cliff, while relatively open, is sloped awkwardly downhill, and there are no comfortable flat places to get organized (exceptions being the base of **Tier Pressure**, and the rock ledge at the base of **High Plains Drifter**). This, combined with the weeds and prickly plants, make walking left or right along the base slippery and inconvenient.

In many ways, the cliff is still raw and undeveloped. Because the cliff was private, those that climbed here were stealthy, and details weren't published. Hence, the various routes overlap and wander around, and nothing would yet be considered well-traveled. The exception is **Tier Pressure**, which has been compared to **Quadrophenia** or **Hesitation** in quality.

DIRECTIONS

From the intersection of NY 30 and NY 28 in Indian Lake (0.0 mile), go west on the combined NY 30/28. At 2.1 miles, turn left onto Cedar River Road. At 9.9 miles, the pavement ends; from here the road is closed through mud season, opening around mid-May. At 11.7 miles, reach a grassy pulloff on the right 0543832,4844910 with room for many cars. You can just see the upper section of the cliff.

For routes on the right end of the cliff (everything right of **Superman Flake**), park at the grassy pulloff and walk 5 min further on Cedar River Road to where it levels out. Leave the road on the right and follow either of two gullies straight up the hill. At 20 min, you should arrive at the cliff near the route **Return to Sender**.

For routes on the left end of the cliff (**Magic Carpet Ride** to **Superman Flake**), continue on Cedar River Road. At 12.0 miles (and 300' past a hunting camp with a metal gate) park on the side of the road 0543515,4844379 just beyond a deep culvert. The left end of the slab is visible behind the cabin. Skirt the cabin on the left and follow a faint stream uphill. Stay on the right to avoid the talus as long as possible. Continue uphill to the base of the cliff in the vicinity of **Meteorite**, about 10 min from the road.

ACCESS

The land in front of the cliff was owned by former Finch Pruyn timber company and was off-limits to the public. In 2007, The Nature Conservancy purchased the land and transferred it to the state in April 2014. There are several hunting camps along the road in front of the cliff. Until Sep 30, 2018, these camps maintain exclusive use of 1-acre parcels around their structures, so don't approach them. It's easy enough to approach the cliff out of sight of the camps. The camps will be removed by the end of 2019.

The east side of Cedar River Road is conservation easement land with limited public access. Try to park on the cliff-side of the road. A parking area will be built within the next couple years directly across from the cliff.

The unpaved section of Cedar River Road is closed for the winter (unless you have a snowmobile) through mud season, usually opening up mid-May. Unfortunately, this means you can't drive the last 2 miles to the cliff until after the black flies have hatched.

This is a new acquisition and access may be further specified in the future. Check the web site (www.AdirondackRock.com) for updates.

HISTORY

Tom Rosecrans learned of Sugarloaf while hiking on the Northville Lake Placid Trail in 1971. He returned with Doug Leith climbed "two short pitches of slab with tree belays, sparsely protected and fairly featureless". Rosecrans was (and still is) an enthusiastic explorer of new cliffs, and in the 1970s, he developed a special liking for slabs—e.g., Rogers Rock (Lake George) and Moxham Dome, both of which he included in his 1976 rock

SUGARLOAF
1. Magic Carpet Ride (5.8)
9. Superman Flake (5.8)
12. Return to Sender (5.8)
13. Deja View (5.8)
16. Tier Pressure (5.8+)

Indian Lake

Sugarloaf

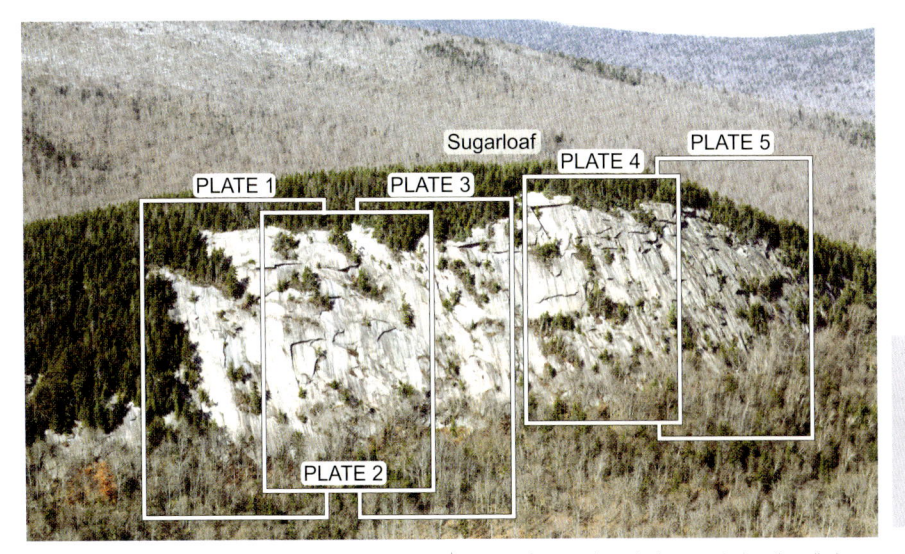

PLATE 1 | PLATE 3 | PLATE 4 | PLATE 5
PLATE 2

climbing guidebook. His visit to Sugarloaf was "not pleasant, scary and steep," and he never returned.

Next to visit were Rick Morse and friends, from 1978-1979. Morse was a school teacher living in Blue Mountain Lake, an active outdoor enthusiast and bicyclist. With very little experience, and armed with a goldline rope, some nuts, and pitons, he and Mike Pinard ascended **Little Finger** at Rogers Rock. Morse had spotted Sugarloaf while on a biking outing, and returned with Pinard and others to establish several full-length routes. Three of their four routes were documented in Mellor's 1983 guidebook. (The cliff was removed from Mellor's later editions due to concerns with private property.)

Tad Welch read the key sentence in Mellor's 1983 guidebook "There is great potential for exploration here." Welch had just developed Echo Cliff (near Piseco), and gained some slab-climbing expertise on Cannon in New Hampshire; he saw Sugarloaf as the Adirondack version of the Cannon slabs. Welch explored the cliff—both solo and with Bill Widrig and Jamie Savage—several times in 1985, then again between 1991 and 1992.

Without knowledge of any previous visitors, Mike Rawdon and friends began visiting in 2000, and have returned nearly every year since. They added many full-length routes, all ground-up with a heightened spirit of adventure. Rawdon's group discovered evidence of prior explorations, but it wasn't until many years of visits that he discovered Mellor's information, then later Welch's route descriptions. Others have visited Sugarloaf, most notably Mark Meschinelli around 1985-86, but have long since forgotten what they did.

Slab climbing exploration often links naturally protectable features with tree islands for belays. The easy lines of weakness at Sugarloaf were obvious to all of the parties through the years, sometimes resulting in overlapping routes. Hence, the various climbing groups have unknowingly repeated entire climbs or sections of climbs, often improving and straightening the lines.

1 Magic Carpet Ride 5.8 X 380' ★ ★ ★ ★
This high quality route ascends the clean sweep of rock on the extreme left end of the cliff. More committing the higher you get. Not only one of the best lines on the cliff, but, unlike many other routes, the first pitch is clean. The original route was direct and ended after three pitches at a tree island; the variation adds another pitch to the top. The route can be tamed by deviating left to protect in trees. Named for a Steppenwolf song.
Start: The most prominent feature on the left end of the cliff is the 100'-wide open, sheer slab of **Sole Fusion**. Begin 75' left at the next open section of slab, left of some mossy streaks. On the right side of this open area is an overlap that begins in the ground 543294,4844612.
P1 5.7 PG: Go straight up unprotected slab to a left-facing, left-leaning edge. Go to its top, make a tricky mantel, then climb good holds to a hollow flake. Wonderful face moves lead to a second flake. Traverse left to a maple tree and belay. (You can continue 40' further left to a comfortable belay in trees.) 150'
P2 5.6 R: Climb a rippled corner past a fixed pin, then run it out to a large detached flake. Go left to an alcove belay. 110'
P3 5.8 X: Move out around the pointed overhang (pins, crux) then (V1) up and right through an obvious ceiling. Continue up to a tree island belay. 120'
V1 5.6 X: Continue up and left with no protection (5.6) to a large detached flake. Above climb easy friction, then head left to trees for a belay, 120'. Regain the slab and friction up to a large spruce tree at the very top, 80'.
Descent: Rappel the route with two 60m ropes.
FA Oct 30, 1985, Tad Welch (roped solo)
FA (V1) Nov 12, 2012, Mike Rawdon, Kim Graves

Indian Lake

Sole Fusion

It's interesting how often life comes full circle. Today, I find myself at the top of Sugarloaf Cliff with two influential and well-respected Adirondack climbers, Tad Welch and Jim Lawyer. Twenty years ago my oldest brother Rob and I purchased land just a few miles down the road. Little did I know then that my journey would take me back to the place where it all began. Still green, and working to become 46ers, Rob and I built a base camp in the heart of this magical place. I remember it as if it were yesterday, looking south from our property, and being struck by the impressive cliffs on Sugarloaf Mountain. Certainly, with a different vision than I have today. Coincidentally, at this same moment in time, Tad was establishing some of the earliest routes on the cliff…roped solo, using hammer-ins. Impressive in any era.

My rock climbing career would start shortly after this. One day, as we were summiting Saddleback Mountain, Rob looked at me and said, "Hey, let's learn to rock climb!" Without hesitation I said, "Definitely!" Over the next few years we would take guided lessons, and build a lead rack. Every weekend would be the same routine: feverishly flipping through the guidebook in search of the next place to explore—Azure Mountain, Shanty Cliff, Moxham Dome, Poko, Good Luck Cliff, Chapel Pond area. This lasted 10 years, but like most good things in life, my traditional climbing career came to an end. Rob slowly lost interest, and I lost my level-headedness, so necessary for lead climbing. Still consumed with a passion for climbing, I turned to bouldering. In retrospect, it was all part of the journey. I soon discovered how much of the park is unexplored. Seeking out first ascents, I began to reap the rewards of route development, and gained a new appreciation for the sport.

This past summer, after 20 years of climbing, I partnered up with Jim Lawyer. Over dinner with mutual friends he convinced me to get back on a rope. Unknowingly, Jim and I have been relative neighbors most of our lives, but somehow never really crossed paths. Despite being only four years older than me, his wealth of climbing knowledge, accomplishments, and experience overwhelms mine, so I jumped at the opportunity. Soon, I would find out that his humble attitude, exceptional climbing ability, and unstoppable work ethic, are second to none. We went on to have a memorable summer, teaming up on a number of first ascents. Beginning at the Lost T crag, our explorations would continue at areas like Little Johnson, Pinnacle Mountain, and a visit to Gull Pond to give our best shot at a long-standing project. Along the way, we also unveiled hidden gems like the "super sweet" Honey Pot, Makomis Mountain Cliff, and Castle Rock. It was a successful season, to say the least.

Two nights ago, Jim called and asked if I wanted to join him and Tad at Sugarloaf Mountain. The plan was to extend a climb Tad had established 20 years ago. How could I pass up on another great opportunity? Topping out on this bluebird day with fall foliage in full bloom is breathtaking. It takes me back 20 years, to the time Rob and I began our Adirondack adventures. Looking down into the valley and out over the vast expanse of forest, I realize how much has yet to be explored. As we rap down, I see Tad look over to his right and I ask him, "Whatcha looking at?" Tad replies, "Oh, just seeing if this other line goes." Yeah, I'm definitely looking forward to the next 20 years.

- David Buzzelli

2 Sole Fusion 5.10c G 600' ★★★★★

If you like friction, every pitch is superb. One of the best, long outings in the central Adirondacks, and a must-do for slab aficionados.

Start: At the left end of the cliff is a 100'-wide section of very smooth slab that goes right into the steep dirt. Begin at the lowest point on this tongue of slab. 25' right (and slightly uphill) is the only feature on this slab—an 8'-tall right-facing corner 20' up (which marks the start of Touch The Earth and It Ain't Over).

● **P1 5.10b G:** Climb straight up the slab (5.8 PG) to gain a left-leaning crack 60' up. Follow the crack to near its top, then step right onto the slab and mantel onto a ledge. Continue straight up the slab above the ledge, move left (crux), then continue straight up to stacked flakes and a fixed anchor. 180'

● **P2 5.10c G:** Go first up and right, then up and left to the base of a black streak. Make a couple hard moves up the black streak (crux), then go up and right to a narrow shelf and fixed anchor. 100'

● **P3 5.10b G:** Continue straight up, then angle up and right to a steep headwall. Up this (crux) to a welcome jug where the angle eases. Move back left along the lip of the headwall, then straight left on pure friction (5.8) to a fixed anchor below a large overlap. 100'

● **P4 5.7 PG:** Go straight up to the overlap, then undercling 20' right to a break at a small flake–nose. Step up onto this, then up onto the slab above (crux). Traverse up and left 60' to belay in a horizontal crack (#1 and #2 Camalot) just left of a vertical tree island. 120'

● **P5 5.8 PG:** Go straight up the clean dimpled face past two steep sections. Weave left to a good crack (#3 Camalot), then back right and up the clean streak to the top. Fixed rappel anchor on trees. 100'

Descent: Three rappels: Angle right 160' to the top of P3 below the overlap; straight down 170' to the block stack at the top of P1; straight down 180' to the ground.

Gear: P1: #0.5, #1 Camalots; P2-P4: quickdraws; P5: quickdraws plus #3 Camalot.

History: Having just received his new Boreal Fire shoes, Welch raced up to Sugarloaf one afternoon and solo-lead up to the top of P2, drilling rivets from stances

Opposite: Tad Welch on P1 (5.10b) of **Sole Fusion** *(5.10c).*

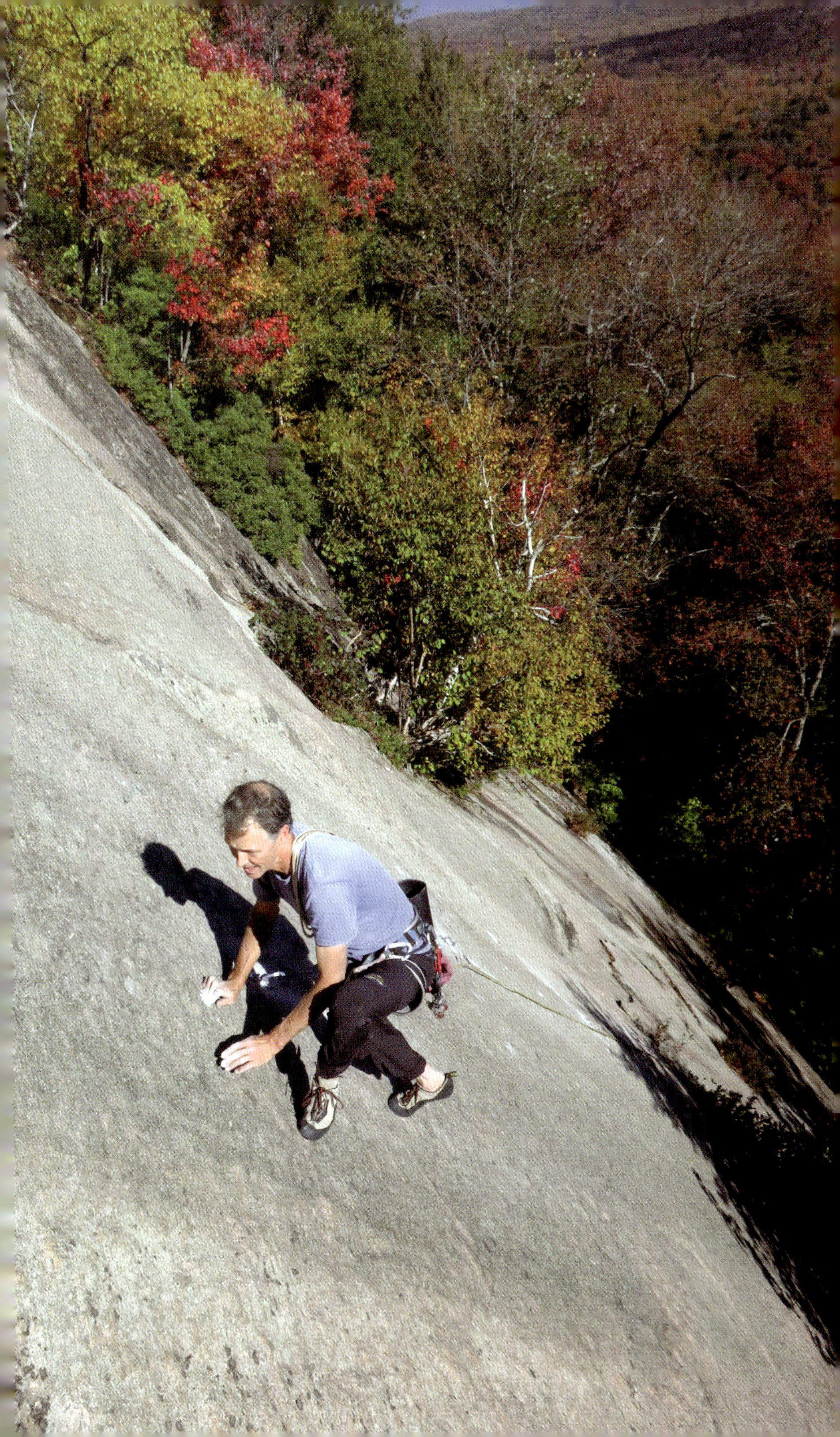

Indian Lake

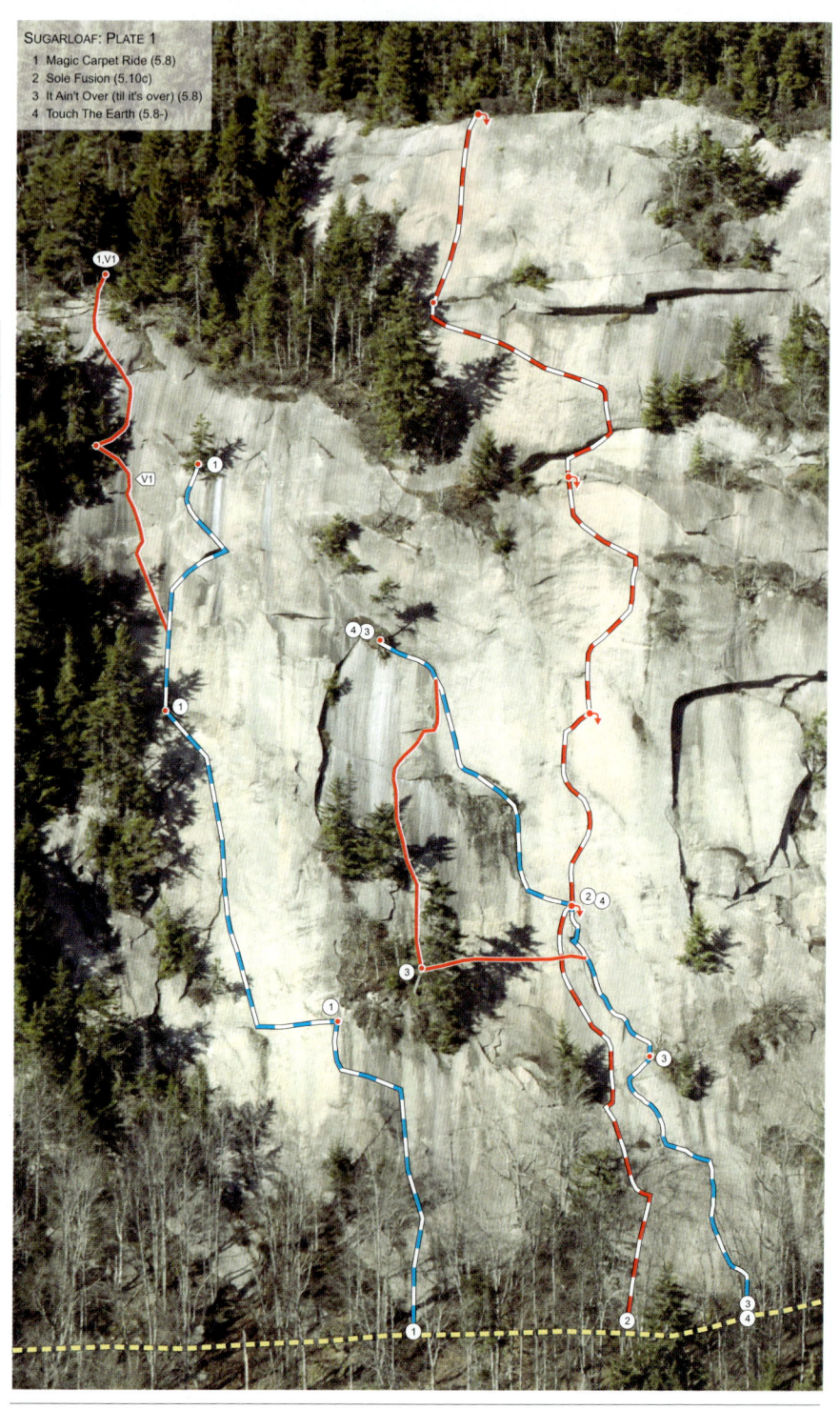

SUGARLOAF: PLATE 1
1 Magic Carpet Ride (5.8)
2 Sole Fusion (5.10c)
3 It Ain't Over (til it's over) (5.8)
4 Touch The Earth (5.8-)

268

along the way for protection. He named the route **For What It's Worth**, and it ranks as one of the boldest solo new route attempts in the park. He reported the route as 5.9; yeah right! Welch returned 27 years later with Lawyer and, over two days, they replaced much of the ancient hardware and extended the route to the top. A week later, the pair returned and straightened out P1, moving it left to make it completely independent of the neighboring routes.
FA (P1: 5.8 X, P2: 5.10c) Nov 19, 1985, Tad Welch (roped solo)
FA (P3-P5) Sep 20, 2013, Jim Lawyer, Tad Welch
FA (P1 redirected) Sep 26, 2013, Tad Welch, Jim Lawyer, David Buzzelli

3 It Ain't Over (til it's over) 5.8 R 350' ★★
Start: Same as **Touch The Earth**.
P1 5.7 X: Climb P1 of **Touch The Earth** to the clump of birch trees. 100'
P2 5.7 PG: Climb clean slab up and left (5.7) to a shallow, right-facing, left-leaning corner system of **Touch The Earth**. Go up this until you can traverse directly left across four shallow, left-facing corners to the top corner of a forested ledge. 110'
P3 5.8 R: Go straight up a narrow face between opposing corners. Move out right when the trees crowd in from the left, and follow shallow black ramps. Stay right of two small overhangs (5.8 R) to a small right-facing corner that rounds off to become a flake (may take small gear). Traverse left from this until it is possible to make a dicey step (crux) to a ledge at the bottom of a left-facing corner. Belay at the spruce tree directly above. 140'
Gear: Double ropes and micronuts helpful.
Descent: Two double-rope rappels straight down.
FA Aug 31, 2001, Mike Rawdon, Bill Bitting, Brad Austin, Eldeva Tofte

4 Touch The Earth 5.8- R 300'
Start: 25' right of **Sole Fusion** (and slightly uphill) is an 8'-high right-facing flake–corner 20' up, the only feature on this slab. Begin 15' to the right at a head-high horizontal edge.
P1 5.7 X: Mantle onto the ledge, then up several scoops until you can traverse left to the right-facing flake–corner (first gear). Go up this, then follow a fragile right-facing, right-leaning flake to a narrow ledge. Traverse left 15', then climb another fragile right-facing flake to its top. Foot traverse right to a birch clump, then friction up and left to a jug (runout) to gain a shallow, right-facing, left-leaning corner system. Up this to its top, then up perched flakes to a good stance at the top of the blocks; fixed anchor. 150'
P2 5.7 PG: Face climb up and left past a blueberry ledge to a small ceiling. Thin moves (crux) lead to better holds and a spruce tree (shared with **It Ain't Over**). 150'
FA Sep, 1985, Tad Welch (roped solo)

Indian Lake

5 The Pusher 5.9 G 90' ★★
Named for another Steppenwolf song. This is a great feature, but ends in the middle of nowhere. A good candidate for extending.
Start: Scramble 4th class to the top of the left-rising ramp of **Fistful of Stoppers**, then up to the highest point on the vegetated ledges above. Belay on the left side.
P1 5.9 G: Traverse left to a position just right of a blueberry ledge and below a thin crack. Follow this crack to its top. Fixed anchor. 90'
FA 1986, Tad Welch, Bill Widrig, Jamie Savage, Jim Lawyer

6 Fistful of Stoppers 5.8 PG 220' ★★★
Start: Locate the left-rising ramp at the start of **Meteorite**, then scramble up and left to a spruce tree belay. Begin where faint horizontal dike bands extend horizontally to the right from the ramp across. About 25' along these bands is a 12'-tall, shallow, left-facing corner.
P1 5.8 G (5.5 R): Traverse right following thin dikes to the 6'-high, shallow, left-facing corner. Up this corner, then up a black face with good edges to an overlap (first gear). Traverse left 12' on steep friction, then up a crack to another overlap. Over this at a sharp tips crack. Follow this for 50' as it gradually widens to hands, to an alcove at the base of a right-arching roof, marked by a scary, 8' wide, cantilevered flake held in place by magic. An adequate belay can be established (finger-sized cams) without using the flake. 140'
P2 5.5 G (5.2 R): Go straight up the arête (taking care not to touch the flake) past an hourglass flake and several horizontals to a slab. Angle up left on the clean dimpled slab to right-facing corner, then up to a tree ledge. 80'
FA Nov 10, 1991, Bill Widrig, Tad Welch

7 Quarter-Inch 5.5 410'
Seems to climb some of the same terrain as **Fistful of Stoppers**, but avoids the clean dramatic cracks of that route. It also adds a pitch to the top. Needs a modern ascent to confirm route details.
Start: Same as **Fistful of Stoppers**.
P1: Traverse right following thin dikes to the 6'-high, shallow, left-facing corner of **Fistful of Stoppers**. Continue right to the next left-facing corner (join **Meteorite** here) and follow this past the **Meteorite** belay to a high tree. 130'
P2 5.5 G (5.2 R): Push left though bushes across easy friction to an alcove at the left end of an overlap (the P1 belay alcove for **Fistful of Stoppers**). Follow P2 **Fistful of Stoppers** to the tree island. 130'
P3: Surmount overlap and friction up to mossy cracks. Climb up and left to 2"-wide, short, vertical crack (last protection). Friction up 30' (crux) and an easier 20' to a small spruce, then up the last 20' to the top. 150'
FA Aug 26, 1978, Mike Pinard, Rick Morse

Indian Lake

SUGARLOAF: PLATE 2
5 The Pusher (5.9)
6 Fistful of Stoppers (5.8)
7 Quarter-Inch (5.5)
8 Meteorite (5.8)

Indian Lake

SUGARLOAF: PLATE 3
9 Superman Flake (5.8)
10 Superman Flake Alternative Finish (5.10)
11 High Plains Drifter (5.10-)

271

Indian Lake

8 Meteorite 5.8 PG 220' ★★★

The surface of the slab here is "thermally responsive"—the vertical crack at and just above the first belay will close significantly as the sun warms the slab.

Start: On the left end of the cliff is a clean wide slab of It Ain't Over. Walk right 150', then steeply uphill and right another 100', and locate a left-rising ramp 543331,4844664. Where the ramp begins is a left-facing, left-leaning corner that arches left into an overlap that becomes a brushy break that extends for 60'. Begin 15' left along this left-rising ramp.

P1 5.8- PG: Go straight up to an overlap (5.7 PG), over this to the brushy break. Continue up a black streak (5.8-) to another overlap using tiny right-facing edges. Break the overlap at a right-facing corner, then move up and left to an "eye" hole in the rock that suggests the route's name, then continue up and left to a vegetated island with a tree. 90'

P2 5.8 PG: Climb the corner to its top, step out right, go past a stance, then work back up left to an obvious large left-facing flake, staying right of bushes. From the top of the flake, climb a shallow, left-facing corner (5.7+). At its top, traverse right and work up to a right-facing corner. Layback up the corner crack as it thins to fingertips (5.8 PG, small wires of questionable strength). Traverse right and climb up into the tree island. There is gear to back up the single solid tree. 130'

Descent: Rappel straight down. Double 60m ropes just make it.

Gear: Micronuts and screamers helpful.

FA (P1) Jul 3, 2000, Mike Rawdon, Scott Rawdon, Brad Austin
FA (complete) Jul 29, 2001, Mike Rawdon, Kevin Moyles

9 Superman Flake 5.8 PG (5.4 R) 360' ★★★

Start: 100' right of Meteorite and 450' left of Return to Sender below a large, 5-sided flake 15' up and shaped like the emblem on Superman's chest 543356,4844683. Higher up you can see P2—two V-shaped blocks stuck in the large, arching overhang and a prominent large spruce tree above the arch. The second pitch climbs past the right block to the tree. There are two ways to finish from there: a single pitch of 5.5 (5.4 R), or a two pitch 5.10 line to the very top of the slab.

P1 5.7 PG: Climb a curvy crack to the right side of the flake, then go left to a couple of trees and a grassy ramp. Work up to a short, right-facing corner that arches slightly to the right. Don't climb up this; rather, step out right to a left-rising ledge (just below black rock) and then up past vague horizontal edges until it is possible to step right to a maple tree. 130'

P2 5.8 PG: Climb up past a white birch to the double overlap (fixed pin). Step up to the rightmost V-shaped block (the left V-shaped block appears to be dangerously loose), undercling this right, and surmount the second tier of the overlap. Up the face (bolt), then angle up left to the large spruce tree. 110'

P3 5.5 PG (5.4 R): Layback a left-facing corner for 30' (the Superman Flake Alternative Finish continues up this corner) until it is easy to step over it. Move easily out right onto the face, then go straight up well-featured rock (5.4 R); aim for a broad depression that leads to a tree at the edge of the woods above. 120'

Descent: Three rappels with double 60m ropes.
FA Oct 11, 2010, Mike Rawdon, Ryan Smith

10 Superman Flake Alternative Finish 5.10 PG 250' ★★★

Start: The top of P2 of Superman Flake.

P1 5.6 G: Layback a left-facing, left-arching corner to its end. Clip the lower bolt, and step down to belay in a stand of birch trees. 80'

P2 5.10 PG: Climb the face past 2 bolts to easier ground. Angle slightly left and past a couple small trees to the top of the slab (5.4 R). 170'

FA Jul 7, 2011, Mike Rawdon, Dolgio Nergui

11 High Plains Drifter 5.10- PG 415' ★★★

Start: 200' right of Superman Flake on top of a comfortable rock ledge below an overhang 15' up. The left side of the overhang has a right-facing open book corner. Needs a modern ascent to confirm details of the upper pitches.

P1 5.10- PG: Go up a left-leaning crack on the slab to the overhang. Over this at one of two possible breaks with good protection, then up and left to a spruce that sits just below the highest point on a ledge. 50'

P2: An excellent pitch. Follow a hairline crack past a fixed pin to thin face moves (crux) and a bucket. Layback a beautiful thin flake and continue up and left (loose flakes here) to spacious ledge. 75'

P3: Climb the fingertip crack over bulge to hand jams and block. Push through shrubs and go up a low-angle left-facing corner to tree belay above. 140'

P4: Continue up and right on low-angle rock to summit. 150'

FA (cleaning on aid) Apr, 1992, Tad Welch, Bill Widrig
FFA May, 1992, Bill Widrig, Jamie Savage

12 Return to Sender (aka Open Shutter) 5.8 R 480' ★★★★

Start: 250' right of High Plains Drifter, and 550' right Meteorite at a prominent, reasonably clean, left-facing, left-leaning corner that begins at a clump of several white birch trees 20' up 543423,4844749. There is a 3" crack splitting the corner a short way up.

P1 5.5 G: Climb the corner to its top. Move right to a mantel move in pink rock at a 2-3" horizontal crack. Weave up easy slab past small trees and vertical grooves to the belay at a tree below a TCU seam. 170'

P2 5.8 PG: Follow the TCU seam to the ledge above. Traverse right past 2 small trees to a right-arching overlap. Step over this near its right end and work up past a bolt, then follow a fingercrack to a small belay stance at a 0.5"–1" horizontal crack. This is about 15' below another bolt, which you can use as part of the anchor. 100'

P3 5.7 R: Climb the face above (bolt), then continue up for 35' (5.7, no protection). Step left to a right-arching corner-overhang, continue to the next overhang, then traverse right to belay at some trees under the left end of a prominent, triangular roof. 90'

P4 5.5 G: Climb a dihedral past a small tree, then up an hourglass-shaped feature on the right face to a stance with perched blocks and an outstanding view. Go up and left, passing just right of a long ceiling, to the summit. 120'

Descent: Rappel back to the third and first belays with two 60m ropes.

History: A new camera was accidentally dropped from the top, christening the route and leading to the original name, Open Shutter, as reported in Mellor's 1983 guide. Due to confusion in reporting, the name should have been Return to Sender. It was climbed 23 years later and, thinking it was a new route, named Bees Three. The route described here is slightly different than the original line: P2 is more direct (with a bolt) instead of moving right to a tree island, and the bolt on P3 resolves a serious runout (both were placed without knowledge of the previous ascent).
FA Aug 5, 1979, Rick Morse, Mike Traynor
FA (P2) Sep, 2002, Mike Rawdon, Nate Bryant, Dawn Alguard, Tim Cochran

13 Deja View 5.8 R 430' ★★★★

A really good climb except for the tree-tunneling at each belay. Named for the shameless previewing of the first pitch on rappel.

Start: 225' right of Return to Sender 543449,4844794 at an attractive, left-facing, clean open book with a good layback crack. There's a toaster-oven sized flake at the base of the corner, and 30' right is a sharp, left-facing corner which forms a prow 40' up (Another Botanical Wonder).

P1 5.8 R: Layback the crack-edge until it ends (5.6), then continue up to a bolt. Angle right (5.8) to some welcome edges in the greenish rock (small gear possible) then back left on black rock above a grassy island to a shallow, right-facing corner. Climb this until it ends, then make a long reach left to a square block-flake. Belay at a spruce tree above. Extra finger-size cams recommended. 150'

P2 5.7 PG: Angle left onto the face above the belay tree, then climb well-featured, pink rock past a bolt to a ledge. Skirt the large ceiling directly above at its left end (watch for pinched rope here), then follow a long, left-facing corner (5.7, small wires) until it ends at a smaller ceiling. Step left into the bushes and wade 20' up to the P3 belay of Return to Sender under the left end of the large triangular roof. 160'

P3 5.6 PG: Follow a right-angling seam to the right end of the triangular roof until clean, coarse rock leads a few feet further right to an A-shaped break. Step up to a black overhang with an alarming patch of lichen under it, and undercling around the left end. Follow a vertical crack which becomes a vegetated left-facing corner to rough, water-streaked, black rock at the top of the slab (Return to Sender joins here) 120'
FA (initial crack) Aug, 2005, Jeremy Morgan, Mike Rawdon
FA (upper P1) Sep 13, 2007, Mike Rawdon, Matt Shoemaker, Ian Guertin
FA (complete) Sep 26, 2008, Mike Rawdon, Mike McGrath

14 Another Botanical Wonder 5.8 R 450'

The start needs to be dry to be climbable.
Start: Same as Deja View.

P1 5.6 G: Walk right to the left-facing corner. Layback this to a large spruce tree. 80'

P2 5.5 G: Continue up the corner above, then follow dirt ramps, blocks, and corners to belay at another spruce tree out left. Rappel is possible from here with 2 ropes. 90'

P3 5.8 R: Tunnel through the trees at the belay, and follow a line of bushes up 35', perhaps climbing the clean rock to their left. Once past the higher of two small maple trees, traverse straight out left to the base of a left-facing corner (almost meeting Deja View). Follow the corner until it arches left, then step right onto the lichen-covered face and climb up (5.8 R) to a belay at a stout tree on the left. The best climbing may be a few feet right of the trees, then grab a branch and swing in. 100'

P4 5.6 PG: Tunnel through or around the tree. Climb out left and up to a single spruce. Climb up to join Deja View's last pitch at the small undercling overhang, pass this around its left end, then follow a left-facing corner up to a grassy stance (loose block out left). Go straight to the top. 180'

Descent: Rappel as for Return to Sender.

History: This route is a contender for being one of the original routes on the cliff, Why (Kris Solem, Rick Morse, 8/7/1979), named for the Y branch at the top. The only documented landmark for Why is that it's 70' right of Return to Sender, which it clearly isn't. The climbing description, however, roughly matches this route.
FA (P1-P2) Aug 31, 2007, Mike Rawdon, Ian Guertin
FA (P3) Sep 13, 2007, Ian Guertin, Matt Shoemaker, Mike Rawdon
FA (P4) Sep 29, 2007, Mike Rawdon, Todd Paris

15 Heroes 5.8 PG 400' ★★★

After a typically grungy P1, this route has some of the most delightful climbing on the cliff up a long, dramatic wall which is well-featured with cracks of all sizes. The direct finish is a blast.

Start: 100' left of Tier Pressure at a level spot below a thin strip of slab with a clear view of the full height of the cliff above 543450,4844877.

P1 5.8 G: Wade up the ferns and brush on the left side of the slab past a long vertical root. Step out onto the rock when it's clean enough. Get some gear at a square-ish, orange block in the middle of the depression above, then make a big step right (5.8). Follow blocky features up to a belay at the higher of two clumps of maple trees. 120'

P2 5.6 G: Follow a vertical crack through a bulge above the belay to a left-facing corner, the signature feature of the route with a delightful finger crack. Above are two spruce trees; step left above the left tree to continue up the left-facing corner to a belay on a small but pleasant ledge. 100'

P3 5.8 G: Follow the corner directly above, then break an overhang at its right edge (crux). Continue another 50' to a bolt, (V1) then make a pendulum-protected downclimb into the trees on the left for the belay. 100'

Indian Lake

SUGARLOAF: PLATE 4
12 Return to Sender (5.8)
13 Deja View (5.8)
14 Another Botanical Wonder (5.8)

*Ben Brooke follows P3 of **Heroes** (5.8).*
Photo by Mike Rawdon.

Indian Lake

SUGARLOAF: PLATE 5
15 Heroes (5.8)
16 Tier Pressure (5.8+)
17 Blind Date (5.7)
18 Psychotic (5.10+)

P4 5.7 PG: Go around the left end of the ceiling, then up the right side of a large, scary block somewhat wedged in the cliff. Make an undercling traverse right (exciting 5.7) then up into the trees. 80'

V1 Direct Finish 5.9 G: From the bolt, aim for the middle of the ceiling. Get solid gear (blue Alien), then undercling out right to the end of the overhang. Continue straight up slab to top. Grade depends on finger size.

History: Climbed on the 10th anniversary of the 9/11 attacks.

Gear: Bring extra finger-size gear.

Descent: Rappel to P3, then straight down two more raps with double ropes.

FA (P1-P3) Sep 11, 2011, Mike Rawdon, Jane Pike
FA (P4) Jul 30, 2012, Mike Rawdon, Ben Brooke
FA (V1) Sep 17, 2012, Mike Rawdon

16 Tier Pressure 5.8+ R 420' ★★★★

Climbs through the maze of arches which dominate the right side of the cliff. The first pitch, while good, is dirty (and grows in quickly). V1 provides a reliable way to avoid this, and gain access to the remarkable climbing above.

Start: 450' right of **Return to Sender** (and 100' right of **Heroes**), at a low-angle, left-facing corner with a 2'-wide triangular ceiling 7' up 543479,4844874. The crack up the corner is usually sporting a line of ferns, with moss on the lower section. Another landmark is a nearly level 3'x5' rock on the ground just back from the base which provides a good bench for changing shoes and sorting gear.

P1 5.8+ PG: (V1) Layback the left-facing corner to its top. Step right to a fixed anchor. (Note: the pitch is significantly harder if damp or if the crack is wet or heavily vegetated.) 80'

P2 5.7 PG: Follow a shallow, right-facing groove above, stay right at the first fork and left at the second (do not climb up to the diamond-shaped roof). Follow an arching left-facing corner, step over it near its top to a fixed anchor. 110'

P3 5.7 G: Move up and left for 25', then follow a right-facing open book straight up into a corner-alcove and a fixed piton belay. 70'

*Elaine Matthews follows P2 (5.7) of Deja View (5.8).
Photo by Mike Rawdon.*

P4 5.8 R: Stem the corner directly above the anchor (5.8) until it is possible to swing over onto the slab above the left wall. (V2) Get some gear on the slab, then angle up and right and cross the first overlap at the right end of an 8'-wide horizontal section of overlap (tight purple TCU above this step). Continue up and right to pass the next overlap at a small, pointed corner (fixed knifeblade) with a fun "turn around" move. (V3) Continue rightwards past a block and tree, then friction straight up and climb a pointed flake to the trees. 160'

V1 5.7+ PG: The line of the original ascent: Begin 25' left in a triangular depression that narrows into a left-facing, right-arching corner. Climb easily up the depression to a short handcrack. Up this, then right to an incipient crack and stance with fixed anchor. 90'

V2 5.7 PG: Follow a leftwards line past a couple of knifeblades and a bolt and continue sideways to a belay in the trees. 150'

V3 5.8 R: A high-quality alternative finish. Angle left across the slab past a bolt; aim for the wide crack (#3, #4 Camalots) at the base of the right-facing corner that leads steeply to the top. Climb up one overlap here (dirty), then undercling dramatically out right until you can reach over the lip and gain the upper crack to move back left into the corner to a fixed anchor. 160'

History: Yet another route that saw multiple parties thinking their ascent was the first. Although originally climbed using V1, the route is now climbed as described with the V3 finish. Portions of this route could be part of the lost route **Unfinished Business** (Rick Morse and Mike Pinard, 9/1/1978); the description provided for that route is ambiguous, so we may never know with any degree of certainty. Suffice to say, this is the most logical line on this end of the cliff, so it's seems most likely.

Descent: From the top of V2, rappel as for **Heroes**. For V3, rappel to the top of P2, then to the ground.

Gear: Double ropes.

FA (complete with V1) May, 1985, Tad Welch, Bill Widrig
FA (P1 as described) 1992, Tad Welch, Jim Lawyer, Bill Widrig, Jamie Savage
FA (V1) May, 1985, Tad Welch, Bill Widrig
FA (V2) Sep 5, 2003, Mike Rawdon, Peter Borden
FA (V3) Aug 31, 2007, Ian Guertin, Mike Rawdon

17 Blind Date 5.7 PG (5.5 R) 170' ★★

Start: At the top of P2 of **Tier Pressure**.

P1 5.7 PG: Angle up and left a few steps, then traverse directly left about 40' to a small ledge of blueberries at the base of a left-facing corner-ramp. Follow this for 50' until it steepens and narrows, then exit out right on good holds to a spruce tree belay (1"-2" crack here also). 110'

P4 5.5 R: Follow a black slab up to the trees. 60'

Descent: Rappel as for **Heroes**.

FA Aug 18, 2011, Mike Rawdon, Mitchel Hoffman

18 Psychotic 5.10+ TR 80' ★★★

Smear up the clean buttress directly under the P1 anchor of **Tier Pressure**. This will take your friction climbing to a whole new level!

FA (TR) Aug 21, 2003, Andrew Kratz, Mike Rawdon

Indian Lake

CEDAR RIVER CRAG

Location	Off Cedar River Road, accessed from NY 28 / NY 30 west of Indian Lake
Aspect	Southeast
Height	100'
Quality	
Approach	5 min, easy
Summary	A small roadside crag with one good toprope route.

Located on Water Barrel Mountain, Cedar River Crag was first visited as a consolation prize when the first ascentionists realized that the neighboring cliffs of Sugarloaf Mountain were on private property. This is a steep, sheer cliff with several right-facing corners that begin on a tree-covered ledge that rises to the right, dividing the right end of the cliff in two.

DIRECTIONS (MAP PAGE 264)
The cliff is located on Cedar River Road, which begins 2.1 miles north of Indian Lake (from the intersection of NY 28 and NY 30).

From the intersection of NY 28 / NY 30 and Cedar River Road (0.0 mile), drive west on Cedar River Road. Winter maintenance ends at 7.1 miles, the pavements ends at 7.8 miles, and the state land boundary is reached at 10.2 miles. At 10.4 miles, you reach a parking area along the shoulder of the road 543399,4843666, next to a culvert, before the height of land and before the Wakely Dam (at 11.0 miles).

Hike 5 min uphill and northwest toward talus beneath the cliff 543319,4843760.

1 Fritzie's Honor 5.9+ TR 85' ★

Locate the right-rising ledge that splits the right end of the cliff in two. From the left end of the ledge, this is the third right-facing corner that begins above a shoulder-high ceiling. Move over the ceiling, then up the corner to a right-rising, stepped overhang. Go left to a vertical crack and follow it to the top.
FA (TR) Sep 16, 2000, Steve Adler, Mike Caruso

LEDGE MOUNTAIN

Location	East of NY 28 / NY 30 north of Indian Lake
Aspect	South
Height	70'
Quality	
Approach	40 min, moderate
Summary	A few short routes on a clean wall that is surrounded by lots of mediocre cliffs.

	2		1		3
-5.6	5.7	5.8	5.9	5.10	5.11	5.12	5.13+	total

Visible to the north when you cross the bridge over the Cedar River, 1.9 miles north of Indian Lake on NY 28 / NY 30, Ledge Mountain has many cliffbands, and a few have decent potential for climbing. The lowest cliffband is approximately 200' long and includes the White Wall, a clean, dry buttress with less than vertical face climbing above a level base area. Further exploration would reveal lots of rock in every direction, OK bouldering potential, and a few crack lines.

HISTORY
Mike Caruso and Steve Adler reported toproping a few face climbs on a lower cliffband in 2000. Lack of natural protection and easy toprope access convinced them that lead climbing made little sense at the time.

DIRECTIONS (MAP PAGE 264)
From Indian Lake (at the intersection of NY 28 and NY 30), drive 4.0 miles north on the combined NY 28 / NY 30. Park on the east side of NY 28 / NY 30 next to the northernmost of two culverts (with guardrails) 554988,4850500. The Sawyer Mountain Trailhead is 0.4 mile farther north on the west side of the road.

From the guardrail (0 hr 0 min), bushwhack northeast on a bearing of 64°, cross a brook, and continue to a snowmobile trail that is reached at 10 min. Locate a small brook that crosses the snowmobile trail at a log-filled ditch. Enter the woods left (north) of the small brook and continue on the 64° bearing. Traverse the side of a hill before dropping down to a brook, reached at 20 min, that has a 50' by 50' clearing upstream of a forest of dense conifers. Cross the brook, continue on the bearing, and follow a herd path uphill past conifers and into open woods. You'll encounter a second small clearing and minor boulderfield at 30 min. Turn right and contour east across the hillside and beneath small cliffs. Resist the temptation to hike uphill toward larger cliffs. You'll encounter the left end of the lowest cliffband at 40 min. The White Wall is halfway along the cliffband and has a narrow traverse ledge 30' up 555847,4850992.

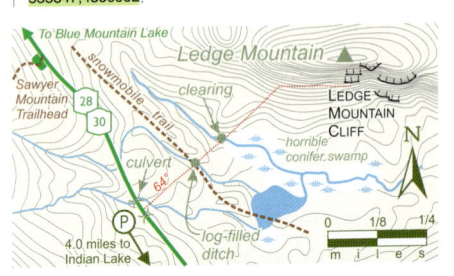

DESCENT OPTIONS
On top of the White Wall is a tree with a fixed anchor that is shared by all three routes. Hiking off (left) is easy.

White Wall

1 Invincible Machine 5.8+ PG 70' ★★

Start: Beneath a wedged flake 10' up.
P1 5.8+ PG: Up a left-rising crack to the flake. Carefully climb past the flake, then up another left-rising crack (crux) to the narrow traverse ledge. Foot-traverse to the right, then up the center of the face and top out at left-leaning cracks. 70'
Gear: To 4".
FA Jul 12, 2007, Jeremy Haas, Stuart Linke

Indian Lake

2 Stretch Armstrong 5.11a G 70' ★★
Start: At the center of the wall, at a left-rising ledge at chest height.
P1 5.11a G: Up the face to a horizontal crack at 12'. Stretch to a higher horizontal crack (crux) and mantel to the narrow traverse ledge. Up the face and top out at left-leaning cracks as for Invincible Machine. 70'
Gear: To 4".
FA Jul 12, 2007, Jeremy Haas

3 Intelligent Design 5.8+ G 70' ★★
Start: At the right end of a left-rising ledge at chest height.
P1 5.8+ G: Out a right-rising fingercrack, then up a vertical seam. Climb up a scoop and top out on a blunt arête. 70'
FA Jul 12, 2007, Stuart Linke, Jeremy Haas

CASTLE ROCK

Location	Blue Mountain Lake, accessed from the combined NY 30 / NY 28N
Aspect	South
Height	120'
Quality	★★
Approach	30 min, easy
Summary	Small cliff with a couple hard routes; some potential for new routes, and a great scrambling destination.

1				1	1		3
-5.6	5.7	5.8	5.9	5.10	5.11	5.12	5.13+	total

Castle Rock is a very popular mini-summit that sits above the northwest shore of Blue Mountain Lake. There's a DEC trail to the cliff and an open-rock summit from which there are views in all directions, especially of Blue Mountain Lake.

Despite the excellent rock quality, the roped climbing potential is small, as the cliff is broken up into ledges and short discontinuous faces. But it's a great destination for scrambling in the house-sized boulders that make up the lower section of the cliff. There are passageways into hidden rooms, 4th class chimneys that lead through holes to perches, and many isolated, hard-to-reach ledges with views and privacy. This is a great destination if you're in the area and need a half-day diversion.

Sassafras and I Can't Believe It's Not Butter are located on summit directly below the popular viewpoint. There are no cracks for natural protection on the top, so you'll need 30' of extra rope to anchor back to trees, which is awkward if there are 20 hikers picnicking on top.

HISTORY
Hikers have been scrambling among the boulders for a long time, and, as evidenced by the rubber marks on the rock, even up many of the 4th class chimneys. Jordan Wemett visited in 2006 and reported several boulder problems.

DIRECTIONS
From Blue Mountain Lake, at the intersection of NY 28 and NY 30 (0.0 mile), follow the combined NY 30 / NY 28N north (towards Long Lake). At 0.6 mile, turn left onto Maple Lodge Road, also signposted for "Minnowbrook Conference Center." Follow the road to its end at 1.7 miles; there are signs for trailhead parking on the left, and there's a DEC kiosk on the right with signs for Castle Rock and Upper Sargent Pond 0544108,4857908.

From the kiosk (0 hr 0 min), follow the trail, which at first is actually a dirt road that provides access to more private homes, marked with red discs. Stay to the right at all intersections. At 7 min the trail splits; straight (red discs) goes the long way to Castle Rock and Sargent Pond, and left (yellow discs) goes to Castle Rock the short way. Go left and cross a bridge. At 16 min, reach an intersection with a trail that goes left to the lake (blue discs), and continue straight, following the yellow discs. At 30 min the trail reaches the cliff at an amphitheater where you walk between the cliff and a large boulder below an enormous roof, 20' deep, and 15' up 542780,4858188. This amphitheater is a popular spot for scrambling and bouldering.

1 I Can't Believe It's Not Butter 5.11b G 50' ★★★
More like "I can't believe it's not 5.8." This snaking finger- and hand-crack looks easy, but don't be deceived—it's a beast. Great jams and fingerlocks, but sustained with no feet. Use plenty of gear because the route leans left above a rising slab that makes every piece seem like you're placing your second piece.
Start: This route is located on the west face of the summit block. From the summit overlooking Blue Mountain Lake, scramble west down a slab, then back to the base of the wall. Begin in a shallow right-facing corner at the base of a snaking crack.
P1 5.11b G: Go up the corner for 6', then hand traverse left in the crack to a fist-sized pod where the crack turns vertical and pinches to fingers. Up this (crux) to where the crack snakes left. Move left to a decent foot rest, then up the easier handcrack to the top. 50'
Gear: Cams: 1 ea #0.4, #3, #2; 2 ea #0.5, #0.75.
FA May 11, 2011, Jim Lawyer, Martine Schaer
FFA Aug 3, 2013, Jim Lawyer, David Buzzelli

2 Side Boob 5.12a G 40' ★★★
A short, naturally clean line with a couple of difficult sections, a baseball-shaped key hold, and a super-cool topout.
Start: Same as I Can't Believe It's Not Butter.
● **P1 5.12a G:** Go up the corner to a good stance with a baseball hold. Make a hard move onto this hold (crux), the mantel onto some friction slopers to top out. 40'
Gear: 1 ea #4 Camalot (or a large nut).
FA Aug 3, 2013, David Buzzelli, Jim Lawyer

3 Enjoy the Little Things 5.4 G (5.1 R) 120' ★★
Easy climbing, naturally clean rock, and great views.
Start: The route begins on the highest forested ledge

Indian Lake

Jim Lawyer on the first free ascent of **I Can't Believe It's Not Butter** *(5.11b).*

above the huge roof that you walk under on the hiking trail. There are many hidden chimneys and passageways that link up to this ledge. The easiest is to walk 30' left from the giant roof to a person-sized slot that leads into a hidden room. Instead of going through the slot, walk 15' left and scramble up a chimney to a forested ledge below a slab. From the upper right side of this ledge, make a puzzling move up another slot to a higher forested ledge. Begin at a shallow, right-facing corner with a good crack. Another landmark is a very long, right-leaning, right-facing, fern-filled flake that begins 2' to the right.

P1 5.4 G (5.1 R): Up the crack in the shallow corner to a good horizontal on the left. Continue up the corner to a good stance at its top. Step left and friction up a clean slab to gain a left-rising, shallow blueberry ramp-ledge. Move left 6' on the ramp-ledge to an unlikely bulge and pull over using an amazing bucket. Step right and follow good jugs to a tree ledge. 120'
Gear: To 3".
Descent: Contour 75' left to the base of a slab that sits directly below the summit viewpoint. Scramble up and right around this slab to the summit, then follow the hiking trail back to the base.
ACB Oct 19, 2010, Jim Lawyer (solo)

TIRRELL POND

Location	East of NY 30, accessed from the Blue Mountain Trailhead
Aspect	West
Height	250'
Quality	
Approach	1 hr 45 min, moderate
Summary	Run-out slab routes on an overgrown cliff in a beautiful setting above a pond.

3							3
-5.6	5.7	5.8	5.9	5.10	5.11	5.12	5.13+	total

Tirrell Pond is a popular hike from the well-known trailhead for Blue Mountain. Although the climbing is not exceptional, the setting of boreal forests along a sandy-shored pond is outstanding. Campsites are plentiful, as are the seaplane arrivals (hence the route name **No Nuts, No Seaplanes**). The cliff is a steep slab with no obvious cracks. It is very dirty, and only **Chicken Soup** can be recommended. However, a very clean (and un-climbed) 5th-class slab is located 200' right (south) of the start of **Chicken Soup**.

HISTORY

The first known climbers to ascend the slabs at Tirrell Pond were Dave and Lois Legg in the late 1970s. They would wander through the woods with a Goldline rope and toprope exposed bits of rock—no harnesses, no rock shoes. They discovered Shanty Cliff in this same delightfully casual manner.

Twenty years later, Emmett Dwyer saw the slab from Blue Mountain and decided to organize, in his mind, a Shackleton-style expedition to explore it. He recruited complete strangers on the Internet and, armed with an elaborate menu, spent a weekend in 1999 climbing new routes.

DIRECTIONS

Park at the Blue Mountain Trailhead 545853,4858013 on NY 30, 0.4 mile north of the Adirondack Museum in the town of Blue Mountain Lake and 9.3 miles south of the town of Long Lake (at the intersection of NY 28N and NY 30). The Tirrell Pond Trail marked with yellow discs leaves from the north end of the parking lot. Hike on the level trail, and at 1 hr, you'll reach the intersection with the Northville-Placid Trail (blue blazes), 3.3 miles from the road. The cliff is visible from the trail junction. Go right (south) and hike a short distance to a lean-to where several herd paths head left (east) to the sandy shore on the north end of Tirrell Pond, reached at 1 hr 15 min. Go left along the shore to a "No Camping" sign and a yellow-marked trail that heads left into the woods and circles the pond. At 1 hr 20 min, the trail crosses a creek; leave the trail to the left and follow the creek upstream. You'll immediately encounter a beaver dam followed by meadows with views of the cliff ahead. Bushwhack due east on a bearing of 90° to the base of the cliff 550945,4859952, reached at 1 hr 45 min. Climbs are described left to right, but locating the start of Chicken Soup is necessary in order to locate the other routes.

DESCENT OPTIONS

Rappel from trees at the left (north) end of the cliff.

1 Alien Shrimp 5.6 R 220'
Start: From the start of Chicken Soup on the right side of the cliff, traverse left across an exposed slab with clumps of soil and grass for 80' to a tree belay common with No Nuts, No Seaplanes. An alternative start, on the high vegetation on the lower left side of the cliff, is 20' below the recommended start.

P1 5.5 R: From the tree belay, make a rising left ascent on small ledges to the left side of the lower wall. This pitch follows the easiest, and somewhat clean, rock just right of the line of trees. 120'

P2 5.6 R: Traverse left beneath the more significant traverse dike, cross a black water streak, and belay at trees at the left end of the cliff. 100'
FA Oct 9, 1999, Steven Cherry, Bob Monty

2 No Nuts, No Seaplanes 5.5 R 290'
Start: From the start of Chicken Soup on the right side of the cliff, traverse left across an exposed slab with clumps of soil and grass for 80' to a tree belay beneath a 4'-long overlap 10' above the highest vegetation.

P1 5.5 R: A clean start climbs straight up the middle of the face until the angle eases. Climb a left-rising traverse on the obvious traverse dike to a tree belay. 70'

P2 5.5 R: Traverse left in the dike (poor protection but secure climbing), cross a black water streak, and belay at trees at the left end of the cliff. 100'

P3 5.4 R: Climb water grooves to the top. 120'
FA Oct 9, 1999, Emmett Dwyer, Brad Austin

3 Chicken Soup 5.6 X 250' ★
Start: At the lowest part of the cliff is a right-facing, right-rising band of rock with a cairn at its base. Hike up and right toward the right end of the cliff, then traverse back left to a tree-covered ledge 150' above the lowest part of the cliff. The mossy cliff is broken by a clean strip of rock that is immediately left of a large scoop 60' above the tree ledge.

P1 5.6 X: Clean rock (crux) leads to the scoop, then steepens. Climb on positive holds to a right-facing flake (protectable) that is visible from the tree ledge. Angle up and left to a belay in a corner. 80'

P2 5.3 PG: Continue up the lower-angle slab to a tree belay on the left. 100'

P3 5.3 PG: Continue up the slab to the trees at the top of the cliff. 70'
FA Oct 9, 1999, Mike Rawdon, Julie Haas

MCGINN MOUNTAIN

Visible from the NY 28 bridge over Lake Abernaki, east of Indian Lake, McGinn Mountain has two south-facing cliffbands beneath its summit. A left-facing corner on the upper cliffband is the only reported ascent on the mountain, called McWiessner (5.7 G; 120'; 2000; Steve Adler, Mike Caruso). Other left-facing corners on this cliffband, including the one at the right end where the cliff is tallest, remain unclimbed.

Trails on this mountain, including a ski trail that passes between the cliffbands, are no longer maintained. The approach begins from the Bullhead Pond Trailhead 561906,4850145, which is located on Chain Lakes Road 1.3 miles north of its intersection with NY 28. Follow the red-marked trail to its intersection with a yellow-marked trail at 15 min. Turn right onto the yellow-marked trail, which descends to the outlet stream from Bullhead Pond at a small dam. Cross the dam and hike west along the north shore of the pond. Cross a stream and, 30 min from the road, reach a second stream. Leave the shore and bushwhack northeast (on a bearing of 45°) following the second stream high above its bank on the right side. Continuing on that bearing leads to another drainage area on the right, then through open woods, eventually traversing up and right across level slabs and small ledges to the false summit. From here, head due north and descend gently toward the right (east) end of the lower cliffband 561049,4851758. Total hiking time to the cliff is 1 hr.

Indian Lake

STARBUCK MOUNTAIN

Location	Between North River and Indian Lake, accessed from NY 28
Aspect	South
Height	75'
Quality	★★
Approach	15 min, easy
Summary	Good selection of moderate crack routes on high-quality rock; shaded, buggy, and wet.

1	2	6	2	2		13
-5.6	5.7	5.8	5.9	5.10	5.11	5.12	5.13+	total

There's a good amount of exposed rock on the south face of Starbuck Mountain facing NY 28, most of it junk. On the southeast side of the mountain, low down in the woods, in front of the jumbled mass of the main cliff, is this little gem containing moderate off-vertical crack climbs. It's small, but the approach is short, the cliff is mostly shaded, the base is open and comfortable, and it's easy to hike to the top to set topropes.

The cliff is roughly 300' wide, but the left end is broken and scruffy. There's a large, black chimney (the route **Perseid**) that marks the left end of the good rock. Just right of this is a 20'-tall block–tower that forms a left-facing corner. 25' from the right end of the cliff is a 5'-deep right-facing corner (the route **Gemini**).

The cliff suffers from seepage, which is what makes it a good ice climbing venue. Many of the quality lines have been generously cleaned, but with the seepage and the shade of the tree canopy they may revegetate more quickly than elsewhere, and be slow to dry. Starbuck is also an epicenter for biting insects, so visiting in the spring and summer may require a head net and repellent. The cliff is 0.5 mile from the road, so you'll hear distant vehicle traffic.

The cliff is a work-in-progress, and has a number of closed projects that are actively being worked.

DIRECTIONS (MAP PAGE 282)

Access to Starbuck Mountain is from NY 28. Park at the intersection of NY 28 and Cleveland Road 572837,4846568, 9.3 miles east of Indian Lake (measured from the intersection of NY 30 and NY 28 when driving towards North Creek) and 8.0 miles west of North Creek (measured from the intersection of NY 28 and NY 28N when driving towards Indian Lake). There is a giant, 8'-tall, red Adirondack chair on the south side of the road at this intersection with "Indian Lake" in yellow lettering.

Cross NY 28 directly across from Cleveland Road, hop the guard rail, and locate a well-worn herd path (0 hr 0 min). Follow the path northeast on a bearing of 31°. At 1 min, cross Raquette Brook, and at 2 min, walk under some power lines. At 15 min, reach the right end of the cliff just left of the right-facing corner of **Gemini** 573370,4847107.

HISTORY

In the winter of 2013, Mike Prince, Jay Harrison, and Ben Brooke explored the area for ice routes. Recognizing the potential for rock routes, they returned in the spring with Tom Lane and others to begin work, which is ongoing.

Perseid Area7

1 Unnamed1 Project

Closed project. Scramble up a few rock steps to at a crack 10' left of **Perseid**. Climb the crack to a stance below the left end of a bulge broken by parallel vertical seams 6" apart. Go over the bulge using the seams, then follow a crack straight up. Needs cleaning.

2 Perseid 5.7 G 60'

Climbs the big chimney. Slow to dry.
Start: Below the offset black chimney, 15' left of a 20'-tall block–tower that forms a clean left-facing corner.
P1 5.7 G: Up the chimney to a roof, step left, and continue up the chimney past some wide slots to a slab. Sling some trees, and climb the slab to the top. 60'
Gear: 1 ea #2, #3, #4, #5, #6 Camalot, plus a few runners for slinging trees on the upper slab.
FA Aug 19, 2013, Jay Harrison, Tom Lane

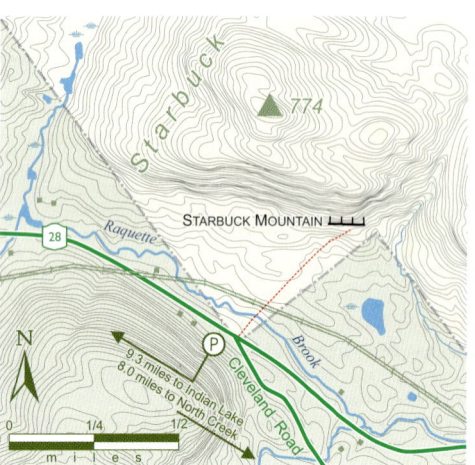

Ledge Area

The following routes begin on a ledge 12' above the cliff. Walk left to **Perseid** and the 20'-tall block-tower, then up right onto the ledge.

3 Asterisk 5.8 PG 60' ★

Start: From the base of **Perseid**, walk up and right to a wide ledge. Look for a 3'-tall pedestal protruding from the face at ground level, 5' left of a 40'-tall vertical crack (**Starline**) and 10' right of a 20'-tall, wide, brown crack.
P1 5.8 PG: Climb the face above the pedestal, move up and slightly left, then up to a thin crack (first pro: micro cams). Continue up to a right-rising crack under

Opposite: Matt Nuaman on Gemini (5.9). Photo by Ben Brooke.

an overhanging flake. Follow it to a left-facing corner and climb to its top. Move through a bulge, go up along the top of a left-rising flake, step up to a fist-sized pod, then move right to a vertical seam. Follow the seam to the top. 60'

FA Oct 10, 2013, Jay Harrison, Tom Lane

4 Starline 5.10b PG 60' ★★★

Start: 5' right of Asterisk below an attractive crack that disappears 40' up.

P1 5.10b PG: Climb the crack to its end. Mantel a sloping ledge (crux, microcams) below a bolt. Go up and left, and weave through the final bulge to the top and a tree anchor. 60'

Gear: A #00 C3 or equivalent is a crucial and strenuous placement at the crux.

FA Oct 2, 2013, Jay Harrison, Tom Lane

Indian Lake

5 Sagittarius 5.8 PG 60' ★★

Sustained; you should be solid at 5.8 face climbing before attempting a lead.
Start: A few feet left of Aquarius at a thin vertical crack.
P1 5.8 PG: A hand jam in a sharp pocket gets you off the deck. Follow the crack past a blank section to a second pod. Follow the crack up and left through a steep section, then make a long move to a horizontal ledge (first crux, #3 Camalot helpful). Go up and right on a short slab, then up the steep headwall trending left to a nice hueco. Crimpy moves (second crux) lead to the top and a fixed anchor on a tree. 60'
FA Oct 4, 2013, Ben Brooke, Tom Lane

6 Aquarius 5.6 G 60' ★★

Easiest route at Starbuck, and good for a new leader.
Start: 20' right of Asteroid at a vertical hand crack in black rock.
P1 5.6 G: Pull over a small bulge on hand jams. Continue up on more jams and jugs to a small foot ledge. Straight in hand- and foot-jams lead up 10' to a horizontal break in the wall. Mantel onto the ledge (crux), then up easier jams to the top. Fixed anchor on a tree. 60'
Gear: To 4"; doubles in hand sizes.
FA Oct 4, 2013, Ben Brooke, Tom Lane

7 Cosmic Ray 5.7 G 60' ★★

Fingerlocks and Tricam pockets.
Start: 8' right of Aquarius at a thin vertical crack.
P1 5.7 G: Climb crack to a bulge; over this using face holds. Finish on a sparsely-protected, easy slab. 60'
Gear: To 1"; doubles of 3/4" to 1", and a .125 Tricam.
FA Nov 6, 2013, Jay Harrison, Tom Lane

Right End

8 Starboard Tack 5.10a PG 75' ★

Start: Below a large tree on the right end of the Ledge Area.
P1 5.10a PG: Go up a face past a horizontal crack to the ledge. Go behind the tree and follow a vertical seam-crack past a short, bulging, left-facing corner to a horizontal overlap. Swing right over this and follow a crack to the top. 75'
FA Jun 5, 2013, Tom Lane, Mike Prince

9 Starstruck 5.8 G 75' ★

Start: 5' right of Starboard Track, and 18' left of Gemini's right-facing corner, below a wide bulging crack 12' up. At the ground is a short 4'-high left-facing V-corner.
P1 5.8 G: Go up the V-corner to a stance below the bulging crack. Go up the crack through the bulge past the left side of a triangular ceiling and into a left-facing corner. At its top, go through an overlap, then up the crack system to the top. 75'
FA May 12, 2013, Jay Harrison, Tom Lane

10 Unnamed2 Project

Closed project. Begin 6' right of Starstruck at a flared pod at ground level. Go up the flared pod, then up a beautiful series of discontinuous seams in the face to a fixed anchor. In the 5.10+ range.

11 O'Ryan's Belt 5.8 G 75' ★★

The initial moves can be protected using the first bolt of Andromeda.
Start: 6' right of Unnamed2 at a slab where the trail meets the cliff, 4' left of Gemini's right-facing corner below a wide crack that begins 20' up.
P1 5.8 G: Go up a slab to a stance, then up a face to gain seams which widen to a flared crack. Up this to the top, step left to the crack's continuation and go up this to the top. 75'
FA Oct 2, 2013, Tom Lane, Jay Harrison

12 Andromeda 5.8 G 75' ★★★

Start: At the outside edge of the large right-facing corner near the right end of the wall (Gemini).
P1 5.8 G: Climb the attractive arête that forms the right-facing corner of Gemini to a position where it meets the left end of the Gemini roof. Step left and finish up a short flared crack to a fixed anchor shared with Gemini. 75'
FA Nov 9, 2013, Jay Harrison, Tom Lane

13 Gemini 5.9 G 75' ★★★

Climbs the giant right-facing corner near the right end of the cliff.
Start: Below the 5'-deep right-facing corner, 25' from the right end of the cliff.
P1 5.9 G: Go up the corner to the square 8'-deep roof. Traverse right in a horizontal under the roof to the arête, then up and right to a fixed anchor. 75'
FA May 14, 2013, Ben Brooke, Jay Harrison

14 Unnamed4 Project

Closed project. Climb the crack right of Gemini to its juncture with Quantum Entanglement. Climb the face left of the crack and chimney to a tenuous stance at an overhanging orange wall. Climb the right edge of this wall to a niche below an overhang. Ascend the overhang via a crack in a bottomless right-facing corner to reach the top.

15 Quantum Entanglement 5.8 G 75' ★★

Start: At a clean crack system 10' right of Gemini's right-facing corner.
P1 5.8 G: Climb the crack for 30', step left into a shallow chimney. Up this to a position below a wide crack in a right-facing corner (V1). Up the crack and corner to a fixed anchor on the left wall. 75'
Gear: Big cams.
V1 5.6 PG: Hand-traverse right along the ledge, mantel, then climb up and left to the top on good holds.
FA Jun 5, 2013, Mike Prince, Tom Lane, Jay Harrison

16 Gamma Ray Arête 5.9+ G 75' ★★

Start: At the far right edge of the lowest point of the cliff, beside the path that leads up to the top.
P1 5.9+ G: Climb the face right of Quantum Entanglement to a stance under an overhang on the arête. Over this, then up right around the arête to the top of the cliff. 75'
FA Nov 9, 2013, Tom Lane, Jay Harrison

BLACK MOUNTAIN CLIFF

Location	Near North River, accessed from NY 28
Aspect	South
Height	235'
Quality	
Approach	30 min, moderate
Summary	Seldom-visited cliff with two routes.

2							2
-5.6	5.7	5.8	5.9	5.10	5.11	5.12	5.13+	total

The center of the main face is split by a wide low-angle gully, visible from NY 28 when you're driving west of North River. The existing routes are right of the gully, with **Home after Dark** starting near its base. The right end of the face has long, horizontal roofs above smooth slabs. **Goodfellows** climbs the tallest section of cliff, which is between the roofs and a steep gully to the left.

HISTORY

The climbs were pioneered by members of Central New York Climbers, who climbed at many of the cliffs in this section of the Adirondacks. It is doubtful that their routes have seen a repeat ascent, although Jay Harrison reported scrambling on this cliff. Because their report stated that the climbs were on Casey Mountain, a peak farther west on NY 28, the actual location of the routes remained a mystery until now.

DIRECTIONS (MAP PAGE 285)

From the intersection of NY 28 and Thirteenth Lake Road (0.0 mile) in North River, drive west on NY 28 (toward Indian Lake) and park on the right (north) side of the road at 1.5 miles 574280,4846060. (From Indian Lake at the intersection of NY 30 and NY 28, drive east towards North River 10.7 miles and park on the left.)

Hike downhill and northwest on a bearing of 308°. Cross a stream and continue uphill, staying to the right of the yellow-blazed state boundary. The right end of the cliff comes into view near a wet depression on a bench beneath the cliff. Traverse left (west) under low cliffbands to their left end beneath a wide, low-angle gully that bisects the higher main cliff. Hike uphill steeply to the steep, deep squeeze chimney of **Home after Dark** 574134,4846791.

DESCENT OPTIONS

Rappel from trees.

1 Home after Dark 5.4 G 110'

P1 of this route appears to have been altered by rockfall and looks much harder than the reported grade.
Start: Begin 200' right of the wide, low-angle gully and beneath a steep, deep chimney with a chockstone 30' above the ground.
P1 5.4 G: Up the chimney to the chockstone, then traverse left beneath an overhang to a left-facing corner. Climb the corner to a belay on a ledge. 50'
P2 5.4 G: Go up a short left-facing corner and a vertical crack to a slab, then climb the slab to the top of the cliff. 60'
FA Jun 1, 1991, Jim Vermeulen

2 Goodfellows 5.6 G 230' ★

The first ascentionists reported P1 to be "one of the most interesting and sustained moderate pitches in the southern Adirondacks."
Start: Hike right (east) 300' along the steep, wooded slope above the lower cliffband to a steep gully. Start 100' right of the gully, along an exposed, vegetated ledge beneath a clean, smooth slab 30' above the ground.
P1 5.6 G: Go up the left-facing corner at the right end of the slab to a short vertical crack on the right wall. Up the crack to a stance, then up another short wall to a left-rising ramp. Follow the ramp to a 10'-long ceiling, passing it on the right to a stance at a small pine tree. Traverse right toward a large pine tree, then up a depression behind the tree to a tree belay on the left. 150'
P2 5.4 G: An easy face pitch leads to the top of the cliff. 80'
FA Jun 22, 1991, Jim Vermeulen, Bill Morris, Mike Cross

PEAKED MOUNTAIN

Peaked Mountain is a very popular open summit west of Thirteenth Lake, accessed from NY 28 in North River. You can approach it by making a short paddle on Thirteenth Lake (or a short hike), then following the trail to Peaked Mountain Pond. From the pond, the trail leads northeast to the summit of Peaked Mountain 568535,4841885. There is considerable rock here that consists mostly of blocks, bulges, and smooth faces; nothing very high. The mountain was explored by Dick Tucker and Dave Legg, who climbed a route on the narrow face just below the summit that faces east, toward Thirteenth Lake called **Summit Route** (5.5; 50'; Jul 27, 1980).

Indian Lake

GORE MOUNTAIN

Location	Gore Mountain Ski Center
Aspect	South and southwest
Height	50' to 80'
Quality	★
Approach	40 min, moderate
Summary	Several small crags scattered in gladed ski trails.

	1	2	1		2	1		7
	-5.6	5.7	5.8	5.9	5.10	5.11	5.12	5.13+	total

The large boulders and small cliffs that dot these popular ski trails are familiar to the skiers and snowboarders who ride down Twister and Cirque Glades. Several defunct hiking and biking trails criss-cross this area and make navigation a bit easier. While the cragging is barely developed, the rock quality is very good and there is significant potential for new routes, especially in the upper section of the Cirque Glade. The glades are a refreshing change from the typically claustrophobic forests of the Adirondacks.

HISTORY
Veteran ski coach Patrick Purcell did the first reported ascents of the crack climbs on the Ski Tracks Wall in 1991. Later, in 1998, Dick Tucker and Jay Harrison did some exploratory toproping at the Calligraphy and Rampart Cliffs, as well as the upper section of the Cirque Glade, which is perhaps the best find.

ACCESS
Access at Gore is unclear. The mountain is state land designated intensive use, but the ski center is operated by a private company. No access is allowed anywhere near maintenance operations; outside of that, it's unclear whether summer recreation can be restricted. Lift service is offered to mountain bikers and hikers, so if in doubt, pay for a lift ticket and shorten the approach. Call 518.251.2411 for lift hours.

DIRECTIONS (MAP PAGE 287)
From NY 28 at the town of North Creek, turn west onto Peaceful Valley Road (0.0 mile) and drive 0.5 mile to the Gore Mountain Access Road. Turn right, and drive to the parking area next to the ski lodge, reached at 2.1 miles. There is a large ski trail map on a board outside the ski lodge, which is handy for locating the ski trails. Directions to the specific cliffs begin from here.

Gore Mountain
TWISTER GLADE AREA

DIRECTIONS (MAP PAGE 287)
From the parking, locate the Twister Trail and Twister Glades on the ski trail map. Hike past the Northwoods gondola, then up the slope beneath Adirondack Express chairlift. At the first junction, hike up and right. This is Twister Trail, and the woods to the right are Twister Glades.

Follow Twister Trail past the intersection with the 1A Trail on the left, to reach a gravel service road at 40 min. Turn right, walk 320' to the height of land, and locate an unmarked trail that crosses the road. It's hard to find; once you find it, there are blue DEC markers on trees. This is the old Schaefer Trail, which has been relocated to the other side of the mountain.

Gore Mountain ● Twister Glade Area
PAUL'S LEDGE

Aspect	South
Height	40'
Quality	
Approach	45 min, difficult
Summary	Beautiful open ledges with potential for more routes.

These beautiful open ledges have great views of Gore and the mountains to the south and east. There is potential for new routes.

DIRECTIONS (MAP PAGE 287)
From the service road, follow this old Schaefer Trail downhill (east) for 3 min to the top of Paul's Ledge 578839,4836928. Just before you get to the "Caution Cliffs" sign, there is a spur trail on the left to a clearing and the site of a burned lean-to.

1 Paul's Gondola Ride 5.4 G 45'
Start: From the viewpoint on Paul's Ledge, walk (skier's) left along the cliff edge to a 5'-deep fissure. Scramble down into the fissure, then walk (climber's) left 75' along base of the cliff to a giant left-facing corner directly below the lookout. The right wall of the corner is orange, and has a horizontal 15' up. Begin 25' left of the corner, at a shallow right-rising scoop 5' right of a double-trunked birch tree.
P1 5.4 G: Friction up the scoop to a horizontal, then continue up and right to where the scoop becomes a ramp filled with vegetation. Up the ramp to a flared crack in a left-facing corner formed by a block. Over this and into the main corner, then continue up this to the top. 45'
FA Sep 5, 2009, Daniel Mosny, Kate Mosny

Pauls Ledge.

Indian Lake

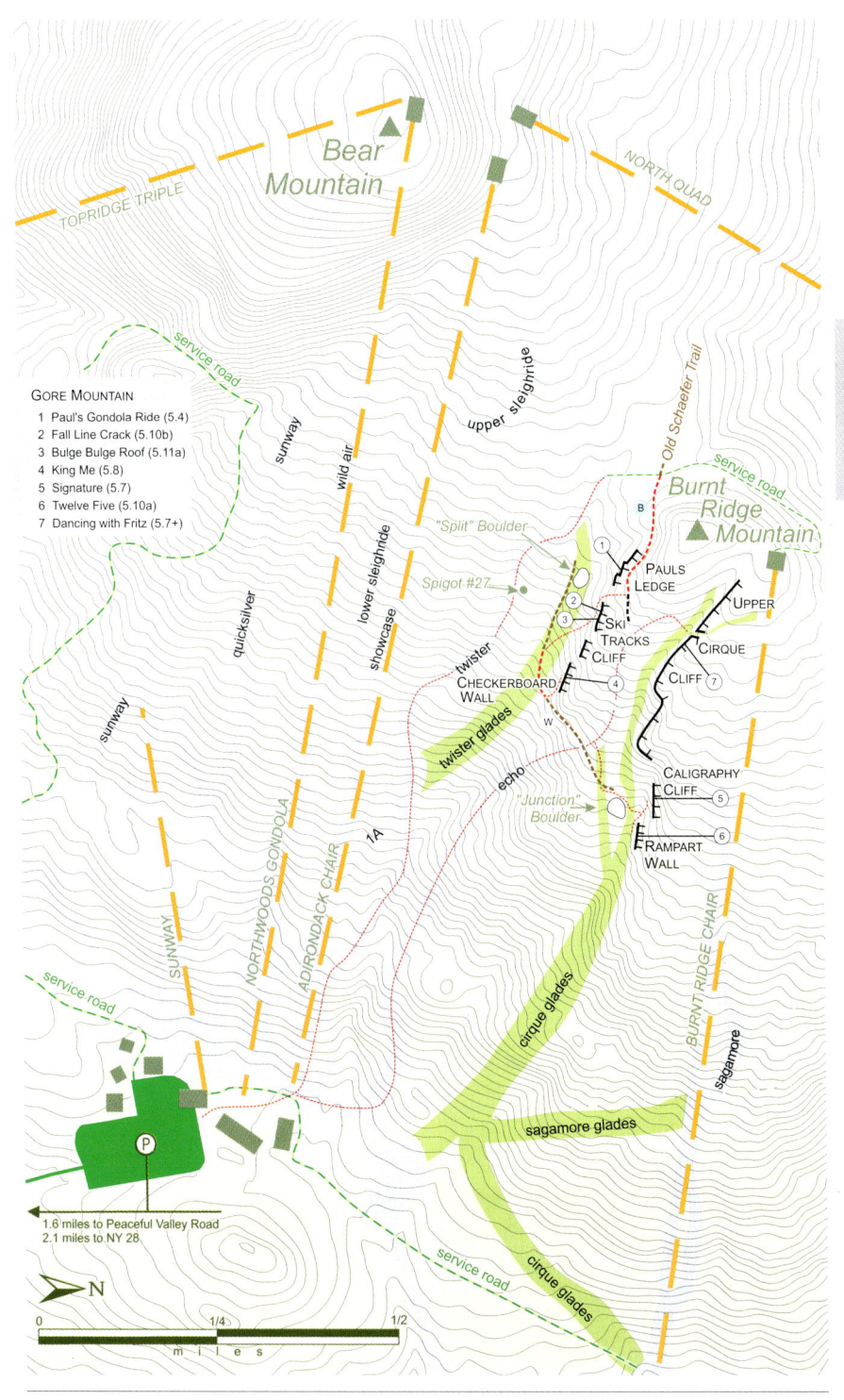

Gore Mountain
1. Paul's Gondola Ride (5.4)
2. Fall Line Crack (5.10b)
3. Bulge Bulge Roof (5.11a)
4. King Me (5.8)
5. Signature (5.7)
6. Twelve Five (5.10a)
7. Dancing with Fritz (5.7+)

1.6 miles to Peaceful Valley Road
2.1 miles to NY 28

Indian Lake

Gore Mountain • Twister Glade Area
SKI TRACKS CLIFF

Aspect	South
Height	80'
Quality	★★★
Approach	50 min, difficult
Summary	A superb cliff with two amazing cracks.

DIRECTIONS   (MAP PAGE 287)
From the viewpoint at Paul's Ledge, continue down the old Schaefer Trail another 200' to a cedar tree growing on top of a boulder. Just beyond is a cut glade on the right. Walk downhill (south) 150' to a constriction in the cliff. Continue downhill in the glade to the base of the wall. The two cracks are impossible to miss 0578939,4836820.

2 Fall Line Crack 5.10b G 80' ★★★
Start: 40' from the left end of the cliff, beneath a J-shaped crack 20' up. There's some moss at the base.
P1 5.10b G: Up the face to a continuous fingercrack, then follow the crack to the top. 80'
FA Aug, 1991, Patrick Purcell, Ann Eastman

3 Bulge Bulge Roof 5.11a G 70' ★★★
Start: 25' right of Fall Line Crack beneath a ceiling 50' up, at a fingercrack with a hand-sized flare 4' up.
P1 5.11a G: Up the steep fingercrack past a bulge (crux) to the left end of a ceiling. Continue in a hand-crack through the ceiling to the top. 70'
FA Aug, 1991, Patrick Purcell, Ann Eastman

Gore Mountain • Twister Glade Area
CHECKERBOARD WALL

Aspect	South
Height	80'
Quality	★★★
Approach	1 hr, difficult
Summary	Naturally clean wall crisscrossed with seams and cracks; good potential for routes.

This impressive tan-colored wall is crisscrossed with a grid pattern of seams and cracks. It's naturally clean, and has potential for new routes. The base of the cliff is flat and pleasant.

DIRECTIONS   (MAP PAGE 287)
From the Ski Tracks Wall, walk downhill into the main Twister Glade and locate the White Disk Trail, an old ski trail clearly marked with 6"-diameter white disks on the uphill side of the trees, which leaves the main glade on the left. Follow this downhill until you can see the cliff about 50' left 579066,4836775. It's the last cliff, and if you go too far, you'll reach the Echo Trail; backtrack and look for the cliff on your right, 10 min from Ski Tracks Cliff.

For a shorter approach, walk up the Echo Trail (as for the Cirque Glade Area). After 30 min, on the right,

Bulge Bulge Roof (5.11a).

look for a spot where the two water pipes span a large gap, and the attached spigot is high in the air. On the other side of the pipe, you can see the 6"-diameter white disks of the White Disk Trail heading downhill. Now for the hard part: on the left side of the Echo Trail, locate the White Disk Trail (you can't see the markers because they are on the uphill side of the trees) and follow this uphill about 300' to the Checkerboard Wall on the right.

4 King Me 5.8 TR 80' ★

Begin 30' from the left end of the clean checkerboard wall, at the third-from-the-left crack-seam, directly below a vertical crack 25' up. Face-climb between horizontal cracks and finish in the vertical crack.
FA (TR) 2003, Josh Bingham, Shawn Martin

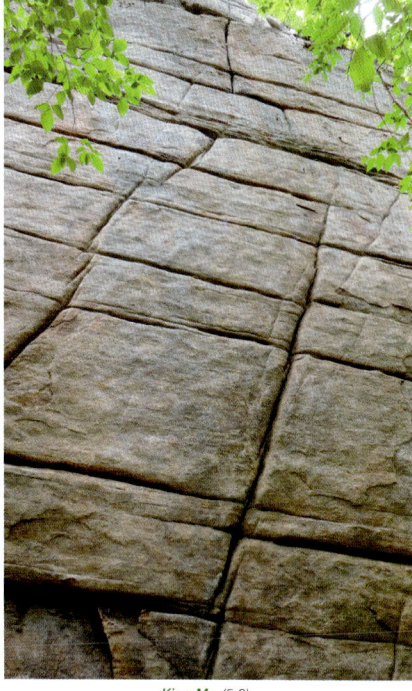

King Me (5.8).

Gore Mountain
CIRQUE GLADE AREA

The Cirque Glade provides access to the Calligraphy Cliff, Rampart Cliff, and Upper Cirque Cliffs.

DIRECTIONS   (MAP PAGE 287)
From the parking, locate the Echo Trail and Cirque Glades on the ski trail map. Hike past the Northwoods gondola to the Adirondack Express Chairlift. The Echo Trail is the second ski trail on the left beyond the chairlift. Follow this uphill, steeply at times, for 40 min. On the right, watch for the "Cirque Glades, Echo Trail Entrance" sign.

Indian Lake

Gore Mountain • Cirque Glade Area
CALLIGRAPHY CLIFF

Aspect	South
Height	70'
Quality	
Approach	50 min, difficult
Summary	Many cracks, but very dirty.

Another impressive cliff with many cracks, but unfortunately very dirty, with lichen-covered faces, and fern-filled cracks. The right side is especially steep.

DIRECTIONS   (MAP PAGE 287)
At the intersection of the Echo Trail and the "Cirque Glades, Echo Trail Entrance", turn right, and follow the trail downhill towards the Cirque Glades. On the left is a large boulder—"Junction" boulder 579340,4836884. Turn left here in front of the boulder and bushwhack north following the contour to the Cirque Glades. Calligraphy Cliff 579341,4836969 and Rampart Cliff are directly in front of you.

5 Signature 5.7 TR 70'

Probably not climbable in its present state. Begin 30' left of the low point of the terrain. Climb 2 right-rising cracks to a single fern-choked right-rising crack. Follow this to a left-rising horizontal. Traverse left, then up a vegetated vertical crack to the top.
FA (TR) Dec 5, 1998, Dick Tucker, Jay Harrison

Gore Mountain • Cirque Glade Area
RAMPART CLIFF

Aspect	South
Height	50'
Quality	
Approach	50 min, difficult
Summary	Wide cliff split by horizontal cracks; dirty.

An off-vertical face covered with lichen and split by long horizontal cracks. The only feature that breaks the face vertically is an offwidth crack in the center.

DIRECTIONS   (MAP PAGE 287)
Walk 300' downhill and right of the Calligraphy Cliff. You can clearly see this from the Cirque Glade, and navigation to the cliff is open and easy 579391,4836933.

6 Twelve Five 5.10a TR 50'

Presently super dirty. Locate the right-leaning handcrack that begins 10' up and 40' left of the offwidth in the center of the cliff. Begin a few feet to the right at a right-leaning seam. Go up the seam to a horizontal, hand traverse left 4' and climb the right-rising handcrack to the top.
FA (TR) Dec 5, 1998, Dick Tucker, Jay Harrison

Indian Lake

Gore Mountain • Cirque Glade Area
UPPER CIRQUE CLIFF

Aspect	Southwest
Height	80'
Quality	
Approach	1 hr, difficult
Summary	Wide cliff with many subsections; excellent potential for routes.

This cliff is located near the summit of Burnt Ridge Mountain alongside the Cirque Glade. On the right side, the vegetation near the cliff has been cut back for the glade, and access is easy. The forest on the left side hasn't been cleared, and the vegetation is tighter up to the cliff base. Being mostly clean, the many vertical cracks and sheer faces split by horizontals make this a great cliff for new routes.

DIRECTIONS   (MAP PAGE 287)
Continue up the Echo Trail to near the very top of Burnt Ridge Mountain. The cliffs are visible about 300' right of the ski trail 578860,4837097; the ski trail is raised and has a great view of them. Scramble down the embankment and bushwhack 200' through the brambles and weeds to the cliff.

Alternatively (and longer), hike up the Cirque Glade from Calligraphy Wall for 20 min.

7 Dancing with Fritz 5.7+ TR 60'
There are several sheer cliffs split by long horizontal cracks. This cliff has a parallel-sided offwidth crack on the right end that starts in a boxed alcove 578972,4837053. Walking uphill, the Cirque Glade makes a right turn up a chimney-like gully on the left end of this cliff. Climb the offwidth crack past two horizontals to the top.
FA (TR) Aug 25, 2000, Dick Tucker, Jay Harrison

DUTTON MOUNTAIN

This area is still being explored and the potential for rock routes seems limited. Even so, at least one route has been reported here.

DIRECTIONS
From Minerva, at the intersection of NY 28N and CR 37, follow 14th Road (CR 37) west 3.0 miles to where the road makes a sharp turn to the southwest, and crosses a major stream 578137,4847458. Find a yellow pipe that marks the state land boundary, then follow the property boundary northwest to Dutton Mountain, about 0.6 miles. The cliff faces southwest, and is on the southwest-most corner of the mountain 577244,4848516.

1 Lunatic Fringe 5.5 PG 120'
This route was climbed two days before several new ice routes on a cliff 1/4 mile to the west.
Start: Left of center, below a dirty open book.
P1 5.5 PG: Climb the open book, then up through a small overhang. Continue up a low-angle offwidth crack to a horizontal crack below a steep bulge. Rail left to another open book (presently has a tiny birch at your feet), traverse farther left to an outside corner, then up easier corners and pine-needle-covered slabs to belay off the first secure tree you can find. 120'
FA Mar 29, 2011, Jay Harrison

HAYES MOUNTAIN

Location	In the Hoffman Notch Wilderness west of Schroon Lake, accessed from US 9
Aspect	Southeast
Height	250'
Quality	
Approach	1 hr, moderate
Summary	Large wilderness cliff with a moderate approach and two incomplete routes.

This is a large, tall cliff with two incomplete routes. The center of the cliff is a steep buttress with clean rock and somewhat broken rock to the right. Left of the buttress is a small ledge beneath a large tree-covered ledge above which chimneys extend to the top of the cliff.

HISTORY
Rick Beardsley, Mike Emelianoff, and Dick Tucker explored the area briefly on a sunny day during the winter of 1998. Tucker returned with Jay Harrison in 1999 to climb Hayeburner, although they found a fixed anchor at their high point. Colin Maury climbed here around the same time and put up Big White Guy and attempted another route.

There's definitely more here than these two partial routes, as climbers report finding evidence of earlier activity. Additionally, this cliff is a major ice climbing destination.

DIRECTIONS   (MAP PAGE 291)
From the central school in the village of Schroon Lake (0.0 mile), drive south on US 9 to its intersection with Hoffman Road at 0.6 mile. Turn right onto Hoffman Road and drive west to its intersection with Loch Muller Road, reached at 6.8 miles. Turn right onto Loch Muller Road and drive to a parking area, reached at 9.3 miles, with a sign for Bailey Pond 589263,4857838.

From the parking area (0 hr 0 min), hike the trail marked with blue discs for 1 mile to the Bailey Pond outlet stream, where a short side trail, reached at 20 min, heads left (west) to the pond. Cliffs are visible across the pond, but the crag is farther left (west) and out of sight. Continue west, bushwhacking now, and follow the south shore of the pond to its inlet stream. Follow the inlet stream, and drainage area above, west to the height of land, which is reached at 40 min. Traverse west across the deciduous hillside of Hayes Mountain (on the right). Continue past an 80'-tall vertical cliffband to a level bench to a small clearing beneath the crag that is reached at 1 hr 587053,4857704.

Indian Lake

DESCENT OPTIONS
Rappel the routes from fixed anchors and trees.

1 Hayeburner 5.7 PG 230'
Start: Hike up talus to the high point along the base of the cliff and left of the steep buttress. Begin in a wide gash with a car-sized wedged flake.
P1 5.0 G: Up the gash and exit right onto a spacious ledge. Belay at its right end. 50'
P2 5.7 PG: Climb the depression that begins as a left-facing corner, then up and left on steps to an opposing right-facing corner. Gain a left-leaning crack that becomes a left-rising ramp before it arches right to a belay ledge with fixed protection. 180'
ACB 1999, Jay Harrison, Dick Tucker

2 Big White Guy A2 80'
Start: 100' uphill from and left of the base of the steep buttress, beneath a triangle roof 20' above the ground and left of orange rock at head height. This is 100' right of the wide gash of **Hayeburner**.
P1 A2: Up left-leaning cracks to a ledge beneath a vertical seam. Follow the seam to parallel, flared left-leaning cracks and a fixed anchor. 80'
FA 1999, Colin Maury, Glen Whiteman

HAYES MOUNTAIN
1 Hayeburner (5.7)
2 Big White Guy (A2)

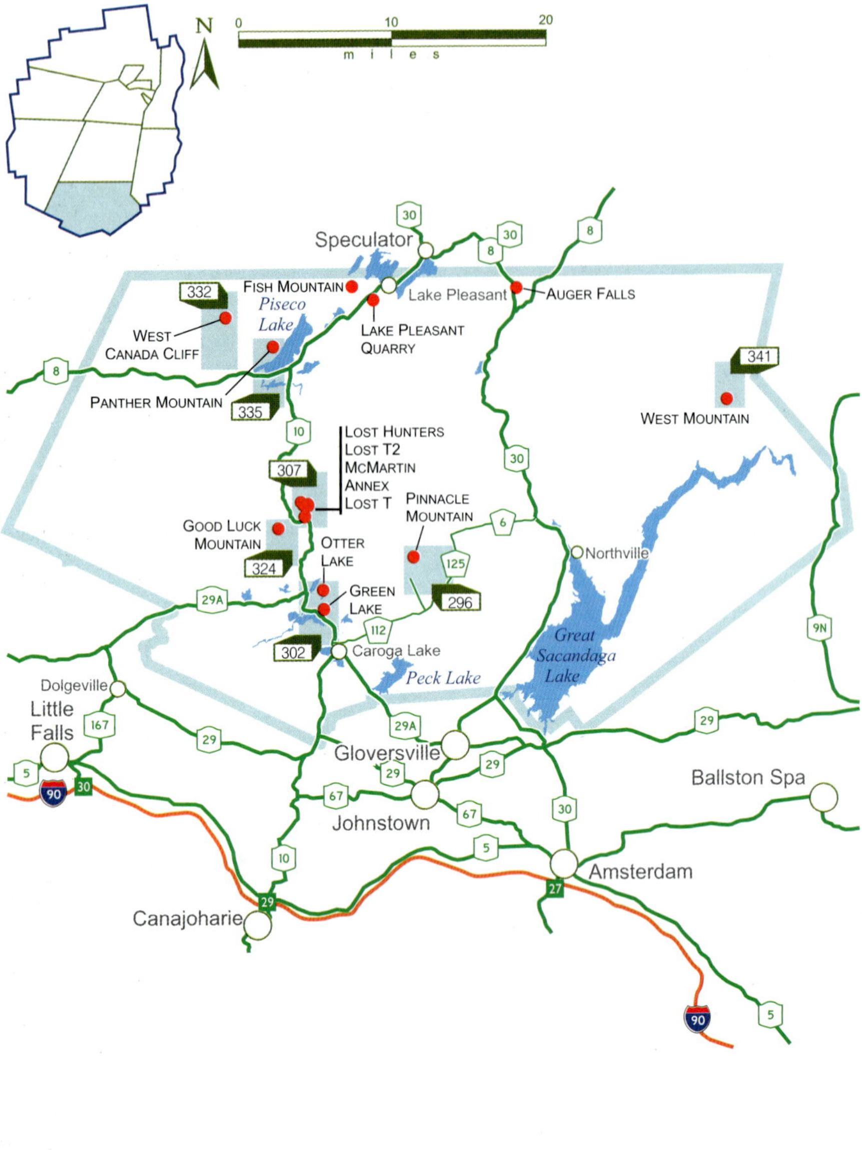
N
0
10
20
miles
Speculator
FISH MOUNTAIN
Piseco Lake
Lake Pleasant
AUGER FALLS
332
WEST CANADA CLIFF
LAKE PLEASANT QUARRY
PANTHER MOUNTAIN
335
341
WEST MOUNTAIN
LOST HUNTERS
LOST T2
MCMARTIN
ANNEX
LOST T
307
PINNACLE MOUNTAIN
GOOD LUCK MOUNTAIN
324
OTTER LAKE
Northville
GREEN LAKE
296
302
Caroga Lake
Great Sacandaga Lake
Peck Lake
Dolgeville
Little Falls
Gloversville
Ballston Spa
Johnstown
Amsterdam
Canajoharie
8
30
10
6
125
29A
112
167
29
9N
5
90
67
27

Southern Mountains

The Southern Mountains region stretches from the cliffs the Sacandaga River Valley along NY 10 northward to the NY 8 corridor near Lake Pleasant and Speculator. It includes about 15 areas that share a similar rock composition, and the gneiss found at several of these areas is outstanding. Hard rock has produced hard climbs, of which this region has plenty: in total, there are 40 routes between 5.11 and 5.13. The region contains many small mountains on state land that hint at the potential for more high-caliber cliffs in the future. Since the first edition, climbers have explored several semi-remote cliffs, but many more backcountry crags remain for those willing to penetrate the remote sections of the Silver Lake Wilderness, West Canada Wilderness, and the Wilcox Lake Wild Forest.

The southernmost climbing area in this guide is Green Lake Cliff, located north of Caroga Lake. Also nearby are Pinnacle Mountain (with excellent cracks) and Otter Lake (mostly compact face climbing). Continuing north on NY 10, you'll come to the trailheads for the Lost Crags and Good Luck Mountain Cliff. Good Luck is a well-developed cliffband with a good selection of moderate routes and high-quality hard face and crack routes. The Lost Crags (Lost Hunters Cliff, Lost T, Lost T2, and McMartin) are outstanding cliffs scattered on or around Sherman Mountain. The once-difficult approach to the Lost Crags has become much better defined, making these cliffs easier to access. Lost T is noteworthy for outstanding routes with a good range of grades, and is now considered the most popular cliff in the region.

At the north end of NY 10 is Piseco Lake, with the cliffs of Panther Mountain on its north shore. Panther Mountain is a short hike and passes near the small, sheer wall of Echo Cliff, with several excellent, seldom-visited crack lines. Just east along NY 8 are the small cliffs around Speculator: Lake Pleasant Quarry (great for toproping), Fish Mountain, and Auger Falls.

The final offering in this region is West Canada Cliff, a very large, wilderness cliff guarded by a long, arduous bushwhack. Surely more routes will be added here in the future.

SEASON
Being the southernmost region and low in elevation, this is a good place to finish out the season. The region is within the lake-effect snowbelt and can be choked with snow into April.

DIRECTIONS (MAPS PAGES 4 AND 292)
To reach the NY 10 corridor from the south, take I-90 to Exit 28 and find your way to Gloversville, then west on NY 29A, past Caroga Lake, to the intersection with NY 10. Coming from the west, it is faster to get off I-90 at Little Falls (Exit 29A) and make your way to NY 167; follow NY 167 to Dolgeville, left onto NY 29, then east on NY 29A to NY 10.

WHERE TO STAY
There are many options for camping along NY 10. The trailheads are all on state land, and the approach trails to Good Luck Lake and the Lost Crags pass many campsites. The summit of Good Luck Mountain makes an excellent camping/climbing destination (provided you bring water). DEC campgrounds are located on Caroga Lake (518.835.4241) and Piseco Lake: Point Comfort (518.548.7586), Poplar Point (518.548.8031), Little Sand Point (518.548.7585).

AMENITIES
The city of Gloversville is 15 miles south of the NY 10 / NY 29A intersection near the trailhead to Nine Corners Lake. The village of Speculator is 12 miles east of Piseco Lake, on NY 8, and has a gas station, grocery, bank, and general store at the intersection with NY 30.

DIVERSIONS
The Northville–Placid hiking trail begins in this region, passes through the Silver Lake Wilderness, crosses NY 8 at Piseco Lake, then continues north into the West Canada Lakes Wilderness. Good swimming and sand beaches can be found at the campgrounds on Caroga Lake and Piseco Lake.

Jeremy Haas on the first ascent of
Joy Crack *(5.11b), Pinnacle Mountain.*

Southern Mountains

Climb All of New York!

Professional instruction and guided trips throughout the Adirondacks and all New York

In addition to years of experience, *all* of our guides have been trained and are certified through the American Mountain Guides Association as Alpine Guides, Rock Guides, Rock Instructors, and/or Single Pitch Instructors.

877-486-5769
AlpineEndeavors.com

Climb with us in the Shawangunk and Catskills, or join us on one of our guided trips to unique locations abroad.

Greg Catton on The Matrix, Roger's Rock, NY

Southern Mountains

PG	CLIFF	QUALITY	ASPECT	APPROACH		GRADES	#
295	Pinnacle Mountain	★★★	E	40 min	moderate		11
301	Green Lake Cliff	★★★	W	5 min	easy		7
301	Otter Lake Cliff	★★★	S	30 min	moderate		13
306	The Lost Crags Lost T Cliff	★★★★	W	20 min	easy		24
314	The Lost Crags The Annex	★	W	15 min	easy		6
315	The Lost Crags Lost Hunters Cliff	★★★★★	W	52 min	moderate		17
319	The Lost Crags McMartin Cliff	★★★	W	42 min	moderate		14
322	The Lost Crags Lost T2 Cliff	★★	W	35 min	moderate		5
323	Good Luck Mountain	★★★★	W	45 min	moderate		24
331	West Canada Cliff	★★	SW	2 hr 5 min	difficult		1
335	Panther Mountain Echo Cliff	★	SE	20 min	easy		9
337	Panther Mountain The Grotto	★	SE	30 min	easy		1
337	Panther Mountain Summit Cliff	★	SE	30 min	easy		1
337	Fish Mountain Crag	★	SW	15 min	easy		4
338	Lake Pleasant Quarry	★★★	SE	3 min	easy		14
342	West Mountain Rods & Guns Wall	★★★	W & S	1 hr 10 min	difficult		21

PINNACLE MOUNTAIN

Location	Between NY 30 and NY 10, east of Caroga Lake
Aspect	East
Height	100'
Quality	★★★
Approach	40 min, moderate
Summary	Steep, remote wall with many excellent, difficult routes, including one of the best cracks in the park, Release The Kraken.

		2		1	7	1		11
-5.6	5.7	5.8	5.9	5.10	5.11	5.12	5.12+	total

This remote and excellent cliff has two distinct sections: the left-hand section known as the Peninsula, and the sheer right-hand Main Face. No easy routes here: the cliff has mostly high-quality, difficult crack routes on excellent rock. Most of the routes are equipped with lower-off anchors.

DIRECTIONS (MAP PAGE 296)

From the east: locate the intersection of NY 30 and the Benson Road (CR 6) (0.0) just north of Northville. Follow the Benson Road west 5.8 miles to a triangular intersection; stay on the main road which goes left (south) and becomes CR 125. At 11.3 miles, reach the intersection with Pinnacle Road on the right.

From the west: locate the intersection of NY 10 and NY 29A in Caroga Lake (0.0). Drive north on the combined NY10 / NY 29A for 0.8 mile, then turn right onto CR 112. At 5.5 miles, the road forks (CR 112 goes right); go straight on CR 125. At 7.3 miles, reach the intersection with Pinnacle Road on the left.

From the intersection of CR 125 and Pinnacle Road (0.0), drive north on Pinnacle Road. At 1.2 miles, the road turns to gravel and crosses a one-lane bridge. At 1.6 miles, reach the end of the road, the trailhead for Chase Lake and County Line Lake 0549516,4783982.

From the trailhead (0 hr 0 min), follow the red-marked trail towards Chase Lake. The trail goes through a wet section, crosses a bridge, then follows a stream which is to the left. The trail swings away from the stream, ascends briefly, then levels out. There is a dinner-table-sized sunken boulder on the right; 100' past this boulder, at 8 min (0549912,4784347), turn left off the trail (cairn) and follow a herd path northeast staying relatively level. At 30 min, the trail makes a sharp left turn and goes directly up the hillside. At 40 min, arrive at the cliff at the front (east-facing) wall of the Peninsula 550152,4785580.

HISTORY

On a tip from a boulderer, Bill Griffith, Gary Thomann, Jaysen Henderson and others (aka " Arietta Climbing"), visited the cliff in the winter of 2012. They returned in

295

Southern Mountains

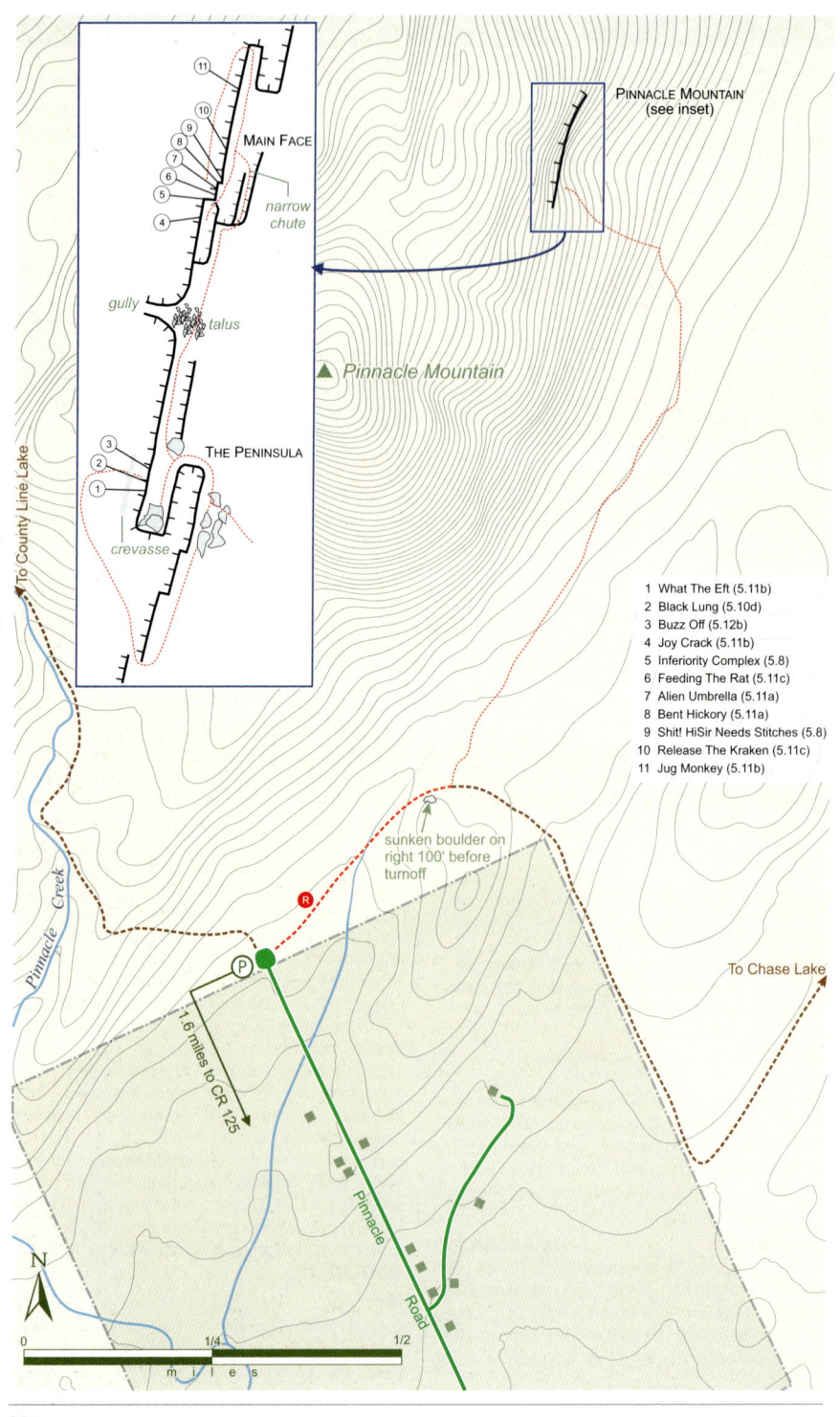

Pinnacle Mountain (see inset)

Main Face
narrow chute
gully
talus
The Peninsula
crevasse

To County Line Lake
Pinnacle Creek
sunken boulder on right 100' before turnoff
To Chase Lake
1.6 miles to CR 125
Pinnacle Road

1. What The Eft (5.11b)
2. Black Lung (5.10d)
3. Buzz Off (5.12b)
4. Joy Crack (5.11b)
5. Inferiority Complex (5.8)
6. Feeding The Rat (5.11c)
7. Alien Umbrella (5.11a)
8. Bent Hickory (5.11a)
9. Shit! HiSir Needs Stitches (5.8)
10. Release The Kraken (5.11c)
11. Jug Monkey (5.11b)

the summer of 2012 to climb **Bent Hickory** and to-prope **Release The Kraken**. Jaysen Henderson was particularly captivated by this route and made several visits logging many falls in attempting to lead this fine line. Afterwards, a group from Glens Falls made several visits and added many routes.

The Peninsula

This feature is unusual in that it has cliffs on three sides and no easy walk-up. Several lines have been toproped on the blocky front (east) side by the same Arietta Climber's Group that discovered Pinnacle Mountain. The climbs listed here are in the box canyon behind the main east-facing wall.

DIRECTIONS (MAP PAGE 296)

To reach the box canyon, walk around the right end of the cliff and up into the canyon. When facing into the canyon, the climbs are on the right (east-facing) wall.

To reach the top of the routes (**What The Eft** et al), go out of the box canyon to the front (east-facing) wall of the Peninsula, then walk left 200 yards until you can break through the cliff barrier. Bushwhack right, then downhill until you can see the Peninsula below you. There is a deep crevasse that separates the slope from the top of the routes.

To reach the top of the 3-sided Peninsula, go into the box canyon and scramble (3rd class) up the backside directly in front of **Buzz Off**. Nowhere else in the park is there such an excellent perch from which to photograph climbing action.

1 What The Eft
5.11b G 60' ★★★★

Great crack climbing, especially given the ample footholds on the ripples unique to this wall.
Start: On the right-hand wall of the box canyon are two full-length cracks. This is the left-hand crack.
P1 5.11b G: Climb up a short unprotected section to the crack (#1 Camalot backed up by a #4 Camalot critical), past a brief fist-sized section, then up a handcrack to its top where the crack pinches and flares. Go up this (crux) to a good horizontal, then up a final fingercrack to a fixed anchor. 60'
Gear: #1 Camalot, #4 Camalot, #1 Camalot, #3 Camalot, #.75 Camalot; grey Alien, green Alien; #.5 Camalot.
FA Aug 4, 2013, Jim Lawyer, David Buzzelli

2 Black Lung 5.10d G 60' ★★★★

This is the right-hand crack, 6' right of **What The Eft**. Excellent and varied.
Start: Same as **What The Eft**.

*Jim Lawyer on the first ascent of **Black Lung** (5.10d). The left crack is **What the Eft**.
Photo by David Buzzelli.*

P1 5.10d G: Follow a thin seam up and right to a good horizontal below the right-hand crack. Reach past the wide section (5" cam here), then up perfect hands to where the crack turns into a groove. Go up the groove (crux), then up a tight V-chimney to the trees. 60'
Gear: to 5".
FA Aug 10, 2013, Jim Lawyer, Craig Vollkommer

3 Buzz Off 5.12b G 70' ★★★★

Varied line that climbs a short crack, then a crimpy face, some overhanging horizontals, then an amazing 20'-tall tips crack in a smooth vertical headwall. Super pumpy, saving the best for the last couple moves.
Start: At a short, right-leaning crack that begins at the lowest point on the wall, 17' right of **What The Eft**.
P1 5.12b G: Go up the right-leaning crack to its top, then step left onto the steep face. Work up and left to a shallow, right-facing corner, up this past an overlap to a sloping ledge and right-facing corner. Move up and right past a couple horizontals to a position below the headwall tips crack. Up this (crux) to a fixed anchor. 70'
Gear: 1 ea red Alien, grey Alien, #0.4 Camalot, #0.5 Camalot, #1 C3, green Alien.
FA (A0) Aug 10, 2013, David Buzzelli
FFA Aug 15, 2013, Jim Lawyer, David Buzzelli

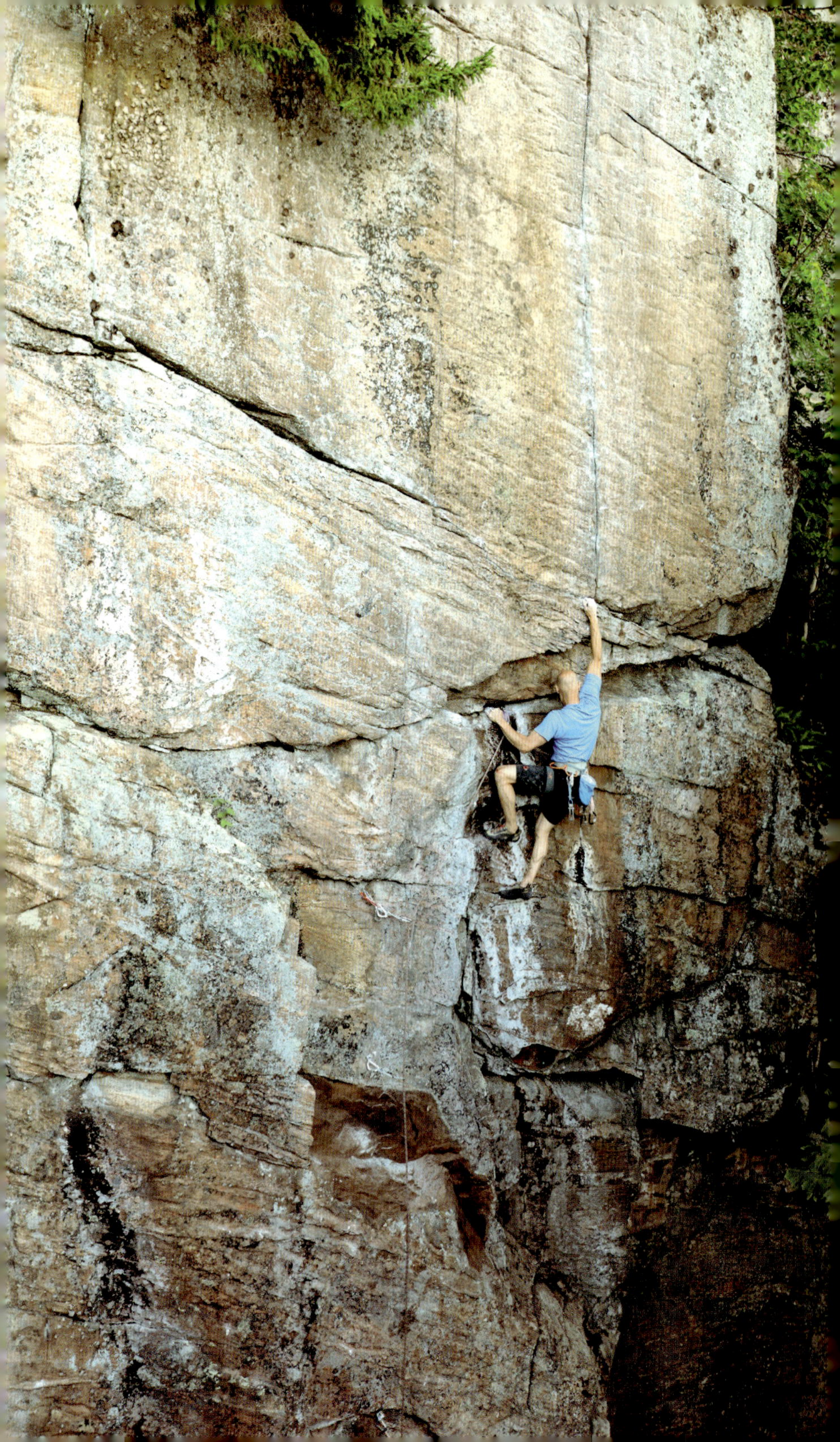

Southern Mountains

PINNACLE MOUNTAIN
4 Joy Crack (5.11b)   6 Feeding The Rat (5.11c)   8 Bent Hickory (5.11a)   10 Release The Kraken (5.11c)
5 Inferiority Complex (5.8) 7 Alien Umbrella (5.11a)   9 Shit! HiSir Needs Stitches (5.8) 11 Jug Monkey (5.11b)

To The Peninsula

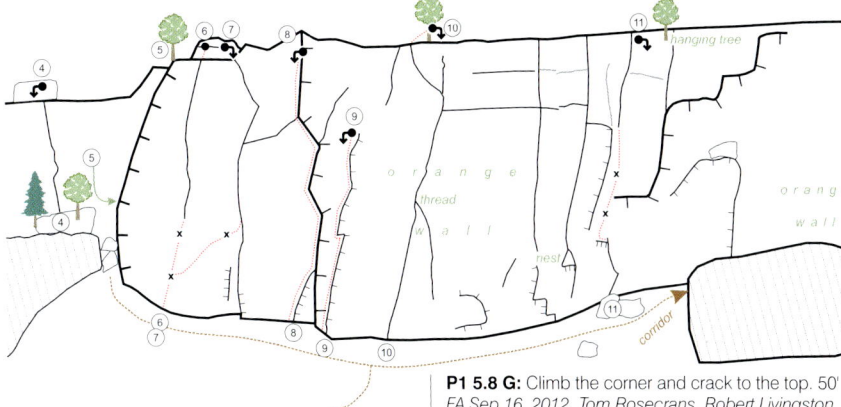

Main Face

Roughly 140' wide and 100' tall, this sheer face is steep and split by two obvious lines: the left-facing, left-leaning corner of **Bent Hickory**, and the dramatic crack **Release The Kraken** that splits the steepest, smoothest part of the main wall.

The cliff is reminiscent of the steep section of Lost Hunters Cliff, only less featured. That said, there is potential for several more difficult lines. The base of the cliff is relatively flat, open, and pleasant.

DIRECTIONS **(MAP PAGE 296)**
From the box canyon behind the Peninsula, get onto the excellent ledge right of **Buzz Off**. Walk right along the base of the cliff (staying above some a lower cliffband), cross a talus gully, then continue right on another ledge. Go up a dirt chute to arrive at the Main Face directly in front of **Release The Kraken** 0550181,4785724. It takes about 2 min to walk here from the box canyon.

4 Joy Crack 5.11b G 35' ★★★

Excellent steep crack climbing from hands to fingers that packs a wallop in its short length. It's best to belay from the top to keep the rope out of the crack.
Start: At the left end of the main face is a steep dirt cone that leads around a corner to a short wall. Make a move up the wall (easier without a pack) to a large ledge. Begin below the center of a head-high ledge with a block below a beautiful left-leaning crack. This is 15' left of the large corner of **Inferiority Complex**.
P1 5.11b G: Go up the crack to a wide pod. Continue with increasing difficulty to the top. There is a fixed anchor on a short wall just above. 35'
Gear: To 3".
FA Sep 16, 2012, Jeremy Haas

5 Inferiority Complex 5.8 G 50' ★★

Start: On the ledge of **Joy Crack**, below the large corner with a handcrack on the wall right of the corner.

Opposite: David Buzzelli on Buzz Off (5.12b).

P1 5.8 G: Climb the corner and crack to the top. 50'
FA Sep 16, 2012, Tom Rosecrans, Robert Livingston

6 Feeding The Rat 5.11c G 60' ★★★

Sustained finger jamming and technical laybacking.
Start: 25' uphill and left of the prominent left-facing corner of **Bent Hickory**, and 5' right of an arête that forms the left end of the cliff, below a fingercrack in black rock that begins 20' up.
P1 5.11c G: Go up a steep face on crimps and incuts to a jug below the crack. Make a hard move to gain the crack (crux), then climb the crack to a ledge. 60'
Gear: To 1". Take a couple of 2" cams for the anchor.
Descent: Walk right 10' to the fixed anchor on **Alien Umbrella**.
History: Named for Al Alvarez's book about Mo Antoine and his lifelong obsession with seeking adventure.
FA Aug 26, 2012, Jim Lawyer

Tom Rosecrans on the first ascent of Inferiority Complex (5.8).

299

Southern Mountains

Jim Lawyer on the first free ascent of Release the Kraken (5.11b). Photo by Colin O'Connor.

7 Alien Umbrella 5.11a G 60' ★★★★
A beautiful crack that awaits a free lead.
Start: Same as **Feeding The Rat**.
P1 5.11a G: Climb **Feeding The Rat** for 5' to the first bolt, then move rightwards across the face past another bolt to gain the bottom of a curving crack. Climb the crack to its top, and mantel a ledge with a fixed anchor just above. 60'
FA (5.10 A0) Sep 16, 2012, Robert Livingston

8 Bent Hickory 5.11a G 100' ★★★★
Start: Up and left of the low point of the terrain below a large, obvious, 5'-deep, left-facing corner.
P1 5.11a G: Climb the corner to where it leans dramatically left forming a roof-corner. Work out left under the roof-corner and break it on its left end. Easier climbing on the slab on the right leads to a fixed anchor. 100'
FA Sep, 2011, Arietta Climbing

9 Shit! HiSir Needs Stitches 5.8 PG 45' ★
Start: 5' right of the **Bent Hickory** corner below a shallow left-facing corner.
P1 5.8 PG: Up the corner that leans right and becomes a left-facing, orange flake. There is a fixed anchor at the top of the flake on the left. 45'
FA Jul, 2012, Jeff Erickson

10 Release The Kraken 5.11c G 100' ★★★★★
An amazing, jaw-dropping crack that breaks a sheer, orange, overhanging wall. One of the finest crack lines of its grade in the Adirondack Park, with a fine position, excellent rock, unique holds, and good rests. Not a move harder than .11b, but with a 5.12 pump. The top of the route is sometimes wet.
Start: Just left of center of the low point of the terrain, below a right-leaning crack that runs the full height of the cliff (the only such crack to do so).
P1 5.11c G: Boulder up a short face and gain the crack. Go up the crack to near the top of the cliff. Angle left to finish in parallel cracks. There is a fixed anchor on a large tree set back from the edge. 100'
History: The route was a project of Jaysen Henderson, who moved away before he was able to complete it. Lawyer freed and named the route. A kraken is a mythical squid-like sea monster. The expression "release the kraken" was popularized by the 2010 film *Clash of the Titans*, and has come to mean "kicking ass".
Gear: Nuts, triple cams to 1.5", 2 ea #3 Camalot.
FA (A1) Aug 14, 2012, Jaysen Henderson
FFA Sep 16, 2012, Jim Lawyer, Colin O'Connor

Craig Vollkommer on the first ascent of Jug Monkey (5.11b).

Southern Mountains

11 **Jug Monkey 5.11b G 100'** ★★★★

Start: Uphill and right of Release The Kraken at an upturned boulder, below the middle of three crack systems. The rightmost crack begins on the ground and goes up through a left-facing corner to a hanging oak tree.

P1 5.11b G: Move up to a bird-poop-stained hold, then make a hard move to gain an overhanging crack (#0.75 Camalot). Up the crack to grab a ledge, then layback up (#1 Camalot) onto the ledge. Move left to a jug, then up to a large ledge and thankful rest. Continue up easy rock to a crack, then make big moves on sidepulls and horizontals to a stance below parallel cracks. A couple of layback moves up these cracks to gain a fixed anchor. 100'

Gear: To 2".

FA Sep 16, 2012, Craig Vollkommer, Jeremy Haas

GREEN LAKE CLIFF

Location	North of Caroga Lake, accessed from NY 10
Aspect	West
Height	40'
Quality	★★★
Approach	5 min, easy
Summary	A small cliff, close to the road, with excellent rock and no easy routes.

-5.6	5.7	5.8	5.9	5.10	5.11	5.12	5.13+	total
				5	1	1		7

DESCRIPTION

This small cliff is one of the many scattered through the woods in this region. It's steep, about 75' wide, has excellent rock and a communal, open cliff base. The routes have seen very little traffic, so there will inevitably be adjustments on grades as consensus develops.

The cliff is known to locals as Target Rock, as it has been used for generations as a backdrop for gun sight adjustment. In fact, the entire Pine Mountain area is a major hunting destination. During hunting season, it is recommended that climbers wear orange and be respectful of hunters in the area.

This cliff is presently the southernmost roped climbing in the Adirondack Park.

DIRECTIONS (MAP PAGE 302)

From the triangle intersection of NY 10 and NY 29A (0.0 mile), drive south on NY 10 (NY 10 is combined with NY 29E at this point). At 2.0 miles, turn left onto Green Lake Road, a dirt road; the lake is right next to the road here. The road follows the shoreline around the northeast end of the lake. At 2.9 miles, reach the end of the road and park at an unpaved turnaround loop in the road 0540387,4780442. This is next to the last camp on the road, and the owner has given permission to park on the road, just make sure there is room for other vehicles to turn around.

Walk back on Green Lake Road for 150' yards to a stream that crosses under the road in a culvert, across the road from camp #270. Leave the road and walk east, following the left side of the stream for 300 yards to the cliff, about 5 minutes from the road 540755,4780482. As you approach, veer slightly to the north away from the stream, as the cliff is about 180' north of the stream.

HISTORY

The first climbers to visit this cliff were Caroga Lake locals Jay and Eric Manning, who did some toproping here between 2001 and 2005. Later, in January, 2009, Justin Sanford "discovered" this cliff while on a cross-country skiing reconnaissance. He began work in early spring, with the bulk later that June. The major project, Incredible Hulk, went unclimbed for months, linked on TR, then after several more months, led.

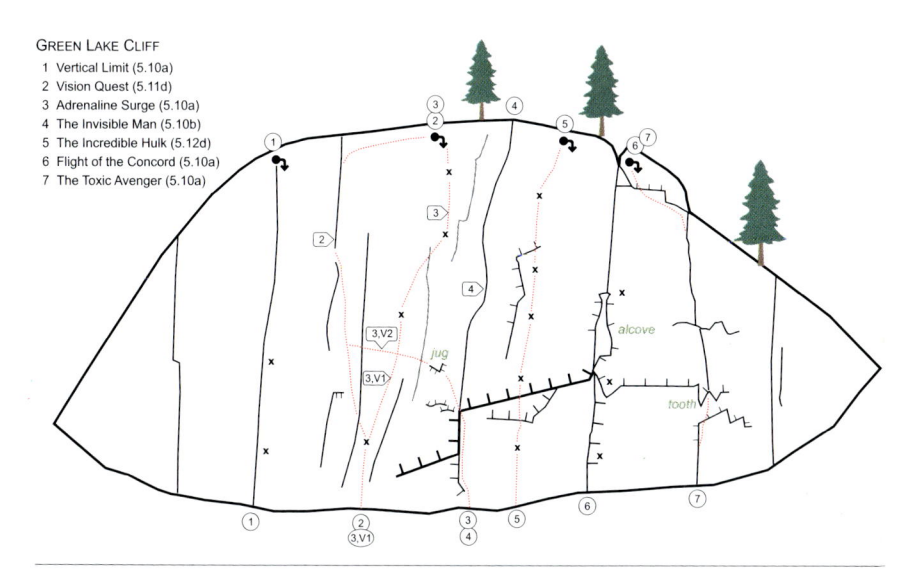

GREEN LAKE CLIFF
1 Vertical Limit (5.10a)
2 Vision Quest (5.11d)
3 Adrenaline Surge (5.10a)
4 The Invisible Man (5.10b)
5 The Incredible Hulk (5.12d)
6 Flight of the Concord (5.10a)
7 The Toxic Avenger (5.10a)

Southern Mountains

Southern Mountains

1 Vertical Limit 5.10a G 35' ★
Start: At the left end of the cliff is an offwidth crack that runs the full height of the cliff. Begin 4' right of the offwidth crack at a thin seam in black rock that begins at chest height.
P1 5.10a G: Follow the seam, which becomes a left-facing edge, then changes back to a seam again. There is a fixed anchor at the top of the seam. 35'
FA Jun, 2009, Justin Sanford

2 Vision Quest 5.11d G 40' ★
Start: 8' right of Vertical Limit below parallel seams in orange rock. There is a 4"-wide pocket at waist height.
P1 5.11d G: Stick clip, then make a technical boulder problem to gain easier crack climbing above with great gear. Step right at the top to a fixed anchor (shared with Adrenaline Surge). 40'
FA Jun, 2009, Justin Sanford

3 Adrenaline Surge 5.10a G 40' ★★
Start: At a right-facing corner in the center of the cliff, 8' right of Vision Quest.
P1 5.10a G: (V1) Climb good juggy holds until you can access the large jug on the face left of the corner. From the jug, (V2) go straight up the face to a fixed anchor. 40'
V1 Ghost Rider 5.10d G ★★: Start as for Vision Quest. Follow vertical seams trending slighting right up the face to two incut triangle holds. From here, a big move gets you to the large jug of the normal route.
V2 Stretch Armstrong 5.10b G ★★: Traverse left to access the upper crack of Vision Quest. A hand-heel match on the jug allows you to slap sidepulls out left to make it over to the crack (easier for tall climbers).
FA Jun, 2009, Justin Sanford

4 The Invisible Man 5.10b G 40' ★
Start: Same as Adrenaline Surge.
P1 5.10b G: Climb good juggy holds up the corner system to its top, then follow a crack system trending up and right to a fixed anchor. 40'
Gear: Standard rack.
FA Jun, 2009, Justin Sanford

5 The Incredible Hulk 5.12d G 40' ★★★★
A stout route worthy of a five minute hike any day; basically a 40'-tall V6 boulder problem.
Start: 3' right of the right-facing corner of Adrenaline Surge, at a steep, black face with an overhang 10' up.
● **P1 5.12d G:** Go up the steep, black face to an overhang. Work over the overhang and follow a right-leaning seam that becomes a short, shallow, right-facing corner. At its top, work straight up the face to a bulge and a fixed anchor just above. 40'
FA May 15, 2010, Justin Sanford

6 Flight of the Concord 5.10a G 35' ★★
Start: Right of center, at a prominent right-leaning crack that goes through an overhang 10' up.
P1 5.10a G: Step up into a slot, then follow a crack through an overhang to a triangular alcove. Continue up the crack to a fixed anchor (shared with The Toxic Avenger). 35'
FA Jun 5, 2010, Justin Sanford

7 The Toxic Avenger 5.10a G 35' ★
Start: 8' right of Flight of the Concord at a seam with a black rock 2' to its right.
P1 5.10a G: Follow a vertical crack up the face to two ceilings, the upper of which has a downward-pointing tooth. Above the ceilings, work up and left to a fixed anchor (shared with Flight of the Concord). 35'
FA Jun 6, 2010, Justin Sanford

OTTER LAKE CLIFF

Location	North of Caroga Lake, accessed from NY 10
Aspect	South
Height	45'
Quality	★★★
Approach	30 min, moderate
Summary	A small, steep sport cliff with compact, crimpy rock and many roofs.

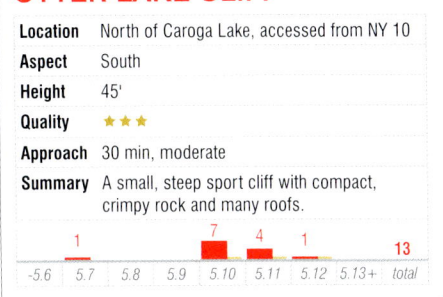

	1			7	4	1		13
-5.6	5.7	5.8	5.9	5.10	5.11	5.12	5.13+	total

DESCRIPTION
Otter Lake Cliff is a small cliff that sits on the lower slopes of Pine Mountain facing Otter Lake. It's a small cliff, but what it lacks in height it more than makes up for in difficulty. The rock is clean, compact, steep, and crimpy. There are a number of steep, technical faces and several large roofs.

The base is level, open, and pleasant. Unfortunately, the cliff seeps and takes some time to dry out after rain. The cliff is 300' wide, but all the climbs are clustered together in a 150'-wide section.

In the center of the cliff is a right-facing corner that forms a deep alcove; the route White Arête is located here. On the left end of the cliff is a huge, 7'-deep roof 6' above the ground. Tucked under the right side of this roof is a large, flat-topped boulder known as the Belay Boulder.

The Pine Mountain area is a major hunting destination. During hunting season, it is recommended that climbers wear orange and be respectful of hunters in the area. There is a frequent "watching post" for deer on top of Otter Lake Cliff.

HISTORY
Caroga Lake locals Jay and Eric Manning did some toproping here between 2001 and 2005. After seeing "some bouldering videos on YouTube," Jay contacted Ken Murphy about the cliff, who then contacted Justin Sanford. Sanford and Murphy developed most of the climbs here in 2010.

DIRECTIONS   (MAP PAGE 302)
From the triangle intersection of NY 10 and NY 29A (0.0 mile), drive south on NY 10 (NY 10 is combined with NY 29E at this point). At 2.0 miles, turn left onto Green Lake Road; the lake is right next to the road here. At 2.5 miles the pavement ends; turn left onto a small dirt road marked with a several small signs: "Kane MT," "Fire Tower," and "Parking Area," as well as a giant boulder

Southern Mountains

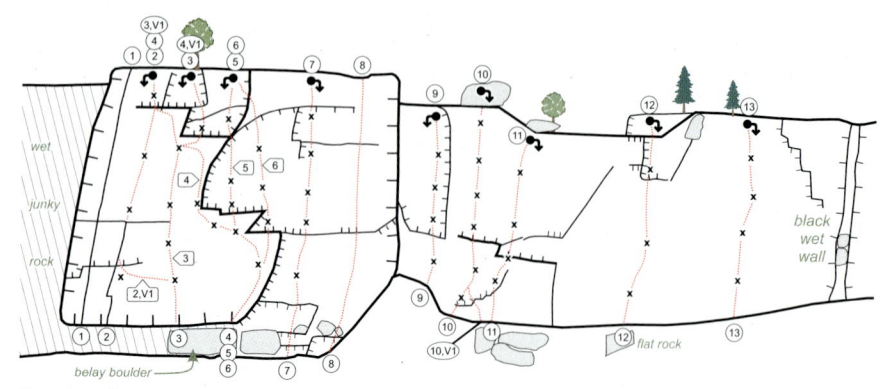

Otter Lake Cliff

1. Contradiction Crack (5.7)
2. Porcupine Prelude (5.10a)
3. Harvest Moon (5.11b)
4. Roof Traverse (5.10b)
5. Roof Direct (5.12a)
6. Rubber Knumbchuck (5.10a)
7. Pandora's Box (5.11a)
8. Burgundy Color Lily Crack (5.10a)
9. White Arête (5.10c)
10. Independence Pass (5.10a)
11. Approach Shoe Assassin (5.10d)
12. Crimp Scampi (5.11a)
13. Dukes of Hazard (5.11d)

with "Kane MT" faintly painted on it. At 2.6 miles, reach the trailhead parking 540265,4780943.

At the north end of the parking area is the trail to Kane Mt, and another to Stuart Lake (0.0 min). Continue on the dirt road (towards Stuart Lake) for 200' to a three-way intersection (left is the Pine Lake X-C Ski Trail, straight is the continuation of the dirt road, and right goes to Stuart Lake). Go left onto the Pine Lake X-C Ski Trail marked with yellow discs.

Follow the ski trail (a bit muddy) to a large cairn on the right, reached at 4 min. From here, veer off the trail 45° to the right, heading towards the sound of water; this is the outlet of Otter Lake. Once you reach the water, follow this north, and eventually the stream will merge into the lake; reached at 11 min; there's a cabin on the opposite shore, on a small piece of private land that touches the lake here. Continue northeast along the shoreline of the lake following a good network of paths through open hemlock forest, sometimes right next to the shore, while other times inland 50'. Eventually, but not quite at the north end of the lake, you'll find a large cairn (and maybe some flagging) 540775,4782018 about 15' from the water, reached at 21 min. Go 40' beyond the cairn, then head directly north away from the lake, at first uphill, then level, across a stream, and up to the cliff, reached at 30 min 540673,4782428.

1 Contradiction Crack 5.7 PG 40'
An all-gear route; a little dirty on the topout.
Start: 4' left of **Porcupine Prelude** at a crack that begins at the roof and runs the full height of the cliff.
P1 5.7 PG: Pull through the roof and follow the crack to the top. Tree anchor. 40'
FA May 19, 2012, Mitchel Hoffman, Jae Zhong

2 Porcupine Prelude 5.10a G 40' ★★
Start: At the left end of the cliff is a huge, 7'-deep roof 6' above the ground. Begin in the center of the roof below a right-facing flake in the face above the roof.
● **P1 5.10a G:** (V1) Pull up the flake to get established on the wall above the roof. Follow the right-leaning flake and crack to its end, then up past a bulge to the left side of a roof. Pull over this to a fixed anchor. 40'
● **V1 5.9 G ★:** To avoid the strenuous pull at the start, begin as for **Harvest Moon**. Go up 8' to the first bolt, then traverse left on good holds to the normal route.
Gear: Gear needed for the right-leaning flake.
FA Apr 10, 2010, Justin Sanford
FA (V1) Apr 10, 2010, Justin Sanford

3 Harvest Moon 5.11b G 40' ★★
The first ascent was at 1:30 AM by headlamp and lanterns.
Start: On top of (and on the left side of) the Belay Boulder.
● **P1 5.11b G:** Climb straight up the face to the second highest roof. (V1) Traverse right under the roof, then pull over the roof and up the face to a fixed anchor. 40'
● **V1 5.10b G:** Step left and go up to the highest roof. Traverse left, then pull over the overhang to the fixed anchor on **Porcupine Prelude**.
FA Jun 24, 2010, Justin Sanford

4 Roof Traverse 5.10b G 55' ★★★
Start: On the right side of the Belay Boulder.
● **P1 5.10b G:** Climb up and right on a ramp to the lowest roof. Work your way up and left on the underside of the stepped roofs to (V1) the highest roof. Traverse left, then pull over the overhang to the fixed anchor on **Porcupine Prelude**. 55'
● **V1 Roof Traverse Variation 5.10b G ★★:** Combines the **Roof Traverse** with the finish of **Harvest Moon**. At the second highest roof, traverse right under the roof, then pull over the roof and up the face to a fixed anchor.
FA Jun 26, 2010, Ken Murphy
FA (V1) Aug 7, 2010, Justin Sanford

Southern Mountains

5 Roof Direct 5.12a G 40' ★★★★

Directly climbs the most prominent feature on the cliff—the overlapping roof.
Start: Same as Roof Traverse.
● **P1 5.12a G:** Go up Roof Traverse to the second bolt. Pull straight through the roof and up to the fixed anchor of Rubber Knumbchuck. 40'
FA May 19, 2012, Justin Sanford

6 Rubber Knumbchuck 5.10a G 40' ★
Start: Same as Roof Traverse.
● **P1 5.10a G:** Climb up the ramp to the lowest roof (as for Roof Traverse). Step right and break through the low roof onto the face above. Up the face to a fixed anchor. 40'
FA Jun 12, 2010, Justin Sanford

7 Pandora's Box 5.11a G 45' ★★★★

Perhaps the best route here.
Start: At a 5'-tall right-facing corner 15' right of the Belay Boulder at the tallest part of the cliff.
● **P1 5.11a G:** Climb up horizontals to the highest ledge, then up the face to some shallow left-facing corners, through an overlap, and up to a fixed anchor. 45'
FA Jun 12, 2010, Justin Sanford

8 Burgundy Color Lily Crack
5.10a R 40'
A bold trad lead.
Start: Right of Pandora's Box and just left of the rounded arête that divides this wall from the alcove with White Arête, below a discontinuous 2" crack formed by a block with a horizontal on top.
P1 5.10a R: Go up the 2" crack for 15', then wander up the face. A critical nut in a horizontal constriction protects the crux, followed by marginal gear to the top. 40'
FA May, 2012, Mitchel Hoffman, Jae Zhong

9 White Arête 5.10c G 30' ★
Start: In the back of the depression formed by the huge right-facing corner that divides the cliff, a few feet right of the corner.
● **P1 5.10c G:** Work up an overhanging wall to a clean face and small arête in the back of the depression to a fixed anchor. 30'
FA Jun 26, 2010, Ken Murphy

10 Independence Pass 5.10a G 30' ★★
Start: On the right side of the depression in the center of the cliff, 10' right of White Arête.
● **P1 5.10a G:** (V1) Boulder up the bulging black face to a good jug. Mantel this, then up the black face to a fixed anchor. 30'
● **V1 5.9 G:** Avoid the crimpy start by starting 10' right and work up left to the good jug. Might want to stick clip the second bolt.
FA Jul 3, 2010, Justin Sanford
FA (V1) Jul 3, 2010, Mitchel Hoffman

Tim Poulterer on Contradiction Crack (5.8), with ropes hanging on various other routes. Photo by Justin Sanford.

11 Approach Shoe Assassin 5.10d G 40' ★★
Start: Just right of the huge right-facing corner and depression that divides the cliff is a pile of flat-topped boulders. Begin on top of these boulders, 10' right of Independence Pass.
● **P1 5.10d G:** Climb up a right-leaning flake to a roof. Pull the roof, then up the steep face to a fixed anchor. 40'
FA Jul 3, 2010, Justin Sanford

12 Crimp Scampi 5.11a PG 40' ★★
Watch the second clip.
Start: 20' right of Approach Shoe Assassin, and 10' right of a pile of flat-topped boulders, on top of a small boulder just right of a 4'-tall, left-facing, right-leaning corner that begins 4' up.
● **P1 5.11a PG:** Crimp up the face on edges and incuts to a large horizontal (gear). Over this to a fixed anchor at the top. 40'
FA May 9, 2010, Justin Sanford

13 Dukes of Hazard 5.11d G 40' ★★
Start: 15' right of Crimp Scampi.
● **P1 5.11d G:** Up the orange face to a good horizontal 8' up. Continue straight up the face, over a bulge, to a fixed anchor at the top. 40'
FA Aug 7, 2010, Justin Sanford

Southern Mountains

THE LOST CRAGS

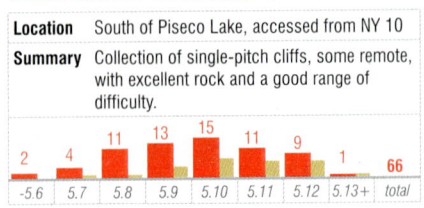

Location	South of Piseco Lake, accessed from NY 10
Summary	Collection of single-pitch cliffs, some remote, with excellent rock and a good range of difficulty.

2	4	11	13	15	11	9	1	66
-5.6	5.7	5.8	5.9	5.10	5.11	5.12	5.13+	total

Tucked in the Silver Lake Wilderness are a number of excellent cliffs. (Not to be confused with the Silver Lake climbing area north of Wilmington.) The remote Lost Hunters Cliff on Sherman Mountain was the first to be discovered, and now boasts some of the region's most difficult routes. Lost T and The Annex on Chub Mountain are immensely popular, with well-protected crack and face routes, and an easy approach. McMartin and Lost T2 are more remote, located on a sub-summit between Sherman Mountain and Trout Lake Mountain. All of the cliffs have excellent rock—coarse and textured with excellent friction properties—and share a common network of approach paths.

Cliffs are still being discovered in this area.

CAMPING
There is a good campsite across the road from the west end of the parking area. There's also a good spot on Chub Lake, about 5 min from the road, with a great swimming beach.

DIRECTIONS (MAP PAGE 307)
Park 0.2 mile east of the Good Luck Mountain Trailhead at a paved pullout on the north side of the road 538088,4789289. This parking area is 11.8 miles south of NY 8 (on the left), and 5.8 miles north of NY 29A (on the right). There is room for many cars.

The Lost Crags
LOST T CLIFF

Aspect	West
Height	80'
Quality	★★★★
Approach	20 min, easy
Summary	Excellent, off-vertical cliff laced with cracks; great crack and face routes.

1	3	3	6	5	4	2		24
-5.6	5.7	5.8	5.9	5.10	5.11	5.12	5.13+	total

Tucked in the forest above Chub Lake near the summit of Chub Lake Mountain is yet another gem. This 300'-wide wall stands between 40' and 80', is tilted at a comfortable 80°, and is laced with cracks. The rock is especially coarse and textured with excellent friction properties; hence, there is a good mixture of face climbs and crack routes, many of which are equipped with lower-off anchors. The base of the cliff rises gently uphill to the left and is pleasant, open and airy.

The cliff is located across the road from Good Luck and has easy access—the straight line distance from the road is less than 2000'. With the short approach, the cliff is sure to be popular. To reach the top, walk around the left end of the cliff.

The cliff was developed in a style similar to Shanty Cliff, meaning a mix of trad and fixed gear, well-cleaned routes, and good access for groups. Many of the routes are designed to be stick-clipped (there's often a pole stashed on a ledge at the base of the cliff).

HISTORY
Lost T cliff was discovered by accident by Gary Thomann (the "T" for Thomann) in July 2008. Routes were added that summer by the Arietta Climbing group (page 308).

*Paul Roberts at the crux on **Flavor of the Day** (5.12a).*

Southern Mountains

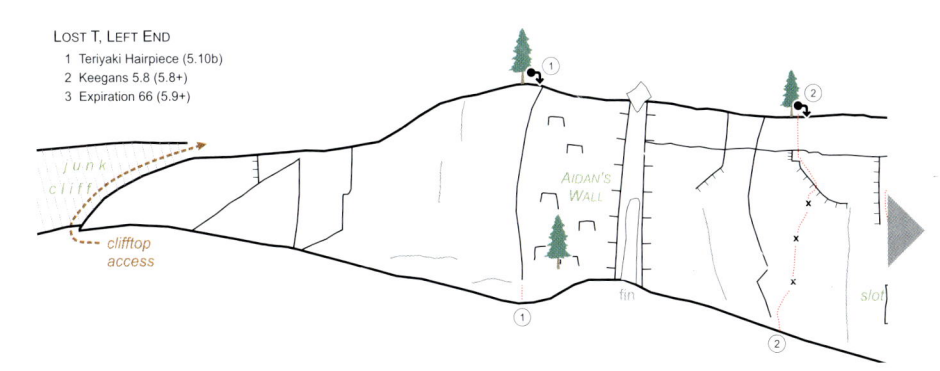

LOST T, LEFT END
1. Teriyaki Hairpiece (5.10b)
2. Keegans 5.8 (5.8+)
3. Expiration 66 (5.9+)

DIRECTIONS (MAP PAGE 307)

From the east end of the parking pullout, locate an obvious trail in the trees (0.0 min) and follow this east, parallel to the road. At 3 min, reach a T intersection; go left (downhill) towards Chub Lake (right goes to NY 10, the old approach). About 100' before the lake, turn right onto a small path and follow this as it contours around the east side of Chub Lake. The path crosses a small stream, then makes a short climb to a Y intersection at 9 min. The left branch goes to Lost Hunters Cliff, McMartin, and Lost T2; you go right. Walk steeply uphill through open forest to the crest of a ridge. The Annex sits below the trail here. Continue along the mostly level trail another few minutes to the cliff **538748,4789866**.

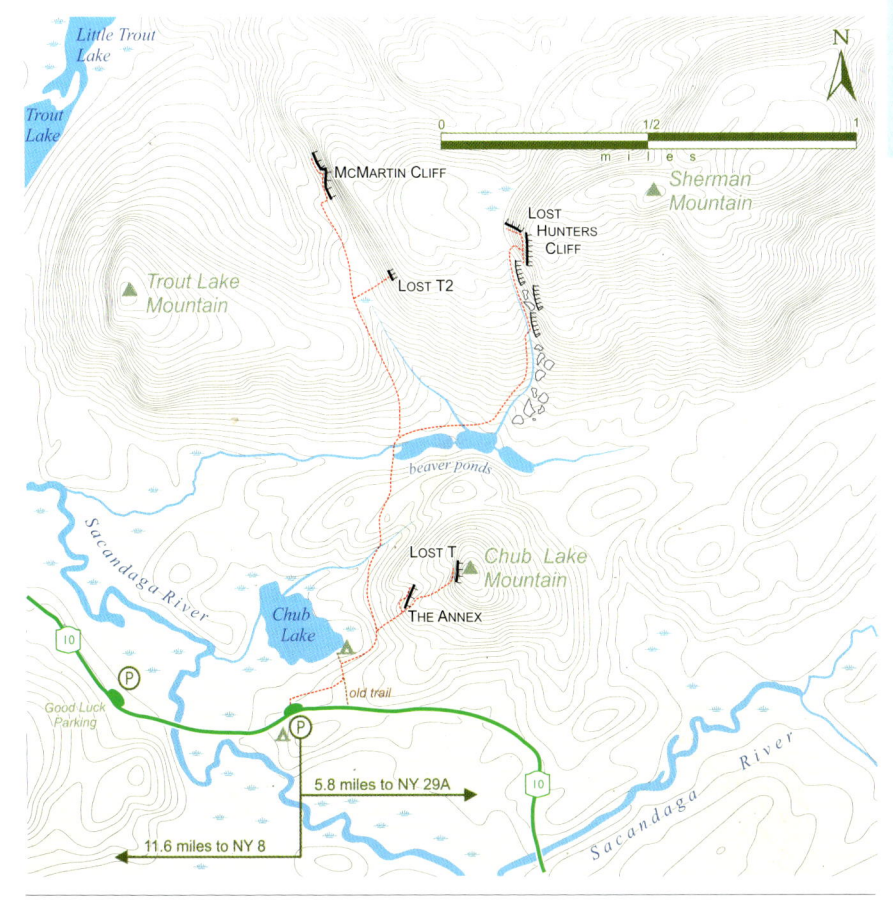

Southern Mountains

LOST T, MIDDLE
4 CB Love Grannys (5.12a)
5 Ten B (5.11a)
6 Freckles and No Lipstick (5.9)
7 The Beauty to Come (5.10c)
8 Spelunking Midget (5.10b)
9 The Keyhole (5.11a)
10 Courtney Marie's Boobies (5.10a)
11 Crimps are for Pimps (5.11a)

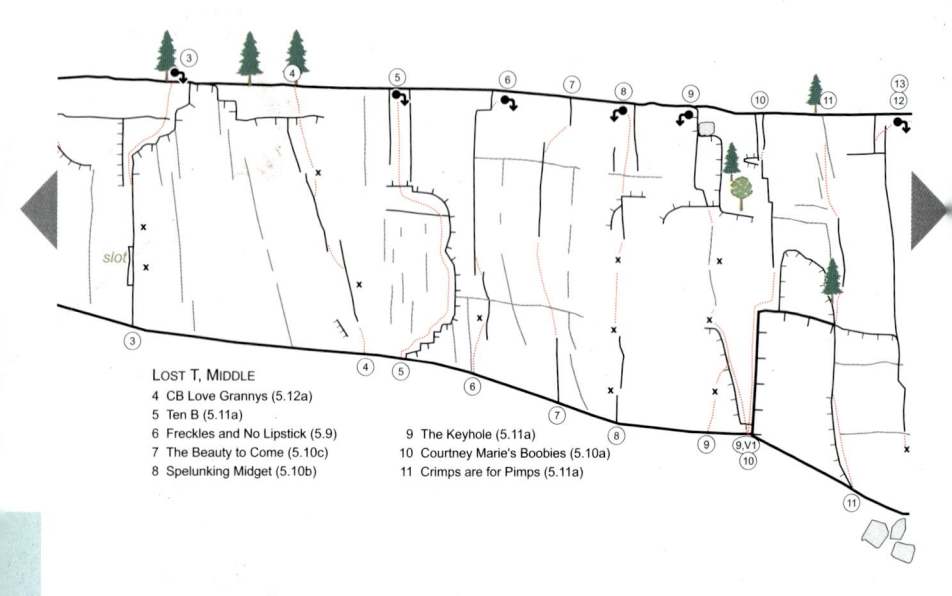

Arietta Climbing

"Arietta Climbing" is a group of climbers and route developers whose activity has been centered near the town of Arietta in the Southern Adirondacks. Their mission is to create new routes for climbers of all levels, skilled and novice alike, and "make the Southern Adirondacks a major destination area for climbers."

The group began with Bill Griffith and Jimmy Diliberto, who visited Shanty Cliff in 2007 while searching for cliffs appropriate for the youth groups they took climbing. They spent three days building a trail, and another 25 days cleaning routes. Over time, many others joined the development group, beginning with Gary Thomann, who became a central figure, and created mini-guides for the cliffs developed by the group.

Bill had been climbing for 20 years, and pursued cliff development as a way to give back to the climbing community. He preferred to remain semi-anonymous, so the group broke with the tradition of crediting individuals for first ascents; instead, they credit them to the group as a whole.

Bill has fond recollections of these times. Many high-quality, fun climbs at Shanty were added that put this dormant cliff back on the climbing map. Despite a river crossing in the approach—a challenge in cold weather—it is very popular.

After their work at Shanty Cliff, Bill and Gary had the new-routing bug, and Lost Hunters Cliff was their next project. Like Shanty Cliff, this remote cliff lay dormant, protected by a long, blind bushwhack and offering only difficult routes. They spent 15 days cleaning the cliff, and making path improvements that cut 20 minutes off the approach. While working out the path one day, Gary missed his target and stumbled upon Lost T, a cliff near the top of another mountain altogether that turned out to be a gem of the Adirondacks for routes between 5.7 and 5.11. They spent another 20 days cleaning there, and another 7 at the nearby Annex.

Included in Gary's discoveries is McMartin Cliff, which he read about in a 1974 Barbara McMartin guide. Bill considers McMartin the group's best contribution to the climbing scene, with good lines in a beautiful, remote setting.

Pinnacle and The Peninsula were identified and developed more recently, thanks to a tip from a boulderer who was searching for new boulders.

Many other climbers contributed to the development of all these cliffs, including Jonathan Nickel, Nicole Nowick, Weston Griffen, Gray Watkins, Keith Matuszyk, Keegan Griffith, Priscilla Cassidy, Rachel Smith, Rachel Breidster, Carlton (aka "Coach") Maricle, Mary Giehl, Greg Boyer, Sarah Weiss, John Lubrant, Rachael Brugeman, Eric Brugeman, Ping-Kwan Keung, Brett Olsen, Jeff Erickson, Dave Garber, and Kelsey Lane.

Arietta Climbing wants more than to simply add new routes: they create destination crags that attract climbers of all abilities. Over time, they have developed a signature style for cliff development: build a trail, create a comfortable cliff base, clean the routes, and install protection and anchors. The results are fun, safe, clean, approachable routes where none existed before.

Southern Mountains

Lost T, Right End
12 Little Kisses (5.9)
13 Parthenope (5.11d)
14 Five Star Crack (5.7)
15 Dixie Normus (5.9)
16 Wide Crack (5.7)
17 Limp Stick (5.9)
18 The Dike (5.8)
19 Mean Sister (5.10b)
20 Coach and Mary (5.7)
21 Emily Doesn't Have a Clue (5.8)
22 Flavor of the Day (5.12b)

1 Teriyaki Hairpiece 5.10b G 40'

Start: 60' left of **Keegans 5.8**, and 40' left of a full-height chimney (the bottom half of which is stuffed with a fin of rock protruding 1' from the cliff) below a crack that leans right and flares in the middle and runs the full height of a sheer face.

P1 5.10b G: Go up easy, mossy holds to gain the crack. Follow the crack past a flared section (easier on the face to the right) to a horizontal. A couple of layback moves gain the jugs at the top. 40'

Gear: Small nuts and cams to yellow Alien. Green Alien critical at the crux.

History: Despite the forest having been cleared, the route was unreported. Perhaps it was left as a toprope problem?

ACB Jul 31, 2012, Jim Lawyer, Jeremy Haas

2 Keegans 5.8 5.8+ G 40' ★

Start: At the left and uphill end of the wall, 20' right of a full-height chimney (the bottom half of which is stuffed with a fin of rock protruding 1' from the cliff) and 10' left of a large pine tree growing on top of a sunken boulder.

P1 5.8+ G: Up the face to a good horizontal crack, then up more face to a pine tree. 40'

FA Aug, 2008, Keegan Griffith

3 Expiration 66 5.9+ G 40' ★★

Trickier than it looks as good stances are scarce. A few small cams are helpful.

Start: 15' right of **Keegans 5.8** and 5' right of a large pine tree growing on top of a sunken boulder, below a seam and crack that runs the full height of the cliff.

P1 5.9+ G: A small cam protects the opening moves to gain a seam. Go up the seam past a hand slot to the top. 40'

FA Aug, 2008, Arietta Climbing

4 CB Love Grannys 5.12a PG 45'

An exercise in smearing on a steep face. Requires small gear.

Start: 15' right of **Expiration 66** and 12' left of the shallow left-facing left-arching corner that marks the start of **Ten B**, at a face with a left-slanting seam that begins 8' up.

P1 5.12a PG: Up the face on good holds to gain the left-leaning seam. Up the seam to its top, then switch left to another left-leaning seam which is followed to the top. 45'

FA Sep, 2008, Bill Griffith

5 Ten B 5.11a G 45' ★★★

Clean rock with good moves and a short crux. The name does not align with the rating.

Start: 50' downhill and right of a full-height chimney (the bottom half of which is stuffed with a fin of rock protruding 1' from the cliff) at a shallow left-facing left-arching corner.

P1 5.11a G: Move up and right on staircase holds to gain the left-facing corner. Up the corner as it arches left into an overlap. Traverse left in a horizontal crack below the overlap to its left end, then up to parallel seams in the face. Up the seams past a horizontal crack (crux), then up the short face to the top. 45'

FA Aug, 2008, Jimmy Diliberto

309

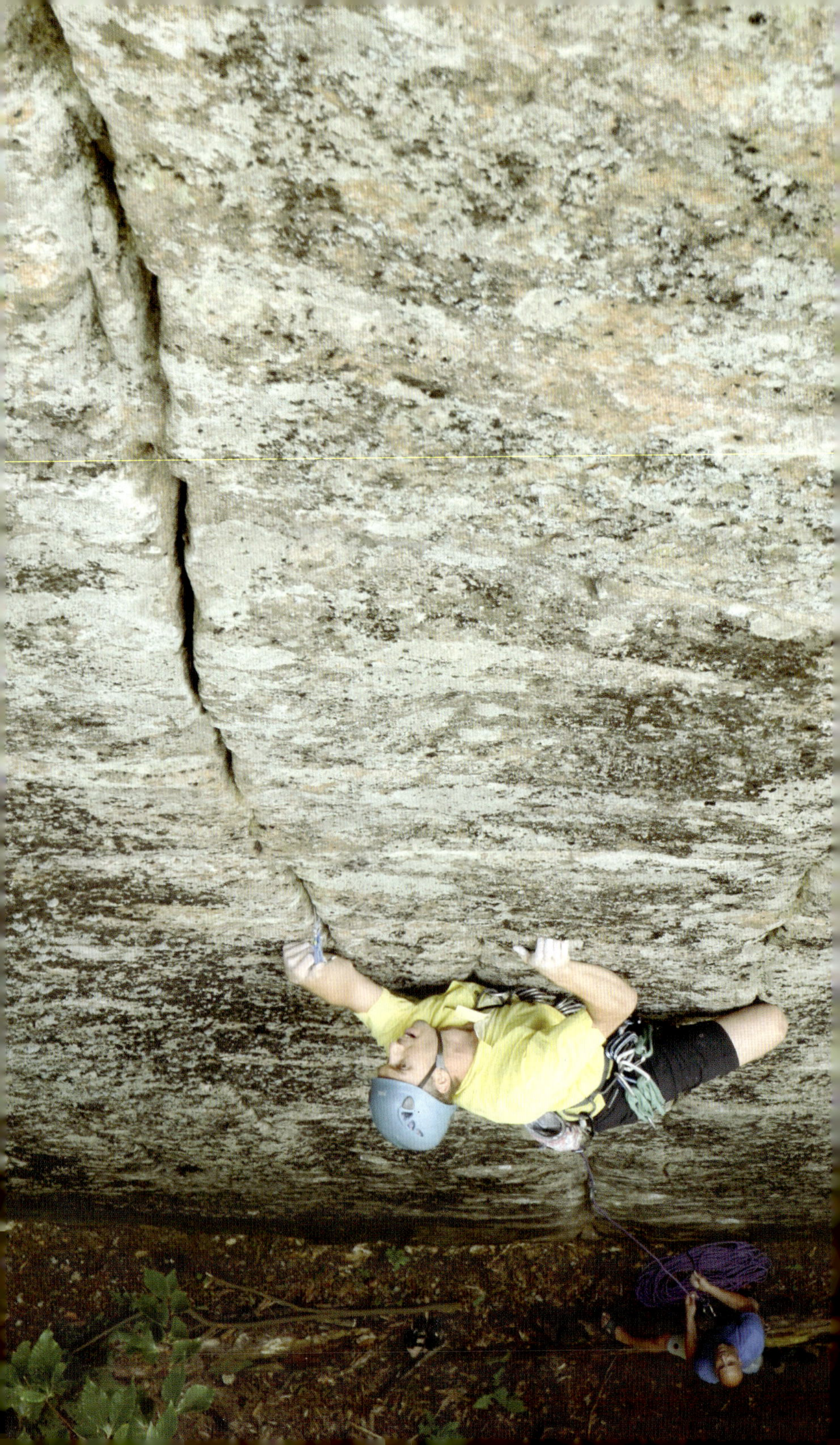

Southern Mountains

6 Freckles and No Lipstick 5.9 G 50' ★★
An excellent crack climb.
Start: 5' downhill and right of the shallow left-facing left-arching corner of Ten B and 45' left of the large left-facing corner of The Keyhole, below a face with seams.
P1 5.9 G: A small nut protects the opening moves to an excellent crack. Up the face with seams to a crack and flared pod, then up more crack to a fixed anchor at the top. 50'
FA Aug, 2008, Arietta Climbing

7 The Beauty to Come 5.10c PG 45' ★★
The sister route to Spelunking Midget with similar (and slightly more difficult) climbing.
Start: 6' left of Spelunking Midget and 15' downhill and right of Freckles and No Lipstick at a thin left-leaning seam.
P1 5.10c PG: Up the left-leaning seam to a horizontal, then up the face to a good vertical crack. Follow this past an 18"-wide overlap to its top. Move right and go up a handcrack to a fixed anchor. 45'
Gear: Nuts, microcams to 3/4".
FA Jul 19, 2013, Ben Cook, David Buzzelli

8 Spelunking Midget 5.10b G 45' ★★★
Start: In a shallow groove.
P1 5.10b G: Up the groove and vertical seams to a small overlap at mid-height. Continue up intermittent cracks to the top. 45'
FA Apr 3, 2010, Justin Sanford, Ryan Pooler

9 The Keyhole 5.11a PG 55' ★★
Start: Centered on the cliff (and just left of the highest section of cliff) is a stepped, 3'-deep, 40'-tall, left-facing corner. Begin 10' left of the corner at a brown mossy face.
P1 5.11a PG: (V1) Up the face to a horizontal crack (scary clip), then straight up a thin crack to an overhang below a right-facing corner. Step left and go over the overhang, then up and left in a good crack past horizontals to a fixed anchor on the left. 55'
V1 5.9 G: Begin 10' right in the left-facing corner. Step left onto the face, and climb a mossy, shallow, right-facing, left-leaning ramp to gain the thin crack. This reduces the overall grade to 5.10c G.
FA Aug, 2008, Arietta Climbing

10 Courtney Marie's Boobies 5.10a PG 60' ★★★
Start: In the left-facing corner 10' right of The Keyhole (and same as The Keyhole V1).
P1 5.10a PG: Go up the left-racing corner past a ledge to its top. Step left onto the face and climb a thin crack system to where it disappears, make a move left to a jug, then a bigger move right to finish up a fingercrack. 60'
FA Jul 22, 2012, Jeff Erickson

Opposite: Ben Cook on the first ascent of The Beauty to Come (5.10c), belayed by David Buzzelli.

11 Crimps are for Pimps 5.11a PG 80' ★★
Start: At a right-facing corner 12' left of Little Kisses.
P1 5.11a PG: Up a handcrack in the corner to a tree on a ledge 20' up. Go up a blocky section to reach a handcrack on the right. Protect here, move left on small edges for 15' to reach a seam. Up seam for 25' past two horizontals (sustained crux) to a big jug. Continue up an easy handcrack to a fixed anchor on a tree. 80'
Gear: Some small cams (#000, #00) are necessary to protect the crux.
FA Jul 25, 2012, Paul Roberts, Jeff Erickson

12 Little Kisses 5.9 G 80' ★★★★
This is the first of three parallel climbs on the tallest section of the cliff. This crack is a contender for the best 5.9 in the southern section of the park. The crack is fingers and tight hands with many hidden horizontals for rests.
Start: At the tallest section of cliff, 30' downhill and right of the stepped left-facing corner that marks the start of The Keyhole, and 8' right of a 12'-high right-facing corner (Crimps are for Pimps), below a seam in chocolate-colored rock.
P1 5.9 G: Go up the seam and face to gain the crack, then follow this incredible feature to its top. Move left and finish in a short handcrack to a fixed anchor on the right (shared with Parthenope). 80'
Gear: To 2", with doubles in the finger size range.
FA Aug, 2008, Arietta Climbing

Jeff Erickson on the first ascent of Courtney Marie's Boobies (5.10a).

311

Southern Mountains

*Ben Cook on **Spelunking Midget** (5.10b).*

13 **Parthenope** 5.11d PG 80' ★★★

Start: 4' right of **Little Kisses**, exactly between **Little Kisses** and **Five Star Crack**, at the left end of a blocky ledge 2' up.

○ P1 5.11d PG: Up the face to a thin seam in the face. Go up the seam and face (crux) to a good horizontal. A thin crack on the right (very close to **Five Star Crack**) protects more face climbing to another horizontal, then hard moves past a final horizontal (5.11b) lead to a fixed anchor shared with **Little Kisses**. 80'
Gear: Small cams, nuts.
FA Aug, 2008, Arietta Climbing

14 **Five Star Crack** 5.7 G 70' ★★★

Sustained at the grade with good moves and excellent protection.

Start: The right-hand crack at the tallest section of cliff, 3' left of a large, broken birch tree 4' up.

P1 5.7 G: Go up to a small overlap to gain the left-leaning crack. Up the crack past many horizontals to a fixed anchor. 70'
Gear: To 2".
FA Aug, 2008, Arietta Climbing

15 **Dixie Normus** 5.9 G 70' ★★

Start: Same as **Wide Crack**.
P1 5.9 G: Go up **Wide Crack** for 10', then traverse left 5' (almost to **Five Star Crack**) and climb a series of thin cracks straight up to the top. 70'
FA Aug 7, 2012, Jeff Erickson

16 **Wide Crack** 5.7 G 60' ★

Somewhat marred by a chossy finish.
Start: 12' right of **Five Star Crack** below a chossy overhang 5' up, above which is a crack that runs to the top of the cliff.
P1 5.7 G: Layback through the initial overhang to gain the crack which is climbed to the top. 60'
FA Aug, 2008, Jimmy Diliberto, Nicole Norwick

17 **Limp Stick** 5.9 PG 60'

Climbs the face via a thin, flared seam between **Wide Crack** and **The Dike**.
Start: Same as **Wide Crack**.
P1 5.9 PG: Go up **Wide Crack** to a horizontal crack on the right. Traverse right 5' to a thin crack, then climb straight up the face to an overlap. Over this via a crack on the left, then up to the trees. 60'
FA Jul 25, 2012, Jeff Erickson, Paul Roberts

18 **The Dike** 5.8 G 55' ★

This is the crack and dike 20' right of **Wide Crack**.
Start: Same as **Wide Crack**.
P1 5.8 G: Go up **Wide Crack** to a horizontal crack on the right. Foot traverse right 20' to the dike, then follow it to its top. Go past a tree, then up a deep, flared crack to a fixed anchor at the top. 55'
FA Aug, 2008, Arietta Climbing

19 **Mean Sister** 5.10b G 55' ★★★★

A harder version of **Little Kisses**, and one of the best fingercracks here.
Start: Halfway between **The Dike** and **Coach and Mary** below roof at head height.
P1 5.10b G: (V1) Move over the roof to a triangular incut hold, then up a crack that leans left to its top. Move right and continue up another crack to a fixed anchor at the top. 55'

*Leslie Ackerman on **Five Star Crack** (5.7).*

Southern Mountains

Leslie Ackerman on Emily Doesn't Have a Clue (5.8).

V1 5.8 G: Go up **Coach and Mary** to just past the first horizontal. Move left across the face to reach the thin crack of the normal route.
FA Oct, 2011, Arietta Climbing

20 Coach and Mary 5.7 G 55' ★

Start: On the right end of the cliff, 40' right of **Wide Crack**, 20' right of **The Dike**, and 10' left of the right end of the main face (where the terrain rises to the start of **Emilie Doesn't Have a Clue**).
P1 5.7 G: Go up the wide crack to the top. 55'
FA Oct, 2011, Arietta Climbing

21 Emily Doesn't Have a Clue 5.8 G 45' ★

Start: Near the right end of the wall is a boulder pile above which is a right-facing corner capped by a roof. Begin at a large birch tree at the top of a left-rising ramp below the right-facing corner.
P1 5.8 G: Up the wide crack in the right-facing corner past the left edge of the roof to a fixed anchor shared with **Flavor of the Day**. 45'
FA Aug, 2008, Arietta Climbing

22 Flavor of the Day 5.12b G 45' ★ ★ ★

Start: Same start as **Emily Doesn't Have a Clue**.
● **P1 5.12b G:** Stick-clip! Move right to a jug below the roof, then go directly over the roof (a toe-heel cam works well) onto a horizontal rail on the face. Bump up to the arête, then follow this to a fixed anchor shared with **Emily Doesn't Have a Clue**. 45'
FA Aug, 2008, Arietta Climbing

Jeff Erickson on the megaclassic Little Kisses (5.9).

Southern Mountains

23 Fat People Are Harder To Kidnap
5.9 G 45' ★★

A nice finish crack, but mediocre climbing below.
Start: On the right side of the boulder pile, above which is the ramp that leads to Flavor of the Day, and 40' right of that route, at blocky chaotic terrain with a cleaned strip through moss below a ledge 10' up.
P1 5.9 G: Move up to the ledge, then up a crack to another ledge. Move left past a small tree and gain a seam and crack that snakes up a clean face. At the top of the crack, go up to a horizontal crack, then up the short face (crux) to the top. 45'
FA Aug, 2008, Arietta Climbing

24 Waiting for the Sun 5.5 G 60'
Start: 30' right of Fat People Are Harder To Kidnap at a mossy, blocky, vague depression below a 2' x 3' projecting block at the top of the cliff.
P1 5.5 G: Climb the blocky depression, then over the projecting block to the top. 60'
Gear: To 2".
FA Aug 28, 2012, Mike Rawdon, Dawn Alguard

The Lost Crags
THE ANNEX

Aspect	West
Height	50'
Quality	★
Approach	15 min, easy
Summary	Small cliff with several crack and face routes.

-5.6	5.7	5.8	5.9	5.10	5.11	5.12	5.13+	total
	1	1	1	3				6

A smaller version of Lost T Cliff (and probably an extension of that cliff), this 150'-wide wall has several crack and face routes. The left end has a large left-facing corner capped by a stepped roof, the location of Chocolate Left and Chocolate Right.

Like its parent, Lost T, the routes here are designed to be stick-clipped.

DIRECTIONS (MAP PAGE 307)
From the east end of the parking pullout, locate an obvious trail in the trees (0.0 min) and follow this east parallel to the road. At 3 min reach a T intersection (going right goes to NY 10, the old approach); go left (downhill) towards Chub Lake. About 100' before the lake, turn right onto a small path and follow this as it contours around the east side of Chub Lake. The path crosses a small stream, then makes a short climb to a Y intersection at 9 min. The left branch goes to Lost Hunters Cliff, McMartin, and Lost T2; you go right.

Walk steeply uphill through open forest to the crest of a ridge. The trail traverses within 20' of the top of The Annex (you can see the opening in the forest on your left when the trail reaches the ridge), then continues on to Lost T. Leave the trail and walk (skier's) left along the top of the cliff to a short down scramble to reach the base of the cliff, then turn (skier's) right and follow a trail to the base of the cliff.

HISTORY
The Annex was developed by the Arietta Climbing group (page 308) in the summer of 2009.

1 Chocolate Left 5.8 G 45' ★★
Start: At the far left end of the cliff, uphill and left of the large overhang.
● **P1 5.8 G:** Stick-clip the first bolt. Work right across the face to the hanging left-facing corner on the left side of the buttress. Up the corner almost to its top, then work right around the arête onto the face to a fixed anchor. 45'
FA 2009, Arietta Climbing

2 Chocolate Right 5.9 G 40' ★★
A 5.8 route with a boulder-move start.
Start: Below the large roof at the left end of the cliff, at a shallow trough below a 4'-high right-facing corner 5' up, and 8' left of the left-facing corner (this left-facing corner is 20' left of Welcome to Arietta).
● **P1 5.9 G:** Make a boulder move up the trough (crux), then up to the left end of the large roof. Step right around the arête and climb the face and shallow left-facing corner to a fixed anchor shared with Chocolate Left. 40'
FA 2009, Arietta Climbing

3 Welcome to Arietta 5.10c G 50' ★★
Start: 12' right of the large left-facing corner at the left end of the cliff, below flakes with a thin seam just above. A gnarled birch tree provides a seat at the base.
P1 5.10c G: Scramble up the flakes, then up a thin seam. Face climb up past several short vertical cracks and excellent horizontals (crux) to a final long reach move to a pocket. Mantel into the moss above. 50'
FA Jul 6, 2009, Jim Lawyer, Leslie Ackerman

4 Toolbox Woody 5.7 G 50' ★★
Start: 6' right of Welcome to Arietta below a crack that runs the full height of the cliff.
P1 5.7 G: Up and right on a large blocky flake to gain a crack just left of a shallow left-facing corner. Follow the crack system to the top. 50'
FA Jul 6, 2009, Leslie Ackerman, Jim Lawyer

5 Shirtless In November 5.10d PG 50'
Start: 18' right of Toolbox Woody below the left end of a blocky right facing, right-arching corner 15' up.
P1 5.10d PG: Climb the face up to the corner, then up the corner to its top where it becomes an overlapping flake. Make face moves up and left to a good horizontal, then more face moves to a finishing handcrack (crux), the left of two parallel handcracks. 50'
Gear: To 2".
FA Nov, 2010, Lyle Farren

6 Criss Cross 5.10c G 45' ★★
Start: On the right end of the cliff below a shallow vertical trough with parallel seams, just right of a square, box-shaped hole 8' up, 20' right of a left-facing corner that arches left into a roof, and 20' left of a giant oak growing 2' from the cliff face.
● **P1 5.10c G:** Up the groove using incut flakes and seams and intermittent cracks to a fixed anchor. 45'
FA 2009, Arietta Climbing

Southern Mountains

The Lost Crags
LOST HUNTERS CLIFF

Aspect	West
Height	90'
Quality	★ ★ ★ ★ ★
Approach	52 min, moderate
Summary	Steep cracks and face climbs on near-perfect rock.

	1	3	3	3	6	1	17
-5.6	5.7	5.8	5.9	5.10	5.11	5.12	5.13+	total

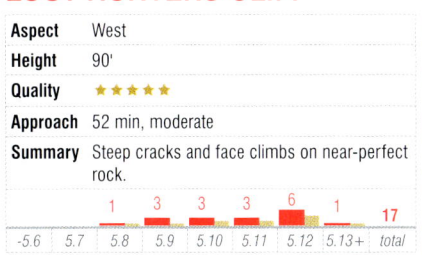

Lost Hunters Cliff contains a collection of high-quality crack and face routes, several of which are among the best single pitches in the park. The crag is located near the broad summit of Sherman Mountain, not far from Good Luck Mountain, accessed from NY 10 south of Piseco Lake.

The cliff is very steep and sheer, with impeccable rock. The two obvious cracks (**Lost Hunters Crack** and **Father Knows Best**) are some of the best in the region for the grade. For hard face climbing, there is no better cliff.

The Main Face is the primary attraction, and was the first section of cliff to be developed. Left of this is a descent gully that provides access to the top of the cliff. Left of this is a cliff with several prominent left-facing corners, the Mountain Bruin Wall. Further left still is the Corkscrew Buttress, with several sport routes.

HISTORY

The crag derives its name from the way in which it was discovered. Fred Abbuhl and his father were deer hunting and became separated and lost. Abbuhl came across his father's footprints in the snow and followed them for several hours until he finally found him having lunch at the base of this crag, where his father said, "Howdya like this crag I found for ya?" Well, as the saying goes, "Father knows best," which inspired the name of one of the first crack routes done here.

Abbuhl returned with various partners to climb almost every route here.

The first edition of *Adirondack Rock* sparked interest, and several new routes were added, beginning with the Mountain Bruin Wall, then much further left at the Corkscrew Buttress. On the Main Face, Justin Sanford and Ken Murphy equipped some of Abbuhl's toprope routes, establishing several top-quality lead routes.

CAMPING

There is a campsite next to Chub Lake, about 5 min from the road. There's also a good campsite across the road from the west end of the pullout.

DIRECTIONS   (MAPS PAGES 307 AND 315)

From the east end of the parking pullout, locate an obvious trail in the trees (0.0 min) and follow this east parallel to the road. At 3 min reach a T intersection (going right goes to NY 10, the old approach); go left (downhill) towards Chub Lake. About 100' before the lake, turn right onto a small path and follow this as it contours around the east side of Chub Lake. The path crosses a small stream, then makes a short climb to a Y intersection at 9 min. The right branch goes to Lost T; you go left.

Follow the path as it meanders north, making several brief bends to the east. At 21 min, cross two large streams that drain a beaver pond on the right 538557,4790326. Just after the second stream is another intersection. The left fork leads to McMartin Cliff; you go right. Follow the path along the shore of the beaver pond for 5 min, then break away to the north, and follow a stream up the side of Sherman Mountain. As the path rises, you can see short cliffbands on the right. Eventually you'll find a distinctive 40'-wide, 30'-high clean face with two prominent horizontals. This is key to locating the crag, as the main face sits hidden just

LOST HUNTERS CLIFF
1 Corkscrew (5.11c)
2 Hot Compress (5.12a)
3 Sideways (5.10a)
4 Mountain Bruin (5.9+)
5 Terapia (5.12a)
6 Trigger Finger (5.11a)
7 The Weasel Climb (5.9)

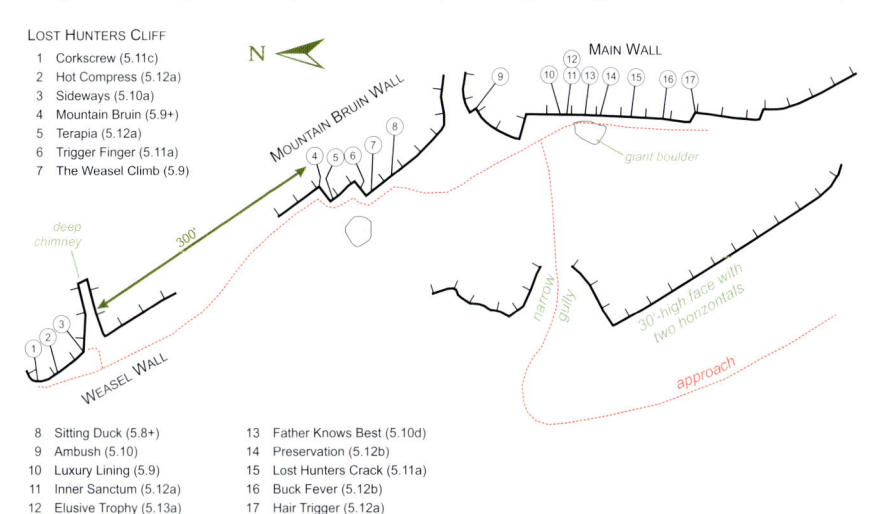

8   Sitting Duck (5.8+)
9   Ambush (5.10)
10 Luxury Lining (5.9)
11 Inner Sanctum (5.12a)
12 Elusive Trophy (5.13a)
13 Father Knows Best (5.10d)
14 Preservation (5.12b)
15 Lost Hunters Crack (5.11a)
16 Buck Fever (5.12b)
17 Hair Trigger (5.12a)

Southern Mountains

above. Follow along the left side of this cliff and into a steep gully (fixed rope). At the top of the gully, the main face is visible directly in front of you 539096,4790967, reached at 52 min.

DESCENT OPTIONS
Most routes have fixed anchors, and you can lower with a single 60m rope. The gully on the left of the main face is used to access the cliff top.

Corkscrew Buttress

Walk left from Mountain Bruin, and stay below the broken cliffs. In 300', arrive at a buttress, the left side of which has a distinctive left-facing yellow corner (the route Corkscrew), and the right side of which has a very deep, dramatic chimney hidden above a steep, cone-shaped dirt slope. The base of this cliff is steeply sloped and somewhat uncomfortable 539053,4791153.

1 Corkscrew 5.11c G 50' ★★★
Start: On the left side of the buttress, at an arête below the distinctive, left-facing, yellow corner.
● **P1 5.11c G:** Climb up and right onto a beautiful yellow face with a shallow, left-facing corner. Up the corner to its top, then over two overlaps to a fixed anchor. 50'
FA 2009, Arietta Climbing

2 Hot Compress 5.12a G 50' ★★★
A large roof with a steep, bulging, upper headwall. Unique, with no crimps; only sidepulls.
Start: In the middle of this buttress, about 35' right of Corkscrew, on top of a right-rising ramp at a left-facing corner. This is below a giant square roof 35' up and above a 20'-tall slab.
● **P1 5.12a G:** Stick-clip the first bolt (or use trad gear to climb the 2" corner crack). Go up a left-facing corner to a good ledge, then up to a roof. Go past the roof on the right, then up an overhanging face using slopey sidepulls to a final mantel and a fixed anchor. 50'
FA Sep 26, 2010, James Otey

3 Sideways 5.10a G 100' ★★★
Watch for rope drag on the first section. Great view from the top.
sStart: Scramble up towards the chimney on the right side of the buttress. Belay on a ledge with a birch downhill and left of the mouth of the chimney, 30' right of Hot Compress, below a short, overhanging face above a slab.
● **P1 5.10a G:** Move left 10' under an overhanging face, then back right up a ramp above the overhanging face. Large holds lead to a midway ledge, just left of a small pine tree. Walk 40' across the ledge and move up to the left of a large block that forms a roof. Continue into a corner between a slab and block, step right onto left side of block and up to a fixed anchor. 100'
FA 2009, Jimmy Diliberto

Mountain Bruin Wall

These routes are on the rock face and corners just left of the gully used to access the cliff top, or about 200' left of the main face 539097,4791073.

4 Mountain Bruin 5.9+ G 50' ★★
An attractive corner climb with good rests.
Start: At a flat area at the base of the obvious chiseled left-facing corner 150' left of the descent gully.
P1 5.9+ G: Stem, jam, and layback up the corner past the small roof to its top. Fixed anchor on the right. 50'
Gear: Standard rack to 3.5".
Descent: Rappel from the large pine tree on a ledge at the top of the corner.
FA May 19, 2001, Don McGrath, Fred Abbuhl, Doug Morse

5 Terapia 5.12a G 50' ★★★★
Start: On the arête 10' right of Mountain Bruin.
● **P1 5.12a G:** Climb the arête and beautiful orange-yellow face just right of the arête to a fixed anchor. 50'
FA Apr 2, 2010, Justin Sanford, Brad Wenskoski

6 Trigger Finger 5.11a G 50' ★
An overhanging finger exercise marred somewhat by the remnants of a bird's nest before the final crack.
Start: On top of a blocky ledge beneath the overhanging wall that forms the left edge of the face just left of the descent gully.
P1 5.11a G: Climb the overhanging fingercrack to the ledge, then up the handcrack above. 50'
Gear: Extra small cams and TCUs; a 4" cam for the top crack.
FA Apr 30, 2006, Jim Lawyer, Chris Yenkey

7 The Weasel Climb 5.9 G 50' ★★★★
Start: 18' left of Sitting Duck, just right of an arête, at a short handcrack. This is right of, and just around the corner from Trigger Finger.
P1 5.9 G: Up the handcrack, then step right to a bolt. Go up and right over a bulge, then up left to a stepped ceiling. Over this at a thin seam, then work up the face just right of the arête to a fixed anchor. 50'
Gear: Medium cams.
FA Apr, 2009, Bill Griffith, Keegan Griffith, Gary Thomann

8 Sitting Duck 5.8+ G 50' ★★★
The easiest route on the cliff.
Start: On the clean face just left of the descent gully, at a right-facing corner at the base of an obvious crack.
P1 5.8+ G: Climb the right-facing corner, through a small roof, then up a beautiful handcrack to a double-crack finish. Fixed anchor up and left. 50'
FA Apr 30, 2006, Simeon Warner, David Le Pagne, Jim Lawyer

Watercolor by Lucie Wellner.

316

Southern Mountains

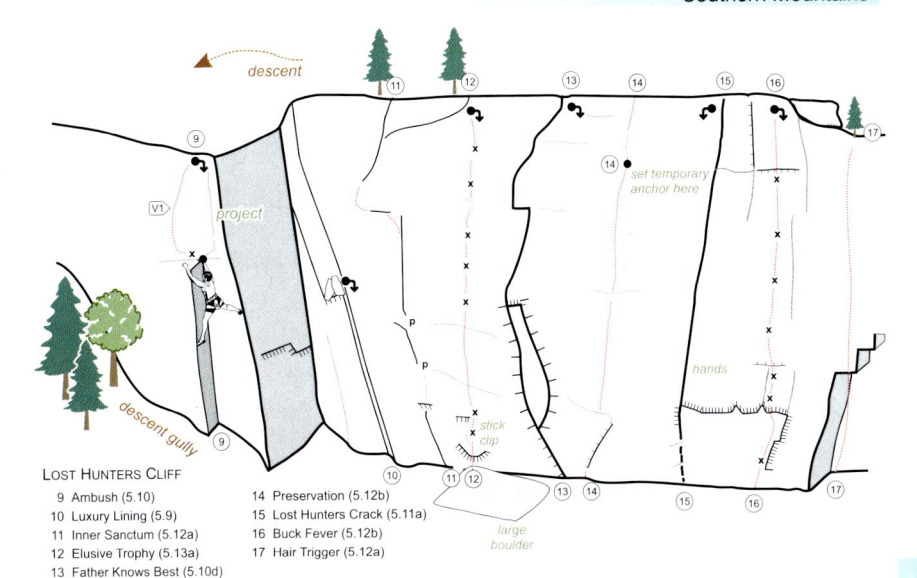

LOST HUNTERS CLIFF

9 Ambush (5.10)
10 Luxury Lining (5.9)
11 Inner Sanctum (5.12a)
12 Elusive Trophy (5.13a)
13 Father Knows Best (5.10d)
14 Preservation (5.12b)
15 Lost Hunters Crack (5.11a)
16 Buck Fever (5.12b)
17 Hair Trigger (5.12a)

Main Face

This is the main, sheer face at the top of the approach trail.

9 Ambush 5.10 G 45' ★★

This beautiful-looking corner ends in the middle of the face. The first ascent party lowered from an anchor and retrieved their gear later via rappel. There's a right-hand finish being prepared (a closed project) that makes the overall grade 5.11a.
Start: At the left side of the cliff, on the face that forms the right wall of the descent gully, at a well-defined right-facing corner with a thin crack in the back.
P1 5.10 G: Climb the crack in the right-facing corner to the horizontals at the top. There's a good no-hands rest here. (V1) 45'
V1 5.12d PG ★★: At the corner (no hands rest), climb up and left a bit, then head up a blank face (crux) for 15' to a good horizontal (adequate gear placements). Trend up and right to a fixed anchor (80').
FA (to top of corner) May 19, 2001, Fred Abbuhl, Don McGrath, Doug Morse
FA (V1) Sep, 2013, Justin Sanford

10 Luxury Lining 5.9 G 60' ★★

This route is the first section of an in-progress project that continues up the rounded arête to the top.
Start: Just left of **Inner Sanctum** at a dirty left-leaning fistcrack that leads to a ledge with pointy block-flakes.
P1 5.9 G: Follow the crack to the ledge. There's a fixed anchor on the face right of the crack. 60'
Gear: To 4".
FA Jul, 2012, Mitchel Hoffman, Jae Zhong

11 Inner Sanctum 5.12a PG 80' ★★★★★

One of the best pitches in the Adirondacks and definitely worth the hike.
Start: On top of the boulder several feet right of the left-leaning, dirty fistcrack of **Luxury Lining**, and below a smaller left-leaning crack.
P1 5.12a PG: Climb the left-leaning crack to a bulge, then face-climb up to the amazing fingercrack. At the top of the fingercrack, reach left to a horizontal crack (excellent gear). Move up and left to the arête and follow the thin crack to the woods. Another crack that diagonals off to the right near the top provides an alternative finish. 80'
Gear: Extra TCUs, a few RPs, nuts, and cams to 2".
FA Sep 1, 1994, Fred Abbuhl

12 Elusive Trophy 5.13a G 80' ★★★★★

A spectacular and technical face climb, perhaps one of the best hard pitches in the Adirondacks. Mostly bolted but requires a few key pieces for the timid.
Start: Same as **Inner Sanctum**.
P1 5.13a G: Stick-clip the first bolt, then climb the bouldery start (5.12) to the first bolt. Continue up the beautiful, gently overhanging wall to a fixed anchor. 80'
Gear: The lower half of the route has some horizontal cracks with excellent gear. At three-quarters height, there is a small nut placement that may be helpful.
FA Sep 30, 1995, Fred Abbuhl

13 Father Knows Best 5.10d G 80' ★★★★

A nice hand- and fingercrack that snakes its way to the top of the cliff. This crack, along with **Lost Hunters Crack**, is the most obvious feature on the main face.
Start: At a left-leaning, right-facing corner-ramp, at the base of the large boulder, and beneath a small 1' overlap.
P1 5.10d G: Climb the corner to a flared chimney-alcove. At the top of the alcove, follow a snaking crack through a crux to good holds at a break. Angle right up the crack (often wet) to a fixed anchor at the top. 80'
Gear: Extra finger- and hand-sized cams.
FA Jul 17, 1994, Fred Abbuhl, Guy Haas

Southern Mountains

*Chris Yenkey in the flared alcove on **Father Knows Best** (5.10d).*

14 Preservation 5.12b TR 60'
Just right of the previous route is a short, right-leaning crack behind a flake. Climb the flake, then diagonal up left 10' before climbing straight up the technical face above. The climb ends at a prominent horizontal crack 20' below the top, where the rock becomes lichen-covered. A toprope can be set by climbing right from the top of the fingercrack of **Father Knows Best**.
FA (TR) Oct 1, 1995, Fred Abbuhl

15 Lost Hunters Crack 5.11a PG 80' ★★★
An excellent crack that actually offers a pure hand-jam crux. The upper crack is often wet.
Start: At the lowest part of the cliff, below the crack that more or less splits the center of the wall 20' right of **Father Knows Best**.
P1 5.11a PG: Climb the broken crack to the overlap on the right at 20', then continue straight to a fixed anchor at the top. 80'
Gear: Extra hand-sized cams to 3.5".
FA Jul 9, 1995, Fred Abbuhl, Don McGrath

16 Buck Fever 5.12b G 80' ★★★★★
One of the best sport routes of its grade in the park. No single move is as hard as **Elusive Trophy**, but it is more sustained.
Start: 15' right of **Lost Hunters Crack** is a left-facing corner below roofs.
● **P1 5.12b G:** Climb the face and cracks next to this corner to the roofs. Pull the roofs, moving slightly left. Face-climb straight up the face following the most prominent holds and features to a fixed anchor. 80'
FA Aug 24, 2001, Fred Abbuhl
FFA Jul 7, 2012, Ken Murphy

17 Hair Trigger 5.12a TR 50'
At the right end of the wall is a prominent right-facing corner capped by a roof. This route climbs up the corner, over the roof, and up past smaller right-facing corners to the top.
FA (TR) Aug 24, 2001, Fred Abbuhl, Doug Morse

*Ken Murphy cops a rest on **Buck Fever** (5.12b).*
Photo by Jobi Gabrielli.

Southern Mountains

The Lost Crags
MCMARTIN CLIFF

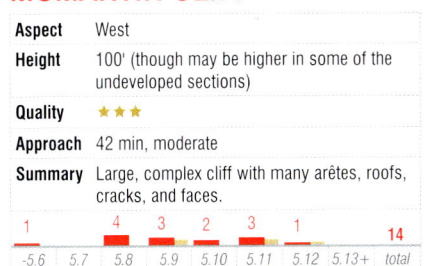

Aspect	West
Height	100' (though may be higher in some of the undeveloped sections)
Quality	★★★
Approach	42 min, moderate
Summary	Large, complex cliff with many arêtes, roofs, cracks, and faces.

1	4	2	3	1	14
-5.6	5.7	5.8	5.9	5.10	5.11	5.12	5.13+	total

This cliff is located in the Sacandaga River Valley along NY 10 in the same general area as Good Luck Mountain, Lost Hunters Cliff, and Lost T. It shares the excellent rock found at Lost Hunters Cliff—super textured, coarse rock, split by cracks. The cliff has a complex geometry consisting of many dihedrals, arêtes, overhangs, and steep overhanging faces. The base of the cliff is generally open and comfortable.

There are currently two groupings of routes. The first grouping is located above the dirt-scramble used to access the terrace at the base of the climbs; this is directly below a huge fin-like arête and the route Suomi. The second grouping is 100' uphill and left of the fin routes, at the height of land, where there are two large, flat-topped boulders, directly below the route Welcome to McMartin. Just right of the height-of-land is a large ledge 15' up with a boulder-tower sitting in a huge corner; no routes here yet. Left of this second grouping, the terrain drops steeply downhill along the base of the cliff, which continues for hundreds of feet of unexplored goodness.

The cliff is perhaps 500' or more wide, so there's good potential for more routes, although the rock is fairly dirty and may require considerable work.

HISTORY
Fred Abbuhl originally visited these cliffs, but it was Gary Thomann and the Arietta Climbing group (page 308) that were first to put in the work and climb here in 2010. Like many other cliff discoveries, it was Barbara McMartin's writings[1] that led Thomann to this cliff.

DIRECTIONS (MAP PAGE 307)
From the east end of the parking pullout, locate an obvious trail in the trees (0.0 min) and follow this east parallel to the road. At 3 min reach a T intersection (going right goes to NY 10, the old approach); go left (downhill) towards Chub Lake. About 100' before the lake, turn right onto a small path and follow this as it contours around the east side of Chub Lake. The path crosses a small stream, then makes a short climb to a Y intersection at 9 min. The right branch goes to Lost T; you go left.

Follow the path as it meanders north, making several brief bends to the east. At 21 min, cross two large streams that drain a beaver pond on the right 538557,4790326. Just after the second stream is another intersection. The right fork leads to Lost Hunters Cliff; you go straight. Proceed north following the trail; climb steadily uphill and stay well uphill (and west) of a narrow valley with a stream. Eventually, the terrain levels and you will come to a boggy section. Just after the bog is the turnoff for Lost T2; continue straight and slightly downhill. At 37 min, you will see the first mini-cliff about 50' right of the trail. At 39 min, turn right to the base of another mini-cliff with two large left-facing corners; make a switchback to the right and walk uphill around the right end of this mini-cliff, then back left to the top of this mini-cliff. Continue north following the contour to reach the right end of main face—the Southern Wall—at 42 min 538307,4791339.

Continue left along the base of the cliff to a short dirt-scramble up to a tree terrace and the Griffith Wall, directly below a 100'-tall buttress of rock (and the routes Suomi and Mikkihiiri). This area contains the highest concentration of routes.

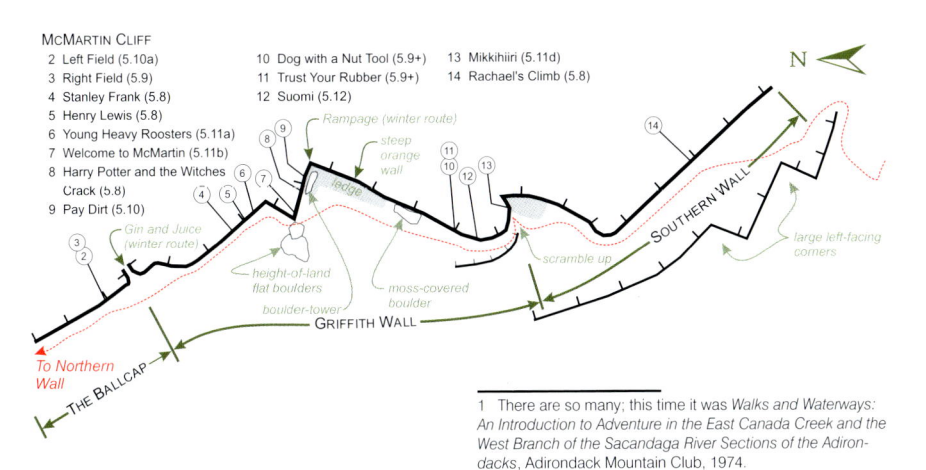

MCMARTIN CLIFF
2 Left Field (5.10a)
3 Right Field (5.9)
4 Stanley Frank (5.8)
5 Henry Lewis (5.8)
6 Young Heavy Roosters (5.11a)
7 Welcome to McMartin (5.11b)
8 Harry Potter and the Witches Crack (5.8)
9 Pay Dirt (5.10)
10 Dog with a Nut Tool (5.9+)
11 Trust Your Rubber (5.9+)
12 Suomi (5.12)
13 Mikkihiiri (5.11d)
14 Rachael's Climb (5.8)

[1] There are so many; this time it was *Walks and Waterways: An Introduction to Adventure in the East Canada Creek and the West Branch of the Sacandaga River Sections of the Adirondacks*, Adirondack Mountain Club, 1974.

Southern Mountains

Northern Wall

This is the section of cliff downhill and left of the Ball Cap—the orange buttress capped by roofs.

1 Ownership 5.4 G 70'

An attractive route, if not for the dirt and plants growing from the crack.
Start: From the Ball Cap, continue approximately 90' downhill to the low point of the terrain. Contour left along the base of the cliff for 200' to a slab with a hand-crack, 20' left of a deep, left-facing chimney.
P1 5.4 G: Step up onto sloped holds and climb a 4'-tall, shallow, left-facing corner to gain the crack. Follow the crack to ledge with a 18"-diameter spruce tree with a fixed anchor. 70'
History: The route was named to reflect the desire for exclusive ownership of the cliff expressed by the Arietta Climbing group in not wanting outsiders adding routes to the cliff.
FA Aug 9, 2010, David Hyney, Patrick Berg

Ball Cap

Left and downhill from the main face is a distinctive orange buttress with two left-facing corners capped by large roofs. There are two routes on this feature with a shared start.

2 Left Field 5.10a PG 160'

Start: From the height of land, walk left along the cliff. After you walk past **Stanley Frank**, the terrain drops, and about 70' from the height of land there is a shallow chimney that runs the height of the cliff (the winter route **Gin and Juice**). Begin 20' downhill and left of this chimney, and 6' left of a large birch growing up against the cliff, below a shallow crack system with two wedged chockstones 15' up.
P1 5.6 G: Go up the crack system past an overlap. Follow the wide, shallow crack past two chockstones to a slab. Angle up and left to a fixed anchor. 60'
P2 5.10a PG: Go straight up into a large, orange, left-facing corner. Up the corner to a roof; go left under the roof, up a crack, then move right across a face and around an arête to the front face of the buttress. Continue straight up to a fixed anchor on top of the Ball Cap. 100'
FA 2011, Arietta Climbing

3 Right Field 5.9 PG 160'

Start: Same as **Left Field**.
P1 5.6 G: Same as **Left Field**. 60'
P2 5.9 PG: Go up and right to the right margin of the orange rock. Climb a wide crack in a left-facing corner to an alcove below roofs. Follow a crack straight through multi-tiered roofs. Continue straight up the face to a fixed anchor at the top of the Ball Cap. 100'
FA 2011, Arietta Climbing

Griffith Wall

Once you reach the cliff, contour left, then scramble up a dirt slope and short slab to a tree-covered terrace, directly below a 100'-tall fin of rock (and the routes **Suomi** and **Mikkihiiri**). This is the right (southern) end of the Griffith Wall.

4 Stanley Frank 5.8 PG 50' ★

Start: 30' left of the high point of the terrain, below the left of two cracks. The crack doesn't quite reach the ground.
P1 5.8 PG: Up the crack past the left end of an overlap 12' up. Continue up the crack past a small left-facing corner to a fixed anchor (shared with **Henry Lewis**). The anchor sits below and left of a 50'-tall arête with a square roof at the bottom. 50'
Gear: To 3".
FA Aug, 2010, Arietta Climbing

5 Henry Lewis 5.8 G 50' ★★

Start: 15' right of **Stanley Frank**, below a left-leaning crack that begins as a seam, and widens to fists 8' up.
P1 5.8 G: Up the crack past a left-facing corner to a small ceiling. Step left to a fixed anchor shared with **Stanley Frank**. 50'
Gear: To 3".
FA Aug, 2010, Arietta Climbing

Tribute to Barbara McMartin

As you scan the history of many cliffs in the park, especially those outside the High Peaks, Lake Placid, and Keene Valley areas, you'll find that they were uncovered by a small cadre of adventure seekers—climbers who took a perverse pleasure in thrashing through the woods in search of the next climbing gem, places where new routes were in plain sight and where they had the cliff to themselves. In many cases, these explorers cheated, armed with the backcountry hiking guides published by the late Barbara McMartin. Her guides describe approaches—often bushwhacks—to seldom-visited pools, waterfalls, pristine lakes, and, most important, cliffs and open peaks, most likely for the pretty views they afford. She inadvertently opened up the Adirondack Park to rock climbers as never before.

Ironically, McMartin was a self-acknowledged nonclimber, and more often than not, her "cliffs" turned out to be uninteresting lumps of exposed ledge rock. And, too, her directions were often suspect, at least early on. But like [Bradford] Washburn's photos of the Alaska Range, to the amateur Adirondack adventurer—the likes of Jim Vermeulen, Dave and Lois Legg, Jay Harrison, Tad Welch, Neal Knitel, and Karl Swisher—her books were like gold, and without that currency, who's to say whether Shanty Cliff, Long Pond, Good Luck, Crane, and Huckleberry would have remained, to this day, the undiscovered country.

It is remarkable that a nonclimber is responsible for so much route development in the Adirondacks.

- Dick Tucker

Southern Mountains

6 Young Heavy Roosters 5.11a G 100' ★ ★ ★
Usually climbed in one pitch, but the first pitch makes a good route by itself.
Start: 4' right of Henry Lewis, and 12' left of a large left-facing corner at the height of the terrain, below a white face that overhangs for the first 6'.
● **P1 5.10b G ★ ★ ★:** Up the face to a horizontal seam 10' up. Continue up the face to a fixed anchor. 50'
● **P2 5.11a G:** Move up and right to the left end of a ceiling, then up a short left-facing corner to a larger left-facing corner. At its top, climb a face on the left, then up through tan-colored rock just right of a large arête. Up an inside corner to a roof, step right and up to the top. 50'
Descent: Lower with a 60m rope.
FA Aug, 2010, Arietta Climbing

7 Welcome to McMartin 5.11b G 100' ★ ★ ★ ★
Usually climbed in one pitch, but the first pitch makes a good route by itself.
Start: At the height of land, on the right side of a large arête, 20' left and downhill from the boulder-tower that sits on a ledge 15' up (the boulder-tower is a landmark for the route Pay Dirt).
● **P1 5.9 G ★ ★:** Climb the face to a horizontal (fixed wire). Continue up the face and arête to the left to a fixed anchor under the large roof. 50'
● **P2 5.11b G:** Step left to clear the roof on its left side. Continue straight up to a short open book, then angle up and right to a steep orange face. Up this to a fixed anchor below the top. 50'
Descent: Lower with a 60m rope.
FA Aug, 2010, Arietta Climbing

8 Harry Potter and the Witches Crack 5.8 G 50'
Start: 6' right of Welcome to McMartin below a wide crack in an 8'-high left-facing corner.
P1 5.8 G: Up the crack and into a large left-facing corner. Climb the crack to a roof, then step left to a fixed anchor (shared with P1 of Welcome to McMartin). 50'
Gear: To 6".
FA Aug, 2010, Arietta Climbing

9 Pay Dirt 5.10 PG 100'
Start: Same as Harry Potter and the Witches Crack.
P1 5.10 PG: Go up Harry Potter and the Witches Crack for a few feet, then scramble up and right to the a large ledge with a boulder-tower that forms a hallway with the main face (it may be wise to move the belay here). From the hallway, climb a left-leaning crack in the black rock on the main face to a ledge at its top. Continue up the crack line to a V-groove (bolt on right). Trend right through a fractured bulge to a ceiling. Over this, then up and left to a fixed anchor at the top of the cliff. 100'
FA 2011, Arietta Climbing

10 Dog with a Nut Tool 5.9+ G 80' ★ ★ ★
Positive edges on the face and some secure jams make this one approachable.
Start: 30' uphill and left of the dirt-scramble are two, shallow, left-facing corners: the left corner is 7' high,

Peter Whitmore, on the left, on P1 (5.9) of Welcome to McMartin (5.11b), and Tim Trezise, on the right, on Harry Potter and the Witches Crack (5.8). Photo by Jay Harrison.

and the right corner is 12' high and scooped like a right-parenthesis. Begin in the right-hand corner.
P1 5.9+ G: Up the crack in the corner to a ledge at its top. Continue up a left-leaning crack in the face to where it thins and overhangs at its top (crux) where it meets the right side of a large, triangular roof. Continue up a large right-facing corner and the face to its right to a fixed anchor (shared with Trust Your Rubber). 80'
Gear: To 2".
FA Aug, 2010, Arietta Climbing

11 Trust Your Rubber 5.9+ G 80' ★ ★ ★
Good climbing, but presently very dirty.
Start: Same as Dog with a Nut Tool.
P1 5.9+ G: Climb the corner of Dog with a Nut Tool to the ledge at its top. Step right and climb the face straight up to a fixed anchor (shared with Dog with a Nut Tool). 80'
Gear: To 0.5".
FA Aug, 2010, Arietta Climbing

12 Suomi 5.12 G 70' ★ ★ ★
This dramatic line climbs the outside face of the fin above the dirt-scramble. Needs a stick-clip.
Start: 15' right of Trust Your Rubber at an overhanging face with a chest-high horizontal crack above which is a jagged seam and crack with angular holds.
● **P1 5.12 G:** Up the overhanging face (crux) to where it turns vertical, then up to a horizontal break below an overhang. Over this, then up the outside face of the huge fin to a fixed anchor. 70'
FA Aug, 2010, Arietta Climbing

Southern Mountains

13 Mikkihiiri (aka Musse Pigg)
5.11d G 80' ★★

Climbs the right side of the fin. Sustained, exposed, and difficult.

Start: On the right side of the fin, directly above the dirt-scramble, on a small ledge with a birch tree, below an ugly chimney that defines the right side of the fin.

● **P1 5.11d G:** Up the chimney a few feet until you can step left onto a clean face. Up the face to an overhang on the nose. Step right onto a tower, then back onto the face, over and overlap (crux), and up to a fixed anchor. 80'
FA Aug, 2010, Arietta Climbing

Southern Wall

This is the short cliff where the trail meets the cliff, just right of the dirt scramble up to the tree-covered terrace below the Griffith Wall.

14 Rachael's Climb 5.8 G 50' ★

Start: 100' right of the dirt-scramble, at a face with a right-rising ramp that starts at the ground and goes to about head height. This is 15' left of a poplar tree that has grown into the face.

P1 5.8 G: Climb the ramp up and right to a good horizontal. Move right to a vertical crack, and climb this to a ledge 30' up with a small pine tree on the left. Continue up to another ledge with a fixed anchor. 50'
FA Aug, 2010, Arietta Climbing

The Lost Crags

LOST T2 CLIFF

Aspect	West
Height	60'
Quality	★★
Approach	35 min, moderate
Summary	Very small, steep crag with two really good routes.

	2		2	1		5
-5.6	5.7	5.8	5.9	5.10	5.11	5.12	5.13+	total

This cliff lies just south of McMartin Cliff, and is actually an extension of that cliff line. Due to the jumbled non-cliff terrain between Lost T2 and McMartin Cliff, the developers thought it worthy of its own name. The cliff is sheer, steep, with a couple of obvious crack lines. There are two really good 5.10s here: one trad, and one sport.

Lost T2 is similar to Green Lake Cliff in size and shape—it's about 60' tall, 50' wide, and has a flat, open base. The rock quality is good.

HISTORY

The cliff was another discovery of Gary Thomann, who came upon it while wandering around McMartin Cliff in 2010. The routes were put in during July and August of 2011 by the Arietta Climbing group (page 308).

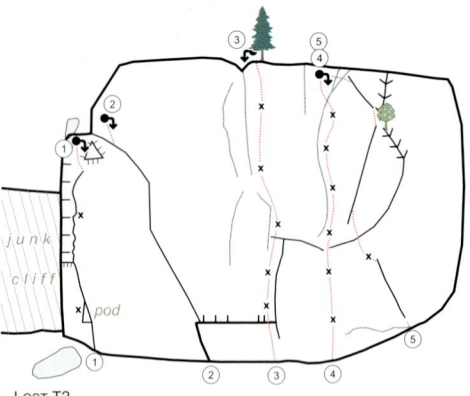

LOST T2
1 Cedar Dog (5.8+)
2 Welcome to America (5.10d)
3 Locust Posts (5.11d)
4 Airtime (5.10a)
5 Public Service (5.8+)

DIRECTIONS (MAP PAGE 307)

From the east end of the parking pullout, locate an obvious trail in the trees (0.0 min), and follow this east, parallel to the road. At 3 min, reach a T intersection and go left (downhill) towards Chub Lake (going right takes you to NY 10, the old approach). About 100' before the lake, turn right onto a small path, and follow this as it contours around the east side of Chub Lake. The path crosses a small stream, then makes a short climb to a Y intersection at 9 min. The right branch goes to Lost T; you go left.

Follow the path as it meanders north, making several brief bends to the east. At 21 min, cross two large streams that drain a beaver pond on the right 538557,4790326. Just after the second stream is another intersection. The right fork leads to Lost Hunters Cliff; you go straight. Proceed north following the trail; climb steadily uphill, and stay well uphill (and west) of a narrow valley with a stream. Eventually, the terrain levels, and you come to a boggy section at 30 min 538422,4790951. Just after the bog is the turnoff for Lost T2. Straight ahead goes to McMartin; go right (east) and walk 300' through open, flat woods to where the terrain rises abruptly. Continue 300' steeply uphill to reach the cliff at 35 min 538565,4791022. As of 2013, there is flagging on the approach trail, and the various intersections are clearly marked.

1 Cedar Dog 5.8+ G 45' ★

Start: On the left side of the cliff, just before the terrain rises uphill to the left, at a large boulder below a crack on a rounded arête.

P1 5.8+ G: Follow a left-leaning crack up to the rounded arête, then straight up the crack on the arête to a fixed anchor. Climbing directly to the anchor is pumpy, and made easier by stepping right to a rest. 45'
Gear: Thin gear.
FA Aug, 2011, Arietta Climbing

Southern Mountains

2 Welcome to America 5.10d G 55' ★★★

The route ascends the most obvious feature on the cliff—a full-height, left-leaning crack, reminiscent of the Spider's Web.
Start: 20' right of Cedar Dog at a left-leaning crack that runs to the top of the cliff.
P1 5.10d G: Go up the left-leaning crack to an overlap 10' up. Continue up the crack to a fixed anchor. The crux comes at mid-height where the crack pinches down, requiring some face climbing on the left. 55'
History: Named for two French hikers that wandered to the cliff during the first ascent. When you consider the remoteness of this cliff, the likelihood of such an encounter is extremely small.
FA Aug, 2011, Arietta Climbing

3 Locust Posts 5.11d G 60' ★★

Start: 10' right of Welcome to America, below a V-groove that begins 7' up.
● **P1 5.11d G:** Go straight up the face to a fixed anchor at the top. 60'
FA Aug, 2011, Arietta Climbing

4 Airtime 5.10a G 50' ★★★

Start: 4' right of Locusts Posts, just left of mossy rock, and just left of a good, head-high horizontal.
● **P1 5.10a G:** Go straight up to a slight V-groove capped by an overlap. Move right and up to another V-groove and follow this to a fixed anchor. 50'
FA Aug, 2011, Arietta Climbing

5 Public Service 5.8+ G 50'

Start: 10' right of Airtime, near the right end of the cliff just before the terrain begins to climb up right, below a left-leaning fingercrack.
P1 5.8+ G: Climb the fingercrack to a bolt. Make a big move up and left (crux, easier if tall), then straight up past two right-leaning cracks to a crack in a left-rising overlap. Move left to the fixed anchor of Airtime. 50'
FA Aug, 2011, Arietta Climbing

GOOD LUCK MOUNTAIN

Location	South of Piseco Lake, accessed from NY 10
Aspect	West
Height	100'
Quality	★★★★
Approach	45 min, moderate
Summary	High-quality cliff with generally clean routes and a partially open summit with good views; quality routes tend to be in the upper grades.

2	2	2	5	8	2	2	1	24
-5.6	5.7	5.8	5.9	5.10	5.11	5.12	5.13+	total

Good Luck Mountain Cliff is a continuous cliffband that runs below the summit of Good Luck Mountain. The Main Face is 200' wide and framed with a buttress on either end—Broken Mirror Buttress on the left and Medicine Man Buttress on the right. Additional routes are found above the Broken Mirror Buttress (the Summit Cliff), north of the Broken Mirror Buttress (the Far Left End), and on a boulder near the approach trail (the Good Luck Boulder). Another smaller 70' cliff is found downhill from and right of the Medicine Man Buttress.

DIRECTIONS (MAP PAGE 324)

Park at the paved trailhead 537481,4789344 on NY 10 (DEC trailhead signposted for Good Luck Lake, Dexter Lake, and the Potter Homestead), located 6 miles north of NY 29A and 11.4 miles south of NY 8. Follow the trail to Good Luck Lake. At 30 min, just past the lake, the trail reaches two bridges. A herd path before the second bridge heads right (north), crosses a creek, and heads steeply up a hillside parallel to low cliffbands. At 45 min, the cliff will appear on the right 536364,4788332, and the Good Luck Boulder is reached (20 yards off the trail on the right). To reach the base of the cliff, continue on the path past the cliff to the height of land 535906,4788654, then turn back along the base of the cliff; this avoids the large boulderfield.

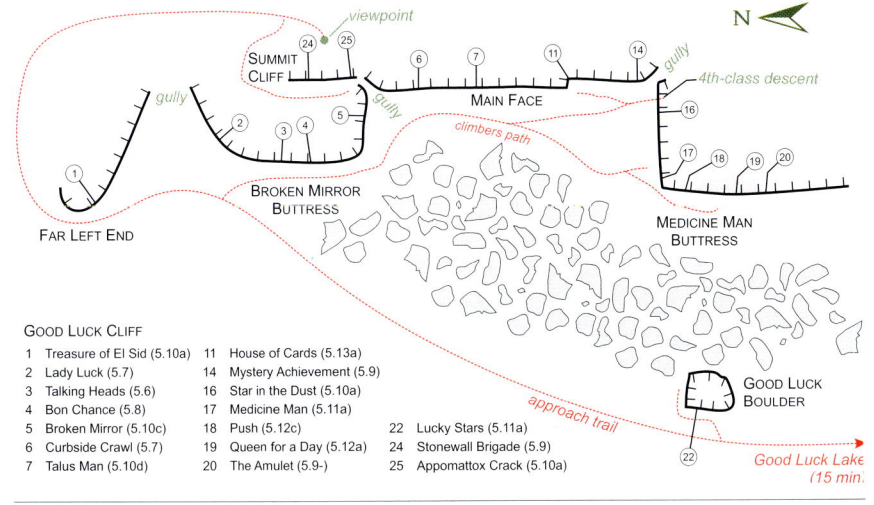

GOOD LUCK CLIFF
1 Treasure of El Sid (5.10a)
2 Lady Luck (5.7)
3 Talking Heads (5.6)
4 Bon Chance (5.8)
5 Broken Mirror (5.10c)
6 Curbside Crawl (5.7)
7 Talus Man (5.10d)
11 House of Cards (5.13a)
14 Mystery Achievement (5.9)
16 Star in the Dust (5.10a)
17 Medicine Man (5.11a)
18 Push (5.12c)
19 Queen for a Day (5.12a)
20 The Amulet (5.9-)
22 Lucky Stars (5.11a)
24 Stonewall Brigade (5.9)
25 Appomattox Crack (5.10a)

323

Southern Mountains

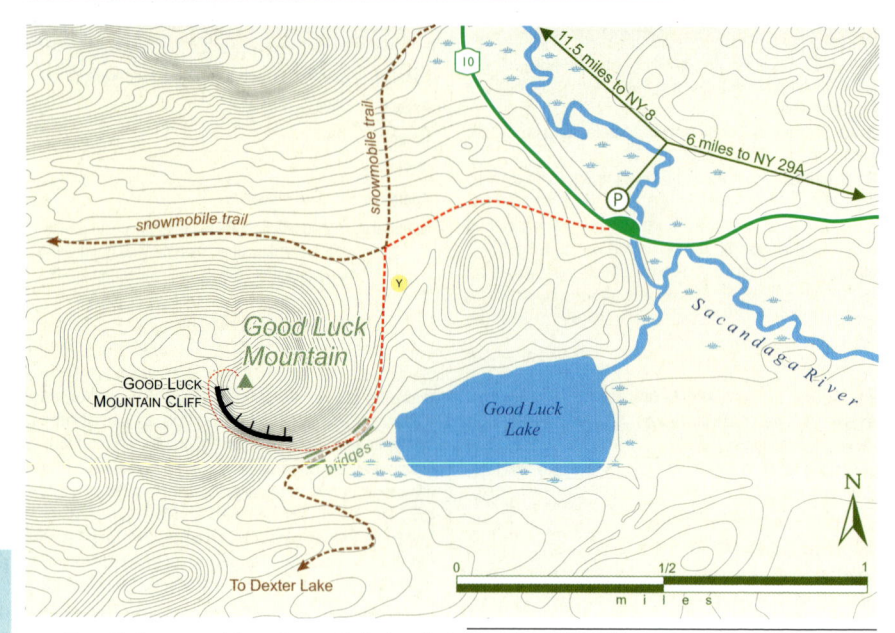

Alternatively, approach by water—put in just south of the trailhead and paddle to the far end of Good Luck Lake, then join the approach where the herd path leaves at the second bridge described above.

HISTORY

There are vague stories of climbing here prior to 1982, but the first reported climbing at Good Luck Mountain was in 1986 by Jim Vermeulen and Bill Morris, who found the cliff using Barbara McMartin's Discover the Adirondacks series. On their first visit in November, they climbed **Talking Heads** on the left end of the cliff. The next year, Vermeulen brought Tad Welch and Jim Lawyer to the cliff, who added the plumb-line handcrack **Mystery Achievement** and the intricate face **Star in the Dust**. Routes continued to be added through the 1990s, now with Bill Widrig and a brief appearance by Don Mellor. Toward the end of the 90s, Karl Swisher arrived with Frank Minunni, Richard Felch, and Sid Perkins. The influx of talent resulted in **Push**, a route reported as the "best 5.12 anywhere," and **House of Cards**, one of the few completely trad 5.13s in the park (see page 33).

DESCENT OPTIONS

The approach herd path wraps around to the north, then cuts back to the actual summit of Good Luck Mountain. This makes a good descent. Alternatively, there is a 4th-class descent where the Main Face meets Medicine Man Buttress, just left of **Star in the Dust**. There are also fixed anchors above **Medicine Man** and above the project left of **House of Cards**.

Far Left End

1 Treasure of El Sid 5.10a G 80' ★★★

At the far left end of the cliff is a small buttress, separated from the main cliff by a steep gully. **Treasure of El Sid** ascends this buttress.

Start: At the toe of the buttress, on top of a sloping ledge 5' above the ground.

P1 5.10a G: Climb to a stance (bolt), then follow a right-rising fingercrack until it disappears near the top. Move left and follow a vertical crack to the top 80'
FA 2000, Sid Perkins, Richard Felch, Andrew Hopson

2 Lady Luck 5.7 G 50' ★★★★

A quality climb for the grade, although a bit short.

Start: At the far left end of the cliff is a small buttress, separated from the main cliff by a steep gully. Begin at the first right-facing corner right of the gully.

P1 5.7 G: Climb the right-facing corner to the roof. Break the roof on the right and scramble to the top. 50'
FA 1990, Jim Lawyer, Stuart Williams

3 Talking Heads 5.6 PG 150'

An exploratory route that initiated development at the cliff. According to Vermeulen, on the first ascent, "verglas and vertical bushwhacking left the first-ascent party mumbling to themselves," hence the name.

Start: 20' left of **Bon Chance** at a deep, dirty crack with a pine tree at the base growing on top of a wedged block, just right of the obvious parallel off-width cracks on the upper face.

P1 5.6 PG: Up the dirty crack, bushwhacking past several cedars (V1) to a ledge. Continue up the line through more trees and brush to the summit. Yuck. 150'

V1 J.J.'s 5.7 G: Traverse left to the base of the parallel off-width cracks, then climb the cracks to the summit. A direct start to these cracks is also possible (5.10).
FA Nov 30, 1986, Jim Vermeulen, Bill Morris
FA (V1) May 9, 1987, Jim Vermeulen, Jim Lawyer

4 Bon Chance 5.8 PG 100' ★★★
An interesting feature with good climbing on clean rock.
Start: At the base of the chimney, 10' left of the orange face on the arête.
P1 5.8 PG: Wiggle up the chimney for 20' to the top of the large block. Follow a crack on the right wall out of the chimney and onto the face just right of the chimney (small gear), then move up to the right-angling crack and follow it to the flat summit. 100'
Gear: Up to 3", including some small wires and small cams.
FA Aug 1, 1993, Don Mellor, Brian Ballantine, Ed Ballantine

Broken Mirror Buttress

The Main Face is bordered on the left by the Broken Mirror Buttress and on the right by the Mystery Man Buttress. The Broken Mirror Buttress is distinguished by a giant orange face near the arête and a flat summit area with nice views. Above the Broken Mirror Buttress is the Summit Cliff.

5 Broken Mirror 5.10c R 90' ★★
Nice climbing once you're out of the gully and onto the face proper with solid gear. (Otherwise, this would receive four stars.)

Bill Widrig on Lady Luck (5.7), belayed by Jim Lawyer.

Frank Minunni on House of Cards (5.13a). Photo by Karl Swisher.

Start: In the large, tree- and block-filled gully on the left side of the Main Face.
P1 5.10c R: Climb the corner in the gully for 20' (or scramble up the gully) and make a very committing move left onto the face. Up the left-leaning thin crack to good horizontals, then slightly right following a larger crack with better gear to the flat summit. 90'
FA May, 1996, Karl Swisher, Courtney Black

Main Face

The Main Face of Good Luck Mountain is framed on the left by the Broken Mirror Buttress and on the right by the Mystery Man Buttress.

6 Curbside Crawl 5.7 G 90'
Looks more appealing than it really is.
Start: At the far left side of the Main Face, above a brushy ledge and beneath a dead tree in a crack.
P1 5.7 G: Follow the brushy, dirty crack past two trees to the top. 90'
FA May 9, 1987, Tad Welch, Jim Lawyer, Jim Vermeulen

7 Talus Man 5.10d G 100' ★★★★
Bring your talisman for this one. Superb climbing on the largest section of unbroken rock on the Main Face; one of the best routes at Good Luck, despite being a bit dirty.

Southern Mountains

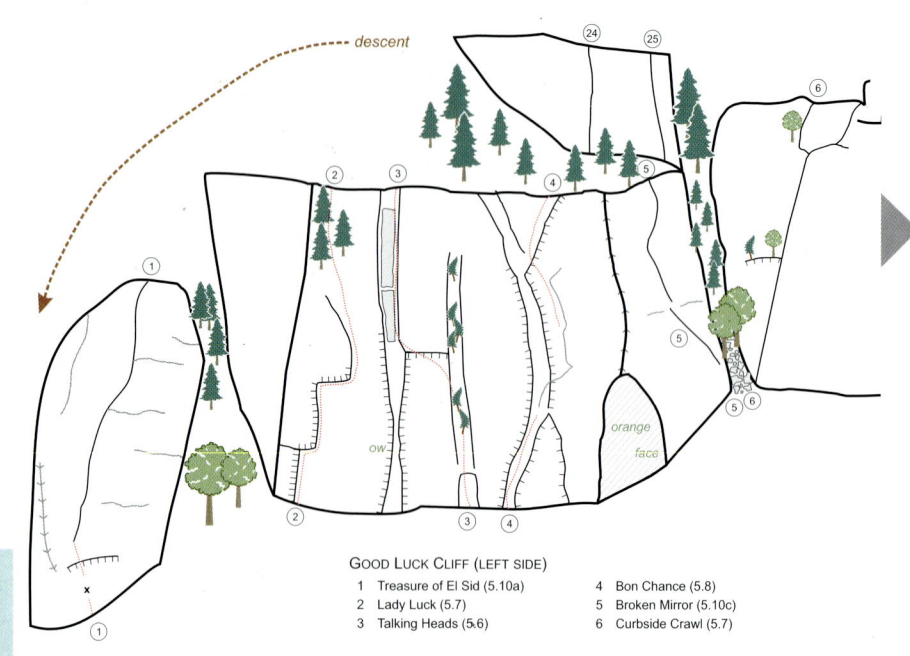

GOOD LUCK CLIFF (LEFT SIDE)
1. Treasure of El Sid (5.10a)
2. Lady Luck (5.7)
3. Talking Heads (5.6)
4. Bon Chance (5.8)
5. Broken Mirror (5.10c)
6. Curbside Crawl (5.7)

Start: At a fingercrack 50' from the left end of the main cliff, below a shallow right-facing, right-leaning corner. There is a tree very close to the cliff at the start.
P1 5.10d G: Work up the fingercrack in the face (easy if you cheat using the tree), then up to the right-facing corner 15' up. Climb past this corner (crux) and into an off-width pod. Go up cracks in the face, finishing rightward on flakes to the tree ledge of Cleveland. 100'
Gear: Standard rack plus double small TCUs.
FA Apr 27, 1996, Jim Lawyer, Tad Welch

8 S.O.L. 5.10b G 130'
Start: Same as Cleveland.
P1 5.10b G: Traverse left following a horizontal crack. At its end, the crack turns vertical, passes an inconvenient tree, then becomes off-width before it reaches the traverse ledge of Cleveland. 130'
FA Apr 27, 1996, Karl Swisher, Courtney Black

9 Cleveland 5.8 G 150' ★★★
Climbs the off-width crack just left of the right-facing, right-leaning red dihedral of House of Cards.
Start: 50' from the right end of the Main Face, at the left end of the spacious ledge beneath House of Cards—the right-facing, right-leaning red dihedral.
P1 5.8 G: Climb the off width in the right-facing corner, past a wedged flake at midheight, to a ledge (V1). Continue left on ledges and blocks to a trees. 150'
V1 5.9 PG: From the ledge, climb a fingercrack, angling slightly left through a bulge to the top.
Gear: Up to 4".
FA Apr 11, 1987, Tad Welch, Jim Vermeulen
FA (V1) Aug, 1995, Jim Lawyer, Mike Cross

Will Mayo on Mystery Achievement (5.9).

Southern Mountains

GOOD LUCK CLIFF (RIGHT SIDE)
- 7 Talus Man (5.10d)
- 8 S.O.L. (5.10b)
- 9 Cleveland (5.8)
- 10 Project
- 11 House of Cards (5.13a)
- 12 Go Fish (5.10b)
- 13 The Reach (5.10a)
- 14 Mystery Achievement (5.9)
- 15 The Wicked Weed Route (4th class)
- 16 Star in the Dust (5.10a)
- 17 Medicine Man (5.11a)
- 18 Push (5.12c)
- 19 Queen for a Day (5.12a)
- 20 The Amulet (5.9-)
- 24 Stonewall Brigade (5.9)
- 25 Appomattox Crack

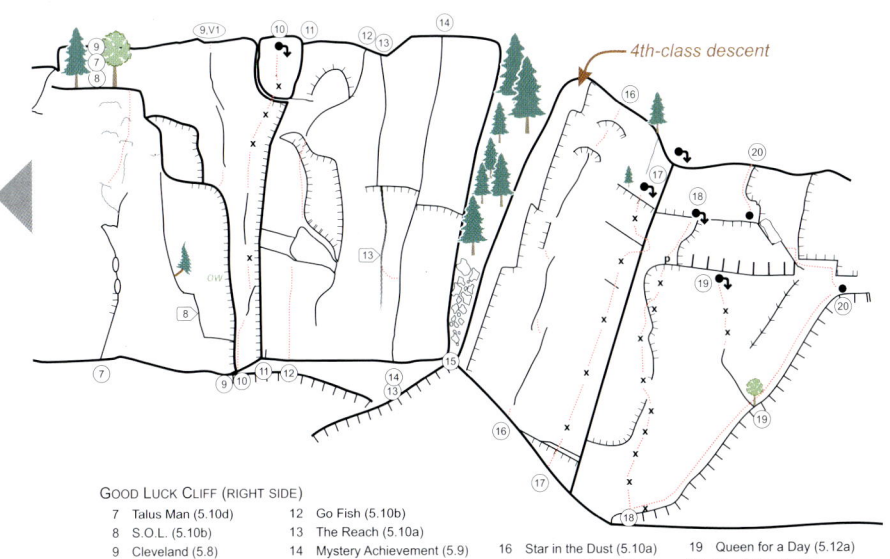

10 Project

This unfinished project climbs **Cleveland** for 10', then angles right following a crack just left of the **House of Cards** arête.

11 House of Cards 5.13a PG 100' ★★★★

Climbs the obvious right-facing, right-leaning red corner in the center of the Main Face. An extremely continuous and demanding climb that required considerable effort over many days. One of the few completely trad 5.13 route in the Adirondacks (see page 33).w

Start: At the obvious right-facing, right-leaning dihedral at the base of **Cleveland**.
P1 5.13a PG: Climb the corner to the top. 100'
Gear: Small wires (RPs) and several small TCUs at the start. According to the first-ascent party, "The most important piece of equipment leading to success was a soccer shin pad to protect the right shin when the critical foot came off the crux."
FA 2002, Karl Swisher, Frank Minunni

12 Go Fish 5.10b PG 120'

Climbs the crack, flakes, and blocks right of **House of Cards**.
Start: 5' right of **House of Cards** at a thin crack.
P1 5.10b PG: Up the thin crack, angling right at the top to flakes and blocks, then up the flakes and blocks to the top. 120'
Gear: Small wires for the crux.
FA 2002, Karl Swisher, Frank Minunni

Jim Lawyer on Star in the Dust *(5.10a).*

Southern Mountains

House of Cards

I first visited Good Luck with Courtney Black. The place looked spectacular from the approach, and up close we found beautiful unclimbed lines. I got on one, jammed up a corner, got a good hex, and headed left toward a thin crack and flake. I placed some small nuts behind the flake, moved up, reached around a bulge to the next crack, and fell . . . and kept falling, headfirst through tree branches. I stopped upside down with my hair brushing the dirt. The flake had blown out, but the hex held. Courtney and I just laughed nervously. After I quit shaking, I got back on it. We called the route Broken Mirror. That same day, I studied the overhanging corner that splits the main face. The feature blew me away, but I knew I couldn't climb it then. A couple of years later at a climbing gym, I met Frank Minunni. I hadn't forgotten that corner, and Frank seemed like someone who might have a shot at getting up it.

I took Frank to the cliff, and he was hooked. We put up Medicine Man, with Dick Felch, and Push and Queen for a Day. These routes were prizes in their own right, but we also needed to get really strong before trying the corner. We got to the point of being able to do laps on Push, so we went for it. We got shut down hard. Eventually we figured out how to high-step past the overhang (a soccer shin pad prevented broken shinbones). Then above the hang came desperate stemming and sternum-cracking palm moves; here written notes helped establish a sequence for the chaotic slapping and kicking. All gear was placed on lead, mostly by Frank, who seems to enjoy climbing above sketchy RPs. Finally, after days of brutal failures, I managed to link the whole thing from the ground up. Frank led it shortly after. We called it House of Cards . . . one wrong touch and the whole thing tumbles. We completed it around the time Courtney and I got married. Both events signaled the end of any Broken Mirror bad luck and proved that the cliff was indeed Good Luck.

- Karl Swisher

13 The Reach 5.10a PG 90' ★★

A fine handcrack with a problematic entry. The top of **Mystery Achievement** is often wet, in which case you can move left at the ledge at two-thirds height and finish on **The Reach**.
Start: Same as **Mystery Achievement**.
P1 5.10a PG: Climb **Mystery Achievement** until you can make a long reach to gain the parallel crack 10' to the left. Climb this fine crack to the summit. 90'
Gear: Cams to 3".
FA Apr, 1991, Tad Welch, Bill Widrig

14 Mystery Achievement 5.9 G 80' ★★★★★

As perfect a handcrack as can be found in the southern Adirondacks; very clean and very straight. Named for a song by The Pretenders.
Start: On the right side of the Main Face, 20' left of the brushy, tree-filled corner, just above a rotting stump.
P1 5.9 G: Climb the handcrack to the top, past a ledge at two-thirds height. 80'
Gear: Hand and finger size, up to 3".
FA May 9, 1987, Tad Welch, Jim Lawyer

15 The Wicked Weed Route 4th class 80'

During the early exploration of the cliff, the rack was mistakenly left in the car; this was the "route" that got climbed sans rack.
Start: On the right side of the Main Face is a horrible tree-filled corner, right of **Mystery Achievement** and left of the 4th-class descent.
P1 4th class: Climb the gully to the summit. 80'
FA 1986, Mike Cross (and crew)

Medicine Man Buttress

One of the most distinctive features of Good Luck Mountain is the arête **Medicine Man**, the outside corner right of the Main Cliff. There is a good 4th-class descent just left of **Star in the Dust**.

16 Star in the Dust 5.10a PG (5.8 R) 80' ★★★

Considerable cleaning revealed this gem—technical thin-crack climbing.
Start: On the steep slope below **Mystery Achievement**, at the base of the north-facing wall between the 4th-class descent and the arête.
P1 5.10a PG (5.8 R): Climb a thin crack until it disappears. Move left to the next thin crack and climb it until it disappears. A long reach leads to easier climbing. 80'
Gear: Small wires and TCUs.
FA May, 1988, Tad Welch, Jim Lawyer

17 Medicine Man 5.11a G 100' ★★★★

A brilliant pitch that ascends the clean arête right of **Star in the Dust**.
Start: Just right of and downhill from **Star in the Dust**, and just left of the arête.
● **P1 5.11a G:** Up the face left of the arête, step right around the arête, then back before continuing to the top at a fixed anchor. 100'
Gear: 1 ea 1", 1 ea 3".
History: The first-ascent party was about to climb the route when Doc (Richard Felch) got appendicitis. They waited for him to recover before doing it, and, since Doc is an MD, it was called **Medicine Man** in his honor.
FA 2001, Richard Felch, Frank Minunni, Karl Swisher

18 Push 5.12c G 100' ★★★★★

Considered by those who have climbed it to be one of the best routes of its grade—anywhere. The moves are varied and continuous, and the rock is impeccable.
Start: 20' right of the arête of **Medicine Man**, on top of a ledge with a bolt at your feet, under an overhanging right-facing corner.
● **P1 5.12c G:** Climb the face to the overhanging right-facing corner, then up the corner to a stance at the base of a shallow left-facing corner. Up the left-facing corner and, just before its top, step right around the arête onto

Opposite: Richard Felch on **Mystery Man** (5.11a).
Photo by Karl Swisher.

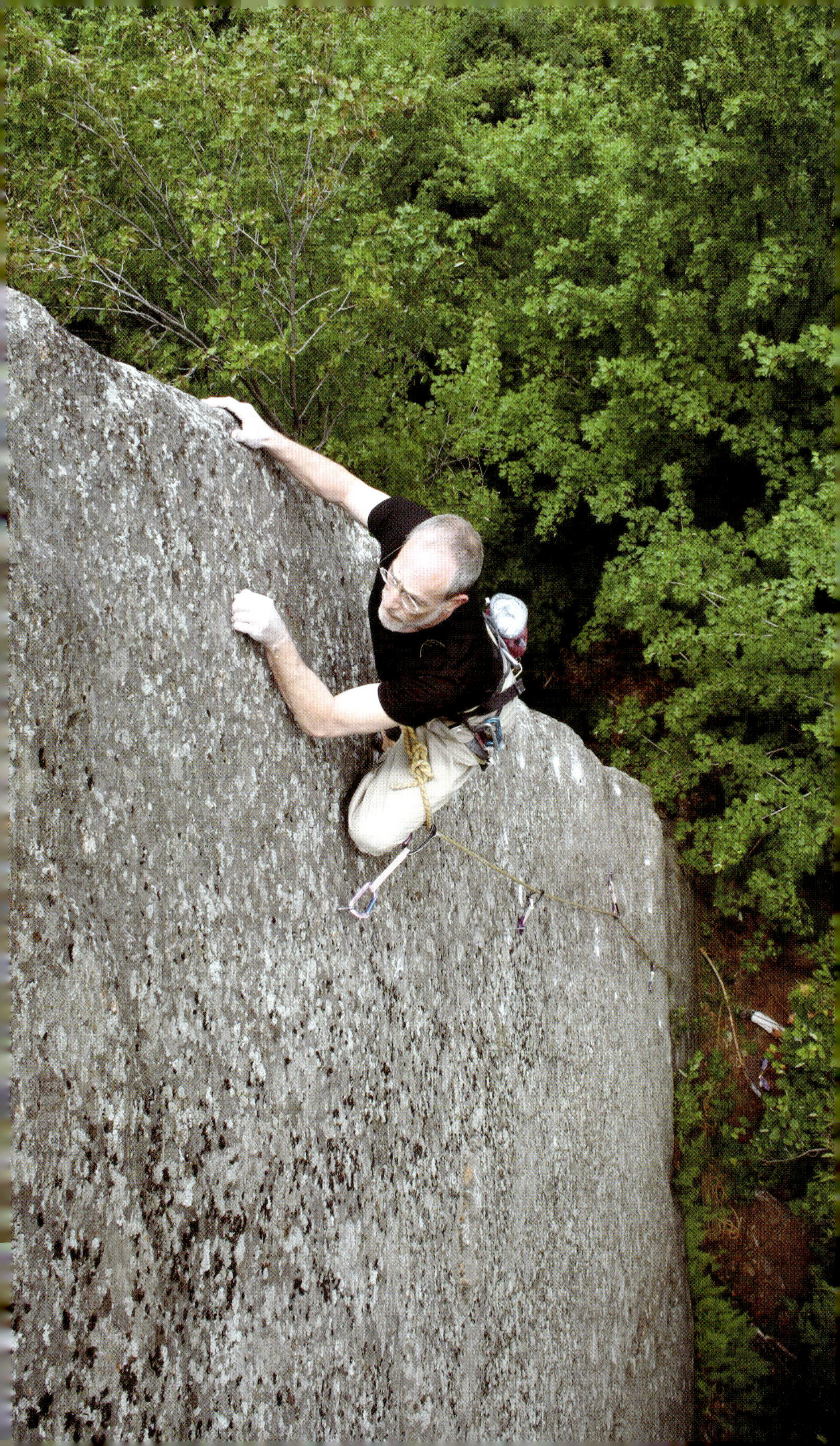

Southern Mountains

the face; then up to the left end of the large roof system. Finish up the crack in the left-facing open book to a fixed anchor above an overhang. 100'
FA 2001, Frank Minunni, Karl Swisher

19 Queen for a Day (aka Suicide King) 5.12a G 70' ★★★

Start: 20' up a right-rising ramp at blocks with a small tree in a crack. This is where the obvious crack meets the ramp, 30' right of Push.
P1 5.12a G: Climb the crack and bulge to a stance at the end; the crack is much more difficult—and nicer (i.e., doesn't shred the hands)—than it appears. Continue up the face past two bolts to an anchor below the roofs. 70'
History: Originally known as Suicide King because Minunni was hell-bent on doing it without bolts. After some exciting gear-ripping falls, the first ascentionists added the bolts. It was climbed on Gay Pride Day, so it was changed to Queen for a Day.
FA Jun 28, 2001, Karl Swisher, Frank Minunni

20 The Amulet 5.9- PG 80' ★

Climbs the ceiling at the top of the Queen for a Day ramp; unlikely terrain for its grade.
Start: Climb up the ramp at the start of Queen for a Day to a spacious belay beneath the ceiling.
P1 5.9- PG: Traverse left 8' under the ceiling, then pull over the lip on hidden buckets (no-hands rest). Make an awkward step left into the short left-slanting jamcrack (crux), then up a corner to a tricky and poorly protected mantel onto a spacious ledge. 60'
P1 5.7 G: A short pitch climbs the left-facing corner around the small ceiling to the top. 20'
History: A metal bookshelf support was found jammed beneath the roof like a piton on the first ascent.
FA 1994, Tad Welch, Bill Widrig

21 Get a Grip 5.9 G 70' ★★

A nice zigzag crack with interesting moves and great finger slots. This route is located on a cliffband below and right of the Medicine Man Buttress.
Start: Located at the far right end of the cliff, and best reached from the approach path by heading right from the first cluster of large boulders encountered; the boulder pile has a distinctive chimney that you can squeeze through. (Walking along the base of the cliff to find this route is arduous and not recommended.) It is the only solid rock in this section of cliff. Begin in an open area close to the stream, on a face 15' right of a right-facing corner, at the base of a groove capped by a triangular ceiling 20' up.

Justin Sanford on Push (5.12c). Photo by Mitch Hoffman.

P1 5.9 G: Climb the tree-filled groove to the roof. Step left and follow a continuous finger-sized crack through many turns to a tree with a fixed anchor. 70'
FA Nov, 1993, Bill Widrig, Tad Welch

Good Luck Mountain
GOOD LUCK BOULDER

In front of the Main Face, just right of the approach trail as you reach the cliff, is a large boulder with two short routes. The right side of the boulder facing the approach path has a perfect fingercrack, which doesn't quite reach the ground (**Lucky Stars**).

The routes can be toproped by lassoing a tree on the back side of the boulder and hand-over-handing to the summit. The inconvenience of this maneuver is probably why these routes are now a bit overgrown.

Southern Mountains

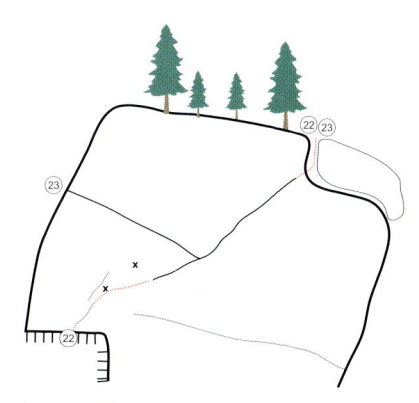

GOOD LUCK BOULDER
22 Lucky Stars (5.11a)
23 Grape Juice (5.9+)

22 Lucky Stars 5.11a G 50' ★★★

A difficult start gains the perfect fingercrack on the front side of the boulder (facing the approach trail). The route was cleaned on rappel, then led ground-up with bogus RPs. The bolts were added later by the first-ascent party to make the route more approachable (a G rating instead of R/X). The route would get four stars if it weren't for the small saplings that have taken root in the crack since the first ascent.
Start: On the left side of the boulder (as it faces the approach path), on top of a ledge with some trees.

Tad Welch on the first ascent of Grape Juice (5.9). Photo by Bill Widrig.

P1 5.11a G: Climb up the face past a bolt (no hanger; sling with a nut). Move right (crux; bolt) to the base of the fingercrack, then follow the fingercrack to the summit. 50'
FA 1994, Jim Lawyer, Tad Welch, Bill Widrig

23 Grape Juice 5.9+ G 50' ★

This route provides an alternative approach to the fingercrack of **Lucky Stars**.
Start: Around the corner on the left side of the boulder.
P1 5.9+ G: Follow the downward-sloping fingercrack past a pin to the fingercrack of **Lucky Stars**. 50'
FA 1994, Tad Welch, Jim Lawyer, Bill Widrig

Good Luck Mountain
SUMMIT CLIFF

This is the small cliff immediately below the viewpoint at the top of Good Luck Mountain and directly above the finishes to **Bon Chance** and **Broken Mirror**. Approach by hiking to the top of the mountain, then drop down the side to the base of the cliff. It can also be reached by thrashing up the unpleasant gully that separates Broken Mirror Buttress and the Main Cliff.

The climbs here are well worth the effort. They are described left to right.

24 Stonewall Brigade 5.9 G 40' ★★★

Start: 30' left of **Appomattox Crack** at an obvious crack.
P1 5.9 G: Climb the crack, thin at the top. 40'
Gear: To 0.75".
FA 1987, Tad Welch (roped solo)

25 Appomattox Crack 5.10a G 30' ★★★

Another pure, high-quality handcrack that doesn't quite make it to the ground.
Start: At the right side of the Summit Cliff, just before the land drops down the steep gully. (The stump that was originally used to gain the crack has long since rotted away.)
P1 5.10a G: A hard move gains the handcrack, then climb the crack to the top. 30'
Gear: To 2".
FA 1987, Tad Welch (roped solo)

WEST CANADA CLIFF

Location	North of Hoffmeister, accessed from NY 8
Aspect	Southwest
Height	200'
Quality	★★
Approach	2 hr 5 min, difficult
Summary	Large, remote cliff with several quality routes, and significant potential for more.

The West Canada Cliff rises above the South Branch of West Canada Creek in a very remote section of the park. At 200' tall and nearly 1/2 mile wide, it's the largest cliff yet explored on the western side of the park. The views from the cliff are open and nice, but somewhat

Southern Mountains

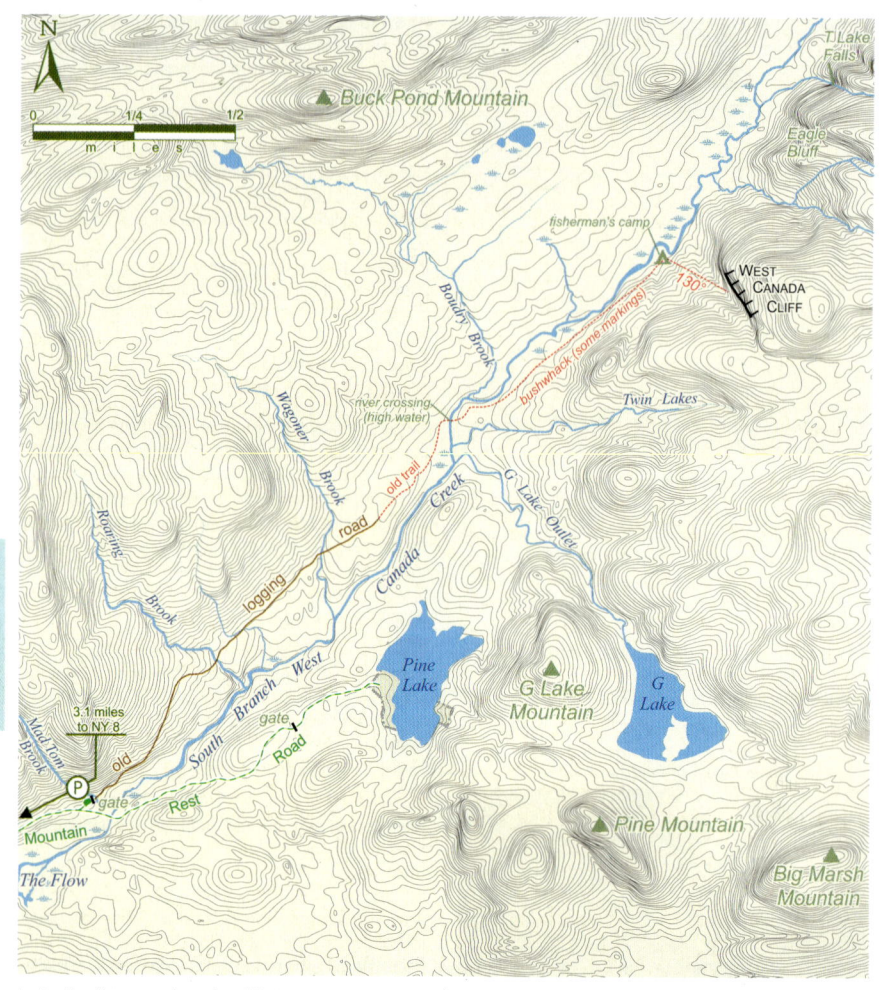

limited in distance, since the cliff sits low on the mountain.

With only 3 routes, the potential for more routes is enormous. Just north of this cliff, and facing the river is Eagle Bluff, totally unexplored.

West Canada Cliff is intimidating, with acres of steep, clean faces, roofs, large corners, huge arêtes, and some cracks. Almost all the rock is near vertical, with very few low-angle slabs. There is one, very imposing, bottom-to-top wet chimney, left of center. There are many enormous corners and arêtes; the most prominent left-facing corner has a large, north-facing, jet-black wall with a clear open area at its base, the bombardment zone for falling ice, and the only open, communal area along the cliff base. This is the Black Wall, and it is the key for locating the routes.

The cliff is located in the West Canada Lake Wilderness, the second largest wilderness area in the park, and contains very few trails, providing some of the most remote and hard-to-reach areas in the park. T Lake Falls, the highest waterfall in the park, is located near here, about 1 mile further upstream from the cliff.

DIRECTIONS (MAP PAGE 332)

The approach herein is from the south, from NY 8 near Hoffmeister. This is one of the approaches for T Lake Falls, and is also described in Barbara McMarttin and Bill Ingersoll's *Discover the West Central Adirondacks*. It's quite long and arduous with some moderate route finding and bushwhacking. You can save weight by bringing a water purifier, as there is water at the fisherman's camp 30 minutes before the cliff, and there's a trickle running through the talus below the cliff.

From the intersection of NY 8 and NY 365 (0.0 mile), which is just east of Hinckley Reservoir, drive east on NY 8 (towards Speculator). At 11.5 miles turn left on Mountain Home Road. This intersection is 1.5 miles west of Hoffmeister, a settlement that is somewhat easy to miss, although there is a post office.

Southern Mountains

WEST CANADA CLIFF
1 Call of the Wild (5.6)
2 Sausage Science (5.11a)
3 Cowboy Up (5.9)

At 13.5 miles the pavement ends at a snow plow turnaround with many posted signs. Not to worry, as these are to prevent you from parking and blocking the turnaround. Continue straight on a one-lane dirt road, currently suitable for low-clearance 2WD vehicles (although this could change, especially early season); there is one small creek crossing that isn't a problem. At 14.6 miles reach a fork where a logging road branches to the left; there is a small forest service sign on a tree. Take the left fork and immediately find a place to park 0525192,4806088; there is room for just a couple cars. (If you miss the fork, going straight leads to a ford across South Branch of West Canada Creek.)

From the parking area (0 hr 0 min), hike on the logging road to reach a barricade at 1 min; just beyond is a sign-in register and foot bridge across Mad Tom Brook. After this, you're on your own, as there are no markers or official trail improvements. Follow the abandoned logging road, at first uphill, then over rolling terrain. The logging road is straight, wide and easy to follow, but very muddy in sections, even in a dry summer. At 55 min the road narrows to a trail, but is still easy to follow. At 1 hr reach the South Branch of West Canada Creek and cross it 0528071,4809054. This "creek" is actually a river, and drains more watershed than most New York State rivers; in high water, the crossing is treacherous and extra shoes are recommended. In low water, you can simply rock hop across.

Once across the river, follow a trail upstream along the east bank of the river. There is some flagging, but don't count on it. After a couple minutes the path veers away from the river and at 1 hr 8 min you reach a vague fork in the trail. (Going straight leads east to Twin Lakes Outlet.) Take the left fork, which is totally overgrown at first, but opens up and becomes a better-defined trail very quickly. In addition to some flagging, there are occasional markings on trees—red paint spots and red, diamond-shaped aluminum markers. The path is well-defined in sections, while other sections are completely obliterated by deadfall. At 1 hr 27 min you reach the river again, and at 1 hr 37 min you reach a fork in the path with a view of a very large boggy area of the river just beyond (this is the beginning of a very long stretch of meandering stillwater). The left fork leads 150' to a fisherman's camp and fire ring 0529700,4810325 on the shore of the river, where you can see acres of flooded alders. If you wander west out into the alders, you can see the top of the cliff to the southeast.

From the fisherman's camp, bushwhack uphill on a bearing of 130°. The forest is mostly open and easy going until you're directly below the cliff, which is choked with large talus. Arrive at the cliff base at 2 hr 5 min 0530359,4810030.

HISTORY

In 1993, Neal Knitel saw this cliff from a plane while on an aerial reconnaissance of Long Pond and T Lake Falls. He snapped a quick photo, then forgot about it for years. In 2010, with rekindled enthusiasm, Knitel worked out the approach and found the cliff. Finding such a large, unexplored cliff, Knitel gave a celebratory howl, which was answered by a nearby pack of coyotes. Yes, this is a remote and wild place. He returned later that year with friends to put up the first routes.

1 Call of the Wild 5.6 PG 175' ★

An exploratory, varied, and somewhat dirty line, that creatively links protectable features—slabs, corners, and cracks. With a little effort, the line could be straightened and improved. Cleaning on lead, the first ascent was a 3.5 hour marathon.

Start: 50' left of the north-facing black wall is a wide chimney formed by a large left-facing corner and an orange tower. Begin 25' downhill and left of the chimney at a clean slab with a crack on the right.

P1 5.6 PG: Up the face, then move right to the crack for gear. Reach a ledge 40' up, then angle left to a right-facing corner with a balanced block on top. Continue angling left to an inverted V-groove. Up this to a ledge with a large bush. Move left to a vertical crack system, which is followed to the top at a giant pine tree on the very edge of the cliff, clearly visible from the base of the cliff. 175'

Gear: Standard rack plus an extra set of cams to 3". Double ropes helpful.

Descent: Rappel 150' from the large pine.

FA Sep 11, 2010, Neal Knitel, Simeon Warner

West Canada Cliff

THE BLACK WALL

This north-facing, black wall has rock that is pressure-washed clean with a pleasant, open, flat-rock area below. Since it's the only black, north-facing wall, and has the only open area along the entire cliff base, it should be easy to locate. It's right of center on the cliff.

There are two routes on the wall that share a fixed anchor. After climbing one of the routes, the other can be toproped from this anchor.

It is possible (but strongly discouraged) to access the fixed anchor at the top of the routes by traversing in from the left, starting from a ledge that you can walk onto (and take incredible photos from). This traverse route, called **Sketchy Shit Suck**, goes at about 5.7, and is wet, loose, terrifying and dangerous.

2 Sausage Science 5.11a G 75' ★★★★

Clean, elegant, and pumpy climbing with excellent holds and delicious moves.

Start: Centered on the Black Wall, 10' left of the arête on top of a block.

P1 5.11a G: Go straight up the face to a good horizontal 12', then use two tiny pockets to reach the next horizontal. Move right 5' to the base of a thin fingercrack and follow this with increasing difficulty to the top. There is a fixed anchor on a large ledge. 75'

Gear: 1 ea #2 Camalot, 0.75 Camalot, medium nuts.

FA Sep 11, 2010, Jim Lawyer, Martin von Arx

3 Cowboy Up 5.9 G 75' ★★★★

Incredible position, great moves, good rock, and excellent photo opportunities. This route and its neighbor **Sausage Science** make the approach worthwhile... almost.

Start: At the right side of the north-facing, black wall, below the toe of the arête.

P1 5.9 G: Move up a few feet to a block, then directly up the arête and wall on the left to a good horizontal crack at two-thirds height. Traverse right around the arête to a short left-facing corner, then up over two bulges to the top. The fixed anchor is shared with **Sausage Science**. 75'

Gear: 1 ea #2 Camalot, 0.75 Camalot, 0.5 Camalot, #0 TCU, medium nuts.

FA Sep 11, 2010, Jim Lawyer, Martin von Arx, Simeon Warner, Neal Knitel

PANTHER MOUNTAIN

Location	West side of Piseco Lake, accessed from NY 8
Summary	Two small summit crags and a larger single-pitch cliff with somewhat dirty routes.

3	1	3	1	1	1	1	11
-5.6	5.7	5.8	5.9	5.10	5.11	5.12	5.13+	total

Panther Mountain is a lovely little summit situated above Piseco Lake, with views of the lake and surrounding mountains. There are some good routes here, although they don't command the same scenic position as the summit viewpoint, and they aren't as clean as one would hope.

DIRECTIONS (MAP PAGE 335)

Parking for the cliffs on Panther Mountain is off West Shore Drive, also labeled Old Piseco Road. From Speculator (at the intersection of NY 30 and NY 8), drive east on NY 8. Continue through Lake Pleasant and Piseco, and at 11.0 miles, you'll reach the intersection with NY 10. At 13.9 miles, turn right onto West Shore Drive. Continue 2.5 miles to a pullout on the right (the lake side) 535838,4806635; there is a DEC sign across the road for the trail to Panther Mountain.

If you're coming from the west, the intersection of West Shore Drive and NY 8 is 19.1 miles east of the intersection of NY 8 and NY 365.

*Jim Lawyer on the first ascent of **Cowboy Up** (5.9). Photo by Neal Knitel.*

Southern Mountains

Panther Mountain
ECHO CLIFF

Aspect	Southeast
Height	130'
Quality	★
Approach	20 min, easy
Summary	Vertical to overhanging cracks on the main face; very dirty.

1	1	3	1	1	1	1		g
-5.6	5.7	5.8	5.9	5.10	5.11	5.12	5.13+	total

Echo Cliff is a scenic, semisecluded crag located on the side of Panther Mountain above Piseco Lake. The cliff is made up of a series of small corners and towers that rise from a steep slope of talus. The primary interest here is a single steep face with several attractive crack lines.

HISTORY
The routes on this cliff were originally climbed in the mid-1980s by Tad Welch and various partners. 15 years later, the climbs were recleaned and anchors installed on various trees. The routes have once again grown in and are in need of cleaning.

DIRECTIONS   (MAP PAGE 335)
From the parking area (0 hr 0 min), follow the trail to Panther Mountain to where the trail levels out at 15 min, just before the shoulder of Panther Mountain. Leave the trail 535303,4806905 and traverse the slope to the right and upward through some talus to the base of the cliff 535345,4807079, reached at 20 min.

DESCENT OPTIONS
Most routes have fixed anchors.

1 West End Brewery 5.8 G 40'
Start: The authors were unable to locate this route, which reportedly begins left of and uphill from the main face.
P1 5.8 G: Climb a handcrack to a ledge, then around blocks to the top. 40'
FA May 10, 1985, Tad Welch, Jamie Savage

2 Misspent Youth 5.8+ G 40' ★★
Nice crack climbing, although a bit short.
Start: Just left of the main face and slightly uphill; behind Yax Crack.
P1 5.8+ G: Climb the cracks just left of the arête to a fixed anchor on a tree. 40'
FA May 8, 1986, Tad Welch, Pat Clark

3 Yax Crack 5.10a G 70' ★
A nice crack initially but with an unappealing finish.
Start: 8' right of the left end of the main face and 20' left of Prisoner in Disguise; at the rightmost of two attractive fingercracks.
P1 5.10a G: Climb the fingertip crack into a shallow right-facing corner. Continue into a box chimney, exiting left onto a ledge near the top. 70'
FA 1985, Tad Welch (rope solo)

4 Prisoner in Disguise 5.9 G 100' ★★
Good climbing on interesting rock, although in need of a good brushing (it would have three or four stars otherwise). The final moves from the second slot are tricky. Named for a Linda Ronstadt album.
Start: At a blocky area 30' left of Life during Wartime, below a rectangular slot 15' up.
P1 5.9 G: Climb into the slot and mantel onto the ledge above. Climb the right-facing shallow corner to parallel cracks and into a second slot, exiting right and up to a fixed anchor at a giant white pine. 100'
FA Nov 2, 1985, Tad Welch (rope solo)

5 Brown and Serve 5.12a TR 90' ★
An excellent toprope begins 6' left of Life during Wartime at a short right-leaning crack that ends after 8'. Boulder up the crack, then up the beautiful orange face to the top. A directional can be arranged from the anchor on Life during Wartime.
FA (TR) Sep 10, 2000, Fred Abbuhl, Don McGrath (toprope)

6 Life During Wartime 5.11a G 90' ★★★
Excellent, steep crack climbing. The original ascent was made in snowmobile boots, as Widrig forgot his rock shoes in the car. Named for a Talking Heads song with the well-known lyrics "This ain't no party, this ain't no disco."
Start: Below the hourglass-shaped crack stuffed with chockstones, which is below a 6" overlap, 60' from the left end of the main face.
P1 5.11a G: Climb past the chockstones, then up the thin crack with crumbly rock on the face to a stance. Continue through the pod and fingercrack above (fixed bong) to a fixed anchor. 90'
FA (A1) Mar 31, 1985, Tad Welch, Bill Widrig
FFA Oct 16, 1999, Jim Lawyer, Simon Catterall

7 Carrion and Crawl 5.8 G 130'
An adventure route, or in other words, wet, mossy, dirty, and full of shrubs and loose rock. On the first ascent, Knitel stuck his head over the ledge and found himself staring into the eyes of a dead, rotting raven. Higher, there is a cavelike alcove into which a scared climber naturally crawls.

335

Southern Mountains

ECHO CLIFF
2 Misspent Youth (5.8+)
3 Yax Crack (5.10a)
4 Prisoner in Disguise (5.9)
5 Brown and Serve (5.12a)
6 Life During Wartime (5.11a)
7 Carrion and Crawl (5.8)
8 Dental Hygienist (5.4)
9 Tennis, Anyone (5.7)

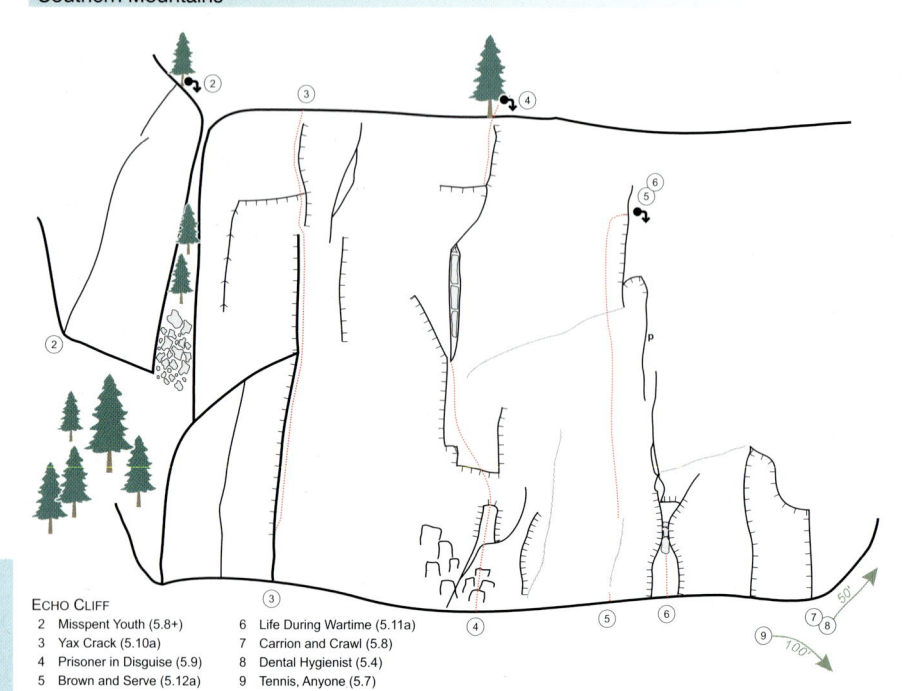

Start: 50' right of **Life during Wartime**, scramble up to a sloped, grassy ledge below the tallest section of the main face. Begin at an A-frame-shaped cave.
P1 5.7 G: Up the crack above the cave and over blocks to a tree beneath a major right-facing corner. 40'
P2 5.8 G: Up the right-facing, block-filled corner. 90'
FA 1993, Neal Knitel, Mykel Ruvola

8 Dental Hygienist 5.4 G 140'
Start: Right of **Carrion and Crawl** at a 5'-high flake that forms a 4" crack.
P1 5.4 G: Up the flake, then up and right through several big fern-covered ledges to a belay ledge with a pine tree on its right end. 90'
P2 5.3 G: Follow a crack up and left to the top. 50'
FA Jun, 2007, David Hyney, Ray Cool

9 Tennis, Anyone 5.7 G 60'
Yet another route that would be much nicer if cleaned.
Start: 100' right of and downhill from the main face. This section of cliff is separated from the main face by the huge gully right of **Carrion and Crawl**.
P1 5.7 G: Climb the right side of a flake to a small 1' roof; angle up and right following cracks to a large pine tree. 60'
FA Nov 2, 1985, Tad Welch, Mike Cross

Tad Welch on *Prisoner in Disguise* (5.9).
Photo by Jamie Savage.

Southern Mountains

Panther Mountain
THE GROTTO

Aspect	Southeast
Height	40'
Quality	★
Approach	30 min, easy
Summary	Very similar to the Summit Cliff but a little longer and more challenging.

The Grotto, named as such to distinguish it from the Summit Cliff, is hidden in the trees near the summit of Panther Mountain. The Grotto and Summit Cliff offer more moderate and accessible routes than on the main Echo Cliff below. The routes can be toproped.

DIRECTIONS (MAP PAGE 335)
Hike the trail to the summit of Panther Mountain. As you near the summit, there is a new water bar just before where the trail negotiates a short steep section of rock. Turn right off the trail at the water bar and follow the indistinct herd path down and to the left for less than 1 min. Veer right to get around a small 10'-high cliff, then head down and left to the base of the routes.

There is a distinct trail to the ledge at the top of the climbs that leaves the main trail just below the summit.

10 Zack's Sunspot 5.6 G 40' ★
Start: At the left-hand crack below a pine 20' up.
P1 5.6 G: (V1, V2) Climb the crack up to a pine, then step right to crescent-shaped flakes and cracks. Up the cracks to a steep slab, then into a dirty minichimney to the top. 40'
V1 5.7 G: Adds a difficult start, beginning on the farthest right crack that starts 4' off the ground. Start up this thin crack and move left 1' when it runs out into the beginning of another crack about 10' up. Follow the crack straight up onto a slab and chimney as for the main route.
V2 5.5 G: Stem between the two crack systems to gain the steep slab and dirty minichimney above.
ACB Oct, 2006, Daniel Mosny, Kate Mosny

Panther Mountain
SUMMIT CLIFF

Aspect	Southeast
Height	30'
Quality	★
Approach	30 min, easy
Summary	A small cliff just below the hikers' lookout on the summit of Panther Mountain with a few short moderate routes.

The routes here are short and can be easily toproped. Beware of hikers throwing rocks off the cliff above.

DIRECTIONS (MAP PAGE 335)
Follow the Panther Mountain Trail nearly to the summit ledge. A few yards before you come onto the ledge, there is a trail that goes right; follow it down to the base of the cliff.

11 Look Out Above 5.6 G 30' ★
Start: At base of the cliff, identify obvious right- and left-hand crack systems; this route begins below the right-hand crack.
P1 5.6 G: (V1, V2) Climb the right-hand crack until you reach a short, steep slab below a block. Step around left or go over the block and continue to the top. 30'
V1 5.5 G: Climb the left-hand crack up to horizontal cracks left of the block that caps the slab on the main route. Step right and up to the top.
V2 5.4 G: Stem both crack systems up to the block, then climb to the top as for the main route.
ACB Oct, 2006, Daniel Mosny, Kate Mosny

FISH MOUNTAIN CRAG

Location	Lake Pleasant NY, accessed from Fish Mountain Road
Aspect	Southwest
Height	50'
Quality	★
Approach	15 min, easy
Summary	Small cliff with a mix of face, crack, and small slab.

	1	1	2					4
-5.6	5.7	5.8	5.9	5.10	5.11	5.12	5.13+	total

Fish Mountain Crag is a small cliff with good quality rock on the southwest aspect of Fish Mountain overlooking Oxbow Lake. For the most part, the rock is dirty, but a few clean sections can be found. The cliff has a mix of short faces, cracks, and even a mini-slab. Additionally, from the top there is a decent view of Piseco Lake and Oxbow Lake to the southwest.

The base of the cliff is level and semi-open, and the cliff is wide, although the existing routes are located on a 60'-wide section.

DIRECTIONS
Locate the intersection of NY 8 and Tamarack Road. This intersection is 1.7 miles from South Shore Road in Lake Pleasant, when traveling towards Piseco.

From the intersection (0.0), turn onto Tamarack Road. At 0.6 mile at a 4-way intersection, turn left onto Fish Mountain Road and drive to its end at 1.2 miles. Park at the snow plow turn-around next to the Fish Mountain Cemetery **543972,4812768**.

On the north side of the cemetery (0 hr 0 min), follow a gravel road heading northeast towards Sacandaga Lake. Go 75' past the DEC gate with a faded metal stop sign, then switchback left onto a well-maintained hiking trail that heads gently up the hill (west). Follow this trail for about 0.25 mile to a point where the trail begins to lose elevation. At 6 min, leave the trail and walk rightwards into the woods, heading over a small hill, then down to cross a wet area. Head north and walk up the shoulder of the mountain to reach the crag at 15 min **543700,4813128**.

337

Southern Mountains

Neal Knitel on an unfinished project at Fish Mountain. Photo by Jay Harrison.

1 Just Chum-me 5.7+ PG 55'
Start: At the left end of the cliff, 15' right of a mossy slab 10' up, and below a horizontal break 20' up. Just right (and 5' up) are two pasted-on block-flakes, one above the other, and just left of a mossy crack system.
P1 5.7+ PG: Go up the face left of the pasted-on block-flakes, then up a thin crack in a face to the horizontal break 20' up. (V1) Move right to a short, gently-overhanging, right-leaning fingercrack that leads to a ledge in a right-facing corner with a small tree. Pull around left (watch the rope drag in the finger crack below the corner) onto a slab and move left about 5' to a vertical crack. Follow this crack to the top. 55'
V1 5.9 G: Much better than the normal finish: go straight up the face to a vertical crack 5' left of the right-facing corner. Finish on the normal route.
FA Apr, 2012, Neal Knitel, Dereck Nabozney
FA (V1) May 6, 2012, Neal Knitel, Neal Lamphear

2 Balls In Space 5.8 TR 55'
Begin 22' right of **Just Chum-me** and 6' left of **With Brook Trout Eyes**, at a sometimes-wet vertical crack that leads to a boxed alcove 10' up. Go up the crack to the alcove, then up a flared crack. At its top, move left onto a face-slab to a nice left-facing flake, then up lower-angled, dirty terrain to the trees. The moss has been cleaned out of the crack above the offwidth making a more pure crack climb straight up.
FA (TR) May 6, 2012, Neal Lamphear, Neal Knitel

3 With Brook Trout Eyes 5.9 TR 50'
Begin 6' right of **Balls in Space** below a flared handcrack that begins 9' up and snakes up the face. Climb steps and face holds to gain the flared handcrack. Follow this to a good ledge with good gear.
FA (TR) May 6, 2012, Neal Knitel, Neal Lamphear

4 Royal Coachman 5.9 G 60' ★★
Start: 12' right of **With Brook Trout Eyes** at a short, 5'-high, right-facing corner, which is 2' left of a vertical seam that gradually increases to hand width.
P1 5.9 G: Go up the corner to a good stance 7' up. Reach right and climb the gradually-widening fingercrack. Finish on a very low angle slab at the top. 60'
FA May 11, 2012, Neal Knitel, Tom Lane, Jay Harrison

LAKE PLEASANT QUARRY

Location	Near Lake Pleasant, accessed from NY 8
Aspect	Southeast
Height	45'
Quality	★★★
Approach	3 min, easy
Summary	An old quarry with an excellent wall for toproping, but limited for leading.

2	6	3	1	2		14
-5.6	5.7	5.8	5.9	5.10	5.11	5.12	5.13+	total

The Lake Pleasant Quarry is an abandoned quarry near Lake Pleasant, long used as a toproping spot by local climbers. The area has some evidence of industrial use, but it's now so overgrown that the environment is actually quite pleasant. The climbing is in a small amphitheater with a meadow of grass and larch trees. The most obvious rock in the amphitheater is a 20'-high black wall on top of a talus slope; there may be climbing here, but it's short, blasted, and not recommended. The better climbing is on the Toy Story Wall—the right side of the amphitheater (as you walk in) hidden in the trees, and at the same level as the meadow, where the

A busy day at the Quarry. Photo by Jay Harrison.

Southern Mountains

rock is compact, with many features (vertical seams, small ceilings, some cracks), and shows no signs of having been blasted.

The Toy Story Wall is the orange and black wall about 125' wide and between 20' and 40' tall, with an open flat base and toprope anchors peppered along the top. To access the top, walk right. Topropes can be arranged by carefully reaching over the edge and threading the rope through any of the many chain anchors. The climbing is a mix of smooth crimpy face climbing, horizontal blocks and cracks, and small roofs, resulting from blasted rock. Many of the climbs have toprope anchors, but even so, several are good for leading.

Looking at the cliff from the open meadow in front, there are 12 sets of anchors. The leftmost four anchors are for the first four routes Barrel of Monkeys, Sarge, Buzz, and To Infinity and Beyond! The anchors on these routes are difficult to access from the top (use a short rappel or lead Barrel of Monkeys). The crag's main features are the "Iron Curtain," a smooth face to a ledge 8' up spanning the first five routes, and the "Rock Fall Area," just left of center, where many large loose blocks have come down.

There is a wonderful swim spot in Sacandaga Lake near the Quarry parking area. The beach is owned by NYS and open to the public. From the parking area, drive southwest (away from Lake Pleasant) on NY 8 for 0.2 mile, and turn right onto Tamarack Road. Follow it to its end, and turn left onto Fawn Lake Road. At its end, turn right onto Forest Trail.

HISTORY

The quarry has had surges of popularity, mostly as a place for local climbers to toprope after work, as well as an area for the local ski patrol to practice rappelling. In the late 1980s, the area was frequented by Neal Knitel and friends, including Jim and Neal Lamphear, and Mykel and Ann Ruvola. In 1994, Knitel and Lamphear created a single lead route with two bolts which they named Bullseye, although Lamphear later removed the hangers when he noticed that locals were using them for target practice.

In 2008, the area was resurrected (i.e., cleaned, groomed, and equipped) by Tim Trezise, outdoor director at *Camp of the Woods* in Speculator with help from Jay Harrison, and Todd Paris. They began naming routes after characters in the 1995 animated movie *Toy Story*.

DIRECTIONS

Parking for the Lake Pleasant Quarry is on NY 8 at a paved entrance (the old entrance to the quarry) 545547,4812195 with a gate, stop sign, and gravel barrier, 3.9 miles from Old Piseco Road in Piseco on the right (when you're traveling toward Lake Pleasant), and 1.4 miles from South Shore Road in Lake Pleasant on the left (when you're traveling toward Piseco).

From the parking area, walk over the barrier to a section of exposed asphalt patch. On the right end of this is a distinct path; follow this directly to the Toy Story Wall 545622,4812075.

Lake Pleasant Quarry
TOY STORY WALL

1 Barrel of Monkeys 5.4 G 35' ★

A good introduction to the area.
Start: 25' left of Sarge at a left-facing corner just right of a large, dirty chimney-crack.
P1 5.3 G: Up low-angled, highly-featured rock to a large ledge, then angle right to a fixed anchor. 35'
FA Mar, 2009, Todd Paris

2 Sarge 5.7+ G 42' ★

The fixed anchor is accessible from the top; use a short rappel to avoid unstable rock.
Start: Near the left end of the cliff is an orange nose near the top. Begin just right of the nose, 55' left of Bullseye and 10' left of Buzz, below a horizontal crack 8' up.
P1 5.7+ G: (V1, V2) Climb up two small vertical cracks to the left of a smooth face. Continue up thin seams to a ledge with a fixed anchor. 42'
V1 5.6+ G: Begin by climbing the left-arching corner on the right of the smooth face to a great jug, then pull onto a small ledge. Join the normal route to the top.
V2 Stinky Pete 5.10c TR: Just right of the normal start, climb the smooth face using a horizontal crack.
FA Jul, 2008, Todd Paris
FA (V2) Apr, 2009, Peter Whitmore

3 Buzz 5.8 G 40' ★★★

Start: At a face just right of a left-facing corner that arches left into a small ceiling.
P1 5.8 G: (V1) Go directly up the face, staying out of the left-arching corner, to a ledge at mid-height. Continue up a thin, broken crack to a fixed anchor. 40'
V1 5.6+ G: Begin just left in the left-facing corner that arches left into a small ceiling. Move up the corner to a high jug at the end of the arch, then up to a horizontal crack. Step right, and climb a thin crack to a good ledge with a fixed anchor.
FA Jul, 2008, Tim Trezise

4 To Infinity and Beyond! 5.9 G 35' ★★★★

Despite appearances of being thin and crimpy, this is a fun climb that has a lot more available than meets the eye.
Start: 6' right of Buzz at a black face with shattered rock.
P1 5.9 G: (V1) Climb the black face to a good horizontal, then follow a straight-up seam to a fixed anchor. 35'
V1 Wheezy 5.10b G: Go up the smooth rock face to the right of the bolts using face crimps, avoiding use of the side pulls on Woody. Higher up, move diagonally right up small footholds, then lunge from a crimp to a horizontal crack.
FA (V1) Jul, 2009, Eric Jacobson
FA Jul, 2008, Tim Trezise, Jay Harrison

Southern Mountains

5 Woody 5.7 PG 35' ★★

Perhaps the most obvious crack at the cliff. There is no fixed anchor; use "woody" (trees) for toprope anchors. Beware of large, loose, unstable rock at the bottom overhang, and loose blocks at the top ledge area. When setting up as a toprope, there is a bolt around the corner from the main face to serve as a directional to keep the belay end of the rope out of a crack.
Start: 5' right of **To Infinity and Beyond!** and at the left end of a low ceiling 4' up with some lighter-colored unstable blocks in it.
P1 5.7 PG: Climb straight up black rock to a left-leaning orange seam that becomes a right-facing corner, then up to a ledge. 35'
FA Jun, 2008, Tim Trezise

6 Squeaky Toy Aliens 5.7 G 35' ★★

Use caution with the large unstable blocks at the overhang.
Start: At the right side of large hanging blocks.
P1 5.7 G: Go up the hanging blocks, then straight up using horizontal cracks to finish on a large ledge at a fixed anchor around the corner of the face. 35'
FA Oct, 2011, Tim Trezise

7 Emperor Zurg 5.10a G 37' ★★★★

The fixed anchor is easily accessible from the top.
Start: On the right end of the low ceiling 4' up at a thin seam in black rock.
P1 5.10a G: (V1) Up the seam in the smooth face to a ledge in a small right-facing corner. Work up and left for 4', then straight up the orange face to a fixed anchor. 37'
V1 The Project 5.12 TR: Start just right of **Squeaky Toy Aliens** in the center of the low ceiling 4' up. Climb over the ceiling, then up the smooth face to a second ceiling. Over this, then up to the **Emperor Zurg** fixed anchor.
FA Jul, 2008, Jay Harrison

8 Rex 5.8+ TR 35' ★★★

Start as for **Emperor Zurg** and step up and right onto a black face with good incut, crimpy holds. Up the face to a ledge, then over a ceiling and onto an orange face. Continue up some overlapping blocks to a fixed anchor. The fixed anchor is easily accessible from the top.
FA (TR) Jun, 2008, Tim Trezise

9 I Am Not a Toy! 5.10b TR 30' ★★★

Begin 10' right of **Rex** at a 5'-wide ceiling 4' up in black rock. Up the black face, then over a small ceiling to a fixed anchor. The fixed anchor is easily accessible from the top.
FA (TR) Jul, 2008, Jay Harrison

10 Bullseye 5.8 G 30' ★★

This route has two bolts and no top anchor, but you can reach left and use the fixed anchor on **I Am Not a Toy**.
Start: 5' right of **I Am Not a Toy**, and just right of a 5'-wide ceiling 4' up, 40' from the right end of the cliff.
● **P1 5.8 G:** Up past a ledge on the right to a ceiling (bolt), then up past a V-shaped pod to the top. 30'
FA 1994, Neal Knitel, Neal Lamphear

11 Tour Guide Barbie 5.7+ TR 28' ★

Start as for **Bullseye**. Climb up and right through shattered rock to a horizontal crack, then to a vertical seam that leads to a fixed anchor. The fixed anchor is easily accessible from the top.
FA (TR) Jun, 2008, Tim Trezise

12 Psycho Sid 5.7 TR 25' ★

Begin 25' from the right end of the cliff at the 4th crack from the right end of the cliff, and the first crack right of **Bullseye**. Up the crack to a good ledge, step right and follow a seam to a fixed anchor. The fixed anchor is easily accessible from the top.
FA (TR) Jun, 2008, Tim Trezise

13 Mutant Toy 5.6 TR 20'

This is the second crack (which is more of a seam) from the right end of the cliff, and 15' from the right end of the cliff. Up the thin crack past horizontals to a ledge, then past a small alcove to a fixed anchor. The fixed anchor is easily accessible from the top.

14 Mr. Potato Head 5.7 TR 16'

(V1) Begin 6' from the right end of the cliff. Up a face with thin holds in a seam to an 8"-wide vertical slot with a fixed anchor just above. The fixed anchor is easily accessible from the top.
V1 Mrs. Potato Head TR: Begin further right at a large blocky crack near the right end of the crag.

AUGER FALLS

Auger Falls is a narrow gorge on the Sacandaga River just upstream of its junction with the East Branch, where the river becomes much more substantial. The river makes a short drop, then augers steeply down through angled slabs and potholes. Near the downstream end of the falls—and on the east side—is a small, steep, northwest-facing crag with potential for a few routes. It's a noisy, dark place, (great for hot days). Since it's also northwest facing, bring a wire brush.

DIRECTIONS

From Speculator (the intersection of NY 30 and NY 8), drive southeast on the combined NY 30 / NY 8. At 8.0 miles, turn left on a hidden dirt road. Turn immediately right and drive 600' to the trailhead 560573,4813027. Follow the yellow-marked trail for 5 minutes to the falls. At the end of the trail, walk downstream 400'; the cliff is directly across the river 560911,4812948.

Crossing the river may be a problem, especially if the water is cold and you are unwilling to wade. If you are unable to cross the river, you may find a more reasonable crossing upstream about 1/4 mile. Otherwise, you'll have to approach from Griffin. From the intersection where NY 8 and NY 30 split (0.0 mile), follow NY 8 north 2.5 miles to Teachout Road—a hidden, unsigned dirt road on the left (this is 0.1 mile after a large paved pullout on the right). Turn left and, at 2.7 miles, cross a bridge over the East Branch Sacandaga River, then bear left. Follow this to its end at 3.1 miles; a high-clearance 2WD vehicle is sufficient.

Southern Mountains

There is room for a few cars; make sure not to block the road 562177,4813357. Walk past the yellow gate and follow the red-marked trail to the falls, about 20 min. Once near the river, leave the trail on the left and follow a good herd path downstream along the high bank above the river. Before the end of the river canyon, follow a seasonal tributary down a gully to the lower part of the falls. Traverse a short ledge downstream to the base of the cliff 560911,4812948.

1 Knightfire 5.10a TR 50'
On the left end of the cliff is a clean face that forms the left wall of a large left-facing corner. Begin 20' right of this corner behind a semi-flat boulder with ferns, at a left-facing, right-leaning corner that leads to a roof 12' up. There's an 18"-diameter birch at the base touching the rock. Go up the corner to the roof, step left, then up a right-leaning crack to an overlap. Traverse left under the overlap, then up the face to a horizontal. Step left again to a crack in a shallow, right-facing corner and follow this to a giant white pine at the top.
FA (TR) Sep 10, 2011, Andrew Cardin

WEST MOUNTAIN

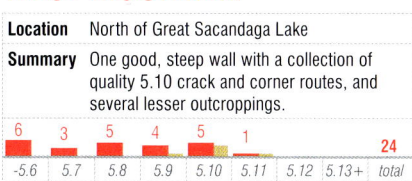

Location	North of Great Sacandaga Lake
Summary	One good, steep wall with a collection of quality 5.10 crack and corner routes, and several lesser outcroppings.

6	3	5	4	5		1	24
-5.6	5.7	5.8	5.9	5.10	5.11	5.12	5.13+	total

Located north of Great Sacandaga Lake, West Mountain is a long ridge of peaks, the primary one being Hadley Mountain, one of the most popular hikes in the southern Adirondacks. The reported climbing so far is located on the steep south-facing slopes near the southern end of the range, on the ridge running south of the Hadley Mountain Trail. When there are no leaves, the cliffs are visible from Hadley Hill Road.

The main attraction here is the Rod & Guns Wall, a steep 80'-tall wall with a high concentration of quality routes in the 5.10 range and potential for even more difficult routes; the roof area is especially interesting. The other cliffs have exploratory routes and are included for those seeking new terrain.

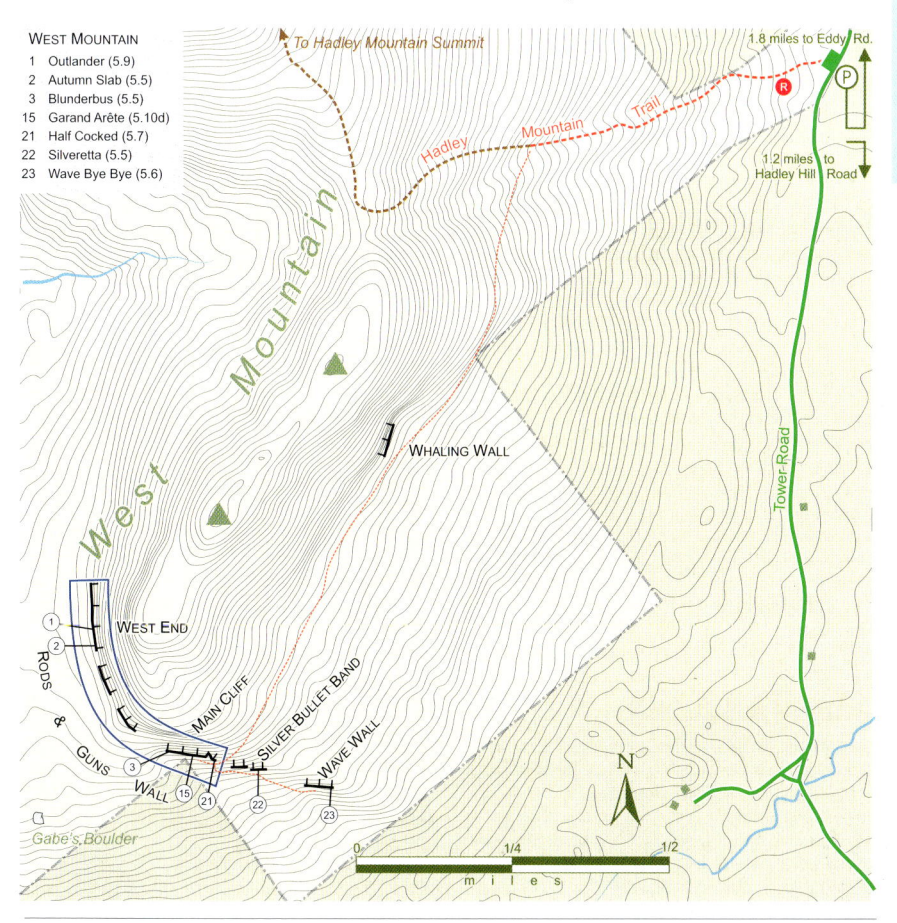

WEST MOUNTAIN
1 Outlander (5.9)
2 Autumn Slab (5.5)
3 Blunderbus (5.5)
15 Garand Arête (5.10d)
21 Half Cocked (5.7)
22 Silveretta (5.5)
23 Wave Bye Bye (5.6)

341

Southern Mountains

HISTORY

Tom Lane, who lives nearby, saw these cliffs while driving on Hadley Hill Road. Lane was mostly retired from climbing, but a chance meeting with Jay Harrison changed everything. They made their first visit in April 2011 with their ascent of **Kalashnikov Corner**. Because of the long approach, Lane joined a nearby gun club primarily to get easier access to the cliffs, and it's for this reason that most of the routes are named after hunting and guns.

DIRECTIONS   (MAP PAGE 341)

The cliffs are on state land, but all of the land between the cliffs and the Hadley Hill Road is owned by several hunting clubs. Hence, you must approach from the Hadley Mountain Trail.

From the south and west: Locate the intersection of NY 30 and Bridge Street in Northville (0.0 mile). Follow Bridge Street to its end at 0.7 mile, then turn right on South Main Street (CR 152). Follow this to its end at a 4-way intersection at 2.0 miles. Turn right onto Ridge Road (CR 113) and follow this to a fork at 2.7 miles. Bear left onto Northville Road (CR 4) and follow this to a 4-way intersection at 5.1 miles. Turn left onto North Shore Road (CR 4). At 13.8 miles turn left onto Hadley Hill Road. At 19.1 miles, turn left onto Tower Road, a gravel road. At 20.3 miles, turn left into the Hadley Mountain Trailhead 585014,4802878.

From the east: From the Northway (I-87) Exit 21 (0.0), go south on NY 9N toward Lake Luzerne. At 10.2 miles, turn right onto School Road. Follow this to its end at Bay Road; turn right, then an immediate left onto Bridge St / Rockwell St. At 10.7 miles turn right onto Stoney Creek Road (CR 1). At 13.8 miles turn left onto Hadley Hill Road. At 18.1 miles, turn right onto Tower Road, a gravel road. At 19.5 miles, park at the Hadley Mountain Trailhead on the left 585014,4802878.

Follow the trail for 0.5 mile to the #3 marker (these numbers coincide with the brochures available at the parking lot). Leave the trail 584268,4802668 and contour south/southwest (left) to a private property boundary. Go around this, staying on the state land side, then continue southwest through talus below a 50'-tall cliff. Drop down slightly, and continue south/southwest along a wide, sparsely wooded bench to the southern end of the mountain. Descend along the eastern edge of the bench, then turn west. The Rods & Guns Wall is positioned just east of the southernmost end of the ridge 583315,4801177. The hike is about 1.6 miles and takes about 1 hr 10 min.

West Mountain
GABE'S BOULDER

Located southwest of the Rods & Guns Wall is a lone, tall boulder in the woods split by a crack 582999,4801014. The existing route, **Gabe's Boulder** (5.7; 20'; Jun 26, 2013; Gabe Linncourt), climbs the crack in corner on the southwest side of the boulder. There's a large shard of rock at the base of the corner. Descend by lowering off the opposite side of the boulder.

West Mountain
RODS & GUNS WALL

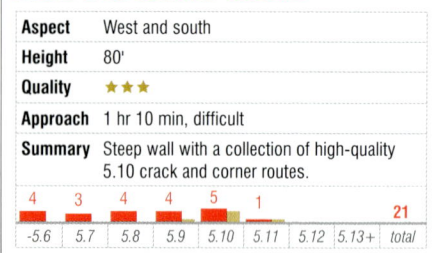

Aspect	West and south
Height	80'
Quality	★★★
Approach	1 hr 10 min, difficult
Summary	Steep wall with a collection of high-quality 5.10 crack and corner routes.

4	3	4	5	1		21
-5.6	5.7	5.8	5.9	5.10	5.11	5.12	5.13+	total

The most distinctive, highest, and desirable wall on the mountain is the Rod & Guns Wall. The roof section in the middle makes this wall easy to identify, but in the thick foliage of summer, it may prove difficult to locate. A GPS is recommended.

West End

DIRECTIONS   (MAP PAGE 341)

From the Main Cliff, descend to the bench below the talus. Contour west for 8 min staying below the talus. Keep an eye on the hillside at the top of the talus, and head up when you see rock. A series of broken buttresses marks where the slope of the mountain turns northward. These are the walls of the West End 583126,4801417.

There's potential for additional short routes on these walls.

1 Outlander 5.9 G 65' ★

Start: Locate a steep buttress with a broken steep left side. Begin in an orange right-facing corner 12' uphill and left of the low point of the terrain. There's a crack in the corner than snakes around 3 overhangs.

P1 5.9 G: Climb the face right of the corner (avoid choss on the left face), then up the corner for 15' to where it becomes a tight V-notch (There's a large block perched on a ledge to the right here.) Up the V-notch to a stance below a bulge. Go through a hanging notch to easier climbing that leads to a large ledge sparingly festooned with scraggly birch and poplar. 65'

Descent: Rappel off anemic trees or scramble up (climber's) left to reach a 3rd class gully.
FA Nov 2, 2011, Jay Harrison, Tom Lane

2 Autumn Slab 5.5 G 70'

Looks awful, but Jay insists it's fun. Really.

Start: Locate **Outlander**, which is much easier to identify. Walk right 90' and locate the lowest point on a tongue of slab. Begin 10' up and right from this low point.

P1 5.5 G: Climb up and left to a crack breaking through an overhang. Continue upward to finish on a right-rising crack that goes through a small, left-rising overhang. 70'

Descent: Go down class 3rd class gully to the (climber's) right.
FA Oct 7, 2011, Jay Harrison (solo)

Southern Mountains

Main Cliff

The Main Cliff is hidden by large hardwoods, and is 300' wide and 85' tall 583315,4801177. To either side lie several smaller outcrops. In the center of the Main Cliff is a major roof 30' and 50' wide up that blocks access to the upper portion of the cliff, and to date, no routes break this barrier.

To descend, rappel from a fixed anchor on a tree directly over the roof. Or, walk west (climber's left) until you can scramble down to the base of the cliff just left of Blunderbus.

3 Blunderbus 5.5 G 55'

Mildly awful.
Start: Near the left end of the cliff at a foot-wide channel that begins as a shallow, right-facing corner. The channel is just behind an oak tree, and there's a large pine 25' up.
P1 5.5 G: Climb the channel past the pine tree, then, from a large block, continue up a final steep wall. 55'
FA Jun 15, 2011, Jay Harrison

4 Misfire 5.9- PG 60'

Looks like 5.7.
Start: At stacked boulders 15' right of Blunderbus, and 4' left of Scattershot's right-facing corner, below a thin crack in an overhang.
P1 5.9- PG: Climb blocks to overhang, go through this using the crack and outside corner, then climb up right of a giant boulder and scramble up easy rock, joining Scattershot to the top of the cliff. 60'
FA Aug 24, 2011, Jay Harrison, Tom Lane

5 Scattershot 5.4 R 55'

Good pro in bad rock, this route ascends a choss pile, originally thought to be a quick way to the top. Nobody should climb this.
Start: At a dirty, right-facing corner just left of a fresh slab. A 10'-tall stone needle is tilted against the corner 20' up.
P1 5.4 R: Climb the slab just right of the corner until a tricky move to somewhat stable rock is possible. Clamber up the corner behind the needle onto a ledge. Climb the brushy face above this to the top. 55'
FA Jun 15, 2011, Jay Harrison

6 Colt 45 Corner 5.10a G 55' ★

Start: 30' right of Scattershot and 40' left of Chuting Lane, at a distinct right-facing corner with an offwidth slot at the base, and a tree growing against the left wall of the corner.
P1 5.10a G: Scramble up a broken pile of dirt and rocks to the corner, then up a wide offwidth crack to a bulging tips layback on a thick, square-edged rock fin. A small ledge offers some rest before finishing up a corner with small gear (small nuts and cams) through another bulge to the top. 55'
FA Nov 12, 2011, Jay Harrison, Tom Lane

7 Chuting Lane 5.6 G 55' ★

Start: At a very large, left-facing corner 15' above the trail. 40' left is the opposing corner of Colt 45 Corner.

P1 5.6 G: Climb the corner to a ledge on its top, then climb through the final headwall via a wide crack and corner system. 55'
FA Aug 9, 2011, Jay Harrison

8 Daisy BBs 5.8 G 70' ★★

Start: At a short, vertical crack in a face 12' left of the bookend alcove where Pump Action and Lever Action begin and 25' downhill and right of Chuting Lane.
P1 5.8 G: Climb the crack system to its end at a ledge. Work up the left of two thin cracks to another ledge below an offwidth crack. Up the offwidth crack past a birch tree to a ledge. Climb directly up the crack and face to the top, left of an 8'-long block. 70'
FA Aug 9, 2011, Tom Lane, Jay Harrison

9 Squeezing Miss Daisy 5.8- PG 70' ★

A squeeze job.
Start: At a waist-high concavity in the face just right of a short vertical crack (the start of Daisy BBs), left of a right-facing corner (the start of B.A.R.).
P1 5.8- PG: Climb to a sloping stance, then move up and left to holds just right of the thin crack of Daisy BBs. Climb up onto a ledge at its right end, up a vertical crack for a few feet, then traverse 5' right to a small, short, right-facing corner. Go up above this to a sloping stance below a hand- and fist-crack. Climb the crack past a birch tree to a ledge, then up a final headwall to finish at the right end of an 8' long block. 70'
FA Aug 9, 2011, Jay Harrison, Tom Lane

10 B.A.R. 5.10b G 65' ★★★

Start: At an 10'-tall right-facing corner 7' left of the right-facing corner of the Pump Action.
P1 5.10b G: Climb up the corner to stance, then up and right to a right-rising, right-facing, stepped flake system. Up this to a horizontal under a steep wall, then up a sharply-defined vertical tips crack (4' left of Pump Action). Use face holds and another vertical crack to reach a good ledge. Go up a flaring notch in a final steep face to the top. 65'
Gear: Tricams are helpful for protecting several of the difficult moves.
FA Nov 12, 2012, Tom Lane, Jay Harrison

11 Pump Action 5.10a PG 70' ★★★

Strenuous climbing with good (but pumpy to place) protection.
Start: On the left side of a 12'-wide, level platform at the foot of the cliff, at a 15'-tall, 2'-deep, right-facing corner with a crack continuing above it. This corner faces the left-facing corner of Lever Action 12' right.
P1 5.10a PG: Climb the right-facing corner and crack to a large ledge 45' up, then continue up the shallow, right-facing corner to the top. 70'
Gear: Small to medium cams, tricams.
FA Jul 1, 2011, Tom Lane, Jay Harrison

Southern Mountains

12 Lever Action 5.8- G 70' ★★
Hidden protection makes this easier than it looks.
Start: At a 4'-deep left-facing corner 12' right of Pump Action.
P1 5.8- G: (V1) Climb the corner to a stance, then up a seam, swing left along a left-pointing flake and back right to continue up the crack system to a large ledge 45' up. Climb a left-facing corner to the top. 70'
V1 5.8 G: Begin 12' downhill and right of the corner at a crack in a steep face. Climb the crack, then go up and left to meet the normal route at the beginning of the crux section.
FA May 26, 2011, Jay Harrison, Tom Lane
FA (V1) Nov 12, 2011, Jay Harrison, Tom Lane

13 Trigger Finger 5.11a G 85' ★★★
Start: Around the corner (and down) from Lever Action (and 8' right of Lever Action V1) below the left end of an overhang 10' up. This is located 10' left of a right-facing corner that defines the left end of the major roof system.
P1 5.11a G: Climb to an overhang, then up a left-facing flake to a right-facing flake. Continue up to an overhanging face with a solitary vertical seam. Go up this, then follow an easier crack system to the top. 85'
FA Jul 27, 2011, Michael Farnsworth

14 Winchester Dihedral 5.9+ G 80' ★★★
Stretchy stemming, a tricky traverse, and strenuous crack climbing. The direct finish awaits a free ascent.
Start: At a 2'-deep left-facing corner at the right end of the major roof system, below a large, overhanging, bottomless, flared, orange corner.
P1 5.9+ G: Climb the left-facing corner to a stance below the bottomless right-facing corner. Go up this corner to its top, then use hidden holds to escape left and up to a sloping ledge. Go up a shallow right-facing corner, then angle up right to the top. 80'
FA Jul 1, 2011, Tom Lane, Jay Harrison

15 Garand Arête 5.10d G 80' ★★★★
Hard moves on the arête, and exciting exposure pulling through the hanging slot above.
Start: 4' right of Winchester Dihedral below a small ledge 8' up and a bolt 15' up.
P1 5.10d G: Climb up the steep face to a horizontal crack. Traverse right to the arête, then go straight up the arête to a hanging slot; go past this to left or right, to easier climbing. 80'
FA Aug 24, 2011, Tom Lane, Jay Harrison

Tom Lane on the first ascent Winchester Dihedral (5.9+).
Photo by Jay Harrison.

16 Kalashnikov Corner 5.8 PG 80' ★★
The first route here.
Start: 20' right of Winchester Dihedral at parallel seams in a shallow dike.
P1 5.8 PG: Go up the parallel seams and blocky rock to the right-facing corner and continue up this to a stance at the top of the block forming the corner. Continue up lower-angle rock to the trees. 80'
FA Apr 9, 2011, Tom Lane, Jay Harrison

17 Tommy Gun 5.10c G 65' ★★★★
Excellent laybacking.
Start: 10' right of Kalashnikov Corner, at a steep slab with a wide overlap 8' up and a bolt 10' up.
P1 5.10c G: Make a couple of hard slab moves past the overlap to a steep headwall with a small triangular overhang. On the right end of the triangular overhang, layback up a right-facing flake, then make a long reach to a ledge. Rail up right to another stance, then up and left to the top. 65'
FA Nov 12, 2011, Tom Lane, Jay Harrison

18 Chute to Kill 5.9- PG 45'
The first ascent almost ended fatally for the spectators below. This will be a good route if cleaned.
Start: 50' right of the right end of the major roof system, at a right-facing corner below the left end of a roof 8' up.

344

Southern Mountains

P1 5.9- PG: Climb up the right-facing corner to gain a crack left of the overhang. Go up a thin vertical crack in the slab above to a blocky ledge, step onto a block and climb through a shallow cleft on the right to a sloping finish. 45'
FA Jul 27, 2011, Jay Harrison, Michael Farnsworth

19 Trajectory Crack 5.7 G 50' ★

Start: Right of Chute to Kill is a gully that defines the right end of the Main Cliff. Begin in a small niche below an attractive finger- and handcrack on the left side of the gully. There are some stacked blocks 15' up on the left side of the crack.

P1 5.7 G: Climb up to a stance at the start of the vertical crack, then follow this feature to its end on a ledge. Step left and climb the face to the top. 50'
FA Aug 24, 2011, Jay Harrison, Tom Lane

The Slab

The Slab is directly right of the Main Cliff, separated by a dirty, loose 5th class gully. Trajectory Crack starts on the lower left-hand side of this gully.

DESCENT OPTIONS
Rappel off trees.

20 Off Target 5.7 PG 70'

Start: At an 8'-high left-facing corner 20' uphill and left of the low point of the slab.

P1 5.7 PG: Climb the good holds on the right edge of the corner, then follow a crack up through bulge to the top. 70'
FA Nov 2, 2011, Jay Harrison, Tom Lane

21 Half Cocked 5.7 PG 75'

Start: At the low point of the slab, 60' right of the 5th class gully that defines the right end of the Main Cliff. There is a shallow 2'-high V-groove 4' up, and parallel seams in the slab above.

P1 5.7 PG: Climb up the V-groove and up the slab. Stay right of a right-facing corner to the top. 75'
FA Oct 7, 2011, Jay Harrison, Doug Allcock, Tom Lane

West Mountain
SILVER BULLET BAND

More of a landmark than a destination, this small, south-facing outcrop lies 750' downhill and right of the Rods & Guns Wall. It is 70'-wide and composed entirely of a compact, gray rock. An attractive left-facing corner lies near the left end (the route Silveretta), which is about 12' right of a steep gully that leads to the top.

DIRECTIONS (MAP PAGE 341)
From the Rods & Guns Wall, descent into the woods to the other side of the talus, then walk southeast along the talus for 10 min past several short cliffbands. This wall has a distinctive left-facing corner, just left of a bulging wave of rock 583534,4801132.

22 Silveretta 5.5 G 35' ★

If only it were longer. Several very hard topropes are to the right of this route.

Start: At a left-facing corner with a 3" crack, 40' right of the left side of the cliff.

P1 5.5 G: Climb the left-facing corner 7', then follow a vertical crack up and onto the arête to its right. Ascend it to the top. 35'
FA Apr 12, 2011, Jay Harrison, Tom Lane

West Mountain
WAVE WALL

This small, south-facing, 40'-tall, concave-shaped wall has an overhang at mid-height and many horizontal striations (which are, unfortunately, useless for protection). That, combined with ease of setup, makes it better for toproping than lead climbing, and several toprope routes ranging from 5.9 to 5.11 have been done here.

DIRECTIONS (MAP PAGE 341)
From the Rods & Guns Wall, descent into the woods to the other side of the talus, then walk 0.25 mile southeast along the talus for 15 min past several short cliffbands including the Silver Bullet Band to reach this wall 583699,4801081.

23 Wave Bye Bye 5.6 PG 40'

Yuck.

Start: At a dirty, stepped slab at the low point of the terrain on the right end of the cliff, just right of the concave section and 10' downhill and left of a giant oak.

P1 5.6 PG: Climb up the stepped mossy slab to a steep wall, then up and left to the left end of a large horizontal block. Over this, then up more slab to the top. 40'
FA Sep 14, 2011, Jay Harrison (solo)

West Mountain
WHALING WALL

This 90'-tall, east-facing cliff is closer to the Hadley Mountain trail. Much of the cliff is frightfully chossy, as the one route here exemplifies all too well.

DIRECTIONS (MAP PAGE 341)
From the Hadley Mountain trail locate the westernmost corner of the private property. From here, walk about 8 minutes further south to the cliff 583893,4801914.

24 Whale Ship 5.8 G 90'

A more appropriate name would require changing one letter; it is likely to fall down soon.

Start: At the broken left end of the right side of the cliff, at a left-facing corner, just right of a blocky area below an obvious broken cleft 15' up. Currently, there is a large ash tree growing below this cleft; the belayer may want to use it as a shield.

P1 5.8 G: Climb up right face and corner to a wide crack by a pile of huge blocks. Climb crack to a stance below an overhang with a crack formed by a giant block separated from the cliff. Climb through this to easier rock and belay at trees. 90'

Descent: Rappel off trees.
FA Sep 22, 2011, Tom Lane, Jay Harrison

N
0
10
20
miles
Lake Lila
Little Tupper
Long Lake
Soft Maple Reservoir
Eagle Falls
Beaver Lake
Stillwater Reservoir
Number 4 Road
365
Big Moose Lake
Raquette Lake
Fox Mountain
30
28N
Blue Mountain Lake
30
Moss Lake Slab
Eagle Bay
28
356
Bald Mountain
Inlet
Fulton Chain Lakes
Old Forge
Cedar River Flow
Middle Settlement Lake
Thendara
Mount Tom Cliff
354
Flatrock Mountain
Mitchell Ponds Mountain
350
Ice Cave Mountain
North Lake
Sacandaga Lake
Boonville
Lake Pleasant
28
12
Forestport
Piseco Lake
Ledge Mountain
8
Hoffmeister
28
12
Hinkley Reservoir
365
Barneveld
10
Arietta
365
8

Old Forge

On the western side of the park, buried in a maze of lakes, rivers, and small mountains, is a collection of crags with single-pitch routes. Despite their easy access from NY 28—the western gateway to the interior of the park—they remain raw and unvisited. They are close to Old Forge, a popular resort town in an area replete with attractive hiking and also known for its vast network of lakes.

Bald Mountain has a high concentration of routes and is the only cliff with a long history of climbing. The other cliffs in this section are recent discoveries, and there's plenty more awaiting those with a penchant for long marches and smallish, often dirty cliffs. Approaches vary in difficulty from easy (Bald Mountain) to inconvenient, sometimes requiring a canoe (Mitchell Ponds Mountain), a river crossing (Eagle Falls), or a long hike (Middle Settlement Lake, Ice Cave Mountain). The rock quality varies from exceptionally clean (Ice Cave Mountain) to dirty (Bald Mountain) to brittle (Eagle Falls). Over the last six years, Eagle Falls has proven to be the most popular crag in the region with many excellent routes, especially in the higher grades.

SEASON

Due to its location east of Lake Ontario, the Old Forge area is well known for snow. In the spring, when the Chapel Pond Pass crags are bare and climbable, many of the seasonal roads on the western side of the park are still inaccessible. During the summer, the area is equally known for pesky insects—blackflies, mosquitoes, and deerflies.

DIRECTIONS (MAPS PAGES 4 AND 346)

The cliffs around Old Forge are best reached from the west via NY 28, either by coming north on NY 12 / NY 28 from Utica or coming south through Lowville and Boonville. If you're coming from the east, going through the park is slow, so it's best to go around and come in via NY 28.

WHERE TO STAY

The NY 28 corridor through Old Forge is brimming with campgrounds, motels, B&Bs, and state land: the Visitor Information Center website (www.oldforgeny.com) has good information on lodging. Some noteworthy options are the car-camping sites along the north shore of North Lake (see page 350); car-camping sites on the Cedar River Road, outside of Inlet (see pages 360 and 263); Nicks Lake State Campground, in Old Forge (315.369.3314); and Limekiln Lake State Campground, in Inlet (315.357.4401).

AMENITIES

Major towns in this region are Lowville and Old Forge, which offer ample choices for gas and groceries.

DIVERSIONS

The area has plenty of opportunities for other activities, including mountain biking (stop in at Pedals and Petals in Inlet for information), hiking (simply too much to list here), and boating—for white water, try the Moose River, Beaver River, and Independence River, and for flat water, try the Fourth Lake / McKeever linkup or Stillwater Reservoir, with its excellent lakeside and island camping.

Watercolor by Lucie Wellner.

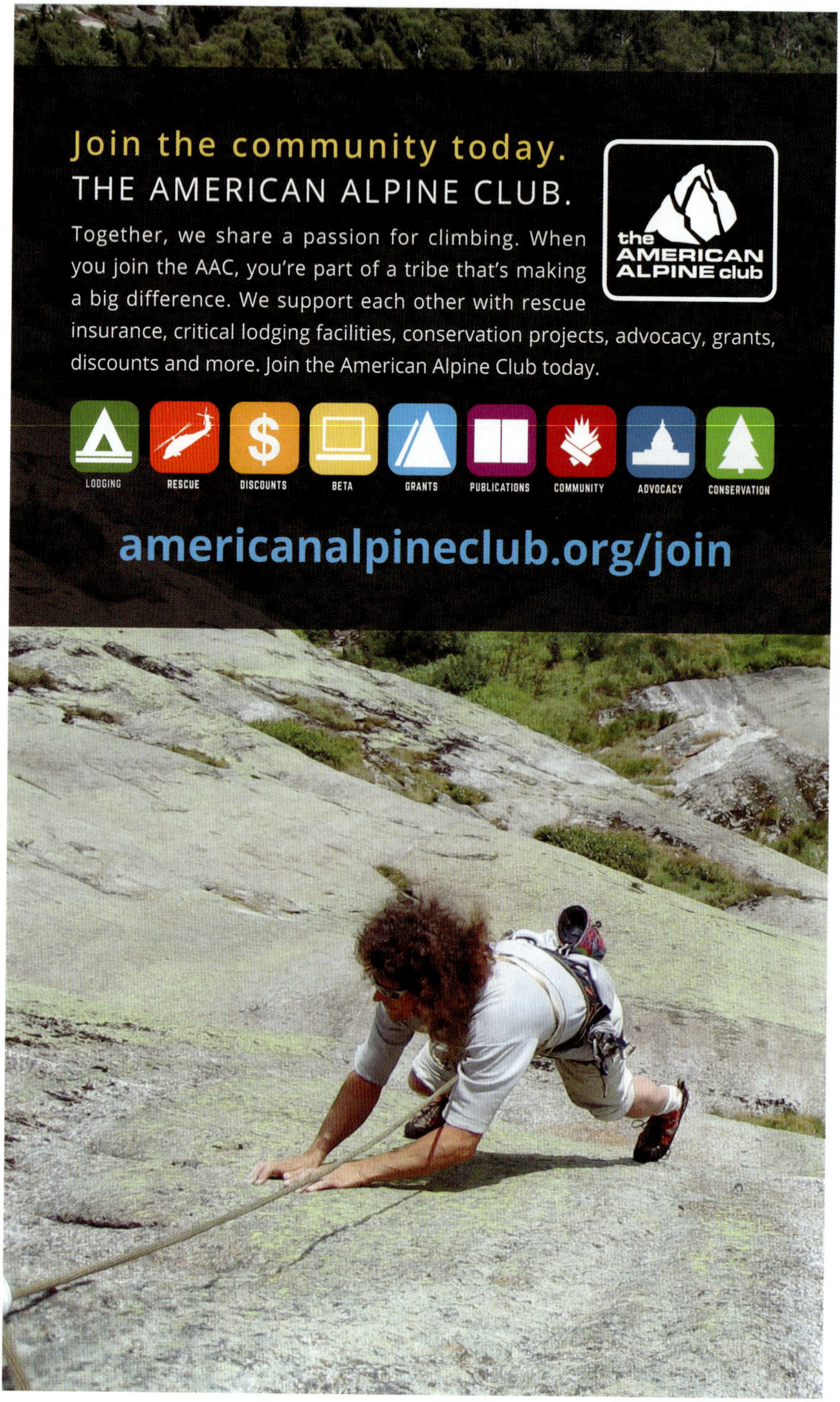

Old Forge

PG	CLIFF	QUALITY	ASPECT	APPROACH		GRADES	#
351	Ice Cave Mountain Fissure Face	★★★	SE & SW	50 min	easy	.6 .7 .8 .9 .10 .11 .12 .13	6
353	Ice Cave Mountain Raven Wall	★	W	1 hr 30 min	difficult	.6 .7 .8 .9 .10 .11 .12 .13	3
353	Middle Settlement Lake	★★	S	1 hr 10 min	easy	.6 .7 .8 .9 .10 .11 .12 .13	6
355	Flatrock Mountain		NW	2 min	easy	.6 .7 .8 .9 .10 .11 .12 .13	3
356	Bald Mountain Main Face	★★	S	10 min	easy	.6 .7 .8 .9 .10 .11 .12 .13	19
360	Moss Lake Slab	★★	SE	40 min	easy	.6 .7 .8 .9 .10 .11 .12 .13	4
362	Mount Tom Cliff		S	10 min	easy	.6 .7 .8 .9 .10 .11 .12 .13	1
362	Mitchell Ponds Mountain		S	1 hr 20 min	difficult canoe required	.6 .7 .8 .9 .10 .11 .12 .13	1
364	Fox Mountain Crag		SE	20 min	easy	.6 .7 .8 .9 .10 .11 .12 .13	2
364	Eagle Falls	★★★★	SW	15 min	easy river crossing	.6 .7 .8 .9 .10 .11 .12 .13	39

LEDGE MOUNTAIN (NOBLEBORO)

Location	Near Nobleboro, accessed from NY 8
Aspect	South
Height	55'
Quality	
Approach	15 min, easy
Summary	A small cliff with several topropes in the 5.8 range.

This cliff, on the small hill locally known as Ledge Mountain, is perhaps the closest Adirondack rock to Utica (less than 30 min). It's small, with the potential for several routes. There is a state hiking trail that ascends to a pretty viewpoint at the top of the mountain; the routes are directly below the viewpoint.

A steep slab with several routes is located right under the viewpoint. The leftmost route is **Moksha** (5.4 G; 65'; Oct 25, 2007; Neal Knitel), which begins at the lowest point and climbs a right-facing corner to a left-leaning ramp, then traverses left 8' and up a right-leaning crack. The route **Lady Bug** (5.9; TR; 55'; Oct 18, 2007; Neal Knitel, Justin Ernst) climbs **Moksha** to the left-leaning ramp, then up a seam to a hanging block, passing it on the right. The last route (5.8) begins on a large boulder on the right side of the slab, directly below a right-facing, right-leaning corner. Step out left onto a good ledge and flake, then follow a shallow right-leaning ramp to a fixed anchor at the top. Right of the large boulder is a steeper wall with a short but steep fingercrack.

HISTORY

Tad Welch explored the area in the 1980s and came away unimpressed. Neal Knitel and Daniel Mosny, reinvigorated by Barbara McMartin's Discover the Adirondacks series, explored the area in 2007 and cleaned several lines.

DIRECTIONS

From the intersection of NY 8 and NY 365, drive north on NY 8 for 2.2 miles to a gravel pit on the left 506640,4802713. Just past the gravel pit, turn left onto a narrow dirt lane, and drive for 0.3 mile (stay left at the fork) to the first grassy area on the left 506596,4803192; there is a large sign that reads "Vista Trail Trailhead." The road is passable with a high-clearance 2WD vehicle, but it's just as easy to park on NY 8 and walk a few minutes to the parking area.

Follow the state hiking trail (yellow disks) for 15 min to the top of the mountain at the small viewpoint. The trail is well marked, but seldom used. Backtrack about 100' and scramble down to the base of the cliff 506227,4803767.

DESCENT OPTIONS

Walk right and scramble down to the base of the cliff.

ICE CAVE MOUNTAIN

Location	South of Old Forge, accessed from North Lake Road near Forestport
Summary	Two remote, small cliffs, one of which is freakishly clean.

1	3	2	1	1		1		9
-5.6	5.7	5.8	5.9	5.10	5.11	5.12	5.13+	total

Ice Cave Mountain, accessed from NY 28 at Forestport, is a popular hiking destination with deep chimneys in the forest floor on the summit that hold snow and ice well into the summer. The deep chimneys would make an interesting refrigerated climbing venue were it not for the complete lack of climbable features on the smooth walls.

The main attractions for the climber are the cliffs scattered along the long ridge that constitute Ice Cave Mountain. There are several short, high-quality, stout routes, with the potential for many more. The cliffs are virtually invisible from afar, as only a few manage to break the forest canopy. There is a good trail to the top of the first summit and Fissure Face, but accessing the

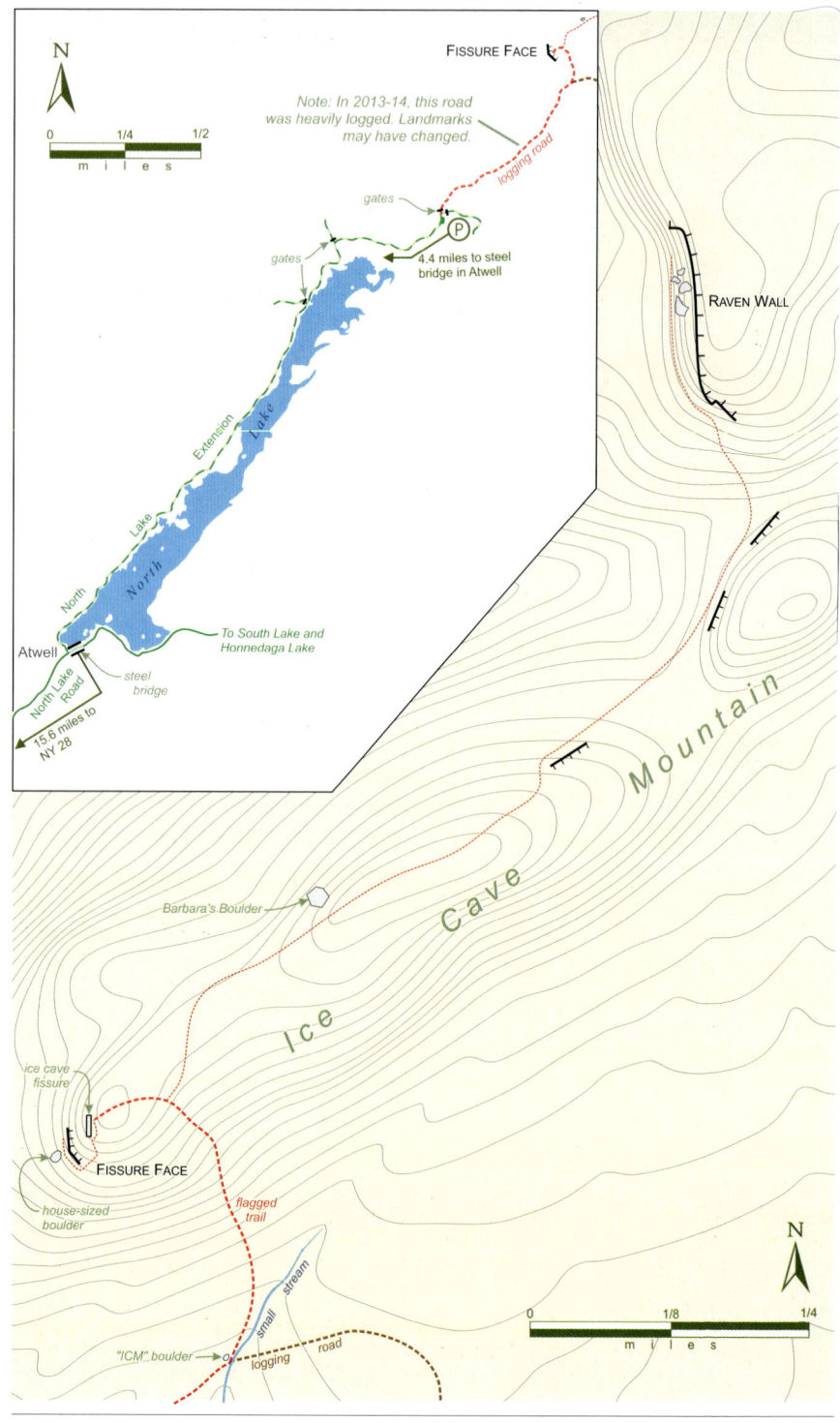

Old Forge

Old Forge

other cliffs, including Raven Wall, requires moderate bushwhacking along the ridge.

ACCESS
The cliff is located on the J. P. Lewis Tract, an area formerly posted by the Adirondack League Club. The state has purchased recreation rights, allowing the public access with the same rules as for other state-owned parcels. The owner has the right to manage the property for timber harvest and may close certain sections when doing so.

CAMPING
Very nice car-accessible lakeside camping is available along the shore of North Lake. The area is justifiably popular with the party types, but the shoreline is several miles long, so there's plenty of space for everyone.

HISTORY
Neal Knitel was the first to explore these cliffs for climbing, having seen them mentioned in one of Barbara McMartin's books. He found the Fissure Face and, with Jim Lawyer and Daniel Mosny, did the first climbing here in 2007. They found the rock on the Fissure Face to be unusually clean, and a flurry of routes was added that same day. Knitel went on to explore the other cliffs on the ridge and uncovered the Raven Wall.

DIRECTIONS   (MAP PAGE 350)
From NY 28 in Forestport (0.0), go east on Woodhull Road. At 1.2 miles, you reach the end of Woodhull Road at Forestport Station, and a split in the road; the Buffalo Head Restaurant, famous for its beef and large portions, is located at this intersection. Go straight (the left fork) onto North Lake Road (CR 73) and follow it across the railroad tracks to reach a steel bridge at 15.6 miles and the small settlement of Atwell; the last half of this road is unpaved. Just before the steel bridge, turn left onto a dirt road (the North Lake Extension, although it's unmarked). The dirt road winds along the west shore of North Lake, past numerous attractive campsites and trailheads, and is passable with a low-clearance 2WD vehicle. At 19.1 miles, there is a fork; take the right branch, staying on the main road. A large football field–sized parking area is reached at 20.0 miles; park here 508232,4823313. This is the end of the road.

The path from here follows old logging roads and is not maintained. It is possible to mountain-bike the next section, although there are a couple of fallen trees.

The dirt road continues past the parking area for 50', then forks. The left branch goes straight to a gate with a large triangular boulder on its left side, and the right branch turns 90° right to another gate. Take the left branch past the gate and hike for 30 min to a small stream that crosses the road. There is a large boulder on the left with faint graffiti that reads "ICM" (for Ice Cave Mountain). Turn left here onto a herd path with considerable flagging and follow this uphill with several steep sections for 15 min. The trail reaches the first summit of Ice Cave Mountain and is marked by a 90'-deep fissure in the earth 509403,4825066 in a north-south orientation. You can scramble into the fissure (4th-class) to reach the bottom, which has ice throughout the summer.

Directions to the cliffs are provided from this first summit.

Ice Cave Mountain
FISSURE FACE

Aspect	Southeast and southwest
Height	50'
Quality	★★★
Approach	50 min, easy
Summary	A small, remote cliff with amazingly clean rock and a good selection of short, stout routes.

1	2	1	1	1		6
-5.6	5.7	5.8	5.9	5.10	5.11	5.12	5.13+	total

The cliff's most impressive feature is the total lack of moss, dirt, lichen, or any other detritus that hinders climbing, as if the rock exudes some type of antigrowth agent. The rock is porous, almost volcanic in nature, but denser than other rock in the park. The faces often hold little treasures, like edges and rounded incut buckets perfectly sculpted for your hands. Expect short routes on clean, steep rock with strenuous climbing.

The cliff is formed by two walls: the left wall faces southwest and has the route Team America, and the right wall faces southeast and has the remaining routes. The lowest point of the cliff is where these two walls meet; there is a large house-sized boulder downhill 40' from the base here.

The top of the cliff is accessible for setting toprope anchors, although the bushwhacking is tight.

DIRECTIONS   (MAP PAGE 350)
The approach trail ends at the fissure on top of the first summit of Ice Cave Mountain. From the south end of the fissure, follow a trail downhill to the southeast for 75', then turn to the southwest for another 120' to a prominent 20'-high triangular boulder perched on the edge of a small cliff; this triangular boulder marks the right end of the cliff. Drop down in front of the boulder, then down two squeeze steps to reach the base of the cliff 509375,4825021.

1 Day of a Thousand Disasters
5.6+ G 35' ★★★

Start: 50' uphill and left of Team America, below a clean, left-leaning fingercrack that starts above a blocky ledge 5' up.
P1 5.6+ G: Climb the blocks and crack to the top. 35'
History: The first ascentionists started the day with a broken bike chain, got lost several times, and arrived at the crag at 3 PM. After completing this climb, Ackerman sliced her leg open on a sharp rock.
FA Jul 19, 2008, Leslie Ackerman, Shawn Higbee

2 Team America 5.7+ G 50' ★★★
Start: 30' uphill from and left of the toe of the buttress (on the southwest face) is an arête. This route begins 2' left of the arête at a chimney with a large jammed flake at the bottom.

Old Forge

P1 5.7+ G: Awkward moves over the flake gain the chimney, then follow it to a horizontal. Move right around the arête to a small ledge, then up the arête using a small crack and left-facing flake (crux). Hand-traverse up and right across the face (bolt) to its right side, then up a short crack in a corner to the top. 50'
Descent: Walk left to a large tree in a small cut viewpoint and rappel.
FA Aug 9, 2007, Jim Lawyer, Neal Knitel

3 Deciphering the Wonderfulness 5.9+ G 40' ★★★

Great moves on the overhanging handcrack through the roof.
Start: At the toe of the buttress where the southeast and southwest faces meet, below a short V-slot 6' up, which is below a roof 20' up.
P1 5.9+ G: Up the V-slot to the roof. Break through the roof at the handcrack (crux) to a sloping ledge. Up a fingercrack in a left-facing corner to another ledge, then up a 6'-high overhanging corner to a tree at the top. 40'
Gear: Cams up to 1", double 1" cams.
FA Aug 9, 2007, Jim Lawyer

4 Atwell's Revenge 5.8 G 35' ★★★★

Secure hand jams, clean rock, and amazing buckets on the face make this one surprisingly accessible. Stellar . . . too bad it's not 200'. Named for Atwell Martin, the hermit of North Lake.
Start: 15' left of Vanilla Ice at a triangular niche 4' up, below an overhanging snaking handcrack. This is also 15' right of the toe of the cliff where, to the left, it bends toward the southwest.
P1 5.8 G: Up the handcrack past two wedged flakes, then past two flared sections to a fixed anchor on a tree. 35'
Gear: 3 ea 2" cams, 1 ea 3".
FA Aug 9, 2007, Jim Lawyer, Daniel Mosny, Neal Knitel

5 Find Us Another Cliff, Barbara 5.10b G 35' ★★★

Great climbing up hidden incut horizontals on a steep wall, finished by a thin crimpy move over a bulge. Named for Barbara McMartin's Discover series, the books that opened up climbing in the remote areas of the Adirondack Park.
Start: Same as Vanilla Ice.
P1 5.10b G: Climb up to the crack for 5' (high gear), then reach far left across an overhanging wall to a bucket and fingercrack. Move 5' left onto a ledge, then straight up the face using hidden incut buckets to good ledge (1" and 3" cams). Hard moves up and right past a bolt (crux) lead to the top. 35'
Gear: To 2".
FA Aug 9, 2007, Jim Lawyer

6 Vanilla Ice 5.7 G 35' ★★★

One of the more obvious routes, and made easy by the numerous hidden footholds.
Start: 100' downhill from and left of the triangular boulder that marks the right end of the cliff and 15' left of a downhill squeeze step, below a V-groove with a finger-crack capped by a triangular roof with a V-slot.
P1 5.7 G: Climb to a ledge 8' up, then up the finger- and handcrack in the corner to the roof. Move up through the V-slot in the roof to the trees at the top. 35'
FA Aug 9, 2007, Jim Lawyer, Daniel Mosny, Neal Knitel

Jim Lawyer on the first ascent of **Deciphering the Wonderfulness** *(5.9+). Photo by Neal Knitel.*

Ice Cave Mountain
RAVEN WALL

Aspect	West
Height	90'
Quality	★
Approach	1 hr 30 min, difficult
Summary	A very remote cliff with great views and one very good route.

	1	1				1		3
-5.6	5.7	5.8	5.9	5.10	5.11	5.12	5.13+	total

This is the highest section of rock along the long ridge of Ice Cave Mountain. The base is a chaotic mess of large talus boulders. Once you're on the ridge, however, the views into this remote section of the park are spectacular.

There are several impressively steep walls here. At the left end of the cliff is a 50'-tall sheer wall split by a horizontal break; this is the marker for **Scarecrow** and **Corvus Crack**. About 140' right is a buttress, the left wall of which is sheer and orange; this marks the start of **The Shaman**. Just right of the orange wall is Lunch Rock, a large, comfortable flat boulder.

There is a 4th-class chimney between **The Shaman** and **Scarecrow** that provides access to the top.

DIRECTIONS   (MAP PAGE 350)

Just before the trail reaches the height of land at the top of the first summit of Ice Cave Mountain, break right and bushwhack along the crest of the ridge on a bearing of 65° for 30 min. Some old flagging marks the way and weaves back and forth on the ridge avoiding the thickest sections. Along the way, you'll pass many perched boulders, including Barbara's Boulder, a 50'-tall balanced boulder just down from the ridge on the left mentioned in one of McMartin's books.[1] You'll pass many more odd boulders on the ridge. After 30 min, you come to a viewpoint where you can just see the cliff to the north. Continue due north on a bearing of 14° for another 10 min, past many small cliffs, to arrive at Raven Wall, 40 min after leaving the first summit. At the right end of the cliff is a large low-angle right-facing corner: its left wall forms a low-angle arête, and its right wall is smooth and sheer. Continue along the base of the cliff (easier to stay in the woods below the talus) to reach the field of large talus boulders beneath the highest section of rock. Weave through the talus to find a buttress, the left wall of which is sheer, orange, and overhanging—the location of **The Shaman**. 510263,4826263.

7 Corvus Crack 5.8 G 60' ★
Start: At the left end of the cliff is a sheer 50'-tall vertical face split by a horizontal break halfway up. This route begins at the left-facing corner that defines the left edge of this face, and 5' downhill from and right of a deep chimney full of chockstones.

---
[1] Barbara McMartin and Bill Ingersoll, *Discover the Southwestern Adirondacks* (2002), p. 96.

P1 5.8 G: Up the stepped ledges in the steep corner to its top. Step right onto the ledge, then walk right 15' to a large tree with a fixed anchor. 60'
Gear: Up to 1".
FA Sep 21, 2007, Jim Lawyer, Daniel Mosny, Neal Knitel

8 Scarecrow 5.12a TR 60' ★★★★
Great moves on an overhanging steep wall with clean rock. This would be an incredible route with a couple of bolts to supplement the trad gear. At the left end of the cliff is a sheer 50'-tall vertical face split by a horizontal break halfway up. This route begins 10' from the left end of the face at some left-rising seams. Climb the seams to the horizontal break, then up a few feet. Reach far right to a shallow crack to gain some face holds that lead to a set of discontinuous shallow cracks. Awkward and strenuous flared jams and laybacking lead to the ledge at the top. There is a fixed anchor on a tree shared with **Corvus Crack**.

9 The Shaman 5.7 G 80' ★★★
This high-quality route climbs a steep corner, then an airy face to the very top of the cliff. Great views from the top.

Start: 140' right of the **Scarecrow** sheer face is a buttress, the left wall of which is overhanging, sheer, and orange; this route climbs an inside corner that defines the left edge of this face. Start at the height of the terrain on the left side of this orange face.
P1 5.7 G: Up a groove with jammed blocks, then step right onto a face with a jug (bolt). Mantel onto a ledge at the base of the inside corner, then up the leaning orange corner to its top. Step right out of the corner to a ledge, then up a right-leaning crack to finish on a steep face with horizontals and knobs. There is a good ledge at the top with a fixed anchor. 80'
Gear: Up to 3", with TCUs to 0.5" for the corner.
FA Sep 21, 2007, Neal Knitel, Jim Lawyer

MIDDLE SETTLEMENT LAKE

Location	West of Old Forge, accessed from NY 28
Aspect	South
Height	50'
Quality	★★
Approach	1 hr 10 min, easy
Summary	A small cliff with some toproping and a few quality crack, corner, and face routes.

2		2		1	1			6
-5.6	5.7	5.8	5.9	5.10	5.11	5.12	5.13+	total

Middle Settlement Lake, located in the Ha-De-Ron-Dah Wilderness, is an extremely popular overnight destination for hikers, with one of the best lean-tos and campsites in the area. The lake is picturesque with great swimming. Unfortunately, the cliff isn't on the lake but just northeast of it, above a field of house-sized boulders. Even so, the lake is within a 10-min walk, so it's easy to combine climbing, swimming, and perhaps some camping.

Old Forge

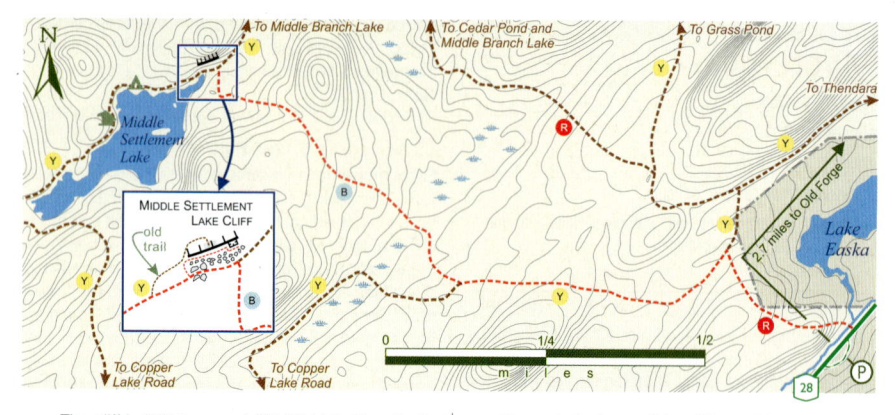

The cliff is 300' long and 30'–50' high. Despite its modest size, it packs a punch, with roofs, corners, and a few steep cracks. The cliff's central features are two buttresses with low roofs under which you can walk; between the buttresses is a high roof with an awesome roof crack, just waiting to be freed. On the right end of the cliff is a detached tower that forms a large left-facing corner; **Amanita Muscaria** climbs the corner, and **I Wish** climbs the outside face of the tower. In the talus in front of the tower is a huge house-sized boulder split in half.

From the end of the lake, if you continue toward the lean-to on Middle Settlement Lake, there is an old red-marked trail, the Vista Trail, now slightly overgrown, which goes to the top of the cliff to a nice flat, rocky viewpoint on top of the most overhanging section. There is a filtered view of the lake from here.

HISTORY

The cliff has been used by local summer camps for rappelling and some toproping. Daniel Mosny did some exploration of the cliff in 2006, toproping several lines. The routes listed here were climbed on a reconnaissance trip by Jim Lawyer and Neal Knitel in 2007.

DIRECTIONS   (MAP PAGE 354)

Parking for Middle Settlement Lake is at a parking loop on the south side of NY 28 495753,4835836, 2.7 miles southwest of Old Forge (measured from the Thendara Railroad Station) and 5.8 miles northeast of the bridge over the Moose River. The parking loop looks more like a rest area than a trailhead parking lot.

From the parking area, cross the road and walk toward Old Forge about 200' to a sign that reads "To State Land" but is otherwise unmarked. Follow the red-marked trail (Scusa Access Trail); at 20 min, you'll reach a T-intersection. Go left on the yellow-marked trail (Browns Tract Trail); you'll reach another intersection at 40 min. Take the right fork, now on blue markers (the Middle Settlement Lake Access Trail). At 60 min, you'll reach another intersection; straight ahead is a field of large boulders, above which is the cliff 492542,4837265.

To reach the base of the cliff, turn left at the last intersection and walk toward Middle Settlement Lake. At the far side of the house-sized boulders and just before the lake, head uphill on the left margin of the boulders to the cliff, reaching it on its left end.

DESCENT OPTIONS

An easy walk around the left end of the cliff returns you to the base.

1 Mycelia 5.5 G 30' ★★

A worthwhile corner with cool exit moves.

Start: At the left end of the cliff is a sheer orange 20'-tall wall with a triangular block on its right end. This route begins 20' right of the triangular block at a shallow left-facing, right-leaning corner.

P1 5.5 G: Climb up the corner to the right end of a ceiling. Break through the ceiling on the right to the trees at the top. 30'
ACB Jul 31, 2007, Neal Knitel, Jim Lawyer

2 Hissing Fauna 5.8 G 35' ★★★

Interesting palming and stemming moves. Harder than it looks.

Start: 20' right of **Mycelia** at the base of a large left-facing corner capped by a large triangular roof. This is 20' left of a section of giant roofs.

P1 5.8 G: Climb the corner past a bolt to its top. Step right onto a ledge, then up through a notch on the right side of the triangular roof to the trees. 35'
FA Jul 31, 2007, Jim Lawyer, Neal Knitel

3 Deciphering the Dirtyness 5.8+ G 60' ★

Cool moves; would be 3 stars if cleaned.

Start: In a recessed alcove with a very prominent right-facing corner, about 20 feet right of the prominent roof crack.

P1 5.8+ G: Climb the crack line in the right-facing corner: first over a bulge (sometimes wet) to a ledge, then up to the roof and out left (crux), then up a steep, tricky face to lower angle rock. Belay in shrubbery. 60'
FA Apr 26, 2008, Rayko Halitschke, Leslie Ackerman

Old Forge

4 Eyes on the Prize 5.11a G 40' ★★★
Start: 60' right of the two low roofs is a sheer wall, bounded on its right side by a detached tower that forms a large left-facing corner. This route begins 30' left of the left-facing corner, 10' right of a right-leaning crack that comes to the ground, below a second right-leaning crack that starts 15' up. Another locator is a maple tree 12' to the right growing up against the face.
P1 5.11a G: Boulder up 10' to a good jug (good TCU crack), then follow the right-leaning crack with several off-width pods and sustained flared jams to the top. 40'
Gear: To 0.75", plus 1 ea 4" and 3" cams.
FA Jul 31, 2007, Jim Lawyer, Neal Knitel

5 Amanita Muscaria 5.4 G 50' ★
Start: At the right end of the cliff is a detached tower that forms a large left-facing corner. Begin below this corner below stacked blocks.
P1 5.4 G: Climb up the blocks past a large birch and into the chimney. Follow a hidden vertical crack deep in the chimney to the top of the tower. Step across to the main face and scramble up to the trees. 50'
Gear: To 2".
FA Jul 31, 2007, Neal Knitel, Jim Lawyer

6 I Wish 5.10c G 50' ★★★
Steep climbing with some interesting moves. Remember to bring some cams for the fingercrack on top. The final moves to the top of the tower are lichen-covered but secure. Named for a Stevie Wonder song.
Start: At the right end of the cliff is a detached tower that forms a large left-facing corner. This route begins on the outside face of the tower, 4' right of the corner and at the right end of a 4'-high ceiling.
● P1 5.10c G: Climb up the overhanging wall with an orange streak to a final mantel move (crux) onto a flat ledge. Up a fingercrack to the top of the tower. Step across to the main face and scramble up to the trees. 50'
Gear: Cams to 0.75" for the topout.
FA Jul 31, 2007, Jim Lawyer

FLATROCK MOUNTAIN

Location	West of Old Forge, accessed from NY 28
Aspect	Northwest
Height	35'
Quality	
Approach	2 min, easy
Summary	Short dirty cliff with great rock, easy access and good potential.

	1	2		3
-5.6	5.7	5.8	5.9	5.10	5.11	5.12	5.13+	total

Flatrock Mountain is primarily a bouldering area south of Old Forge on NY 28. Rope climbing so far has been concentrated on a short—but very wide—cliffband near the parking and parallel to the road. The rock is excellent with good friction, but also quite dirty in places.

DIRECTIONS
Parking for Flatrock Mountain is at an unmarked loop road that parallels the south side of NY 28, 3.8 miles from southwest of Old Forge (measured from the Thendara Railroad Station) and 4.8 miles northeast of the bridge over the Moose River. The loop road is 0.2 mile northeast of Scusa Road. Park at the southeast end of the loop road (the end furthest from Old Forge) 494756,4835123.

The cliff is about 300' into the woods and parallels the road (although you can't see it through the dense foliage). From the parking area, walk away from the road (southeast): step over the ditch and go up the bank and under a phone line. Continue into the woods in the same direction, veering to the right as necessary to avoid bogs. Once you reach the cliff, go to its right end at a clean arête that forms a large right-facing corner—**Flatrock Arête**—that is the landmark for locating the other routes 494681,4834959.

ACCESS
Flatrock Boulders is located in the Flatrock Mountain Demonstration Forest, a working forest owned by the Northeast Loggers Association (NELA). New York State has an easement for public recreation (called the Flatrock Mountain Easement) that allows public access with the same regulations as for state land. For example, you can camp here as long as you're more than 150' from a road or stream.

Regarding exploration and development along this section of NY 28, a majority of the roadside land is private property. It is best to look for posted signs, and check the county tax maps, before investing time in development.

HISTORY
The area was developed by Neal Knitel, a hydro dam operator in nearby Forestport. Being so close, this became Knitel's after-work exercise area.

1 The Cobbler 5.8 G 30' ★★
Start: 5' left of **Flatrock** at a 5'-high mossy alcove with a fistcrack coming out of the top.
P1 5.8 G: Climb the crack (hands to fist to cups) to trees. 30'
Gear: To 4".
FA Jun 1, 2009, Neal Knitel, Joe Pfeiffer

2 Flatrock Arête 5.10c TR 35' ★★★
Begin at the right end of the cliff, at a clean arête that forms a 20'-deep right-facing corner. Just left of the arête are three boulders, and another, larger, slanted, moss-covered boulder facing the cliff. Go up the arête with sidepulls to where the angle diminishes. Finish on the right side of the arête up slab and steps to the trees.
FA (TR) Jun 1, 2009, Neal Knitel, Joe Pfeiffer

3 Indirecto 5.10a TR 35' ★
Begin 7' right of **Flatrock Arête** and climb the face with sloping holds angling left to join that route at the top.
FA (TR) Jun 1, 2009, Neal Knitel, Joe Pfeiffer

355

Old Forge

BALD MOUNTAIN

Location	Near Old Forge on the north side of NY 28
Summary	A large cliff low on the mountain, and a pretty summit cliff with excellent views of the Fulton Chain Lakes.

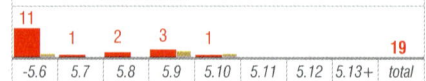

11	1	2	3	1		19
-5.6	5.7	5.8	5.9	5.10	5.11	5.12	5.13+	total

The Main Face of Bald Mountain (aka Rondaxe Mountain) has a long history of climbing dating back to the early 1970s. It sits on the south side of Bald Mountain with commanding views of the Fulton Chain Lakes and the surrounding forested hills.

The base of the cliff is a bit overgrown, and the terrain, although sloping away from the cliff, is relatively level. There are several landmarks used to locate climbs. First is the point where the property boundary meets the cliff, which marks the leftmost route, **Spring Fever**. Moving right, you walk down and around a giant boulder leaning up against the cliff, behind which is a chimney-cave; this is referred to in the route descriptions as the "boulder-cave." Right of this is a clean slab (**Branches**), then a 100'-long section of roofs 25' up. Next is a huge open book, the left wall of which is orange, referred to in the route descriptions as the "orange face." Right of the orange face is a steep section of corners and the routes **Projection** and **Pine Climb**. Finally, at the right end of the cliff are two left-facing corners separated by a section of roofs 20' up; each corner has an obvious crack (**King Crack** and **Cardiac Corner**).

Many of the climbs on Bald Mountain have sat idle for nearly 30 years and are predictably dirty but still climbable; with some traffic, they should clean up nicely. There is also considerable potential for more routes.

ACCESS
The approach follows a boundary with property owned by the town of Webb, which is leased during hunting season (from September 14 through the second Monday of December). The far left end of the cliff is on this parcel, and is closed during that period. Most of the climbing—in fact, every route except **Spring Fever**—is on state land.

HISTORY
The first documented climbing on the Main Face of Bald Mountain was done in 1976 by Bruce Bandorick and his high school chum Scott Wade. The rock, so close to Syracuse, intrigued 46ers Bruce and his father (Art) into investigating it after encountering Bald Mountain during their hiking days. Later, Bruce and Scott thoroughly explored the area, climbing and documenting many lines. However, they were not alone (R.L. Stolz and Woody Carroll visited around the same time, as did Jamie Savage, Kevin Walker, and Tad Welch), nor were they the earliest (they found old pitons on at least one route). The cliff has seen attention since that time, as evidenced by the bolts of unknown origin on the high-quality route **Ceremony of Innocence**.

The cliff has received more recent attention by Neal Knitel and Daniel Mosny, two local climbers. They focused on the area at the right end and around the **Branches** boulder-cave, and claim it's possible these lines were climbed earlier.

Bald Mountain
MAIN FACE

Aspect	South
Height	200'
Quality	★★
Approach	10 min, easy
Summary	Long single-pitch cracks, corners, and face routes in a pretty setting above the Fulton Chain Lakes.

11	1	2	3	1		19
-5.6	5.7	5.8	5.9	5.10	5.11	5.12	5.13+	total

DIRECTIONS (MAP PAGE 356)
Park at the dirt pullout on NY 28 at the intersection with Hollywood Street (CR 216), 3.2 miles from Old Forge (when driving toward Blue Mountain Lake, measured from the Tourist Information Center) and 5.8 miles from Eagle Bay (when driving toward Old Forge, measured from Big Moose Road). Across the road from the parking area is the entrance to a snowmobile trail that immediately branches left and right. Take the left branch, going uphill parallel to the road toward Old Forge for 100 yards to a sign that reads "Danger Sharp Curves, Blind Curves, Steep Hills, Caution." Turn right 20 yards after the sign and follow the Moose River Gun Club's well-posted property boundary, which leads directly to the cliff at the route **Spring Fever** 506564,4842462.

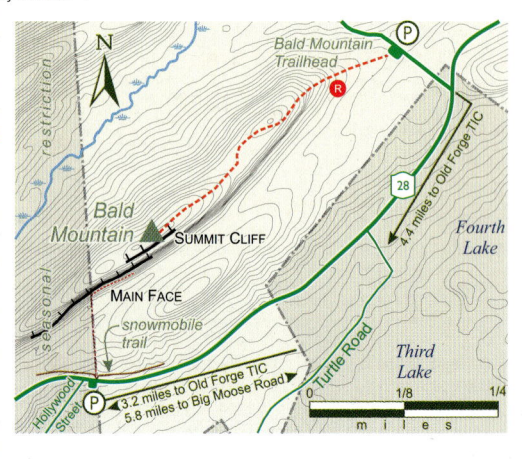

Opposite: Lynn Yenkey follows the upper section of Branches (5.6).

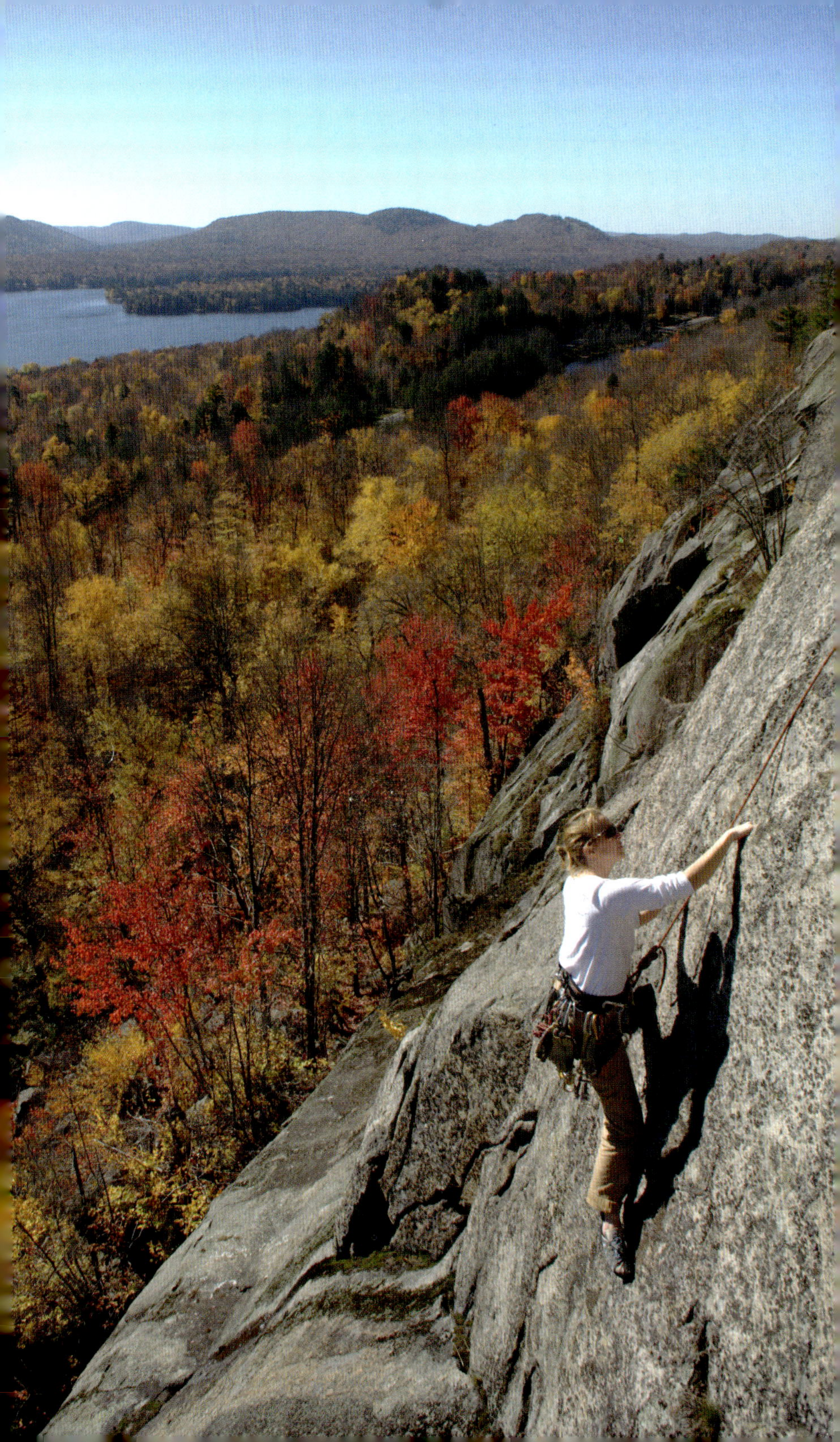

Old Forge

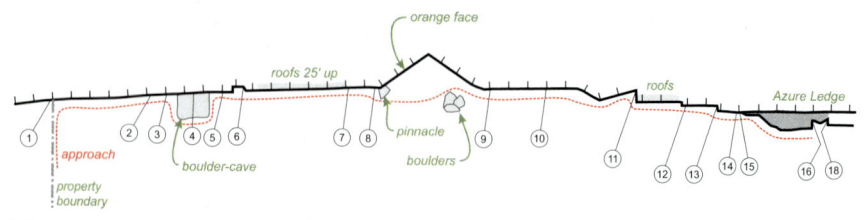

1 Spring Fever 5.5 G 180'

One of the shorter climbs, this makes the best route of descent using two rappels down the route. It was first climbed in the snow.

Start: The property boundary meets the cliff at a sharp-edged right-facing, right-leaning corner that begins 10' up and is capped by a triangular roof. This route begins 5' left on a clean face.

P1 5.5 G: Climb up the face to a shallow overlap 12' up. Step right and climb a crack in an open book to a right-facing corner, over a small ceiling, then step right (crux) to a line of cracks, which are followed to a tree belay. 105'

P2 5.4 G: From the tree, climb diagonally left 60' over blocky slabs to belay on top. 75'

FA 1976, Bruce Bandorick, Scott Wade

2 Crystal Wall 5.9 R 190'

Start: 100' right of where the property boundary meets the cliff and 35' left of the left side of the **Branches** boulder-cave, at a vertical crack in a black slab.

P1: Climb up the crack and slab to a small bulge. Over the bulge and up a clean tan-colored stripe of rock. Angle up and right to some trees and belay. 60'

P2: Climb a short left-facing corner above a tree to perched blocks. Traverse left 20' to easier slabs leading to beneath a very large overhanging flake. 50'

P3: Up over the flake at its right side, then to the top on an exposed slab. 80'

FA 1976, Bruce Bandorick, Scott Wade

3 Woodsman's Field Days 5.5 G 175'

Considerable vegetation but has some sections with nice climbing. Named for the field day of cleaning required to unearth this route.

Start: 12' left of the left side of the **Branches** boulder-cave at a 15'-high broken chimney-corner and arching roof just off the ground.

P1 5.5 G: Climb the chimney-corner to its top, then through a vegetated section. Follow a right-leaning ramp to just below an arête, then make a funky move left and up off the ramp to a large ledge with small trees. Step left about 8' to a blocky right-facing corner with cracks ranging from finger to off width. Climb this to a fingercrack at the top, then up a couple of more blocks to the top, staying just left of the arête. 175'

Gear: Up to 3".

Descent: Rappel from trees.

FA Aug 25, 2007, Neal Knitel (roped solo)

4 Phinding Phalaris 5.3 G 180'

Start: On top of the **Branches** boulder-cave. (Some 4th-class scrambling is required to get to the top.)

BALD MOUNTAIN: MAIN FACE

1. Spring Fever (5.5)
2. Crystal Wall (5.9)
3. Woodsman's Field Days (5.5)
4. Phinding Phalaris (5.3)
5. Branches (5.6)
6. Lichen or Not (5.5)
7. Sprucification (5.7)
8. Easy Squeeze (5.3)
9. Projection (5.8)
10. Pine Climb (5.8)
11. King Crack (5.9)
12. Ceremony of Innocence (5.10c)
13. Cardiac Corner (5.9+)
14. Zigzag (5.6)
15. Where's the Booty? (5.5)
16. Missin' Moe (5.6)
18. Azure (5.4)

P1 5.3 G: Climb a left-leaning fingercrack with nice textured footholds for 8' to a dirty slab, then head up and slightly left to a right-facing corner (this right-facing corner is the right side of the ramp of **Woodsman's Field Days**). Follow the corner system through a couple of overlaps (going 10' past an arête on the left) to a 4" ledge leading back down to the slab, then up increasingly easier ground, angling up and right to the fixed anchor of **Branches**. 180'

FA Aug 28, 2007, Neal Knitel, Justin Ernst

5 Branches 5.6 PG 190' ★★★★

This slab climb is *the* best climb at Bald Mountain, featuring good protection, clean featured rock, and some of the best views.

Start: Below a slab with flakes and a shallow right-facing corner that begins 6' up and leads to a bulging ceiling 15' up. This slab is 20' right of the boulder-cave, a large house-sized boulder leaning up against the face that forms a deep chimney-cave at its point of contact. 50' right is a 100'-long section of roofs 25' up.

P1 5.6 PG: Climb up the flakes and the short right-facing corner to a bulging ceiling. Over this via a crack, then up flakes and knobs to an old piton (can be backed up with a slung flake), then up an unprotected section to a ledge. Step right to a small left-facing flake (gear), then up into a right-facing corner (optional belay). At the top of the corner, climb a steep fingercrack (and face to its right, crux), then straight up easier corners and slab to a good ledge with a fixed anchor. 190'

Gear: To 0.75"; include small TCUs and nuts.

Descent: Rappel with two 60-m ropes to the ground.

FA 1976, Bruce Bandorick, Scott Wade

6 Lichen or Not 5.5 PG 160'

Interesting and varied climbing, although somewhat difficult to protect.

Start: 60' right of the **Branches** boulder-cave at a left-facing open book. The open book is 15' right of a right-facing corner with trees 25' up.

Old Forge

P1 5.5 PG: Up the left-facing open book to a bulge 25' up. Step right to a ledge and mantel to a second ledge and climb the corner past the overhang to a ledge. Traverse right over exposed slab for 20' to a belay ledge beneath a tree. 80'

P2 5.5 PG: Step right and then up a wide crack (V1) to the top. 80'

V1 5.7 G: Traverse right under the summit overhang for 10', then up to the top.
FA 1976, Bruce Bandorick, Scott Wade

7 Sprucification 5.7 G 120'

Start: Just right of a 100'-long section of roofs 25' up, 15' left of **Easy Squeeze**, below an open book with moss, trees, and grass. On the left side of the open book is a short right-facing flake with a downward point at its base, 4' up.

P1 5.7 G: Step onto a block at the base of the open book, move up onto the left face, then traverse 10' left to the left end of a ledge below a short right-facing corner. Up the right-facing corner, then up right-facing flakes to a vegetated groove. Up the groove and easier rock to the top. 120'
FA 1976, Bruce Bandorick, Scott Wade

8 Easy Squeeze 5.3 G 120' ★

Although easy and a bit manky-looking, this climb is spectacular and worth doing.

Start: 20' left of the orange face (just left of the arête formed by the left side of the orange face) at a slab, below a left-leaning sharp-edged chimney-slot 25' up.

P1 5.3 G: (V1) Climb squeeze slab to the chimney-slot and up into a blocky area. Continue up the large squeeze chimney to a square ledge. 120'

V1 5.3 G: Begin 15' to the right on the right side of the pinnacle. Climb up a chimney with a jammed flake. Move left behind the pinnacle to join the normal route.

History: Old pitons were found in 1976, making this the oldest known route on the face.
FA (V1) 1976, Bruce Bandorick, Scott Wade

9 Projection 5.8 G 110'

Start: 20' right of the orange face is a grouping of boulders sitting in front of a broad open-book corner. This route begins 10' right of the boulders directly below an overhanging blade of rock 30' up.

P1 5.8 G: Up the face to gain a chimney whose right side is formed by protruding flakes. Continue straight up the cracks and chimney around a blocky ceiling and up to a ledge. Continue up the chimney past a large chockstone to the top. 110'

History: In 1976, new pitons were found.

10 Pine Climb 5.8 G 110' ★★

An excellent and convoluted line that weaves its way up corners, chimneys, and slabs.

Start: 20' right of the orange face is a grouping of boulders sitting in front of a broad open-book corner. This route begins 50' right of the boulders on a ledge 6' up, below a broken left-facing corner that leads to a chimney-slot. Another locator is a large tan-colored open-book corner capped by a triangular roof that sits 8' left of the chimney-slot.

P1 5.8 G: Climb up into the chimney, step right at its top into a large right-facing corner. Up the corner to a roof, then undercling to its left end (3.5" cam) and up into a squeeze chimney. Instead of climbing the chimney, step left onto a slab with a jagged crack. Up and left on the slab to a 10'-high mossy open-book corner, which is followed to sloping ledges at the top. 110'

Gear: To 3.5".

Descent: Walk right and rappel from trees using a single 60-m rope.
FA 1976, Bob Look

11 King Crack 5.9 G 80' ★★★

A beautiful sustained crack in a corner that is often wet. If only it were cleaner.

Start: At the base of a deep left-facing corner; in the corner is a 2" crack rising above a 10'-high chimney at the bottom. The face left of the corner is wide, off-vertical, smooth, and capped by a ceiling at its top. The right wall of the corner tapers to 6' deep at half height.

P1 5.9 G: Up through the chimney and up the excellent corner to a tree. 80'

Gear: To 4".

12 Ceremony of Innocence 5.10c G 100' ★★★

This quality route combines hard face climbing with an excellent fingercrack. The route has four bolts. Named for a 1997 adventure game based on Nick Bantock's *Griffin & Sabine Trilogy*.

Start: Right of the **King Crack** corner is a series of roofs 20' up with a broken left-facing corner at its right end. This route begins 6' right of this broken left-facing corner and 30' right of **King Crack**, at a steep face with two bolts. Another landmark for the start is the large left-facing corner of **Cardiac Corner** 15' to the right.

● **P1 5.10c G:** Climb up to a bolt in a black streak, then up to a shallow left-facing open book. Make hard moves up and right to some good right-facing flakes. Traverse right 10' to the base of a left-facing corner, then up the corner with an amazing fingercrack up to a ledge. Follow a crack and ramp up and right to the top. 100'

Descent: Rappel from trees.

13 Cardiac Corner 5.9+ G 60' ★★★

Climbs the beautiful corner crack. The off-width section in the middle is a real brute.

Start: 15' uphill and right of **Ceremony of Innocence** and 45' right of **King Crack** at a left-facing, left-leaning corner with a wide crack, wider at the bottom. At the top of the cone-shaped slope below the corner is a giant birch tree.

P1 5.9+ G: Chimney up the initial wide section to where the crack narrows to finger size. Above, the crack bulges and widens to off width (crux). A final mantel move leads to a ledge with a large pine tree. 60'

Gear: To 4" plus 2 ea 3".
FA 1976, Bruce Bandorick, Scott Wade

Old Forge

14 Zigzag 5.6 PG 120' ★★

A great climb with clean rock and solid jamming. The zigzag crack of this route ends on the left end of Azure Ledge, a large forested ledge.

Start: 15' right of **Cardiac Corner** on a platform 10' up, beneath a wide crack that jogs right at half height. This crack is 5' left of a large left-facing open-book corner of **Where's the Booty?**.

P1 5.6 G: Up the wide crack to a jog right, then up to a wedged block at the top. Over the wedged block to a ledge with a large spruce tree (same tree as for **Cardiac Corner**). 60'

P2 5.5 PG: Rappel, or step right and climb a 3" crack in a left-facing corner for 15' to a ledge, then up nondescript dirty slabs to the top. 60'

Gear: To 4".

FA 1976, Bruce Bandorick, Scott Wade

15 Where's the Booty? 5.5 G 60'

Start: Same as for **Zigzag**.

P1 5.5 G: Traverse right 10' to the left-facing open book, then climb the handcrack just left of the open-book corner to the Azure Ledge. Step left to a fixed anchor on a large spruce tree (shared with **Zigzag**). 60'

Gear: To 4".

FA Sep 5, 2007, Neal Knitel, Justin Ernst

16 Missin' Moe 5.6 G 175' ★★

A direct line to the top of the cliff. The lower section of this route looks unappealing, but the cliff above Azure Ledge is of higher quality. The first ascentionists missed the moe.down music festival to climb this route.

Start: Right of **Zigzag** is a low nose with a yellow buttress above. The route begins at a large right-facing corner that forms the right side of this buttress, 150' right of **Zigzag**.

P1 5.6 G: Climb up the right-facing corner through a 6'-wide stem box to the Azure Ledge (5.3), a large forested ledge 85' up. Above the Azure Ledge, the cliff becomes more vertical; climb a crack that widens from hand width to off width 20' up (crux), then up cracks with large face holds straight to the top, staying 10' right of a large right-facing corner. 175'

Gear: To 3"; double 2" and 3" cams.

Descent: Rappel with one rope from trees to Azure Ledge, then to the ground.

FA Aug 31, 2007, Neal Knitel, Daniel Mosny

17 Yard Work 5.4 G 85' ★★

This is a variation to the top section of **Missin' Moe**.

Start: On top of Azure Ledge, 15' right of the **Missin' Moe** crack.

P1 5.4 G: Climb the crack and nice face holds straight to the top. 85'

FA Aug 31, 2007, Daniel Mosny, Neal Knitel

18 Azure 5.4 G 175' ★★

Start: 25' right of **Missin' Moe** at a left-facing open book that is just right of a roof 25' up shaped like the prow of a ship.

P1 5.4 G: Climb the open book to a short chimney and off-width section. Move left onto face holds (thereby avoiding the chimney and off width), then climb the corner straight to the top, passing the right side of Azure Ledge, a large forested ledge 85' up. Continue up the vertical wall following cracks and good face holds straight to the top. 175'

Gear: To 3"; double 2" and 3" cams.

FA Aug 31, 2007, Neal Knitel, Daniel Mosny

19 The Perch 5.6 A1 100'

Start: About 100' right of **Azure** where the cliff begins to angle back, at a shallow open book, below a hanging slot at the top of the cliff.

P1 5.6 A1: Up the shallow open book, then weave up slabs and overlaps to the slot. Through the slot (A1) to the trees. 100'

FA 1979, Jamie Savage, Kevin Walker

Bald Mountain

SUMMIT CLIFF

Aspect	South
Height	50'
Quality	★
Approach	20 min, easy
Summary	A small cliff immediately below an open rocky summit with several toprope and trad routes.

There are several routes on the summit cliffs of Bald Mountain, approach by the hiking trail off Rondaxe Road. They are located directly below the fire tower and reached via rappel. **Shindig** (5.5 G; 70'; 1979; Jamie Savage, Kevin Walker) climbs the crack and face directly below the tower. 40' left of **Shindig** is **Walker's Weave** (5.7 G; 1979; Kevin Walker, Jamie Savage) that climbs a crack up to a roof, around this on the left to a stance, then up easier rock to the summit.

DIRECTIONS   (MAP PAGE 356)

Drive 4.4 miles from Old Forge, turn left on Rondaxe Road, then drive 0.2 mile to the trailhead on the left. Follow the Bald Mountain trail (red markers) 1 mile to the summit, about 20 min.

MOSS LAKE SLAB

Location	Eagle Bay, accessed from Big Moose Rd
Aspect	Southeast
Height	200'
Quality	★★
Approach	40 min, easy
Summary	Disconnected tongues of open, clean slab that extend down into the trees in a picturesque valley.

	3		1					4
	-5.6	5.7	5.8	5.9	5.10	5.11	5.12	5.13+	total

Moss Lake Slab is tucked away in what feels like a remote valley, but is quite close to the road. The approach follows a mountain-bike trail around Moss Lake with some nice canoe-accessible campsites right off the trail on the way in.

Old Forge

*Neal Knitel on the first ascent of **The Iron Heel** (5.4). Photo by* Dereck Nabozney.

The cliffs are located on the steep southeast-facing slopes of a long ridge. The ridge is dotted with open rock that stretches down into the woods in long tongues of slab. Finding the correct slab on the mile-long ridge can be a challenge. The slab with **The Iron Heel** is the largest, cleanest, and most easily identified, as it is capped by a large overlap 510912,4847566. The quality of the routes is enhanced by beautiful sections of dimpled "moon" rock unique to the Adirondacks.

There are more—and larger—slabs located further west on the same ridgeline.

DIRECTIONS
At the intersection of NY 28 and Big Moose Road (CR 1) in Eagle Bay, follow the Big Moose Road north 2.0 miles to the Moss Lake Trailhead on the left (west) side of the road 512512,4848406.

From the kiosk (0 hr 0 min), follow the trail counter-clockwise around the lake for 1 mile. At 15 min, when the trail reaches the western tip of the lake 511479,4847892, head into the woods, and contour southwest along the bottom slope of the mountain through a flat, open hardwood forest. You can see various slabs through the woods up the slope to your right. A GPS will help identify the correct slab.

HISTORY
There had been talk of a cliff in this region, but Neal Knitel was the first to report climbing here in 2011. Being a technology devotee, Knitel used a combination of satellite imagery and USGS topographical data to locate cliffs in this region. Samual Wysocki, a partner of Knitel on the early routes, returned and added additional routes, more than are recorded here.

1 Lychons 5.4 PG 130'
Start: About 600' left of **The Iron Heel** is another, non-descript slab with this route 510715,4847460. The slab has its low point on the right side, and rises gradually up and left. Begin in the middle of the slab, half-way up the left-rising slope.

P1 5.4 PG: Go straight up the slab aiming for a depression left of the trees that border the right side of the slab. Go over a steep, orange-colored bulge, up a tiny left-facing corner, and into the trees at the top of the slab. Break through the trees and continue up another slab (hidden from below) to the top. 130'
FA May 2, 2012, Samuel Wysocki, Neal Knitel

2 Grumpy Rolls 5.4 R 210'
Start: From the base of the main slab with **The Iron Heel**, drop down and walk left under a low tongue of slab. Walk up along the left side of this slab to some scoops and knobs in a steep bulge of black, mossy rock 510859,4847553, about 180' left of **The Iron Heel**.

P1 5.4 R: Go up the scoops and knobs, and surmount the black bulge. Go up and right to an overlap 70' up; break through this at a gap in the vegetation and continue up another steep section of slab to the top. 210'
Descent: Rappel off very poorly-rooted trees.
FA May 2, 2012, Samuel Wysocki, Neal Knitel

3 The Iron Heel 5.4 PG 175' ★★★
When combined with the **Crackberry** finish, it provides a well-protected 5.9 route. Named for a Jack London novel.

Old Forge

Start: 30' up and right from the low point on the slab, below an unmistakable, long, left-facing, left-leaning corner formed by a large flake 510912,4847566.

P1 5.4 PG: Move up and right across the open slab to the corner. Climb the corner (good gear) for 50', then straight up the wonderfully textured, dimpled, low-angle slab (protection every 25' or so) to an overlap 125' up. (From here, you can finish straight through the overlap as for **Crackberry**, 5.9.) Traverse right for 50' below the overlap to the trees. 175'

Gear: To 3".

Descent: Rappel from trees with double 60m ropes.
FA Nov 11, 2011, Neal Knitel, Dereck Nabozney

4 Crackberry 5.9 G (5.3 X) 195' ★★★

Knitel dropped and shattered his Blackberry during the ascent.

Start: On the far right side of the slab, 25' right of **The Iron Heel**, and just left of a short, fern-filled, low-angle, left-facing corner below a wide overlap 12' up.

P1 5.3 X: Go up to the overlap, then undercling left to its left end. Continue left a few more feet, then up featured orange-black rock to the large overlap 125' up (some small gear can be found in a few pockets and cracks by wandering around and looking carefully). Move left at the large overlap to a pinkish, right-facing, rounded flake in the overlap (good gear). 140'

P2 5.9 G: Pull the overlap at the pinkish, right-facing, rounded flake, and finish on the easy slab to the trees at the top. 55'

Gear: To 3".

Descent: Rappel from trees with double 60m ropes.
FA Apr 30, 2012, Samuel Wysocki, Neal Knitel

MOUNT TOM CLIFF

Location	In the Moose River Plains, south of Inlet, accessed from NY 28
Aspect	South
Height	200'
Quality	
Approach	10 min, easy
Summary	Steep wilderness crag with some potential for routes.

Mount Tom Cliff is an easily-accessible wilderness crag, situated near a road on the southern slope of the multi-summited Mount Tom. It's 300' wide and 100' tall, similar to Bald Mountain in Old Forge, but much steeper. There are potential for a few moderate climbs, but on the whole this is a very steep cliff with potential for difficult routes—steep faces and a few crack lines. The bottom of the cliff is easy to negotiate, while the top has some thickets and dense vegetation along the edge. To reach the top, scramble around the left end.

HISTORY

A local forest ranger did some toprope soloing here, but pretty much kept the cliff quiet. Daniel Mosny rediscovered the cliff with his wife Kate, and documented the first full-length route in 2010.

DIRECTIONS

From the post office in the town of Inlet (0.0 mile), drive east on NY 28 (toward Blue Mountain Lake). At 0.8 mile, turn right at the fire station onto Limekiln Lake Road (CR 14). There is a sign for Moose River Wild Forest and the Limekiln Lake Entrance at this intersection. At 2.7 miles, turn left onto a dirt road marked as the Limekiln Lake Entrance and drive 100 yards to the registration booth 516976,4840878. From here the road can be rough, but still suitable for a low-clearance 2WD vehicle, and marked with diamond-shaped mile markers. At 7.3 miles, you'll reach a three-way intersection; turn left following the sign to the South Branch of the Moose River. At 9.5 miles, reach camp site #68 on the left 522936,4836970 (this is 0.1 mile before mile marker 7).

Standing in the road in front of the campsite (and looking over the outhouse), you can glimpse the cliff through the trees. It is possible to walk directly from the campsite to the cliff, but this involves navigating a swamp and huge talus. Instead, walk back on the road 300', then walk due north to the cliff 522917,4836965, staying left of the talus and uphill of the swampy area. Hiking time is about 10 minutes.

1 Spooky Tom 5.5 G 180'

An exploratory route, so expect the typical vegetation and loose rock.

Start: Locate a 100' wide, black, overhanging wall, which is left of center. On the left side are two right-facing open book corners. Begin below the left-hand open book at a right-leaning offwidth crack that opens to a chimney 25' up.

P1 5.5 G: Climb the offwidth crack for 20' to where it widens to a chimney, then move right to an arête and climb up to the first ledge. Move back left carefully, and step across the offwidth chimney (avoid large loose blocks). Make a long traverse left, then move up ledges to the top. Watch rope drag. 180'

History: The name comes from a legend about Mount Tom being haunted—some hunters discovered human torsos in a nearby swamp, and the leg bones were discovered a mile away. Add to that the scary big block that shifted under body weight above the offwidth on the first ascent.
FA Sep 20, 2010, Daniel Mosny, Kate Mosny

MITCHELL PONDS MOUNTAIN

Location	In the Moose River Plain, south of Inlet, accessed from NY 28
Aspect	South
Height	100'
Quality	
Approach	1 hr 20 min, difficult; canoe required
Summary	A remote cliff with one route in an isolated river setting.

Mitchell Ponds Mountain is an isolated bump in a vast plain of meandering rivers, ponds, and forested hills. If you like canoeing in a remote section of the park

Old Forge

combined with a bit of easy climbing, then this cliff is a good choice.

The view from the top of the cliff is to the south, where you can see Beaver Lake (the Mitchell Ponds themselves are on the other side of the mountain from the cliff). To the west in the distance is Blue Mountain. The meandering South Branch of the Moose River can be seen below making loopy slices through a carpet of dense river vegetation.

The cliff is a slab, mostly dirty but with several sections of clean rock, broken by the occasional roof. The right side has a slab below a steeper headwall, and the left side has a wide roof above a higher-angle slab covered by a thick shag carpet of lichen. The route **Moosed You** climbs a naturally clean strip through the carpet. Further exploration is necessary, but at first glance, the climbing potential at the cliff seems limited.

HISTORY
The cliff was explored for climbing by Jim Vermeulen and Bill Morris after they read about the cliff in Barbara McMartin's books.

DIRECTIONS
The cliff is approached by a 2.5-mile paddle down the South Branch of the Moose River. The first 0.5 mile is very shallow and rocky, so you must walk the river and pull the canoe (river shoes or old sneakers are a must). There was once an alternative put-in after a 0.5-mile carry that avoided this shallow section, but the trail seems to have been abandoned and is now heavily overgrown, full of blowdown, and nearly impossible to follow—a bad choice.

*The super inspiring cliff at Mitchell Ponds Mountain. Colin O'Connor follows **Moosed You** (5.3).*

From the post office in the town of Inlet, set the odometer to 0.0 and drive east on NY 28 (toward Blue Mountain Lake) for 0.8 mile, then turn right onto Limekiln Lake Road. There is a sign for Moose River Wild Forest and the Limekiln Lake Entrance at this intersection. At 2.7 miles, turn left onto a dirt road marked as the Limekiln Lake Entrance and drive 100 yards to the registration booth. There are two sign-ins—one for canoeing and the other for your vehicle. At 7.3 miles, you'll reach a three-way intersection; turn left following the sign to the South Branch of the Moose River. At 11.1 miles, you'll reach another three-way intersection; go straight following the sign to the South Branch of the Moose River. At 11.8 miles, there is a campsite on the right where the old portage trail begins (not recommended). At 12.4 miles, the road crosses the South Branch of the Moose River. Park here 0524067,4834037.

Walk and paddle the shallow, rocky river downstream (west) for 0.5 mile to where the river deepens. Continue for approximately 2.0 miles of deeper water along the beautiful, meandering river. The cliff is visible on the mountainside above early on but is obscured later. At the end of a long, wide, straight section of river, and just before the river becomes rocky, beach the boat on the right, after about 1 hr of river travel 0521134,4834010.

Walk on a bearing of 324° through the thick vegetation that borders the river, then steeply uphill through prickers, skirting several slabs, to reach a flat bench. Cross a small stream, then continue up steeply (thankfully with less dense vegetation now), skirting other slabs, to reach the cliff, about 20 min from the river 0520976,4834399.

1 Moosed You 5.3 G 100' ★★
Certainly not a destination, but if you're in the area, this is an acceptable route.

Start: On the left end of the cliff is a section of slab with a wide roof at the top. The left side of the roof narrows to where it merges into the cliff face, and the right side abruptly ends at a right-facing corner. This route begins on the highest vegetated ledge below the right end of this roof, at a 20'-long right-rising bulging overlap with a crack in it.

P1 5.3 G: Climb up the slab to the bulging overlap and follow it up and right to its end. Pull over the bulge on small holds (crux), then up the clean slab to a horizontal. Straight up the face to a crack, follow the crack to its end, then continue straight up on good flakes and edges on a somewhat dirty face to the top. Step left to the large right-facing corner (formed by the right end of the roof) and belay at a good birch tree. 100'

Descent: Rappel from the birch tree.
Gear: To 2".
FA Jul, 1990, Jim Vermeulen, Bill Morris

FOX MOUNTAIN CRAG

Location	West of the village of Raquette Lake overlooking Browns Tract Inlet
Aspect	Southeast
Height	100'
Quality	
Approach	20 min, easy
Summary	Long, broken cliff with a raw, unexplored feel; new routes will require some unearthing.

1	1						2
-5.6	5.7	5.8	5.9	5.10	5.11	5.12	5.13+	total

DESCRIPTION
This long cliff rises above Browns Tract Inlet and is a mix of slabs, roofs, flakes, and cracks. Similar to nearby Bald Mountain, the rock is quite dirty, but a few clean lines have been uncovered. The main face is over 400' wide and 100' tall with good potential for routes for those that persevere.

There is good cell reception at the cliff.

CAMPING
There is a beautiful campground run by the DEC—Brown Tract Pond (315.354.4412)—about 3 miles away.

DIRECTIONS
Park at the Raquette Lake Free Library in the village of Raquette Lake 527592,4851240. Walk (or bike) west on Dillon Road, an old railroad bed and a designated biking trail and snowmobile trail, for 0.2 mile to a locked gate. Continue past the gate for 0.6 mile with good views of the cliff. Once past the cliff (and just west of the swampy area in front of the cliff) 526272,4850872, leave the road and head northeast to the talus. Ascend the left side of the talus, working right to reach the cairn (a cheater stack of stones) at the base of **Outfoxed** 526492,4851172.

You can also reach the cliff from the west by following Dillon Road (the old railroad) from a gate 523846,4849812 near Upper Brown Tract Pond.

HISTORY
There are signs that the cliff has been climbed in the past, but the first to report climbing were Neal Knitel, Neal Lamphear, and Joe Pfeiffer in the summer of 2009. Knitel, like Jim Vermeulen, and Dick Tucker, is an enthusiastic explorer for climbable rock, and saw this cliff while driving on NY 28.

1 Outfoxed 5.8 PG 100' ★★

An unprotected crux start. Most of the dirty rock is avoided by staying on the nicely featured, outside faces of the flakes.

Start: At some stacked blocks 100' left of **Devin Monkey** below a roof 4' up. 50' right is a large open book capped by a roof.

P1 5.8 PG: Boulder up to gain a left-facing flake which is climbed to its top. Move across a vegetated black streak to another left-facing flake and climb to its top. Move left and step over a black streak to right-facing flake which is followed up and left to a sloping ramp. Head up and right up a small buttress with incut holds to a fixed anchor on a very large pine tree. 100'
Gear: To 3".
FA Aug 19, 2009, Neal Knitel, Neal Lamphear

2 Devin Monkey 5.6 PG 90' ★★

Enjoyable flake climbing down low with a grungy finish.

Start: At the highest point along the base of the cliff, on top of a short slab overlooking the open talus field.
P1 5.6 PG: Go up a leaning arête to a tree ledge. Step left onto a block, then up a right-sloping ramp to some flakes. Climb the left-facing flakes system to its top at a large ledge. (V1) Walk right 10' and climb a crack in a very dirty slab to the top. 90'
V1 5.10 TR: Go straight up to gain a horizontal above the ledge, and hand traverse left 10' to holds above a ceiling. Pull through the ceiling, then up a notch to the top.
Gear: To 2".
FA Aug 19, 2009, Neal Lamphear, Neal Knitel, Joe Pfeiffer

EAGLE FALLS

Location	Near Stillwater Reservoir, east of Lowville
Aspect	Southwest
Height	100'
Quality	★★★★
Approach	15 min, easy; river crossing
Summary	Single-pitch face, crack, arête, and corner routes in an amazing riverside location.

11	6	6	4	5	6	1	39
-5.6	5.7	5.8	5.9	5.10	5.11	5.12	5.13+	total

Eagle Falls is a unique area for the Adirondacks. Located in a remote section of the Adirondack Park, the cliff rises above the Beaver River that connects Beaver Lake and Soft Maple Reservoir. The section of the river is well known in the kayaking community as one of the premier steep creek descents in the region.

For the climber, the cliff features angular, sharp, and highly fractured rock, very different from the coarse anorthosite typical elsewhere in the park. The base of the cliff is noisy from the constant pounding of the river, making communication difficult.

The central feature of the cliff is the huge Eagle Buttress, just above the rocky cascade in the river. It has a large, prominent 15'-deep roof, below which is an enormous boulder. It is the most obvious feature on the cliff when you first see it from the river. Right (upstream) of the buttress, the rock is looser and more fractured, whereas to the left, it is more solid. The base of the cliff is well traveled, open, and with an occasional giant boulder. A trail runs around the left end of the cliff, cuts back right up stone steps to the top of the cliff, then follows the top of the cliff to the viewpoint at the top of Eagle Buttress. Many of the routes have giant trees at the top that make excellent toproping anchors.

Old Forge

The rock at Eagle Falls is often blocky and loose. Use care on the older routes, as they could use a good scrubbing as well as some cleaning with a pry bar. The newer routes ascend clean features, but even on these routes the rock is brittle, solid-looking holds sometimes pull off, and cracks are blown apart by cams. Many of the newer routes use fixed protection.

The area offers more than just climbing including canoeing at the nearby lakes, swimming, and picnicking at the open mini-summit on top of Eagle Buttress.

HISTORY

Eric Buzzell and his son Aaron began cleaning and toproping routes in 1988. Buzzell was program director at Beaver Camp, located upriver on Beaver Lake, and toproping became a standard activity at the camp. Many of the routes such as **Ranger Rick** (aka **Crossing the Red Sea**), **Red Book** (aka **Open Book**), **Fipi Lele** (aka **Love Joy**), **Soft Maple Times** (aka **Goliath**), **Face of a Thousand Cracks** (aka **Jacob's Ladder**), **Adsit Arête**, and **Easy Ramp** (aka **Damascus Road**) were toproped by the Buzzells during this period. A few years later, the canyon was closed by its owner, Niagara Mohawk Power Corp. Buzzell worked tirelessly for eight years with the various agencies to secure public access to the cliffs, and eventually the canyon was deeded to the DEC. The area remained under the radar until visited by Rolf Orsagh (who learned of the cliff from a nearby summer camp that his son was attending) and Mike Donahue. They were the first climbers to lead routes here. Jim Lawyer and Neal Knitel began visiting in 2008 to add many high-quality face and arête routes.

DIRECTIONS (MAP PAGE 365)

You can access Eagle Falls from the west (Lowville) or from the east (Eagle Bay). From Lowville, at the intersection of NY 12 and River Street (0.0), go east on River Street (CR 22), which becomes Number Four Road (CR 26). At 4.2 miles turn left staying on Number Four Road. At 17 miles reach the intersection with Stillwater Road. To reach this point from Eagle Bay, take Big Moose Road (which becomes the Stillwater–Big Moose Road) to Stillwater, then follow Stillwater Road west to its intersection with Number Four Road (this latter approach involves miles of rough dirt road).

From the intersection of Stillwater and Number Four Roads near Beaver Lake (0.0), drive north on Buck Point Road. At 0.5 mile, just before the "Dead End" sign, turn left onto a dirt road (this is Soft Maple Road, but there's no sign; there is a small sign here for the Adsit Trail). At 3.0 miles, turn right onto another dirt road marked "Beaver River Canoe Route." Drive down the hill to the dam, bear left, and continue downhill. At 3.5 miles, you reach a small parking area on the left 484056,4861534, just opposite a huge green pipe (a penstock for the hydroelectric power facility). The parking is marked "Beaver River Project Parking Area." There are also signs that read "Fishing Access" and "Beaver River Canoe Route Portage."

Walk across the road and down a set of steps that lead under the green pipe, then turn right and walk upstream parallel to the pipe. After a few minutes, the trail veers away from the pipe and follows yellow disks along the riverbank; eventually it reaches a good swimming hole where the river cascades down some rocky steps. The cliff—specifically, the roofs of Eagle Buttress—is visible on the opposite shore. Cross here and walk up to the cliff 484266,4861346. In the summer, the water is 2' deep and swift-moving; an extra pair of shoes is recommended due to sharp rocks. At times of high water (such as early spring during snowmelt), this crossing is difficult to impossible. There is often a wood plank stashed in the woods 150' upriver from the cascade that is sometimes used to cross the river, but if you use it, be sure to remove it immediately for the

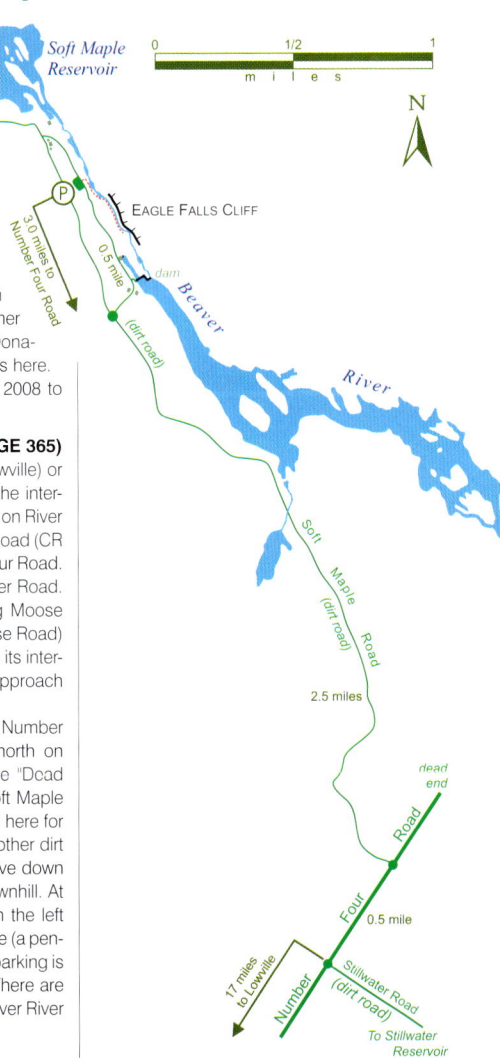

Old Forge

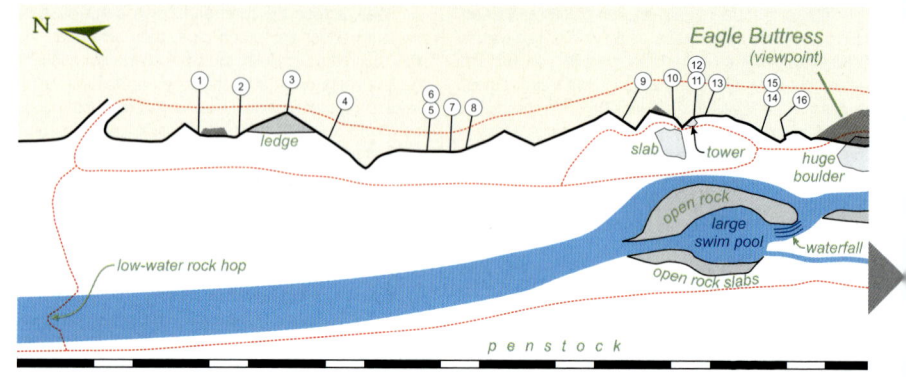

Eagle Falls

1. Ranger Rick (5.6)
2. Tree Hugger (5.10c)
3. Red Book (5.7)
4. Munkey Bars and Geetar Stars (5.7)
5. Fipi Lele (5.6+)
6. Naked Truth (5.9)
7. Soft Maple Times (5.6)
8. Gypsy's Curse (5.5)
9. Face of a Thousand Cracks (5.6)
10. Adsit Arête (5.4)
11. The Tower of Babel (5.4)
12. The Cross (5.8)
13. Hooker Heels and Crimp Pimps (5.11a)
14. Easy Ramp (5.1)
15. Open for Business (5.8)
16. Papa Don't Preach (5.11a)

kayakers. Another option is to bring a boat, put in at the dam launch site, cross to the other side, then walk back along the top of the cliff.

In summer, it might be wise to check the release schedule at www.americanwhitewater.org. During a scheduled release you cannot cross the river without swimming.

CAMPING

Beautiful primitive campsites are available on Basket Factory Road (4.1 miles east on Stillwater Road from the intersection with Number Four Road). The utility company that operates the hydro facilities has a very nice summer campground on Soft Maple Flow about 3 miles downriver from the parking. It has car camping, a canoe boat launch, and a nice beach. It's an easy flatwater paddle from here to Eagle Canyon, and you can take out on the cliff-side of the river. Another option, Beaver Camp, has rooms, cabins, campsites, and meals (315.376.2640, www.beavercamp.org).

DESCENT OPTIONS

A path along the top of the cliff visits various viewpoints. Follow this path to either rappel from the slings above **Random Rope** or **Adsit Arête**, or continue to the left, following the path down to a break in the cliff with large manicured rock steps.

1 Ranger Rick 5.6 PG 50' ★

Start: 30' left of the **Red Book** corner is a large open-book corner. Begin on the right wall of the corner beneath a crack just left of the arête.
P1 5.6 PG: Climb the crack system just left of the arête to the top. 50'
FA Jul, 2007, Rolf Orsagh, Julie Babulski, Mike Donahue

2 Tree Hugger 5.10c G 60' ★★★

Start: Immediately right of **Ranger Rick** and to the left of the **Red Book** face is a buttress, overhanging at the bottom. On the right is a thin crack angling slightly left.
P1 5.10c G: Follow the crack through a point near the top of the buttress where it widens and becomes a flake. 60'
FA Nov 3, 2007, Curtis Howard

3 Red Book 5.7 G 60' ★★★

Start: There is a large red corner 200' right of the descent trail and 100' left of a large orange jutting flake at the top of the cliff that forms a left-facing chimney (the route **Soft Maple Times**). Begin at the base of the red corner on top of a ledge 10' up.
P1 5.7 G: Up the corner to the top at a huge tree. 60'
FA Jul, 2006, Rolf Orsagh, Edward Llado

4 Munkey Bars and Geetar Stars 5.7 G 70' ★★★

Start: At the far end of **Red Book**'s right wall below a wide chimney capped by a roof.
P1 5.7 G: Up the right-hand side of the chimney to the roof. Exit the roof on the right over stacked blocks, then up and left to the top. 70'
FA Sep 29, 2007, Curtis Howard, Mark Chauvin Bezinque

5 Fipi Lele 5.6+ G 60' ★

Start: Same start as **Naked Truth**.
P1 5.6+ G: Up **Naked Truth** for 10' to a ledge, hand traverse 10' left, then straight up to gain the broken double crack system, which is followed to the top. 60'
FA Sep 29, 2007, Mark Chauvin Bezinque, Curtis Howard

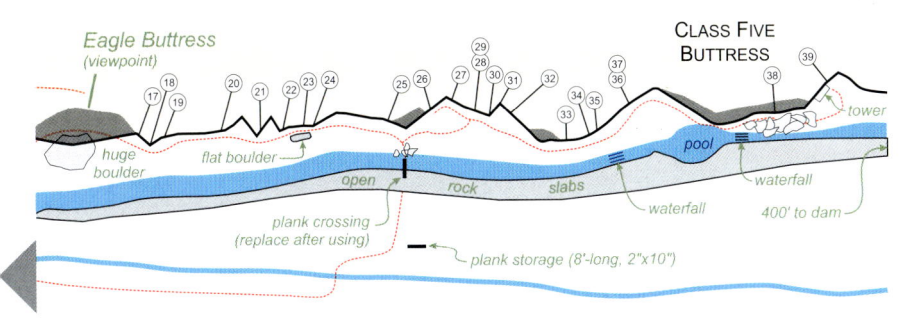

Old Forge

Eagle Buttress (viewpoint) — CLASS FIVE BUTTRESS

- 17 El Supremo (5.11c)
- 18 Random Rope (5.8)
- 19 The Big Donger (5.7)
- 20 Good Housekeeping (5.5)
- 21 Dobsonfly (5.7)
- 22 Stihl Water (5.9+)
- 23 The Eagle Has Landed (5.10d)
- 24 LM (5.10a)
- 25 Ravenous (5.11a)
- 26 Lloyd's of Lowville (5.10a)
- 27 Horizontal Fridge (5.8)
- 28 Shiver Me Timbers (5.8)
- 29 Lichen or Not (5.11c)
- 30 Promiscuous Girl (5.12a)
- 31 Puppies in a Sack (5.5)
- 32 The Tasp (5.9)
- 33 Prey Tell (5.10a)
- 34 Rolling Stone (5.7)
- 35 Seventeen (5.7)
- 36 Analysis Paralysis (5.8)
- 37 Welcome to the Machine (5.9)
- 38 Class Five (5.11c)
- 39 Stacked (5.6)

6 Naked Truth 5.9 G 60' ★★★★

Excellent face climbing on positive incut holds with clean, solid rock. One of the best routes of its grade here.

Start: 15' left of the large orange jutting flake of **Soft Maple Times**, at a short right-leaning V-slot 3' up.

P1 5.9 G: Climb up on good incut holds to a ledge. Make thin face moves (bolt; crux) to a shallow left-facing, left-arching corner, then up a good handcrack to the top. 60'

Gear: To 1".

FA Sep 8, 2007, Jim Lawyer, Simeon Warner, Leslie Ackerman

7 Soft Maple Times 5.6 G 60' ★★

Start: Start at the base of the large orange jutting flake at the top of the cliff that forms a left-facing chimney. There is a cedar on a ledge about 10' up on the right side of the chimney.

P1 5.6 G: Climb the hand- and fingercrack just to the left of the chimney to the top and exit to the left. 60'

FA Jul, 2007, Mike Donahue, Julie Babulski, Rolf Orsagh

EAGLE FALLS
- 2 Tree Hugger (5.10c)
- 3 Red Book (5.7)
- 4 Munkey Bars and Geetar Stars (5.7)
- 5 Fipi Lele (5.6+)
- 6 Naked Truth (5.9)
- 7 Soft Maple Times (5.6)
- 8 Gypsy's Curse (5.5)

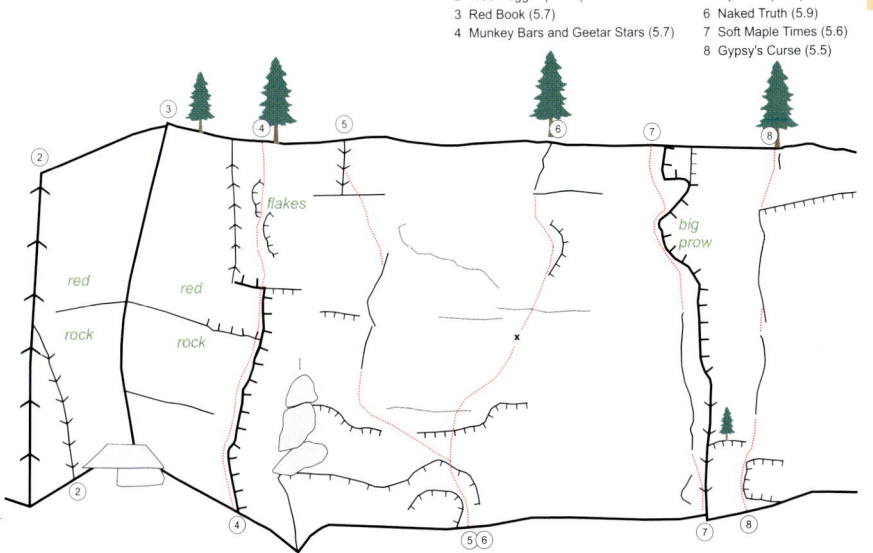

367

Old Forge

EAGLE FALLS
17 El Supremo (5.11c)
18 Random Rope (5.8)
19 The Big Donger (5.7)

8 Gypsy's Curse 5.5 G 60' ★
Start: 15' right of **Soft Maple Times** in a 1'-deep left-facing corner formed by a 10'-high ledge.
P1 5.5 G: Climb up to the ledge, continue on cracks and positive edges past a point higher up where a ramp rises to the right. Finish at the large pine tree that sits directly at the cliff's edge. 60'
FA Oct 21, 2007, Curtis Howard, Carlos Barrios, Jen Indovina, Sarah Van-Cor Hosmer

9 Face of a Thousand Cracks 5.6 G 30' ★★★
An excellent warm-up route with great protection and solid, clean rock. Sometimes wet.

Start: 200' right of **Red Book** (and 100' right of the large orange flake at the top of the cliff that forms the left-facing chimney of **Soft Maple Times**) is an open-book corner with a 4th-class chimney, the right wall of which has a maze of vertical cracks. Begin below the cracks just left of the arête. (25' right is another open-book corner capped by a large roof, the route **Adsit Arête**.)
P1 5.6 G: Climb the cracks in the face to the top. 30'
ACB Sep 8, 2007, Leslie Ackerman, Jim Lawyer, Simeon Warner

368

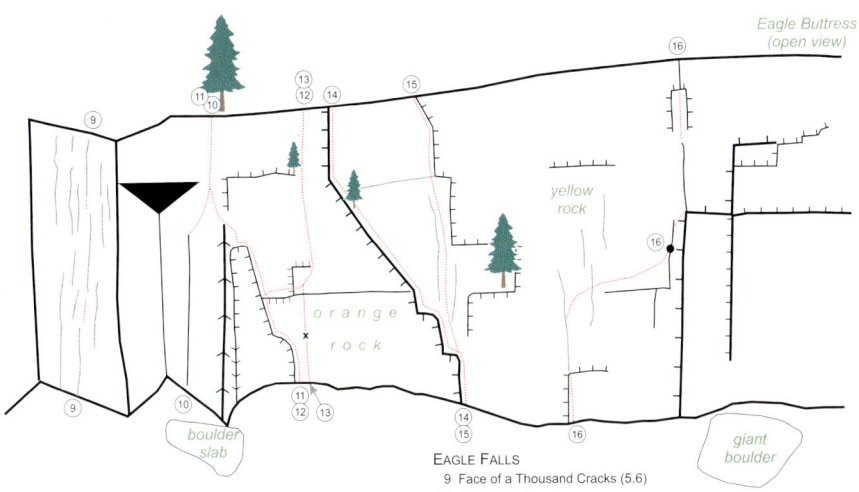

Old Forge

Eagle Buttress (open view)

EAGLE FALLS
9 Face of a Thousand Cracks (5.6)
10 Adsit Arête (5.4)
11 The Tower of Babel (5.4)
12 The Cross (5.8)
13 Hooker Heels and Crimp Pimps (5.11a)
14 Easy Ramp (5.1)
15 Open for Business (5.8)
16 Papa Don't Preach (5.11a)

10 Adsit Arête 5.4 G 40' ★★★

The route has good protection, but the final critical nut placement, although excellent, could prove tricky to find.

Start: 25' right of **Face of a Thousand Cracks** is an open book capped by a ceiling 25' up. Begin on the right wall, 6' left of the arête. (Just right of the open book is a 20'-tall freestanding tower, and just right of this is an overhanging concave red wall.)

P1 5.4 G: Up cracks and angle rightward to the arête, then straight up good incut buckets to the top. 40'
ACB Sep 8, 2007, Jim Lawyer, Simeon Warner, Leslie Ackerman

11 The Tower of Babel 5.4 TR 50' ★★

Great climb for beginners and kids, as even the shortest ones can stand on top of the flat tower and feel victorious. Begin at the base of a free-standing tower at the left end of the overhanging red wall and 25' right of **Adsit Arête**. Climb to the top of the tower, then step left onto the face and finish up **Adsit Arête** on good incut buckets to the top.
FA (TR) 1988, Eric Buzzell, Aaron Buzzell

Martin von Arx on the upper wall of **El Supremo** (5.11c).

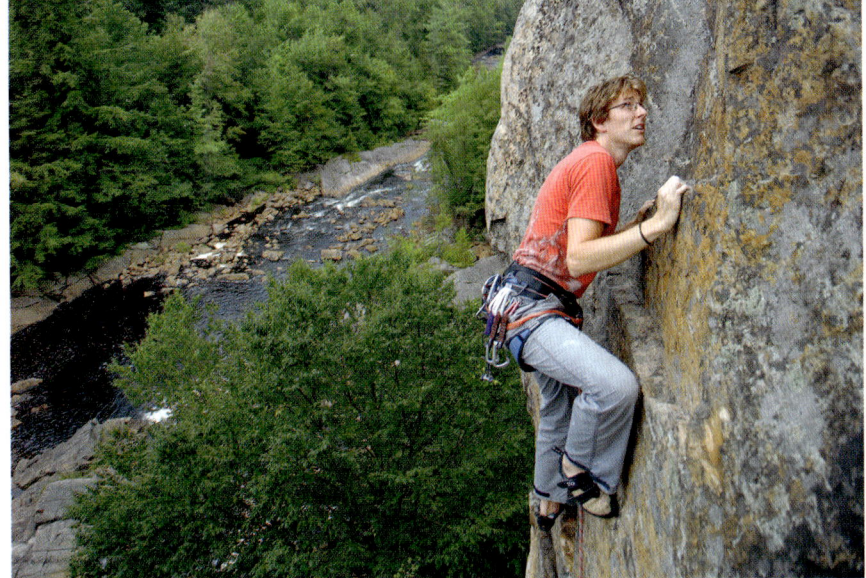

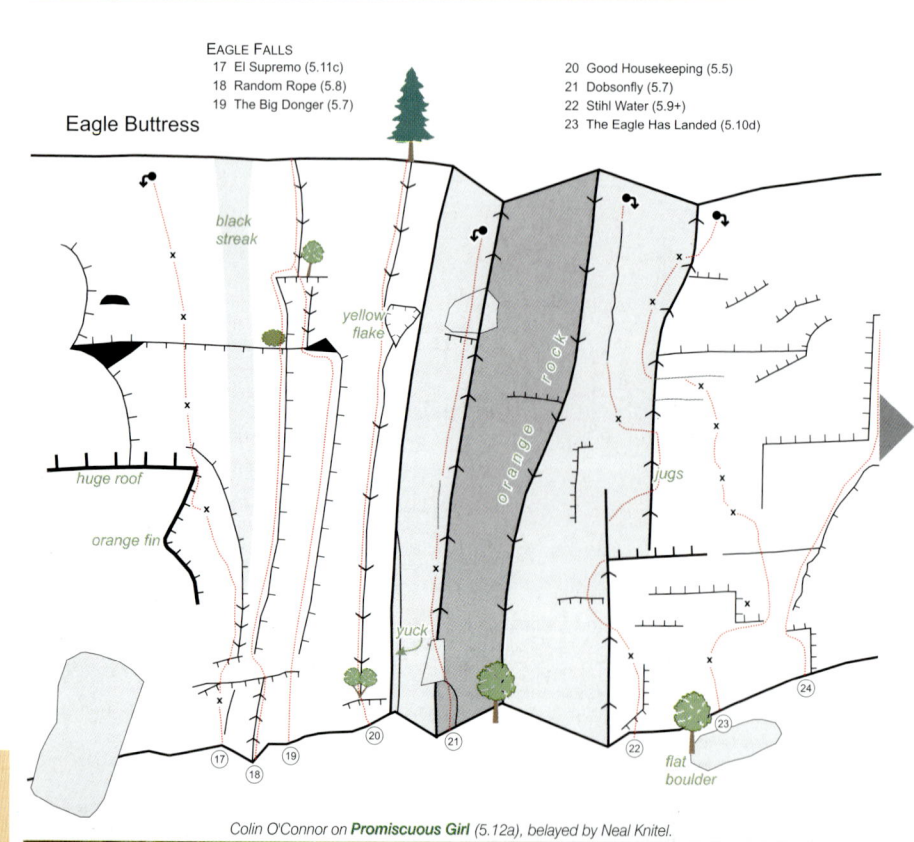

Old Forge

Eagle Buttress

Eagle Falls
17 El Supremo (5.11c)
18 Random Rope (5.8)
19 The Big Donger (5.7)
20 Good Housekeeping (5.5)
21 Dobsonfly (5.7)
22 Stihl Water (5.9+)
23 The Eagle Has Landed (5.10d)

Labels on topo: black streak, yellow flake, huge roof, orange fin, orange rock, yuck, jugs, flat boulder

*Colin O'Connor on **Promiscuous Girl** (5.12a), belayed by Neal Knitel.*

Old Forge

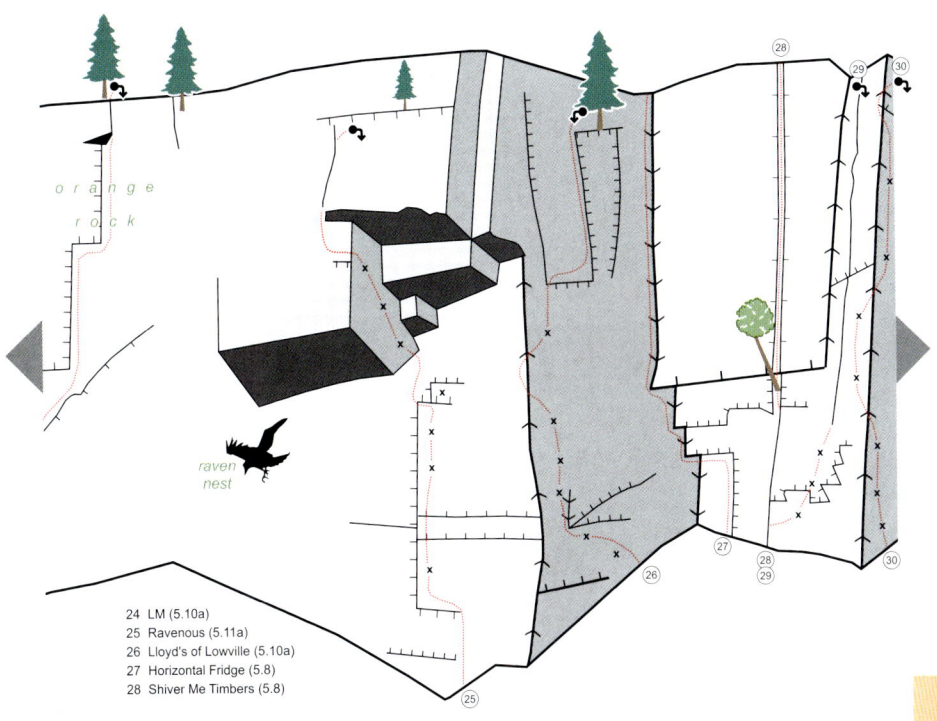

orange rock

raven nest

24 LM (5.10a)
25 Ravenous (5.11a)
26 Lloyd's of Lowville (5.10a)
27 Horizontal Fridge (5.8)
28 Shiver Me Timbers (5.8)

12 The Cross 5.8 G 60' ★★

Due to the overhanging nature of the wall, this route stays fairly dry in the rain except for the last couple moves. Originally a toprope problem, but not super popular as there is a potential for a nasty pendulum.
Start: In the right-facing corner at the base of **The Tower of Babel**.
P1 5.8 G: Up the corner to near its top, then traverse right using a prominent horizontal crack on an overhanging orange wall for 30'. At its end, move up over a bulge to a tree. Lower from here, or continue to the top. 60'
FA (TR) 1988, Eric Buzzell, Aaron Buzzell
FFA Jun 4, 2011, Neal Knitel, Jim Lawyer

13 Hooker Heels and Crimp Pimps 5.11a G 50'

Start: Just right of **The Cross** and **The Tower of Babel**.
P1 5.11a G: Go straight up the overhanging orange wall past a bolt to a good horizontal below a rectangular roof. Stay right past the roof using horizontal cracks, then up a vertical seam with shallow pockets. Move up and left over roof to slabby section, then up to large pine tree on the left. 50'
FA Jul 21, 2013, Andrew Freeman, Chris Todt

14 Easy Ramp 5.1 G 60' ★★

Start: 25' right of **Face of a Thousand Cracks** is an open book capped by a roof, and 30' right of this is an overhanging concave red wall. Begin at a 4'-high block on the right side of this face, 50' left of Eagle Buttress.
P1 5.1 G: Climb onto the block and short right-facing corner to gain a left-rising ramp, then follow it to a tree below a right-facing corner and an off-width crack. Climb the face left of the off width to the top. 60'
FA 2005, Jeff Heintz (solo)

15 Open for Business 5.8 TR 80'

Begin at the same 4'-high block described at the beginning of **Easy Ramp**. Climb straight up from the block to a system of small cracks. Follow the cracks to the left of some overhangs and into a left-facing corner ending at a large pine tree.
FA (TR) Oct 21, 2007, Carlos Barrios, Curtis Howard

16 Papa Don't Preach 5.11a G 120' ★★★

A great climb with a short crux sequence up the highest part of the cliff. Can be done in a single pitch; however, rope drag and communication with the second may become an issue.
Start: 40' right of **Easy Ramp** and 30' left of the boulder under Eagle Buttress in a right facing corner underneath a section of blocky overhanging rock 10' up. There is a large roof 70' above the start.
P1 5.11a G: Climb the right-facing corner for 10' to a large grassy ledge (you can walk onto this ledge starting 25' to the left). Up a small crack and face moves to jugs higher up. Traverse right (crux, missing bolt) to

371

Old Forge

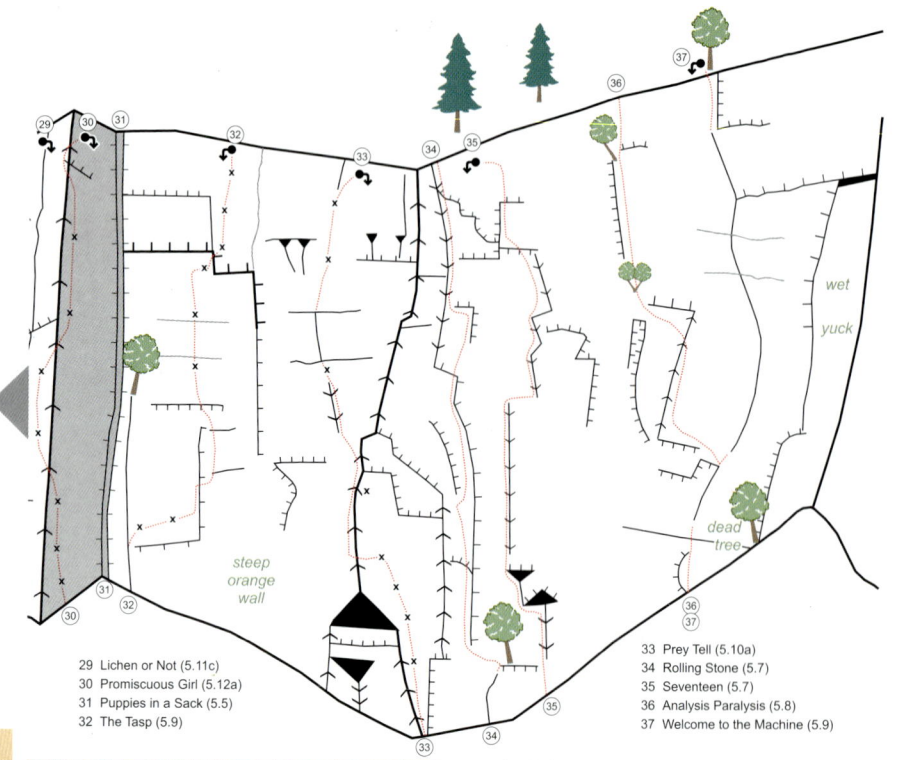

29 Lichen or Not (5.11c)
30 Promiscuous Girl (5.12a)
31 Puppies in a Sack (5.5)
32 The Tasp (5.9)
33 Prey Tell (5.10a)
34 Rolling Stone (5.7)
35 Seventeen (5.7)
36 Analysis Paralysis (5.8)
37 Welcome to the Machine (5.9)

reach a belay stance on a 4'-high detached block. The block sits on the arête at the left side of the smaller of the two Eagle Buttress roofs. 70'

P2 5.8 G: Follow a crack to double cracks which lead to a chimney. Finish in an overhanging off width. 50'
FA Nov 4, 2007, Curtis Howard, Dave Howard

17 El Supremo 5.11c G 90' ★★★★

This scenic route climbs the most prominent feature at Eagle Falls—the buttress with huge roofs, Eagle Buttress, ending at a beautiful bare-rock summit. The crimpy crux is considerably harder if you're short.

Start: On the right side of the open rocky area below the roofs of Eagle Buttress and 15' right of the giant boulder, at a right-leaning crack with pods, below the right side of an orange fin of rock that forms a chimney 20' up.

● **P1 5.11c G:** Up the short crack (5.8), then through a brief blocky section with good incut buckets. Work up the orange fin to its top, then make a long move to a hidden edge on the overhanging orange face above the roofs. Crimp up the face (crux) to a fantastic incut ledge, then up easier jugs (5.5) to a fixed anchor at the top. 90'

Gear: 2 ea 0.5".
FA Jul 30, 2009, Jim Lawyer, Michelle Burlitch, Neal Knitel

Jim Lawyer on the awesome fingercrack of **Lichen or Not** *(5.11c).*

Old Forge

18 Random Rope 5.8 G (5.7 R) 70' ★★

A random length of rope dangling from a tree on the top ledge inspired the route name.
Start: 15' right of **El Supremo**, just right of an arête.
P1 5.8 PG: Climb to the ledge 12' up, then up and right to an unprotected left-facing corner with a crack. Follow the corner past a small ledge with a bush, then past another ledge with a tree on the right. Continue up a fingercrack (crux) to the top. Watch for loose rock. 70'
FA Nov 4, 2007, Curtis Howard, Dave Howard

19 The Big Donger 5.7 PG 90' ★

Start: At a 10'-high open book, 10' right of **Random Rope**.
P1 5.7 G: Up the corner to where it arches left and becomes an overhang. Break the overhang to gain the ledge described in **Random Rope** with a tree. From the tree, traverse down and left to a small ledge that leads to the arête on the right side of Eagle Buttress. Easy moves lead to the top. 90'
FA Oct 21, 2007, Curtis Howard, Carlos Barrios

20 Good Housekeeping 5.5 PG 60'

Start: At a triple-trunked birch tree 8' up and 60' right of the giant boulder that sits beneath the huge roofs of Eagle Buttress, 10' left of a dirty open book, and 20' left of **Dobsonfly**.
P1 5.5 PG: Climb past a big tree, then up and right following a shallow open book with ledges to sharp-edged left-facing orange flakes. Up the flakes, then up an open book to a giant cedar that grows on the lip of the cliff. 60'
FA Aug, 2006, Rolf Orsagh, Adrian Fife

21 Dobsonfly 5.7 G 70' ★★★

Start: 10' left of **Stihl Water** and 10' right of the open book mentioned in the start of **Good Housekeeping**, below a cleaned arête with a ledge 10' up. Start on either side of the arête.
P1 5.7 G: Gain the ledge, then follow the arête (crux) to a large perched block at the top. Over this to another perched block with a fixed anchor on the left. 70'
Gear: To 2", including small cams.
FA Jul 25, 2009, Neal Knitel, Rayko Halitschke

22 Stihl Water 5.9+ G 80' ★★★

Excellent crack and face climbing with a juggy exposed arête thrown in for good measure.
Start: 15' left **The Eagle Has Landed** at an arête capped by a large square roof 20' up. There is a large flat boulder 10' to the right.
P1 5.9+ G: Up the right side of the arête to the roof, then break the roof on its left side via a good crack. Once positioned above the roof, traverse right and climb the large juggy arête to a good stance. Move left onto the face, then up (crux) to a fingercrack and a corner to its left (V1), which are followed to a fixed anchor at the top. 80'
Gear: Standard rack to 2".
FA Jun 21, 2008, Neal Knitel, Rayko Halitschke, Jim Lawyer

EAGLE FALLS
20 Good Housekeeping (5.5)
21 Dobsonfly (5.7)
22 Stihl Water (5.9+)
23 The Eagle Has Landed (5.10d)

23 The Eagle Has Landed 5.10d G 90' ★★★★★

This gem climbs a beautiful, clean, and unlikely orange wall, finishing on an arête with good views of the river.
Start: 10' left of **LM** below two bottomless left-facing corners capped by roofs 15' up. The trail at the base of the cliff run up against the wall here, and there is a large flat boulder 4' back from the cliff.
● P1 5.10d G: (V1) Up the leftmost corner to the roof, then make an intricate traverse right around the second corner (crux) to better holds and up to a prominent 3" horizontal. Work up the face on good edges and flakes to a ceiling, then traverse left following an excellent horizontal crack (no feet) to the arête. Swing around the arête, then climb it to a fixed anchor at the top. 90'
V1 5.8 G: The initial crux can be avoided: start on **LM**, then traverse left onto the face above the horizontal. This reduces the overall difficulty to 5.10b.
Gear: 1 ea 3" cam, 1 ea 3/4" cam.
FA May 21, 2008, Jim Lawyer, Neal Knitel

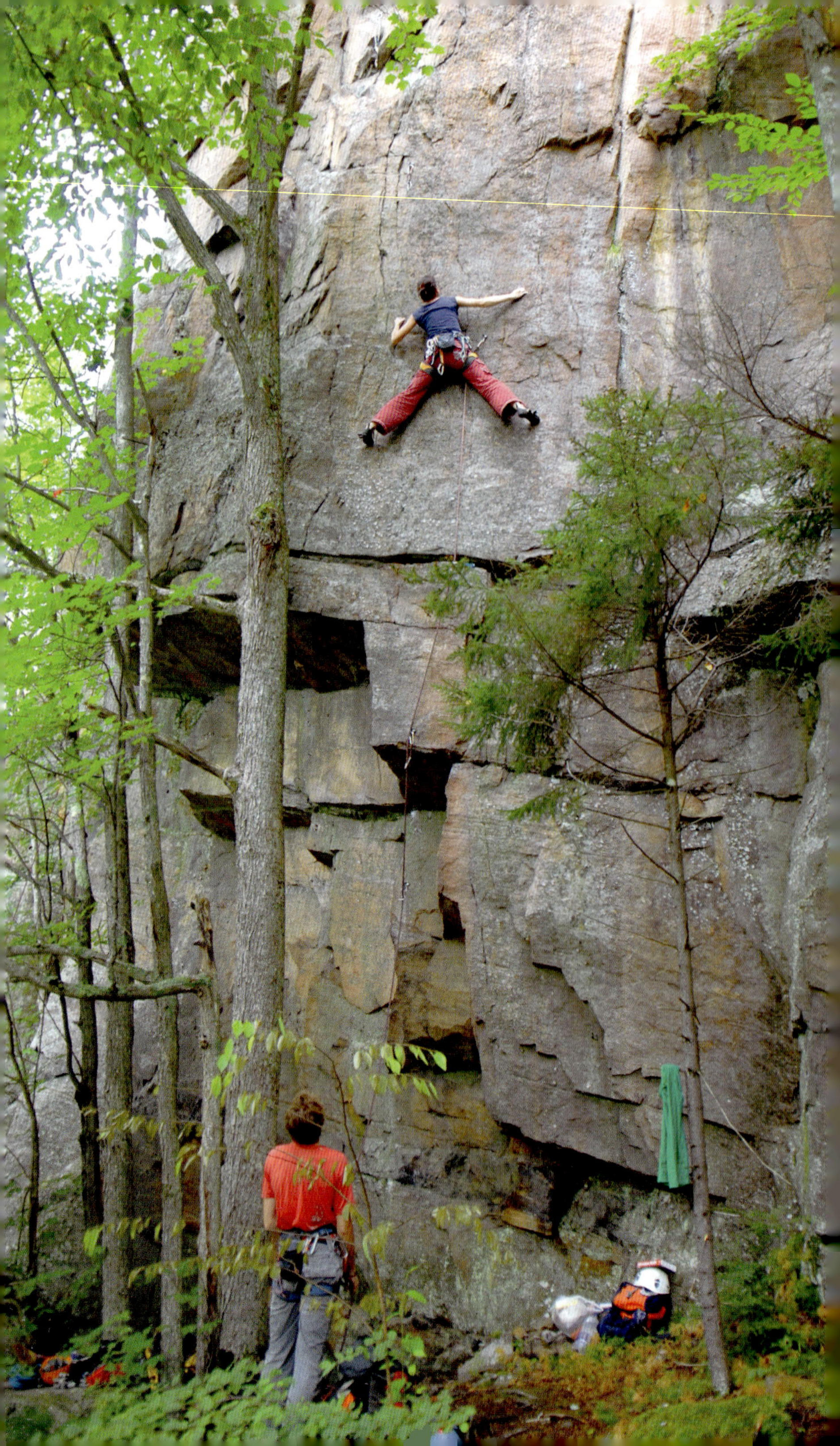

Old Forge

EAGLE FALLS
21 Dobsonfly (5.7)
22 Stihl Water (5.9+)
23 The Eagle Has Landed (5.10d)
24 LM (5.10a)

24 LM 5.10a G 90' ★★★

Climbs through a clean, stepped orange corner. No sleeping on this one—the protection is good, but strenuous to place in the upper corner.

Start: 50' right of the triple-trunked birch of **Good Housekeeping** and 10' right of **The Eagle Has Landed**, at a handcrack in a left-facing open book capped by a triangular ceiling 12' up.

P1 5.10a G: Climb the handcrack to the ceiling. Move left around the ceiling, then follow a right-rising flake to the base of a stepped right-facing orange corner.

Opposite: Martine Schaer on The Eagle Has Landed, belayed by Martin von Arx (5.10d).

Up the corner to a roof, around this on the right (crux), then layback up the next corner to a large tree at the top. 90'

Gear: Up to 3", with a 4" cam for the roof. Small nuts in the upper corner.

FA Aug, 2006, Mark Chauvin Bezinque, Rolf Orsagh

25 Ravenous 5.11a G 90' ★★★★

Incredible climbing up a puzzling corner finishing through an exposed series of roofs.

Start: At the toe of the buttress left of **Lloyd's of Lowville** is a square-roofed alcove below a beautiful right-facing corner that begins 15' up. Begin on the right side of the alcove.

Old Forge

EAGLE FALLS
25. Ravenous (5.11a)
26. Lloyd's of Lowville (5.10a)
27. Horizontal Fridge (5.8)

● **P1 5.11a G:** Climb to a good incut ledge below the corner, then up the corner (crux) to its top. Move left onto a face and thankful stance, then work left under a dramatic series of roofs using hidden sidepulls to an exposed perch on the lip of the large roof. Easy climbing up cracks in a headwall leads to a fixed anchor. 90'
Gear: Cams to 3/4".
History: Named for the raven's nest that sits under the large roofs (and hence not a good climb for the spring), and for Lawyer and Knitel's insatiable appetite for new routes.
FA Jun 21, 2008, Jim Lawyer, Neal Knitel, Ben Currens, Rayko Halitschke

● **26 Lloyd's of Lowville 5.10a G 90'** ★★★★
Clean, solid rock with exposed positions on an arête. Fantastic; one of the best routes here, although the opening moves are considerably more difficult if you're short. Named for a diner in Lowville.
Start: On the left wall of a large open book, 10' left of **Horizontal Fridge**, and just uphill and right of some ceilings below a clean orange arête.
● **P1 5.10a G:** A tricky move off the ground leads to a good stance on the face. Work up and left past an undercling pocket (3" cam) to the arête (crux). Up the arête to a good stance, then move right and up a fingercrack. Swing right on jugs to a shallow left-facing corner that is followed to a fixed anchor on a tree. 90'
Gear: 1 ea 3" cam, 1/2" cam.
FA May 6, 2008, Jim Lawyer, Neal Knitel

*Opposite: Neal Knitel on his route, **Prey Tell** (5.10a), belayed by Shawn Higbee.*

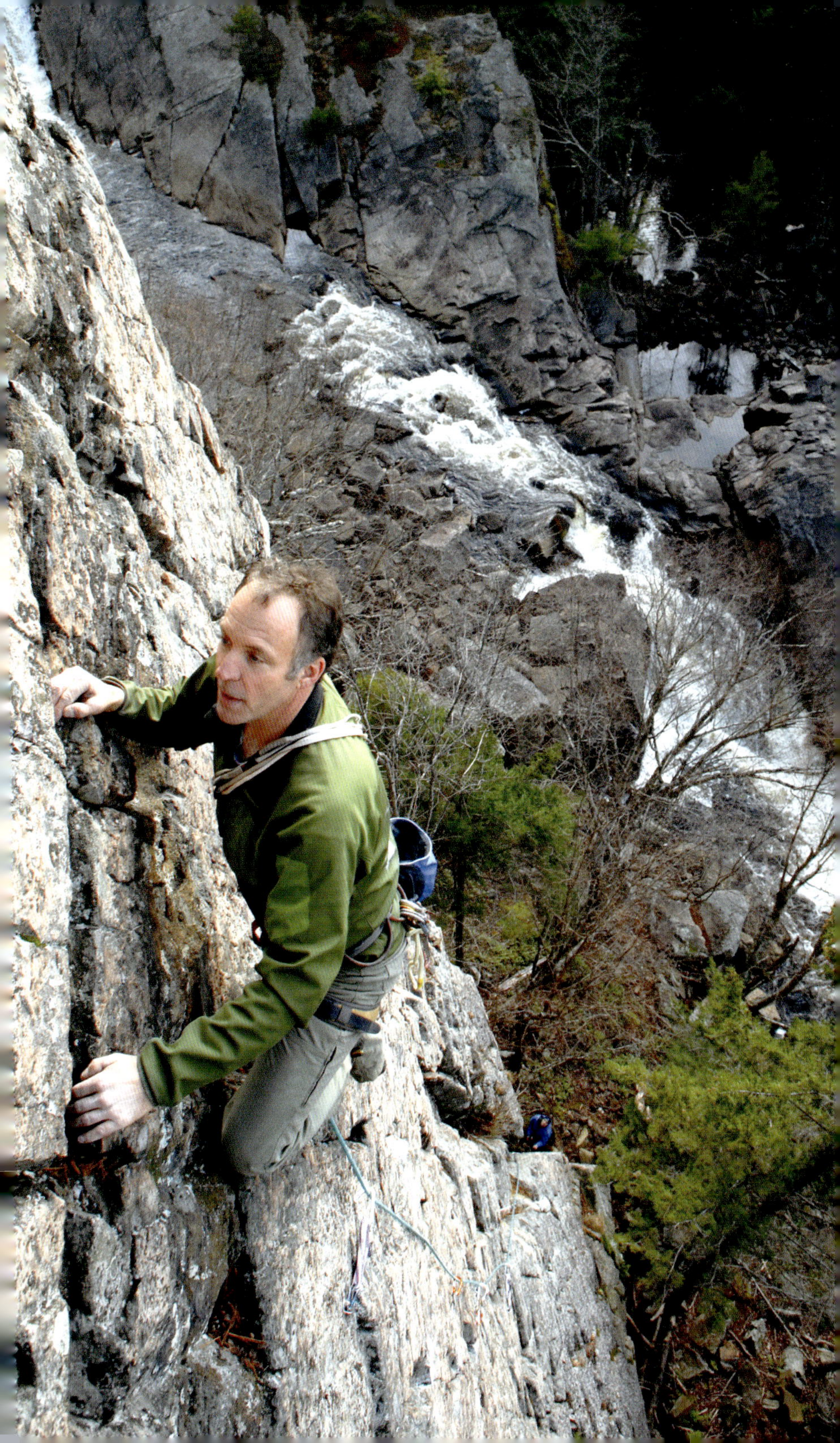

Old Forge

EAGLE FALLS
28 Shiver Me Timbers (5.8)
29 Lichen or Not (5.11c)
30 Promiscuous Girl (5.12a)
31 Puppies in a Sack (5.5)
32 The Tasp (5.9)

27 Horizontal Fridge 5.8 PG 100'
An interesting climb with a tricky crux. The upper section has a fair amount of loose rock and dirt and provides a very different sort of challenge. Recommended belayer position is off to the right, out of the line of fire of the open book.

Start: 35' left of **Puppies in a Sack** and 130' right of the triple-trunked birch of **Good Housekeeping** is an enormous open-book corner whose right wall has large roofs. The first roof, 15' up, is formed by a horizontal, refrigerator-sized orange block split in the middle. The route begins at a shallow left-facing corner below the right end of the orange block, 10' left of **Shiver Me Timbers**.

P1 5.8 PG: Climb up the left-facing corner to the orange blocks. Traverse left under the blocks, then move left onto the face below the open book and up into the corner of the book (crux; 5.8). Continue carefully up the face and open book to the top, avoiding a minefield of loose rock (5.5). 100'

Gear: A small TCU is useful at the crux. Gardening tools are useful up higher to excavate for pro.
FA Jul 20, 2005, Mike Donahue, Peter Harrison

28 Shiver Me Timbers 5.8 G 90' ★

Perhaps the most obvious line at the cliff—a crack that gradually widens from hands to 10". The roof at mid-height is overcome using the tree; otherwise, it would be much more difficult.

Start: 15' right of **Horizontal Fridge** below a crack that runs the full height of the cliff.

P1 5.8 G: Up the crack to the roof, then shimmy up the birch tree over the roof. Continue up the outside of the squeeze chimney to the top. 90'

Gear: Surprisingly, gear to 4", with an emphasis on small TCUs.

FA Aug 30, 2008, Joe Szot, Aya Alt

29 Lichen or Not 5.11c G 90' ★★★★

Devious face climbing followed by high-quality, steep, finger- and hand-cracks. The route was significantly easier until the key hold broke down low; the route still goes, but now starts in the crack to the left, and the second clip is a hard.

Start: Same as **Shiver Me Timbers**.

P1 5.11c G: Up **Shiver Me Timbers** for 5', then traverse right on the delicate face to a series of insecure moves up three left-leaning ramp features to gain a tips crack. Up the tips crack to parallel overhanging cracks, which are followed up a corner to a fixed anchor at the top. 90'

History: Originally a variation to **Promiscuous Girl**, the bottom half was added later making an independent line.

Gear: Normal rack to 2.0", with an emphasis on small to finger-sized cams.

FA (upper section) Oct 12, 2008, Chris Yenkey
FA (complete) Oct 14, 2008, Jim Lawyer, Neal Knitel
FA (post hold break) May 1, 2010, Martin von Arx, Martine Schaer

30 Promiscuous Girl 5.12a G 90' ★★★★

Sustained, technical arête climbing on immaculate rock. It has been done four (!) different ways.

Start: 5' left of **Puppies in a Sack** below an arête that forms a right-facing corner.

🔵 **P1 5.12a G:** Starting on the right side of the arête, mantel onto an obvious hold at head height, then climb the overhanging arête (V1) to a good stance at two-thirds height. The climbing eases now—move right, then back up to the arête, finish on good sidepulls on the left to reach a fixed anchor on the right side of the arête. 90'

Gear: Optional micro cam.

FA Oct 12, 2008, Jim Lawyer, Neal Knitel, Chris Yenkey

31 Puppies in a Sack 5.5 PG 90' ★

A very deep chimney with some loose rock.

Start: 40' left of **Rolling Stone** and at the height of a cone-shaped slope below a huge right-facing chimney with large jammed boulders 25' up.

P1 5.5 PG: Climb up to the jammed boulders, around these on the right, then up a slope to gain the chimney. Secure but unprotected climbing squeezes up the chimney behind two chockstones to the top. 90'

FA Sep 8, 2007, Leslie Ackerman, Jim Lawyer, Simeon Warner

32 The Tasp 5.9 G 80' ★★

Nice face climbing with a high, exposed roof with a heel hook—a one-move wonder.

Start: 10' right of the large right-facing chimney of **Puppies in a Sack** below a crack filled with jammed flakes. This is just left of an overhanging orange wall.

🔵 **P1 5.9 G:** Up the flake-filled groove for 10', then traverse right on a narrow ledge to a shallow left-facing corner. Step right out of the corner and climb a pleasantly juggy face to a roof. Out the roof (crux), then up a face to a fixed anchor. 80'

Gear: 1 ea 2" cam, #6 nut.

FA Jun 30, 2008, Jim Lawyer, Neal Knitel

33 Prey Tell 5.10a G 100' ★★★★

An excellent combination of a thin face, an arête, and a steep intricate face.

Start: 40' right of **The Tasp** and 16' left of **Seventeen**, at a small arête that leads to the right side of a large triangular roof 20' up. There is a wet, mossy open book corner 1' right of the start.

🔵 **P1 5.10a G:** Up the arête (taking care to avoid the wet, mossy corner) to better holds and a good stance on the right side of the large triangular roof 20' up. Go up the face (crux), then step left and ascend a juggy staircase of holds on the large arête above the triangular roof. Begin up a steep face, make long reaches between good holds, trend toward the left then finish up and right at a fixed anchor. 100'

Gear: To 2".

FA Nov 13, 2009, Neal Knitel, Jim Lawyer

34 Rolling Stone 5.7 G 100' ★★

Start: 10' left of **Seventeen**, at a crack 6' right of a 4'-wide ceiling 10' up and 15' right of **Prey Tell**. Another marker 20' to the left is a large arête that begins 20' up, below which are multi-tiered roofs."

P1 5.7 G: Climb up the face into a shallow left-facing corner that leads to a roof. Over the roof, then up a series of orange left-facing flakes. Climb the corner and flakes up to a ceiling, traverse left 6' and into a large left-facing corner, and follow it to the top. 100'

FA Aug, 2006, Mark Chauvin Bezinque, Rolf Orsagh

35 Seventeen 5.7 G 100' ★★★

Start: Upstream from Eagle Buttress is a large pool beneath overhanging rock (the Class Five Buttress). This route is located 150' left of the pool at a narrowing in the river with a small waterfall and 275' right of the giant boulder at Eagle Buttress. Start below a left-facing open book that begins 20' up, and has a right wall of pink rock. Just right of (and below) the open book are two triangular ceilings, and there is a small birch 10' up.

P1 5.7 G: Climb up the face to two small ceilings, around these to the left and up a left-facing open book with a fingercrack to its top at a small tree. Work right and climb the left-facing corner and crack to a ledge at its top. Step left, up a thin crack, then up a right-facing corner to a square ceiling, then move out its right side and follow a thin crack to a fixed anchor at the top. 100'

FA Aug, 2006, Rolf Orsagh, Mark Chauvin Bezinque

Old Forge

EAGLE FALLS
32 The Tasp (5.9)
33 Prey Tell (5.10a)
34 Rolling Stone (5.7)
35 Seventeen (5.7)

36 Analysis Paralysis 5.8 PG 100'

Marginal protection, ample vegetation.
Start: Same as **Welcome to the Machine**.
P1 5.8 PG: Climb to the horizontal, then up the steep face past two sidepull pockets to better holds beneath a fractured crack system 20' up. Move left onto a fern ledge, then up an arête to a 5' triangular roof on the left. Traverse left beneath the roof, then up to a ledge in the main open book corner to the top. 100'
FA Sep 29, 2007, Curtis Howard, Mark Chauvin Bezinque

37 Welcome to the Machine 5.9 PG 90' ★ ★

Good climbing and exposure on the upper section. The bottom section is slightly runout, but the high crux is well-protected. Despite massive cleaning, this route still has a section of questionable rock through an easy section. Named for a Pink Floyd song.
Start: Walk upstream to a wall facing upstream and facing the large pool (the pool beneath the Class Five Buttress). Begin 40' right of **Seventeen** on a flat boulder, below a right-facing scoop, 6' downhill and left of where a horizontal crack meets the dirt.

Old Forge

EAGLE FALLS
34 Rolling Stone (5.7)
35 Seventeen (5.7)
36 Analysis Paralysis (5.8)
37 Welcome to the Machine (5.9)

P1 5.9 PG: Climb to the horizontal, then up the steep face past two sidepull pockets to better holds beneath a fractured crack system 20' up (there is a fern ledge to the left). Work up the crack system to where the wall becomes steeper (crux), then up to a small ceiling. Move left around the ceiling into a short left-facing corner and follow this to a fixed anchor on a birch tree. 90'
FA May 13, 2008, Jim Lawyer, Neal Knitel, Colin O'Connor

38 Class Five 5.11c G 80' ★★★★

Incredibly exposed, intricate, and puzzling climbing through a roof above a Class V rapid in the river (even in low water, the noise here is substantial). Up to the roof is spectacular 5.9.

Start: At the right end of the cliff is a dominate buttress, horizontally fractured with multi-tiered roofs overlooking a large pool in the river. Begin at a flat ledge at the height of land beneath the roofs. This is down, left, and around the corner from **Stacked**.

● **P1 5.11c G:** Walk left on a ledge to a short right-facing corner. A crimp move gains the corner. Work up buckets in the overhanging tiers, then layback up to a good stance on the face beneath the huge 7'-deep roof, below and left of an acute left-facing corner in the roof. Chimney up the acute corner, then make a huge move out right (crux) to an excellent horizontal crack at the lip of the roof. Over the roof and onto the face with parallel cracks. Step left to a fixed anchor. 80'.

Gear: At the top, a 2" cam protects the second for the move over the roof.
FA Sep 3, 2009, Jim Lawyer

Old Forge

39 ▶ Stacked 5.6 G 60' ★

Start: Walk upstream and around the large pool beneath the severely overhanging, horizontally fractured prow of rock. (Getting around this pool may be difficult in high water, in which case you can hike along the top of the cliff and descend a gully just upstream of the prow.) Right around the corner from this prow is a slender detached tower of rock, broken in the middle, that leans up against the main face. Begin at a handcrack in the main face on the right side of the tower.

P1 5.6 G: Climb the narrowing crack up to a stacked pile of blocks at the point where the tower contacts the main wall. Break left onto the face of the tower, then scramble up to the trees at the top. 60'

FA Sep 8, 2007, Simeon Warner, Leslie Ackerman, Jim Lawyer

*Opposite: Chris Yenkey on **Stihl Water** (5.9+), belayed by Neal Knitel. Below: Martin von Arx on **Class Five** (5.11c).*

EAGLE FALLS
38 Class Five (5.11c)

EAGLE FALLS
39 Stacked (5.6)

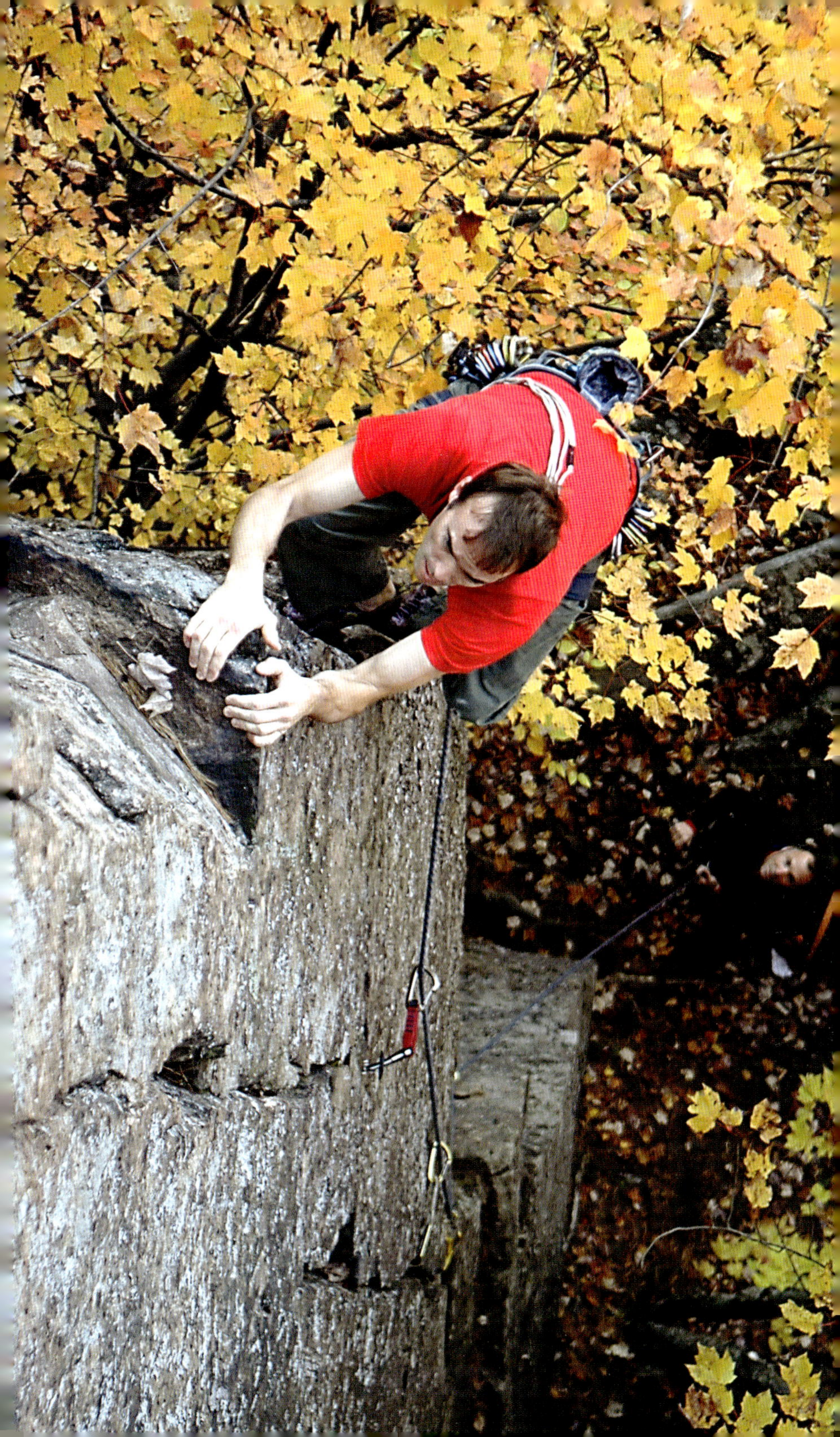

384

Cranberry Lake

If you like canoeing and kayaking in wild places—an activity for which the Adirondacks is well known—and climbing in complete isolation, then focus your attention on the cliffs in the Cranberry Lake section. The central theme here is water—lakes, meandering rivers, wetlands, swamps, and, well, more lakes. Many cliffs in this section can be approached by boat. Lake Lila and Hitchins Pond are accessible by moderate paddles. Grass Pond Mountain is more remote, approached by crossing Cranberry Lake or via a 14-mile paddle up the meandering Bog River. The seclusion is rewarded by excellent camping and a large cliff, virtually undeveloped.

The rock here has a raw and unclimbed feeling, perhaps because there are so few visitors. Cat Mountain was first visited in the 70s, Lake Lila in the 80s, Hitchins Pond in the early 90s, and Grass Pond in 2007. These cliffs may go several years between visits, and the climbs may not have seen second ascents. The exception is the new Twin Falls Cliff, a small crag with excellent routes and a short approach. This and Lake Lila are the most popular cliffs in this region.

Random sections of the forest in this area were moderately to heavily impacted by the microburst windstorm of 1995, making off-trail hiking in those areas nearly impossible.

DIRECTIONS (MAPS PAGES 4 AND 384)

The gateway towns are Tupper Lake and Cranberry Lake. Depending on where you're coming from (and which cliff you're visiting), it may make sense to approach from Watertown on NY 3. Otherwise, the approaches begin on NY 30 between Long Lake and Tupper Lake.

WHERE TO STAY

There are several state campgrounds: Cranberry Lake (315.848.2315); Lake Eaton, in Long Lake (518.624.2641); and Forked Lake (518.624.6646). There are first-come, first-served primitive campsites at Horseshoe Lake, located on NY 421 just south of Tupper Lake (on the approach to Hitchins Pond). In the Cranberry Lake area, a nice option for rooms and meals is Packbasket Adventures in Wanakena (315.848.3488). For other options, refer to the Chamber of Commerce website for Tupper Lake (www.tupperlakeinfo.com) or the tourism website for Long Lake (www.centraladirondacks.com).

AMENITIES

There are numerous opportunities for gas along NY 3: Tupper Lake, Sevey Corner (Ham's, at the intersection with NY 56), Cranberry Lake, and Star Lake. The larger grocery stores are Shaheen's IGA, in Tupper Lake; and Padgetts IGA, in Star Lake. There are many options for boat rentals: Raquette River Outfitters, in Tupper Lake (518.359.3228); the Emporium Marina, in Cranberry Lake (315.848.2140); and the St. Regis Canoe Outfitters, in Saranac Lake (518.891.1838).

Watercolor by Lucie Wellner.

PROTECTING CLIMBING **ACCESS** SINCE 1991

ACCESS FUND
Protect America's Climbing

| JOIN US |
WWW.ACCESSFUND.ORG

Jonathan Siegrist climbs the Third Millenium (14a) at the Monastery, Colorado. Photo by: Keith Ladzinski

Cranberry Lake

PG	CLIFF	QUALITY	ASPECT	APPROACH	GRADES	#
387	Lake Lila	★★★	SE	1 hr 30 min / easy canoe optional	.6 .7 .8 .9 .10 .11 .12 .13	7
390	Hitchins Pond Cliff		SE	1 hr / easy canoe optional	.6 .7 .8 .9 .10 .11 .12 .13	3
392	South Bay Roadcut		NW	0 min / easy	.6 .7 .8 .9 .10 .11 .12 .13	1
392	Grass Pond Mountain	★★★	W	2 hr 15 min / moderate boat required	.6 .7 .8 .9 .10 .11 .12 .13	6
397	Cat Mountain West Cliff		W	1 hr 40 min / moderate	.6 .7 .8 .9 .10 .11 .12 .13	1
398	Cat Mountain Summit Cliff	★★★	SW	1 hr 45 min / moderate	.6 .7 .8 .9 .10 .11 .12 .13	2
399	Cat Mountain Main Face		S	1 hr 45 min / moderate	.6 .7 .8 .9 .10 .11 .12 .13	3
399	Twin Falls Cliff	★★★	W	7 min / easy	.6 .7 .8 .9 .10 .11 .12 .13	8

LAKE LILA

Location	West shore of Lake Lila, accessed from NY 30 between Tupper Lake and Long Lake
Aspect	Southeast
Height	100'
Quality	★★★
Approach	1 hr 30 min, easy; canoe optional
Summary	Crack and face climbing in a wilderness setting.

```
  1     3        1    2                      7
-5.6  5.7  5.8  5.9  5.10  5.11  5.12  5.13+  total
```

The cliff is located on the southeast slopes of Frederica Mountain (formerly Smith Mountain), a hill that sits above the picturesque Lake Lila, the largest lake in the Adirondack Forest Preserve whose shoreline is completely state-owned. Although the center of the cliff is broken and overgrown, you can find attractive cracks through clean, featured rock at both ends.

A trip to Lake Lila is a package deal of canoeing and camping with a nice crag with a small number of excellent routes.

CAMPING

The shores of Lake Lila offer many camping possibilities, and some sites have sand beaches nearby. The most convenient is the lean-to (campsite #7) or any of the tenting sites just south. There is a freshwater spring near these sites, hidden back in the ferns.

ACCESS

Lake Lila and Mt Frederica are in the William C. Whitney Wilderness, purchased by the state in 1997, then designated a wilderness area in 2000. The north shore of Lake Lila (north of the old railroad tracks), which includes the cliff, is designated as the Nehasane Primitive Area. Unfortunately, no bikes are allowed on the trails. There is no parking on the Lake Lila Road, except at its end. Permits are required for camping more than three nights, and lakeside camping is allowed only at sites marked with "Camp Here" disks.

DIRECTIONS (MAP PAGE 387)

From Tupper Lake (where NY 3 and NY 30 split), drive on NY 30 toward Long Lake for 11.2 miles, then turn right on Sabattis Road (CR 10A). Follow this for 3.0 miles to a three-way intersection at the end of Little Tupper Lake. Turn right and drive 1.3 miles to the Little Tupper Lake Headquarters on the left.

From Long Lake (the intersection of NY 28N and NY 30), follow NY 30 toward Tupper Lake for 7.0 miles, then turn left on Sabattis Road (CR 10). Follow this for 2.9 miles to a three-way intersection at the end of Little Tupper Lake. Turn left and drive 1.3 miles to the Little Tupper Lake Headquarters on the left.

From the headquarters (0.0), continue on Sabattis Road. At 3.2 miles, turn left onto Lake Lila Road (aka Charlie Pond Road) and follow it to its end at 8.9 miles 521636,4873982. The last section is a dirt road that is slow going in good condition, suitable for all vehicles.

Hiking approach: From the parking area (0 hr 0 min), hike the continuation of the Lake Lila Road (gated), following blue markers; the going is flat and boring. The road reaches the lake at 1.5 miles, then continues along the shoreline with great views and reaches a lean-to at 1 hr 10 min (campsite #7), 3.2 miles from the parking area 518003,4872054. Be alert, as the lean-to is hidden from the trail, and the sign is easy to miss; the turnoff is

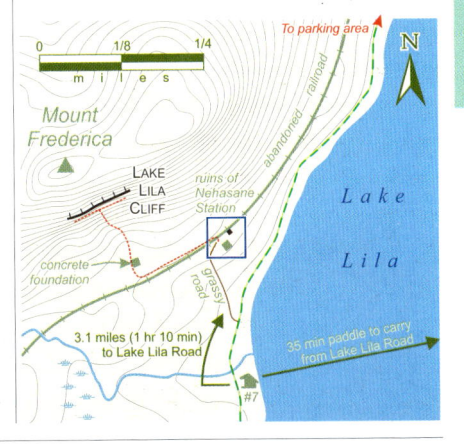

Cranberry Lake

just after you cross a small stream.

From the lean-to, backtrack 160 yards to a grassy road on the left. Follow this to the railroad tracks and two small, dilapidated buildings, reached at 1 hr 20 min. Turn left and follow the tracks for 280 yards to where the railroad goes through a trough and there is a clearing on the right; the top of the cliff is just visible above the trees. Cross the clearing past an old concrete foundation (watch for deep holes through the weeds) and hike up to the cliff, reached at 1 hr 30 min 517630,4872468.

Canoe approach: You can also reach the lean-to (campsite #7) by canoe. From the parking area (0 hr 0 min), do a carry following yellow markers for 0.3 mile to the put-in, reached at 15 min, then paddle west to the opposite end of the lake (about 3.0 miles, reached at 50 min) near the northernmost and tallest pine tree along the west shore. Paddle south along the shore and locate an inlet stream that is next to the lean-to at campsite #7 518003,4872054. Hike 50' up from the shore to reach the trail/road (marked with blue discs), then follow the hiking approach from there.

HISTORY

Not much is known about the history of climbing at this cliff, other than that Patrick Purcell climbed four routes in the mid-80s, two of which are documented here.

DESCENT OPTIONS

Rappel with a single 60-m rope from fixed anchors atop **The Island Marriage** and **Honeymoon in Yosemite**, or walk off either end of the cliff.

1 Road Less Traveled 5.5 PG 110' ★

Start: 150' right of the left end of the cliff at a waist-high rock spike, below a shallow 10'-tall right-facing corner and left of a black streak.

P1 5.5 PG: Climb the unprotected corner, then traverse left along a sloping ledge (small nuts). Up easy slabs to a left-facing corner (gear to the left) and climb it to a detached block. Up and left of the block to a vertical crack, then follow incut holds out right to another left-facing corner. Up the corner to a slab finish and a tree belay. 110'
FA Aug 11, 2007, Jeremy Haas, Erika Schielke

2 Pretty in Pink 5.9 G (5.1 R) 100' ★★★

Climbs the beautiful, clean, pink, pocketed face between the upper cracks of **Island Marriage** and **Honeymoon in Yosemite**. A one-move-wonder.
Start: 5' left of **Island Marriage** and 5' right of the waist-high rock spike of **Road Less Traveled**, below a tan streak with a bolt 12' up.
P1 5.9 G (5.1 R): Up the face to a bolt, then runout straight up (crossing **The Island Marriage**) past a shallow-open book to a large left-facing flake (gear). Continue up the clean pocketed face past a saucer-sized divot to its top. Runout to a fixed anchor. 100'
Gear: Nuts and cams to 0.5".
FA Sep 25, 2008, Tad Welch, Jim Lawyer

3 The Island Marriage 5.7 G 100' ★★

Start: 10' right of a waist-high rock spike of **Road Less Traveled**, at a right-arching fingercrack.
P1 5.7 G: (V1) Up the crack (crux) to a ledge. Step left (gear) and climb with ease to the bottom of a vertical crack 10' right of a prominent black streak. Follow the crack up a steep, featured wall to a slab finish and a fixed anchor on the right. 100'
V1 5.6 G: Begin as for **Pretty in Pink**, climb past the bolt, then slightly left to the base of the crack.
FA 1984, Patrick Purcell, Mary Purcell
FA (V1) Sep 25, 2008, Jim Lawyer, Tad Welch

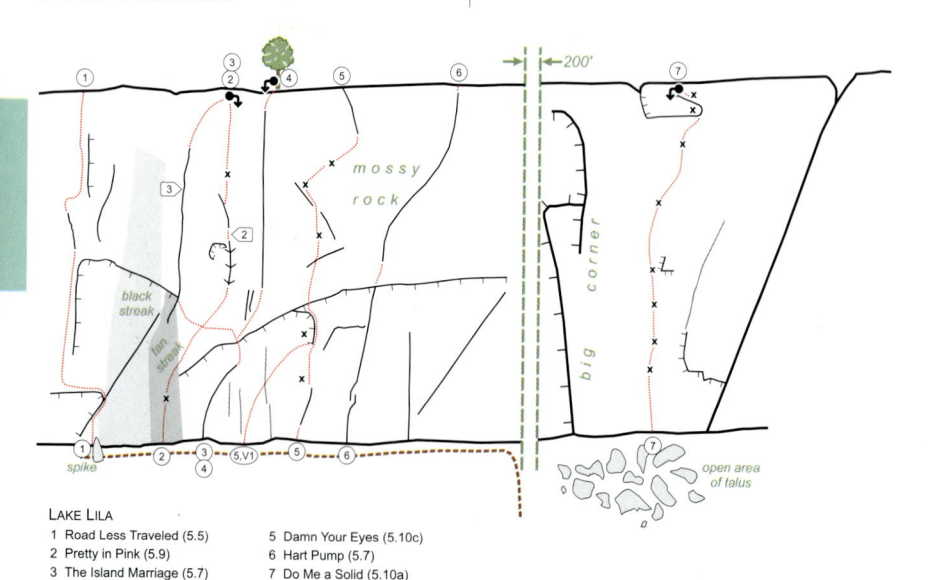

LAKE LILA
1 Road Less Traveled (5.5)
2 Pretty in Pink (5.9)
3 The Island Marriage (5.7)
4 Honeymoon in Yosemite (5.7)
5 Damn Your Eyes (5.10c)
6 Hart Pump (5.7)
7 Do Me a Solid (5.10a)

Cranberry Lake

4 Honeymoon in Yosemite
5.7 G 100' ★★★

A fabulous route that climbs clean, steep rock and a deep, parallel-sided crack.
Start: Same as **The Island Marriage**.
P1 5.7 G: Up the crack (crux) to a ledge. Step right and climb a continuous finger- and handcrack to a slab and belay at a shrub with a fixed anchor. 100'
FA 1984, Patrick Purcell, Mary Purcell

5 Damn Your Eyes
5.10c G 120' ★★★★

Climbs the face between the cracks **Honeymoon in Yosemite** and **Hart Pump**, featuring amazingly clean, pocketed rock, and two distinct, well-protected cruxes.
Start: 15' left of **Hart Pump**, at a seam in tan rock with a good finger-sized slot 7' up, and a bolt 15' up.
P1 5.10c G: Boulder up the seam (crux) to a good jug on a sloped shelf, then step right to a sharp right-facing corner. Layback up to a ledge, then straight up to a pink, pocketed face. Up the face (5.9+) to a stance, then traverse right to a beautiful fingercrack and follow it to the top. 120'
V1 5.3 G: To avoid the crux (and make the overall difficulty 5.9+), begin 15' uphill and left. Follow right-rising, sloping holds to the second bolt of the main route.
Gear: Nuts and cams to 0.5".
Descent: A 60m rope does not reach here, so walk 15' left and rappel from trees.
FA Sep 25, 2008, Jim Lawyer, Tad Welch
FA (V1) Sep 25, 2008, Tad Welch

6 Hart Pump 5.7 G 120' ★★★

Good, sustained, and continuous finger- and hand-crack climbing.
Start: At a handcrack that begins in the ground and shoots up out of view, and 10' left of another handcrack that begins at the ground and disappears 20' up.
P1 5.7 G: Up the handcrack to a ledge, then follow the crack as it angles right to the top. 120'
Descent: Walk (climber's) left and rappel from trees.
History: It is possible that this is one of the four "lost" Purcell routes. Who knows?
FA Sep 15, 1998, Joe Bridges, Barbara Hart

7 Do Me a Solid
5.10a G 110' ★★★★★

Excellent climbing in a remote and scenic location. This route alone is worth the hike/paddle. The rock is extremely compact on this face, but immaculately clean and littered with hidden incuts. Other lines have been toproped on this face.
Start: Uphill and right from the center (or low point) of the cliff is a beautiful, clean, black face, bordered on the left by a broken right-facing corner that runs the height of the cliff, and on the right by a prominent, right-leaning, grass-filled crack. There's a clearing at the base of the wall, an obvious bombardment zone from falling ice. Begin in the center of the face.
● **P1 5.10a G:** Easy climbing leads to the first bolt at 25'. Pull through a steep section at mid-height, then work up and right to a steep headwall. Up through the headwall on a hidden flake and good edges to a fixed anchor. 110'
Descent: Carefully lower with a 60m rope, which just makes it with some down-scrambling.
FA May 11, 2008, Jim Lawyer, Leslie Ackerman, Michelle Burlitch

The approach hike offers excellent views of Lake Lila.

*Tad Welch on the first ascent of **Pretty in Pink** (5.9+).*

Cranberry Lake

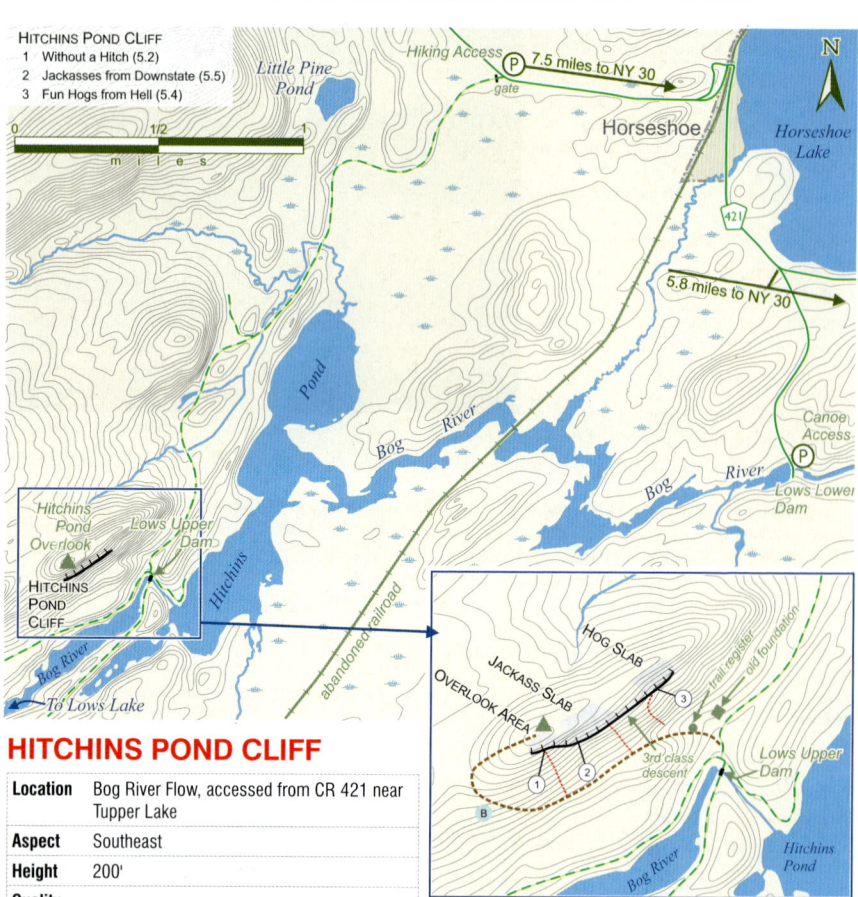

HITCHINS POND CLIFF
1 Without a Hitch (5.2)
2 Jackasses from Downstate (5.5)
3 Fun Hogs from Hell (5.4)

HITCHINS POND CLIFF

Location	Bog River Flow, accessed from CR 421 near Tupper Lake
Aspect	Southeast
Height	200'
Quality	
Approach	1 hr, easy; canoe optional
Summary	Clean, easy slabs that are accessed by an excellent paddle and a short hike.

3								3
-5.6	5.7	5.8	5.9	5.10	5.11	5.12	5.13+	total

Visible above the Bog River Flow, a popular canoe route to Lows Lake, is a series of slabs beneath the rocky ridge of Hitchins Pond Overlook. A maintained trail to the overlook, and access to the slabs, begins at Lows Upper Dam, which is just above Hitchins Pond. The right end of the cliff has clean slabs that are mostly 3rd- and 4th-class, with **Fun Hogs from Hell** ascending a short stretch of 5th-class rock to the far right. Steeper rock, beneath the top of the Overlook Trail, can be found at the left end of the cliff, but it is dirty and undeveloped. The hike (or bike) is along a flat road; however, this is canoe country, and the paddle approach along the Bog River passes through bogs and boreal forests and offers the chance of seeing loons on Hitchins Pond.

DIRECTIONS (MAP PAGE 390)
Begin at the intersection of CR 421 and NY 30 between Tupper Lake and Long Lake. From Tupper Lake (where NY 3 and NY 30 split), drive on NY 30 toward Long Lake for 8.4 miles, then turn right on CR 421. From Long Lake (the intersection of NY 28N and NY 30), follow NY 30 toward Tupper Lake for 13.0 miles, then turn left on CR 421.

Canoe Approach: From the beginning of CR 421 (0.0 mile), drive to the end of the pavement at 5.8 miles, then turn left on a dirt road and follow it to Lows Lower Dam canoe access at 6.5 miles.

From the put-in at Lows Lower Dam, paddle upstream along the winding Bog River for 3 miles (40 min) to Hitchins Pond. Paddle south across the pond to the inlet brook and follow it to the base of Lows Upper Dam and a portage. From the road that crosses the top of the dam, hike right (north) and uphill, past a clearing with an old foundation, for 200' to the trailhead and register for Hitchins Pond Overlook.

Hiking Approach From the beginning of CR 421 (0.0 mile), drive to the end of the pavement at 5.8 miles, then

Cranberry Lake

to a gated road on the left at 7.5 miles 528291,4886840. There is no sign or blazes to suggest that the road is the trail to Hitchins Pond.

Hike south along the flat road to its intersection with the dirt road that crosses over Upper Lows Dam (2.6 miles, 40 min). Hike right (north) and uphill, past a clearing with an old foundation, for 200' to the trailhead and register for Hitchins Pond Overlook.

HISTORY
The area is the result of yet another exploration by Jim Vermeulen, who, armed with Barbara McMartin's Discover the Adirondacks books, explored many remote cliffs in the park. On the approach, you pass numerous foundations; the Lows Upper Dam was the site of a maple-sugaring and timber facility, belonging to Augustus Low, which was destroyed by fires in 1911.

Overlook Area

DIRECTIONS (MAP PAGE 390)
From the register, follow the trail marked with blue discs uphill and south. At 20 min, the trail ends at an overlook at the top of the Jackass Slab.

1 Without a Hitch 5.2 G 35' ★
An easy climb in a spectacular setting below where the trail emerges at the overlook.
Start: Approach from the top: where the trail meets the cliff, scramble down ramped ledges to the (skiers) right (3rd class). Begin below a fingercrack at a flat slab backed by trees.
P1 5.2 G: Climb the fingercrack straight to the overlook above. 35'
FA Sep 1, 2008, Daniel Mosny, Kate Mosny

View from Hitchins Pond Cliff. Photo by Barb Schielke.

Jackass Slab

DIRECTIONS (MAP PAGE 390)
From the register, follow the trail marked with blue discs uphill and south. At 8 min, you reach open woods with fern-covered slopes. Bushwhack uphill and right (north), and, at 16 min, you arrive at the cliff near its center. Go left along the base to its left end and beneath a tree-covered ledge 80' up 525989,4884204.

DESCENT OPTIONS
Hike down and (climber's) left of **Without a Hitch**, through trees and ledges, to the start of the route.

2 Jackasses from Downstate 5.5 R 200'
This route was inadvertently climbed when one of the guidebook authors was trying to find **Fun Hogs from Hell**. The clean rock that is above the start, and left of the tree-covered ledge, would be a nice toprope route.
Start: Beneath the left end of the tree-covered ledge at an 8'-tall right-facing flake.
P1 5.4 PG: Up a dirty slab to a sloping ledge beneath a 6'-tall overlap. Break the overlap at a left-facing flake, then up dirty rock to the tree-covered ledge. Traverse the ledge toward its right end. 100'
P2 5.5 R: Up and right to a right-facing detached flake (last protection for the crux). Up past the flake and bulges to a long reach (crux) to a horizontal crack. Traverse left along the crack, then up past an overlap to a belay at the hiking trail where it crosses a narrow rocky ridge. 100'
FA Aug 12, 2007, Jeremy Haas, Erika Schielke

Hog Slab

DIRECTIONS (MAP PAGE 390)
From the register, follow the trail marked with blue discs for 50', then leave the trail and cross a streambed on the right. Hike 100' uphill (north) to a herd path, then follow it up and left to open slabs at 10 min 526187,4884294. The highest rock that is visible up and right is the top of **Fun Hogs from Hell**. Traverse right (east) for 300' and stay in the woods beneath the open slabs.

DESCENT OPTIONS
Traverse left (west) along the rocky ridgeline to its low point and descend the open slabs (3rd-class) to the herd path.

3 Fun Hogs from Hell 5.4 R 200' ★
An exploratory climb that was part of a wilderness canoe trip.
Start: At a short, steep wall at the right end of the slab.
P1 5.4 R: Up the steep slab (crux; no protection) to a vertical seam in a broad slab. Climb the seam to a belay in a left-rising tree-covered ramp. 120'
P2 5.1 G: Traverse the ramp down and right to a crack in a right-facing corner, then climb the crack to the top. 80'
FA Oct, 1990, Jim Vermeulen, Bill Morris, Willard Moulton

Cranberry Lake

SOUTH BAY ROADCUT

Location	On NY 3, at the south end of Tupper Lake
Aspect	Northwest
Height	70'
Quality	
Approach	0 min, easy
Summary	A roadcut with a single bolted route and easy toproping.

This cliff, which rises above the road next to the shore of Tupper Lake, is a roadcut, meaning that the cliff has been drilled and blasted to make the road. If you don't mind the traffic and vertical grooves left over from blasting holes, then this cliff is for you.

The cliff can be used for toproping. There is a good trail on the right end of the cliff, and there are large trees set back from the edge of the cliff.

HISTORY
This cliff has long been used for toproping by Boy Scout camps on Long Lake. The single lead route, **The Last Tupper**, is of unknown origin.

ACCESS
The cliff is next to the road but, according to one state trooper, far enough away to be legal.

DIRECTIONS
From Tupper Lake (where NY 3 and NY 30 split), drive on NY 30 toward Long Lake for 8.3 miles to a large parking area on the right; there is a historic sign here, and it's right next to the lake. The cliff is across the road 537012,4885935.

From Long Lake (at the intersection of NY 28N and NY 30), follow NY 30 toward Tupper Lake for 13.5 miles to the parking area on the left.

DESCENT OPTIONS
Walk right.

1 The Last Tupper 5.8 G 70' ★★
This is a good route, perhaps as good as roadcut climbing can be. A high-angle face route that climbs natural features of the rock. The old 0.25" bolts are unsafe (one snapped off by hand, and one has no hanger).
Start: At the highest point of the cliff below the left side of a rib of rock, at a shallow 4'-high right-facing corner.
P1 5.8 G: Climb past two bolts on the left side of the rib to its top. Trend right following four more bolts to the top. 70'

GRASS POND MOUNTAIN

Location	North shore of Lows Lake, accessed from Cranberry Lake or from CR 421 near Tupper Lake
Aspect	West
Height	120'
Quality	★★★
Approach	2 hr 15 min, moderate; boat required
Summary	An undeveloped cliff with amazing potential in an extremely remote wilderness setting.

	3	2	1			6
-5.6	5.7	5.8	5.9	5.10	5.11	5.12	5.13+	total

This cliff is a real gem and one of the more remote cliffs in the Adirondack Park. The existing routes are located on the shorter, less imposing right end; so far, no routes have been done on the good-looking overhanging faces of the main cliff. The established climbs are short, but they're all pretty good.

The left (north) end of the cliff has two bands (a

The cliff on Grass Pond Mountain. The established climbs are on the right end, in the trees. Photo by Simeon Warner.

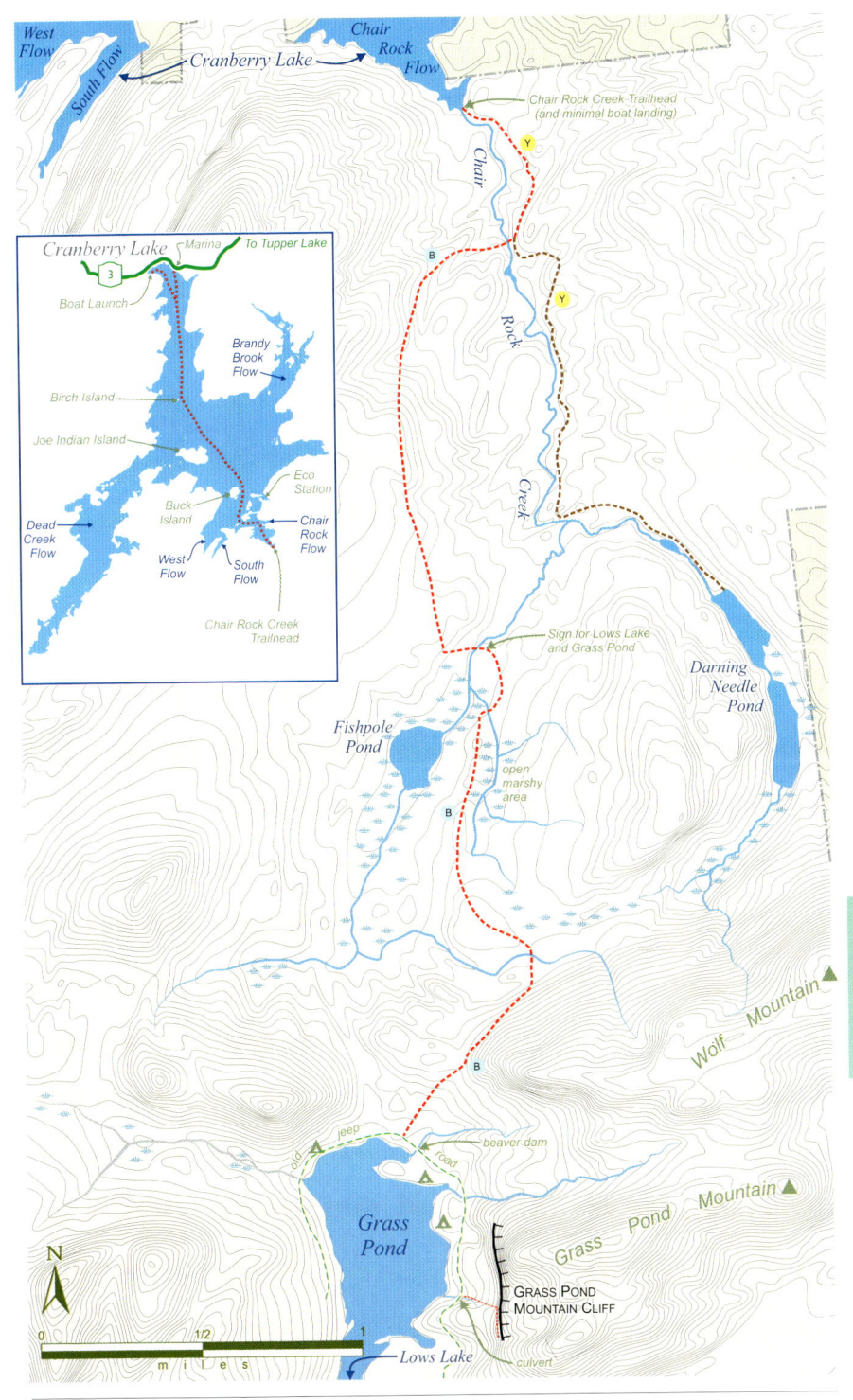

Cranberry Lake

Cranberry Lake

lower and an upper), both of which are dirty but offer several obvious possibilities. The main cliff is steep and relatively clean (quite clean in some spots) and stretches about 0.25 mile. It is consistently 80–120' high. There is good potential for new rock routes here, mostly 5.8 and above, on steep to overhanging rock.

The trail reaches the cliff near a 20'-tall pointed orange tower of rock known as Leaning Tower. Just right of the tower is a section of overhanging orange rock. To reach the existing routes, walk right from Leaning Tower past a low nose of rock to a giant flake that leans up against the cliff and forms a cave. This flake is the landmark for locating the routes.

HISTORY

The cliff was first reported by Jamie Savage, a teacher at the Ranger School in Wanakena, and Tad Welch. During their first visit, they found evidence of previous climbers on **Lost Horizon** and **Lunatic Hares**, perhaps from nearby Boy Scout groups' toproping. The cliff and the ice caves in the talus seem to be a popular destination for Boy Scouts in the Sabattis area.

DIRECTIONS (MAP PAGE 393)

The shortest way to this cliff is to boat 6 miles to the southeast end of Cranberry Lake, then hike 4 miles or so to the cliff.

Start in the town of Cranberry Lake 513048,4896520. The easiest way across the lake is by motorboat, as Cranberry Lake is very large, and the open-water sections can be quite windy and rough. There is a public boat launch in town: from the center of town, go 1.1 miles east on NY 3 and turn left onto Colombian Road; the boat launch is 0.4 mile on the left. The Emporium Marina (315.848.2140) runs a water taxi and rents kicker boats ($60.00 per day in 2007). Either way, from town, aim for the left side of Birch Island, then the left side of Joe Indian Island, then the left side of Buck Island. Continue past Buck Island heading toward a remote grouping of lake houses. Bear left into Chair Rock Flow and follow it as it winds its way around a point and through a minefield of submerged stumps. At the very end of the flow is a trailhead, just left of where Chair Rock Creek drains into the lake 516340,4887491. It takes 40 min to reach the trailhead from town, assuming you don't get lost in the maze of false bays and islands.

From the landing (0 hr 0 min), hike the yellow trail that follows the left side of Chair Rock Creek. At 4 min, an unexplained blue-marked trail merges from the left; stay straight on the yellow trail. At 11 min, the trail forks; the left fork (yellow markers) goes to Darning Needle Pond. Take the right fork (marked with blue markers and yellow "canoe carry" markers) for Grass Pond and cross Chair Rock Creek. (Note that the mileages on the signs are very wrong.) At 40 min, cross a stream with a sign for Grass Pond but no intersection. At 45 min, the trail reaches a marshy area on the left (with Fishpole Pond barely visible through the trees to the right) and continues along its side. At 1 hr 15 min, the trail hits a T-intersection with the old jeep road that circles Grass Pond, a large pinched-off bay on the north side of Lows Lake.

From the T-intersection, you can walk right for 5 min to the end of the blue-marked trail. Continue on the jeep road for 2 min to a beautiful campsite (#32) 515647,4882483 with views of the cliff, a sandy beach, and an outhouse.

From the T-intersection, turn left and walk across a beaver dam, then follow the old jeep road as it rings the pond. At 1 hr 27 min, the jeep road crosses a large culvert that drains an obvious creekbed (dry in the summer). (This is the second culvert; you'll also pass a smaller, somewhat hidden culvert that drains a wet area.) Just before the creek is an excellent herd path marked with tape and a cairn that heads up to the cliff at 1 hr 35 min. The trail meets the cliff just right of the aptly named Leaning Tower, a 20'-high orange feature in the talus 516452,4881730.

The herd path is maintained by a local Boy Scout group and leads to "ice caves," holes in the talus slope beneath the cliff that hold ice throughout the year.

Alternate Approach: Begin at the intersection of CR 421 and NY 30 between Tupper Lake and Long Lake. From Tupper Lake (where NY 3 and NY 30 split), drive on NY 30 toward Long Lake for 8.4 miles, then turn right on CR 421. From Long Lake (the intersection of NY 28N and NY 30), follow NY 30 toward Tupper Lake for 13.0 miles, then turn left on CR 421.

From the beginning of CR 421 (0.0 mile), drive to the end of the pavement at 5.8 miles, then turn left on a dirt road and follow it to Lows Lower Dam canoe access at 6.5 miles.

From the put-in at Lows Lower Dam, paddle upstream along the winding Bog River for 3 miles (40 min) to Hitchins Pond. Paddle south (left) across the pond to the inlet brook and follow it to the base of Lows Upper Dam and a portage. (The Hitchins Pond Cliff, page 390, is up and right.) Carry over the dam and continue on the Bog River to Lows Lake. Paddle along the north shore, around a large point, then north into Grass Pond, the pinched-off bay to the north. This is a long paddle (about 14 miles), requiring about half a day.

1 Lost Horizon 5.8 G 50' ★★★

Sustained crack climbing.

Start: At the right end of the cliff is a giant flake that leans up against the cliff forming a cave, below a long sharp-edged ceiling 30' up. 10' right of the flake is a roof 15' up. This route begins 3' right of the right end of the roof, at an obvious straight-up crack.

P1 5.8 G: Up the crack through a flared section to a V-slot below a tiny triangular ceiling. Climb out right to a ledge, then step left and climb up to the top. Walk right to a pine tree. 50'
FA Sep, 2006, Tad Welch, Jamie Savage

2 Take the Power Back 5.9 G 50' ★★

An unlikely start is made easier by hidden incut buckets. Named for a Rage Against the Machine song.

Start: 6' right of **Lost Horizon** is a right-facing corner that sits below a shallow right-facing open book that begins 15' up.

P1 5.9 G: Climb the corner through some bulges on good incut buckets to a stance below the open book.

Cranberry Lake

Up the open book to a ledge (crux). Move left and join **Lost Horizon** to the top; walk right to a pine tree. 50'
Gear: To 0.75", including small TCUs.
FA Jul 16, 2007, Jim Lawyer, Colin O'Connor

3 The Dharma Initiative 5.9+ G 50' ★★★

Good climbing through the roof. The route is named for a fictional research project in the television series *Lost*.
Start: Right of **Take the Power Back** and above some blocks is a large box-shaped alcove formed by large opposing corners 10' apart and capped by a large roof 30' up. This route begins in the left-facing corner that forms the right side of the box-shaped alcove.
P1 5.9+ G: Up a chimney up to the roof, then out right (crux) and into the shallow left-facing corner above. Work up the corner to the top and a good pine tree anchor. 50'
Gear: To 2".
FA Jul 16, 2007, Jim Lawyer, Colin O'Connor

4 Dirtbag Dharma 5.10b G 40' ★★★

This route climbs the crack in the face just right of the box-shaped alcove of **The Dharma Initiative**. Awkward jamming with poor feet.
Start: On the high blocks on the right side of the box-shaped alcove of **The Dharma Initiative**.
P1 5.10b G: Step right from the alcove on a narrow ledge 15' above the ground to the base of a crack. Up the hand- and fingercrack to a tree at the top. 40'
FA Sep, 2006, Jamie Savage, Tad Welch

5 Pema 5.8- G 40' ★

Start: 20' right of the box-shaped alcove of **The Dharma Initiative** is a low roof that you can walk under. Just right is a large right-facing corner. Begin at a handcrack in a large inside corner below the arête of the larger right-facing corner.
P1 5.8- G: Up the handcrack, moving right onto the left wall of the large right-facing corner. Up the crack past a pointed flake to the top. 40'
FA Sep, 2006, Tad Welch, Jamie Savage

6 Lunatic Hares 5.8- G 40' ★★

Start: At the right end of the cliff is a large right-facing corner with cracks on the right wall. The left wall of the corner has a 2'-wide chimney with a chockstone at its top. Begin 5' right of the corner at parallel cracks.
P1 5.8- G: Up the parallel cracks to where they meet at a birch tree, then up a left-leaning wide crack to a ledge. (V1, V2) Step right to a right-facing corner, which is climbed to the top. Step left to a large pine. 40'
V1 5.10a G: Starting at a hand slot, climb a left-leaning fingercrack through a steep face to the tree.
V2 5.9 G: Step left to the large orange corner, which is climbed to the top.
FA Sep, 2006, Jamie Savage, Tad Welch
FA (V1, V2) Sep, 2006, Tad Welch, Jamie Savage

*Tad Welch on the first ascent of **Lost Horizon** (5.8). Photo by Jamie Savage.*

CAT MOUNTAIN

Location	Five Ponds Wilderness Area, accessed from NY 3 near Wanakena
Summary	An isolated and remote summit with several good higher-end crack climbs and some exploratory routes on cliffs with good potential.

-5.6	5.7	5.8	5.9	5.10	5.11	5.12	5.13+	total
	2		1	1	2			6

Cat Mountain is a very isolated bump that rises above rolling forests, ponds, and swamps deep in the Five Ponds Wilderness Area south of Cranberry Lake. There are only a few established climbs, but the area has excellent potential for more. There are three separate cliffs on the mountain: the Summit Cliff, the West Cliff, and the Main Face.

The approach to Cat Mountain is long, but easy because it's nearly flat. The first section (2.8 miles) follows an old railroad grade through a swamp and is notoriously buggy. Recent beaver activity has flooded several sections, which can easily be waded through. An alternative that avoids this first leg is to use a boat, launching at the public boat launch in Cranberry Lake and landing at Janacks Landing at the end of the Dead Creek Flow. A short 0.2-mile connector is used to reach the first junction described below.

In comparison with the approach, the cliff is breezy and relatively bug free. The views are excellent.

CAMPING

There's a beautiful campsite right off the trail on the Dead Creek Flow 508318,4884591, a lean-to at Janacks Landing, and a campsite along the trail at Glasby Pond 509408,4882908. A final option is on the summit of Cat Mountain: walk east along the summit ledges to a large, round boulder, then walk 30' into the woods to a beautiful grassy site with a fire ring (no water).

HISTORY

Cat Mountain was first explored in the late 1970s by Bill Widrig and Tad Welch. Widrig's family has a camp on Cranberry Lake and thus a familiarity with the Five Ponds Wilderness. This led Widrig and Welch to explore the cliff, where they toproped several routes and aided Catatonic. Since then, Jamie Savage and various partners from the Ranger School in Wanakena have visited the cliff and explored the lower cliff, making an attempt on a route there. Research for this book focused on free-climbing Catatonic, which was freed by Will Mayo in the fall of 2007.

DIRECTIONS (MAP PAGE 396)

Parking is at the Dead Creek Flow Trailhead in Wanakena. From Tupper Lake (where NY 30 and NY 3 split), drive west on NY 3 for 32.9 miles (or 7.7 miles west of Cranberry Lake) to Wanakena Road (CR 61).

The road is marked with a large sign for the Ranger School (0.0). At 0.8 mile go right at the fork onto Main Street. At 1.1 miles there's a traffic triangle; there is a trailhead at this intersection for the Moore Trail. Go straight onto South Shore Road and cross a bridge. At 1.2 miles there is a trailhead for High Falls on the right (this doesn't lead to Cat Mountain); continue straight past the tennis courts to the Dead Creek Flow Trailhead at 1.6 miles on the right. There is a dirt pullout here, but the DEC sign is hidden in the woods up some wood steps 506778,4886677.

The approach to Cat Mountain is 5.6 miles each way and mostly flat. From the trailhead, hike the red-marked Dead Creek Flow Trail along an old railroad bed (and directly through a swamp) and, at 32 min, reach two campsites on the left 508318,4884591 on the shore of Dead Creek

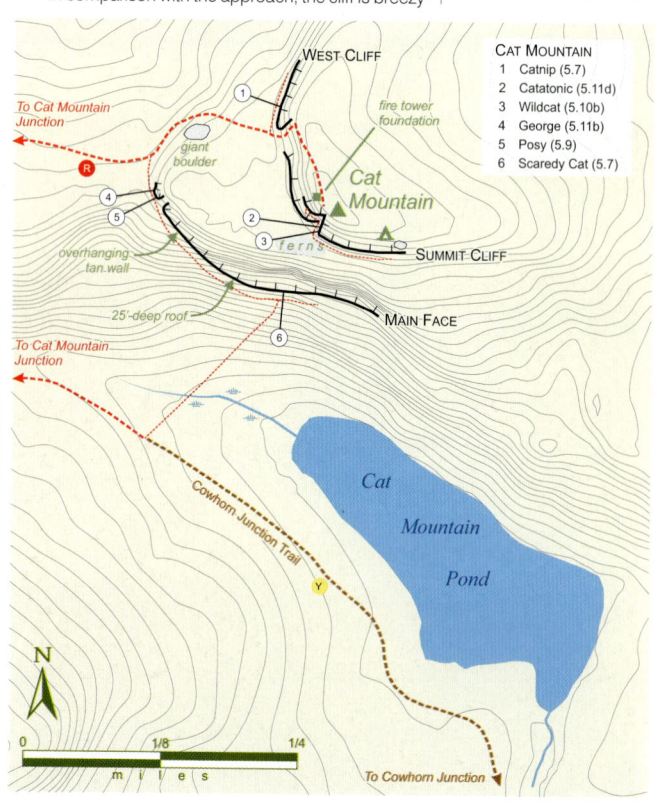

CAT MOUNTAIN
1. Catnip (5.7)
2. Catatonic (5.11d)
3. Wildcat (5.10b)
4. George (5.11b)
5. Posy (5.9)
6. Scaredy Cat (5.7)

Cranberry Lake

Flow (a deep bay of Cranberry Lake). At 50 min, you reach the first junction with the trail from Janacks Landing. Continue on the red-marked trail for Cat Mountain, now going gently uphill. At 1 hr 6 min, you reach Sand Hill Junction—the intersection with the trail to High Falls. Continue on the yellow-marked trail for Cat Mountain; this section of trail is shared with the "Cranberry Lake 50", a 50-mile long trail that circumnavigates Cranberry Lake, and uses distinctive blue "50" markers. At 1 hr 13 min, you reach Glasby Pond on the left and a second camp site on the shore of the lake 509408,4882908. (You can see cliffs on the hill across the lake; they look interesting, but are not the Cat Mountain cliffs.) At 1 hr 24 min, you reach Cat Mountain Junction—the intersection with the Cowhorn Junction Trail. Directions to the three cliffs are provided from this junction.

Cat Mountain
WEST CLIFF

Aspect	West
Height	70'
Quality	
Approach	1 hr 40 min, moderate
Summary	Broken cliff next to the trail with good potential for routes.

The cliff ranges between 40'–70' tall and a few hundred feet wide, with some potential for more routes. West Cliff is a continuation of the Summit Cliff, but separated by a wide broken section where the hiking trail is located.

DIRECTIONS (MAP PAGE 396)
From the Cat Mountain Junction, follow the red-marked trail towards the summit of Cat Mountain. The trail climbs, levels, climbs again (there's a giant boulder on the right), then levels. At the end of this level section, and just before the final steep rise to the summit, you'll pass the right end of this cliff 510742,4883114. This is 3 min before the summit of Cat Mountain, and 2 minutes above the giant boulder.

The hiking trail goes up the right side of the cliff to its top, then makes a sharp right turn towards the summit. A small herd path goes to a viewpoint on top of West Cliff.

1 Catnip 5.7 G 70'
Start: 80' left of the hiking trail at a right-facing open book that leads to a 2"-deep triangular ceiling 15' up. Up and left of this ceiling is a giant, triangular perched flake. The left side of the open book extends down to a slabby tongue in the woods.
P1 5.7 G: Go up the S-crack in the right-facing open book to the triangular ceiling. Go past the ceiling on the left, and up a wide crack formed by the right side of the triangular flake. At the top of the flake, step left to an unpleasant offwidth; follow this to a treed ledge below a slab. Avoid the slab by tree-pulling to the top. 70'
Descent: Walk up, then right to join the hiking trail. Follow this back around the right end of the cliff.
Gear: Large cams helpful.
FA May 7, 2011, Simon Thompson, Ben Botelho

*Colin O'Connor at the start of **Catatonic** (5.11d).*

Cranberry Lake

Cat Mountain
SUMMIT CLIFF

Aspect	Southwest
Height	70'
Quality	★★★
Approach	1 hr 45 min, moderate
Summary	Steep cliff directly below the open, flat summit with one excellent crack and potential for more.

			1	1		2
-5.6	5.7	5.8	5.9	5.10	5.11	5.12	5.13+	total

This is the cliff on the actual summit of Cat Mountain. Routes can be toproped (cams to 2" for an anchor). The rock is clean, the climbing is hard, and the views and ambiance are superb. There's good potential for additional routes.

The Summit Cliff has two beautiful open, flat viewpoints. The first viewpoint has concrete mounts of an old fire tower as well as some solar-powered equipment. The second viewpoint is larger, flat, and separated from the first viewpoint by a deep cleft. The entire cliff faces roughly southwest, but the established climbing is on the west-facing wall of the second viewpoint. The upper section of the Catatonic crack is clearly visible from the first viewpoint. To reach the climbs, scramble down slabs and ledges below the old fire tower, aiming for the cleft separating the two viewpoints.

DIRECTIONS (MAP PAGE 396)
From Cat Mountain Junction, continue on the red-marked trail to Cat Mountain, now uphill. At 1 hr 45 min (21 min from Cat Mountain Junction), you reach the summit of Cat Mountain 510811,4883012.

2 Catatonic 5.11d G 70' ★★★★★
The Supercrack of the Adirondacks—the best and most continuously demanding fingercrack in the Adirondacks, perhaps more at home at Indian Creek. It's better than it looks from the old fire tower, as the lower half is obscured by trees. The crack is mostly clean, but there are some friable edges on the left wall that will clean up with a few more ascents.
Start: Scramble down to the base of the wall below the cleft that separates the two summit viewpoints. The route begins below the obvious overhanging fingercrack and a triangular block 5' up.
P1 5.11d G: Climb into a shallow pod above the triangular block, then up the unrelenting off fingers to a tight-hands crack to the summit. 70'
Gear: 4 ea 1", 1.25"; 2 ea 1.5"; 1 ea 1.75".
FA (A1) Sep 2, 1978, Tad Welch, Bill Widrig
FFA Oct 9, 2007, Will Mayo, Katy Klutznick

3 Wildcat 5.10b G 30' ★★
Start: 12' right of Catatonic at a V-groove that leads to a stem box.
P1 5.10b G: Climb the tips crack in the back of the V-groove to the right-facing corner, then up the handcrack to the top at a ledge with pine trees. 30'
FA Jul 23, 2007, Jim Lawyer, Colin O'Connor

Cat Mountain
MAIN FACE

Aspect	South
Height	150'
Quality	
Approach	1 hr 45 min, moderate
Summary	Rather large, steep cliff above Cat Mountain Pond with good potential for new routes.

	1		1		1			3
-5.6	5.7	5.8	5.9	5.10	5.11	5.12	5.13+	total

This cliff 510716,4882920 sits below the Summit Cliff and above Cat Mountain Pond. The cliff has seen little exploration, but has excellent potential for new routes. It's larger than the other cliffs—roughly 150' high at its highest, and 0.25 mile wide—and has amazing features. On the left is a tan-colored overhanging wall with a narrow ledge along the base. In the middle is a 25'-deep roof 60' up, right of which is a large left-facing corner, the left wall of which is a slab. Right of this is a tall amphitheater (the location of **Scaredy Cat**).

DIRECTIONS (MAP PAGE 396)

It's possible to approach from Cat Mountain Pond. From Cat Mountain Junction, follow the yellow-marked Cowhorn Junction Trail for 20 minutes (this section is also marked with blue "50' markers). Before you reach Cat Mountain Pond, leave the trail on the left 510557,4882715 on a bearing of 28°. Cross a stream and wet area, then continue uphill to reach the cliff on its right end near **Scaredy Cat**.

A faster approach is from the Cat Mountain trail. From Cat Mountain Junction, follow the red-marked trail toward Cat Mountain. After the first uphill section, the trail levels, then begins to climb again. Watch for a large boulder on the right; once you find it, backtrack 300' on the trail to the level section, then leave the trail and walk south. Immediately you'll encounter rocky terrain on your left. Follow along the base of this as it bends towards the east and becomes a substantial cliff. The first landmark is a stand-alone lump of rock, the Molar, with a couple topropes. Right of this is the main wall proper 510599,4882968.

The Molar

This is a stand-alone lump of rock on the left end, separated from the Main Face by a broad tree-covered slope. There are some scattered remains of the old firetower at the top 510584,4883021.

4 George 5.11b TR 50' ★★

Begin on the left side of the face, 25' left of **Posy**, and climb the overhanging wall using a staircase of slopers. Go past a triangular slot, then up the face to the top.
FA (TR) Oct 4, 2013, Jim Lawyer

5 Posy 5.9 TR 50' ★★

Begin on the right side of the wall, just left of the broad tree slope that separates The Molar from the Main Face,

Opposite: **Catatonic** *(5.11d). Yes, it's really that good.*

at a 10'-high overhanging finger- and handcrack. Go up the crack to a good stance. Move right to a ledge, then left up flakes to a razor-thin crack in a scooped slab. Up this past a good jug to the top.
FA (TR) Oct 4, 2013, Jim Lawyer, Tad Welch

End of The Molar

6 Scaredy Cat 5.7 G 50'

Start: On the right end of the cliff (and approximately 300' right of a 25'-deep roof 60' up) is a steep, tall wall above an open fern-covered slope. High up there are multi-tiered roofs on the right, and a pointed triangular roof on the left. Along the bottom, and centered in the amphitheater, is a short left-facing corner, the upper part of which is formed by a triangular, black block. From the top of this corner is a distinctive low-angle, right-rising, sharp-edged, light-colored flake. Walk left 20' and scramble onto a ledge, then move right to the left-facing corner formed by the block, about 15' above the ground.

P1 5.7 G: Work up the corner and follow the right-rising, sharp-edged flake to its top, then up and right into a giant open book. Traverse right around a corner to a ledge with a fixed anchor. 50'

Gear: Standard rack with many long runners.
FA May 7, 2011, Simon Thompson, Ben Botelho

TWIN FALLS CLIFF

Location	Accessed from the west end of Tooley Pond Road, near Twin Falls
Aspect	West
Height	50'
Quality	★★★
Approach	7 min, easy
Summary	Small cliff with easy approach and one exceptional crack.

2		1		2		1	2		8
-5.6	5.7	5.8	5.9	5.10	5.11	5.12	5.13+	total

This small, vertical cliff is about 50' high and 150' wide, has excellent rock, and is laced with thin vertical seams and cracks. It's in a pretty location, rising abruptly from an otherwise flat hardwood forest, with a flat, open cliff base and several fire rings. Along with South Colton, this cliff is a great destination for climbers living north of the park.

ACCESS

This cliff is on the Santa Clara Tract, which is open year round to the public.

CAMPING

There are many places along Tooley Pond Road to camp, including several pullouts near Twin Falls and the trailhead to Allen Pond (this is 0.9 mile east of Twin Falls, on the north side of the road, at an open yellow gate marked with #4 on the gate post; drive 0.4 mile to the end of this road.)

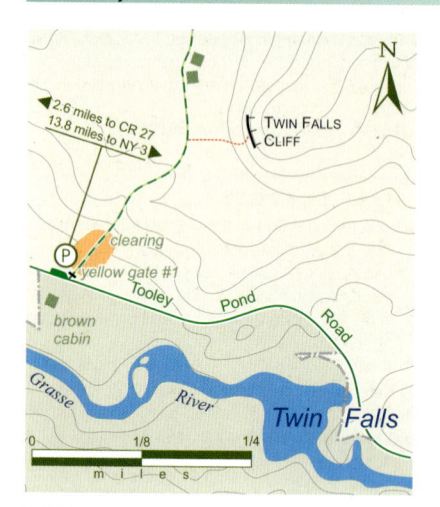

Cranberry Lake

DIRECTIONS (MAP PAGE 400)

The cliff is located near the west end of Tooley Pond Road, which goes from NY 3 in Cranberry Lake northwest to Degrasse.

From the east, from the post office in the center of Cranberry Lake (0.0), drive west on NY 3 for 0.9 mile, then turn right onto Tooley Pond Road. This road is paved for a while, then turns to dirt, then back to pavement. At 14.7 miles you reach Twin Falls on the left (Twin Falls is unmarked, but the Grasse River is very near the road and plunges down an obvious waterfall. At 15.1 miles you reach a logging road on the right (the second logging road on the right after Twin Falls) with a yellow gate and #1 painted on the gate post 0497438,4909104.

From the west, from the intersection of CR 27 and Tooley Pond Road in Degrasse (0.0 mile), go east on Tooley Pond Road. At 1.9 miles you reach Lake George Road on the right. At 2.6 miles you reach a logging road on the left with a yellow gate and #1 painted on the gate post 0497438,4909104.

The correct logging road is directly across from a hidden brown cabin set back 100' from the road. There is a grassy clearing on the other side of the yellow gate, and the logging road is visible going up a steep hill. Plenty of parking is available on the wide shoulders; make sure not to block the cabin or logging road.

From the parking (0 hr 0 min), walk up the logging road and, at 5 min, the road levels out and there is a clearing on the right. Walk 150' further, then turn right (small cairn here, 0497669,4909372) and walk straight east to reach the cliff at 7 min 0497767,4909345. Due to the foliage, the cliff remains hidden until you are very close.

1 Jake's Route 5.8 G 75' ★★

One of the better routes here, as it goes to the top of a second tier of rock. The route is 5.6, excluding the 5.8 opening moves. Great views of Twin Falls from the top.
Start: At the left end of the cliff at the base of a large, left-facing, left-leaning open book with a good crack.

P1 5.8 G: Go up the crack for 25' (crux) to its top. Step back right over the top of the crack to a small ledge with a birch, then go straight up the rounded buttress past several horizontals to the top. 75'
FA Apr, 2010, Jake Colony, Grant Watkins

2 The Afternoon Matinee 5.10c G 40' ★★

Start: 15' left of a snaking V-groove that begins 12' up, 45' left of **Elusive Bastard**, at a right-leaning seam that begins at the ground.
P1 5.10c G: Go up the fingertip crack (crux) to a horizontal with great, thank-god jugs. Go up the easier handcrack to a mantel finish. Belay off small trees. 40'
Gear: To 2".
FA Apr, 2011, Conor Cliffe

3 Bugged Out 5.12a G 55' ★★

Not a pretty climb, but great moves. It overhangs 5'. Named for the "shitty black flies that day."
Start: At the highest point on the cliff, at a thin crack 5' left of **Jeff-James** and 5' right of a dirty flare.
P1 5.12a G: Tough thin moves up the crack lead to easier climbing and gear placements. (Alternatively, begin slightly right on crimps trending left into the crack.) A painful mono and powerful moves guard the top. 55'
FA Sep 15, 2012, Conor Cliffe

4 Jeff–James 5.12d G 70' ★★

Start: 12' left of **Elusive Bastard** below a thin crack. The cliff is at its highest here, and overhangs 5'.
P1 5.12d G: Several 5.11d/5.12a moves lead to a good hold out left 25' up. Step right, then make a series of powerful layback moves. A strenuous-to-place—and critical—#4 nut protects the lower part of the crux, and a #1 TCU protects the upper part. Continue up the crack to the top. 70'
FA Sep 13, 2012, Conor Cliffe

5 Elusive Bastard (aka The Whipping Post) 5.11b G 50' ★★★★

Most prominent route at the cliff and a North Country gem. Sequency and sustained.
Start: 110' right of **Jake's Corner**, at the lowest point on the steepest part of the face, at a left-leaning crack in orange rock that leads to a flared open book 25' up.
P1 5.11b G: Climb up the crack to the flared open book (#3 Camalot in the bottom). Move up the open book to the horizontal crack just above (small cam). A hard move up the fingertip crack (crux) leads to stance, followed by another hard move to a fixed anchor. 50'
Gear: To 1", and a #3 Camalot.
FA Apr, 2010, Forrest Schwab
FFA Oct, 2010, Grant Watkins

6 Fancy Feet 5.10a PG 45'

Start: 20' right of **Elusive Bastard** below a flared slot 6' up. This is 1.5' right of a waist-high, mossy seasonal spring.
P1 5.10a PG: Go up the crack into the flare capped by a roof. Up the flare and over the roof at its top (#00 TCU critical), layback past a hidden hold to a ledge, then easier to the top. 45'
FA Nov 1, 2011, Conor Cliffe

Cranberry Lake

7 Trundle Bundle 5.6 G 35' ★
Start: 28' right of **Elusive Bastard**, 3' left of a left-facing corner that has a birch 15' up, below a face with left-facing flakes.
P1 5.6 G: Up left-facing flakes into a crack to a ledge, then up parallel cracks to the top. 35'
FA Apr, 2010, Ben Partridge, Jake Colony

8 Tool-less Wonder 5.6 G 60'
Start: 40' right of **Trundle Bundle**, in a left-facing corner with a birch 12' up, below a stem box with small roofs 40' up.
P1 5.6 G: Up left-facing corner to tree ledge at 12' through some blocky stuff into a right-facing corner with nice crack. Follow corner and crack through small roof with larger roof to the right (stem box), up a few more feet then move left to the top. 60'
FA Jun 17, 2011, Neal Knitel, Joe Pfeiffer

*Forrest Schwab near the top of **Elusive Bastard** (5.11b).*

401

N
0
10
20
miles
CANADA
Border Crossing
Lacolle / Champlain
Champlain
Malone
Potsdam
Plattsburgh
Keeseville
Colton
South Colton
Saranac Lake
Lake Placid
Tupper Lake
Cranberry Lake
Paul Smiths
Jay
Keene
Keene Valley
Elizabethtown
Upper Chateaugay Lake
Chazy Lake
Carry Falls Reservoir
Cranberry Lake
431
Panther Hill
492
Titusville Mountain
Inman Slab
Deer Pass
County Line Mountain
409
Azure Mountain
Lost Key Crag
416
421
406
South Colton
Jenkins Mountain
Charcoal Kiln Quarry
Blue Hill
Silver Lake
436
Catamount Mountain
434
Baker Mountain
Bluff Island
425
Clements Pond Trail
11
11B
30
458
3
56
86
73
9N
9
87
42
37
34
33
31

Northern Mountains

Wrapping across the north end of the park, this region forms the boundary between the lowlands of the St. Lawrence Valley and the High Peaks to the south. Much of the region is private land.

The big news here is the opening of the Black Brook Tract to climbers, known to climbers as "Silver Lake". The slopes of Silver Lake and Potter Mountains have a jaw-dropping amount of exposed rock from multi-pitch slabs, steep cracks, and steep, overhanging testpieces. With a long history of climbing and many enthusiastic locals, the area now boasts more than 150 routes, some of which are among the best in the park.

Other cliffs in the region are generally remote, buried deep in a wild area of rolling hills; forests; broad, swampy river valleys; and smaller mountain ranges. These have pockets of quality climbing but generally not in the concentrations found elsewhere in the park. Azure Mountain and the vast rock reserves of the Santa Clara Tract represent a large potential for future development in this region, although the approaches are involved. For short approaches, try the smaller cliffs such as Baker Mountain and South Colton, both of which have high-quality, short climbs.

Several of the cliffs are popular with college students (e.g., Paul Smiths, Clarkson, SUNY Potsdam and St. Lawrence). However, most of these crags are considered to be inconvenient and are often overlooked in favor of the roadside cliffs to the south. As a result, the Northern Mountains remain a secluded locale, and on any given day, you may be the only climber in this colossal region.

SEASON
Saranac Lake ranks among the top-ten places in the continental United States for the coldest temperatures, although these conditions aren't representative of this region as a whole. As with the rest of the park, expect early snow and a heavy snowpack until late in the spring.

DIRECTIONS   (MAPS PAGES 4 AND 402)
NY 3 runs east–west through this region and provides access from Watertown (I-81) and Plattsburgh (I-87). NY 30, the north–south road in the center of the park, enters the park south of Malone and intersects NY 3 to the west of Saranac Lake. Aside from the crags of the Santa Clara Tract, Silver Lake, and those clustered around Saranac Lake, the travel time between cliffs in the Northern Mountains can be measured in hours.

WHERE TO STAY
Excellent camping can be found around Azure Mountain, the Santa Clara Tract, Bluff Island, and Second Pond. There are some designated car-camping sites located off NY 30, on Floodwood Road, 5.5 miles north of Wawbeek.

Campgrounds: Fish Creek Pond (518.891.4560) and Rollins Pond (518.891.3239) are west of Saranac Lake. Meadowbrook (518.891.4351) is near Ray Brook. Taylor Pond (518.647.5250) is north of Wilmington and convenient for climbing at Silver Lake. Buck Pond (518.891.3449) is north of Bloomingdale. Meacham Lake (518.483.5116) is north of Paul Smith's.

AMENITIES
Saranac Lake is the largest town in the Adirondacks and has plenty to offer. Otherwise, stock up on supplies before you arrive, because options are limited to gas stations along NY 3. Be aware that there is no longer a gas station in Wilmington.

DIVERSIONS
Saint Regis, the largest wilderness canoe area in the Northeast (19,000 acres), is located in this region. Motorboats and seaplanes are prohibited from this network of more than 50 lakes, which are connected by short portages. Recommended short hikes include Azure Mountain, Silver Lake Mountain, Lyon Mountain, and Catamount Mountain.

Liam Schneider on P1 of **Where the Wild Things Are** *(5.10b), Potter Mountain.*

Northern Mountains

This Rock and Snow original tee & many others, as well as a great selection of climbing gear at

rockandsnow.com

Also in the Gunks at one of the oldest and wisest climbing shops in the country

ROCK AND SNOW

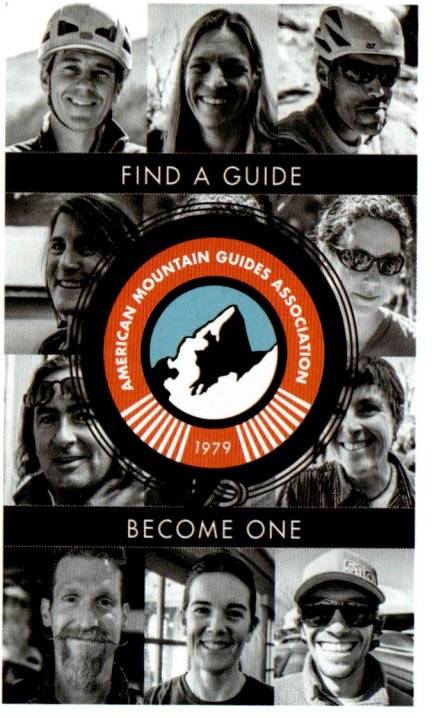

FIND A GUIDE

AMERICAN MOUNTAIN GUIDES ASSOCIATION 1979

BECOME ONE

FREE CLIMBERISM.COM

climberism
THE NORTHEAST CLIMBING MAGAZINE

Peter Kamitses on *Moonshine and Chronic* (5.13+) at Mud Pond, belayed by Pat Dyess.

404

Northern Mountains

PG	CLIFF	QUALITY	ASPECT	APPROACH	GRADES	#
406	South Colton	★★	SW	5 min	easy	12
409	Azure Mountain Main Face	★	SW	1 hr	moderate	16
414	Azure Mountain Planet Terror Face		SW	15 min	easy	2
414	Azure Mountain Equinox Face	★★	S	15 min	easy	5
417	Santa Clara Tract Deer Pass	★	W	1 hr 35 min	difficult	7
419	Santa Clara Tract Lost Key Crag		SW	1 hr 35 min	difficult	1
420	Santa Clara Tract County Line Mountain		S	55 min	moderate	5
420	Jenkins Mountain		S	1 hr 30 min	difficult	9
423	Charcoal Kiln Quarry		SE	3 min	easy	9
425	Baker Mountain	★★★	W	12 min	easy	11
428	Inman Slabs	★	E	0 min	easy	11
430	Panther Hill Cliff	★★★	SE	1 hr	moderate	8
433	Catamount Mountain		S	1 hr	moderate	3
439	Silver Lake C Chimney Cliff	★★★★	S	40 min	moderate	19
445	Silver Lake Never Never Land	★★★	S	50 min	moderate	4
446	Silver Lake Purple Rain Wall	★★	S	1 hr	moderate	6
447	Silver Lake Summit Cliff	★★★★	S & SW	1 hr	difficult	23
453	Silver Lake Center of Progress Cliff	★★★	S & SW	30 min	moderate	28
461	Silver Lake Tsunami Wall	★	S	30 min	moderate	4
464	Silver Lake Midway Cliff	★★	S	40 min	easy	12
467	Silver Lake Outback Slab	★★★★	S	1 hr	difficult	6
469	Silver Lake Wayback Cliff		SW	1 hr 45 min	difficult	2
470	Silver Lake Potter Mountain Cliff	★★★★★	S	35-50 min	easy	27
484	Silver Lake The Burrow		W	1 hr 10 min	moderate	1
485	Silver Lake Hydrogen Wall	★★	S	35 min	moderate	2
486	Silver Lake Mud Pond Cliff	★★★★	S & SW	25 min	easy	15
490	Clements Pond Trail The Towers of the Teeth		SW	20 min	easy	3
491	Clements Pond Trail Fisherman's Wall	★	SW	20 min	easy	2
492	Titusville Mountain		SE	20 min	moderate	4

405

SOUTH COLTON

Location	South of Potsdam, accessed from NY 56 near South Colton
Aspect	Southwest
Height	50'
Quality	★★
Approach	5 min, easy
Summary	A great spot for toproping and short, single-pitch lead climbing at moderate grades.

3	1	3	4	1		12
-5.6	5.7	5.8	5.9	5.10	5.11	5.12	5.13+	total

The cliffs at South Colton are located in the Snow Bowl State Forest, just south of South Colton on NY 56. Although the land adjoins the Adirondack Park (the cliff is within 0.5 mile of the park), it is not technically within the park's boundary. It is included, however, because it serves as an important niche for climbers in that area. The name "Snow Bowl" comes from a defunct ski area of St. Lawrence University on the eastern side of the state forest.

The crag, though small in size, is located in a pretty setting—shaded by hardwoods with an open base and a quiet, remote feeling. The rock is pink and quite solid, and there is a good mixture of easy routes. The cliff has been equipped for toproping with fixed anchors above every route and is therefore ideal for groups and teaching. Additionally, several of the trad routes have been equipped with bolts for "students who are more motivated than they are prudent."

On the left side of the wall is a chossy red-colored buttress. There's a mossy face in the middle, then a more appealing crack-riddled buttress on the right.

Questions about the Snow Bowl State Forest are handled by the DEC, Region 6 (315.265.3090).

HISTORY

Dave Furman, who discovered the cliff while skiing, was the first to report climbing here in 1992, while he was attending school in Potsdam. The first route was an ice climb (**Wicked World**, Feb, 1992). It was early in Furman's climbing career, and some of these routes required repeated attempts and falls. Since then, the cliffs have become very popular with college groups from nearby Clarkson, St. Lawrence University, and SUNY Potsdam. More recently, developers have bolted the previously-led crack lines; this should not be used as an example for other cliffs in the park.

DIRECTIONS (MAP PAGE 406)

At the post office in South Colton, set your odometer to 0.0 and drive south on NY 56 for 0.6 mile, then turn left onto East Hill Road. At the 1.9-mile mark, turn right onto Scovill Road. This road is paved at first, then turns to gravel. At 3.0 miles, Scovill Road makes a 90° right turn; continue straight on a smaller dirt road, reaching a grassy clearing at 3.2 miles where you can park 511715,4926001. At the clearing, the road bends left and downhill, and another road continues straight.

From the parking area, walk downhill (east) along a 4WD track to a stream. Cross the stream and turn left on a trail that heads northeast (this left turn is just before the 4WD track goes uphill in a deep track with high banks). Follow the trail uphill parallel to the stream and, at the top of the hill, turn right. After 30 yards, the crag will be seen on the left 511958,4926021.

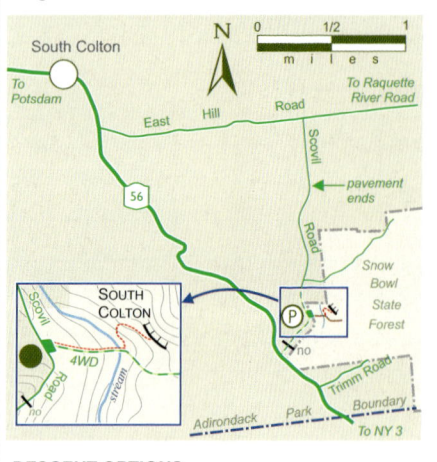

DESCENT OPTIONS

Walk right.

1 Sport Climbing Is Neither 5.8 G 30' ★

Start: Uphill from and left of the main wall, at a shallow pink right-facing corner below the right side of a ceiling 15' up.
P1 5.8 G: Climb up the overhanging corner to the ceiling, then up to three triangular ledges and up to a fixed anchor. 30'
FA 1994, Sean Kullman

2 GK's First BJ 5.9+ G 35' ★

"Bolt Job", that is.
Start: 15' uphill and left from **Climb It**, right of a blocky section and below a triangular roof 20' up.
● **P1 5.9+ G:** Up orange rock to a right-leaning crack. Follow this to the right side of the triangular roof. Break the roof on the right, then go up and left to a fixed anchor. 35'
FA Apr, 2012, Matt Hosmer, Greg Kuchyt

3 Climb It 5.9 G 40'

Start: In the middle of the mossy face below a thin crack that starts 4' up, 5' left of **Love It**.
P1 5.9 G: Climb the dirty, shallow crack to a horizontal, step right, and continue up the vertical crack to the top. Step right to the fixed anchor for **Love It**. 40'
FA 1994, Andrew Bentley

4 Love It 5.7 G 40' ★

Start: At a huge tree below stacked blocks on the left side of the face, just right of the mossy wall.
● **P1 5.7 G:** Climb up blocky rock to a triangular niche, then up a crack to a fixed anchor. 40'
FA 1994, Andrew Bentley

Northern Mountains

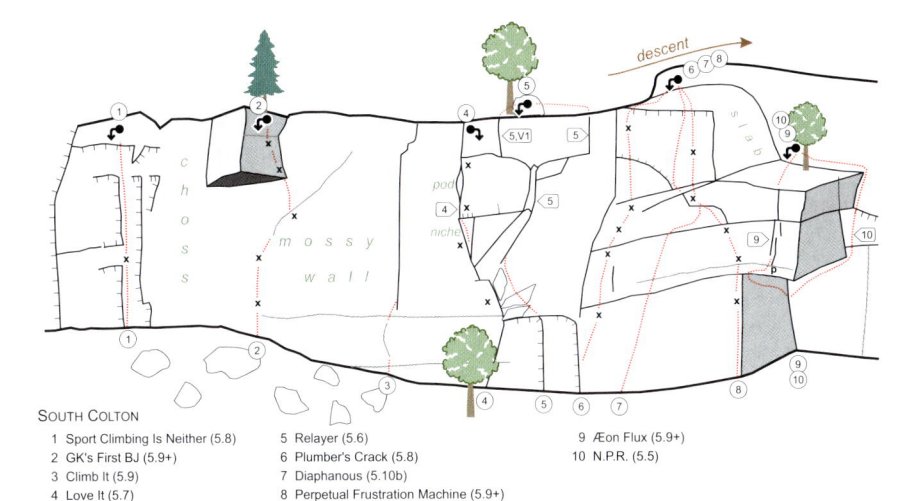

SOUTH COLTON

1 Sport Climbing Is Neither (5.8)
2 GK's First BJ (5.9+)
3 Climb It (5.9)
4 Love It (5.7)
5 Relayer (5.6)
6 Plumber's Crack (5.8)
7 Diaphanous (5.10b)
8 Perpetual Frustration Machine (5.9+)
9 Æon Flux (5.9+)
10 N.P.R. (5.5)

5 Relayer 5.6 G 40' ★★

Start: At a 10'-high off-width crack in a right-facing corner.

P1 5.6 G: Climb up the crack and corner to a ledge, then up blocks to two parallel right-leaning cracks. Up the right-leaning cracks to where they fork. (V1) Climb the right-hand crack to the top; step left to the fixed anchor. 40'

V1 5.8 G: Step left and climb the left-hand crack to the fixed anchor.
FA Mar, 1993, Dave Furman

6 Plumber's Crack 5.8 G 40' ★★★★

Start: 4' right of Relayer's off-width crack at a shallow 10'-high right-facing flaky corner, 15' left of the huge right-facing corner on the right end of the face.

● **P1 5.8 G:** Up to the first bolt, then follow a right-arching crack and corner to a straight-up crack. Follow the straight-up crack to a ledge with a fixed anchor. 40'
History: The bolts were added by an unknown party after the first ascent.
FA Mar, 1993, Clark Woodward
FFA Mar, 1993, Dave Furman

7 Diaphanous 5.10b PG 40' ★★★

Start: 3' right of the shallow right-facing flaky corner of Plumber's Crack.

P1 5.10b PG: Climb up flakes to a horizontal, then up to the next horizontal. Traverse right 3', then up cracks to another horizontal. From here, you can step right to a ledge with a fixed anchor (making the grade 5.9) or continue up a slab to a fixed anchor. 40'
FA Apr, 1993, Dave Furman

8 Perpetual Frustration Machine 5.9+ G 40' ★★

Start: On the arête just left of the Æon Flux corner.
● **P1 5.9+ G:** Up the left side of the arête to a horizontal crack. Layback up a right-facing edge to another horizontal, then up to a third horizontal. Go up a slab angling left to the fixed anchor of Diaphanous. 40'
FA May, 2012, Zach O'Neil, Julia Robinson

9 Æon Flux 5.9+ G 30' ★★★

Named for an animated science fiction series on MTV's Liquid Television.

Start: At the base of the right-facing corner at the right end of the cliff.

P1 5.9+ G: Up the corner to the roof, then around this to the left (piton) and up a right-facing edge to a good horizontal. Twin cracks lead to a ledge with a fixed anchor. 30'
FA Mar, 1993, Dave Furman

10 N.P.R. 5.5 G 30' ★★★

Start: Same as Æon Flux.

P1 5.5 G: Climb up the corner to the roof, then out right under the roof and continue up the right-facing corner to the ledge with a fixed anchor. 30'
FA Apr, 1993, Nat Patridge

11 Up Your Bum 5.8 G 30'

Start: 25' right of the Æon Flux corner,

P1 5.8 G: Scramble up a left-rising dirt ramp, (V1) then up and left on a rock ramp to a small tree. Go up a right-leaning crack past a small ceiling to a fixed anchor. 30'

V1 5.9 G: Go up an arête to a left-leaning crack. Follow this to the right end of a 10' wide ceiling. Move left, and join the normal route.
FA 2012, Chris Foster

12 Where Frenchmen Dare 5.5 G 25'

Could use some cleaning.

Start: 25' right of the previous route, below a short corner.

P1 5.5 G: Climb the corner to a fixed anchor. 25'
FA 2012, Bill Beauchamp

Northern Mountains

AZURE MOUNTAIN

Location	Southwest of Santa Clara, accessed from Blue Mountain Road off NY 458
Summary	Mostly moderate routes in a very remote setting with good potential for high-end routes.

8	5	4	1	2	2		23
-5.6	5.7	5.8	5.9	5.10	5.11	5.12	5.13+	total

Azure Mountain is the easternmost bump on a long range of mostly unexplored rock that includes Brushy Top Mountain, Lost Mountain, Flat Top Mountain, County Line Mountain, and Weller Mountain. With its close proximity to several universities and colleges, it is also one of the most popular hikes in this region.

Azure Mountain, when seen from the parking area, is nothing more than an unimpressive wooded knob. The southwest side, however, is cleaved off, leaving a steep 250'-high wall with roofs that rises above a slope of large talus blocks. With such a striking feature, this face should be riddled with routes, but the massive roofs, friable rock, and lack of protectable features have curbed route exploration.

On the south side are three less imposing walls with a collection of moderate routes. The rock routes are located on the middle of three cliffs, the Equinox Face.

HISTORY

The reported routes were the result of early explorations by the Clarkson Outing Club, which first arrived on the scene in the early 1970s. Club activity diminished, but the work was picked up enthusiastically in the mid-80s by Jon Bassett, Andy Legg (son of David and Lois Legg that first explored many other cliffs including Shanty Cliff), Chris Moratz (formerly Bill Moratz), Kevin Steele, and Mike Rawdon. In the early 1990s, the cliff was visited by Andy Tuthill, who picked off its two plums, including **Côte d' Azure**, the only route to break the most impressive section of the Main Face.

Andy Tuthill.

DIRECTIONS (MAP PAGE 409)

Approach the cliffs via the Azure Mountain Trailhead 540861,4931758. From Santa Clara (at the intersection with Center Street), drive 2.3 miles northeast on NY 458 to Blue Mountain Road and turn left. This is 3.8 miles south of the blinking red light in Saint Regis Falls. On Blue Mountain Road, drive 6.9 miles to the trailhead on the right, marked by a small DEC sign. Park along this small dead-end side road.

A more scenic drive from the south begins at the intersection of NY 86 and NY 30 at the entrance to Paul Smiths. From here, follow NY 30 north for 100 yards, then turn left on Keese Mills Road (unmarked) and follow it 17.5 miles to the trailhead on the left. (The name of the road changes to Blue Mountain Road after some distance.)

From the parking area, follow the main hiking trail, a dirt road really, for 5 min to a clearing with a picnic table, fireplace, and the remains of the foundation of an old ranger cabin. The various approaches are described relative to this clearing 540354,4931876.

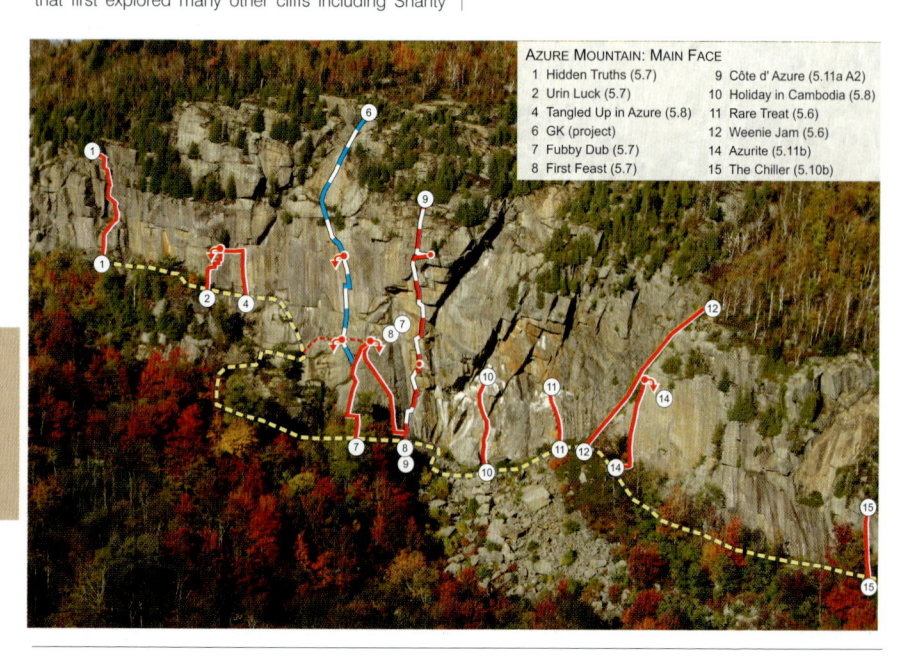

AZURE MOUNTAIN: MAIN FACE
1 Hidden Truths (5.7)
2 Urin Luck (5.7)
4 Tangled Up in Azure (5.8)
6 GK (project)
7 Fubby Dub (5.7)
8 First Feast (5.7)
9 Côte d' Azure (5.11a A2)
10 Holiday in Cambodia (5.8)
11 Rare Treat (5.6)
12 Weenie Jam (5.6)
14 Azurite (5.11b)
15 The Chiller (5.10b)

408

Northern Mountains

Azure Mountain
MAIN FACE

Aspect	Southwest
Height	250'
Quality	★
Approach	1 hr, moderate
Summary	A huge face with a few moderate routes and one exceptional arête.

4	4	4		2	1		16
-5.6	5.7	5.8	5.9	5.10	5.11	5.12	5.13+ · total

One of the more impressive features in the park, the central section of the Main Face overhangs and is capped by enormous orange roofs. One route is known to breach this wall, **Côte d' Azure**. The wall is out of character with its surroundings of relatively flat terrain of forests and bogs with only moderately sized hills.

The Main Face has several sections. The Upper Left End is the section of routes that begins above slabs above **Fubby Dub** below a sheer, featureless headwall. The Dinner Table is the off-vertical wall just left of the Amphitheater that begins above a flat slab of rock and ends just below the featureless headwall. The Amphitheater is in the center of the cliff beneath the enormous orange overhangs. Right of this is the Right End, with the **Weenie Jam** ramp and the enormous left-facing corner of **Planet Claire**.

DIRECTIONS (MAP PAGE 409)

From the clearing near the former ranger cabin, the main trail continues straight and a faint trail branches left through the grass. Follow the faint trail (which improves significantly) for 10 min past a switchback to gain the crest of a ridge. From here, turn left off the trail and pick up a line of cairns that drops down a bit, then contour around the mountain to the southwest side. There are many cairns but virtually no trail; however, the woods are fairly open, and the going is easy. The line of cairns eventually heads uphill to the base of a small cliff; walk left along it to reach **Border Crossing Fugitive**, then **Azurite**, after which you finally emerge into the talus in the center of the cliff **539436,4931922**.

If you lose the cairns (which is likely), simply continue contouring left around the mountain. The immense open area formed by the talus and cliff are very difficult to miss.

Upper Left End

The left end of the cliff, left of the Amphitheater, has a less traumatic slab that leads to a featureless, sheer headwall with many wet streaks. The routes begin at the top of this slab below the headwall.

DIRECTIONS (MAP PAGE 409)

At the highest point in the talus on the left side of the Amphitheater (and 50' left of **Holiday in Cambodia**) is a flat ledge known as the Dinner Table. Approach this from the right (through a thick but avoidable crop of poison ivy), then, from its left end, walk left 150'. Reach some slabs via 3rd-class tree pulling, walk right, then zigzag up the slabs (3rd class) to the base of a steep, featureless wall. (The anchor for **Fubby Dub** and **First Feast** is on the far right end of this slabby area.)

1 Hidden Truths 5.7 G 135'

Start: From the base of the featureless headwall, walk left past a tan-colored open-book corner (**Tangled Up in Azure**), through some trees, and behind a large boulder to a distinctive featureless orange open book capped by a ceiling. Continue another 60' left on slabs and boulders to a high ledge that drops off on its left side. The route begins on this ledge below a dirty face with parallel grungy cracks, just below and left of a balanced boulder 15' up.

P1 5.3 G: Climb the parallel cracks, up behind the balanced boulder, then around the back of a freestanding tower to a belay at the base of the corner. 85'

P2 5.7 G: Go up the grungy corner (crux), past a small overlap, to its top. Angle up and left to the summit. 50'

FA Sep 27, 1987, Jim Olsen, Jon Bassett

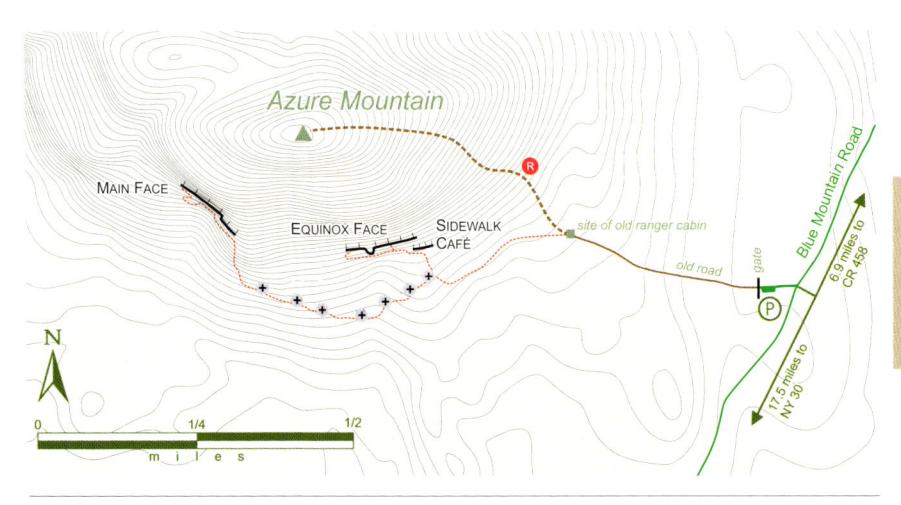

Northern Mountains

2 Urin Luck 5.7 G 50' ★★
Intricate climbing up right-arching flakes provides a nice introduction to this section of the cliff.
Start: On a fern-covered open ledge, 30' left of **Tangled Up in Azure**, at the base of a shallow right-facing flake that forms a right-facing V-slot. This is 50' right of the featureless orange open book used as a landmark for **Hidden Truths**.
P1 5.7 G: Climb up the right-facing flake as it arches right to an overhang. Break around the right side of the overhang and continue up the right-arching flake to the next overhang. Break around the right side of this second overhang, then straight up to a large cedar with a fixed anchor. 50'
FA 2004, Sarah Councell, Jay Kullman

3 Walking Disaster 5.8 G 50'
Not recommended.
Start: At the dirty, left-facing corner between **Urin Luck** and **Tangled Up in Azure**, the only feature between the two routes.
P1 5.8 G: Up the dirty crack to a much cleaner crack above. Anchor shared with **Urin Luck**. 50'
FA Apr, 2012, James Armstrong

4 Tangled Up in Azure 5.8 G 70' ★★★
Makes a nice top pitch for the Dinner Table Routes.
Start: On the left side of the sheer, featureless wall at a 20'-tall right-facing, tan-colored open book that gradually narrows at its top to a point. There is a jagged crack in the open book.
P1 5.8 G: Climb the open book and large right-facing flake to the point at its top. Continue up the right-facing corner (or, cleaner on the knobby face to its left) to its top, then traverse left 20' on a foot ledge to a cedar with a fixed anchor. 70'
FA 2004, Jay Kullman, Sarah Councell

Dinner Table Routes
The left end of the cliff, left of the Amphitheater, has a less traumatic slab that leads to a sheer, featureless headwall. The routes thus far climb the low-angle wall and slab below the headwall.

DIRECTIONS   (MAP PG 409)
At the highest point in the talus on the left side of the Amphitheater (and 50' left of **Holiday in Cambodia**) is a flat ledge known as the Dinner Table. Approach this from the right (through a thick but avoidable crop of poison ivy).

DESCENT OPTIONS
For the routes that end at the base of the steep, featureless wall (**Fubby Dub** and **First Feast**), rappel from the anchor or scramble/zigzag down the slabs (3rd class), then angle left to a final 3rd-class downclimb in trees.

5 The Window 5.1 PG 60'
Once a popular toprope by the Clarkson Outing Club.
Start: 50' left of **Fubby Dub** on a large ledge below the middle of a slab.
P1 5.1 PG: Climb the slab and a short, wide crack in the low-angle face. 60'
FA 1970, Clarkson Outing Club

6 GK Project
This open project ascends the fingercrack in the imposing steep wall above the finish of **Fubby Dub**. From the top of **Fubby Dub**, move left 35' to another fixed anchor. Go up easy terrain and a left-facing corner to a roof. Over this, then up a steep bolt-protected face (crux) to gain the left-leaning seam-crack. The rock is somewhat friable, and bits of the route have broken off. As a result, a free attempt may require repositioning of some of the fixed protection.

Andy Tuthill on P1 (5.11a) of Côte d' Azure (5.11a A2).

7 Fubby Dub 5.7 G 100' ★

One of the more popular routes on the Main Face, with nice crack climbing.

Start: 10' left of the Dinner Table at a 3" crack.

P1 5.7 G: Climb the crack to where it's split by a horizontal. Traverse left 10' to gain a right-rising crack (filled with bushes), and follow it to its top. Move up a face just left of an angular overhanging rock that projects left until you reach a slabby area with a fixed anchor on blocks in a low-angle left-facing corner (shared with First Feast). 100'

History: The route was previously misspelled "Flubby Dub." The name mimics the sounds Bill Cosby made during one of his comedy routines.

FA Apr, 1985, Chris Moratz, Kevin Steele

8 First Feast 5.7 PG 125' ★

Start: Above the Dinner Table is a series of left-facing corners, the leftmost and largest of which is filled with bushes and trees. This route begins in the next corner to the right, capped by a long triangular overlap 6' up.

P1 5.7 PG: (V1) Climb up the left-facing corner to the overlap, then traverse left to a flared crack just right of the arête. Up the crack and arête to a right-rising overlap. (V2) Use a short right-leaning crack to gain a face with many horizontals (staying left of the right-facing flake), then up to a ledge. Work over a bulge to a small overlap, then follow a left-leaning crack (left of two black streaks) that ends at a horizontal. Traverse right and up another crack that leads to a slabby area with a fixed anchor on blocks. 125'

V1 Forward to Death 5.10 G: Begin 5' right below a left-facing corner. Up the corner to a ledge, then up to the top of a block. Traverse left to a right-facing flake, and climb it to the ledge to join the normal route. Named after a song by the Dead Kennedys, a 1980s punk band.

V2 5.7 G: Continue up the right-rising overlap to a right-facing flake and follow it to the ledge to rejoin the normal route.

ACB Apr, 1987, Russ Marvin, Jon Bassett
FA (V1) Apr 19, 1986, Chris Moratz

Amphitheater

This is the central section of cliff below the enormous orange overhangs. The rock is generally friable but, with some work, might yield more popular routes.

9 Côte d' Azure 5.11a A2 250'

The only route to breach the geometric puzzle of roofs and corners in the Amphitheater. The first pitch has been freed, but the impressive middle pitch remains, for now, and aid exercise.

Start: Same as First Feast.

P1 5.11a G: Up the left-facing corner to the overlap, over this the up to the top of the pedestal (same as for Forward to Death). Work up and right on a steep wall with loose rock to gain a ledge with a perched block and copious bird shit. Up a crack in a right-facing corner to a ceiling (5.10b) and break this on its left end to a stemmed stance just above. Move right and follow an S-shaped crack up and right across a rust-colored wall to an arête. Swing around the arête into a right-facing corner, then up to a belay at a small stance in the corner (1/4" bolt, piton). 100'

P2 Triple Roofs Pitch 5.10 A2: Continue up the right-facing corner (bolt) to an overlap at its top, then up a seam in a headwall. Halfway up the headwall, follow a horizontal crack system to the right to gain a ledge, then move up and left to the first roof where it is broken by a thin crack. Over the roof and into a right-facing corner which is followed to the second roof. Over this and up cracks in another headwall to the third roof; break this via a handcrack which is followed to a ledge with a pine tree on its right end. 100'

P3 5.6 G: Scramble up easier rock to the top. 50'

FA May 8, 1993, Andy Tuthill, Susan Frankenstein

10 Holiday in Cambodia 5.8 G 50'

Named for a Dead Kennedys song.

Start: 100' left of Weenie Jam below the left end of a very large talus block that forms a squeeze against the cliff.

P1 5.8 G: Climb a crack in a shallow boxed chimney capped by a ceiling 30' up. Step right around the ceiling and up a crack in a large open book to a spacious ledge. 50'

FA Apr 19, 1986, Chris Moratz

11 Rare Treat 5.6 PG 50'

An unappealing section of rock, whose name may have been inspired by the copious bird shit that drips from the finishing ledges.

Start: 60' left of the Weenie Jam ramp and 20' left of a splash of orange lichen on the rock, at a short, bulging buttress with bits of orange lichen.

P1 5.6 PG: Climb up the bulges and mossy, lichen-covered face to ledges adorned with white bird shit below the overhanging bands of orange rock. 50'

FA Mar 8, 1986, Chris Moratz, Kevin Steele

Right End

This is the section of cliff right of the overhangs, starting with the obvious right-rising ramp of Weenie Jam. The far right end of the cliff, right of Azurite, is sheer and has seen some activity but has only one recorded route. Old anchors and the occasional piton indicate a more extensive, but unknown, exploration.

Walk right to access the top.

12 Weenie Jam 5.6 PG 165' ★★★

The first route climbed on the Main Face, it offers good friction and low-angle face climbing. Named for the third appendage used as a climbing aid.

Start: Right of the Amphitheater on some blocks below an obvious right-rising ramp.

Route Description: Climb up the ramp to birches at the top. If you stay left, the route is more pure friction (around 5.6). Keep to the right for easier climbing (5.1) and better protection, notwithstanding some vegetation, on steps and shallow corners.

FA 1970, Clarkson Outing Club

Northern Mountains

13 Planet Claire (aka Shuffle and Grunt) 5.5 G 165' ★

An impressive corner, although it needs some pruning. The route was originally named **Shuffle and Grunt**, but it was reported later by Chris Moratz, who named it after a B-52's song.

Start: 50' right of the right-rising ramp of **Weenie Jam** is a large left-facing corner. The left wall has an orange strip, and the corner itself has a narrow chimney and crack. Begin below the chimney.

P1 5.5 G: Climb up the wide crack in the corner (gear in the crack in the left wall), past several wedged blocks, then claw through trees to a ledge on the left wall. Step left to belay in trees near the **Weenie Jam** ramp. 70'

P2 5.5. G: Step back into the corner and onto the right wall, then follow a right-leaning crack to a cedar with a fixed anchor (the top of **Azurite**). Work up a right-leaning crack behind the cedar to a horizontal formed by a huge block. Traverse left and climb to the top of the chimney-slot. Step left onto the blunt arête and climb easy slabs above to the top. 95'
FA 1975, Frank Zupancic, Mike Rawdon

14 Azurite 5.11b G 100' ★★★★★

A beautiful and demanding arête climb and one of the best single pitches in the park.

Start: At a large pointed boulder just uphill from the base of the arête downhill and right of the deep corner of **Planet Claire**.

P1 5.11b G: From the right end of a boulder, step right into a shallow left-facing open book and up to a small overlap. Clear the overlap on the left and gain a handcrack left of the arête. Follow the crack to where it disappears, then up to a bolt (crux). Swing around the arête to a hidden orange jug, then back to the left side to gain another crack, which is followed to a ledge. Work up a wide crack right of the arête to its top, then step left to a cedar tree with a fixed anchor (shared with **Planet Claire**). 100'

Gear: Standard rack from small TCUs to 3".
FA Mar 27, 1993, Andy Tuthill, Susan Frankenstein

15 The Chiller 5.10b G 50' ★★★

The wall right of the **Azurite** arête has some good possibilities. Not as imposing as the Amphitheater, it has the potential for many steep 50'–90' routes. This is one of the better lines.

Start: 75' right of the **Azurite** arête is a large boulder that forms a squeeze chimney with the Main Face. 35' right of this is a 20'-high boulder-flake that leans up against the Main Face and forms a covered passage through which you can walk. 35' right of the covered passage is an open area with a right-facing, left-leaning corner that begins 10' up. 110' right of the covered passage is another, smaller open area with a 1'-deep, clean, 50'-high right-facing corner with a fingercrack. This route begins on blocks 5' right of the corner.

P1 5.10b G: Up the blocks, then traverse left on a sloped ledge to gain the corner (first protection) and climb it to its top. Walk right 10' to a fixed anchor on a tree. 50'

*Joe Szot on **Planet Claire** (5.5)*

Gear: To 3".
History: The route was climbed solo on aid by Steele during the winter, hence the name. It was perhaps free-climbed earlier, but this is the first reported lead.
FA (A2) Nov 22, 1985, Kevin Steele (roped solo)
FFA 2000, Kevin Boyle, Jay Kullman

16 Chalk Full O' Nuts 5.10b G 50' ★★★

Seeps after a rain.

Start: At a head-high ledge below a fingercrack, 30' left of **Coffee Shop Panorama** and 40' right of **The Chiller**.

P1 5.10b G: Boulder onto the ledge, then climb the fingercrack and small crimps until the crack closes. Transition into another fingercrack just above and to the right. Go up to a horizontal crack halfway up, then continue up a handcrack to the top. 50'
FA Sep, 2013, Will Leith, Matt Kahabka

17 Coffee Shop Panorama 5.8+ G 40' ★★★

Start: 70' right of **The Chiller** at a crack in an arête below a right-facing corner 15' up.

P1 5.8+ G: Go up the finger- and handcrack and up to the right wall of the large corner. Go up two parallel fingercracks to the top of the wall, then up a short slab for 15' to a clump of birch trees. 40'

Descent: Rappel from a cedar tree to the left.
FA 2013, Will Leith, Matt Kahabka

*Opposite: Will Mayo on **Azurite** (5.11b).*

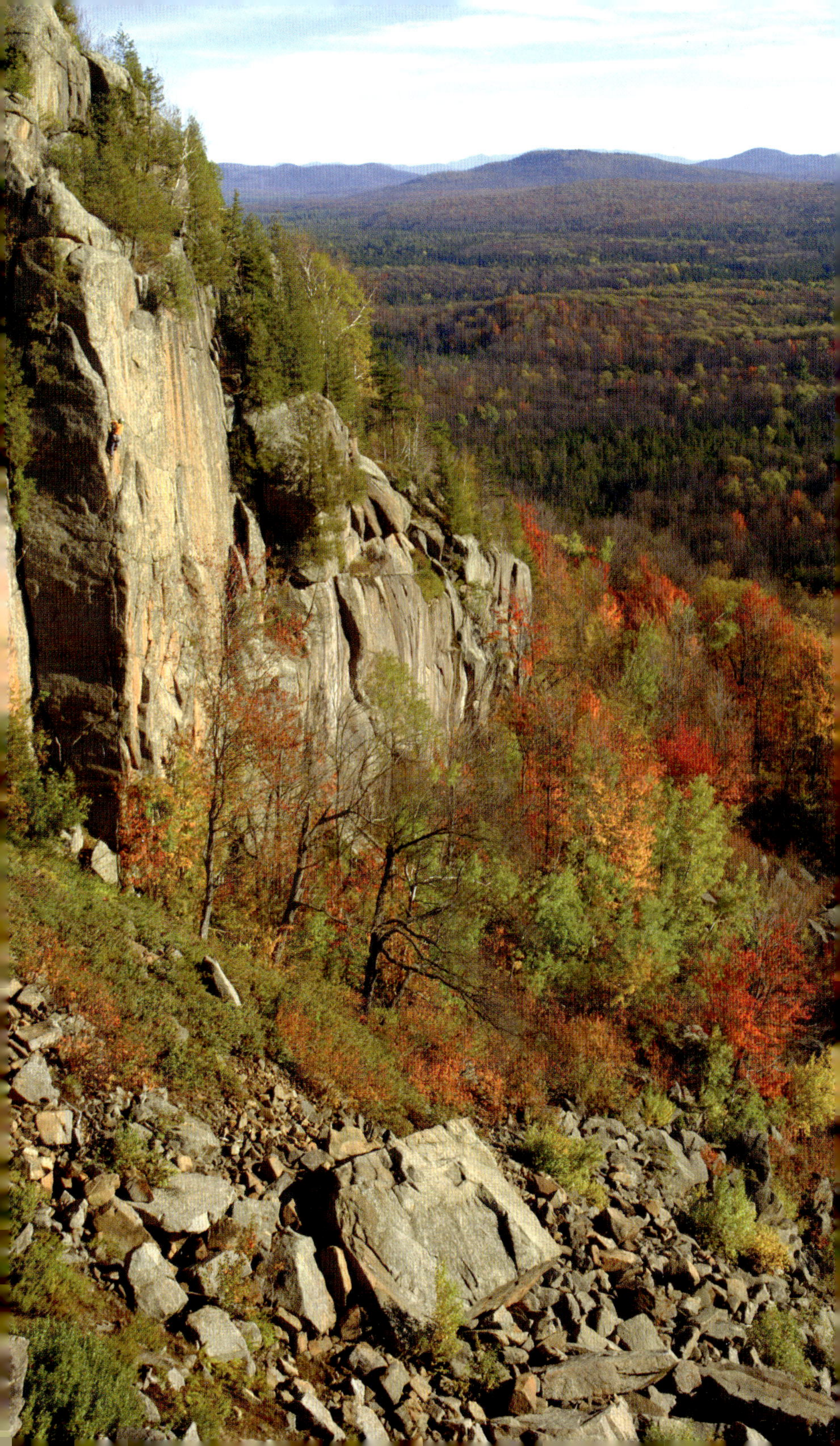

Northern Mountains

Azure Mountain
PLANET TERROR FACE

Aspect	Southwest
Height	70'
Quality	
Approach	15 min, easy
Summary	Two steep, interesting routes in orange rock.

			1		1			2
-5.6	5.7	5.8	5.9	5.10	5.11	5.12	5.13+	total

DIRECTIONS (MAP PAGE 409)
Where the trail to the Equinox Face makes its last right-hand switchback up to the base of the face, there is a smaller trail that contours left below broken cliffs. Proceed 200' on this trail to where the path fades below an orange face. Continue past the face, then scramble back right to the base of the face.

18 Planet Terror 5.9 G 70'
Named for one of the two horror-film segments that comprise the anthology film *Grindhouse*.
Start: About 50' uphill and left of a low broken buttress, and just right of the left end of the face, below a V-chimney in orange rock that leads to a roof 20' up. Right of the chimney is an orange face with a dirty, jagged right-leaning crack on its right margin; below this is a stepped, blocky right-rising ramp.
P1 5.9 G: Climb the chimney to the roof at its top, then out the ceiling via a right-leaning off-width crack. Follow the crack past the right end of a roof, then up large wedged flakes in a right-facing corner to a good stance in a chimney. 1"–2" cams make a belay. 70'

Descent: Walk back in the chimney, then scramble down and left, and follow a gully that returns to the base of the cliff.
FA 2004, Jay Kullman, Sarah Councell

19 Death Proof 5.11a TR 60'
20' right of **Planet Terror** is a jagged right-leaning crack on the right margin of an orange wall. Just left of this is a right-facing edge in orange rock. This route climbs the orange face to a fixed anchor above and right of the finish of **Planet Terror**.
FA (TR) 2004, Jay Kullman, Sarah Councell

Azure Mountain
EQUINOX FACE

Aspect	South
Height	120'
Quality	★★
Approach	15 min, easy
Summary	A collection of quality face routes densely packed into a small area; great for first-time leading.

4	1							5
-5.6	5.7	5.8	5.9	5.10	5.11	5.12	5.13+	total

Of the several cliffs on south-facing slopes of Azure Mountain, this one has the best rock climbing. The rock is clean, well protected for the most part, and highly featured with knobs in places (the route **You're No Spring Chicken Head**). The main feature is a large left-facing, left-leaning corner that sits 30' above the lowest point on the face; the route **Diamond C** climbs this corner. At the highest point of the terrain is a clearing,

PLANET TERROR FACE

EQUINOX FACE

AZURE MOUNTAIN
18 Planet Terror (5.9)
20 Diamond C (5.7)
23 Equinox (5.3)
24 The Other One (5.6)

414

Northern Mountains

below which is a large boulder with another clearing and a fire ring.

The top of the cliff overlooks spectacular vistas of vast greenness and marshes with no signs of human impact.

The area doesn't lend itself to toproping, as you must lead something to set up a rope. These routes are densely packed, and you can climb pretty much anywhere.

DIRECTIONS   (MAP PAGE 409)
From the clearing near the former ranger cabin, the main trail continues straight and a faint trail branches left through the grass. Follow the faint trail (which improves significantly) for 10 min past a switchback to gain the crest of a ridge. Continue up the ridge to the left end of a brown wall known as the Sidewalk Café. The trail bears left along the base of the cliff, up a rock step to its end at the Equinox Face 539880,4931841.

The trail splits just before it reaches the Equinox Face. It's tempting to take the left fork to reach the Main Face, but this trail quickly fades (just below the Planet Terror Face), and it's too high on the mountain (nearly level with the top of the Main Face).

DESCENT OPTIONS
You'll need two ropes to rappel from the fixed anchor on top of the face. Walking right is possible, but it's not straightforward and may require a short rappel.

20 Diamond C 5.7 G (5.4 R) 125' ★★★
Start: Uphill and left of the lowest point of the terrain is a small platform. The route starts on the platform directly below the lower right end of a large left-facing, left-leaning corner that begins 30' up.
P1 5.7 G (5.4 R): Climb up right on knobby, mossy rock to the left end of a broken ledgy area, then angle up left to a left-facing corner and follow it to the large left-leaning corner above. Up the large leaning corner about halfway, then swing right around the corner on jugs to the face. Work straight up to the top on well-featured face. 125'
FA Sep 8, 1988, Jon Bassett, Andy Legg

21 Sunshine Daydream 5.4 PG 135' ★★
Start: At the lowest point of the terrain where the approach trail meets the cliff, 4' left of You're No Spring Chicken Head.
P1 5.4 PG: Climb up the face to a ledge below a left-rising ceiling. Up to the ceiling, then left to a shallow left-facing corner on its left end. Up the corner, then straight up the face, staying right of a black streak and left of the knobby rock (of You're No Spring Chicken Head). At the top of the face, step left to a right-leaning crack, then up to trees with a fixed anchor. 135'
FA May 6, 1988, Jon Bassett, Jim Olsen

22 You're No Spring Chicken Head 5.4 G 125' ★★★
The upper face has unique knobs.
Start: 4' right of the low point of the terrain and directly below the apex of an A-shaped overlap.
P1 5.4 G: Climb up the A-shaped overlap and onto a ledge below a left-rising ceiling. Break through the ceiling in the center, then straight up the featured face with knobs to its top. Work up and left on a slab to a ledge, over a bulge with a crack, then scramble up to the fixed anchor on trees. 125'
FA Jun 8, 1988, Jon Bassett, Andy Legg

23 Equinox 5.3 G 125' ★★
The first route on the face, climbed just after the spring equinox.
Start: At the highest point of the terrain below a 3'-high left-leaning open book that begins 4' up.
P1 5.3 G: Up past the open book to a ledge. Work left around a ceiling, then straight up a steep crack to slabs left of a birch. Up the orange slab to a steep headwall, then step left and climb a crack around the left side of the headwall up to trees with a fixed anchor. 125'
FA Mar 24, 1988, Jon Bassett, Rob Washbourne

24 The Other One 5.6 G 50' ★★
Start: 15' right of the high point of the terrain, below a shallow zigzag left-facing corner that begins 10' up at a triangular pod.
P1 5.6 G: Move up good edges and crack to the triangular pod, then up the left-facing corner to its top. Climb through the highest A-shaped break in the ceiling above via a left-leaning crack and proceed up to a birch tree with a fixed anchor at the top. 50'
FA Jun 12, 1988, Jon Bassett, Tripp Leiby

SANTA CLARA TRACT

Location	Southwest of Santa Clara, accessed from Blue Mountain Road off NY 458
Summary	Several cliffs, one of them very large, that are raw and virtually undeveloped.

3	4	2	2	1	1		13
-5.6	5.7	5.8	5.9	5.10	5.11	5.12 5.13+	total

There is a wealth of rock west of Azure Mountain on the summits of Brushy Top Mountain, Lost Mountain, Flat Top Mountain, and County Line Mountain. Due to its inaccessibility, the area has seen limited exploration.

ACCESS
The land is part of the Santa Clara Tract and is one of the more remote sections of the Adirondacks. It has been owned by a number of large timber companies since the 1870s. The land is currently owned by Heartwood Forest Fund, and the state has purchased public recreation rights to the property. The limitations are the same as those for other state land (the same camping rules, etc.).

The numerous hunting camps and various other structures on the land are private and should not be approached.

The state has an easement to the Santa Clara Tract through the McCavanaugh Pond Club property, with the stipulation that you stay on the road as described.

A full description of the special rules and regulations can be found on New York State's DEC website (search for "NYS DEC Santa Clara Tract").

Northern Mountains

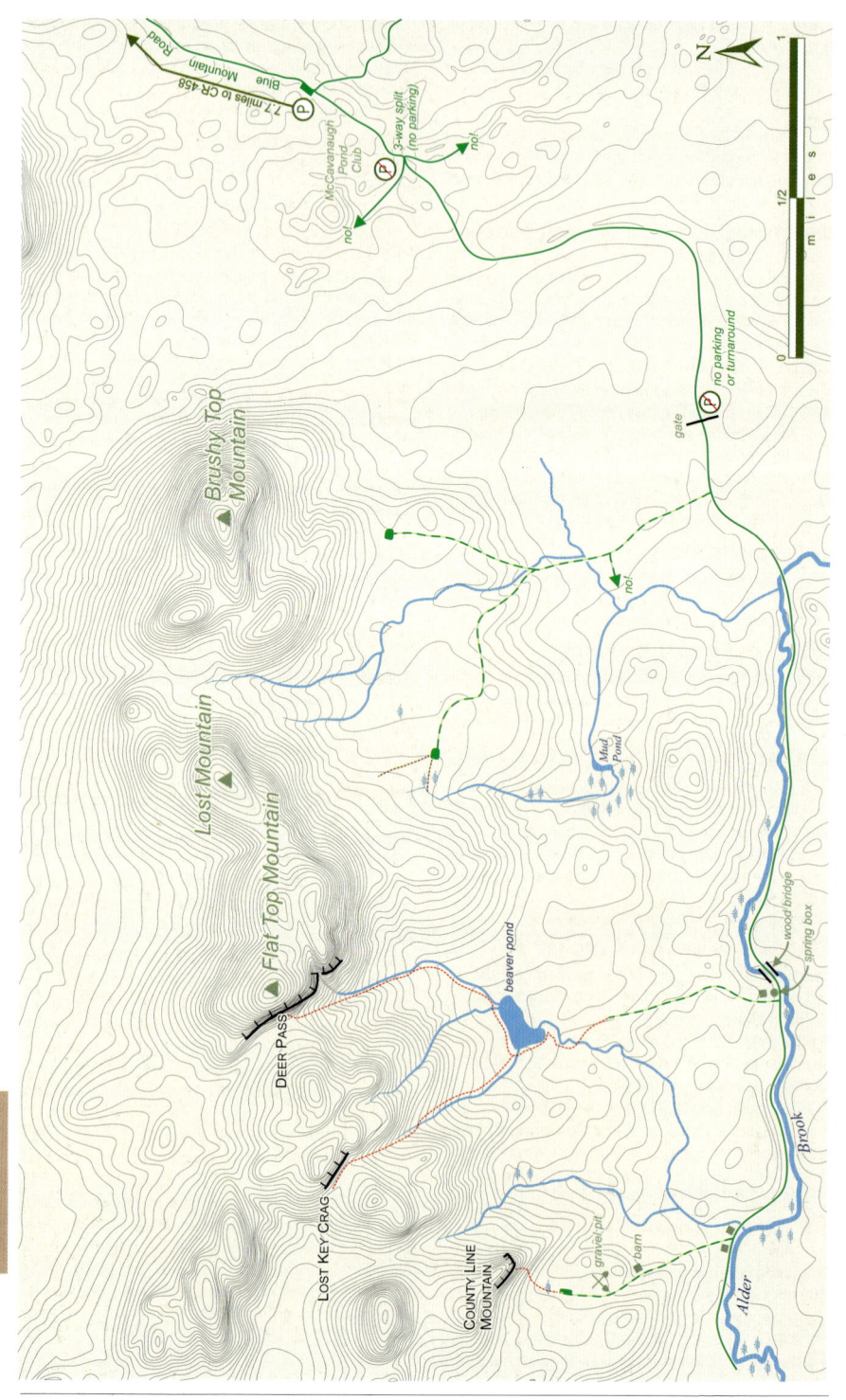

Northern Mountains

Santa Clara Tract
DEER PASS

Location	West side of Flat Top Mountain
Aspect	West
Height	300'
Quality	★
Approach	1 hr 35 min, difficult
Summary	A long, high, complex cliff that is virtually undeveloped; impressive features, although dirty.

2	1	1	1	1	1		7
-5.6	5.7	5.8	5.9	5.10	5.11	5.12	5.13+	total

This large cliff sits on the west side of Flat Top Mountain in a very isolated part of the park. The cliff is extensive, 300' high in places and spanning more than 0.5 mile in width, and virtually unexplored. The routes done so far represent only a small fraction of the potential here.

The cliff sits on a hillside that rises to the height of the pass. The existing climbs are located in the center (Twain Town Area) and the right end (Deer Hunter Area).

HISTORY

The earliest known rock climber at Deer Pass was Jared Thayer, who heard of the cliff from Hubert Clark, a woodsman and longtime hunter in the area. Thayer explored several of the cliffs before returning with Jeff Edwards to climb the first route, Twain Town. Thayer continued exploration with Steve Harris and the Ohio Boys (Scott Blanchard, John Mansperger, et al.), climbing a few routes at Deer Pass and County Line Mountain. The cliff has seen other explorations, by Jay Kullman and Mark Simon, but their routes aren't known.

DIRECTIONS   (MAP PAGE 416)

This remote cliff is best approached with a mountain bike, as getting there will involve about 5 miles of biking and an hour of hiking.

From Santa Clara (at the intersection with Center Street), drive 2.3 miles northeast on NY 458 to Blue Mountain Road and turn left. This is 3.8 miles south of the blinking red light in Saint Regis Falls. Reset the odometer to 0. At 2.7 miles, you lose the pavement; at 7.0 miles, you pass the trailhead to Azure Mountain; and at 7.7 miles, you reach a widening or large open lot on Blue Mountain Road 540271,4930350. The main road bends to the left, and straight ahead is a smaller dirt road marked "McCavanaugh Pond Club, Inc.," with many warning signs about private property. There is a public easement for nonmotorized use of this road.

A more scenic drive from the south begins at the intersection of NY 86 and NY 30 at the entrance to Paul Smiths. From here, Follow NY 30 north for 100 yards, then turn left on Keese Mills Road (unmarked) and follow it 16.5 miles to the McCavanaugh Pond Club, Inc., entrance on the left. (The road changes name to Blue Mountain Road after some distance.)

Park in the open lot on Blue Mountain Road and walk or bike the McCavanaugh Pond Club road heading south. After 0.4 mile, there is a three-way split; take the middle branch. About 2.0 miles from the three-way split is a locked gate where you enter state land. 2.0 miles past the gate is a right turn 535695,4927862, this is 0.2 mile after a good-sized wood bridge and 180' after a small rectangular spring box with a curved roof on the right side of the road. Turn right onto a grassy logging road and proceed straight to its end (don't take any of the right forks). The road eventually fades into a trail; leave the bike and continue straight ahead on foot following the trail with occasional survey flagging. Follow the trail to its end at a beaver pond. Bushwhack around the beaver pond to the left (west) to the opposite side of the pond (circling around the pond is farther than it looks) and find the inlet stream. Follow the inlet stream north and uphill for 20 min to the height of the pass. The cliff is obvious on the right side of the pass 535524,4930625.

It takes about 35 min to reach the end of the road

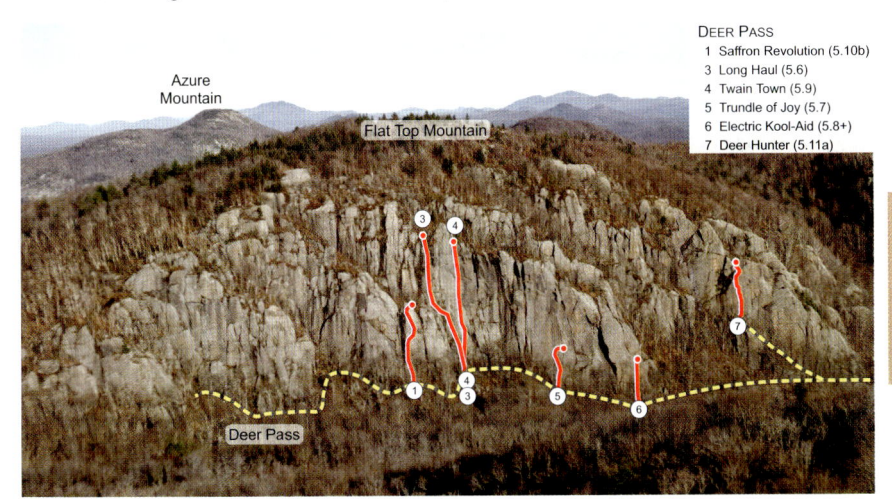

DEER PASS
1 Saffron Revolution (5.10b)
3 Long Haul (5.6)
4 Twain Town (5.9)
5 Trundle of Joy (5.7)
6 Electric Kool-Aid (5.8+)
7 Deer Hunter (5.11a)

417

by bike: 15 min to the locked gate, 10 more min to the turnoff after the spring box, then 10 more min. to the end of the grassy logging road. There are some sections of soft sand on the main road, especially around the locked gate.

Twain Town Area

In the center of the cliff and at the high point of the terrain is a sloped grassy clearing. In the center of the clearing is a tipped-up boulder with a maple tree growing up against it, about 20' from the base of the cliff and 20' left of a narrow 50'-high chimney. This tipped-up boulder serves as a landmark to locate routes in this section.

1 Saffron Revolution
5.10b G (5.6 R) 160' ★★★
Named for the political protests occurring in Myanmar at the time of the first ascent.
Start: Walk downhill and left of Twain Town to another wall with roofs 25' up broken by a distinctive chimney. Begin 30' left of the chimney at a clean crack that leads to a left-facing corner that starts 30' up.
P1 5.10b G (5.6 R): Up the handcrack to a small square overhang, then step right into the left-facing corner. Up the corner (crux) to its top, then move right to a left-facing flake. Mantel the flake, then move right and make another mantel to gain a short crack. Move left to the top of a right-facing flake (last gear), then run out a slab with grooves, working up and left to a hidden 3" crack on its upper left side. Work back right to a large birch cluster with a fixed anchor. 160'
FA Sep 29, 2007, Jim Lawyer, Tad Welch, Josh Hancock

2 Two Nuts and a Cam 5.3 G 90'
Originally climbed with a rack that consisted of two nuts and one cam and broken into three very short pitches.
Start: 15' left of Twain Town below a mossy right-facing corner.
P1 5.3 G: Up the corner broken by many ledges, trees, and blueberry bushes to a tree ledge. 90'
FA Sep 29, 2007, Josh Hancock, Jared Thayer

3 Long Haul 5.6 G 170'
Start: Same as Twain Town.
P1 5.6 G: Up the slab to gain a crack in a bulge on the left. Up the bulging crack (crux), then follow a long vegetated crack in a right-facing corner to its top. Step left to a tree ledge (possible belay), then continue up through a series of cracks, flakes, and blocks to a higher sloping ledge. Move up and left 30', then up to a third ledge just below mossy corners. 130'
P2 5.6 G: Traverse left 15' to avoid the mossy corners, then around to the left side of an arête. Follow discontinuous fingercracks straight to the top. 40'
FA Sep 29, 2007, Steve Harris, Neal Knitel, Roland Barr

Leslie Ackerman on the first ascent of Trundle of Joy (5.7).

4 Twain Town 5.9 G 180' ★★
Reportedly an excellent route, and one of the more obvious lines at the cliff. Named for the country singer Shania Twain, who briefly owned a house near Saint Regis Falls in the Adirondacks.
Start: 40' left of the tipped-up boulder at a cluster of birches below a clean slab. This slab sits below a large right-facing corner that dominates this section.
P1 5.9 G: Climb up the left edge of the slab and into a right-facing corner. The corner steepens through a bulge, then merges with a larger right-facing corner; climb the crack in the larger corner through an overhanging section to a ledge with a tree. Up the steep wall through a notch on the skyline to the top. 180'
FA 1998, Jeff Edwards, Jared Thayer

Northern Mountains

5 Trundle of Joy 5.7 G 70' ★

This climb of exploration ends at a ledge but could be extended up a dirty off-width crack. Named for the large unstable boulder trundled from the ledge.

Start: 50' right of the tipped-up boulder at the base of a left-facing, left-arching corner.

P1 5.7 G: Climb the crack in the corner, then make an airy move left out to another thin crack. Continue up right a few more feet, then scramble onto a ledge. 70'

Descent: There is no fixed anchor on the ledge. The first-ascent party downclimbed right (5.3; loose) to a large grassy ledge and rappelled from tiny unstable trees.

FA May 6, 2007, Leslie Ackerman, Neal Knitel, Jim Lawyer, Jared Thayer

6 Electric Kool-Aid 5.8+ G 80' ★★

This nice corner is relatively clean with solid protection. The climb can be extended above. The name was inspired by a Tom Wolfe book.

Start: 80' right of Trundle of Joy (and 130' right of the tipped-up boulder) at a right-facing corner on the right end of an orange ceiling 15' up. There is a tree growing up against the arête formed by the corner.

P1 5.8+ G: Climb up the corner past a wide section with a couple of chockstones to a bulge. Continue in the wide crack through the bulge (crux; dirty) to a birch tree. 80'

Descent: Rappel from the birch tree.

FA May 6, 2007, Jim Lawyer, Leslie Ackerman, Neal Knitel

Deer Hunter Area

At the right end of the cliff is a gully that separates the main cliff from Hubert's Brow, the knob of rock to the right. Left of the gully is a sheer, clean face broken by cracks that rises above a left-rising tree slope. At the highest point of the left-rising tree slope is a pile of boulders with the route Deer Hunter. At the lower right end of the face are several cracks that have been toproped (Sep 30, 2007, Kyle Schaefer, Josh Hancock, Neal Knitel, Jared Thayer, Roland Barr, Steve Harris).

7 Deer Hunter 5.11a G 100' ★★★

Start: 6' right of the height of the left-rising tree slope, below a shallow 5'-long right-rising ramp that leads to a straight-in crack.

P1 5.11a G: Up the short ramp, then follow the tight, gnarly handcrack to a sloped stance on the left. Up parallel cracks to where they converge at another stance, then up the crack to its end. Crux face moves up and left gain a fingercrack. Follow the fingercrack to a ledge. Mantel up right onto another ledge, then up to a headwall with a 4" left-slanting crack. Up this to a tree or step right around the headwall and up an easy ramp to the top. 100'

Gear: To 3"; a 4" cam is helpful for the topout.

FA Sep 29, 2007, Jim Lawyer, Tad Welch

Santa Clara Tract

LOST KEY CRAG

Location	On a knoll west of Deer Pass, accessed from Blue Mountain Road off NY 458
Aspect	Southwest
Height	120'
Quality	
Approach	1 hr 35 min, difficult
Summary	A recently discovered cliff with crack lines, corners, and some roofs; provides nice views of Train Pond.

Lost Key Crag is positioned on the southwest side of a knoll west of Deer Pass, about halfway between Flat Top Mountain to the east and County Line Mountain to the west. It's about 750' wide and has a lot of unexplored rock, although much of it is dirty. The rock is the same quality as that in Deer Pass, but more vertical with more horizontal cracks.

There is a good camping area at the base.

HISTORY

Neal Knitel and Jim Lawyer saw the cliff during a reconnaissance flight for this book. Knitel returned the next day with friends and climbed the route Keyed In.

DIRECTIONS (MAP PAGE 416)

Follow the approach to Deer Pass to the beaver pond. Hike around the pond, then follow the westernmost (leftmost) stream that flows into the beaver pond. Hike up the drainage area past many boulders on a bearing of 353° into a notch. The cliff will be obvious on your right 534853,4930177.

8 Keyed In 5.7 G 100'

Start: 330' from the left side of the cliff at the high point along the base at a large right-facing corner split by a ledge. This is 60' right of a right-facing corner with a chimney at the top and just right of an orange wall that rises above a ledge 10' up.

P1 5.7 G: Up the corner with a hand- and fistcrack in the back (and using ample face holds on the right) to a cramped ledge beneath a ceiling. Pull around the right side of the ceiling, reach up and right to a jug (crux), and continue up the corner to a perched boulder. Scramble up to the top and belay at good trees. 100'

FA Nov 3, 2007, Neal Knitel, Jared Thayer, Josh Hancock, Greg Williams

LOST KEY CRAG
8 Keyed In (5.7)

Northern Mountains

Santa Clara Tract
COUNTY LINE MOUNTAIN

Location	West of Deer Pass, accessed from Blue Mountain Road off NY 458
Aspect	South
Height	80'
Quality	
Approach	55 min, moderate
Summary	A number of short single-pitch crack and face routes on an off-vertical face.

1	2	1	1				5
-5.6	5.7	5.8	5.9	5.10	5.11	5.12	5.13+	total

This small crag is located on a subsummit of County Line Mountain, west of Deer Pass. The cliff has an easier approach than Deer Pass, in that it's less difficult to find and involves only 15 min of bushwhacking. The established climbing is all single-pitch and is located on a south-facing off-vertical wall. The climbs are very close together and can be toproped by walking right (past **Woo Hoo!**) to access the top of the cliff. The cliff is in a wooded setting with thick foliage around the base. The top offers good views.

The cliff has a continuous wall that faces west, then turns uphill facing south, then turns again to face east. There are no reported routes on the more extensive west-facing wall, although evidence of climbing does exist and the potential for short routes is obvious. The south-facing section of the cliff is sloped uphill and, in the center, has a ledge 10' up with trees; the routes **Groovy Monkey Love** and **Home and Garden Center** begin on top of this ledge.

DIRECTIONS (MAP PAGE 416)
From the turnoff to Deer Pass, continue on the main road another 0.75 mile to the next right turn (the first right turn that's not a driveway to a camp). The turn is between two camps on the right 534503,4928106. Follow the road steeply uphill at first, past a small barn on the right, then past a gravel pit on the right, and finally to the end of the road. The cliff is visible through the trees on the hillside above as you approach the end of the road. Hike on a bearing of 40°, through a marshy section, then steeply uphill to reach the base of the cliff 534343,4929246, about 15 min.

The cliff is best approached by mountain bike. On a bike, it takes about 55 min to reach the cliff: 25 min to the turnoff to Deer Pass, 15 more min to the end of the road, then 15 min of bushwhacking.

9 With a Little Help from My Friends
5.6 G 80' ★

Start: 3' left of the chimney of **Push, Bob, Push!**, below a clean crack that ends 20' up.
P1 5.6 G: Climb the crack to its end, step left to the next crack, and climb it to its end. Step left again to a third crack and climb it to a cedar. Step left and finish in a deep V-slot to the top. 80'
FA Sep 8, 2002, Josh Dowd, Anthony Stacy, Scott Blanchard

10 Push, Bob, Push! 5.7 PG 75'
Lamaze class might be an added benefit for this chimney/off-width combination.
Start: At the base of the 2'-wide chimney that begins left of the wide ledge from which **Home and Garden Center** and **Groovy Monkey Love** start.
P1 5.7 PG: Climb up the chimney to where it narrows and sanity forces you left onto the face. Climb a mossy crack on the face to the top. 75'
FA Sep 8, 2002, Bob Schopis, Andy Feilen

11 Home and Garden Center 5.8+ G 70' ★
Need some mulch? This one required extensive cleaning on lead.
Start: In the center of the south-facing cliff is a ledge 10' up with trees. Begin at the left end of the ledge, 20' left of **Groovy Monkey Love**, 2' right of the chimney of **Push, Bob, Push!**, at the base of a right-leaning crack.
P1 5.8+ G: Climb up the crack to a 10'-high flake (the "chopping block"). Up the right side of the flake to a left-facing, right-leaning corner, then follow the corner to the top. 70'
FA Sep 8, 2002, John Mansperger, Mike Palasek

12 Groovy Monkey Love 5.7 G 65' ★★★
Start: In the center of the south-facing cliff is a ledge 10' up with trees. Begin on the ledge 5' left of a right-leaning vegetated crack that is 10' left of the left-facing corner that defines the right end of the ledge.
P1 5.7 G: Boulder up the face and mantel onto a small ledge at the base of the crack. Follow the crack as it angles right to the top. 65'
FA Sep 8, 2002, Steve Harris, Jared Thayer

13 Woo Hoo! 5.9+ G 20' ★
Start: Walk right along the base of the cliff to a corner where the cliff bends left and becomes east-facing. Begins 30' uphill below a right-leaning handcrack.
P1 5.9+ G: Jam the crack to a lichen-covered slab. 20'
FA Sep 8, 2002, Scott Blanchard, Josh Dowd

JENKINS MOUNTAIN

Location	Near Paul Smiths, accessed from Keese Mills Road
Aspect	South
Height	200'
Quality	
Approach	1 hr 30 min, difficult
Summary	Very dirty moderate routes on a remote cliff with a scenic approach.

7		1	1				9
-5.6	5.7	5.8	5.9	5.10	5.11	5.12	5.13+	total

Jenkins Mountain is located near Paul Smiths, about 20 min north of Saranac Lake. The mountain has two summits, and this cliff sits below the easternmost knoll of the north summit. The approach is long but with fantastic scenery along the shores of two wilderness ponds, Black Pond and Long Pond.

420

Northern Mountains

The cliff is not as appealing, however, with dense vegetation at its base and no real summit, as the climbs seem to end on vegetated islands on a steep slab. The exceptions are several sections that overhang at the bottom with excellent rock, then turn to ugly slab just above. If you are prepared for short, severe routes, this overhanging section offers numerous possibilities (**Bong Hits 4 Jesus** and **Lost in Paradise** are two such examples).

The ice climbing on Jenkins Mountain is at a different location on the northeast side, closer to NY 30.

On the southwest face of the north summit near the notch is another cliff with some potential.

HISTORY

The first reported exploration of the cliffs of Jenkins was in the late 1960s by Ken Nichols and Steve Hall, then students at Paul Smiths. As beginners, they pounded some pitons, hung in aiders, and practiced rappelling but never really climbed anything. The area was rediscovered by Dick Tucker in 1988 while he was looking for glacial features typical of the area—potholes and a very prominent esker that goes nearly to NY 30. He climbed **Sennet** as a solo adventure, then returned four years later with Tim Riley, his childhood climbing buddy, to climb several routes. The cliff has seen little attention since then.

ACCESS

The north (and lower) summit of Jenkins Mountain is located on state lands, but the south summit and the approach are on lands owned by Paul Smiths College and leased to the state of New York for the Visitor Interpretive Center (VIC). This means that camping is not allowed at the lean-tos, but camping at the base of the cliff is OK.

DIRECTIONS (MAP PAGE 421)

From the intersection of NY 86 and NY 30 at the entrance to Paul Smiths, drive north on NY 30 for 100', then turn left on Keese Mills Road (unmarked, but there is a large traffic triangle at this intersection) and follow it 2.4 miles to the trailhead on the right marked for "Black and Long Pond Access."

From the parking area, follow Black Pond Trail (orange disks) for 20 min (1 mile) to the intersection with Long Pond Trail (red disks). Go straight on Long Pond Trail past a beautiful lean-to with a dock 556469,4921974, then to the intersection with Jenkins Road (aka Jenkins Mountain Road), 1.6 miles (35 min) from the parking area.

An alternative approach to this point (same distance, but far less scenic) follows Jenkins Road from the Visitor Interpretive Center on NY 30, 0.8 mile north of the intersection of NY 86 and NY 30 at the entrance to Paul Smiths. The VIC is open from 9:00 a.m. to 5:00 p.m. and is otherwise gated, so it may be wise to park on NY 30. From the VIC, follow Jenkins Road for 1.6 miles to the intersection with Long Pond Trail.

From the intersection of Long Pond Trail and Jenkins Road, follow Jenkins Road (blue markers) 0.4 mile to an area of beaver activity. Just before the swamp, the road passes an outhouse on the right and makes a hard left turn to the south. The road continues on a small ridge parallel to a beaver swamp and, within 200', the road ends, narrowing to a trail; at this point, leave the road and bushwhack downhill to the beaver swamp and cross it. (In high water, you may need to contour around the ends of the swamp.) On the far side, pick up a small stream that feeds the swamp and follow it uphill. Within 100' of the swamp, the steam pours over a 15'-high, 30'-wide rock wall; this is a good marker for finding the correct stream.

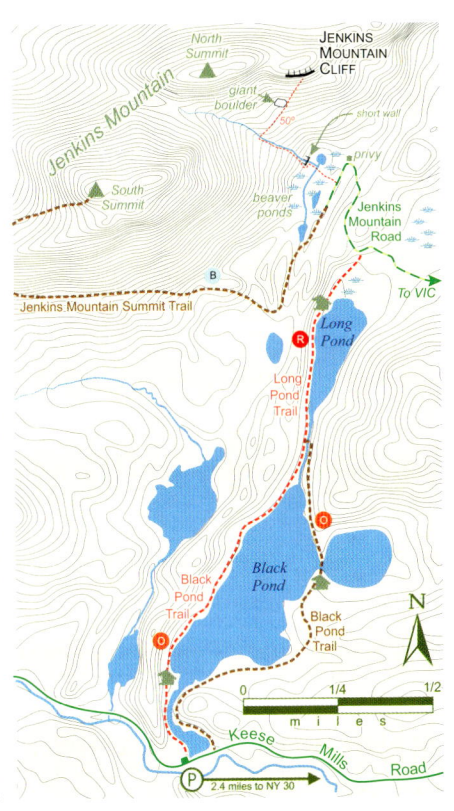

Follow the stream uphill for 10 min to a cairn, then turn right on a bearing of 50°. A large boulder (with the footprint of a house) is reached after 5 min, then the cliff is reached within another 5 min 556337,4922915. The forest along the stream and beneath the cliff is thick and the leaves significantly reduce visibility, so expect to do some hunting around for the cliff.

1 Sennet 5.2 G 50'

A little climbing at the bottom but nothing noteworthy after that.

Start: At the left end of the cliff is a low 40'-wide overhanging gray wall that eventually diminishes into the dirt. This route begins at the right end of this wall below two steps 3' up. Just right of the steps is a right-leaning groove.

Northern Mountains

P1 5.2 G: Climb up the steps, then straight up mossy rock in a right-facing V-groove to a ledge. Step over a small wall and up a slab to some trees. 50'
FA Jun 18, 1988, Dick Tucker (solo)

2 The Slot 5.4 G 25'
Like Sennet, this route has a little climbing at the bottom, then up vegetated slabs to trees.
Start: 30' right of Sennet in a wide, shallow chimney with a V-slot in the back and a right-leaning handcrack to its right.
P1 5.4 G: Climb up the slot and onto the slab above to some trees. 25'
FA Jul 26, 1992, Dick Tucker (solo)

3 Fly Away 5.4 G 60'
Start: 50' right of the wide, shallow chimney of The Slot, and on the left end of a bulging wall, below a V-groove that begins 6' up.
P1 5.4 G: Climb the mossy V-groove, then step left to a bulge and climb it via a left-leaning wide crack. At its top, step left into a shallow right-facing open book with a crack. At its top, step right to trees. 60'
FA Jul 25, 1992, Dick Tucker, Tim Riley

4 Amnesia 5.5 G 130'
Start: 30' left of the V-groove of Draining the Beaver, at a 6'-high bulge below a slab-ledge, above which is a deep left-leaning V-groove. There is a triangular pod at the base of the V-groove and a short, steep overhanging wall to its right.
P1 5.5 G: Up the bulge onto the slab, then up the face left of the V-groove on ledges to a slab above. Up the slab and blueberry bushes to a crack that breaks the left end of a ceiling, just right of a birch. Up the crack and onto a dirty slab, which is followed to the top. 130'
FA Jul 25, 1992, Dick Tucker, Tim Riley

5 Draining the Beaver 5.6 G 70' ★★
Start: At an obvious V-groove just right of an overhanging black wall and 20' left of another deep, mossy V-groove. There is a thimble-sized finger hole 7' up on the left wall of the V-groove and a 2'-high pedestal at its base.
P1 5.6 G: Climb up the crack past a wide section to a ledge, then over a vegetated bulge to a pine tree. 70'
Descent: Rappel from the pine tree.
FA Jul 1, 2007, Leslie Ackerman, Jim Lawyer

6 Lost in Paradise 5.8 G 70' ★★
Protects well with small TCUs. Named for the epic of finding the cliff.
Start: 5' right of Draining the Beaver below a steep brown wall littered with angular holds.
P1 5.8 G: Climb the face to its top, then step left over a bulge and up to a pine tree (same as Draining the Beaver). 70'
History: This was cleaned by Dick Tucker, who never returned to complete it.
FA Jul 1, 2007, Jim Lawyer, Leslie Ackerman

7 Bong Hits 4 Jesus 5.9 G 80' ★★
Named after the banner at issue in the free-speech case *Morse v. Frederick*, which was in the news at the time.
Start: 45' right of Draining the Beaver is an overhanging black wall with a crack, just left of a large right-facing corner. 75' right of this corner is the most overhanging section of the cliff, with a nice flat base. Begin on the right side of this overhanging section at a discontinuous black crack that starts 6' up, just above a shallow A-shaped alcove, 15' right of a large tree with three intertwined trunks.
P1 5.9 G: Climb the cracks to the top, then up a slab to a short bulge with a handcrack. Over the bulge, then up slab and vegetation to trees. 80'
Descent: Rappel from the trees.
FA Jul 1, 2007, Jim Lawyer, Leslie Ackerman

8 Forty Winks 5.6 G 240'
Start: 50' right of Bong Hits 4 Jesus, at the right end of roofs, below a right-facing mossy corner that begins 4' up.
P1 5.6 G: Climb the corner, up through some blueberry bushes, over a bulge, and onto a slab. Continue up a dirty crack and belay at its top. 120'
P2 5.4 G: Continue up easy slabs to the top. 120'
FA Jul 25, 1992, Dick Tucker, Tim Riley

Leslie Ackerman on the first ascent of Draining the Beaver (5.6).

9 Epilogue 5.5 G 240'

Start: 50' right of Bong Hits 4 Jesus, at the right end of roofs, is the right-facing mossy corner of Forty Winks. Right of this is another low-angle 25'-high right-facing corner, and right of this is a third 5'-high right-facing corner capped by a left-arching overlap. This route begins at the base of the third corner.

P1 5.5 G: Climb up and left on clean rock to a bulge with two cracks. Over the bulge at the vertical crack and onto an easy slab. Belay to the right of a tree island. 130'

P2 5.4 G: Continue up easy slabs to the top. 110'

Descent: You can rappel from trees or walk left (bring your shoes).

FA Jul 26, 1992, Dick Tucker, Tim Riley

CHARCOAL KILN QUARRY

Location	Near Paul Smiths, accessed from Keese Mills Road
Aspect	Southeast
Height	50'
Quality	
Approach	3 min, easy
Summary	A small, historically interesting cliff with an easy approach, with an unpleasant semi-urban feel.

6	1		1	1				9
-5.6	5.7	5.8	5.9	5.10	5.11	5.12	5.13+	total

Charcoal Kiln Quarry is a long-abandoned quarry with mostly solid rock and easy access. The rock has a quarried feel—some drill marks, and friability. Once a popular practice area with local climbers, it became vegetated and littered with garbage, making it an uninviting destination. In 2011, the cliff was cleaned up and equipped with 1/2" bolts for leading. All routes have fixed anchors, making this a good spot for toproping.

The cliff's most prominent feature, on its right end, is a right-rising ramp that provides a 4th-class approach to the top. As you look up from the base of the ramp, there is a left-facing corner (the start of Burke's Path), to the left of which is a larger right-facing corner.

HISTORY

Climbers have been using the quarry for years for practice. Stanley Smith, who grew up in Saranac Lake, recalls climbing here in the late 1940s with Donald Lebeau using their homemade pitons. The charcoal kiln was removed in the 1980s.[1]

In 2010, Tony Turfano, the climbing coach at Paul Smiths, added a number of routes. They serve as the closest climbing for Paul Smiths' students, and for training for his climbing team.

[1] Dr. Michael Kudish, *Historical Update: Paul Smith's College Lands, Forests, and Buildings 1981 to 2004* (Paul Smith's College, Paul Smiths, NY, 2004), pp 13, 69.

DIRECTIONS

From the intersection of NY 86 and NY 30 at the entrance to Paul Smiths, drive north on NY 30 for 100', then turn left on Keese Mills Road (unmarked, but there is a large traffic triangle at this intersection), and follow it 0.6 mile to a pullout on the right 558557,4920739, just after a small bridge. The pullout is an entrance to a gated dirt road that leads into the Visitor Interpretive Center property.

Proceed through the gate onto the dirt road. Bear left at the first fork and walk 75' to a grassy open area. The cliff is through the trees 100' on the left 558527,4920858, just before the next fork in the road. When approaching from the clearing, aim for the far right side of the cliff and pick up a good herd path. This avoids the tangle of trees, rocks, and other debris directly in front of the cliff.

1 Capstone 5.10+ TR 65'

Begin on the left side of the quarry just before the terrain drops down left, on a ledge below three small, clean overhangs. Climb over the overhangs, then step right and join A Cold Draft...Horse to a fixed anchor just left of a large perched boulder on the skyline at the top of the cliff.

2 A Cold Draft...Horse 5.6 G 65'

Start: Below the right end of three small overhangs, right of Capstone, where the ledge merges into the ground, at a drill-tube in black rock at head height.

● **P1 5.6 G:** Follow the crack above the drill tube to a short right-facing corner. Up the corner past a small ceiling to another short corner, then up easier terrain to a fixed anchor shared with Capstone. 65'

FA 2011, Dylan Shows

3 Burke's Path 5.4 G 65'

Start: In the center of the quarry, at the height of land, is the beginning of a long, right-rising ramp that goes to the top of the cliff. Begin at the lower left end of this ramp.

● **P1 5.4 G:** Move up some ledges, then step left to the base of a shallow, right-facing open book. Go straight up (V1) staying left of the bolts to a ledge with small birches. Go up and right to a fixed anchor at the top of a cliff. 65'

● **V1 Learning the Steps 5.5 G:** Staying right of the bolts increases the grade a bit. 65'

4 Stager's Arête 5.6 G 65'

Start: Same as Burke's Path.

● **P1 5.6 G:** Go up Burke's Path for 10', then veer right to an arête. Up the arête (stay out of the corner) to a ledge, then join Burke's Path to the top. 65'

5 Dunce In the Corner 5.5 G 65'

Start: Same as Burke's Path.

● **P1 5.5 G:** Go up Burke's Path for 10', then veer right beneath Stager's Arête to the large, black, right-facing open book. Up the corner to a ledge, then angle left to finish on Stager's Arête. 65'

Northern Mountains

6 Back on the Horse 5.9 G 65'
Start: Same as **Burke's Path**.
● **P1 5.9 G:** Go up **Burke's Path** for 10', then veer right beneath **Stager's Arête** to the large, black, right-facing open book. Go up the face right of the corner to a ledge below a black wall. Angle up and right to a fixed anchor at the rim, about 6' left of a prominent, left-facing nose with a birch tree. The crux is 15' below the top. 65'
FA 2011, Dustin Ulrich

7 The Smell of B.O. 5.4 G 65'
The very first route climbed on top rope.
Start: Same as **Burke's Path**.
● **P1 5.4 G:** Climb up and right on the ramp to below the prominent, left-facing nose at the top of the cliff. Climb straight up left-facing, broken flakes to the birch tree on the nose, then step left to a fixed anchor shared with **Back on the Horse**. 65'

8 Ted's Has It All 5.7 G 65'
Start: 20' right of **Burke's Path**, below the ramp, at the bottom of a large, boulder-looking bulge.
● **P1 5.7 G:** Go straight up the face to the ramp. Step across the ramp and climb over two large ledges to a shallow scooped feature on the main face. Up this to a high ledge below an orange headwall. Go up the left side of the headwall to the top; step right to a fixed anchor. 65'
FA 2011, Tony Tufano

9 No M.D. for You 5.6 G 65'
Start: 5' right of **Ted's Has It All**.
● **P1 5.6 G:** Climb up to meet the ramp, then move up right, and climb a crack moving up left to the right side of the high ledge beneath the orange headwall. Up the headwall to a fixed anchor. 65'
FA 2011, Matt Baer

BLUE HILL

There is a long, low cliff on the southwest side of Blue Hill, northeast of Gabriels. The cliff lies at about the 650-meter contour and well south of the partially vegetated west face 567795,4921500. The approach involves a long bushwhack, made more difficult by the Great Ice Storm of 1998. There are several cliffs grouped into two bands, the lower of which is taller, reaching 150'. Dick Tucker and Tim Riley explored the area and climbed a single route, **Black Dog Chimney** (5.2; 30'; Oct 22, 1977), located at the northern end of the cliff, which ascends the obvious 18"-wide chimney with two large chockstones.

BLUFF ISLAND

Location	In Lower Saranac Lake, accessed from NY 3 west of Saranac Lake
Aspect	South
Height	70'
Quality	★★★
Approach	20 min, easy; boat required
Summary	An island cliff rising from the water, used mostly for toproping.

This 70'-high cliff is located on Bluff Island in Lower Saranac Lake. It's a great setting for climbing, as the lake, surrounded mostly by state land, has a remote feeling and is dotted with islands, many of which have campsites. It's one-star climbing in a five-star location.

Unfortunately, the logistics of the cliff make leading inconvenient—there are no ledges at the bottom, the protection isn't great, and you can't traverse in from the sides. You have to start from a boat, and calm lake conditions are required. Toproping, however, is highly recommended, as there are large trees for anchoring (although they are set back a bit), and you can't beat the setting. Such an outing is made even more complete when combined with island camping, exploring the lake by canoe, a picnic lunch, swimming, cliff jumping, and perhaps some deep-water soloing. The climbing isn't necessarily for beginners, as there is nothing easy, and they might find it scary to be lowered over the water.

On the left side of the cliff, and starting from a small ledge, are two right-leaning cracks that go at about 5.7. The central crack system is about 5.8. Right of this is some difficult face climbing on a blank upper section

Bluff Island, seen from the approach from First Pond.

424

Northern Mountains

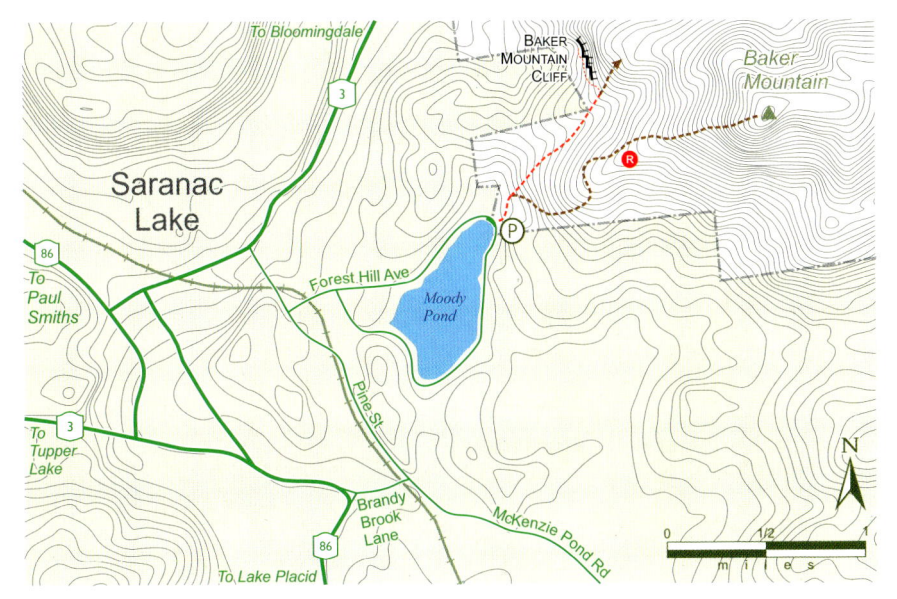

that rises above a triangular niche 20' up. On the right end of the cliff is a series of left-leaning cracks, about 5.8. On the far right end of the cliff is a large ledge that can be reached by scrambling down the right end of the cliff; this is a popular diving platform. (Jumping from the top isn't recommended and has resulted in numerous injuries.)

The rock is a little dirty, but that's not a major hindrance to climbing.

HISTORY
Little is known of the climbing history on Bluff Island. There is, however, a long history of jumping off the top. Bluff Island was even featured in the silent movie *Perils of Pauline*, filmed in 1914, in which actors Crane Wilbur and Pearl White took the plunge.

DIRECTIONS
The parking and boat access for Bluff Island are at the Second Pond Fishing Access Site, also called the Saranac Lake Islands Public Campground 565048,4904119. This is located on NY 3, 4.2 miles from Saranac Lake (when driving toward Tupper Lake, measured from the intersection of NY 3 and NY 86).

From the put-in, paddle northwest under NY 3 and into First Pond. Cross the pond and follow the channel to the lake. The cliffs of Bluff Island are straight ahead across a short section of open water and can't be missed 564073,4905250.

You can paddle around either side of the cliff to the other side of the island, where the water is calm and it is possible to pull your boat onto shore. Many herd paths lead to the top of the cliff.

BAKER MOUNTAIN

Location	In Saranac Lake
Aspect	West
Height	80'
Quality	★★★
Approach	12 min, easy
Summary	A small crag close to town with several good crack lines and two beautiful arêtes; good for toproping.

3	1	1	3	1	1	1	11
-5.6	5.7	5.8	5.9	5.10	5.11	5.12	5.13+	total

This small crag is located very near Saranac Lake and makes a good spot for communal cragging, similar to the Jewels and Gem wall. The pretty orange rock, quality lines, variety of grades, and proximity to town have made this popular for locals for nearly 70 years. The upper sections of the routes tend to be sandy, as dirt washes down over the face.

HISTORY
There is a long history of climbing at Baker Mountain. The earliest visitors are unknown, perhaps Dave Bernays, but old photos exist of climbers using Baker as a testing ground for aid climbing. The proximity to town and popularity with local climbers have obscured much of the first-ascent information for the obvious lines. Some noteworthy routes were added by Patrick Purcell in the late 80s and early 90s, and the most difficult lead was added by Mark Polinski in 2006 during his stint as a scuba diving instructor in Saranac Lake.

425

Northern Mountains

DIRECTIONS (MAP PAGE 425)

When you drive into Saranac Lake from Lake Placid on NY 86, the road makes a sharp bend to the left with an NBT Bank on the corner. Turn right onto Brandy Brook Lane. Cross the railroad tracks, then turn left at the T-intersection onto Pine Street (the right turn is McKenzie Pond Road, which leads to McKenzie Pond Boulders). Cross the tracks again, then turn right onto Forest Hill Avenue and follow this around Moody Pond to the far side of the pond. Parking for several cars is available on the pond side of the road; the trailhead is opposite the parking 570487,4909064.

From the pond, follow the main hiking trail for 2 min, under the high-tension wires to where the trail splits. The main trail goes right, and access to the cliff continues straight. Follow this trail for 8 min to a boggy area with some fallen trees; look for a climbers' path that branches off to the left. The climbers' path is followed for 2 min to the base of the crag 570831,4909631; total time about 12 min.

ACCESS

The land running along the base of the cliff is private, so extra care should be taken to preserve the property around the cliff.

DESCENT OPTIONS

On top of the Main Face is a large pine tree on the left. Just right of the pine is a large block set back from the edge with a fixed anchor. You can also walk right back to the trail.

Left End

To find the Left End, from the Main Face, walk left, downhill at first, then back uphill, a total of 200'. The features to look for are two facing corners capped by a roof near the top of the cliff. The corner on the left is **Doctor Y's**, and the arête formed by the right corner is **Saranac Saber**.

1 Mountain Boots and Pitons 5.5 G 70'

An exploratory route.

Start: 25' left of **Doctor Y's** is a large, irregular, overhanging right-facing corner left of a smooth steep face.

P1 5.5 G: Climb the inside corner, moving right under the roofs to gain the large grassy ledge. There is an old pin in the back corner. 40'

P2 5.5 G: Climb a series of blocks and ledges to a large corner, then on to the top. There is a large flake sitting precariously on a small ledge halfway up. 30'

ACB Sep 2, 1978, Dick Tucker, Tim Riley

2 Doctor Y's 5.9 G 60' ★★

A very nice-looking corner but presently a little dirty. Named after a once-popular drinking establishment in Saranac Lake, which is now Morgan's 11. The "Y" stands for the last name of the owner, Yanchitis, who owns the famous Tail O' the Pup BBQ in Ray Brook.

Start: 5' left of **Saranac Saber** at the base of a right-facing corner.

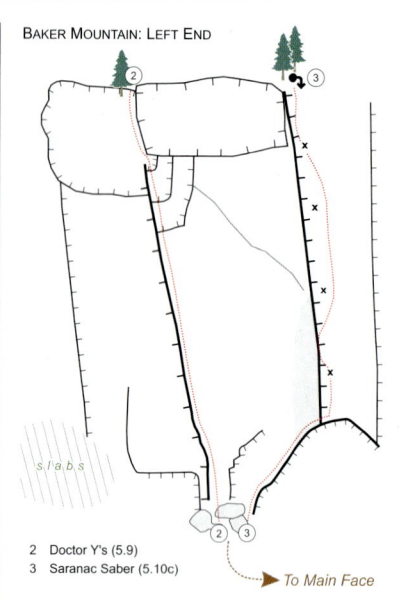

P1 5.9 G: Step up left to the base of a shallow right-facing, left-leaning corner with a crack. Up this corner (piton) to three roofs, stepping left around the third (and largest) roof into a large left-facing corner, which is followed to the top. 60'

FA Oct 4, 1990, Patrick Purcell, Dominic Eisinger

3 Saranac Saber 5.10c PG 60' ★

Another good arête climb, but a scary second clip.

Start: Below and just left of the obvious arête on the right end of the face.

● **P1 5.10c PG:** Climb the lichen- and moss-covered buttress rightward to the base of the arête, which is followed to the top. 60'

FA Aug 14, 1990, Patrick Purcell, Jeff Edwards

Main Face

This is the largest section of rock, the most obvious (and shocking) feature being Cure Cottage Block, a precariously wedged block the size of a refrigerator about 25' up. (The block seems to defy gravity until you climb it and realize it's cammed in at the top.) On the left side of the face are some stepped left-rising ceilings and overlaps.

4 Saranac 1888 5.9+ PG 80'

Saranac 1888 was the brand name of a line of hand-crafted nonalcoholic soft drinks made by Matt Brewing Company in the 1930s.

Start: At the left end of the Main Face, on the face directly below the prominent hanging arête.

P1 5.9+ PG: Climb up the face to gain the left-facing corner (the arête formed by this corner is the route **Bubba Does Baker**), which is followed past a pointed block to the top. 80'

Northern Mountains

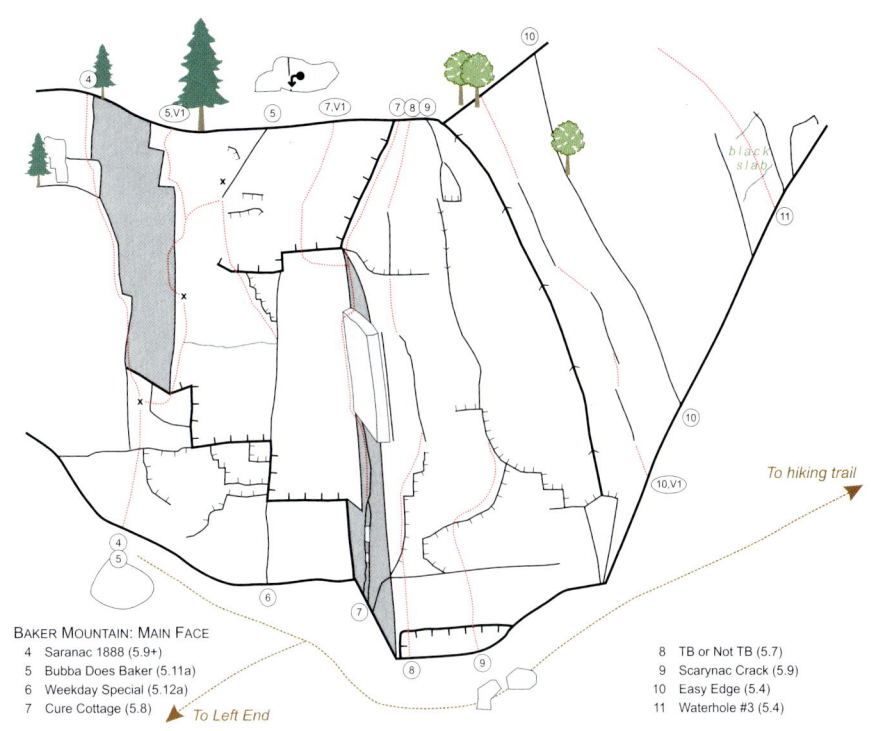

BAKER MOUNTAIN: MAIN FACE
4 Saranac 1888 (5.9+)
5 Bubba Does Baker (5.11a)
6 Weekday Special (5.12a)
7 Cure Cottage (5.8)

◀ To Left End

8 TB or Not TB (5.7)
9 Scarynac Crack (5.9)
10 Easy Edge (5.4)
11 Waterhole #3 (5.4)

Bill Coton, on aid at Baker Mountain in 1979. Photo by Jim Cunningham.

5 Bubba Does Baker 5.11a G 80' ★★★

Very good arête climbing; the regular route and the variation are both good.
Start: Same as Saranac 1888.
P1 5.11a G: Climb some face holds to a horizontal and past a bolt, then hand-traverse right to the arête. Up the arête past another bolt, (V1) then right onto the steep face at the base of a right-angling fingercrack. Crux face moves up the face lead to the top. 80'
V1 5.10a G: Clip the high bolt and move up left on blocks, then up the face to the top, just left of the large pine tree.
FA May 5, 1989, Patrick Purcell, Jeff Edwards

6 Weekday Special (aka Saranac Face) 5.12a R 80' ★

Technical climbing with barely adequate gear. This was an established toprope problem before led by Polinski.
Start: Just left of the large left-facing corner of Cure Cottage, at a crack below the left end of a low ceiling.
P1 5.12a R: Climb up the crack to the left end of the low ceiling, then up through tiered overlaps to gain a face with a thin crack. Work left to a shallow left-facing open book capped by a small triangular ceiling; over this to gain the right-angling finishing fingercrack of Bubba Does Baker. 80'
FA May, 2006, Mark Polinski

427

Northern Mountains

7 Cure Cottage 5.8 G 80' ★★★

Saranac Lake was once a world-renowned center for the treatment of tuberculosis (TB). A "cure cottage" was a small two-story cottage with an enclosed porch where TB patients were placed to breathe fresh air.

Start: At the base of a large left-facing corner in the center of the Main Face at its lowest point are two cracks; the route begins in the left-most of these cracks, which is filled with vertical flakes.

P1 5.8 G: Climb up the crack with wedged flakes to the left side of the Cure Cottage Block—a refrigerator-sized block cammed into the cliff 25' up. Jam up the left side, mount it, then continue straight up to the large roof, (V1) breaking out right at a right-facing, right-slanting dihedral. 80'

V1 5.10b G: Traverse left under the roof and break through the roof at the widest section using jugs to a thin, spicy finish.

Gear: To 4".

8 TB or Not TB 5.7 G 80' ★★

The name is yet another reference to Saranac Lake as a tuberculosis (TB) treatment center.

Start: On top of a flat shelf 4' up, on the right side of the Main Face just before going uphill. This shelf is just right of the large left-facing corner of **Cure Cottage**.

P1 5.7 G: From the left end of the shelf, climb up the orange face to two parallel cracks, the left of which is formed by the Cure Cottage Block. Climb these cracks to the top of the flake and up to a small, dirty overlap broken by a crack. Finish on the face just right of the right-leaning, right-facing dihedral (the finish is contrived due to the close proximity to **Cure Cottage** and **Scarynac Crack**). 80'

9 Scarynac Crack 5.9 G 80' ★★★

Once listed as a variation, this excellent route is distinct for all but the last 10'.

Start: Same as **TB or Not TB**.

P1 5.9 G: From the middle of the shelf, climb the orange face past a horizontal to a left-facing, right-slanting flake. Up this to a triangular slot, then up a curvy handcrack to its top. Step right to an orange left-facing open book, which is followed to the arête, merging with **TB or Not TB** to the top. 80'

Gear: To 1".

10 Easy Edge 5.4 G 70' ★

This easy route provides a good way to get to the top and set topropes for climbs on the Main Face.

Start: Uphill and right of the Main Face is a slab on a hillside, perpendicular to the Main Face. This route begins on the left side of this slab below a tree-filled crack.

P1 5.4 G: Scramble up some blocks to the base of the crack. (V1) Climb the crack to the top. 70'

Alex Pellman on Cure Cottage (5.8). Photo by Forrest Schwab.

V1 5.6 PG: Climb the face just left of the crack, following discontinuous cracks past several horizontals to the top.

11 Waterhole #3 5.4 PG 70'

Named after a well-known bar in Saranac Lake across the street from the town hall.

Start: 50' up the sloped hillside and 30' right of the tree-filled crack of **Easy Edge**, at the base of a black slab with horizontals.

P1 5.4 PG: Climb the black slab past many horizontals and several vertical crack features to a ledge system, then up leftward through dirty nondescript terrain to the top. 70'

INMAN SLABS

Location	Loon Lake, accessed from NY 3 north of Bloomingdale
Aspect	East
Height	90'
Quality	★
Approach	0 min, easy
Summary	Two small slabs with many quality moderate slab routes, most of which unfortunately are badly overgrown.

6	3	1	1				11
-5.6	5.7	5.8	5.9	5.10	5.11	5.12	5.13+	total

Inman Slabs are located near the north end of Loon Lake close to the settlement of Inman, the site of two long-gone railroad stations. The cliffs face an old railroad grade, now a right-of-way for National Grid power transmission lines. Despite the remote location, it has an urban feel due to its close proximity to the power lines and the fact that it's within earshot of the camps that ring the pond below the slabs.

You can drive right up to Blackfly Slab—one of the few cliffs where you can literally belay from your car bumper.

Northern Mountains

The area is reported to be a breeding ground for all things bad in the insect community (e.g., blackflies, deerflies, mosquitoes), hence the names of the various slabs.

The route descriptions in this section were adapted with permission from Dick Tucker's meticulous notes.[2]

HISTORY

Dick Tucker, then living in Gabriels, first visited the slabs in the 1970s, mostly for bouldering at an area about 100 yards south of the slabs at a railroad cut. He returned several times in the early 1990s, mostly with his childhood friend Tim Riley, but initially found the cliffs to be too overgrown. They persevered and unearthed the excellent rock beneath the moss and lichen. Several of the routes are listed as topropes; they were Tucker's projects and are awaiting leads . . . but they must be cleaned first.

ACCESS

The property is owned by Lyme Timber Company of Hanover, N.H. New York State has a Working Forest Conservation Easement that allows recreational opportunities beginning April 22, 2009.

DIRECTIONS

From Bloomingdale, take NY 3 north approximately 9.5 miles to the intersection on the left with CR 26 (formerly CR 99, also known as Port Kent–Hopkinton Turnpike, also labeled Merrill Road). On the right is the Alder Brook Park Road. Turn left onto CR 26 (0.0 miles). At 5.4 miles, you reach the intersection on the left with Kushaqua Mud Pond Road. At 5.9 miles, there are several dirt road entrances to a power line area on the left. Turn left and follow the power lines left (southeast) to reach the base of the cliff at 6.3 miles (at a point where the cliff comes within 25' of the power line). This is the base of Blackfly Slab 572201,4935358. There is a widening in the dirt road 100' farther where you can pull a vehicle off to the side.

DESCENT OPTIONS

Rappel from trees.

Inman Slabs

DEERFLY SLAB

This slab would make a worthwhile cleaning project. It has some good routes—handcracks and steep friction—but they are currently totally overgrown and unclimbable. The large trees along the base of the cliff have lower branches that lean up against the cliff and shade the lower portion of the slab from light, thereby creating a vertical moss garden to 20'. Above this, the cracks have grown in with grass and saplings.

The most distinctive feature is **Crystalline Entity**, the unbroken sheet of rock with several bolts.

About 75' yards above the top of the slab is an outcropping of bedrock with two easy cracks. The right crack is 5.3, and the irregular mossy crack on the left is 5.2 (both climbed by Dick Tucker, Jun 14, 1992).

---

2 Richard E. Tucker, "Inman Slabs" (typescript, Adirondack Research Library, Niskayuna, NY, 1997).

DIRECTIONS

This slab is situated up from and left of Blackfly Slab, about 75' from the dirt road. To approach, walk up the steep embankment to the forested area at the base of the slab.

1 One-Trick Pony 5.5 G 70'

This is the leftmost route on the slab and is currently completely obscured by moss and saplings.

Start: 15' right of the left end of the open section of slab below a crack that leads to a tree 30' up.

P1 5.5 G: Up the crack for 30' to a tree, then up to a ledge. Continue up a steep slab to the summit boulder. 70'

FA Jul 4, 1992, Dick Tucker (roped solo)

2 Crystalline Entity 5.9 G 90'

Some steep friction leads to a nice crack. The route and its variation are clearly the best lines here and would get three or four stars if cleaned. The name (taken from the large, snowflake-shaped life-form that consumed all living things in the *Star Trek: The Next Generation* episode "Datalore") refers to the extremely hard crystals embedded in the anorthosite slab, which makes climbing this route possible.

Start: In the center of the slab below a crack that begins 30' up, 2' right of a large birch tree and below bolts.

P1 5.9 G: (V1) Friction up the face for 30' to a crack. Up the crack and right-facing flake to a bushy ledge, then up a vertical crack in a slab to the top. 90'

V1 Prom Night Entity 5.7 G: Start as for **Prom Night Trickery**. Climb up the crack to 15', then friction left to a thin seam and a bolt. Continue up and left to the bolt line of the normal route.

FA (TR) Jul 5, 1993, Dick Tucker
FA (V1) Jul 4, 1994, Dick Tucker, Tim Riley

3 Prom Night Trickery 5.5+ G 90'

A nice crack line that would get three stars if cleaned.

Start: 12' right of **Crystalline Entity** and 2' right of a large maple, at a handcrack that has some small pods at the bottom and runs to the top of the cliff.

P1 5.5+ G: Climb the handcrack to its top, then move slightly left at the horizontals to another vertical crack that breaks the upper slab. 90'

FA Jun 14, 1992, Dick Tucker, Tim Riley

4 Otto Sells Lemons 5.5 G 90'

Start: 15' right of the handcrack of **Prom Night Trickery** and 10' left of the right end of the slab, at a right-leaning handcrack with a zigzag at the bottom.

P1 5.5 G: Up the handcrack, then left to gain two vertical cracks, which are followed to the top. 90'

FA Jul 4, 1994, Dick Tucker, Tim Riley

Inman Slabs

BLACKFLY SLAB

This is the first slab you see when driving in on the dirt road. It is 25' right of the dirt road, separated from the road by raspberry bushes (yummy in season, but scratchy). The sunny aspect and lack of trees around the base make for cleaner rock.

The most distinguishing feature is the right-facing,

429

Northern Mountains

right-leaning low-angle corner. The leftmost routes begin below the left end of this corner. If you look carefully along the base of the slab, there is a large 6"-diameter rusted ring bolt 1' above the ground, a useful locator for the routes.

5 Unbroken 5.7 G 70' ★★

Start: First locate the right-facing, right-leaning low-angle corner that begins 20' up, the most obvious feature on the slab. This route begins 6' right of the base of the corner, at a clean slab with a left-leaning, right-facing edge 7' up. This is also 8' left of the large ring bolt at the base of the slab.

P1 5.7 G: Unprotected friction leads straight up (crux) to a good ledge 10' up. Step left 6' to the base of the right-facing corner, then up good edges to a bolt. Break left around the corner at a horizontal crack and (V1) climb a crack straight up to another horizontal (jug). Spicy friction moves (5.7) lead to the top. 70'

V1 Dick's Nose 5.8+ TR: Friction straight up the arête to the top.

Gear: Cams to 0.75".
FA Jul 29, 2007, Simeon Warner, Jim Lawyer
FA (V1) Jul 5, 1997, Dick Tucker

6 Torment Direct 5.8 G 70' ★

After the first couple of moves, the climb is 5.3.
Start: Same as **Unbroken**.
P1 5.8 G: Unprotected friction leads straight up (crux) to a good ledge 10' up. Step left 6' to the base of the right-facing corner, then up good edges to a bolt. Continue up the right-leaning, right-facing corner to the top. 70'

Gear: Cams to 0.5".
FA Jul 6, 1997, Dick Tucker, Tim Riley

7 Torment 5.7 TR 70'

Start at the large rusted ring bolt driven into the base of the slab. Climb straight up to a ledge 10' up, then move left 4' and climb straight up the slab paralleling the right-facing corner to the top.
FA (TR) 1980, Dick Tucker, Tim Riley

8 Feeding Frenzy 5.7 TR 70'

Start as for **Torment**, directly below the lower left end of a prominent right-rising overlap. Climb straight up to a ledge 10' up, move up to the right-rising overlap and follow it up and right to its top, then join **Bad Brains** to the top.
FA (TR) May 24, 1992, Dick Tucker

9 Simulium Venustum 5.5 PG 70'

The name is the genus and species of the dreaded blackfly, which is so prevalent here in the summer.
Start: 4' right of the large rusted ring bolt driven into the base of the slab, below a bolt 25' up.
P1 5.5 PG: Climb straight up the slab to the bottom of a right-rising seam (bolt), then straight up to the prominent right-rising, right-facing overlap. Follow the overlap up and right to a horizontal (piton), then join **Bad Brains** up a slab and past a bolt to the top. 70'
FA Oct 12, 1997, Dick Tucker, Tim Riley

10 Bad Brains 5.5 PG 70' ★★★

Start: 8' right of the large rusted ring bolt driven into the base of the slab, below the left end of a narrow ledge 10' up.
P1 5.5 PG: Climb up to the ledge, then friction straight up to a bolt. Up the face to a right-rising, right-facing edge and follow it up and right to another bolt. Continue straight up the face to a horizontal (piton), then up a slab past another bolt to a large tree at the top. 70'
FA May 29, 1993, Dick Tucker, Tim Riley

11 Dinner Guest 5.5 TR 80'

Start 15' right of **Bad Brains** below a right-rising, right-arching overlap 60' up. Climb up the overlap, then up to a horizontal. Continue up the slab (currently carpeted with lichen) past a bolt, (V1) then move over a bulge and pass left of a horizontal ribbing of trees and grass. Finish on a right-leaning crack to the top.

V1 5.7 TR: Move up and left to a horizontal, then straight up through a bulge at a crack next to a white streak.
FA (TR) Jul 6, 1997, Dick Tucker, Tim Riley

PANTHER HILL CLIFF

Location	North of Merrill and Upper Chateaugay Lake, accessed from NY 374
Aspect	Southeast
Height	100'
Quality	★★★
Approach	1 hr, moderate
Summary	A long, mostly unexplored cliff with several high-quality routes.

4	1		1	2			8
-5.6	5.7	5.8	5.9	5.10	5.11	5.12	5.13+	total

This cliff sits on the slopes of Panther Hill with outstanding views of Lyon Mountain and Lake Chateaugay to the south. The cliff has only recently seen activity, and vast sections remain untouched. Route development here is more involved than at other cliffs, as the rock is generally shattered, loose, and dirty.

The cliff is divided into two halves, split by a deep, steep, scree-filled gully known as Devil's Channel. This is the first gully that you come to on the approach, and there is a fixed rope to facilitate the topmost 12'. On the cliff to the left of the gully (and just left of the gully's mouth) is the first route, **Frosted Flake**. Near the mouth of the gully on the right side is a deep chimney that sits below the viewpoint and has a fixed rope to facilitate passage. **The Buffaloed Panther** begins just left of this chimney, and **A Shot in the Dark** begins in the chimney. Around the corner to the right of the gully's mouth is **Pink Panther**, the real gem of the cliff. The cliff continues for some distance to the left and right of the gully.

It should be noted that the cliff's entire base is horribly unstable talus that slides with just the slightest provocation. Perhaps this is why the routes so far are clustered near the approach chimney and gully.

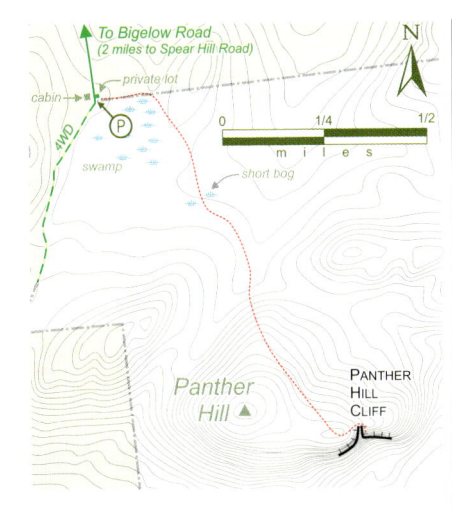

Northern Mountains

DIRECTIONS (MAP PAGE 416)

From Lyon Mountain (at the Mobil station at the intersection of NY 374 and Standish Road), follow NY 374 northeast for 7.3 miles to the intersection with Spear Hill Road. Turn right on Spear Hill Road, resetting your odometer to 0.0. At 2.1 miles, the road forks; take the right branch, staying on Spear Hill Road. At 3.5 miles, there is a four-way intersection (Peets Road on the left, Bigelow Road on the right, Steam Mill Road straight ahead); turn right onto Bigelow Road, and, at 5.5 miles, there is a cabin on the right (very close to the road) and a dirt pullout on the left. The pullout is private, so park on the left side of the road just after the pullout. Be sure to get your car off the road 583017,4961928.

From the dirt pullout, walk east 200' following the state land property boundary (marked with yellow blazes on the trees). There is flagging here that marks the trail to the cliff; veer right to a beaver swamp and follow the shoreline to a substantial beaver dam. Cross this and follow the trail on a bearing of roughly 167° to near the top of a wooded subsummit of Panther Hill (about 50 min from the car). The path turns east, reaching the cliff at the top of a gully with a fixed rope on a tree. This gully splits the cliff in two halves. You can descend this gully, but it is steep, loose scree. Continue on the path to the viewpoint (the only viewpoint on the cliff) 584071,4960648, which sits directly above a hidden chimney. Descend the chimney with a fixed rope, reaching the base of the cliff on the right side of the mouth of the gully that splits the cliff.

ACCESS

Although it is possible to approach from the south on Bigelow Road, this crosses private property. Bigelow Road can be reached directly from NY 374, but requires a high-clearance 4WD vehicle and is unreliable.

DESCENT OPTIONS

The routes are equipped with lower-off anchors. Optionally, you can descend the fixed rope in the chimney or the fixed rope in the gully that splits the cliff.

HISTORY

The early settlers of the Chateaugay Lakes region named Devil's Channel. According to their written accounts, a hunter escaped from an attacking panther by scrambling partway up the cliff. Luckily for him, his companion came upon the scene and shot the animal.

The first climber to visit was Steve Jervis in the 1960s, although no routes were recorded. He returned in 1975 with Tad Welch, a teenager just starting out, but, again, no routes were recorded. Their early visits involved throwing off loose rock and sod, but usually coming away empty-handed. It wasn't until 1977 that Welch returned with Chuck Yax and Jamie Savage to climb Toad's Traverse. A breakthrough in development occurred at the hands of Charles Pechousek, who invested the time and energy to unearth the best lines. When he was visiting his family's camp on Lake Chateaugay, the cliff was visible from the porch and became the inspiration for afternoon projects.

Michelle Burlitch at the top of Panther Hill, looking towards Upper Chateaugay Lake.

Northern Mountains

1 Frosted Flake 5.6 G 80' ★★★

Ascends a high left-facing flake. Despite appearances, it takes only small gear. The route was originally encrusted in a forest of lichen, hence the name.

Start: Locate the large, deep, loose gully that splits the cliff. This route begins left of the gully's mouth at a short chimney capped by a ceiling 12' up, below an enormous left-facing flake.

P1 5.6 G: Climb up the shallow chimney to the roof, then left into opposing sharp flakes (bolt), then up the enormous left-facing flake to its top. Step right and climb a broken corner another 10' to a fixed anchor below some ceilings. 80'

Gear: Small gear up to 1".

FA Sep, 2006, Charles Pechousek, Benoit Tessier

2 The Buffaloed Panther 5.5 G 50'

The first ascentionists were fooled (hence the name), as it's hard to understand why anyone would climb this route.

Start: On the right wall of the gully that splits the cliff is a deep hidden chimney. This route begins just uphill from the chimney on a platform, below an open book with a chimney filled with stacked flakes.

P1 5.5 G: Climb up the corner and chimney to a triangular block with a crack on either side; climb the left crack to the fixed anchor at the top. 50'

FA Jun 24, 2007, Tom Yandon, Michelle Burlitch, Jim Lawyer

3 A Shot in the Dark 5.10c G 50' ★★★

Steep, sustained face climbing. Named for the second Pink Panther film.

Start: On the right wall of Devil's Channel is a deep hidden chimney. This route begins in the chimney on the left wall (as you face into the chimney), 10' uphill from and right of a 20'-high V-chimney, across from a good ledge on the opposite wall, at some thin seams in the face.

Tom Yandon on Frosted Flake (5.6).

P1 5.10c G: Starting uphill, gain a good finger slot, traverse left into a flared orange groove, then up to an orange horn in the groove. Continue straight up the crack, then angle left to a flared handcrack and follow it to a short left-facing corner capped by a ceiling. Over this on its right side via a crack, then follow the crack to a fixed anchor at the top. 50'

Gear: To 3".

FA Jun 24, 2007, Jim Lawyer, Charles Pechousek, Michelle Burlitch, Tom Yandon

Charles Pechousek on his route Pink Panther (5.10a).

Northern Mountains

4 Mentor 5.2 G 50'
Start: On the right wall of Devil's Channel is a deep hidden chimney. Begin just right of this chimney, facing into Devil's Channel, below a short, wide crack on a narrow low-angle face.
P1 5.2 G: Up the crack to a ledge. Finish on a nose right of a spruce tree. 50'
FA Sep 14, 2007, Tad Welch, Steve Jervis

5 It's Come to This 5.7 PG 50'
Interesting in that this ascends some of the same ground as **Pink Panther**, sans bolts.
Start: Same as **Pink Panther**.
P1 5.7 PG: Climb up to the first bolt, then step right past a jutting block to orange lichen and good holds, 10' right of the second bolt. Go straight up past a small ceiling to a ledge with berry bushes. Exit up and left to a spruce tree. 50'
FA Jun 11, 1989, Tad Welch, Steve Jervis

6 Pink Panther 5.10a G 90' ★★★★
The excellent pink rock, good moves, and sustained climbing of this route demonstrate this cliff's potential.
Start: 40' downhill from and right of the mouth of the gully that splits the cliff, at pink rock just right of an inverted triangle roof. This is directly below a large left-facing corner at the top of the cliff.
● **P1 5.10a G:** Climb up to the first bolt, then trend right to a short right-facing corner, over a bulge (crux), then work right aiming for a notch on the right side of a small ceiling. Step left and climb a face straight up to the large left-facing corner. Tricky moves gain the corner, then follow it to a fixed anchor just above. 90'
FA Jul, 2006, Charles Pechousek, Eric Paquet

Tad Welch on the first ascent of Toad's Traverse in 1977. Photo by Jamie Savage.

7 Fledgling Flight 5.9 G 60' ★★
Named for a young bald eagle cared for by Welch.
Start: Halfway along the cliff right of Devil's Channel, uphill from and left of the obvious **Toad's Traverse** at a large left-facing corner.
P1 5.9 G: Up a sharp-edged fingercrack to a ledge and bolt at midheight. Finish up the inside corner to a birch. 60'
FA Sep 23, 2007, Tad Welch, Bill Widrig

8 Toad's Traverse 5.5 G 60' ★
Start: Below large multitiered roofs, 50' left of a large left-facing chimney-corner that marks the right end of the cliff.
P1 5.5 G: Good rock streaked with orange lichen leads to a wide crack formed by a giant block. Up this, then hand-traverse right to a mantel, then up to the top. 60'
History: A photo of this appeared in *Adirondack Life* with the mysterious caption, "Strenuous climbing at an 'undiscovered' crag north of Lake Placid."[3]
FA Jul, 1977, Tad Welch, Jamie Savage, Chuck Yax

CATAMOUNT MOUNTAIN

Location	North of Wilmington, accessed from NY 3 or NY 86
Aspect	South
Height	450'
Quality	
Approach	1 hr, moderate
Summary	Scrambles on ledges and slabs of a low peak with an excellent hiking trail.

3							3
-5.6	5.7	5.8	5.9	5.10	5.11	5.12	5.13+	total

Once considered an obscure destination, Catamount Mountain has become popular with hikers. For the climber, it affords a good alpine scramble on a low peak. The hiking trail skirts around the right (east) side of two rock outcroppings on the south face of the mountain, one on the lower south summit and the other beneath the main summit. The cliff on the south summit is directly above the hiking trail and is both steeper and taller than the slabs beneath the main summit. Several routes and variations exist on these easy, broken cliffs.

HISTORY
Dick Tucker and Tim Riley explored on Sep 2, 1979, and reported three climbs on the South Summit: **Second Face**, a 40'-tall slab to a vertical wall; **Aid Crack**, a dihedral, possibly the one left of **South Summit Route**; and **First Face**, a series of easy slabs 100' left of the hiking trail. The details, however, are insufficient to make a positive identification. First ascent information for the other routes remains a mystery.

ACCESS
Some climbing has been reported on a steep cliff closer to the road on the southwest end of the mountain. This cliff is unfortunately on private land.

---
3 Jim Cunningham, "On Belay," *Adirondack Life* 16, no. 3 (May–Jun 1985), pp. 38–43.

Northern Mountains

The Main Summit of Catamount Mountain.

DIRECTIONS (MAP PAGE 434)

The trailhead is on the north side of Forestdale Road and is marked with red paint on a tree. The parking area is a widened shoulder of the road 589108,4921650.

From the north: From Plattsburgh, follow NY 3 southwest to Clayburg. Turn left on Silver Lake Road (0.0) and drive southeast to Taylor Pond State Campground at 8.0 miles. Continue southeast to Nelson Road at 8.6 miles. Turn right onto Nelson Road and follow this to Forestdale Road at 9.5 miles. Turn right onto Forestdale Road and drive to the trailhead at 14.3 miles.

From the south: From NY 86 in Wilmington (0.0 mile), drive north on the Whiteface Mountain Veterans Memorial Highway (CR 431). At 2.8 miles, turn right onto Whiteface Mountain Road–Gillespie Drive (CR 72) toward Franklin Falls. At 6.1 miles, turn right onto Roseman Road and follow this to Plank Road at 6.9 miles. Turn right and follow Plank Road (which changes name to Forestdale Road) to the parking area at 9.1 miles.

From the parking area, follow the hiking trail (unmarked, but obvious) to a clearing where the path crosses some open slabs beneath the cliffs of the south summit, reached at 45 min. There is a large table-like boulder perched on the slab here. The approach to the South Summit Route begins here 589802,4922914. To approach the main summit, continue along the hiking trail.

Catamount Mountain
SOUTH SUMMIT

DIRECTIONS (MAP PAGE 434)

From the clearing, walk back on the trail 300', then bushwhack directly to the cliff through open forest. The forest on the right end of the cliff is thick with cedar-covered boulders; the climbs are more in the center of the cliff, which is more easily approached in this way.

1 Three Blind Mice 5.5 G 130'
Start: 130' left of South Summit Route is a level, relatively-open section of forest in front of the cliff. Begin at a 6'-high, right-facing corner directly below a 10'-high slot 589763,4923022.
P1 5.5 G: Climb the corner, then step left onto a slab. Move left on the slab to a shallow open book (right of a tan streak, and 3' left of a shallow left-facing left-leaning edge used for gear). Go up the open book (crux), then trend right to a tree thicket below a 30'-tall right-facing corner-chimney 50' up. (The corner-chimney is 25' left of a sharp-edged left-facing corner.) Up the corner, then up an excessively lichen-covered face, emerging onto a rolling slab that takes you to the top of the technical climbing. 130'
Descent: From the top of the technical climbing, scramble and cedar-pull up and right another 100' to reach the hiking trail.
ACB Jul 19, 2008, Mike Stanislaw, Sam Vona, Harry Young

Northern Mountains

2 South Summit Route 5.6 G 450' ★

Starts with a steep pitch and climbs a couple of the prominent features that are visible from the clearing: the broad slab on the upper left side and the clean vertical cracks near the top.

Start: Locate a large 30'-tall open book above a large, triangular, sloping shelf. Begin 10' right at a left-facing open book 8' up 589778,4922980.

P1 5.6 G: Up the corner, then follow a left-rising ramp, past cedar trees, to a short, steep open book (this is just above and right of the large 30'-tall open book). Climb the open book to a tree belay on the right. 90'

P2 5.0 PG: Go right past vegetation and climb a short, steep wall and slab to a bulge with flakes. Climb over the bulge to the right side of a perched block. Move over the block, then climb the left side of a broad, dirty slab to a tree belay. 180'

P3 4th class: Go through vegetation for 60' to the base of a clean wall with vertical cracks. Climb the wall and continue over a second wall to a belay at the south summit. 180'

Descent: Follow the hiking trail, which is 100' to the right (east), and descend around the east side of the cliff.

Catamount Mountain
MAIN SUMMIT

DIRECTIONS (MAP PAGE 434)

From the clearing beneath the cliffs of the south summit, continue on the hiking trail as it ascends steeply up the right end of the cliff. Pass over the south summit and descend to a wooded col between the two summits, 1 hr from the road 589814,4923257. Leave the trail and bushwhack left (west) and downhill for 200', then turn right (north) and hike uphill, staying left of cliffs on the right. At 1 hr 5 min, turn left (west) and cross over vegetated slabs to reach the main slab at its right side. Hike down along the slab to a 200'-long left-facing overlap that is reached at 1 hr 10 min.

3 Main Summit Route 5.0 G 380'

When viewed from the south summit, the slabs and left-rising cracks of the main summit look steep and enticing. In this case, looks are deceiving, as the slabs and cracks are barely 4th-class.

Start: At a zigzag crack that is right of a long left-facing overlap.

P1 4th class: Up the zigzag crack that diagonals left across a slab and goes over an overlap. Above the overlap, continue in the crack toward trees, then move up and right to a belay on a ledge with trees. 200'

P2 5.0 G: Go left onto an easy slab and follow it to tiered overlaps with vertical cracks, then climb the cracks to a tree belay at the top of the cliff. 180'

Descent: Scramble up and right to reach the main summit, then follow the hiking trail back down the east side of the slab.

SILVER LAKE

Location	North of Whiteface and Wilmington, accessed from Silver Lake Road
Summary	Vast area of many cliffs from 500'-tall slabs to multi-pitch cracks; good potential for new routes.

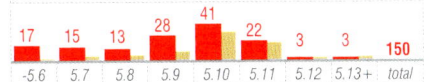

17	15	13	28	41	22	3	3	150
-5.6	5.7	5.8	5.9	5.10	5.11	5.12	5.13+	total

Silver Lake Mountain and Potter Mountain are located north of Wilmington and Whiteface Mountain on a parcel of land known as the Black Brook Tract. For years, the area has been referred to by local climbers as "Silver Lake," which is slightly confusing seeing that the actual Silver Lake is not near the climbing, and the Silver Lake Wilderness is located south of Speculator in the Southern Adirondacks.

As you drive northwest on Silver Lake Road and round the corner near the Taylor Pond Campground the cliffs, all seventeen and counting, come into view. Try not to ditch the car as you stare, jaw dropped, at the sheer quantity of exposed rock on these mountains. For obvious reasons—and despite the posted property—these cliffs have not escaped the attention of climbers through the years. The area has it all: overhanging walls with extreme routes, 500'-tall slabs, multi-pitch cracks, arêtes, buttresses, and chimneys. Some cliffs have 50+ pitches of climbing, while others have only one, so there is significant potential for new routes. The cliffs rise out of the forested lowlands, a view dotted with marshes, ponds, and the distant summits of Catamount and Whiteface. There's no screaming traffic, and no other people.

The most popular cliffs (so far) are Potter Mountain, C Chimney Cliff, and Mud Pond. The once-arduous approaches to these cliffs, while still long, are now well-traveled and straightforward. Next in popularity are the Summit Cliffs and Center of Progress, both of which have fantastic cracklines. The Outback Slab, Midway, and Purple Rain Wall are noteworthy destinations, but a little harder to get to. One of the most impressive walls in the park, the Tsunami Wall, is home to the first all-trad 5.14 route in the eastern US, **Oppositional Defiance Disorder**.

Aside from the hiking trail to the summit of Silver Lake Mountain and the sign-in registers at the trailheads, few improvements have been made to the property. There are no parking lots, marked trails, outhouses, or trail signs. There is, however, an extensive network of logging roads, skid paths, and logging headers, remnants of the most recent logging activity. In fact, the area has been extensively logged for many years, and the land has been thoroughly ravaged. In some cases, the logging roads and skid paths provide for excellent and speedy hiking, but just as often they are overgrown with chest-high weeds and prickly plants, deeply rutted, steep and washed out, and often muddy. There are endless braided skid paths with many intersections, so walking in a straight line often

Northern Mountains

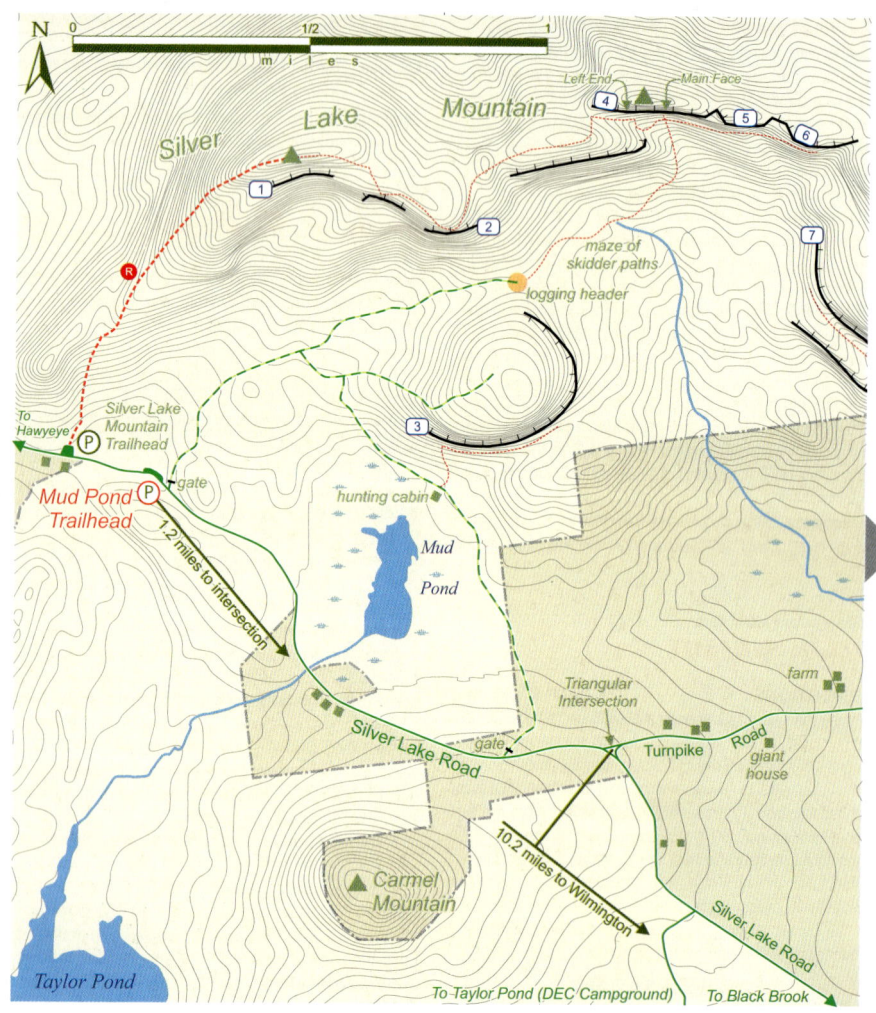

means making a confusing series of turns from one path to another. As a result, there are flags and cairns everywhere as hikers try to make sense of it all. Not to mention the paint on the trees from forestry work. On top of that, for the most part, the forest is young growth with dense foliage at head height, restricting visibility to just a few body lengths. Bring a compass and map or GPS, and try to keep the cliffs in sight. Durable clothing is essential.

The insect populations are more abundant here than anywhere else. A typical summer day includes swarms of deer flies (especially on the logging roads), black flies, mosquitoes, and bees (mostly in the flowering logging headers). For some reason, these cliffs have more ants than elsewhere. A head net, long-sleeved shirt, and DEET are strongly recommended.

Since 2009, climbing visitation has steadily increased and the approaches are getting consolidated and better defined. Once you're at a cliff, it feels like any other seldom-visited Adirondack cliff. The rock is generally dirty and unspoiled, and the cliff bases are wild with dense foliage. There are cliffs that have many routes, while others have just one. Best of all, you're likely to be alone.

There is strong cell phone reception at the cliffs (line of site to Whiteface), although coverage at the trailheads is poor.

ACCESS

The property is owned by Lyme Timber (formerly owned by International Paper) and, due to a conservation easement with the state, is open for non-motorized public recreation including hiking, skiing, horseback riding, mountain biking, fishing, trapping, and, of course, climbing. There is currently no camping, but aside from that, all other state land use regulations are in effect.

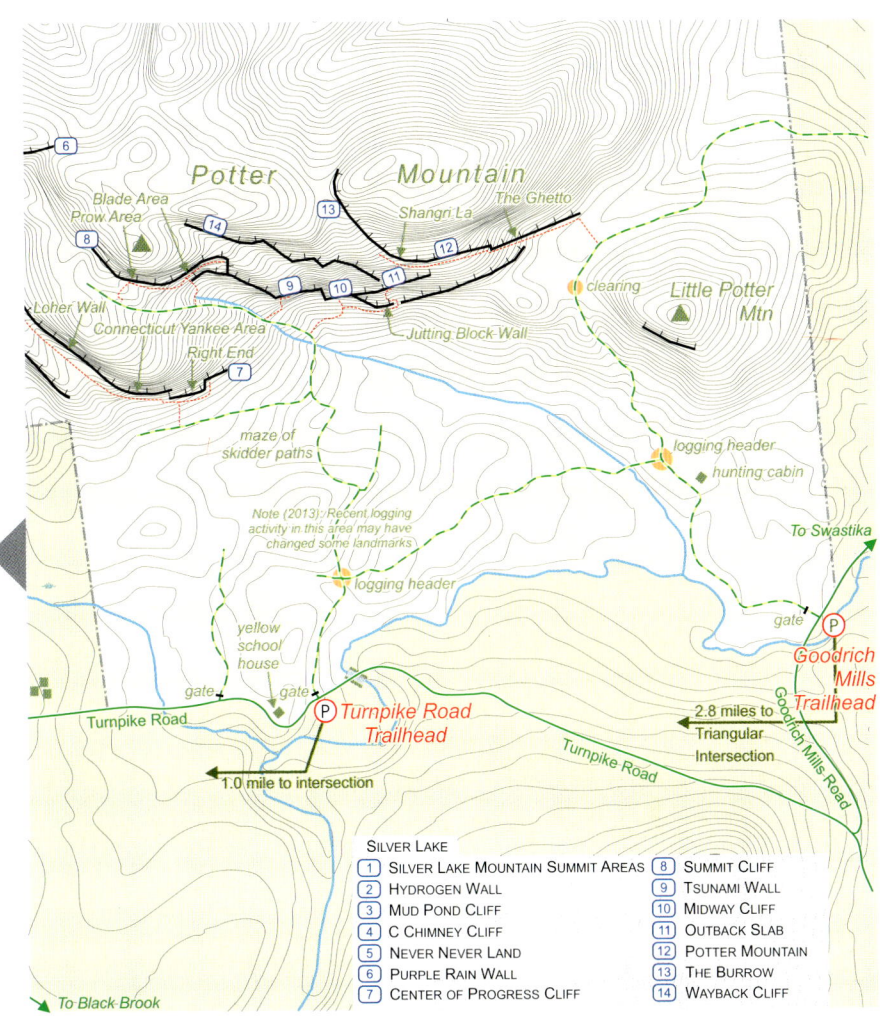

Northern Mountains

SILVER LAKE

1. Silver Lake Mountain Summit Areas
2. Hydrogen Wall
3. Mud Pond Cliff
4. C Chimney Cliff
5. Never Never Land
6. Purple Rain Wall
7. Center of Progress Cliff
8. Summit Cliff
9. Tsunami Wall
10. Midway Cliff
11. Outback Slab
12. Potter Mountain
13. The Burrow
14. Wayback Cliff

The state has installed sign-in registers at each of the trailheads. We recommend that you use these, as the usage stats determine how the DEC allocates funds for infrastructure development.

CAMPING
Use DEC Taylor Pond Campground (518.647.5250) or Douglas Resort (http://www.douglasresort.com) (800.201.8061) on Silver Lake. There is no camping on the Silver Lake properties at this time, although this may change soon.

DIRECTIONS (MAP PAGE 436)
From Wilmington (0.0) at the "four corners"—the intersection of NY 86, NY 431, and Bonnie View Road—go north on Bonnie View Road (CR 19A) to its end at a T junction with Silver Lake Road (CR 1) at 6.0 miles. Turn left and go west on Silver Lake Road. At 9.8 miles is the entrance to Taylor Pond Campground on the left. At 10.2 miles you reach the triangular intersection with Turnpike Road on the right. The various trailheads are described from this intersection. There are other access points, but those described here are public and provide easy access to the cliffs. If you choose another access point, be sure that it's not on private property.

Although it may be possible and tempting to drive on the various logging roads, this is illegal, and doesn't save you much time. Several of the logging roads seem excellent, but quickly deteriorate and would only save 5 or 10 minutes.

On several approaches you will pass near several hunting camps. These camps are set on 1-acre parcels and are private; do not approach them. The camp owners have gate keys and permission to drive vehicles on the forest roads to and from their camps. Don't be tempted even if you find an open gate and see other motorized vehicles using the logging roads.

437

Northern Mountains

SILVER LAKE
1. SILVER LAKE MOUNTAIN SUMMIT AREAS
2. HYDROGEN WALL
3. MUD POND CLIFF
4. C CHIMNEY CLIFF
5. NEVER NEVER LAND
6. PURPLE RAIN WALL

Silver Lake Mountain Trailhead: From the triangular intersection (the intersection of Silver Lake Road and Turnpike Road), drive west on Silver Lake Road for 1.4 miles to the Silver Lake Mountain Trailhead on the right. The parking area is difficult to see from the road, but is marked with a DEC sign on the road 591419,4929265, and is directly across the street from Island Road.

Mud Pond Trailhead: The logging road for Mud Pond Cliff is 0.2 miles before the Silver Lake Mountain Trailhead (and 1.2 miles west of the intersection of Silver Lake Road and Turnpike Road), on the north side of the road next to a sign that reads "Driveways Next 3/4 Mile" 591763,929161. Parking here saves a little walking. Be sure to avoid blocking the logging road and park your vehicle completely off the pavement. There is a sign-in register within 100' of the road next to the gate.

Turnpike Road Trailhead: From the triangular intersection (the intersection of Silver Lake Road and Turnpike Road), drive east on Turnpike Road for 1.0 mile to a gated logging road on the left 594973,4928499. This is 300' after a yellow schoolhouse-style house on the left, and sharp left turn in the road. 600' beyond the parking area is a bridge where the road crosses Black Brook–Taylor Pond Outlet. There is ample room on the shoulder on either side of the road for many cars. Don't block the gate, and park your vehicle completely off the pavement. There is a sign-in register within 100' of the road.

Goodrich Mills Trailhead: From the triangular intersection (the intersection of Silver Lake Road and Turnpike Road), drive east on Turnpike Road to a hairpin turn in the road. Stay on the paved road, which changes name to Goodrich Mills Road. After the hairpin turn, at 2.8 miles, there is a logging road on the left with an orange gate set back 200'; park on the shoulder on either side of Goodrich Mills Road 596668,4928750. The logging road is directly across the road from a yellow highway sign that shows a 90° turn to the right. Don't block the logging road, and park your vehicle completely off the pavement. There is a sign-in register on the other side of the gate.

HISTORY

The earliest reported climbers to explore Silver Lake were those from Tanager Lodge, a summer camp on Upper Chateaugay Lake. Associated with this camp was Steve Jervis, known for climbing with the Appies in the Gunks in the 1950s. In the mid-1970s, he took the young staffers Tad Welch, Bill Widrig, Jamie Savage, and Chuck Yax here to climb. Over the ensuing years, the Welch–Widrig team became a new routing force, establishing routes at nearly every cliff, and naming them all in the process. Some of their best achievements were **Green Mountain Boys** and **Great Northern Diver** at the Summit Cliff, **Mine Shaft** at the C Chimney Cliff, **Bimathalon** at the Outback Slab, **Tooth & Nail** and **African Barking Spiders** at Center of Progress, and nearly every route at Midway Cliff. It's difficult to grasp the sheer number of routes and the area they covered at such an early time in Adirondack climbing.

The Welch–Widrig duo weren't completely alone, however. In 1979, Dick Tucker and friends also made visits, adding adventure-style routes at the Summit Cliff, Wayback Cliff, Center of Progress, and the Tsunami Wall. In the early 1980s, the north country "regulars" also made appearances, including Mark Meschinelli, Todd Eastman, Dave Szot, Tom Yandon, Don Mellor, and Tom Rosecrans. And of course the prolific Patrick Purcell, although there are insufficient details to know what he did.

Piecing together who did what at this time is a difficult task. FAers often report discovering pitons and other breadcrumbs left by earlier climbers, so clearly more has happened here than we know. Clouding the past is the fact that climbers weren't allowed here and had to sneak around, and therefore kept their explorations to themselves. Further, no guidebook meant no reporting, and routes simply got lost. The exception was the well-documented ascent of **Connecticut Yankee** by Ken Nichols and Mike Heintz that appeared in Climbing Magazine in 1985[4].

These early explorations lasted nearly ten years until 1984, after which the cliffs went dormant. Perhaps nobody visited because it was too dirty, too much work, too remote, or too risky. Maybe there

---

[4] *Climbing*, no. 90 (Jun 1985), pp. 10–11.

Northern Mountains

- ⑦ CENTER OF PROGRESS CLIFF
- ⑧ SUMMIT CLIFF
- ⑨ TSUNAMI WALL
- ⑩ MIDWAY CLIFF
- ⑪ OUTBACK SLAB
- ⑫ POTTER MOUNTAIN
- ⑬ THE BURROW
- ⑭ WAYBACK CLIFF

were better projects elsewhere, or people just didn't remember. Don Mellor recalls days of walking around endlessly and not finding anything suitable to climb—the style at that time was ground up, which precluded routes too dirty to climb, or those without adequate removable protection. Whatever the reason, new routing stalled nearly twenty years until 2003.

But did new routing really stall? Some have described Adirondack climbing as "backwater", which means Silver Lake is back-backwater; it's really out there. Some local climbers such as Willard Race and Aaron Stredny have been active at Silver Lake for some time, but chose not to contribute route information in an effort to preserve this feeling.

In 2004, the state purchased recreation easements from International Paper (now Lyme Timber) in one of the biggest land preservation deals in the park's history. The agreement was slow to be enacted—climbers had to wait until 2009—but the publicity surrounding this agreement brought Silver Lake back into the consciousness of the local community. Development picked up once again, starting with Welch and Jamie Savage's appropriately named route **Easement** at Midway. Also active were local climbing guides Colin Loher, Will Roth, Chad Kennedy, and Mike LeBlanc at the C Chimney Cliff and Center of Progress.

In 2009, the year the area opened to recreation, a small group of St. Lawrence graduates collected in a small apartment in Wilmington with the sole purpose of developing new routes at Silver Lake. In between odd jobs, Jesse Littleton, Matt Way, and Richard Wilson—aka "Team Nasty" (page 490)—spent evenings, weekends, and pretty much every available moment at the cliffs, beginning with the Summit Cliff, then Center of Progress, and finally The C Chimney Cliff. They added a long list of brilliant new lines, and unbeknownst to them, eliminated aid from many of the Welch–Widrig routes.

After 2009, development intensified. Potter Mountain, originally thought as a low-angle pad-up-in-your-sneakers cliff, was visited and found to be a water-streaked heaven of climbable, clean, dimpled rock. Mud Pond was rediscovered, its overhanging right side the stage for ultra-hard projects. One of the most exciting events was the free ascent of the ski track cracks on the 110° overhanging wave of rock on the Tsunami Wall by Pete Kamitses, creating the first all-gear 5.14a route in the eastern U.S. That's pretty good for a back-backwater place like Silver Lake.

Silver Lake
C CHIMNEY CLIFF

Aspect	South
Height	200'
Quality	★★★★
Approach	40 min, moderate
Summary	Steep, wide wall with mostly difficult, excellent routes; somewhat dirty rock, though.

3	1		1	7	6	1		19
-5.6	5.7	5.8	5.9	5.10	5.11	5.12	5.13+	total

Sitting high on the Silver Lake Mountain–Potter Mountain ridgeline is this steep wall broken by a single C-shaped chimney, visible from the road. Once thought to be impenetrable, this cliff was slow to reveal its secrets. It now boasts some excellent cracklines and faces. Especially noteworthy is the pure-trad **Zoinks**, the face of **Tears of Gaia**, and the amazing overhanging crack of **Flying Buddha**.

The cliff is separated into two parts, divided by a rocky buttress that extends down into the woods. This buttress forms a large right-facing corner on the left end of the Main Face. Scramble up the left side of this buttress to access the right-rising tree gully that splits the cliff—a good descent route from the top of the cliff. On top of this buttress is an excellent open ledge—Lunch Ledge—a great place to escape the canopy of the forest, out of the bugs. Left of the buttress is the Left End with a couple of good routes.

The top of the cliff is also easily accessed by hiking to the right end of the cliff and ascending a gully that separates the C Chimney Cliff from Never Never Land. It's a beautiful summit, and worth the hike even if you're not climbing.

Northern Mountains

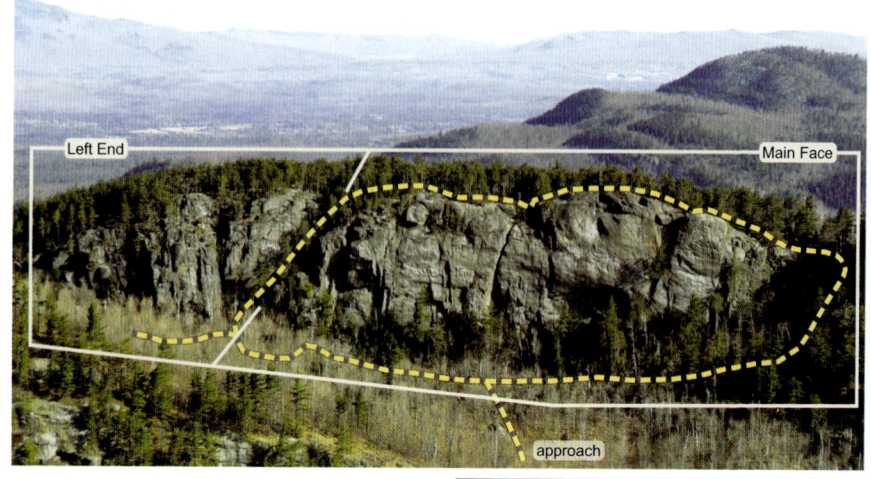

DIRECTIONS (MAP PAGE 436)

Park at the Mud Pond Trailhead (0 hr 0 min). Follow the logging road to a large clearing choked with raspberries and other unpleasantries at 15 min. This clearing is directly below the Hydrogen Wall to your left (north). Continue straight across the clearing and head east, following a logging road through some dense brush and prickers, and past a wet section. Descend slightly to reach a boggy clearing at 25 min, then turn left and pick up a trail on the other side of the bog. Continue northeast, cross a stream, and arrive at a giant boulder with a handcrack. Go north and arrive at the cliff at 40 min, near its right end 593430,4930394.

If you really like bushwhacking, you can reach the cliff by following the Silver Lake Mountain ridgeline. From the top of the Hydrogen Wall, continue east along the ridge through extremely dense spruce and blowdown—pretty rough going. After you cross the old property boundary (which will most likely go unnoticed), head northeast into a notch. From the notch, you can easily regain the ridge that runs along the top of the cliff, or walk right along the cliff base, again rough going. Not recommended.

HISTORY

There are several reports of climbing the "C" chimney, but the earliest found so far was in 1981 by the Tanager crew—Steve Jervis, Tad Welch, Bill Widrig, and Jamie Savage. It wasn't until 2003 that another route was reported, although others definitely visited before then. In 2010, development really exploded with the self-named "Climbing Rebels"[5] Jesse Littleton, Matt Way, Richard Wilson; they showed what was possible here with their routes **Zoinks**, **Haroom Baroom**, **Bearded Munchkin**, **Seeking Enlightenment**, and **Hippie Sticks and Black Flies**. They also cleaned the dramatically overhanging cracks **Flying Buddha** and **Jenga** which were later freed by Conor Cliffe.

[5] David Crothers, "Silver Lake and Potter Mountain Climbing Rebels Interview," *Climberism* (Jun 8, 2010).

Left End

1 C+ 5.7 G 140'

Start: The distinctive feature on the Left End is an 8'-wide chimney that runs the height of the cliff, and begins just left of the right-rising tree-filled ramp that divides the cliff. Begin 20' left of the chimney on top of blocks in a right-facing corner with a ceiling at head height.

P1 5.7 G: Climb over the roof on its left side to a ledge with a pine tree. Continue up the crack in the right-facing corner to the top. 140'
FA Jun 8, 2009, Don Mellor, Justin Norton

2 The Norton Anthology 5.10b G 120' ★★★

Start: 20' right of **C+** is a deep, dark, 8'-wide chimney. From the base of the chimney scramble up and right onto a ledge. Begin 10' right of the edge of the chimney at a thin seam below a short fistcrack 9' up. (The start should not be confused with the more prominent hand- and finger-crack in dark rock 10' to the right that begins 20' up, which is the route **Cliff Notes**.)

P1 5.10b G: Up the thin seam in the face, past the fist slot, then move left across a face to a fragile, shallow, right-facing flake (crux, small gear). Follow a left-facing corner to the top. 120'
FA Jun 8, 2009, Don Mellor, Justin Norton

3 Cliff Notes 5.10d PG 60' ★★

To make the route safe, you have to chimney up between the rock and a tree and place a sling high in the tree; double ropes work best here.

Start: 10' right of **The Norton Anthology** on a dark face with a seam that widens to fingers 18' up, and widens to hands 25' up.

P1 5.10d PG: Go up the face and mantel onto a small ledge (crux) 12' up. Place RP in seam, then continue up face to fingercrack, which becomes hands, and eventually 4". Finish at a ledge with a fixed anchor. 60'
FA Sep 3, 2011, Will Roth, Colin Loher

Northern Mountains

C CHIMNEY CLIFF: LEFT END
1 C+ (5.7)
2 The Norton Anthology (5.10b)
3 Cliff Notes (5.10d)

Main Face

4 Shaggy's Secret Stash 5.10c PG 135'
Better than it looks, and way better than the start.
Start: 15' left of **Mystery Machine** at a chimney–gully with a birch 15' up.
P1 5.10c PG: Up the gully until it is possible to escape out right. Climb a ramp to gain a left-facing flake, then go straight up past ledges, aiming for a finger-size crack. Avoid the huge detached blocks on the right. 135'

Gear: Doubles of cams through 2", extra small stuff.
FA May 16, 2010, Jesse Littleton, Richard Wilson

5 The Purist 5.10b G 105' ★★★
Start: Climb **Mystery Machine** (5.6) and build belay up and right in the base of the large attached flake.
P1 5.10b G: Traverse left 10' to gain large right-facing corner. Climb a hand-crack through a bulge and continue up crack. Trend right towards small clusters of trees. Anchor on excellent foot-ledge below large, right-facing flake. 65'

Jim Lawyer belays Martine Schaer on the arête right of Velma's Snatch. Photo by Emilie Drinkwater.

441

Northern Mountains

C Chimney Cliff: Main Face

- 4 Shaggy's Secret Stash (5.10c)
- 5 The Purist (5.10b)
- 6 Mystery Machine (5.6)
- 7 Zoinks!! (5.11a)
- 8 Double Fisting Blueberries (5.9)
- 9 If You Don't Like It, Leave (5.11b)
- 10 Tears of Gaia (5.10b)
- 11 Mine Shaft (5.4)
- 12 Haroom Baroom (5.11d)
- 13 Bearded Munchkin (5.10b)
- 14 Seeking Enlightenment (5.11a)
- 15 Flying Buddha (5.12a)
- 16 Hippie Sticks and Black Flies (5.11a)
- 17 Jenga (5.11b)
- 18 Velma's Snatch (5.3)
- 19 I See You (5.10b)

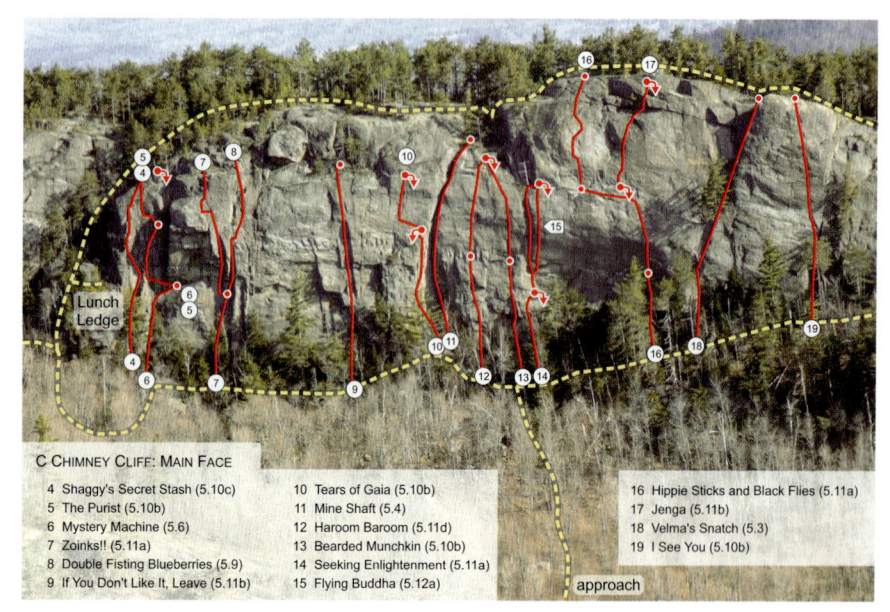

P2 5.9+ G: Climb the right-facing flake, heading for a wide crack. Climb this up to a small tree and pull up out of the pool onto the slab. Continue up slab to anchor on tree. 40'
Gear: Doubles of cams to 5".
FA Oct, 2007, Chad Kennedy, Michael LeBlanc, Colin Loher

6 Mystery Machine 5.6 G 45' ★★
An exploratory climb with several promising possibilities above. Good climbing.
Start: 25' right of the huge right-facing corner formed by the buttress that defines the left end of the Main Face, below a shallow chimney box with parallel cracks.
P1 5.6 G: Up the parallel cracks to slab, then up and right to belay under the roof system. 45'
FA 2003, Chad Wawrzyniak, Kevin Thompson

7 Zoinks!! 5.11a G 180' ★★★★★
A classic plumb line with non-stop fun and good movement up an obvious feature. Perhaps sandbagged.
Start: 75' right of Mystery Machine at two pointed boulders at the left end of a long, low overhang, below a shallow, hanging, right-facing open book 10' up.
P1 5.10c G: Step on the boulders and move up into the open book. Follow a crack in the open book (crux) straight up to a stance. Continue up right-leaning cracks in facing corners until just below roofs. Hanging belay (3" cam handy). 40'
P2 5.11a G (5.6R): Step left 4' and into a left-facing corner. Up the corner, then up a short fingercrack in black rock to roofs. Gulp down some Scooby Snacks, then angle up and right through the roofs (pumpy, spectacular) via underclings and strenuous-to-place gear to a final small overlap (crux). Make a long reach up into a crack. Follow the crack up a left-facing corner to its top (last gear). Traverse left 6' on a slab, then work back up and right into the line, then straight up mossy rock to the top. Tree anchor. 140'
Gear: Singles to 2.5", doubles through finger sized cams, #3 Camalot for P1 anchor.
Descent: Walk left 50' to a wooded gully, then down this to the base of the cliff.
FA May 10, 2010, Jesse Littleton, Richard Wilson
FFA May 31, 2010, Jesse Littleton, Richard Wilson

8 Double Fisting Blueberries 5.9 G 120'
The chimney is reportedly better than it looks.
Start: Climb P1 of Zoinks.
P1 5.9 G: From the belay, move right and up into a chimney and climb this until blocked by a large moss and tree island. Exit right onto slabs, then follow an incipient crack (crux) to the top. 120'
FA Jul, 2011, Tom Wright, Will Roth

9 If You Don't Like It, Leave 5.11b PG 200' ★★★
Start: On top of a finely constructed pedestal below a 3" crack in an imposing low overhang, downhill and left of Tears of Gaia.
P1 5.11b PG: Crank through an unusual, hard, bouldery start to easier climbing on delicate rock that gives access to a V-slot. Make strenuous moves through V-slot to a roof. Break the roof on the right (place gear before you do so), then make some hard moves right to a fingercrack (crux). Follow the fingercrack to the base of a long, left-facing corner. Go up the corner with a few more spicy, hard moves for another 50' to a small ledge; belay here (2" cam, green Alien, nut), which is left of a gargoyle-like formation on your right. 100'
P2 5.10b PG: Continue up corner to small overhang. Break the overhang on the right and move out to the arête of the corner—super fun and exposed. Follow water-worn fingercracks to a slab finish. 100'

Gear: From RPs up to 2"; doubles up to #0.75. Do not place a cam in the opening 3" crack, as it may break a key hold! If you don't like it...

History: The route is a tribute to Joe Szot and named after his code of conduct for guests at his bunkhouse, The Bivy. Joe Szot died of a heart attack while climbing in the Shawangunks in 2012, and in his memory a large local crew gathered to clean this route, including Nick Gulli, John Lacky, Jeremy Haas, and Tom Wright.
FA Apr 17, 2012, Colin Loher, Dominic Eisinger, Emilie Drinkwater

10 Tears of Gaia 5.10b G 150' ★★★★

This route ascends a convex wall on incut jugs; the steeper the wall, the bigger the jugs. Some of the holds feel fragile, but will improve with traffic; fortunately, the protection is excellent.

Start: The C Chimney (aka Mine Shaft) is recessed in the back of a giant right-facing open book. Begin on the left wall of the open book at the top of the debris cone below the mouth of the chimney.

● **P1 5.10b G:** Scramble easily up to a ledge, then move left and up to a shallow, left facing corner. Trend up and left towards the arête, then up and right to where the wall overhangs. Pumpy climbing on incut jugs leads past the right side of a choss tower (best not to touch this), then up to a stance. Step left to some cracks, then straight up the steep face using horizontal cracks to a long stab for a jug on a smile-shaped scoop with a fixed anchor. 100'

P2 5.9 G: Go straight up to a good slot (yellow Alien), then move left 10' (crux) using a sidepull to parallel cracks. Follow these through a bulge to a small ledge with a fixed anchor below blueberry slabs. 50'
Gear: Minimal rack to 1" for P2.
FA Sep 10, 2011, Jim Lawyer, Neal Knitel, Tad Welch

11 Mine Shaft (aka C Crack, aka Jervis's Joke) 5.4 PG 200'

This spectacular feature unfortunately offers less than spectacular climbing. Much loose rock has been removed with more to come. Currently, there is a very unstable monster block in the topout. Although not recommended as a summer route, this is an excellent winter route. This route, along with Old Route at Hurricane Cliff, are the largest known chimneys in the Adirondack Park. The route was originally climbed in two pitches, but with a 60m rope, only one pitch is required.

Start: Near the center of the cliff at the obvious curving chimney.

P1 5.4 PG: Up the shattered dike deep within the chimney, behind a large chockstone, and up to the sunlight, eventually emerging in a gully that leads to a large pine. 200'

Descent: Walk around either side of the cliff, or rappel with two ropes from the fixed anchor of Haroom Baroom.
FA Aug, 1981, Steve Jervis, Jamie Savage, Bill Widrig, Tad Welch

12 Haroom Baroom 5.11d G 180' ★★★★★

The name is Berber for "cheers." This route has it all: underclings, crimps, slopers, pinches, a tufa, a crystal jug, fingers to fists and overhung rock to a slabby

Martine Schaer on P1 of Tears of Gaia (5.10b)

Northern Mountains

top. Bouldery for the first 80' until the angle kicks back. Then tricky gear up a water grooved crack. Led in two pitches but should be linked.
Start: 50' right of **Mine Shaft** at an obvious stem box created by two facing corners.
● **P1 5.11d G:** Climb up the stem box, then up through tiered overlaps and roofs. At the third clip step left and make a hard move over the roof (crux), then step back right and continue up to the crack. Gear belay. 80'
P2 5.9 PG: Follow the crack until it fades. After you pull onto the slab (crux), continue up to a fixed anchor. 100'
Gear: Doubles through 0.75 Camalot, plus #1 and #2 Camalots.
FA Oct 11, 2010, Matt Way, Jesse Littleton, Richard Wilson

13 Bearded Munchkin 5.10b G 185' ★★★★
Another beautiful pitch. With work, an excellent second pitch is possible.
Start: 40' right of **Haroom Baroom** and 30' left of **Seeking Enlightenment** below a left-slanting dihedral capped by a large roof.
● **P1 5.10b G:** Climb up to a ramp and dihedral. Near its top step right and pull past the roof (wild, crux). Continue up until the dihedral ends and then step right. Continue up a crack to a foot-sized block and a fixed nut belay. 75'
P2 5.10c PG: Continue up into a left-facing corner with some loose blocks. Tread lightly past this and continue up the mostly finger-size crack until it ends. Make a few moves up the slab and then step left and head to the fixed anchor. 110'
Gear: Double rack up to 0.5", extra small stuff helpful.
Descent: Rappel. Gear can be collected by rappelling **Haroom Baroom**.
FA Nov 7, 2010, Jesse Littleton, Richard Wilson

14 Seeking Enlightenment 5.11a G 160' ★★★
The first pitch is used as an approach to several stunning cracks.
Start: 75' right of **Haroom Baroom** beneath a cow's-mouth roof 40' up.
● **P1 5.10d G:** Move up to the roof. Pull the roof to good cracks just above, then work right up a slab to a fixed anchor. 50'
P2 5.11a G: Go straight up the slab (first crux) to a good horizontal below a thin, overhanging crack. Work up the overhanging crack to surprising holds, then up the thin tips crack to where it pinches off. Continue up to where the crack opens to hands (second crux), and follow this to big jugs. Continue the crack through another bulge, then step right to a fixed anchor. 110'
Gear: P1: 1 ea 2" cam; P2: doubles to 2".
Descent: A double-rope rappel returns to the ground.
FA (P1) Oct 28, 2010; Jesse Littleton, Richard Wilson
FA (P2, A0) May 23, 2011, Colin Loher, Jim Lawyer, Will Roth
FFA (P2) Sep 3, 2011, Colin Loher, Will Roth

15 Flying Buddha 5.12a G 110' ★★★★
This beautiful splitter overhangs 10'. It's the obvious overhanging crack to the right of the second pitch of **Seeking Enlightenment**.
Start: Top of P1 of **Seeking Enlightenment**.
P1 5.12a G: Head up the slab past the first 2 bolts of **Seeking Enlightenment**, then move right to the base of a right-facing corner with the crack above. Pull though a small roof and up to a horizontal. Rest, then jam your way from fingers to hands to fists for 15'. Make a big move, followed by several harder ones. Finish up the crack more easily on lower-angled rock. 110'
FA Jun 18, 2012, Conor Cliffe, Tom Wright

*Forrest Schwabb on an early attempt of **Jenga** (5.11b), belayed by Matt Way and Phoebe Wolcott-MacCausland. Photo by Richard Wilson.*

Northern Mountains

16 Hippie Sticks and Black Flies
5.11a G (5.5 R) 280' ★★★

The last pitch is reportedly one of the best at Silver Lake.

Start: 150' right of Mine Shaft in front of a birch tree stump at an obvious, large, left-facing corner capped by a roof 50' up.

P1 5.11a G: Up the initial corner (crux) up to the roof. Traverse left under the roof and continue up flake to a shrubby ledge. Large cams helpful for the anchor (4" to 5"). 60'

P2 5.9 G (5.5 R): Gain the top of the left-facing corner. Climb the railroad track cracks (crux) and head for easier terrain to a slight ledge system. Traverse left 30' (passing the fixed anchor of Jenga) to a comfy belay at the base of a thin crack. 110'

P3 5.10d G ★★★★★**:** Climb the crack until it fades. Step left to another thin seam and climb this to a right-rising crack–flake. When this ends, go up and left (crux) to a rounded corner. Climb a slab to the top. 110'

Gear: Double rack plus large cams for the P1 anchor.
Descent: Walk right and rappel Jenga.
FA May 16, 2010, Jesse Littleton, Mark Scott, Richard Wilson

17 Jenga 5.11b PG 80' ★★★

Insecure jamming and imbalance characterize this pitch.

Start: Climb P1-P2 of Hippie Sticks and Black Flies (5.11a), but stop the P2 traverse at a comfy belay and fixed anchor.

P1 5.11b PG: Move up and slightly left, then back right to a flared crack. Follow the crack until it disappears, then move right and aim for the impressive-looking hand crack in a block. Surmount this, then go up to a fixed anchor. 80'

Descent: Two rappels: the first is 30m and the second is 35m.
FFA Jun 16, 2012, Conor Cliffe, Tom Draper

18 Velma's Snatch 5.3 X 190'

Climbs the second-most obvious feature on the cliff, the right-leaning ramp on the right side of the main face. Looks much better than it is.

Start: 55' right of Hippie Sticks and Black Flies below a large open book with a dark, dirty, and wet chimney at its center.

P1 5.3 X: Climb the chimney for 40' to a jumble of detached blocks. Over these, then up the surprisingly steep gully filled with pine needles to the top. 190'

Gear: 1 ea #4 Camalot, 0.5 Camalot, slung pine tree.
Descent: Walk left and rappel Jenga.
FA Oct 18, 2010, Forrest Schwab, Alex Pellman

19 I See You 5.10b G 230' ★★★

A really fun, long route that needs a little cleaning. The first ascent was climbed as one long pitch with 30' of simul-climbing; could easily be done as two separate pitches. The route ends at a fine perch—one of the nicest craggy summits in the Adirondacks.

Start: At the obvious 90' stem box on the right side of the cliff, approximately 100' right of Black Flies and Hippie Sticks.

P1 5.10b G: Head up the stem box for 90' making interesting moves that corkscrew up this feature. Step left at the top of the stem box and make some harder face moves (crux) to a beautiful crack. Follow the crack that eventually narrows to an incredible left-rising fingercrack which is climbed to the top. 230'

History: Drinkwater cleaned the route over 4 days. On one day, she left the cliff in the evening and returned the next morning to find a pine-cone face next to her fixed line; a little creepy.
FA May 2, 2012, Emilie Drinkwater, Colin Loher

Silver Lake
NEVER NEVER LAND

Aspect	South
Height	80'
Quality	★★★
Approach	50 min, moderate
Summary	Small wall with several difficult, high-quality cracks.

			1	2	1		4
-5.6	5.7	5.8	5.9	5.10	5.11	5.12	5.13+	total

This cliff sits high on the Silver Lake Mountain–Potter Mountain ridgeline, between the larger C Chimney Cliff on the left and the Purple Rain Wall on the right. It's characterized by steep, short cracks. Bring a brush.

DIRECTIONS (MAP PAGE 436)
Follow the approach to the C Chimney Cliff (40 min), then walk right along the base to its far right end. Continue across a gully to this cliff 593631,4930341.

HISTORY
You get a great view of this cliff from the routes on the C Chimney Cliff, which is what led climbers here in 2010. First to visit was the St. Lawrence crew, then Colin Loher and Joe Szot.

1 Hammerhead 5.10b G 80' ★★★

Excellent views of Taylor Pond, Silver Lake, C Chimney Cliff, and Center of Progress.

Start: 200' left of Blockus is a grassy, tiered, tree-covered ledge system. Walk to its left end, directly in front of (and 70' below) a splitter handcrack. Scramble up the tiered ledge system (3rd class) to a red pine belay below the handcrack; there is a hammerhead-shaped flake formation just to its right.

P1 5.10b G: Go up the crack a few moves than follow large face holds left, then back right to a small overhang where the crack pinches down to a seam. At the overhang, gently use the hammerhead-shaped flake to advance past the seam, then follow the splitter handcrack (somewhat overhanging) to a fixed anchor on a tree. 80'

Descent: A single 60m rappel from tree. Be careful not to get the rope stuck!
FA Oct 5, 2010, Colin Loher, Richard Wilson

Northern Mountains

2 Second Crimp to the Right, Keep on Climbing Till Morning 5.9 G 70' ★★

Sustained and fun with sequential hand and finger jams peppered with good feet. A little dirty.
Start: Same as Blockus.
P1 5.9 G: Begin as for Blockus: climb a left-rising dirt ramp below the offwidth to a small right-facing flake. Climb past the flake, then go straight up the splitter crack to a fixed anchor (shared with Blockus). 70'
History: This was Joe Szot's last new rock route before he died in the spring of 2012. Named for the directions to the fictional Neverland in the works of J. M. Barrie.
FA Oct 24, 2010, Joe Szot, Colin Loher

3 Blockus 5.10a G 70' ★★★

Start: At an offwidth crack formed by the left side of a tractor-trailer-sized, detached block.
P1 5.10a G: Climb a left-rising dirt ramp below the offwidth to a small right-facing flake. Climb past the flake and traverse right into the offwidth. Get sucked in as the crack gradually widens and spits you out on a good ledge. Follow a hand- and fist-crack to its top, then scramble up 10' to a fixed anchor shared with Always. 70'
Gear: Doubles of 5" and 6" cams recommended.
FA Oct 5, 2010, Matt Way, Jesse Littleton

4 Happy Thoughts and Chalk Dust 5.11a PG 80' ★★★

Every move gets continually harder until the top, but with good rests. Would get 5 stars if longer, and if the top was cleaner.
Start: At a handcrack in a small left-facing corner, underneath the right side of the Blockus formation.
P1 5.11a PG: Up the corner for 10', then move right on small crimps to a fingercrack that lies just left of an arête. Up fingercrack to its end. Plug in gear, then make exciting moves up the arête to an awkward mantel onto a stance. Up increasingly difficult fingercrack just right of the arête, then dive out right to the top of a left-facing corner. Make another hard mantel move to a nice rest, then up the super thin fingercrack in a mini-corner (crux). Break left to a thin slab topout, moving left to the fixed anchor shared with Blockus. 80'
FA Oct 24, 2010, Colin Loher, Joe Szot

Silver Lake
PURPLE RAIN WALL

Aspect	South
Height	150'
Quality	★★
Approach	1 hr, moderate
Summary	Good collection of multi-pitch moderate routes in a remote setting.

	2	1	2	1		6
-5.6	5.7	5.8	5.9	5.10	5.11	5.12	5.13+	total

This is the rightmost in a series of three cliffs that sit high on the Silver Lake Mountain–Potter Mountain ridgeline. It has good quality rock—but a bit dirty, so bring a brush—with good potential for additional routes. The left end is slabby, the middle is steeper, and the right end is broken up. The base is very user-friendly with flat terrain that is not overgrown. On the right side of the cliff is the ice route Way Up Yonder.

DIRECTIONS (MAP PAGE 436)

Follow the approach to the C Chimney Cliff (40 min), then walk right past Never Never Land to this cliff 593874,4930287.

HISTORY

Kevin Thompson began visiting this cliff in 2003 and is responsible for most of the routes here.

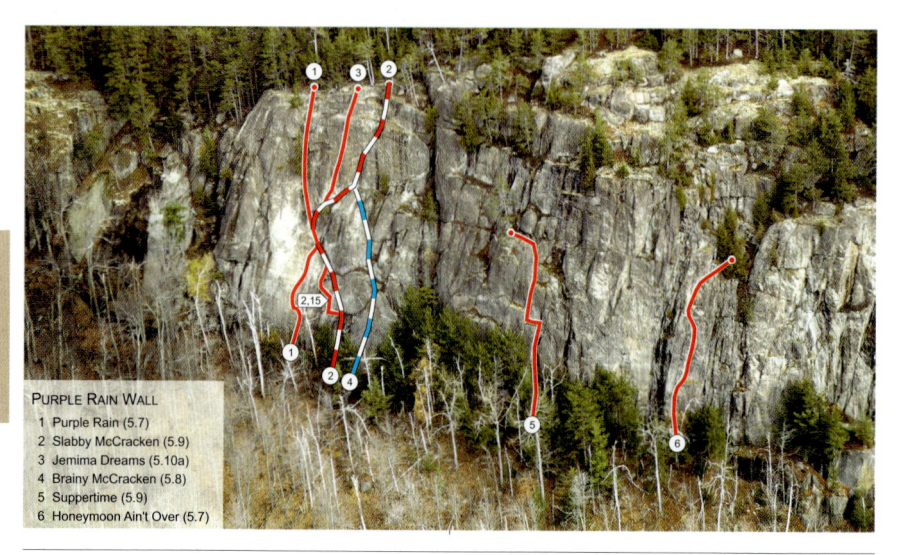

PURPLE RAIN WALL
1 Purple Rain (5.7)
2 Slabby McCracken (5.9)
3 Jemima Dreams (5.10a)
4 Brainy McCracken (5.8)
5 Suppertime (5.9)
6 Honeymoon Ain't Over (5.7)

Northern Mountains

1 Purple Rain 5.7 G 165' ★★★

Start: Left end of the cliff, in a depression left by a recently uprooted birch tree below a head-high overhang with horizontal cracks just above. When approaching from the C Chimney Cliff, this route is just past the top-to-bottom slabs that dominate the left end of the cliff.

P1 5.7 G: Work up through the overhang, then up 15' of easier terrain. Move up and right to a small overlap with an undercling. Over this, then up left to a handcrack in a slab. Up the handcrack to its end, then up an easier unprotected slab to a small pine. Head left along a low-angle, left-facing corner to a sloped belay ledge below a large cedar. 115'

P2 5.7 G: Climb past the cedar, then fun climbing up a blocky right-facing corner leads to the top. 50'

FA Jul 6, 2009, Kevin Thompson, David Dietzgen

2 Slabby McCracken 5.9 G 175' ★★★

The initial crack is very good, and P2 is excellent.

Start: 30' right of Purple Rain below a 20'-tall right-leaning crack.

P1 5.8 G: (V1) Up the crack to its end, then wander up and left on lower-angled terrain to the small pine of Purple Rain. At the pine, move up and right out of the left-facing corner to a belay at the base of a right-facing right-leaning corner which deepens higher up. 115'

P2 5.9 G: Up the right-facing corner which becomes harder as the angle diminishes. Continue to the top. 60'

V1 5.8 G: Up the initial crack to a horizontal (#0.75 Camalot), then traverse left 10' to a handcrack (#2 Camalot). Up the handcrack, then step left into a brown water stream on the slab and up into the leaning corner and pine tree of Purple Rain.

FA 2003, Matt Bresler, Kevin Thompson
FA (V1) Apr 11, 2012, Greg Kuchyt

3 Jemima Dreams 5.10a TR 60' ★★

This route climbs a crack in a steep face between the top pitches of Purple Rain and Slabby McCracken.

FA (TR) Jul 25, 2009, Jeff Cohen, Kevin Thompson

4 Brainy McCracken 5.8 G 115' ★★★

A nice alternative start to Slabby McCracken.

Start: 20' right of the Slabby McCracken, at a right-leaning, right-facing corner capped by a roof 25' up.

P1 5.8 G: Up the crack and right-facing corner to its end, then up easier terrain for 60'. Angle left on a slab to a belay at the base of a right-facing, right-leaning corner which deepens higher up (same belay as for P1 of Slabby McCracken). 115'

FA Jul 6, 2009, Kevin Thompson, David Dietzgen

5 Suppertime 5.9 G 100' ★★

A bouldery start; would be 4 stars if clean.

Start: 100' right of Jemima Dreams at the rightmost of four right-leaning cracks.

P1 5.9 G: Climb the hand- and fingercrack to its end. Move up and left past a scary dinner-table-sized detached flake, then straight up an open book for 15'. Continue up, then left on a big ledge to belay at a pine tree. 100'

FA Jul 25, 2009, Kevin Thompson, Jeff Cohen

6 Honeymoon Ain't Over 5.7 PG 115' ★

A little bit dirty but with some cleaning it could earn a few more stars. There is some space between gear on easier sections of rock.

Start: 15' right of a very dirty, overgrown open book corner below a V-slot with a crack in it and a ledge 10' up and right.

P1 5.7 PG: Climb up 30' to a decent size ledge. Step right and up a corner–crack and follow this to the top. Diagonal left, then follow discontinuous cracks trending right to a rappel cedar tree. 115'

Descent: 70m rope required to rappel.

FA Apr 29, 2013, Jesse Littleton, Margaret Littleton

Silver Lake

SUMMIT CLIFF

Aspect	South and southwest
Height	200'
Quality	★★★★
Approach	1 hr, difficult
Summary	Very wide cliff with many excellent cracks in the Prow Area.

-5.6	5.7	5.8	5.9	5.10	5.11	5.12	5.13+	total
4	3	2	5	8	1			23

This long cliff has a high concentration of quality cracks. The primary feature you can see from the road is a buttress—the Prow Area—on the left end of the cliff with a splitter crack; this is the route Tales of Weakness. Most of the quality climbing is in the vicinity of this buttress, which is positioned near the height of land. As you move downhill and right from the Prow Area, the terrain becomes slabby. On the right side of the cliff and positioned near the top is a right-arching blade of rock—the Blade Area. Just right of this is a wet black wall with the winter route Twilight Falls.

Getting to the top of the cliff is a challenge. It's easiest to walk left and scramble up the Silver Lake Chimney. You can also walk right and climb North Dike (5.2).

DIRECTIONS (MAP PAGE 436)

The approach takes about 1 hour. It's strenuous but with easy navigation.

Park at the Turnpike Road Trailhead. Follow an excellent logging road for 4 minutes to a huge field (an old logging header) where many smaller arteries branch off. There's a good view of the cliffs here. Bear slightly left and uphill, following occasional cairns. There are many intersections along this road, but stay on the main (most improved) logging road with cairns; you can occasionally see the cliffs, and you're aiming for the Tsunami Wall, the unmistakable wall with an overhanging wave-like feature at its top. Once directly in front of the Tsunami Wall, the logging road turns uphill and becomes more of a skid path that grows increasingly unpleasant (poor footing, steep, high weeds). The logging road ascends the wide forested bench in front of the Summit Cliff, so you can turn off to the right just

Northern Mountains

about anywhere and reach the cliff. To reach the most popular area, just before the height of land, look for a herd path on the right, which is followed for 2 minutes to the cliff, reaching the cliff at the base of **Handlebarbarism** and **Green Mountain Boys** 594368,4929859.

To reach the right end, look for the Blade feature—a 100'-high, right-arching arête that dominates the upper section of the cliff. Once level with this feature (which you can see from the approach road), look for a cairn and flagged trail on the right; this takes you to the right end in the vicinity of **Crackus Interuptus** 594544,4929892.

Left End

1 Silver Lake Chimney 3rd class
The preferred approach to the top of the cliff, and an excellent destination for a hike. From **Green Mountain Boys** (where the trail reaches the cliff), walk left past **Burnt Toast**, hugging the main cliff. After several hundred feet the terrain rises steeply; continue uphill along the base of the cliff to a hidden 4'-wide chimney. This chimney has several giant chockstones; the most impressive is bridge formed by two leaning boulders at the top. Scramble up the chimney to emerge from the forest floor above.

2 Racoon Eyes 5.7 G 100' ★
Start: 30' left of **Scooped By Fritz**, scramble up a steep dirt slope. Begin below a deep mossy cleft.
P1 5.0 G: Scramble up the gully to gain a large tree ledge. 50'
P1 5.7 G: Step right and climb a fingercrack that widens to hands. Step right and belay at a tree with a fixed anchor. 50'
FA May, 2013, Tom Wright, Will Roth

3 Scooped By Fritz 5.9 G 140' ★★
Start: Scramble up a 3rd-class ramp 20' to a good belay stance at the left end of the **Hot Tamale** tree ledge.
P1 5.9 G: Up a fingercrack for 20', then step right to a right-facing corner. Jam up the corner to a tree ledge. Optional belay. Go up another corner (past a ring piton!) past an overhanging block (appears solid). Scramble up and left 30' to a sloping ledge and belay at a flimsy tree. 140'
Descent: Rappel with a 70m rope, or make two rappels with a 60m rope.
FA May, 2013, Tom Wright, Will Roth

4 Hot Tamale 5.9 G 80' ★★
Start: 100' left of **Handlebarbarism** is a large 8'-deep, right-facing corner that rises above a narrow ledge with large cedars 10' up. Begin on the left end of the ledge where the low-angle rock leads up to the right-facing corner.
P1 5.9 G: Follow a series of small right-facing corners, flakes, and small ledges heading for a prominent vertical crack 15' right of the right-facing corner. Follow the crack to a small ledge, and then climb a right-facing corner–crack to the top. 80'
FA Aug 15, 2009, Kevin Crowl, Adam Crofoot

5 Caspian Corner 5.9+ G 80' ★★★
Start: At the very right end of the narrow ledge (as described for **Hot Tamale**).
P1 5.9+ G: Follow a crack system up and slightly left to gain a sharp left-facing corner. Up the corner to its top, then finish up cracks through a blocky section to a ledge with a "surfboard" and a belay tree behind it. 80'
FA Aug 15, 2009, Adam Crofoot, Jenny Mugrace, Kevin Crowl

Northern Mountains

SUMMIT CLIFF: LEFT END
1 Silver Lake Chimney (3rd class)
2 Racoon Eyes (5.7)
3 Scooped By Fritz (5.9)
4 Hot Tamale (5.9)
5 Caspian Corner (5.9+)
6 Burnt Toast (5.7)
7 Beginner's Route (5.2)
8 Handlebarbarism (5.10b)
11 Great Northern Diver (5.10d)
12 Hairy Upper Lip Drip (5.10b)

Prow Area

6 Burnt Toast 5.7 G 260'

Start: 60' left of Handlebarbarism below an open book corner with a giant cedar 15' up. On the left wall of the open book corner (and 4' right of the toe of the arête that forms the left wall of the open book) is a fingercrack.

P1: (V1) Move up to the cedar and thrash past this to gain a left-leaning corner with a wide crack. Up the corner onto small holds on the face beyond. A few steps upward bring one to a large ledge with trees. Belay at birch tree. 60'

P2: Climb a short slab to the obvious layback crack above. Jam and layback to better holds at the cedar. Harder than it looks. Scruffy going ends at the mammoth terrace. Belay anywhere. 100'

P3: On the left side of the terrace is a stepped, left-facing dihedral. Straightforward climbing up the corner and cracks over much lichen finishes just short of the attractive summit. 100'

V1 5.9 G: Climb the thin fingertip crack on the left wall of the open book corner to an arête. Up the arête to join the regular route at the top of the left-leaning corner.

Descent: Walk off left and scramble down the class II chimney.

History: On the FA, Bill fell while leading the crack on P2 and was stopped short of the ledge in an undignified upside-down position.
FA Sep, 1983, Tad Welch, Bill Widrig

7 Beginner's Route 5.2 PG 80'

Start: Same as for Burnt Toast.

P1 5.2 PG: Climb up to the cedar, then work out right onto a slab, staying right of the tree-choked corner and left of the steeper section of the slab. A short fun crack ends at the lovely Window Box Ledge atop P1 of Green Mountain Boys. 80'

Descent: Rappel or downclimb the route.
FA Sep, 1983, Tad Welch (solo)

8 Handlebarbarism 5.10b G 90' ★★★★

Tenuous vertical crack that starts as fists and narrows to fingers, then offwidth.

Start: 12' left of Green Mountain Boys, at a handcrack that begins on a ledge 10' up with a cedar tree.

P1 5.10b G: Climb up onto a small ledge with a tree, then up a vertical crack, fists at first, then fingers, then opening to offwidth (#5 Camalot helpful) to a ledge. Continue up and left in the crack with a tree to a large ledge. Move up and right onto some low-angle slabs to a shared anchor with Green Mountain Boys on Window Box Ledge (an excellent, flat ledge system). 90'

Gear: Singles to 6".
FA Apr 22, 2009, Richard Wilson, Matt Way
FFA May 12, 2009, Richard Wilson, Devin Berberich

9 Green Mountain Boys 5.10a G 70' ★★★★

Start: 60' left of Great Northern Diver, where the trail meets the cliff, are two parallel crack lines 12' apart. This is the right-hand crack that begins above an overhanging bulge.

449

Northern Mountains

SUMMIT CLIFF: PROW AREA

- 6 Burnt Toast (5.7)
- 7 Beginner's Route (5.2)
- 8 Handlebarbarism (5.10b)
- 9 Green Mountain Boys (5.10a)
- 10 Turning 21 Again (5.10c)
- 11 Great Northern Diver (5.10d)
- 12 Hairy Upper Lip Drip (5.10b)
- 13 Tales of Weakness (5.9)
- 14 Finger Lickin' Good (5.10d)
- 15 Snapperhead (5.9)
- 16 Cedar Run (5.6)
- 17 Blueberry Buttress (5.8)
- 18 Skinny Cat (5.7)
- A Window Box Ledge

P1 5.10a G: Climb the handcrack through the bulge to a small ceiling. Continue up the handcrack in a left-facing corner to a second bulge, then up to a ledge. Another short corner past a bush ends at Window Box Ledge (an excellent, flat ledge system). 70'
Descent: Rappel from tree down the slab to the left.
History: This route may have had an earlier ascent by a party from Vermont (Tim Beaman and company), hence the name.
FA (5.8 A1) Sep, 1983, Tad Welch, John Thackray
FFA Apr 29, 2009, Matt Way, Colin Loher, Jesse Littleton

10 Turning 21 Again 5.10c G 90' ★★

Start: Below the obvious squeeze chimney between **Green Mountain Boys** and **Great Northern Diver**.
P1 5.10c G: Climb the slightly overhanging handcrack (crux) to the offwidth squeeze chimney that is followed to the top. 90'
Gear: To 5".
FA (A0) Sep 5, 2009, John Armstrong, James Armstrong
FFA Oct 8, 2011, John Armstrong, James Armstrong

11 Great Northern Diver 5.10d G 210' ★★★★★

A thoroughly enjoyable climb. Indeed, the first pitch is on par with anything at the Battle of the Bulge buttress at Indian Creek.
Start: Below the right side of a dirty slab, above which is an unmistakable huge left-facing dihedral with an overhanging left wall. In front of this route, but set back from the cliff is a huge boulder (may be difficult to find mid-summer).
P1 3rd class: Scramble up the dirty slab (pulling on trees, etc.) and set a belay below the corner. 30'
P2 5.10d G: Climb the relentlessly steep, immaculate corner to a fixed anchor (back up with a 3" cam). 70'
P3 5.6 G: Continue up the crack, then left-facing corner to a large ledge system with a fixed anchor on a tree. 110'
Descent: Rappel.
History: Bill Widrig gave this his highest rating, deeming it "better than sex."
FA (A1) Oct, 1982, Bill Widrig, Tad Welch
FFA May, 2009, Jesse Littleton, Matt Way, Colin Loher

12 Hairy Upper Lip Drip 5.10b G 100' ★★★★★

Named for the constant drip of water that comes from the roof.
Start: From Window Box Ledge. Reach this ledge by climbing **Beginner's Route**, **Handlebarbarism**, or **Green Mountain Boys**.
P1 5.10b G: Up the handcrack in a corner to an impressive triangular-shaped overhang. Follow the crack

Northern Mountains

*In 1982, Bill Widrig on the first ascent of **Great Northern Diver** (5.10d). Photo by Tad Welch.*

...almost 30 years later, Devin Berberich on the same route, belayed by Matt Way. Photo Richard Wilson.

on the right side of the overhang until it diminishes, then switch to the left crack (tight hands). Follow this crack as it widens (strenuous) to a stembox chimney (some loose rock) to the top. 100'

Descent: Three rappels starting from the fixed anchor on top of **Finger Lickin' Good**. 70m rope required.
FA Apr, 2009, Matt Way, Jesse Littleton
FFA May, 2009, Jesse Littleton, Matt Way

13 Tales of Weakness 5.9 G 100' ★★★

This is the proud line you can see from the road—a striking crack splitting the buttress on the upper left side of the cliff.

Start: On a ledge below the base of the crack. There are many ways to access the crack, the most direct being **Great Northern Diver**. It can also be reached from the Window Box Ledge. (The first ascent climbed **Snapperhead**, then traversed way left to access the crack.)

P1 5.9 G: Climb the striking right-leaning crack to a low angle slab. Gear anchor. 100'

Descent: Scramble right to the fixed anchor on top of **Finger Lickin' Good**. Three rappels with a 70m rope are required.
FA 1981, Mark Meschinelli, Todd Eastman

14 Finger Lickin' Good 5.10d G 110' ★★★★

This is the prominent right-rising fingercrack right of **Tales of Weakness**. This excellent project awaits a clean lead (and maybe some cleaning in the upper crack).

Start: At the large cedar at the end of P3 of **Great Northern Diver**.

P1 5.10d G: Step down to a ledge and traverse left to the base of a handcrack. Straight up the handcrack for 10', then follow the right-angling crack to a tree. Go straight up a crack to a fixed anchor. 110'

15 Snapperhead 5.9 G 80' ★★

Start: 100' right of Great Northern Diver and right of a small "toe" of cliff is a slabby wall with a wide tree-filled crack near the middle and a left-facing corner system on the right. Begin in the left-facing corner.

P1 5.9 G: Follow the left-facing corner over several budges heading to a short finger crack beside a large roof. Finish to the cedar tree. 80'
FA Jun 6, 2009, Kevin Crowl, Julia Gronski

16 Cedar Run 5.6 PG 80'

Start: 20' right of **Snapperhead** is a right-facing open book with a medium-sized oak tree growing 2' from the cliff. Begin a few feet left of this corner at a wide crack that leads into a cedar tree 20' up.

P1 5.6 PG: Climb the crack, then climb the cedars until they end. An obvious belay ledge is on your left. 80'
FA Jul 11, 2009, Micah Stewart, Kevin Crowl

17 Blueberry Buttress 5.8 G 170' ★★★

This crack splits a high buttress, which is easily seen from the trail, but completely invisible from the base of the cliff.

Start: 75' right of **Snapperhead** at a splitter, 30'-tall off-hands crack. There is a large oak tree 2' from the cliff face.

P1 5.7 G: Follow the crack to its top, then up a slabby corner to the trees. 70'

P1 5.8 G: Climb the left-facing corners to a large cedar–shrub–mat–mess. Continue up the offwidth and follow the fingercracks to the top. 100'
FA (P1) Sep 14, 2010, Kevin Crowl, Julia Gronski, Micah Stewart
FA (P2) Aug 9, 2009, Kevin Crowl, Adam Crofoot

Northern Mountains

Pavlova (winter route)
Violent Stems (winter route)
Twilight Falls (winter route)
WAYBACK CLIFF
Blade
Grand Traverse Ledge
Viewpoint

SUMMIT CLIFF: BLADE AREA
19 Crackus Interuptus (5.10a)
20 It Goes to Eleven (5.11a)
21 Tusk (5.8)
22 Queen of the Jungle (5.10c)
23 North Dike (5.2)

18 Skinny Cat 5.7 PG 240'

Climbs the up the center of the left side of the main slab.

Start: 90' downhill and right from **Blueberry Buttress** is a large slab that leads to a huge, left-facing, open book corner at the top of the cliff. Begin on the left side of a cave at the base of the slab.

P1 5.7 PG: Follow a crack through a roof on its left side (or stand on a block and step right into the crack). Up the crack for 10' to a small spruce on a ledge. 20'

P2 5.7 PG: Move to the right end of the ledge to gain the slab, then wander up the slab to the top. 220'

History: The first ascent climbed the route in three pitches, as it's difficult to find a belay beyond the horizontal 20' up.

ACB Jun, 2010, Kevin Crowl, Julia Gronski

Blade Area

High on the right end of the cliff is The Blade—a 100'-high, right-arching arête.

19 Crackus Interuptus 5.10a G 170' ★★★

Start: Begin directly below the left side of The Blade at a fingertip crack in black rock, 10' right of a right-facing corner.

P1 5.10a G: Up the crack 40' to a bulge. Over the bulge to a pod (crux). Continue up the crack past a hanging cedar to a ledge below a headwall. Work up the steep crack in the headwall to an awkward move onto a slab. Up the slab and left-facing corner to a good ledge with an oak tree belay. 140'

P2 5.8+ G: Up a left-facing corner to a ledge, which is the left end of the Grand Traverse Ledge, and directly below the left side of The Blade. 30'

Descent: Walk right along the Grand Traverse Ledge.

Gear: To 3", emphasis on small cams and nuts.

FA Sep 6, 2009, Tom Yandon, Tad Welch, Jim Lawyer

20 It Goes to Eleven 5.11a G 100' ★★★

Start: At the left end of the black wall (described in **Tusk**), 15' uphill and left from the low point of the dip, below a good horizontal 10' up.

● **P1 5.11a G:** Up to a fragile block 10' up, then power up sidepulls and good buckets to the top of the black wall. A hard move gains the friction slab. Move up the slab to a dike, then up good edges in the slab to another dike. Foot traverse left 10', then over a black bulge to the left end of an overlap (gear). Move up and right to the Grand Traverse Ledge and a clump of oak trees on the left. 100'

Gear: 1 ea yellow Alien.

FA Sep 6, 2009, Jim Lawyer, Tom Yandon, Tad Welch

21 Tusk 5.8 PG 70' ★★★

Start: Walk right from **Crackus Interuptus** to where the terrain dips below an overhanging black wall, 50' downhill and left of where you can walk left onto the Grand Traverse Ledge. Begin near the right end of the black wall, 10' up and right from the low point of the dip (The winter route **Pavlova** also begins here.)

● **P1 5.8 PG:** Climb up good incut buckets and sidepulls to a dike with a tooth-like spike (sling this for critical gear). Traverse left on the dike for 25', then

452

friction up the face (some pods for protection) to the Grand Traverse Ledge and oak tree belay. 70'
Gear: Long sling for the tooth, yellow Alien, #0 TCU.
FA Sep 6, 2009, Jim Lawyer, Tom Yandon, Tad Welch

22 Queen of the Jungle 5.10c G 100' ★★★★
Start: The route begins on the Grand Traverse Ledge that horizontally splits the right end of the cliff. To access the ledge, walk up and right along the base of the cliff, past the Viewpoint, past an overhanging black wall (the location of **It Goes to Eleven** and **Tusk**) until below a deep, wet, groove that begins 30' up (the winter route **Violent Stems**). Cut back left onto a narrow tree-covered ledge (3th class) for 150' to a 30'-high, 3'-deep, left-facing corner with a 5" crack that narrows to hand size. There is a gnarled cedar 60' up in the crack, a huge cedar 10' below the ledge growing out of the cliff, and 20' right of a large healthy pine on the ledge with a fixed anchor.
P1 5.10c G: Power layback up a wide crack and then jam the handcrack which quickly narrows to finger tips to a good rest at 30'. Above, the crack widens again to hand size, then back to fingers (crux) to a second rest. Continue up crack through an offwidth roof to a tree anchor. 100'
Gear: Up to a 4", doubles in the 1"–3" sizes.
Descent: 100' rappel back to ledge, then another 100' rappel to the base of the cliff (or reverse the 3rd class Grand Traverse Ledge).
FA Sep, 2006, Colin Loher, Bob Starinsky

23 North Dike 5.2 G 120'
This route provides access to the broad ramp below Wayback Cliff, reportedly more enjoyable than the **Dirty Gully** (imagine that). The route has a first pitch that begins at the actual cliff base, but it's nondescript vertical 4th class bushwhacking; the cleaner, well-defined upper portion of the route is described here.
Start: 200' right of the "switchback" (the point along the cliff base where you cut left onto the Grand Traverse Ledge to approach **Queen of the Jungle**) at a 3'-wide parallel-sided, low-angle chimney in a huge left-facing corner. (This is just right of the winter route **Twilight Falls** described in *Blue Lines*.)
P1 5.2 G: Climb the dike to the top. 120'
FA Sep 30, 1979, Dick Tucker, Eric T. Laurin, Tim Riley

Silver Lake
CENTER OF PROGRESS CLIFF

Aspect	South and southwest
Height	250'
Quality	★★★
Approach	30 min, moderate
Summary	Large cliff with mostly crack climbs, some multi-pitch.

2	3	5	3	7	3		28
-5.6	5.7	5.8	5.9	5.10	5.11	5.12 5.13+	total

Another of Silver Lake's gems, this large cliff is one of the easier to reach. On the left end is the Loher Wall with some short single-pitch crack routes down in the trees. Left of center is the Tooth & Nail Area, a large corner area sitting above a terrace. The Silver Flake Area is right of center, and has a number of moderate multi-pitch routes. The Connecticut Yankee Area is the impressive shield of rock on the right end, bound on its right side by a right-rising gully used to access the top of the cliff and for descent. **Sinner Repent** is the difficult-to-miss offwidth crack that begins in a cave, and **Connecticut Yankee** is the crack system 50' right; both routes run the full height of the cliff. Downhill and right of the descent gully, the cliff continues with a number of short, demanding single-pitch routes.

DIRECTIONS (MAP PAGE 436)
Park at the Turnpike Road Trailhead. Follow an excellent logging road for 4 minutes to a huge field (an old logging header) where many smaller arteries branch off. There's a good view of the cliffs here. Bear slightly left and uphill, following occasional cairns. There are many intersections along this road, but stay on the main (most improved) logging road with cairns; you can occasionally see the cliffs, and you're aiming for the Tsunami Wall, the unmistakable wall with an overhanging wave-like feature at its top. After a marshy area (and before the trail begins to climb) there is a fork in the road. The Summit Cliff approach, which is the larger road, bears right. Take the left fork and follow logging roads as they contour the slope (some flagging here)

CENTER OF PROGRESS CLIFF
1. LOHER WALL
2. TOOTH & NAIL AREA
3. SILVER FLAKE AREA
4. CONNECTICUT YANKEE AREA
5. RIGHT END

*Will Roth stands below **Another Crack in the Wall** (5.9). Photo by Colin Loher.*

to the west. Turn right (north) at a cairn and follow a well-cairned path uphill to the cliff in the vicinity of **Connecticut Yankee** 0594460,4929514.

Loher Wall

Walk left from **Connecticut Yankee** about 10 minutes, uphill, following the cliff line until the terrain levels. The cliff diminishes in height. Look for the wet, 20' deep, right-facing corner that marks the start of **Another Crack in the Wall** 594129,4929634.

1 Another Crack in the Wall 5.9 G 60'

Start: At the top of a cone-shaped sloped covered in pine needles, below an attractive crack.

P1 5.9 G: Follow the crack to a ledge, then up to another ledge below a left-facing corner capped by a small triangular ceiling. Up the corner and over the ceiling, then jam a crack up to a tricky finish. Lower from a fixed anchor on a pine tree. 60'
FA Oct 26, 2006, Colin Loher, Will Roth

2 Mo'in The Mud 5.7+ G 60'

Start: 20' to the left of **Franklin's Tower**.

P1 5.7+ G: Climb a left-arching crack (crux) to a rest ledge. Continue up the crack to a steep, 10'-tall headwall. Climb the crack through the headwall and finish at a fixed anchor on a pine tree. 60'
FA Aug 29, 2010, Kris O'Connor, Monique Wicks
FFA Sep 4, 2010, Will Roth, Kris O'Connor

3 Franklin's Tower 5.8+ G 80'

Start: 200' right of **Another Crack in the Wall** is a 20' deep, right-facing corner with wet, mossy cracks in the corner. Begin 12' right of the corner below a shallow right-facing corner with a handcrack. There is a large maple 6' back from the start of the route.

P1 5.8+ G: Up the crack, then up the right side of a small tower that vibrates alarmingly. Finish in a crack in a right-facing corner to a fixed anchor on a pine tree. 80'
FA Oct 26, 2006, Will Roth, Colin Loher

4 The Dirty Mattress 5.8 G 70'

The flake stuck in the crack that makes the thin crux section is solid even though at first it looks hollow.

Start: 40' right of **Franklin's Tower** at a wide crack at the end of the buttress just behind a large oak tree.

P1 5.8 G: Climb the wide crack on its right side. After 10', step left to the start of a left-arching crack and climb to its top. There is a fixed anchor on a pine set back from the edge of the cliff to the right. 70'
FA Aug 29, 2010, Will Roth, Kris O'Connor
FFA Sep 4, 2010, Will Roth, Monique Wicks

5 Angry Hemorrhoid Chimney 5.4 G 60'

Reported as "a piece of shit." Perhaps better left as a winter route.

Start: Left of the Tooth & Nail Terrace, follow a ribbon of trees up and left to a position below a chimney breaking the upper wall.

P1 5.4 G: Follow the chimney to the top. 60'
FA Jun, 2008, Colin Loher, Aaron Pfenler

*Bill Widrig ties in to complete P1 on the first ascent of **Tooth & Nail** (5.10b) in 1979. Photo by Tad Welch.*

Northern Mountains

CENTER OF PROGRESS CLIFF:
TOOTH & NAIL AREA
5 Angry Hemorrhoid Chimney (5.4)
6 African Barking Spiders (5.11a)
7 Tooth & Nail (5.10b)
8 Oral Surgery (5.11b)

Tooth & Nail Area

The Tooth & Nail Area is accessed from the Tooth & Nail Terrace, a slab positioned above the cliff base and below an unmistakable, 30'-wide, 15'-deep, rectangular roof 25' up. Approach from the right by scrambling up several ledges chocked with cedar trees.

6 African Barking Spiders 5.11a PG 80' ★★★

The gear takes up your hand holds making this a tricky lead. Very barn-doory.
Start: On the Tooth & Nail Terrace and below the rectangular roof is a large open book corner with a cedar tree. Begin 10' left of the corner at a crack in the left wall and below the left lip of the rectangular roof.
P1 5.11a PG: Make a few free moves up a thin crack, then continue up a series of cracks 20' to the left end of the rectangular roof (crux, small wired nuts). Move around the roof and layback over easier rock to a rest (larger nuts). Above, the wall steepens and the crack thins leading to some tricky climbing before a ledge with a fixed anchor. 80'
Descent: Rappel.
FA (5.7 A2) Jul 30, 1981, Tad Welch, Nathan Blum
FFA Sep 1, 2009, Jesse Littleton, Richard Wilson

7 Tooth & Nail 5.10b G 200' ★★★★★

Start: On the Tooth & Nail Terrace, 25' right of **African Barking Spiders**, at a shallow left-facing corner 10' right of the right end of the rectangular roof 25' up.
P1 5.10b G: Go up the strenuous handcrack in the left-facing corner to a stance, then rail up and left following a very thin crack (crux) to a small right-facing corner. Follow perfect finger locks in corner to a roof. Climb through roof and continue up incredible corner (easier climbing) to a beautiful ledge with a fixed anchor. 90'
P2 5.7 G: Traverse right and climb a dirty chimney to cliff top. 110'
FA (5.6 A2) Sep, 1979, Bill Widrig, Tad Welch
FFA Aug 10, 2009, Colin Loher, Matt Way, Devin Berberich, Tom Wright

455

Northern Mountains

8 Oral Surgery 5.11b PG 90' ★★★★
Start: Same as Tooth & Nail.
P1 5.11b PG: Up the strenuous fingercrack in the left-facing corner to a stance (same as Tooth & Nail). Continue straight up through some overlaps and a small left-facing corner to a ceiling. Traverse left under the ceiling, cross Tooth & Nail, and continue traversing left following a crack to reach an arête. Continue the traverse another 25' left to African Barking Spiders and finish on that route.
Gear: Small gear, doubles to 1.5".
FA Aug 10, 2009, Jesse Littleton, Matt Way

Silver Flake Area

9 Silver Flake 5.8 G 270'
Start: Walk downhill past Wish You Were Here to a break in the cliff offering easy climbing though broken rock and spruce trees to large terrace with an oak tree.
P1: Climb easily past spruce trees to belay at large oak on terrace. 60'
P2: Walk back down to lichen-covered jam crack splitting a short wall (possible belay). Climb hand- and fist-crack up and around outside corner. The crack now becomes a spectacular hand traverse (the silver flake). Continue for 30' to belay stance on block. An especially fine pitch. 80'
P3: Traverse up and right over easier, though dirty, rock. Continue past small cedars to belay at the base of a large inside corner (big white cedar). 90'
P4 5.8 G: Up the wide crack in the corner until you can exit right onto a large ledge. 40'
FA Jun 23, 1981, Tad Welch, Nathan Blum

10 Heroes Are Hard To Find 5.8 G 200'
The route is so-named because the first ascent party went left on P2 rather than climbing the strenuous alternative which is the line of Mystery to Me.
Start: At a shallow inside corner marked by three hardwoods close to the rock, 40' left of Cedar Root. Far above is P3 of Silver Flake.
P1: A few difficult moves off the ground and up the corner bring one to gradually easier climbing. Stem up widening corner on good horizontal holds to a fine belay on a block on the left. 80'
P2: Step right onto sloping terrace and make friction moves to jam crack leading to obvious downward facing flakes. Jam a few feet, then layback a sharp-edged flake (V1) until it's possible to stretch left to a rest at a balanced block. A hidden layback up a left-facing corner brings you to the area of the cedars on P3 of Silver Flake. Friction climb up into final corner. 80'
P3 5.8 G: (Same as P3 of Silver Flake) Up the wide crack in the corner until you can exit right onto a large ledge. 40'

V1 Mystery To Me 5.9- G: Take a deep breath and undercling the flake's fragile edge rightwards. As the flake trends upwards, the climbing eases and a rest is possible. A hidden finger traverse leads back left and the angle eases. Climb to final corner.
FA Oct, 1982, Bill Widrig, Tad Welch
FA (V1) Sep, 1983, Tad Welch (toprope solo)

11 Cedar Root 5.9- G 190'
A major feature, but unfortunately far less inspiring than it looks.
Start: About 150' left of Connecticut Yankee, below a huge left-facing corner system that begins 80' up. This is 20' left of a white spire of rock leaning up against the main face, at a 5'-high left-facing corner with a shallow chimney-depression. There is an 8'-high block on the top of the left-facing corner.
P1 Crap is King (aka Dirty Laundry) 5.8 G: Climb up the chimney-depression past a dangerous chockstone to a sloped ledge, then up a wide crack past a cedar tree on your right to a large sloped ledge in a huge, left-facing corner system. Gear belay. 90'
P2 5.9- G: Continue up a crack in a left-facing corner to a slab, then up this to a very large cedar, belay on top. 60'
P3 5.8 G: (Same as P3 of Silver Flake) Up the wide crack in the corner until you can exit right onto a large ledge. 40'
Gear: Standard rack up to 3.5".
FA (P1) Aug 22, 1982, Tad Welch, Nathan Blum
FA (P2, complete) 1983, Dave Szot, Tom Yandon
FA (P3) Jun 23, 1981, Tad Welch, Nathan Blum

Jesse Littleton aiding Abracadabra (5.11d), a route he freed three years later with Matt Way. Photo Richard Wilson.

Northern Mountains

CENTER OF PROGRESS CLIFF:
SILVER FLAKE AREA
9 Silver Flake (5.8)
10 Heroes Are Hard To Find (5.8)
11 Cedar Root (5.9-)

Connecticut Yankee Area

12 Bromancing the Stone 5.10d PG 200' ★★★
P2 is amazing with near-perfect rock. P1 and P3 are not. After the crux it is well protected.
Start: 80' left of Abracadabra at a very large boulder leaning against the cliff.
P1 5.6 G: Climb up boulder and straight up some dirty rock. Traverse right for 30' following obvious feature. Belay just past a right facing corner. 50'
P2 5.10d PG ★★★: Climb up the short corner (crux; small hard-to-place wires) and step around onto the slab. Follow obvious cracks, trend right at the top. Belay at a gnarly cedar and good stance. 120'
P3 5.0 G: An unfortunate finish to a great climb: scramble left around cedar and then back right to a big tree with a rap anchor on it. 30'
Descent: Three rappels with a 60m rope
FA Jul 25, 2013, Matt Way, Jesse Littleton

457

Northern Mountains

CENTER OF PROGRESS CLIFF:
CONNECTICUT YANKEE AREA
11 Cedar Root (5.9-)
12 Bromancing the Stone (5.10d)
13 Abracadabra (5.11d A0)
14 Dreamweaver (5.11d)
15 Sinner Repent (5.10)
16 Connecticut Yankee (5.10d)

13 Abracadabra 5.11d A0 230' ★★★★

After the start this is a well-protected climb up a magnificent chunk of stone. The second pitch will likely go free at hard 11+/12-.
Start: 80' left of **Connecticut Yankee** at a small crack that begins 15' up and leads to an overhang 30' up.
P1 5.11d PG: Boulder up to a stance at the base of the crack. Up this and straight over the roof. Move slightly right to an anchor. 50'
P2 5.9 A0: Climb up the slab following the crack. Move up the headwall pulling on some gear. Then traverse left and go up the corner. Escape right onto the face 10' before the top of the corner to a fixed anchor. 90'
P3 5.11b G: Traverse right following fixed protection. Up a discontinuous finger crack to the top and fixed anchor. 90'
Descent: Three rappels with a 60m rope
FA Mar 11, 2010, Jesse Littleton, Richard Wilson
FFA (P1, P3) Jul 26, 2013, Jesse Littleton, Matt Way

14 Dreamweaver 5.11d TR 80' ★★★★

This high-quality line needs to be equipped. Begin at the top of P2 of **Abracadabra**. Climb up to an obvious left-facing corner, then up this with hard stem moves and an "elevator door" move. Continue up an easier crack, then step right at its top to a fixed anchor (shared with **Abracadabra**).
FA (TR) Jul 26, 2013, Jesse Littleton, Matt Way

15 Sinner Repent 5.10 G 250' ★★

Watch for ropes getting stuck in the crack. The first pitch can be used as an alternative to P1 of **Connecticut Yankee**.
Start: At a cave left of **Connecticut Yankee** with a 5" crack in the roof.
P1 5.10a G: Chimney up to crack. Traverse out left 12' under roof to a layback on the right side of the offwidth. Up the offwidth and chimney for 50' to a ledge (shared with **Connecticut Yankee**). Strenuous. 80'
P2 5.9 G: Continue up the chimney system until possible to traverse right to the right-hand of two cracks that split the headwall left of **Connecticut Yankee**. 170'
Gear: Doubles up to 6".
History: The first ascent climbed a tree to bypass the crux opening cave to gain the offwidth above.
FA Bob Bushart, Mark Bon Signor
FFA Sep, 1984, Don Mellor, Mark Meschinelli

16 Connecticut Yankee (aka Interloper) 5.10d G 280' ★★★★★

A dramatic, obvious, and elegant line that finds a direct path to the top of the cliff.
Start: 100' left of the right-rising descent gully and 50' right of the cave start of **Sinner Repent** at a left-facing corner with cracks, 15' right of the major right-facing flake system 25' up.
P1 5.10d G: (V1) Follow the cracks to a small left-curving arch, then undercling and hand traverse left to a stance below a huge right-facing flake above. (V2) Continue up the right-facing corner formed by the flake to a comfortable 3'-deep ledge. 100'
P2 5.10a G: Up a thin, flaring fingercrack for 50' to a right-facing corner. Up corner for another 15' to a handcrack, which turns into a left-facing corner. Up corner (easier) to overhang, over this to roof (piton). Over roof, then move up and right to an oak belay. 180'
V1 5.11+ G: Begin at a thin crack directly below the right-facing flakes above. Climb the difficult crack to join the normal route at the stance below the right-facing flakes.

458

V2 5.9 G: Work your way left on a small ledge to another stepped right-facing corner. Climb the jam crack at its back to a broad ledge. Scramble left, then back right to the belay ledge.
Gear: Doubles up to 3".
Descent: Two rappels to ground.
History: Several parties reported climbing this route, the earliest being Tad Welch and Bill Widrig, taking a roundabout variation on the first pitch, and ending two-thirds up the wall at a piton anchor. Naming the route **Interloper**, Welch wrote, "This climb has the potential to become a committing and demanding undertaking." Around 1983, Dave Szot, Tom Rosecrans, and Tom Yandon also climbed this line, calling it **Fadrus**, but it's not known whether they extended the route to the summit. Both the early ascents report using aid. The undeniable first free (and complete) ascent was by Nichols and Heintz, who published their route in Climbing[6]. They reported 5 fixed pitons on the route.
FA (with V2) Jul, 1982, Tad Welch, Bill Widrig
FFA Sep, 1984, Ken Nichols, Mike Heintz
FA (V1) 2009, Will Mayo, Sarah Tonin

Right End

This is the minor buttress that begins immediately right of the descent gully at the right end of the Main Face. The buttress is approximately 200' right of **Connecticut Yankee**.

17 Whale Crack A2 40'
An attractive practice route that is easily toproped.
Start: Immediately right of the descent route and facing the main cliff, below a right-leaning crack that begins 6' up, just above an indistinct whale-shaped feature.
P1 A2: A tricky start gives way to more straightforward nutting higher up. 40'
History: This was the first route climbed at Silver Lake by the Tanager crew, and their second FA in the park.
FA Jun, 1977, Chuck Yax, Bill Widrig, Tad Welch

18 Princess Leia A1+ 60'
An amazing line that has seen free attempts by some strong parties.
Start: Downhill and right from **Whale Crack**, 20' right of the outside corner in a dry cave, below a crack that breaks a large roof 8' up.
P1 A1+: Climb to the roof, then out to jug at the lip. Follow a fingertip seam to the left side of a second roof. Go past the roof on the left and into a left-facing corner. Free climbing (5.10) leads to the top. 60'
FA Sep 14, 2009, Jesse Littleton, Matt Way

19 Atomic Vomit A2 60'
Start: 10' right of **Princess Leia** at a crack in a small buttress 4' left of the left-facing corner of **Early Onset Dementia**.
P1 A2: Up the crack to a ledge, then up parallel crack to a large roof 25' up. Out the roof via a thin seam to the lip. Continue on aid for a few more moves past a tree leaning against the rock, then free climb to the top. 60'
FA Sep 14, 2009, Matt Way, Jesse Littleton

---
6 *Climbing*, no. 90 (Jun 1985), pp. 10–11.

20 Early Onset Dementia 5.8 G 60'
Start: At a left-facing open book corner below a crack and chimney system that runs the full height of the cliff.
P1 5.8 G: Up the corner through a squeeze section and into a 4'-wide chimney which leads to the top. 60'
FA Sep, 1984, Don Mellor, Mark Meschinelli

21 Tiguidou Pack-Sack 5.9+ G 70' ★★★
An attractive corner climb named for a song that references the Adirondacks by La Bottine Souriante that, roughly translated, means "let's go backpack."
Start: 15' right of **Early Onset Dementia** (and the next open book corner right), at a crack that leads past two small ceilings. There's a suitcase-sized triangular boulder at the base.
P1 5.9+ G: Boulder the initial open book onto a ledge using a spooky but solid block. Stem and layback up the steep, undulating corner and pull onto a small ledge (crux) below the overhang. Move to the right under the overhang onto the face. Moderate cracks (5.7) lead to a fixed anchor. 70'
Gear: To 3".
FA Apr, 2009, Mark Bealor
FFA Aug 12, 2009, Mark Bealor, Royce Van Evera

22 Rolls Royce 5.7+ G 70' ★★★
A nice face start that finishes on the same cracks as the previous route. Sections of this route have been climbed previously as evidenced by a pin in the crack to the right.
Start: 5' right of **Tiguidou Pack-Sack** at a 12'-high, 2'-wide rib with pasted-on cubes.
P1 5.7+ G: Climb easily to the top of the rib, then place a good TCU under the overhang and step onto the face. Climb the face and arête to the left past a bolt. Head for a fingercrack (old pin easily backed up) and climb the crack and face to the left (crux) to a stance at the base of the upper cracks. Up the cracks (5.7) to a fixed anchor. 70'
Gear: To 3".
FA May, 2009, Royce Van Evera, Michelle Sirois, Mark Bealor
FFA Aug 3, 2009, Mark Bealor, Royce Van Evera

23 In Hiding 5.10 PG 95' ★★★
Named for a Pearl Jam song, and the fact that this excellent route ended up climbing much differently than anticipated. Good gear but tricky to place.
Start: 40' right of **Rolls Royce** and 15' left of a rubble-filled, left-facing chimney is a lighter-colored wall laced with horizontal seams. Begin at the only vertical seam on the wall below a good horizontal crack 8' up.
P1 5.10 PG: Boulder the reachy start to the stance. Climb the steep, sustained face (crux) using the thin crack and good horizontal holds. Aim for right-facing flakes that eventually lead left to the obvious crack–groove. Climb the crack and right-hand face, then mantel onto a ledge. Step up to a thin crack in a bulging wall, then climb the crack and cleaned face on the left (5.9). Climb easily to the top when the crack ends. 95'

Northern Mountains

CENTER OF PROGRESS CLIFF: RIGHT END
17 Whale Crack (A2)
18 Princess Leia (A1+)
19 Atomic Vomit (A2)
20 Early Onset Dementia (5.8)
21 Tiguidou Pack-Sack (5.9+)
22 Rolls Royce (5.7+)
23 In Hiding (5.10)
24 The Chipmunk Waltz (5.11a A0)
25 Trub (5.0+)
26 Rock Hangers (5.10b)
27 Snarling Spiders (5.7)
28 Oops! I'm Pregnant (5.10c)

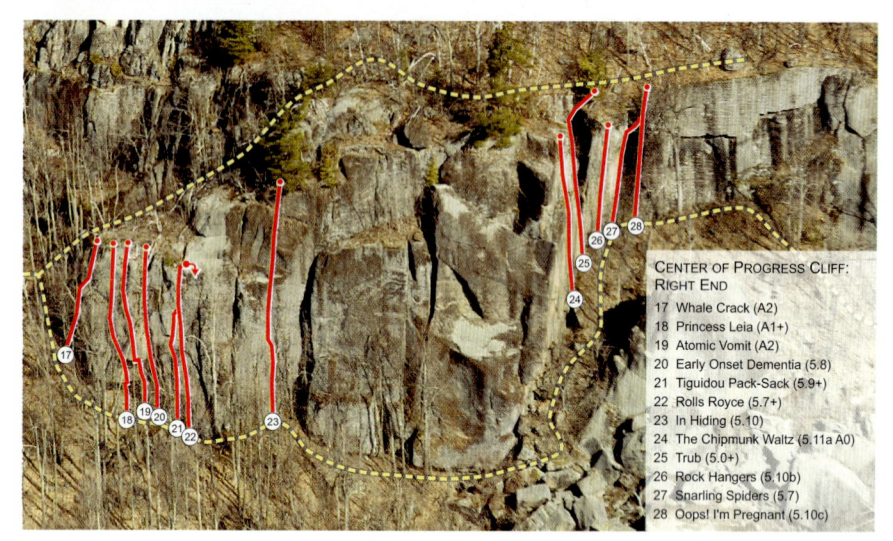

Gear: To 3" with extra small and med TCU's and micro nuts. Also helpful are pink and red tri-cams.
Descent: Rap with a single 60m from the white pine at the top.
FA Apr, 2009, Mark Bealor
FFA Aug 12, 2009, Mark Bealor, Royce Van Evera

24 The Chipmunk Waltz 5.11a A0 80'
A work-in-progress, and reportedly pretty stiff.
Start: 50' downhill and left from the right-facing corner and chimney of **Snarling Spiders** below a right-leaning crack in an otherwise blank face, and in front of a large overhung boulder.
P1 5.11a A0: Work up the right-leaning crack that splits the blank face (be mindful of the overhung boulder behind you). At the fork, bear hug and slap your way up the cracks and steep face to a ledge. (The left fork seems to be the path of least resistance for the last 15'.) 80'
FA Sep 20, 2009, Jesse Littleton, Matt Way

25 Trub 5.0+ X 80'
Used to access the top of the cliff.
Start: In an corner 15' left of **Snarling Spiders**.
P1 5.0+ X: Up the gully, which quickly turns into 5th class terrain. 80'
FA Sep 3, 2009, Jesse Littleton

26 Rock Hangers 5.10b G 70' ★★★
The name is a term used by a local to refer to climbers.
Start: 10' right of **Trub** and 20' downhill and around the corner behind **Snarling Spiders** and below an obvious crack line front and center on the buttress.
P1 5.10b G: A steep start leads to beautiful hand jams and unique dike-rock jugs. 70'
Descent: Rappel from **Ooops! I'm Pregnant**.
History: This was a former toprope route (4/09, Mark Bealor) named **Dacker Slacker**.
FA Nov 18, 2009, Matt Way, Jesse Littleton

27 Snarling Spiders 5.7 PG 80'
The first ascent used a headlamp to inspect the gear placements. Named for the large spiders inhabiting the chimney.
Start: Directly above the boulder field at the right end of the cliff, at an obvious right-facing corner formed by a free-standing block leaning against the main cliff. In the corner is a chimney–offwidth.
P1 5.7 PG: Up the chimney by climbing the fractured face tucked inside. When the chimney narrows, continue up the offwidth until forced onto the face. Finish on the face and through an overlap. 80'
History: There was evidence of previous climbers.
ACB Sep 3, 2009, Richard Wilson, Michael Leblanc

460

Northern Mountains

28 Oops! I'm Pregnant 5.10c TR 80'
A deceivingly difficult face climb—it looks 5.6. Climbs the face 10' right of **Snarling Spiders**. (This is the location of the winter route of the same name.)
FA (TR) Sep 3, 2009, Jesse Littleton, Richard Wilson, Michael Leblanc

*Richard Wilson deep in the chimney of **Snarling Spiders** (5.7), belayed by Mike Leblanc. Photo by Jesse Littleton.*

Silver Lake
TSUNAMI WALL

Aspect	South
Height	220'
Quality	★
Approach	30 min, moderate
Summary	A slab with good potential, above which is an immense overhanging wall with one super hard route.

1	1					1	4
-5.6	5.7	5.8	5.9	5.10	5.11	5.12	5.13+	total

Easily visible from the road, this cliff is the most distinctive and unusual cliff at Silver Lake—a black slab capped by a tan-colored 100'-tall overhanging wave of rock. The cliff holds good potential for routes, such as the various cracks on the slab and the buttress left of the wave feature. The wave itself holds one of the most outrageous lines in the northeast, **Oppositional Defiance Disorder**.

You can reach the top by climbing **Dirty Gully**.

DIRECTIONS   (MAP PAGE 436)
Park at the Turnpike Road Trailhead. Follow an excellent logging road for 4 minutes to a huge field (an old logging header) where many smaller arteries branch off. There's a good view of the cliffs here. Bear slightly left and uphill, following occasional cairns. There are many intersections along this road, but stay on the main (most improved) logging road with cairns; you can occasionally see the cliffs, and you're aiming for the Tsunami Wall, the unmistakable wall with an overhanging wave-like feature at its top. Once directly in front of the Tsunami Wall, the logging road turns uphill and becomes more of a skid path.

Head uphill towards the Summit Cliff for several hundred feet (until about level with the base of the cliff), then cut right aiming for the left side of the slab. Avoid the talus directly below the slab, as it is a Bolivian jungle: 5'-tall poison ivy plants with 6" diameter leaves, some of the most healthy-looking PI in the park. Go uphill staying left of the talus to reach the cliff on its left side at a large right-facing corner beneath the left end of the wave. You can walk along the base taking exceptional care to avoid the amazing PI plants.

Due to the PI and complexity of the terrain, it is not recommended that you walk to Midway Cliff from here. Even though it looks close, you'll get cliffed and be forced to navigate PI-infested boulders. It's better to return to the logging road and follow the approach to Midway Cliff.

1 Dirty Gully 5.0 G 100'
This is a dike providing access through the lower cliff band (the nondescript cliff between Tsunami Wall and the Summit Cliff) to the top of the Tsunami Wall and the broad ramp below Wayback Cliff. It is dirty and messy, but reasonable enough for both up and down. It is located 200' uphill and left of the Tsunami Wall.
FA Sep 30, 1979, Dick Tucker, Eric T. Laurin, Tim Riley

*Opposite: Jesse Littleton on **The Chipmunk Waltz** (5.11a A0). Photo by Leah Shaw*

461

Northern Mountains

TSUNAMI WALL
1 Dirty Gully (5.0)
2 Two Socks (5.7)
4 Oppositional Defiance Disorder (5.14a)

MIDWAY CLIFF

2 Two Socks 5.7 G 220' ★★
Reported to be better than it looks.
Start: 20' left of the large right-facing corner that leads to the left end of the wave, below a small right-leaning ramp in a slab.
P1 5.7 G: Up the ramp to its end. A steep move up a crack gains a lower-angled, heavily vegetated crack. Follow this for 40' to another 40' of easier terrain, then up a right-facing corner for 60'. Belay below a gully in a bottomless left-facing corner next to a large overhang on the right. 150'
P2 5.6 G: Go straight up the gully in the left-facing corner to the top. The right side of the gully is cleaner and more enjoyable, with good protection available in the right wall. 70'
FA Jul 26, 2009, Jeff Cohen, Kevin Thompson

3 Dead End 5.5 A1 150'
Follows one of the cracks (which one is still unknown) in the slab to the base of double cracks that break the wave feature.
FA 1983, Tad Welch, Bill Widrig

4 Oppositional Defiance Disorder 5.14a G 100' ★★★★★
A candidate for the most difficult pure trad climb in the northeast: other than La Zébrée in Val-David in Quebec, this is the only all-gear 5.14 in the east. The route climbs the often-wet double cracks on the 100'-tall, 30 degree overhanging, wave-like wall.

Start: At the fixed anchor at the top of the slab, below the double cracks in the overhanging wall. (The first ascent party rappelled into this station, then fixed a static rope from here to the ground to facilitate repeated attempts on the upper wall.)
P1 5.14a G: Climb up slab 10' and pull into the crack system at a roof with a few chimney moves. Go up the techy crack 30', then move right into the other crack to "loaf" jug. Place a couple of cams and punch it 15' slapping up both cracks thru the crux until you get a good side pull jug and a big rest. Layback and jam up to small roof–overlap, pull the roof, then exit straight up. 100'
Gear: Doubles on some pieces singles in others, from blue TCU to #2 Camalot. Quite a variety of placement options. The rock is solid except a crumbly section at the start, which may require placing cams close together.
History: The first ascent required efforts (4 days of leading, 10 days of toproping) spread over two seasons. Towels and a blow torch were used to dry the crack.
FA Sep 18, 2011, Peter Kamitses

*Opposite: Peter Kamitses on **Oppositional Defiance Disorder** (5.14a), on the overhanging Tsunami Wall. Photo by Tomás Donoso.*

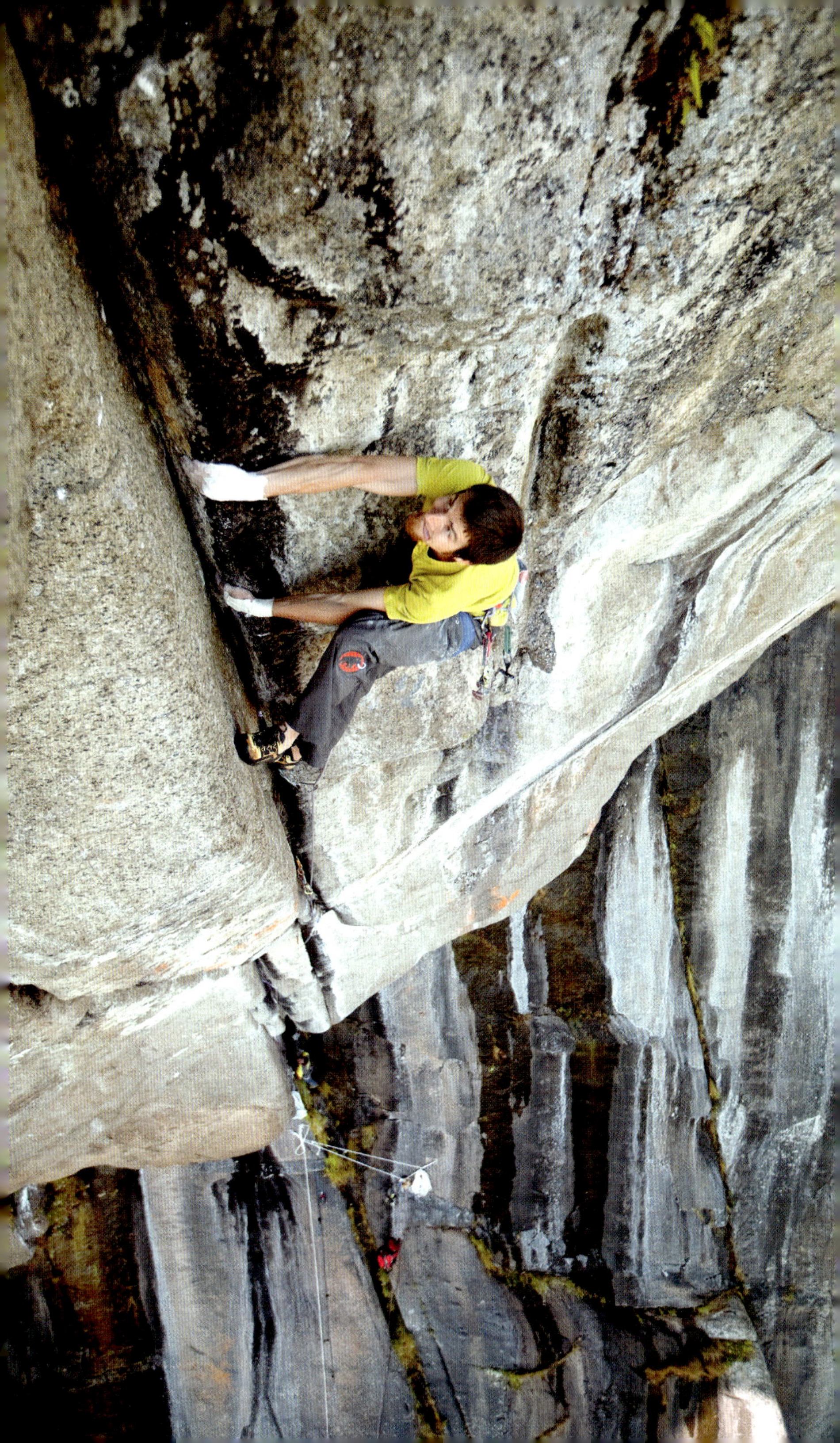

Oppositional Defiance Disorder

I first heard about the Tsunami Wall at Silver Lake from Will Mayo: "There is this one wall over there, it's like the Web on steroids!" The Spider's Web is close to the natural state of things as far as rock steepness in the Dacks is concerned, but the Tsunami Wall is definitely on the juice. My interest was piqued.

As soon as I got home to Vermont, I rallied across the lake for a recon mission. As any climber who has driven down Silver Lake Road will attest, the first view you get of the cliffs is enough to make even the most diligent driver clip a mailbox. That glorious mountain side is virtually covered in a patchwork of rock: big walls, little crags, sweeping multi-pitch slabs— tier upon tier of climbing terrain. And then you notice something different, out of place, and slightly alien in nature. Low at the foot of the mountain, just above the trees, is an impossibly steep, 100'-high sweeping wave of rock perched on top of a slab.

I got goose bumps. If that wall had lines that were climbable, it would be a dream come true. Projects for years!

The approach was full-on Dacks style, complete with swarms of microscopic flying vampires (aka black flies), neck-high brambles on overgrown logging roads, and bushwhacking through thick groves of saplings. Accessing the top required a chossy 4th-class gully scramble, ensuring that we were properly warmed up.

On the first rappel, I located the stunning crack system splitting the Tsunami Wall, and concluded that it was the only free-climbable line on the wall. It was disappointing that the rest of the wall lacked features, but that made this crack system even more special. Descending was an amazing core workout—swinging acrobatically into the wall and deadpointing cams in the crazy-steep crack as directionals. I spent that first day swinging around, trying to figure out how the middle and upper sections (the obvious cruxes) would be climbed. At the end of the day, I wasn't sure the line was doable, as there were more than a couple of spots where the crack could not be jammed.

The beautiful thing about climbing, is making the impossible become possible. After many sessions hanging around on toprope sussing beta, I had reasonable sequences put together for the crux sections. This line went beyond my expectations on many levels: 100'-long, 45 degrees overhung, and requiring all kinds of crazy beta. It starts with a couple of chimney moves, then up some funky, physical crack moves to a flat jug, where you get a shake, and plug in a couple of cams. The crux features a huge lock off from a painful finger jam to get into a series of wild compression moves between two cracks that would be more at home on a boulder problem. I had to fully turn it on and punch it through this section, as it's impossible to stop to place gear. After taking a sizable whip from the end of this sequence, and coming a little too close to the slab below, I figured out a way to put in a slightly higher cam: I put it between my teeth while doing the finger lock, and rapidly fired it in just before the first compression move.

Reducing the size of that runout by just a few feet gave me the mental edge I needed. On my next redpoint attempt, I was able to sneak through that bit, then the slopey layback crux up higher, and finally the little boulder problem guarding the anchor ledge. I named it "Oppositional Defiance Disorder" due both to the physical nature of the sidepull-slapping twin-crack section, and the mental battle of defying my mind so that I could shut it off, let it flow and climb with clear focus.

This was one of the best leads of my life, and I doubt I'll ever have a chance to do another FA of such a wild trad route of this difficulty. Once again, the Dacks delivered a gift of incomparable value. For this, and many other reasons understood by each and every climber who gets to know this region, the Adirondack Park remains one of my favorite places on earth.

- Peter Kamitses

Silver Lake
MIDWAY CLIFF

Aspect	South
Height	350'
Quality	★★
Approach	40 min, easy
Summary	Nice selection of moderate crack routes with a relatively easy approach.

3	2	1	3	2			12
-5.6	5.7	5.8	5.9	5.10	5.11	5.12	5.13+	total

This nondescript cliff is located immediately right of the Tsunami Wall and holds a good selection of routes concentrated in a small area. The best route appears to be **After the Bash**, which has attracted many parties, each of which reported this as a "first ascent".

The reported routes are all located on the clean buttress on the left side of the cliff, just right of the talus field below the Tsunami Wall. At the highest point of the terrain on the left side is a prominent left-facing corner with a shallow, flared chimney and handcrack—this is **Hangover Corner**.

This is the only cliff at Silver Lake suitable for toproping.

Uphill and right of Midway Cliff is the winter route **Freezer Burn** (also known as **Confessional** described in *Blue Lines*).

DIRECTIONS   (MAP PAGE 436)
Park at the Turnpike Road Trailhead. Follow an excellent logging road for 4 minutes to a huge field (an old logging header) where many smaller arteries branch off. There's a good view of the cliffs here. Bear slightly left

Northern Mountains

MIDWAY CLIFF
1. Upsidaisium (5.8 A2)
2. Curve Like a Wave (5.10a)
3. Schadenfreude (5.10b)
4. Fearless Leader (5.9-)
5. Static Cling (5.9+)
6. Hangover Corner (5.4)
7. Arête's Syndrome (5.4)
8. After the Bash (5.7)

and uphill, following occasional cairns. There are many intersections along this road, but stay on the main (most improved) logging road with cairns; you can occasionally see the cliffs, and you're aiming for the Tsunami Wall, the unmistakable wall with an overhanging wave-like feature at its top. Once directly in front of the Tsunami Wall, the logging road turns uphill and becomes more of a skid path.

From the last small clearing in front of the Tsunami Wall, before the trail begins climbing in earnest, and just after a white boulder in the path (the size of a mini-fridge), turn right (east) and follow flagging. Cross a seasonal creek (that drains the Tsunami Wall) staying below the talus. After the talus, angle uphill to the cliff, aiming for the highest point on the terrain below the left side; about 10 min from the logging road 595044,4929804.

Laundromat Ledge

On the left side of the cliff, 180' up, facing the Tsunami Wall, is a large ledge with a giant white pine growing on the prow, known as Laundromat Ledge. It is reached by climbing the first two pitches of **After the Bash**.

465

Northern Mountains

1 Upsidaisium 5.8 A2 135'

Has been freed, but needs a modern ascent to confirm grade and other details.

Start: Walk to the left end of Laundromat Ledge, past a huge white pine, until beneath exciting-looking ceilings.

P1: Walk right from belay on wet mossy ledge to its end. Make an awkward mantel onto a spacious ledge with a juniper tree. 35'

P2: The first roof. Nail crack at left end of ledge 10' to ceiling. Aid out right beneath overhang 4' to its lip (2" to 2.5" bongs). Layback the steep crack above (5.8) to low-angle ramp. Belay. 50'

P3: The second roof—similar climbing but more exposed. Bongs straight up under roof bring you into the final lichen-filled dihedral. Climb free and aid to poplar tree belay at the top. 50'

Descent: Walk off right or make 2 short rappels from trees back to Laundromat Ledge.

History: Welch once wrote, "...with some extensive gardening (and better climbers) much more of the route will go free." Indeed it did. It's interesting to note that both roofs are actually partially detached from the rest of the cliff. From the final dihedral it is possible to peer down the crack to the bottom of P1. Described by Mellor as similar to the roofs on **Quadrophenia** (at Hurricane Cliff) but much harder.

FA Jun 10, 1981, Bill Widrig, Tad Welch
FFA Don Mellor, Mark Meschinelli

Main Face

2 Curve Like a Wave 5.10a G 100' ★★

Start: 50' down and left from **Hangover Corner** is a 4'-wide chimney stuffed with trees and flakes. Scramble up the chimney for 30' to its top and belay from flakes that are stuffed into the top of the chimney, which is also the end of a wide tree ledge.

P1 5.10a G: Mantel past tiny red pine and onto low-angled arête. Follow cracks for pro through scoops to a finger-tip crack through a steep short headwall (crux). Cross a horizontal dike and belay in cracks just above. 100'

FA Sep 2, 2006, Tad Welch, John Thackray, Bill Widrig

3 Schadenfreude 5.10b TR 100'

Left of **Fearless Leader** is a right-facing corner below a tree-filled gully; left of this is a clean shield of rock. Begin below the clean shield and climb a black streak to a right-rising horizontal crack. Wander up to the anchor of **Curved Like a Wave**.

FA (TR) Sep 2, 2006, John Thackray, Bill Widrig, Tad Welch

4 Fearless Leader 5.9- PG 80' ★★

Start: At the height of the terrain, 8' left of **Hangover Corner** and 6' right of a clean shield of rock.

P1 5.9- PG: Up the perfect black rock on left side of slab past solitary bolt. Continue straight up, stay right of lower-angle, right-leaning groove to belay at overlap beneath an overhang. 80'

FA Oct, 2004, Tad Welch, Bill Widrig

5 Static Cling 5.9+ TR 70' ★★

The slab is devoid of any natural protection; with some bolts, it will become a fine lead up smooth, clean granite. Begin 5' left of **Hangover Corner** and climb clean, tan-colored rock for 40'. Step right into **Hangover Corner**, which is followed to a ledge with an oak tree (this tree can be reached by scrambling in from the right). (There is a full-length winter route that begins here, confusingly named **After the Bash**.)

FA (TR) Aug, 1983, Bill Widrig, Tad Welch

6 Hangover Corner 5.4 G 60'

Involves stemming, chimneying, and jamming; easier and more pleasant than it appears.

Start: From the height of the terrain on the left side of the cliff, at an obvious left-facing corner with a flared chimney pod and handcrack.

P1 5.4 G: Up the corner. At the top, move right to a ledge with an oak tree. 60'

History: On the first ascent, the leader's hangover was cured when he fell head-over-heels out of a crack above Laundromat Ledge.

FA Aug, 1979, Chuck Yax, Bill Widrig

7 Arête's Syndrome (aka Before The Fall) 5.4 G 70'

Start: Same as **Hangover Corner**.

P1 5.4 G: Up the corner a few feet, then step right on good foot edges, following cracks to the arête. Up the arête for 30', then work back left into **Hangover Corner**, which is followed to a ledge with an oak tree. 70'

History: The first ascent was actually an unroped, solo descent, which preceeded Chuck's spectacular head-first, backwards fall above Laundromat Ledge.

FA Aug, 1980, Chuck Yax (solo downclimb)

8 After the Bash 5.7 G (5.4 R) 370' ★★★

The first route done on the cliff. The third pitch is highly recommended.

Start: 20' down and right from the height of the terrain at **Hangover Corner**, below an open book corner with a left-facing layback crack.

P1 5.7 G: Up a wide crack to an "A"-shaped overhang to gain the layback crack. Follow the layback crack through a pink bulge to a belay on a ledge with an oak tree (shared with **Hangover Corner**). 90'

P2 5.5 PG: (V1) From the left side of the terrace, scramble up easy rock, then make a few thin moves to gain a 4th class slab. Continue up slab to another large ledge with trees, Laundromat Ledge. 130'

P3 5.7 G (5.4 R): On the wall at the right rear of the terrace is an obvious, right-leaning crack leading to a hole. Super fun and acrobatic moves (improbable but with good gear) lead to a slab above. Traverse right (watch rope drag) into corner, then up an easy corner-chimney to a final 4th class topout in shrubs. 150'

V1: Traverse left across dike, level with belay ledge, until it is possible to climb through an overhang (above the finish of **Fearless Leader**) and up sloping rock onto Laundromat Ledge. Although better climbing, this pitch is poorly protected.

Northern Mountains

Descent: Walk left and rappel from trees with two 60m ropes. First rappel leads to giant pine tree on Laundromat Ledge with a fixed anchor. Second rappel, 210', trends right to leave you 10' up **Fearless Leader** where you can scramble down.
FA Aug, 1980, Tad Welch, Jamie Savage, Steve Jervis

9 Face Dances 5.8 R 90'
Start: 15' downhill and right of **After the Bash**.
P1 5.8 R: Step up easily onto the slab, then follow a left-rising ramp to a scooped overlap. Over this, then up the lichen-covered face to a ledge with an oak tree (shared with **Hangover Corner**). 90'
FA Jun 10, 1981, Tad Welch (toprope solo)

10 Attachment 5.9- TR 40'
Begin 6' left of **Easy Listening** and climb a mossy slab to the tree ledge.
FA (TR) Sep 2, 2006, John Thackray, Bill Widrig, Tad Welch

11 Easy Listening 5.7+ G 90' ★
Start: 100' right of **After the Bash** at a low-angle slab below a tapering left-facing corner with a fingercrack.
P1 5.7+ G: Up the corner to its top, step right to a scoop. Up the scoop, then scramble to a tree ledge. From the back of the tree ledge, move up a crack in an open book corner to a ledge at its top, then traverse left to the top. 90'
FA Oct, 2004, Bill Widrig, Tad Welch

12 Easement 5.3 G 70'
Start: 25' right of **Easy Listening** at a 5'-high open book corner with a left-leaning finger crack just above.
P1 5.3 G: Up the open book to gain the fingercrack. Up the crack to its top. 70'
FA Jun, 2004, Tad Welch, Jamie Savage

Silver Lake
OUTBACK SLAB

Aspect	South
Height	300'
Quality	★★★★
Approach	1 hr, difficult
Summary	Excellent slab climbing on clean, dimpled rock.

2	1		1	2			6
-5.6	5.7	5.8	5.9	5.10	5.11	5.12	5.13+	total

Also referred to as The Brown Slab, this wall has a steep bottom, then after 80', the angle eases, changing character to a moderate slab with water streaks and some of the best friction anywhere. It has a flat, 40'-wide open area at the base where you can step back and admire the imposing 300'-tall slab in front of you. Much of the rock is super clean, especially in the water streaks.

Several of the established routes (such as **Bimathalon** and **Morticia**) have fixed protection where the climbing is difficult, then runout friction on easier terrain. The other routes wander over the moderate upper portion of the slab using sparse natural flakes and cracks for protection. It's easy to escape the forest canopy on this cliff, as you can wander up and right near the base of **Pugsley** and begin climbing from a high ledge. You are guaranteed solitude and excellent views.

DIRECTIONS (MAP PAGE 436)
From Midway Cliff, walk downhill and right in semi-open forest with boulders. Stay below a scrappy cliffband,

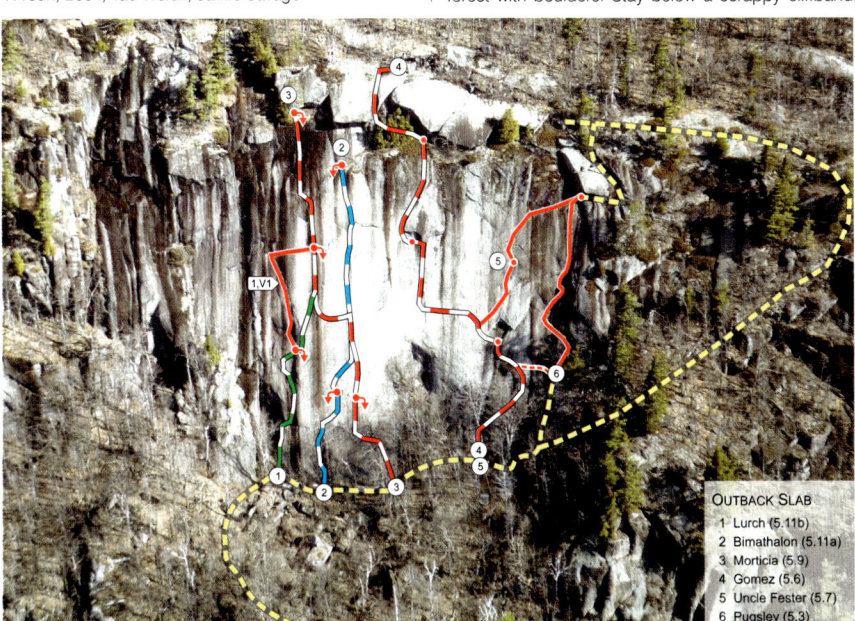

OUTBACK SLAB
1. Lurch (5.11b)
2. Bimathalon (5.11a)
3. Morticia (5.9)
4. Gomez (5.6)
5. Uncle Fester (5.7)
6. Pugsley (5.3)

467

Northern Mountains

the right side of which has a huge block jutting from a chimney (the Jutting Block Wall). From the right side of this cliff, continue another 50', then scramble straight uphill for 200' until you can cut back left on top of the Jutting Block Wall. The Outback Slab can be seen through the trees above. Continue left (avoiding the thicket immediately above), then go straight uphill to meet the Outback Slab on its far left side. Walk downhill and right along the base to the beautiful open area at the lowest point 595233,4929847.

HISTORY

Tad Welch and Bill Widrig visited this cliff in 1981 and added three multi-pitch moderate routes on the right end, starting the Addams Family naming theme. They also aided their way up **Bimathalon** to practice hand drilling (much like their route **Sole Fusion** at Sugarloaf). A few years later, and completely by chance, Mike Heintz and Mark Meschinelli walked by, saw the dowels, and climbed to the Welch–Widrig high point. Then they extended the route to the top of the cliff, creating a classic, long crack–face–slab route.

In 2009, Jim Lawyer visited with various partners and added **Morticia** and **Lurch**.

1 Lurch 5.11b G 200' ★★★★

Start: On the left side of the slab is an alcove. Begin below the super clean arête that forms the right side of the alcove, 40' uphill and left of **Bimathalon** (this is the location of the winter route **Snow Queen**).

● **P1 5.11b G:** Up the arête, then move right onto the face. Work up the face (crux) to a good edge, then to a 3" crack. Move left to a scoop, then work rightwards to a fixed anchor. 100'

● **P2 5.7 G (5.6 R):** (V1) Step right and climb the bulging face straight up to where the angle eases. Join P2 of **Morticia** at the end of the traverse and run out easy friction to a fixed anchor. 100'

V1 5.6 PG: Follow a left-leaning crack system in clean black rock to the top of the protectable section of the crack. Traverse right on friction with no gear 40' to the fixed anchor of **Morticia**. Minimal rack to 3". 140'

Descent: Rap the route in two 100' rappels.
History: The route was originally climbed using V1 as the second pitch. Later, a more direct P2 was added.
FA Sep 5, 2009, Jim Lawyer, Lori Crowningshield, Tom Yandon
FA (P2) Sep 11, 2011, Bill Widrig, Tad Welch, Neal Knitel, Jim Lawyer

2 Bimathalon (aka Silver Slab) 5.11a G (5.6 R) 275' ★★★★

This highly recommended line has short, well-protected cruxes, excellent rock, and ascends an intimidating section of cliff. The top of P2 is dirty; best to finish on **Morticia**.
Start: At the left side of the flat area at the lowest point on the slab, below a crack in a left-leaning open book corner that begins 6' up.

P1 5.11a G: Make a layback move off the ground to gain the crack. Up the crack to its top (5.8), then move up to a dike (crux). Face climb up and right to a small, left-facing flake, then straight up a textured face to gain a stance with a fixed anchor. 80'
P2 5.10a G (5.6 R): Step left to a left-facing flake (dubbed Lawnchair Flake) and climb this to its top. Move up and right, then straight right (crux) to knobs and the line of **Morticia**. Go straight up on excellent holds to a shallow left-facing flake, then straight up to a tree island. 195'
Descent: 100' rappel down and left to the P2 anchor on **Morticia**, then a 100' down and left to the P1 anchor on **Lurch**, then 100' to the ground.
Gear: To 2". Double up on #1 and #2 Camalots.
History: Named by Widrig who was taking Calc 3 and Differential Equations at the same time. The first ascent was practice for aid climbing and drilling dowels, actually bits from a shelving bracket purchased from a local hardware store. Heintz and Meschinelli came upon this "bolt ladder" and climbed it to the top, drilling 3 additional bolts on lead. Later, they were talking about it with "some guys" in a local restaurant, who coincidentally were Welch and Widrig. The route was repeated later by Don Mellor and dubbed **Silver Slab**. The route was re-equipped in 2011 with the old dowels remaining in place.
FA 1981, Bill Widrig, Tad Welch
FFA 1985, Mike Heintz, Mark Meschinelli

Jim Lawyer at the top of the initial crack on ***Bimathalon*** *(5.11a). Photo by Neal Knitel.*

Northern Mountains

3 Morticia 5.9 G (5.6 R) 370' ★★★★

Excellent face and slab climbing, with some of the best friction anywhere—the water streak on P2 and P3 is "sand blasted" clean and has been climbed without hands. The route begins right of Bimathalon, joins that route on P2 for a few feet, then crosses to its left to ascend a parallel water streak.

Start: 10' uphill and right of the flat area at the lowest point on the slab, below a left-leaning open book corner with a pinched-off thin crack. This is 50' right of Bimathalon.

P1 5.7 G: Up the corner to its top at a horizontal dike. Traverse left 15' (a 2" cam placed high in a crack protects the traverse) on knobby holds in the dike, then up a featured face with knobs and edges to a ledge with a fixed anchor. 80'

● **P2 5.9 G (5.6 R):** Straight up from the belay to a fragile, right-facing flake. Continue up the excellent knobby face, then a long runout to a bolt (shared with P2 of Bimathalon). Traverse directly left 20' to a black water streak which is followed straight up (amazing friction) to a belay seat and fixed anchor. Long runners are necessary to reduce rope drag. 150'

P3 5.3 R: Continue straight up the excellent water streak to a large pine tree at the top. 140'

Gear: A few small cams to 0.25" and one 2" cam.

Descent: Rappel with double ropes to the P2 anchor, then a single 200' rappel just makes it to the ground (or a 100' rappel to the Lurch P1 anchor, then another 100' to the ground).

FA Jul 15, 2009, Jim Lawyer, Emilie Drinkwater
FA (P3) Sep 5, 2009, Tom Yandon, Jim Lawyer, Lori Crowningshield

4 Gomez 5.6 PG (5.4 R) 390' ★★

Start: 100' uphill and right from the flat area at the lowest point on the slab, below some blocks, stacked 12' high, above which is a right-leaning crack, the only crack in this area (and difficult to see in heavy foliage). These blocks are at the height of the tree slope. The first pitch can be avoided by starting as for Pugsley.

P1 5.6 G: Clamber up the blocks to gain the right-leaning crack. Follow this to its end, then scramble up the slab to a spacious, sloped ledge and a tiny tree belay (backed up with small cams in an overlap). 90'

P2 5.6 PG: This pitch climbs to the prominent lichen-covered headwall in the center of the slab. Climb up and left on large holds to a small flake with a piton, then traverse straight left aiming for a good right-facing flake. From its top, work straight up to the headwall. Traverse left under the headwall and belay 6' from its left end (cams to 1.5" for the belay). 150'

P3 5.4 R: Move left and climb directly over the headwall at a good crack. Continue up dirty slab to belay beneath summit overhangs. 100'

P4 5.4 PG: Escape left through mossy chimney. 50'
FA May 31, 1981, Bill Widrig, Tad Welch

5 Uncle Fester 5.7 PG 300' ★★★

Start: Same as for Gomez.
P1 5.6 G: Climb P1 of Gomez. 90'

P2 5.7 PG: Step left, then up over delicate friction until you can work right to reach obvious parallel cracks and protection (crux). Jam and undercling for a few feet up the perfect crack until it's possible to stand up and gain the second crack. Move up to a hidden sickle-shaped ledge (large nut needed for belay). Excellent pitch. 60'

P3 5.4 R: Run it out up and right over moderate friction on lichen-covered rock. Finish at the base of the Pugsley boulder. 150'
FA May 31, 1981, Tad Welch, Bill Widrig

6 Pugsley 5.3 R 100' ★★★

Fun climbing, but poor protection.

Start: From the start of Gomez, walk right 40' and scramble up a short buttress, then up steep easy terrain to a three-trunked oak tree beneath a jet-black, left-leaning crack on the extreme right side of the slab.

P1 5.3 R: Climb up to the black crack and follow this as it leans left to its end. Gain the wide, winding, trough-shaped, super-clean water groove, and follow this to the huge jutting boulder at the top-right side of the slab. Belay at the base of the boulder. 100'

Descent: Walk off right to the trees and scramble back to the base of the route.
FA May 31, 1981, Tad Welch, Bill Widrig

Silver Lake
WAYBACK CLIFF

Aspect	Southwest
Height	250'
Quality	
Approach	1 hr 45 min, difficult
Summary	A long, broken cliff with lots of potential, but guarded by a long, complex approach.

1	1						2
-5.6	5.7	5.8	5.9	5.10	5.11	5.12	5.13+	total

Sitting above (and behind) the Summit Cliff, this extensive cliff is a complex assortment of broken buttresses, slabs and corners with a very long approach. There is definite potential for routes, but perhaps not the quality lines that exist on the other cliffs, and so far nothing obvious justifies the long approach. The route Mr. Peabody ascends the most obvious large feature.

DIRECTIONS (MAP PAGE 436)

Since Wayback Cliff sits above the right end of Summit Cliff, the easiest approach would seem to be through a weakness at the right end of the Summit Cliff. Here are the known options:

Option 1: Climb Dirty Gully on the Tsunami Wall. This gets you above the Tsunami Wall, at which point you walk uphill to the cliff.

Option 2: Approach the right end of the Summit Cliff, then climb the obvious North Dike to the top of the cliff. Hike downhill along the open cliff top, then turn left into the forest; several minutes of bushwhacking bring you to the Wayback Cliff, just left of Mr. Peabody.

Northern Mountains

WAYBACK CLIFF
1 Mr. Peabody (5.7)

THE BURROW

SUMMIT CLIFF RIGHT END

Blade

MIDWAY CLIFF

Dirty Gully

TSUNAMI SLAB

Option 3: Approach the left end of the Summit Cliff, then scramble up **Silver Lake Chimney**. At the top, turn right through open forest to reach the open summit area (above **Tales of Weakness**, etc). Continue hiking downhill staying on the open slabs near the edge. After 5 min or so, when you can look back and see a good portion of the Summit Cliff behind you, turn left and bushwhack for several minutes to the cliff.

1 Mr. Peabody 5.7 PG 360'
Needs a modern ascent to confirm grade.
Start: Just left of the lowest point of a smooth, narrow slab which is below a huge left-facing corner with trees.
P1: Crux. Friction upwards staying right of the bushy groove. From the little cedar, traverse right on a small dike to a rest. Continue over better holds, while heading toward a birch on the right. Belay on flakes. 100'
P2: Straight up on thin holds (no protection) until the angle eases. Aim for blocks in the lower corner of the dihedral below the short chimney. Belay at trees. 80'
P3: Climb 8' up the chimney past a cedar and walk up the corner past more blocks to a belay on moss. 60'
P4: Walk left to a clean slab. Friction upwards over solution pockets with little protection. Thrash through dirty and awkward, but short overhangs at a cedar the top. 120'
Descent: Walk left and rappel.
FA Jun 1, 1981, Tad Welch, Bill Widrig

2 Spelunker 5.4+ PG 160'
It's not known exactly where this route is, or even if it's on this cliff, but the few available details place it here. It leads directly to the summit. A black bear strolled past the foot of this climb while the first ascent party was still on the first pitch.
Start: At a pair of open book corners leading upward to a ledge.

P1: Climb the left open book corner past the tree to the ledge. Follow a rising diagonal crack rightward to a small ledge with trees and brush. 100'
P2: Crawl through the cave behind the belay ledge to a larger ledge. Climb to the summit. 60'
FA Sep 30, 1979, Eric T. Laurin, Tim Riley, Dick Tucker

Silver Lake
POTTER MOUNTAIN CLIFF

Aspect	South
Height	500'
Quality	★★★★★
Approach	35-50 min, easy
Summary	Excellent long face climbs on amazing dimpled rock; some cracks in The Ghetto on the right end.

1	4	5	12	3	1		27
-5.6	5.7	5.8	5.9	5.10	5.11	5.12	5.13+	total

Located below the summit of Potter Mountain, this cliff looks low angle, as though one can romp up in sneakers. Don't be deceived! It's as high as the main face at Poke-O Moonshine, steep, and with no obvious bottom-to-top natural lines. Shangri La is the water streaked section on the left side and is unique—one of the best faces in the park—with acres of clean, dimpled rock, as though someone had scoured the face with a pressure washer. The climbs are dramatic and exposed, but never desperate, with spacious belay ledges and straightforward rappels (although, be aware that several rappels are just over 100' and require two ropes).

Best of all, the summit of this cliff is wide, flat, open rock—a stunning setting—remote, private, and one of the best views anywhere.

To access the top of the cliff, hike left along the base to a short 4th class step up. Up the step, then head left to a low-angle slab which is followed to the top.

Northern Mountains

POTTER MOUNTAIN CLIFF
3 Pothead (5.12a)
19 Never Again, Again (5.7)
25 Hold It Like a Hamburger (5.11d)
26 Pox (5.11c)
27 Vaccination (5.9)

DIRECTIONS (MAP PAGE 436)

From the Goodrich Mills Trailhead (0 hr 0 min), follow the logging road to a large clearing at 15 min, an old logging header, with good views of the cliffs ahead. This serves as a hub for many smaller roads; angle 45° to the right across the clearing and continue on a good, grassy logging road to the height of land between Potter Mountain and Little Potter Mountain at 30 min. There is a clearing here with views of the cliff. Continue along the road another minute of level walking to where you can see the base of the cliff on your left. There is a brush pile on the left 595939,4929981 and a small path with a cairn. Turn left following the herd path towards the cliff. The forest is fairly open and the going is easy to the base of the cliff at 35 min.

The trail reaches the cliff near the right end of the Ghetto 595744,4930076; walk left. The cliff is 1/2 mile wide and the terrain goes uphill through intermittent jungle. Continue walking left to reach Shangri La 595460,4930004 at 50 min.

HISTORY

The earliest climbers to visit were Dave Szot and Tom Rosecrans, but exactly where is a mystery. The first reported route was climbed by Don Mellor and Mark Bealor in 2009 in an attempt to reach the prominent **Partition**-like corner in the center of the cliff. Their route was a disappointment (never making it to the **Partition**-like corner) with poor rock and little to recommend it. A more concerted effort was conducted later that fall by Tad Welch, Jim Lawyer, and Tom Yandon who explored the extensive water streaks on the left side. Their first route, **Stop Making Sense**, finds a moderate way up an impressive wall, and was used to explore the upper reaches of the cliff. Within a couple weeks they added more than 15 pitches of climbing to the Shangri La sector. Later that fall they were joined by Colin Loher, Neal Knitel, and Jesse Littleton to add even more pitches. The quality of these routes is outstanding, mostly because of the amazing texture of the rock—**Once in a Lifetime** and the second pitch of **Positive Latitude** are unlike anything else in the park and not to be missed.

At the same time, Yandon, Joe Szot, and Aya Alt explored the crack climbs at the Ghetto. Their ground-up efforts followed natural features to their logical end, often in the middle of the wall.

After 2009, activity diminished to a trickle, but quality routes were still uncovered by Lawyer and Loher, such as **Honeybadger**, **Pothead**, **Scary Potter Traverse**, and **Hold It Like a Hamburger**.

Left End

1 Where's Ian 5.8 X 375' ★★★

An excellent pitch with no bottom. The cleanest approach, described here, requires 5.10 climbing and a long traverse. Not a good choice if 5.8 is your leading limit.

Start: At the oak tree at the top of P1 of **Bears, Beets, Battlestar Galactica**. Alternatively, you can approach P2 by hiking up the left side of the cliff, then traversing right on the ledge to the right-facing flake system; vegetated 4th class.

P1 4th class: Traverse left along the ledge to a right-facing flake system rising off the ledge. 180'

P2 5.8 X: Climb the flake to its top, then go up a slab to a horizontal at a chicken head. Creative gear leads to spicy climbing up a black streak to base of a finger-crack. Follow finger crack to its top and break out left onto a slab. Head for the hand crack to the left which is followed to its top where it disappears. Easy slab leads to the top with no obvious anchor (i.e., lasso a boulder). 195'

471

Northern Mountains

POTTER MOUNTAIN CLIFF: LEFT END
1 Where's Ian (5.8)
2 Bears, Beets, Battlestar Galactica (5.10d)

Descent: Walk (climber's) left and scramble down the left side of the cliff, or walk right and rappel **Bears, Beets, Battlestar Galactica**.

History: The route was toprope soloed by Tad Welch in 2009. In 2010 the route was further inspected, but given no bottom pitch, it was abandoned and never led. Now approached from **Bears, Beets, Battlestar Galactica**, it was led in a bold gesture, ground up without preinspection by Matt Way.
FA Oct 4, 2010, Matt Way, Richard Wilson, Colin Loher

2 Bears, Beets, Battlestar Galactica (aka Three B's) 5.10d G (5.4 R) 280' ★★★

The last pitch is a prize of sustained complexities. The other pitches are fun, one-move wonders. P3 is often wet.

Start: Walk left from the left end of the tree terrace of **Piece Out** to an open area with large boulders and recent rockfall. This is the only clear, open area in the vicinity with good views to the top of the cliff. Begin on a ledge 10' up with a huge oak tree.

● **P1 5.10a G:** Go straight up the slab on good holds, then make a desperate friction move to a large ledge. Walk left, then climb blocky terrain with good cracks up and left to a ledge with an oak tree. 90'

● **P2 5.9 G (5.4 R):** Go straight up the steep face. Traverse right (crux) to a good stance, then wander up and right on easy terrain to a fixed anchor at the base of a black, left-facing corner in the headwall above. 90'

● **P3 The Black Corner 5.10d G:** A great pitch: go straight up the corner, then move left under a ceiling to a final mantel move. Step back right over the ceiling, then go straight up to a large pine tree with a fixed anchor. 100'

Gear: A few cams up to 3/4".
Descent: Rappel 100' to the top of P2, then 120' to the ground. For the last rappel, a 60m rope just makes it to the ledge where you can walk right.
FA Aug 8, 2010, Jim Lawyer, Martine Schaer

Shangri La

Near the center of the cliff are two prominent, wide, full-height water streaks of clean rock. The right-hand streak is nearly pink in color and has a 12'-high rock pancake leaning up against the base. Below the left-hand streak is a large open area with a pile of car-sized boulders leaning up against the face—**Brazilian** and **Stop Making Sense** begin here.

The dimpled climbing here is the best of its type in the northeast. It's dimpled and clean for a reason—it's often wet from water flowing out of huge horizontal cracks below the summit. On the positive side, some pitches are quick to dry. The driest routes are **Garden of Leadin'**, **Jug-Or-Not**, **Poker Face**, **Piece Out**, P1–P3 of **Stop Making Sense**, P1 of **Groovitational Pull**, and **Where the Wild Things Are**.

The cliff is broken at mid height by a large traverse ledge, making it very easy to move about and link together pitches from various routes. Parties have been known to haul a pack with water and lunch to the mid-height ledge and spend the day climbing just the top pitches.

Shangri La faces south and receives full sun making this an ideal cold-weather crag. If it's sunny, even if it's 15 degrees at the car, you can still climb in a T-shirt.

Northern Mountains

Gear: Bring a single rack of nuts and cams up to 3" to the cliff. Although most pitches have fixed protection, nearly every pitch requires one or two trad placements as noted in the descriptions. There are many long pitches here, so two 60m ropes are required for most rappels.

3 Pothead 5.12a G 80' ★★★★

This atypical Potter route climbs a steep, juggy wall with dynamic, crimpy moves. The top anchor is accessible by easy climbing left from the P3 anchor of Stop Making Sense.

Start: 50' left of Garden of Leadin' at a large white pine. (Reach this ledge by climbing P1 of Piece Out or Poker Face.)

● **P1 5.12a G:** Move up to a stance and a good jug 15' up. Make a big move to a horizontal edge. Mantel and crimp onto the edge (crux), then make a series of big moves between good edges straight up until the angle eases. Continue straight up to a fixed anchor. 80'
FA Oct 9, 2011, Jim Lawyer, Colin Loher

4 Garden of Leadin' 5.10d G 130' ★★★★

Technical, steep face and flake climbing characterizes this gem, that is if you can pull the first mantel move. (You can traverse left on a ledge from the start of P2 of Piece Out to avoid the crux mantel, making the overall grade 5.10b.)

Start: On the sloped ledge accessed by climbing P1 of Piece Out or Poker Face, 20' left of the clump of trees at the start of P2 of Piece Out. A few 1" and smaller cams are needed for the belay.

● **P1 5.10d G:** Mantel onto a ledge (crux), then up good holds to a right-facing flake. Up the flake to its top, then wander up the face, first to the right, then back left under an island of perched boulders. Continue up the face to a sloped ledge. Walk 25' right to a fixed anchor (shared with Piece Out, P3 of Stop Making Sense, Jug-Or-Not, and Poker Face). 130'

Descent: Rappel Piece Out, or climb the last pitch of Stop Making Sense.
FA Nov 18, 2009, Colin Loher, Jim Lawyer

5 Piece Out 5.9+ G 170' ★★★★★

High-quality face climbing on incut edges and flakes.

Start: Walk 250' left from the pile of car-sized boulders that marks the start of Stop Making Sense, then back right onto a tree-covered terrace. Begin near the right end of the terrace below a short right-facing corner 7' up.

P1 5.7 G: Up the corner, then up buckety goodness to a horizontal dike. Traverse left, then mantel onto the dike (crux). Continue left in the dike to gain a large sloping ledge. Belay at the top of the ledge at a clump of trees (at the time of this writing, there is a large, dead tree hanging down this ledge, the stump of which is well anchored in the clump of trees). This ledge can also be reached by walking left from the top of P1 or V1 of Brazilian, or climbing P1 of Poker Face. 70'

Ed Ward nears the crux on P1 of Positive Latitude (5.10b).

● **P2 5.9+ G ★★★★★:** Wander up the steep face on fantastic incut holds and flakes to a fixed anchor (shared with P3 of Stop Making Sense). A great pitch. 100'

Descent: Finish on Stop Making Sense, or make two rappels with a single 60m rope (which barely makes it).

History: This and the previous route were established in late November during a rare spell of sunny, warm weather.

Gear: 1 ea #1 Camalot, yellow Alien.
FA Nov 17, 2009, Jim Lawyer, Neal Knitel

6 Jug-Or-Not 5.11c G 120' ★★★★

Intricate, puzzling, and stellar.

Start: On the sloped ledge accessed by climbing P1 of Piece Out or Poker Face, 20' right of the clump of trees at the start of P2 of Piece Out, and 15' left of the start of P2 of Poker Face, beneath an obvious flake-jug 8' up, and just right of a small oak tree.

● **P1 5.11c G:** Grab the jug and make a high, shoulder-ripping undercling to reach a good hold (crux), then go straight up the face, eventually angling left to a fixed anchor (shared with P3 of Stop Making Sense). 120'
FA May 9, 2011, Jim Lawyer, Martine Schaer, Emilie Drinkwater, Jesse Littleton

Northern Mountains

POTTER MOUNTAIN CLIFF, SHANGRI LA

- 4 Garden of Leadin' (5.10d)
- 5 Piece Out (5.9+)
- 6 Jug-Or-Not (5.11c)
- 7 Poker Face (5.9+)
- 8 Brazilian (5.10a)
- 9 Once in a Lifetime (5.10d)
- 10 Stop Making Sense (5.8)
- 11 Groovitational Pull (5.10a)
- 12 Where the Wild Things Are (5.10b)
- 13 Positive Latitude (5.10b)
- 14 Every Inch Counts (5.10a)
- 15 First? Really? (5.8)
- 16 Scary Potter Traverse (5.10c)
- 17 Honeybadger (5.10a)

Northern Mountains

cave

pink waterstreak

easy traverse

smile-shaped ledge

3rd class

pancake

475

Northern Mountains

7 Poker Face 5.9+ G 210' ★★★

Another quality face climb. The first pitch ends at a huge ledge, and is the best way to approach P2 of **Peace Out** (and **Garden of Leadin'**, **Jug-Or-Not**, and **Pothead**).

Start: At the left side of the open boulder pile, in front of the leftmost boulder leaning up against the cliff.

P1 5.9 G: Scamper the outside face of the boulder to a position just left of its high point. At a horizontal on the cliff (#3 Camalot), foot traverse left 5', then climb straight up the black face and mantel onto a horizontal dike. Continue straight up with a pure friction move and up to a ceiling. Pull over this onto a ledge with interesting white crystals. Step left and belay at an oak tree. 70'

P2 5.9+ G: Move the belay 15' left to another oak tree. Climb a steep face straight up to where the angle eases. Continue up and left (runout, but very easy) to join P3 of **Stop Making Sense** to a fixed anchor. 140'

Gear: 1 ea #3 Camalot.

Descent: Rappel **Peace Out** (2 rappels with one 60m rope).

FA Oct 9, 2010, Jim Lawyer, Leslie Ackerman, Erica Loher

8 Brazilian 5.10a G 240' ★★★★

The first hard, direct line to the top of the cliff with a little of everything—chimney, fingercrack, and amazing face climbing on dimpled rock. The first two pitches can be combined with attention towards rope management. (**Brazilian** ascends the same line as the winter route **Same As It Ever Was**, also named **Siamese Left** in *Blue Lines*).

Start: Same as **Stop Making Sense**.

P1 5.10a G: (V1) From the back of the boulder cave, move up behind blocks and into a left-facing, left-arching, bombay chimney. Up the chimney to where it narrows to fingers. Go through a bulge (crux), then up a left-facing corner to its top. Angle up and left to a perched boulder. 60'

P2 5.10a G: Straight up the black face above the perched boulder to a crack below a left-rising overlap. Over the overlap on cool edges, then straight up the black face (crux, stay right of a naturally trimmed bush) to a fixed anchor on Belly Button Ledge. 50'

P3 5.10a G: Move right from the belay and step up to a black wall below a crack that begins 6' higher in a right-facing corner. Up the crack to its top, step right, then go up and right to a right-facing, pointed flake. Work left on a rail, then up the crimpy face (crux) to where the angle eases. Run up the dimpled slab to a final tricky move to the fixed anchor. An excellent pitch. 130'

V1 5.5 R: An alternative to the first pitch. From the top of the boulder pile (described in **Stop Making Sense**), step up onto left-trending dike, then walk left along the dike to a 10'-high right-facing flake. Up the flake to a ledge, then up unprotected friction to an overlap (gear). Move right, then up onto a ledge. Walk right to the perched, protruding boulder. 110'

Gear: P1: to 5"; P2: 1 ea #3 Camalot. P3: yellow Alien, large nut, red Alien.

Descent: A 120' rappel returns to Belly Button Ledge. Another 100' rappel returns to the ground.

FA (V1, P2) Sep 7, 2009, Tom Yandon, Tad Welch, Jim Lawyer
FA (P1) Sep 16, 2009, Tom Yandon, Colin Loher, Jesse Littleton
FA (P3) Sep 16, 2009, Jim Lawyer, Tad Welch

*Michelle Burlitch on P2 (5.9) of **Positive Latitude** (5.10b).*

Northern Mountains

Emilie Drinkwater on Every Inch Counts *(5.10a).*

9 Once in a Lifetime 5.10d G 110' ★★★★★
One of the purest dimpled face climbs to date—very sustained with few rests. If you climb it perfectly, it may be 5.10b, but in the sea of polished black dimples, that's really hard to do on sight.
Start: At the fixed anchor on Belly Button Ledge.
● **P1 5.10d G:** Move up to the overhanging wall above the belay and make a boulder move over a bulge onto another ledge. Follow a hollow undercling flake up and left to its top, then step right onto the black, dimpled face. Go straight up the amazing, sustained, black face to where the angle eases, then run straight up to join the final move of Brazilian to the fixed anchor. 110'
Gear: Optional #0 TCU.
Descent: Rappel 120' to the Belly Button Ledge.
History: Named for a Talking Heads song.
FA Sep 16, 2009, Colin Loher, Jesse Littleton, Tom Yandon

10 Stop Making Sense 5.8 G 380' ★★★
A full-length moderate with excellent and varied climbing on clean rock with exposed positions. The upper section of the route has several brief sections of 5.7 as it makes long traverses on sloped slabs below rolling waves of clean rock, each time finding an unlikely path upwards. To reach the summit, from the top anchor, scramble left 25' to a ledge with oak trees (excellent bivy-like recess here), then up a brushy right-facing corner to the top.
Start: Locate the pile of car-sized boulders leaning up against the face. Begin in a boulder cave on the right side of the boulder pile, below a left-facing corner and arête.
P1 5.8 G: Stem up the mouth of the cave to gain the arête that forms the left-facing corner. Up the arête (crux) to a good stance on the right-hand face. Climb a shallow left-facing corner, then step right to a black streak and follow this to a ledge with a large oak. 80'
P2 5.4 PG: Traverse left behind and on top of a knobby fin to a wide, right-leaning crack. Up the crack to Belly Button Ledge—a wide comfortable ledge. Walk left to a fixed anchor high on the ledge. 60'
● **P3 5.7+ G (5.2 R):** Move the belay to the left end of Belly Button Ledge (there's a good ledge down and left with a gear belay). Traverse left to The Sausage—a 10' long torpedo-shaped boulder resting on a head-high ledge. Mantel onto the right end of The Sausage, then up a steep face (crux) to where the angle eases. Traverse left 60' on a sloping left-rising ramp, past some cedar bushes, to a fixed anchor below a second steep headwall. 90'
P4 5.7 G: Step right and climb the bulging face and slab above to a headwall. Traverse right on a knobby slab below the headwall to its right end. Continue rightwards on steeper friction for 20', then up and left to a ledge. Step right to an exposed position with a fixed anchor on the right end of a narrow ledge. 150'
Descent: Rappel 120' to the Belly Button Ledge, then 100' to the ground.
Gear: Minimal rack to 1.5".
History: The first route established in Shangri La, and named in typical Tad Welch style after a Talking Heads song.
FA Sep 8, 2009, Tad Welch, Tom Yandon, Jim Lawyer

477

Northern Mountains

11 Groovitational Pull 5.10a G 260' ★★★★★

Amazing, sustained face climbing for 2 pitches. The second pitch has outstanding position.
Start: 4' left of **Where the Wild Things Are**, at the left end of a horizontal crack at chest height. The first 60' is trad.

● **P1 5.10a G:** Up the face to a pod in the prominent left-rising crack (3" cam). Up the face to a thin seam, then up to a crack which leads to a ledge. (With 50' of rope out, there is a danger of hitting this ledge from the next set of moves; if you're worried, move the belay up to here.) Step left and work straight up the steep wall to a good ledge (with an amazing belay seat) and a fixed anchor. 140'

● **P2 5.9+ G:** Work up and left on black flakes, then straight up to the top of a right-facing flake. Angle up and right to the base of a steep wave in the water groove; over this (crux, brilliant moves), then straight up to a fixed anchor below the lichen-covered summit headwall. 120'

Gear: P1: small nut, 1 ea 0.75" cam, 0.25" cam, 3" cam.
Descent: Two rappels (120', 140') to the ground.
History: The name comes from Bowie's *In Space*, a song by Flight of the Conchords.
FA Sep 19, 2009, Jim Lawyer, Jesse Littleton, Tad Welch, Matt Way, Bill Widrig

12 Where the Wild Things Are 5.10b G 330' ★★★

Another full-length route with a dramatic topout that finishes on the flat table-like summit.
Start: Right of the **Stop Making Sense** clearing and boulder pile is a low slab topped by a left-rising 4th class ledge. Start in the center of the slab below the right end of a left-rising crack that begins 5' up.

● **P1 5.10b G ★★★★★:** An especially fine and varied pitch; use long slings to reduce rope drag. Move up the wall past the right end of the left-rising crack, then up and right to a stance. Go up and right on pure friction to a bulge, then straight up to the 4th class ledge at the top of the slab. (With 40' of rope out, there is a danger of hitting this ledge from the next set of moves; if you're worried, move the belay up to here.) Go straight up the headwall on crimps (crux), then traverse right to a right-facing flake. Up the flake to its top, then straight up nippled rock to an oak tree belay. 170'

P2 5.6 G: Move 4' left of the oak tree and climb a left-facing corner to a hanging cedar. Move right to a horn on the arête, then up the arête to a dirt ledge at its top. Gear belay (cams to 1") in a good horizontal above the ledge. Can be combined with the next pitch. 40'

P3 5.8 G: Go straight up the unlikely dimpled face (sustained 5.7+) above the belay to the summit headwall, aiming for a left-facing, lichen-covered corner with many horizontal cracks. Go up and right into a cave (the Hermitage). Move left out of the cave's mouth onto a nose, then step left into the lichen-covered left-facing corner. Up the corner to the flat table-like summit. Gear to 3" for the belay. 120'

Gear: P2-P3: sparse rack to 3".
Descent: Walk left and downclimb the brushy corner above **Brazilian** (4th class), then rappel that route.
History: Named for the 1963 children's book by Maurice Sendak, and for the mythical creatures living in the Hermitage cave below the summit.
FA (P1) Sep 16, 2009, Tad Welch, Jim Lawyer
FA (P2, P3) Sep 17, 2009, Jim Lawyer, Tad Welch, Jesse Littleton

Shangri La: Pink Waterstreak

The pink-colored water streak (the one above the 12'-high rock pancake leaning up against the base) is split horizontally in the middle by a wide, deep, smile-shaped ledge, completely hidden from below. The upper pitches here have some of the best dimpled face anywhere (and the location of the winter route **Siamese Right** described in *Blue Lines*). To access this ledge, climb P1 of **Positive Latitude**. Alternatively, you can climb the P1 of **Where the Wild Things Are** or **Groovitational Pull** (or any route that goes to Belly Button Ledge), then traverse right to the left-facing corner at the top of P1 of **Where the Wild Things Are**. Continue right to where the ledge ends, then step down 6' on a slab (5.1) to a hidden foot ledge. Continue rightwards on a narrow ledge that leads to the major smile-shaped ledge that splits the pink-colored water streak. This point is 200' right of the fixed anchor on Belly Button Ledge.

Both routes finish at a somewhat hidden fixed anchor at the top of the wall. From here, you can walk right, then back left to reach the table-flat summit.

DESCENT OPTIONS

Rappel 190' to the smile-shaped ledge. A second rappel from the fixed anchor on the left side (the P1 belay for **Positive Latitude**) returns to the ground. Or, reverse the traverse (5.1) back to the top of P1 of the other routes.

13 Positive Latitude 5.10b G 320' ★★★★★

The second pitch has the best dimple climbing in the park, or perhaps anywhere for that matter. A very special route.
Start: At the left side of the pink water streak 100' right of **Where the Wild Things Are** and 40' uphill and left of the pancake leaning up against the main face, below a shallow, 20'-tall, right-facing corner that begins 15' up.

● **P1 5.10b G:** Up the right-facing corner to its top, then step right and climb straight up the face past some creaky flakes to a headwall where the angle steepens to vertical. Angle right through the steep wall (crux) to the smile-shaped ledge. Set a directional (#1 Camalot), then scramble easily up and left to an oak tree on the upper left side of the ledge. 160'

● **P2 5.9 PG:** Climb up and right on the black face to a stance. Traverse right a few feet, then go straight up a sea of dimpled rock, past a right-facing flake, to a right-rising ribbon of knobs (aka "The Triple R-K"). Follow the knobs up and right to another right-facing flake,

Opposite: Jim Lawyer on the first ascent of Scary Potter Traverse (5.10c). Photo by Colin O'Connor.

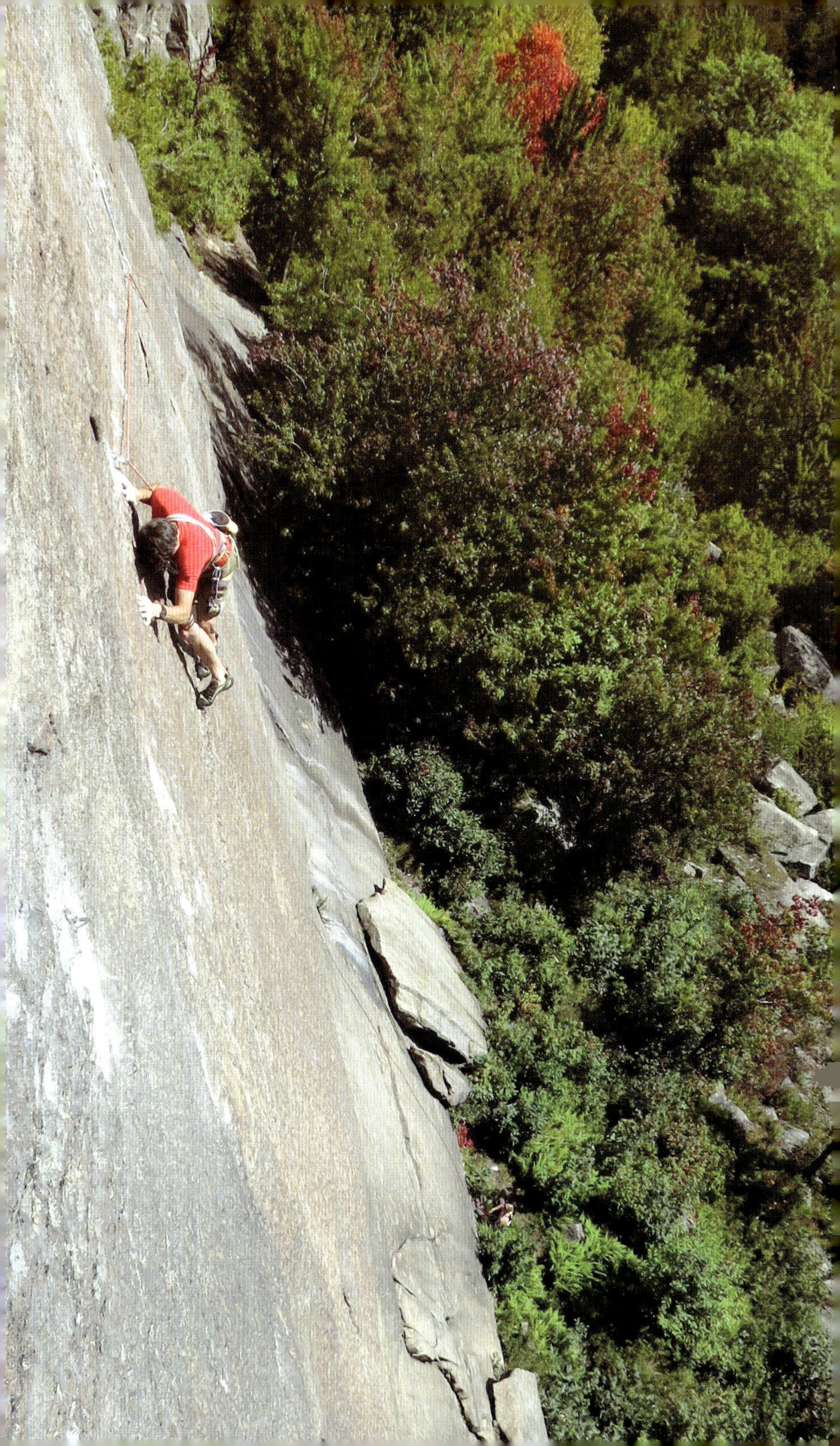

up this to its top, then step into a rust-colored pocket. Continue straight up the dimpled black face to where the angle eases, then run up the slab to the headwall. Climb the headwall (2" or 3" cam) to a fixed anchor (shared with Every Inch Counts). 160'
Gear: P1: 1 ea #1 Camalot, #2 Camalot, medium nut; P2: 1 ea 2" or 3" cam.
Descent: Rappel the route with two 60m ropes.
FA (P2) Sep 25, 2009, Jim Lawyer, Tad Welch, Colin Loher
FA (P1) Oct 19, 2009, Jim Lawyer, Colin Loher, Emilie Drinkwater

14 Every Inch Counts 5.10a G 190' ★★★★★

A rope stretcher and another amazing, sustained line on varied, dimpled rock. This route has no lower pitch and is accessed from the smile-shaped ledge.
Start: On the right side of the smile-shaped ledge is a clean left-facing corner. Belay here (a 3"–4" cam provides the only belay protection), and begin 5' left of the corner.
P1 5.10a G: Go straight up the dimpled face to a shallow, right-facing corner that arches right at its top. Up the corner, then move right out the arch to a good undercling at its right end. Move over the arch on crimps (crux), then go straight up the dimpled face to where the angle eases. Run up the slab to the headwall (joining Positive Latitude here), then up (2" or 3" cam) to a fixed anchor (shared with Positive Latitude). 190'
Gear: 1 ea red Alien, blue TCU, 2" or 3" cam.
Descent: Rappel Positive Latitude with two 60m ropes.
FA Sep 25, 2009, Colin Loher, Jim Lawyer, Tad Welch

15 First? Really? 5.8 PG 170' ★★

Start: Same as Every Inch Counts.
P1 5.6 G: Go up the left-facing corner system. Where the corner widens, climb the face left of the corner to a roof (beware of suspect blocks in the roof, #4 Camalot). Move left around the roof and up the corner to its top and gear anchor. 50'
P2 5.8 PG: Walk right on the ledge 20' to a short right-facing corner with a fingercrack. Climb this past a technical move to where the crack widens to hands and transitions to easy terrain. Follow this to a dirty, right-facing corner (medium stopper). Go up the corner a few feet, then move left onto the face. Wander up the face to belay on a ledge below overlap, 50' left of (and level with) a large pine tree. 120'

Monica Wormald, getting it done on Honeybadger (5.10a), belayed by Liam Schneider.

Descent: On the right side of the overlap, scramble up a short right-facing corner to the top. Walk left, find the fixed anchor for Positive Latitude, and rappel that route.

History: Named for the surprise that this obvious, natural line was one of the last lines to be climbed here.
FA Nov 18, 2012, Greg Kuchyt, Matt Hosmer

16 Scary Potter Traverse 5.10c G 160' ★★★★

Well-protected, but it is, after all, a traverse, and scary for both the leader and the follower. Spectacular.
Start: Same as Honeybadger.
● **P1 5.10c G:** Climb Honeybadger to the shallow, right-facing corner. Once in the corner, move left to another left-leaning, shallow corner and follow this cool feature to its top. Traverse 40' left using barely perceptible crystals for feet and no hands. At the end of the traverse, undercling a flake and reach up to better holds; follow these to the top where Positive Latitude joins in from the left. Run up and left on easy ground to the fixed anchor on Positive Latitude. 160'
Gear: Bring long runners to reduce rope drag.
FA Sep 3, 2012, Jim Lawyer, Emilie Drinkwater, Colin O'Connor

17 Honeybadger 5.10a G 90' ★★★★★

Varied and well-protected. The route unfortunately doesn't reach the smile-shaped ledge, but the climbing is so good, who cares?
Start: On the left side of the "pancake" (between the "pancake" and the "sausage"), 40' right of Positive Latitude.

● **P1 5.10a G:** Go to the top of the "sausage," then up a clean face, angling left to a good hold at the left end of an overlap. Undercling right 6' (crux), then move up to a stance just left of a large, triangular, held-on-by-magic flake. Go straight up and mantel onto an edge, then up a shallow, right-facing corner to its top. Move up and right to a jug, then up and right to another jug (aka the "double rightwards whammy"), then go straight up the black face on great holds to a fixed anchor. 90'

History: Within an hour of the first ascent, this route saw five leads by different climbers at the cliff.
FA Oct 8, 2011, Jim Lawyer

Main Face

18 Morningside Heights 5.10a G (5.4 X) 80'

Much harder than it looks, especially if you're short.
Start: At a right-leaning ramp, 180' left of the large left-facing corner of Never Again, Again.
P1 5.10a G (5.4 X): Hard moves and good gear near the ground lead to the corner. Up the corner (5.4, no pro) to its top, then angle back left on a steep face with increasingly better holds to a good ledge with trees. 80'
FA Sep 26, 2009, Joe Szot, Aya Alt

19 Never Again, Again 5.7 PG 300'

A typical recon route—"shit line with death blocks"—this route explores the tallest section of cliff and ends less than halfway up the wall. The start seems appealing, but despite being ascended by two separate parties, the route has poor belays and crap rock and is

POTTER MOUNTAIN CLIFF: MAIN FACE
14 Every Inch Counts (5.10a)
15 First? Really? (5:8)
17 Honeybadger (5.10a)
18 Morningside Heights (5.10a)
19 Never Again, Again (5.7)
20 Bonanza Lunchbox (5.10b)

481

not recommended. Positioned right of center at a point just left of where the terrain rises steeply uphill to the left, is a large, broken left-facing corner, the right wall of which forms an appealing arête. Begin here and climb to the top of the corner to a small ledge below a clean face with a right-facing corner and a crack to its right, 50' below a distinct left-facing, left-rising dihedral. Up the crack in the face to trees at the base of the corner. Follow the corner (or face below) to a tree ledge. Two rappels from trees return to the ground.

History: The first rock route established on Potter Mountain. Since it climbs the most obvious feature on the cliff, it was ascended by two parties, each thinking it was a "first". Mellor thought it unworthy of a name, so it was named by the second ascent party (Tom Yandon and Joe Szot) "Never Again"; finding that it was already climbed, they modified the name to "Never Again, Again".
FA Jul 30, 2009, Don Mellor, Mark Bealor

20 Bonanza Lunchbox 5.10b PG 160' ★★★
Start: Same as Never Again, Again.
P1 5.10b PG: Stem up between the gully and the arête to arrange some solid RPs, then move up to large holds on the arête to gain a stance (crux). Move right to a crack and follow this over a steep bulge-ceiling, then continue up semi-loose (but moderate) blocks and cracks to trees. Belay in an off-vertical hand- and fist-crack. 160'

Descent: Rappel from small trees to the ground.
FA Oct 14, 2010, Patrick Mulhern, Willard Race

The Ghetto

The Ghetto is the first section of cliff you reach on the approach trail. It's 100' tall and very steep with only a few lines of weakness. It is separated from the main cliff by a right-rising ramp that leads to the top of this section of cliff.

The Ghetto's crack lines are a bit dirty, but with some cleaning this could become a worthwhile destination.

21 Leroy Brown A1 100' ★★★
Sustained and gymnastic crack climbing under a roof. It's presently a clean aid route and awaits a clean lead, estimated at 5.11+ G.
Start: 25' left of Zebra in a small cave below the left end of a horizontal crack that shoots out right, around a bulging arête, then angles up and right across a brown wall.
P1 A1: Climb the large right-trending horizontal crack under the roof to a bulging arête. Negotiate the arête, then move back into the crack that now rises up and right. Jam and layback the crack until you can break the roof feature up to a ledge. Climb a handcrack to a ledge with a refrigerator-sized block–flake. Step right and follow a crack to a fixed anchor on the ledge. 100'
Gear: Rack to 6" with doubles of #1,#2 and #3 Camalots.
FA (A1) Sep 30, 2009, Richard Wilson, Jesse Littleton

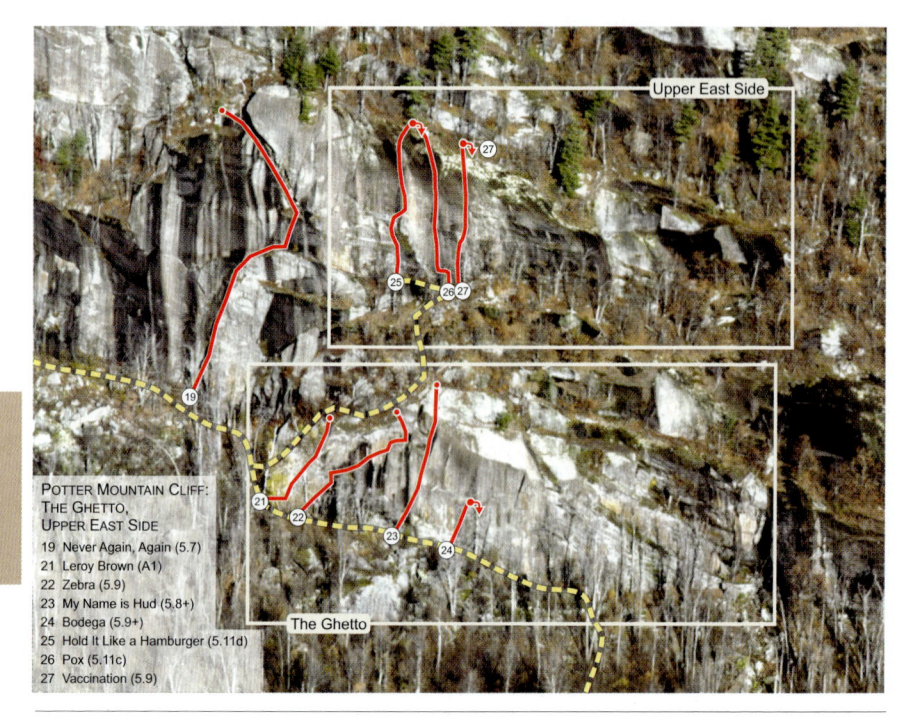

POTTER MOUNTAIN CLIFF:
THE GHETTO,
UPPER EAST SIDE
19 Never Again, Again (5.7)
21 Leroy Brown (A1)
22 Zebra (5.9)
23 My Name is Hud (5.8+)
24 Bodega (5.9+)
25 Hold It Like a Hamburger (5.11d)
26 Pox (5.11c)
27 Vaccination (5.9)

22 Zebra 5.9 G 130' ★★★

Start: First locate a prominent right-facing, right-leaning corner that starts at the ground, wraps around a bulge, and shoots up and right at a 45° angle. Begin 40' right of this corner at a second right-leaning fingertip crack in black and white striped "zebra" rock.

P1 5.9 G: Up the fingertip crack and over bulge to the left-hand end of a large ledge. Follow ledge and crack system at base of headwall to its right end at a left-facing corner capped by a protruding finger of rock. Surmount finger to a ledge with huge, detached, 8'-high block. Over the top of the block, then finish up a stepped face with cracks to a tree ledge. 130'

Gear: To 3" with an emphasis on small to medium.
FA Sep 17, 2009, Tom Yandon, Joe Szot

23 My Name is Hud 5.8+ G 130'

Start: 30' right of Zebra below a left-facing right-leaning corner with a fingercrack.

P1 5.8+ G: Boulder up to the corner (no pro), then follow the corner to its top. Fight your way over a birch tree, go up a chimney, then up ledges. Finish up a short left-facing corner to low-angle slab and trees. 130'
FA Sep 26, 2009, Joe Szot, Aya Alt

24 Bodega 5.9+ G 50' ★★

Start: 150' left of where the trail meets the cliff, and 200' right of Zebra, below a left-facing right-leaning corner with a fingertip crack.

P1 5.9+ G: Climb the corner to a hanging stance at its top. Rappel from fixed gear. 50'
FA Sep 19, 2009, Joe Szot, Tom Yandon

Upper East Side

The Upper East Side is the wall above the tree-covered, sloped terrace on top of the Ghetto. Mostly difficult crimpy face and dimple pulling here.

DIRECTIONS (MAP PAGE 436)

Follow the trail leftwards along the base of the Ghetto to where it ascends steeply up and left. Look for an easy ramp that breaks up and right to the tree slope at the top of the Ghetto. Locate an orange wall with several right-leaning crack-like features; the left "crack" is left of a black streak (Hold It Like a Hamburger), and the right crack is left of a tan streak (Pox) 595712,4930100.

You can walk to the top of this wall (and the top of Never Again, Again) by continuing rightwards along the terrace, then cutting back left above the wall. Just left of the top of Pox is an amazing, flat, open ledge.

25 Hold It Like a Hamburger
5.11d G (5.1 R) 160' ★★★

A masterpiece of steep climbing on positive crimps and small footholds.

Start: Walk 25' left from Pox on a narrow, grass-covered ledge above a steep, mossy slab and begin at a shallow, short, left-facing corner with a ledge 7' up.

● **P1 5.11d G:** Climb up to a ledge, then make several high-steps up a cleaned face. At its top, run out a slab to the left side of a large, hanging, black block. Move up and right across the top of the hanging block, then follow desperate crimps straight up the orange face to where the angle eases. Run out up and right to a fixed anchor on a large pine (shared with Pox). 160'

Jim Lawyer on the first ascent of Hold It Like a Hamburger (5.11d). Photo by Colin O'Connor.

Northern Mountains

History: This route was prepped in 2010, but it took two years before the right conditions: cooler temps and conditioning. Lawyer got the first successful lead, immediately followed by Loher.
FA Sep 1, 2012, Jim Lawyer, Colin Loher, Colin O'Connor

26 Pox 5.11c G (5.1 R) 140' ★★★
Perhaps the easiest-looking route of its grade anywhere, this route has the hardest dimple climbing yet at Potter combined with a hard "crack," which is actually a connected series of flared water pockets on an overhanging wall. Yikes!
Start: Below a tan streak at a shallow, black, right-facing open book that begins 5' up.
● **P1 5.11c G (5.1 R):** Go up the right-facing open book, then step left onto a narrow ledge. Shuffle left and climb a narrow ribbon of dimples (5.10d) to reach the base of a right-leaning "crack". Desperate moves up the steep water pockets lead to a hand jam, and the end of the difficulties. Run out the clean, textured slab to a fixed anchor on a large pine. 140'
Gear: 1 ea #1 Camalot, #2 Camalot.
FA Aug 30, 2010, Jim Lawyer, Colin Loher, Aaron Pfenler

27 Vaccination 5.9 G 140' ★★
The "cure" to the hard climbing on this wall; consists of a couple awkward mantels and a puzzling friction crux. It can be used to access the top of **Pox** and **Hold It Like a Hamburger**.
Start: 15' right of **Pox**.
● **P1 5.9 G:** Follow the obvious weakness up the face heading towards a scoop-like feature. Break right (crux), then up an easier slab to a tree at the top. 140'
Gear: Optional #1 or #2 Camalot.
Descent: Two rope rappel from tree.
FA Sep 23, 2010, Colin Loher, Matt Way, Richard Wilson

Silver Lake
THE BURROW

Aspect	West
Height	80'
Quality	
Approach	1 hr 10 min, moderate
Summary	Short, broken cliff with many cracks, but interrupted by ledges.

This cliff is mostly broken, but with a couple short, steep walls laced with cracks. The cracks have great finger locks, but they're also short and a bit dirty; some potential for short, powerful routes. The cliff base is moderately open and comfortable.

DIRECTIONS **(MAP PAGE 436)**
Follow the approach to the Shangri La sector of Potter Mountain (50 min). Continue along the base of the cliff past **Bears, Beets, Battlestar Galactica** to the far end of low roofs and locate a broken, 4th-class, left-facing corner. Scramble up this and continue following the base of the slab as it bends to the west and diminishes. Continue west to reach the cliff at 1 hr 10 min.

Colin Loher in the water groove of Pox (5.11c)

1 Ledge You To Believe 5.9- G 80'
An excellent initial handcrack, but the route is broken by several large ledges.
Start: On the right side of the cliff is a broad, open gully that leads to the top of the cliff (the only easy access to the top of the cliff). 75' left of the gully is a 30'-high, acute, right-facing, tapering corner with a mossy crack. Begin 20' left of this corner at a larger right-facing corner with a good, clean, black handcrack in the left wall, 4' left of the corner. Further left is a deep, narrow, boulder-capped chimney with a good fingercrack in the left wall.
P1 5.9- G: Go up the handcrack in the left wall to a final difficult mantel (crux) onto a terrace with a tree belay. 30'
P2 5.8 G: Climb a crack in a corner with a pod stance at mid-height to another broad ledge. Continue up a crack in a right-facing corner to a final crux mantel. Tree belay. 50'
Gear: To 3".
FA Sep 28, 2011, Jim Lawyer, Tad Welch

Northern Mountains

Silver Lake
HYDROGEN WALL

Aspect	South
Height	220'
Quality	★★
Approach	35 min, moderate
Summary	Holds two quality crack routes; some potential for new routes on the left side.

			1		1			2
-5.6	5.7	5.8	5.9	5.10	5.11	5.12	5.13+	total

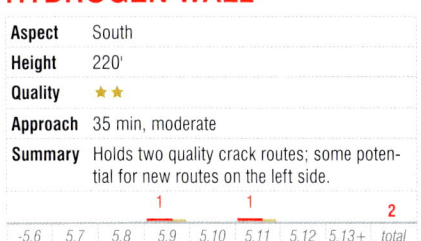

Situated high on the Silver Lake Mountain ridgeline, this cliff has seen some exploration for climbing. The cliff is about 220' tall. 80' below the top is Supper Ledge, a beautiful ledge that spans the width of the cliff. You can reach Supper Ledge by rappelling in on the right side, or by climbing Sam I Am.

DIRECTIONS (MAP PAGE 436)
This cliff can be approached from top or bottom.
To approach from the top: From the Silver Lake Mountain Trailhead, follow the red-blazed trail for 30 minutes to the summit of Silver Lake Mountain 592134,4930357, then continue east on a good path. The first slabby open summit area is the top of Pandorum 592471,4930118 (no routes here yet). Continue along the ridge to the next open slabby summit of the Hydrogen Wall 592717,4930011.
To approach from the bottom: Park at the Mud Pond Trailhead. Follow the logging road for 15 minutes to a large clearing choked with raspberries and other unpleasantries. This clearing is directly below the Hydrogen Wall. Follow your nose (best assisted with a compass), aiming for the open talus area on the far right side of the cliff.

From the open talus, you can scramble straight up to the ridge, then follow open ledges back left to the top of the cliff 592717,4930011.

HISTORY
This cliff was the playground for local climber Kevin Crowl, who spent many afternoons by himself cleaning these pitches.

1 The Cement Mixer 5.11 G 80' ★★★
Start: In the middle of Supper Ledge below a prominent (and only) crack that breaches the upper wall.
P1 5.11 G: Work up the crack (crux) to a ledge 25' up. Move over a steep bulge using a flake that forms double cracks. Pull through the double cracks to a slab, then up a pretty white slab to a good ledge with a tree. 80'
FA May, 2010, Kevin Crowl, Micah Stewart

2 Sam I Am 5.9 G 140' ★★★
Bring small gear. The route ends at Supper Ledge, and provides access to The Cement Mixer on the upper headwall.
Start: To find the route, start at the base of the cliff near the right end (near the large open talus field). Follow the base of the cliff down and left until you come to "The Gate"—a large, 10'-high flake positioned far enough away from the cliff to walk through. Walk through The Gate and onto a tree-covered ledge. Follow the ledge down and left until you come to a large, square, head-high boulder blocking the ledge. The route begins on top of this boulder.
P1 5.9 G: Follow a weakness straight up, passing a small cedar to a ledge 30' up. Directly above, follow a crack line that begins in a small right-facing corner, then continue straight up to the double red pines on the Super Ledge. 140'
FA Jul 28, 2009, Kevin Crowl, Julia Gronski

HYDROGEN WALL
1 The Cement Mixer (5.11)
2 Sam I Am (5.9)

485

Silver Lake
MUD POND CLIFF

Aspect	South and southwest
Height	200'
Quality	★★★★
Approach	25 min, easy
Summary	A wide cliff with two section of overhanging rock; lots of difficult routes here.

1			4	2	5	1	2	15
-5.6	5.7	5.8	5.9	5.10	5.11	5.12	5.13+	total

This cliff sits apart from the other cliffs at Silver Lake, in front of Mud Pond. It has an easy approach and is fairly popular.

On the left end is a low-angle slab capped by a steep, roof headwall. Right of this is an impressive overhanging amphitheater; **Born To Run** is on its left side. Moving right is a collection of corners and faces with the routes **Rico's Roughnecks** through to **Dirty Uncle**. Right of this is a very overhanging section of rock with futuristic lines. Finally, on the right end is a large talus area with a few more extreme routes.

DIRECTIONS (MAP PAGE 436)
Park at the Mud Pond Trailhead (0 hr 0 min). Follow the logging road and turn right at 8 min at the first, well-used logging road 592201,4929610. Follow this for to a fork at 10 min; turn right again (downhill) on another well-used logging road. Follow the logging road to a hunter's cabin at 15 min. About 400' past the cabin, turn left into an open, logged area, and follow an open skid path up to the cliff 592828,4929320 at 25 min.

HISTORY
Tim Beaman added two brutal, thuggy routes here in 1983: **Born to Run**, and **Gizmo**. Originally rated 5.10, like many Beaman routes, they are far more difficult, and each have a single, unusual 1/2" bolt.

After that, like the other Silver Lake cliffs, Mud Pond went off the radar for 25 years until 2009 when Jim Lawyer and Don Mellor got the ball rolling with **Rico's Roughnecks**. They were followed by the trio Karl Swisher, Frank Minunni, and Richard Felch who added 7 routes here in 2010. They also explored the overhanging wall on the right end and even equipped several projects before Minunni moved away from the region.

Rumors of these fantastic overhanging cracks spread, drawing Pete Kamitses and Matt McCormick over from Vermont in 2011. While there's been some success, such as **The Sword of Deception**, and **Moonshine and Chronic**, other projects are open and await suitors.

Left End

1 Last Grasp 5.9 G 90'
Start: On the left end of the cliff, and 250' left of **Born To Run**, is an 80'-tall slab, the only large slab on the cliff, capped by an overhanging, roofy headwall. About 50' left of the right end of this section is a left-leaning crack that starts as a seam, then becomes a left-facing corner 60' up. Begin at a black slab 12' right of the crack and 5' left of a 10'-tall, left-facing corner.

P1 5.9 G: Friction up the black slab to a ledge, then follow a 1'-thick right-facing flake to a small overlap at its top. Traverse 10' left, then follow the left-leaning crack to the left-facing corner, then up this to a tree below the overhanging headwall. Rappel. 90'
FA 1983, Tad Welch, David Fisher, John Thackray

2 Born To Run 5.11+ PG 80'
The crux crack climbing is difficult to protect with ledge fall potential if you don't work the pro.

Start: In the center of the cliff is an open, cleared, grassy area with house-sized talus blocks set back in the woods. The cliff here forms an amphitheater—sheer and overhanging, often dripping, with a distinctive pinkish shield of rock on the left side, and a prominent, left-leaning, full-height, 1'-wide chimney–dike on the right.

MUD POND: LEFT END
1 Last Grasp (5.9)
2 Born To Run (5.11+)

Begin below the pinkish shield at an overhanging, crumbly, left-facing flake at head height.

P1 5.11+ PG: Boulder up the crumbly pink flake and make a tricky mantel onto a ledge (5.9+, R). Step right and climb to a second ledge. Traverse 12' right to a crack which is followed to an overhang at its top. Follow the crack through the left side of the overhang, then up an open book to a sloped ledge on the right and fixed anchor. 80'
FA 1983, Tim Beaman, Sylvia Lazarnick

Right End

3 Waiting For The Weather 5.9+ G 90' ★★

The initial slab seeps, hence the name. Would be better if cleaned up.

Start: 200' right of Born To Run at a slab, above which is a crack that begins 6' up.

P1 5.9+ G: Climb the slab for 6' to gain the crack. Go up the crack, which pinches off at head level (crux), and follow it 30' to a ledge. Continue up the crack as it trends left past ledges with a few hard moves. Finish on a large, grassy ledge with a cedar tree and a fixed anchor. 90'
FA Aug 8, 2011, Will Roth, Sara George

4 Rico's Roughnecks 5.10c G 200' ★★★★

The first pitch is especially good.

Start: On the right side of the cliff is a wide section of overhanging rock with a dark band of dike rock running horizontally along the base. Begin 300' left at an obvious handcrack in a right-facing wall. The crack doglegs right 60' up. This is 300' right of the left-leaning chimney–dike that marks the right side of the amphitheater with Born To Run.

P1 5.10c G: Up the handcrack to an overhang. Traverse right 8' under the overhang (crux, small cams), then continue up a handcrack in a right-facing corner to a good belay ledge with a fixed anchor. 100'

P2 5.7 G: Traverse right into open book and follow this straight up to a cedar in a chimney just below the top. 100'

Gear: To 3.5", including 2 ea #0.75, #1, #2.

Descent: Two raps with a 60m rope.
ACB Jun 23, 2009, Jim Lawyer, Don Mellor

5 Big Brother 5.9+ G 60' ★★

Start: Same as Little Sister.

P1 5.9+ G: Climb up 8', then move up and left along a ramp to a thin crack in the face. Follow the thin crack to a right-facing corner. At its top, continue up a thin crack in the face to a ledge with a fixed anchor shared with Little Sister. 60'

Gear: Small wires and cams to 1.5".
FA Oct 11, 2010, Richard Felch, Frank Minunni, Karl Swisher

6 Little Sister 5.11c G 60' ★★★

Great rock, great climbing, and continuous.

Start: 30' right of Rico's Roughnecks at a face with a pair of right-facing corners. Begin below the left-hand corner.

P1 5.11c G: Climb up into the left of two parallel corners and follow it to its top. Continue up the face (crux) to a ledge with a fixed anchor. 60'

Gear: To 2".
FA Oct 11, 2010, Frank Minunni, Richard Felch, Karl Swisher

7 Evil Twin 5.10c G 60' ★

Much harder than it looks.

Start: Locate an open book with a good crack that leads past two cedar trees. Begin 10' right of the open book.

P1 5.10c G: Climb up to a sloped ledge, then step left into the open book. Up the crack in the open book past the cedar trees to a ledge with a fixed anchor on a tree. 60'
FA Sep, 2010, Frank Minunni, Richard Felch

MUD POND: RIGHT END

4 Rico's Roughnecks (5.10c)
5 Big Brother (5.9+)
6 Little Sister (5.11c)
7 Evil Twin (5.10c)
8 Dirty Uncle (5.9)
9 The Sodomizer (project)
10 Moonshine and Chronic (5.13+)
11 The Sword of Deception (5.13)
12 Gizmo (5.11)
13 The Mideast Solution (5.11d)
14 Crispy Critters (5.12a)
15 Plan C (5.11c)
16 Rear Entry (5.6)

Northern Mountains

8 Dirty Uncle 5.9 PG 100'

An incomplete project with pitons of unknown origin. Recent ascents traverse right at the triangular ceiling, then climb a crappy corner to the top; not recommended. A fixed anchor has been installed at the top of the corner, but remains an open project.

Start: 30' right of Evil Twin in a large open book corner with splashes of orange lichen on the walls. The corner leads to a triangular ceiling below a hanging cedar.

P1 5.9 PG: Up the corner with hidden pitons to the square roof. Traverse 25' right on a good ledge. 100'

9 The Sodomizer Project

Another amazing crack on the most overhanging section of the wall on the right end of the cliff. The crack begins above a roof system 30' up. Start from the right and climb a crack to a roof, then traverse left under the roof. Swing over the roof and into the seam at the lip. Climb the seam and crack to a fixed anchor. An open project.

10 Moonshine and Chronic 5.13+ PG 90' ★★★★★

Reported as "super exciting mega classic". The steepness and "rad-ness" of the moves are rare for the Adirondacks. There's a V8 boulder problem on the face, followed by a 5.13 crack. The last 15' are often wet.

Start: 20' left of The Sword of Deception.

P1 5.13+ PG: Stick-clip the first bolt. Climb through a loose, dark band of dike rock for 10', then up a difficult, thin, tan-colored face (V8 boulder problem) to gain a crack–seam and first bolt. Climb up the crack–seam (bolts and gear), then runout to a fixed anchor. 90'

Gear: Nuts 1 ea #7, #9; 2 ea 1" cam.

FA Oct, 2013, Peter Kamitses

11 The Sword of Deception 5.13 R 90' ★★★

Climbs an awesome, overhanging crack. After an initial loose rock band, the route has good to excellent rock. The initial moves require some boulder pads, or pre-placed gear 15' up. Higher up, a long runout over good gear requires the belayer to take in rope to keep the leader off the ground.

Start: 15' left of Gizmo below an overhanging crack.

P1 5.13 R: After initial moves up to the first gear, punch up though the first crux (powerful moves, minimal features, bad feet) to gain a good left-hand jug. Place a tiny nut or cam in a good constriction (pumpy), then work past some dicey moves to a solid finger lock. Next piece in a flare, then make techy foot smears up to a horizontal with a good rest. Make a big dynamic move, then a substantial runout (ground fall potential). The finish is steep, pumpy, but has good gear and cool moves. Fixed anchor. 90'

History: The route was first explored by Frank Minunni in 2010 and named The Sword of Damocles for the ominous, spear-shaped tree overhanging the belayer. Minunni moved away soon after and opened the project. Kamitses worked the route thinking it would be "no big deal", but it turned out to be deceptively more difficult and serious to send, especially considering the hot, sticky conditions.

FA Jul 22, 2012, Peter Kamitses

12 Gizmo 5.11 G 90'

An impressive, old-school line that awaits a modern ascent and needs cleaning. Hands and fists pulling the bulge.

Start: On the right side of the cliff is a wide section of overhanging rock with a dark band of dike rock running horizontally along the base. Begin on the right side at a crack that leads to a hanging cedar. This is downhill and left of an open area of large talus boulders.

P1 5.11 G: Up the crack and past a bulge (crux). Continue in the crack through the roof (bolt) to a fixed anchor. 90'

FA 1983, Tim Beaman, Sylvia Lazarnick

13 The Mideast Solution 5.11d G 50' ★★

Once considered 5.10c, the hold "shaped like Africa" came off, making the route considerably more difficult.

Start: 30' uphill and right of Gizmo in an area of open talus, at a pointed boulder that leans up to within 6" of the cliff face, below an overhanging, right-facing open book corner.

● **P1 5.11d G:** From the top of the pointed boulder, move up and left into the corner. Layback strenuously up the open book to a good ledge. Finish with fun mantel moves to a fixed anchor. 50'

Gear: A few pieces to 0.5".

FA Sep, 2010, Frank Minunni, Richard Felch, Karl Swisher

14 Crispy Critters 5.12a G 50' ★★

A brief crux, and a scary flake.

Start: 20' right of The Mideast Solution. The wall is undercut here with good holds in black rock, and there's a large boulder–slab at the base.

● **P1 5.12a G:** Stick-clip the first bolt of Plan C. Move up Plan C for 8', then move left to an arête with a skinny fragile flake on its nose (you can see behind this flake to Silver Lake). Continue up the nose of the arête to a fixed anchor. 50'

FA Sep, 2010, Frank Minunni, Karl Swisher

15 Plan C 5.11c G 50' ★★★

Start: Same as Crispy Critters.

● **P1 5.11c G:** Stick-clip the first bolt, then climb up a right-leaning, shallow open book corner to a fixed anchor below a ledge. 50'

FA Sep, 2010, Frank Minunni, Karl Swisher, Richard Felch

16 Rear Entry 5.6 G 70'

Use primarily to access the fixed anchors of the routes to the left.

Start: At the right end of the cliff, 40' right of Plan C and on the right side of an open talus area, at a 6'-high, right-facing corner that begins 4' up. There is a clump of maple trees at the base.

● **P1 5.6 G:** Go up the corner, then up blocky terrain to the right end of a left-rising ledge. Scramble left along the ledge and pick a fixed anchor. 70'

FA Sep, 2010, Karl Swisher, Frank Minunni, Richard Felch

Peter Kamitses sets up for "the best boulder problem I've done on a trad route", on Sword of Deception (5.13).
Photo by David Crowthers.

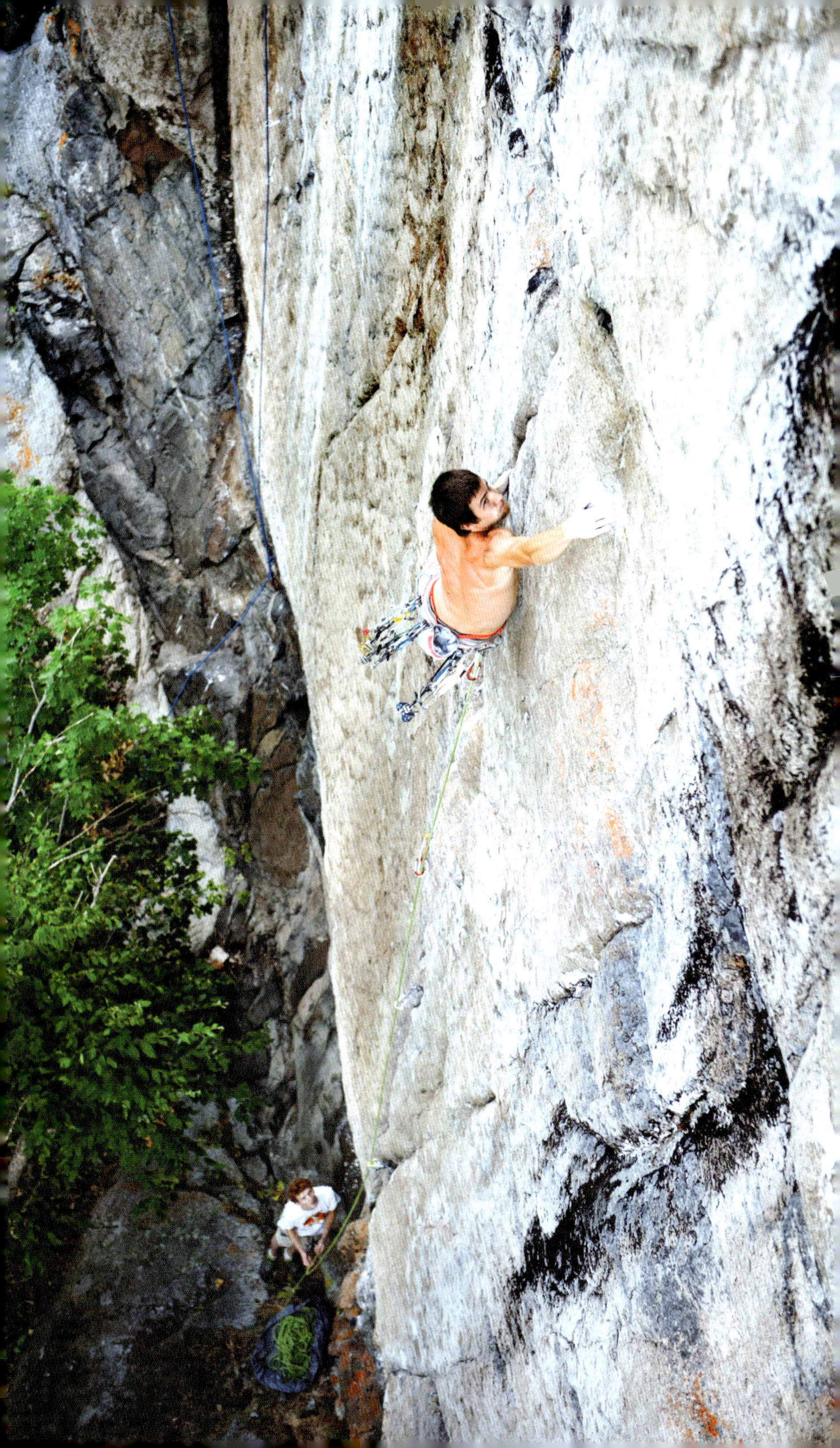

Northern Mountains

Team Nasty

Earth Day, April 22, 2009. The day I've been anticipating for five years has finally arrived. The cliffs are open and I am standing next to my car, super amped, pack shouldered with its arsenal of climbing gear. I even have backup: Team Nasty, or as my daughter Cecy calls them, The Lost Boys: Matt Way, Jessie Littleton, and Rich Wilson. Whatever the name, it's undeniable they are talented climbers, uber-psyched, and just plain fun to be around. If you don't believe me, just ask my kids.

I first met these guys a year ago, downstate, at the legendary Mac Wall. We did a few pitches there, and I ended up at their house that evening. I noticed a magazine on the coffee table addressed to Team Nasty. "Who's Team Nasty?" I asked. "Oh, that's just us," Jesse responded. "All of our magazines are addressed to us that way." I liked them immediately. The relationship was cemented when Jesse said he "wanted to do a first ascent somewhere." I knew just the place, and dropped some Silver Lake knowledge on him.

A week before Earth Day, I did a Silver Lake recon flight with Jim Lawyer. Based on what I saw—a concentration of architecturally beautiful splitter cracks—I decided to take Team Nasty there. After a good hour of arduous bushwhacking on old, muddy, heavily vegetated skidder paths, we finally made it to the base of the cliff. It was better than we hoped: multitudes of splitter cracks of all sizes. We hit pay dirt, literally, as the cracks were choked with dirt. Team Nasty aided up, and we began cleaning. Welcome to the Adirondacks.

The first route we tried was an amazing, overhanging corner crack, reminiscent of something you would find at the Battle of the Bulge Buttress at the Creek. I was first up, and right off the deck I'm completely absorbed, trying to read with my hands and feet a billion year old story written in the ancient rock. I made it about 15', fell, and lowered. We took turns throwing ourselves at the climb, each person going a little higher than the last. It became a game, a really fun game. Who's going to crack this crack? The only rule was: you fall, you come down. In the end, I'm not really sure who won (I know it wasn't me), but I did know that I had made some good friends.

They moved up later that summer, working restaurant jobs, spending every free minute at the cliffs of Silver Lake: Summit Cliff, Center of Progress, Potter, and eventually the C Chimney Cliff. I joined them when I could.

They've since moved away, but I still have hopes that someday I will be inducted into their team...   - Colin Loher

---

Silver Lake

SILVER LAKE MOUNTAIN SUMMIT AREAS

Aspect	South
Height	50'
Quality	
Approach	40 min, easy
Summary	Broken, mostly unexplored cliffs near a pretty mountain summit.

These are the smaller cliffs and slabs nestled in the blowdown that lies directly below the ridge near the summit of Silver Lake Mountain. The area could use more exploration.

1 The Mercury Program 5.9+ PG 50'

Start: From the open rocky viewpoint at the top of Silver Lake Mountain, walk about 100' further along the ridge on a good herd path. At the first area with a view, follow a path down around some small ledges which get larger if you follow the wall. This leads to a slab with a ledge and a small overhang with a couple of boulders wedged in between. Begin below and 10' left of these small boulders. To the left is a chimney and a 30'-high column of stacked boulders.

P1 5.9+ PG: Follow small holds to a small shelf, then friction with no protection to the top of a slab. Go right 5' to the wedged boulders and follow a dirty crack straight up. 50'

FA Apr 3, 2012, Eric Bretthauer

CLEMENTS POND TRAIL

Location	Keene, accessed from NYS 9N and Styles Brook Road
Summary	Collection of cliffs along the newly constructed Clements Pond Trail.

1	1	1	2					5
-5.6	5.7	5.8	5.9	5.10	5.11	5.12	5.13+	total

The Clements Mountain tract is part of the Wilmington Wild Forest, featuring Clements Mountain and some rolling country to its west, including Clements Pond. Two cliffs have been identified and developed within this tract. The DEC has recently routed a fishing access trail from Styles Brook Road to Clements Pond, which provides convenient access to these cliffs. The rock is somewhat similar to the Pitchoff Chimney cliff, in that it is sandy, red, sometimes fragile, and has horizontal features.

HISTORY

The cliffs were located by Tom DuBois in May, 2010 during his routine explorations of the area. The extremely convenient state trail was constructed in 2009, as part of the UMP for the Wilmington Wild Forest.

Matt Way of "Team Nasty".
Photo by Jessica Gladdis.

Northern Mountains

DIRECTIONS (MAP PAGE 436)

From Keene (0.0), go north on NYS 9N. At 3.0 miles, turn right on Styles Brook Road (labeled Glen Road on some maps). Climb the steep hill until the road levels off. You will pass the driveway of the Keene Farm (the hut owned by the Alpine Club of Canada) on your left. At 4.0 miles (and 600' past the driveway), park on the right (south) side of the road, at a pullout that will accommodate 3 cars. There is a DEC sign at the trailhead.

Enter the woods on the north side of the road. The trail is marked with blue discs and begins flat, then climbs moderately, crossing and re-crossing a small brook.

Clements Pond Trail
THE TOWERS OF THE TEETH

Aspect	Southwest
Height	80'
Quality	
Approach	20 min, easy
Summary	Two promontories of rock with exploratory routes.

The Towers of the Teeth are two promontories of rock extending from the hillside, joined by a sandy neck of land. The upper tower is to the left, and the lower tower is below it to the right. Access to the tops of the towers is to climbers left of the upper tower, or by scrambling up between the towers. The tops of the towers have panoramic views extending from Giant around to Sentinel.

DIRECTIONS

Follow the trail for 17 minutes to where you can glimpse a cliff through the trees on the right. Continue on the trail as it goes slightly downhill to a low point. There is a large three-trunked oak tree left of the trail here (with one dead trunk), and a small cairn right of the trail. (There is another large three-trunked oak tree about 50' further along the trail.) When there are no leaves, the cliff is visible through the trees on the right. Leave the trail at a cairn at the low point and walk easily downhill a couple hundred feet through open woods to the cliff 598498,4906928.

Upper Tower

1 Thangorodrim 5.8- PG 50'

Start: At a clean, right-facing, low-angle corner with an extremely thin crack, which widens to hands 20' up.
P1 5.8- PG: Climb the corner, initially on balancy face moves with very tiny gear, until the crack opens up and the climbing and the gear become much easier. Finish on a large, pleasant ledge. 50'
Descent: Rappel from the fixed anchor for the neighboring route, or scramble up blocks to the top of the tower
Gear: Standard rack plus thin nuts.
FA May 16, 2010, Tom DuBois, Ellen DuBois

2 Hobbit's Way 5.6 G 50'

Start: At a wide crack–chimney, 8' right of Thangorodrim.
P1 5.6 G: Up the chimney for 6', then up a short, left-rising ramp to a crack. Up the crack to a large ledge and a tree with a fixed anchor. 50'
FA May 16, 2010, Tom DuBois, Ellen DuBois

3 The Silmaril 5.7 G 70'

Start: From Hobbit's Way, walk downhill and right 35' past a blocky, broken, right-facing corner to a reddish right-facing corner with a large, rotten-looking crack that widens to an alcove 15' up. Above the alcove are two dihedrals (the upper left dihedral is moderately steep and capped by a roof, the lower right dihedral is lower-angled and disappears out of sight). Begin at the large, rotten looking crack. There is a big, freshly-fallen, orange-red block (the "Silmaril") on the ground near the base.
P1 5.7 G: Climb the crack to the alcove. Pull up and left (crux) into the upper-left dihedral, and climb this. Step right around the roof at the top, and then up to a small birch tree cluster. 70'
Descent: Go left and rappel Hobbit's Way.
Gear: Standard rack plus a 3"-4" cam for the crux.
FA Jul 5, 2010, Tom DuBois, Ellen DuBois

4 The Oath of Fëanor Project

An open project. Like Fëanor's Oath, this starts out looking reasonable and then becomes a problem. Begin the large rotten-looking crack as for The Silmaril, climb to the alcove, and continue in the lower right dihedral as it narrows, and then finally inverts and becomes a rising hand traverse under a large roof. Once past the right end of the roof, climb straight up a few feet, then back left to the same finish as The Silmaril.

Lower Tower

The left end of the lower tower begins 75' right of The Silmaril, past an outcrop and a brushy side hill. Find some broken ledges and cracks, and then a left-facing corner capped by a roof 15' up. 20' right of the left-facing corner is a vertical, straight-up crack which overhangs slightly for the first 10'; this is Morannon.

5 Morannon Project

This open project begins 20' right of a left-facing corner at a vertical, overhanging crack. A strenuous start leads to easier crack climbing into a left-facing corner and a blocky finish. About 45' long.

Clements Pond Trail
FISHERMAN'S WALL

Aspect	Southwest
Height	80'
Quality	★
Approach	20 min, easy
Summary	Two routes on a trailside cliff.

This wall also has wonderful views from its top, and nu-

Northern Mountains

merous blueberries in season. The key to finding the routes on this wall is the obvious recent rockfall at the foot of the center of the wall. The two routes are on either side of this rockfall area.

DIRECTIONS
Follow the trail for 20 minutes to the base of the cliff, which sits about 30' off to the right. This is about 3 minutes past the turnoff for The Towers of the Teeth, and just after a switchback in the trail 598302,4906020. Past this point, the trail continues another half mile mostly downhill to Clements Pond.

6 Fish Story 5.9 PG 80' ★★
Start: About 20' left of the recent rockfall (which is at the foot of the center of the wall), at some easy blocks, with a 4" birch tree growing out of the cliff 12' up to (climber's) left.

P1 5.9 G: Scramble up the blocks, and then left past the birch tree onto a left-rising ledge. Walk up the ledge to the pile of blocks below the spectacular headwall. Climb straight up the headwall on a series of disjointed cracks to a fine ledge, and then up the last crux bit for 10' to the top. 80'

Gear: Standard rack with micro nuts or ball nuts for the last section.
FA Jul 3, 2010, Tom DuBois, Ellen DuBois

7 Fishin' Cruise 5.9 G 70' ★
Start: About 20' right of the rockfall (which is at the foot of the center of the wall), a roof line develops about 12' up. Begin at the obvious flaring crack that splits the center of the roof.

P1 5.9 G: A strenuous start through the roof (crux) leads to easier climbing as the crack swings left past a small birch tree, and then up to the top. 70'

Descent: There is a fixed anchor on a tree 10' to the right.
FA Jul 3, 2010, Tom DuBois, Ellen DuBois

TITUSVILLE MOUNTAIN

Location	In Titusville Mountain State Forest, south of Malone off NY 30
Aspect	Southeast
Height	300'
Quality	
Approach	20 min, moderate
Summary	A barely explored slab with high-quality rock located in a wild and scenic area just outside the Adirondack Park boundary.

	1	1	1	1				4
-5.6	5.7	5.8	5.9	5.10	5.11	5.12	5.13+	total

This cliff lies just outside the northern boundary of the Adirondack Park in Titusville Mountain State Forest. The cliff sits in a beautiful setting high on Titusville Mountain with an unspoiled view. The high-quality rock is grippy and low-angled, offering good potential for long, traditionally-protected crack and slab climbs.

There's good car camping in the grassy clearings along the Lee Road Truck Trail, a rough dirt road that provides access to the cliff.

Climbers have so far used the route **Titusville Express** to access Tomahawk Ledge, the starting point for all the routes on the Tomahawk Wall. The Tomahawk Wall is a clean, dry face with quality routes. It has a large tomahawk-shaped block perched on a horizontal in the middle of the wall with a perfect 60'-tall handcrack directly above it.

To the right of **Titusville Express**, the cliff base is difficult to navigate, with broken ledges that fade into the ravine. There is an ever-steepening, 300'-tall slab with water streaks that go up to a blocky headwall; the winter route **Milking Time** (M4 WI3+) is located here and follows the leftmost water streak. To the left of **Titusville Express** is additional route potential.

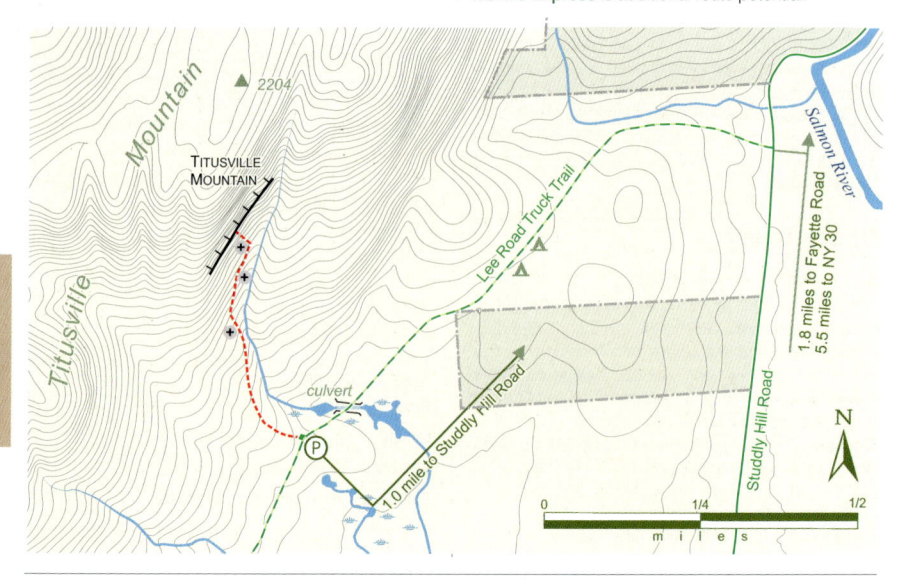

492

Northern Mountains

DIRECTIONS (MAP PAGE 492)

Locate the junction (0.0 mile) of NY 30 and Fayette Road (CR 41), 23.8 miles north of Paul Smiths (the intersection of NY 86 and NY 30) and roughly 17 miles south of Malone. Go east on the Fayette Road, past the Upper Titus Mountain Ski Area at 2.9 miles. At 3.7 miles, turn right on Studdly Hill Road (aka Duane Road), just before the dam in Chasm Falls. Go south on Studdly Hill Road. Just past a red house, at 5.5 miles, turn right on the Lee Road Truck Trail (aka Tamarack Trail, aka "Secondary 78") 0561734,4952672.

Lee Road is a seasonal road that turns into a 4WD trail. The parking is exactly one mile down this road, and it's in relatively good condition to that point. With care, a high clearance 2WD vehicle can make the trip, but expect some loose gravel and overgrown sides. At 6.0 miles, reach some grassy clearings with the first view of the cliff to the right. Good car camping here 561175,4952414. Continue downhill and at 6.4 miles, reach a low point with a beaver pond on the left (which you can see through a sparse screening of trees) and a muddy area on the right. You can see the cliff up and right. Continue uphill to where the road begins to level at 6.5 miles, and park at the first place possible on the right, room for 1 car 0560565,4951984. You can also park before the beaver pond.

Head into the woods behind the parking, and locate an old overgrown logging road. (There is some random blue flagging around; don't follow this.) About 400' up the logging road, head right, and walk downhill to a small stream that feeds the beaver pond. Follow this drainage upstream staying on its left. The stream bends to the north and a low, moss-covered cliff band and talus field will appear on the left. Just after the stream enters the talus, look for cairns that head uphill towards the cliff. Follow the cairns west to reach the "Wall of Horizontals"—a 40'-wide, 20'-tall wall, the left half of which is mossy, the right half laced with horizontal cracks. Walk around this on the left, and claw up a steep grass and fern slope to the cliff 0560352,4952432. Walk 40' right, staying above the Wall of Horizontals to a low tongue of slab; the route **Titusville Express** begins here.

DESCENT

Rappel from the maple tree anchor at top of the **Tomahawk Crack** with a 70m rope to Tomahawk Ledge.

HISTORY

Having grown up nearby, Michael Miletich explored the area as a kid. On a winter visit home in 2008 he rediscovered the cliff and realized the area's potential to hold a large number of quality ice climbs. He returned in 2009 to climb the winter route **Milking Time** with Mike and Amelia Whalen. Further exploration revealed cracks up high that Miletich felt deserved a ground-up attempt. Several years passed with no partners, so he finally just threw a rope down and cleaned and climbed all the routes by self belay. In 2012 he returned with Emily Butler and led all the routes.

1 Titusville Express 5.9 G 125' ★★★

This route provides access to Tomahawk Ledge where other routes begin.

Start: At the toe of the cliff with a large cherry tree on a ledge 25' up.

P1 5.9 G: Go up low-angle rock to a stance below a bolt. Move left to an arête and climb this past more bolts to a left-rising fingercrack. Climb this, then head up and right to an overlap and another left-rising crack. Follow this to a triangular ledge with a large spruce tree—Tomahawk Ledge. 125'

History: The original route started up and right by climbing a tree, then swinging on branches to gain the rock.
FA Oct 12, 2012, Mike Miletich, Emily Butler

2 The Chopping Block 5.10a G 125' ★★★

A fun variation to approach the handcrack on **Tomahawk Crack**.

Start: On Tomahawk Ledge. (Climb **Titusville Express** to gain this ledge.)

P1 5.10a G: Head up and left past a small maple to a series of folds in a left-facing corner. Make a well-protected move though the folds to a splitter crack and a fun pull up onto the left side of a tomahawk-shaped block beneath a short crack. Climb the short crack past a bolt to an overlap. Undercling left to a short corner and a perch beneath another bolt. Foot traverse the thin seam to a crack finish. 125'
FA Oct 12, 2012, Mike Miletich, Emily Butler

3 The Tomahawk Crack 5.7 G 125' ★★★★★

Start: On Tomahawk Ledge. (Climb **Titusville Express** to gain this ledge.)

P1 5.7 G: (V1) Head straight up a stepped corner to a stance under a flake. Climb a solid flake to its end, then make a committing slab move (harder if you're short) to a stance under a tomahawk-shaped block. Move easily around the right side of the block and up to a perfect handcrack. At its top, foot traverse right to another short, fun, flaring crack to a slab move topout. 125'

V1 5.8 G: Climb the first half of chopping block and step right to the tomahawk crack.
FA Oct 12, 2012, Mike Miletich, Emily Butler

4 Crack of the Titans 5.8 G 150' ★★★

Climbs the obvious "hex munching" handcrack system right of **Tomahawk Crack**.

Start: Same as **Tomahawk Crack**.

P1 5.8 G: Head directly out right onto a slab. Climb up and right, passing over a crack to an outside corner. Move into the corner and up through the "rhino horn" to a roof. Pull the roof and climb a fistcrack heading towards blocky left-facing flakes. Gain the serpentine hex-munching crack system, and climb this to a flared crack finish. 150'
FA Oct 12, 2012, Mike Miletich, Emily Butler

Appendix A: Grade Conversion

YDS	V	UIAA	FR	AUS	SAX	SCA	BRA	UK			
5.2		II	1	7-8	II	3		D difficult			
5.3		III	2	9-10	III	3+			VD very difficult		
5.4		IV- / IV	3	11-12		4				HVD hard very difficult	
5.5		IV+		13		4+					S severe
5.6		V-	4	14		5-		HS hard severe	4a		
5.7		V / V+		15	VIIa	5			VS	4c	
5.8		VI-	5a	16	VIIb	5+	4 / 4+		5a very severe		
5.9	V0	VI	5b	17	VIIc	6-	5 / 5+			HVS hard very severe	5a / E1
5.10a		VI+	5c	18	VIIIa	6	6a	5b		5b	5c
5.10b		VII-	6a	19	VIIIb	6+	6b		5c		
5.10c		VII	6a+	20	VIIIc		6c	E2 6a	E3 6a	6a	
5.10d	V1	VI+	6b	21	IXa	7-	7a			E4 6a	6a
5.11a		VIII-	6b+	22	IXb	7	7b				
5.11b	V2		6c	23	IXc	7+	7c	6b		6b	E5
5.11c		VIII	6c+	24							
5.11d	V3	VIII+	7a	25	Xa	8- / 8	8a		6c		6c
5.12a		IX-	7a+	26	Xb	8+	8b	E6			
5.12b	V4		7b	27			8c				
5.12c	V5	IX	7b+	28	Xc	9-	9a		E7		7a
5.12d	V6	IX+	7c	29			9b	6c			
5.13a	V7	X-	7c+	30		9	9c	7a	7a	E8	
5.13b	V8	X	8a	31	XIa		10a				E9
5.13c	V9	X+	8a+	32	XIb	9+	10b		7a		
5.13d	V10	XI-	8b	33			10c	E10	7a		
5.14a	V11	XI	8b+	34	XIc		11a			E11	7b
5.14b	V12	XI+	8c	35			11b				
5.14c	V13	XII-	8c+	36			11c	7b			
5.14d	V14		9a	37			12a		7b		
5.15a	V15		9a+				12b				
5.15b	V16		9b								

safe (G protection)
bold (R or X protection)

Appendix B: Cliffs by Category

Canoe Approach Crags

A boat is required, or highly recommended, to reach these cliffs:

CLIFF	REGION	PAGE
Baldface Mountain	Indian Lake	253
Bluff Island	Northern Mountains	424
Grass Pond Mountain	Cranberry Lake	392
Jolly Roger Slab	Lake George	87
Long Pond	Indian Lake	240
Pulpit Rock	Wilmington Notch	386
Rogers Rock, Rogers Slide	Lake George	92

Canoe-Optional Crags

These cliffs have paddling opportunities nearby, or an approach by water is preferred to hiking the entire distance. In many cases, the boat approach is faster and more pleasant.

CLIFF	REGION	PAGE
Barn Rock	Lake Champlain	145
Cat Mountain	Cranberry Lake	396
Good Luck Mountain	Southern Mountains	323
Henderson Cliff	High Peaks	428
Hitchins Pond Cliff	Cranberry Lake	390
Lake Lila	Cranberry Lake	387
Mitchell Ponds	Old Forge	362
Palisades	Lake Champlain	141

Backpacking and Climbing

These destinations offer the opportunity to backpack into a campsite near the cliff—at the base or on the top. While it is possible to camp nearly anywhere and at almost every cliff, these destinations are far from the road and have excellent camp spots. Most of the cliffs in the High Peaks make excellent backpacking destinations.

CLIFF	REGION	PAGE
Barn Rock	Lake Champlain	145
Barton High Cliff	Lake George	117
Cat Mountain	Cranberry Lake	396
Good Luck Mountain	Southern Mountains	323
Grass Pond Mountain	Cranberry Lake	392
Huckleberry Mountain	Indian Lake	214
Long Pond	Indian Lake	240
Middle Settlement Lake	Old Forge	353
Pharaoh Mountain	Lake George	122
Snowy Mountain, Main Face	Indian Lake	248
Washbowl Pond	Chapel Pond Pass	250
West Canada Cliff	Southern Mountains	331

Areas Near Water

These cliffs, and areas, are close to water and afford the opportunity to combine climbing and swimming.

CLIFF	REGION	PAGE
Avalanche Lake	High Peaks	507
Between The Lakes	Keene	372
Bluff Island	Northern Mountains	424
Boquet Canyon	Chapel Pond Pass	181
Boxcar	Chapel Pond Pass	183
Buck Mountain	Lake George	67
Chapel Pond Gully Cliff	Chapel Pond Pass	223
Chapel Pond Slab	Chapel Pond Pass	213
Eagle Falls	Old Forge	364
Grass Pond Mountain	Cranberry Lake	392
Gull Pond Cliff	Lake George	132
Hitchins Pond Cliff	Cranberry Lake	390
Hudson River Crag	Lake George	79
Lake Lila	Cranberry Lake	387
Middle Settlement Lake	Old Forge	353
Otter Lake	Southern Mountains	303
Pilot Knob	Lake George	74
Pitchoff Chimney Cliff	Keene	352
Roaring Brook Falls	Chapel Pond Pass	316
Rogers Rock	Lake George	87
Shelving Rock	Lake George	38
Tilmans Arete	Chapel Pond Pass	234
Washbowl Pond	Chapel Pond Pass	250
Whitewater Walls	Chapel Pond Pass	183

Toprope Areas

The areas listed here have easy access to the top for setting topropes, an accessible cliff base, and few obstructions for dropping ropes. Plan on building your own anchors with long cord and/or protection. Review the regulations in the relevant section regarding group size, and be sure to share the cliff with others.

CLIFF	REGION	PAGE
Baker Mountain	Northern Mountains	425
Beer Walls	Chapel Pond Pass	285
Bluff Island	Northern Mountains	424
Brain, The	Lake George	78
Chapel Pond Viewpoint	Chapel Pond Pass	251
County Line Mountain	Northern Mountains	420
Courthouse, The	High Peaks	491
Crane Mountain, Measles Group	Indian Lake	164
Crane Mountain, The Prows	Indian Lake	159
Creature Wall	Chapel Pond Pass	236
Eagle Falls	Old Forge	364
Flatrock Mountain	Old Forge	213

Appendix B

CLIFF	REGION	PAGE
Grass Pond Mountain	Cranberry Lake	392
Jewels and Gem Wall	Chapel Pond Pass	*198*
King Philip's Spring Wall	Lake Champlain	*147*
Lake Pleasant Quarry	Southern Mountains	338
Ledge Mountain (Nobleboro)	Old Forge	349
Lost T	Southern Mountains	306
Middle Settlement Lake	Old Forge	353
New Buck	Lake George	69
Noonmark Mountain	High Peaks	*480*
Notch Mountain, The Slabs	Wilmington Notch	*389*
Outlet Wall	Chapel Pond Pass	256
Owls Head Mountain	Keene	*349*
Panther Mountain	Southern Mountains	334
Pitchoff Chimney Cliff, Practice Wall	Keene	*362*
Silver Lake, Midway Cliff	Northern Mountains	464
South Bay Roadcut	Cranberry Lake	392
South Colton	Northern Mountains	406
Spruce Hill Crag	Keene	*330*
Stewarts Ledge	Lake George	74
Tanager Face	Chapel Pond Pass	*230*
Wright Peak Cliff	High Peaks	*525*

Mountaintop Destinations

These cliffs are positioned on top of a mountain or pointed viewpoint. In other words, when you reach the top of the climb, you're on top of a summit.

CLIFF	REGION	PAGE
Bald Mountain, Summit Cliff	Old Forge	360
Castle Rock	Indian Lake	279
Cat Mountain	Cranberry Lake	396
Catamount Mountain	Northern Mountains	433
Chimney Mountain	Indian Lake	257
Crane Mountain, Summit Cliffs	Indian Lake	153
Good Luck Mountain	Southern Mountains	323
Gothics	High Peaks	*468*
Hitchins Pond Cliff	Cranberry Lake	390
Mt Colden	High Peaks	*509*
Noonmark Mountain	High Peaks	*480*
Notch Mountain, The Slabs	Wilmington Notch	*389*
Owls Head Lookout	High Peaks	*463*
Owls Head Mountain	Keene	*349*
Poke-O Moonshine, Summit Cliff	Lake Champlain	*115*
Rooster Comb	High Peaks	*485*
Silver Lake, C Chimney Cliff	Northern Mountains	447
Silver Lake, Potter Mountain	Northern Mountains	470

CLIFF	REGION	PAGE
Silver Lake, Summit Cliff	Northern Mountains	447
Wright Peak Cliff	High Peaks	*525*

Multipitch Climbing Areas

These cliffs offer mostly multipitch climbing, or have at least one noteworthy multipitch climb. Note that many scrambling routes in the High Peaks should be treated as multipitch climbs (for example, Mt Colden, Giant Mountain, Basin Mountain, Marcy East Face, and Dix Mountain).

CLIFF	REGION	PAGE
Avalanche Lake	High Peaks	*507*
Barton High Cliff	Lake George	117
Big Slide Mountain	High Peaks	*494*
Chapel Pond Gully Cliff	Chapel Pond Pass	223
Chapel Pond Slab	Chapel Pond Pass	*213*
Crane Mountain, Bellavista Slab	Indian Lake	174
Crane, Beaverview	Indian Lake	146
Deer Pass	Northern Mountains	417
Gothics, South Face	High Peaks	*473*
Hurricane Crag	Keene	*321*
Marcy, Panther Gorge	High Peaks	*498*
Moss Cliff	Wilmington Notch	*392*
Pharaoh Mountain	Lake George	122
Pitchoff Chimney Cliff	Keene	*352*
Poke-O Moonshine, Main Face	Lake Champlain	*31*
Poke-O Slab	Lake Champlain	*106*
Porter Mountain	High Peaks	*502*
Rogers Rock, Rogers Slide	Lake George	92
Silver Lake, Center of Progress	Northern Mountains	453
Silver Lake, Outback Slab	Northern Mountains	467
Silver Lake, Potter Mountain	Northern Mountains	470
Silver Lake, Summit Cliff	Northern Mountains	447
Sugarloaf Mountain	Indian Lake	263
Upper Washbowl	Chapel Pond Pass	*240*
Upper Wolfjaw Cliff	High Peaks	*482*
Wallface	High Peaks	*431*

Slab Climbing Areas

These cliffs offer friction climbing.

CLIFF	REGION	PAGE
Avalanche Lake	High Peaks	*507*
Basin Mountain	High Peaks	*487*
Big Slide Mountain	High Peaks	*494*
Chapel Pond Slab	Chapel Pond Pass	*213*
Crane Mountain, Bellavista Slab	Indian Lake	174
Crane, Beaverview	Indian Lake	146

496   Page numbers in this volume   *Page numbers in Volume 1*

Appendix B

CLIFF	REGION	PAGE
Emperor Slab	Chapel Pond Pass	*209*
Giant Mountain, West Face	High Peaks	*465*
Gothics, Rainbow Slide	High Peaks	*477*
Marcy East Face	High Peaks	*501*
Moss Lake Slab	Old Forge	360
Mt Colden	High Peaks	*509*
Notch Mountain, The Slabs	Wilmington Notch	*389*
Poke-O Slab	Lake Champlain	*106*
Rogers Rock, Rogers Slide	Lake George	92
Silver Lake, Outback Slab	Northern Mountains	467
Silver Lake, Potter Mountain	Northern Mountains	470
Snowy Mountain, Lower Slabs	Indian Lake	252
Sugarloaf Mountain	Indian Lake	263

Quick-to-Dry Areas

These cliffs dry quickly after a rain.

CLIFF	REGION	PAGE
Ark Wall	Lake George	60
Beer Walls	Chapel Pond Pass	*285*
Chimney Mountain	Indian Lake	257
Deadwater	Lake Champlain	*155*
Lake Pleasant Quarry	Southern Mountains	338
Notch Mountain, The Slabs	Wilmington Notch	*389*
Owls Head Mountain	Keene	*349*
Pitchoff Chimney Cliff	Keene	*352*
Potash Cliff	Lake George	80
Shelving Rock	Lake George	38
Silver Lake, C Chimney Cliff	Northern Mountains	447
Silver Lake, Potter Mountain	Northern Mountains	470
Snowy Mountain, Main Face	Indian Lake	248
Spider's Web	Chapel Pond Pass	*258*
Stewarts Ledge	Lake George	74
Tilmans Arete	Chapel Pond Pass	*234*
Typhoon Wall, Ward Cleaver Buttress	Keene	*331*

Areas with Sport Routes

These cliffs have several sport routes or at least one notable sport route.

CLIFF	REGION	PAGE
Ark Wall	Lake George	60
Beaver Brook	Wilmington Notch	*420*
Beer Walls	Chapel Pond Pass	*285*
Brain, The	Lake George	78
Charcoal Kiln Quarry	Northern Mountains	423

CLIFF	REGION	PAGE
Crane Mountain, Measles Group	Indian Lake	164
Eagle Falls	Old Forge	364
Good Luck Mountain	Southern Mountains	323
Gothics, South Face	High Peaks	*473*
Green Lake	Southern Mountains	301
Honey Pot, The	Lake Champlain	*145*
Huckleberry, Hard Guy Wall	Indian Lake	226
King Wall	Chapel Pond Pass	*200*
Little Crow Mountain	Keene	*337*
Little Johnson	Lake Champlain	*169*
Lost Hunters	Southern Mountains	315
Makomis Mountain	Lake Champlain	*151*
Martini Wall	Chapel Pond Pass	*236*
McMartin Cliff	Southern Mountains	319
New Buck	Lake George	69
Otter Lake	Southern Mountains	303
Poke-O Moonshine, Main Face	Lake Champlain	*31*
Potash Cliff	Lake George	80
Rogers Rock, Campground Wall	Lake George	88
Santa Claus Hill	Wilmington Notch	*418*
Shanty Cliff	Indian Lake	231
Shelving Rock	Lake George	38
Silver Lake, Mud Pond	Northern Mountains	486
Silver Lake, Potter Mountain	Northern Mountains	470
Snowy Mountain, Main Face	Indian Lake	248
Spanky's Wall	Chapel Pond Pass	*190*
Stewarts Ledge	Lake George	74
Typhoon Wall, Ward Cleaver Buttress	Keene	*331*
Wild Pines	Lake George	106

Areas with Good Cracks

These cliffs have excellent cracks, or at least one exceptional crack.

CLIFF	REGION	PAGE
Alcatraz	Wilmington Notch	*408*
Avalanche Lake, The Fin	High Peaks	*520*
Bald Mountain	Old Forge	356
Barkeater Cliff	Keene	*339*
Bear Den, right side	Wilmington Notch	*418*
Beer Walls	Chapel Pond Pass	*285*
Cat Mountain	Cranberry Lake	396
Crane Mountain	Indian Lake	140
Creature Wall	Chapel Pond Pass	*236*
Deadwater	Lake Champlain	*155*
High Falls Crag	Wilmington Notch	*410*
Hurricane Crag	Keene	*321*
Jewels and Gem Wall	Chapel Pond Pass	*198*
Long Pond	Indian Lake	240

Appendix B

CLIFF	REGION	PAGE
Lost Hunters	Southern Mountains	315
Lost T	Southern Mountains	306
Moss Cliff	Wilmington Notch	*392*
Noonmark Mountain	High Peaks	480
Owls Head Mountain	Keene	*349*
Pinnacle Mountain	Southern Mountains	295
Pitchoff Chimney Cliff	Keene	*352*
Poke-O Moonshine, Main Face	Lake Champlain	*31*
Poke-O Moonshine, Upper Tiers	Lake Champlain	*114*
Polar Soldier Wall	Wilmington Notch	*415*
Silver Lake, Mud Pond	Northern Mountains	486
Silver Lake, Summit Cliff	Northern Mountains	447
Silver Lake, Tsunami Wall	Northern Mountains	461
Spider's Web	Chapel Pond Pass	*258*
Starbuck Mountain	Indian Lake	282
Tongue Mountain	Lake George	111
Twin Falls	Northern Mountains	399
Upper Washbowl	Chapel Pond Pass	*240*

Bug-Free Areas

Unfortunately, there's no such thing as bug free, but these areas have fewer bugs due to insect control, elevation, or wind.

CLIFF	REGION	PAGE
Chapel Pond Pass	Chapel Pond Pass	*177*
Eagle Falls	Old Forge	364
Owls Head Mountain	Keene	*349*
Pitchoff Chimney Cliff	Keene	*352*
Rogers Rock, Rogers Slide	Lake George	92
Shelving Rock	Lake George	38
Stewarts Ledge	Lake George	74

Areas to Visit When it's Hot

These areas have shade and stay cooler.

CLIFF	REGION	PAGE
Avalanche Lake	High Peaks	*507*
Barkeater Cliff	Keene	*339*
Lost Hunters	Southern Mountains	315
Lost T	Southern Mountains	306
Martini Wall	Chapel Pond Pass	*236*
McMartin Cliff	Southern Mountains	319
Notch Mountain, The Slabs	Wilmington Notch	*389*
Pinnacle Mountain	Southern Mountains	295
Tanager Face	Chapel Pond Pass	*230*
Wild Pines	Lake George	106

Areas to Visit When It's Cold

These areas are good when it's cold due to sun exposure, elevation, or protection from wind. On a sunny, windlesss day, you can climb at many of these late or early in the season. Check the cliff's aspect to determine the best time of day.

CLIFF	REGION	PAGE
Beaver Brook	Wilmington Notch	*420*
Deadwater	Lake Champlain	*155*
Eagle Falls	Old Forge	364
Gull Pond Cliff	Lake George	132
Hurricane Crag	Keene	*321*
Pitchoff Chimney Cliff	Keene	*352*
Poke-O Moonshine, Main Face	Lake Champlain	*31*
Poke-O Slab	Lake Champlain	*106*
Potash Cliff	Lake George	80
Rogers Rock, Rogers Slide	Lake George	92
Shelving Rock	Lake George	38
Silver Lake, Potter Mountain	Northern Mountains	470
Spider's Web	Chapel Pond Pass	*258*
Stewarts Ledge	Lake George	74

Areas to Visit in Light Rain

These cliffs stay dry in a light rain.

CLIFF	REGION	PAGE
Ark Wall	Lake George	60
Beer Walls, Clutch and Cruise Cave	Chapel Pond Pass	*309*
King Wall	Chapel Pond Pass	*200*
Moss Cliff, Aid Wall		*392*
Potash Cliff	Lake George	80
Shelving Rock	Lake George	38
Shelving Rock, Main Face	Lake George	44
Silver Lake, Mud Pond	Northern Mountains	486
Spider's Web	Chapel Pond Pass	*258*

Areas with Clean Aid Routes

These areas are good for clean aid climbing.

CLIFF	REGION	PAGE
Beer Walls, Upper Beer Wall	Chapel Pond Pass	*289*
High Falls Crag	Wilmington Notch	*410*
Moss Cliff	Wilmington Notch	*392*
Poke-O Moonshine, Main Face	Lake Champlain	*31*
Spider's Web	Chapel Pond Pass	*258*
Wallface	High Peaks	*431*

Page numbers in this volume   *Page numbers in Volume 1*

Appendix C: Private Land Crags

The cliffs listed below are not documented in this book but have a known climbing history. All of these cliffs are on private land. Access to these cliffs requires permission from the landowner, whether it be an organization, a hunting club, a paper company or an individual. A few cliffs, such as Mt. Jo (Adirondack Mountain Club) and Indian Head (Ausable Club), are of historic significance, and climbing is permitted by membership in those clubs. Other cliffs are frequently visited because climbers have been granted permission by the landowner.

Do not trespass at these cliffs. Trespassing may compromise the access for those climbers who were mindful enough to contact the landowners beforehand. If you ask permission, the worst that can happen is a "no" from the landowner. If you are declined access, respect the landowner's decision and go climb somewhere else. This book has no shortage of destinations that are accessible to the public.

Some of these cliffs may become accessible in the future through conservation easements or direct acquisition by the state. Be sure to check www.AdirondackRock.com for updates.

- 8 Eyes Wall
- Anthony's Nose
- Antone Mountain
- Aunt Mary's Kitchen
- Broughton Ledge
- Cartehena Cliff
- Cartoon Cliff
- Clear Pond
- Crane Mountain, Northernmost Wall
- Crane Mountain: Putnam Farm Wall
- Diameter Mountain
- Ebenezer Mountain
- Hadley Pond
- Knob Mountain
- Mosher Cliff
- Moxham Quarry
- Otis Mountain
- Realty Wall
- Sherwood Forest
- Shippee's Ledge
- South Bay
- Super Face Wall
- The New New
- Willsboro

Private cliffs described in previous guidebooks

- Cobble Hill
- East Keene Hill
- Haystack Mountain
- Indian Head
- Moxham Dome
- Mountain Shadows
- Mt Gilligan
- Mt Jo
- Petit Mountain

Appendix D: Advertiser Index

Access Fund . . . . vol. 2, 386	Mountain Skills . . . . vol. 1, 424
Alpine Adventures . . . . vol. 1, 16	Outdoor Gear Exchange . . . . Cover flaps
Alpine Development Knocepts . . . . vol. 2, 16	Outdoor Research . . . . vol. 1, 178
Alpine Endeavors . . . . vol. 1, 28; vol. 2, 294	Patagonia . . . . Inside front cover
American Alpine Club . . . . vol. 2, 348	Paul Smiths . . . . vol. 1, 180
AMGA . . . . vol. 2, 404	Petra Cliffs . . . . vol. 2, 16
Bounding Bee . . . . vol. 2, 519	Petzl . . . . vol. 1, 320
Climberism . . . . vol. 2, 404	Plattsburgh Shoe Hospital . . . . vol. 1, 58
Cloudsplitter . . . . vol. 1, 180	Rock and Snow . . . . vol. 1, 16; vol. 2, 404
DMM . . . . Back cover	Rocksport . . . . vol. 1, 424; vol. 2, 36
Five Ten . . . . vol. 1, 16	Scarpa . . . . vol. 1, 384
Fountain Square Outfitters . . . . vol. 2, 138	St. Lawrence University . . . . vol. 1, 178; vol. 2, 16
High Peaks Cyclery . . . . vol. 1, 490	SUNY Adirondack . . . . vol. 2, 36
La Cordée . . . . vol. 1, 259	The Crux . . . . vol. 1, 57
MEC . . . . vol. 1, 537; vol. 2, 501	The Edge . . . . Inside back cover
Mountainside Adventures . . . . vol. 2, 162	The Mountaineer . . . . vol. 1, 178

Appendix E: Local Resources

Gear Shops
These gear shops are located in the Adirondack Park:

Eastern Mountain Sports: Lake Placid, www.ems.com (518.523.2505)

High Peaks Cyclery (vol. 1, 490): Lake Placid, www.highpeakscyclery.com (518.523.3764)

The Mountaineer (vol. 1, 178): Keene Valley, www.mountaineer.com (518.576.2281)

Near the park are the following shops:

Eastern Mountain Sports: Saratoga, www.ems.com (518.580.1505)

Fountain Square Outfitters (vol. 2, 138): Glens Falls, www.fountainsquareoutfitters.com (518.932.8355)

Outdoor Gear Exchange (see cover flaps): Burlington, www.gearx.com (802.860.0190)

Rock and Snow (vol. 1, 16; vol. 2, 404): New Paltz, www.rockandsnow.com (845.255.1311)

Wear on Earth: Potsdam, www.wearonearth.com (315.265.3178)

Climbing Gyms
Gyms are a good place for partners, limited gear, posting, and perhaps cliff updates.

Albany Indoor Rock Gym: Albany, www.airrockgym.com (518.459.7625)

The Crux (vol. 1, 57): Willsboro, www.ClimbTheCrux.com (518.963.4646)

The Edge Halfmoon (see inside back cover): www.theedgehalfmoon.com (518.982.5545)

Petra Cliffs (vol. 2, 16): Burlington, www.petracliffs.com (866.657.3872)

Rocksport (vol. 1, 424; vol. 2, 36): Queensbury, www.rocksportny.com (518.793.4626)

Guide Services
There are many guide services for the park, all of which have licensed guides.

Adirondack Mountain Guides: www.adirondackmountainguides.com (518.576.9556), Ian Osteyee

Adirondack Rock and River Guide Service, Inc.: www.rockandriver.com (518.576.2041), Ed Palen

Alpine Adventures: www.alpineadven.com (518.576.9881), R.L. Stolz

Alpine Development Koncepts (vol. 2, 16): www.alpinedevelopmentkoncepts.com (518.524.3328), Stephen Mergenthaler

Alpine Endeavors (vol. 1, 28; vol. 2, 294): www.alpineendeavors.com (845.658.3094), Marty Molitoris

Cloudsplitter Mountain Guides (vol. 1, 180): www.cloudsplitterguides.com (518.569.8910), Jesse Williams

Eastern Mountain Sports: www.emsclimb.com (800.310.4504), Matt Wiech

High Peaks Mountain Adventures (vol. 1, 490): www.hpmountainguides.com (518.523.3764), Brian Delaney

Mountainside Adventures (vol. 2, 162): www.mtnsideview.com (518.623.2062), Jay Harrison

Mountain Skills (vol. 1, 424): www.mountainskills.biz (845.853.5450), Doug Ferguson

Petracliffs (vol. 2, 16): www.petracliffs.com (518.657.3872), Steve Charest

Rocksport (vol. 1, 424; vol. 2, 36): www.rocksportny.com (518.793.4626) Tom Rosecrans`

MEC

SEND BIG

Burn down big projects with lightness, speed and efficiency. Find ropes, helmets and the widest selection of climbing gear in Canada at MEC.

MEC.CA/CLIMB

Get the MEC app	Available on the App Store	Follow us	Like us	Read us	Sarah Hart
mec.ca/iphone		@mec	fb.com/mec	blog.mec.ca	MEC Climbing Envoy

Andrew Querner, Squamish BC

501

Graded List of Climbs

Aid Routes

Kingdom Come ..... ★★★★★	209
Abracadabra......... ★★★★★	458
Buckwheat .... ★★★★	251
Climb Control to Major Bob .... ★★★★	52
Crown Crack........ ★★★★	150
Psalm 32 .... ★★★★	76
Roof of All Evil....... ★★★★	45
Keep Off Flake .... ★★★	102
Leroy Brown .... ★★★	482
Mission to Mars, The ... ★★★	442
No Man's a Pilot ...... ★★★	446
Wedlock .... ★★★	389
Blinded by Rainbows .... ★★	49
Children and Alcohol .... ★★	404
Crack of Despair........ ★★	117
Mosscalito............ ★★	404
Pan Am .... ★★	406
Positive Progression .... ★★	103
Ramps of Deception..... ★★	104
Adirondack Black Fly Rancher........... ★	402
Dangle 'n Whack Lad ...... ★	90
Gourmet .... ★	448
Grace and Commitment.... ★	91
Mad Cow Disease .... ★	68
Stanley................ ★	483
To Bee or Not to Bee....... ★	153
Atom Smasher	144
Atomic Vomit............	459
B.M.Z., The	462
Because Dogs Can	347
Big White Guy............	291
Catch a Wave	154
Chipmunk Waltz, The	460
Chuting Star	363
Côte d' Azure...........	411
Dead End	462
Desi's Misery...........	187
Direct Start, variation to Knights in Armor	64
Dog's Breakfast............	220
Elusive Dream...........	207
Excitable Boy	72
Huff 'n Puff................	440
Jagger-Richards	447
King of Spades	207
Mortal Strife.............	157
Nettle Crack	109
Neurosis Direct	91
Nutcracker, The..........	278
Perch, The..............	360
PF Flyers' Flying Circus	362
Pharaoh Ocean Wall........	131
Porcelain Forest	207
Princess Leia............	459

Right Place, but Must Have Been the Wrong Time........	463
Scream from on High, A.....	407
Split Beaver.............	381
Sportsmanship, variation to Gamesmanship	73
Upsidaisium	466
Wags on the Wall	441
Whale Crack	459
White Lightning...........	92

3rd class

Bottle, The............. ★★★	466
Corner Scramble..........	217
Lunch Rock Scramble	217
Silver Lake Chimney........	448

4th class

Trap Dike.......... ★★★★★★	515
Eagle, The.......... ★★★	466
East Face .... ★★	488
Summit Direct........... ★	488
Blueberry Scramble	218
Broken Shovel Gully	220
Goodwin-Stanley Route, Gothics Mountain	478
Hunter's Pass Slide.........	528
Old Route, Gothics Mountain.	472
Seagull	334
Tanager Gully	232
Wicked Weed Route, The....	328

5.0

Hollyrock............... ★★	339
Social Climber........... ★	171
Bullhead	261
Dirty Gully	461
Main Summit Route	435
Robin's Rainy Day Route	184
Trub	460

5.1

Walk in the Sky, A ..... ★★★★	228
Easy Ramp .... ★★	371
Journey through the Past . ★★	136
Lead 101 .... ★★	171
New Finger Slide.......... ★	473
Standard Route........... ★	259
Another Walk in the Sky	228
Barbara's Fault	336
Coffee Break	69
Cooties	171
Escalator to Heaven	184
Little Fever..............	169
Stepping-stone	145
Window, The	410

Metacomet .... ★★★	149
And She Was .... ★★	391
Chapel View Arête ..... ★★	232
Joe Hill................ ★★	240
Rickety Pinnacle .... ★★	278
Bogus Dent............ ★	236
Lead 102.............. ★	171
Sleepwalk .... ★	232
Without a Hitch .... ★	391
Beginner's Route...........	449
Black Dog Chimney	424
Daybreak................	149
Falaise.................	221
Fizzle, variation to Gullet.....	234
Golden Sheaves, variation to Morning Stars	150
Gullet	234
Howdy Doody............	235
Le Petit Chien	217
Malaise	221
Mentor.................	433
New Beginning	150
New Finger Connector, variation to North Face Direct	472
North Dike...............	453
Paltry Show	156
Pasta Galore	149
Return Home.............	391
Scruffy	153
Second Lead	198
Sennet.................	421
Sky High	176
Sorcerer's Stone	198
Sword Breaker, variation to Badinage............	150
Zero Gravity Bella	154

5.3

Bob's Knob Standard ... ★★★	220
Pugsley .... ★★★★	469
Wright Wrong Chimney . ★★★	526
Basti .... ★★	240
Contos................ ★★	194
Equinox............... ★★	415
Hydrophobia, Crane Mountain .... ★★	170
Le Jour de Bon Heures... ★★	174
Moosed You .... ★★	363
Morning Stars .... ★★	150
Up on the Mountain ..... ★★	149
Cross-Eyed Orphan .... ★	234
Dirty Diana............. ★	379
Easy Squeeze........... ★	359
Jugs of Beer .... ★	312
Mountain Mist........... ★	230
No Name............... ★	331

502   Page numbers in this volume   *Page numbers in Volume 1*

Graded List of Climbs

Old Route, Hurricane Mountain	★	329
Walk on the Easy Side	★	185
Badinage		150
Child's Play		166
Crack Chimney		480
Dark Streets		160
Easement		467
Fatal Ease		148
Feeble		152
Garden Alone		148
Guide's Gift		164
Heart Thrills		148
I Didn't Give It a Name		331
Irene		278
Jay's Solo		229
Juliet		222
Lane–Harrison		179
Lap Dog		217
Little Ado		243
Margin Slide, The		502
Measly Little Corner		168
Mill Mountain Route		229
Parenthood		348
Phinding Phalaris		358
Pig in a Poke		72
Pine Tree Corner		152
Rock Hop		186
Scout About		211
Sibiletto		221
Silly		149
Silly Willy		148
Slippery Needles		391
Social Pariah		171
Sunshine Slab		351
Tablerock Corner		152
Third-Quarter Profit		149
Tilly's Trench		208
Two Nuts and a Cam		418
Velma's Snatch		445
Willy		229

5.4

Buttress Slide	★★★★	528
Adsit Arête	★★★	369
Colden Slide	★★★	517
Iron Heel, The	★★★	361
Old Route, Rooster Comb	★★★	486
Shipton's Voyage	★★★	235
Snake, The	★★★	45
You're No Spring Chicken Head	★★★	415
3.2	★★	290
Azure	★★	360
Dark Speed	★★	147
Enjoy the Little Things	★★	279
First Lead	★★	196
Glee Club Crack	★★	173
Let Sleeping Bats Lie	★★	193
No Bats Here	★★	193
Ormus the Viking God	★★	389
Paris Parody, A	★★	185
Puzzle	★★	151
Spire Route	★★	274
Sunshine Daydream	★★	415
Tower of Babel, The	★★	369
Yard Work	★★	360
Alter Weg	★	371
Amanita Muscaria	★	355
Barrel of Monkeys	★	339
Black Plague, King Wall	★	201
Bun in the Oven	★	72
Cheap Date	★	229
Circuitous Shit	★	234
Easy Edge	★	428
Folly-Stricken	★	158
Fun Hogs from Hell	★	391
Groupies	★	379
Half-Baked Flake	★	388
It's a Boy	★	80
Let's Go Golfing	★	390
Nervy	★	158
Old Route, Noonmark Mountain	★	481
Overlap It Up	★	259
Short Sharp Shocked	★	164
Solitude, Washbowl Pond	★	253
To Do	★	185
Wiessner Route, Wallface	★	457
Zigzag, Notch Mountain	★	389
Angry Hemorrhoid Chimney		454
Arête's Syndrome		466
Barn Buttress		145
Before The Fall		466
Bo Peep		232
Burke's Path		423
C Crack		443
Caveman's Hairy Backside		260
Chess Club Crack		173
CLN		73
Cozy Corner		276
Dad's Day Off		150
Dental Hygienist		336
Diagonal Chockstone Chimney		307
Dzelarhons		175
Eddy		186
Father's Day		150
Fly Away		422
Foretaste		160
Forgotten Days		147
French Spoof, The		185
Gev's Tree		314
Gnarly		158
Grumpy Rolls		361
Hangover Corner		466
Hangover Direct		193
Home after Dark		285
Hydraulic		185
Jervis's Joke		443
Kristin		193
Little Corner		169
Little Jam, Huckleberry Mountain		216
Lychons		361
Middle Earth		281
Mine Shaft		443
Moksha		349
Ominous Chimney		191
Original Route		475
Ownership		320
Paul's Gondola Ride		286
Plumber's Crack, The Aquarium		222
Pronged Again		341
River Run		186
Route Number 1		184
Scattershot		343
Slot, The		422
Smell of B.O., The		424
Spelunker		470
Sunday Stroll		148
Sunday Stroll		166
Tallywhacker		225
Unfair		118
Wanderer, variation to Gullet		234
Wandering Window		256
Waterhole #3		428
Wretched Wanderer		155

5.5

Catharsis	★★★★★	107
Empress	★★★★★	217
Little Finger	★★★★★	98
Regular Route	★★★★★	219
Afternoon Delight	★★★★	302
Bad Brains	★★★	430
Bottleneck	★★★	466
Cornerstone	★★★	161
Cruise Crack	★★★	158
High Anxiety	★★★	253
N.P.R.	★★★	407
Nescafé	★★★	189
Redrum	★★★	304
Standard Deviation	★★★	519
Backs against the Wall	★★	310
Brinksmanship	★★	95
Case Route	★★	458
Chili Pepper Arête	★★	190
Chocolate Rain	★★	140
Cracklosis	★★	168
Dairy Aire	★★	158
Dragonfly	★★	184
Drama Queen	★★	72
East Face Direct	★★	468
Every Creature's Theme	★★	150
Good Dough	★★	349
Guinness	★★	290
Junior Varsity	★★	45
Left-Hand Route	★★	227
Mycelia	★★	354
New Route	★★	330
Northeast Shoulder Slide	★★	488

Graded List of Climbs

Climb	Rating	Page
On the Fence	★★	182
Over the Rainbow	★★	479
Silent Spring	★★	230
Tourista	★★	63
After Ireland	★	330
Amateur's Edge	★	315
Bailey–Bolliger Route	★	221
Blueberry Flapjacks, variation to Madame Blueberry	★	179
Cross-examination	★	494
Dome Arête	★	169
Every Which Way and Loose	★	163
Four Plus	★	491
Gypsy's Curse	★	368
In the Chimney	★	342
Joshua Climb	★	342
Men of Iron	★	390
Moon Unit	★	438
Planet Claire	★	412
Puppies in a Sack	★	379
Rasputin	★	331
Road Less Traveled	★	388
Rudolph	★	419
Silveretta	★	345
Spiral Staircase	★	186
Team Rocksport	★	69
Toad's Traverse	★	433
Train Wreck	★	71
Trouser Flute	★	158
Ulluwatu	★	175
Wounded Knee	★	184
5.58		289
Ahhh Autumn		255
Amnesia		422
Annie's Crack		72
Autumn Slab		342
Bastille Day		196
Beat the Crowd		147
Blunderbus		343
Bog Spavin		147
Buffalo Soldier		249
Buffaloed Panther, The		432
C & E		236
Caterpillar Chimney		214
China Grove		235
Coors Corner		304
Craterface		169
Daddy, Where Are You?		390
Deep Cleanser		335
Demitasse		229
Dinner Guest		430
Dunce In the Corner		423
Easter's Bunny		169
Easy Monkey		165
Epilogue		423
Exit Lite		158
Fenris		390
Fire Starter		237
Five Small Stones		160
Flu, The		167
Flume		186
Fly in the Ointment		71
Friction Finish		116
Good Housekeeping		373
Goodwin-Stanley Route, Porter Mountain		506
Great Escape, The, Whitewater Walls		184
Gunpowder Corner		315
Hypoxia		168
Jackasses from Downstate		391
Learning the Steps, variation to Burke's Path		423
Learning to Fly		212
Lichen or Not, Bald Mountain		358
Little Chimney		190
Lucille		222
Lunatic Fringe		290
Mister Buzzárd		222
Moosehead		310
Mountain Boots and Pitons		426
New Moon		98
No Nuts, No Seaplanes		281
Nut 'n Left		243
One-Trick Pony		429
Otto Sells Lemons		429
Pimples		170
Princess Bride		51
Prom Night Trickery		429
Quarter-Inch		269
Ray's Ascent		261
Right-Hand Route		228
Rope Toss Wall		277
Runway		116
Scratch		313
Shantyclear		236
Shindig		360
Short Order		274
Shuffle and Grunt		412
Simulium Venustum		430
Slipshod		74
Spooky Tom		362
Spring Fever		358
Sugar Plum Fairy		278
Summit Route		285
Sweeper		154
Taytay Corner		120
Thing 2		232
Three Blind Mice		434
Too Shallow for Diving, variation to Roaring Brook Falls		317
Travels with Travis		437
Tribulations		202
Turd Ferguson Can Suck It		154
Ugly as Sin		133
Waiting for the Sun		314
Wanderlust, Avalanche Lake		507
Wanderlust, Summit Cliff, Poke-O Moonshine		120
Way in the Chimney		342
Wayout Chimney		145
Weenie's Way		222
Where Frenchmen Dare		407
Where's the Booty?		360
Whirlpool, variation to Flume		186
White Pine Fever		257
Wiessner-Austin Route		496
Woodsman's Field Days		358

5.6-

Climb	Rating	Page
Belle Bottom Crack	★★★	174
Yodellaybackloon	★★	189

5.6

Climb	Rating	Page
After Irene	★★★★	317
Bozeman Bullet	★★★★	158
Branches	★★★★	358
Mr. Toad's Wild Ride	★★★★	220
North Country Club Crack	★★★★	200
Sword	★★★★	304
Aunt Polly	★★★	222
Chock Full O' Nuts	★★★	189
Diamond and Coal	★★★	200
E-Stim	★★★	198
Face of a Thousand Cracks	★★★	368
Fine Line, A	★★★	107
Frosted Flake	★★★	432
Full Recovery	★★★	199
Gothic Arch	★★★	476
Grand Game, The	★★★	94
Great Chimney	★★★	365
Greensleeves	★★★	217
Helms-Jolley	★★★	388
Li'l Sebastian, variation to Regular Route	★★★	219
Pug Love	★★★	238
Puppies on Edge	★★★	42
Roast 'n Boast	★★★	391
Sunfall	★★★	261
Weenie Jam	★★★	411
Wiessner Route, Upper Washbowl	★★★	245
Aquarius	★★	284
Armistice	★★	196
Benediction	★★	175
Big Bertha	★★	345
BlueCross BlueShield	★★	185
Bon Chance, Crane Mountain	★★	175
Brightly Colored Males	★★	230
Cream Puffer	★★	263
CWI	★★	300
Devin Monkey	★★	364
Devine	★★	72
Dewey, Cheetham, and Howe!	★★	492
Disappearing Act, Wright Peak	★★	526
Drag Queen	★★	72
Draining the Beaver	★★	422
El Muerte Rojo	★★	170

504 — Page numbers in this volume · *Page numbers in Volume 1*

Graded List of Climbs

Fudge Brownie a la Mode ★★ *337*
Gomez. . . . . ★★ **469**
Hipster. . . . . ★★ *317*
Kerr Route . . . . ★★ *481*
Little Gem Diner . . . . ★★ **235**
Malfeasance . . . . ★★ *196*
Missin' Moe . . . . ★★ **360**
Mystery Machine. . . . . ★★ **442**
N.O.C. Route. . . . . ★★ *352*
Necessary Risk . . . . ★★ *442*
No Lead . . . . ★★ *198*
No Picnic. . . . . ★★ *235*
Other One, The . . . . ★★ **415**
Ranger Danger . . . . ★★ *525*
Ranger on the Rock . . . . . ★★ *501*
Relayer . . . . ★★ **407**
Shanty Girl. . . . . ★★ **238**
Smoking Jacket . . . . ★★ *187*
Soft Maple Times . . . . ★★ **367**
Solar Energy . . . . ★★ *121*
Southwest Ridge. . . . . ★★ **259**
Storming the Tower. . . . . . ★★ *196*
Ten-Point Buck . . . . ★★ **71**
WMD . . . . ★★ **59**
Zigzag, Bald Mountain . . . ★★ **360**
As She Is . . . . ★ *391*
Autopilot . . . . ★ **70**
Blueberry Tafone . . . . ★ **179**
Call of the Wild . . . . ★ **333**
Central AC. . . . . ★ *350*
Chicken Soup . . . . ★ **281**
Chuting Lane. . . . . ★ **343**
Corner In Out . . . . ★ *184*
Crossway . . . . ★ **208**
Dodder . . . . ★ *225*
Fat-Free Warrior . . . . ★ *390*
Freeway. . . . . ★ *175*
Goodfellows . . . . ★ **285**
Goodwin Route. . . . . ★ *476*
Here I Go Again . . . . ★ **200**
Hooters . . . . ★ *350*
Jack Straw. . . . . ★ *284*
Last Lead . . . . ★ *198*
Lonely, The . . . . ★ *363*
Look Out Above . . . . ★ **337**
Madame Blueberry . . . . ★ **179**
Marjory . . . . ★ *222*
Mr. Dirty . . . . ★ *346*
Owl Crack . . . . ★ *350*
Providence . . . . ★ **210**
Ranger Rick . . . . ★ **366**
Rockhound . . . . ★ *138*
Run for Rabies . . . . ★ **168**
Shelving Rock Earth
    Penetrator . . . . ★ **59**
Shock and Awe . . . . ★ **59**
Slim Pickins, Crane Mountain ★ **147**
South Summit Route . . . . . . ★ **435**
Stacked . . . . ★ **382**
Stagger and Swerve . . . . . . ★ *256*
Teetotaler. . . . . ★ *289*

Trundle Bundle . . . . ★ **401**
Vernal Imperatives . . . . ★ **236**
Viewpoint Crack . . . . ★ **151**
Waterfall Left . . . . ★ **211**
Well Now, That's Better . . . . . ★ *169*
When Clouds Part. . . . . ★ **131**
Wind Song . . . . ★ *350*
With a Little Help from My
    Friends. . . . . ★ **420**
Withheld Pay . . . . ★ *370*
Zack's Sunspot. . . . . ★ **337**
Afternoon Tea **148**
Alien Shrimp **281**
Beautiful Dreamer. **174**
Beehive *378*
Best of Friends, variation to
    Helms-Jolley *388*
Big Man's Bane, variation to
    Induhvidual **191**
Birthday Route *143*
Blue Toes. **236**
Bone Games, variation to
    Standing Room Only . . . *315*
Brighter Visions. **156**
Broil 'n' Brag, variation to
    Roast 'n Boast. *391*
Bushwhacker **218**
Cedar Run. **451**
Chik'n Garbonzo, variation to
    The Snake *45*
Chilblain **170**
Chossmonaut **210**
Codswallop, variation to
    Tallywhacker **225**
Cold Draft...Horse, A. **423**
Cold Hands, variation to Steel
    Breeze **120**
Colden's Corner **255**
Columbine Crack **121**
Cruisin' with Joey, variation to
    Clutch and Cruise **310**
Demolition *415*
Devil Dogs. **218**
Deviled Eggs. **218**
Direct Start, variation to
    Wiessner Route. *457*
Double Vision **218**
Down in the Mall **228**
Dryer Weather **77**
Easier Than Expected. **67**
Etiquette *369*
First Taste **111**
Fits and Arms **210**
For Once a Great Notion *228*
Forty Winks **422**
Frankenpine **76**
Free for All **157**
Grommet *175*
Guermantes **105**
Gusto Crack *122*
H2 Alpine **177**

Hands That Work **211**
Heel and Toe, Heel and Toe,
    Heel and Toe. Slide, Slide,
    Slide. *212*
Hobbit's Way **491**
Indecisive **216**
Iron in the Fire **71**
Jaredtol *190*
Jonah Rocks *370*
Josey Wales *163*
Last Dance **224**
Le Poisson *112*
Leave Your Wallet At Home . . **229**
Let It Dry *255*
Lizard Head, variation to
    The Hole *526*
Long Haul **418**
Lookout Crack *116*
Lost in the Thicket *525*
Malarkey Direct *377*
Malcontent **242**
Méséglise **105**
More Than One Way to Skin a
    Cat, variation to Wiessner
    Route. *457*
Mountain Sunshine. *479*
Mutant Toy. **340**
Nameless Corner *335*
Neurosis **89**
No Dogs Allowed **217**
No M.D. for You **424**
North-End Route *463*
Old Route, Chapel Pond Gully
    Cliff. *228*
Opening Moves **229**
Penguin's Progress, A. **256**
Philippine Connection. *119*
Prone to Wander **210**
PSOC, variation to
    Wiessner Route. *457*
Raging Queen **88**
Rare Treat **411**
Rear Entry **488**
Roger That **102**
Schwartz's Ridge, variation
    to Roaring Brook Falls . . *317*
Short-Term Memory **243**
Sizzle Me **66**
Snooker. *313*
Son of Circuitous Shit **234**
Sōt Torn **122**
Spaghetti Western *163*
Stager's Arête **423**
Steptoe *89*
Strike Zone **247**
Sunday Funnies *279*
SWAPS **73**
Table Scraps *527*
Talking Heads **324**
Thing 1 . . . . **232**
TL *390*

Page numbers in this volume   *Page numbers in Volume 1*   505

Graded List of Climbs

Tool-less Wonder	401
Trundle Fodder	377
Underhanging Garter	376
Unpoplar	*188*
Up and Over, variation to Zig-Zag	*289*
Vogel	*279*
Wall of Desires	*507*
Waterfall Center	212
Wave Bye Bye	345
Way of the Peckerheads	247
Where's the Sun, Bob Kovachick?	145
Wolfshack Corner	59
Woodland Idiot	189
Yard Sale	*417*

5.6+

Bill Route	★★★	100
Crucible of War, The	★★★	95
Day of a Thousand Disasters	★★★	351
Yakapodu	★★★	*348*
Hour of Prayer	★★	220
Le Petit Slab	★★	94
Solar Grace	★★	*179*
Asher Crack	★	79
Chunga's Revenge	★	*275*
Fipi Lele	★	366
Peasant's Toehold		*196*
Trav-Ass, variation to Hour of Prayer		220
Trick or Treat, Huckleberry Mountain		216
Victoria		*218*

5.7-

Stand Your Ground	★★★★	184
Teddy's Trauma	★★★	*478*
Blueberry Crumble	★	*179*
North Face Direct	★	*472*

5.7

Fun City	★★★★	*347*
Lady Luck	★★★★	324
Opening Statement	★★★★	*493*
Pete's Farewell	★★★★	*364*
Pot of Gold	★★★★	*479*
Roaring Brook Falls	★★★★	*316*
Seven Ounces	★★★★	*290*
Tilman's Arête	★★★★	*235*
Tomahawk Crack, The	★★★★	*493*
After the Bash	★★★	466
Beam Me Up	★★★	*232*
Bella Vista	★★★	*175*
Calamity Crack	★★★	*428*
Caramel Chasm	★★★	*337*
Diamond C	★★★	415
Dobsonfly	★★★	*373*
Easter's Force	★★★	*168*
Escape from Haiti	★★★	243
Five Star Crack	★★★	312
Flying Friends	★★★	233
Gob Hoblin	★★★	*239*
Groovy Monkey Love	★★★	420
Hart Pump	★★★	389
Heart of Gold	★★★	*137*
Honeymoon in Yosemite	★★★	389
In the Buff	★★★	250
King and I	★★★	146
Labatt-Ami	★★★	*296*
Lichen Delight	★★★	*376*
Lichenbräu	★★★	*309*
Motoring with Mohammed	★★★	218
Munkey Bars and Geetar Stars	★★★	366
Prince	★★★	*204*
Purple Rain	★★★	446
Recuperation Boulevard	★★★	195
Red Book	★★★	366
Seventeen	★★★	*379*
Shaman, The	★★★	353
Thank You, Cindy	★★★	157
Thanksgiving	★★★	218
Touché	★★★	63
Tuesday Layback	★★★	70
Turbulescence	★★★	*183*
Two Bits	★★★	100
Uncle Fester	★★★	469
Vanilla Ice	★★★	352
Wright Crack, The	★★★	*525*
B-47	★★	*526*
Betty Is a Klepto	★★	*339*
Big In Munchkin Land	★★	133
Black Lectroids	★★	*335*
Blind Date	★★	277
Burton Birch Route	★★	*168*
Center Climb	★★	*481*
Climber's Yodel #7	★★	*239*
Cosmic Ray	★★	284
Cowpoke Chimney	★★	*156*
Cross Dresser	★★	72
Dark of the Sun	★★	224
Drumthwacket	★★	147
Firecracker	★★	184
Fireworks	★★	182
Fogbound	★★	*525*
Forked Tongue	★★	115
French Curve	★★	*117*
Full Moon Fever	★★	170
Garter	★★	*45*
Island Marriage, The	★★	388
Ladder	★★	*42*
Last Chance	★★	*109*
Last Swim or Dive	★★	*315*
Mean Low Blues	★★	238
Octo-Pussy	★★	*237*
On the Leash	★★	*345*
Opplevelsen	★★	155
Out with the Boys Again	★★	*438*
Pacifier	★★	*169*
Peanut Butter Pandemonium	★★	*337*
Provando	★★	*182*
Rangers' Run	★★	90
Right Way, The	★★	176
Rolling Stone	★★	*379*
Rum Doodle	★★	*222*
Scenic Slip	★★	150
Shaky Flake	★★	238
Slide Rules	★★	*497*
Space Cowboy	★★	*158*
Split Rock	★★	*174*
Spruce Crack	★★	*525*
Spur of the Moment	★★	*293*
Squeaky Toy Aliens	★★	340
Start Again	★★	68
Sub-Dude	★★	51
TB or Not TB	★★	428
Telepathy	★★	*117*
Toolbox Woody	★★	314
Topknot	★★	*430*
Traverse of the Climbing Gods	★★	*153*
Two Socks	★★	462
Unbroken	★★	*430*
Urin Luck	★★	*410*
Whaamburger	★★	*489*
Woody	★★	340
5th Season, The	★	*330*
Bachelors and Bowery Bums	★	*349*
Baywatch	★	113
BBC	★	*244*
Bidonville	★	*239*
Big Donger, The	★	*373*
Black and Tan	★	*189*
Breeze Crack	★	*350*
Carl's Climb	★	*158*
Chicken Flake	★	*159*
Coach and Mary	★	*313*
Cool Water	★	*185*
Deep Cover	★	*117*
Diet Coke Crack	★	*289*
Dos	★	*302*
El Niño	★	*254*
Fat Crack	★	65
Fee, Fie, Foe, Fum	★	*468*
Figaro	★	*331*
First Feast	★	*411*
Fledgling	★	*335*
Fubby Dub	★	*411*
Gold Wall	★	*136*
Good Intentions	★	*110*
Hat Rabbit	★	*222*
Honeymoon Ain't Over	★	*447*
Horses in Armor	★	*202*
Induhvidual	★	*191*
Jam Session	★	*117*
Jump Back Jack Crack	★	*121*
Lakeview	★	*139*
Love It	★	*406*
Mint Marcy	★	*337*

506   Page numbers in this volume   *Page numbers in Volume 1*

Graded List of Climbs

Natural English	★ 313
Never Alone	★ 182
No Parking	★ 174
Nose Traverse	62
NS Gauche	★ 351
Nuke the Nite	★ 392
Permafrost	★ 380
Pillar	★ 50
Psycho Sid	★ 340
Racoon Eyes	★ 448
Robbed	★ 275
Rock of Ages	★ 160
Rumble Strips	★ 164
Scary Lead	★ 198
Snake Slide	53
Snakeskin	★ 166
Steve's Flakes	★ 253
Sunset Arête	★ 118
Synchronized Swimming	★ 258
Trajectory Crack	★ 345
Trickagnosis	★ 167
Trundle of Joy	★ 419
Tubular Bells	★ 282
Virginia Reel	★ 380
Wednesday Wisecrack	★ 70
Weird Science	★ 334
Wide Crack	★ 312
Wobbly Crack	★ 120
A. Minor Mellor Route	506
AG	450
Also Ran	174
Animal Logic	120
Ankle Bruise	169
B Gentle	278
Bag It or Buy It	256
Bats and Bird Vomit, variation to Look, Roll, and Fire	328
Ben's Bump	176
Black Plague, Wallface	445
BLC	179
Block Party	304
Bowling for Simon	108
Buddy of Bradour, variation to Labatt-Ami	298
Burnt Toast	449
C+	440
Catnip	397
Cave Finish, variation to Regular Route	219
Cedar Corner, variation to Roaring Brook Falls	317
Chocolate City	280
Climb Free or Die Trying	314
Clutchin' the Bräu, variation to Clutch and Cruise	310
Contact Buzz	330
Contradiction Crack	304
Crowley Cream Cheese	190
Curbside Crawl	325
Dangerous Game, variation to Thanksgiving	219

Desperate Passage	220
Digging for Gold	119
Don't Kill The Client	352
Dugal, The	472
Eagle Crack	221
Everywhere That Man Can Be, variation to Carl's Climb	158
Fade and Flee	147
Fat Toad	68
Fawn Crack	71
Feeding Frenzy	430
Forty-niner	458
Full Moon	480
Gabe's Boulder	342
Golf Balls through Garden Hoses	349
Great Job	184
Green Streak: Portside	479
Green Thumb	71
Half Cocked	345
Happiness Is a Warm Belay Jacket	323
Hayeburner	291
Hidden Truths	409
Homo	53
Hummingbird	276
I Ain't a Marching Anymore	472
In the Beginning	210
Indecision '08	58
It's a Puzzle	229
It's Come to This	433
J.J.'s, variation to Talking Heads	325
Jealous Dogs	222
Keep Your Powder Dry, Ranger	316
Keyed In	419
King Kan Variation, variation to Mental Blocks	462
King of Guides	204
Knitel's Route	157
Lady's Route	377
Leap of Flake	242
Left In, variation to Left Out	51
Leftover	175
Leila's Line, variation to Empress	217
Lick 'Em & Stick 'Em	256
Looking for Mr. Goodhold	185
Loon Roof	243
Lost and Weary	161
Lost in the Crowd, variation to Cornerstone	161
Mad Dogs and Englishmen	105
Made In The Shade	273
McWiessner	281
Mr. Peabody	470
Mr. Potato Head	340
Never Again, Again	481
New Rubber, variation to Thanksgiving	219

Off Target	345
Once a New, variation to Flying Friends	233
One Hold	74
Only the Lonely	176
Overhanging Gutter	377
Palm Sunday, variation to Thanksgiving	219
Pantless Phenom	283
Paris–Harrison	190
Perseid	282
Pink Lynch	415
Poodles Are Just Like Little Sheep	130
Pringles, variation to Victoria	218
Prom Night Entity, variation to Crystalline Entity	429
PSOC	326
Push, Bob, Push!	420
Pustulence	170
Pyromania	242
Rain Delay	230
Reckless Endangerment	120
River View	232
Roast Turkey, variation to Thanksgiving	219
Root Explosion	524
Rope Burn	192
Ruby Star, variation to Diamond and Coal	200
Rum Doodle Direct, variation to Rum Doodle	223
Scaredy Cat, Cat Mountain	399
Shaky Flakes Traverse	524
Shemtastic	63
Shiling Was Willing	233
Signature	289
Silmaril, The	491
Skillyabuda	348
Skinny Cat	452
Snarling Spiders	460
Solid Rock	175
Solo, Gracias	182
Sprucification	359
Standing Room Only	315
Static Cringe	59
Summer Rules	529
Superstition Traverse	51
Surf and Turf, variation to Slide Rules	497
Swamp Arête	285
Sweaty April	67
Ted's Has It All	424
Tennis, Anyone	336
Thousand Faces of a Hundred People	234
Thrash	312
Time Trials	236
Timeline	515
Tommy, variation to Look, Roll, and Fire	328

Page numbers in this volume   *Page numbers in Volume 1*   507

Graded List of Climbs

Tone-Bone Tennys		94
Too Much Chop		*145*
Torment		430
Tougastan		63
Vertical Ag & Tech		212
Walker's Weave		360
We Should Have Taken a Left		*504*

5.7+

Quadrophenia	★★★★★	*327*
ASPCA	★★★	*345*
Carpenter & Das	★★★	195
Cat's Meow, The	★★★	*500*
Darmok	★★★	225
FM, The	★★★	*59*
Grips of Wrath	★★★	239
I'd Rather Be in Iowa	★★★	225
Raindance Corner	★★★	116
Rolls Royce	★★★	459
Team America	★★★	351
WMP	★★★	*194*
Buffalo Bob	★★	*162*
Crab Soccer	★★	*257*
Crackerbox Palace	★★	133
Death Penalty	★★	*494*
Kill It Before It Spreads	★★	193
O'Tom's Tick Twister	★★	173
Prima Facie	★★	*59*
Snake Free	★★	116
Sundowner	★★	65
Touran	★★	63
Crane Fang	★	186
Crooks and Nannies	★	187
Cul-de-Sac	★	*244*
Dweezil	★	51
Easy Listening	★	467
Half Mile	★	*65*
In the Rough	★	*200*
Pink Dayglo Tootsies	★	*370*
Sarge	★	*339*
Tour Guide Barbie	★	*340*
Bara Bara		*327*
Dancing with Fritz		290
Direct Finish, variation to Little Finger		100
Fig Fuckin' Newton		*376*
Fool in the Forest		189
Just Chum-me		338
Mo'in The Mud		454
Nasty Seven		200
Running on Empty		*274*
SARS Right, variation to SARS		169

5.8-

Snake Charmer, Tongue Mountain	★★★★	114
Matrix, The	★★★	98
Pieces of Eight	★★★	100
Poplar Climb, A	★★★	*188*
Straits of Fear	★★★	210
Cold Bare Rapport, The	★★	58
Discovered Check	★★	173
Fast and Furious	★★	*312*
Hand Therapy	★★	*138*
Lever Action	★★	344
Lunatic Hares	★★	395
Requiem Pro Patris	★★	146
Seam Ripper	★★	158
Hail Mary, variation to Moehammed, Larry, & Curly	★	192
Lakeview Arête	★	122
No Regrets Coyote	★	*189*
Pema	★	395
Pretty Good Dihedral, The	★	*529*
Second Chance	★	*252*
Shake and Bake	★	50
Squeezing Miss Daisy	★	343
Upper Level Disturbance	★	213
Amid the Flood		157
Black Moriah		238
Blueberry Pie		185
Cripple Creek		154
Doe Si Doe		71
Impulse Drive, variation to Pinch an Inch		202
Jug, Tug, and Jam		185
Line of Fire, variation to Little Finger		100
Mike's Mountaineering Route		176
October Crack		145
Owl Tail		*464*
Renegade		206
Swept Away, Backwater Wall		*186*
Ta Da		186
Thangorodrim		491
Touch The Earth		269
Troublemaker		230

5.8

El, The	★★★★★	*363*
Sting, The	★★★★★	72
Arachnid Traction	★★★★	*238*
Atwell's Revenge	★★★★	352
Bee Hold	★★★★	*194*
Caveman Crack	★★★★	260
Deja View	★★★★	273
Diagonal	★★★★	*442*
Fairview	★★★★	*119*
Habeas Corpus	★★★★	*493*
Hole, The	★★★★	*526*
Lake Champlain Monster	★★★★	*143*
Lost Arrow—Southeast Face	★★★★	*279*
Magic Carpet Ride	★★★★	265
Paralysis	★★★★	*99*
Plumber's Crack, South Colton	★★★★	407
Return to Sender	★★★★	272
Rockaholic	★★★★	*302*
Samboneparte	★★★★	*337*
Screaming Meaney	★★★★	98
Springtime	★★★★	*149*
Still Bill	★★★★	100
Andromeda	★★★	284
Anopheles	★★★	82
Anteater	★★★	*307*
Asteroid	★★★	251
Blueberry Buttress	★★★	451
Bon Chance, Good Luck Mountain	★★★	325
Brainy McCracken	★★★	447
Buzz	★★★	339
Chalk-Up Matilda	★★★	*524*
Cleveland	★★★	326
Crack of the Titans	★★★	493
Cure Cottage	★★★	428
Devo	★★★	52
Entertainer, The	★★★	76
Entrance	★★★	*522*
Equis	★★★	*302*
Excalibur, Lower Washbowl	★★★	*276*
Fistful of Stoppers	★★★	*269*
Freak Gasoline Fight Accident	★★★	*195*
Frick	★★★	65
Frippery	★★★	*414*
Geronimo	★★★	*158*
Goodwin-Eastman Route	★★★	*503*
Heroes	★★★	*273*
Hesitation	★★★	*248*
Hissing Fauna	★★★	354
Incognito	★★★	*156*
Jump Bat Crack	★★★	*237*
Lost Horizon	★★★	394
Mellor–Hyson	★★★	*504*
Meteorite	★★★	272
Mr. Rogers' Neighborhood	★★★	*267*
Opplevelsen Direct, variation to Opplevelsen	★★★	155
Otherwise Normal People	★★★	*234*
Parallel Dreams	★★★	98
Pearl Necklace	★★★	*200*
Porter Party	★★★	*503*
Second Job	★★★	208
Silent Flight	★★★	*419*
Sleepy Hollow	★★★	206
Soweto	★★★	235
Spider Biter	★★★	*135*
Sports Psychology	★★★	*333*
Squeeze Box	★★★	*323*
Stairway to Heaven	★★★	187
Stop Making Sense	★★★	477
Sunburst Arête	★★★	*100*
Superman Flake	★★★	272
Tangled Up in Azure	★★★	410
Toma's Wall	★★★	*499*
Tone-Boneparte	★★★	*212*
Tusk	★★★	452
Up Yanda	★★★	110

508   Page numbers in this volume   *Page numbers in Volume 1*

Graded List of Climbs

Climb	Rating	Page
Water Streak	★★★	250
Welcome to the Jungle	★★★	183
Where's Ian	★★★	471
Yellow Paddles	★★★	244
Afraid of the Dark	★★	329
Barking Spider	★★	76
Beanstalk	★★	468
Big Dack Attack	★★	128
Bullseye	★★	340
C'est la Vie	★★	428
Chimney Variation	★★	329
Chocolate Left	★★	314
Cobbler, The	★★	355
Cross, The	★★	371
Cujo	★★	239
Daisy BBs	★★	343
Detoxification	★★	302
Dig It	★★	156
Disputed, The	★★	365
Dorsal Fin	★★	523
First? Really?	★★	480
Frack	★★	65
Good, the Bad, and the Ugly, The	★★	157
Gorillas in the Mist	★★	525
Gunky Route	★★	236
Handcrack Boulder	★★	134
Henry Lewis	★★	320
Inferiority Complex	★★	299
J.E. 26	★★	257
Jake's Route	★★	400
Kalashnikov Corner	★★	344
Kings and Desperate Men	★★	95
Last Tupper, The	★★	392
Life and Debt	★★	235
Lost in Paradise	★★	422
Meltdown	★★	380
Monkey	★★	165
New Year's Day	★★	274
Norman's Crack of Joy	★★	193
Old School	★★	57
O'Ryan's Belt	★★	284
Outfoxed	★★	364
Pine Climb	★★	359
Polar Vortex	★★	212
Poseidon Adventure	★★	512
Quantum Entanglement	★★	284
Raindance Roof	★★	186
Random Rope	★★	373
Sagittarius	★★	284
Screams of the Primitive	★★	174
Seams Poplar	★★	188
Sergeant Pepper	★★	275
Sidewinder	★★	113
Simon	★★	195
Spring Equinox	★★	330
Squirrelless Journey	★★	233
Stemtastic	★★	63
Swampoodle	★★	239
Tang Corner	★★	65
Walking Fern Face	★★	109
Why Did I Fall for That	★★	322
Yes, Virginia	★★	419
5756 in Service	★	131
Asterisk	★	282
Bad Advice	★	281
Carbohydrate	★	190
Carnivore Crack	★	185
Caught in the Act	★	254
Corvus Crack	★	353
Diamondback	★	238
Dike, The	★	312
Disappearing Act, Eagle Cliff	★	72
Discord	★	44
Dreams of the Desert	★	80
Emily Doesn't Have a Clue	★	313
Fake ID	★	290
Far Side, The	★	396
Frosted Fern	★	165
Giuoco Piano	★	173
Gray–Harrison	★	187
Halitosis	★	170
Hoedown	★	156
Howdy, Hiker	★	253
Iditarod	★	253
Instigator	★	230
Joey Baggadonuts	★	310
King Me	★	289
Left Out	★	51
Life Aquatic	★	511
Low-Rise Thong	★	70
Morsel Line	★	189
Nobber	★	255
On Appeal	★	493
P8tience	★	108
Pet Cemetery	★	239
Pharaoh Winds	★	131
Poke-O Pup	★	138
Pringsheim Chimney	★	491
Protractor	★	45
Quest	★	304
Rachael's Climb	★	322
Rainy Night Road Toads	★	360
Recital	★	277
Scab Slab	★	389
Shit! HiSir Needs Stitches	★	300
Shiver Me Timbers, Eagle Falls	★	379
Slab Happy	★	150
Slave Labor	★	202
Slipped Bits	★	102
Slippy Sliden' Away	★	131
Solitude, Flowed Lands	★	428
Spectacular Rising Traverse	★	62
Sport Climbing Is Neither	★	406
Stanley Frank	★	320
Starstruck	★	284
Swept Away, Crane Mountain	★	154
Tardis Traveler	★	230
Tie Me Up	★	289
Timbuk-2	★	63
Torment Direct	★	430
Uncontrollable Desires	★	356
Varsity	★	45
Weather Clown	★	213
Whoops	★	244
Woolsey Route	★	485
Worse Than Real	★	89
Xenolith	★	327
1968 Offwidth Pants, variation to Frippery		415
Adirondack High		125
A-Frame		308
Amnesia Chasm		200
Analysis Paralysis		380
Another Botanical Wonder		273
Arch Traverse		110
Arrested Development		194
Balls In Space		338
Barista		229
Barking up the Wrong Climb		349
Beam Us Up, Scotty, variation to The El		363
Beardsley Buttress		148
Bender's Chasm		222
Blue Streaks		151
Bogeyman		369
Bully Pulpit		386
Bulwark		145
Butterflies Are Free, variation to Mastercharge		244
Carrion and Crawl		335
CCD Route		509
Chameleon		254
Crow's Nest		230
Curb Your Enthusiasm		336
Darker Dreams		156
Dartmouth Notch		156
Dexter's Dugout, variation to Pinch an Inch		202
Direct Finish, variation to Gamesmanship		73
Directissima		98
Dirty Little Corner		134
Dirty Mattress, The		454
Dodge and Dangle		281
Don't Give Guns to Children		407
Dream of Frozen Turkeys		442
Early Onset Dementia		459
Easy Off		360
Eight Shit		76
Face Dances		467
Felony in Georgia, A		334
For the Birds		144
Freeze-Thaw Cycle		175
Friends in Business		341
Fruit Stripe		170
Fugarwe, variation to Beehive		378
Führer		211
Gone Fishin'		145
Good Book, The		150
Grand View		522
G-String		220

Page numbers in this volume   Page numbers in Volume 1

Graded List of Climbs

Climb	Page
Handle with Care	326
Harrison–Haas, variation to Gray–Harrison	187
Harry Potter and the Witches Crack	321
Heroes Are Hard To Find	456
Holiday in Cambodia	411
Holyfield & Foreman	70
Horizontal Fridge	378
Indian Summer	*174*
Intensive Care	195
Isosceles	118
It'll Probably Be Mostly a Scramble	*472*
Johnsburg Red	229
Kaibob	*37*
Knock Before Entering	489
Land of the Little People	333
Left-Hand Direct, variation to Left-Hand Route	*228*
Linkup, variation to The El	*363*
Little Buttress	158
Little Finger Direct Start	100
Machinist	*119*
Matt Finish	*116*
Misty Mountain Hop	186
Moonstruck	*121*
My Pleasure	*166*
Na-my	*462*
Night Mare	*237*
Not Long For This World	66
Nothing We Bailed	*273*
Off Route, The	*213*
Old Route, Third Tier, Poke-O Moonshine	*137*
Open for Business	371
Open Shutter	272
Opposition	*35*
Ornithologists from Hell	*334*
P.T. Pillar Right	*70*
Pain and Pleasure	159
Path to Iowa	225
Persecution, variation to Bloody Mary	*77*
Pinus Strobus	*152*
Piton Route	*145*
Pollen Junkies	*135*
Prelude	*248*
Projection	359
Scared for Life, variation to Cracklosis	*168*
Seamly Route	*151*
Shanty 101	239
Short Person's Disease	169
Silver Flake	456
Small Craft Advisory	*333*
Split Personality, variation to Raindance Roof	186
SRT	*62*
Stone Cross	160
Storm Warning	*334*
Strip Mine	*119*
Swamp Gas	285
Sweeping up to Glory	159
Sword, The	*128*
Teeth	*372*
Tempest, variation to Heart of Gold	*137*
This, Too, Shall Pass	*255*
Three Way	*529*
Tita U. Assol	*314*
Tripping Karen	*365*
Up Your Bum	407
Walking Disaster	410
Wear Four	*280*
West End Brewery	335
Whale Ship	345
Wiessner Route, Avalanche Lake	*515*
Yoyodyne, variation to Oscillation Overthruster	*336*

5.8+

Climb	Stars	Page
Gamesmanship	★★★★★	73
Eat Yourself a Pie	★★★★	*345*
Lifelong Affliction	★★★★	*230*
Panther's Fang	★★★★	*501*
Tier Pressure	★★★★	277
Wiessner Route, Noonmark Mountain	★★★★	*481*
Breaking Bad	★★★	51
Bunny Slope	★★★	84
Clutch and Cruise	★★★	*310*
Coffee Shop Panorama	★★★	412
Dark Lord	★★★	*126*
Dark Venomous Dreams	★★★	115
Dudeman	★★★	*431*
Final Frontier	★★★	121
Hard Going	★★★	257
Jack in the Pulpit	★★★	*386*
Le Chat Noir	★★★	*501*
Obama Mama	★★★	59
Pick Pocket	★★★	69
Poplar Mechanics	★★★	*188*
Rex	★★★	340
Sitting Duck	★★★	316
Warpath	★★★	*157*
Affliction	★★	*522*
Chewing on Balloons	★★	*225*
Chokin' Chickens	★★	184
Electric Kool-Aid	★★	419
Excalibur, Tongue Mountain	★★	114
Family Jewels	★★	*199*
Grin and Bear It, Shelving Rock	★★	46
H1N1	★★	169
Intelligent Design	★★	279
Invincible Machine	★★	278
Maiden Voyage	★★	*138*
Misspent Youth	★★	335
P.T. Pillar	★★	69
Paradise Now	★★	*255*
Peney for Your Freedom, A	★★	189
Pulled Tooth	★★	82
Too Close for Comfort	★★	244
Tun Tavern	★★	193
Two Lefts Don't Make It Right	★★	63
Welcome Matt	★★	71
Winds of Change	★★	58
Cedar Dog	★	322
Day of Madness	★	*331*
Deciphering the Dirtyness	★	354
Dole Me	★	*254*
Home and Garden Center	★	420
Keegans 5.8	★	309
Leader Line	★	73
Lives of the Hunted	★	*314*
Lunar Manscape	★	45
Pine Tree Crack	★	77
Pump It Up	★	342
Son of Cirrhosis	★	118
Soup Kitchen, Upper Washbowl	★	*249*
Tour Arête Syndrome	★	63
40 Oz. to Freedom		*290*
Dick's Nose, variation to Unbroken		430
Dog Eat Dog		*342*
Franklin's Tower		454
Get Over It		235
I'm Committed, variation to Mastercharge		244
Knock the Cairn Down		*526*
Mirror Image		*450*
My Name is Hud		483
Outpatient		195
Pee Wee Pillar		69
Public Service		323
Rugosity		*368*

5.9-

Climb	Stars	Page
Gong Show, The	★★★★	46
Mr. Clean	★★★★	*345*
Partition	★★★★	*244*
Lager-Rhythm	★★★	*299*
Another Beer Walls Black Streak	★★	*303*
Darmok Indirect	★★	225
Doodle Bug	★★	47
Excellent Adventure, The	★★	120
Fearless Leader	★★	466
Jammer	★★	184
Metatarsal Opportunity	★★	*186*
Toucan	★★	63
Wandering and Pondering	★★	*370*
Amulet, The	★	330
Felonious Mopery	★	193
Fishes on a Landscape	★	*222*
Homegrown	★	*136*
Jackrabbit	★	*174*
Trapped in the Dike	★	*516*
Attachment		467

Graded List of Climbs

Climb	Stars	Page
Cedar Root		456
Chute to Kill		344
Dancin' Buckwheat		*194*
Highway Patrol		*174*
Kissing Pigs		188
Ledge You To Believe		484
Little Jam, Crane Mountain		185
Misfire		343
Mystery To Me, variation to Heroes Are Hard To Find		456
Pythagoras		118
Suicidal Sidney		208
Traffic Engineer		*181*

5.9

Climb	Stars	Page
Frosted Mug	★★★★★	296
Mystery Achievement	★★★★★	328
American-Russian-Chinese Route	★★★★	*117*
Amphitheater Crack	★★★★★	202
Arch Madness	★★★★	*440*
Cock-a-doodle-doo	★★★★	*486*
Cowboy Up	★★★★	334
Freudian Slip	★★★★	*497*
Great Sail, The	★★★★	*430*
Little Kisses	★★★★	311
Morticia	★★★★	469
My Favorite Martian	★★★★	*379*
Naked Truth	★★★★	367
Overdog	★★★★	*343*
Prints of Darkness	★★★★	100
Shantytown	★★★★	238
Slip Tease–Skid Row	★★★★	102
Something Wicked	★★★★	*520*
Taste Buds	★★★★	113
To Infinity and Beyond!	★★★★	339
Vertebrae	★★★★	252
Weasel Climb, The	★★★★	316
Autumn Gold	★★★	*138*
Bodhi Tree	★★★	191
Chiquita	★★★	*254*
Cloudsplitter, The	★★★	*500*
Corktown	★★★	239
Crack 'n Corner	★★★	66
Crackberry	★★★	362
Day's End	★★★	*293*
Don We Know Wears Gay Apparel	★★★	*419*
Dynamo Hum	★★★	*362*
Flexi-Flier	★★★	*346*
Flight of the Falcon	★★★	65
Force Nine	★★★	*333*
Fossil Formation Buttress	★★★	*464*
Gemini	★★★	284
Glass Ceilings	★★★	*141*
Green Onion	★★★	*94*
Hammerdog	★★★	222
King Crack	★★★	359
Lentil Beans	★★★	*190*
Lewis Elijah	★★★	*447*
Pegasus	★★★	*308*
Pharaoh's Phallus	★★★	128
Pretty in Pink	★★★	388
Rearview Mirror	★★★	*138*
Re-Entry	★★★	*519*
Rubicon	★★★	*460*
Sam I Am	★★★	485
Scales	★★★	133
Scarynac Crack	★★★	428
Side Show, variation to Hoops and Yo Yo	★★★	66
Silk Road, The	★★★	*369*
Sky Traverse	★★★	*62*
Slabby McCracken	★★★	447
Snake Charmer, Shelving Rock	★★★	45
Space Walk	★★★	*112*
Stonewall Brigade	★★★	331
Sundance	★★★	*160*
Tales of Weakness	★★★	451
Teddy Ruxpin	★★★	116
Titusville Express	★★★	493
Twist Off	★★★	*293*
Up In Smoke	★★★	133
Virgin Sturgeon	★★★	*276*
Waterloo	★★★	*37*
Zebra	★★★	483
Adonis	★★	*42*
Bee's Knees	★★	*135*
Bong Hits 4 Jesus	★★	422
Cat Scratch Fever	★★	170
Chocolate Right	★★	314
Crotalusly Challenged	★★	114
Dividing Line	★★	155
Dixie Normus	★★	312
Do You Feel Lucky	★★	*163*
Doctor Y's	★★	426
Draught Dodger	★★	*303*
Eating Tripe and Lichen It	★★	205
Fat People Are Harder To Kidnap	★★	314
Fish Story	★★	492
Fledgling Flight	★★	433
Freckles and No Lipstick	★★	311
Get a Grip	★★	330
Get Up, Stand Up	★★	222
Give It a Name, Man	★★	229
Gray–Sointio, variation to Gray–Harrison	★★	187
Greenhouse Effect	★★	*174*
Halfway Handcrack	★★	*147*
Happy Trails to You	★★	525
High Noon	★★	*481*
Hooligans	★★	328
Hot Saw	★★	*121*
Hot Tamale	★★	448
Knuckle-Dragger	★★	53
Lichenstorm	★★	*103*
Little Secret	★★	*255*
Luxury Lining	★★	317
Mixamotosis	★★	167
More Tea, Vicar	★★	*280*
Octoberfast	★★	*303*
Odd Nine	★★	*129*
Original Exploit	★★	157
Pere-o-grins	★★	90
Posy	★★	399
Prisoner in Disguise	★★	335
Psychosis	★★	*48*
Pull Up Your Pants	★★	134
Pusher, The	★★	269
Rough Cut	★★	*231*
Royal Coachman	★★	338
Scooped By Fritz	★★	448
Second Crimp to the Right, Keep on Climbing Till Morning	★★	446
Shaken, Not Stirred	★★	*236*
Shiver Me Timbers, Rogers Slide	★★	94
Smallville Left	★★	*37*
Snapperhead	★★	451
Straight A's	★★	*524*
Strangers in Paradise	★★	*118*
Strict Time	★★	*174*
Suppertime	★★	447
Take the Power Back	★★	394
Tasp, The	★★	379
Twain Town	★★	418
Vaccination	★★	484
Wald-Calder Route	★★	*358*
Welcome to the Machine	★★	380
Worlds in Collision	★★	*127*
Wrong Crack, The	★★	*526*
Yvonne	★★	*271*
Ape X	★	185
Backer Line	★	73
Bandaloop Dancers	★	113
Bathtub Virgin	★	*44*
Belleview	★	*173*
Better Place to Be, A	★	*153*
Cooler, The	★	*79*
Cosmo Cracks	★	*72*
Crosstown Traffic	★	*369*
Decathlon	★	240
Drive	★	200
Festus	★	*162*
Fire-Tower Crack	★	*117*
First Aid	★	*115*
Fishin' Cruise	★	492
Flapper	★	*389*
Flying Dutchman, The	★	*523*
Goes Both Ways	★	86
Group Therapy	★	*42*
Guillotine	★	*196*
Harvest	★	*137*
High and Dry	★	*36*
Hochschartner Highway	★	*516*
Hydrophobia, Upper Tiers, Poke-O Moonshine	★	*124*
Ice Point	★	*175*
Indi's Arête	★	77
Jury Duty	★	*493*

Graded List of Climbs

Climb	Page
Key, The.	★ 269
Kirby Corner	★ 377
Lightning	★ 96
Medulla Oblongata	★ 78
Muckraker	★ 192
National Federation of the Blind	★ 78
NCS Crack	★ 516
Outlander	★ 342
Pajama Sam	★ 153
Post Op	★ 198
Raindance	★ 53
Rolling Rock	★ 303
Schizophrenia	★ 329
Sharp Bridge	★ 164
Summer Party	★ 79
Vanishing Species	★ 230
Watch My Bolt	★ 100
Yabba Dabba Do	★ 53
Along the Watchtower	129
Another Crack in the Wall	454
Another Crack, variation to Great Chimney	366
Aspaguass	242
Atlantis	130
Ausable Arête	407
Back on the Horse	424
Badminton 101	258
Bandit, The	124
Barbecued Dogs, variation to Wald-Calder Route	358
Barstool Direct	311
Cabin 6, Capacity 10	449
Canine	342
Canoes for Feet	342
Climb It	406
Cream on Top	407
Crystal Wall	358
Crystalline Entity	429
Dalek Connection	230
Day-Tripper	164
Dicentra	96
Direct Finish, variation to Heroes	277
Direct Finish, variation to Lichen Delight	377
Dirty Uncle	488
Double Fisting Blueberries	442
Drawing Mustaches on Dangerous Dogs, variation to Wald-Calder Route	358
Explorers' Club	128
False Advertising	336
FM Direct, The, variation to The FM	59
From Switzerland With Hate	481
Graphite Corner	212
Haley's Nose	86
Half Man, Half Wit	189
Hamburger Helper	221
In the Buff, variation to In the Rough	200
Kid Rock	51
Lady Bug	349
Last Grasp	486
Lazy Crack	133
Lessons in Guiding	256
Life's a Beach	198
Limp Stick	312
Low Plains Drifter	369
Manic Depression	252
Mann Act	250
McNeill–Harrison	176
Misadventures on Ausable Arête	407
Mother Mantel	307
Mrs. Clean	519
Mustard Sandwich	496
My Little Johnson	172
New Suede Shoes	70
Normal People, variation to Land of the Little People	333
Old Guys Having Fun	430
Panorama	251
Pearly Gates	37
Planet Terror	414
Plumb Line, Little Crow Mountain	339
Pointless and Hard, variation to The El	363
Rare Earth	103
Refrainer, The	76
Right Field	320
Rock of Aegis, variation to Rock of Ages	160
Romper Room	66
Roof	358
Rules	369
Rumney but Crumbly	58
Schnapps	111
Skyline Arête	110
Snap, Crackle, and Pop	129
Snatch It, variation to The Snatch	64
Stalking Caribou	520
Tempest, The	212
To Pass Or Not To Pass	509
Tomb of the Falcon	130
Tom's Daring-Do	179
Trolls in Hiding, variation to Pay the Troll's Bridge	203
Twenty-one	225
Twinflower Traverse	121
Underage Drinking	289
Way Hairball	342
With Brook Trout Eyes	338
Wrong Side of the Tracks	235
Wronged Again	341
Zig-Zag	289
Zone X	96

5.9+

Climb	Page
Bloody Mary	★★★★★ 76
California Flake	★★★★★ 510
Hard Times, Moss Cliff	★★★★★ 397
Piece Out	★★★★★ 473
Touch of Class	★★★★★ 399
Black Market	★★★★ 135
Brrright Star	★★★★ 368
Great Dihedral	★★★★ 64
Gridlock	★★★★ 116
King and I, The	★★★★ 206
Original Route, The	★★★★ 144
Slim Pickins, Spider's Web	★★★★ 265
Æon Flux	★★★ 407
Arch, The	★★★ 111
Bronze	★★★ 418
Cardiac Corner	★★★ 359
Caspian Corner	★★★ 448
Cirrhosis	★★★ 96
Crumbs Along the Mohawk	★★★ 337
Deciphering the Wonderfulness	★★★ 352
Dharma Initiative, The	★★★ 395
Dog with a Nut Tool	★★★ 321
Ectoplasmic Remains	★★★ 235
French Kiss	★★★ 113
High Wire	★★★ 66
Hysteria	★★★ 106
Last Hurrah	★★★ 102
Live Free or Die	★★★ 312
Moehammed, Larry, & Curly	★★★ 192
Optimist, The	★★★ 371
Poker Face	★★★ 476
PR	★★★ 284
Rock Lobster	★★★ 47
Scorpion Bowl	★★★ 72
Slime Line	★★★ 45
Stihl Water	★★★ 373
Sun Dogs	★★★ 145
Swept Away, The Ticket, Lower Washbowl	★★★ 280
Tiguidou Pack-Sack	★★★ 459
Transplant	★★★ 172
Trust Your Rubber	★★★ 321
Willie's Danish Prince	★★★ 192
Winchester Dihedral	★★★ 344
7 Year Itch	★★ 45
After the Gold Rush, variation to Gold Wall	★★ 136
Almost Rectum	★★ 420
Battle Fatigue	★★ 143
Beating to North	★★ 143
Big Brother	★★ 487
Bodega	★★ 483
Crackatoa	★★ 76
Dackdation	★★ 392
Dirty Boy	★★ 248
Expiration 66	★★ 309

512   Page numbers in this volume   Page numbers in Volume 1

Graded List of Climbs

Galapagos . . . . ★★ *229*	Mother's Day Variation, variation to Phase III *42*	Airtime . . . . ★★★ *323*
Gamma Ray Arête . . . . . . ★★ *284*	Muscinae *385*	Appomattox Crack . . . . . ★★★ *331*
Gotta Go . . . . ★★ 56	No Fear Is Queer *312*	Aquaman . . . . ★★★ *370*
Great Spoof, The . . . . ★★ *175*	On the Beach *136*	Areticus Maximus . . . . . . ★★★ 116
Homecoming . . . . ★★ *52*	Pillar of Strength, variation to Wild Blue *56*	Blockus . . . . ★★★ 446
Mountain Bruin . . . . ★★ 316	Positive Thinking *69*	Bond Girls . . . . ★★★ *236*
Not Tell Wife, OK? . . . . ★★ *164*	Real 208, The *102*	Brothers in Arms . . . . ★★★ 90
Padanarum Crack . . . . ★★ 108	Saranac 1888 426	Caribou Barbie . . . . ★★★ 59
Perpetual Frustration Machine . . . . ★★ 407	Sister Sarah *163*	Cave Artist, The . . . . ★★★ *380*
Phase III . . . . ★★ *39*	Some Things Considered *333*	Chopping Block, The . . . ★★★ 493
Reproof . . . . ★★ 184	Stone Face *274*	Christine . . . . ★★★ *239*
Retrograde Motion . . . . . . ★★ *127*	Tarantula, variation to Fire Starter *237*	Colossus of Tongue . . . . ★★★ 116
Ricochet . . . . ★★ *160*	Three Stooges, Beer Walls . . . *311*	Courtney Marie's Boobies ★★★ *311*
Road Trip . . . . ★★ *149*		Crackus Interuptus . . . . . ★★★ 452
Static Cling, Silver Lake . . ★★ 466	**5.10-**	Criminal Lawyer . . . . ★★★ *493*
Too Early Spring . . . . ★★ *358*	High Plains Drifter . . . . . . ★★★ 272	Darklord . . . . ★★★ 104
Tough Act to Follow, A . . . ★★ 254	Dead Dog *221*	Desperado . . . . ★★★ *160*
Waiting For The Weather . ★★ 487		Dutch Masters Direct . . . ★★★ *123*
Arc of a Climber . . . . ★ *153*	**5.10a**	F.B.W . . . . ★★★ 224
Banana Republic . . . . ★ *254*	Blacksmith . . . . ★★★★★ *309*	Finger It Out . . . . ★★★ *342*
Blueberry Jam . . . . ★ 184	Do Me a Solid . . . . ★★★★★ 389	Flash Flood . . . . ★★★ *126*
Coal Miner . . . . ★ *199*	Every Inch Counts . . . ★★★★★ 480	Geriatric Profanity Disorder . . . . ★★★ 225
Cro-Magnon . . . . ★ 53	Fastest Gun . . . . ★★★★★ *78*	Getcher Breakfast . . . . ★★★ 169
Divide By Zero . . . . ★ 156	Fear of Gravity . . . . ★★★★★ *123*	Great Northern . . . . ★★★ *121*
Flashback Crack . . . . ★ *116*	Flying & Drinking and Drinking & Driving . . . . ★★★★★ *296*	Grin and Bear It, Bear Den . . . . ★★★ *417*
Fritzie's Honor . . . . ★ *278*	Groovitational Pull . . . . ★★★★★ 478	Hair of the Dog . . . . ★★★ *342*
GK's First BJ . . . . ★ 406	Honeybadger . . . . ★★★★★ 481	High Falls . . . . ★★★ *412*
Grape Juice . . . . ★ 331	On the Loose . . . . ★★★★★ 269	Hoops and Yo Yo . . . . . . ★★★ 66
Hidden Gem . . . . ★ *200*	Tombstone . . . . ★★★★★ *157*	I Am Lesion . . . . ★★★ 168
Lane Change . . . . ★ 197	TR . . . . ★★★★★ 265	Jim's Faith . . . . ★★★ *447*
Limelight . . . . ★ 76	Bear Necessities . . . . . . ★★★★ *417*	Kielbasy Posse . . . . ★★★ 193
On Tap: Special Brew . . . . . ★ *302*	Berry Good . . . . ★★★★ *417*	Lithium . . . . ★★★ 76
Rotator Complications . . . . ★ *380*	Brazilian . . . . ★★★★ 476	LM . . . . ★★★ 375
Splitting Headache . . . . ★ 78	Cascade Lichen Dance ★★★★ *378*	Lost Chance . . . . ★★★ *90*
Sumo Fly . . . . ★ *310*	Cenotaph, The . . . . ★★★★ 44	Macrobiotic . . . . ★★★ *99*
Woo Hoo! . . . . ★ 420	Critical Crimps . . . . ★★★★ 206	Mechanical Hydraulic Control . . . . ★★★ *122*
Amphibious Moat Monsters . . *203*	Emperor Zurg . . . . ★★★★ 340	Millennium . . . . ★★★ *428*
Bengal Tiger *347*	Esthesia . . . . ★★★★ *262*	Naughty or Nice . . . . ★★★ *419*
Bushy Pussy *501*	Gold . . . . ★★★★ *418*	No Ifs, Ands, or Bolts . . . ★★★ *371*
Changing of the Guard, variation to Great Dihedral *65*	Green Mountain Boys . . ★★★★ 449	Overture . . . . ★★★ *248*
Cheap Money *256*	Hackett Corner . . . . ★★★★ 46	Pinch an Inch . . . . ★★★ 202
Cue Ball *311*	Hot Metal and Methedrine . . . . ★★★★ *454*	Pine Shadow . . . . ★★★ *308*
Fang Time, variation to Tun Tavern 193	Lloyd's of Lowville . . . . . ★★★★ 376	Pinnacle of Success . . . . ★★★ *129*
Fifty-Foot Fright Fest 150	Long Play . . . . ★★★★ 192	Puma Concolor . . . . ★★★ *501*
Gale Force *334*	Parallel Passage . . . . . . ★★★★ 206	Pump Action . . . . ★★★ 343
Ginger Tea 111	Pink Panther . . . . ★★★★ 433	Rodeo . . . . ★★★ 247
Goombay Finish, variation to Fastest Gun *78*	Power of Attorney . . . . . ★★★★ *494*	Shining, The . . . . ★★★ *239*
Horror Show 226	Prey Tell . . . . ★★★★ 379	Sideways . . . . ★★★ 316
I Don't Need No Doctor *187*	Scallion . . . . ★★★★ *94*	Slumlord . . . . ★★★ 238
Kat Nap *500*	Son of Slime . . . . ★★★★ *69*	Stake and Cake . . . . ★★★ 50
Land of the Lost *283*	Three Degrees of Separation . . . . ★★★★ 44	Star in the Dust . . . . ★★★ 328
Lichenbräu Dark, variation to Lichenbräu *309*	Turbocharge . . . . ★★★★ *307*	Stoned in a Crowded Corner, variation to Cornerstone . . . . . . ★★★ 161
Look, Roll, and Fire 328	Veracity . . . . ★★★★ *230*	Tea and Biscuits . . . . ★★★ *476*
McCarthy Off Width, variation to Fastest Gun *78*	Wake and Bake . . . . ★★★★ 50	Toiling Men . . . . ★★★ 161
Mercury Program, The 490	Adirondack Rehab . . . . . ★★★ 195	Trailblazer . . . . ★★★ *129*
		Treasure of El Sid . . . . . . ★★★ 324

Page numbers in this volume   *Page numbers in Volume 1*   513

Graded List of Climbs

Climb	Stars	Page
Two Camels, One Hump	★★★	61
Updraft	★★★	128
Variety Crack	★★★	210
Walk the Plank	★★★	94
War and Peace	★★★	523
War of the Worlds	★★★	67
Welcome to Bedrock	★★★	339
Adrenaline Surge	★★	303
Birthday Corner	★★	200
Body Snatcher, The	★★	62
Curve Like a Wave	★★	466
Democralypse Now	★★	58
Diva	★★	52
El Kabong	★★	59
End of the Line	★★	187
Flight of the Concord	★★	303
Get Reborn	★★	134
Gopher Wood	★★	62
Gun Show	★★	203
High-Rise Tightie Whities	★★	70
Hoar–Horovitz	★★	283
Independence Pass	★★	305
Jemima Dreams	★★	447
Lick It Up	★★	342
Lost Arrow—Southwest Face	★★	279
Nevermore	★★	77
O'Barrett Factor, The	★★	57
Pebbles and Bamm Bamm	★★	339
PF Flyers	★★	364
Porcupine Prelude	★★	304
Reach, The	★★	328
Red Zinger	★★	397
Roofer Madness	★★	186
Thunderbolt	★★	123
Ukiah	★★	52
Zippity Doo-Dah	★★	90
Beaver Fever, Beaver Brook	★	420
Beechnut	★	171
Boob Job	★	84
Breathe Easy	★	156
Buck Hunter	★	71
Colt 45 Corner	★	343
Curly Shuffle, The	★	74
Indirecto	★	355
Kaiser Friedrich	★	206
Little Black Book	★	199
Lost Ark	★	62
Mr. Spaceman	★	379
Not My Moss to Bear	★	222
Pay the Troll's Bridge	★	203
Pockets R Us	★	71
Railroad Dickie	★	239
Rubber Knumbchuck	★	305
Shipwrecked	★	94
Soup Kitchen, Shanty Cliff	★	236
Starboard Tack	★	284
Toxic Avenger, The	★	303
Vertical Limit	★	303
Wahlnut	★	127
Yax Crack	★	335

Climb	Stars	Page
Arch Crack, The, variation to Pilgrim's Progress		87
Atlas Shrugged, variation to Eastern Shield		451
Bad Karma		524
Battle Creek		37
Black Watch		90
Burgundy Color Lily Crack		305
Captain Chips Traverse, variation to Drop, Fly, or Die		267
Death Trap Lite, variation to Death Trap		304
Deviant Finish, variation to The Key		269
Direct Start, variation to Frosted Mug		296
Downtown Brown		524
Drifter		158
Dunn Finish, variation to Fastest Gun		78
English Channel		189
Fancy Feet		400
Fun Country, variation to Fun City		347
GPD		225
Hamburger Face		168
Hershey Squirt, variation to Chocoholic		192
Jay's Affliction, variation to Critical Crimps		208
Keystone		193
Knightfire		341
Leapin' Louie		193
Left Field		320
Morningside Heights		481
Natural, The		90
Nestlings, variation to Touch of Class		399
Not Quite Geiko		171
Orchestra		99
Pepé Le Pew		256
Perseverance		129
Razor's Edge		113
Snowballing		131
Sweet Sunday		94
Takes All Kinds		347
Teamwork		131
Twelve Five		289
Up		91
Wandering Wizard		440
Whip It Bad		274
Wish You Were Here		513

5.10b

Climb	Stars	Page
Black Arch Arête	★★★★★	206
Freedom Flight	★★★★★	50
Hairy Upper Lip Drip	★★★★★	450
Positive Latitude	★★★★★	478
Roaches on the Wall	★★★★★	358
Tequila Mockingbird	★★★★★	295
Tooth & Nail	★★★★★	455

Climb	Stars	Page
3D	★★★★	524
Ancient of Days	★★★★	89
Bearded Munchkin	★★★★	444
Coffee Achievers	★★★★	366
Cooney-Norton Face	★★★★	70
Fear of Flying	★★★★	399
Forever Wild	★★★★	326
Grand Ole Osprey	★★★★	414
Handlebarbarism	★★★★	449
Infinity and Beyond	★★★★	48
Johnny Tsunami	★★★★	56
Karate Crack	★★★★	104
Mean Sister	★★★★	312
Neutron Brew	★★★★	294
Oddy's Crack of Horror	★★★★	189
Old Guy Shootin' Powder	★★★★	420
Perfect Pitch	★★★★	139
Radioactive	★★★★	294
Raw Tips	★★★★	195
Reach for the Sky	★★★★	162
Rescue Breathing	★★★★	113
Roaring Twenties	★★★★	294
Route of Oppressive Power	★★★★	411
Second Amendment	★★★★	179
Snatch, The	★★★★	64
Son of a Mother	★★★★	39
Space Odyssey	★★★★	113
Tears of Gaia	★★★★	443
To Catch a Wave	★★★★	430
Torcher	★★★★	205
B.A.R.	★★★	343
Bonanza Lunchbox	★★★	482
Certified Raw	★★★	38
Chalk Full O' Nuts	★★★	412
Chiller, The	★★★	412
Chronic Fixation	★★★	209
Coming of Age	★★★	151
Crossfire	★★★	131
Dark Venomous Reality	★★★	115
Diaphanous	★★★	407
Dirtbag Dharma	★★★	395
Dog Pounder	★★★	76
Dr. Livingstone, I Presume	★★★	485
Eighteen-Wheeler	★★★	150
Fall Line Crack	★★★	288
Find Us Another Cliff, Barbara	★★★	352
Hammerhead	★★★	445
Heat Wave	★★★	183
Home Rule	★★★	91
Huckleberry Hound	★★★	224
I Am Not a Toy!	★★★	340
I See You	★★★	445
I'll Fly Away	★★★	212
Keira's Thumbs	★★★	255
Land of Make-Believe	★★★	128
Lex Luther	★★★	38
Monty Python	★★★	48
Mossiah, The	★★★	396

Graded List of Climbs

Climb	Rating	Page
Norton Anthology, The	★★★	440
Pandemonium	★★★	43
Park and Ride	★★★	150
Purist, The	★★★	441
Puzzle Rue	★★★	86
Rock Hangers	★★★	460
Roof Traverse	★★★	304
Saffron Revolution	★★★	418
Spelunking Midget	★★★	311
Starline	★★★	283
Three Stooges, Shelving Rock	★★★	42
Time Jumpers	★★★	38
Trick Move	★★★	138
True North	★★★	139
Two Pots to Piss In	★★★	61
Vendetta, variation to War of the Worlds	★★★	67
Where the Wild Things Are	★★★	478
Animal Farm	★★	184
Asteroid Belt	★★	129
Black Streak	★★	115
Boiler Maker	★★	298
Bouncer	★★	290
Cleopatra	★★	125
Corpus Callosum	★★	78
Cranium	★★	206
Fracture Zone	★★	128
Ghost Boner	★★	51
Goat's Foot on Rock	★★	35
Hunter's Moon	★★	110
J.D. Memorial Route	★★	71
No Más	★★	396
Pomme de Terre	★★	94
Pox, Crane Mountain	★★	168
Riprovando	★★	182
Roof Traverse Variation, variation to Roof Traverse	★★	304
Royal Savage	★★	90
SARS Right	★★	169
Side Show, variation to Gun Show	★★	203
Stretch Armstrong, variation to Adrenaline Surge	★★	303
Ten Even	★★	129
This is Spinal Tap	★★	78
Too Burly Bulls	★★	360
Walk Like an Egyptian	★★	126
Wildcat	★★	398
Carl's New Baby	★	79
Conveyor Belt	★	154
Eastman-Kodak Crack	★	133
Fifi Fingers	★	211
Gyroscopic Tendencies	★	56
Hipster Handbook	★	416
Incision	★	115
Invisible Man, The	★	303
Midsummer Night's Frustration, A	★	153
Revolver	★	74

Climb	Rating	Page
Rosemary's Baby	★	79
Sentry	★	202
Thin Soles	★	69
Travisty	★	134
Where's My Cane?	★	78
Winter's Tale	★	280
Ali-Kat		121
Beam Me to Leoni's		343
Bloodroot		121
Cold Stone Sober		313
Controversial Midgets		202
County Route 40		349
Crime, Fools, and Treasure		415
Dennis' Demise		129
Detour on Route 73		213
Direct Start, variation to Smear Campaign		90
Don's Toprope		302
Duty Free		302
Eastern Shield		450
Fang, The		283
Fifth Metacarpal		462
Free Swing		90
Go Fish		327
Intrusion		517
Mad Cows		182
Mule Kick		314
Not for Love or Lust, variation to Slim Pickins		265
Pine Cone Eaters, variation to Too Early Spring		359
Psycho Slut		88
P-Town Approach		449
Rattlesnake		49
S.O.L.		326
Schadenfreude		466
Shaky Spider		200
Speakeasy		314
Tanks of Beer, variation to Tita U. Assol		314
Tequila Mockingbird Direct, variation to Tequila Mockingbird		295
Teriyaki Hairpiece		309
Third Time for Mrs. Robinson		246
Tunnel Vision		129
Weekend Warrior		246
Welcome to Deadwater, variation to Tombstone		157
Wheezy, variation to To Infinity and Beyond!		339
Whips and Chains		274
Wild Man from Borneo		368
Your Anus		128

5.10

Climb	Rating	Page
In Hiding	★★★	459
Superman Flake Alternative Finish	★★★	272
Ambush	★★	317
Sinner Repent	★★	458

Climb	Rating	Page
Trick or Treat, Pharaoh Mountain	★★	130
Banana Splitter		254
Cosmic Thing		379
Forward to Death, variation to First Feast		411
Golden Dreams		151
Jay's Job		148
Pay As You Go		456
Pay Dirt		321
Pulpitted		386

5.10c

Climb	Rating	Page
El Regalo	★★★★★	83
Maestro	★★★★★	99
Sole Fusion	★★★★★	266
Barney Is the Antichrist	★★★★	226
Cosmopolitan Wall	★★★★	70
C-Tips	★★★★	65
Damn Your Eyes	★★★★	389
Die by the Drop	★★★★	56
Jackal	★★★★	130
Menace to Sobriety	★★★★	96
My Generation	★★★★	328
No Comments from the Peanut Gallery	★★★★	294
Orange Crush	★★★★	338
Queen of the Jungle	★★★★	453
Rico's Roughnecks	★★★★	487
Rule of the Bone	★★★★	346
Scary Potter Traverse	★★★★	481
Tommy Gun	★★★★	344
Tongue and Groove	★★★★	115
Animal Charm	★★★	185
Arachnophobic Reaction	★★★	238
Bouncy Bounce	★★★	66
Boyz in the Hood	★★★	171
Carhartt Confidentials	★★★	42
Ceremony of Innocence	★★★	359
Coy Dog	★★★	347
Dacker Cracker	★★★	260
Devil Wears Prana	★★★	70
Diamonds Aren't Forever	★★★	194
Dill Pickle	★★★	127
Enduro Man	★★★	56
Favela	★★★	238
Flashdance	★★★	248
Flatrock Arête	★★★	355
I Wish	★★★	355
Keep the Faith	★★★	130
Lawyers, Guns, and Money	★★★	174
Line of Fire	★★★	51
Mayflower	★★★	86
Messiah, Ark Wall	★★★	61
New Star	★★★	112
Noah's Ark	★★★	62
Oracle	★★★	62
Pining for More	★★★	257
Rocinha	★★★	235
Rock and Roll Star	★★★	358

Graded List of Climbs

Climb	Stars	Page
Sauron's Bolt of Horror	★★★	188
Shot in the Dark, A	★★★	432
Star Sailor	★★★	365
Static Cling, Poke-O Moonshine	★★★	38
Supercharged	★★★	307
Thorn Forest	★★★	67
Tree Hugger	★★★	366
Wall Ruler	★★★	206
Afternoon Matinee, The	★★	400
Beauty to Come, The	★★	311
Beckerheads	★★	59
Broken Mirror	★★	325
Charming Hackett	★★	45
Continental Drift	★★	125
Criss Cross	★★	314
Death Trap	★★	304
Doc Holiday	★★	156
Falcon Free	★★	36
Gold Digger	★★	200
Gunga Din Chin	★★	156
Justin Time	★★	255
No Ifs, Ands, or Buts	★★	244
Octoberfest	★★	133
Profusion	★★	106
Reducto Adductor	★★	208
Standard	★★	296
Thunder Down Under	★★	46
Turning 21 Again	★★	450
Welcome to Arietta	★★	314
B.O. Plenty	★	59
Back to School	★	80
Evil Twin	★	487
Golden Road	★	230
Holy Grail	★	50
Hung Jury	★	492
Saranac Saber	★	426
Skeleton Key	★	269
Spit and Drivel	★	120
White Arête	★	305
A.S.		94
Anniversary Waltz		356
Crunchy on the Outside, Chewy on the Inside		77
Delirium Tremens		302
Destined for Obscurity		412
Domingo		102
Jungle Rot		168
Oops! I'm Pregnant		461
Passion Corner		304
Roped Bouldering		169
Shaggy's Secret Stash		441
Stinky Pete, variation to Sarge		339
Straight and Narrow		120
Suspect Terrane		127
Tarsal Grinder		187
Upright and Locked		368
V for Victory		133
Vermontville Redneck		356
Zigzag Crack, variation to Out with the Boys Again		438

5.10d

Climb	Stars	Page
Anaconda	★★★★★	113
Connecticut Yankee	★★★★★	458
Eagle Has Landed, The	★★★★★	373
Flapjack	★★★★★	128
Great Northern Diver	★★★★★	450
Once in a Lifetime	★★★★★	477
Plate Tectonics	★★★★★	126
Redneck on a Rope	★★★★★	252
Save a Tree, Eat a Beaver	★★★★★	420
Sheer Failure	★★★★★	522
Black Lung	★★★★	297
Father Knows Best	★★★★	317
Finger Lickin' Good	★★★★	451
Garand Arête	★★★★	344
Garden of Leadin'	★★★★	473
Knights in Armor	★★★★	64
Macintosh	★★★★	94
Perfect Storm	★★★★	126
Perilous Journey	★★★★	526
South Face Direct	★★★★	476
Talus Man	★★★★	325
Two Evil Deeds	★★★★	62
Under the Influence	★★★★	96
Wolfman	★★★★	485
Bears, Beets, Battlestar Galactica	★★★	472
Beaver Fever, Beaver Wall, Poke-O Moonshine	★★★	141
Bromancing the Stone	★★★	457
Double Diamond	★★★	84
Eternity	★★★	271
Falling Kaiser Zone	★★★	67
Fifty Grades of Spray	★★★	191
Footloose	★★★	47
Hooverville	★★★	238
It Don't Come Easy	★★★	85
Morning Star	★★★	87
Out for the Boyz	★★★	415
Pat Tricks	★★★	309
Protruding Forehead	★★★	53
Ripples	★★★	223
Santa Crux	★★★	419
Smallville Right	★★★	38
Snowbound	★★★	120
Thunderhead	★★★	95
Time Bomb	★★★	160
Wandering Lunatic	★★★	304
Welcome to America	★★★	323
Yabba Dabba Doo	★★★	339
Ace of Diamonds	★★	175
Approach Shoe Assassin	★★	305
Bandito	★★	157
Bird's Nest	★★	260
Birthday Spanking	★★	79
Cliff Notes	★★	440
Cosmic Arrest	★★	131
Crack in the Woods	★★	316
Eat Dessert First	★★	81
Edge of the Valley	★★	256
Ghost Rider, variation to Adrenaline Surge	★★	303
Good to the Last Drop	★★	421
Gu-man-chu	★★	91
Ku Klux Who?, variation to White Knight	★★	269
Silver	★★	418
Sinful Ways	★★	76
Tartar Control	★★	113
There Be Dragons	★★	412
Where Beagles Dare	★★	377
D Squared	★	68
Dirty Dancing	★	47
End Game	★	96
Foam Flower	★	133
Halloween Cracks	★	130
Morse Code	★	117
Plunge, The	★	90
Steel Breeze	★	120
Wilderness Work	★	131
Autumn Flare		50
Avalauncher, variation to Dorsal Fin		523
Dutchman's Britches		140
Fastest Shark, variation to Shark Week		79
Flying & Drinking Direct, variation to Flying & Drinking and Drinking & Driving		296
Frosty Edge, variation to Frosted Mug		296
Gull Pucky		133
Hangover		309
Interloper		458
Isotope, variation to Radioactive		294
Paper Walls		102
Pardon Me, Boy		225
Pegasus Direct		308
Radioactive Direct Direct, variation to Radioactive		294
Radioactive Direct, variation to Radioactive		294
Rainbow Crack		120
Shark's Fin, The		256
Shirtless In November		314
Sound System		50
Sweat Man		331
Tenacity		230
Three B's		472
Toodeloo		232
Wipe It Off		342

5.10+

Climb	Stars	Page
Psychotic	★★★	277
Call Me Gone		211
Capstone		423

Graded List of Climbs

5.11a

Climb	Rating	Page
Drop, Fly, or Die	★★★★★	267
Endless Journey	★★★★★	83
Free Ride	★★★★★	455
Zoinks!!	★★★★★	442
Alien Umbrella	★★★★	300
Amongst the Crowd/Clouds	★★★★	96
Bear Claw	★★★★	116
Bent Hickory	★★★★	300
Bimathalon	★★★★	468
Casual Observer	★★★★	77
Inner Space	★★★★	111
Insomnia	★★★★	226
Macho	★★★★	69
Medicine Man	★★★★	328
Pandora's Box	★★★★	305
Plumb Line, Crane Mountain	★★★★	206
Ravenous	★★★★	375
Sausage Science	★★★★	334
Stones of Shame	★★★★	127
WISWIG	★★★★	156
African Barking Spiders	★★★	455
Beyond Reason	★★★	192
Bubba Does Baker	★★★	427
Bulge Bulge Roof	★★★	288
Code Breaker	★★★	128
Coronary Country	★★★	404
Cover Charge	★★★	293
Crux Capacitor	★★★	38
Darkest Africa	★★★	130
Deer Hunter	★★★	419
Enigma	★★★	127
Eyes on the Prize	★★★	355
Falconer	★★★	396
Flight into Emerald City	★★★	250
Happy Thoughts and Chalk Dust	★★★	446
Hippie Sticks and Black Flies	★★★	445
It Goes to Eleven	★★★	452
Judge Judy, variation to Hung Jury	★★★	492
Life During Wartime	★★★	335
Lost Hunters Crack	★★★	318
Lucky Stars	★★★	331
Mummy, The	★★★	126
Nettle Highway	★★★	248
Papa Don't Preach	★★★	371
Peter Croft and the Crime-Fighting Bear	★★★	371
Price is Right, The	★★★	46
Ragtime	★★★	70
Seeking Enlightenment	★★★	444
Skid Row	★★★	236
Slabmeister	★★★	210
Spirit of Adventure	★★★	398
Ten B	★★★	309
Trigger Finger, West Mountain	★★★	344
Young Heavy Roosters	★★★	321
Annie's Dilemma	★★	99
Apollo Tucker	★★	226
Banana Hammock	★★	254
Big Purple Rat	★★	226
Bootlegger Variation, variation to Scarface	★★	410
Breadline	★★	236
Bulging Smear	★★	185
Castor Canidensis	★★	420
Crimp Scampi	★★	305
Crimps are for Pimps	★★	311
Crispy Critter	★★	239
Divine Wind	★★	120
Foosa Territory	★★	116
Here Come the Pigs	★★	128
Keyhole, The	★★	311
Master Craft	★★	244
Monkey See, Monkey Do	★★	267
Moonshine	★★	100
Playing Stick	★★	70
Resistant Strain	★★	168
Scorpion	★★	53
Stretch Armstrong	★★	279
Tongue-Lashing	★★	114
Tough Act, A	★★	254
True Grit	★★	72
Bastard	★	42
Dushara	★	229
Libido	★	53
Magic Flute	★	522
Mouth That Roared, The	★	293
Shredded Wheat	★	131
Toss Me My Nuts	★	134
Trigger Finger, Lost Hunters Cliff	★	316
Wide Supremacy	★	86
Wild Blue	★	53
Wrong Again, Chalkbreath Bear	★	260
		156
Black Crack		133
Cogito, The, variation to Fastest Gun		78
Death Proof		414
Freestyle		418
Greenhouse Defect		173
Greenhouse Effect Direct, variation to Greenhouse Effect		174
Hooker Heels and Crimp Pimps		371
Microwave		48
Pine Nuts		67
Placid Es Pontas		386
Pod Puller		88
Silver Slab		468
TAO, variation to Watch My Bolt		100
Time Piece		312
Traverse City		341
Trilogy, variation to Darkest Africa		130

5.11b

Climb	Rating	Page
Azurite	★★★★★	412
Earthly Night	★★★★★	89
Keep, The	★★★★★	206
Running of the Bulls	★★★★★	360
Cara Bonita	★★★★	83
Chocoholic	★★★★	192
Claim Jumper	★★★★	48
Creation of the World	★★★★	403
Elusive Bastard	★★★★	400
Fear and Loathing in Keene Valley	★★★★	265
Flying Squirrels	★★★★	358
Hang Time	★★★★	205
Honey Dipper	★★★★	146
Jug Monkey	★★★★	301
Karmic Kickback	★★★★	59
Lurch	★★★★	468
Oral Surgery	★★★★	456
Oscillation Overthruster	★★★★	335
Prelude to Gravity	★★★★	440
Raging Raven	★★★★	360
Run Higher, Jump Faster	★★★★	362
Rusty Lumberjack	★★★★	47
Smear Campaign	★★★★	90
Space Race	★★★★	368
Tennessee Excursion	★★★★	225
Twilight	★★★★	112
Welcome to McMartin	★★★★	321
What The Eft	★★★★	297
Anal Retention	★★★	56
Bigger Than Jesus	★★★	275
Deuteronomy	★★★	50
Firing Line	★★★	48
Foreplay	★★★	85
Grapes of Wrath	★★★	94
Home Run Derby	★★★	56
I Can't Believe It's Not Butter	★★★	279
If You Don't Like It, Leave	★★★	442
Jenga	★★★	445
Joy Crack	★★★	299
Jumpin' Jack Flash	★★★	124
Katrina	★★★	50
Knights That Say Neigh	★★★	50
Letting Go	★★★	85
Master of the Flying Guillotine	★★★	332
Mastercharge	★★★	244
Prohibition	★★★	296
Sailor's Dive	★★★	84
Satisfaction Guaranteed	★★★	88
Talons of Power	★★★	335
TG Farm	★★★	523
Thrill Ride	★★★	106
Till the Fat Lady Sings	★★★	250
George	★★	399
Harvest Moon	★★	304
Juicy Fruit	★★	170
La Spirale	★★	95

Graded List of Climbs

Climb	Stars	Page
Medieval Times	★★	206
Raven	★★	122
Rope Monster	★★	189
Scaredy Cat, Crane Mountain	★★	197
Teflon Wall	★★	224
Telegraph Crack	★★	117
Tighter than Two	★★	186
Tuesdays	★★	300
Tuna Fish Crack	★★	131
Valium	★★	76
Verdon	★★	52
Gravity Grave	★	77
Jelly Arms	★	260
Mother Nature	★	256
Pocket Pool	★	69
Super Cell	★	377
Waiting for the Son	★	358
Adirondack Crack		122
Crazy Fingers		311
Direct Start, variation to Drop, Fly, or Die		267
Exit Cracks		74
Foot Patrol		224
Forget Bullet		49
Gun Control		77
James and the Giant Boulder		437
Miller Time		234
Patent-Proof Roof		135
Quo Vadis		95
Radio Flier, variation to Flexi-Flier		346
Red Hill Mining Town		290
Retrograde		259
Silver Chicken		256
Snow Blue		87
Sour Grapes		94
Statute of Rights		412
Thunder and Lichen		192
Turbocharge Direct Finish, variation to Turbocharge		307
Whipping Post, The		400
Wright Stuff, The		526

5.11

Climb	Stars	Page
Cement Mixer, The	★★★	485
Gizmo		488
Passing By		256
Summit Snacks		527

5.11c

Climb	Stars	Page
Born Ready	★★★★★	128
Gathering, The	★★★★★	80
Iron Cross	★★★★★	86
Release The Kraken	★★★★★	300
Shark Week	★★★★	79
Borderline	★★★★	85
Bushido	★★★	36
Class Five	★★★	381
Connoisseur	★★★	130
El Supremo	★★★	372

Climb	Stars	Page
Fear of a Flat Planet	★★★★	86
Jug-Or-Not	★★★★	473
La Frontera	★★★★	83
Lichen or Not, Eagle Falls	★★★★	379
Pilgrim's Progress	★★★★	87
Pleasure Victim	★★★★	454
Resurrection	★★★★	84
Romano's Route	★★★★	269
Stones of Shame Direct	★★★★	127
Vagtastic Voyage	★★★★	42
Ward Cleaver	★★★★	331
Cinnamon Girl	★★★	282
Corkscrew	★★★	316
Feeding The Rat	★★★	299
Four Guns Blazing	★★★	209
Good and Plenty	★★★	65
Hard Times, Shanty Cliff	★★★	235
Hop on Pop	★★★	414
Little Sister	★★★	487
N.R.A.	★★★	192
Plan C	★★★	488
Plumb Line Direct, variation to Plumb Line	★★★	206
Pox, Silver Lake	★★★	484
Pumpernickel	★★★	265
Radio Face	★★★	119
Tumbler	★★★	235
Unforgiven	★★★	70
Air Male	★★	39
Chattanooga Choo-Choo	★★	225
Dark Horse Ail	★★	296
Eurotech	★★	364
Flake 'n Bake	★★	90
Piece of Snatch	★★	64
Wimp Crack	★★	333
Womb with a View, A	★★	44
Only the Good Die Young	★	265
All the King's Men, variation to Kingdom Come		209
Black Triangle Right		89
D1		200
Doc Theo		347
Five Hundred Rednecks with Guns		260
Gun Control Now, variation to Gun Control		77
Matrix, variation to Pilgrim's Progress		87
Sirloin Tips		190
Smoke Signal		131
Solarium, The		70
Tommy's Climb		130
What about Bob		347

5.11d

Climb	Stars	Page
Catatonic	★★★★★	398
Haroom Baroom	★★★★★	443
It's Only Entertainment	★★★★★	261
Dreamweaver	★★★★	458
Easy Street	★★★★	70

Climb	Stars	Page
Extreme Unction	★★★★	80
Hidden Constellation	★★★★	365
Just Take It	★★★★	47
Monkey Pump	★★★★	146
Crack Mechanic	★★★	366
Hang 'Em High	★★★	42
Hold It Like a Hamburger	★★★	483
In Vivo	★★★	103
Normal Route	★★★	267
Parthenope	★★★	312
Potato-Chip Flake	★★★	225
Ten Plagues, The	★★★	126
Defiant Eyes	★★	138
Devotee	★★	130
Dukes of Hazard	★★	305
Gauntlet, The	★★	126
Locust Posts	★★	323
Mideast Solution, The	★★	488
Mikkihiiri	★★	322
Pete's Wicked Flail	★★	299
Swamp Thang	★★	285
Chicken Wire	★	261
Rapture, The	★	87
Sands of Time	★	130
Vision Quest	★	303
Watch Crystal	★	312
Direct Start, variation to Pomme de Terre		94
Feet of Fire		250
Hit by a Car, variation to Jelly Arms		260
Jamie Lee Curtis		392
Kamikaze Heart		70
Musse Pigg		322
Porcelain Mechanic, The		366
Silver Streak		62
Spooks		52

5.11+

Climb	Stars	Page
Machine Gun Kelly	★★	408
Born To Run		486
Slash and Burn		360

5.12a

Climb	Stars	Page
Another Wack and Dangle Job	★★★★★	206
Center Stage	★★★★★	293
Fancy Cat, The	★★★★★	41
Inner Sanctum	★★★★★	317
Mental Blocks	★★★★★	461
Aerie	★★★★	398
Awesome Sauce	★★★★	171
Bitter End	★★★★	130
Bushmaster	★★★★	36
Flying Buddha	★★★★	444
Infinity Crack	★★★★	48
Mistah Luthah	★★★★	403
Munchky Microarête, variation to Earthly Night	★★★★	89
Pothead	★★★★	473
Promiscuous Girl	★★★★	379

Graded List of Climbs

Climb	Stars	Page
Rhinoplasty	★★★★	84
Roof Direct	★★★★	305
Scarecrow	★★★★	353
Southern Hospitality	★★★★	73
Summer Break	★★★★	53
Terapia	★★★★	316
White Knight	★★★★	269
Austin City Limits	★★★	134
Black Dog	★★★	86
Bonnie and Clyde	★★★	282
Crazy Horse	★★★	160
Cross to Bear, A	★★★	417
Daughter of the Moon	★★★	151
Escape from Iowa	★★★	224
Grand Hysteria	★★★	269
Hot Compress	★★★	316
Kodiak	★★★	116
Pinching One Off	★★★	56
Project X	★★★	48
Queen for a Day	★★★	330
Side Boob	★★★	279
Sphinx in the Face	★★	126
Bugged Out	★★	400
Crispy Critters	★★	488
Parabolic Cats	★★	103
Walking the Tightrope	★★	360
Working Wives	★★	203
Brown and Serve	★	335
Chingacrack	★	72
Feed the Beast	★	117
Little Rascals	★	340
Uncle Remus	★	89
Weekday Special	★	427
Captain Hooks, variation to It's Only Entertainment		261
CB Love Grannys		309
Counting Coup		347
Fear of Frogs		130
Hair Trigger		318
Saranac Face		427
Save the Rock for Uncle Sam		72
Suicide King		330
Too Wet to Plow		250
Touch of Gray, A, variation to Rough Cut		231
Trouser Gallery, variation to Frippery		414
Twelve-Step Program		298

5.12b

Climb	Stars	Page
Buck Fever	★★★★★	318
Battle of Alcatraz	★★★★★	409
Beavers Taste Like Wood	★★★★	421
Big Buddha	★★★★	36
Buzz Off	★★★★	297
Like a Boss	★★★★	172
Mogster	★★★★	69
Remembering Youth	★★★★	50
Tsunami Slap-Up	★★★★	332
Cosmic Ripple	★★★	42
Flavor of the Day	★★★	313
Pat's Blue Ribbon, variation to Miller Light	★★★	310
Atmospheric Pressure	★★	377
Slip of the Tongue	★★	114
Jungle Fever	★	262
BOA		409
Free the Slaves		202
Preservation		318
Widow Maker		362

5.12

Climb	Stars	Page
Suomi	★★★	321
Rasp		256
The Project, variation to Emperor Zurg		340
Unfinished Business		332

5.12c

Climb	Stars	Page
Calvary Hill	★★★★★	84
Push	★★★★★	328
Urgent Fury	★★★★★	146
Bodacious	★★★★	37
Connection	★★★★	385
Messiah, Poke-O Moonshine	★★★★	85
Miller Light	★★★★	310
Northern Revival	★★★★	245
Pentecostal	★★★★	52
Raptor's Scream	★★★★	90
Scarface	★★★★	410
Sea of Seams	★★★★	65
Howling, The	★★★★	52
Lycanthropia	★★★	267
Tachycardia	★★★	100
Peace in Our Climbs	★	261
Black Widow, variation to Pumpernickel		265
Ku Klux Ken, variation to White Knight		269
Separate Denialty		135

5.12d

Climb	Stars	Page
Brass Balls, Steel Nuts, and Sticky Rubber	★★★★★	402
Four Ounces to Freedom	★★★★	202
Incredible Hulk, The	★★★★	303
They Never Recognized Me	★★★	310
Jeff–James	★★	400
Captain Crimper	★	68
Northern Inhospitality, variation to Southern Hospitality		73
Reciprocity		385

5.12+

Climb	Stars	Page
Godfather, The	★★★	410

5.13 and Above

Climb	Stars	Page
Elusive Trophy	★★★★★	317
Fire in the Sky	★★★★★	406
Great Escape, The, Alcatraz	★★★★★	409
Highline, The	★★★★★	406
Illuminescence	★★★★★	406
Moonshine and Chronic	★★★★★	488
Oppositional Defiance Disorder	★★★★★	462
Wheelin' N' Dealin'	★★★★★	267
Bookmaker's Variation, variation to The Godfather	★★★★	410
Dope-a-Mean	★★★★	134
House of Cards	★★★★	327
Leap of Faith	★★★★	151
Mark's Blue Ribbon, variation to They Never Recognized Me	★★★★	310
Mushu	★★★★	171
Salad Days	★★★★	52
Zabba	★★★★	265
Sasquatch Hunting	★★★	84
Sword of Deception, The	★★★	488
Raging Asian		171

STATIONERY & GIFTS

featuring artwork by

Lucie Wellner

boundingbee.com

Available at:
The Mountaineer, Keene Valley
Adirondack Museum Store,
Blue Mountain Lake

Martin von Arx on *The Eagle Has Landed* (5.10d), Eagle F...

*Jeremy Haas on **Rhinoplasty** (5.12a) at Potash Cliff, belayed by Jeremy Morgan. Photo by Drew Haas.*

Index

1968 Offwidth Pants,
    variation to Frippery *415*
3.2 . . . . *290*
3D *524*
40 Oz. to Freedom *290*
5.10 WALL , THE, Upper Beer
    Wall, Beer Walls. *293*
5.58 . . . . *289*
5756 in Service **131**
5th Season, The *330*
7 Year Itch *45*

A

A. Minor Mellor Route. *506*
A.S. *94*
ABOVE-THE-MEASLES WALL,
    Crane Mountain **166**
Abracadabra. **458**
Access Slot **159**
Ace of Diamonds *175*
Adirondack Black Fly Rancher . *402*
Adirondack Crack *122*
Adirondack High *125*
Adirondack Rehab **195**
Adonis *42*
Adrenaline Surge **303**
Adsit Arête. **369**
Æon Flux **407**
Aerie *398*
Affliction. *522*
Afraid of the Dark *329*
A-Frame *308*
African Barking Spiders **455**
After Ireland. *330*
After Irene *317*
After the Bash **466**
After the Gold Rush,
    variation to Gold Wall *136*
Afternoon Delight *302*
Afternoon Matinee, The *400*
Afternoon Tea **148**
AG *450*
AGHARTA WALL, Panther
    Gorge, Mt Marcy *499*
Ahhh Autumn **255**
Aid Crack **433**
AID WALL, Moss Cliff *403*
Air Male *39*
Airtime **323**
ALCATRAZ *408*
Alien Shrimp **281**
Alien Umbrella **300**
Ali-Kat **121**
All the King's Men, variation
    to Kingdom Come **209**
Almost Rectum *420*
Along the Watchtower *129*
Also Ran **174**

Alter Weg. *371*
Amanita Muscaria **355**
Amateur's Edge *315*
Ambush **317**
American-Russian-Chinese
    Route *117*
Amid the Flood **157**
Amnesia **422**
Amnesia Chasm **200**
Amongst the Crowd/Clouds . . *96*
AMPERSAND MOUNTAIN **526**
Amphibious Moat Monsters . . **203**
Amphitheater Crack **202**
AMPHITHEATER OF THE
    OVERHANGS, Chapel
    Pond Gully Cliff *224*
AMPHITHEATER, Black Arches
    Wall, Crane Mountain **200**
Amulet, The **330**
Anaconda **113**
Anal Retention **56**
Analysis Paralysis **380**
Ancient of Days *89*
And She Was *391*
Andromeda **284**
Angry Hemorrhoid Chimney . . **454**
Animal (5.10c) **188**
Animal Charm **185**
ANIMAL CHARM WALL, Upper
    Walls, Crane Mountain . . . **185**
Animal Farm **184**
Animal Logic **120**
Ankle Bruise *169*
ANNEX, THE, The Lost Crags . *314*
Annie's Crack **72**
Annie's Dilemma *99*
Anniversary Waltz *356*
Anopheles **82**
Another Beer Walls Black
    Streak *303*
Another Botanical Wonder . . . **273**
Another Crack in the Wall **454**
Another Crack, variation to
    Great Chimney *366*
ANOTHER ROADSIDE
    DISTRACTION *153*
Another Wack and
    Dangle Job *206*
Another Walk in the Sky **228**
Anteater *307*
Antivenom **113**
Ape X **185**
Apollo Tucker **226**
Appomattox Crack **331**
Approach Shoe Assassin **305**
Aquaman *370*
AQUARIUM, THE *221*
Aquarius **284**
Arachnid Traction *238*

Arachnophobic Reaction *238*
Arc of a Climber *153*
Arch Crack, The, variation to
    Pilgrim's Progress *87*
Arch Madness *440*
Arch Traverse *110*
Arch, The *111*
Arête's Syndrome **466**
Areticus Maximus **116**
ARK WALL **60**
Armistice *196*
Arrested Development *194*
As She Is *391*
Asher Crack **79**
Aspaguass **242**
ASPCA **345**
Asterisk **282**
ASTERISK, Washbowl Pond . . *254*
Asteroid **251**
Asteroid Belt *129*
Atlantis *130*
Atlas Shrugged, variation to
    Eastern Shield *451*
Atmospheric Pressure *377*
Atom Smasher *144*
Atomic Vomit **459**
Attachment **467**
Atwell's Revenge **352**
AUGER FALLS **340**
Aunt Polly **222**
AUSABLE #4 . . . . **336**
Ausable Arête *407*
AUSABLE ARETE, Moss Cliff . *407*
AUSABLE BUTTRESS,
    Moss Cliff *407*
Austin City Limits **134**
Autopilot **70**
Autumn Flare *50*
Autumn Gold *138*
Autumn Slab **342**
AVALANCHE LAKE *507*
AVALANCHE PASS,
    Avalanche Lake *509*
Avalauncher, variation to
    Dorsal Fin *523*
Awesome Sauce *171*
Azure **360**
AZURE MOUNTAIN **408**
Azurite **412**

B

B Gentle *278*
B.A.R. **343**
B.M.Z., The *462*
B.O. Plenty **59**
B-47 . . . . *526*
BABY DOME *168*
Bachelors and Bowery Bums . . *349*

Index

Back on the Horse **424**
Back to School **80**
Backer Line **73**
Backs against the Wall *310*
BACKWATER WALL, Boquet
    River Crags *185*
Bad Advice *281*
Bad Brains **430**
Bad Karma *524*
Badinage. **150**
Badminton 101 . . . . *258*
Bag It or Buy It **256**
Bailey–Bolliger Route *221*
BAKER MOUNTAIN **425**
BALCONY CLIFF,
    Lower Washbowl *280*
BALD MOUNTAIN **356**
BALDFACE MOUNTAIN **253**
Balls In Space **338**
BANANA BELT,
    Washbowl Pond *253*
Banana Hammock *254*
Banana Republic *254*
Banana Splitter *254*
Bandaloop Dancers **113**
Bandit, The *124*
Bandito *157*
BANZAI WALL, Peregrine
    Pillar Area *335*
Bara Bara *327*
Barbara's Fault *336*
Barbecued Dogs, variation
    to Wald-Calder Route *358*
Barista **229**
BARKEATER CLIFF *339*
Barking Spider **76**
Barking up the Wrong Climb . . *349*
Barn Buttress *145*
BARN ROCK *145*
Barney Is the Antichrist **226**
Barrel of Monkeys *339*
Barstool Direct *311*
BARTON HIGH CLIFF **117**
BASIN MOUNTAIN *487*
BASS LAKE HILL CRAG *165*
Bastard *42*
Basti **240**
Bastille Day *196*
Bathtub Virgin *44*
Bats and Bird Vomit, variation
    to Look, Roll, and Fire *328*
Battle Creek *37*
Battle Fatigue *120*
Battle of Alcatraz *409*
Baywatch **113**
BBC *244*
Beam Me to Leoni's *343*
Beam Me Up *232*
Beam Us Up, Scotty, variation
    to The El *363*
Beanstalk *468*

Bear *156*
Bear Claw **116**
BEAR DEN, Olympic Acres . . . *416*
Bear Necessities *417*
Bearded Munchkin **444**
Beardsley Buttress **148**
BEARDSLEY BUTTRESS,
    Beaverview Cliff,
    Crane Mountain **148**
Bears, Beets, Battlestar
    Galactica **472**
Beat the Crowd **147**
Beating to North *143*
Beautiful Dreamer **174**
Beauty to Come, The **311**
BEAVER BROOK *420*
Beaver Fever, Beaver Brook . . *420*
Beaver Fever, Beaver Wall,
    Poke-O Moonshine *141*
BEAVER WALL,
    Poke-O Moonshine *141*
Beavers Taste Like Wood *421*
BEAVERVIEW CLIFF,
    Crane Mountain **146**
Because Dogs Can *347*
Beckerheads **59**
Bee Hold *194*
Beechnut *171*
Beehive *378*
BEER WALLS *285*
Bee's Knees *135*
Before The Fall **466**
Beginner's Route **449**
Bella Vista **175**
BELLAVISTA SLAB,
    Crane Mountain **174**
Belle Bottom Crack **174**
Belleview **173**
BELLEVIEW AREA,
    Crane Mountain **171**
BELLEVIEW SLAB,
    Crane Mountain **173**
BELOW-THE-MEASLES WALL,
    Crane Mountain **170**
Bender's Chasm **222**
Benediction **175**
Bengal Tiger *347*
Ben's Bump **176**
Bent Hickory **300**
Berry Good *417*
Best of Friends, variation
    to Helms-Jolley *388*
Better Place to Be, A *153*
Betty Is a Klepto *339*
BETWEEN THE LAKES *372*
Beyond Reason *192*
Bidonville **239**
Big Bertha *345*
Big Brother **487**
Big Buddha *36*
Big Dack Attack *128*

Big Donger, The **373**
Big In Munchkin Land **133**
Big Man's Bane, variation to
    Induhvidual **191**
Big Purple Rat **226**
BIG SLIDE MOUNTAIN *494*
BIG WALL AREA, Main Face,
    Poke-O Moonshine *80*
Big White Guy **291**
Bigger Than Jesus *275*
BIKINI ATOLL *198*
Bill Route **100**
Bimathalon **468**
BIRCH WALL, Spanky's Wall,
    Spanky's Area *191*
Birdman *410*
Bird's Nest *260*
Birthday Corner **200**
Birthday Route *143*
Birthday Spanking **79**
Bitter End *130*
Black and Tan *189*
Black Arch Arête **206**
BLACK ARCHES WALL,
    Crane Mountain **194**
Black Crack *133*
Black Dog **86**
Black Dog Chimney **424**
Black Lectroids *335*
Black Lung **297**
Black Market *135*
BLACK MARKET WALL, Second
    Tier, Poke-O Moonshine . . *134*
Black Moriah *238*
BLACK MOUNTAIN CLIFF . . . **285**
Black Plague, King Wall *201*
Black Plague, Wallface *445*
Black Streak **115**
Black Triangle Right **89**
BLACK TRIANGLE WALL,
    Campground Wall,
    Rogers Rock **88**
BLACK WALL, THE,
    West Canada Cliff **334**
Black Watch **90**
Black Widow, variation
    to Pumpernickel *265*
BLACKFLY SLAB,
    Inman Slabs **429**
Blacksmith *309*
BLC **179**
Blind Date **277**
Blinded by Rainbows *49*
Block Party *304*
Blockus **446**
Bloodroot **121**
Bloody Mary *76*
BLUE HILL **424**
Blue Streaks **151**
Blue Toes **236**
Blueberry Buttress **451**

Page numbers in this volume   Page numbers in Volume 1   523

Index

Blueberry Crumble 179
Blueberry Flapjacks, variation to
    Madame Blueberry 179
Blueberry Jam. 184
Blueberry Pie. 185
Blueberry Scramble 218
Blueberry Tafone. 179
BlueCross BlueShield. *185*
BLUFF ISLAND. 424
Blunderbus 343
Bo Peep 232
BOA. *409*
Bob's Knob Standard *220*
Bodacious *37*
Bodega .483
Bodhi Tree. 191
Body Snatcher, The *62*
Bog Spavin 147
Bogeyman. *369*
Bogosity (5.8+) *368*
Bogus Dent. 236
Boiler Maker *298*
Bon Chance, Crane Mountain .175
Bon Chance,
    Good Luck Mountain 325
Bonanza Lunchbox. 482
Bond Girls *236*
Bone Games, variation to
    Standing Room Only *315*
BONEYARD, Huckleberry
    Mountain 216
Bong Hits 4 Jesus. 422
Bonnie and Clyde. *282*
Bonus Mule. *163*
Boob Job. 84
Bookmaker's Variation, variation
    to The Godfather *410*
Bootlegger Variation, variation
    to Scarface *410*
BOQUET CANYON, Boquet
    River Crags *182*
BOQUET RIVER CRAGS *181*
Borderline *85*
Born Ready. 128
Born To Run 486
Bottle, The. *466*
Bottleneck *466*
Bouncer. *290*
Bouncy Bounce 66
Bowling for Simon. 108
BOXCAR, Boquet River Crags .*183*
Boyz in the Hood *171*
Bozeman Bullet. *158*
BRAIN, THE, Pilot Knob
    Mountain 78
Brainy McCracken 447
Branches. 358
Brass Balls, Steel Nuts, and
    Sticky Rubber *402*
Brazilian. 476
Breadline. 236

Breaking Bad 51
Breathe Easy. 156
Breeze Crack *350*
Brighter Visions. 156
Brightly Colored Males *230*
Brinksmanship 95
Broil 'n' Brag, variation to
    Roast 'n Boast *391*
Broken Broom (5.10a) 202
Broken Mirror 325
Broken Shovel Gully 220
Bromancing the Stone 457
Bronze *418*
Brothers in Arms. 90
BROTHERS, THE. *489*
Brown and Serve 335
BROWN MOUNTAIN CLIFF . . .102
BROWN SLAB,
    Crane Mountain 148
Brrright Star *368*
Bubba Does Baker. 427
Buck Fever 318
Buck Hunter 71
BUCK MOUNTAIN 67
Buckwheat 251
Buddy of Bradour, variation
    to Labatt-Ami *298*
Buffalo Bob *162*
Buffalo Soldier *249*
Buffaloed Panther, The 432
Bugged Out 400
Bulge Bulge Roof 288
Bulging Smear *185*
Bullhead 261
Bullseye. 340
Bully Pulpit 386
Bulwark .145
Bun in the Oven 72
Bunny Slope 84
Burgundy Color Lily Crack 305
Burke's Path 423
Burnt Toast 449
BURROW, THE, Silver Lake . . .484
Burton Birch Route *168*
Bushido. *36*
Bushmaster. *36*
Bushwhacker 218
Bushy Pussy *501*
Butterflies Are Free, variation
    to Mastercharge *244*
Buttress Slide *528*
Buzz 339
Buzz Off. 297

C

C & E. .236
C CHIMNEY CLIFF, Silver Lake 439
C Crack 443
C+ 440
Cabin 6, Capacity 10 . . . .*449*
Calamity Crack *428*

California Flake *510*
Call Me Gone 211
Call of the Wild 333
CALLIGRAPHY CLIFF,
    Gore Mountain 289
Calvary Hill *84*
CAMEL'S HUMP *166*
CAMPGROUND WALL,
    Rogers Rock 88
Canine *342*
Canoes for Feet *342*
Capstone 423
Captain Chips Traverse, variation
    to Drop, Fly, or Die *267*
Captain Crimper 68
Captain Hooks, variation to It's
    Only Entertainment *261*
Cara Bonita. 83
Caramel Chasm *337*
Carbohydrate *190*
Cardiac Corner 359
Carhartt Confidentials. 42
Caribou Barbie 59
CARL MOUNTAIN CIRQUE,
    Poke-O Moonshine *140*
Carl's Climb. 158
Carl's New Baby 79
Carnivore Crack 185
Carpenter & Das. 195
Carrion and Crawl 335
CASCADE CLIFF,
    Between the Lakes *372*
Cascade Lichen Dance *378*
Case Route *458*
CASE WALL, Beer Walls *314*
Caspian Corner 448
Castaways 94
CASTLE ROCK 279
Castor Canidensis *420*
Casual Observer. *77*
CAT MOUNTAIN 396
Cat Scratch Fever 170
CATAMOUNT MAIN FACE,
    Fly Brook Valley 109
CATAMOUNT MOUNTAIN 433
Catatonic 398
Catch a Wave *154*
Caterpillar Chimney 214
CATERPILLAR CLIFF,
    Crane Mountain 213
Catharsis. *107*
Catnip 397
Cat's Meow, The *500*
Caught in the Act 254
Cave Artist, The. *380*
Cave Finish, variation
    to Regular Route *219*
Caveman Crack 260
CAVEMAN WALL,
    Chimney Mountain 259
Caveman's Hairy Backside 260

Index

CB Love Grannys 309
CCD Route *509*
Cedar Corner, variation to
    Roaring Brook Falls. *317*
Cedar Dog **322**
CEDAR RIVER CRAG **278**
Cedar Root **456**
Cedar Run. **451**
Cement Mixer, The **485**
Cenotaph, The **44**
Center Climb *481*
CENTER OF PROGRESS
    CLIFF, Silver Lake **453**
Center Stage. *293*
Central AC. *350*
CENTRAL CRANE,
    Crane Mountain **148**
Ceremony of Innocence **359**
Certified Raw. *38*
C'est la Vie. *428*
Chalk Full O' Nuts **412**
Chalk-Up Matilda *524*
Chameleon *254*
Changing of the Guard,
    variation to Great Dihedral .*65*
CHAPEL POND GULLY CLIFF .*223*
CHAPEL POND SLAB *213*
CHAPEL POND VIEWPOINT,
    Washbowl Pond *251*
Chapel View Arête *232*
CHARCOAL KILN QUARRY . . .**423**
Charming Hackett. **45**
Chattanooga Choo-Choo *225*
Cheap Date. *229*
Cheap Money *256*
CHECKERBOARD WALL,
    Gore Mountain **288**
Chess Club Crack **173**
Chewing on Balloons *225*
Chicken Flake **159**
Chicken Soup **281**
Chicken Wire *261*
Chik'n Garbonzo, variation
    to The Snake *45*
Chilblain **170**
Children and Alcohol *404*
Child's Play *166*
Chili Pepper Arête *190*
Chiller, The. **412**
CHIMNEY MOUNTAIN **257**
CHIMNEY SUMMIT, Chimney
    Mountain **258**
Chimney Variation *329*
China Grove *235*
Chingacrack **72**
Chipmunk Waltz, The **460**
Chiquita. *254*
Chock Full O' Nuts *189*
Chocoholic *192*
Chocolate City *280*
Chocolate Left. **314**

Chocolate Rain *140*
Chocolate Right **314**
Chokin' Chickens **184**
CHOKIN' CHICKENS WALL,
    Upper Walls,
    Crane Mountain **184**
Chopping Block, The **493**
Chossmonaut **210**
Christine *239*
Chronic Fixation *209*
Chunga's Revenge *275*
Chute to Kill **344**
Chuting Lane. **343**
Chuting Star *363*
Cinnamon Girl *282*
Circuitous Shit. **234**
CIRQUE GLADE AREA,
    Gore Mountain **289**
Cirrhosis *96*
CITADEL, THE,
    The Peasant Crags *195*
Claim Jumper **48**
Class Five **381**
CLEAVER, THE,
    Lower Washbowl *279*
CLEMENTS POND TRAIL **490**
Cleopatra **125**
Cleveland **326**
Cliff Notes **440**
Climb Control to Major Bob *52*
Climb Free or Die Trying *314*
Climb It **406**
Climber's Yodel #7 . . . .**239**
CLN **73**
CLOUDSPIN CLIFF *412*
Cloudsplitter, The **500**
Clutch and Cruise **310**
CLUTCH AND CRUISE CAVE,
    Lower Beer Wall,
    Beer Walls *309*
Clutchin' the Bräu, variation
    to Clutch and Cruise *310*
Coach and Mary **313**
Coal Miner. *199*
COBBLE CLIFF *385*
Cobbler, The **355**
Cock-a-doodle-doo *486*
Cockpit, The **529**
Code Breaker *128*
Codswallop, variation
    to Tallywhacker **225**
Coffee Achievers *366*
Coffee Break **69**
Coffee Shop Panorama **412**
Cogito, The, variation to
    Fastest Gun. *78*
Cold Bare Rapport, The **58**
Cold Draft...Horse, A **423**
Cold Hands, variation to
    Steel Breeze *120*
Cold Stone Sober *313*

Colden Slide *517*
Colden's Corner **255**
Colossus of Tongue **116**
Colt 45 Corner **343**
Columbine Crack **121**
COLUMBINE TERRACE WALL,
    Barton High Cliff **121**
Coming of Age *151*
Commotion **106**
CONCAVE WALL,
    Lower Washbowl *281*
Connecticut Yankee **458**
Connection *385*
Connoisseur *130*
Contact Buzz *330*
Continental Drift *125*
Contos *194*
Contradiction Crack **304**
Controversial Midgets *202*
Conveyor Belt *154*
Cool Water *185*
Cooler, The *79*
Cooney-Norton Face *70*
Coors Corner *304*
Cooties **171**
Coprophagia **56**
Corkscrew **316**
Corktown **239**
CORNER CLIFF,
    Huckleberry Mountain **220**
Corner In Out *184*
CORNER POCKET, Beer Walls *313*
Corner Scramble. **217**
Cornerstone **161**
CORNERSTONE BUTTRESS,
    The Prows,
    Crane Mountain **160**
Coronary Country *404*
Corpus Callosum **78**
Corvus Crack **353**
Cosmic Arrest *131*
Cosmic Ray **284**
Cosmic Ripple **42**
Cosmic Thing *379*
Cosmo Cracks *72*
Cosmopolitan Wall *70*
Côte d' Azure **411**
Counting Coup *347*
COUNTY LINE MOUNTAIN,
    Santa Clara Tract **420**
County Route 40. . . . .*349*
COURTHOUSE, THE *491*
Courtney Marie's Boobies **311**
COVE WALL, Rogers Rock **91**
Cover Charge *293*
Cowboy Up **334**
Cowpoke Chimney *156*
Coy Dog *347*
Cozy Corner **276**
Crab Soccer **257**
Crack Chimney *480*

Index

Crack in the Woods *316*
CRACK IN THE WOODS
    CLIFF, Beer Walls *315*
Crack Mechanic *366*
Crack 'n Corner. **66**
Crack of Despair. *117*
Crack of the Titans **493**
Crackatoa *76*
Crackberry **362**
Crackerbox Palace **133**
Cracklosis **168**
Crackus Interuptus **452**
CRANE EAST,
    Crane Mountain **163**
Crane Fang. **186**
CRANE MOUNTAIN **140**
CRANE WEST,
    Crane Mountain **144**
Cranium. **206**
Craterface **169**
Crazy Fingers *311*
Crazy Horse *160*
Creaking Wall *49*
Cream on Top *407*
Cream Puffer. **263**
Creation of the World *403*
CREATURE WALL. *236*
Crime, Fools, and Treasure . . .*415*
Criminal Lawyer *493*
Crimp Scampi **305**
Crimps are for Pimps **311**
Cripple Creek **154**
Crispy Critter *239*
Crispy Critters **488**
Criss Cross **314**
Critical Crimps **206**
Cro-Magnon **53**
Crooks and Nannies. **187**
Cross Dresser. **72**
Cross to Bear, A *417*
Cross, The. **371**
Cross-examination *494*
Cross-Eyed Orphan **234**
Crossfire *131*
Crossing the Red Sea **365**
Crosstown Traffic *369*
Crossway **208**
Crotalusly Challenged **114**
Crowley Cream Cheese *190*
Crown Crack **150**
CROWN, THE. *150*
Crow's Nest. **230**
Crucible of War, The **95**
Cruise Crack **158**
Cruisin' with Joey, variation to
    Clutch and Cruise *310*
Crumbs Along the Mohawk . . .**337**
Crunchy on the Outside,
    Chewy on the Inside **77**
Crux Capacitor **38**
Crystal Wall **358**

Crystalline Entity **429**
C-Tips **65**
Cue Ball. *311*
Cujo. *239*
Cul-de-Sac *244*
Curb Your Enthusiasm **336**
Curbside Crawl **325**
Cure Cottage **428**
Curly Shuffle, The **74**
Curve Like a Wave **466**
CWI *300*

D

D Squared. **68**
D1 . . . .*200*
Dackdation *392*
Dacker Cracker. **260**
Daddy, Where Are You? **390**
Dad's Day Off **150**
Dairy Aire. **158**
Daisy BBs **343**
Dalek Connection **230**
Damascus Road. **365**
Damn Your Eyes **389**
Dancin' Buckwheat *194*
Dancing with Fritz **290**
Dangerous Game, variation
    to Thanksgiving. *219*
Dangle 'n Whack Lad **90**
Dark Horse Ail. *296*
Dark Lord *126*
Dark of the Sun **224**
Dark Speed. **147**
Dark Streets **160**
Dark Venomous Dreams **115**
Dark Venomous Reality **115**
Darker Dreams **156**
Darkest Africa *130*
Darklord. **104**
Darmok **225**
Darmok Indirect **225**
Dartmouth Notch **156**
Daughter of the Moon *151*
Day of a Thousand Disasters. .**351**
Day of Madness *331*
Daybreak. **149**
Day's End *293*
Day-Tripper *164*
Dead Dog *221*
Dead End **462**
DEADWATER *155*
DEADWATER WAY LEFT *162*
Death Penalty *494*
Death Proof. **414**
Death Trap. *304*
Death Trap Lite, variation
    to Death Trap. *304*
Decathlon **240**
Deciphering the Dirtyness **354**
Deciphering the
    Wonderfulness **352**

Deep Cleanser *335*
Deep Cover. *117*
Deer Hunter. **419**
DEER LEAP. **104**
DEER PASS,
    Santa Clara Tract. **417**
DEERFLY SLAB, Inman Slabs .**429**
Defiant Eyes *138*
Deja View **273**
Delirium Tremens *302*
Demitasse. **229**
Democralypse Now **58**
Demolition. *415*
Dennis' Demise. *129*
Dental Hygienist **336**
Desi's Misery *187*
Desperado *160*
Desperate Passage **220**
Destined for Obscurity *412*
Detour on Route 73 . . . .*213*
Detox (5.10d) *96*
Detoxification *302*
Deuteronomy *50*
Deviant Finish, variation
    to The Key *269*
Devil Dogs. **218**
Devil Wears Prana. **70**
Deviled Eggs. **218**
DEVIL'S WASHDISH CLIFF . . . **134**
Devin Monkey **364**
Devine **72**
Devo **52**
Devotee. *130*
Dewey, Cheetham,
    and Howe!. *492*
Dexter's Dugout, variation
    to Pinch an Inch **202**
Dharma Initiative, The. **395**
Diagonal *442*
Diagonal Chockstone
    Chimney *307*
DIAGONAL RAMP WALL,
    Crane Mountain **192**
Diamond and Coal *200*
Diamond C **415**
Diamondback *238*
Diamonds Aren't Forever *194*
Diaphanous. **407**
Dicentra. *96*
Dick's Nose, variation
    to Unbroken **430**
Die by the Drop. **56**
Diet Coke Crack *289*
Dig It *156*
Digging for Gold *119*
Dike, The. **312**
Dill Pickle. *127*
Dinner Guest **430**
Direct Finish, variation
    to Gamesmanship *73*

Index

Direct Finish, variation
    to Heroes. 277
Direct Finish, variation
    to Lichen Delight *377*
Direct Finish, variation to
    Little Finger 100
Direct Start, variation to
    Drop, Fly, or Die *267*
Direct Start, variation to
    Frosted Mug *296*
Direct Start, variation to
    Knights in Armor *64*
Direct Start, variation to
    Pomme de Terre *94*
Direct Start, variation to
    Smear Campaign *90*
Direct Start, variation to
    Wiessner Route. *457*
Directissima 98
Dirtbag Dharma 395
Dirty Boy 248
Dirty Dancing 47
Dirty Diana. *379*
Dirty Gully 461
Dirty Little Corner 134
Dirty Mattress, The 454
Dirty Uncle. 488
Disappearing Act, Eagle Cliff . . .72
Disappearing Act,
    Wright Peak. *526*
Discord *44*
Discovered Check 173
Disputed, The *365*
Diva. .52
Divide By Zero. 156
Dividing Line 155
Divine Wind. *120*
DIX MOUNTAIN *527*
Dixie Normus 312
Do Me a Solid 389
Do You Feel Lucky *163*
Dobsonfly 373
Doc Holiday *156*
Doc Theo *347*
Doctor Y's 426
Dodder *225*
Dodge and Dangle. *281*
Doe Si Doe 71
Dog Eat Dog. *342*
Dog Pounder. 76
Dog with a Nut Tool. 321
Dog's Breakfast. *220*
Dole Me. *254*
Dome Arête. *169*
Domingo. *102*
Don We Know Wears Gay
    Apparel *419*
Don's Toprope. *302*
Don't Give Guns to Children. . .*407*
Don't Kill The Client. *352*
Doodle Bug. 47

Dope-a-Mean 134
Dorsal Fin *523*
Dos *302*
Double Diamond 84
Double Fisting Blueberries 442
Double Recracker. 106
Double Vision 218
Down in the Mall 228
Downtown Brown *524*
Dr. Livingstone, I Presume *485*
Drag Queen 72
Dragonfly. *184*
Draining the Beaver 422
Drama Queen. 72
Draught Dodger *303*
Drawing Mustaches on
    Dangerous Dogs, variation
    to Wald-Calder Route *358*
Dream of Frozen Turkeys *442*
Dreams of the Desert 80
Dreamweaver 458
DREGS WALL, Beer Walls 289
Drifter. *158*
Drive 200
Drop, Fly, or Die *267*
Drumthwacket. 147
DRY WALL, Beer Walls. *313*
Dryer Weather 77
Dudeman *431*
Dugal, The. *472*
Dukes of Hazard. 305
Dunce In the Corner 423
Dunn Finish, variation to
    Fastest Gun. *78*
Dushara. *229*
Dutch Masters Direct *123*
Dutchman's Britches. *140*
DUTTON MOUNTAIN 290
Duty Free. *302*
Dweezil 51
Dynamo Hum *362*
Dzelarhons *175*

E

EAGLE CLIFF, Buck Mountain . .72
Eagle Crack *221*
EAGLE FALLS. 364
Eagle Has Landed, The 373
Eagle, The. *466*
Early Onset Dementia. 459
Earthly Night *89*
Easement 467
Easier Than Expected. 67
East Face *488*
East Face Direct *468*
EAST FACE OF AVALANCHE
    MOUNTAIN, Avalanche
    Lake. *518*
EAST FACE, Basin Mountain . .*487*
EAST FACE, Giant Mountain . .*467*
EAST FACE, Mt Marcy *501*

EAST NOSE, Crane Mountain .*212*
Eastern Shield. *450*
Easter's Bunny *169*
Easter's Force *168*
Eastman-Kodak Crack *133*
Easy Edge. 428
Easy Listening. 467
Easy Monkey. *165*
Easy Off. *360*
Easy Ramp 371
Easy Squeeze. 359
Easy Street *70*
Eat Dessert First 81
Eat Yourself a Pie *345*
Eating Tripe and Lichen It 205
ECHO CLIFF,
    Panther Mountain 335
Ectoplasmic Remains. *235*
Eddy *186*
Edge of the Valley. *256*
Edgeucation *192*
Eight Shit. 76
Eighteen-Wheeler *150*
EIGHTH WALL,
    Lower Washbowl. *283*
El Kabong 59
El Muerte Rojo 170
El Niño. *254*
El Regalo. 83
El Supremo 372
El, The *363*
Electric Kool-Aid 419
Elusive Bastard. 400
Elusive Dream. *207*
Elusive Trophy. 317
Emily Doesn't Have a Clue 313
EMPEROR SLAB *209*
Emperor Zurg 340
Empress *217*
End Game. 96
End of the Line 187
Endless Journey 83
Enduro Man 56
English Channel 189
Enigma *127*
Enjoy the Little Things. 279
Entertainer, The. 76
Entrance *522*
ENTRANCE WALL,
    Beer Walls *288*
Epilogue *423*
Equinox 415
EQUINOX FACE,
    Azure Mountain. 414
Equis *302*
Escalator to Heaven 184
Escape from Haiti 243
Escape from Iowa. 224
Esthesia. *262*
E-Stim 198
Eternity *271*

Index

Etiquette *369*
Eurotech *364*
Every Creature's Theme **150**
Every Inch Counts. **480**
Every Which Way and Loose . . *163*
Everywhere That Man Can Be,
    variation to Carl's Climb . . **158**
Evil Twin. **487**
Excalibur, Lower Washbowl . . .*276*
Excalibur, Tongue Mountain . . .**114**
Excellent Adventure, The **120**
Excitable Boy *72*
Exit Cracks **74**
Exit Lite **158**
Expiration 66 . . . .**309**
Explorers' Club *128*
Extreme Unction *80*
Eyes on the Prize **355**

F

F.B.W.. . . . .**224**
Face Dances. **467**
Face of a Thousand Cracks . . .**368**
FACTORY SLABS,
    Huckleberry Mountain. . . .**229**
Fade and Flee. **147**
Fairview. *119*
Fake ID *290*
Falaise. **221**
Falcon Free. *36*
Falconer *396*
Fall Line Crack **288**
Falling Kaiser Zone **67**
False Advertising *336*
FALSE ARROW FACE,
    Lower Washbowl. *274*
Family Jewels *199*
FAN, THE, Lower Washbowl . . .*280*
Fancy Cat, The **41**
Fancy Feet **400**
Fang Time, variation
    to Tun Tavern **193**
Fang, The *283*
Far Side, The. *396*
Fast and Furious. *312*
Fastest Gun. *78*
Fastest Shark, variation
    to Shark Week. *79*
Fat Crack. **65**
Fat People Are Harder
    To Kidnap **314**
Fat Toad **68**
Fatal Ease **148**
Fat-Free Warrior *390*
Father Knows Best **317**
Father's Day **150**
FATHER'S DAY SLAB, Brown
    Slab, Crane Mountain. . . .**150**
Favela **238**
Fawn Crack. **71**

Fear and Loathing in Keene
    Valley *265*
Fear of a Flat Planet **86**
Fear of Flying *399*
Fear of Frogs. *130*
Fear of Gravity. *123*
Fear of Touching Aerie (5.10b) .*398*
Fearless Leader **466**
Fee, Fie, Foe, Fum **468**
Feeble **152**
Feed the Beast *117*
Feeding Frenzy **430**
Feeding The Rat **299**
Feet of Fire *250*
FELINE WALL, Panther Gorge,
    Mt Marcy. *500*
Felonious Mopery **193**
Felony in Georgia, A *334*
Fenris. *390*
FERN CUBBY *370*
Festus *162*
Fifi Fingers. **211**
Fifth Metacarpal *462*
Fifty Grades of Spray **191**
Fifty-Foot Fright Fest **150**
Fig Fuckin' Newton *376*
Figaro *331*
Final Frontier **121**
Find Us Another Cliff, Barbara .**352**
Fine Line, A. **107**
Finger It Out *342*
Finger Lickin' Good. **451**
Finger Slides *527*
Fipi Lele. **366**
Fire in the Sky *406*
Fire Starter. *237*
FIRECAMP WALL,
    Crane Mountain **156**
Firecracker **184**
Fire-Tower Crack *117*
Fireworks. **182**
Firing Line *48*
First Aid *115*
First Face **433**
First Feast **411**
First Lead *196*
FIRST LEAD SLAB **196**
First Taste **111**
First? Really?. **480**
FISH MOUNTAIN CRAG. **337**
Fish Story **492**
FISHERMAN'S WALL,
    Clements Pond Trail **491**
Fishes on a Landscape *222*
Fishin' Cruise. **492**
FISSURE FACE,
    Ice Cave Mountain **351**
Fistful of Stoppers. **269**
Fits and Arms **210**
Five Hundred Rednecks
    with Guns *260*

Five Small Stones **160**
Five Star Crack **312**
Fizzle, variation to Gullet **234**
FLAILING WALL, Beer Walls. . .*299*
Flake 'n Bake. **90**
Flapjack. **128**
Flapper *389*
Flash Flood *126*
Flashback Crack *116*
Flashdance *248*
Flatrock Arête **355**
FLATROCK MOUNTAIN **355**
Flavor of the Day. **313**
Fledgling **335**
Fledgling Flight **433**
Flexi-Flier *346*
Flight into Emerald City. *250*
Flight of the Concord **303**
Flight of the Falcon **65**
FLOWED LANDS *427*
Flu, The **167**
Flume *186*
Fly Away **422**
FLY BROOK VALLEY **107**
Fly in the Ointment **71**
Flying & Drinking and
    Drinking & Driving *296*
Flying & Drinking Direct, variation
    to Flying & Drinking and
    Drinking & Driving *296*
Flying Buddha **444**
Flying Dutchman, The *523*
Flying Friends **233**
Flying Squirrels *358*
FM Direct, The, variation
    to The FM *59*
FM, The. *59*
Foam Flower. *133*
Fogbound *525*
Folly-Stricken. **158**
Fool in the Forest **189**
Foosa Territory. **116**
Foot Patrol. *224*
Footloose **47**
For Once a Great Notion *228*
For the Birds **144**
For What It's Worth **266**
Force Nine. *333*
Foreplay *85*
Foretaste. **160**
Forever Wild *326*
Forget Bullet *49*
Forgotten Days **147**
Forked Tongue **115**
Forty Winks **422**
Forty-niner. *458*
Forward to Death, variation
    to First Feast **411**
Fossil Formation Buttress *464*
Four Guns Blazing **209**
Four Ounces to Freedom **202**

Index

FOUR PINES BUTTRESS,
    Boneyard, Huckleberry
    Mountain 218
Four Plus *491*
FOURTH TIER,
    Poke-O Moonshine *138*
FOX MOUNTAIN CRAG 364
Frack 65
Fracture Zone *128*
Frankenpine 76
Franklin's Tower 454
Freak Gasoline Fight Accident .*195*
Freckles and No Lipstick 311
Free for All 157
Free Ride *455*
Free Swing *90*
Free the Slaves *202*
FREE WALL, Moss Cliff *396*
Freedom Flight *50*
Freestyle *418*
Freeway *175*
Freeze-Thaw Cycle *175*
French Curve *117*
French Kiss 113
French Spoof, The *185*
Freudian Slip *497*
Frick 65
Friction Finish *116*
Friends in Business *341*
Frippery *414*
Fritzie's Honor 278
From Switzerland With Hate . . .*481*
Frosted Fern *165*
Frosted Flake 432
Frosted Mug *296*
Frosty Edge, variation
    to Frosted Mug *296*
Fruit Stripe *170*
Fubby Dub 411
Fudge Brownie a la Mode *337*
Fugarwe, variation to Beehive .*378*
Führer *211*
Full Moon *480*
Full Moon Fever 170
Full Recovery 199
Fun City *347*
Fun Country, variation to
    Fun City *347*
Fun Hogs from Hell 391
FUN-DA-GA-O CLIFF *336*
FUTURE WALL, Washbowl
    Pond *252*

G

Gabe's Boulder 342
GABE'S BOULDER,
    West Mountain 342
Galapagos *229*
Gale Force *334*
Gamesmanship *73*
Gamma Ray Arête 284

Garand Arête 344
Garden Alone 148
Garden of Leadin' 473
Garter *45*
Gathering, The *80*
Gauntlet, The *126*
Gemini 284
George .399
Geriatric Profanity Disorder 225
Geronimo *158*
Get a Grip 330
Get Over It 235
Get Reborn 134
Get Up, Stand Up *222*
Getcher Breakfast 169
Gev's Tree *314*
Ghost Boner 51
Ghost Rider, variation to
    Adrenaline Surge 303
GIANT MOUNTAIN *464*
GIANT'S SECRET,
    Washbowl Pond *255*
Ginger Tea 111
Giuoco Piano 173
Give It a Name, Man *229*
Gizmo 488
GK 410
GK's First BJ 406
Glass Ceilings *141*
Glee Club Crack 173
Gnarly 158
Go Fish .327
Goat's Foot on Rock *35*
Gob Hoblin *239*
Godfather, The *410*
God's Grace (5.11b) *56*
Goes Both Ways 86
Gold *418*
Gold Digger *200*
Gold Wall *136*
Golden Dreams 151
Golden Road *230*
Golden Sheaves, variation to
    Morning Stars 150
Golf Balls through
    Garden Hoses *349*
Goliath 365
Gomez .469
Gone Fishin' *145*
Gong Show, The 46
Good and Plenty 65
Good Book, The 150
Good Dough *349*
Good Housekeeping 373
Good Intentions *110*
GOOD LUCK BOULDER,
    Good Luck Mountain 330
GOOD LUCK MOUNTAIN 323
Good to the Last Drop *421*
Good, the Bad, and
    the Ugly, The *157*

Goodfellows 285
Goodwin Route *476*
Goodwin-Eastman Route *503*
Goodwin-Stanley Route,
    Gothics Mountain *478*
Goodwin-Stanley Route,
    Porter Mountain *506*
Goombay Finish, variation to
    Fastest Gun *78*
Gopher Wood 62
GORE MOUNTAIN 286
Gorillas in the Mist *525*
Gothic Arch *476*
GOTHICS MOUNTAIN *468*
Gotta Go .56
Gourmet *448*
GPD 225
Grace and Commitment 91
Grand Game, The 94
Grand Hysteria *269*
Grand Ole Osprey *414*
Grand View *522*
GRAND VIEW CLIFF *369*
Grape Juice 331
Grapes of Wrath *94*
Graphite Corner 212
GRASS POND MOUNTAIN . . .392
Gravity Grave 77
Gray–Harrison 187
Gray–Sointio, variation to
    Gray–Harrison 187
Great Chimney *365*
Great Dihedral *64*
Great Escape, The, Alcatraz . . .*409*
Great Escape, The,
    Whitewater Walls *184*
Great Job *184*
Great Northern *121*
Great Northern Diver 450
Great Sail, The *430*
Great Spoof, The *175*
GREEN HILL 145
GREEN LAKE CLIFF 301
Green Mountain Boys 449
Green Onion *94*
Green Streak: Portside *479*
Green Thumb 71
Greenhouse Defect *173*
Greenhouse Effect *174*
Greenhouse Effect Direct,
    variation to
    Greenhouse Effect *174*
GREENHOUSE, THE,
    Northway Express Wall . . .*173*
Greensleeves *217*
Gridlock .116
Grin and Bear It, Bear Den *417*
Grin and Bear It, Shelving Rock .46
Grips of Wrath *239*
Grommet *175*
Groovitational Pull *478*

Index

Groovy Monkey Love **420**
GROTTO, THE,
    Panther Mountain **337**
Group Therapy *42*
Groupies *379*
Grumpy Rolls **361**
G-String **220**
Guermantes **105**
Guide's Gift *164*
Guillotine *196*
Guinness *290*
GULL POND CLIFF **132**
Gull Pucky **133**
Gullet **234**
Gu-man-chu *91*
Gun Control *77*
Gun Control Now, variation
    to Gun Control *77*
Gun Show **203**
Gunga Din Chin **156**
Gunky Route **236**
Gunpowder Corner *315*
Gusto Crack *122*
Gypsy's Curse **368**
Gyroscopic Tendencies **56**

H

H1N1 . . . . **169**
H2 Alpine **177**
Habeas Corpus *493*
Hackett Corner **46**
Hail Mary, variation to
    Moehammed, Larry, &
    Curly **192**
Hair of the Dog *342*
Hair Trigger **318**
Hairy Upper Lip Drip **450**
Haley's Nose **86**
Half Cocked **345**
Half Man, Half Wit **189**
Half Mile **65**
Half-Baked Flake *388*
Halfway Handcrack *147*
HALFWAY HANDCRACK *147*
Halitosis **170**
Halloween Cracks **130**
Hamburger Face **168**
Hamburger Helper **221**
Hammerdog **222**
Hammerhead **445**
Hand Therapy *138*
Handcrack Boulder *134*
Handle with Care *326*
Handlebarbarism **449**
Hands That Work **211**
Hang 'Em High *42*
Hang Time **205**
Hangover *309*
Hangover Corner **466**
Hangover Direct *193*

Happiness Is a Warm
    Belay Jacket *323*
Happy Thoughts and
    Chalk Dust **446**
Happy Trails to You *525*
Hard Going **257**
HARD GUY WALL, Main Cliff,
    Huckleberry Mountain **226**
Hard Times, Moss Cliff *397*
Hard Times, Shanty Cliff **235**
Haroom Baroom **443**
Harrison–Haas, variation to
    Gray–Harrison **187**
Harry Potter and the
    Witches Crack **321**
Hart Pump **389**
Harvest *137*
Harvest Moon **304**
Hat Rabbit **222**
Hayeburner **291**
HAYES MOUNTAIN **290**
HEADWALL,
    Poke-O Moonshine *120*
Heart of Gold *137*
HEART OF GOLD BUTTRESS,
    Second Tier,
    Poke-O Moonshine *136*
Heart Thrills **148**
Heat Wave *183*
Heel and Toe, Heel and Toe,
    Heel and Toe. Slide,
    Slide, Slide *212*
HEIGHT OF LAND WALL,
    Crane Mountain **185**
Helms-Jolley *388*
HENDERSON CLIFF *428*
Henry Lewis **320**
Here Come the Pigs **128**
Here I Go Again **200**
Heroes **273**
Heroes Are Hard To Find **456**
Hershey Squirt, variation
    to Chocoholic *192*
Hesitation *248*
Hidden Constellation *365*
Hidden Gem **200**
Hidden Truths **409**
High and Dry *36*
High Anxiety *253*
High Falls *412*
HIGH FALLS CRAG *410*
High Noon **481**
High Plains Drifter **272**
High Wire **66**
Highline, The *406*
High-Rise Tightie Whities **70**
HIGHWAY BLUES SLAB *149*
Highway Patrol *174*
Hippie Sticks and Black Flies . . **445**
Hipster *317*
Hipster Handbook *416*

Hissing Fauna **354**
Hit by a Car, variation
    to Jelly Arms *260*
HITCHINS POND CLIFF **390**
Hoar–Horovitz *283*
Hobbit's Way **491**
Hochschartner Highway *516*
Hoedown **156**
HOFFMAN NOTCH **528**
Hold It Like a Hamburger **483**
Hole, The *526*
Holiday in Cambodia **411**
Hollyrock *339*
Holy Grail **50**
Holy Grail, The *209*
Holyfield & Foreman *70*
Home after Dark **285**
Home and Garden Center **420**
Home Rule *91*
Home Run Derby *56*
Homecoming *52*
Homegrown *136*
Homo **53**
Honey Dipper *146*
HONEY POT, THE *145*
Honeybadger **481**
Honeymoon Ain't Over **447**
Honeymoon in Yosemite **389**
Hooker Heels and
    Crimp Pimps **371**
Hooligans *328*
Hoops and Yo Yo **66**
Hooters *350*
Hooverville **238**
Hop on Pop *414*
Horizontal Fridge **378**
Horror Show **226**
Horses in Armor *202*
HOSPITAL ROCK,
    Poke-O Moonshine **115**
Hot Compress **316**
Hot Metal and Methedrine *454*
Hot Saw **121**
Hot Tamale **448**
Hour of Prayer **220**
House of Cards **327**
Howdy Doody **235**
Howdy, Hiker **253**
Howling, The *52*
Huckleberry Hound **224**
HUCKLEBERRY MOUNTAIN . . **214**
HUDSON RIVER CRAGS **79**
Huff 'n Puff *440*
HUMBLE PIE WALL **186**
Hummingbird *276*
HUMPHREY MOUNTAIN
    CLIFF **247**
Hung Jury **492**
Hunter's Moon *110*
Hunter's Pass Slide *528*
HURRICANE CRAG *321*

Index

Hydraulic *185*
HYDROGEN WALL, Silver
    Lake **485**
Hydrophobia,
    Crane Mountain **170**
Hydrophobia, Upper Tiers,
    Poke-O Moonshine . . . *124*
Hypoxia **168**
Hysteria **106**

I

I Ain't a Marching Anymore *472*
I Am Lesion **168**
I Am Not a Toy! **340**
I Can't Believe It's Not Butter . . . **279**
I Didn't Give It a Name *331*
I Don't Need No Doctor *187*
I See You **445**
I Wish **355**
ICE AGE WALL,
    Between the Lakes *380*
ICE CAVE MOUNTAIN **349**
Ice Point *175*
I'd Rather Be in Iowa **225**
Iditarod **253**
If You Don't Like It, Leave . . . **442**
Ill Fire (5.14a) *407*
I'll Fly Away **212**
Illuminescence *406*
I'm Committed, variation
    to Mastercharge *244*
Impulse Drive, variation to
    Pinch an Inch **202**
In Hiding **459**
In the Beginning **210**
In the Buff **250**
In the Buff, variation to
    In the Rough **200**
In the Chimney *342*
In the Rough *200*
In Vivo *103*
Incision *115*
Incognito *156*
Incredible Hulk, The **303**
Indecision '08 . . . . **58**
Indecisive **216**
Independence Pass **305**
Indian Summer *174*
Indirecto **355**
Indi's Arête **77**
Induhvidual **191**
Inferiority Complex **299**
Infinity and Beyond **48**
Infinity Crack **48**
INMAN POND BLUFF **73**
INMAN SLABS **428**
Inner Sanctum **317**
Inner Space *111*
Insomnia **226**
Instigator **230**
Intelligent Design **279**

Intensive Care **195**
Interloper **458**
Intrusion *517*
Invincible Machine **278**
Invisible Man, The **303**
IOWA WALL, Main Cliff,
    Huckleberry Mountain . . . **224**
Irene *278*
Iron Cross **86**
Iron Heel, The **361**
Iron in the Fire **71**
Island Marriage, The **388**
ISOBUTTRESS, Black Arches
    Wall, Crane Mountain . . . **194**
Isosceles **118**
Isotope, variation
    to Radioactive *294*
It Ain't Over (5.8) **269**
It Can Only Get Better **111**
It Don't Come Easy **85**
It Goes to Eleven **452**
It'll Probably Be Mostly
    a Scramble *472*
It's a Boy **80**
It's a Puzzle **229**
It's Come to This **433**
It's Only Entertainment *261*

J

J.D. Memorial Route **71**
J.E. 26 . . . . *257*
J.J.'s, variation to
    Talking Heads **325**
Jack in the Pulpit *386*
Jack Straw *284*
JACK STRAW WALL,
    Lower Washbowl *284*
Jackal *130*
Jackasses from Downstate . . . **391**
Jackrabbit *174*
Jacob's Ladder **365**
Jagger-Richards *447*
Jake's Route **400**
Jam Session *117*
James and the Giant Boulder . *437*
Jamie Lee Curtis *392*
Jammer **184**
JAMMER WALL, Upper Walls,
    Crane Mountain **184**
Jaredtol *190*
JAWS WALL, Between
    the Lakes *372*
Jay's Affliction, variation to
    Critical Crimps **208**
Jay's Job **148**
Jay's Solo **229**
Jealous Dogs **222**
Jeff–James **400**
Jelly Arms *260*
Jemima Dreams **447**
Jenga **445**

JENKINS MOUNTAIN **420**
Jervis's Joke **443**
JEWELS AND GEM *198*
Jim's Faith *447*
Joe Hill **240**
Joey Baggadonuts *310*
JOHN POND CLIFFS **255**
Johnny Tsunami **56**
Johnsburg Red **229**
JOLLY ROGER SLAB, Rogers
    Slide, Rogers Rock **93**
Jonah Rocks *370*
Josey Wales *163*
Joshua Climb *342*
Journey through the Past *136*
Joy Crack **299**
Judge Judy, variation
    to Hung Jury *492*
Jug Monkey **301**
Jug, Tug, and Jam **185**
Jug-Or-Not **473**
Jugs of Beer *312*
Juicy Fruit *170*
Juliet **222**
Jump Back Jack Crack *121*
Jump Bat Crack *237*
Jumpin' Jack Flash *124*
Jungle Fever **262**
Jungle Rot **168**
Junior Varsity *45*
Jury Duty *493*
Just Chum-me **338**
Just Take It **47**
Justin Time **255**

K

Kaibob *37*
Kaiser Friedrich *206*
Kalashnikov Corner **344**
Kamikaze Heart **70**
Karate Crack **104**
Karmic Kickback *59*
Kat Nap **500**
Katrina *50*
Keegans 5.8 . . . . **309**
Keep Off Flake *102*
Keep the Faith **130**
Keep Your Powder Dry,
    Ranger *316*
Keep, The *206*
Keira's Thumbs **255**
Kerr Route *481*
Key, The **269**
Keyed In **419**
Keyhole, The **311**
Keystone **193**
Kid Rock **51**
Kielbasy Posse **193**
Kill It Before It Spreads **193**
King and I **146**
King and I, The *206*

Index

King Crack 359
King Kan Variation, variation
    to Mental Blocks *462*
King Me. **289**
King of Guides *204*
King of Spades. *207*
KING PHILIP'S SPRING WALL.*147*
KING WALL. *200*
Kingdom Come *209*
Kings and Desperate Men **95**
KINGS FLOW CLIFF. **255**
Kirby Corner **377**
Kissing Pigs **188**
Knightfire. **341**
Knights in Armor. *64*
Knights That Say Neigh **50**
Knitel's Route **157**
Knock Before Entering *489*
Knock the Cairn Down *526*
Knuckle-Dragger. **53**
Kodiak **116**
Kristin *193*
Ku Klux Ken, variation to
    White Knight *269*
Ku Klux Who?, variation to
    White Knight *269*

L

La Frontera **83**
La Spirale *95*
Labatt-Ami. *296*
LABOR DAY WALL *392*
Ladder. *42*
LADDER AREA, True Summit,
    Crane Mountain **159**
Lady Bug. **349**
Lady Luck **324**
Lady's Route *377*
Lager-Rhythm *299*
Lake Champlain Monster *143*
LAKE LILA. *387*
LAKE PLEASANT QUARRY . . .**338**
Lakeview *139*
Lakeview Arête **122**
Land of Make-Believe. *128*
LAND OF OVERHANGS,
    Crane Mountain **186**
Land of the Little People. *333*
Land of the Lost *283*
Lane Change **197**
Lane–Harrison. **179**
Lap Dog **217**
Last Chance *109*
Last Dance **224**
Last Grasp **486**
Last Hurrah **102**
Last Lead *198*
Last Swim or Dive *315*
Last Tupper, The **392**
LAST WALL,
    Huckleberry Mountain. . . .**229**

Lawyers, Guns, and Money . . .**174**
Lazy Crack *133*
Le Chat Noir *501*
Le Jour de Bon Heures. **174**
Le Petit Chien **217**
Le Petit Slab **94**
Le Poisson *112*
Lead 101 . . . .**171**
Lead 102 . . . .**171**
Leader Line **73**
Leap of Faith *151*
Leap of Flake **242**
Leapin' Louie. **193**
Learning the Steps, variation
    to Burke's Path **423**
Learning to Fly **212**
Leave Your Wallet At Home . . . *229*
LEDGE MOUNTAIN **349**
LEDGE MOUNTAIN **278**
Ledge You To Believe **484**
Left Field **320**
Left In, variation to Left Out. **51**
Left Out **51**
Left-Hand Direct, variation to
    Left-Hand Route *228*
Left-Hand Route *227*
Leftover **175**
Leila's Line, variation
    to Empress *217*
Lentil Beans *190*
Leroy Brown **482**
Lessons in Guiding. *256*
Let It Dry *255*
Let Sleeping Bats Lie *193*
Let's Go Golfing *390*
Letting Go *85*
Lever Action **344**
Lewis Elijah *447*
Lex Luther *38*
Libido *53*
Lichen Delight. *376*
Lichen or Not, Bald Mountain. .*358*
Lichen or Not, Eagle Falls. **379**
Lichenbräu *309*
Lichenbräu Dark, variation
    to Lichenbräu *309*
Lichenstorm *103*
Lick 'Em & Stick 'Em **256**
Lick It Up *342*
Life and Debt **235**
Life Aquatic *511*
Life During Wartime **335**
Lifelong Affliction. *230*
Life's a Beach *198*
Lightning *96*
Like a Boss *172*
Li'l Sebastian, variation to
    Regular Route *219*
Limelight *76*
Limp Stick **312**
Line of Fire **51**

Line of Fire, variation to
    Little Finger **100**
Linkup, variation to The El . . . *363*
Lithium. **76**
Little Ado. **243**
Little Black Book *199*
Little Buttress **158**
Little Chimney *190*
Little Corner. *169*
LITTLE CROW MOUNTAIN . . .*337*
Little Fever. **169**
Little Finger **98**
Little Finger Direct Start **100**
Little Gem Diner **235**
Little Jam, Crane Mountain. . . .**185**
Little Jam,
    Huckleberry Mountain. . . .**216**
LITTLE JOHNSON *169*
Little Kisses. **311**
Little Rascals. *340*
Little Secret *255*
Little Sister. **487**
Live Free or Die. *312*
Lives of the Hunted. *314*
Lizard Head, variation
    to The Hole *526*
Lloyd's of Lowville **376**
LM **375**
Locust Posts **323**
Lonely, The *363*
LONG BUTTRESS,
    Lower Washbowl. *281*
Long Haul **418**
Long Play **192**
LONG PLAY WALL,
    Crane Mountain **190**
LONG POND CLIFF **240**
LONG WALL, Hoffman Notch .*529*
Look Out Above **337**
Look, Roll, and Fire. *328*
Looking for Mr. Goodhold. *185*
Lookout Crack *116*
LOOKOUT ROCK,
    Chimney Mountain **259**
Loon Roof **243**
Lost and Weary. **161**
LOST AND WEARY SLAB, The
    Prows, Crane Mountain . .**161**
Lost Ark. **62**
LOST ARROW FACE,
    Lower Washbowl. *275*
LOST ARROW, Lost Arrow Face,
    Lower Washbowl. *278*
Lost Arrow—Southeast Face .*279*
Lost Arrow—Southwest Face .*279*
Lost Chance *90*
LOST CRAGS, THE. **306**
Lost Horizon **394**
LOST HUNTERS CLIFF,
    The Lost Crags **315**
Lost Hunters Crack. **318**

Lost in Paradise 422
Lost in the Crowd, variation
   to Cornerstone 161
Lost in the Thicket. *525*
LOST KEY CRAG,
   Santa Clara Tract. 419
LOST T1 CLIFF, The Lost Crags .306
LOST T2 CLIFF,
   The Lost Crags 322
Love It .406
Love Joy 365
Low Plains Drifter *369*
LOWER BEER WALL,
   Beer Walls *300*
LOWER CLIFFBAND,
   Hudson River Crags 79
LOWER DOME, Pitchoff
   Ridge Trail Domes. *351*
LOWER MEASLES WALL,
   Crane Mountain 168
LOWER SLABS,
   Snowy Mountain 252
LOWER SUMMIT CLIFF,
   Pharaoh Mountain. 131
LOWER WASHBOWL *272*
LOWER WOLFJAW CLIFF *479*
Low-Rise Thong 70
Lucille .222
Lucky Stars 331
Lunar Manscape. 45
LUNAR WALL, THE,
   Poke-O Moonshine. *131*
Lunatic Fringe 290
Lunatic Hares 395
Lunch Rock Scramble 217
Lurch 468
LUTHER WALL, Main Face,
   Poke-O Moonshine. *38*
Luxury Lining. 317
Lycanthropia *267*
Lychons. 361

M

Machine Gun Kelly *408*
Machinist. *119*
Macho. *69*
Macintosh *94*
Macrobiotic *99*
Mad Cow Disease 68
Mad Cows. 182
MAD COWS WALL, Upper
   Walls, Crane Mountain . . .182
Mad Dogs and Englishmen . . .105
Madame Blueberry 179
Made In The Shade *273*
Maestro. *99*
Magic Carpet Ride 265
Magic Flute *522*
Maiden Voyage. *138*
MAIN CLIFF, Huckleberry
   Mountain 221

MAIN FACE, Azure Mountain . .409
MAIN FACE, Bald Mountain . . .356
MAIN FACE,
   Baldface Mountain 254
MAIN FACE, Cat Mountain. . . .399
MAIN FACE, Pharaoh
   Mountain 124
MAIN FACE,
   Poke-O Moonshine. *31*
Main Summit Route 435
MAIN SUMMIT,
   Catamount Mountain 435
MAKOMIS MOUNTAIN CLIFF .*151*
Malaise 221
Malarkey Direct. *377*
Malcontent 242
Malfeasance *196*
MALFUNCTION JUNCTION
   CLIFF *181*
Manic Depression. *252*
Mann Act. *250*
March Magma (5.8) *330*
Margin Slide, The *502*
Marjory *222*
Mark's Blue Ribbon, variation to
   They Never
   Recognized Me. *310*
MARTINI WALL *236*
Master Craft *244*
Master of the Flying Guillotine .*332*
Mastercharge *244*
Matrix, The. 98
Matrix, variation to
   Pilgrim's Progress *87*
Matt Finish. *116*
Mayflower *86*
McCarthy Off Width, variation to
   Fastest Gun. *78*
MCGINN MOUNTAIN 281
MCMARTIN CLIFF,
   The Lost Crags 319
McNeill–Harrison. 176
McWiessner 281
MEADOW HILL CLIFF *166*
Mean Low Blues 238
Mean Sister. 312
MEASLES GROUP,
   Crane Mountain 164
Measly Little Corner 168
Mechanical Hydraulic Control .*122*
Medicine Man 328
Medieval Times. *206*
Medulla Oblongata. 78
Mellor–Hyson *504*
Meltdown. 380
Men of Iron *390*
Menace to Sobriety. *96*
Mental Blocks *461*
MENTAL BLOCKS
   BUTTRESS, Wallface *460*
Mentor. 433

Mercury Program, The 490
Méséglise 105
Messiah, Ark Wall 61
Messiah, Poke-O Moonshine . . .*85*
Metacomet *149*
Metatarsal Opportunity. *186*
Meteorite. *272*
Microwave. *48*
Middle Earth *281*
MIDDLE SETTLEMENT LAKE .353
Mideast Solution, The. 488
Midsummer Night's
   Frustration, A. *153*
MIDWAY CLIFF, Silver Lake . . .464
Mike's Mountaineering Route . .176
Mikkihiiri. 322
MILL MOUNTAIN 229
Mill Mountain Route 229
Millennium. *428*
Miller Light. *310*
Miller Time. *234*
Mine Shaft. 443
MINEVILLE SLAB *154*
Mint Marcy *337*
Mirror Image *450*
Misadventures on
   Ausable Arête *407*
Misfire .343
Missin' Moe 360
Mission to Mars, The *442*
Misspent Youth 335
Mistah Luthah *403*
Mister Buzzárd 222
Misty Mountain Hop 186
MITCHELL PONDS
   MOUNTAIN 362
Mixamotosis 167
Moehammed, Larry, & Curly. . .192
Mogster. *69*
Mo'in The Mud 454
Moksha 349
Monkey *165*
Monkey Pump. *146*
Monkey See, Monkey Do *267*
Monty Python 48
Moon Unit *438*
Moonshine *100*
Moonshine and Chronic. 488
Moonstruck. *121*
Moosed You 363
Moosehead. *310*
Morannon 491
More Tea, Vicar *280*
More Than One Way to Skin
   a Cat, variation to
   Wiessner Route. *457*
Morning Star *87*
Morning Stars 150
Morningside Heights 481
Morse Code *117*
Morsel Line *189*

Index

Mortal Strife **157**
Morticia **469**
MOSS CLIFF *392*
MOSS LAKE SLAB **360**
Mosscalito *404*
Mossiah, The *396*
Mother Mantel *307*
Mother Nature *256*
Mother's Day Variation,
    variation to Phase III *42*
Motoring with Mohammed **218**
MOUNT TOM CLIFF **362**
Mountain Boots and Pitons . . . **426**
Mountain Bruin **316**
Mountain Mist **230**
Mountain Sunshine *479*
Mouth That Roared, The *293*
Mr. Clean *345*
Mr. Dirty *346*
Mr. Peabody **470**
Mr. Potato Head **340**
Mr. Rogers' Neighborhood . . . *267*
Mr. Spaceman *379*
Mr. Toad's Wild Ride **220**
Mrs. Clean *519*
Mrs. Potato Head, variation to
    Mr. Potato Head **340**
MT FREDERICA **387**
MT MARCY *497*
Muckraker **192**
MUD POND CLIFF,
    Silver Lake **486**
Mule *163*
Mule Kick *314*
Mummy, The **126**
Munchky Microarête, variation
    to Earthly Night *89*
Munkey Bars and Geetar Stars **366**
Muscinae *385*
Mushu *171*
Musse Pigg **322**
Mustard Sandwich *496*
Mutant Toy **340**
My Favorite Martian *379*
My Generation *328*
My Little Johnson *172*
My Name is Hud **483**
My Pleasure *166*
Mycelia **354**
Mystery Achievement **328**
Mystery Machine **442**
Mystery To Me, variation to
    Heroes Are Hard To Find . **456**

N

N.O.C. Route *352*
N.P.R. **407**
N.R.A. *192*
Naked Truth **367**
Nameless Corner *335*
NAMELESS KNOB **229**

Na-my *462*
Nasty Seven **200**
National Federation of the Blind . **78**
Natural English *313*
Natural, The *90*
Naughty or Nice *419*
NCS Crack *516*
NEAR BEER WALL,
    Beer Walls *289*
Necessary Risk *442*
Nervy **158**
Nescafé *189*
NESTLE WALL, Spanky's Area . *189*
Nestlings, variation to
    Touch of Class *399*
Nettle Crack **109**
Nettle Highway **248**
Neurosis *89*
Neurosis Direct *91*
Neutron Brew *294*
Never Again, Again **481**
Never Alone **182**
NEVER NEVER LAND,
    Silver Lake **445**
Nevermore **77**
New Beginning **150**
NEW BUCK, Buck Mountain . . **69**
New Finger Connector, variation
    to North Face Direct *472*
New Finger Slide *473*
New Moon **98**
New Route *330*
New Rubber, variation to
    Thanksgiving *219*
New Star *112*
New Suede Shoes **70**
New Year's Day *274*
Night Mare *237*
No Bats Here *193*
No Comments from the
    Peanut Gallery *294*
No Dogs Allowed **217**
No Fear Is Queer *312*
No Ifs, Ands, or Bolts *371*
No Ifs, Ands, or Buts **244**
No Lead *198*
No M.D. for You **424**
No Man's a Pilot *446*
No Más *396*
No Name *331*
No Nuts, No Seaplanes **281**
No Parking *174*
No Picnic *235*
No Regrets Coyote *189*
Noah's Ark **62**
Nobber *255*
NO-NAME WALL,
    Huckleberry Mountain . . . **228**
NOONMARK MOUNTAIN . . . *480*
Normal People, variation to
    Land of the Little People . *333*

Normal Route *267*
Norman's Crack of Joy **193**
North Country Club Crack . . . *200*
North Dike **453**
NORTH END,
    Huckleberry Mountain . . . **216**
North Face Direct *472*
NORTH FACE, Gothics
    Mountain *469*
NORTH HUDSON DOME *167*
Northeast Shoulder Slide . . . *488*
North-End Route *463*
Northern Inhospitality, variation
    to Southern Hospitality . . *73*
NORTHERN KNOB,
    Crane Mountain **148**
Northern Revival *245*
NORTHWAY EXPRESS WALL . *172*
NORTHWEST FACE,
    Dix Mountain *527*
Norton Anthology, The **440**
NOSE APRON, Main Face,
    Poke-O Moonshine *51*
Nose Traverse *62*
Not for Love or Lust, variation to
    Slim Pickins *265*
Not Long For This World *66*
Not My Moss to Bear *222*
Not Quite Geiko *171*
Not Tell Wife, OK? *164*
NOTCH MOUNTAIN *388*
Nothing We Bailed *273*
NS Gauche *351*
NUBBLE CLIFF,
    Washbowl Pond *253*
Nuke the Nite *392*
NURSERY, THE *371*
Nut 'n Left **243**
Nutcracker, The *278*

O

Oath of Fëanor, The **491**
Obama Mama **59**
O'Barrett Factor, The **57**
October Crack **145**
Octoberfast *303*
Octoberfist *133*
Octo-Pussy *237*
Odd Nine *129*
Oddy's Crack of Horror **189**
Off Route, The *213*
Off Target **345**
Old Guy Shootin' Powder . . . *420*
Old Guys Having Fun *430*
Old Route, Chapel Pond
    Gully Cliff *228*
Old Route, Gothics Mountain . *472*
Old Route,
    Hurricane Mountain *329*
Old Route,
    Noonmark Mountain *481*

534   Page numbers in this volume   Page numbers in Volume 1

Index

Old Route, Rooster Comb *486*
Old Route, Third Tier,
    Poke-O Moonshine *137*
Old School **57**
OLYMPIC ACRES *415*
Ominous Chimney *191*
On Appeal *493*
On Tap: Special Brew *302*
On the Beach *136*
On the Fence **182**
On the Leash *345*
On the Loose *269*
Once a New, variation to
    Flying Friends **233**
Once in a Lifetime **477**
One Hold **74**
One-Trick Pony **429**
Only the Good Die Young **265**
Only the Lonely **176**
Oops! I'm Pregnant **461**
Open Book **365**
Open for Business **371**
Open Shutter **272**
Opening Moves **229**
Opening Statement *493*
Opplevelsen **155**
Opplevelsen Direct, variation
    to Opplevelsen **155**
Opposition *35*
Oppositional Defiance
    Disorder **462**
Optimist, The **371**
Oracle **62**
Oral Surgery **456**
Orange Crush *338*
Orchestra *99*
Original Exploit **157**
Original Route *475*
Original Route, The *144*
Ormus the Viking God **389**
Ornithologists from Hell **334**
O'Ryan's Belt **284**
Oscillation Overthruster *335*
Other One, The *415*
Otherwise Normal People *234*
O'Tom's Tick Twister **173**
OTTER LAKE CLIFF **303**
Otto Sells Lemons **429**
Out for the Boyz *415*
Out with the Boys Again *438*
OUTBACK SLAB, Silver Lake . . **467**
Outfoxed **364**
Outlander **342**
OUTLET WALL *256*
Outpatient **195**
Over the Rainbow *479*
Overdog *343*
Overhanging Gutter **377**
Overlap It Up **259**
Overture *248*
Owl Crack *350*

Owl Tail *464*
OWLS HEAD LOOKOUT *463*
OWLS HEAD MOUNTAIN *349*
Ownership **320**

P

P.E. WALL **256**
P.T. Pillar *69*
P.T. Pillar Right *70*
P8tience **108**
Pacifier *169*
PADANARUM CLIFF **109**
Padanarum Crack **108**
Pain and Pleasure **159**
Pajama Sam **153**
PALISADES *141*
Palm Sunday, variation
    to Thanksgiving *219*
Paltry Show **156**
Pan Am *406*
Pandemonium *43*
Pandora's Box **305**
Panorama *251*
PANTHER DEN, Panther
    Gorge, Mt Marcy *501*
PANTHER GORGE, Mt Marcy . *498*
PANTHER HILL CLIFF **430**
PANTHER MOUNTAIN **334**
Panther's Fang *501*
Pantless Phenom *283*
Papa Don't Preach **371**
Paper Walls *102*
Parabolic Cats *103*
Paradise Now *255*
Parallel Dreams **98**
Parallel Passage **206**
Paralysis *99*
Pardon Me, Boy *225*
Parenthood *348*
Paris Parody, A *185*
Paris–Harrison **190**
Park and Ride *150*
Parthenope **312**
Partition *244*
Passing By *256*
Passion Corner *304*
Pasta Galore **149**
Pat Tricks *309*
Patent-Proof Roof *135*
Path to Iowa **225**
Pat's Blue Ribbon, variation to
    Miller Light *310*
Paul's Gondola Ride **286**
PAUL'S LEDGE,
    Gore Mountain **286**
Pay As You Go *456*
Pay Dirt **321**
Pay the Troll's Bridge *203*
Peace in Our Climbs *261*
PEAKED MOUNTAIN **285**
Peanut Butter Pandemonium . . *337*

Pearl Necklace *200*
Pearly Gates *37*
PEASANT CRAGS, THE *195*
PEASANT WALL, King Wall . . . *201*
Peasant's Toehold *196*
Pebbles and Bamm Bamm . . . *339*
Pee Wee Pillar *69*
Pegasus *308*
Pegasus Direct *308*
Pema **395**
Peney for Your Freedom, A. . . . **189**
Penguin's Progress, A. **256**
Pentecostal *52*
Pepé Le Pew *256*
Perch, The **360**
Peregrine *529*
PEREGRINE PILLAR AREA . . . *333*
PEREGRINE PILLAR,
    Peregrine Pillar Area *333*
Pere-o-grins **90**
Perfect Pitch *139*
Perfect Storm *126*
Perilous Journey *526*
Permafrost **380**
Perpetual Frustration Machine . **407**
Persecution, variation to
    Bloody Mary *77*
Perseid **282**
Perseverance *129*
Pet Cemetery *239*
Peter Croft and the Crime-
    Fighting Bear **371**
Pete's Farewell **364**
Pete's Wicked Flail *299*
PF Flyers **364**
PF Flyers' Flying Circus *362*
PHARAOH MOUNTAIN **122**
Pharaoh Ocean Wall **131**
Pharaoh Winds **131**
Pharaoh's Phallus **128**
Phase III *39*
Philippine Connection *119*
Phinding Phalaris **358**
Pick Pocket **69**
Piece of Snatch *64*
Piece Out **473**
Pieces of Eight **100**
Pig in a Poke **72**
PILGRIM WALL, Main Face,
    Poke-O Moonshine *86*
Pilgrim's Progress *87*
Pillar *50*
Pillar of Strength, variation
    to Wild Blue *56*
PILOT KNOB MOUNTAIN **74**
Pimples **170**
Pinch an Inch **202**
Pinching One Off **56**
Pine Climb **359**
Pine Cone Eaters, variation to
    Too Early Spring *359*

Index

Pine Nuts....................67
PINE PEAK CLIFF...........256
Pine Shadow................*308*
Pine Tree Corner............152
Pine Tree Crack.............77
Pining for More.............257
Pink Dayglo Tootsies........*370*
Pink Lynch..................*415*
Pink Panther................433
PINNACLE MOUNTAIN.........295
Pinnacle of Success.........*129*
PINNACLE OVERLOOK,
    Crane Mountain.........193
Pinus Strobus...............*152*
PIPELINE WALL, Northway
    Express Wall............*175*
PITCHOFF CHIMNEY CLIFF.....*352*
PITCHOFF NORTH FACE....*381*
PITCHOFF RIDGE TRAIL
    DOMES..................*350*
Piton Route.................*145*
Placid Es Pontas............*386*
Plan C......................488
Planet Claire...............412
Planet Terror...............414
PLANET TERROR FACE,
    Azure Mountain.........414
Plate Tectonics.............*126*
Playing Stick...............70
Pleasure Victim.............*454*
Plumb Line Direct, variation
    to Plumb Line..........206
Plumb Line, Crane Mountain..206
Plumb Line,
    Little Crow Mountain....*339*
Plumber's Crack,
    South Colton...........407
Plumber's Crack,
    The Aquarium..........222
Plunge, The.................90
Pocket Pool.................69
Pockets R Us................71
Pod Puller..................88
Pointless and Hard, variation
    to The El..............*363*
POKE-O MOONSHINE..........*29*
Poke-O Pup..................*138*
POKE-O SLAB,
    Poke-O Moonshine......*106*
Poker Face..................476
POLAR SOLDIER WALL,
    Olympic Acres..........*415*
Polar Vortex................212
Pollen Junkies..............*135*
Pomme de Terre.............*94*
PONDVIEW WALL,
    Crane Mountain........153
Poodles Are Just Like
    Little Sheep...........*130*
Poplar Climb, A.............*188*
Poplar Mechanics............*188*

POPLAR WALL,
    Spanky's Area..........*188*
Porcelain Forest............*207*
Porcelain Mechanic, The.....*366*
Porcupine Prelude...........304
PORTER MOUNTAIN..........*502*
Porter Party................*503*
Poseidon Adventure..........*512*
Positive Latitude...........478
Positive Progression........103
Positive Thinking...........*69*
Post Op.....................198
Posy........................399
Pot of Gold.................*479*
POTASH CLIFF...............80
Potato-Chip Flake...........225
Pothead.....................473
POTTER MOUNTAIN CLIFF,
    Silver Lake............470
Power of Attorney...........*494*
Pox, Crane Mountain.........168
Pox, Silver Lake............484
PR..........................*284*
PRACTICE WALL AREA,
    Pitchoff Chimney Cliff...*362*
Prelude.....................*248*
Prelude to Gravity..........*440*
Preservation................318
Pretty Good Dihedral, The...*529*
Pretty in Pink..............388
Prey Tell...................379
Price is Right, The.........46
Prima Facie.................59
Prince......................*204*
Princess Bride..............51
Princess Leia...............459
Pringles, variation to Victoria..*218*
Pringsheim Chimney..........*491*
Prints of Darkness..........100
Prisoner in Disguise........335
Profusion...................106
Prohibition.................*296*
Project X...................48
Projection..................359
Prom Night Entity, variation to
    Crystalline Entity.....429
Prom Night Trickery.........429
Promiscuous Girl............379
Prone to Wander.............210
Pronged Again...............*341*
Protractor..................45
Protruding Forehead.........53
Provando....................182
PROVANDO WALL, Upper
    Walls, Crane Mountain...182
Providence..................210
PROWS, THE,
    Crane Mountain........159
Psalm 32....................*76*
PSOC.......................*326*

PSOC, variation to
    Wiessner Route.........*457*
Psycho Sid..................340
PSYCHO SLAB, Campground
    Wall, Rogers Rock......88
Psycho Slut.................88
Psychosis...................*48*
Psychotic...................277
P-Town Approach.............*449*
Public Service..............323
PUFFER MOUNTAIN CLIFF...261
Pug Love....................238
Pugsley.....................469
Pull Up Your Pants..........134
Pulled Tooth................82
PULPIT ROCK...............*386*
Pulpitted...................*386*
Puma Concolor...............*501*
Pump Action.................343
Pump It Up..................*342*
Pumpernickel................*265*
Puppies in a Sack...........379
Puppies on Edge.............*42*
Purist, The.................441
Purple Rain.................446
PURPLE RAIN WALL,
    Silver Lake............446
Push........................328
Push, Bob, Push!............420
Pusher, The.................269
Pustulence..................170
Puzzle......................151
Puzzle Rue..................*86*
Pyromania...................242
Pythagoras..................118

Q

Quadrophenia................*327*
Quantum Entanglement........284
Quarter-Inch................269
Queen for a Day.............330
Queen of the Jungle.........453
Quest.......................*304*
Quo Vadis...................*95*

R

Rachael's Climb.............322
Racoon Eyes.................448
Radio Face..................119
Radio Flier, variation to
    Flexi-Flier............*346*
Radioactive.................*294*
Radioactive Direct Direct,
    variation to Radioactive..*294*
Radioactive Direct,
    variation to Radioactive..*294*
Raging Asian................*171*
Raging Queen................88
Raging Raven................*360*
Ragtime.....................*70*
Railroad Dickie.............239

Index

Rain Delay 230
Rainbow Crack 120
RAINBOW SLIDE,
    Gothics Mountain 477
Raindance 53
Raindance Corner 116
Raindance Roof 186
Rainy Night Road Toads 360
RAMPART CLIFF,
    Gore Mountain 289
Ramps of Deception 104
Random Rope 373
Ranger Danger 525
Ranger on the Rock 501
Ranger Rick 366
Rangers' Run 90
Raptor's Scream 90
Rapture, The 87
Rare Earth 103
Rare Treat 411
Rasp 256
Rasputin 331
Rattlesnake 49
Raven 122
RAVEN WALL,
    Ice Cave Mountain 353
Ravenous 375
Raw Tips 195
Ray's Ascent 261
Razor's Edge 113
Reach for the Sky 162
Reach, The 328
Real 208, The 102
Rear Entry 488
Rearview Mirror 138
Reciprocity 385
Recital 277
Reckless Endangerment 120
Recuperation Boulevard 195
Red Book 366
Red Hill Mining Town 290
Red Zinger 397
Redneck on a Rope 252
Redrum 304
Reducto Adductor 208
Re-Entry 519
Refrainer, The 76
Regular Route 219
Relayer 407
Release The Kraken 300
Remembering Youth 50
Renegade 206
Reproof 184
Requiem Pro Patris 146
Rescue Breathing 113
Resistant Strain 168
Resurrection 84
Retrograde 259
Retrograde Motion 127
Return Home 391
Return to Sender 272

Revolver 74
Rex 340
Rhinoplasty 84
Rickety Pinnacle 278
Ricochet 160
Rico's Roughnecks 487
Right Field 320
Right Notion, The (5.5) 228
Right Place, but Must Have
    Been the Wrong Time 463
Right Way, The 176
Right-Hand Route 228
Ripples 223
Riprovando 182
River Run 186
River View 232
Roaches on the Wall 358
ROACHES TERRACE,
    Pitchoff Chimney Cliff 356
Road Less Traveled 388
Road Trip 149
Roaring Brook Falls 316
ROARING BROOK FALLS 316
Roaring Twenties 294
Roast 'n Boast 391
Roast Turkey, variation
    to Thanksgiving 219
Robbed 275
Robin's Rainy Day Route 184
Rocinha 235
Rock and Roll Star 358
Rock Hangers 460
Rock Hop 186
Rock Lobster 47
Rock of Aegis, variation to
    Rock of Ages 160
Rock of Ages 160
ROCK OF AGES BUTTRESS,
    The Prows,
    Crane Mountain 160
Rockaholic 302
Rockhound 138
Rodeo 247
Rodeo Man 53
RODS & GUNS WALL,
    West Mountain 342
Roger That 102
ROGERS ROCK 87
ROGERS SLIDE, Rogers Rock . 92
Rolling Rock 303
Rolling Stone 379
Rolls Royce 459
Romano's Route 269
Romper Room 66
Roof 358
Roof Direct 305
Roof of All Evil 45
Roof Traverse 304
Roof Traverse Variation,
    variation to Roof Traverse . 304
Roofer Madness 186

ROOSTER COMB 485
Root Explosion 524
Rope Burn 192
Rope Monster 189
Rope Toss Wall 277
Roped Bouldering 169
Rosemary's Baby 79
Rotator Complications 380
Rough Cut 231
Route Number 1 184
Route of Oppressive Power . . . 411
Royal Coachman 338
Royal Savage 90
Rubber Knumbchuck 305
Rubicon 460
Ruby Star, variation to
    Diamond and Coal 200
Rudolph 419
Rugosity 368
Rule of the Bone 346
Rules 369
Rum Doodle 222
Rum Doodle Direct, variation
    to Rum Doodle 223
Rumble Strips 164
Rumney but Crumbly 58
Run for Rabies 168
Run Higher, Jump Faster 362
Running of the Bulls 360
Running on Empty 274
Runway 116
Rusty Lumberjack 47

S

S.O.L. 326
Saffron Revolution 418
Sagittarius 284
Sailor's Dive 84
Salad Days 52
Sam I Am 485
Samboneparte 337
Sands of Time 130
SANTA CLARA TRACT 415
SANTA CLAUS HILL 418
Santa Crux 419
Saranac 1888 426
Saranac Face 427
Saranac Saber 426
Sarge 339
SARS Left, variation
    to SARS Right 169
SARS Right 169
Sasquatch Hunting 84
Satisfaction Guaranteed 88
Sauron's Bolt of Horror 188
Sausage Science 334
Save a Tree, Eat a Beaver . . . 420
Save the Rock for Uncle Sam . . 72
Scab Slab 389
Scales 133
Scallion 94

Index

Scarecrow................353
Scared for Life, variation
   to Cracklosis...........168
Scaredy Cat, Cat Mountain...399
Scaredy Cat, Crane Mountain.197
Scarface.................*410*
SCARFACE MOUNTAIN......527
Scary Lead..............*198*
Scary Potter Traverse.......481
Scarynac Crack..........428
Scattershot..............343
Scenic Slip..............150
Schadenfreude...........466
Schizophrenia............*329*
Schnapps................111
Schwartz's Ridge, variation
   to Roaring Brook Falls...*317*
Scooped By Fritz.........448
Scorpion.................*53*
Scorpion Bowl.............72
Scout About.............211
Scratch.................*313*
Scream from on High, A....*407*
Screaming Matrix (5.7).....98
Screaming Meaney.........98
Screams of the Primitive....*174*
Scruffy.................153
Sea of Seams............*65*
Seagull..................*334*
Seam Ripper.............158
Seamly Route............151
Seams Poplar............*188*
Second Amendment........179
Second Chance..........*252*
SECOND CHANCE WALL,
   Washbowl Pond.......*252*
Second Crimp to the Right,
   Keep on Climbing
   Till Morning............446
Second Face.............433
Second Job..............208
Second Lead.............*198*
SECOND TIER,
   Poke-O Moonshine......*134*
Seeking Enlightenment......444
Sennet..................421
Sentry..................*202*
Separate Denialty........*135*
SERAC WALL.............*255*
Sergeant Pepper..........*275*
Seven Ounces...........*290*
Seventeen...............379
Shaggy's Secret Stash......441
Shake and Bake...........50
Shaken, Not Stirred.......*236*
Shaky Flake.............238
Shaky Flakes Traverse....*524*
Shaky Spider...........*200*
Shaman, The.............353
Shanty 101..............239
SHANTY CLIFF...........231

Shanty Girl..............238
SHANTY KNOB, Shanty Cliff..232
SHANTY SLAB, Shanty Cliff...240
SHANTY SPORTS ARENA,
   Shanty Cliff...........239
Shantyclear.............236
Shantytown.............238
Shark Week.............*79*
Shark's Fin, The.........*256*
Sharp Bridge...........*164*
SHARP BRIDGE
   CAMPGROUND........*163*
Sheer Failure.............*522*
SHELVING ROCK..........38
Shelving Rock Earth Penetrator.59
Shemtastic..............*63*
Shiling Was Willing.......*233*
Shindig.................360
Shining, The............*239*
SHIPTON'S ARÊTE, Chapel
   Pond Gully Cliff........*235*
Shipton's Voyage........*235*
Shipwrecked............94
Shirtless In November.....314
Shit! HiSir Needs Stitches....300
Shiver Me Timbers,
   Eagle Falls............379
Shiver Me Timbers,
   Rogers Slide..........94
Shock and Awe..........59
Short Order.............*274*
Short Person's Disease....*169*
Short Sharp Shocked.....*164*
Short-Term Memory......243
Shot in the Dark, A.......432
SHOTGUN FACE, Case Wall,
   Beer Walls...........*315*
Shredded Wheat........131
Shuffle and Grunt........412
Sibiletto................221
Side Boob..............279
Side Show, variation
   to Gun Show.........203
Side Show, variation to
   Hoops and Yo Yo......66
Sideways..............316
Sidewinder.............113
Signature..............289
Silent Flight............*419*
Silent Spring...........*230*
Silk Road, The..........*369*
Silly...................149
Silly Willy..............148
Silmaril, The............491
Silver.................*418*
SILVER BULLET BAND,
   West Mountain......345
Silver Chicken..........*256*
Silver Flake............456
SILVER LAKE...........435
Silver Lake Chimney.....448

SILVER LAKE MOUNTAIN
   SUMMIT AREAS,
   Silver Lake...........490
Silver Slab..............468
Silver Streak............*62*
Silveretta..............345
Simon.................*195*
Simulium Venustum.....430
Sinful Ways.............*76*
Sinner Repent..........458
Sirloin Tips.............*190*
Sister Sarah............*163*
Sitting Duck............316
Sizzle Me...............66
Skeleton Key..........*269*
SKI TRACKS CLIFF,
   Gore Mountain......288
Skid Row..............236
Skillyabuda............*348*
Skinny Cat.............452
Sky High..............176
Sky Traverse..........*62*
Skyline Arête..........110
Slab Happy...........150
Slab with a View......*255*
Slabby McCracken.....447
Slabmeister...........210
SLANTING CRACKS WALL,
   Crane Mountain.....209
Slash and Burn........*360*
Slave Labor...........*202*
SLEEPING BEAUTY MOUNTAIN 64
Sleepwalk............*232*
Sleepy Hollow........206
Slide Rules...........*497*
Slim Pickins, Crane Mountain..147
Slim Pickins, Spider's Web....*265*
Slime Line.............*45*
Slip of the Tongue.....114
Slip Tease–Skid Row...102
Slipped Bits..........102
Slippery Needles......*391*
Slippy Sliden' Away...131
Slipshod.............74
Slot, The............422
Slumlord............238
Small Craft Advisory..*333*
Smallville Left.........*37*
Smallville Right.......*38*
Smear Campaign.....*90*
Smell of B.O., The....424
Smoke Signal........*131*
Smoking Jacket......*187*
Snake Charmer, Shelving Rock.45
Snake Charmer,
   Tongue Mountain....114
Snake Free..........116
SNAKE LEDGE, Main Face,
   Poke-O Moonshine...*45*
Snake Slide..........*53*
Snake, The..........*45*

Index

Snakeskin *166*
Snap, Crackle, and Pop *129*
Snapperhead 451
Snarling Spiders 460
Snatch It, variation
    to The Snatch *64*
Snatch, The. *64*
Snooker. *313*
Snow Blue 87
Snowballing. *131*
Snowbound. *120*
SNOWY MOUNTAIN. 248
Social Climber. 171
Social Pariah 171
Sodomizer, The 488
Soft Maple Times 367
Solar Energy *121*
Solar Grace. 179
Solarium, The 70
Sole Fusion 266
Solid Rock. *175*
SOLITUDE WALL,
    Washbowl Pond *253*
Solitude, Flowed Lands *428*
Solitude, Washbowl Pond. . . . *253*
Solo, Gracias 182
Some Things Considered. . . . *333*
Something Wicked *520*
Son of a Mother *39*
Son of Circuitous Shit 234
Son of Cirrhosis 118
Son of Slime 69
Sorcerer's Stone *198*
Söt Torn 122
Sound System *50*
Soup Kitchen, Shanty Cliff 236
Soup Kitchen,
    Upper Washbowl 249
Sour Grapes *94*
SOUTH BAY ROADCUT 392
SOUTH COLTON 406
SOUTH CORNER CLIFFS,
    Crane Mountain 175
SOUTH FACE AMPHITHEATER,
    Basin Mountain 488
South Face Direct *476*
SOUTH FACE,
    Gothics Mountain *473*
South Summit Route. 435
SOUTH SUMMIT,
    Catamount Mountain 434
SOUTHEAST FACE,
    Basin Mountain *488*
Southern Hospitality *73*
SOUTHWEST FACE,
    Poke-O Moonshine *114*
Southwest Ridge. 259
Soweto 235
Space Cowboy *158*
Space Odyssey *113*
Space Race *368*

Space Walk. *112*
Spaghetti Western *163*
SPANKY'S AREA *187*
SPANKY'S WALL,
    Spanky's Area *190*
Speakeasy *314*
SPECTACLE PONDS CLIFF. . .121
Spectacular Rising Traverse . . . *62*
Spelunker 470
Spelunking Midget 311
Sphinx in the Face 126
Spider Biter *135*
SPIDER'S WEB *258*
Spiral Staircase 186
Spire Route *274*
Spirit of Adventure *398*
Spit and Drivel. 120
Split Beaver. *381*
Split Personality, variation
    to Raindance Roof 186
Split Rock *174*
Splitting Headache 78
SPOOF WALL, Northway
    Express Wall *174*
Spooks *52*
Spooky Tom 362
Sport Climbing Is Neither 406
Sports Psychology *333*
SPORTSMAN CRAG,
    Notch Mountain. *388*
Sportsmanship, variation
    to Gamesmanship *73*
Spring Equinox *330*
Spring Fever 358
Springtime. *149*
Spruce Crack *525*
SPRUCE HILL CRAG *330*
Sprucification 359
Spur of the Moment *293*
SQUATTER WALL, Shanty Cliff 239
Squeaky Toy Aliens 340
Squeeze Box. *323*
Squeezing Miss Daisy 343
Squirrelless Journey *233*
SRT *62*
Stacked 382
Stager's Arête 423
Stagger and Swerve *256*
Stairway to Heaven. 187
Stake and Cake 50
Stalking Caribou *520*
Stand Your Ground 184
Standard *296*
Standard Deviation *519*
Standard Route 259
Standing Room Only *315*
Stanley. *483*
Stanley Frank 320
Star in the Dust 328
Star Sailor *365*
Starboard Tack 284

STARBUCK MOUNTAIN 282
Starline 283
Starstruck 284
Start Again. 68
Static Cling, Poke-O Moonshine *38*
Static Cling, Silver Lake 466
Static Cringe 59
Statute of Rights *412*
Steel Breeze *120*
Stemtastic 63
Stepping-stone 145
Steptoe *89*
Steve's Flakes *253*
STEWART'S LEDGE,
    Pilot Knob Mountain 74
Stihl Water 373
Still Bill .100
Sting, The *72*
Stinky Pete, variation to Sarge .339
Stone Cross 160
Stone Face *274*
STONE FACE RIB,
    Lower Washbowl. *273*
Stoned in a Crowded Corner,
    variation to Cornerstone . .161
Stones of Shame 127
Stones of Shame Direct 127
Stonewall Brigade. 331
Stop Making Sense 477
Storm Warning *334*
Storming the Tower. *196*
Straight and Narrow *120*
Straight A's *524*
Straits of Fear 210
Strangers in Paradise *118*
Stretch Armstrong. 279
Stretch Armstrong, variation
    to Adrenaline Surge 303
Strict Time *174*
Strike Zone 247
Strip Mine *119*
Sub-Dude 51
Sugar Plum Fairy *278*
SUGARLOAF MOUNTAIN 263
Suicidal Sidney 208
Suicide King 330
Summer Break *53*
Summer Party 79
Summer Rules *529*
Summer Solstice. *53*
SUMMIT CLIFF,
    Bald Mountain. 360
SUMMIT CLIFF,
    Baldface Mountain 254
SUMMIT CLIFF, Cat Mountain .398
SUMMIT CLIFF,
    Good Luck Mountain 331
SUMMIT CLIFF,
    Panther Mountain 337
SUMMIT CLIFF,
    Poke-O Moonshine *115*

Page numbers in this volume   *Page numbers in Volume 1*   539

Index

SUMMIT CLIFF, Silver Lake . . . 447
SUMMIT CLIFF,
    Snowy Mountain 250
SUMMIT CLIFFS,
    Crane Mountain 153
SUMMIT CLIFFS,
    Pharaoh Mountain. 130
Summit Direct *488*
Summit Route 285
Summit Snacks. 527
Sumo Fly *310*
Sun Dogs 145
SUN WALL, THE,
    Poke-O Moonshine. *133*
Sunburst Arête *100*
Sundance *160*
Sunday Funnies *279*
Sunday Stroll. 148
Sunday Stroll *166*
Sundowner 65
Sunfall 261
SUNRISE MOUNTAIN SLAB . . *387*
Sunset Arête 118
Sunset Crack 82
SUNSHINE CITY, Spanky's
    Wall, Spanky's Area. *193*
Sunshine Daydream 415
Sunshine Slab. 351
Suomi 321
Super Cell *377*
Supercharged. *307*
Superman Flake 272
Superman Flake
    Alternative Finish. 272
Superstition Traverse *51*
Suppertime 447
Surf and Turf, variation
    to Slide Rules *497*
Suspect Terrane *127*
Swamp Arête 285
Swamp Gas 285
SWAMP ROCK *349*
SWAMP ROCK,
    Lower Washbowl. *284*
Swamp Thang. 285
Swampoodle. 239
SWAPS .73
Sweat Man *331*
Sweaty April 67
Sweeper 154
SWEEPER WALL,
    Crane Mountain 154
Sweeping up to Glory 159
SWEET FERN HILL. *165*
Sweet Sunday. 94
Swept Away, Backwater Wall . . *186*
Swept Away, Crane Mountain .154
Swept Away, The Ticket,
    Lower Washbowl. *280*
Sword *304*

Sword Breaker, variation
    to Badinage. 150
Sword of Deception, The 488
Sword, The *128*
Synchronized Swimming *258*

T

Ta Da 186
Table Scraps *527*
Tablerock Corner. 152
TABLEROCK CRAG,
    Crane Mountain 152
Tachycardia. *100*
Take the Power Back 394
Takes All Kinds 347
Tales of Weakness 451
Talking Heads 324
Tallywhacker 225
Talons of Power. *335*
Talus Man 325
TANAGER FACE, Chapel
    Pond Gully Cliff *230*
Tanager Gully *232*
Tang Corner 65
Tangled Up in Azure 410
Tanks of Beer, variation to
    Tita U. Assol *314*
TAO, variation to
    Watch My Bolt *100*
Tarantula, variation to
    Fire Starter. *237*
Tardis Traveler 230
Tarsal Grinder *187*
Tartar Control. 113
Tasp, The. 379
Taste Buds 113
Taytay Corner *120*
TB or Not TB 428
Tea and Biscuits 476
Team America 351
Team Rocksport 69
Teamwork *131*
Tears of Gaia. 443
Teddy Ruxpin 116
Teddy's Trauma *478*
Ted's Has It All 424
TEEPEE WALL,
    Crane Mountain 188
Teeth *372*
Teetotaler. 289
Teflon Wall 224
Telegraph Crack *117*
Telepathy *117*
Tempest, The 212
Tempest, variation to
    Heart of Gold. *137*
Ten B 309
Ten Even *129*
Ten Plagues, The 126
Tenacity *230*
Tennessee Excursion 225

Tennis, Anyone 336
Ten-Point Buck 71
Tequila Mockingbird *295*
Tequila Mockingbird Direct,
    variation to Tequila
    Mockingbird *295*
Terapia. 316
Teriyaki Hairpiece 309
TG Farm 523
Thangorodrim 491
Thank You, Cindy 157
Thanksgiving. *218*
The Project, variation to
    Emperor Zurg 340
There Be Dragons. *412*
They Never Recognized Me . . . *310*
Thin Soles 69
Thing 1 232
Thing 2 232
THIRD TIER,
    Poke-O Moonshine. *137*
Third Time for Mrs. Robinson . . *246*
Third-Quarter Profit 149
This is Spinal Tap 78
This, Too, Shall Pass *255*
Thorn Forest 67
Thousand Faces of a
    Hundred People 234
Thrash *312*
Three Blind Mice. 434
Three B's 472
Three Degrees of Separation . . .44
Three Stooges, Beer Walls *311*
Three Stooges, Shelving Rock . .42
Three Way 529
Thrill Ride 106
Thunder and Lichen *192*
Thunder Down Under 46
Thunderbolt. *123*
Thunderhead *95*
TICKET, THE,
    Lower Washbowl. *279*
Tie Me Up *289*
Tier Pressure. 277
Tighter than Two 186
Tiguidou Pack-Sack 459
Till the Fat Lady Sings. 250
Tilly's Trench 208
Tilman's Arête *235*
TILMAN'S ARÊTE, Chapel
    Pond Gully Cliff *234*
Timbuk-2 63
Time Bomb *160*
Time Jumpers 38
Time Piece *312*
Time Trials 236
Timeline *515*
TIRRELL POND 280
Tita U. Assol *314*
Titusville Express. 493
TITUSVILLE MOUNTAIN 492

540   Page numbers in this volume   *Page numbers in Volume 1*

Index

TL. *390*
To Bee or Not to Bee. 153
To Catch a Wave. *430*
To Do. .185
To Infinity and Beyond! **339**
To Pass Or Not To Pass *509*
Toad's Traverse 433
Toiling Men 161
Tomahawk Crack, The 493
Toma's Wall *499*
Tomb of the Falcon 130
Tombstone *157*
Tommy Gun. 344
Tommy, variation to Look,
    Roll, and Fire 328
Tommy's Climb *130*
Tom's Daring-Do 179
Tom's Roof. 186
Tone-Bone Tennys. 94
Tone-Boneparte *212*
Tongue and Groove 115
TONGUE MOUNTAIN CLIFF . .111
Tongue-Lashing 114
Too Burly Bulls. *360*
Too Close for Comfort. 244
Too Early Spring *358*
Too Much Chop *145*
Too Shallow for Diving, variation
    to Roaring Brook Falls . . .*317*
Too Wet to Plow *250*
Toodeloo *232*
Toolbox Woody 314
Tool-less Wonder 401
Tooth & Nail. 455
Topknot *430*
TOP-O-THE-MEASLES WALL,
    Crane Mountain 170
Torcher 205
Torment 430
Torment Direct. 430
Toss Me My Nuts 134
Toucan. .63
Touch of Class *399*
Touch of Gray, A, variation to
    Rough Cut. *231*
Touch The Earth 269
Touché. .63
Tougastan 63
Tough Act to Follow, A 254
Tough Act, A 254
Tour Arête Syndrome 63
Tour Guide Barbie. 340
Touran 63
Tourista .63
Tower of Babel, The 369
TOWERS OF THE TEETH,
    THE, Clements Pond Trail.490
Toxic Avenger, The 303
TOY STORY WALL,
    Lake Pleasant Quarry 339
TR *265*

Traffic Engineer. *181*
Trailblazer *129*
Train Wreck 71
Trajectory Crack 345
Transplant *172*
Trap Dike. *515*
Trap Dike Slide *515*
Trapped in the Dike. *516*
Trav-Ass, variation to
    Hour of Prayer. 220
Travels with Travis *437*
Traverse City *341*
Traverse of the Climbing Gods.*153*
Travisty 134
Treasure of El Sid 324
Tree Hugger 366
Tribulations 202
Trick Move. *138*
Trick or Treat,
    Huckleberry Mountain. . . .216
Trick or Treat, Pharaoh
    Mountain 130
Trickagnosis 167
Trigger Finger,
    Lost Hunters Cliff. 316
Trigger Finger, West Mountain .344
Trilogy, variation to
    Darkest Africa *130*
Tripping Karen. *365*
Trolls in Hiding, variation to
    Pay the Troll's Bridge. *203*
Troublemaker 230
Trouser Flute 158
Trouser Gallery, variation
    to Frippery. *414*
Trub 460
True Grit. *72*
True North *139*
TRUE SUMMIT SLABS,
    Chimney Mountain 260
TRUE SUMMIT, Crane
    Mountain 158
Trundle Bundle 401
Trundle Fodder *377*
Trundle of Joy 419
Trust Your Rubber 321
TSUNAMI CRAG. *153*
Tsunami Slap-Up *332*
TSUNAMI WALL, Silver Lake . .461
Tubular Bells *282*
TUCKER WALL, Main Cliff,
    Huckleberry Mountain. . . .222
Tuesday Layback 70
Tuesdays. *300*
Tumbler 235
Tun Tavern 193
Tuna Fish Crack 131
Tunnel Vision *129*
Turbocharge *307*
Turbocharge Direct Finish,
    variation to Turbocharge . .*307*

Turbulescence. *183*
Turd Ferguson Can Suck It. . . .*154*
Turning 21 Again. 450
Tusk. 452
Twain Town 418
Twelve Five 289
Twelve-Step Program *298*
Twenty-one 225
Twilight. *112*
TWIN FALLS CLIFF 399
Twinflower Traverse. 121
Twist Off. *293*
TWISTER GLADE AREA,
    Gore Mountain 286
Two Bits 100
Two Camels, One Hump 61
Two Evil Deeds 62
Two Lefts Don't Make It Right. . .63
Two Nuts and a Cam 418
Two Pots to Piss In 61
Two Socks. 462
TYPHOON WALL *331*

U

UFO WALL, Between
    the Lakes. *379*
Ugly as Sin 133
Ukiah *52*
Uluwatu *175*
UNBALANCED ROCK CLIFF .*380*
Unbroken 430
Uncle Fester 469
Uncle Remus 89
Uncontrollable Desires *356*
Under the Influence *96*
Underage Drinking *289*
Underhanging Garter *376*
Unfair. *118*
Unfinished Business. *332*
Unforgiven. *70*
Unnamed1 282
Unnamed2 284
Unnamed4 284
Unpoplar. *188*
Untammed Stimulation. 106
Up. 91
Up and Over, variation to
    Zig-Zag *289*
Up In Smoke. 133
Up on the Mountain 149
Up Yanda 110
Up Your Bum. 407
Updraft 128
UPPER BEER WALL,
    Beer Walls. *289*
UPPER BUCK, Buck Mountain .67
UPPER CIRQUE CLIFF,
    Gore Mountain 290
UPPER CLIFFBAND,
    Hudson River Crags 79

Index

UPPER DOME, Pitchoff
    Ridge Trail Domes......*351*
Upper Incisor...............*192*
Upper Level Disturbance.....**213**
UPPER MEASLES WALL,
    Crane Mountain.......**169**
UPPER SUMMIT CLIFF,
    Pharaoh Mountain......**131**
UPPER TIERS, Poke-O
    Moonshine..............*114*
UPPER WALLS,
    Crane Mountain........**176**
UPPER WASHBOWL........*240*
UPPER WOLFJAW CLIFF.....*482*
Upright and Locked..........**368**
Upsidaisium................**466**
Urgent Fury................**146**
Urin Luck..................**410**

V

V for Victory................**133**
Vaccination................**484**
Vagtastic Voyage............**42**
Valium.....................**76**
Vanilla Ice..................**352**
Vanishing Species...........*230*
VANITY FACE, Spanky's Wall,
    Spanky's Area..........**190**
Variety Crack...............**210**
Varsity.....................*45*
Velma's Snatch.............**445**
Vendetta, variation to War
    of the Worlds...........**67**
Veracity....................*230*
Verdon.....................*52*
Vermontville Redneck.......*356*
Vernal Imperatives..........**236**
Vertebrae..................*252*
Vertical Ag & Tech..........**212**
Vertical Limit...............**303**
Victoria....................*218*
VIEWPOINT CLIFF,
    Crane Mountain........**150**
Viewpoint Crack.............**151**
Virgin Sturgeon.............*276*
Virginia Reel................**380**
Vision Quest................**303**
Vogel......................*279*

W

Wags on the Wall...........*441*
Wahlnut...................*127*
Waiting for the Son..........*358*
Waiting for the Sun..........**314**
Waiting For The Weather....**487**
Wake and Bake..............**50**
Wald-Calder Route..........*358*
Walk in the Sky, A...........**228**
Walk Like an Egyptian.......**126**
Walk on the Easy Side.......*185*
Walk the Plank..............**94**

Walker's Weave............**360**
Walking Disaster...........**410**
Walking Fern Face..........**109**
Walking the Tightrope.......*360*
WALL #1, Boquet River Crags.*184*
WALL #2, Boquet River Crags.*184*
WALL #3, Boquet River Crags.*185*
Wall of Desires.............*507*
WALL OF SORROWS,
    Washbowl Pond........*251*
Wall Ruler..................*206*
Wall Ruler–King and I ' (5.10c)..*206*
WALLFACE.................**431**
Wanderer, variation to Gullet..**234**
Wandering and Pondering....*370*
Wandering Lunatic..........*304*
Wandering Window..........**256**
Wandering Wizard..........*440*
Wanderlust, Avalanche Lake..*507*
Wanderlust, Summit Cliff,
    Poke-O Moonshine.....**120**
War and Peace.............*523*
War of the Worlds...........**67**
Ward Cleaver...............*331*
WARDSBORO CLIFF,
    Fly Brook Valley.........**108**
Warpath...................*157*
WASHBOWL POND..........*250*
WASHBOWL POND SLAB,
    Washbowl Pond........*254*
Watch Crystal..............*312*
Watch My Bolt.............**100**
Water Streak...............**250**
Waterfall Center............**212**
Waterfall Left...............**211**
WATERFALL WALL,
    Crane Mountain........**211**
Waterhole #3...............**428**
Waterloo...................**37**
Wave Bye Bye..............**345**
WAVE WALL, West Mountain..**345**
Way Hairball................*342*
Way in the Chimney.........*342*
Way of the Peckerheads.....*247*
WAYBACK CLIFF, Silver Lake..**469**
Wayout Chimney............**145**
WAYOUT WALL,
    Crane Mountain........**144**
We Should Have Taken a Left.*504*
Wear Four..................*280*
Weasel Climb, The...........**316**
Weather Clown.............**213**
Wedlock...................*389*
Wednesday Wisecrack........**70**
Weekday Special...........**427**
Weekend Warrior...........*246*
Weenie Jam................**411**
Weenie's Way...............**222**
Weird Science..............*334*
Welcome Matt...............**71**
Welcome to America........**323**

Welcome to Arietta..........**314**
Welcome to Bedrock.........*339*
Welcome to Deadwater,
    variation to Tombstone..*157*
Welcome to McMartin.......**321**
Welcome to the Jungle......*183*
Welcome to the Machine....**380**
Well Now, That's Better......*169*
WEST CANADA CLIFF.......**331**
WEST CLIFF, Cat Mountain..**397**
West End Brewery..........**335**
WEST FACE OF MT COLDEN,
    Avalanche Lake.........**509**
WEST FACE, Dix Mountain...*528*
WEST FACE, Giant Mountain.*465*
WEST FACE,
    Gothics Mountain.......**479**
WEST MOUNTAIN...........**341**
WEST SLAB,
    Poke-O Moonshine.....*139*
Whaamburger..............*489*
Whale Crack...............**459**
Whale Ship................**345**
WHALING WALL,
    West Mountain.........**345**
What about Bob............*347*
What The Eft...............**297**
Wheelin' N' Dealin'..........*267*
Wheezy, variation to To Infinity
    and Beyond!............**339**
When Clouds Part...........**131**
Where Beagles Dare........*377*
Where Frenchmen Dare....**407**
Where the Wild Things Are..**478**
Where's Ian................**471**
Where's My Cane?...........**78**
Where's the Booty?.........**360**
Where's the Sun,
    Bob Kovachick?........**145**
Whip It Bad.................*274*
WHIP IT WALL,
    Lower Washbowl.......*274*
Whipping Post, The.........**400**
Whips and Chains..........**274**
Whirlpool, variation to Flume..*186*
White Arête................**305**
White Knight...............**269**
White Lightning.............**92**
White Pine Fever............**257**
WHITE SLAB,
    Huckleberry Mountain...**228**
WHITE WALL,
    Ledge Mountain........**278**
WHITEWATER WALLS,
    Boquet River Crags......*183*
Whoops...................*244*
Why Did I Fall for That.......**322**
Wicked Weed Route, The....**328**
Wide Crack................**312**
Wide Supremacy...........**86**
Widow Maker..............*362*

542   **Page numbers in this volume**   *Page numbers in Volume 1*

Index

Wiessner Route, Avalanche Lake 515
Wiessner Route, Noonmark Mountain 481
Wiessner Route, Upper Washbowl 245
Wiessner Route, Wallface 457
Wiessner-Austin Route 496
Wild Blue 53
Wild Man from Borneo 368
WILD PINES 106
Wild Rumpus 106
Wildcat 398
Wilderness Work 131
Willie's Danish Prince 192
Willy 229
Wimp Crack 333
Winchester Dihedral 344
Wind Song 350
Window, The 410
Winds of Change 58
Winter's Tale 280
Wipe It Off 342
Wish You Were Here 513
WISWIG 156
With a Little Help from My Friends 420
With Brook Trout Eyes 338
Withheld Pay 370
Without a Hitch 391
WMD 59
WMP 194
Wobbly Crack 120
Wolfman 485
Wolfshack Corner 59
Womb with a View, A 44
Woo Hoo! 420
Woodland Corner 104
Woodland Idiot 189
Woodsman's Field Days 358
Woody 340
Woolsey Route 485
Working Wives 203
Worlds in Collision 127
Worse Than Real 89
Wounded Knee 184
Wretched Wanderer 155
Wright Crack, The 525
WRIGHT PEAK 525
Wright Stuff, The 526
Wright Wrong Chimney 526
Wrong Again, Chalkbreath 260
Wrong Crack, The 526
Wrong Side of the Tracks 235
Wronged Again 341

X

Xenolith 327

Y

Yabba Dabba Do 53
Yabba Dabba Doo 339
Yakapodu 348
YANDO WALL, Headwall, Poke-O Moonshine 129
Yard Sale 417
Yard Work 360
Yax Crack 335
Yellow Paddles 244
Yes, Virginia 419
Yodellaybackloon 189
Young Heavy Roosters 321
Your Anus 128
You're No Spring Chicken Head 415
Yoyodyne, variation to Oscillation Overthruster . . 336
Yvonne 271

Z

Zabba 265
Zack's Sunspot 337
Zebra 483
Zero Gravity Bella 154
Zig-Zag 289
Zigzag Crack, variation to Out with the Boys Again 438
Zigzag, Bald Mountain 360
Zigzag, Notch Mountain 389
Zippity Doo-Dah 90
Zoinks!! 442
Zone X 96

Drawing by Colin O'Connor.

Acknowledgments

Producing this guide was a monumental effort, involving the collaboration of many individuals.

Those who made first ascents deserve the ultimate credit. It's because of their dedication and perseverance that we have so many routes to climb. We contacted many first ascentionists, who have our deep appreciation for accepting our cold calls and dredging their memories to recount route details of long-ago climbs.

We thank those who helped with background research. Don Mellor was always accessible and willing to share his insights, opinions, and historical recollections. Without his "blue bin"—and, no, not the recycling bin, but rather his collection of notes, correspondence, and route reports dating back to Trudy Healy— this project would not have been possible.Ced Dick Tucker deserves special mention for his generous diligence in uncovering historical gems.

Since the first edition, many people have contributed material that has served as a basis for our work. Special thanks to Kevin "MudRat" MacKenzie and his excellent photos of the High Peaks; Justin Sanford and his topos of the Southern Adirondack areas; and Gary Thomann and his online mini-guides.

Of our many contributors, Jay Harrison tops them all. Not only is he a prolific route developer, but he spent many countless hours poring over aerial photos, editing and reediting route descriptions, and running up to the cliff from his house to confirm route details. If you see him at the cliff, be sure to shake his hand, and thank him for his many years of scrubbing routes.

Many climbers contributed essays to the first edition that portrayed Adirondack climbing in a variety of voices. This second edition offers new additional essays from Tad Welch, Tom Rosecrans, Peter Kamitses, Dick Tucker, Conor Cliffe, David Buzzelli, Dave Hough, and Colin Loher. Thanks guys!

The Department of Environmental Conservation was very helpful with their contributions on peregrines and timber rattlesnakes, and their reviews of backcountry rules and regulations. In the 6 years since the first edition, New York State has purchased huge tracts of land, and coincidentally many cliffs. Special thanks to Dan Levy, Robert Daley, and Allison Buckley, who, along with Connie Prickett at The Nature Conservancy, kept us in the loop, assisted with field research, and reviewed draft materials.

A special thanks goes to our production team: Karen Kwasnowski for her GIS expertise; Sara Catterall and Sue Cohan for copy editing; and Colin O'Connor, Tad Welch and Lucie Wellner for their drawings and watercolors. Lucie Wellner in particular went above and beyond by color correcting hundreds of photos and assisting with nearly every aspect of book design.

There's also a long list of photographers, many of whom donated their photos. Those that deserve special recognition are Jim Cunningham, Joel Dashnaw, Drew Haas, Keenan Harvey (www.kennanharvey.com), David Le Pagne (www.davidlepagne.com), Rick Levinson (www.rlphoto.com), Mark Meschinelli, Olaf Sööt (www.osphoto.com), Dave Vuono (www.davevuono.com), Carl Heilman II (www.carlheilman.com), and Tomás Donoso (www.tomasdonoso.com).

We thank those who accompanied us on forays into the mountains to research this guide. Like all climbing partnerships, we depended upon you to show up, navigate the woods, share the rope, and be willing to do it again (and again).

Lastly, we offer the deepest gratitude to our wives who know us well enough to realize that our bellyaching was mostly a facade, and for being on call as both editors and therapists. Lucie and Erika, you knew you were marrying climbers, but this was a whole new level. Thank you both.

About the Authors

JIM LAWYER

Jim began bagging peaks in the Adirondacks at the age of 5, during a family vacation in 1970. His love of wild places and the escape they offer led him to long-distance hiking in his teens. After that, rock climbing was a natural extension. Over the last 30 years, he has dedicated his life to climbing extensively around the world. With an education in computer science from Syracuse University, he helped found Summit Software in 1989. He and his wife Lucie split their time between Pompey, NY, and their hut in the High Peaks.

JEREMY HAAS

Jeremy began climbing at the age of 14, and promptly abandoned his childhood dream of becoming an Olympic gymnast. His first Adirondacks weekend was an epic: wasp nests on Poke-O; freaky runouts on Big Slide; and a struggle up Wallface after he'd left all the slings in the car. A graduate of the University of New Hampshire, with a Masters in Education from Cornell, he teaches science at Saratoga Springs High School, and in his spare time is a guide for Adirondack Rock and River. Jeremy and his wife Erika live in Glens Falls, NY.

GET TIED IN
With the Area's Leading Rock Climbing Facility!

Looking for a rainy day or off-season workout? How about your weekly after work training sessions?

The Edge Halfmoon is the place for Upstate climbers to stay on top of the sport we love.

- Build new partnerships as you tackle enjoyable and challenging routes up to 5.13+ and V10
- Stay fit on our steep lead climbing and top out bouldering
- Get strong in our dedicated pull up, finger board and campus training area

For more information check us out at **theedgehalfmoon.com**, or call **518.982.5545**.

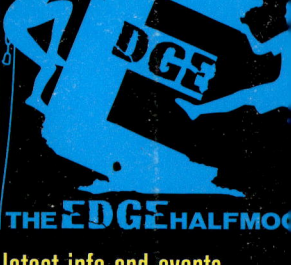

THE EDGE HALFMOON

And be sure to "friend us" on Facebook for all of the latest info and events.